Fodor's 200

Germany

The Guide
for All Budgets

Completely
Updated

Where to Stay, Eat,
and Explore

On and Off
the Beaten Path

When to Go,
What to Pack

Maps, Travel Tips,
and Web Sites

Fodor's Travel Publications • New York, Toronto, London, Sydney, Auckland
www.fodors.com

Fodor's Germany 2003

EDITOR: Christina Knight

Editorial Contributors: Jennifer Abramsohn, Uli Ehrhardt, Satu Hummasti, Marton Radkai, Jürgen Scheunemann, Inez Sharp, Ted Shoemaker, Kerry Brady Stewart
Editorial Production: Taryn Luciani
Maps: David Lindroth, *cartographer;* Robert Blake and Rebecca Baer, *map editors*
Design: Fabrizio La Rocca, *creative director;* Guido Caroti, *art director;* Jolie Novak, *senior picture editor;* Melanie Marin, *photo editor*
Cover Design: Pentagram
Production/Manufacturing: Colleen Ziemba
Cover Photo: Owen Franken

Copyright

ISBN 1-4000-1058-6

ISSN 1525-5034

Important Tip

Although all prices, opening times, and other details in this book are based on information supplied to us at press time, changes occur all the time in the travel world, and Fodor's cannot accept responsibility for facts that become outdated or for inadvertent errors or omissions. So **always confirm information when it matters,** especially if you're making a detour to visit a specific place.

Special Sales

Fodor's Travel Publications are available at special discounts for bulk purchases for sales promotions or premiums. Special editions, including personalized covers, excerpts of existing guides, and corporate imprints, can be created in large quantities for special needs. For more information, contact your local bookseller or write to Special Markets, Fodor's Travel Publications, 1745 Broadway, New York, NY 10019. Inquiries from Canada should be directed to your local Canadian bookseller or sent to Random House of Canada, Ltd., Marketing Department, 2775 Matheson Boulevard East, Mississauga, Ontario L4W 4P7. Inquiries from the United Kingdom should be sent to Fodor's Travel Publications, 20 Vauxhall Bridge Road, London SW1V 2SA, England.

PRINTED IN THE UNITED STATES OF AMERICA

10 9 8 7 6 5 4 3 2 1

CONTENTS

Maps

ON THE ROAD WITH FODOR'S

A TRIP TAKES YOU OUT OF YOURSELF. Concerns of life at home completely disappear, driven away by more immediate thoughts—about, say, what marvels will beguile the next day, or where you'll have dinner. That's where Fodor's comes in. We make sure that you know all your options, so that you don't miss something that's around the next bend just because you didn't know it was there. Mindful that the best memories of your trip might have nothing to do with what you came to Germany to see, we guide you to sights large and small all over the country. You might set out to cruise by the castles on the Rhine, but back at home you find yourself unable to forget the hours you whiled away at a beer garden or the suspenseful climb up a winding staircase to an ancient tower's balcony. With Fodor's at your side, serendipitous discoveries are never far away.

About Our Writers

Our success in showing you every corner of Germany is a credit to our extraordinary writers. Although there's no substitute for travel advice from a good friend who knows your style, our contributors are the next best thing—the kind of people you would poll for travel advice if you knew them.

Jennifer Abramsohn left a fast-paced life in financial journalism in New York in order to move to Cologne, Germany, where she is a freelance journalist and mother of two. She produces news and feature programs for Germany's official state radio, Deutsche Welle, and edits and writes for various U.S. publications.

Uli Ehrhardt, a native German, has had a long career in the travel and tourism fields. He began as an interpreter and travel consultant in the United States, and then for 20 years served as director of the State Tourist Board Bodensee–Oberschwaben (Lake Constance–Upper Swabia). He now makes his home in the city of Ulm as a tourism consultant, writer, and teacher at a state college for tourism.

Marton Radkai is a native New Yorker of Bavarian/Hungarian descent and lives in Munich. Since 1985 he has lived in Germany and Austria working as a travel photographer, translator, editor, and writer for radio and print media.

Jürgen Scheunemann grew up in Hamburg and fell in love with Berlin 15 years ago when he moved there to study North American history and German literature. Since then, he has worked as a journalist and editor, and has written, published, and translated a number of books on Berlin and the United States.

Inez Sharp first came (very unwillingly) to Germany in 1984 as part of a university teaching course from her home in London, England. She fell in love and settled (willingly) in Bavaria. She works as a journalist, translator, and travel writer from her base in Munich.

Ted Shoemaker settled in Germany more than 40 years ago when, as a U.S. Army officer, he married a German. He has been editor of three English-language magazines in Germany and a correspondent for many American publications. He lives in Frankfurt.

Kerry Brady Stewart was born in St. Louis, Missouri, and now lives in Wiesbaden. After working at the German Wine Information Bureau in New York, she moved to Germany in 1981 to coordinate the activities of the European and overseas press services of the German Wine Institute, Mainz. Today she runs Fine Lines, a public relations agency specializing in wine, food, and travel. Her latest books are *The Hungry Traveler: Germany,* and *A Traveller's Wine Guide to Germany.*

How to Use This Book

Up front is Smart Travel Tips A to Z, arranged alphabetically by topic and loaded with tips, Web sites, and contact information. Destination: Germany helps get you in the mood for your trip. Subsequent chapters in Germany are arranged regionally. All city chapters begin with exploring information, with a section for each neighborhood (each recommending a good tour and listing sights alphabetically). All regional chapters are divided geographically; within each area, towns are covered in logical geographical order, and attractive stretches of road between them are indicated by the designation En Route. To help you decide what you'll have time to visit, all chapters begin with our writers' favorite itineraries. (Mix itineraries from several chapters, and you can put together a really exceptional trip.) The A to Z section that ends every chapter lists additional resources. At the end of the book you'll find Background and Essentials, including a chronology of German history, German vocabulary, and a menu guide.

Icons and Symbols

- ★ Our special recommendations
- ✕ Restaurant
- 🏨 Lodging establishment
- ✕🏨 Lodging establishment whose restaurant warrants a special trip
- 🦆 Good for kids (rubber duck)
- ☞ Sends you to another section of the guide for more information
- ✉ Address
- ☎ Telephone number
- ⏲ Opening and closing times
- 🎫 Admission prices (those we give apply to adults; substantially reduced fees are almost always available for children, students, and senior citizens)

Numbers in white and black circles ③ ❸ that appear on the maps, in the margins, and within the tours correspond to one another.

For hotels, you can assume that all rooms have private baths, phones, TVs, and air-conditioning unless otherwise noted and that all hotels operate on the European Plan (with no meals) if we don't specify another meal plan. We always list a property's facilities but not whether you'll be charged extra to use them, so when pricing accommodations, do ask what's included. For restaurants, it's always a good idea to book ahead; we mention reservations only when they're essential or are not accepted. All restaurants we list are open daily for lunch and dinner unless stated otherwise; dress is mentioned only when men are required to wear a jacket or a jacket and tie. Look for an overview of local dining-out habits in Smart Travel Tips A to Z and in the Pleasures and Pastimes section that follows each chapter introduction.

You can rest assured that you're in good hands—and that no property mentioned in the book has paid to be included. Each has been selected strictly on its merits, as the best of its type in its price range.

Don't Forget to Write

Your experiences—positive and negative—matter to us. If we have missed or misstated something, we want to hear about it. We follow up on all suggestions. Contact the Germany editor at editors@fodors.com or c/o Fodor's at 1745 Broadway, New York, NY 10019. And have a fabulous trip!

Karen Cure

Karen Cure
Editorial Director

Germany
DENMARK
Baltic Sea
North Sea
POLAND
THE NETHERLANDS
0 100 miles
0 150 km
KEY
Ferry Lines
N
Sylt
Niebüll
Flensburg
Husum
Kiel
Fehmarn
Rügen
Stralsund
Greifswald
Usedom
Anklam
SCHLESWIG-HOLSTEIN
Rendsburg
Neustadt
Rostock
MECKLENBURG-VORPOMMERN
East Frisian Islands
Cuxhaven
Wismar
Lübeck
Güstrow
Teterow
Neubrandenburg
Elbe
HAMBURG
Hamburg
Schwerin
Waren
Norden
Wilhelmshaven
Bremerhaven
Emden
Ludwigslust
Neustrelitz
Oder
Bremen
Oldenburg
BREMEN
FORMER BORDER BETWEEN EAST AND WEST GERMANY
Wittenberge
Oranienburg
LOWER SAXONY
Ems
Stendal
Berlin
Brandenburg
Potsdam
Hanover
Osnabrück
Braunschweig
BRANDENBURG
Frankfurt-an-der-Oder
Odra
Magdeburg
Bielefeld
Hildesheim
Lübben
Münster
Halberstadt
Dessau
Wittenberg
Cottbus
NORTH RHINE-WESTPHALIA
SAXONY-ANHALT
Saale
Essen
Göttingen
HARZ MOUNTAINS
Nordhausen
Dortmund
Halle
Kassel
Hagen
Leipzig
Neisse
Görlitz

Buchenwald
Cologne/Köln
Siegen
Erfurt
Weimar
Gera
SAXONY
Dresden
Aachen
Bonn
Marburg
Eisenach
Bad Hersfeld
Ilmenau
Chemnitz
Zwickau
Rhine
Alsfeld
Thüringer Wald
THURINGIA
HESSEN
Fulda
Meiningen
BELGIUM
Koblenz
Plauen
Hof
Coburg
RHINELAND-PALATINATE
Wiesbaden
Mainz
Frankfurt-am-Main
Münchberg
Mosel
Bamberg
Bayreuth
CZECH REPUBLIC
LUX.
Trier
Darmstadt
Würzburg
Main
Mannheim
Ludwigshafen
SAARLAND
Heidelberg
Rothenburg-o-d-Tauber
Fürth
Nuremberg
Saarbrücken
Heilbronn
BAVARIA
Karlsruhe
Regensburg
Deggendorf
Stuttgart
Baden-Baden
Ingolstadt
Passau
Danube (Donau)
Isar
Tübingen
Danube
Rhine (Rhein)
Ulm
Augsburg
Offenburg
BADEN-WÜRTTEMBERG
Munich
Black Forest
Inn
Biberach
Memmingen
Freiburg
Tuttlingen
BAVARIAN ALPS
FRANCE
Ravensburg
Wangen
Rheinfelden
Konstanz
Bodensee
Friedrichshafen
Garmisch-Partenkirchen
Berchtesgaden
Füssen
Mittenwald
AUSTRIA
SWITZERLAND

ESSENTIAL INFORMATION

ADDRESSES

In this book the words for street (*Strasse*) and alley (*Gasse*) are abbreviated as str. and g. within italicized service information. Brüdergasse will appear as Brüderg., for example.

AIR TRAVEL

BOOKING

When you book **look for nonstop flights** and **remember that "direct" flights stop at least once.** Try to avoid connecting flights, which require a change of plane. Two airlines may operate a connecting flight jointly, so ask if your airline operates every segment of the trip; you may find that the carrier you prefer flies you only part of the way. To find more booking tips and to check prices and make on-line flight reservations, log on to www.fodors.com.

CARRIERS

Lufthansa, a privatized company, is Germany's leading carrier and has shared mileage plans and flights with Air Canada and United, among other airlines.

Germany's internal air network is excellent, with frequent flights linking all major cities in little more than an hour. Services are operated by Lufthansa and two other carriers in which it has an interest—Condor, a subsidiary, and Eurowings. Also in the market, mainly for charter service and regional service to smaller airports, are Deutsche BA, a subsidiary of British Air, LTU, Hapag-Lloyd, Aero-Lloyd, Air Berlin, and Germanair.

➤ TO AND FROM GERMANY: **Air Canada** (☎ 888/247–2262). **American** (☎ 800/433–7300). **Continental** (☎ 800/525–0280). **Delta** (☎ 800/241–4141). **LTU International Airways** (☎ 800/888–0200). **Lufthansa** (☎ 800/645–3880). **Northwest** (☎ 800/225–2525). **United** (☎ 800/241–6522). **US Airways** (☎ 800/428–4322).

➤ WITHIN GERMANY: **Aero-Lloyd** (☎ 06171/62500). **Air Berlin** (☎ 01801/737800). **Condor** (☎ 06107/982888). **Deutsche BA** (☎ 089/9759–1500). **Eurowings** (☎ 0231/92450). **LTU** (☎ 0211/941–8888). **Lufthansa** (☎ 0180/380–3803). **Hapag-Lloyd** (☎ 0511/97270).

➤ FROM THE U.K.: **British Airways** (☎ 0345/222–111). **Lufthansa** (☎ 0345/737–747). **Ryanair** (☎ 0870/1–569–569, WEB ryanair.com).

CHECK-IN AND BOARDING

Always **ask your carrier about its check-in policy.** Plan to arrive at the airport about two hours before your scheduled departure time for domestic flights and two to three hours before international flights.

Germany has flight safety rules similar to the ones in effect in the United States. Security is especially tight on transatlantic flights and on flights by British and American airlines. Several airlines, including Lufthansa, have announced that cockpit doors will be electronically locked, and that air marshals will be aboard flights. Assuming that not everyone with a ticket will show up, airlines routinely overbook planes. When everyone does, airlines ask for volunteers to give up their seats. In return, these volunteers usually get a certificate for a free flight and are rebooked on the next flight out. If there are not enough volunteers, the airline must choose who will be denied boarding. The first to get bumped are passengers who checked in late and those flying on discounted tickets, so **get to the gate and check in as early as possible,** especially during peak periods.

Always **bring a government-issued photo I.D. to the airport;** even when it's not required, a passport is best.

CUTTING COSTS

The least expensive airfares to Germany are priced for round-trip travel and must usually be purchased in advance. Airlines generally allow you to change your return date for a fee; most low-fare tickets, however, are nonrefundable. A super-cheap way of flying to Germany from the British Isles is through the "no frills" Irish airline, Ryanair. Fares range €15 from Bournemouth and Glasgow (Prestwick), €25 from London (Stansted) and €35 from Shannon. Lufthansa, by contrast, might charge €432 from London (Heathrow). The catch is that the Ryanair flights are into Hahn, a remote former U.S. Air Force base in Rhineland-Pfalz, 100 mi and a two-hour bus ride west of Frankfurt.

It's smart to **call a number of airlines,** and when you are quoted a good price, **book it on the spot**—the same fare may not be available the next day. Always **check different routings** and look into using alternate airports. Also, price off-peak flights, which may be significantly less expensive than others. Travel agents, especially low-fare specialists (☞ Discounts and Deals), are helpful.

Consolidators are another good source. They buy tickets for scheduled international flights at reduced rates from the airlines, then sell them at prices that beat the best fare available directly from the airlines. Sometimes you can even get your money back if you need to return the ticket. Carefully read the fine print detailing penalties for changes and cancellations, purchase the ticket with a credit card, and **confirm your consolidator reservation with the airline.**

When you **fly as a courier,** you trade your checked-luggage space for a ticket deeply subsidized by a courier service. There are restrictions on when you can book and how long you can stay. Some courier companies list with membership organizations, such as the Air Courier Association and the International Association of Air Travel Couriers; these require you to become a member before you can book a flight.

➤ CONSOLIDATORS: **Cheap Tickets** (☎ 800/377–1000 or 888/922–8849, WEB www.cheaptickets.com). **Discount Airline Ticket Service** (☎ 800/576–1600). **Unitravel** (☎ 800/325–2222, WEB www.unitravel.com). **Up & Away Travel** (☎ 212/889–2345, WEB www.upandaway.com). **World Travel Network** (☎ 800/409–6753).

➤ COURIER RESOURCES: **Air Courier Association** (☎ 800/282–1202, WEB www.aircourier.org). **International Association of Air Travel Couriers** (☎ 352/475–1584, WEB www.courier.org). **Now Voyager Travel** (☎ 212/431–1616).

ENJOYING THE FLIGHT

State your seat preference when purchasing your ticket, and then repeat it when you confirm and when you check in. For more legroom, you can request one of the few emergency-aisle seats at check-in, if you are capable of lifting at least 50 pounds—a Federal Aviation Administration requirement of passengers in these seats. Seats behind a bulkhead also offer more legroom, but they don't have under-seat storage. Don't sit in the row in front of the emergency aisle or in front of a bulkhead, where seats may not recline.

If you have dietary concerns, **ask for special meals when booking.** These can be vegetarian, low-cholesterol, or kosher, for example. It's a good idea to pack some healthy snacks and a small (plastic) bottle of water in your carry-on bag. On long flights, try to maintain a normal routine, to help fight jet lag. At night, **get some sleep.** By day, **eat light meals, drink water** (not alcohol), and **move around the cabin** to stretch your legs. For additional jet-lag tips consult *Fodor's FYI: Travel Fit & Healthy* (available at bookstores everywhere).

Smoking policies vary from carrier to carrier. Many airlines prohibit smoking on all of their international flights; others allow smoking only on certain routes or certain departures. Ask your carrier about its policy.

FLYING TIMES

Flying time to Frankfurt is 1½ hours from London, 7½ hours from New York, 10 hours from Chicago, and 12 hours from Los Angeles.

HOW TO COMPLAIN

If your baggage goes astray or your flight goes awry, complain right away. Most carriers require that you **file a**

claim immediately. The Aviation Consumer Protection Division of the Department of Transportation publishes *Fly-Rights,* which discusses airlines and consumer issues and is available on-line. At PassengerRights.com, a Web site, you can compose a letter of complaint and distribute it electronically.

➤ AIRLINE COMPLAINTS: **Aviation Consumer Protection Division** (✉ U.S. Department of Transportation, Room 4107, C-75, Washington, DC 20590, ☎ 202/366–2220, WEB www.dot.gov/airconsumer). **Federal Aviation Administration Consumer Hotline** (☎ 800/322–7873).

RECONFIRMING

Check the status of your flight before you leave for the airport. You can do this on your carrier's Web site, by linking to a flight-status checker (many Web booking services offer these), or by calling your carrier or travel agent. Always confirm international flights at least 72 hours ahead of the scheduled departure time.

AIRPORTS

Frankfurt is Germany's air hub, with nonstop flights connecting its airport to New York, Washington, Boston, Philadelphia, Atlanta, Miami, Chicago, Detroit, Denver, Houston, Dallas/Fort Worth, Phoenix, San Francisco, Los Angeles, Toronto, and Vancouver. There are also a few direct connections from North America to Munich and Düsseldorf, but none to Berlin. The Frankfurt airport has the convenience of its own long-distance train station.

➤ AIRPORT INFORMATION: Berlin: **Flughafen Tegel (TXL), Tempelhof (THF), Schönefeld (SXF)** (☎ 0180/500–0186, WEB www.berlin-airport.de). Düsseldorf: **Flughafen Düsseldorf** (DUS, ☎ 0211/421–2223, WEB www.duesseldorf-international.de). Frankfurt: **Flughafen Frankfurt Main** (FRA, ☎ 069/6900, WEB www.frankfurt-airport.de). Hamburg: **Fuhlsbüttel International Airport** (HAM, ☎ 040/50750, WEB www.ham.airport.de). Köln: **Flughafen Köln/Bonn** (CGN, ☎ 02203/404–001, WEB www.airport-cgn.de). Munich: **Flughafen München** (MUC, ☎ 089/97500, WEB www.munich-airport.de).

BIKES IN FLIGHT

Most airlines accommodate bikes as luggage, provided they are dismantled and boxed; check with individual airlines about packing requirements. Airlines sell bike boxes, which are often free at bike shops, for about $15 (bike bags start at $100). International travelers often can substitute a bike for a piece of checked luggage at no charge; otherwise, the cost is about $100. Domestic and Canadian airlines charge $40–$80 each way.

DUTY-FREE SHOPPING

You can purchase duty-free goods when traveling between any EU country, such as Germany, and a non-EU country. The big sellers at duty-free (also called tax-free) shops are perfumes and cosmetics, liquor, tobacco products, and chocolates.

BOAT AND FERRY TRAVEL

Eurailpasses and German Rail Passes (☞ Train Travel) are valid on all Rhine River services of the Köln-Düsseldorfer Deutsche Rheinschiffahrt (KD Rhine Line) and on the Mosel River between Trier and Koblenz (if you use the fast hydrofoil, a supplementary fee is required). The railroad follows the Rhine and Mosel rivers most of their length, meaning you can go one way by ship and return by train. Cruises generally operate between April and October (☞ Cruise Travel).

The MS *Admiral of Scandinavia* carries passengers and cars three times a week for the 19½-hour run between Hamburg and Harwich, England.

➤ CAR FERRY: **MS *Admiral of Scandinavia,*** DFDS Seaways (☎ 040/389–0371).

BUSINESS HOURS

Catholicism gives Bavaria more religious holidays than the other states of Germany. Otherwise, business hours are consistent throughout the country. Many visitor information offices close by 4 during the week and might not be open on weekends.

BANKS AND OFFICES

Banks are generally open weekdays from 8:30 or 9 to 3 or 4 (5 or 6 on Thursday), sometimes with a lunch break of about an hour at smaller branches. Banks at airports and main train stations open as early as 6:30 AM and close as late as 10:30 PM. *See* Mail and Shipping, for post office hours.

GAS STATIONS

Along the autobahn and major highways, gas stations and their small convenience shops are often open late, if not around the clock.

MUSEUMS AND SIGHTS

Most museums are open from Tuesday to Sunday 10–5. Some close for an hour or more at lunch. Many stay open until 8 or 9 on Wednesday or Thursday.

PHARMACIES

Most pharmacies are open 9–6 weekdays and 9–1 on Saturday. Those in more prominent locations often open an hour earlier and/or close an hour later. A list of pharmacies in the vicinity that are open late or on Sunday is posted on the door.

SHOPS

Department stores and larger stores are generally open from 9 or 9:30 to 8 weekdays and until 4 on Saturday. Smaller shops and some department stores in smaller towns close at 6 or 6:30 on weekdays and as early as 1 on Saturday. Visit a department store in the morning or early afternoon to avoid crowds. Shops in train stations are allowed to stay open later during the week and to open on Sunday.

BUS TRAVEL

Germany has good local bus service but no proper nationwide network. A large portion of services is operated by Deutsche Touring, a subsidiary of the railroad that has offices and agents country-wide. Rail tickets are valid on its lines. Regional lines coordinate with the railroad to reach remote places.

One of the best services is the Romantic Road bus between Würzburg (with connections to and from Frankfurt) and Füssen (with connections to and from Munich, Augsburg, and Garmisch-Partenkirchen). Buses, with an attendant on board, offer one- or two-day tours in each direction in summer, leaving in the morning and arriving in the evening. Eurailpasses and German Rail Passes (☞ Train Travel) are good on this and other Deutsche Touring scenic routes.

All towns of any size have local buses, which often link up with trams (streetcars) and electric railway (S-bahn) and subway (U-bahn) services. Fares vary according to distance, but a ticket usually allows you to transfer freely between the various forms of transportation. Most cities issue 24-hour tickets at special rates.

There is direct service from London's Victoria Coach Station to some 50 German cities. Many departures are daily, some three times a week. Some go via the Channel Tunnel and some still take the ferry. However, there is no difference in fare and little difference in the time the trip takes. Times from London are: Cologne (12 hours), Frankfurt (13 hours), Stuttgart/Nürnberg (17 hours), and Munich (20 hours).

➤ INTERCITY BUSES: **Deutsche Touring** (✉ Am Römerhof 17, D–60486 Frankfurt/Main, ☎ 069/790–350, FAX 069/790–3219, WEB www.deutsche-touring.com).

➤ FROM THE U.K.: **Eurolines** (☎ 0990/143–219).

CAMERAS AND PHOTOGRAPHY

German law protects the right of individuals not to be photographed against their will; this only applies to situations in which individuals are recognizable, not to landscapes or photographs of groups of people. The cost of film varies greatly according to the brand and where you shop. A 36-exposure roll of ASA color film, for example, can cost anywhere from €3 to €6. You can save at least 50% on developing costs by choosing an overnight service at a drugstore such as Schlecker or Drospa. The *Kodak Guide to Shooting Great Travel Pictures* (available at bookstores everywhere) is loaded with tips.

➤ PHOTO HELP: **Kodak Information Center** (☎ 800/242–2424, WEB www.kodak.com).

EQUIPMENT PRECAUTIONS

Don't pack film and equipment in checked luggage, where it is much more susceptible to damage. X-ray machines used to view checked luggage are becoming much more powerful and therefore are much more likely to ruin your film. Try to **ask for hand inspection of film,** which becomes clouded after repeated exposure to airport X-ray machines, and **keep videotapes and computer disks away from metal detectors.** Always **keep film, tape, and computer disks out of the sun.** Carry an extra supply of batteries, and **be prepared to turn on your camera, camcorder, or laptop** to prove to airport security personnel that the device is real.

VIDEOS

The German standard for video is VHS–PAL, which is not compatible with the U.S. VHS–NTSC standard.

CAR RENTAL

Rates with the major car-rental companies begin at about €75 per day and €300 per week, including value-added tax, for an economy car with a manual transmission and unlimited mileage. Volkswagen, Opel, and Mercedes are some standard brands of rentals; most rentals are manual, so if you want an automatic, be sure to **request one in advance.** If you're traveling with children, don't forget to **arrange for a car seat** when you reserve.

➤ MAJOR AGENCIES: **Alamo** (☎ 800/522–9696; 0800/181–9226 in Germany; WEB www.alamo.com). **Avis** (☎ 800/331–1084; 800/879–2847 in Canada; 02/9353–9000 in Australia; 09/526–2847 in New Zealand; 0870/606–0100 in the U.K.; 0180/555–7755 in Germany; WEB www.avis.com). **Budget** (☎ 800/527–0700; 0870/156–5656 in the U.K.; 01805/244–388; WEB www.budget.com). **Dollar** (☎ 800/800–6000; 0124/622–0111 in the U.K., where it's affiliated with Sixt; 02/9223–1444 in Australia; WEB www.dollar.com). **Hertz** (☎ 800/654–3001; 800/263–0600 in Canada; 020/8897–2072 in the U.K.; 02/9669–2444 in Australia; 09/256–8690 in New Zealand; 01805/333–535 in Germany; WEB www.hertz.com). **National Car Rental** (☎ 800/227–7368; 020/8680–4800 in the U.K.; 0180/580–000 in Germany, where it is also known as Europcar InterRent; WEB www.nationalcar.com).

CUTTING COSTS

For a good deal, **book through a travel agent who will shop around.**

Do **look into wholesalers,** companies that do not own fleets but rent in bulk from those that do and often offer better rates than traditional car-rental operations. Prices are best during off-peak periods. Rentals booked through wholesalers often must be paid for before you leave home.

➤ LOCAL AGENCIES: **Sixt** (☎ 01805/252–525).

➤ WHOLESALERS: **Auto Europe** (☎ 207/842–2000 or 800/223–5555, FAX 207/842–2222, WEB www.autoeurope.com). **Europe by Car** (☎ 212/581–3040 or 800/223–1516, FAX 212/246–1458, WEB www.europebycar.com). **Destination Europe Resources** (DER; ✉ 9501 W. Devon Ave., Rosemont, IL 60018, ☎ 800/782–2424, WEB www.der.com). **Kemwel** (☎ 800/678–0678 or 800/576–1590, FAX 207/842–2124, WEB www.kemwel.com).

INSURANCE

When driving a rented car you are generally responsible for any damage to or loss of the vehicle. Collision policies that car-rental companies sell for European rentals typically do not cover stolen vehicles. Before you rent—and purchase collision or theft coverage—see what coverage you already have under the terms of your personal auto-insurance policy and credit cards.

REQUIREMENTS AND RESTRICTIONS

In Germany your own driver's license is acceptable, but an International Driver's Permit is a good idea; it's available from the American or Canadian automobile association and, in the United Kingdom, from the Automobile Association or Royal Automobile Club. These international permits are universally recognized, and having one in your wallet may save you a problem with the local authorities. In Germany you usually must be 21 to rent a car. Nearly all agencies will allow you to drive the car to Germany's neighboring countries, and it's frequently possible to return the car in another West European neighbor. East European neighbors, like Poland and the Czech Republic, are more of a problem. You can usually drive to them, but it's rarely possible to return there.

SURCHARGES

Before you pick up a car in one city and leave it in another, **ask about drop-off charges or one-way service fees,** which can be substantial. Note, too, that some rental agencies charge extra if you return the car before the time specified in your contract. To avoid a hefty refueling fee, **fill the tank just before you turn in the car,** but be aware that gas stations near the rental outlet may overcharge. It's almost never a deal to buy the tank of gas in the car when you rent it; the understanding is that you'll return it empty, but some fuel usually remains.

CAR TRAVEL

Entry formalities for motorists are few: all you need is proof of insurance, an international car-registration document, and a U.S., Canadian, Australian, or New Zealand driver's license. If you or your car are from an EU country, Norway, or Switzerland, all you need is your domestic license and proof of insurance. *All* foreign cars must have a country sticker. There are three principal automobile clubs in Germany that provide roadside assistance.

➤ AUTO CLUBS: ADAC (Allgemeiner Deutscher Automobil-Club; ✉ Am Westpark 8, D–81373 Munich, ☎ 089/76760, FAX 089/7676–2801, WEB www.adac.de). ACE (✉ Schmidener Str. 233, D–70374 Stuttgart, ☎ 0711/53030, FAX 0711/5303–288, WEB www.ace-online.de). AvD (Automobilclub von Deutschland; ✉ Lyonerstr. 16, D–60528 Frankfurt, ☎ 069/66060, FAX 069/660–6260, WEB www.avd.de).

EMERGENCY SERVICES

ADAC and AvD (☞ Auto Clubs) operate tow trucks on all autobahns; they also have emergency telephones every 2 km (1 mi). On minor roads **go to the nearest call box and dial 01802/222–222** (if you have a mobile phone, just dial 222–222). Ask, in English, for road-service assistance. Help is free (with the exception of materials) if the work is carried out by the ADAC. If the ADAC has to use a subcontractor for the work, charges are made for time, mileage, and materials.

GASOLINE

Gasoline (petrol) costs are slightly below €1 per liter—which is higher than in the United States. Most German cars run on lead-free fuel. Some models use diesel fuel, so if you are renting a car, **find out which fuel the car takes.** Some older vehicles cannot take unleaded fuel. German filling stations are highly competitive, and bargains are often available if you shop around, but *not* at autobahn filling stations. Self-service, or *SB-Tanken,* stations are cheapest. Pumps marked *Bleifrei* contain unleaded gas.

PARKING

Daytime parking in cities is very difficult. Parking restrictions are not always clearly marked and can be hard to understand when they are. Larger parking lots have parking meters (*Parkautomaten*). After depositing enough change in a meter, you will be issued a timed ticket to display on your dashboard. Parking-meter spaces are free at night. In German garages you must **pay immediately on returning to retrieve your car,** not when driving out. Put the ticket you got on arrival into the machine and pay the amount displayed. Retrieve the ticket, go to your car, and upon exiting, insert the ticket in a slot to get the barrier raised.

ROAD CONDITIONS

Roads in both the western and eastern part of the country are generally excellent. *Bundesstrasse* are two-lane highways, abbreviated "B," as in B–38. Autobahns are high-speed thruways abbreviated with "A," as in A–7.

ROAD MAPS

The best-known road maps of Germany are put out by the automobile club ADAC, by Shell, and by the Falk Verlag. They're available at gas stations and bookstores.

RULES OF THE ROAD

Germans **drive on the right,** and road signs give distances in kilometers. There *are* posted speed limits on autobahns, and drivers are advised to keep below 130 kph (80 mph). Speed limits on country roads vary from 80 kph to 100 kph (50 mph to 60 mph). Alcohol limits on drivers are equivalent to two small beers or a quarter of a liter of wine (blood-alcohol level .05%). Note that **seat belts must be worn at all times by front- *and* back-seat passengers.** Passing is permitted on the left side only. Headlights, not parking lights, are required during inclement weather. Don't enter streets with signposts bearing a red circle with a white horizontal stripe—they are one-way streets. The blue sign *EINBAHNSTRASSE* (one-way) indicates you have the right of way. A right turn on a red light is permitted only if there is also a green arrow.

SCENIC ROUTES

Germany has many specially designated tourist roads. The longest is the *Deutsche Ferienstrasse*, the German Holiday Road, which runs from the Baltic to the Alps, a distance of around 1,720 km (1,070 mi). The most famous, however, is the *Romantische Strasse* (the Romantic Road, ☞ Chapter 5), which runs from Würzburg to Füssen in the Alps, covering around 355 km (220 mi).

Among other notable touring routes are the *Strasse der Kaiser und Könige* (Route of Emperors and Kings), running from Frankfurt to Passau (and on to Vienna and Budapest); the *Burgenstrasse* (Castle Road), running from Mannheim to Bayreuth; the *Deutsche Weinstrasse* (German Wine Road, ☞ Chapter 11), running through the Palatinate wine country; and the *Deutsche Alpenstrasse* (German Alpine Road, ☞ Chapter 3), running the length of the country's Alpine southern border from near Berchtesgaden to Bodensee. Less well-known routes are the *Märchenstrasse* (Fairy-tale Road, ☞ Chapter 13), the *Weser Renaissance Strasse,* and the *Deutsche Fachwerkstrasse* (German Half-Timber Road).

CHILDREN IN GERMANY

Almost every city in Germany has its own children's theater, and the country's puppet theaters rank among the best in the world. Playgrounds are around virtually every corner, and there are about a half-dozen major theme parks around the country. Many tourist offices have booklets for younger visitors. For general advice about traveling with children, consult *Fodor's FYI: Travel with Your Baby* (available in bookstores everywhere).

BABY-SITTING

For recommended local sitters, **check with your hotel desk.** Updated lists of well-screened baby-sitters are also available from most local tourist offices. Rates are usually between €8 and €13 per hour. Many large department stores in Germany provide baby-sitting facilities or areas where children can play while their parents shop.

FLYING

If your children are two or older, **ask about children's airfares.** As a general rule, infants under two not occupying a seat fly at greatly reduced fares or even for free. When booking, **confirm carry-on allowances** if you're traveling with infants. In general, for babies charged 10% of the adult fare you are allowed one carry-on bag and a collapsible stroller; if the flight is full, the stroller may have to be checked or you may be limited to less.

Experts agree that it's a good idea to use safety seats aloft for children weighing less than 40 pounds. Airlines set their own policies: U.S. carriers usually require that the child be ticketed, even if he or she is young enough to ride free, since the seats must be strapped into regular seats. Do **check your airline's policy about using safety seats during takeoff and landing.** Safety seats are not allowed everywhere in the plane, so get your seat assignments as early as possible.

When reserving, **request children's meals or a freestanding bassinet** (not available at all airlines) if you need them. But note that bulkhead seats, where you must sit to use the bassinet, may lack an overhead bin or storage space on the floor.

LODGING

Many hotels in Germany allow children under three to stay in their parents' room at no extra charge. Beyond that age they may be charged half price or even be considered extra adults; be sure to **find out if the cutoff age applies.**

SIGHTS AND ATTRACTIONS

Places that are especially appealing to children are indicated by a rubber-duckie icon (🐤) in the margin.

SUPPLIES AND EQUIPMENT

Supermarkets and drugstores (not pharmacies) carry disposable diapers (*Windeln*). Baby formula is available in powder form and comes in two types: *Anfangsmilch/nahrung* is labeled with a big number 1, and is suitable for infants ages 0–4 months; *Folgemilch/nahrung* is labeled with a big number 2 and is suitable for infants from 4 months. *Dauermilch/nahrung* is suitable for all ages. Coloring books (*Malbücher*) and crayons (*Buntstifte*) are widely available, as is modeling clay (*Knetmasse*).

COMPUTERS ON THE ROAD

Larger German hotels now have Internet centers from which, for a fee, you can call up a Web site or send an e-mail message. There are also cyber-cafés in the cities, at which you can go on-line, either with their equipment or your own laptop. To access a phone line in your hotel room, buy a German standard adaptor, available at many stores. Most notebooks with a modem or single modems will have a plug-in to match the German Telekom socket. If you're plugging into a phone line, you'll need a local access number for a connection.

➤ ACCESS NUMBERS: **AOL** (☎ 01914). **CompuServe** (☎ 01033–019–160).

CONSUMER PROTECTION

Whether you're shopping for gifts or purchasing travel services, **pay with a major credit card** whenever possible, so you can cancel payment or get reimbursed if there's a problem (and you can provide documentation). If you're doing business with a particular company for the first time, **contact your local Better Business Bureau and the attorney general's offices** in your state and (for U.S. businesses) the company's home state as well. Have any complaints been filed? Finally, if you're buying a package or tour, always **consider travel insurance** that includes default coverage (☞ Insurance).

➤ BBBs: **Council of Better Business Bureaus** (✉ 4200 Wilson Blvd., Suite 800, Arlington, VA 22203, ☎ 703/276–0100, FAX 703/525–8277, WEB www.bbb.org).

CRUISE TRAVEL

The Viking River Cruises company tours the Rhine, Main, Elbe, and Danube rivers, with 4- to 13-day itineraries. The cruises, especially on the Elbe and Danube, are in great demand, so **reserve several months in advance.** Köln–Düsseldorfer Deutsche Rheinschiffahrt (KD Rhine Line) offers trips of one day or less on the Rhine and Mosel. Between Easter and October there's Rhine service between Köln and Mainz, and Mosel service between Koblenz and Cochem.

To learn how to plan, choose, and book a cruise-ship voyage, consult *Fodor's FYI: Plan & Enjoy Your Cruise* (available in bookstores everywhere).

➤ CRUISE LINES: **KD Rhine Line** (✉ Frankenwerft 35, D–50667 Köln, ☎ 0221/208–8318, WEB www.k-d.com; in the U.S., JFO Cruise Service Corp., ✉ 2500 Westchester Ave., Purchase, NY 10577, ☎ 800/346–6525). **Viking River Cruises** (✉ Hohe Strasse 68–82, D–50667 Köln, ☎ 0221/25860, WEB www.vikingkd.com; in the U.S., ✉ 21820 Burbank Blvd., Los Angeles, CA 91367, ☎ 877/668–4546).

CUSTOMS AND DUTIES

When shopping abroad, **keep receipts** for all purchases. Upon reentering the country, **be ready to show customs officials what you've bought.** If you feel a duty is incorrect, appeal the assessment. If you object to the way your clearance was handled, note the inspector's badge number. In either case, first ask to see a supervisor. If the problem isn't resolved, write to the appropriate authorities, beginning with the port director at your point of entry.

IN AUSTRALIA

Australian residents who are 18 or older may bring home A$400 worth of souvenirs and gifts (including jewelry), 250 cigarettes or 250 grams of tobacco, and 1,125 ml of alcohol (including wine, beer, and spirits). Residents under 18 may bring back A$200 worth of goods. Prohibited items include meat products. Seeds, plants, and fruits need to be declared upon arrival.

➤ INFORMATION: **Australian Customs Service** (Regional Director, ✉ Box 8, Sydney, NSW 2001, ☎ 02/9213–2000 or 1300/363263, FAX 02/9213–4043, WEB www.customs.gov.au).

IN CANADA

Canadian residents who have been out of Canada for at least seven days may bring in C$750 worth of goods duty-free. If you've been away fewer than seven days but more than 48 hours, the duty-free allowance drops to C$200; if your trip lasts 24 to 48 hours, the allowance is C$50. You may not pool allowances with family members. Goods claimed under the C$750 exemption may follow you by mail; those claimed under the lesser exemptions must accompany you. Alcohol and tobacco products may be included in the seven-day and 48-hour exemptions but not in the 24-hour exemption. If you meet the age requirements of the province or territory through which you reenter Canada, you may bring in, duty-free, 1.5 liters of wine *or* 1.14 liters (40 imperial ounces) of liquor *or* 24 12-ounce cans or bottles of beer or ale. If you are 19 or older you may bring in, duty-free, 200 cigarettes and 50 cigars. Check ahead of time with the Canada Customs and Revenue Agency or the Department of Agriculture for policies regarding meat products, seeds, plants, and fruits.

You may send an unlimited number of gifts (only one gift per recipient, however) worth up to C$60 each duty-free to Canada. Label the package UNSOLICITED GIFT—VALUE UNDER $60. Alcohol and tobacco are excluded.

➤ INFORMATION: **Canada Customs and Revenue Agency** (✉ 2265 St. Laurent Blvd. S, Ottawa, Ontario K1G 4K3, ☎ 204/983–3500; 506/636–5064; 800/461–9999 in Canada, WEB www.ccra-adrc.gc.ca/).

IN GERMANY

Since a single, unrestricted market took effect within the European Union (EU) early in 1993, there have no longer been restrictions for persons traveling among the 15 EU countries. However, there are restrictions on what can be brought in without declaration. For example, if you have more than 800 cigarettes, 90 liters of wine, or 10 liters of alcohol, it is considered a commercial shipment and is taxed and otherwise treated as such.

For anyone entering Germany from outside the EU, the following limitations apply: (1) 200 cigarettes or 100 cigarillos or 50 cigars or 250 grams of tobacco; (2) 2 liters of still table wine; (3) 1 liter of spirits over 22% volume or 2 liters of spirits under 22% volume (fortified and sparkling wines) or 2 more liters of table wine; (4) 50 grams of perfume and 250 milliliters of toilet water; (5) 500 grams of roasted coffee or 200 grams of instant coffee; (6) other goods to the value of €175.

Tobacco and alcohol allowances are for visitors age 17 and over. Other items intended for personal use can be imported and exported freely. If you bring in cash, checks, securities, precious metals, or jewelry with a value of more than €15,000, you must tell the customs people where you got it and what you intend to do with it. This is a new measure for fighting money laundering.

If you have questions regarding customs or bringing a pet into the country, contact the Zoll-Infocenter, preferably by mail or e-mail.

➤ INFORMATION: **Zoll-Infocenter** (✉ Hansaallee 141, D–60320 Frankfurt am Main, ☎ 069/469976-00, FAX 069/469976-99, info@zoll-infocenter.de).

IN NEW ZEALAND

All homeward-bound residents may bring back NZ$700 worth of souvenirs and gifts; passengers may not pool their allowances, and children can claim only the concession on goods intended for their own use. For those 17 or older, the duty-free allowance also includes 4.5 liters of wine or beer; one 1,125-ml bottle of spirits; and either 200 cigarettes, 250 grams of tobacco, 50 cigars, *or* a combination of the three up to 250 grams. Meat products, seeds, plants, and fruits must be declared upon arrival to the Agricultural Services Department.

➤ INFORMATION: **New Zealand Customs** (✉ Head Office, The Customhouse, 17–21 Whitmore St., Box 2218, Wellington, ☎ 09/300–5399 or 0800/428–786, WEB www.customs.govt.nz).

IN THE U.K.

If you are a U.K. resident and your journey was wholly within the European Union, you probably won't have to pass through customs when you return to the United Kingdom. If you plan to bring back large quantities of alcohol or tobacco, check EU limits beforehand. In most cases, if you bring back more than 200 cigars, 800 cigarettes, 10 liters of spirits, and/or 90 liters of wine, you have to declare the goods upon return.

➤ INFORMATION: **HM Customs and Excise** (✉ Portcullis House, 21 Cowbridge Rd. E, Cardiff CF11 9SS, ☎ 029/2038–6423 or 0845/010–9000, WEB www.hmce.gov.uk).

IN THE U.S.

U.S. residents who have been out of the country for at least 48 hours may bring home, for personal use, $400 worth of foreign goods duty-free, as long as they haven't used the $400 allowance or any part of it in the past 30 days. This exemption may include 1 liter of alcohol (for travelers 21 and older), 200 cigarettes, and 100 non-Cuban cigars. Family members from the same household who are traveling together may pool their $400 personal exemptions. For fewer than 48 hours, the duty-free allowance drops to $200, which may include 50 cigarettes, 10 non-Cuban cigars, and 150 milliliters of alcohol (or perfume containing alcohol). The $200 allowance cannot be combined with other individuals' exemptions, and if you exceed it, the full value of all the goods will be taxed. Antiques, which the U.S. Customs Service defines as objects more than 100 years old, enter duty-free, as do original works of art done entirely by hand, including paintings, drawings, and sculptures.

You may also send packages home duty-free, with a limit of one parcel per addressee per day (except alcohol or tobacco products or perfume worth more than $5). You can mail up to $200 worth of goods for personal use; label the package PERSONAL USE and attach a list of its contents and their retail value. If the package contains your used personal belongings, mark it PERSONAL GOODS RETURNED to avoid paying duties. You may send up to $100 worth of goods as a gift; mark the package UNSOLICITED GIFT. Mailed items do not affect your duty-free allowance on your return.

➤ INFORMATION: **U.S. Customs Service** (for inquiries, ✉ 1300 Pennsylvania Ave. NW, Washington, DC 20229, WEB www.customs.gov, ☎ 202/354–1000; for complaints, ✉ Customer Satisfaction Unit, 1300 Pennsylvania Ave. NW, Room 5.5A, Washington, DC 20229; for registration of equipment, ✉ Office of Passenger Programs, 1300 Pennsylvania Ave. NW, Room 5.4D, Washington, DC 20229, ☎ 202/927–0530).

DINING

Almost every street of Germany has its *Gaststätte,* a sort of combination diner and pub, and every village its *Gasthof,* or inn. The emphasis in either is on *gutbürgerliche Küche,* or good home cooking—simple food at reasonable prices. A *Bierstube* (pub) or *Weinstube* (wine cellar) may also serve light snacks or meals. Italian restaurants are about the most popular of all ethnic restaurants in Germany.

Service can be slow, but you'll also never experience being rushed out of your seat. Something else that may seem jarring at first: people can, and do, join other parties at a table in a restaurant if seating is tight. It is common courtesy to ask first, though.

Regional specialties are given in the dining sections of individual chapters. The restaurants we list are the cream of the crop in each price category. Properties indicated by a ✕🏨 are lodging establishments whose restaurant is recommendable.

BUDGET EATING TIPS

Imbiss (snack) stands can be found in almost every busy shopping street, in parking lots, train stations, and near markets. They serve *Würste* (sausages), grilled, roasted, or boiled, and rolls filled with cheese, cold meat, or fish. Prices range from €1.50 to €2.50 per portion. It's acceptable to bring sandwich fixings to a beer garden and order a beer there.

Butcher shops, known as *Metzgerei,* often serve warm snacks. Try *Warmer Leberkäs mit Kartoffelsalat,* a typical Bavarian specialty, which is a sort of baked meat loaf with sweet mustard and potato salad. In northern Germany try *Bouletten,* small meatballs, or *Currywurst,* sausages in a piquant curry sauce.

Restaurants in department stores are especially recommended for wholesome, appetizing, and inexpensive lunches. Kaufhof, Karstadt, and Horton are names to note. Germany's vast selection of Turkish, Italian, Greek, Chinese, and Balkan restaurants are often inexpensive.

MEALS AND SPECIALTIES

Most hotels serve a buffet-style breakfast (*Frühstück*) of rolls, cheese, cold cuts, eggs, cereals, yogurt, and spreads, which is often included in the price of a room. Cafés offer a similar choice, accompanied by coffee, tea, or *Milchkaffee*—a milky coffee that is rarely available at other times of the day.

Lunch (*Mittagessen*) is generally light. You can get sandwiches from most cafés and from bakeries, and many restaurants have special lunch menus that are often cheaper than in the evenings.

Dinner (*Abendessen*) is usually an à la carte affair. A substantial salad often comes with the main dish.

MEALTIMES

Gaststätte normally serve hot meals from 11:30 AM to 9 PM; many places stop serving hot meals between 2 PM and 6 PM, although you can still order cold dishes. Unless otherwise noted, the restaurants listed in this guide are open daily for lunch and dinner.

PAYING

You will need to call for the bill in order to get it from the waiter, the idea being that the table is yours for the evening. Credit cards are generally accepted only in moderate to expensive restaurants, so check first before sitting down.

RATINGS

The restaurants in our listings are divided by price (representing the average cost of a dinner entrée) into four categories: $$$$, $$$, $$, and $. Nearly all restaurants display their menus, with prices, outside; all prices shown will include tax and service charge. Prices for wine also include tax and service charge.

RESERVATIONS AND DRESS

Reservations are always a good idea; we mention them only when they're essential or not accepted. Book as far ahead as you can, and reconfirm as soon as you arrive. (Large parties should always call ahead to check the reservations policy.) We mention dress only when men are required to wear a jacket or a jacket and tie.

Note, though, that even when Germans dress casual, the look is generally crisp and neat.

SMOKING

Non-smoking sections in restaurants are almost unheard of, although in summer, this problem is alleviated by the fact that many restaurants have outdoor seating.

WINE, BEER, AND SPIRITS

Chapter 11, which follows the German Wine Road, and Chapter 12, which covers the Rhine and Mosel valleys, have the most information regarding wines and wine estates. The German Wine Information Bureau (GWIB) promotes the wines of all 13 German wine regions and can supply you with general background information and such invaluable free brochures as the German wine festivals schedule and *Vintners to Visit* (a roster of visitor-friendly wineries).

➤ WINE INFORMATION: **German Wine Information Bureau** (✉ 245 Park Ave., 39th floor, New York, NY 10167, ☎ 212/792–4134, FAX 212/792–4001, WEB www.Germanwineusa.org). **Deutsche Wein Institut** (✉ Gutenbergpl. 3–5, 55116 Mainz, ☎ 06131/282–933, WEB www.deutscheweine.de).

DISABILITIES AND ACCESSIBILITY

Many cities and towns issue special guides for visitors with disabilities, which offer information, usually in German, about how to get around destinations and suggestions for places to visit.

LODGING

All the major hotel chains (Hilton, Sheraton, Marriott, Holiday Inn, Steigenberger, and Kempinski) have special facilities for guests with disabilities. Some leading privately owned hotels also cater to travelers with disabilities; local tourist offices can provide lists of these hotels and additional information.

RESERVATIONS

When discussing accessibility with an operator or reservations agent, **ask hard questions.** Are there any stairs, inside *or* out? Are there grab bars next to the toilet *and* in the shower/tub? How wide is the doorway to the room? To the bathroom? For the most extensive facilities meeting the latest legal specifications, **opt for newer accommodations.** If you reserve through a toll-free number, consider also calling the hotel's local number to confirm the information from the central reservations office. Get confirmation in writing when you can.

TRAIN TRAVEL

The Deutsche Bahn (☞ Train Travel) provides a complete range of services and facilities for travelers with disabilities. All InterCity Express (ICE) and InterRegio trains and most EuroCity and InterCity trains have special areas and toilets for wheelchair users, and the larger stations have a portable device for lifting wheelchairs aboard. Reservations for wheelchair users are free of charge. A service called the Bahnhofs-Mission (Railway Station Mission) has support facilities at all major and many smaller regional stations. It assists with boarding, leaving, and changing trains and also helps with reservations. Local trams and buses are also becoming more disability-conscious, with sections that can accommodate a wheelchair and entrances that are, if not flush with the platform, at least quite low to the ground.

Deutsche Bahn issues a booklet, with an English section, detailing its services. For access to train platforms that are not wheelchair accessible, **call Deutsche Bahn's 24-hour hot line three working days before your trip.** The German Railroad's ReisePacket Komfort (☞ Train Travel) may also be of interest.

➤ COMPLAINTS: **Aviation Consumer Protection Division** (☞ Air Travel) for airline-related problems. **Departmental Office of Civil Rights** (for general inquiries, ✉ U.S. Department of Transportation, S-30, 400 7th St. SW, Room 10215, Washington, DC 20590, ☎ 202/366–4648, FAX 202/366–3571, WEB www.dot.gov/ost/docr/index.htm). **Disability Rights Section** (✉ U.S. Department of Justice, Civil Rights Division, Box 66738, Washington, DC 20035-6738, ☎ 202/514–0301 or 800/514–0301, for ADA inquiries; WEB www.usdoj.gov/crt/ada/adahom1.htm).

➤ HOT LINE: **Deutsche Bahn** (☎ 01805/996–633).

TRAVEL AGENCIES

In the United States, the Americans with Disabilities Act requires that travel firms serve the needs of all travelers. Some agencies specialize in working with people with disabilities.

➤ TRAVELERS WITH MOBILITY PROBLEMS: **Access Adventures** (✉ 206 Chestnut Ridge Rd., Scottsville, NY 14624, ☎ 716/889–9096, dltravel@prodigy.net), run by a former physical-rehabilitation counselor. **Care Vacations** (✉ No. 5, 5110–50 Ave., Leduc, Alberta T9E 6V4, Canada, ☎ 780/986–6404 or 877/478–7827, FAX 780/986–8332, WEB www.carevacations.com), for group tours and cruise vacations. **Flying Wheels Travel** (✉ 143 W. Bridge St., Box 382, Owatonna, MN 55060, ☎ 507/451–5005, FAX 507/451–1685, WEB www.flyingwheelstravel.com).

DISCOUNTS AND DEALS

Be a smart shopper and **compare all your options** before making decisions. A plane ticket bought with a promotional coupon from travel clubs, coupon books, and direct-mail offers or purchased on the Internet may not be cheaper than the least expensive fare from a discount ticket agency. And always keep in mind that what you get is just as important as what you save.

Several German cities sell discount passes that grant free or reduced admission to major attractions and discounts on public transportation. The passes are usually available at tourist offices or participating museums.

DISCOUNT RESERVATIONS

To save money, **look into discount reservations services** with Web sites and toll-free numbers, which use their buying power to get a better price on hotels, airline tickets, even car rentals.

When booking a room, always **call the hotel's local toll-free number** (if one is available) rather than the central reservations number—you'll often get a better price. Always ask about special packages or corporate rates.

When shopping for the best deal on hotels and car rentals, **look for guaranteed exchange rates,** which protect you against a falling dollar. With your rate locked in, you won't pay more, even if the price goes up in the local currency.

➤ AIRLINE TICKETS: ☎ **800/AIR-4LESS.**

➤ HOTEL ROOMS: **International Marketing & Travel Concepts** (☎ 800/ 790–4682, WEB www.imtc-travel.com). **Steigenberger Reservation Service** (☎ 800/223–5652, WEB www.srs-worldhotels.com). **Travel Interlink** (☎ 800/888–5898, WEB www.travelinterlink.com). **Turbotrip.com** (☎ 800/473–7829, WEB www.turbotrip.com).

PACKAGE DEALS

Don't confuse packages and guided tours. When you buy a package, you travel on your own, just as though you had planned the trip yourself. Fly/drive packages, which combine airfare and car rental, are often a good deal. If you **buy a rail/drive pass,** you may save on train tickets and car rentals. All Eurail- and Europass holders get a discount on Eurostar fares through the Channel Tunnel. A German Rail Pass is also good for travel aboard some KD German Rhine Line steamers and includes discounts on some Deutsche Touring/Europabus routes.

ELECTRICITY

To use electric-powered equipment purchased in the United States or Canada, **bring a converter and adapter.** The electrical current in Germany is 220 volts, 50 cycles alternating current (AC); wall outlets take Continental-type plugs, with two round prongs.

If your appliances are dual-voltage, you'll need only an adapter. Most laptops operate equally well on 110 and 220 volts and so require only an adapter.

EMBASSIES

➤ AUSTRALIA: ✉ Friedrichstr. 200, Berlin, ☎ 030/880–0880, WEB www.australian-embassy.de.

➤ CANADA: ✉ Friedrichstr. 95, Berlin, ☎ 030/213–120, WEB www.canada.de.

➤ IRELAND: ✉ Friedrichstr. 200, Berlin, ☎ 030/220–720.

➤ NEW ZEALAND: ✉ Friedrichstr. 60, Berlin, ☎ 030/206–210, WEB www.nzembassy.com.

➤ SOUTH AFRICA: ✉ Friedrichstr. 60, Berlin, ☎ 030/220–730, WEB www.suedafrika.org.

➤ UNITED KINGDOM: ✉ Wilhelmstr. 70–71, Berlin, ☎ 030/204–570, WEB www.britischebotschaft.de.

➤ UNITED STATES: ✉ Neustädtische Kirchstr. 4–5, Berlin, ☎ 030/83050, WEB www.us-botschaft.de.

EMERGENCIES

Throughout Germany call ☎ 110 for police, and ☎ 112 for an ambulance or the fire department.

ENGLISH-LANGUAGE MEDIA

The *International Herald Tribune* is widely available at newsstands, as are such Americans publications as *USA Today, Time,* and *Newsweek,* and such British publications as the *Daily Mail, Daily Telegraph,* and *Times.* The international newsstands at main train stations and airports carry hundreds of English-language newspapers, magazines, and paperbacks.

RADIO AND TELEVISION

In Frankfurt, the American Forces Network presents American news, sports, and music. Its AM broadcast (primarily talk) is at 873; the FM signal (primarily music) is at 98.7. You can pick up the BBC World Service in Berlin at 90.2 FM, and local station Rock Star FM (at 87.9 FM) has regular news bulletins, current affairs reports, and music programs from American networks.

Most hotels have a range of American cable TV channels on offer including CNN, NBC, and MTV. BBC World broadcasts free.

ETIQUETTE AND BEHAVIOR

Being on time for appointments, even casual social ones, is very important. Germans are more formal in addressing each other than Americans. Always address acquaintances as Herr (Mr.) or Frau (Mrs.) plus their last name; do not call them by their first name unless invited to do so. The German language has an informal and formal pronoun for "you": Formal is "*Sie*," informal is "*du*." Even if adults are on a first-name basis with one another, they may still keep the *Sie* form between them. A handshake is expected upon meeting someone for the first time and is often customary when simply greeting acquaintances.

In restaurants, shops, and department stores, you are unlikely to be offered help unless you ask for it. The presumption is that you would prefer to be alone unless you indicate otherwise.

Germans are less formal when it comes to nudity: a sign that reads FREIKÖRPER or FKK indicates a park or beach allows nude sunbathing.

GAY AND LESBIAN TRAVEL

Though only a few of the German states have laws banning discrimination on the basis of sexual orientation, the German people are very tolerant.The law recognizes gay marriages and property rights, and it is unlikely that same-sex couples will have trouble at hotel front desks, even in rural areas.

➤ GAY- AND LESBIAN-FRIENDLY TRAVEL AGENCIES: **Different Roads Travel** (✉ 8383 Wilshire Blvd., Suite 902, Beverly Hills, CA 90211, ☎ 323/651–5557 or 800/429–8747, FAX 323/651–3678, lgernert@tzell.com). **Kennedy Travel** (✉ 314 Jericho Turnpike, Floral Park, NY 11001, ☎ 516/352–4888 or 800/237–7433, FAX 516/354–8849, WEB www.kennedytravel.com). **Now, Voyager** (✉ 4406 18th St., San Francisco, CA 94114, ☎ 415/626–1169 or 800/255–6951, FAX 415/626–8626, WEB www.nowvoyager.com). **Skylink Travel and Tour** (✉ 1006 Mendocino Ave., Santa Rosa, CA 95401, ☎ 707/546–9888 or 800/225–5759, FAX 707/546–9891, WEB www.skylinktravel.com), serving lesbian travelers.

GUIDEBOOKS

Plan well and you won't be sorry. Guidebooks are excellent tools—and you can take them with you. You may want to check out color-photo-illustrated *Fodor's Exploring Germany,* thorough on culture and history. Pocket-size *Citypack Berlin* and *Citypack Munich* include foldout maps. All are available at on-line retailers and bookstores everywhere.

HOLIDAYS

The following national holidays are observed in Germany: January 1; January 6 (Epiphany—Bavaria, Saxony-Anhalt, and Baden-Württemberg only); April 18 (Good Friday); April 21 (Easter Monday); May 1 (Workers' Day); May 29 (Ascension); June 9 (Pentecost Monday); June 19 (Corpus Christi, southern Germany only); August 15 (Assumption Day—Bavaria and Saarland only); October 3 (German Unity Day); November 1 (All Saints' Day—Baden-Württemberg, Bavaria, North Rhine-Westphalia, Rhineland-Pfalz and Saarland only); December 24–26 (Christmas).

INSURANCE

The most useful travel-insurance plan is a comprehensive policy that includes coverage for trip cancellation and interruption, default, trip delay, and medical expenses (with a waiver for pre-existing conditions).

Without insurance you will lose all or most of your money if you cancel your trip, regardless of the reason. Default insurance covers you if your tour operator, airline, or cruise line goes out of business. Trip-delay covers expenses that arise because of bad weather or mechanical delays. Study the fine print when comparing policies.

If you're traveling internationally, a key component of travel insurance is coverage for medical bills incurred if you get sick on the road. Such expenses are not generally covered by Medicare or private policies. U.K. residents can buy a travel-insurance policy valid for most vacations taken during the year in which it's purchased (but check pre-existing-condition coverage). British and Australian citizens need extra medical coverage when traveling overseas.

Always **buy travel policies directly from the insurance company**; if you buy them from a cruise line, airline, or tour operator that goes out of business you probably will not be covered for the agency or operator's default, a major risk. Before making any purchase, **review your existing health and home-owner's policies** to find what they cover away from home.

➤ TRAVEL INSURERS: In the U.S.: **Access America** (✉ 6600 W. Broad St., Richmond, VA 23230, ☎ 800/284–8300, FAX 804/673–1491 or 800/346–9265, WEB www.accessamerica.com). **Travel Guard International** (✉ 1145 Clark St., Stevens Point, WI 54481, ☎ 800/826–1300 or 715/345–0505, FAX 800/955–8785, WEB www.travelguard.com).

➤ INSURANCE INFORMATION: In the U.K.: **Association of British Insurers** (✉ 51 Gresham St., London EC2V 7HQ, ☎ 020/7600–3333, FAX 020/7696–8999, WEB www.abi.org.uk). In Canada: **RBC Travel Insurance** (✉ 6880 Financial Dr., Mississauga, Ontario L5N 7Y5, ☎ 905/791–8700 or 800/668–4342, FAX 905/813–4704, WEB www.rbcinsurance.com). In Australia: **Insurance Council of Australia** (✉ Level 3, 56 Pitt St., Sydney, NSW 2000, ☎ 02/9253–5100, FAX 02/9253–5111, WEB www.ica.com.au). In New Zealand: **Insurance Council of New Zealand** (✉ Level 7, 111–115 Customhouse Quay, Box 474, Wellington, ☎ 04/472–5230, FAX 04/473–3011, WEB www.icnz.org.nz).

LANGUAGE

English is spoken in most hotels, restaurants, airports, stations, museums, and other places of interest. However, English is not widely spoken in rural areas; this is especially true of the eastern part of Germany.

Unless you speak fluent German, you may find some of the regional dialects hard to follow, particularly in Saxony and Bavaria. However, most Germans can speak "high" or standard German.

LANGUAGES FOR TRAVELERS

Two word endings that appear frequently on vacation itineraries are *-burg*, and *-berg*. A Burg (*u* as in "burr") is a fortress; a Berg (*e* as in *ea* of "bear") is a mountain.

A phrase book and language-tape set can help get you started. *Fodor's German for Travelers* (available at bookstores everywhere) is excellent.

LODGING

The standards of German hotels are very high, down to the humblest inn. You can nearly always **expect courteous and polite service and clean and comfortable rooms.** In addition to hotels proper, the country has numerous *Gasthöfe* or *Gasthäuser*, which are country inns that serve food and also have rooms, and pensions, or *Fremdenheime* (guest houses). Most hotels have restaurants, but those listed as *Garni* provide breakfast only. At the lowest end of the scale are *Fremdenzimmer*, meaning simply "rooms," normally in private houses. (Look for the sign reading ZIMMER FREI or ZU VERMIETEN on a green background, meaning "to rent"; a red sign reading BESETZT means there are no vacancies.)

The hotels in our listings are divided by price into four categories: $$$$, $$$, $$, and $. The lodgings we list are the cream of the crop in each price category. Properties are assigned price categories based on the range from their least-expensive standard double room at high season (excluding holidays) to the most expensive. Properties marked ✕🏨 are lodging establishments whose restaurants are recommendable. We always list the facilities that are available—but we don't specify whether they cost extra. **Ask about breakfast and bathing facilities** when booking. A Continental breakfast is often included in the rate. All hotels listed have a private bath or shower unless otherwise noted.

Room rates are by no means inflexible and depend very much on supply and demand. You can save money by inquiring about reductions: many resort hotels offer substantial ones in winter, except in the Alps, where rates often rise then. Likewise, many $$$$ and $$$ hotels in cities cut their prices on weekends and when business is quiet. If you have booked and plan to arrive late, let the hotel know. And if you have to cancel a reservation, inform the hotel as soon as possible, otherwise you may be charged the full amount for the unused room.

Tourist offices will also make bookings for a nominal fee, but they may have difficulty doing so after 4 PM in high season and on weekends, so **don't wait until too late in the day to begin looking for your accommoda-**

tions. If you do get stuck, ask someone—like a mail carrier, police officer, or waiter, for example—for directions to a house renting a Fremdenzimmer or a Gasthof.

A list of more than 10,000 lodgings is available from the Deutsche Hotel- und Gastättenverband (DEHOGA). Regional and local tourist offices also have lists. Although there is no nationwide grading system for hotels in Germany, the DEHOGA's guide has one- to five-star ratings based on amenities offered.

➤ LODGING LISTINGS: **Deutsche Hotel- und Gastättenverband** (DEHOGA; ✉ An Weidendamm 1a, D–10117 Berlin, ☎ 030/7262–5200, FAX 030/7262–5242, WEB www.dehoga.de).

APARTMENT AND VILLA (OR HOUSE) RENTALS

If you want a home base that's roomy enough for a family and comes with cooking facilities, **consider a furnished rental.** These can save you money, especially if you're traveling with a group. Home-exchange directories sometimes list rentals as well as exchanges.

➤ INTERNATIONAL AGENTS: **Drawbridge to Europe** (✉ 98 Granite St., Ashland, OR 97520, ☎ 541/482–7778 or 888/268–1148, FAX 541/482–7779, WEB www.drawbridgetoeurope.com). **Interhome** (✉ 1990 N.E. 163rd St., Suite 110, N. Miami Beach, FL 33162, ☎ 305/940–2299 or 800/882–6864, FAX 305/940–2911, WEB www.interhome.com). **Villas International** (✉ 4340 Redwood Hwy., Suite D309, San Rafael, CA 94903, ☎ 415/499–9490 or 800/221–2260, FAX 415/499–9491, WEB www.villasintl.com).

CAMPING

Campsites are scattered across the length and breadth of Germany. The DCC, or German Camping Club, produces an annual listing of some 8,000 sites Europe-wide, of which some 5,500 are in Germany. It also lists a number of sites where you can rent trailers and mobile homes. Similarly, the German Automobile Association (ADAC) (☞ Car Travel) publishes a listing of campsites.

The majority of sites are open year-round, and most are crowded during high season. Prices at ordinary campsites range from around €10 to €25 for a car, tent, or trailer and two adults, though prices at fancier ones, with pools, sports facilities, and entertainment, can be considerably more. If you want to camp elsewhere, you must **get permission from the landowner beforehand;** ask the police if you can't track him or her down. Drivers of mobile homes may park for a limited time on roadsides and in autobahn parking-lot areas, but may not set up camping equipment there.

➤ CAMPSITES: **DCC** (German Camping Club; ✉ Mandlstr. 28, D–80802 Munich, ☎ 089/380–1420, FAX 089/334–737, WEB www.camping-club.de).

CASTLE-HOTELS

Germany's atmospheric castle-, or *Schloss,* hotels are all privately owned and run. The simpler ones may lack some amenities, but the majority combine four-star luxury with valuable antique furnishings, four-poster beds, stone passageways, and a baronial atmosphere. Some offer full resort facilities. Nearly all are in the countryside (☞ Chapters 9 and 12, in particular, have several castle-hotel reviews). The European Castle Hotels & Restaurant Association issues a brochure listing 74 European castle-hotels, of which 42 are in Germany. Euro-Connection also has a brochure listing about 26 castle-hotels in Germany, and can advise you on castle-hotel packages, including four- to six-night tours.

➤ CONTACTS: **Euro-Connection** (✉ 7500 212th St. SW, Suite 103, Edmonds, WA 98026, ☎ 800/645–3876, WEB www.euro-connection.com). **European Castle Hotels & Restaurants** (✉ Weinpalais, Postfach 1111, Deidesheim/Weinstr., D–67412 Germany, ☎ 06326/7000, FAX 06326/700–022, WEB www.european-castle.com).

FARM VACATIONS

Almost every regional tourist office has a brochure listing farms that offer bed-and-breakfasts, apartments, and entire farmhouses to rent ("Ferienhöfe"). Staying in such a rural setting is referred to as *Urlaub auf dem Bauernhof* (vacation down on the farm). The German Agricultural Association provides an illustrated brochure covering more than 1,500 inspected and graded farms, from the

Alps to the North Sea. It costs €10.50 whether in bookstores or postpaid.

➤ GERMAN AGRICULTURAL ASSOCIATION: **DLG Reisedienst, Agratour** (German Agricultural Association; ✉ Eschborner Landstr. 122, D–60489 Frankfurt/Main, ☎ 069/247–880, FAX 069/247–881–1466, WEB www.dlg.org).

HOME EXCHANGES

If you would like to exchange your home for someone else's, **join a home-exchange organization,** which will send you its updated listings of available exchanges for a year and will include your own listing in at least one of them. It's up to you to make specific arrangements.

➤ EXCHANGE CLUBS: **HomeLink International** (✉ Box 47747, Tampa, FL 33647, ☎ 813/975–9825 or 800/638–3841, FAX 813/910–8144, WEB www.homelink.org; $106 per year). **Intervac U.S.** (✉ Box 590504, San Francisco, CA 94159, ☎ 800/756–4663, FAX 415/435–7440, WEB www.intervacus.com; $93 yearly fee includes one catalog and on-line access).

HOSTELS

No matter what your age, you can **save on lodging costs by staying at hostels**—rates run €10–€13 for people under 27 and €13–€19 for those older (breakfast included). Accommodations can range from single-sex, dorm-style beds to rooms for couples and families. Germany's more than 600 *Jugendherbergen* (youth hostels) are among the most efficient and up-to-date in Europe, and many are in castles. There's an age limit of 27 in Bavaria; elsewhere, there are no age restrictions, though those under 20 take preference if space is limited. The DJH Service GmbH provides a complete list of German hostels and has information on regional offices around the country. Hostels must be reserved well in advance for midsummer, especially in eastern Germany. To book a hostel, you must call the particular lodging directly, and be a member of a national hosteling association or Hostelling International (HI).

Membership in any HI national hostel association, open to travelers of all ages, allows you to stay in HI-affiliated hostels at member rates; one-year membership is about $25 for adults (C$35 for a two-year minimum membership in Canada, £12.50 in the U.K., A$52 in Australia, and NZ$40 in New Zealand); hostels run about $10–$25 per night. Members have priority if the hostel is full; they're also eligible for discounts around the world, even on rail and bus travel in some countries.

➤ IN GERMANY: **DJH Service GmbH** (✉ D–32754 Detmold, ☎ 05231/74010, FAX 05231/740–149, WEB www.jugendherberge.de).

➤ ORGANIZATIONS: **Hostelling International—American Youth Hostels** (✉ 733 15th St. NW, Suite 840, Washington, DC 20005, ☎ 202/783–6161, FAX 202/783–6171, WEB www.hiayh.org). **Hostelling International—Canada** (✉ 400–205 Catherine St., Ottawa, Ontario K2P 1C3, ☎ 613/237–7884; 800/663–5777 in Canada, FAX 613/237–7868, WEB www.hihostels.ca). **Youth Hostel Association of England and Wales** (✉ Trevelyan House, 8 St. Stephen's Hill, St. Albans, Hertfordshire AL1 2DY, U.K., ☎ 0870/8708808, FAX 01727/844126, WEB www.yha.org.uk). **Youth Hostel Association Australia** (✉ 10 Mallett St., Camperdown, NSW 2050, ☎ 02/9565–1699, FAX 02/9565–1325, WEB www.yha.com.au). **Youth Hostels Association of New Zealand** (✉ Level 3, 193 Cashel St., Box 436, Christchurch, ☎ 03/379–9970, FAX 03/365–4476, WEB www.yha.org.nz).

HOTELS

Many major American hotel chains—Hilton, Sheraton, Holiday Inn, Best Western, Marriott—have hotels in German cities. European chains are similarly well represented.

Most hotels in Germany do not have air-conditioning, nor do they need it given the climate and the German style of building construction that uses thick walls and recessed windows to help keep the heat out. Smaller hotels do not provide much in terms of bathroom amenities. You may have to request a washcloth. Hotels often have no-smoking rooms or even no-smoking floors, so it's always worth asking for one when you reserve. Note that the beds in double rooms often consist of two twin mattresses placed side by side within a frame. When you arrive, if you don't like the room you're offered, ask to see another.

➤ RESERVATIONS: **Tourimus Service GmbH** (✉ Yorckstr. 23, D–79110 Freiburg im Breisgau, ☎ 0761/885–810, FAX 0761/885–8129, WEB www.tibs.de).

RESERVING A ROOM

Most hotels can process a letter or fax asking for a reservation in English, but here are sample phrases in German:

Sehr geehrte Damen und Herren! (Dear Sir/Madam,)

Ich möchte ein Doppelzimmer/ Zweibettzimmer mit Bad reservieren. (I would like to reserve a double/ twin room with bath.)

und zwar vom. bis. (from. until.; dates are written day/month/year.)

Ich hätte gern ein Zimmer auf der oberen Etage/auf der unteren Etage/ mit Ausblick/in ruhiger Lage. (I would like a room on a high floor/a low floor/with a view/a quiet room.)

Könnten Sie mir bitte weitere Informationen auf Englisch über Ihr Hotel zuschicken. (Please send me more information in English about your hotel.)

Mit freundlichen Grüssen, (Kind regards,).

➤ TOLL-FREE NUMBERS: **Best Western** (☎ 800/528–1234, WEB www.bestwestern.com). **Choice** (☎ 800/221–2222, WEB www.choicehotels.com). **Clarion** (☎ 800/252–7466, WEB www.clarionhotel.com). **Comfort Inn** (☎ 800/228–5150, WEB www.comfortinn.com). **Four Seasons** (☎ 800/332–3442, WEB www.fourseasons.com). **Hilton** (☎ 800/445–8667, WEB www.hilton.com). **Holiday Inn** (☎ 800/465–4329, WEB www.basshotels.com). **Hyatt Hotels & Resorts** (☎ 800/233–1234, WEB www.hyatt.com). **Inter-Continental** (☎ 800/327–0200, WEB www.interconti.com). **Kempinski Hotels & Resorts** (☎ 800/426–3135; 0800/868–588 in the U.K.; 00800/4263–1355 in Germany). **Marriott** (☎ 800/228–9290, WEB www.marriott.com). **Le Meridien** (☎ 800/543–4300, WEB www.lemeridien-hotels.com). **Nikko Hotels International** (☎ 800/645–5687, WEB www.nikkohotels.com). **Quality Inn** (☎ 800/228–5151, WEB www.qualityinn.com). **Radisson** (☎ 800/333–3333, WEB www.radisson.com). **Ramada** (☎ 800/228–2828; 800/854–7854 international reservations, WEB www.ramada.com or www.ramadahotels.com). **Renaissance Hotels & Resorts** (☎ 800/468–3571, WEB www.renaissancehotels.com/). **Ritz-Carlton** (☎ 800/241–3333, WEB www.ritzcarlton.com). **Sheraton** (☎ 800/325–3535, WEB www.starwood.com/sheraton). **Steigenberger** (☎ 800/223–5652, WEB www.srs-worldhotels.com). **Westin Hotels & Resorts** (☎ 800/228–3000, WEB www.starwood.com/westin).

ROMANTIK HOTELS

Among the most delightful places to stay—and eat—in Germany are the aptly named Romantik Hotels and Restaurants. The Romantik group has 204 establishments throughout Europe, with 92 in Germany. All are in atmospheric and historic buildings—a precondition of membership—and are personally run by the owners, with the emphasis on excellent food and service. Prices vary considerably but in general represent good value, particularly the special weekend and short-holiday rates. A three- or four-day stay, for example, with one main meal, is available at about €150–€250 per person. A detailed brochure listing all Romantik Hotels and Restaurants is available by mail.

➤ CONTACTS: **Romantik Hotels and Restaurants** (✉ Lyoner Stern, Hahnstr. 70, D–60528 Frankfurt/M, ☎ 069/661–2340, FAX 069/6612–3456, WEB www.romantikhotels.com). **Euro-Connection** (✉ 7500 212th St. SW, Suite 103, Edmonds, WA 98026, ☎ 800/645–3876, WEB www.euro-connection.com).

SPAS

Taking the waters in Germany, whether for curing the body or merely beautifying it, has been popular since Roman times. More than 300 health resorts, mostly equipped for hot mineral, mud, or brine treatments are set within pleasant country areas or historic communities. The word *Bad* before the name of a town usually means it's a spa destination.

There are four main groups of spas and health resorts: the mineral and moorland spas, where treatments are based on natural warm-water springs; those on the Baltic and North Sea coasts; hydropathic spas, which use an invigorating cold-water process developed during the 19th century; and climatic health resorts, usually in the mountains, which depend on their climates and fresh air for their health-giving properties.

Using saunas, steam baths, and other hot room facilities is done "without textiles" in Germany—in other words, naked. Wearing a bathing suit is frowned upon in a sauna and sometimes even prohibited. The average cost for three weeks of treatment is from €1,500 to €2,500. This includes board and lodging, doctors' fees, treatments, and tax.

➤ CONTACTS: **Deutsche Heilbäderverband** (German Health Resort and Spa Association; ✉ Postfach 190 147, D–53037 Bonn, ☎ 0228/201–200, FAX 0228/201–2041, WEB www.deutscher-heilbaederverband.de).

MAIL AND SHIPPING

Post offices (*Deutsche Post*) are recognizable by the postal symbol, a black bugle on a yellow background. Stamps (*Briefmarken*) can also be bought at some news agencies and souvenir shops. Letters take approximately 3–4 days to the United Kingdom, 7–8 days to the United States, and 7–10 days to Australia and New Zealand. Post offices are generally open weekdays 8–6, Saturday 8–1.

OVERNIGHT SERVICES

The Deutsche Post has an express international service that will deliver your letter or package the next day to countries within the EU, within 1–2 days to the United States, and slightly longer to Australia. A letter or package to the United States weighing less than 200 grams costs €48.57. You can drop off your mail at any post office, or it can be picked up for an extra fee. International carriers tend to be slightly cheaper (€35–€45 for the same letter) and provide more services.

➤ MAJOR SERVICES: **Deutsche Post Express International** (☎ 08105/2711, WEB www.deutschepost.de). **DHL** (☎ 0800/225–5345, WEB www.dhl.de). **FedEx** (☎ 0800/123–0800, WEB www.fedex.com). **UPS** (☎ 0800/822–6630, WEB www.ups.com).

POSTAL RATES

Airmail letters to the United States, Canada, Australia, and New Zealand cost €1.53; postcards, €1.02. All letters to the United Kingdom cost €.66; postcards, €.51.

RECEIVING MAIL

You can arrange to have mail sent to you in care of any German post office; **have the envelope marked "Postlagernd."** This service is free, and the mail will be held for 14 days. Or you can have mail sent to any American Express office in Germany. There's no charge to cardholders, holders of American Express traveler's checks, or anyone who has booked a vacation with American Express.

SHIPPING PARCELS

Most major stores that cater to tourists will also ship your purchases home. You should check your insurance for coverage of possible damage. The companies listed under ☞ Overnight Services also have international shipping services, although these are quite expensive.

MONEY MATTERS

Germany has an admirably high standard of living. Lots of things—gas, food, hotels, and trains, to name but a few—are more expensive than in the United States. A good way to budget is to visit lesser-known cities and towns. All along the Main and Neckar rivers, for example, are small towns as charming as, but significantly less expensive than, the likes of Rothenburg and Heidelberg. Wine lovers can explore the Pfalz and Rhine Terrace area's German Wine Road instead of the classic Rhine-Mosel tour.

The five states (Brandenburg, Mecklenburg-Vorpommern, Saxony, Saxony-Anhalt, and Thuringia) of the former East Germany still have a lower standard of living than does the former West Germany. Outside large cities, public transportation and dining are cheaper than in, say, the Black Forest or the Rhineland. Prices in leading hotels and restaurants in Dresden and Leipzig match rates in

Frankfurt and Munich. As the standard of living in the new states continues to rise, so will the cost of traveling in them.

Prices throughout this guide are given for adults. Substantially reduced fees are almost always available for children, students, and senior citizens. For information on taxes, *see* Taxes.

ATMS

Twenty-four-hour ATMs (*Geldautomaten*) can be accessed with PLUS or Cirrus credit and banking cards. Some German banks exact €2–€5 fees for use of their ATMs. Your PIN number should be set for four digits; if it's longer, change it at your bank before the trip. Since some ATM keypads show no letters, know the numeric equivalent of your password.

CREDIT CARDS

All major U.S. credit cards are accepted in Germany. If you have a four-digit PIN number for your card, you can use it at German ATMs.

Throughout this guide, the following abbreviations are used: **AE**, American Express; **DC**, Diners Club; **MC**, MasterCard; and **V**, Visa.

➤ REPORTING LOST CARDS: **American Express:** ☎ 01805/840–840. **Diners Club:** ☎ 05921/861–234. **MasterCard:** ☎ 0800/819–1040. **Visa:** ☎ 08008/149–100.

CURRENCY

Germany shares a common currency, the euro (€), with 11 other countries: Austria, Belgium, Finland, France, Greece, Ireland, Italy, Luxembourg, Netherlands, Portugal, and Spain. The euro is divided into 100 cents. There are bills of 5, 10, 20, 50, 100, and 500 euros and coins of €1 and €2, and 1, 2, 5, 10, 20, and 50 cents.

CURRENCY EXCHANGE

At press time, you could get €1.03 for a U.S. dollar, €.65 for a Canadian dollar, €1.57 for a British pound, €.55 for an Australian dollar, €.46 for a New Zealand dollar, and €.10 for a South African rand.

For the most favorable rates, **change money through banks.** Although ATM transaction fees may be higher abroad than at home, ATM rates are excellent because they are based on wholesale rates offered only by major banks. You won't do as well at exchange booths in airports or rail and bus stations, in hotels, in restaurants, or in stores. To avoid lines at airport exchange booths, **get a bit of local currency before you leave home.**

➤ EXCHANGE SERVICES: **International Currency Express** (☎ 888/278–6628 orders, WEB www.foreignmoney.com). **Thomas Cook Currency Services** (☎ 800/287–7362 orders and retail locations, WEB www.us.thomascook.com).

TRAVELER'S CHECKS

Do you need traveler's checks? It depends on where you're headed. If you're going to rural areas and small towns, go with cash; traveler's checks are best used in cities, where even dollar denomination checks can be easily cashed. Lost or stolen checks can usually be replaced within 24 hours. To ensure a speedy refund, buy your own traveler's checks—don't let someone else pay for them: irregularities like this can cause delays. The person who bought the checks should make the call to request a refund.

OUTDOORS AND SPORTS

Germans are very active and constantly organize themselves into sports teams and clubs. Hiking trails abound throughout the country.

BIKING

There are many long-distance bicycle routes in Germany. Among the best river bike paths are those along the Danube River, which you can meet at Regensburg or Passau, and along the Weser River, which you can meet at Hannoversch-Münden. Another route, somewhat rugged, is along the Baltic Coast, mainly in the state of Mecklenburg-Vorpommern. The *Radfährerkarten,* issued by the Bielefelder Verlaganstalt and by Haupka Verlag, are good bike travel maps available at bookstores.

Bicycles can be rented in or near more than 230 train stations throughout Germany, mainly from April through October, though some are offered year-round. The cost is from €3 to €12.70 per day. You may have to leave cash or your passport or other identification as a deposit, depending on the arrangement with the private contractors who now handle the service. You must return the bike to the station at which you rented it. Special types, such as mountain bikes at Alpine stations, children's bikes and rickshaws, are also available. Most bike shops have rentals for about €10 per day or €5 a week.

Bikes cannot be transported on Inter-City Express trains or on most Inter-City and EuroCity trains. Trains that do carry them have a little bicycle symbol on the timetable. Bike transportation costs €3 on local trains. On all other trains **you must make advance reservations** and pay €8. Bikes can usually be transported without charge on municipal suburban trains, trams, and buses.

➤ CLUBS: **Allgemeiner Deutscher Fahrrad-Club** (The German Cycle Club; ✉ Postfach 107747, D–28077 Bremen, ☎ 0421/346–290, FAX 0421/3462–950, WEB www.adfc.de). **Deutsche Bahn bicycle hot line** (☎ 01805/151–415).

GOLF

The countryside along the Romantic Road is ideal golf territory, and clubs exist throughout the country.

➤ GOLF: **Deutscher Golf-Verband** (German Golf Association; ✉ Viktoriastr. 16, D–65189 Wiesbaden, ☎ 0611/990–200, WEB www.golf.de).

FISHING

Anglers **must obtain a license** (€4–€6 a day) from local town halls or tourist offices.

HIKING

The Deutscher Alpenverein maintains more than 50 mountain huts and about 15,000 km (9,300 mi) of Alpine paths. In addition, it can provide courses in mountaineering and route suggestions. Foreigners may become members. Various mountaineering schools offer weeklong courses ranging from basic techniques for beginners to advanced mountaineering. Tourist offices in all Bavarian Alpine resorts have details.

➤ CONTACTS: **Deutscher Alpenverein** (✉ Von-Kahr-Str. 2–4, D–80997 Munich, ☎ 089/140–030, FAX 089/140–0312, WEB www.alpenverein.de). **Verband Deutscher Gebirgs- und Wandervereine e.V.** (✉ Wilhelmshöhe Allee 157–159, D–34121 Kassel, ☎ 0561/938–730).

SKIING

The Black Forest has many cross-country ski trails, and downhill is most popular in the Bavarian Alps.

PACKING

What you pack depends more on the time of year than on any particular dress code. Winters can be bitterly cold; summers are warm but with days that suddenly turn cool and rainy. In summer **take a warm jacket or heavy sweater** for the Bavarian Alps, where the nights can be chilly even after hot days.

For cities, **pack as you would for an American city**: dressy outfits for formal restaurants and nightclubs, casual clothes elsewhere. Jeans are as popular in Germany as anywhere else and are perfectly acceptable for sightseeing and informal dining. In the evening men will probably feel more comfortable wearing a jacket and tie in more expensive restaurants, although it is almost never required. Many German women wear stylish outfits to restaurants and the theater, especially in the larger cities.

To discourage purse snatchers and pickpockets, **carry a handbag with long straps** that you can sling across your body bandolier style and with a zippered compartment for money and other valuables.

For stays in budget hotels, **take your own soap.** Many provide no soap at all or only a small bar.

In your carry-on luggage, **pack an extra pair of eyeglasses or contact lenses and enough of any medication** you take to last a few days longer than the trip. You may also ask your doctor to write a spare prescription using the drug's generic name, since brand names may vary from country to country. In luggage to be checked, **never pack prescription drugs or valuables.** And don't forget to carry with you the addresses of offices that handle refunds of lost traveler's checks. Check *Fodor's How to Pack* (available in bookstores everywhere) for more tips.

To avoid customs and security delays, carry medications in their original packaging. Don't pack any sharp objects in your carry-on luggage, including knives of any size or material, scissors, manicure tools, and corkscrews, or anything else that might arouse suspicion.

CHECKING LUGGAGE

You are allowed one carry-on bag and one personal article, such as a purse or a laptop computer. Make sure that everything you carry aboard will fit under your seat or in the overhead bin. Get to the gate early, so you can board as soon as possible, before the overhead bins fill up.

If you are flying internationally, note that baggage allowances may be determined not by piece but by weight—generally 88 pounds (40 kilograms) in first class, 66 pounds (30 kilograms) in business class, and 44 pounds (20 kilograms) in economy.

Airline liability for baggage is limited to $2,500 per person on flights within the United States. On international flights it amounts to $9.07 per pound or $20 per kilogram for checked baggage (roughly $640 per 70-pound bag) and $400 per passenger for unchecked baggage. You can buy additional coverage at check-in for about $10 per $1,000 of coverage, but it excludes a rather extensive list of items, shown on your airline ticket.

Before departure, **itemize your bags' contents** and their worth, and label the bags with your name, address, and phone number. (If you use your home address, cover it so potential thieves can't see it readily.) Inside each bag, **pack a copy of your itinerary.** At check-in, **make sure that each bag is correctly tagged** with the destination airport's three-letter code. If your bags arrive damaged or fail to arrive at all, file a written report with the airline before leaving the airport.

PASSPORTS AND VISAS

When traveling internationally, **carry your passport** even if you don't need one (it's always the best form of I.D.) and **make two photocopies of the data page** (one for someone at home and another for you, carried separately from your passport). If you lose your passport, promptly call the nearest embassy or consulate and the local police.

U.S. passport applications for children under age 14 require consent from both parents or legal guardians; both parents must appear together to sign the application. If only one parent appears, he or she must submit a written statement from the other parent authorizing passport issuance for the child. A parent with sole authority must present evidence of it when applying; acceptable documentation includes the child's certified birth certificate listing only the applying parent, a court order specifically permitting this parent's travel with the child, or a death certificate for the non-applying parent. Application forms and instructions are available on the Web site of the U.S. State Department's Bureau of Consular Affairs (www.travel.state.gov).

ENTERING GERMANY

U.S., Canadian, Australian, New Zealand, and British citizens need only a valid passport to enter Germany for stays of up to 90 days.

PASSPORT OFFICES

The best time to apply for a passport or to renew is in fall and winter. Before any trip, check your passport's expiration date, and, if necessary, renew it as soon as possible.

➤ AUSTRALIAN CITIZENS: **Australian State Passport Office** (☎ 131–232, WEB www.passports.gov.au).

➤ CANADIAN CITIZENS: **Passport Office** (to mail in applications: ✉ Department of Foreign Affairs and International Trade, Ottawa, Ontario K1A 0G3, ☎ 819/994–3500 or 800/567–6868, WEB www.dfait-maeci.gc.ca/passport).

➤ NEW ZEALAND CITIZENS: **New Zealand Passport Office** (☎ 04/474–8100 or 0800/22–5050, WEB www.passports.govt.nz).

➤ U.K. CITIZENS: **London Passport Office** (☎ 0870/521–0410, WEB www.passport.gov.uk).

➤ U.S. CITIZENS: **National Passport Information Center** (☎ 900/225–5674, 35¢ per minute for automated service or $1.05 per minute for operator service, WEB www.travel.state.gov).

REST ROOMS

It's customary to leave a gratuity in a rest room if it has an attendant. He or she will likely have a plate out "primed" with €.50 coin.

SAFETY

Germany has one of the lowest rates of violent crime in Europe. The best advice is to take normal precautions. Put valuables in the hotel safe. Don't carry a shoulder bag or purse in such a way that it can be easily snatched. Avoid remote areas late at night. And then, don't worry too much.

WOMEN IN GERMANY

Don't wear a money belt or a waist pack, both of which peg you as a tourist. If you carry a purse, choose one with a zipper and a thick strap that you can drape across your body; adjust the length so that the purse sits in front of you at or above hip level. Store only enough money in the purse to cover casual spending. Distribute the rest of your cash and any valuables (including credit cards and your passport) between a deep front pocket, an inside jacket or vest pocket, and a hidden money pouch. Do not reach for the money pouch once in public.

SENIOR-CITIZEN TRAVEL

In Germany the number of citizens over 60 is growing; this section of the population has also become more affluent and even has its own political party, the Gray Panthers. The strength of this special-interest age group has won it special privileges—such as discounts on the railways and in museums—and elderly visitors from abroad can also take advantage of these discounts. The German Railroad's ReisePacket Komfort (☞ Train Travel) may also be of interest to a senior citizen.

To qualify for age-related discounts, **mention your senior-citizen status up front** when booking hotel reservations (not when checking out) and before you're seated in restaurants (not when paying the bill). Be sure to have identification on hand. When renting a car, ask about promotional car-rental discounts, which can be cheaper than senior-citizen rates.

If your mobility is impaired at all, be aware that ancient hotels might not have elevators, and beds are fairly low to the floor in Germany.

➤ EDUCATIONAL PROGRAMS: **Elderhostel** (✉ 11 Ave. de Lafayette, Boston, MA 02111-1746, ☎ 877/426–8056, FAX 877/426–2166, WEB www.elderhostel.org). **Interhostel** (✉ University of New Hampshire, 6 Garrison Ave., Durham, NH 03824, ☎ 603/862–1147 or 800/733–9753, FAX 603/862–1113, WEB www.learn.unh.edu).

STUDENTS IN GERMANY

Most museums and modes of transportation have reduced prices for students, so have your student I.D. card handy. *See* Lodging for hosteling information.

➤ I.D.S AND SERVICES: **STA Travel** (☎ 212/627–3111 or 800/781–4040, FAX 212/627–3387, WEB www.sta.com). **Travel Cuts** (✉ 187 College St., Toronto, Ontario M5T 1P7, Canada, ☎ 416/979–2406 or 800/667–2887, FAX 416/979–8167, WEB www.travelcuts.com).

TAXES

VALUE-ADDED TAX

Most prices you see on items already have Germany's 16% value-added tax (VAT) included. When traveling to a non-EU country, you are entitled to a refund of the VAT you pay (multiply the price of an item by .138 to find out how much VAT is embedded in the price). Some goods, such as books and antiquities, carry a 7% VAT as a percentage of the purchase price. An item must cost at least €25 to qualify for a VAT refund.

When making a purchase, **ask for a VAT refund form** and find out whether the merchant gives refunds—not all stores do, nor are they required to. Have the form stamped like any customs form by customs officials when you leave the country or, if you're visiting several European Union countries, when you leave the EU. Be ready to show customs officials what you've bought (pack purchases together, in your carry-on luggage); budget extra time for this. Take the form to a refund-service counter for an on-the-spot refund, or mail it back to the store or a refund service after you arrive home.

A refund service can save you some hassle, for a fee. Global Refund is a Europe-wide service with 130,000 affiliated stores and more than 700 refund counters—located at every major airport and border crossing. Its refund form is called a Shopping

Cheque. The service issues refunds in the form of cash, check, or credit-card adjustment, minus a processing fee. If you don't have time to wait at the refund counter, you can mail in the form instead.

If you are departing from Terminal 1 at Frankfurt Airport, bring your purchases to one of two areas, depending on how you've packed the goods. Bring items packed in check–in luggage to the customs office in the baggage claim areas of Arrivals Halls A, B, and C (access through the Terminal Supervisor Desk); or bring your baggage to Level 3 near the Sky Line Station, Hall B. For goods you are carrying on the plane with you, go to the customs office at Gates A 15/17, Transit Area B, near the passport control; or baggage claim area, Hall C. If you are departing from Terminal 2, bring goods in luggage to be checked to the customs office in Hall D, Level 2 (opposite the Delta Airlines check-in counters). For goods you are carrying on the plane with you, go to the customs office in Hall E, Level 3 (near security control).

At Munich's airport, go to a VAT refund counter between areas A and B or B and C, in each case right next to the customs office.

➤ VAT REFUNDS: **Global Refund** (✉ 99 Main St., Suite 307, Nyack, NY 10960, ☎ 800/566–9828, FAX 845/348–1549, WEB www.globalrefund.com).

TELEPHONES

AREA AND COUNTRY CODES

The country code for Germany is 49. When dialing a German number from abroad, drop the initial "0" from the local area code. The country code is 001 for the United States and Canada, 0061 for Australia, 0064 for New Zealand, 0044 for the United Kingdom, 00353 for Ireland, and 0027 for South Africa.

DIRECTORY AND OPERATOR ASSISTANCE

The German telephone system is fully automatic, and it's unlikely you'll have to employ the services of an operator unless you're seeking information. If you have difficulty reaching your number, call 0180/200–1033. You can book collect calls through this number to the United States but not to other countries. For information in English dial 11837 for numbers within Germany, and 11834 for numbers elsewhere. But first **look for the number in the phone book or on the Web** (www.teleauskunft.de), because directory assistance is costly. Calls to 11837 and 11834 cost at least €.50, more if the call lasts more than 30 seconds.

INTERNATIONAL CALLS

International calls can be made from just about any telephone booth in Germany. It costs only €.13 per minute to call the United States, day or night, no matter how long the call lasts. Use a phone card. If you don't have a good deal with a calling card, there are many stores that offer international calls at rates well below that which you will pay from a phone booth. At a hotel, rates will be at least double the regular charge, so **avoid making international calls from your room.**

LOCAL CALLS

A local call from a telephone booth costs €.10 per minute. You can drop the local area code.

LONG-DISTANCE CALLS

Dial the zero before the area code when making a long-distance call within Germany.

LONG-DISTANCE SERVICES

AT&T, MCI, and Sprint access codes make calling long distance relatively convenient, but you may find the local access number blocked in many hotel rooms. First ask the hotel operator to connect you. If the hotel operator balks, ask for an international operator, or dial the international operator yourself. One way to improve your odds of getting connected to your long-distance carrier is to travel with more than one company's calling card (a hotel may block Sprint, for example, but not MCI). If all else fails, call from a pay phone.

➤ ACCESS CODES: **AT&T Direct** (☎ 0800/225–5288). **MCI WorldPhone** (☎ 0800/888–8000). **Sprint International Access** (☎ 0800/888–0013).

MOBILE PHONES

The standard mobile phones used in the United States and Canada are *not* compatible with Germany's GSM digital cellphone network. Because public phones are not nearly as ubiquitous as in North America, you should seriously consider renting a GSM cellphone if you intend to make calls regularly. You can rent a cellphone at the The Airport Communications Service at Frankfurt's airport. It's located in the Frankfurt Airport Center, opposite Terminal I and near the Sheraton Hotel. Rates are €13 a day, including €6.50 worth of calls. At Munich's airport the V2 Connect shop rents cellphones.

➤ PHONE RENTALS: **The Airport Communications Service** (☏ 069/6959–1163, WEB www.aircom.de). **V2 Connect** (☏ 089/973–5110).

PHONE CARDS

A phone card is a must if you think you'll be using public phones. You can purchase one, among other places, at post offices, newsstands, and exchange places. Most phone booths have instructions in English as well as German. Another advantage of the card: it charges only what the call costs.

PUBLIC PHONES

Most telephone booths in Germany are card-operated, so **buy a phone card.** Coin-operated phones, which take €0.10, €0.20, €0.50, €1, and €2 coins, don't make change. Telephone booths are not a common feature on the streets, so be prepared to ask locals where to find one; you might have to walk a bit out of your way.

TIME

Germany is on Central European Time, which is six hours ahead of Eastern Standard Time and nine hours ahead of Pacific Standard Time. Germans use military time (1 PM is indicated as 13:00) and write the date before the month, so October 3 will appear as 03.10.

TIPPING

The service charges on bills is sufficient for most tips in your hotel, though you should **tip bellhops and porters**; €1 per bag or service is ample. It's also customary to leave a small tip (a euro or so per night) for the room-cleaning staff. Whether you tip the desk clerk depends on whether he or she has given you any special service.

Service charges are included in all restaurant checks (listed as *Bedienung*), as is tax (listed as *MWST*). Nonetheless, it is customary to **round up the bill to the nearest euro or to leave about 5%** (give it to the waiter or waitress as you pay the bill; don't leave it on the table, as that's considered rude). Bartenders and servers also expect a 2%–5% tip.

In taxis **round up the fare about a euro** as a tip. Only give more if you have particularly cumbersome or heavy luggage.

TOURS AND PACKAGES

Because everything is prearranged on a prepackaged tour or independent vacation, you spend less time planning—and often get it all at a good price.

BOOKING WITH AN AGENT

Travel agents are excellent resources. But it's a good idea to collect brochures from several agencies, as some agents' suggestions may be influenced by relationships with tour and package firms that reward them for volume sales. If you have a special interest, **find an agent with expertise in that area**; the American Society of Travel Agents (ASTA; ☞ Travel Agencies) has a database of specialists worldwide.

Make sure your travel agent knows the accommodations and other services of the place being recommended. Ask about the hotel's location, room size, beds, and whether it has a pool, room service, or programs for children, if you care about these. Has your agent been there in person or sent others whom you can contact?

Do some homework on your own, too: local tourism boards can provide information about lesser-known and small-niche operators, some of which may sell only direct.

BUYER BEWARE

Each year consumers are stranded or lose their money when tour operators—even large ones with excellent reputations—go out of business. So **check out the operator.** Ask several travel agents about its reputation, and try to **book with a company that has a consumer-protection program.** (Look for information in the company's brochure.) In the United States, members of the National Tour Association and the United States Tour Operators Association are required to set aside funds to cover your payments and travel arrangements in the event that the company defaults. It's also a good idea to choose a company that participates in the American Society of Travel Agents' Tour Operator Program (TOP); ASTA will act as mediator in any disputes between you and your tour operator.

Remember that the more your package or tour includes the better you can predict the ultimate cost of your vacation. Make sure you know exactly what is covered, and **beware of hidden costs.** Are taxes, tips, and transfers included? Entertainment and excursions? These can add up.

➤ TOUR-OPERATOR RECOMMENDATIONS: **American Society of Travel Agents** (☞ Travel Agencies). **National Tour Association** (NTA; ✉ 546 E. Main St., Lexington, KY 40508, ☎ 859/226–4444 or 800/682–8886, WEB www.ntaonline.com). **United States Tour Operators Association** (USTOA; ✉ 275 Madison Ave., Suite 2014, New York, NY 10016, ☎ 212/599–6599 or 800/468–7862, FAX 212/599–6744, WEB www.ustoa.com).

TRAIN TRAVEL

Deutsche Bahn (DB—German Rail) is a very efficient, privatized railway. Its high-speed InterCity Express (ICE), InterCity (IC), and EuroCity (EC) trains make journeys between the centers of many cities—Munich–Frankfurt, for example—faster by rail than by air. It's also possible to sleep on the train and save a day of your trip. There are CityNightLine (CNL) trains to distant locations, and many overnight D-Class trains also have sleepers. The high-speed trains have a first-class service that includes breakfast in bed. All InterCity and InterCity Express trains have restaurant cars and trolley service. RE trains are regional trains.

With the high-speed expresses you often only have to cross to the other side of the station platform to change trains. Special train maps on platform notice boards give details of the layout of trains arriving on that track, showing the locations of first- and second-class cars and the restaurant car, as well as where they will stop along the platform. Large railroad stations have English-speaking staff handling information inquiries.

Always **check that your ticket is valid for the type of train you are planning to take.** If you have the wrong type of ticket you will have to pay the difference in the train, in cash.

BAGGAGE SERVICE

Most major train stations have luggage lockers (in four sizes). By inserting coins into a storage unit, you release the unit's key. Prices range from €1 for a small locker to €3 for a "jumbo" one. Smaller towns' train stations may not have any storage options.

Throughout Germany you can use the Deutsche Bahn *KurierGepäck* service to deliver your baggage from a private residence or hotel to any of six large airports. Buy a *KurierGepäck* ticket at any DB ticket counter and call 01805/4884 to schedule a pickup. The service costs €14.30 for the first two suitcases (with a valid ticket) and €9.20 for each additional piece. Delivery to the airports at Berlin, Frankfurt, Leipzig-Halle, Munich, Hamburg, and Hannover is guaranteed on the second weekday following pickup.

German railway's ReisePacket Komfort service is for travelers who are inexperienced, elderly, disabled, or just appreciative of extra help. It costs €10 and provides, among other things, for help in boarding, disembarking, and transferring on certain selected trains that serve the major cities and vacation areas. It also includes a seat reservation and a voucher for an on-board snack.

CLASSES

The difference between first and second class seats is that first-class passengers pay approximately 1.5% more for a bit more legroom and the convenience of having meals delivered directly to their seats. Most people find second class entirely adequate.

CUTTING COSTS

InterCity Express trains are the most expensive. A €3.60 surcharge (€7.20

round-trip) is added to the ticket price on all InterCity and EuroCity journeys irrespective of distance. The charge is €4.60 if paid on board the train.

To save money, **look into rail passes.** But be aware that if you don't plan to cover many miles you may come out ahead by buying individual tickets. Under a price structure introduced in the fall of 2002, you save 10% off the ticket price if you book a day in advance, 25% if you book three days in advance, and 40% if you book at least seven days in advance. There are a few catches. Especially during times of peak travel, only a limited number of seats are set aside for these cut-rate tickets. The 25% and 40% reductions are only for round trips, and to get 40% off you must have a Sunday between the outward and return journeys.

The *Guten Abend Ticket* (Good Evening Ticket) provides great savings between 7 PM and 2 AM on all trains except sleepers, and the *Schönes Wochenend Ticket* (Happy Weekend Ticket) provides unlimited weekend travel for up to five persons for as little as €3.50 per person. Rail passengers with a valid round-trip air ticket can **buy a heavily discounted "Rail and Fly" ticket for DB trains** connecting with 14 German airports and two airports outside Germany (Basel and Amsterdam).

If Germany is your only destination in Europe, **consider purchasing a "flexi" German Railpass,** which allows 4–10 days of unlimited first- or second-class travel within a one-month period on any DB train, up to and including the ICE. A Twin Pass does the same for two people traveling together and is even cheaper per person. A Youth Pass, sold to those 12–25, is also much the same but for second-class travel only. You can also **use these passes aboard KD Rhine Line** (☞ Cruise Travel) along certain sections of the Rhine and Mosel rivers. Prices begin at $180 for a single traveler in second class and $260 in first class. Twin Passes begin at $270 in second class and $390 in first class, and Youth Passes begin at $142. Additional days may be added to either pass.

Germany is one of 17 countries in which you can **use Eurailpasses,** which provide unlimited first-class rail travel in all participating countries for the duration of the pass. If you plan to rack up the miles, get a standard pass. These are available for 15 days ($572), 21 days ($740), one month ($918), two months ($1,298), and three months ($1,606).

If your plans call for only limited train travel, **look into a Europass,** which costs less money than a EurailPass. Unlike with Eurailpasses, however, you get a limited number of travel days in a limited number of countries during a specified time period. For example, the cheapest two-month pass ($360) allows five days of rail travel but costs $200 less than the least expensive EurailPass. Keep in mind, however, that the Europass is good only in France, Germany, Italy, Spain, and Switzerland, though it can be extended through the purchase of up to two additional zones.

In addition to standard Eurailpasses, **check out special rail-pass plans.** Among these are the Eurail Youthpass (for those under age 26, from $401 to $1,126), the Eurail Saverpass (which gives a discount for two people traveling together, from $486 to $1,366 per person) and a Eurail Flexipass (which allows a certain number of travel days within a set period). Eurailpasses and some of the German Railpasses **must be purchased before you leave** for Europe.

➤ INFORMATION AND PASSES: **DER Travel Services** (✉ 9501 W. Devon Ave., Rosemont, IL 60018, ☎ 800/782–2424, FAX 800/860–9944 to request a brochure; 888/337–8687 fax on demand service, WEB www.dertravel.com). **Deutsche Bahn** (German Rail; ✉ Stephanstr. 1, D–60313 Frankfurt am Main, ☎ 01805/996–633 for 24-hr hot line; €0.12 per minute, WEB www.bahn.de). **Europe On Rail** (✉ 725 Day Ave., Suite 1, Ridgefield NJ 07657, ☎ 877/667–2457, FAX 866/329–7245, WEB www.europeonrail.com). **German Rail Passenger Services** (☎ 08702/435–363 in the U.K.).

FARES AND SCHEDULES

You have to pay by the minute for fare and schedule information on the Deutsche Bahn information phone line, and you may have to wait a few moments before someone can help you in English. On the DB Web site, which can be a bit tricky to figure out, click on "Int. Guests" and then "Travel Service" to enter your departure and arrival points.

FROM THE U.K.

There are several ways to reach Germany from London on British Rail. Travelers coming from the United Kingdom should **take the Channel Tunnel to save time, the ferry to save money.** Fastest and most expensive is the route via the Channel Tunnel on Eurostar trains. They leave at two-hour intervals from Waterloo and require a change of trains in Brussels. Cheapest and slowest are the 8–10 departures daily from Victoria using the Ramsgate–Ostend ferry, jetfoil, or SeaCat catamaran service.

➤ TRAIN AND PASS INFORMATION: **Eurostar** (☎ 0870/518–6186).

RESERVATIONS

Many travelers assume that rail passes guarantee them seats on the trains they wish to ride. Not so. You need to **book seats ahead even if you are using a rail pass**; seat reservations are required on some European trains, particularly high-speed trains, and are a good idea during summer and on popular routes. If you board the train without a reserved seat, you take the chance of having to stand. You'll also need a reservation if you purchase sleeping accommodations. Seat reservations on all but InterCity Express and EuroCity trains cost €2.60.

To avoid standing in lines at the station, **make an advance reservation and purchase** by calling the 24-hour Deutsche Bahn hot line or booking on-line at their Web site (☞ Information and Passes). You will then be able to collect your seat ticket from a special counter without having to wait in line.

SENIOR-CITIZEN PASSES

Holders of British Rail Senior Citizens' Rail Cards can buy an "add-on" European card that permits a 30% reduction on train travel in most European countries, including Germany. Unfortunately it can't be had at just any ticket office. Call 0207/904–0540 to order it.

TRANSPORTATION AROUND GERMANY

The Deutsche Bahn, Germany's privatized railway, is by far the best way to travel around the country. The basic ticket prices are not cheap, but several special offers can reduce ticket prices by as much as half. The carefully structured network of services—from the super-high-speed InterCity Express to slower D-trains and local trains—ensures fast connections between cities and good access to rural areas; very few villages are more than 10 km (6 mi) or so from a railroad station.

The country's airlines—principally Lufthansa—are far more expensive than train travel and not always speedier. The Deutsche Bahn "Sprinter" business special, for instance, gets its passengers between Frankfurt and Munich or Berlin faster than a plane, by the time city-to-airport travel and check-in requirements are taken into account. The Frankfurt–Munich "Sprinter" stops only in Mannheim; the Frankfurt–Berlin one doesn't stop at all.

There are few long-distance bus services in Germany. Those buses that do cross the country are either tourist services covering routes such as the Romantic Road or long-distance companies originating outside Germany. In rural areas local bus companies complement rail services, making even the most remote community accessible. If you must save as much money as possible, take local buses, which are generally less expensive than trains, but take much longer.

All major German cities have multi-structure urban transportation systems, incorporating subway (U-bahn) and metropolitan suburban (S-bahn) trains, trams, and buses. Public transportation in cities is invariably fast, clean, and efficient.

TRAVEL AGENCIES

A good travel agent puts your needs first. Look for an agency that has been in business at least five years, emphasizes customer service, and has someone on staff who specializes in your destination. In addition, **make sure the agency belongs to a professional trade organization.** The American Society of Travel Agents (ASTA)—the largest and most influential in the field with more than 24,000 members in some 140 countries—maintains and enforces a strict code of ethics and will step in to help mediate any agent-client disputes involving ASTA members if necessary. ASTA (whose motto is "Without a travel agent, you're on your own") also maintains a Web site that includes a directory of agents. (If a travel agency is also acting as your tour operator, *see* Buyer Beware *in* Tours and Packages.)

A very large travel agency, Deutsches Reisebüro (DER), has 353 offices in just about every section of every German city (check the telephone book). All offer a full range of travel services, from tours and hotel bookings to car rentals, and rail and plane tickets. The tours it organizes are also sold by travel agents.

➤ DER: **DER Travel Services** (✉ 9501 W. Devon Ave., Rosemont, IL 60018, ☎ 800/782–2424, FAX 800/860–9944 to request a brochure; 888/337–8687 fax on demand service, WEB www.dertravel.com).

➤ LOCAL AGENT REFERRALS: **American Society of Travel Agents** (ASTA; ✉ 1101 King St., Suite 200, Alexandria, VA 22314, ☎ 800/965–2782 24-hr hot line, FAX 703/739–3268, WEB www.astanet.com). **Association of British Travel Agents** (✉ 68–71 Newman St., London W1T 3AH, ☎ 020/7637–2444, FAX 020/7637–0713, WEB www.abtanet.com). **Association of Canadian Travel Agents** (✉ 130 Albert St., Suite 1705, Ottawa, Ontario K1P 5G4, ☎ 613/237–3657, FAX 613/237–7052, WEB www.acta.ca). **Australian Federation of Travel Agents** (✉ Level 3, 309 Pitt St., Sydney, NSW 2000, ☎ 02/9264–3299, FAX 02/9264–1085, WEB www.afta.com.au). **Travel Agents' Association of New Zealand** (✉ Level 5, Tourism and Travel House, 79 Boulcott St., Box 1888, Wellington 6001, ☎ 04/499–0104, FAX 04/499–0827, WEB www.taanz.org.nz).

VISITOR INFORMATION

Local tourist offices are listed in the A to Z sections of the individual chapters. Staff at the smaller offices, especially in eastern Germany, might not speak English. Many offices keep shorter hours than normal businesses, and you can expect some to close during weekday lunch hours, and as early as noon on Friday.

➤ TOURIST INFORMATION: **U.S. Nationwide** (German National Tourist Office, ✉ 122 E. 42nd St., New York, NY 10168, ☎ 212/661–7200, FAX 212/661–7174, WEB www.visits-to-germany.com). **Canada** (✉ 175 Bloor St. E, Suite 604, Toronto, Ontario M4W 3R8, Canada, ☎ 416/968–1570, FAX 416/968–1986). **U.K.** (✉ 18 Conduit St., London W1R ODT, U.K., ☎ 020/7317–0908, FAX 020/7495–6129). **Australia** (✉ Box A980, Sydney, NSW 1235, Australia, ☎ 9267–8148, FAX 9267–9035). **Germany** (✉ Beethovenstr. 68, D–60325 Frankfurt, ☎ 069/974–640, FAX 069/751–903).

➤ U.S. GOVERNMENT ADVISORIES: **U.S. Department of State** (✉ Overseas Citizens Services Office, Room 4811, 2201 C St. NW, Washington, DC 20520, ☎ 202/647–5225 interactive hot line or 888/407–4747, WEB www.travel.state.gov); enclose a business-size SASE.

WEB SITES

Do check out the World Wide Web when planning your trip. You'll find everything from weather forecasts to virtual tours of famous cities. Be sure to **visit Fodors.com** (www.fodors.com), a complete travel-planning site. You can research prices and book plane tickets, hotel rooms, rental cars, vacation packages, and more. In addition, you can post your pressing questions in the Travel Talk section. Other planning tools include a currency converter and weather reports, and there are loads of links to travel resources. One site that goes in-depth regarding international telephone systems and modem hook-up troubleshooting is www.kropla.com.

Many German tourism-related Web sites have an English-language version, usually indicated by an icon of the American or British flag. For general information on Germany, visit www.visits-to-germany.com, the German National Tourist Office's site.

WHEN TO GO

The tourist season in Germany runs from May to late October, when the weather is at its best. In addition to many tourist events, this period has hundreds of folk festivals. The winter sports season in the Bavarian Alps runs from Christmas to mid-March. Prices everywhere are generally higher during the summer, so **consider visiting out of season to save money.** Most resorts offer between-season (*Zwischensaison*) and edge-of-season (*Nebensaison*) rates, and tourist offices can provide lists of hotels that offer special low-price inclusive weekly packages (*Pauschal-angebote*). Many winter ski resorts have lower rates early in the season, from mid-December to mid-January. High season runs from mid-January to Easter. The disadvantages of visiting in winter are that the weather is often cold and gloomy and some attractions, especially in rural areas, are closed or have shorter hours. Ski resorts are the exception.

It's wise to **avoid cities at times of major trade fairs,** when attendees commandeer all hotel rooms and prices soar. Among the fairs to avoid are Green Week in Berlin (January), the radio-TV fair in Berlin (August and September in odd-number years), the boat fair in Düsseldorf (January), the computer fair in Hannover (February and March), and the auto fair in Frankfurt (September in odd-number years). You can check trade fair schedules with the German National Tourist Office.

CLIMATE

Germany's climate is temperate, although cold spells can plunge the thermometer well below freezing, particularly in the Alps, the Harz region of Lower Saxony and Saxony-Anhalt, the Black Forest, and the higher regions of northern Franconia. Summers are usually sunny and warm, though you should **be prepared for a few cloudy and wet days,** especially in the north half of the country. The south is normally always a few degrees warmer than the north. As you get nearer to the Alps, however, the summers get shorter, often not beginning until the end of May. Fall is sometimes spectacular in the south—warm and soothing. The only real exception is the strikingly variable weather in South Bavaria caused by the *Föhn,* an Alpine wind that gives rise to clear but very warm conditions. The Föhn can occur in all seasons. Sudden atmospheric pressure changes associated with the Föhn give some people headaches. Germans measure temperature in Celsius.

➤ FORECASTS: **Weather Channel Connection** (☎ 900/932–8437), 95¢ per minute from a Touch-Tone phone.

The following are the average daily maximum and minimum temperatures for Berlin, Frankfurt, and Munich.

BERLIN

Jan.	35F	2C	May	66F	19C	Sept.	68F	20C
	26	−3		47	8		50	10
Feb.	37F	3C	June	72F	22C	Oct.	56F	13C
	26	−3		53	12		42	6
Mar.	46F	8C	July	75F	24C	Nov.	45F	7C
	31	0		57	14		36	2
Apr.	56F	13C	Aug.	74F	23C	Dec.	38F	3C
	39	4		56	13		29	−1

FRANKFURT

Jan.	39F	4C	May	69F	20C	Sept.	69F	21C
	30	−1		49	9		52	11
Feb.	43F	6C	June	74F	23C	Oct.	57F	14C
	31	1		55	13		44	7
Mar.	51F	11C	July	75F	24C	Nov.	45F	7C
	37	3		58	15		37	3
Apr.	59F	15C	Aug.	76F	24C	Dec.	40F	4C
	41	5		57	14		32	0

MUNICH

Jan.	35F	1C	May	64F	18C	Sept.	67F	20C
	23	– 5		45	7		48	9
Feb.	38F	3C	June	70F	21C	Oct.	56F	14C
	23	– 5		51	11		40	4
Mar.	48F	9C	July	74F	23C	Nov.	44F	7C
	30	– 1		55	13		33	0
Apr.	56F	14C	Aug.	73F	23C	Dec.	36F	2C
	38	3		54	12		26	– 4

FESTIVALS AND SEASONAL EVENTS

Germany's efforts to draw foreign visitors in 2003 are targeted on the business traveler. The country ranks number one in the world in the number of foreign visitors attending fairs and exhibitions, and it also looms large as a center of international business and as a venue for conferences and seminars.

Top seasonal events include Carnival festivities in January and February, spring festivals around Easter and Pentecost, Bayreuth's Richard Wagner Festival in August, wine festivals throughout the southern half of the country in late summer and fall, the Oktoberfest in Munich in late September and early October, the Frankfurt Book Fair in October, and December's Christmas markets. For event listings see the German National Tourist Office's Web site (www.germany-tourism.de).

➤ DEC.: **Christmas Markets,** outdoor festivals of light, choral and trumpet music, handcrafted gift items, and hot wine are held in just about every German city. Nürnberg's is the most famous.

➤ JAN.: **Fasching season.** The Rhineland is Germany's capital of Carnival events, including proclamations of Carnival princes, street fairs, parades, masked balls, and more. Some of the main Carnival cities are Koblenz, Köln, Mainz, Bonn, and Düsseldorf, although there's also plenty of activity in Munich and throughout southern Germany. Festivities always run through February, finishing on Fasching Dienstag (Shrove or Fat Tuesday, or Mardi Gras).

➤ FEB.: **Frankfurt International Fair** is a major consumer-goods trade fair.

International Filmfestspiele, in Berlin, is one of Europe's leading film festivals.

The **International Toy Fair** takes place in Nürnberg.

➤ MAR.: **ITB,** one of Europe's largest international tourism fairs, takes place in Berlin.

Strong Beer Season in Munich brings out the bands and merrymaking in all the beer halls.

➤ APR.: **Walpurgis** festivals. Towns in the Harz Mountains celebrate with spooky, Halloween-like goings on the night before May Day.

➤ MAY: **Medieval Festival.** By downing a huge tankard of wine in one gulp, the 17th-century mayor of Rothenburg-ob-der-Tauber saved the town from sacking. On Pentecost weekend his Meistertrunk is reenacted.

Religious Processions, featuring hundreds of horses, giant candles, and elaborate statues, are particularly spectacular in Catholic Eastern Bavaria during the Pentecost weekend. The best ones are at Bogen, Sankt Englmar, and Kötzting.

➤ MAY–SEPT.: **Pied Piper** plays are performed at Hameln each Sunday at noon, from May through mid-September. The children of the town first portray the rats, then themselves as they are piped to parts unknown.

Rhine in Flames highlights the river with fireworks, Bengal lights along the bank, floodlighted castles, and a fleet of illuminated boats; it takes place around Bonn (May), Rüdesheim (July), Koblenz (August), and St. Goar (September).

➤ JUNE: **Kiel Week** is an international sailing regatta and cultural festival in the town of Kiel in Schleswig-Holstein.

➤ JUNE–SEPT.: **Castle Illuminations,** with spectacular fireworks, are presented in Heidelberg in June, July, and September.

The Schleswig-Holstein Music Festival takes place over six weeks in July and August. World-famous and young musicians perform in cities and towns throughout Schleswig-Holstein.

➤ JULY: **Kinderzeche** is Dinkelsbühl's medieval pageant and festival. It reenacts an incident from the Thirty Years' War, in which the children stood at the gate and pleaded with the conquerors to spare their homes.

Love Parade (WEB www.loveparade.de), a huge street party of techno-music and ravers, draws a million revelers to Berlin the second weekend in July.

➤ AUG.: **Festivals Along the Main River** take place in Frankfurt in early and late August.

Kulmbach Beer Festival takes place in Franconia.

Richard Wagner Festival unfolds the Wagner operas in Bayreuth.

The Student Prince, the noted Sigmund Romberg operetta set in Heidelberg, is performed in English in the Heidelberg's castle courtyard.

➤ SEPT.: **Berlin Festival Weeks** feature classical music concerts, exhibits, and many special events.

Folk and Beer Festival at Stuttgart/Bad Cannstatt, is said to be just as big and raucous as Munich's Oktoberfest (September and October).

Oktoberfest (late September–early October) in Munich draws millions of visitors to cavernous beer tents, each with two bands, and to fairgrounds with every kind of carnival attraction imaginable.

Wine Festivals. More than a thousand of these harvest-time events take place in September and October, mainly in the valleys of the Rhine River and three of its tributaries—the Mosel, Main, and Neckar, plus the Pfalz.

Wurstmarkt, the world's biggest wine festival, is held in a field at Bad Dürkheim.

➤ OCT.: **Berlin Jazz Festival.**

Bremen Freimarkt is a centuries-old folk festival and procession in Bremen.

Frankfurt Book Fair is a famous annual literary event and a browser's paradise.

➤ NOV.: **St. Martin's Festival** includes children's lantern processions, and is celebrated throughout the Rhineland and Bavaria.

1 DESTINATION: GERMANY

Relax, It's Not as Serious as You Think

What's Where

Pleasures and Pastimes

Fodor's Choice

Great Itineraries

RELAX, IT'S NOT AS SERIOUS AS YOU THINK

GERMANY HAS A REPUTATION of being a hard-working country of *Dichter und Denker* (poets and philosophers), a nation of serious-minded people, not as romantic as the French, not as charming as the Italians, and not as polite as the British. If we use translated fairy tales and literature as a cultural barometer—*Faust, Hansel and Gretel, Death in Venice, The Metamorphosis, All Quiet on the Western Front, The Tin Drum*—Germans seem to be fascinated by dark and haunted themes. And if you can read German newspapers and eavesdrop on conversations, you'll notice the country revels in endlessly debating politics and culture without ever finding a consensus.

The healthy balance to this intellectual heaviness is a tradition of easy-going hospitality and friendliness, embodied in traits called *Gemütlichkeit* and *Geselligkeit*. Germans' preferred way to spend their free time is to gather friends, co-workers, or family to quaff beer in the pub or restaurant, or even on the street or park bench (consuming alcohol in public at any time of the day is no offense here). This love of a good time, with fine food, good entertainment and, sometimes, deep conversations, is shared by people from all walks of life. When out in a bar, beer garden, or park, you might feel like you're not the only one on vacation, shaking off the daily grind.

The people who coined the term *Wanderlust* tend to be outdoorsy and hearty, and athletic activities are the best way to take in the diverse German landscapes. In the north, the dry, sandy lowlands are dotted with heaths and moors, lakes and deciduous forests. The North Sea and Baltic coasts draw summer vacationers who prefer its windblown dunes to the heat of the Mediterranean. The snow-covered Alps and their foothills in Bavaria provide a playground of ski resorts and lakes for sports enthusiasts. The terraced hills and vineyards of the Rhine and Mosel rivers, and the central mountain ranges, whose evergreen forests have had such an impact on German imagination and folklore, provide the country's psychological and physical North–South divide. And all of this is found within 375,000 square km, a land mass approximately the size of Montana.

Germans subscribe to the idea that a daily dose of fresh air is the key to good health and building up the immune system. Go to any forest or park on Sunday after the midday meal, and you'll see families out for their regular stroll—before they stop at a café to take part in another German Sunday ritual, *Kaffee und Kuchen* (coffee and cake). The sweets, beer, and generally heavy national cuisine seem to have little negative effect on the populace—many keep fit through bicycling as a mode of transportation, from the briefcase-toting commuter to the woman carting her child to daycare.

The image that many foreigners have of Germans—tall, strapping blondes with icy blue eyes and chiseled features—is largely a type cast in Hollywood films and 1930s Nazi propaganda. The fact is Germans descended from various ethnic peoples such as the Franks, the Saxons, the Swabians, and the Bavarians. Today's 16 states, or *Länder*, loosely correspond to the regions these groups settled, and their traditions and dialects live on. Saxons are said to be hardworking, Swabians thrifty, Rhinelanders happy-go-lucky, and Mecklenburgers reserved. Whether true or not, the stereotypes make for steady joke material.

There *are* generalizations to keep in mind about Germany and the Germans. Northerners are more likely to be Protestant, politically liberal, and socially reserved. Southerners are more likely to be Catholic, conservative, warm and outgoing. The five former Eastern states form another category altogether. These states, under Communist rule from 1945 to 1990, are less populous, poorer, and some have substandard infrastructure to their western counterparts. Even more than a decade after re-unification, East and West look at each other with deep suspicion and even remorse: many Westerners think of the *Ossis*, their Eastern brothers and sisters, as annoying relatives subsidized by their hard-earned money. Many Easterners still view the West as a greedy bunch of capitalists, arrogant, and disrespectful of the completely different, Eastern way of life. This Eastern resentment is blatantly expressed in Eastern state and local elections, which have made the Communist party there one of the strongest political forces.

Germans' foremost loyalty lies with their hometown regions, and their states are ruled by a democratically elected federal government (with two houses of representatives similar to the U.S. Congress). Germany had remained monarchic, with a patchwork of hundreds of small states, counties, and cities until 1871. Following a harrowing war with the country's arch enemy, France, the German states assembled under the hovering wings of the Prussian eagle, which became the symbol of the new German Empire. It was the iron fist of Prussia, the country's strongest state, which ratified this unification. The new empire proved to be a blessing for science and technical progress; many of the most renowned German companies such as Siemens, Mercedes-Benz, AEG, Krupp, and Thyssen were established in the early 20th century and scientists such as Robert Koch, Albert Einstein, and Theodor Mommsen made Germany a focal point for scientific development. Germany would pioneer or invent the first space rocket, radio and television, nuclear fusion, astrophysics, modern microbiology, and ground-breaking medications such as penicillin. Unfortunately, a similar resolve was also brought into play when the German superiority complex instigated two world wars and the Holocaust.

After 1945 the two German states flourished in the shadows of their big brothers in the East (the Soviet Union) and the West (the United States). With the aid of the Marshall Plan, West Germany emerged as a *Wirtschaftswunder,* an unprecedented miracle of economic recovery and success. Its social market economy became a model for Europe and the gains of the German middle class obliterated a social system once based on class and heritage. The only thing Germans now lack is self-respect for what they have accomplished. Talk to a Frenchman, Italian, or Dutchman (or Belgian, for that matter) about their homeland, and you'll probably hear some heartfelt ode to the language, the land, the food, or the culture. But ask one of today's young Germans how he feels about being German, and he will most likely answer: "I don't feel German, I feel European."

Considering 20th-century history, it's no wonder that national pride is in short supply here. Patriotism—especially displays such as flag waving or anthem singing—seem too close to nationalism for comfort. Germany, with Europe's largest population of 82 million, instead plays a strong role in international organizations such as the European Union with its European Central Bank, NATO, and the United Nations. One glance at the map shows why stability in Europe is such an important goal. Germany sits right in the middle of the continent, bordered by Denmark to the north, the Netherlands, Belgium, Luxembourg, and France to the west, Switzerland and Austria to the south, and the Czech Republic and Poland to the East. Especially since reunification in 1990, Germany is more than ever a link between East and West.

Though dialects are alive within each state, the lingua franca of Germany is High German, or *Hochdeutsch.* It is the language taught in schools, enunciated by TV announcers, and used in commerce. (For the record, natives of Hannover are said to speak the purest Hochdeutsch.) Mark Twain, in his 1880 essay "The Awful German Language," comically vents his frustration with the grammar, citing it has "more exceptions to the rule than instances of it." Those who, like Twain, "would rather decline two drinks than one German adjective," should not despair: one can get by in Germany without being fluent in the language, thanks to the fact that many Germans speak English quite well.

The ribbing Germans receive most is for the high value they place on *Ordnung* (order), which relates to putting the good of the whole before the desire of the individual. Take Quiet Time (*Ruhezeit*), for example. All of Sunday, and the hours between 1 and 3 in the afternoon, and nights from 10 PM until 7 AM, Monday through Saturday, are officially designated as Quiet Time. This is meant to prevent neighbors from disturbing each others' peace through such mundane activities as mowing the lawn, drilling the wall, playing loud music, vacuuming, washing the car, or even shouting. These and other civil ordinances may seem silly or extreme, but the fact that they are so widely adhered to helps keep the country's densely populated towns and cities livable—the generally high standard of living in Germany is more than just a measure of material goods.

In the face of rules, order, and work ethics flies Germany's role as host to two of the most massive public parties in Europe—Munich's beer-based Oktoberfest in September, and Berlin's techno music-themed Love Parade in July. Millions of Europeans pour in for these two-week and weekend-long events that put a halt to business-as-usual. Either festival is worth avoiding if you don't like crowds, but don't feel shy if in a quaint medieval town like Rothenburg-ob-der-Tauber or a city like Bremen, a group of merrymakers invites you over to their table. On the island of Rügen you could be biking through the marshes and suddenly find yourself discussing environmental issues with a local riding next to you. In Cologne, let yourself be jostled by the jolly Rhineländer celebrating the pre-Lenten weeks of Carnival with costumes, parades, and mischief. The country may have a reputation for seriousness, but the value Germans place on carefree relaxation is a tradition that can make a visitor feel right at home.

WHAT'S WHERE

Munich

Hands and beer steins down, the easygoing and fun-loving capital of Bavaria is the favorite city of both natives and visitors from abroad. Class and kitsch coexist amicably here—the former embodied in the glorious city palaces of the art-loving Wittelsbach dynasty, and the latter the stuff of Oktoberfest, a fort-night-long tribute to beer and its consequences. The city's fashionable burghers support some of the best restaurants in the country, but the *Gemütlichkeit* is nowhere stronger than in the city's many beer halls, of which surely the best-known is the venerable Hofbräuhaus, deafening and perennially packed. A much more tranquil refuge is the Englischer Garten, where you can cross-country ski or sunbathe nude, depending on the season. There's also the 500-year-old late-Gothic Frauenkirche, whose twin domes are a city emblem.

Bavarian Alps

Majestic peaks, rocky pastures, and frescoed houses further brightened by window boxes overflowing with geraniums make for Germany's most photogenic region. Year-round you can find the country's finest skiing in Garmisch-Partenkirchen and scenic hikes above mountain lakes such as Tegernsee, Schliersee, or the pristine Königsee, near Berchtesgaden. "Mad" King Ludwig let loose his architectural fantasies on the island palace Schloss Herrenchiemsee, modeled on Versailles. Craftmanship continues in towns such as Mittenwald, where violin makers have worked since the 17th century, and in Oberammergau, where many residents are woodcarvers.

Bavarian Forest

Hikers, anglers, and nature lovers head to this idyllic mountainous retreat on the border of the Czech Republic. The region is part of Europe's largest and most dense forest and had long been inaccessible to outsiders. People living here have their own distinctive accent, and unlike Southern Germans, a quiet reserve. They do take great pride in their handcrafts such as glass-making. The region's only larger and well-known city is Passau, almost Mediterranean in its appearance. A gateway city to the west of the forest is the wonderfully medieval Regensburg.

The Romantic Road

Picturesque beyond words, the Romantic Road is more than 200 mi of castles and walled villages, half-timber houses and imposing churches, set in pastoral countryside. The rivers Tauber, Lech, and Main are never distant. Though it looks like a fairy-tale version of a medieval town, Rotenburg-ob-der-Tauber is authentic and Europe's best-preserved one. A total fantastical construction of a castle is King Ludwig II's Schloss Neuschwanstein, which even Walt Disney looked to for inspiration. The baroque era still lives in the city of Würzburg. Powerful prince-bishops spared little expense in creating astonishing opulence, hiring Tiepolo to paint the ceiling frescoes above the grand split staircase of their Residenz. Altars and sculptures by the renown Tilman Riemenschneider grace chapels and museums throughout the area.

Franconia

The region of Franconia is rich in ancient and cultural cities, making this a small but immensely interesting area. The countryside is dotted with old villages and a few historic and very prosperous cities such as Bayreuth, Nürnberg, and Bamberg, which have played a significant role in German cultural history. The former imperial city of Nürnberg, in the heart of the hilly Franconian Switzerland, greets visitors with one of Europe's most beautiful medieval downtowns, but it is also where the Nazi party held its rallies in the 1930s. Today however, it is better known for its *Lebkuchen,* the sweet candy-like gingerbread cookies baked for Christmas and the *Christkindlmarkt,* the nation's most famous and beautiful Christmas fair. Equally tasty are the *Rostbratwürstl,* small roasted sausages from this region. Bamberg, Coburg, and Krombach are little-known treasure troves with quiet streets and breathtaking churches or cloisters. Bayreuth, on the other hand, is a national shrine, where Germany's elite come each year, to applaud the dramatic operas of Richard Wagner, who once lived here.

Bodensee

The Bodensee, or Lake Constance, is the warmest area in Germany, and though a popular vacation area, no tourist developments have spoiled its historic atmosphere. The scenery is enchanting, especially when viewed from the shoreline promenades or from ferries traveling between towns like terraced Meersburg and beautifully preserved Konstanz, a half-hour distant. Formal gardens of tulips, hyacinths, and narcissi thrive on the colorful island of Mainau. The maze of streets in the island town of Lindau carry a history that takes back to Roman Gaul. Bike routes circle the lake; pedal long enough and you'll cross into Switzerland or Austria.

The Black Forest

The Black Forest is synonymous with cuckoo clocks and primeval woodland: certainly thousands of acres are cloaked in pines, and at least one entire town, little Triberg, goes all atwitter every hour. The area also gave its name to one of Germany's most favorite cakes and the *Schwarzwälder Schinken,* a smokey ham. For many Germans, the Black Forest is the epitome of a healthy vacation filled with hikes and fresh mountain air. A world apart from the quaint villages is the stately spa and casino resort of Baden-Baden. Westward through the deep Hell Valley gorge is the beautifully restored university town of Freiburg, the region's largest city.

Heidelberg and the Neckar Valley

For most American and Japanese tourists, good old Heidelberg is quintessential Germany—the medieval town is full of cobblestone alleys, half-timber houses, vineyards, castles, and Germany's oldest university. Heidelberg is the country's most romantic town in a very literal sense, as it was from here that artists like Hölderlin, Schumann, and von Weber shaped the German Romantic movement in the 19th century. The Castle Road makes its way through the Neckar Valley, passing fortresses and villages all the way south to the *Schwabenländle,* the German nickname for the Swabian cities Stuttgart, Heilbronn, and Tübingen. It's the home of hard-working people, speaking with one of the country's most distinctive dialects, a singing and soft version of Southern German. It is also one of most affluent areas in Europe, with a brand-new Mercedes standing in nearly every garage. The area's largest employer is DaimlerChrysler, headquarted in Stuttgart. The Swabians are also famous for their pastamania: everything here is served with curly egg noodles called *Spätzle.*

Frankfurt

You wouldn't know from its skyline of skyscrapers that Frankfurt's history is ancient. More important, the city holds many international trade fairs, is home to Germany's leading stock exchange, the Börse, and is the seat of the new European Central Bank, which controls the euro. Prosperity here has left the art museums flush with works by Dürer, Vermeer, Rembrandt, Rubens, Monet, and Renoir, among others. The city has Germany's oldest jazz cellar and an annual jazz festival. But not everything is modern here. The Römerberg square is lined with historic buildings and writer Goethe's home is a popular attraction. Frankfurters relax in traditional ways—they head for the nearby Taunus Hills for a hike, or stop for

Apfelwein (hard cider) at taverns in the district of Sachsenhausen, on the south bank of the Main River.

The Pfalz and the Rhine Terrace

Wine reigns supreme here. Bacchanalian festivals pepper the calendar between July and October, and wineries welcome drop-ins for tastings year-round. Once you've had your fill of looking at the bottom of a wine glass, head for Worms, whose streets were ancient even when Charlemagne and Luther walked them. Its Jewish cemetery has been in use for more than a millennium. Three great cathedrals are found in Worms, Speyer, and Mainz. Mainz is also where Johannes Gutenberg printed the first bible and where Germany's powerful public television station *ZDF* is headquartered. People here are known for their tolerance and relaxed attitude. The region's most famous son is former German chancellor Helmut Kohl, the longest reigning German head of state in the 20th century.

The Rhineland

Although it is part of westernmost Germany, the Rhineland is the country's spiritual heart. Stories that originated here—of the Nibelungen and the Loreley—have become national legends, and tourists have been enthralled for centuries by the mighty Rhine River and the Mosel, the tributary with improbable twists and turns. Cruises on either river last anywhere from a few hours to a week, passing riverbanks terraced with castles, villages, and vineyards (the world's best Rieslings are produced here). Rüdesheim, the region's unofficial wine capital, has plenty of cozy wine taverns and the entire area has castle hotels. Ancient Trier, on the Mosel, was 1,300 years old when Caesar's legions arrived. Wiesbaden, on the Rhine, was founded by Roman soldiers who discovered its hot springs, prized once again by Europe's elite in the 19th century. Farther north, in vibrant Köln (Cologne), a certain 18th-century eau de cologne is still for sale on Glockengasse at the address for which it is named, No. 4711. However, the city may be most famous as the site of the country's largest and finest Gothic cathedral, and for the German version of Mardi Gras, the *Karneval* in February.

The Fairy-Tale Road

The Fairy-Tale Road, stretching 370 mi between Hanau and Bremen, is also the Road Less Traveled. (All the better for those who choose it.) This is Brothers Grimm Country, the area that the great compilers of folklore mined for their sometimes-dark tales of magic and miracles. The Grimms' imaginations were nourished during a childhood in Steinau an der Strasse, a medieval beauty of a town where their stories delight children today at the Steinauer Marionettentheater. In Hameln (Hamelin), sculptures, plaques, and even rat-shaped pastries recall the tale of the Pied Piper. Bremen is fabled to have been saved by a quartet of animal musicians. Their statues can be seen against the backdrop of a medieval downtown, a historic reminder of Bremen's proud membership in the Hanseatic League. All along the Fairy-Tale Road, misty woodlands and small towns full of half-timber houses look as if they have mysterious and compelling tales to tell. When you pass this way, it's not hard to see how the area spawned the legends that the Grimms shared with the world.

Hamburg

With its international port, rusty brick warehouses, fish market, and Reeperbahn red-light district, Hamburg is undeniably gritty. But its downtown is truly elegant, laced with canals spanned by small bridges. The Inner and Outer Alster Lakes, bordered with parks and shopping arcades and big enough for sailing, form the city's heart, and a 9-mi footpath lines the Elbe River banks. Despite World War II bombings, the city's architecture is diverse, encompassing the neo-Renaissance Rathaus, on a square not unlike Venice's Piazza San Marco, and turn-of-the-century art nouveau buildings.

Schleswig-Holstein and the Baltic Coast

Schleswig-Holstein and the former East Germany's Baltic coast share a windswept landscape scattered with medieval towns, fishing villages, long white beaches, and summer resorts. The Ahlbeck pier dates from the 19th century, and charming Stralsund has a 14th-century redbrick Rathaus. Schwerin, the area's second-largest town after Rostock, has an amazing castle, and striking chalk cliffs edge remote, quiet Rügen island. In Schleswig-Holstein, major draws are chic Sylt island and medieval Lübeck, a stronghold of the powerful Hanseatic merchants who controlled trade on the Baltic beginning in the 13th century.

Berlin

By night this capital is saucy, and culture thrives in its opera houses, concert halls, and theaters. Two cities' worth of world-class museums compete for your daylight hours, as do the shops along 2-mi Kurfürstendamm, which ends at a sobering World War II memorial, the Kaiser-Wilhelm-Gedächtniskirche. One can't forget modern history at other landmarks such as the Brandenburger Tor, which stood alone in divided Berlin's no-man's land until jubilant Berliners flocked here the night the wall fell. Originally the capital of Prussia, the city displays its royal finery and grand collections at Schloss Charlottenburg, and at Potsdam's magnificent palace of Sanssouci, the most beautiful and largest palace complex east of Versailles.

Saxony, Saxony-Anhalt, and Thuringia

Much of Germany's cultural contributions to the world stem from these eastern states. Weimar was home to the poets Goethe and Schiller. The Bach family home and the Thomaskirche, where Johann Sebastian served as choirmaster for 27 years, are in Leipzig, where Richard Wagner was born. Both he and Richard Strauss had premieres at the Semper Opera House in Dresden, whose Brühlsche Terrasse above the Elbe River was once called "Europe's balcony." It was in Meissen that an 18th-century alchemist discovered how to make fine porcelain. And Martin Luther nailed his 95 theses to the door of Wittenberg's Schlosskirche, inching closer to a break with Rome. Near Eisenach you can also see the Wartburg fortress where the excommunicated Luther spent a year in refuge.

PLEASURES AND PASTIMES

Beer and Wine

Germany is the world's largest producer and consumer of beer. Each of its high-quality brands are brewed in accordance with the strict German *Reinheitsgebot* (legislation governing purity of ingredients). Drinking beer, even in public and at any time of the day, is socially quite acceptable. North Germans favor *Pils,* a light lager-like beer. *Alt* is a dark, bitter, English-style ale popular in the northwest. Bavaria prefers the rather heavy *Bockbier* (a type of malt beer), and the typical summer beer *Hefeweizen,* brewed with yeast, also called *Weissbier.* These are usually served in tall half-liter glasses.

The old German national anthem doesn't extol the country's beer, but rather its wine. For many European palates, German wine is either too bitter or too sweet, and has too much sulphur or gas, but the Germans love their vintages, and rightly so. Fine Rieslings have some of the most subtle, spicey tastes of European whites. The country's most prominent wine regions are the Rhine valley terraces, Hesse, Baden, Württemberg, and Franken as well as Saxony in the east. Good wines are labeled *Auslese* or *Qualitätswein*; the addition *mit Prädikat* (with award) indicates an exceptionally good harvest. Some of the (mostly white) wines you should try are *Riesling, Grauburgunder* (Pinot Gris), and *Weissburgunder* (Pinot Blanc) and also the drier *Silvaner* and *Rivaner (Müller-Thurgau)* wines, often bottled in flagon-shaped bottles. Baden produces Germany's best heavy red wines called *Burgunder* or *Spätburgunder.*

Castles and Palaces

Watching over nearly any town that ends in -burg is a medieval fortress or Renaissance palace, often now serving the populace as a museum, a restaurant, and sometimes, a hotel. Grand 18th- and 19th-century palaces are the pride of almost every *Residenzstadt,* a city that once was a king's, duke's or bishop's seat, such as Würzburg. Holy Roman Emperors made their home in Nürnberg's Kaiserburg and renegade Martin Luther spent most of the year 1521 within the hulking Wartburg in Eisenach, hiding from the pope. The castle ruins along the Rhine River are the result of ceaseless fighting with the French, but even their remains were picturesque enough to inspire 19th-century Romantic poets and painters. Other fine castles can be found lurking along the Burgenstrasse (Castle Road) in the Neckar Valley and in mountainous Saxony. The north and northwest is dotted with Renaissance-style *Wasserschlösser* (water palaces), a peculiar variety rarely seen outside Germany. They're built in the middle of a lake or surrounded by an ingenious canal system. Some picture-perfect palaces such as Ludwig the II's Neuschwanstein in Bavaria are not really castles, but were built for show. Berlin, Potsdam, Dresden, Meissen, Schwerin, Munich, and Regensburg have some of the finest palaces in Germany.

Museum Treasures

Germans value education more highly than wealth or social status and regularly bring their children to museums to glean some appreciation of art, history, and the world's achievements. Cities such as Frankfurt and Berlin have nurtured a *Museumslandschaft* (museum landscape), presenting expansive complexes of museums at a single location. Berlin's Museum Island holds monuments of antiquity from around the world and is probably the most amazing museum complex you will ever see. Among the fine art museums not to miss are those in Hamburg, Munich, Frankfurt, and Cologne. Other museums typical for Germany are those showcasing technological inventions, such as the Deutsche Museum in Munich or the Zeppelin Museum on the shore of the Bodensee. Even small towns have *Heimatmuseen* (local museums), which detail the history and cultural contributions of a particular region. Another quirky sort of museum in Germany is the tiny one that exposes Germans' peculiar and often amusing *Sammelleidenschaft* (passion for collecting things)—such as a thimble, creche, or miniature toy soldier museum.

Music

Germany has a lively and centuries-old musical tradition. Though the country is primarily known for its love of the classics such as Bach, Mozart, Beethoven, Brahms, Haydn, Händel, Wagner, and others, there is also a legion of modern classical composers. Masters like Schönberg, Richard Strauss, Mahler, Orff, and Stockhausen are hugely popular. Germans don't just like to listen carefully at classical concerts (avoid any opportunity for your neighbor or the whole row to shush you), but also like to perform themselves. Practically every small town has a music school or *Musikverein* (music association) that regularly present concerts. This tradition has formed some of the world's leading orchestras, such as the Berlin Philharmonic, and opera houses, as in Berlin, Munich, and Hamburg. Equally important in daily life (just check the local newspapers) are choral societies, mainly church or folk choirs, who appear are on stage more often than complete orchestras. The German label *Deutsche Grammophon* is the leading producer of classical music.

Walks and Hikes

German history, literature, and folk songs are full of *Wanderlust,* the passion for hiking and walking. From the leisurely Sunday afternoon stroll to the more strenuous ramble, walks and hikes are a favorite national pastime in this densely populated land. A retreat into nature is never far off as an expansive network of trails crisscross the whole country. Many towns, communities, and states have carefully laid out their hiking trails to connect points of natural or historic interest. Most paths lead through forests or mountain ranges, but there are also numerous trails along the coast and marshlands. Tourist information offices are a good source for maps and arranging packages in which you can hike from inn to inn while someone else transports your luggage.

FODOR'S CHOICE

Even with so many special places in Germany, Fodor's writers and editors have their favorites. Here are a few that stand out.

Museums

Domschatzkammer, Aachen. Sacred art from late antiquity and the Carolingian, Ottonian, and Hohenstaufen eras fill one of the richest cathedral treasuries in Europe.

Glyptothek, Munich. Louis I of Bavaria, who launched Munich's trajectory as an art center, began this wonderful collection of Greek and Roman sculptures. Most famous is the sensuous Barberini faun, also called the Sleeping Satyr (200 BC).

Kunsthalle, Hamburg. German Romantic painters Caspar David Friedrich and Philip Otto Runge are featured here, as are masters like Holbein, Rembrandt, Van Dyck, and Tiepolo.

Museum der Bildenden Künste, Leipzig. Cranach the Elder's works are a highlight of the thousands of paintings here.

Pergamonmuseum, Berlin. Within this world-class museum are the Greek Pergamon Altar, the market gate of Miletus, and the Babylonian processional way.

Zwinger, Dresden. Explore the baroque magnificence of this palace as well as its galleries with paintings by Raphael, Vermeer, and Rubens.

Dining

Bareiss, Baiersbronn. The cuisine and champagne selection at this Black Forest mountain resort attract even the French from across the border. $$$$

Im Schiffchen, Düsseldorf. Wear your jacket and tie for a special meal at this favorite of the Rhineland. The chef offers a lower-priced menu of local specialties at the ground-floor restaurant, Aalschokker. $$$$

Residenz Heinz Winkler, Aschau. The reverence paid to herbs and spices here makes for sumptuous and healthy, French-leaning cuisine. Well-heeled Müncheners know the trip to the chef's Alpine inn is worth it. $$$$

Margaux, Berlin. Let the sommelier help you choose one of the 750 bottles of wine at this hip eatery across from the Brandenburg Gate. The imaginative menu makes Margaux the talk of the town. $$$–$$$$

Aurum, Hamburg. The menu changes weekly at this small restaurant with minimalist design and innovative German cuisine. $–$$$

Dukatz, Munich. If you aren't flush with funds, you don't have to miss out on Munich's highly praised dining scene. Casual but stylish Dukatz excels at German nouvelle cuisine. $–$$$

Wein- und Speisehaus zum Stachel, Würzburg. This restaurant in the Franken wine region's capital serves its own vintages and hearty Franconian fare. $

Lodging

Dornröschenschloss, Sababurg. A wild animal preserve and dense woods surround the small castle-hotel said to have inspired *Sleeping Beauty.* $$$$

Kempinski Hotel Vier Jahreszeiten, Munich. This Four Seasons hotel known for luxury and excellent service is perfectly placed among the premier shops of Maximilianstrasse. $$$$

Schlosshotel Bühlerhöhe, Bühl. High on a Black Forest mountain, this resort pampers guests with everything from aromatherapy and seaweed wraps to horseback riding. $$$$

Burghotel Auf Schönburg, Oberwesel. This intimate hotel in a 900-year-old castle provides spectacular views of the Rhine from the terrace restaurant and many of the rooms. $$$–$$$$

Hotel Adlon, Berlin. No other hotel in Berlin can match the Adlon's history or its prestigious location near the Brandenburger Tor. It's the government's unofficial guesthouse. $$$–$$$$

Art Hotel Robert Mayer, Frankfurt. Artists have outfitted the 11 rooms of this 1905 art nouveau villa with cool minimalist style—and a sense of humor. $$$

Romantik Hotel zum Ritter St. Georg, Heidelberg. Heidelberg's only Renaissance building has a stunning facade, three restaurants, and comfortably modern rooms. $$$

Towns Where Time Stands Still

Bad Wimpfen. Romans founded this ancient hill town in the 1st century AD. The remains of Barbarossa's imperial palace and a picture-postcard ensemble of Gothic and Renaissance buildings are part of the town's marked walking tour.

Bernkastel-Kues. Early Renaissance facades surround the market square of this town that straddles the Mosel River.

Quedlinburg. A UNESCO World Heritage site, this Harz Mountains town has more than 1,600 half-timber houses, the oldest dating from the early 1300s.

Rothenburg-ob-der-Tauber. This walled town on the Romantic Road is a treasure of medieval towers and turrets.

St. Martin. Grapevines garland ancient houses in one of the most charming wine villages of the Pfalz region.

Wasserburg. What was born as a fortress on the site of a Roman watchtower is now a car-free island town on the Bodensee.

GREAT ITINERARIES

Highlights of Germany

12 to 18 days. Germany offers everything from opera houses to oompah bands and from seaside villages to snowcapped mountains. For a parade of early German architecture, cruise the steeply banked, vineyard-terraced Rheingau between Mainz and Koblenz, full of riverside castles. The Romantic movement, a product of this evocative setting, flourished in the university town of Heidelberg. Munich, Germany's most laid-back city and the capital of Bavaria and of beer, is the gateway to the Alps and foothill lakes. In Nürnberg, relics of the Holy Roman Empire coexist with ruins of the Third Reich. Leipzig and Dresden are the pearls of what was East Germany, and just to the north of these is the racy capital of Berlin, which overwhelms with entertainment, culture, and vivid reminders of 20th-century history.

Rhine Valley from Mainz to Koblenz *(three to four days).* From Frankfurt take the short train ride over the Rhine to see Mainz's Dom, one of Europe's greatest Romanesque cathedrals. Continue by train through Rheingau vineyards to Bingen and stay in a castle hotel. In the morning take a leisurely river cruise as far as Koblenz, breaking up your journey to overnight in a riverside inn. Allow a day for exploring Koblenz, setting aside an hour to visit the scenic Deutsches Eck, the point where the Mosel flows into the Rhine, and the site of monuments to Germany's unity and division. (☞ The Rhine Terrace in Chapter 11 and the Mittelrhein in Chapter 12.)

Heidelberg *(one to two days).* Generations of artists, composers, writers, and romantics have crossed the Alte Brücke, spanning the Neckar River, and climbed up the steep, winding Schlangenweg to the aptly named Philosophers' Path. At the top you'll have a view of Germany's archetypal university city and its ruined Renaissance castle. Don't leave Heidelberg without eating (and drinking) in a centuries-old student tavern. (☞ Heidelberg and the Neckar-Rhine Triangle in Chapter 9.)

Munich and the Alps *(three to four days).* Visit the Wittelsbach palaces Schloss Nymphenburg and Residenz, reminders that Bavaria once was the second most powerful kingdom in Germany. Follow that with an evening in a beer hall, which will confirm everything you've ever heard about beer, pork, and potato consumption in Bavaria. Relax on the morning train to Berchtesgaden, the Bavarian Alps a soothing cyclorama beyond the window. Not far away from Berchtesgaden Hitler's Obersalzberg retreat takes priority, but find time for the most beautiful corner of Germany, the mountain-ringed Königsee. (☞ Chapters 2 and 3.)

Nürnberg *(one to two days).* In Nürnberg you'll see the full spectrum of German history. The city's massive fortress, dating from 1050, was the residence of successive Holy Roman Emperors. The former home of Renaissance artist Albrecht Dürer is now a fascinating museum. Ride the S-2 suburban rail line to the Zeppelinfeld, the enormous parade grounds where Hitler addressed the Nürnberg rallies. (☞ Southern Franconia in Chapter 6.)

Leipzig and Dresden *(two to three days).* To understand the enormous political and social changes brought about by German reunification you have to visit Leipzig or Dresden—both, if possible. Deteriorated after nearly a half century of communism, they have returned to commercial and cultural prominence. A choral concert in Leipzig's Thomaskirche, where Johann Sebastian Bach was choirmaster, or a walk high above the Elbe River along Dresden's Brühlsche Terrasse is completely enchanting. (☞ Saxony in Chapter 17.)

Berlin *(two to three days).* Reunited and rebuilt, Berlin races forward. The German parliament is back in the Reichstag, and world-renowned architects have changed the city's face. Hip restaurants and bars fill the courtyards and alleyways of Mitte, which is also home to many museums. Sights recalling World War II and the

Cold War are everywhere, and antiquities steal the spotlight on Museum Island. The Zoologischer Garten, Tiergarten, and Ku'damm cafés offer the relaxation you'll need after being swept up in this city's energy. (☞ Chapter 16.)

By Public Transportation

Mainz is a 30-minute train ride from Frankfurt, and Bingen is 40 minutes farther by train or bus. Cruise boats leave Bingen daily for the Rhine journey to Koblenz. Catch an InterCity train in Koblenz for the return trip south, changing at Mannheim for Heidelberg (3 hrs). Return to Mannheim by a local train (10 min) and change to an InterCity or Eurocity train to Munich (about 3 hrs). InterCity Express and Eurocity services link Munich and Nürnberg (1 hr, 45 min). InterCity and InterRegio services link Nürnberg and Leipzig (3 hrs, 40 min) and Leipzig and Dresden (1 hr). There are hourly InterCity and other express services from Dresden to Berlin (1 hr). Return from Berlin to Frankfurt by InterCity Express (3 hrs) or fly back (1 hr).

Castles in Wine Country

Six to nine days. Centuries of German culture unfold on a medieval castle tour through the valleys of the Rhine and its tributaries. Today castle guest rooms and restaurants provide panoramic views as well as glasses of crisp Riesling and velvety Spätburgunder (pinot noir), Germany's finest white and red wines. Wine estates often post signs near their entrances that announce WEINVERKAUF (wine for sale) or HEUTE WEINPROBE (wine tastings today). Come during summer or autumn, when the wine-festival season is in full swing and many a castle courtyard hosts theater and concerts.

Mittelrhein and Mosel *(three to four days).* The Mittelrhein wine town of St. Goar is an ideal base for excursions into the Rhine and Mosel valleys. The terrace of the hotel-restaurant opposite Burg Rheinfels, the Rhine's largest fortress ruin, is a superb vantage point. Ferry across the river to catch a train to Rüdesheim, the liveliest town in the Rheingau wine region. Return to St. Goar on a KD Rhine steamer, and savor a glass of delicate Mosel wine or its fuller-bodied Rhine counterpart. Set aside a full day to tour the Rhine's only impregnable castle, the Marksburg, followed by a jaunt through the lower Mosel valley from Koblenz to the fairy-tale castle Burg Eltz. En route you'll pass breathtakingly steep vineyards and dozens of wine estates. (☞ The Mittelrhein and the Mosel Valley in Chapter 12.)

Neckar Valley *(two to three days).* Spend one day in Heidelberg's Old Town and massive castle ruins, but beware the crowds of summer. The town straddles the Hessische Bergstrasse and northern Baden wine regions. The white varietals Riesling, Grauburgunder (Pinot Gris), and Weissburgunder (Pinot Blanc) yield the finest wines. On the Burgenstrasse (Castle Road), have lunch on the castle terrace in Hirschhorn. Neckarzimmern's Burg Hornberg, residence of a celebrated 16th-century knight, is the perfect stopover. Atop its own terraced vineyards in the Württemberg wine region, the 12th-century castle includes guest rooms with splendid views of the Neckar Valley as well as good food and wine (try the spicy white varietals Traminer and Muskateller). There's a museum and falconry at Burg Guttenberg, and medieval Bad Wimpfen has a former imperial palace and a Benedictine monastery. (☞ Heidelberg and the Neckar-Rhine Triangle, and the Burgenstrasse in Chapter 9.)

Tauber and Main Valleys *(two to three days).* The Baden, Württemberg, and Franken wine regions converge in the peaceful Tauber Valley. Foremost are the earthy, robust, dry white Silvaner and Rivaner (Müller-Thurgau) wines, often bottled in the flagon-shaped Bocksbeutel. Bad Mergentheim, a pretty spa and former residence of the Knights of the Teutonic Order, lies in the heart of the valley. In neighboring Weikersheim, tour the Renaissance hunting palace of the counts of Hohenlohe, after which you can sample the local wines in the shop at the gateway. Follow the course of the Tauber to its confluence with the Main River at Wertheim, also known as "little Heidelberg" because of its impressive hilltop castle ruins. In Würzburg, your next stop, you'll see many Gothic and baroque masterpieces plus the Marienberg fortress and its successor, the opulent Residenz. Three first-class wine estates here have wine pubs and shops. (☞ Northern Romantic Road in Chapter 5.)

By Public Transportation

Fast, frequent train service from Frankfurt to St. Goar, Koblenz, Heidelberg, or Würzburg, supplemented by local train and bus service, gets you to the above destinations within two hours. The Deutsche Touring company's Europabus travels the Burgenstrasse, including Heidelberg and the Neckar Valley, as well as the Romantic Road, serving Würzburg, Bad Mergentheim, and Weikersheim. Sights are open and boats cruise the Rhine, Mosel, Neckar, and Main rivers from Easter through October.

The Great German Outdoors

7 to 10 days. Germans love the outdoors, and the autobahns are often jammed with families on their way to the countryside. News of a cold front on its way from Russia sets Germans to dusting off their skis, and the prediction of a high-pressure zone moving up from the Mediterranean fills the beds in hiking retreats. The mountains and lakes of Bavaria are southern Germany's playground. The Black Forest and Bodensee (Lake Constance), also in the south, are popular spa and recreation destinations. The gateway to all of them is Munich.

Bavarian Alps and Lakes *(three to four days).* The Ammersee, ringed by cycling paths and walking trails, is a short ride from Munich. Most of the lakes in the Alps are warm enough for swimming in summer, and boatyards rent small sailboats and windsurfing boards. There are hiking trails in the mountains above Tegernsee; for more challenging walking head to Garmisch-Partenkirchen. It's one of Bavaria's three leading ski centers, with skiing virtually year-round on the glacier atop the Zugspitze, Germany's highest mountain. From here, wind your way down to the warmer clime of the Bodensee via the Deutsche Alpenstrasse. (☞ Side Trips from Munich in Chapter 2 and Chapter 3.)

Bodensee *(two to three days).* The Bodensee area is great for bicycling. An uninterrupted cycle path follows the shore of the lake, which you and your bike can cross via ferries. Bikes are rented at shops and some hotels. The climate here is unusually warm for Germany. Vineyards and orchards fill the hillsides, and rare and exotic plants decorate the tiny island of Mainau. On the rural island Reichenau you can hike or pedal between Romanesque churches dating back to the year 816. Bird-watchers should head to the Mettnau Peninsula. (☞ Chapter 7.)

The Black Forest *(two to three days).* The Black Forest has wide open spaces for walking, horseback riding, cycling, and even golf. In winter, meadows become ski slopes, and forest paths are meticulously groomed as cross-country ski trails. This is also spa country, where you can rest your weary limbs in hot springs in Baden-Baden, while rubbing elbows with high society. (☞ Northern Black Forest in Chapter 8.)

By Public Transportation

The lakes near Munich are easily accessible both by S-bahn suburban services and via local trains that run hourly between Munich and Garmisch-Partenkirchen. The Bodensee towns are all within three hours of Munich by train, and local buses and trains travel the north shore of the lake. Baden-Baden is about 6½ hours from Munich by train via Stuttgart or Karlsruhe, and 3–4 hours from Friedrichshafen. Local buses and trains link Baden-Baden with most Black Forest resorts.

2 MUNICH

Chic and cosmopolitan, carefree and with a distinct touch of provincial charm. As Bavaria's capital and one of Germany's biggest cities, Munich has more than its share of great museums, architectural treasures, historic sites, and world-class shops, restaurants, and hotels. The same could be said of its abundance of lederhosen and oompah bands. But it's the overall feeling of *Gemütlichkeit*—loosely translated as conviviality—that makes the city so special, with an open-air market here, a park there, and beer halls everywhere.

Updated by
Marton Radkai

IN THE RELAXED AND SUNNY SOUTH, Munich (*München*) is the proud capital of Bavaria. Even Germans come here to vacation, mixing the city's pleasures with those of the inviting landscapes surrounding it. The very likeable city bills itself as *Die Weltstadt mit Herz* (the cosmopolitan city with heart), but in rare bouts of self-deprecatory humor, friendly Bavarians will remind you that Munich is hardly anything more than a world village.

The *Innenstadt,* or city center, is younger than some of the surrounding neighborhoods, such as Heuhausen or Haidhausen. Munich was created in the 12th century as a market town on the "salt road" connecting mighty Salzburg and Augsburg, and it has never lost its sense for business and marketing. It continues to exist between two poles, tradition and high-tech, or as the locals say "laptops and lederhosen." It's a city of ravishing baroque and smoky beer cellars, of grand 19th-century architecture and sleek steel-and-glass office buildings, of millionaires and farmers. Germany's favorite city is a place with extraordinary ambience and a vibrant lifestyle all its own, in a splendid setting within view—on a clear day—of the towering Alps. The city is the stomping grounds of all kinds of media, from traditional publishing houses to top-notch digital postproduction companies. The concentration of electronics and computer firms—Siemens, IBM, Apple, and the like—in and around the city has turned it into the Silicon Valley of Europe.

One thing deserves special mention: Munich is the world capital of beer and beery culture. Between visits to the world-class museums, drop into one of those equally renowned cavernous beer halls, filled with the deafening clanking of beer mugs, brass bands, and conversations in gravelly Bavarian, and where the beer is often served by busty Fräuleins in flaring dirndl dresses. No sooner have the first spring rays of sun started warming the atmosphere, than Müncheners from all walks of life flock outside to their beer gardens in the shade of huge chestnut trees. Munich's most famous festival isn't on any arts calendar: the beer-soaked Oktoberfest started as an agricultural fair held on the occasion of a royal marriage.

The *other* Munich is one of charm, refinement, and sophistication, populated by museum goers who shop in high-fashion boutiques and dine in five-star restaurants. Various "long nights" throughout the year celebrate museum-going, books, and musical peformances. The city's appreciation of the arts began under the kings and dukes of the Wittelsbach Dynasty, which ruled Bavaria for over 750 years until 1918. The Wittelsbach legacy is alive and well in the city's fabulous art museums, the Opera House, the Philharmonic, and much more.

Munich is a big and rich city, but its cleanliness, safety, and comfortable pace give it an ever so slightly rustic feeling. This, combined with broad sidewalks, endless shops and eateries, view of the Alps, and a huge green heart, the English Garden, make Munich one of Germany's most enjoyable cities.

Pleasures and Pastimes

Beer and Beer Gardens

Munich has more than 100 beer gardens, ranging from huge establishments that seat several hundred to small terraces tucked behind neighborhood pubs and taverns. Beer gardens are such an integral part of Munich life that a council proposal to cut down their hours provoked a storm of protest in 1995, culminating in one of the largest mass demonstrations in the city's history. They open whenever the thermometer creeps above 10°C (42°F) and when the sun filters through the chestnut trees that are a necessary part of beer-garden scenery. Most—but not all—allow you to bring along your own food, but if you do, don't defile this hallowed territory with something so foreign as pizza or a burger from McDonald's.

Dining

Old Munich inns (*Gaststätten*) feature solid regional specialties and *gutbürgerliche Küche,* loosely translated as good homey fare. The settings for such victuals include boisterous brewery restaurants, beer halls, beer gardens, rustic cellars, and *Weinstuben* (wine taverns).

The city's snacking tradition is centuries old and a tempting array of food is available almost anytime day or night. The generic term for snacks is *Imbiss,* and thanks to growing internationalism, these come in all shapes, sizes, and national flavors, from the generic *Wiener* (hot dog), to the Turkish *Döner* sandwich (pressed and roasted lamb, beef, or turkey). Following a spate of Chinese places is a small but quality-minded community of sushi bars. Virtually every butcher offers some sort of *Brotzeit* snack, which can range from a modest sandwich to a steaming plate of goulash with potatoes and salad.

Some edibles come with social etiquette attached. Before noon, during what is sometimes called *Frühschoppen* ("early mug"), one eats *Weisswurst,* a tender minced-veal sausage—made fresh daily; steamed; and served with sweet mustard, a crisp roll or a pretzel, and *Weissbier* (wheat beer). As legend has it, this white sausage was invented in 1857 by a butcher who had a hangover and mixed the wrong ingredients. A plaque on a wall in Marienplatz marks where the "mistake" was made. At one time sausage was available only in and around Munich and served only between midnight and noon. Thanks to refrigeration and preservatives, Weisswurst can now be eaten all day in Munich, though some places stop selling them at noon. The better folk use knife and fork to remove the edible part from the skin. The rougher crowd might indulge in *auszuzeln,* using tooth and jaw to suck the innards of the Weisswurst out.

Another favorite Bavarian specialty is *Leberkäs*—literally "liver cheese," although neither liver nor cheese is among its ingredients. It is a spicy meat loaf baked to a crusty turn each morning and served in succulent slabs throughout the day. A *Leberkäs Semmel*—a wedge of the meat loaf between two halves of a crispy bread roll slathered with a slightly sharp mustard—is the favorite Munich on-the-hoof snack. After that comes the repertoire of sausages indigenous to Bavaria, including short thick ones from Regensburg and short thin ones from Nürnberg.

More substantial dishes include *Tellerfleisch,* boiled beef with freshly grated horseradish and boiled potatoes on the side, served on wooden plates (there is a similar dish called *Tafelspitz*). Among roasts, sauerbraten (beef) and *Schweinebraten* (roast pork) are accompanied by dumplings and sauerkraut. *Hax'n* (ham hocks) are roasted until they're crisp on the outside, juicy on the inside. They are served with sauerkraut and potato puree. Game in season (venison or boar, for instance) and duck are served with potato dumplings and red cabbage. As for fish, the region has not only excellent trout, served either smoked as an hors d'oeuvre or fried or boiled as an entrée, but also the perchlike Rencke from Lake Starnberg.

You'll also find soups, salads, casseroles, hearty stews, and what may well be the greatest variety and the highest quality of baked goods in Europe, including pretzels. And for dessert, put aside the fears of cholesterol and indulge in a bowl of Bavarian cream, apple strudel, or *Dampfnudel,* a fluffy leavened dough dumpling served usually with vanilla sauce. No one need ever go hungry or thirsty in Munich.

Music and Opera

Munich and music complement each other marvelously. The city has two world-renowned orchestras (one, the Philharmonic, is directed by the American conductor James Levine), the Bavarian State Opera Company (managed by an ingenious British director, Peter Jonas), wonderful choral ensembles, a rococo jewel of a court theater, and a modern Philharmonic concert hall of superb proportions and acoustics—and that's just for starters.

Shopping

Munich has three of Germany's most exclusive shopping streets. At the other end of the scale, it has a variety of flea markets to rival that of any other European city. In between are department stores, where acute German-style competition assures reasonable prices and often produces outstanding bargains. Artisans and artists bring their wares of beauty and originality to the Christmas markets. Collect their business cards—in the summer you're sure to want to order another of those little gold baubles that were on sale in December.

EXPLORING MUNICH

Munich is a wealthy city—and it shows. Everything is extremely upscale and up-to-date. At times the aura of affluence may be all but overpowering. But that's what Munich is all about these days and nights: a new city superimposed on the old; conspicuous consumption; a fresh patina of glitter along with the traditional rustic charms. Such are the dynamics and duality of this fascinating town.

Numbers in the text correspond to numbers in the margin and on the Munich map.

Great Itineraries

IF YOU HAVE 2 OR 3 DAYS

Visit the tourist information office at the *Hauptbahnhof* (main railway station) and make for one of the cafés of the nearby pedestrian shopping zone to get your bearings (try the cafeteria at the Hertie department store on the square opposite the train station or at the Mövenpick in the beautiful Künstlerhaus on Lenbachplatz). You can see the highlights of the city center and royal Munich in one day. Plan an eastward course across (or rather under) Karlsplatz and into Neuhauserstrasse and Kaufingerstrasse, plunging into this busy center of commerce. You can escape the crowds inside one of the three churches that punctuate the route: the Bürgersaal, the Michaelskirche, or the Frauenkirche, a soaring Gothic cathedral. Try to arrive in the city's central square, Marienplatz, in time for the 11 AM performance of the glockenspiel in the tower of the neo-Gothic Neues Rathaus (City Hall). Proceed to the city market, the Viktualienmarkt, for lunch, and then head a few blocks north for an afternoon visit to the Residenz, the rambling palace of the Wittelsbach rulers. End your first day with coffee at Munich's oldest café, the Tambosi, or an early evening cocktail at Käfer's, both on Odeonsplatz. Set aside days two and three for Munich's leading museums in the Maxvorstadt district. Also find time for a stroll east to the Englischer Garten, Munich's city park, for an outdoor lunch or an evening meal at one of its beer gardens or in the Seehaus, on the northern shore of the Kleinhesseloher See (lake).

IF YOU HAVE 4 OR 5 DAYS

For the first three days follow the itinerary described above. On the fourth day venture out to suburban Nymphenburg for a visit to Schloss Nymphenburg, the Wittelsbachs' summer residence. Allow up to a whole day to view the palace's buildings and its museums and to stroll through its lovely park, breaking for lunch at the restaurant in the botanical garden. A tour of the Olympiapark can be fit into half a day. Ride to the top of the Olympic Tower for the best view of Munich and the surrounding countryside. Then either take a walk along the surprisingly quiet city banks of the Isar River, its rapid waters a translucent green from its mountain sources, or visit one of the two villa-museums, the Museum Villa Stuck or the Städtische Galerie im Lenbachhaus. The latter is huge and has a popular café.

The City Center

Munich's Old Town has been rebuilt so often over the centuries, that it no longer has that homogeneous look that one finds in many other old German towns. Postwar developments often separate clusters of buildings that date back to Munich's origins—and not always to harmonious effect. The outer perimeter of this tour is defined more by your stamina than by ancient city walls.

A Good Walk

Begin your walk through the city center at the **Hauptbahnhof** ①, the main train station and site of the city tourist office, which is next to the station's main entrance. Pick up a detailed city map here. Cross Bahnhofplatz, the square in front of the station (or take the underpass), and walk toward Schützenstrasse, which marks the start of Munich's pedestrian shopping mall, the *Fussgängerzone,* 2 km (1 mi) of traffic-free streets. Running virtually the length of Schützenstrasse is Munich's largest department store, Hertie. At the end of the street you descend via the pedestrian underpass into a vast underground complex of boutiques, shops, and snack bars. Above you is the busy traffic intersection, **Karlsplatz** ②, always referred to as Stachus after an inn and beer garden that stood here back in the 19th century. Its fountain area is a favorite place to hang out. Just make sure your wallet is safe.

Ahead stands one of the city's oldest gates, the Karlstor, first mentioned in local records in 1302. Beyond it lies Munich's main shopping thoroughfare, Neuhauserstrasse, and its extension, Kaufingerstrasse. On your left as you enter Neuhauserstrasse is another attractive fountain: a late-19th-century figure of Bacchus. This part of town was almost completely destroyed by bombing during World War II. Great efforts were made to ensure that the designs of the new buildings harmonized with the old city, although some of the modern structures are little more than functional. Though this may not be an architectural showplace, there are redeeming features to the area. Haus Oberpollinger, on Neuhauserstrasse, is one; it's a department store hiding behind an imposing 19th-century facade. Notice the weather vanes of old merchant ships on its high-gabled roof.

Shopping is not the only attraction on these streets. Worldly department stores rub shoulders with two remarkable churches. The first is the **Bürgersaal** ③, which dates to the early 18th century. Farther on comes the **Michaelskirche** ④, a Renaissance construction originally built in the 16th century and entirely redone after the war. A part of the pavement near the Michaelskirche is alive with hundreds of tulips in spring. The fountain here features Salome, in honor of the opera of the same name by Munich's famous son Richard Strauss. The massive building next to Michaelskirche was once one of Munich's oldest

Alte Pinakothek **41**
Alter Botanischer Garten **34**
Alter Hof **14**
Altes Rathaus **9**
Antikensammlungen **39**
Archäologische Staatssammlung . . . **32**
Asamkirche **12**
Bayerisches Nationalmuseum . . . **30**
Bürgersaal **3**
Deutches Jagd- und Fischereimuseum **5**
Deutsches Museum **16**
Dreifaltigkeitskirche . **35**
Englischer Garten **28**
Feldherrnhalle **24**
Frauenkirche **6**
Gasteig Kulturzentrum **17**
Glyptothek **38**
Hauptbahnhof **1**
Haus der Kunst **29**
Hofbräuhaus **18**
Hofgarten **23**
Karlsplatz **2**
Karolinenplatz **36**
Königsplatz **37**
Kunsthalle der Hypo-Kulturstiftung . . **27**
Marienplatz **7**
Maximilianstrasse . . **19**
Michaelskirche **4**
Münchner Stadtmuseum **11**
Münze **15**
Museum Villa Stuck **33**
Nationaltheater **21**
Neue Pinakothek . . . **42**
Neues Rathaus **8**
Peterskirche **13**
Pinakothek der Moderne **43**
Residenz **22**
Schack-Galerie **31**
Siegestor **25**
Staatliches Museum für Völkerkunde **20**
Städtische Galerie im Lenbachhaus . . . **40**
Theatinerkirche **26**
Viktualienmarkt **10**

Munich (München)

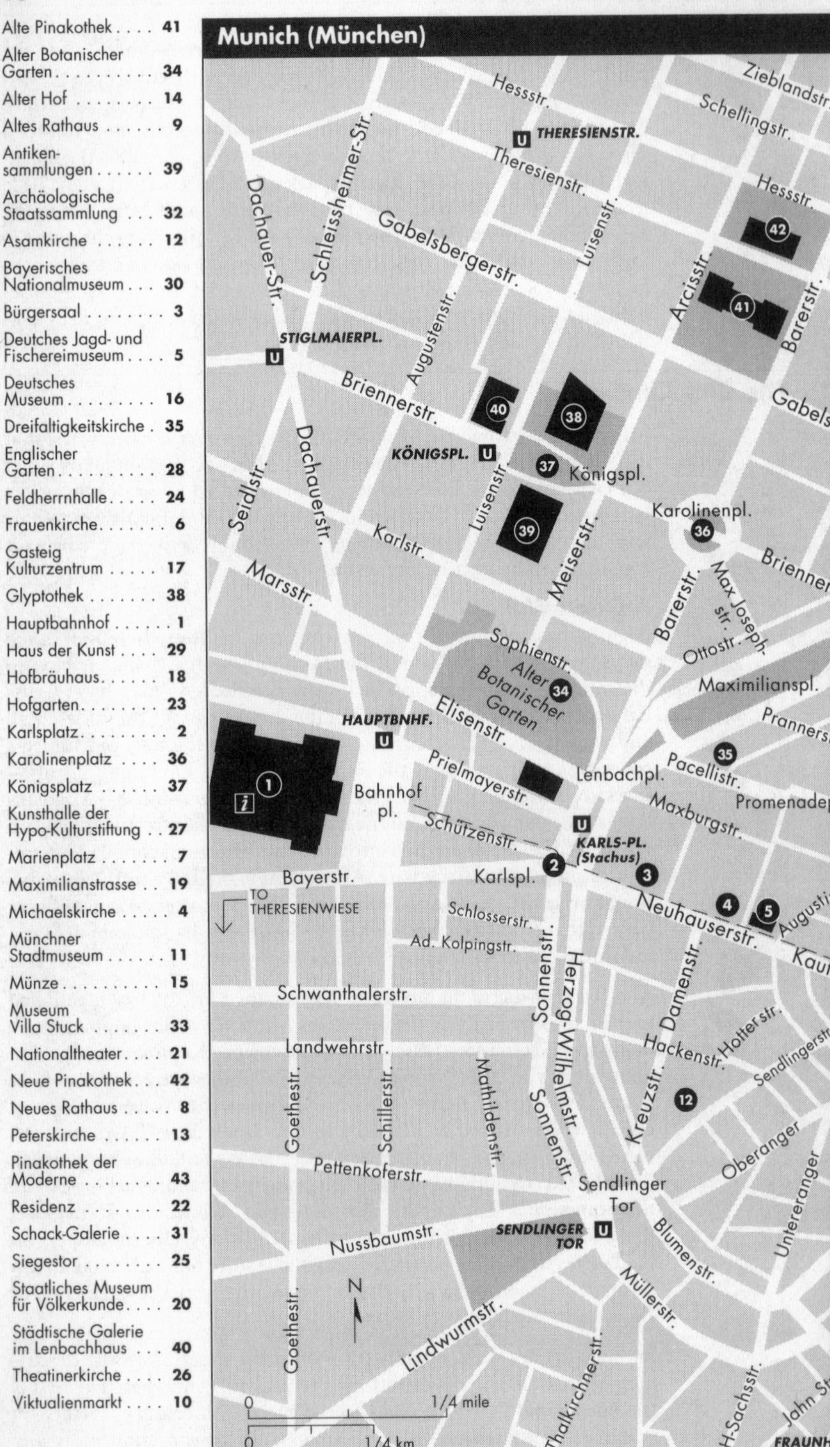

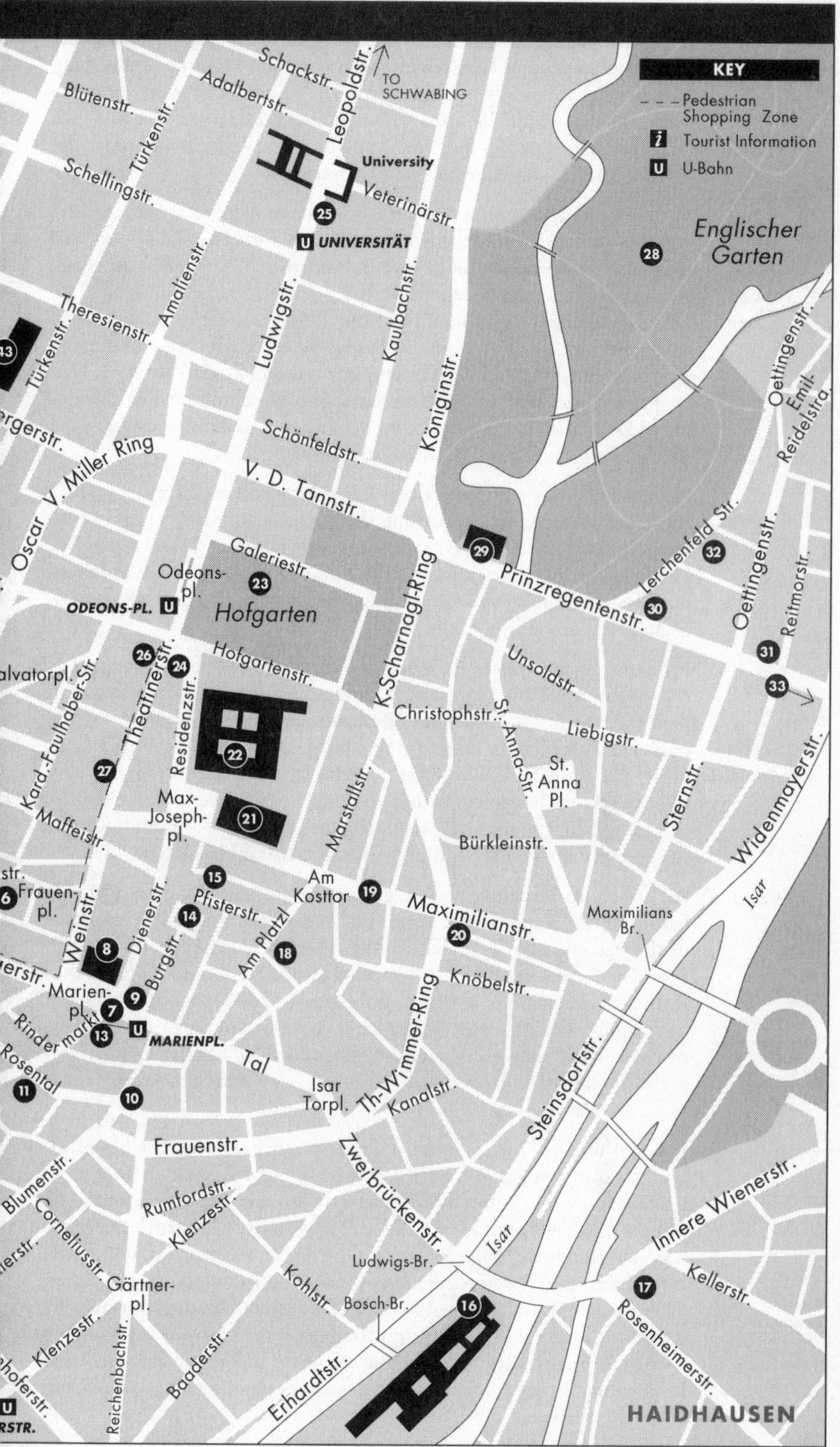

KEY
Pedestrian Shopping Zone
Tourist Information
U-Bahn
Schackstr.
Leopoldstr.
TO SCHWABING
Blütenstr.
Adalbertstr.
Türkenstr.
University
Schellingstr.
Veterinärstr.
UNIVERSITÄT
Englischer Garten
Amalienstr.
Ludwigstr.
Kaulbachstr.
Theresienstr.
Türkenstr.
Königinstr.
Oettingenstr.
Emil-Reidelstr.
Schönfeldstr.
Oscar V. Miller Ring
V. D. Tannstr.
Galeriestr.
Odeons-pl.
ODEONS-PL.
Hofgarten
K.-Scharnagl-Ring
Prinzregentenstr.
Lerchenfeld Str.
Oettingenstr.
Reitmorstr.
Hofgartenstr.
Theatinerstr.
Residenzstr.
Kard.-Faulhaber-Str.
Unsoldstr.
Christophstr.
St.-Anna-Str.
Liebigstr.
St. Anna Pl.
Sternstr.
Widenmayerstr.
Max-Joseph-pl.
Maffeistr.
Marstallstr.
Bürkleinstr.
Frauen-pl.
Weinstr.
Dienerstr.
Pfisterstr.
Am Kosttor
Maximilianstr.
Maximilians Br.
Isar
Burgstr.
Am Platzl
Knöbelstr.
Marien-pl.
Rindermarkt
MARIENPL.
Tal
Th.-Wimmer-Ring
Steinsdorfstr.
Rosental
Isar Torpl.
Kanalstr.
Frauenstr.
Zweibrückenstr.
Blumenstr.
Corneliusstr.
Rumfordstr.
Klenzestr.
Innere Wienerstr.
Isar
Ludwigs-Br.
Kellerstr.
Gärtner-pl.
Kohlstr.
Bosch-Br.
Rosenheimerstr.
Klenzestr.
Reichenbachstr.
Baaderstr.
Erhardtstr.
HAIDHAUSEN

churches. Originally built in the 13th century for Augustine monks, the edifice was secularized in the early 19th century and today is the **Deutsches Jagd- und Fischereimuseum** (German Hunting and Fishing Museum) ⑤. Opposite is one of Munich's famous brewery inns, the Augustiner Bierhalle. Behind its Renaissance and baroque facade—the establishment occupies two buildings—are vaulted ceilings and a delightful little courtyard decorated with frescoes.

Turn left at the museum onto crescent-shape Augustinerstrasse, and you will soon arrive in Frauenplatz, a quiet square with a shallow, sunken fountain. Towering over it is the **Frauenkirche** ⑥, Munich's cathedral, whose twin onion domes are the city's main landmark and its symbol. From the cathedral follow any of the alleys heading east, and you'll reach the very heart of Munich, **Marienplatz** ⑦, which is surrounded by stores and dining spots. Marienplatz is dominated by the 19th-century **Neues Rathaus** ⑧; the **Altes Rathaus** ⑨, a rebuilt medieval building of assured charm, sits more modestly at the eastern entrance of the square. Its pretty tower houses a toy museum.

Hungry? Thirsty? Help is only a few steps away. From the Altes Rathaus, cross the street, passing the Heiliggeistkirche, an early Munich church with a rococo interior added between 1724 and 1730. Heiliggeiststrasse brings you to the jumble known as the **Viktualienmarkt** ⑩, the city's open-air food market, where you can eat a stand-up lunch at any of the many stalls.

From the market follow Rosental and turn left onto Sendlingerstrasse, one of the city's most interesting shopping streets. On the way you'll pass the rear of the **Münchner Stadtmuseum** (City Museum) ⑪ at the corner of Oberangerstrasse. As you head down Sendlingerstrasse, on your right is the remarkable **Asamkirche** ⑫. The exterior fits so snugly into the street's housefronts that you might easily overlook the church were it not for the somewhat incongruous rocks it was built upon. At the end of the street is Sendlinger Tor, a medieval brick gate.

Backtrack up Sendlingerstrasse and turn right onto Rindermarkt (the former cattle market), and you'll be beneath the single, square tower of the **Peterskirche** ⑬, the city's oldest and best-loved parish church. From the Peterskirche reenter Marienplatz and pass in front of the Altes Rathaus once again to step into Burgstrasse. You'll soon find yourself in the quiet, airy **Alter Hof** ⑭, the inner courtyard of the original palace of Bavaria's Wittelsbach rulers. A short distance beyond its northern archway, on the north side of Pfisterstrasse, stands the former royal mint, the **Münze** ⑮.

If you'd like to visit some museums, extend your walk by about 10 minutes, returning down Burgstrasse to broad Tal, once an important trading route that entered Munich at the Isartor, a gate restored to its original medieval appearance. A frieze depicts the 1322 battle of Ampfing, during which Munich was saved from an Austrian attack. Cross Isartorplatz into Zweibrückenstrasse, and you'll come to the Isar River. There, on an island, is the massive bulk of the **Deutsches Museum** ⑯, with a gigantic thermometer and barometer on its tower showing the way to the main entrance. Budding scientists and young dreamers will be delighted by its many interactive displays with buttons to push and cranks to turn.

On a sunny day join the locals for ice cream and a stroll along the Isar River, where the more daring sunbathe nude on pebble islands. On a rainy day you can splash around in the Müllersches Volksbad, a restored art nouveau indoor swimming pool at Ludwigsbrücke, opposite the Deutsches Museum. The massive glass-and-brick facade on the hill above the Volksbad belongs to the **Gasteig Kulturzentrum** ⑰, home of the Munich Philharmonic Orchestra, the main city library, and a variety of theaters, galleries, and cafés.

TIMING

Set aside at least a whole day for this walk, hitting Marienplatz when the glockenspiel plays at 11 AM or noon. Prepare for a big spectator crowd, and try to avoid shopping in the pedestrian zone between noon and 2, when workers on lunch break make for the department stores. The churches along the route each deserve some contemplation inside. Aficionados of hunting or engineering could spend hours in the Deutsches Jagd- und Fischereimuseum and Deutsches Museum.

Sights to See

⓮ **Alter Hof** (Old Palace). This palace was the original residence of the Wittelsbachs, the ruling dynasty established in 1180. The palace now serves as local government offices. Something of a medieval flavor survives in the Alter Hof's quiet courtyard in the otherwise busy downtown area. Don't pass through without turning to admire the medieval oriel (bay window) that hides on the south wall, just around the corner as you enter the courtyard. ✉ *Burgstr., City Center.*

❾ **Altes Rathaus** (Old City Hall). This was Munich's first city hall, built in 1474. Its great hall—destroyed in 1944 but now fully restored—was the work of architect Jörg von Halspach. It is used for official receptions and is not normally open to the public. The tower provides a fairy-tale-like setting for the **Spielzeugmuseum** (toy museum) accessible via a winding staircase. Its toys and dolls are joined by quite a few Barbies visiting from the United States. ✉ *Marienpl., City Center,* ☎ *089/294–001.* *Museum €3.* ⏲ *Daily 10–5:30.*

★ ⓬ **Asamkirche** (Asam Church). Munich's most unusual church has a suitably extraordinary entrance, framed by raw rock foundations. The insignificant door, crammed between its craggy shoulders, gives little idea of the opulence and lavish detailing within the small, 18th-century church (there are only 12 rows of pews). Above the doorway St. Nepomuk, a 14th-century Bohemian monk who drowned in the Danube, is being led by angels from a rocky riverbank to heaven. The church's official name is Church of St. Johann Nepomuk, but it is known as the Asamkirche for its architects, the brothers Cosmas Damian and Egid Quirin Asam, who lived next door. Inside you'll discover a prime example of true southern German, late-baroque architecture. Frescoes by Cosmas Damian Asam and rosy marble cover the walls. The sheer wealth of statues and gilding is stunning—there's even a gilt skeleton at the sanctuary's portal. ✉ *Sendlingerstr., City Center.* ⏲ *Daily 9–5:30.*

❸ **Bürgersaal** (Citizens' Hall). Beneath the modest roof of this unassuming church are two contrasting levels. The Oberkirche (upper level)—the church proper—is a richly decorated baroque oratory. Its elaborate stucco foliage and paintings of Bavarian places of pilgrimage project a distinctly different ambience from that of the Unterkirche (lower level), reached by a double staircase. This gloomy, cryptlike chamber contains the tomb of Rupert Mayer, a Jesuit priest renowned for his energetic and outspoken opposition to the Nazis. ✉ *Neuhauserstr. 14, City Center,* ☎ *089/219–9720.* ⏲ *Oberkirche only during services; Unterkirche Mon.–Sat. 6:30 AM–7 PM, Sun. 7–7.*

❺ **Deutsches Jagd- und Fischereimuseum** (German Museum of Hunting and Fishing). Fans of the thrill of the chase will be fascinated by this museum. It contains the world's largest collection of fishhooks, some 500 stuffed animals (including a 6½-ft-tall North American grizzly bear), a 12,000-year-old skeleton of an Irish deer, and a valuable collection of hunting weapons. Here you can find the elusive *Wolpertinger*, a legendary Bavarian animal. The brass boar outside the front door is a favorite place for parents to photograph children. ✉ *Neuhauserstr. 2, City Center,* ☎ *089/220–522.* 🎫 *€3.50.* ⏲ *Daily 9:30–5; until 9 on Mon. and Thurs.*

★ ⓰ **Deutsches Museum** (German Museum of Science and Technology). Within a monumental building on an island in the Isar River, this museum—filled with aircraft, vehicles, locomotives, and machinery—is an engineering student's dream. The immense collection is spread out over 19 km (12 mi) of corridors, six floors of exhibits, and 30 departments. Not all exhibits have explanations in English, which is why you should skip the otherwise impressive coal-mine labyrinth. The most technically advanced planetarium in Europe has up to six shows daily, and includes a Laser Magic display. An IMAX theater—with a wraparound screen six stories high—shows nature and adventure films. The Internet Café on the third floor is open daily 9–3. To arrange for a two-hour tour in English, call ☎ 089/217–9252 two weeks in advance. In mid-2003 a subsidiary Center for Transportation will open on the fairgrounds at the Theresienhöhe (where Oktoberfest is held). By 2005, all the transportation exhibitions will be exhibited in the new halls. ✉ *Museumsinsel 1, City Center,* ☎ *089/21790; 089/2112–5180 to reserve tickets at planetarium and IMAX,* WEB *www.fdt.de.* 🎫 *Museum €5, Planetarium €6.25, IMAX €5.95; combined ticket for planetarium and IMAX €10.25 (admission for some performances is higher).* ⏲ *Daily 9 AM–11 PM.*

OFF THE BEATEN PATH

FRANZISKANERKLOSTERKIRCHE ST. ANNA (FRANCISCAN MONASTERY CHURCH OF ST. ANNE) – This striking example of the two Asam brothers' work is in the Lehel district. Though less opulent than the Asamkirche, this small Franciscan monastery church, consecrated in 1737, impresses with its sense of movement and its heroic scale. It was largely rebuilt after wartime bomb damage. The ceiling fresco by Cosmas Damian Asam glows in all its original vivid joyfulness. The ornate altar was also designed by the Asam brothers. Towering over the delicate little church, on the opposite side of the street, is the neo-Romanesque bulk of the 19th-century church of St. Anne. You can get to Lehel on Tram 17 or U-bahn 4 or 5 from the city center. ✉ *St.-Anna-Str., Lehel,* ☎ *089/212–1820.*

★ ❻ **Frauenkirche** (Church of Our Lady). Munich's *Dom* (cathedral) is a distinctive late-Gothic brick structure with two towers that are the city's chief landmark. Each is more than 300 ft high, and both are capped by onion-shape domes. The towers are an indelible feature of the skyline and a Munich trademark by now—some say because they look like overflowing beer mugs.

The main body of the cathedral was completed in 20 years (1474–94)—a record time in those days. The towers were added, almost as an afterthought, in 1524–25. Jörg von Halspach, the Frauenkirche's original architect, is buried here. The building suffered severe damage during Allied bombing and was lovingly restored between 1947 and 1957. Inside, the church combines most of von Halspach's original features with a stark, clean modernity and simplicity of line, emphasized by slender, white octagonal pillars that sweep up through the nave to the tracery ceiling. As you enter the church, look on the stone floor for the dark imprint of a large foot—the *Teufelstritt* (Devil's Footprint). According to lore, the devil challenged von Halspach to build a nave without windows. The architect accepted the challenge. When he completed the job, he led the devil to the one spot in the well-lit church from which the 66-ft-high windows could not be seen. The devil stomped his foot in rage and left the Teufelstritt. The cathedral houses an elaborate 15th-century black-marble tomb guarded by four 16th-century armored knights. It is the final resting place of Duke Ludwig IV (1302–1347), who became Holy Roman Emperor Ludwig the Bavarian in 1328. The Frauenkirche's great treasure, however, is the collection of 24 carved wooden busts of the Apostles, Saints, and Prophets above the choir, by the 15th-century Munich sculptor Erasmus Grasser.

The observation platform high up in one of the towers offers a splendid view of the city. But beware—you must climb 86 steps to reach the tower elevator! ✉ *Frauenpl., City Center,* ☎ *089/290–0820.* 🎫 *Tower €2.* ⏲ *Tower elevator Apr.–Oct., Mon.–Sat. 10–6.*

17 **Gasteig Kulturzentrum** (Gasteig Culture Center). Sitting high above the Isar River, this striking postmodern, brick cultural complex for music, theater, and film has an open-plan interior and a maze of courtyards and plazas. The center has two theaters, where plays in English are occasionally staged. ✉ *Rosenheimerstr. 5, Haidhausen,* ☎ *089/480–980.*

1 **Hauptbahnhof** (Main Train Station). A renovation here has made room for a host of rather fancy sandwich bars. On the underground level you'll find all sorts of shops that remain open even on Sundays and holidays. The city tourist office here has maps and helpful information on events around town. ✉ *Bahnhofpl., Leopoldvorstadt,* ☎ *089/2333–0256 or 089/2333–0257.*

2 **Karlsplatz.** In 1755, Eustachius Föderl opened an inn and beer garden here, which became known as the Stachus. The beer garden is long gone, but the name has remained. This busy intersection has one of Munich's most popular fountains, a circle of water jets that acts as a magnet on hot summer days when city shoppers and office workers seek a cool place to relax. A semicircle of yellow buildings with tall windows and delicate, cast-iron balconies back the fountain.

★ 7 **Marienplatz.** Bordered by the Neues Rathaus, shops, and cafés, this square is named after the gilded statue of the Virgin Mary that has watched over it for more than three centuries. It was erected in 1638 at the behest of Elector Maximilian I as an act of thanksgiving for the city's survival of the Thirty Years' War, the cataclysmic religious struggle that devastated vast regions of Germany. When the statue was taken down from its marble column for cleaning in 1960, workmen found a small casket in the base containing a splinter of wood said to be from the cross of Christ. ✉ *Bounded by Kaufingerstr., Rosenstr., Weinstr., and Dienerstr., City Center.*

4 **Michaelskirche** (St. Michael's Church). A curious story explains why this sturdy Renaissance church has no tower. Seven years after the start of construction the principal tower collapsed. Its patron, pious Duke Wilhelm V, regarded the disaster as a heavenly sign that the church wasn't big enough, so he ordered a change in the plans—this time without a tower. Completed seven years later, the Michaelskirche was the first Renaissance church of this size in southern Germany. The duke is buried in the crypt, along with 40 other Wittelsbachs, including the eccentric King Ludwig II. A severe neoclassical monument in the north transept contains the tomb of Napoléon's stepson, Eugene de Beauharnais, who married one of the daughters of King Maximilian I and died in Munich in 1824. You'll find the plain white-stucco interior of the church and its slightly barnlike atmosphere soothingly simple after the

lavish decoration of the nearby Bürgersaal. ✉ *Neuhauserstr. 52, City Center,* ☎ *089/231–7060.* 🎟 *€1.* 🕓 *Daily 8–7, except during services.*

11 **Münchner Stadtmuseum** (City Museum). Wedged in by Oberanger, Rosental, and St.-Jakobsplatz, this museum is as eclectic within as the architecture is without. Though the entire complex was rebuilt in several stages after World War II, the original building dates to 1491 (the front on St.-Jakobsplatz). Inside are instrument collections, international cultural exhibits, a film museum showing rarely screened movies, a photo and fashion museum, a puppet theater, and one of the most pleasant cafés in town. ✉ *St.-Jakobspl. 1, City Center,* ☎ *089/2332–2370,* WEB *www.stadtmuseum-online.de.* 🎟 *€2.50; €4 for special exhibitions.* 🕓 *Tues.–Sun. 10–6.*

15 **Münze** (Mint). Originally the royal stables, the Münze was created by court architect Wilhelm Egkl between 1563 and 1567 and now serves as an office building. A stern neoclassical facade emblazoned with gold was added in 1809; the interior courtyard has Renaissance-style arches. ✉ *Pfisterstr. 4, City Center.* 🎟 *Free.* 🕓 *Mon.–Thurs. 8–4, Fri. 8–2.*

8 **Neues Rathaus** (New City Hall). Munich's present city hall was built between 1867 and 1908 in the fussy, turreted, neo-Gothic style so beloved by King Ludwig II. Architectural historians are divided over its merits, though its dramatic scale and lavish detailing are impressive. Perhaps the most serious criticism is that the Dutch and Flemish style of the building seems out of place amid the baroque and rococo of so much of the rest of the city. The tower's 1904 glockenspiel (a chiming clock with mechanical figures) plays daily at 11 AM, noon, and 9 PM, with an additional performance at 5 PM June–October. As chimes peal out over the square, the clock's doors flip open and brightly colored dancers and jousting knights go through their paces. They act out two events from Munich's past: a tournament held in Marienplatz in 1568 and the *Schäfflertanz* (Dance of the Coopers), which commemorated the end of the plague of 1517. When Munich was in ruins after World War II, an American soldier contributed some paint to restore the battered figures, and he was rewarded with a ride on one of the jousters' horses, high above the cheering crowds. You, too, can travel up there, by elevator, to an observation point near the top of one of the towers. On a clear day the view is spectacular. ✉ *Marienpl., City Center.* 🎟 *Tower €1.50.* 🕓 *Mon.–Thurs. 9–4, Fri. 9–1.*

13 **Peterskirche** (St. Peter's Church). Munich's oldest and smallest parish church traces its origins to the 11th century and has been restored in a variety of architectural styles. The rich baroque interior has a magnificent late-Gothic high altar and aisle pillars decorated with exquisite 18th-century figures of the apostles. In clear weather it's well worth the climb up the 300-ft tower—the view includes glimpses of the Alps. The Peterskirche has a Scottish priest who is glad to show English-speaking visitors around. ✉ *Rindermarkt, City Center,* ☎ *089/260–4828.* 🎟 *Tower €1.50.* 🕓 *Mon.–Sat. 9–6, Sun. 10–7.*

OFF THE BEATEN PATH

THERESIENWIESE – The site of Munich's annual beer festival—the notorious Oktoberfest—and of the most hip Christmas market (the Tollwood) is only a 10-minute walk from the Hauptbahnhof or a single stop away by subway (U-4 or U-5). The enormous exhibition ground is named after Princess Therese von Sachsen-Hildburghausen, who celebrated her marriage to the Bavarian Crown Prince Ludwig—later Ludwig I—here in 1810. The accompanying agricultural fair was such a success that it became an annual event. Beer was served then as now, but what began as a night out for the locals has become a 16-day international bonanza at the end of September and the beginning of October, attracting more than 6 million people each year (it qualifies as an *Oktober* fest by ending the first Sunday in October).

Overlooking the Theresienwiese is a 19th-century hall of fame—one of the last works of Ludwig I—and a monumental bronze statue of the maiden **Bavaria**, more than 100 ft high. The statue is hollow, and 130 steps take you up into the braided head for a view of Munich through Bavaria's eyes. *€2.50. Dec.–Oct., Tues.–Sun. 10–noon and 2–4.*

★ 10 **Viktualienmarkt** (Victuals Market). The city's open-air food market has a wide range of produce, German and international foodstuffs, and tables and counters for eating and drinking, which make the area a feast for the eyes as well as the stomach. It's also the realm of the garrulous, sturdy market women who run the stalls with dictatorial authority. Whether here, or at a bakery, *do not* try to select your pickings by hand; ask for help.

OFF THE BEATEN PATH

Valentin-Karlstadt Musäum – This museum devoted to the fabulous cabaret artists Karl Valentin (1892–1948) and Liesl Karlstadt (1892–1960) lies within the tower of the Isartor. It's a must to get a flavor of local culture and color. Valentin, a spookily thin man, was a Munich original, whose absurd humor bashed all conventions. A statue of him and Karlstadt are at Viktualienmarkt. Though much of his wit involves linguistic games, there is much here to catch a sense of genuine, upscale Munich humor, notably a fabulous amount of knickknacks, statues, photographs of Valentin in various off-the-wall poses, and costumes. *Tal 50, City Center/Isarvorstadt, 089/223–266. 199 Bavarian cents/€1.99. Fri., Sat., Mon. Tues. 11:01–5:29, Sun. 10:01–5:29.*

ZAM – Nestled in a passageway just off the Isartor, the ZAM (which stands for Center for Unusual Museums) consists of the private collections belonging to the late Manfred Klauda, a Munich lawyer. There is no specific guiding theme, except perhaps the obsession of a single individual. Exhibitions include collections of chamber pots and bourdaloues (a convenience for women in 17th- and 18th-century clothing), corkscrews, locks, Easter bunnies, pedal cars, perfume bottles, and ephemera relating to Empress Elisabeth of Austria (known as Sissi, the cousin of Ludwig II). *Westenriederstr. 41, City Center, 089/290–4121,* WEB *www.zam-museum.de. €4. Daily 10–6.*

Royal Munich

From the relatively modest palace of the Alter Hof, the Wittelsbachs expanded their quarters northward, where more space was to be found than in the jumble of narrow streets of the old quarter. Three splendid avenues radiated outward from their new palace and garden grounds and fine homes arose along them. One of them—Prinzregentenstrasse—marks the southern end of Munich's huge public park, the Englischer Garten—also the creation of a Wittelsbach ruler. Lehel is an upmarket residential neighborhood that also serves as Munich's museum quarter.

A Good Walk

A good way to start this very long walk is to stoke up with a Bavarian breakfast of Weisswurst, pretzels, and beer at the **Hofbräuhaus** (18), perhaps Munich's best-known beer hall, on Am Platzl. Turn right from the Hofbräuhaus for the short walk along Orlandostrasse to **Maximilianstrasse** (19), Munich's most elegant shopping street. Right opposite you is a handsome city landmark: the Hotel Vier Jahreszeiten, a historic host to traveling princes, millionaires, and the expense-account jet set. Maximilianstrasse was named after King Maximilian II, whose statue you'll see far down on the right. This wide boulevard has many grand buildings, which contain government offices and the city's ethnological museum, the **Staatliches Museum für Völkerkunde** ⑳. The Maximilianeum, on a rise beyond the Isar River, is an impressive mid-19th-century palace where the Bavarian state government now meets.

Turn left on Maximilianstrasse and you'll arrive at Max-Joseph-Platz, a square dominated by the pillared portico of the 19th-century **Nationaltheater** ㉑, home of the Bavarian State Opera Company. The statue in the square's center is of Bavaria's first king, Max Joseph. Along the north side is the lofty and austere south wall of the **Residenz** ㉒, the royal palace of Wittelsbach rulers for more than six centuries.

Directly north of the Residenz, on Hofgartenstrasse, lies the former royal garden, the **Hofgarten** ㉓, which was started in the 16th century and eventually achieved its Italian Renaissance look. The plaza in front of the Hogarten is Odeonsplatz. The monument on the southern end is the 19th-century **Feldherrnhalle** ㉔, modeled after the familiar Loggia dei Lanzi in Florence. Looking north up Ludwigstrasse, the arrow-straight avenue that begins at the Feldherrnhalle, you'll see the **Siegestor** ㉕, or victory arch, which marks the beginning of Leopoldstrasse. Completing this impressively Italianate panorama is the great yellow bulk of the former royal church of St. Kajetan, the **Theatinerkirche** ㉖, an imposing baroque structure across from the Feldherrnhalle. A few steps down Theatinerstrasse is the **Kunsthalle der Hypo-Kulturstiftung** ㉗.

Now head north up Ludwigstrasse. Court architect Leo von Klenze designed this first stretch of the generous avenue to give the road to the village of Schwabing a look befitting what had become a kingdom after the Napoleonic wars. In much the same way that Baron Haussmann would later demolish many of the old streets and buildings in Paris, replacing them with stately boulevards, von Klenze swept aside the small dwellings and alleys that stood here and replaced them with severe neoclassical structures such as the Bayerische Staatsbibliothek (Bavarian State Library), the Universität (University), and the peculiarly Byzantine Ludwigskirche. Müncheners either love or hate the architect's high-windowed and formal buildings, which end just before Ludwigstrasse becomes Leopoldstrasse. Another leading architect, Friedrich von Gärtner, took over construction here with more delicate structures that are a pleasant backdrop to the busy street life in summer. Once the hub of the legendary artists' district of Schwabing, Leopoldstrasse still throbs with life from spring to fall, exuding the atmosphere of a Mediterranean boulevard, with cafés, wine terraces, and artists' stalls. In comparison, Ludwigstrasse is inhabited by ghosts of the past.

At the south end of Leopoldstrasse lies the great open quadrangle of the university. A circular area divides into two piazzas named after anti-Nazi resistance leaders: Geschwister-Scholl-Platz and Professor-Huber-Platz. From the University, Leopoldstrasse then continues into Schwabing itself, once Munich's bohemian quarter but now distinctly upscale and chic to the point of being monotonous. Explore the streets of old Schwabing around Wedekindplatz to get the feel of the place. Or enjoy the shops and cafés in the student quarter parallel to Leopoldstrasse. (Those in search of the bohemian mood that once animated Schwabing should head to Haidhausen, on the other side of the Isar River, though it is about to end there, too, owing to gentrification and high rents.)

Bordering the east side of Schwabing is the **Englischer Garten** ㉘. Five kilometers (3 mi) long and 1½ km (about 1 mi) wide, it's Germany's largest city park, stretching from Prinzregentenstrasse, the broad avenue laid out by Prince Regent Luitpold at the end of the 19th century, to the city's northern boundary, where the lush parkland is taken over by the rough embrace of open countryside. Dominating the park's southern border is one of the few examples of Hitler-era architecture still standing in Munich: the colonnaded **Haus der Kunst** ㉙, a leading art gallery and home to Munich's most fashionable nightclub, the P 1.

A few hundred yards farther along Prinzregentenstrasse are two other leading museums, the **Bayerisches Nationalmuseum** ㉚ and the **Schack-Galerie** ㉛, and around the first left-hand corner, on Lerchenfeldstrasse, is a museum of prehistory, the **Archäologische Staatssammlung** ㉜, in a modern concrete building appropriately covered with rusting steel Cor-Ten plates.

On a hill at the eastern end of Prinzregentenstrasse, just across the Isar River from the Schack-Galerie, is Munich's well-loved Friedensengel (Angel of Peace), a gilt angel crowning a marble column. Beyond the Friedensengel is another historic home that became a major Munich art gallery—the **Museum Villa Stuck** ㉝, a jewel of an art-nouveau fantasy wrapped in a sober, neoclassical shell.

TIMING

You'll need a day (and good walking shoes) for this stroll. Set aside at least two hours for a tour of the Residenz. If the weather is good, return to the southern end of the Englischer Garten at dusk, when you'll be treated to an unforgettable silhouette of the Munich skyline, black against the retreating light.

Sights to See

32 **Archäologische Staatssammlung** (State Archeological Collection). This is Bavaria's principal record of its prehistoric, Roman, and Celtic past. The perfectly preserved body of a ritually sacrificed young girl, recovered from a Bavarian peat moor, is among the more spine-chilling exhibits. Head down to the basement to see the fine Roman mosaic floor. ✉ *Lerchenfeldstr. 2, Lehel,* ☎ *089/211–2402.* 🎫 *€4.50; free Sun.* ⏲ *Tues.–Sun. 9–4:30.*

30 **Bayerisches Nationalmuseum** (Bavarian National Museum). Although the museum places emphasis on Bavarian cultural history, it has art and artifacts of outstanding international importance and regular exhibitions that attract worldwide attention. The highlight for some will be the medieval and Renaissance wood carvings, with many works by the great Renaissance sculptor Tilman Riemenschneider. Tapestries, arms and armor, a unique collection of Christmas crèches (the *Krippenschau*), and Bavarian and German folk art compete for your attention. ✉ *Prinzregentenstr. 3, Lehel,* ☎ *089/211–2401,* WEB *www.bayerisches-nationalmuseum.de.* 🎫 *€3, €5 for special exhibitions.* ⏲ *Tues.–Sun. 9:30–5.*

★ 28 **Englischer Garten** (English Garden). This virtually endless park, which melds into the open countryside at Munich's northern city limits, was designed for the Bavarian prince Karl Theodor by Benjamin Thompson, later Count Rumford, from Massachusetts, who fled America after having taken the wrong side during the War of Independence. The open, informal nature of the park—reminiscent of the rolling parklands with which English aristocrats of the 18th century liked to surround their country homes—gave the park its name. It has a boating lake, four beer gardens, and a series of curious decorative and monumental constructions, including the Monopteros, a Greek temple designed by von Klenze for King Ludwig I and built on an artificial hill in the southern section of the park. In the center of the park's most popular beer garden is a Chinese pagoda erected in 1789. It was destroyed during the war and then reconstructed. The Chinese Tower beer garden is world famous, but the park has prettier places for nursing a beer: the Aumeister, for example, along the northern perimeter. The Aumeister's restaurant is in an early 19th-century hunting lodge. At the Seehaus, on the shore of the Kleinhesseloher See (lake), choose between a smart restaurant or a cozy *Bierstube* (beer tavern).

The Englischer Garten is a paradise for joggers; cyclists; musicians; soccer players; sunbathers; dog owners; and, in winter, cross-country skiers. The Munich Cricket Club grounds are in the southern section—and spectators are welcome. The park has designated areas for nude sunbathing—the Germans have a positively pagan attitude toward the sun—so don't be surprised to see naked bodies bordering the flower beds and paths. ✉ *Main entrances at Prinzregentenstr. and Koniginstr., Schwabing and Lehel.*

24 **Feldherrnhalle** (Generals' Hall). This open-sided, pavilionlike building was modeled after the 14th-century Loggia dei Lanzi in Florence and honors three centuries worth of Bavarian generals. Two huge Bavarian lions are flanked by the larger-than-life statues of Count Johann Tserclaes Tilly, who led Catholic forces in the Thirty Years' War, and Prince Karl Philipp Wrede, hero of the 19th-century Napoleonic Wars. The imposing structure was turned into a militaristic shrine in the 1930s and '40s by the Nazis, who also found significance in the coincidence that it marked the site of Hitler's abortive coup, or putsch, which took place in 1923. All who passed it had to give the Nazi salute. Viscardigasse, a tiny alley behind the Feldherrnhalle linking Residenzstrasse and Theatinerstrasse and now lined with exclusive boutiques, was used by those who wanted to dodge the tedious routine. ✉ *South end of Odeonspl., City Center.*

29 **Haus der Kunst** (House of Art). This colonnaded, classical-style building is one of Munich's few remaining examples of Hitler-era architecture and was officially opened by the führer himself. In the Hitler years it showed only work deemed to reflect the Nazi aesthetic. One of its most successful postwar exhibitions was devoted to works banned by the Nazis. It stages exhibitions of art, photography, and sculpture, as well as theatrical and musical "happenings." The survival-of-the-chicest disco, P 1, is in the building's west wing. ✉ *Prinzregentenstr. 1, Lehel,* ☎ *089/211–270,* WEB *www.hausderkunst.de.* 💰 *Admission varies.* ⏲ *Daily 10–10.*

18 **Hofbräuhaus.** Duke Wilhelm V founded Munich's most famous brewery in 1589. Hofbräu means "royal brew," which aptly describes the golden beer poured in king-size liter mugs. If the cavernous downstairs hall is too noisy for you, try the quiet restaurant upstairs. Americans, Australians, and Italians far outnumber Germans, and the brass band that performs here most days adds modern pop and American folk to the traditional German numbers. ✉ *Am Platzl 9, City Center,* ☎ *089/221–676.*

23 **Hofgarten** (Royal Garden). The formal garden was once part of the royal palace grounds. It's bordered on two sides by arcades designed in the 19th century by the royal architect Leo von Klenze. On the east side of the garden stands the new state chancellery, built around the ruins of the 19th-century Army Museum and incorporating the remains of a Renaissance arcade. Its most prominent feature is a large copper dome. Bombed during World War II air raids, the museum stood untouched for almost 40 years as a grim reminder of the war. Nowadays,

it is known as Palazzo Prozzi, an untranslatable joke referring to the huge sums that went into rebuilding it, and its ostentatious look.

In front of the chancellery stands one of Europe's most unusual—some say most effective—war memorials. Instead of looking up at a monument, you are led down to a **sunken crypt** covered by a massive granite block. In the crypt lies a German soldier from World War I. The crypt is a stark contrast to the **memorial** that stands unobtrusively in front of the northern wing of the chancellery: a simple cube of black marble bearing facsimiles of handwritten wartime manifestos by anti-Nazi leaders, including members of the White Rose movement. ⊠ *Hofgartenstr., north of Residenz, City Center.*

27 **Kunsthalle der Hypo-Kulturstiftung** (Hall of the Hypobank's Cultural Foundation). This exhibition hall for art from antiquity to the most modern studios is in the midst of the commercial pedestrian zone. Chagall, Giacometti, Picasso, and Gauguin are among the artists featured in the past. Its success over the years has led to its expansion, designed by the Swiss architect team Herzog and de Meuron, who also designed London's Tate Modern. ⊠ *Theatinerstr. 8, City Center,* ☎ *089/227–817,* WEB *www.hypo-kunsthalle.de.* 🎟 *€14.* ⏲ *Daily 10–8.*

Ludwigskirche (Ludwig's Church). Planted halfway along the severe, neoclassical Ludwigstrasse is this curious neo-Byzantine/early Renaissance–style church. It was built at the behest of Ludwig I to provide his newly completed suburb with a parish church. It's worth a stop to see the fresco of the *Last Judgment* in the choir. At 60 ft by 37 ft, it is one of the world's largest. ⊠ *Ludwigstr. 22, Maxvorstadt,* ☎ *089/288–334.* ⏲ *Daily 7–7.*

19 **Maximilianstrasse.** Munich's sophisticated shopping street was named after King Maximilian II, who wanted to break away from the Greek-influenced classical style of city architecture favored by his father, Ludwig I. With the cabinet's approval, he created this broad boulevard, its central stretch lined with majestic buildings. It culminates on a rise beyond the Isar River in the stately outlines of the **Maximilianeum,** a lavish 19th-century arcaded palace built for Maximilian II and now the home of the Bavarian state parliament. Only the terrace can be visited.

33 **Museum Villa Stuck.** This neoclassical villa is the former home of one of Munich's leading turn-of-the-20th-century artists, Franz von Stuck (1863–1928). Renovation of the upstairs rooms, the artist's former quarters, is expected to be completed in 2004. The downstairs is used for special exhibitions. His work, which is at times haunting, at times erotic, and occasionally humorous, covers the walls of the ground floor rooms. ⊠ *Prinzregentenstr. 60, Haidhausen,* ☎ *089/4555–5125.* 🎟 *Free.* ⏲ *Tues.–Sun. 10–6.*

21 **Nationaltheater** (National Theater). Built in the late 19th century as a royal opera house with a pillared portico, this large theater was bombed during the war but is now restored to its original splendor and has some of the world's most advanced stage technology. ⊠ *Max-Joseph-Pl., City Center,* ☎ *089/2185–1920.*

★ 22 **Residenz** (Royal Palace). Munich's royal palace began as a small castle in the 14th century. The Wittelsbach dukes moved here when the tenements of an expanding Munich encroached upon their Alter Hof. In succeeding centuries the royal residence developed parallel to the importance, requirements, and interests of its occupants. It came to include the Königsbau (on Max-Josef-Platz) and then (clockwise) the Alte Residenz; the Festsaal (Banquet Hall); the Altes Residenztheater/Cuvilliés Theater; the since-destroyed Allerheiligenhofkirche (All Souls' Church); the Residenztheater; and the Nationaltheater.

Building began in 1385 with the **Neuveste** (New Fortress), which comprised the northeast section; most of it burned to the ground in 1750, but one of its finest rooms survived: the 16th-century **Antiquarium,** which was built for Duke Albrecht V's collection of antique statues (today it's used chiefly for state receptions). The throne room of King Ludwig I, the **Neuer Herkulessaal,** is now a concert hall. The accumulated Wittelsbach treasures are on view in several palace museums. The **Schatzkammer** (treasury; €4, a combo ticket with the Residenzmuseum costs €7; Apr.–Oct., Tues., Wed., Fri.–Sun. 9–6, Thur. 9–8; Nov.–Mar., Tues.–Sun. 9–4) has a rich centerpiece in its small Renaissance statue of St. George, studded with 2,291 diamonds, 209 pearls, and 406 rubies. Paintings, tapestries, furniture, and porcelain are housed in the **Residenzmuseum** (€4; Apr.–Oct., Tues., Wed., Fri.–Sun. 9–6, Thur. 9–8; Nov.–Mar., Tues.–Sun. 9–4). Antique coins glint in the **Staatliche Münzsammlung** (Residenzstr. 1; €2, free Sun.; Tues.–Sun. 10–5, Thurs. until 6:45). Egyptian works of art make up the **Staatliche Sammlung Ägyptischer Kunst** (Hofgarten entrance; €2.50, free Sun.; Tues. 9–9, Wed.–Fri. 9–4, weekends 10–5).

During the summer, chamber-music concerts take place in the inner courtyard. Also in the center of the complex is the small rococo **Altes Residenztheater/Cuvilliés Theater** (Residenzstr.; €2; Tues.–Sun. 10–4). It was built by François Cuvilliés between 1751 and 1755, and it still holds performances. The French-born Cuvilliés was a dwarf who was admitted to the Bavarian court as a decorative "bauble." Prince Max Emanuel recognized his latent artistic ability and had him trained as an architect. The prince's eye for talent gave Germany some of its richest rococo treasures. *Max-Joseph-Pl. 3, entry through archway at Residenzstr. 1, City Center, 089/290–671. Closed a few days in early Jan.*

31 **Schack-Galerie.** Those with a taste for florid and romantic 19th-century German paintings will appreciate the collections of the Schack-Galerie, originally the private collection of one Count Schack. Others may find the gallery dull, filled with plodding and repetitive works by painters who now repose in well-deserved obscurity. *Prinzregentenstr. 9, Lehel, 089/2380–5224. €2.50; free Sun. Wed.–Mon. 10–5.*

25 **Siegestor** (Victory Arch). Marking the beginning of Leopoldstrasse, the Siegestor has Italian origins—it was modeled on the Arch of Constantine in Rome—and was built to honor the achievements of the Bavarian army during the Wars of Liberation (1813–15). The writing on the gable facing the inner city reads: DEDICATED TO VICTORY, DESTROYED BY WAR, ADMONISHING PEACE. *Leopoldstr., Schwabing.*

20 **Staatliches Museum für Völkerkunde** (State Museum of Ethnology). Arts and crafts from around the world are displayed in this extensive museum. There are also regular special exhibits. *Maximilianstr. 42, Lehel, 089/210–1360. €3.50; free Sun. Tues.–Sun. 9:30–5:15.*

26 **Theatinerkirche** (Theatine Church). This mighty baroque church owes its Italian appearance to its founder, Princess Henriette Adelaide, who commissioned it in gratitude for the birth of her son and heir, Max Emanuel, in 1663. A native of Turin, the princess distrusted Bavarian architects and builders and thus summoned a master builder from Bologna, Agostino Barelli, to construct her church. He took as his model the Roman mother church of the newly formed Theatine Order. Barelli worked on the building for 11 years but was dismissed before the project was completed. It was another 100 years before the Theatinerkirche

was finished. Its lofty towers frame a restrained facade capped by a massive dome. The superb stucco work on the inside will be covered in scaffolding and dropcloth for part of 2003. The gaping space before the Feldherrnhalle and Theatinerkirche is often used for outdoor stage events. ✉ *Theatinerstr. 22, City Center.*

NEED A BREAK? Munich's oldest café, **Tambosi** (✉ Odeonspl., Maxvorstadt, ☎ 089/224–768), borders the street across from the Theatinerkirche. Watch the hustle and bustle from an outdoor table or retreat through a gate in the Hofgarten's western wall to the café's tree-shaded beer garden. If the weather's cool or rainy, find a corner in the cozy, eclectically furnished interior.

DenkStätte Weisse Rose (Reflecting Place). Siblings Hans and Sophie Scholl, fellow student Alexander Schmorell, and Kurt Huber, Professor of Philosophy, founded the short-lived resistance movement against the Nazis in 1942–43 known as the Weisse Rose (White Rose). All were executed. A small exhibition about their work is in the inner quad of the university, where the Scholls were caught distributing leaflets and denounced by the janitor. ✉ *Geschwister-Scholl-Pl. 1, Maxvorstadt,* ☎ *089/2180–3053.* *Free.* *Weekdays 10–4, Thurs. until 9.*

Maxvorstadt and Schwabing

Here is the artistic center of Munich: Schwabing, the old artists' quarter, and the neighboring Maxvorstadt, where most of the city's leading art galleries and museums are congregated. Schwabing is no longer the bohemian area where such diverse residents as Lenin and Kandinsky were once neighbors, but at least the solid cultural foundations of the Maxvorstadt are immutable. Where the two areas meet (in the streets behind the university), life hums with a creative vibrancy that is difficult to detect elsewhere in Munich.

A Good Walk

Begin with a stroll through the city's old botanical garden, the **Alter Botanischer Garten** ㉞. The grand-looking building opposite the garden's entrance is the Palace of Justice, law courts built in 1897 in suitable awe-inspiring dimensions. On one corner of busy Lenbachplatz, you can't fail to notice one of Munich's most impressive fountains: the monumental late 19th-century Wittelsbacher Brunnen. Beyond the fountain, in Pacellistrasse, is the baroque **Dreifaltigkeitskirche** ㉟.

Leave the garden at its Meiserstrasse exit. On the right-hand side you'll pass two solemn neoclassic buildings closely associated with the Third Reich. The first served as the administrative offices of the Nazi Party in Munich. The neighboring building is the Music Academy, where Hitler, Mussolini, Chamberlain, and Daladier signed the prewar pact that carved up Czechoslovakia.

At the junction of Meiserstrasse and Briennerstrasse, look right to see the obelisk dominating the circular **Karolinenplatz** ㊱. To your left will be the expansive **Königsplatz** ㊲, bordered by two museums, the **Glyptothek** ㊳ and the **Antikensammlungen** ㊴, and closed off by the Propyläen, a colonnade framed by two Egyptian pylons.

After walking by the museums, turn right onto Luisenstrasse, and you'll arrive at a Florentine-style villa, the **Städtische Galerie im Lenbachhaus** ㊵, which has an outstanding painting collection. Continue down Luisenstrasse, turning right on Theresienstrasse to reach Munich's three leading art galleries, the **Alte Pinakothek** ㊶; the **Neue Pinakothek** ㊷, opposite it; and the **Pinakothek der Moderne** ㊸. They are as complementary as their buildings are contrasting: the Alte Pinakothek, severe and serious in style; the Neue Pinakothek, almost frivolously Florentine; and the Pinakothek der Moderne, glass-and-concrete new.

After a few hours immersed in culture, end your walk with a leisurely stroll through the neighboring streets of Schwabing, which are lined with boutiques, bars, and restaurants. If it's a fine day, head for the **Elisabethmarkt,** Schwabing's permanent market.

TIMING

This walk may take an entire day, depending on how long you linger at the major museums en route. Avoid the museum crowds by visiting as early in the day as possible. All of Munich seems to discover an interest in art on Sunday, when admission to most municipal and state-funded museums is free; you might want to take this day off from culture and join the late-breakfast and brunch crowd at the Elisabethmarkt, a beer garden, or at any of the many bars and Gaststätten. Some have Sunday-morning jazz concerts. Many Schwabing bars have happy hours between 6 and 8—a relaxing way to end your day.

Sights to See

★ 41 **Alte Pinakothek** (Old Picture Gallery). The towering brick Alte Pinakothek was constructed by von Klenze between 1826 and 1836 to exhibit the collection of old masters begun by Duke Wilhelm IV in the 16th century. It's now judged one of the world's great picture galleries. Among its most famous works are Dürers, Titians, Rembrandts, Rubenses (one of the world's largest collections), and two celebrated Murillos. ✉ *Barerstr. 27, Maxvorstadt,* ☎ *089/2380–5216,* WEB *www.pinakotheken-muenchen.de.* 🎫 *€5; free Sun.; €8 for a combined ticket for the Alte Pinakothek and Neue Pinakothek, valid for 2 days.* ⏲ *Tues.–Sun. 10–5, Thurs. until 10.*

34 **Alter Botanischer Garten** (Old Botanical Garden). Munich's first botanical garden began as the site of a huge glass palace, built in 1853 for Germany's first industrial exhibition. In 1931 it shared the fate of a similarly palatial glass exhibition hall, London's Crystal Palace, when its garden burned to the ground; six years later it was redesigned as a public park. Two features from the 1930s remain: a small, square **exhibition hall,** still used for art shows, and the 1933 **Neptune Fountain,** an enormous work in the heavy, monumental style of the prewar years. At the international electricity exhibition of 1882, the world's first high-tension electrical cable was run from the park to a Bavarian village 48 km (30 mi) away. ✉ *Entrance at Lenbachpl., Maxvorstadt.*

NEED A BREAK?

On the north edge of the Alter Botanischer Garten is one of the city's central beer gardens. It's part of the **Park-Café** (✉ Sophienstr. 7, Maxvorstadt, ☎ 089/598–313), which at night becomes a fashionable nightclub serving magnums of champagne for €780 a pop. Prices in the beer garden are more realistic.

39 **Antikensammlungen** (Antiquities Collection). This museum, which underwent much-needed renovations in 2002, has a collection of small sculptures, Etruscan art, Greek vases, gold, and glass. ✉ *Königspl. 1, Maxvorstadt,* ☎ *089/598–359.* 🎫 *€3; combined ticket to Antikensammlungen and Glyptothek €5; free on Sun.* ⏲ *Wed., Fri.–Sun. 10–5, Tues. and Thurs. 10–8.*

35 **Dreifaltigkeitskirche** (Church of the Holy Trinity). A local woman prophesied doom for the city unless a new church was erected: this striking baroque edifice was then promptly built between 1711 and 1718.

It has frescoes by Cosmas Damian Asam depicting all sorts of heroic scenes. ✉ *Pacellistr. 10, City Center,* ☎ *089/290–0820.* ⊙ *Daily 7–7, except during services.*

Elisabethmarkt (Elisabeth Market). Schwabing's permanent market is smaller than the popular Viktualienmarkt, but hardly less colorful. It has a pocket-size beer garden, where a jazz band performs every Saturday from spring to autumn. ✉ *Arcistr. and Elisabethstr., Schwabing.*

★ 38 **Glyptothek.** These Greek and Roman sculptures are among the finest collections in Munich. The small café that expands into the quiet courtyard is a favorite for visitors, which include budding artists practicing their drawing skills. ✉ *Königspl. 3, Maxvorstadt,* ☎ *089/286–100.* 🎫 *€3; combined ticket to Glyptothek and Antikensammlungen €5; free Sun.* ⊙ *Wed., Fri.–Sun. 10–5, Tues. and Thurs. 10–10.*

36 **Karolinenplatz** (Caroline Square). At the junction of Barerstrasse and Briennerstrasse, this circular area is dominated by an obelisk unveiled in 1812 as a memorial to Bavarians killed fighting Napoléon. **Amerikahaus** (America House) faces Karolinenplatz. It has an extensive library with many magazines and a year-round program of cultural events. ✉ *Karolinenpl. 3, Maxvorstadt,* ☎ *089/552–5370.*

37 **Königsplatz** (King's Square). This expansive square is lined on three sides with the monumental Grecian-style buildings by Leo von Klenze that gave Munich the nickname "Athens on the Isar." The two templelike structures are now the Antikensammlungen and the Glyptothek museums. In the 1930s the great parklike square was paved with gray granite slabs, which resounded with the thud of jackboots as the Nazis commandeered the area for their rallies. Although a busy road passes through it, the square has regained something of the green and peaceful appearance intended by Ludwig I.

42 **Neue Pinakothek** (New Picture Gallery). This exhibition space opened in 1981 to house the royal collection of modern art left homeless and scattered after its building was destroyed in the war. The exterior of the modern building mimics an older one with Italianate influences. The interior offers a magnificent environment for picture gazing, at least partly due to the natural light flooding in from the skylights. French Impressionists—Monet, Degas, Manet—are all well represented. The 19th-century German and Scandinavian paintings—misty landscapes predominate—are only now coming to be recognized as admirable products of their time. ✉ *Barerstr. 29, Maxvorstadt,* ☎ *089/2380–5195.* 🎫 *€5; free Sun.* ⊙ *Wed., Fri.–Mon. 10–5, Thurs. 10–10, closed Tues.*

43 **Pinakothek der Moderne.** Munich's ever-delayed new museum opened in September 2002. The striking glass-and-concrete complex holds four outstanding art and architectural collections, including modern art, industrial and graphic design, the Bavarian State collection of graphic art, and the Technical University's architectural museum. ✉ *Barer Str. 40, Maxvorstadt,* ☎ *089/2380–5118,* WEB *www.museum-der-moderne.de,* ⊙ *Tues.–Sun. 10–5, Thurs. and Fri. until 8.*

40 **Städtische Galerie im Lenbachhaus** (Municipal Gallery). Inside this delightful late-19th-century Florentine-style villa, former home and studio of the artist Franz von Lenbach (1836–1904), are renowned works from the Gothic period to the present, including an exciting assemblage of art from the early 20th-century *Blaue Reiter* (Blue Rider) group: Kandinsky, Klee, Jawlensky, Macke, Marc, and Münter. The chambers of Lenbach are on view as well. The adjoining **Kunstbau** (art building), a former subway platform of the Königsplatz station, hosts changing exhibitions of modern art. ✉ *Luisenstr. 33, Maxvorstadt,* ☎ *089/*

233–0320. *€6 (prices vary).* *Tues.–Thurs., Sun. 10–6, Fri., Sat. 10–8.*

Outside the Center

Bavaria Filmtour. Munich is Germany's leading moviemaking center, and the local Hollywood-style lot, Geiselgasteig, is on the southern outskirts of the city. The Filmexpress transports you on a 1½-hour tour of the sets of *Das Boot* (*The Boat*), *Die Unendliche Geschichte* (*The Neverending Story*), and other productions. Stunt shows are held at 11:30, 1, and 2:30, and action movies are screened in Showscan, the super-wide-screen cinema. Take U-bahn 1 or 2 from the city center to Silberhornstrasse and then change to Tram 25 to Bavariafilmplatz. The Munich transit authority (MVV) offers its own combined ticket for two adults plus three other people under 18 for €22.50; this includes travel. ✉ *Bavariafilmpl. 7, Geiselgasteig,* ☎ *089/6499–2304,* WEB *www.bavaria-filmtour.de.* *€10; stunt show €5; showscan €4; combined ticket €17.* *Nov.–Feb., daily 10–3 (tours only); Mar.–Apr., daily 9–4; May–Oct., daily 9–5.*

BMW Museum Zeithorizonte. Munich is the home of the famous BMW car firm. Its museum, a circular tower that looks as if it served as a set for *Star Wars,* contains not only a dazzling collection of BMWs old and new, but also items and exhibitions relating to the company's social history and its technical developments. It adjoins the **BMW factory** (☎ 089/3895–3308; weekdays, 10–1) on the eastern edge of the Olympiapark. You can see the factory as well, but only with a tour that begins at the museum's box office. Call ahead of time. ✉ *Petuelring 130, Milbertshofen, U-bahn 3 to Petuelring,* ☎ *089/3882–3307.* *€3.* *Daily 9–5, last entry at 4.*

Botanischer Garten (Botanical Garden). A collection of 14,000 plants, including orchids, cacti, cycads, Alpine flowers, and rhododendrons, makes up one of the most extensive botanical gardens in Europe. The garden lies on the eastern edge of Schloss Nymphenburg park. Take Tram 17 or Bus 41 from the city center. ✉ *Menzingerstr. 65, Nymphenburg,* ☎ *089/1786–1350.* *€2.* *Oct.–Mar., daily 9–4:30; Apr.–Sept., daily 9–7:30; hothouses daily 9–11:45 and 1–4.*

Hellabrunn Zoo. There are many parklike enclosures, but a minimum of cages at this attractive zoo, which was set up in the early 20th century. Some of the older buildings are in typical art-nouveau style. Care has been taken to group animals according to their natural and geographical habitats. One of the latest additions is the **Urwaldhaus** (rain forest house), which offers guided tours at night (call ahead of time). The 170 acres include restaurants and children's areas. Take Bus 52 from Marienplatz or U-bahn 3 to Thalkirchen, at the southern edge of the city. ✉ *Tierparkstr. 30, Harlaching,* ☎ *089/625–0834,* WEB *www.zoo-munich.de.* *€6.* *Apr.–Sept., daily 8–6; Oct.–Mar., daily 9–5.*

Olympiapark (Olympic Park). On the northern edge of Schwabing, undulating circus-tent-like roofs cover the stadiums built for the 1972 Olympic Games. The roofs are made of translucent tiles that glisten in the midday sun and act as amplifiers for the rock concerts held here. Tours of the park are conducted on a Disneyland-style train throughout the day. An elevator will speed you up the 960-ft **Olympia Tower** (€2.30) for a view of the city and the Alps; there's also a revolving restaurant near the top. Take U-bahn 3 to the park. ☎ *089/3067–2414; 089/3066–8585 for restaurant,* WEB *www.olympiapark-muenchen.de.* *Adventure tour €7; stadium tour €4.* *Main stadium daily*

9–4:30; Olympia Tower daily 9 AM–midnight. Tours Apr.–Nov.; grand tour 2 PM, stadium tour 11 AM.

Schloss Blutenburg. An international collection of 500,000 children's books in more than 100 languages fills the shelves in this medieval palace. The library is augmented by collections of original manuscripts, illustrations, and posters. The castle chapel, built in 1488 by Duke Sigismund, has some fine 15th-century stained glass. Take any S-bahn train to Pasing station, then Bus 73 or 76 to the castle gate. The palace is beyond Nymphenburg, on the northwest edge of Munich. ✉ *Blutenberg 35, Obermenzing,* ☎ *089/811–3132.* *Free.* *Weekdays 10–5.*

★ **Schloss Nymphenburg.** Five generations of Bavarian royalty spent their summers in this glorious baroque and rococo palace. Nymphenburg is the largest palace of its kind in Germany, stretching more than 1 km (½ mi) from one wing to the other. The palace grew in size and scope over a period of more than 200 years, beginning as a summer residence built on land given by Prince Ferdinand Maria to his beloved wife, Henriette Adelaide, on the occasion of the birth of their son and heir, Max Emanuel, in 1663. The princess hired the Italian architect Agostino Barelli to build both the Theatinerkirche and the palace, which was completed in 1675 by his successor, Enrico Zuccalli. Within the original building, now the central axis of the palace complex, is a magnificent hall, the **Steinerner Saal,** extending over two floors and richly decorated with stucco and grandiose frescoes. In the summer, chamber-music concerts are given here. One of the surrounding royal chambers houses the famous **Schönheitsgalerie** (Gallery of Beauties). The walls are hung from floor to ceiling with portraits of women who caught the roving eye of Ludwig I, among them a butcher's daughter and an English duchess. The most famous portrait is of Lola Montez, a sultry beauty and high-class courtesan who, after a time as the mistress of Franz Liszt and later Alexandre Dumas, so enchanted King Ludwig I, that he almost bankrupted the state for her sake and was ultimately forced to abdicate.

The palace is in a park laid out in formal French style, with low hedges and gravel walks extending into woodland. Among the ancient tree stands are three fascinating structures. Don't miss the **Amalienburg** hunting lodge, a rococo gem built by François Cuvilliés, architect of the Altes Residenztheater. The silver-and-blue stucco of the little Amalienburg creates an atmosphere of courtly high life, making clear that the pleasures of the chase here did not always take place outdoors. In the lavishly appointed kennels you'll see that even the dogs lived in luxury. The **Pagodenburg** was built for royal tea parties. Its elegant French exterior disguises a suitably Asian interior in which exotic teas from India and China were served. Swimming parties were held in the **Badenburg,** Europe's first post-Roman heated pool.

Nymphenburg contains so much of interest that a day hardly provides enough time. Don't leave without visiting the former royal stables, now the **Marstallmuseum** (Museum of Royal Carriages; €2.50). It houses a fleet of vehicles, including an elaborately decorated sleigh in which King Ludwig II once glided through the Bavarian twilight, postilion torches lighting the way. On the walls hang portraits of the royal horses. Also exhibited are examples of Nymphenburg porcelain, produced here between 1747 and the 1920s.

A popular museum in the north wing of the palace has nothing to do with the Wittelsbachs but is one of Nymphenburg's major attractions. The **Museum Mensch und Natur** (Museum of Man and Nature; ☎ 089/171–382; €1.50, free Sun.; Tues.–Sun. 9–5) concentrates on three areas of interest: the variety of life on Earth, the history of humankind, and our place in the environment. Main exhibits include a huge representation of the human brain and a chunk of Alpine crystal weighing half a ton. Take Tram 17 or Bus 41 from the city center to the Schloss Nymphenburg stop. ✉ *Notburgastr. at the bridge crossing the Nymphenburg Canal, Nymphenburg,* ☎ *089/179–080.* *Schloss Nymphenburg complex (Gesamtkarte, or combined ticket, incl. the Marstall Museum, but not the Museum Mensch und Natur) €7.50; €6.50 in winter, when parts of the complex are closed.* ⏲ *Apr.–Sept., daily 9–6; Oct.–Mar., daily 10–4. All except Amalienburg and gardens closed Mon.*

Schloss Schleissheim (Schleissheim Palace). In 1597 Duke Wilhelm V decided to look for a peaceful retreat outside Munich and found what he wanted at this palace, then far beyond the city walls but now only a short ride on a train and a bus. A later ruler, Prince Max Emanuel, added a second, smaller palace, the **Lustheim.** Separated from Schleissheim by a formal garden and a decorative canal, the Lustheim houses Germany's largest collection of Meissen porcelain. To reach the palace, take the suburban S-bahn 1 line to Oberschleissheim station and then Bus 292 (which doesn't run on weekends). ✉ *Maximilianshof 1, Oberschleissheim,* ☎ *089/315–5272.* *Combined ticket for palaces and porcelain collection €2.50.* ⏲ *Tues.–Sun. 10–12:30 and 1:30–5.*

Südfriedhof (Southern Cemetery). At this museum-piece cemetery you'll find many famous names but few tourists. Four hundred years ago it was a graveyard beyond the city walls for plague victims and paupers. During the 19th century it was refashioned into an upscale last resting place by the city architect Friedrich von Gärtner. Royal architect Leo von Klenze designed some of the headstones, and both he and von Gärtner are among the famous names you'll find there. The last burial here took place more than 40 years ago. The Südfriedhof is a short 10-minute walk south from the U-bahn station at Sendlinger-Tor-Platz. ✉ *Thalkirchnerstr., Thalkirchen.*

DINING

With seven Michelin-starred restaurants to its credit, Munich claims to be Germany's gourmet capital. It certainly has an inordinate number of ritzy French restaurants, some with chef-owners who honed their skills under such Gallic masters as Paul Bocuse. For connoisseurs, wining and dining at Tantris or the Königshof could well turn into the equivalent of a religious experience; culinary creations are accorded the status of works of art on a par with a Bach fugue or a Dürer painting, with tabs equal to a king's ransom. Epicureans are convinced that one can dine as well in Munich as in any other city on the Continent.

However, the genuine Munich cuisine is to be experienced in those rustic places that serve down-home Bavarian specialties in ample portions. The city's renowned beer and wine restaurants offer superb atmosphere, low prices, and as much wholesome German food as you'll ever want. They're open at just about any hour of the day or night—you can order your roast pork at 11 AM or 11 PM.

What to Wear

Many Munich restaurants serve sophisticated cuisine, and they require their patrons to dress for the occasion. Other, usually less expensive, restaurants will serve you regardless of what you wear.

Close-Up

EIN BIER, BITTE

HOWEVER MANY FINGERS you want to hold up, just remember the easy-to-pronounce *Bier* (beer) *Bit-te* (please) when ordering a beer. The tricky part is, Germans don't just produce *one* beverage called beer; they brew more than 5,000 varieties. Germany has about 1,300 breweries, 40% of the world's total. The hallmark of the country's dedication to beer is the purity law, *das Reinheitsgebot,* unchanged since Duke Wilhelm IV introduced it in Bavaria in 1516. The law decrees that only malted barley, hops, yeast, and water may be used to make beer, except for specialty Weiss-, or Weizenbier (wheat beers, which are a carbonated, sharp, and sour brew, often with floating yeast particles). When EU regulations demanded that the German market be opened to beers from abroad, there was momentary panic in Bavaria. But the foreign intruders had to start applying the same purity rules if they had any hope of penetrating the beer market here.

Most taverns have several drafts in addition to bottled beers. The type available depends upon the region you're in, and in southern Germany the choice can also depend on the time of year. The alcohol content of German beers also varies. At the weaker end of the scale is the light Munich Helles (3.7% alcohol by volume); stronger brews are the bitter-flavored Pilsner (around 5%) and the dark Doppelbock (more than 7%).

Germany's biggest breweries are in the city of Dortmund, which feeds the industrial Ruhr region. Popular northern beers are Export Lagers or the paler, more pungent Pilsners. Köln and Düsseldorf breweries in the Rhine region produce "old-fashioned" beers similar to English ales. But Bavaria is where the majority of breweries—and beer traditions—are found. The Bavarians and the Saarlanders consume more beer per person than any other group in the country.

In Munich you'll find the most famous breweries, the largest beer halls and beer gardens, the biggest and most indulgent beer festival, and the widest selection of brews. Even the beer glasses are bigger: a *Mass* is a 1-liter (almost 2-pint) serving; a *Halbe* is half a Mass, and the standard size. The Hofbräuhaus is Munich's most well-known beer hall, but its oompah band's selections are geared more to Americans and Australians than to your average Münchener. You'll find the citizenry in one of the English Garden's four beer gardens. Müncheners see no conflict that their city, a most cosmopolitan place—with great art galleries and museums, an opulent opera house, and chic lifestyles—is internationally recognized as the most beer-drenched city on earth. Postcards are framed with the message "Munich, the Beer City."

Not even the widest-girthed Bavarians can be held wholly responsible for the staggering consumption of beer and food at the annual Oktoberfest, which starts at the end of September and ends in early October. Typically, 5 million liters (1,183,000 gallons) of beer, as well as 750,000 roasted chickens and 650,000 sausages, are put away by revelers of many nationalities. To partake, book lodging by April, and if you're traveling with a group, also reserve bench space with one of the 14 tents. See Munich's Web site, www.muenchen-tourist.de, for beer tent contacts. The best time to arrive at the grounds is lunchtime, when it's easier to find a seat—by 4 PM it's packed. The beer tents are actually huge pavilions, heaving and pulsating with thousands of beer-swilling, table-pounding "serious" drinkers, animated by brass bands pounding it out on boxing-ring-style stages. The grounds close by 11:30 PM. Take advantage of an hour or two of sobriety to tour the fairground rides, which are also an integral part of Oktoberfest. Under no circumstances attempt any of these rides—all of which claim to be the world's most dangerous—after a liter or two of the Oktoberfest beer. The opprobrium from throwing up on the figure eight is truly Germanic in scale.

— Robert Tilley

CATEGORY	COST*
$$$$	over €20
$$$	€15–€20
$$	€10–€15
$	under €10

**per person for a main course at dinner*

City Center

$$$$ ✕ **Am Marstall.** The exciting menu of this Michelin-starred restaurant combines the best of French and German cuisine—lamb bred on the salt-soaked meadows of coastal Brittany, for instance, or venison from the hunting grounds of Lower Bavaria. Book a window seat so you can while away the time between courses by watching Bavaria's well-heeled shoppers promenading on Maximilianstrasse. ✉ *Maximilianstr. 16, City Center,* ☎ *089/2916–5511. Reservations essential. Jacket and tie. AE, MC, V. Closed Sun., Mon., and holidays.*

$$$$ ✕ **Königshof.** A Michelin star recognizes the reliable old hotel restaurant's place among Munich's finest and most traditional dining rooms. The outstanding menu is French influenced, the surroundings elegant—and if you book a window table you'll have a view of Munich's busiest square, the Stachus, an incandescent experience at night. ✉ *Karlspl. 25, City Center,* ☎ *089/5513–6142. Reservations essential. Jacket and tie. AE, DC, MC, V. No lunch in Aug.*

$$$–$$$$ ✕ **Austernkeller.** *Austern* (oysters) are the specialty of this cellar restaurant, although many other varieties of seafood—all flown in daily from France—help fill its imaginative menu. The lobster thermidor surpasses that served elsewhere in Munich, while a rich fish soup can be had for less than €5. The fussy, fishnet-hung decor is a shade too maritime, especially for downtown Munich, but the starched white linen and glittering glassware and cutlery lend a note of elegance. ✉ *Stollbergstr. 11, City Center,* ☎ *089/298–787. AE, DC, MC, V. No lunch.*

$$$–$$$$ ✕ **Halali.** The Halali is an old-style Munich restaurant—polished wood paneling and antlers on the walls—that offers new-style regional specialties, such as venison in juniper-berry sauce and marinated beef on a bean salad. Save room for the homemade vanilla ice cream. ✉ *Schönfeldstr. 22, City Center,* ☎ *089/285–909. Jacket and tie. AE, MC, V. Closed Sun.*

$$$–$$$$ ✕ **Hunsingers Pacific.** Werner Hunsinger, one of Germany's top restaurateurs, has brought to Munich a reasonably priced restaurant serving eclectic cuisine, borrowing from the Pacific Rim of East Asia, Australia, and North and South America. The restaurant's clam chowder is the best in the city, while another praised specialty is the Chilean-style fillet steak, wrapped in a mantle of onion and eggplant-flavored maize. The many "small dishes" will give you a good panoramic taste of the place. Lunchtime two-course meals cost less than €13. ✉ *Maximilianspl. 5, entrance is in Max-Joseph-Str., City Center,* ☎ *089/5502–9741. AE, DC, MC, V. No lunch weekends.*

$$–$$$$ ★ ✕ **Dukatz.** A literary and business crowd mixes at this smart bar and restaurant in the Literaturhaus, a converted city mansion where regular book readings are presented. Food includes German nouvelle cuisine, but there is a strong gallic touch here as well as traditional with dishes such as calves' head and lamb tripe. Note the verbal art, some of it by New York artist Jennifer Holzer, such as the statement at the bottom of your cup saying: "More eroticism, gentlemen!" ✉ *Salvatorpl. 1, City Center,* ☎ *089/291–9600. No credit cards.*

$$–$$$$ ★ ✕ **Spatenhaus.** A view of the opera house and the royal palace complements the Bavarian mood of the wood-paneled and beamed Spatenhaus. The menu is international, however, with more or less everything

from artichokes to *zuppa Romana* (alcohol-soaked, fruity Italian cake-pudding). But since you're in Bavaria, try the Bavarian plate, an enormous mixture of local meats and sausages. ✉ *Residenzstr. 12, City Center,* ☎ *089/290–7060. AE, MC, V.*

$$–$$$ ✕ **Grüne Gans.** This small, chummy restaurant near the Viktualienmarkt is popular with local entertainers, whose photos clutter the walls. International fare with regional German influences dominates the menu, and there are even a few Chinese dishes. Try the chervil cream soup, followed by calves' kidneys in tarragon sauce. ✉ *Am Einlass 5, City Center,* ☎ *089/266–228. Reservations essential. No credit cards. Closed Sun.*

$$–$$$ ✕ **Hackerhaus.** The cozy, upscale restaurant belonging to the Hacker brewery (founded in the 15th century) has three floors of wood-paneled rooms. In summer you can order a cheese plate and beer in the cool, flower-bedecked inner courtyard; in winter you can snuggle in a corner of the Ratsstube and warm up on thick homemade potato broth, followed by schnitzel and *Bratkartoffein* (panfried potatoes), or take a table in the Bürgerstube and admire its proud centerpiece, the world's largest beer mug. ✉ *Sendlingerstr. 14, City Center,* ☎ *089/260–5026. AE, DC, MC, V.*

$–$$$ ✕ **Buxs.** This self-service vegetarian place has a full range of salads, excellent entrées, freshly pressed juices and smoothies, and desserts that are worth the caloric splurge. On warm days you can sit outside and watch the Viktualienmarkt activities. ✉ *Frauenstr. 9, City Center,* ☎ *089/291–9195;* ✉ *Amalienstr. 38, Schwabing,* ☎ *089/280–29940. No credit cards. Closed Sun. No dinner Sat.*

$–$$$ ✕ **Dürnbräu.** A fountain plays outside this picturesque old Bavarian inn. Inside, it's crowded and noisy. Expect to share a table (the 21-ft table in the middle of the place is a favorite); your fellow diners will range from businesspeople to students. The food is resolutely traditional. Try the cream of spinach soup and the boiled beef. ✉ *Dürnbräug. 2, City Center,* ☎ *089/222–195. AE, DC, MC, V.*

$–$$$ ✕ **Erstes Münchner Kartoffelhaus.** In Munich's First Potato House tubers come in all forms, from the simplest baked potato with sour cream to gratin creations with shrimp and salmon. When potatoes were first introduced to Germany, they were dismissed as fodder fit only for animals or the very lowest strata of society. Frederick the Great was largely responsible for putting them on the dining tables of even the nobility, and now the lowly potato is an indispensable part of the German diet. This restaurant is fun and a great value, too. ✉ *Hochbrückenstr. 3, City Center,* ☎ *089/296–331. Reservations essential. AE, MC, V.*

$–$$$ ✕ **Haxenbauer.** This is one of Munich's more sophisticated beer restaurants, with a much greater emphasis on the quality of the food than in similar places. Try the *Schweineshaxn* (pork shanks) cooked over a charcoal fire. The two branches consist of the usual series of interlinking rooms with sturdy yet attractive Bavarian decoration. The restaurant at the corner of Sparkassenstrasse and Ledererstrasse has a big traditional noisy beer hall. The Münzstrasse venue is more intimate. ✉ *Münzstr. 2 and around the corner at Sparkassenstr. and Ledererstr., City Center,* ☎ *089/2916–2100 for both sites. AE, MC, V. Münzstr. Haxenbauer is closed Sun.*

$–$$$ ★ ✕ **Hundskugel.** This is Munich's oldest tavern and also one of the city's smallest. You'll be asked to squeeze together and make room for latecomers looking for a spot at one of the few tables that clutter the handkerchief-size dining room. The tavern dates from 1440 and in many ways doesn't appear to have changed much over the centuries. Even the menu is medievally basic and a bit hit-and-miss, although any

Dining

- Am Marstall **20**
- Augustiner Keller **3**
- Austernkeller **26**
- Bamberger Haus . . . **31**
- Bistro Cezanne. **30**
- Buxs **15**
- Cafe am Beethovenplatz **4**
- Cohen's **29**
- Dukatz **11**
- Dürnbräu. **25**
- Erstes Münchner Kartoffelhaus **24**
- Gasthaus Isarthor . . . **27**
- Grüne Gans. **13**
- Hackerhaus **10**
- Halali **28**
- Haxenbauer. **22**
- Hofbräuhaus **21**
- Hundskugel **8**
- Hunsingers Pacific. **2**
- Königshof **5**
- Leonrod **1**
- Max-Emanuel-Brauerei **32**
- Monaco **14**
- Nürnberger Bratwurst Glöckl am Dom **12**
- Pfälzer Weinprobierstube . . . **19**
- Prinz Myshkin **9**
- Ratskeller. **16**
- Spatenhaus **18**
- Spöckmeier **6**
- Tantris **33**
- Weinhaus Neuner . . . **7**
- Weinstadl **17**
- Weisses Bräuhaus. . . **23**

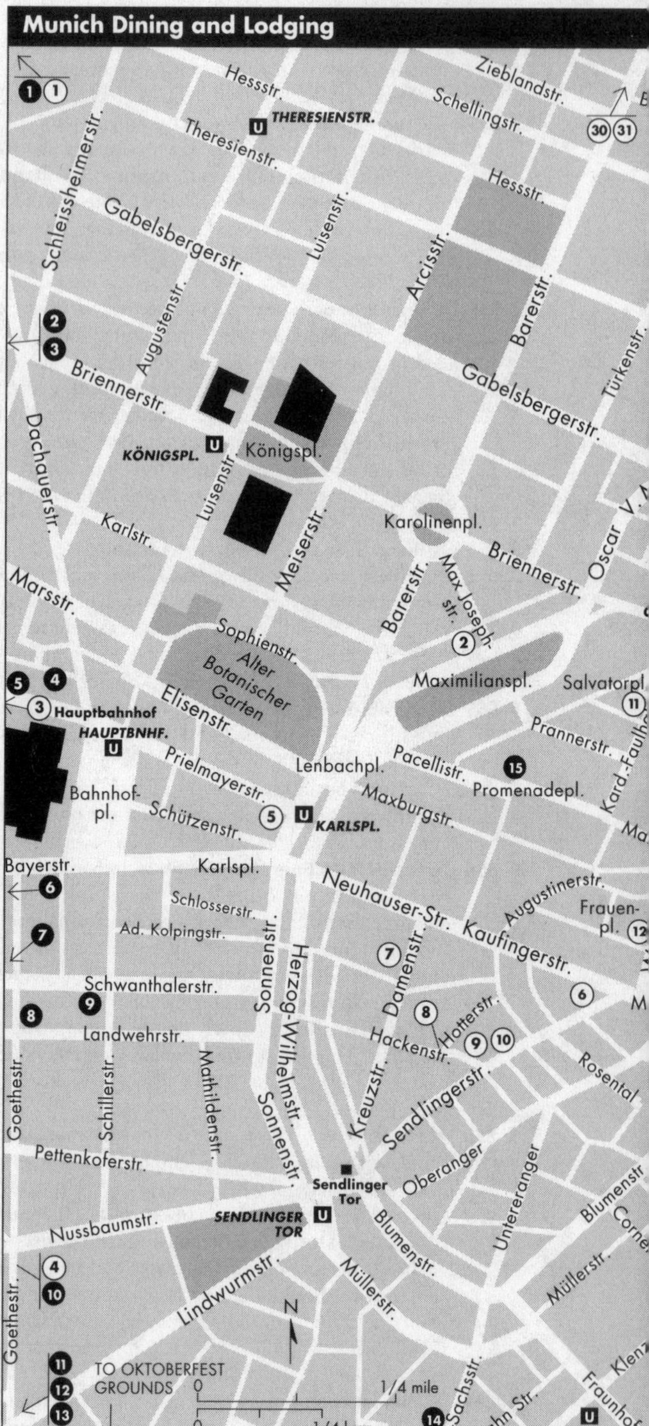

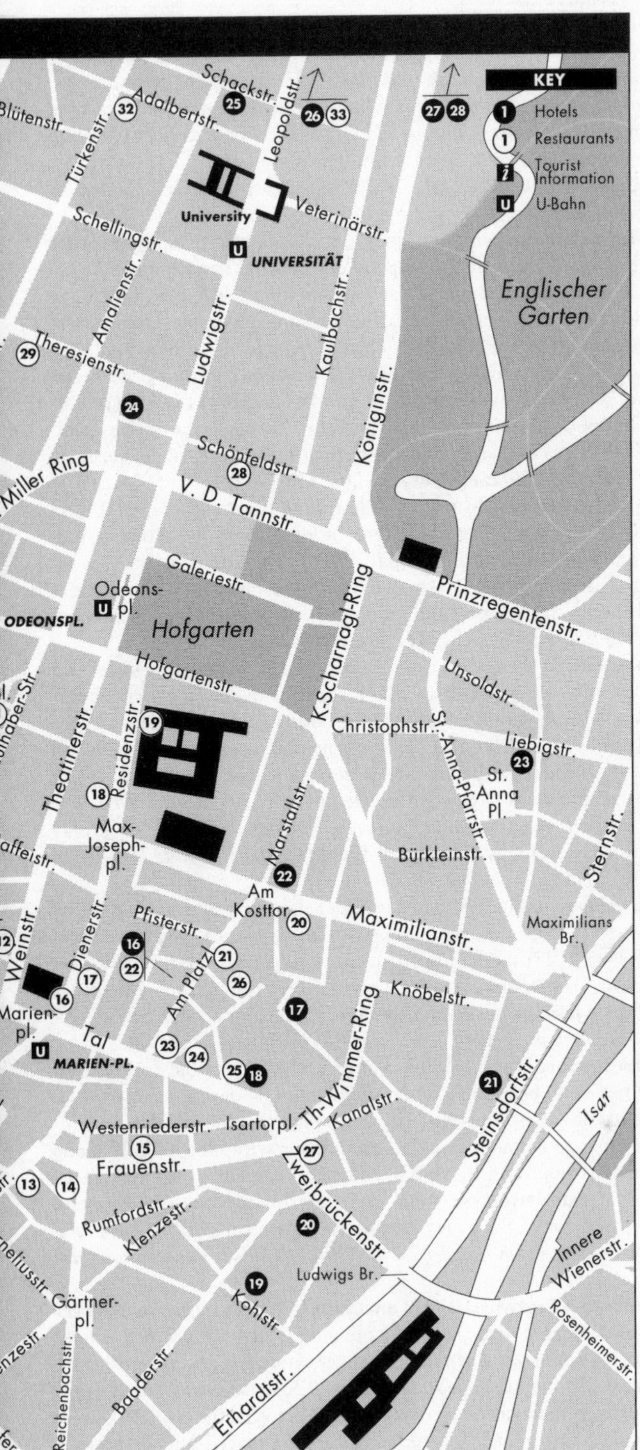

Lodging

Admiral	19
Adria	23
Advokat	20
ArabellaSheraton Grand Hotel	26
Bayerischer Hof	15
Biederstein	28
Brack	11
Carlton	24
Eden Hotel Wolff	5
Erzgiesserei Europe	3
Gästehaus am Englischen Garten	27
Hotel Amba	4
Hotel Concorde	17
Hotel Mirabell	8
Hotel Pension Am Siegestor	25
Hotel Pension Schmellergarten	13
Hotel-Pension Beck	21
Hotel-Pension Mariandl	10
Jagdschloss	6
Kempinski Hotel Vier Jahreszeiten München	22
Kriemhild	3
Kurpfalz	9
Mayer	12
Olympic	14
Park-Hotel Theresienhöhe	7
Platzl	16
Rotkreuzplatz	2
Torbräu	18

combination of pork and potato or sauerkraut can be recommended. ✉ *Hotterstr. 18, City Center,* ☎ *089/264–272. No credit cards.*

$–$$$ ✕ **Monaco.** One of the latest and nicest additions to the Italian scene, the Monaco makes its guests feel at home right away, ensuring returning customers. The decor is simple and unpretentious. Excellent wines on the menu are backed up by a serendipitous selection that the waiter will recommend off the cuff. ✉ *Reichenbachstr. 10, City Center,* ☎ *089/268–141. MC, V.*

$–$$$ ✕ **Spöckmeier.** This rambling, solidly Bavarian beer restaurant spread over three floors, including a snug *Keller* (cellar), is famous for its homemade Weisswurst. If you've just stopped in for a snack and don't fancy the fat breakfast sausage, order coffee and pretzels or, in the afternoon, a wedge of cheesecake. The daily changing menu also offers more than two dozen hearty main-course dishes and a choice of four draft beers. The house *Eintopf* (a rich broth of noodles and pork) is a meal in itself. The Spöckmeier is only 50 yards from Marienplatz; on sunny summer days tables are set outside in the car-free street. ✉ *Rosenstr. 9, City Center,* ☎ *089/268–088. AE, DC, MC, V.*

$–$$$ ✕ **Weinhaus Neuner.** Munich's oldest wine tavern serves good food as well as superior wines in its three nooks: the wood-panel restaurant, the Weinstübl, and the small bistro. The choice of food is remarkable, from nouvelle German to old-fashioned country. Specialties include home-smoked beef and salmon. ✉ *Herzogspitalstr. 8, City Center,* ☎ *089/260–3954. AE, MC, V. Closed Sun.*

$$ ✕ **Weinstadl.** At the end of a small alley off a busy shopping street and overlooked by most passersby, the historic 16th-century Weinstadl is well worth hunting out. In summer the courtyard beer garden is a cool delight. Brass-studded oaken door opens onto a vaulted dining room where traditional Bavarian fare is served at bench-lined tables. A lunchtime menu and a glass of excellent beer costs around €10. The cellar, reached via a winding staircase, features live music on Friday and Saturday evenings. ✉ *Burgstr. 5, City Center,* ☎ *089/2280–7420. AE, DC, MC.*

$–$$ ✕ **Ratskeller.** Munich's Ratskeller under the city hall is known for its goulash soup. Seat yourself—the space is cavernous, and the setting includes vaulted stone ceilings, alcoves, banquettes, and wrought-iron work. An atmospheric tavern serves fine Franconian wine from Würzburg's famous Juliusspital at a price that can't be matched in Munich. ✉ *Marienpl. 8, City Center,* ☎ *089/219–9890. AE, MC, V.*

$–$$ ✕ **Hofbräuhaus.** The pounding oompah band draws the curious into this father of all beer halls, where singing and shouting drinkers contribute to the earsplitting din. This is no place for the fainthearted, although a trip to Munich would be incomplete without a look. Upstairs is a quieter restaurant. In March, May, and September ask for one of the special, extra-strong seasonal beers (Starkbier, Maibock, Märzen), which complement the heavy, traditional Bavarian fare. ✉ *Am Platzl 9, City Center,* ☎ *089/221–676 or 089/290–1360. Reservations not accepted. V.*

$–$$ ✕ **Nürnberger Bratwurst Glöckl am Dom.** Munich's most original beer tavern is dedicated to a specialty from a rival city, Nuremberg, whose delicious *Nürnberger Bratwürste* (finger-size sausages) form the staple dish of the menu. They're served by a busy team of friendly waitresses dressed in Bavarian dirndls, who flit between the crowded tables with remarkable agility. In summer tables are placed outside under a bright awning and in the shade of the nearby Frauenkirche. In winter the mellow dark-paneled dining rooms provide relief from the cold. ✉ *Frauenpl. 9, City Center,* ☎ *089/220–385. V, DC, MC.*

$–$$ ✕ **Pfälzer Weinprobierstube.** A warren of stone-vaulted rooms, wooden tables, flickering candles, dirndl-clad waitresses, and a vast range of wines add up to an experience as close to everyone's image of timeless Germany as you're likely to get. The wines are mostly from the *Pfalz* (Palatinate), as are many of the specialties on the limited menu. Here you'll find former chancellor Kohl's favorite dish, *Saumagen* (meat loaf, spiced with herbs and cooked in a pig's stomach). This place is an excellent value, considering the central location. ✉ *Residenzstr. 1, City Center,* ☎ *089/225–628. Reservations not accepted. No credit cards.*

$–$$ ★ ✕ **Prinz Myshkin.** This sophisticated vegetarian restaurant spices up predictable cuisine by mixing Italian and Asian influences. You have the choice of antipasti, homemade gnocchi, tofu and stir-fried dishes, and excellent wines. If your hunger is only moderate, you can get half portions. The airy room has a majestically vaulted ceiling, and there's always some art exhibited to feed the eye and mind. ✉ *Hackenstr. 2, City Center,* ☎ *089/265–596. MC, V.*

$–$$ ✕ **Weisses Bräuhaus.** If you have developed a taste for Munich's Weissbier, this is the place to enjoy it. The flavorful Weisse (from the Schneider brewery) is served with hearty Bavarian dishes, mostly variations of pork and dumplings or cabbage, by some of Munich's friendlier waitresses, good-humored women in crisp black dresses, who appear to match the art nouveau features of the restaurant's beautifully restored interior. ✉ *Tal 7, City Center,* ☎ *089/299–875. No credit cards.*

Maxvorstadt

$ ✕ **Cohen's.** Reviving the old Jewish Central-European tradition of good, healthy cooking together with hospitality and good cheer seems to be the underlying principle at Cohen's. Dig into a few hearty latkes, a steaming plate of Chulend stew, or a standard gefilte fish doused with excellent Golan wine from Israel. The kitchen is open from 12:30 PM to about 10:30 PM, and if the atmosphere is good, patrons might just be able to hang out chattering until the wee hours. Klezmer singers perform on Friday evenings. ✉ *Theresienstr. 31, Maxvorstadt,* ☎ *089/280–9545. AE, MC, V.*

Lehel

$–$$ ✕ **Gasthaus Isarthor.** The old-fashioned "Wirtshaus," where the innkeeper has his patrons in his sights and keeps the mood going, lives on in this old, wedge-shape dining room. For Rainer Menne, who hails from Salzburg, Austria, having a social mix at his simple wooden tables is the secret of a good establishment—actors, government officials, apprentice craftspersons, journalists, and retirees sit side by side. Besides pork roasts, roast beef with onions, boiled beef, and the like, the house specialty is the Augustiner beer from a wooden barrel, tapped once a day at around 6 PM. When the barrel is empty, that's it for the day. ✉ *Kanalstr. 2, Lehel,* ☎ *089/227–753. No credit cards.*

Schwabing

$$$$ ★ ✕ **Tantris.** Chef Hans Haas has kept this restaurant with a modernist look among the top five dining establishments in Munich. He's been named the country's best chef by Germany's premier food critics in the past. You, too, will be impressed by the exotic nouvelle cuisine on the menu, including such specialties as shellfish and creamed potato soup and roasted wood pigeon with scented rice. But you may wish to ignore the bare concrete surroundings and the garish orange-and-yellow

decor. ✉ *Johann-Fichte-Str. 7, Schwabing,* ☎ *089/361–9590. Reservations essential. Jacket and tie. AE, DC, MC, V. Closed Sun.*

$$–$$$ ✕ **Bistro Cezanne.** You're in for French-Provençal dining at this truly Gallic bistro-restaurant in the heart of Munich's former bohemian quarter, Schwabing. Owner-chef Patrick Geay learned his craft from some of Europe's best teachers. His regularly changing blackboard menu features the freshest market products, with vegetables prepared as only the French can. Among the fish dishes, the scallops melt in the mouth, while the coq au vin will conquer the greatest hungers. Reservations are advised. ✉ *Konradstr. 1, Schwabing,* ☎ *089/391–805. AE, DC, MC, V.*

$–$$ ✕ **Bamberger Haus.** The faded elegance of this historic house on the edge of Schwabing's Luitpold Park disguises an up-to-date kitchen, which conjures up inexpensive dishes of modern flair and imagination. Vegetarians are well catered to with cheap and filling gratins. The cellar beer tavern serves one of the best ales in town. In summer reserve a table on the terrace and eat under chestnut trees with a view of the park. ✉ *Brunnerstr. 2, Schwabing,* ☎ *089/308–8966. AE, DC, MC, V.*

$–$$ ✕ **Max-Emanuel-Brauerei.** This historic old brewery tavern is a great value, with Bavarian dishes rarely costing more than €10; at lunchtime that amount will easily cover the cost of an all-you-can-eat buffet including a couple of beers. The main dining room has a stage, so the bill often covers a cabaret or jazz concert. In summer take a table outside in the secluded little beer garden tucked amidst the apartment blocks. ✉ *Adalbertstr. 33, Schwabing,* ☎ *089/271–5158. AE, MC.*

Leopoldvorstadt

$–$$$ ✕ **Augustiner Keller.** This 19th-century establishment is the flagship beer restaurant of one of Munich's oldest breweries. The decor emphasizes wood—from the refurbished parquet floors to the wood barrels from which the beer is drawn. The menu changes daily and offers a full range of Bavarian specialties, but try to order Tellerfleisch, served on a big wooden board. Follow that with a couple of *Dampfnudeln* (yeast dumpling served with custard), and you won't feel hungry again for 24 hours. ✉ *Arnulfstr. 52, Leopoldvorstadt,* ☎ *089/594–393. AE, MC, V.*

$–$$ ✕ **Café am Beethovenplatz.** Classical music accompanies excellent fare on Mondays and Tuesdays. An international breakfast menu is served daily (on Sunday with live classic music as well), followed by suitably creative lunch and dinner menus. The pork is supplied by a farm where the free-range pigs are fed only the best natural fodder—so the *Schweinsbraten* (roast pig) is recommended. Reservations are advised as a young and intellectual crowd fills the tables quickly. ✉ *Goethestr. 51 (am Beethovenpl.), Leopoldvorstadt,* ☎ *089/5440–4348. AE, MC, V.*

Neuhausen

$–$$ ✕ **Leonrod.** Turkish food is second nature to Munich. This little establishment at the corner of Albrechtstrasse and Leonrodstrasse in the Neuhausen district (U1 to Rotkreuzplatz and then the 33 bus or 12 tram to Albrechtstrasse) attracts many a local for Turkish pizza or a lamb stew, or simply a delicious plate of warm starters. Portions are generous. Adding to the simple decor (a mural depicting a Turkish countryside) is a belly-dancer, who heats up the room on Wednesday and Saturday nights. ✉ *Leonrodstr. 45, Neuhausen,* ☎ *089/123–5661. AE, DC, MC, V.*

LODGING

Though Munich has a vast number of hotels in all price ranges, many are fully booked year-round; this is a major trade and convention city as well as a prime tourist destination. If you're visiting during Mode Wochen (Fashion Weeks), in March and September, or during Oktoberfest at the end of September, make reservations at least six months in advance.

Some of the large, very expensive hotels that cater to expense-account business travelers have very attractive weekend discount rates—sometimes as much as 50% below normal prices. Conversely, regular rates can go up during big trade fairs.

Munich's two tourist information offices—at the main railway station and in the city center (Marienplatz, in the Rathaus)—make hotel bookings. Telephone lines are usually busy, so your best bet is to visit one of the offices personally.

CATEGORY	COST*
$$$$	over €225
$$$	€150–€225
$$	€75–€150
$	under €75

**All prices are for two people in a double room, including tax and service.*

City Center

$$$$ **Bayerischer Hof.** Germany's most respected family-owned hotel, the Bayerischer Hof began its rich history by hosting Ludwig I's guests. Public rooms are grandly laid out with marble, antiques, and oil paintings. Laura Ashley–decorated rooms look out to the city's skyline of towers. Rooms facing the interior courtyard are the least expensive and begin at €254. Nightlife is built into the hotel, with Trader Vic's bar and dancing at the Night Club. ✉ *Promenadepl. 2–6, City Center D–80333,* ☎ *089/21200,* FAX *089/212–0906,* WEB *www.bayerischerhof.de. 306 rooms, 45 suites. 3 restaurants, bar, cable TV with movies and video games, Internet, pool, hair salon, massage, sauna, nightclub, meeting rooms, parking (fee), no-smoking rooms, some pets allowed (fee). AE, DC, MC, V.*

$$$$ ★ **Kempinski Hotel Vier Jahreszeiten München.** The Four Seasons has been playing host to the world's wealthy and titled for more than a century. It has an unbeatable location on Maximilianstrasse, Munich's premier shopping street, only a few minutes' walk from the heart of the city. Elegance and luxury set the tone throughout; many rooms have handsome antique pieces. The Bistro Eck is on the main floor, and the Theater bar/restaurant is in the cellar. The afternoon tea in the poshly decorated foyer is a special treat. ✉ *Maximilianstr. 17, City Center D–80539,* ☎ *089/21250; 516/794–2670 for Kempinski Reservation Service,* FAX *089/2125–2000,* WEB *www.Kempinski-Vierjahreszeiten.de. 268 rooms, 48 suites. 2 restaurants, piano bar, cable TV with movies, pool, health club, massage, sauna, meeting rooms, car rental, parking (fee), no-smoking rooms, some pets allowed (fee). AE, DC, MC, V.*

$$$–$$$$ **Platzl.** The Platzl, which is a privately owned enterprise, has won awards and wide recognition for its ecologically aware management. It stands in the historic heart of Munich, near the famous Hofbräuhaus beer hall and a couple of minutes' walk from Marienplatz and many other landmarks. Its Pfistermühle restaurant, with 16th-century vaulting, is one of the area's oldest and most historic establishments. ✉ *Sparkassenstr. 10, City Center D–80331,* ☎ *089/237–030; 800/448–*

8355 in the U.S., FAX 089/2370–3800, WEB www.platzl.de. 167 rooms. Restaurant, bar, no a/c in some rooms, cable TV with movies, gym, sauna, steam room, parking (fee), no-smoking rooms, some pets allowed (fee). AE, DC, MC, V.

$$$–$$$$ **Torbräu.** In this snug hotel you'll sleep under the shadow of one of Munich's ancient city gates—the 14th-century Isartor. The location is excellent as it's midway between the Marienplatz and the Deutsches Museum (and around the corner from the Hofbräuhaus). The hotel has been run by the same family for more than a century. Comfortable rooms are decorated in a plush and ornate Italian style. Its Italian restaurant, *La Famiglia*, is one of the best in the area. ✉ *Tal 41, City Center D–80331,* ☎ *089/242–340, FAX 089/234–235, WEB www.torbraeu.de. 83 rooms, 3 suites. Restaurant, café, no a/c in some rooms, cable TV, in-room data ports, gym, sauna, bowling, meeting rooms, no-smoking rooms, some pets allowed (fee). AE, MC, V.*

$$ **Olympic.** The English-style entrance lobby, with its leather easy chairs and mahogany fittings, is an attractive introduction to this friendly small hotel, a beautifully converted turn-of-the-20th-century mansion, amid the bars and boutiques of the colorful district between Sendlinger Tor and Isartor. Most of the rooms look out over a quiet interior courtyard. Do not expect constant and fawning care: the style of the hotel is casual, the idea is to make the guest feel really at home. ✉ *Hans-Sachs-Str. 4, City Center D–80469,* ☎ *089/231–890, FAX 089/2318–9199. 38 rooms, 3 apartments. No a/c, cable TV, in-room data ports, parking (fee), some pets allowed (fee). AE, DC, MC, V.*

Isarvorstadt

$$$–$$$$ ★ **Admiral.** The small, privately owned Admiral enjoys a quiet side-street location and its own garden, close to the Isar River and Deutsches Museum. Many of the simply furnished and warmly decorated bedrooms have a balcony overlooking the garden. Bowls of fresh fruit are part of the friendly welcome awaiting guests. The breakfast buffet is a dream, complete with homemade jams, in-season strawberries, and Italian and French delicacies. ✉ *Kohlstr. 9, Isarvorstadt D–80469,* ☎ *089/216–350, FAX 089/293–674, WEB www.hotel-admiral.de. 33 rooms. Bar, no a/c, cable TV, in-room data ports, parking (fee), no-smoking rooms, some pets allowed. AE, DC, MC, V.*

$$–$$$ **Advokat.** Owner Kevin Voigt designed much of his hotel's exquisite furniture, which was then made by Italian craftsmen. The Italian touch is everywhere, from the sleek, minimalist lines of the bedroom furniture and fittings to the choice prints and modern Florentine mirrors on the walls. If you value modern taste over plush luxury, this is the hotel for you. ✉ *Baaderstr. 1, Isarvorstadt D–80469,* ☎ *089/216–310, FAX 089/216–3190, WEB www.hotel-advokat.de. 50 rooms. No a/c, cable TV, in-room data ports, parking (fee), no-smoking rooms, some pets allowed. AE, DC, MC, V.*

Maxvorstadt

$$–$$$$ **Carlton.** This is a favorite of many diplomats, professors, and business executives on tight schedules and in need of a top-notch place to stay: a small, elegant, discreet hotel on a quiet side street in the best area of downtown Munich. Some of the liveliest student bars and restaurants are nearby, as are galleries, museums, and movie theaters. Rooms are on the small side but comfortable. A glass of champagne is included in the complimentary buffet breakfast. ✉ *Fürstenstr. 12, Maxvorstadt D–80333,* ☎ *089/282–061, FAX 089/284–391. 50 rooms. Cable TV with movies, sauna, no-smoking rooms, some pets allowed (fee). AE, DC, MC, V.*

$$ **Erzgiesserei Europe.** Its location on a quiet, residential section of the city is hardly a drawback, because the nearby subway whisks you in five minutes to Karlsplatz, convenient to the pedestrian shopping area and the main railway station. Rooms in this attractive, modern hotel are particularly bright, decorated in soft pastels with good reproductions on the walls. The cobblestone garden café is a haven of peace. ✉ *Erzgiessereistr. 15, Maxvorstadt D–80335,* ☎ *089/126–820,* FAX *089/123–6198,* WEB *www.top-hotels.de/erzeurope. 105 rooms, 1 suite. Restaurant, café, bar, no a/c, cable TV with movies, in-room data ports, parking (fee), no-smoking rooms, some pets allowed (fee). AE, DC, MC, V.*

$ ★ **Hotel Pension Am Siegestor.** This modest but very appealing pension takes up three floors of a fin-de-siècle mansion between the Siegestor monument, on Leopoldstrasse, and the university. An ancient wood-paneled, glass-door elevator brings you to the fourth-floor reception desk. Most of the simply furnished rooms face the impressive Arts Academy across the street. Rooms on the fifth floor are particularly cozy, tucked up under the eaves. ✉ *Akademiestr. 5, Maxvorstadt D–80799,* ☎ *089/399–550 or 089/399–551,* FAX *089/343–050. 20 rooms. No room phones, no TV in some rooms. No credit cards.*

Schwabing

$$–$$$ **Biederstein.** The hotel is not the prettiest from the outside—a modern, uninspired block—but it seems to want to fit into its old Schwabing surroundings. At the rim of the Englischer Garten, the Biederstein has many advantages: peace and quiet; excellent service; and comfortable, well-appointed rooms that were carefully renovated. Guests are requested to smoke on the balconies, not inside. ✉ *Keferstr. 18, Schwabing D–80335,* ☎ *089/389–9970,* FAX *089/3899–97389. 34 rooms, 7 suites. Bar, no a/c, cable TV, free parking, some pets allowed (fee). AE, DC, MC, V.*

$$ ★ **Gästehaus am Englischen Garten.** Reserve well in advance for a room at this popular converted water mill, more than 200 years old, adjoining the Englischer Garten. The hotel is only a five-minute walk from the bars, shops, and restaurants of Schwabing. Be sure to ask for one of the 12 nostalgically old-fashioned rooms in the main building; a modern annex down the road has 13 apartments, all with cooking facilities. In summer breakfast is served on the terrace of the main house, which has a garden on an island in the old millrace. ✉ *Liebergesellstr. 8, Schwabing D–80802,* ☎ *089/383–9410,* FAX *089/3839–4133. 12 rooms, 6 with bath or shower; 13 apartments. No a/c, cable TV, free parking, some pets allowed (fee). AE, DC, MC, V.*

Leopoldvorstadt

$$$–$$$$ **Eden-Hotel Wolff.** Chandeliers and dark-wood paneling in the public rooms contribute to the old-fashioned elegance of this downtown favorite. It's directly across the street from the train station and near the Theresienwiese fairgrounds. The rooms come with plush comforts, and most are spacious. You can dine on excellent Bavarian specialties in the intimate Zirbelstube restaurant. ✉ *Arnulfstr. 4, Leopoldvorstadt D–80335,* ☎ *089/551–150,* FAX *089/5511–5555,* WEB *www.ehw.de. 209 rooms, 7 suites. Restaurant, café, bar, no a/c in some rooms, cable TV with movies, Internet, gym, meeting rooms, parking (fee), some pets allowed (fee). AE, DC, MC, V.*

$$–$$$ **Brack.** Oktoberfest revelers value the Brack's proximity to the beer festival grounds, and its location—on a busy, tree-lined thoroughfare just south of the center—is handy for city attractions. Rooms are furnished in light, friendly veneers and are soundproof (a useful feature

during Oktoberfest) and have amenities such as hair dryers and cable TV. The buffet breakfast will set you up for the day. ✉ *Lindwurmstr. 153, Leopoldvorstadt D–80337,* ☎ *089/747–2550,* FAX *089/7472–5599,* WEB *www.hotel-brack.de. 50 rooms. cable TV with movies, no a/c, free parking, no pets. AE, DC, MC, V.*

$$–$$$ **Hotel Amba.** Don't waste a second with additional travel. The Amba, which is right next to the train station, has clean, bright rooms, good service, no expensive frills, and everything you need to plug and play as it were. No sooner have you enjoyed a solid breakfast at the buffet (with sparkling wine), than you'll be out on the town visiting the nearby sights on foot. ✉ *Arnulfstr. 20, Leopoldvorstadt D–80636,* ☎ *089/545–140,* FAX *089/5451–1555,* WEB *www.hotel-amba.de. 86 rooms. No a/c, cable TV with movies, no-smoking rooms, some pets allowed (fee). AE, DC, MC, V.*

$$ ★ **Hotel Mirabell.** This family-run hotel is used to American tourists who appreciate the friendly atmosphere, central location (between the main railway station and the Oktoberfest fairgrounds), and reasonable room rates. Three apartments are for small groups or families. All rooms have TVs and phones, and are furnished in modern light woods and bright prints. Breakfast is the only meal served, but snacks can be ordered at the bar. Prices are much higher during trade fairs and Oktoberfest. ✉ *Landwehrstr. 42 (entrance on Goethestr.), Leopoldvorstadt D–80336,* ☎ *089/549–1740,* FAX *089/550–3701. 65 rooms, 3 apartments. Bar, cable TV with movies, in-room data ports, no-smoking rooms, some pets allowed (fee). AE, MC, V.*

$–$$ **Hotel-Pension Mariandl.** The American armed forces commandeered this turn-of-the-20th-century neo-Gothic mansion in May 1945 and established Munich's first postwar nightclub, the Femina, on the ground floor (now the charming café-restaurant, Cafe am Beethovenplatz). Most rooms are mansion size, with high ceilings and large windows overlooking a leafy avenue. The Oktoberfest grounds and the main railway station are both a 10-minute walk away. ✉ *Goethestr. 51, Leopoldvorstadt D–80336,* ☎ *089/534–108,* FAX *089/5440–4396. 28 rooms. Restaurant, no a/c, no room phones, no TVs, some pets allowed. AE, DC, MC, V.*

$ **Kurpfalz.** Guests have praised the friendly welcome and service they receive at this centrally placed and affordable lodging. Rooms are comfortable, if furnished in a manner only slightly better than functional, and all are equipped with satellite TV. Breakfast is included. The main train station and Oktoberfest grounds are both within a 10-minute walk, and the area is rich in restaurants, bars, and movie theaters. ✉ *Schwantalerstr. 121, Leopoldvorstadt D–80339,* ☎ *089/540–986,* FAX *089/5409–8811. 44 rooms with shower. Bar, no a/c, in-room data ports, cable TV, some pets allowed, no-smoking rooms. AE, MC, V.*

Isarvorstadt

$ ★ **Hotel-Pension Schmellergarten.** This genuine family business will make you feel right at home, and is very popular with young budget travelers. The little place is on a quiet street just off Lindwurmstrasse, a few minutes walk from the Theresienwiese (Oktoberfest). The Poccistrasse subway station is around the corner to take you into the center of town. ✉ *Schmellerstr. 20, Isarvorstadt D–80337,* ☎ *089/773–157,* FAX *089/725–6886. 14 rooms. No a/c, some pets allowed. No credit cards.*

Lehel

$$–$$$ **Adria.** This modern, comfortable hotel is ideally set in the upmarket area of Lehel, in the middle of Munich's museum quarter. Rooms are large and tastefully decorated, with old prints on the pale-pink walls, Oriental rugs on the floors, and flowers beside the double beds. A spectacular breakfast buffet (including a glass of sparkling wine) is included in the room rate. There's no hotel restaurant, but the area is rich in good restaurants, bistros, and bars. ✉ *Liebigstr. 8a, Lehel D–80538,* ☎ *089/242–1170,* FAX *089/242–117999,* WEB *www.adria-muenchen.de. 43 rooms. No a/c, cable TV, in-room data ports, some pets allowed (fee), no-smoking rooms. AE, MC, V.*

$$ **Hotel Concorde.** The centrally located Concorde wants to do its bit toward relieving traffic congestion, so guests who arrive from the airport on the S-bahn can exchange their ticket at the reception desk for a welcome champagne or cocktail. The nearest S-bahn station (Isartor) is only a two-minute walk away. Rooms are done in pastel tones and light woods. Fresh flowers and bright prints add a colorful touch. A large breakfast buffet is served in its stylish, mirrored Salon Margarita. ✉ *Herrnstr. 38, Lehel D–80539,* ☎ *089/224–515,* FAX *089/228–3282. 67 rooms, 4 suites. Cable TV, in-room data ports, parking (fee), some pets allowed (fee), no-smoking rooms. AE, DC, MC, V.*

$ ★ **Hotel-Pension Beck.** American and British guests receive a particularly warm welcome from the Anglophile owner of the rambling, friendly Beck (she and her pet canary are a regular presence). Bright carpeting, with matching pinewood furniture, gives rooms a cheerful touch. The pension has no elevator, but does have a prime location convenient to the museums on Prinzregentenstrasse and to the Englischer Garten. ✉ *Thierschstr. 36, Lehel D–80538,* ☎ *089/220–708 or 089/225–768,* FAX *089/220–925,* WEB *www.bst-online.de/pension.beck. 44 rooms, 7 with shower. No a/c, cable TV, some in-room data ports, some pets allowed. MC, V.*

Nymphenburg

$$ **Kriemhild.** If you're traveling with children, you'll appreciate this welcoming, family-run pension in a western suburb near parks and gardens. It's a 10-minute walk from Schloss Nymphenburg and around the corner from the Hirschgarten Park, site of one of the city's best beer gardens. The tram ride (No. 16 or 17 to Kriemhildenstrasse stop) from the train station is 10 minutes. The buffet breakfast is included in the rate. ✉ *Guntherstr. 16, Nymphenburg D–80639,* ☎ *089/171–1170,* FAX *089/1711–1755,* WEB *www.kriemhild.de. 18 rooms. Bar, no a/c, cable TV, in-room data ports, free parking, some pets allowed. AE, MC, V.*

Outer Munich

$$–$$$$ **ArabellaSheraton Grand Hotel.** The building itself may raise a few eyebrows. It stands on a slight elevation and is not the most shapely on the Munich skyline. What goes on inside is sheer five-star luxury for the leisure or business traveler. Guests are greeted with a glass of champagne, snacks and drinks are available round the clock in the Towers Lounge. The excellent restaurant Ente vom Lehel has come to roost here, as well. And if you need a special Bavarian flavor to your stay, then book one of the 60 "Bavarian rooms." ✉ *Arabellastr. 5, Bogenhausen D–81925,* ☎ *089/92640,* FAX *089/9264–8699,* WEB *www.arabellasheraton.de. 644 rooms, 31 suites. 2 restaurants, bars, cable TV with movies, Internet, pool, sauna, steam room, hair salon, business services, meeting rooms, parking, some pets allowed (fee), no-smoking rooms. AE, DC, MC, V.*

$$$ **Park-Hotel Theresienhöhe.** The Park-Hotel claims that none of its rooms is less than 400 square ft. Suites are larger than many luxury apartments, and some of them come with small kitchens. The sleek, modern rooms are mostly decorated with light woods and pastel-color

fabrics and carpeting; larger rooms and suites get a lot of light, thanks to the floor-to-ceiling windows. Families are particularly welcome, and a baby-sitting service is provided. There's no in-house restaurant, but you can order in. ✉ *Parkstr. 31, Westend D–80339,* ☎ *089/519–950,* FAX *089/5199–5420. 35 rooms. Bar, no-smoking rooms, cable TV, some in-room data ports, no a/c, baby-sitting, pets allowed. AE, DC, MC, V.*

$$ **Jagdschloss.** This century-old hunting lodge in Munich's leafy Obermenzing suburb is a delightful hotel. The rustic look has been retained, with lots of original woodwork and white stucco. Many of the comfortable pastel-tone bedrooms have wooden balconies with flower boxes bursting with color. In the beamed restaurant or sheltered beer garden you'll be served Bavarian specialties by a staff dressed in traditional lederhosen (shorts in summer, breeches in winter). ✉ *Alte Allee 21, D–81245, München-Obermenzing,* ☎ *089/820–820,* FAX *089/8208–2100,* WEB *www.weber-gastronomie.de. 22 rooms, 1 suite. Restaurant, beer garden, no a/c, cable TV, playground, free parking, some pets allowed. MC, V.*

$$ **Mayer.** If you are willing to sacrifice location for good value, head for this family-run hotel 25 minutes by suburban train from the Hauptbahnhof. The Mayer's first-class comforts and facilities cost about half of what you'd pay at similar lodgings in town. It is furnished in Bavarian country-rustic style—lots of pine and green and red, and check fabrics. The Mayer is a 10-minute walk or a short taxi ride from Germering station on the S-5 line, eight stops west of the Hauptbahnhof. ✉ *Augsburgerstr. 45, D–82110, Germering,* ☎ *089/844–071,* FAX *089/844–094,* WEB *www.hotel-mayer.de. 65 rooms. Restaurant, cable TV, in-room data ports, pool, some pets allowed (fee), no-smoking rooms. AE, DC, MC, V.*

$$ **Rotkreuzplatz.** This small, family-run business on lively Rotkreuzplatz is five minutes by subway (U-1 and U-7) from the main train station. Breakfast in the neighboring café is included in the price. There are no grand amenities, but a pleasant stay is guaranteed. You can watch over one of Munich's most original squares, where people from all walks of life meet around a modern fountain. ✉ *Rotkreuzpl. 2, Neuhausen D–80634,* ☎ *089/139–9080,* FAX *089/166–469. 56 rooms. Cable TV, in-room data ports, parking, pets allowed, no-smoking rooms. AE, DC, MC, V.*

NIGHTLIFE AND THE ARTS

The Arts

Bavaria's capital has an enviable reputation as an artistic hot spot. Details of concerts and theater performances are listed in "Vorschau" and "Monatsprogramm," booklets available at most hotel reception desks, newsstands, and tourist offices. Otherwise, just keep your eye open for advertising pillars and posters. Some hotels will make ticket reservations, or you can book through ticket agencies in the city center, such as **Max Hieber Konzertkasse** (✉ Liebfrauenstr. 1, City Center, ☎ 089/2900–8014). Two **Zentraler Kartenverkauf** ticket kiosks are in the underground concourse at Marienplatz (✉ City Center, ☎ 089/264–620). The **Abendzeitung Schalterhalle** (✉ Sendlingerstr. 10, City Center, ☎ 089/267–024) is a ticket service offered by one of Munich's two rags, the *Abendzeitung*. The **Residenz Bücherstube** (✉ Residenzstr. 1, City Center, ☎ 089/220–868) only sells concert tickets. Tickets for performances at the Altes Residenztheater/Cuvilliés-Theater, Bavarian State Theater/New Residence Theater, Nationaltheater, Prinzregententheater, and Staatheater am Gartnerplatz are sold at the **central box office** (✉

Maximilianstr. 11, City Center, ☎ 089/2185–1920). It's open weekdays 10–6, Saturday 10–1, and one hour before curtain time. One ticket agency, **München Ticket** (☎ 089/5481–8181, WEB www.muenchenticket.de) has a German-language Web site where tickets for most Munich theaters can be booked.

Concerts

Munich and music go together. The first Saturday in May, the **Long Night of Music** (🎫 €10, ☎ 089/5481–8181) is devoted to live performances by untold numbers of groups, from heavy metal bands to medieval choirs at over 100 locations throughout the city and through the night. One ticket covers everything, including transportation on special buses between locations.

Munich's world-class concert hall, the **Gasteig Culture Center** (✉ Rosenheimerstr. 5, Haidhausen, ☎ 089/480–980), is a lavish brick complex standing high above the Isar River, east of downtown. Its Philharmonic Hall is the permanent home of the Munich Philharmonic Orchestra. The city has three other principal orchestras, and the leading choral ensembles are the Munich Bach Choir, the Munich Motettenchor, and Musica Viva—the latter specializing in contemporary music. The choirs perform mostly in city churches.

The Bavarian Radio Symphony Orchestra performs at the **Bayerischer Rundfunk** (✉ Rundfunkpl. 1, Maxvorstadt, ☎ 089/558–080) and also at other city venues. The box office is open Monday–Thursday 9–noon and 2–4, and Friday 9–noon.

The Bavarian State Orchestra is based at the **Nationaltheater** (also called the Bayerische Staatsoper; ✉ Opernpl., City Center, ☎ 089/2185–1920). The Kurt Graunke Symphony Orchestra performs at the romantic art-nouveau **Staatstheater am Gärtnerplatz** (✉ Gärtnerpl. 3, Isarvorstadt, ☎ 089/218–51960).

Herkulessaal in der Residenz (✉ Hofgarten, City Center, ☎ 089/2906–7263) is a leading orchestral and recital venue. Concerts featuring conservatory students are given free of charge at the **Hochschule für Musik** (✉ Arcisstr. 12, Maxvorstadt, ☎ 089/128–901).

Munich's major pop/rock concert venue is the **Olympiahalle** (✉ U-3 Oympiazentrum stop, Georg Brauchle Ring, ☎ 089/3061–3577). The box office, at the ice stadium, is open weekdays 10–6 and Saturday 10–3. You can also book by calling München Ticket (☎ 089/5481–8181).

Opera, Ballet, and Musicals

Munich's Bavarian State Opera Company and its ballet ensemble perform at the **Nationaltheater** (✉ Opernpl., City Center, ☎ 089/2185–1920). The **Staatstheater am Gärtnerplatz** (✉ Gärtnerpl. 3, Isarvorstadt, ☎ 089/218–51960) presents a less ambitious but nevertheless high-quality program of opera, ballet, operetta, and musicals.

Theater

Munich has scores of theaters and variety-show venues, although most productions will be largely impenetrable if your German is shaky. Listed here are all the better-known theaters, as well as some of the smaller and more progressive spots. Note that most theaters are closed during July and August.

Altes Residenztheater/Cuvilliés-Theater (✉ Max-Joseph-Pl.; entrance on Residenzstr., City Center, ☎ 089/2185–1920). This is an intimate stage for compact opera productions such as Mozart's *Singspiele* and classic and contemporary plays (Arthur Miller met with great success here).

Amerika Haus (America House; ✉ Karolinenpl. 3, Maxvorstadt, ☎ 089/343–803). A very active American company, the American Drama Group Europe presents regular productions here.

Bayerisches Staatsschauspiel/Neues Residenztheater (Bavarian State Theater/New Residence Theater; ✉ Max-Joseph-Pl., City Center, ☎ 089/2185–1940). This is Munich's leading stage for classic playwrights such as Goethe, Schiller, Lessing, Shakespeare, and Chekhov.

Deutsches Theater (✉ Schwanthalerstr. 13, Leopoldvorstadt, ☎ 089/5523–4444). Musicals, revues, the Fasching balls, and big-band shows take place here. The box office is open weekdays noon–6 and Saturday 10–1:30.

Feierwerk (✉ Hansastr. 39, Westend, ☎ 089/769–3600). English-language productions are regularly presented at this venue.

The Carl-Orff Saal and the Black Box theaters, in the **Gasteig Culture Center,** occasionally present English-language plays. The box office is open weekdays 10:30–6 and Saturday 10–2.

The **Komödie im Bayerischen Hof** (✉ Bayerischer Hof Hotel, Promenadenpl., City Center, ☎ 089/292–810) offers light theatrical fare. The box office is open Monday–Saturday 11–8 and Sunday 3–8.

Münchner Kammerspiele-Schauspielhaus (✉ Maximilianstr. 26, City Center, ☎ 089/2333–7000). A city-funded rival to the nearby state-backed Staatliches Schauspiel, this theater of international renown presents the classics and new works by contemporary playwrights.

For a spectrum of good jazz, chansons, and café theater, check out the **Pasinger Fabrik** (✉ August-Exter-Str. 1, Pasing, ☎ 089/8292–9079), which also offers live music with breakfasts or late night drinks. To get there is easy: take any S-bahn out to Pasing (exit the station to the north). The box office is open Thursday–Saturday, 4:30–8:30 PM.

Prinzregententheater (✉ Prinzregentenpl. 12, City Center, ☎ 089/2185–2959). Munich's art-nouveau theater, an audience favorite, presents not only opera but musicals and musical gala events.

CHILDREN'S THEATER

Munich has several theaters for children. With pantomime such a strong part of the repertoire, the language problem disappears. Munich is the winter quarters of the big-top **Circus Krone** (✉ Zirkus-Krone-Str. 1–6, Leopoldvorstadt, ☎ 089/545–8000), which performs from Christmas until the end of March. The **Münchner Marionettentheater** (✉ Blumenstr. 32, City Center, ☎ 089/265–712) lets its puppets chew on highbrow material, notably works of Carl Orff. The **Münchner Theater für Kinder** (✉ Dachauerstr. 46, Neuhausen, ☎ 089/595–454) will keep the young ones happy with fairy tales and traditional pieces such as *Pinocchio*. The puppet shows at **Otto Bille's Marionettenbühne** (✉ Bereiterangerstr. 15, Au, ☎ 089/150–2168) are for young children. The **Schauburg Theater der Jugend** (✉ Franz-Joseph-Str. 47, Schwabing, ☎ 089/2333–7171) appeals to older youth, including adults.

Nightlife

Munich's nocturnal attractions vary with the seasons. The year starts with the abandon of Fasching, the Bavarian carnival time, which begins quietly in mid-November with the crowning of the King and Queen of Fools, expands with fancy-dress balls, and ends with a great street party on Fasching Dienstag (Shrove Tuesday) in early March. Men should forget wearing neckties on Fasching Dienstag: women posing as witches make it a point of cutting them off. From spring until late fall the beer garden dictates the style and pace of Munich's nightlife. When it rains, the indoor beer halls and taverns absorb the thirsty like blotting paper.

The beer gardens and most beer halls close at midnight, but there's no need to go home to bed: some bars and nightclubs are open until 6 AM. A word of caution about some of those bars: most are run honestly, and prices are only slightly higher than normal, but a few may intentionally overcharge. The seedier ones are near the main train station. Stick to beer or wine if you can, and pay as you go. And if you feel you're being duped, call the cops—the customer is usually, if not always, right.

Clubs, discos and the like can be a bit of a problem in Munich: the bouncers outside are for the most part there to add to the often specious exclusivity of the inside. Bouncers are usually rude, crude, and somewhat thick, but as such have achieved dubious notoriety throughout Germany. However they are in charge of picking who is "in" and who is "out," and there's no use trying to warm up to them.

Bars

Wait until after midnight before venturing into the **Alter Simpl** (✉ Türkenstr. 57, Schwabing, ☎ 089/272–3083), where a sparkling crowd enlivens the cold glass-and-steel interior. **Eisbach** (✉ Marstallstr. 3, Lehel, ☎ 089/2280–1680) occupies a corner of the Max Planck Institute building opposite the Bavarian Parliament. The bar is among Munich's longest and is overlooked by a mezzanine restaurant area where you can choose from a limited but ambitious menu. Outdoor tables nestle in the expansive shade of huge parasols. The nearby Eisbach Brook, which gives the bar its name, tinkles away like ice in the glass. The Bayerischer Hof's **Night Club** (✉ Promenadepl. 2–6, City Center, ☎ 089/212–0994) has live music, a small dance floor, and a very lively bar (avoid the poorly made mixed drinks). Jazz groups perform regularly there, too. On fashionable Maximilianstrasse, **O'Reilly's Irish Cellar Pub** (✉ Maximilianstr. 29, City Center, ☎ 089/293–311) offers escape from the German bar scene as it pours genuine Irish Guinness. Great cocktails and Irish-German black and tans (Guinness and strong German beer) are made to the sounds of live jazz at the English nautical-style **Pusser's New York Bar** (✉ Falkenturmstr. 9, City Center, ☎ 089/220–500). The pricey sandwiches such as the pastrami is about the only "New York" in Pussers.

Designed to the last corner in modern style, **Scalar** (✉ Seitzstr. 12, Lehel, ☎ 089/2157–9636) attracts a fairly mixed crowd of well-designed people. Its cellar is home to the Blue Oyster Club, where dancing is encouraged. The bartenders are busy shaking cocktails at **Schumann's** (✉ Maximilianstr. 36, City Center, ☎ 089/229–060) after the curtain comes down at the nearby opera house (the bar is closed on Saturday). Exotic cocktails are the specialty of **Trader Vic's** (✉ Promenadenpl. 4, City Center, ☎ 089/226–192), a smart cellar bar in the Hotel Bayerischer Hof. The bar is particularly popular among out-of-town visitors and attracts quite a few Americans. The **Kempinski Vier Jahreszeiten** (✉ Maximilianstr. 17, City Center, ☎ 089/21250) offers piano music until 9 and then dancing to recorded music or a small combo.

Beer Gardens

Each person in Munich has at least one favorite beer garden, so you're in good hands if you ask someone to point you in the direction. You do not need to reserve, that is not the point of the beer garden. No need to phone either: if the weather says yes, then go. Note, however, that Munich has very strict noise laws, so beer gardens tend to close around 11. The two big and famous beer gardens are in the Englischer Garten. The **Biergarten am Chinesischen Turm** (☎ 089/383–8730) is at the five-story Chinese Tower in the Englisher Garten. The Englischer Garten's smaller beer garden, **Hirschau** (☎ 089/369–945), has minigolf to test your skills after a few beers. It's about 10 minutes north of the Kleinhesselohersee. The **Seehaus im Englischen Garten** (☏ 089/381–6130) is on the banks of the artificial lake Kleinhesselohersee, where all of Munich converges on hot summer days (bus line 44, exit at Osterwaldstrasse; you can't miss it). Surprisingly large and green for a place so centrally located is the **Hofbräukeller** (✉ Innere Wiener Str. 19, tramway 18 to Wiener-Pl. or U-bahn 4 or 5 to Max-Weber-Pl., Haidhausen, ☏ 089/459–9250), which is a beer relative of the Hofbräuhaus. Some evenings you can move into the spacious cellar for some live jazz. Out in the district of Laim is the huge **Königlicher Hirschgarten** (☏ 089/172–591), where the crowd is somewhat more blue-collar and foreign. To get there take any S-bahn toward Pasing, exit at Laim, walk down Wotanstrasse, take a right on Winifriedstrasse and then a left into De-la-Paz-Strasse. The crowd at the **Taxisgarten** (☏ 089/156–827) in the Gern district (U-bahn Gern, Line 1 toward "Westfriedhof") is more white collar–oriented and tame, hence less chance of communicating with the natives, as it were, but the food is excellent and while parents refresh themselves, the children can enjoy a nice playground.

Dance Clubs

Schwabing claims more than a dozen dance clubs and live music venues between its central boulevard, Leopoldstrasse, and the area around its central square, the Münchner-Freiheit. Two streets—Feilitzstrasse and Occamstrasse—are lined with clubs, discos, and pubs. Haidhausen is Munich's other "in" area. A former factory hosts the city's largest rave scene: the **Kunstpark Ost** (✉ Grafingerstr. 6, Haidhausen, S-bahn, bus, or to Ostbahnhof, ☏ 089/4900–2928). The venue has no fewer than 17 "entertainment areas," including a Latin dance club among others, bars, and a huge slot-machine and computer-game hall. Kunstpark Ost may be migrating toward the north of Munich. **Muffathalle**'s (✉ Rosenheimerstr. 1, behind the Müllersche Volksbad, Haidhausen, ☏ 4587–5010) burnt orange programs with dates in a purple column are usually posted on advertising pillars. Hodgepodge is the only way to describe the events, but the atmosphere is relaxed, young, and nonchalant. The **Skyline** (✉ Münchner-Freiheit, Schwabing, ☏ 089/333–131) is at the top of the Hertie department store, which towers above a busy square. Bordering the Englisher Garten, **P 1** (✉ Prinzregentenstr., on west side of Haus der Kunst, Lehel, ☏ 089/294–252) is allegedly the trendiest club in town; find out for yourself, and good luck making it past the bouncer. The **Park-Café** (✉ Sophienstr. 7, Maxvorstadt, ☏ 089/598–313) is one of those fashionable places where you'll have to talk yourself past the doorman to join the chic crowds inside.

The **Feierwerk** (✉ Hansastr. 39, Westend, ☏ 089/769–3600) has that oh-so-attractive ramshackle old factory look to it, but it is a genuine institution in the musical scene. Many local bands were launched to fame—and back—here. The big FEST festival in July is one of the city's better alternatives in the night scene. **Nachtwerk** (✉ Landsbergerstr. 185, Westend, ☏ 089/570–7390), in a converted factory, blasts out a range of sounds from punk to avant-garde nightly between 8 PM and 4 AM. Live bands also perform here regularly. The real ravers ride the S-bahn to Munich's Franz-Josef-Strauss Airport, alighting at the Besucherpark station for techno and other beats until dawn at **Night Flight** (☏ 089/9759–7999).

Gay and Lesbian Bars

Munich's growing gay scene stretches between Sendlingertorplatz and Isartorplatz. For an overview check www.munich-cruising.de. The **Nil** (✉ Hans-Sachs-Str. 2, Isarvorstadt, ☏ 089/265–545) is famous for its decent prices and its schnitzel. The **Fortuna** (✉ Maximilianstr. 5, Isarvorstadt, ☏ 089/554–070) is more than just a bar and disco for women, it's also an events venue and organizer (skiing excursions, rafting on the Isar, for example). **Freds Pub** (✉ Reisingerstr. 15, Isarvorstadt, ☏ 089/260–22809) shows gay movies on a large screen for the edification of its patrons. The upscale **Morizz** (✉ Klenzestr. 43, Isarvorstadt, ☏ 089/201–6776) fills with a somewhat ritzy crowd. The **Ochsengarten** (✉ Müllerstr. 47, Isarvorstadt, ☏ 089/266–446) is Munich's leather bar. **Old Mrs. Henderson** (✉ Rumfordstr. 2, Isarvorstadt, ☏ 089/263–469) puts on the city's best transvestite cabaret for a mixed crowd and has various other events.

Jazz

Munich likes to think it's Germany's jazz capital, and some beer gardens have taken to replacing their brass bands with funky combos. Jazz musicians sometimes accompany Sunday brunch at pubs, too. One top club is the tiny **Mr. B's** (✉ Herzog-Heinrich-Str. 38, Isarvorstadt, ☏ 089/534–901), run by New Yorker Alex Best, who also mixes great cocktails, and unlike so many barkeeps, usually sports a welcoming smile on his face. The **Unterfahrt** (✉ Einsteinstr. 42, Haidhausen, ☏ 089/448–2794) is the place for the serious jazzologist, though hip-hop is making heavy inroads into the scene. A haunt with nondescript furnishings rather than chic dilapidation is **Nachtcafé** (✉ Maximilianpl. 5, City Center, ☏ 089/595–900). Food (costly) is served all night, and there's no dancing. Sunday is set aside for jazz at **Waldwirtschaft Grosshesselohe** (✉ Georg-Kalb-Str. 3, Grosshesselohe, ☏ 089/795–088) in a southern suburb. If it's a nice day, the excursion is worth it.

OUTDOOR ACTIVITIES AND SPORTS

The **Olympiapark** (U-bahn: Olympiazentrum), built for the 1972 Olympics, is one of the largest sports and recreation centers in Europe. For general information about sports opportunities in and around Munich contact the sports emporium **Sport Scheck** (✉ Sendlingerstr. 6, City Center, ☏ 089/21660). The big store not only sells every kind of equipment but is very handy with advice.

Beaches and Water Sports

There is sailing and windsurfing on both the Ammersee and the Starnbergersee (☞ Side Trips from Munich). Windsurfers should pay attention to restricted areas at bathing beaches. Information on sailing is available from **Bayerischer Segler-Verband** (✉ Georg-Brauchle-Ring 93, Moosach, ☏ 089/1570–2366). For information on windsurfing, contact **Verband der Deutschen Windsurfing Schulen** (✉ Weilheim, ☏ 0881/5267).

Golf

The **Munich Golf Club** has several courses that admit visitors on weekdays. Visitors must be members of a club at home. It has one 18-hole course (☏ 08123/93080) in Eschenried north of the city. The greens fee is €50 (€80 on weekends and holidays). The **Golfzentrum München-Riem** (☏ 089/9450–0800) to the east of Munich on the way to the congressional center at Riem. The greens fee is €35, €40 on weekends and holidays.

Ice-Skating

Depending on weather conditions, there's outdoor skating in winter on the lake in the Englischer Garten and on the Nymphenburger Canal, where you can also go curling (*Eisstockschiessen*) by renting equipment from little wooden huts, which also sell hot drinks. Players rent sections of machine-smoothed ice on the canal. Watch out for signs reading GEFAHR (danger), warning you of thin ice. Additional information is available from **Bayerischer Eissportverband** (✉ Georg-Brauchle-Ring 93, Moosach, ☎ 089/157–9920). The **Eissportstadion** in Olympiapark (✉ Spiridon-Louis-Ring 3, Schwabing, ☎ 089/3077–2150) has an indoor rink. For outdoor rinks use the **Prinzregentenstadion** (✉ Prinzregentenstr. 80, Haidhausen, ☎ 089/474–808). In the west is another outdoor rink, the **Eisbahn West** (✉ Agnes-Bernauer-Str. 241, Laim, ☎ 8968–9007).

Jogging

The best place to jog is the **Englischer Garten** (U-bahn: Münchner-Freiheit or Universität), which is 11 km (7 mi) around and has lakes and dirt and asphalt paths. You can also jog through **Olympiapark** (U-bahn: Olympiazentrum). The 500-acre park of **Schloss Nymphenburg** (Tramway 12, Romanplatz) and the banks of the **Isar River** are also ideal for running. For a longer jog along the river, take the S-bahn to Unterföhring and pace yourself back to Münchner-Freiheit—a distance of 6½ km (4 mi).

Rowing

Rent a rowboat on the south shore of the **Olympiasee** in Olympiapark or at the **Kleinhesseloher See** in the Englischer Garten.

Swimming

You can try swimming outdoors in the Isar River at Maria-Einsiedel, but because the river flows down from the Alps, the water is frigid even in summer. Warmer lakes near Munich are the **Ammersee** and the **Starnbergersee.** A very relaxing experience is swimming and wellness at one of the metropolitan spas. There are pools at the **Cosima Bad** (✉ Englschalkingerstr. and Cosimastr., Bogenhausen), with man-made waves. The **Dantebad** (✉ Dantestr. 6, Gern) has a huge lawn and is very popular in summer. The **Nordbad** (✉ Schleissheimerstr. 142, Schwabing) has a small, pleasant wellness section. The **Müllersche Volksbad** (✉ Rosenheimerstr. 1, Haidhausen, ☎ 2361–3434) is a grand art-nouveau building right on the Isar. Tuesday and Thursday are reserved for women only in the wellness section. And remember: if you use the saunas and steambaths in these spas, the rules say it's in your birthday suit. The **Olympia-Schwimmhalle** (✉ Olympiapark, Schwabing) not only has an Olympic-size pool, but the sauna area also has a "steam cavern" as an extra delight.

Tennis

There are about 200 outdoor courts all over Munich. Many can be booked via the sports store **Sport Scheck** (☎ 089/21660), which has branches around town. Prices vary from €8 to €13 an hour, depending on the time of day. Full details on tennis in Munich are available from the **Bayerischer Tennis Verband** (✉ Georg-Brauchle-Ring 93, Moosach, ☎ 089/157–030). There are indoor and outdoor courts at Münchnerstrasse 15, in München-Unterföhring; at the corner of Drygalski-Allee and Kistlerhofstrasse, in München-Fürstenried; and at Rothof Sportanlage (✉ Denningerstr., behind the Arabella and Sheraton hotels, Bogenhausen).

SHOPPING

Shopping Districts

Munich has an immense central shopping area, a 2-km (1-mi) *Fussgängerzone* (pedestrian zone) stretching from the train station to Marienplatz and north to Odeonsplatz. The two main streets here are Neuhauserstrasse and Kaufingerstrasse, the sites of most major department stores. For upscale shopping, Maximilianstrasse, Residenzstrasse, and Theatinerstrasse are unbeatable and contain a fine array of classy and tempting stores that are the equal of any in Europe. Schwabing, north of the university, has several of the city's most intriguing and offbeat shopping streets—Schellingstrasse and Hohenzollernstrasse are two to try.

Antiques

Bavarian antiques—from a chipped pottery beer mug to a massive farmhouse dresser—are found in the many small shops around the Viktualienmarkt, including on Westenriederstrasse, just south of the market. At Number 8 Westenriederstrasse, a building houses three antiques shops packed from floor to ceiling with curios, including a great collection of ancient dolls and toys. Also try the area north of the university—Türkenstrasse, Theresienstrasse, and Barerstrasse are all filled with antiques stores.

Strictly for window-shopping—unless you're looking for something really rare and special, and money's no object—are the exclusive shops lining Prannerstrasse, at the rear of the Hotel Bayerischer Hof. Interesting and inexpensive antiques and assorted junk from all over eastern Europe are laid out at the weekend flea markets beneath the Donnersberger railway bridge on Arnulfstrasse (along the northern side of the Hauptbahnhof).

In **Antike Uhren Eder** (✉ Hotel Bayerischer Hof, Prannerstr. 4, City Center, ☎ 089/220–305), the silence is broken only by the ticking of dozens of highly valuable German antique clocks and by discreet negotiation over the high prices. The **Antike Uhren H. Schley** (✉ Kardinal-Faulhaber-Str. 14a, City Center, ☎ 089/226–188) specializes in antique clocks. Nautical items or ancient sports equipment (golf clubs, for instance) fill the **Captain's Saloon** (✉ Westenriederstr. 31, City Center, ☎ 089/221–015). German antique silver and porcelain are the specialty of **Roman Odesser** (✉ Westenriederstr. 16, City Center, ☎ 089/226–388). For Munich's largest selection of dolls and marionettes, head to **Die Puppenstube** (✉ Luisenstr. 68, Maxvorstadt, ☎ 089/272–3267).

Department Stores and Malls

Hertie (✉ Bahnhofpl. 7, Leopoldvorstadt, ☎ 089/55120), commanding an entire city block between the train station and Karlsplatz, is the largest and, some claim, the best department store in the city. The basement has a high-class delicatessen with champagne bar and a standup bistro offering a daily changing menu that puts many high-price Munich restaurants to shame. Hertie's **Schwabing branch** (✉ Münchner-Freiheit, Schwabing, ☎ 089/381–060) is a high-gloss steel-and-glass building. **Karstadt** (✉ Neuhauserstr. 18, City Center, ☎ 089/290–230), in the 100-year-old Haus Oberpollinger, at the start of the Kaufingerstrasse shopping mall, is another upscale department store, with a very wide range of Bavarian arts and crafts. Karstadt also has a Schwabing branch, **Karstadt am Nordbad** (✉ Schleissheimerstr. 93, Schwabing, ☎ 089/13020). **Kaufhof**'s two central Munich stores (✉ Karlspl. 21–24, City Center, ☎ 089/51250; ✉ Corner Kaufingerstr. and Marienpl., City Center, ☎ 089/231–851) offer a variety of goods in the middle price range. The end-of-season sales are bargains.

Ludwig Beck (✉ Marienpl. 11, City Center, ☎ 089/236–910) is considered a step above other department stores by Müncheners. It's packed from top to bottom with highly original wares—from fine feather boas to roughly finished Bavarian pottery. In December a series of booths, each delicately and lovingly decorated, is occupied by craftspeople turning out traditional German toys and decorations. **Hirmer** (✉ Kaufingerstr. 28, City Center, ☎ 089/236–830) has Munich's most comprehensive collection of German-made men's clothes,

Munich Shopping

- Antike Uhren Eder 30
- Antike Uhren H. Schley 31
- Arcade 13
- Barerstrasse 36
- Bayerischer Kunstgewerbe Verein 6
- Captain's Saloon . . . 19
- Dallmayr 25
- Die Puppenstubbe . . . 40
- Galerie Biro 37
- Geschenk Alm 17
- Hermann Geschenke 11
- Hertie 1
- Hertie, Schwabing . . 41
- Hirmer 10
- Hohenzollernstrasse 39
- Johanna Daimer Filze Aller Art 24
- K & L Ruppert 9
- Karstadt 5
- Kaufhof, Karlsplatz . . . 2
- Kaufhof, Marienplatz 14
- Kaufingerstrasse 7
- Kaufinger Tor 8
- Kunstring Meissen . . . 32
- Kunst und Spiel 42
- Lederhosen Wagner 16
- Lehmkuhl 43
- Loden-Frey 29
- Ludwig Beck 22
- Ludwig Mory 21
- Max Krug 12
- Maximilianstrasse . . . 23
- Neuhauserstrasse 4
- Nymphenburg Store 33
- Obletter's, Karlsplatz 3
- Otto Kellnberger's Holzhandlung 17
- Residenzstrasse 28
- Roman Odesser 20
- Schellingstrasse 38
- Sebastian Wesely . . . 15
- Theatinerstrasse 27
- Theresienstrasse 34
- Türkenstrasse 35
- Ulrich Schneider's . . . 18
- Wallach 26

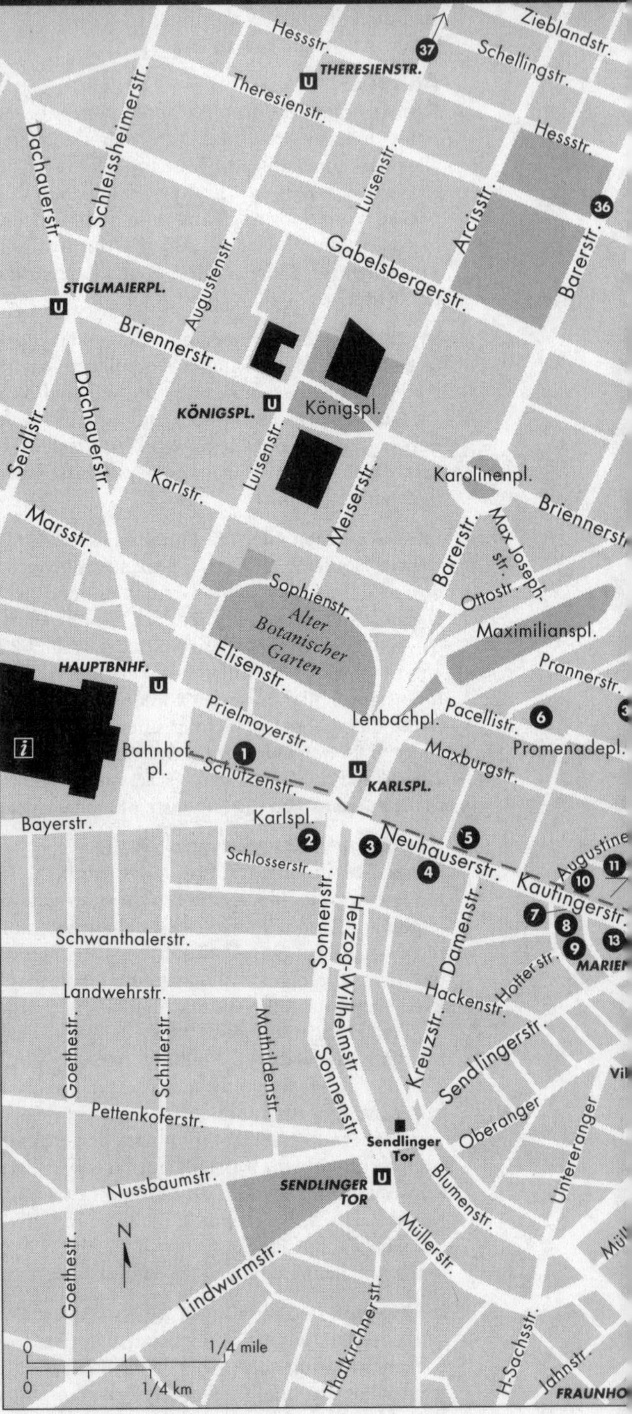

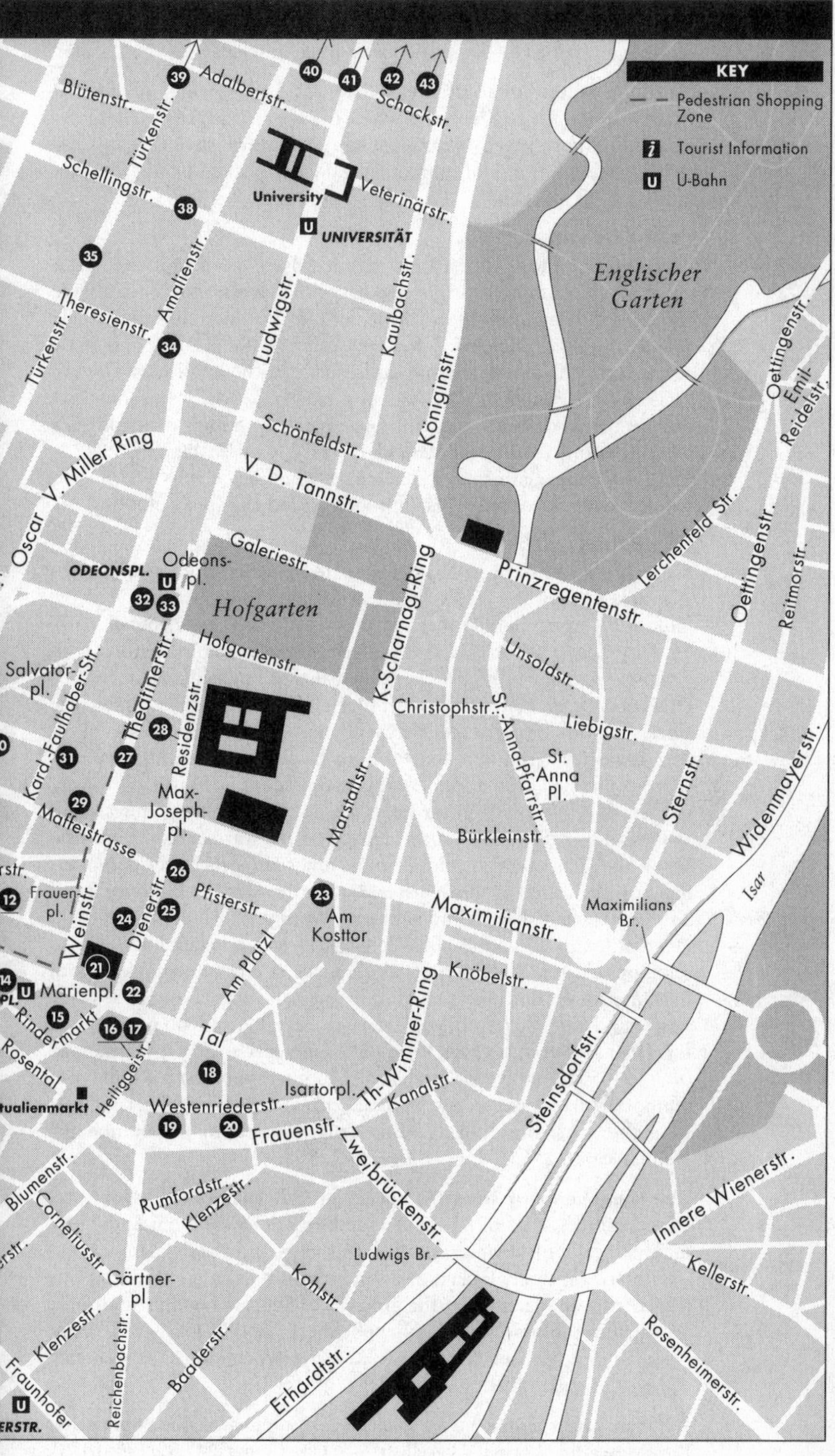
KEY
Pedestrian Shopping Zone
Tourist Information
U-Bahn
Englischer Garten
Hofgarten
University
UNIVERSITÄT
ODEONSPL.
Odeons-pl.
Blütenstr.
Adalbertstr.
Schackstr.
Türkenstr.
Schellingstr.
Veterinärstr.
Amalienstr.
Kaulbachstr.
Theresienstr.
Ludwigstr.
Königinstr.
Schönfeldstr.
Oscar V. Miller Ring
V. D. Tannstr.
Galeriestr.
K-Scharnagl-Ring
Prinzregentenstr.
Lerchenfeld Str.
Oettingenstr.
Emil-Reidelstr.
Reitmorstr.
Hofgartenstr.
Unsoldstr.
Salvator-pl.
Kard.-Faulhaber-Str.
Theatinerstr.
Residenzstr.
Christophstr.
St.-Anna-Pfarrstr.
Liebigstr.
St. Anna Pl.
Sternstr.
Widenmayerstr.
Max-Joseph-pl.
Maffeistrasse
Marstallstr.
Bürkleinstr.
Frauen-pl.
Pfisterstr.
Weinstr.
Dienerstr.
Am Kosttor
Maximilianstr.
Maximilians Br.
Isar
Knöbelstr.
Marienpl.
Am Platzl
Th-Wimmer-Ring
Rindermarkt
Tal
Steinsdorfstr.
Rosental
Heiliggeiststr.
Isartorpl.
Kanalstr.
Westenriederstr.
Frauenstr.
Zweibrückenstr.
Blumenstr.
Rumfordstr.
Klenzestr.
Corneliusstr.
Innere Wienerstr.
Ludwigs Br.
Gärtner-pl.
Kohlstr.
Kellerstr.
Klenzestr.
Reichenbachstr.
Baaderstr.
Erhardtstr.
Rosenheimerstr.
Fraunhofer

with a markedly friendly and knowledgeable staff. **K & L Ruppert** (✉ Kaufingerstr. 15, City Center, ☎ 089/231–1470) has a fashionable range of German-made clothes in the lower price brackets.

The main pedestrian area has two malls. The aptly named **Arcade** (✉ Neuhauserstr. 5, City Center) is where the young find the best designer jeans and chunky jewelry. **Kaufinger Tor** (✉ Kaufingerstr. 117, City Center) has several floors of boutiques and cafés packed neatly together under a high glass roof.

Folk Costumes

If you want to deck yourself out in lederhosen or a dirndl or affect a green loden coat and little pointed hat with feathers, you have a wide choice in the Bavarian capital. Much of the fine loden clothing on sale at **Lodenfrey** (✉ Maffeistr. 7–9, City Center, ☎ 089/210–390) is made at the company's own factory, on the edge of the Englischer Garten. **Wallach** (✉ Residenzstr. 3, City Center, ☎ 089/220–871) has souvenirs downstairs and shoes and clothing upstairs (though no children's wear). The tiny **Lederhosen Wagner** (✉ Tal 2, City Center, ☎ 089/225–697), right up against the Heiliggeist Church, carries lederhosen, woolen sweaters called *Walk* (not loden), and children's clothing.

Gift Ideas

Munich is a city of beer, and items related to its consumption are obvious choices for souvenirs and gifts. Munich is also the home of the famous Nymphenburg Porcelain factory. **Dallmayr** (✉ Dienerstr. 014–15, City Center, ☎ 089/21350) is an elegant gourmet food store, with delights ranging from the most exotic fruits to English jams, served by efficient Munich matrons in smart blue-and-white-linen costumes. The store's famous specialty is coffee, with more than 50 varieties to blend as you wish. There's also an enormous range of breads and a temperature-controlled cigar room. Visit **Ludwig Mory** (✉ Marienpl. 8, City Center, ☎ 089/224–542) for items relating to beer, from mugs of all shapes and sizes and in all sorts of materials, to warmers for those who don't like their beer too cold. Antique mugs and other beer paraphernalia can be found at **Ulrich Schneider's** little shop (✉ Radlsteg 2, off Tal, City Center). Check into **Sebastian Wesely** (✉ Rindermarkt 1 [am Peterspl.], City Center, ☎ 089/264–519) for beer-related vessels and schnapps glasses (*Stampferl*), walking sticks, scarves, and napkins with the famous Bavarian blue-and-white lozenges. If you've been to the Black Forest and forgot to equip yourself with a clock, or if you need a good Bavarian souvenir, try **Max Krug** (✉ Neuhauserstr. 2, City Center, ☎ 089/224–501) in the pedestrian zone. Another specialist for some contemporary Bavarica—pipes, nutcrackers, watch chains, beer mugs—is in the same building as Max Krug: **Herrmann Geschenke** (✉ Neuhauserstr. 2, City Center, ☎ 089/229–308).

The **Nymphenburg store** (✉ corner of Odeonspl. and Briennerstr., Maxvorstadt, ☎ 089/282–428) resembles a drawing room of the Munich palace, with dove-gray soft furnishings and the delicate, expensive porcelain safely locked away in bowfront cabinets. You can buy direct from the factory on the grounds of **Schloss Nymphenburg** (✉ Nördliches Schlossrondell 8, Nymphenburg, ☎ 089/1791–9710). For Dresden and Meissen ware, go to **Kunstring Meissen** (✉ Briennerstr. 4, Maxvorstadt, ☎ 089/281–532).

Bavarian craftspeople have a showplace of their own, the **Bayerischer Kunstgewerbe-Verein** (✉ Pacellistr. 6–8, City Center, ☎ 089/290–1470); here you'll find every kind of handicraft, from glass and pottery to textiles. **Kunst und Spiel** (✉ Leopoldstr. 49, Schwabing, ☎ 089/381–6270) has a fine selection of toys and clothing for children, and various other handcrafted items. **Lehmkuhl** (✉ Leopoldstr. 45, Schwabing, ☎ 089/3801–5013), one of Munich's finest bookshops, also sells beautiful cards. In an arcade of the Neues Rathaus is tiny **Johanna Daimer Filze aller Art** (✉ Dienerstr., City Center, ☎ 089/776–984), a shop selling every kind and color of felt imaginable. For an unusual gift of genuine art made of "alternative materials," try **Galerie Biro** (✉ Zieblandstr. 19, Schwabing, ☎ 089/273–0686). The works are by no means inexpensive, but they are crafted by the top artists working with unusual materials, from Bakelite to plywood. The gallery is closed Sunday through Tuesday.

Otto Kellnberger's Holzhandlung (✉ Heiliggeiststr. 7–8, City Center, ☎ 089/226–479) specializes in wooden crafts. Looking for that pig's-bristle brush to get to the bottom of tall champagne glasses? **Geschenk Alm** (✉ Heiliggeiststr. 7–8, City Center, ☎ 089/226–479) has nooks and crannies filled with brushes of every kind.

Obletter's (✉ Karlspl. 11–12, City Center, ☎ 089/5508–9510) has two extensive floors of toys, many of them handmade playthings of great charm and quality. From November's end until December 24, the open-air stalls of the **Christkindlmarkt** (✉ Marienpl., City Center) are a great place to find gifts and warm up with mulled wine. Two other perennial Christmas market favorites are those in Schwabing (Münchner-Freiheit Square) and at the Chinese Tower, in the middle of the Englischer Garten.

SIDE TRIPS FROM MUNICH

Munich's excellent suburban railway network, the S-bahn, brings several quaint towns and attractive rural areas within easy reach for a day's excursion. The two nearest lakes, the Starnbergersee and the Ammersee, are popular year-round. Dachau attracts overseas visitors, mostly because of its concentration-camp memorial site, but it's a picturesque and historic town in its own right. Landshut, north of Munich, is way off the tourist track, but if it were the same distance south of Munich, this jewel of a Bavarian market town would be overrun. Wasserburg am Inn is held in the narrow embrace of the Inn River, and it's easily incorporated into an excursion to the nearby lake, the Chiemsee (☞ Chapter 2). All these destinations have a wide selection of restaurants and hotels, and you can bring a bike on any S-bahn train. German railways, DB, often has weekend specials during which a family or group of five can travel for as little as €17.50 during certain times. (Inquire at the main train station for the "Wochenendticket.")

Starnbergersee

20 km (12 mi) southwest of Munich.

The Starnbergersee was one of Europe's first pleasure grounds. Royal coaches were already trundling out from Munich to the lake's wooded shores in the 17th century; in 1663 Elector Ferdinand Maria threw a shipboard party at which 500 guests wined and dined as 100 oarsmen propelled them around the lake. Today pleasure steamers provide a taste of such luxury to the masses. The lake is still lined with the small baroque palaces of Bavaria's aristocracy, but their owners now share the lakeside with public parks, beaches, and boatyards. The Starnbergersee is one of Bavaria's largest lakes—20 km (12 mi) long and 5 km (3 mi) wide—so there's plenty of room for swimmers, sailors, and windsurfers. The water is of drinking quality (as with most Bavarian lakes), a testimony to stringent environmental laws. At its deepest point it is 406 ft.

The Starnbergersee is named after its chief resort, **Starnberg,** the largest town on the lake and the nearest to Munich. Pleasure boats set off from the jetty for trips around the lake. The resort has a tree-lined lakeside promenade and some fine turn-of-the-20th-century villas, some of which are now hotels. There are abundant restaurants, taverns, and chestnut-tree-shaded beer gardens.

On the lake's eastern shore at the village of Berg you'll find the **King Ludwig II Memorial Chapel.** A well-marked path leads through thick woods to the chapel, built near the point in the lake where the drowned king's body was found on June 13, 1886. He had been confined in nearby Berg Castle after the Bavarian government took action against his withdrawal from reality and his bankrupting castle-building fantasies. A cross in the lake marks the point where his body was recovered.

The castle of **Possenhofen,** home of Ludwig's favorite cousin, Sisi, stands on the western shore, practically opposite Berg. Local lore says they used to send affectionate messages across the lake to each other. Sisi married the Austrian emperor Franz Joseph I but spent more than 20 summers in the lakeside castle, now a luxury hotel, the **Kaiserin Elisabeth.** ✉ *Tutzingerstr. 2–6, Feldafing,* ☏ *08157/93090,* WEB *www.kaiserin-elisabeth.de.*

Just offshore is the tiny **Roseninsel** (Rose Island), where King Maximilian II built a summer villa. You can swim to its tree-fringed shores or sail across in a dinghy or on a Windsurfer (Possenhofen's boatyard is one of the lake's many rental points).

Dining and Lodging

$$$–$$$$ ✕ **Forsthaus Ilka-Höhe.** This fine old country lodge is set amid meadows above the lake, an uphill stroll from the Tutzing station at the end of the S-6 suburban line. The walk is well worth the effort, for the Ilka-Höhe is one of the region's most attractive restaurants, with a view of the lake. Luncheons are priced in the middle range, dinners are far more exclusive. In summer dine on its vine-clad terrace. Reservations are essential, but dress is casual. ✉ *Auf der Ilkehöhe, Tutzing,* ☏ *08158/8242. Reservations essential. No credit cards. Closed Mon. and Tues., last 2 wks Dec., and weekends Jan.*

$–$$$ ✕ **Seerestaurant Undosa.** This restaurant is only a short walk from the Starnberg railroad station and boat pier. Most tables command a view of the lake, which provides some of the best fish specialties on the international menu. This is the place to try the mild-tasting *Renke,* a perch-type fish. ✉ *Seepromenade 1,* ☏ *08151/998–930. Reservations not accepted. AE, MC, V. Closed Mon., Tues. and most of Jan. and half of Feb.*

$$–$$$$ ✕🏨 **Hotel Schloss Berg.** King Ludwig II spent his final days in the small castle of Berg, from which this comfortable hotel gets its name. It's on the edge of the castle park where Ludwig liked to walk and a stone's throw from where he drowned. The older, century-old main hotel building is on the lakeside, although a modern annex overlooks the lake from the woods. All rooms are spacious and elegantly furnished. The restaurant ($–$$$$) and waterside beer garden are favorite haunts of locals and weekenders. ✉ *Seestr. 17, D–82335 Berg,* ☏ *08151/9630,* FAX *08151/96352,* WEB *www.hotelschlossberg.de. 50 rooms. Restaurant, bar, beer garden, no a/c, Internet, some pets allowed (fee), sauna, bicycles. AE, MC, V.*

$$ ✕🏨 **Forsthaus am See.** The handsome, geranium-covered Forsthaus faces the lake, and so do most of the large, pine-wood furnished rooms. The excellent restaurant ($$$) has a daily-changing international menu, with lake fish a specialty. The hotel has its own lake access and boat pier, with a chestnut-shaded beer garden nearby. ✉ *Am See 1, D–*

82343 Possenhofen, ☎ 08157/93010, FAX 08157/4292. 20 rooms, 1 suite. Restaurant, beer garden, Internet, some pets allowed (fee). AE, MC, V.

Starnbergersee A to Z

TRANSPORTATION TO AND FROM STARNBERGERSEE

Starnberg and the north end of the lake are a 25-minute drive from Munich on the A–95 Autobahn. Follow the signs to Garmisch and take the Starnberg exit. Country roads then skirt the west and east banks of the lake, but most are closed to the public.

The S-bahn 6 suburban line runs from Munich's central Marienplatz to Starnberg and three other towns on the lake's west bank: Possenhofen, Feldafing, and Tutzing. The journey from Marienplatz to Starnberg takes 35 minutes. The east bank of the lake can be reached by bus from the town of Wolfratshausen, the end of the S-bahn 7 suburban line.

VISITOR INFORMATION

The quickest way to visit the Starnbergersee area is by ship. On Saturday evenings, the good ship *Seeshaupt* has dancing and dinner.

➤ TOURIST INFORMATION: ***Seeshaupt*** (☎ 08151/12023). **Tourismusverband Starnberger Fünf-Seen-Land** (✉ Wittelsbacher Str. 2c, D–82319 Starnberg, ☎ 08151/90600, FAX 08151/906–090, WEB www.starnberg.de).

Ammersee

40 km (25 mi) southwest of Munich.

The Ammersee, the "peasant lake," is the country cousin of the better-known, more cosmopolitan Starnbergersee (the prince lake), and, accordingly, many Bavarians (and tourists, too) like it all the more. Munich cosmopolites of centuries past thought it too distant for an excursion, not to mention too rustic. So the shores remained relatively free of villas and parks, and even though upscale holiday homes claim some stretches of the eastern shore, the Ammersee still offers more open areas for bathing and boating than the bigger lake to the west. Bicyclists circle the 19-km-long (12-mi-long) lake (it's nearly 6 km [4 mi] across at its widest point) on a path that rarely loses sight of the water. Hikers can spread out the tour for two or three days, staying overnight in any of the comfortable inns along the way. Dinghy sailors and windsurfers zip across in minutes with the help of the Alpine winds that swoop down from the mountains. A ferry cruises the lake at regular intervals during summer, stopping at several piers. Board it at Herrsching.

Herrsching has a delightful promenade, part of which winds through the resort's park. The 100-year-old villa that sits so comfortably there seems as if it were built by Ludwig II, such is the romantic and fanciful mixture of medieval turrets and Renaissance-style facades. It was actually built for the artist Ludwig Scheuermann in the late 19th century and became a favorite meeting place for Munich and Bavarian artists. It is now a municipal cultural center and the scene of chamber-music concerts on some summer weekends.

The Benedictine monastery of **Andechs,** one of southern Bavaria's most famous pilgrimage sites, lies 5 km (3 mi) south of Herrsching. You can reach it on Bus 951 (which also connects Ammersee and Starnbergersee). This extraordinary ensemble surmounted by an octagonal tower and onion dome with a pointed helmet has a busy history going back over 1,000 years. The church, originally built in the 15th century, was entirely redone in baroque style in the early 18th century. The **Heilige Kapelle** contains the remains of the old treasure of the Benedictines in Andechs, including Charlemagne's "Victory

Cross," and a monstrance containing the three sacred hosts brought back from the crusades by the original rulers of the area, the Counts of Diessen-Andechs. One of the attached chapels contains the remains of composer Carl Orff. The church is being renovated completely in preparation for the 550th anniversary of the monastery in 2005. Crowds of pilgrims are drawn not only by the beauty of the hilltop monastery but by the beer brewed here (600,000 liters annually). The monastery makes its own cheese as well, and it's an excellent accompaniment to the rich, almost black beer. You can enjoy both at large wooden tables in the monastery tavern or on the terrace outside. WEB *www.andechs.de.* ⏲ *Daily 7–7.*

The little town of **Diessen** at the southwest corner of the lake has one of the most magnificent religious buildings of the whole region: the **Augustine abbey church of St. Mary.** No lesser figure than the great Munich architect Johann Michael Fischer designed this airy, early rococo edifice. François Cuvilié the Elder, whose work can be seen all over Munich, did the sumptuous gilt-and-marble high altar. Visit in late afternoon, when the light falls sharply on its crisp gray, white, and gold facade, etching the pencil-like tower and spire against the darkening sky over the lake. Don't leave without at least peeping into neighboring St. Stephen's courtyard, its cloisters smothered in wild roses. But Diessen is not all church. It has attracted artists and craftspeople since the early 20th century. Among the most famous who made his home here is the composer Carl Orff, author of numerous works inspired from medieval material, including the famous *Carmina Burana,* songs based on secular texts. His life and work—notably the pedagogical Schulwerk instruments—are exhibited in the **Carl-Orff-Museum** (✉ Hofmark 3, ☎ 08807/1583, ⏲ weekends 2–5) and visitors are welcome to try them out.

Dining and Lodging

$$ ✕🏨 **Ammersee Hotel.** This very comfortable, modern resort hotel has views from an unrivaled position on the lakeside promenade. Rooms overlooking the lake are in big demand and more expensive. The Artis restaurant ($–$$) has an international menu. ✉ *Summerstr. 32, D–82211 Herrsching,* ☎ *08152/96870,* FAX *08152/5374. 40 rooms. Restaurant, no a/c, cable TV, in-room data ports, some pets allowed (fee), gym, hot tub, sauna. AE, DC, MC, V.*

$$ ✕🏨 **Landhotel Piushof.** In a parklike garden, the family-run Piushof has elegant Bavarian guest rooms, with lots of oak and hand-carved cupboards. The beamed and pillared restaurant ($$–$$$) has an excellent menu of Bavarian specialties, and the open fireplace radiates pure ambience. ✉ *Schönbichlstr. 18, D–82211 Herrsching,* ☎ *08152/96820,* FAX *08152/968–270,* WEB *www.piushof.de. 21 rooms, 3 suites. Restaurant, no a/c, cable TV, in-room data ports, tennis court, pool, massage, sauna, some pets allowed (fee). MC, V.*

$ ✕🏨 **Hotel Promenade.** From the hotel terrace restaurant ($–$$) you can watch the pleasure boats tie up at the pier. The menu satisfies smaller hungers with cheese and ham platters or warm snacks and Alpine appetites with traditional pork dishes (hocks [*Schweinshaxe*] or roast [*Schweinsbraten*]), to more delicate trout dishes (*Forelle*). If you're overnighting, ask for a lake room; they all have geranium-hung balconies. Those under the dormer-broken roof are particularly cozy. ✉ *Summerstr. 6, D–82211 Herrsching,* ☎ *08152/1088,* FAX *08152/5981. 11 rooms. Restaurant, café, no a/c, cable TV, some pets allowed. Closed Jan. DC, MC, V.*

$ 🏨 **Hotel Garni Zur Post.** Families feel particularly at home here, and children amuse themselves at the playground and small deer park. Rooms are in Bavarian country style, with solid pine furnishings, and are clean and functional. A delicious breakfast buffet prepares guests for the long days a-visiting. ✉ *Starnberger Str. 2, D–82346 Andechs,* ☎ *08152/3433,* FAX *08152/2303. 32 rooms, 22 with bath. No a/c, cable TV, Internet, playground, some pets allowed (fee). MC.*

Ammersee A to Z

TRANSPORTATION TO AND FROM AMMERSEE

Take Autobahn 96—follow the signs to Lindau—and 20 km (12 mi) west of Munich take the exit for Herrsching, the lake's principal town.

Herrsching is also the end of the S-bahn 5 suburban line, a 47-minute ride from Munich's Marienplatz. From the Herrsching train station, Bus 952 runs north along the lake, and Bus 951 runs south and continues on to Starnberg in a 40-minute journey.

Getting around on a boat is the best way to visit. Each town on the lake has a pier (*Anlegestelle*).

VISITOR INFORMATION

➤ TOURIST INFORMATION: **Verkehrsbüro** (✉ Bahnhofspl. 2, Herrsching, ☎ 08152/5227, ⏲ Weekdays 8:30–noon).

Dachau

20 km (12 mi) northwest of Munich.

Dachau predates Munich, with records going back to the time of Charlemagne. It's a handsome town, too, built on a hilltop with views of Munich and the Alps. A guided tour of the town, including the castle and church, leaves from the Rathaus on Saturday at 10:30, from May through mid-October. Dachau is better known worldwide as the site of the first Nazi concentration camp, which was built just outside it. Dachau preserves the memory of the camp and the horrors perpetrated there with deep contrition while trying, with commendable discretion, to signal that it also has other points of interest.

The site of the infamous camp, now the **KZ-Gedenkstätte Dachau** (Dachau Concentration Camp Memorial), is just outside town. Photographs, contemporary documents, the few remaining cell blocks, and the grim crematorium create a somber and moving picture of the camp, where more than 30,000 of the 200,000-plus prisoners lost their lives. A documentary film in English is shown daily at 11:30 and 3:30. The former camp has become more than just a grisly memorial: it is now a place where people of all nations meet, to reflect upon the past and on the present. Several religious shrines and memorials have been built to honor the dead, who came from Germany and all occupied nations. To reach the memorial by car, leave the center of the town along Schleissheimerstrasse and turn left into Alte Römerstrasse; the site is on the left. By public transport take Bus 724 or 726 from the Dachau S-bahn train station or the town center. Both stop within a two-minute walk from the site (ask the driver to let you out there). If you are driving from Munich, turn right on the first country road (marked B) before entering Dachau and follow the signs. ✉ *Alte Römerstr. 75,* ☎ *08131/996–880.* 🎫 *Free.* ⏲ *Tues.–Sun. 9–5. Guided English tour June–Aug., Tues.–Sun. 12:30; Sept.–May, weekends 12:30.*

Schloss Dachau, the hilltop castle, dominates the town. What you'll see is the one remaining wing of a palace built by the Munich architect Josef Effner for the Wittelsbach ruler Max Emanuel in 1715. During the Napoleonic Wars the palace served as a field hospital, treating French and Russian casualties from the Battle of Austerlitz (1805). The wars made a casualty, too, of the palace, and three of the four wings were demolished by order of King Max Joseph I. What's left is a handsome cream-and-white building, with an elegant pillared and lantern-hung café on the ground floor and a former ballroom above. About once a month the grand Renaissance hall, with a richly decorated and carved ceiling featuring painted panels depicting figures from ancient mythology, is used for chamber concerts. The east terrace affords panoramic views of Munich and, on fine days, the distant Alps. There's also a 250-year-old *Schlossbrauerei* (castle brewery), which hosts the town's beer and music festival each year in the first two weeks of August. ✉ *Schlosspl.,* ☎ *08131/87923.* 🎫 *€1; tour €2.50.* ⏲ *May–Sept., weekends 2–5; tour of town and Schloss May–mid-Oct., Sat. 10:30.*

St. Jacob, Dachau's parish church, was built in the early 16th century in late-Renaissance style on the foundations of a 14th-century Gothic structure. Baroque features and a characteristic onion dome were added in the late 17th century. On the south wall you can admire a very fine 17th-century sundial. A visit to the church is included in the guided tour of the town. ✉ *Konrad-Adenauer-Str. 7.* ⏲ *Daily 7–7.*

An artists' colony formed here during the 19th century, and the tradition lives on. Picturesque houses line Hermann-Stockmann-Strasse and part of Münchner Strasse, and many of them are still the homes of successful artists. The **Gemäldegalerie** displays the works of many of the town's 19th-century artists. ✉ *Konrad-Adenauer-Str. 3,* ☎ *08131/567–516.* 🎫 *€2.* ⏲ *Wed.–Fri. 11–5, weekends 1–5.*

Dining

$–$$ ✕ **Bräustüberl.** Near the castle, the Bräustüberl has a shady beer garden for lunches and a cozy tavern for year-round Bavarian-style eating and drinking. ✉ *Schlossstr. 8,* ☎ *08131/72553. MC. Closed Mon.*

$–$$ ★ ✕ **Weilachmühle.** You have to drive a ways for this absolute gem of a restaurant–cum–beer garden–cum–stage and exhibition room in the little village of Thalhausen. It's in a farmhouse that was restored the way it should be, the old dark wooden door opening onto a generous dining area paneled in simple, light pine. The food is above reproach, beginning with the benchmark Schweinsbraten. To get to the Weilachmüle drive 26 km (16 mi) north toward Aichach, then take a right toward Thalhausen (2 km [1.25 mi]) in the village of Wollomoos. ✉ *Am Mühlberg 5, Thalhausen,* ☎ *08254/1711,* WEB *www.weilachmuehle.de.* ⏲ *Thurs.–Sat. 5 PM–midnight, Sun. 10:30 AM–11 PM; opens an hr later as of October until mid- to end of Mar. No credit cards.*

$–$$ ✕ **Zieglerbräu.** Dachau's leading beer tavern, once a 17th-century brewer's home, is a warren of cozy, wood-paneled rooms where you'll probably share a table with a party of locals on a boys' night out. The food is solid varieties of pork, potato, and sausages in all forms. In summer the tables spill out onto the street for a very Italian feeling. The restaurant runs the neighboring nightclub. ✉ *Konrad-Adenauer-Str. 8,* ☎ *08131/4073. No credit cards.*

Dachau A to Z

TRANSPORTATION TO AND FROM DACHAU

Take the B–12 country road or the Stuttgart Autobahn to the Dachau exit from Munich. Dachau is also on the S-bahn 2 suburban line, a 20-minute ride from Munich's Marienplatz.

VISITOR INFORMATION

➤ TOURIST INFORMATION: **Verkehrsverein Dachau** (✉ Konrad-Adenauer-Str. 1, ☎ 08131/75286, FAX 08131/84529, WEB www.dachau-info.de).

Landshut

64 km (40 mi) north of Munich.

If fortune had placed Landshut south of Munich, in the protective folds of the Alpine foothills, instead of the same distance north, in the subdued flatlands of Lower Bavaria—of which it is the capital—the historic town would be teeming with tourists. Landshut's geographical misfortune is the discerning visitor's good luck, for the town is never overcrowded, with the possible exception of the three summer weeks when the *Landshuter Hochzeit* (Landshut Wedding) is celebrated. The next celebration is in 2005, and then a visit to Landshut is a must. The festival commemorates the marriage in 1475 of Prince George of Bavaria-Landshut, son of the expressively named Ludwig the Rich, to Princess Hedwig, daughter of the king of Poland. Within its ancient walls, the entire town is swept away in a colorful reconstruction of the event. The wedding procession, with the "bride" and "groom" on horseback, accompanied by pipes and drums and the hurly-burly of a medieval pageant, is held on three consecutive weekends, while a medieval-style fair fills the central streets throughout the three weeks.

Landshut has two magnificent cobblestone market streets. The one in **Altstadt** (Old Town) is one of the most beautiful city streets in Germany; the other is in **Neustadt** (New Town). The two streets run parallel to each other, tracing a course between the Isar River and the heights overlooking the town. A steep path from Altstadt takes you up to **Burg Trausnitz.** This castle was begun in 1204 and accommodated the Wittelsbach dukes of Bavaria-Landshut until 1503. ☎ *0871/22638.* 🎫 *€2.50 including guided tour.* ⏲ *Apr.–Sept., daily 9–noon and 1–5; Oct.–Mar., Tues.–Sun. 10–noon and 1–4.*

The **Stadtresidenz** in Altstadt was the first Italian Renaissance building of its kind north of the Alps. It was built from 1536 to 1537, but was given a baroque facade at the end of the 19th century. The Wittelsbachs lived here during the 16th century. The facade of the palace forms an almost modest part of the architectural splendor and integrity of the Altstadt, where even the ubiquitous McDonald's has to serve its hamburgers behind a baroque exterior. The Residenz includes exhibitions on the history of Landshut. ✉ *Altstadt 79, Altstadt,* ☎ *0871/22638.* 🎫 *€2.* ⏲ *Apr.–Sept., daily 9–noon and 1–5; Oct.–Mar., 10–noon and 1–4.*

The **Rathaus** (Town Hall) stands opposite the Stadtresidenz, an elegant, light-colored building with a typical neo-Gothic roof design. It was originally a set of 13th-century burgher houses, taken over by the town in the late 1300s. The famous bride and groom allegedly danced in the grand ceremonial hall, with its heavy wood paneling and rows of frescoes, during their much celebrated wedding in 1475. The tourist information is on the ground floor. ✉ *Altstadt 315,* ☎ *0871/922–050.* 🎫 *Free.* ⏲ *Mon.–Fri. 2–3, and on official tours.*

The **Martinskirche** (St. Martin's), with the tallest brick church tower (436 ft) in the world, soars above the other buildings with its bristling spire. The church contains some magnificent Gothic treasures and a 16th-century carved Madonna. It is surely the only church in the world to contain an image of Hitler, albeit in a devilish pose. The führer and other Nazi leaders are portrayed as executioners in a 1946 stained-glass window showing the martyrdom of St. Kastulus. In the nave of the church is a clear and helpful description of its history and treasures in English. ✉ *Corner of Altstadt and Kirchg,* ☎ *0871/24277.* ⏲ *Apr.–Sept., daily 7–6:30; Oct.–Mar., daily 7–5.*

Built into a steep slope of the hill crowned by Burg Trausnitz is an unusual art museum, the **Skulpturenmuseum im Hofberg,** containing the entire collection of the Landshut sculptor Fritz Koenig. His own work forms the permanent central section of the labyrinthine gallery. ✉ *Kolpingstr. 481,* ☎ *0871/89021.* *€3.* ⏲ *Tues.–Sun. 10:30–1 and 2–5.*

OFF THE BEATEN PATH

FREISING – Freising (at the end of the S-bahn 1 line, a 45-minute ride from central Munich) is an ancient episcopal seat and its cathedral and Old Town are well worth including in a visit to Landshut, 35 km (22 mi) to the northeast.

Dining and Lodging

There are several attractive Bavarian-style restaurants in the Altstadt and Neustadt, most of them with beer gardens. Although Landshut brews a fine beer, look for a *Gaststätte* offering a *Weihenstephaner,* from the world's oldest brewery, in Freising. Helles (light) is the most popular beer variety.

$$–$$$ **Lindner Hotel Kaiserhof.** The green Isar River rolls outside the bedroom windows of Landshut's most distinctive hotel. Its steep red roof and white facade blend harmoniously with the waterside panorama. The "Herzog Ludwig" restaurant ($$) serves a sumptuous but reasonably priced lunch buffet and is an elegant place for dinner. ✉ *Papiererstr. 2, D–84034,* ☎ *0871/6870,* FAX *0871/687–403,* WEB *www.lindner.de. 144 rooms. Restaurant, no a/c in some rooms, cable TV with movies and video games, in-room data ports, gym, sauna, steam room, meeting rooms, bicycles, pets allowed (fee), no-smoking rooms. AE, DC, MC, V.*

$$ **Hotel Goldene Sonne.** The steeply gabled Renaissance facade of the Golden Sun fronts a hotel of great charm and sleek comfort. It stands in the center of town, near all the sights. Its dining options are a paneled, beamed restaurant ($$–$$$), a vaulted cellar, and a courtyard beer garden, where the service is smilingly, helpfully Bavarian. The menu follows the seasons and toes the "quintessential Bavarian" line, with much pork roast, trout steamed or smoked with horseradish, asparagus in the spring (usually accompanied by potatoes or ham), venison in the fall. ✉ *Neustadt 520, D–84028,* ☎ *0871/92530,* FAX *0871/925–3350,* WEB *www.goldenesonne.de. 55 rooms. Restaurant, beer garden, pub, no a/c, cable TV, in-room data ports, some pets allowed (fee), no-smoking rooms. AE, DC, MC, V.*

$$ **Romantik Hotel Fürstenhof.** This handsome Landshut city mansion had no difficulty qualifying for inclusion in the Romantik group of hotels—it just breathes romance, from its plush little restaurant ($$$) all covered in wood paneling, to the cozy bedrooms. A vine-covered terrace shadowed by a chestnut tree adds charm. ✉ *Stethaimerstr. 3, D–84034,* ☎ *0871/92550,* FAX *0871/925–544,* WEB *www.romantikhotels.com/landshut. 24 rooms. Restaurant, no a/c in some rooms, cable TV, Internet, sauna, no-smoking rooms. AE, DC, MC, V. Restaurant closed Sun.*

$$ **Schloss Schönbrunn.** This country mansion is now a luxurious hotel, with many of the original features intact. Rooms in the most historic part of the building are particularly attractive, with huge double beds, and represent excellent value. The handsome house stands in the Schönbrunn district of Landshut, about 2 km (1 mi) from the center. The journey is worthwhile even for the excellent restaurant ($$–$$$), where the menu includes fish from the hotel's own pond. ✉ *Schönbrunn 1, D–84036,* ☎ *0871/95220,* FAX *0871/952–2222,* WEB *www.hotel-schoenbrunn.de. 33 rooms. Restaurant, café, bar, beer garden, no a/c, cable TV, in-room data ports, some pets allowed (fee), no-smoking rooms. AE, DC, MC, V.*

Landshut A to Z

TRANSPORTATION TO AND FROM LANDSHUT

Landshut is a 45-minute drive northwest from Munich on either the A–92 Autobahn—follow the signs to Deggendorf—or the B–11 highway. The Plattling–Regensburg–Passau train line brings you from Munich in about 50 minutes. A round trip costs about €20.

VISITOR INFORMATION

➤ TOURIST INFORMATION: **Verkehrsverein** (✉ Altstadt 315, ☎ 0871/922–050, WEB www.landshut.de). **Landshut Wedding 2005 celebration** (☎ 0871/22918, FAX 0871/274–653).

Wasserburg am Inn

51 km (30 mi) east of Munich.

Wasserburg floats like a faded ship of state in a lazy loop of the Inn River, which comes within a few yards of cutting the ancient town off from the wooded slopes of the encroaching countryside. Wasserburg was once an important trading post, owing in great part to the still extant Red Bridge (Rote Brücke). Later it was luckily ignored by the industrialization that gripped Germany in the 19th century. You're never more than 100 yards or so from the river in the **Altstadt,** which huddles within the walls of the castle that originally gave the town its name. The almost Italian look is typical of many Inn River towns. Use the north- or east-bank parking lot as the town is expanding the traffic-free zone. It's only a few minutes' walk to the central Marienplatz. There you'll find Wasserburg's late-Gothic brick **Rathaus.** The Bavarian regional government met here until 1804, deliberating in its beautifully decorated Renaissance *Ratsstube* (council chamber). Opposite the Rathaus is the baroque facade of the **Kern Haus**, designed by architect Johann Baptist Zimmermann from Munich. He actually merely pasted two houses together, as it were, and added a glorious front in 1738. ✉ *Marienpl.* 🎫 *€.75.* ⊙ *Guided tour Tues.–Fri. at 10, 11, 2, 3, and 4; weekends at 10 and 11.*

The 14th-century **Frauenkirche** (Church of Our Lady), on Marienplatz, is the town's oldest church. The 213-ft tower was once a city watchtower, and the church was given its baroque style in 1753. The baroque altar frames a Madonna sitting on a throne with a view of Wasserburg in the background. Wasserburg's imposing 15th-century parish church, **St. Jakob** (✉ Kirchhofpl.), has an intricately carved baroque pulpit dating from 1640.

Next to the 14th-century town gate, at the end of Wasserburg's Rote Brücke, is the **Erstes Imaginäres Museum** (First Imaginary Museum). The museum, which is housed in the former Holy Ghost Hospital, has a collection of more than 500 world-famous paintings, but without an original among them; every single one is a precise copy, executed by various artists. This was the idea of the late Günter Dietz, an artist and stage painter, who felt those who couldn't travel the world to see the originals could still appreciate the far-flung masterpieces here. 🎫 *€1.50.* ⊙ *May–Sept., Tues.–Sun. 11–5; Oct.–Apr., Tues.–Sun. 1–5.*

Wasserburg is a convenient base for walks along the banks of the Inn River and into the countryside. A pretty path west leads to the village of **Attel.** Another half hour into the Attel River valley, and you'll reach the enchanting castle-restaurant of **Schloss Hart** (☎ 08039/1774).

Dining and Lodging

$ ✕ **Herrenhaus.** This is one of Wasserburg's oldest houses, with medieval foundations and a centuries-old wine cellar. Pork dishes with dumplings and sauerkraut are served at the oak tables beneath vaulted ceilings. In summer the beer garden opens at 4 PM. ✉ *Herreng. 17,* ☎ *08071/2800. MC. Closed Mon. No dinner Sun.*

$–$$ ✕🏨 **Hotel Fletzinger Bräu.** Wasserburg's leading hotel began as a brewery, and you can sample local ales in its noisy, friendly tavern. Rooms are large and homey; many have original antiques. ✉ *Fletzingerg. 1, D–83512,* ☎ *08071/90890,* FAX *08071/909–8177,* WEB *hotel-fletzinger.com. 40 rooms. Restaurant, beer garden, pub, cable TV, in-room data ports, some pets allowed (fee). AE, MC, V.*

$ ✕🏨 **Paulanerstuben.** If you want to know what living in the glorious Kern Haus is like, try one of the rooms of the remarkable good-value Paulanerstuben. The quieter rear rooms look out onto the river or onto the courtyard. Solid Bavarian cooking welcomes you, with a strong nod to Mediterranean dishes for the vegetarians (ratatouille stuffed pancakes, for example). You will share space with other Wasserburgians. ✉ *Marienpl. 9,* ☎ *08071/3903,* FAX *08071/50474,* WEB *paulanerstuben-wasserburg.de. Restaurant, no a/c, cable TV, some pets allowed. Closed Jan. No credit cards.*

Wasserburg A to Z

TRANSPORTATION TO AND FROM WASSERBURG

Take the B–304 from Munich, which leads directly to Wasserburg. It's a 45-minute drive. The S-bahn 4 suburban line goes to Ebersberg, where you'll have to change to a local train to Wasserburg, or the Salzburg express, changing at Grafing Bahnhof to the local line. Both trips take 90 minutes.

VISITOR INFORMATION

➤ TOURIST INFORMATION: **Verkehrsamt** (✉ Rathauspl. 1, D–83512 Wasserburg am Inn, ☎ 08071/10522, WEB www.wasserburg.de. ⏲ Weekdays 9–3, Sat. 10–1).

MUNICH A TO Z

To research prices, get advice from other travelers, and book travel arrangements, visit www.fodors.com.

AIRPORTS

Munich's International Airport is 28 km (17 mi) northeast of the city center, between the small towns of Freising and Erding. When departing from Munich for home, you can claim your VAT refund for purchases at a counter either between areas B and C, or between C and D.

➤ AIRPORT INFORMATION: **Fluhafen München** (☎ 089/97500, WEB www.munich-airport.de).

AIRPORT TRANSFERS

A fast train service links the airport with Munich's main train station. The S-1 and S-8 lines operate from a terminal directly beneath the airport's arrival and departure halls. Trains leave every 10 minutes, and the journey takes around 40 minutes. Several intermediate stops are made, including the Ostbahnhof (convenient for lodgings east of the Isar River) and such city-center stations as Marienplatz. A one-way ticket costs €8, or €7.20 if you purchase a multiple-use "strip" ticket (you will have two strips left at the end). A family of up to five (two adults and three children under 15) can make the trip for €15 by buying a Tageskarte ticket (which allows travel until around 6 AM the next morning). The bus service is slower than the S-bahn link (€9 one-way, €14.50 round trip). A taxi from the airport costs around €50. During rush hours (7 AM–10 AM and 4 PM–7 PM), allow up to an hour of traveling time. If you're driving from the airport to the city, take route

A–9 and follow the signs for MÜNCHEN STADTMITTE. If you're driving to the city center, head north through Schwabing, join the A–9 Autobahn at the Frankfurter Ring intersection, and follow the signs for the airport (FLUGHAFEN).

BIKE TRAVEL

Munich and its environs are easily navigated on two wheels. The city is threaded with a network of bike paths, and bikes are allowed on the S-bahn (except from 6 AM to 9 AM and from 4 PM to 6 PM). Bicycles on public transportation cost either one strip on a multiple ticket, or € 2.50 for a day ticket, € 0.90 for a single ticket. A free map showing all bike trails is available at all city tourist offices.

Bikes can be rented from April through October at the Hauptbahnhof and at some S-bahn and mainline stations around Munich. A list of stations that offer the service is available from the Deutsche Bahn. The cost is €3.80–€12.50 a day depending on the type of bike.

➤ BIKE RENTALS: **Aktiv-Rad** (✉ Hans-Sachs-Str. 7, Isarvorstadt, ☏ 089/266–506). **the bike and walk company GmbH**(✉ Tal 31, City Center, ☏ 089/5895–8930). **Hauptbahnhof** (✉ Radius Touristik, opposite platform 31, Leopoldvorstadt, ☏ 089/596–113). **Will Fahrradverleih** (✉ Kleinhesselohe 4 [at the Kleinhesselohe Lake in the Englischer Garten], Schwabing, ☏ 089/338–353).

BUS TRAVEL TO AND FROM MUNICH

Long-distance buses arrive and depart from an area to the west of the main train station. The actual office of the bus company, Touring GmbH, is in the northern section of the train station itself, an area referred to as the Starnberger Bahnhof.

➤ BUS STATION: **Zentraler Busbahnhof** (✉ Arnulfstr., Leopoldvorstadt, ☏ 089/545–8700).

CAR RENTAL

All Hauptbahnhof (train station) offices are in the mezzanine-level gallery above the Deutsche Bahn information and ticket center. Airport offices are in the central area, Zentralbereich.

➤ LOCAL AGENCIES: **Avis** (✉ Airport, ☏ 089/9759–7600; ✉ Hauptbahnhof, Leopoldvorstadt, ☏ 089/550–2251; ✉ Nymphenburgerstr. 61, Maxvorstadt, ☏ 089/1260–0020; ✉ Balanstr. 74, Haidhausen, ☏ 089/403–091). **Europcar** (✉ Airport, ☏ 089/973–5020; ✉ Hauptbahnhof, Leopoldvorstadt, ☏ 089/549–0240, WEB www.europcar.de). **Hertz** (✉ Airport, ☏ 089/978–860; ✉ Hauptbahnhof, Leopoldvorstadt, ☏ 089/550–2256; ✉ Nymphenburgerstr. 81, Maxvorstadt, ☏ 089/129–5001). **Sixt** (✉ Airport, ☏ 089/526–2525; ✉ Hauptbahnhof, Leopoldvorstadt, ☏ 089/550–2447; ✉ Seitzstr. 9, Lehel, ☏ 089/223–333).

CAR TRAVEL

From the north (Nürnberg or Frankfurt), leave the autobahn at the Schwabing exit. From Stuttgart and the west, the autobahn ends at Obermenzing, Munich's most westerly suburb. The autobahns from Salzburg and the east, Garmisch and the south, and Lindau and the southwest all join the Mittlerer Ring (city beltway). When leaving any autobahn, follow the signs reading STADTMITTE for downtown Munich.

PARKING

Parking in Munich is nervewracking and not cheap. There are several parking garages throughout the center, but your best bet is to use public transportation, which is exemplary.

CONSULATES

➤ CANADA: **Canadian Consulate** (✉ Tal 29, City Center, ☎ 089/219–9570).

➤ UNITED KINGDOM: **British Consulate General** (✉ Bürkleinstr. 10, Lehel, ☎ 089/211–090).

➤ UNITED STATES: **U.S. Consulate General** (✉ Königinstr. 5, Maxvorstadt, ☎ 089/28880).

EMERGENCIES

Police (☎ 110). **Fire department, ambulance, and medical emergencies** (☎ 112).

ENGLISH-LANGUAGE MEDIA

The monthly English-language magazine *Munich Found* is sold at most newspaper stands and in many hotels. It contains excellent listings, reviews restaurants and shows, and generally gives an idea of life in the city.

The Anglia English Bookshop is the leading English-language bookstore in Munich, although the shop is in incredible disorder, the books are very expensive (even the damaged ones), and the owner tends to make customers feel like intruders. But having overcome the mess, the suspicious looks, and the price, you'll find the selection is unimpeachable. Hugendubel has a good selection geared more toward novels and such. The Internationale Presse store is at the main train station. Words'worth is a well-kept shop with books in English.

Plays, readings, and other events are held in English at the Amerikahaus and at the British Council. They maintain reading rooms with a wealth of books and magazines. Amerikahaus's reading room is sunny and open from 1 to 5.

If you're just looking for some light literature or inexpensive German-language coffee-table books, try texxt; the English language section is in the basement.

➤ BOOKSTORES: **Anglia English Bookshop** (✉ Schellingstr. 3, Schwabing, ☎ 089/283–642). **Hugendubel** (✉ Marienpl. 22, 2nd floor, City Center, ☎ 089/23890 or 01803/484–484; ✉ Karlspl. 3, City Center, ☎ 089/552–2530). **Internationale Presse** (☎ 089/13080). **texxt** (✉ Sendlinger-Str. 24, City Center, ☎ 089/2694–9503). **Words'worth** (✉ Schellingstr. 21a, Schwabing, ☎ 089/280–9141).

➤ ENGLISH-LANGUAGE EVENTS: **Amerikahaus** (✉ Karolinenpl. 3, near Königspl., Maxvorstadt, ☎ 089/552–5370). **British Council** (✉ Rumfordstr. 7, near Isartor, Isarvorstadt, ☎ 089/290–0860).

PHARMACIES

Internationale Ludwigs-Apotheke and Europa-Apotheke, both open weekdays 8–6 and Saturday 8–1, stock a large variety of over-the-counter medications. Munich pharmacies stay open late on a rotating basis, and every pharmacy has a schedule in its window.

➤ CONTACTS: **Internationale Ludwigs-Apotheke** (✉ Neuhauserstr. 11, City Center, ☎ 089/260–3021). **Europa-Apotheke** (✉ Schützenstr. 12, near the Hauptbahnhof, Leopoldvorstadt, ☎ 089/595–423).

TAXIS

Munich's cream-color taxis are numerous. Hail them in the street or phone for one (there's an extra charge of €1 if you call). Rates start at €2.40. Expect to pay €8–€10 for a short trip within the city. There is a €0.50 charge for each piece of luggage.

➤ TAXI COMPANIES: ☎ 089/21610 or 089/19410.

TOURS

For the cheapest sightseeing tour of the city center on wheels, board Streetcar 19 outside the Hauptbahnhof on Bahnhofplatz and make the 15-minute journey to Max Weber Platz. Explore the streets around the square, part of the old Bohemian residential area of Haidhausen (with some of the city's best bars and restaurants, many on the villagelike Kirchenstrasse), and then return by a different route on Streetcar 18 to Karlsplatz. A novel way of seeing the city is to hop on one of the bike-rickshaws. The bike-powered two-seater cabs operate between Marienplatz and the Chinesischer Turm in the Englischer Garten. Just hail one—or book ahead by calling.

City Hopper Touren offers daily escorted bike tours March–October. Bookings must be made in advance, and starting times are negotiable. Radius Touristik has bicycle tours from May through the beginning of October at 10:15 and 2; the cost, including bike rental, is €7.70. Mike's Bike Tours is run by a young American who hires German students to take visitors on a two- to three-hour spin through Munich. The tours start daily at the Old Town Hall, the Altes Rathaus, at 11:20 and 3:50. They cost €14, including bike rental.
➤ FEES AND SCHEDULES: **Bike-rickshaws** (☎ 089/129–4808). **City Hopper Touren** (☎ 089/272–1131). **Mike's Bike Tours** (☎ 089/651–4275). **Radius Touristik** (✉ Arnulfstr. 3, opposite Platforms 30–36 in the Hauptbahnhof, Leopoldvorstadt, ☎ 089/596–113).

BUS TOURS

Bus excursions to the Alps, to Austria, to the royal palaces and castles of Bavaria, or along the Romantic Road can be booked through DER. Next to the main train station, Panorama Tours operates numerous trips, including the Royal Castles Tour (Schlösserfahrt) of "Mad" King Ludwig's dream palaces; the cost is €41, excluding entrance fees to the palaces. Bookings for both companies can also be made through all major hotels in the city. The tours depart from in front of the Hauptbahnhof outside the Hertie department store.

A variety of city bus tours is offered by Panorama Tours. The blue buses operate year-round, departing from in front of the Hertie department store on Bahnhofplatz. A one-hour tour of Munich highlights leaves daily at 10, 11, 11:30, noon, 1, 2:30, 3, and 4. The cost is €11. A 2½-hour city tour departs daily at 10 AM and includes brief visits to the Alte Pinakothek, the Peterskirche, and Marienplatz for the glockenspiel. An afternoon tour, also 2½ hours and starting at 2:30 PM, includes a tour of Schloss Nymphenburg. The cost of each tour is €19. Another 2½-hour tour, departing Saturday, Sunday, and Monday at 10 AM, includes a visit to the Bavaria film studios. The cost is €23. A four-hour tour, starting daily at 10 AM and 2:30 PM includes a visit to the Olympic Park. The cost is €19. The München bei Nacht tour provides 4½ hours of Munich by night and includes dinner and a show at the Hofbräuhaus, a trip up the Olympic Tower to admire the lights of the city, and a final drink in a nightclub. It departs April through November, Friday and Saturday at 7:30 PM; the cost is €60.

Yellow Cab Stadtrundfahrten has a fleet of yellow double-decker buses, in which tours are offered simultaneously in eight languages. They leave hourly between 10 AM and 4 PM from in front of the Elisenhof shopping complex on Bahnhofplatz.
➤ FEES AND SCHEDULES: **DER** (✉ Hauptbahnhofpl. 2, in the main train station building, Leopoldvorstadt, ☎ 089/5514–0100). **Panorama Tours** (✉ Arnulfstr. 8, Leopoldvorstadt, ☎ 089/5490–7560). **Yellow Cab Stadtrundfahrten** (✉ Sendlinger-Tor-Pl. 2, Isarvorstadt, ☎ 089/303–631).

WALKING TOURS

Downtown Munich is only a mile square and is easily explored on foot. Almost all the major attractions in the city center are on the interlinking web of pedestrian streets that run from Karlsplatz, by the main train station, to Marienplatz and the Viktualienmarkt and extend north around the Frauenkirche and up to Odeonsplatz. The two tourist information offices issue a free map with suggested walking tours.

Two-hour tours of the old city center are given daily in summer (March–October) and on Friday and Saturday in winter (November–February). Tours organized by the visitor center start at 10:30 and 1 in the center of Marienplatz. The cost is €8. Munich Walks conducts daily tours of the old city and sites related to the Third Reich era. The cost is €10. Tours depart daily from the Hauptbahnhof, outside the EurAide office by Track 11, and also pick up latecomers outside the McDonalds at Karlsplatz.

➤ FEES AND SCHEDULES: **The Original Munich Walks** (☎ 089/5502–9374, WEB www.radius–munich.com).

TRAIN TRAVEL

All long-distance rail services arrive at and depart from the Hauptbahnhof; trains to and from some destinations in Bavaria use the adjoining Starnbergerbahnhof, which is under the same roof. The high-speed InterCity Express (ICE) trains connect Munich, Augsburg, Frankfurt, and Hamburg on one line; Munich, Nuremberg, Würzburg, and Hamburg on another. Regensburg can be reached from Munich on Regio trains. Call for information on train schedules; most railroad information staff speak English. For tickets and travel information, go to the station information office or try the ABR-DER travel agency, right by the station on Bahnhofplatz.

➤ TRAIN INFORMATION: **ABR-DER** (✉ Bahnhofpl., Leopoldvorstadt, ☎ 089/551–40200). **Hauptbahnhof** (✉ Bahnhofpl., Leopoldvorstadt, ☎ 089/2333–0256 or 089/2333–0257; 01805/996–633 for train schedules).

TRANSPORTATION AROUND MUNICH

Munich has an efficient and well-integrated public transportation system, consisting of the U-bahn (subway), the S-bahn (suburban railway), the Strassenbahn (streetcars), and buses. Marienplatz forms the heart of the U-bahn and S-bahn network, which operates from around 5 AM to 1 AM. An all-night tram and bus service operates on main routes within the city. For a clear explanation in English of how the system works, pick up a copy of *Rendezvous mit München,* available free of charge at all tourist offices.

Fares are uniform for the entire system. As long as you are traveling in the same direction, you can transfer from one mode of transportation to another on the same ticket. You can also interrupt your journey as often as you like, and time-punched tickets are valid for up to four hours, depending on the number of zones you travel through. Fares are constantly creeping upward, but a basic *Einzelfahrkarte* (one-way ticket) costs €2 for a ride in the inner zone and €1 for a short journey of up to four stops. If you're taking a number of trips around the city, save money by buying a *Mehrfahrtenkarte,* or multiple strip ticket. Red strip tickets are valid for children under 15 only. Blue strips cover adults—€9 buys a 10-strip ticket. All but the shortest inner-area journeys (up to four stops) cost two strips (one for young people between 15 and 21), which must be validated at one of the many time-punching machines at stations or on buses and trams. For two to five people on a short stay the best option is the *Partner-Tageskarte* ticket, which

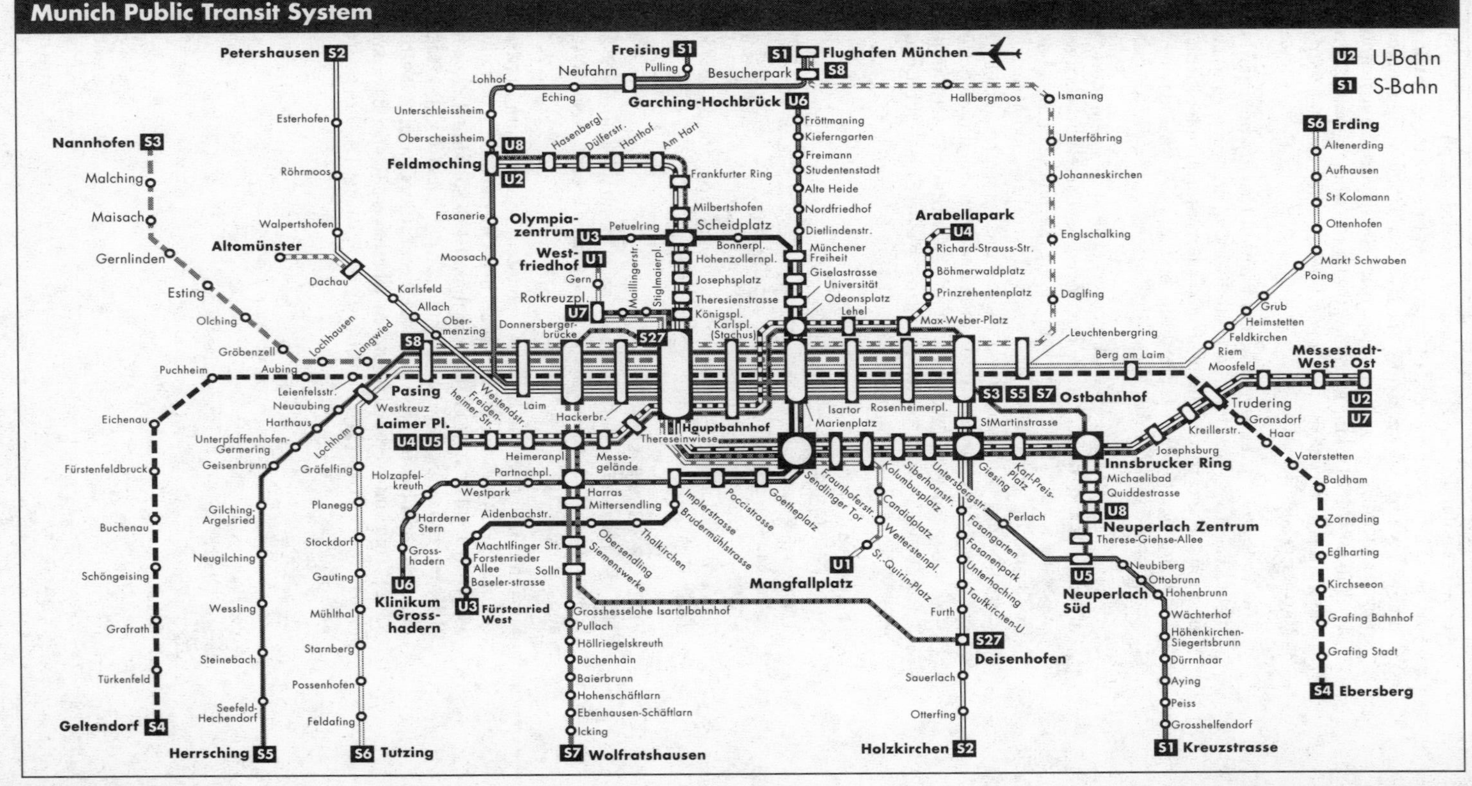
Munich Public Transit System
U2 U-Bahn
S1 S-Bahn
Petershausen S2
Esterhofen
Röhrmoos
Walpertshofen
Altomünster
Dachau
Karlsfeld
Allach
Obermenzing
Nannhofen S3
Malching
Maisach
Gernlinden
Esting
Olching
Gröbenzell
Lochhausen
Langwied
Puchheim
Aubing
Leienfelsstr.
Neuaubing
Harthaus
Eichenau
Fürstenfeldbruck
Buchenau
Schöngeising
Grafrath
Türkenfeld
Geltendorf S4
Unterpfaffenhofen-Germering
Geisenbrunn
Gilching-Argelsried
Neugilching
Wessling
Steinebach
Seefeld-Hechendorf
Herrsching S5
Lochham
Gräfelfing
Planegg
Stockdorf
Gauting
Mühlthal
Starnberg
Possenhofen
Feldafing
S6 Tutzing
S8
Pasing
Westkreuz
Laimer Pl.
U4 U5
Friedenheimer Str.
Westendstr.
Laim
Heimeranpl.
Partnachpl.
Westpark
Holzapfelkreuth
Haderner Stern
Grosshadern
U6
Klinikum Grosshadern
Aidenbachstr.
Machtlfinger Str.
Forstenrieder Allee
Baseler-strasse
U3 Fürstenried West
Solln
Harras
Mittersendling
Obersendling
Siemenswerke
Thalkirchen
Brudermühlstrasse
Implerstrasse
Poccistrasse
Goetheplatz
Grosshesselohe Isartalbahnhof
Pullach
Höllriegelskreuth
Buchenhain
Baierbrunn
Hohenschäftlarn
Ebenhausen-Schäftlarn
Icking
S7 Wolfratshausen
Hackerbr.
Messegelände
Donnersbergerbrücke
S27
Hauptbahnhof
Theresienwiese
Freising S1
Pulling
Neufahrn
Eching
Lohhof
Unterschleissheim
Oberschleissheim
Feldmoching
U8
U2
Hasenbergl
Dülferstr.
Harthof
Am Hart
Frankfurter Ring
Milbertshofen
Scheidplatz
Fasanerie
Moosach
Olympiazentrum U3
Petuelring
Westfriedhof U1
Gern
Rotkreuzpl.
U7
Maillingerstr.
Stiglmaierpl.
Bonnerpl.
Hohenzollernpl.
Josephsplatz
Theresienstrasse
Königspl.
Karlspl. (Stachus)
S1 Flughafen München
Besucherpark S8
Garching-Hochbrück U6
Fröttmaning
Kieferngarten
Freimann
Studentenstadt
Alte Heide
Nordfriedhof
Dietlindenstr.
Münchener Freiheit
Giselastrasse
Universität
Odeonsplatz
Lehel
Isartor
Marienplatz
Rosenheimerpl.
Sendlinger Tor
Fraunhoferstr.
Kolumbusplatz
Candidplatz
Wettersteinpl.
St.-Quirin-Platz
U1
Mangfallplatz
Silberhornstr.
Untersbergstr.
Fasangarten
Fasanenpark
Unterhaching
Taufkirchen-U
Furth
S27
Deisenhofen
Sauerlach
Otterfing
Holzkirchen S2
Giesing
Karl-Preis-Platz
Perlach
StMartinstrasse
Hallbergmoos
Ismaning
Unterföhring
Johanneskirchen
Englschalking
Daglfing
Leuchtenbergring
Berg am Laim
Arabellapark
U4
Richard-Strauss-Str.
Böhmerwaldplatz
Prinzrehentenplatz
Max-Weber-Platz
S3 S5 S7 Ostbahnhof
Innsbrucker Ring
Michaelibad
Quiddestrasse
U8
Neuperlach Zentrum
Therese-Giehse-Allee
U5
Neuperlach Süd
Neubiberg
Ottobrunn
Hohenbrunn
Wächterhof
Höhenkirchen-Siegertsbrunn
Dürrnhaar
Aying
Peiss
Grosshelfendorf
S1 Kreuzstrasse
Josephsburg
Kreillerstr.
Trudering
Gronsdorf
Haar
Vaterstetten
Baldham
Zorneding
Eglharting
Kirchseeon
Grafing Bahnhof
Grafing Stadt
S4 Ebersberg
Moosfeld
Riem
Feldkirchen
Heimstetten
Grub
Poing
Markt Schwaben
Ottenhofen
St Kolomann
Aufhausen
Altenerding
S6 Erding
Messestadt-West
Ost
U2
U7

provides unlimited travel (maximum of two adults, plus three children under 15). It is valid weekdays from 9 AM to 6 AM the following day and at any time on weekends. The costs are €7.50 for an inner-zone ticket and €15 for the entire network. The day card exists in single version for €4.50 for the inner city, €9 for the whole network. A three-day card is also available, costing €11 for a single and €17.50 in the partner version.

The *Welcome Card* covers transport within the city boundaries and includes up to 50% reductions in admission to many museums and attractions. The card, obtainable from visitor information offices, costs €6.50 for one day and €15.50 for three days. A three-day card for two people costs €22.50.

All tickets are sold at the blue dispensers at U- and S-bahn stations and at some bus and streetcar stops. Bus drivers have single tickets (the most expensive kind). There are ticket vending machines in trams, but they don't offer the strip cards. Otherwise tourist offices, and Mehrfahrtenkarten booths (which display a white K on a green background) also sell tickets. Spot checks are common and carry an automatic fine of €30 if you're caught without a valid ticket. Holders of a EurailPass, a Youth Pass, or an Inter-Rail card can travel free on all suburban railway trains the (S-Bahn).

TRAVEL AGENCIES

DER, the official German travel agency, has outlets all over Munich. The two most central ones are in the main railway station building and at the Münchner-Freiheit Square, in Schwabing.

➤ CONTACTS: **American Express** (✉ Promenadenpl. 6, City Center, ☎ 089/290–900). **DER** (✉ Bahnhofpl. 2, Leopoldvorstadt, ☎ 089/5514–0100; ✉ Münchner-Freiheit 6, Schwabing, ☎ 089/336–033).

VISITOR INFORMATION

The Hauptbahnhof tourist office is open Monday–Saturday 9–8 and Sunday 10–6; the Info-Service in the Rathaus is open weekdays 10–8 and Saturday 10–4.

For information on the Bavarian mountain region south of Munich, contact the Tourismusverband München-Oberbayern.

➤ TOURIST INFORMATION: **Hauptbahnhof** (✉ Bahnhofpl. 2, next to DER travel agency, Leopoldvorstadt, ☎ 089/2333–0123, WEB www.munich-tourist.de). **Info-Service** (✉ Marienpl., City Center, ☎ 089/2332–8242). **Tourismusverband München-Oberbayern** (Upper Bavarian Regional Tourist Office; ✉ Bodenseestr. 113, Pasing D–81243, ☎ 089/829–180).

3 THE BAVARIAN ALPS

This region of fir-clad mountains stretches from Munich to the Austrian border. Quaint towns full of half-timber houses—fronted by flowers in summer and by snowdrifts in winter—pop up among the peaks, as do the creations of "Mad" King Ludwig II. Shimmering Alpine lakes abound, and the whole area has sporting opportunities galore.

Updated by Marton Radkai

OBERBAYERN, OR UPPER BAVARIA, is Germany's favorite year-round vacationland and comes closest to what most of us envision as "Germany." Stock images from tourist-office posters—the fairy-tale castles, those too-good-to-be-true villages with brightly frescoed facades, the window boxes abloom, or the sloping roofs heavy with snow—spring to life here. To complete the picture, onion-dome church spires rise out of the mist against the backdrop of the mighty Alps.

This part of Bavaria fans south from Munich to the Austrian border, and as you follow this direction, you'll soon find yourself on a gently rolling plain leading to lakes fed by Alpine rivers and streams and surrounded by ancient forests. In time the plain merges into foothills, which suddenly give way to jagged Alpine peaks. In places such as Königsee, near Berchtesgaden, snowcapped mountains seem to rise straight up from the gemlike lakes.

Continuing south, you'll encounter cheerful villages with richly frescoed houses, churches and monasteries filled with the especially voluble and sensuous Bavarian baroque and rococo, and several minor spas where you can stay to "take the waters" and tune up your system. Sports possibilities are legion: downhill and cross-country skiing, snowboarding, and ice-skating in winter; tennis, swimming, sailing, golf, and, above all (sometimes literally), hiking, paragliding, and ballooning in summer.

Pleasures and Pastimes

Castles

Popping up among the peaks are the curious castles, Schloss Linderhof and Schloss Herrenchiemsee, which were created at the behest of King Ludwig II (1864–1886), one of the last of the Wittelsbachs. No figure riled the Munich taxpayers more. While Bismarck was striving from his Berlin power base to create a modern unified Germany, "Mad" Ludwig—also nicknamed the "Fairytale King"—was bankrupting the royal and public treasury to finance his spate of fanciful castles and remote summer retreats. He was quietly deposed, but history has cleared his name: the castles attract millions to Bavaria each year.

Dining

Designed to pack in the calories after a day's walking or skiing, the food in Bavaria's mountainous areas is understandably hearty and filling. Portions are usually huge, whether they're great wedges of roast pork, dumplings big enough to fire from a cannon, or homemade *Apfelstrudel* (apple-filled pastry), which is a meal in itself. However, thanks to a high standard of living in the area, fine dining and calorie-consciousness are making inroads into the traditional Bavarian kitchen. In lakeside inns and restaurants the day's catch might be plump perch (*Renke*) or freshwater trout (*Forelle, Lachsforelle,* or *Bachsaibling*). Many inns have pools where the trout grow even fatter, although they lack the mountain-water tang. Most districts in the Alps distill their own brand of schnapps from mountain herbs, and you can quaff what is arguably the region's best beer on the banks of the Tegernsee.

CATEGORY	COST*
$$$$	over €20
$$$	€15–€20
$$	€10–€15
$	under €10

**per person for a main course at dinner*

Lodging

With few exceptions, a hotel or *Gasthof* in the Bavarian Alps and lower Alpine regions has high standards and is traditionally styled, with balconies, pine woodwork, and gently angled roofs upon which the snow sits and insulates. Check out the seven-day packages in the larger resort towns. Private homes all through the region offer Germany's own version of bed-and-breakfasts, indicated by signs reading ZIMMER FREI (rooms available). Their rates may be less than €22 per person. As a general rule, the farther from the popular and sophisticated Alpine resorts you go, the lower the rates. In spas and many mountain resorts a "spa tax" is added to the hotel bill. It amounts to no more than €3 per person per day and allows free use of spa facilities and entry to local attractions and concerts.

CATEGORY	COST*
$$$$	over €225
$$$	€150–€225
$$	€75–€150
$	under €75

**All prices are for two people in a double room, including tax and service.*

Outdoor Activities and Sports

BIKING

With its lakeside and mountain trails, this is a mountain biker's paradise. Sports shops rent mountain bikes for around €15 a day.

HIKING AND WALKING

Well-marked and well-groomed hiking trails lead from the glorious countryside, along rivers and lakes, through woods, and high into the Alps. If you just want an afternoon stroll in the champagne air, head for the lower slopes. If you're a serious hiker, make for the mountain trails of the Zugspitze, in Garmisch-Partenkirchen; the heights above Oberammergau, Berchtesgaden, Bad Reichenhall; or the lovely Walchensee. Well-marked trails near the Schliersee or Tegernsee (lakes) lead steadily uphill and to mountaintop inns. A special treat is a hike to the Tatzelwurm Gorge near Bayrischzell.

SAILING

All the Bavarian Alpine lakes have sailing schools that rent sailboards as well as various types of boats. On Tegernsee you can hire motorboats at the pier in front of the Schloss Cafe, in the Tegernsee town center. Chiemsee, with its wide stretch of water whipped by Alpine winds, is a favorite for both sailing enthusiasts and windsurfers. There are boatyards all around the lake and a very good windsurfing school at Bernau. Windsurfing is also a favorite sport on the lakes, where powerful winds can suddenly whip the waters into a veritable lather.

SKIING

Garmisch-Partenkirchen was the site of the 1936 Winter Olympics and remains Germany's premier winter-sports resort. The upper slopes of the Zugspitze and surrounding mountains challenge the best ski buffs and snowboarders, and there are also plenty of runs for intermediate skiers and for families. The slopes above Reit im Winkl (particularly the Winklmoosalm) are less crowded, but the skiing is comparable to the Zugspitze area. All hotels in the region offer skiing packages.

SWIMMING

Bavarian lakes have very fine water, in some cases even drinking quality thanks to environmental regulations. Some of the mountain lakes, such as Kochelsee, Spitzingsee, or deep Lake Starnberg remain quite cold if the summer isn't too hot. The Chiemsee and many of the smaller lakes nearby are shallower and warmer. Public beaches are marked.

EXPLORING THE BAVARIAN ALPS

Numbers in the text correspond to numbers in the margin and on the Bavarian Alps map.

Great Itineraries

Consider basing yourself in one spot (such as Garmisch-Partenkirchen, Berchtesgaden, or a point halfway between, such as the Chiemsee or Tegernsee) and exploring the immediate area—you'll still experience just about everything the Bavarian Alps have to offer. Winter snowfalls can make traveling a nightmare, but if you want to squeeze in as much as possible, come fair weather or foul, the German Tourist Board has a recommended route, the *Deutsche Alpenstrasse* (German Alpine Road). Allow a week to cover it.

IF YOU HAVE 3 DAYS

Choose between the western (Garmisch-Partenkirchen) area and the eastern (Berchtesgaden) corner. If busy little **Garmisch-Partenkirchen** ① is your base, devote a couple of days to exploring the magnificent countryside. Wait for good weather to take the cable car or cog railway to the summit of Germany's highest mountain, the Zugspitze. A comfortable day trip takes in the monastery at **Ettal** ② and one of King Ludwig's loveliest palaces, **Schloss Linderhof** ③. Also worth a visit is **Oberammergau** ④, where villagers stage the famous Passion Play every 10 years (the next performance is in 2010). Allow a third day to visit **Mittenwald** ⑤ and its violin museum, taking in the village of Klais (with Germany's highest railroad station) on the way. If you devote your three days to **Berchtesgaden** ⑳, allow one of them for **Obersalzberg** ㉑, site of Hitler's retreat, called Eagle's Nest, and a second for a boat outing on Königsee, deep in the mountains' embrace. On the third day choose between a trip down into Berchtesgaden's salt mine, the Salzbergwerk, or a cross-border run into the Austrian city of Salzburg.

IF YOU HAVE 5 DAYS

Spend a day or two in **Garmisch-Partenkirchen** ①, and then head for Bavaria's largest lake, **Chiemsee** ⑮ (about a two-hour trip via the autobahn). Overnight in one of the several villages on its western shore (Prien has a main-line railway station and a boat harbor) and take boat trips to **Schloss Herrenchiemsee** Island and to the smaller and utterly enchanting **Fraueninsel.** Round off the journey with two days in **Berchtesgaden** ⑳ and the surrounding countryside.

IF YOU HAVE 7 DAYS

Begin with a day or two based in **Garmisch-Partenkirchen** ① for excursions to **Schloss Linderhof** ③ and **Oberammergau** ④. Next strike out east along the well-signposted Deutsche Alpenstrasse. Leave the route after 20 km (12 mi), at Wallgau, to relax for an hour or two on the southern shore of picturesque Walchensee, doubling back later to compare its dark waters with the fresh mountain green of dammed-up Sylvenstein Stausee, to the east. Then dodge in and out of Austria on a

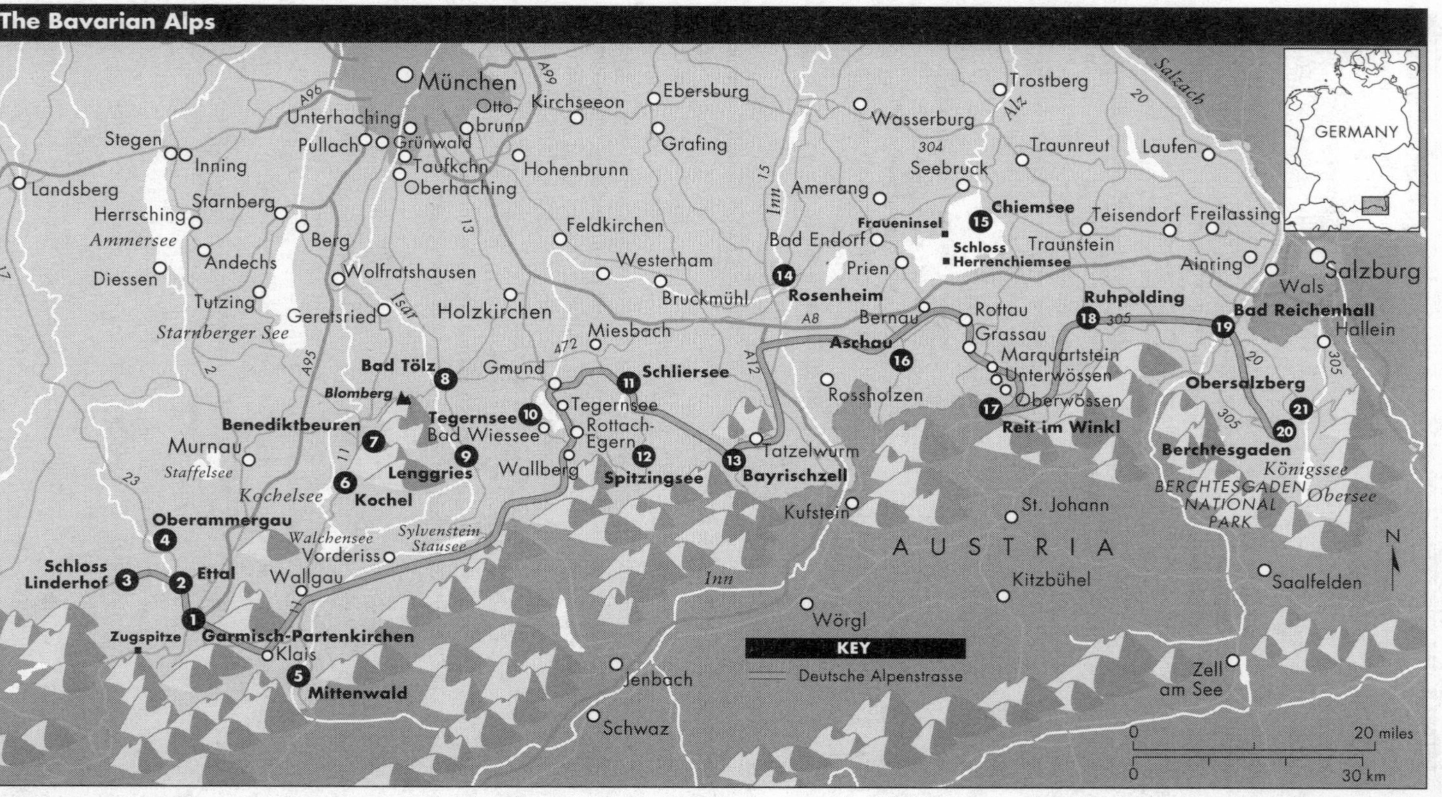
The Bavarian Alps
GERMANY
München
Salzburg
AUSTRIA
KEY
Deutsche Alpenstrasse
BERCHTESGADEN NATIONAL PARK
0
20 miles
0
30 km
N
Schloss Linderhof
Zugspitze
Oberammergau
Ettal
Garmisch-Partenkirchen
Klais
Mittenwald
Kochel
Lenggries
Bad Tölz
Blomberg
Benediktbeuren
Tegernsee
Bad Wiessee
Schliersee
Spitzingsee
Bayrischzell
Rosenheim
Aschau
Chiemsee
Fraueninsel
Schloss Herrenchiemsee
Reit im Winkl
Ruhpolding
Bad Reichenhall
Obersalzberg
Berchtesgaden
Landsberg
Stegen
Inning
Herrsching
Ammersee
Diessen
Starnberg
Andechs
Tutzing
Starnberger See
Berg
Geretsried
Wolfratshausen
Pullach
Unterhaching
Grünwald
Taufkchn
Oberhaching
Otto-brunn
Hohenbrunn
Kirchseeon
Ebersburg
Grafing
Feldkirchen
Westerham
Bruckmühl
Holzkirchen
Miesbach
Gmund
Rottach-Egern
Wallberg
Murnau
Staffelsee
Kochelsee
Walchensee
Vorderiss
Wallgau
Sylvenstein Stausee
Isar
Inn
Bad Endorf
Amerang
Wasserburg
Seebruck
Prien
Bernau
Rossholzen
Tatzelwurm
Kufstein
Wörgl
Jenbach
Schwaz
Rottau
Grassau
Marquartstein
Unterwössen
Oberwössen
Traunstein
Trostberg
Alz
Traunreut
Teisendorf
Laufen
Freilassing
Ainring
Wals
Hallein
Salzach
Königssee
Obersee
St. Johann
Kitzbühel
Saalfelden
Zell am See
A8
A12
A95
A96
A99
472
304
305
20
15
13
2
23
17
11

highland road that snakes through the tree-lined Aachen Pass to **Tegernsee** ⑩, where hills dip from all sides into the lake. Book two or three nights at one of the nearby, moderately priced Gasthöfe, or spoil yourself at one of the luxurious hotels in upscale Rottach-Egern. A day's walk (or a 20-minute drive) takes you to Tegernsee's neighboring lake, the shimmering **Schliersee** ⑪. From there the road becomes a switchback (one stretch is a privately maintained toll road), climbing from narrow valleys to mountain ski resorts and finally plunging to the Inn River valley. Consider leaving the Alpine route here for a stay on the shores of the **Chiemsee** ⑮, where King Ludwig's Schloss Herrenchiemsee stands on one of the three islands. Back on the Alpine route, you'll inevitably head back into the mountains, dropping down again into elegant **Bad Reichenhall** ⑲, another overnight stop. From here it's 30 km (18 mi) to **Berchtesgaden** ⑳, where you can spend your final two days viewing the town, its castle museum, Hitler's mountaintop retreat, and the beautiful Königsee.

When to Tour the Bavarian Alps

This mountainous region is a year-round holiday destination. Snow is promised by most resorts from December through March, although there's year-round skiing on the glacier slopes at the top of the Zugspitze. Spring and autumn are ideal times for mountain walking. November is a between-seasons time, when many hotels and restaurants close down or attend to renovations. Note, too, that many locals take a vacation after January 6th, and businesses may be closed for anywhere up to a month.

Garmisch-Partenkirchen

❶ *90 km (55 mi) southwest of Munich.*

Garmisch, as it's more commonly known, is the undisputed capital of Alpine Bavaria, a bustling, year-round resort and spa. Once two separate communities, Garmisch and Partenkirchen fused in 1936 to accommodate the Winter Olympics. Today, with a population of 28,000, the area is large enough to offer every facility expected from a major Alpine resort but still not overwhelm. Garmisch is walkable but spread out, and the narrow streets and buildings of smaller Partenkirchen hold snugly to each other. In both parts of town pastel frescoes of biblical and bucolic scenes decorate facades.

Partenkirchen was founded by the Romans and you can still follow the road they built between Partenkirchen and neighboring Mittenwald, which was part of a major route between Rome and Germany well into the 17th century. In the early 18th century the region experienced an economic boom thanks to the discovery of iron ore.

Winter sports rank high on the agenda here. There are more than 99 km (62 mi) of downhill ski runs, 40 ski lifts and cable cars, and 180 km (112 mi) of *Loipen* (cross-country ski trails). One of the principal stops on the international winter-sports circuit, the area hosts a week of races every January. You can usually count on good skiing from December through April (and into May on the Zugspitze).

Garmisch-Partenkirchen isn't all sporty, however. In addition to two Olympic stadiums in the Partenkirchen side of the city, there are some other attractions worth seeing. In Garmisch, beautiful examples of Upper Bavarian houses line Frühlingstrasse, and the pedestrian zone begins at Richard-Strauss-Platz. Off Marienplatz, at one end of the car-free zone, is the 18th-century parish church of **St. Martin.** It contains some significant stuccowork by the Wessobrunn artists Schmuzer, Schmidt, and Bader. Across the Loisach River, on Pfarrerhausweg, stands another **St. Martin** church dating from 1280, whose Gothic wall paintings include a larger-than-life-size figure of St. Christopher.

Objects and exhibitions on the town's history can be found in the excellent **Werdenfelser Museum,** which is itself housed in a building with roots going back to around 1200. ✉ *Ludwigstr. 47, Partenkirchen,* ☎ *08821/2134,* 🎫 *€1.50.* ⏲ *Tues.–Fri. 10–1 and 3–6, weekends 10–1.*

On the eastern edge of Garmisch, at the end of Zöppritzstrasse, stands the **villa of composer Richard Strauss,** who lived here until his death in 1949. It's the center of activity during the *Richard-Strauss-Tage,* an annual music festival held in late spring.

The number one attraction in Garmisch is the **Zugspitze,** the highest mountain (9,731 ft) in Germany. There are two ways up the mountain: a leisurely 75-minute ride on a cog railway from the train station in the town center, combined with a cable car ride up the last stretch; or a 10-minute hoist by cable car, which begins its giddy ascent from the Eibsee, 10 km (6 mi) outside town on the road to Austria. If it's summer or autumn (deep snow still clings to the upper slopes in spring), follow one of the well-marked paths to a point where you can pick up the railway to the bottom of the mountain again. There are two restaurants with sunny terraces at the summit and another at the top of the cog railway. A round-trip combination ticket allows you to mix your mode of travel up and down the mountain. Prices are lower in winter than in summer, even though they include use of all the ski lifts on the mountain. You can rent skis at the top. ✉ *Cog railway leaves from Olympiastr. 27,* ☎ *08821/7970,* WEB *www.zugspitze.de.* 🎫 *Funicular or cable car €42, round-trip; parking €3.*

A four-seat cable car goes to the top of one of the lesser peaks: the **Wank** or the **Alpspitze,** some 2,000 ft lower than the Zugspitze. You can tackle both mountains on foot, provided you're properly shod and physically fit.

Dining and Lodging

For information about accommodation packages with ski passes, call the **Zugspitze** (☎ 08821/7970, FAX 08821/797–901, WEB www.zugspitze.de) or get in touch with the tourist office in Garmisch.

$–$$$$ ✕ **Riessersee.** On the shores of a small, green, tranquil lake—a 3-km (2-mi) walk from town—this café-restaurant is an ideal spot for lunch or afternoon tea (on weekends there's live zither music 3–5). House specialties are fresh trout and local game (which fetches the higher prices on the menu). ✉ *Riess 6,* ☎ *08821/95440. AE, MC, V. Closed Mon. and Dec. 1–15.*

$$–$$$ ✕ **Posthotel Partenkirchen.** What makes the Posthotel a delight to the eye and unique in the region is the original old furnishings, beginning with the reception area's 20-ft oak refectory table. A hand-painted ceiling decorates the elegant 500-year-old vaulted cellar restaurant. The menu changes daily, with a focus on international dishes, such as leg of lamb in rosemary sauce, and seasonal specialties, such as asparagus. The café is worth sitting in for its opulently carved paneling and delicious cakes. ✉ *Ludwigstr. 49,* ☎ *08821/93630. AE, DC, MC, V.*

$$$ ✕🏨 **Grand Hotel Sonnenbichl.** This elegant, established lodging on the outskirts of Garmisch captures panoramic views of the Wetterstein Mountains and the Zugspitze, but only from its front rooms—the rear rooms face a wall of rock. The two restaurants ($–$$$) offer differing fare: the Zierbelstube has regional specialties at a lower price, the Blauer Salon serves a variety of German and French dishes, with variations of lamb and Mediterranean fish. ✉ *Burgstr. 97, D–82467,* ☎ *08821/7020,* FAX *08821/702–131. 90 rooms, 3 suites. 2 restaurants, bar,*

cable TV with movies, Internet, pool, gym, hair salon, hot tub, sauna, pets allowed (fee), no-smoking rooms. AE, DC, MC, V.

$$–$$$ ★ **Reindl's Partenkirchner Hof.** Owner Karl Reindl ranks among the world's top hoteliers. His award-winning hotel is a real family concern, with daughter Marianne in charge of the kitchen that cooks up excellent Bavarian specialties (roast of suckling pig) and international gastronomical goodies (coquille St.-Jacques with chanterelles). Each guest room has pinewood furniture and a balcony or patio. Some of the double rooms are huge. If planning to stay for several days, ask about specials. ✉ *Bahnhofstr. 15, D–82467,* ☎ *08821/943–870,* FAX *08821/943–87250,* WEB *www.Reindls.de. 65 rooms, 23 suites. Restaurant, bar, no a/c in some rooms, cable TV with movies, pool, sauna, exercise room, bicycles, no-smoking rooms. AE, DC, MC, V.*

$–$$ **Hotel-Gasthof Drei Mohren.** In the Partenkirchen village you'll find all the simple, homey comforts you'd expect of a 150-year-old Bavarian inn. All rooms have mountain views, and most are furnished with farmhouse-style painted beds and cupboards. A free bus to Garmisch and the cable car stations parks right outside the house. The restaurant ($–$$) serves solid fare, including a series of *Pfanderl,* large portions of meat and potatoes in various guises: fried, roasted, or in sauce. ✉ *Ludwigstr. 65, D–82467,* ☎ *08821/9130,* FAX *08821/18974. 21 rooms, 2 apartments. Restaurant, bar, no a/c, cable TV, Internet, pets allowed (fee). AE, MC, V.*

$$–$$$ ★ **Wittelsbacher Hof.** Dramatic mountain vistas from bedroom balconies and a spacious garden terrace make this hotel especially attractive. Public rooms are elegantly Bavarian, and the restaurant has graceful art nouveau features. The bedrooms are spacious, with corner lounge areas and mahogany or cherrywood furniture. Ask for a room facing south for Zugspitze views. ✉ *Von-Brug-Str. 24, D–82467,* ☎ *08821/53096,* FAX *08821/57312,* WEB *www.wittelsbacher-hof.com. 60 rooms, 2 suites. Restaurant, piano bar, no a/c, cable TV, Internet, pool, sauna, spa, pets allowed (fee), no-smoking rooms. AE, DC, MC, V.*

$$ **Edelweiss.** Like its namesake, the "eternally white" Alpine flower of *Sound of Music* fame, this small, downtown hotel has plenty of mountain charm. Inlaid with warm pinewood, it has Bavarian furnishings and individually decorated rooms. ✉ *Martinswinkelstr. 15–17, D–82467,* ☎ *08821/2454,* FAX *09621/4849,* WEB *www.hoteledelweiss.de. 21 rooms, 2 suites, 2 apartments. No a/c, cable TV, pets allowed (fee), no-smoking rooms. V.*

$$ ★ **Gasthof Fraundorfer.** You can sled your way to dreamland in this beautiful old Bavarian Gasthof—some of the beds are carved like old-fashioned sleighs; others take the form of antique automobiles. The colorfully painted facade, covered for most of the year with geraniums, sets the tone for the interior, where hardly a corner is left unpaneled. The tavern-restaurant presents "Bavarian evenings" of folk entertainment. ✉ *Ludwigstr. 24, D–82467,* ☎ *08821/9270,* FAX *08821/92799,* WEB *www.gasthof-fraundorfer.de. 20 rooms, 7 suites. Restaurant, no a/c, cable TV, in-room data ports, sauna, steam room, pets allowed (fee). AE, MC, V. Closed late-Nov.–early Dec.*

$–$$ **Hotel Hilleprandt.** The Hilleprandt, 500 yards from the train station, is a family enterprise, priding itself on friendliness and good service. A small garden and warmly decorated rooms welcome you—as does a small drink on the house—and will invite you to stay longer than you might have planned. What you put on in the three-course evening meal (€16), you can get sweat off in the sauna. ✉ *Riffelstr. 17, D–82467 Garmisch,* ☎ *08821/943–040,* FAX *08821/745–48,* WEB *www.hotel-hilleprandt.de. 13 rooms, 3 suites. No a/c, cable TV, in-room data ports, sauna, hot tub, some pets allowed. MC, V.*

Hiking and Walking

There are innumerable spectacular walks on 300 km (186 mi) of marked trails through the lower slopes' pinewoods and upland meadows. If you have the time and good walking shoes, try one of the two trails that lead to striking gorges. The **Höllentalklamm** route starts at the Zugspitze Mountain railway terminal (✉ Olympiastr. 27) in town and ends at the mountaintop (you'll want to turn back before reaching the summit unless you have mountaineering experience). The **Partnachklamm** route is quite challenging and takes you through a spectacular, tunneled water gorge (entrance fee), past a pretty little mountain lake, and far up the Zugspitze; to do all of it, you'll have to stay overnight in one of the huts along the way. Ride part of the way up in the **Eckbauer cable car** (€7.50 one-way, €10 round-trip) that sets out from the Skistadion off Mittenwalderstrasse. The second cable car, the **Graseckbahn** takes you right over the dramatic gorges (€3.50 one way, €5 return). There's a handy inn at the top where you can gather strength for the hour-long walk back down to the Graseckbahn station. Horse-drawn carriages also cover the first section of the route in summer; in winter you can skim along it in a sleigh. The carriages wait near the Skistadion. Or you can call the local coaching society, the **Lohnkutschevereinigung** (☎ 08821/942–920) for information. Contact **Deutscher Alpenverein** (✉ German Alpine Association, Von-Kahr-Str. 2–4, D–80997 Munich, ☎ 089/140–030, WEB www.alpenverein.de) for details on hikes and on staying in mountain huts.

Nightlife and the Arts

In season there's a busy **après-ski scene.** Many hotels have dance floors, and some have basement discos that pound away until the early hours. Bavarian folk dancing and zither music is a regular feature of nightlife. During the summer there's entertainment every Saturday evening at the **Bayernhalle** (✉ Brauhausstr. 19). Wednesday through Monday the cozy tavern-restaurant of **Gasthof Fraundorfer** (✉ Ludwigstr. 24, ☎ 08821/9270) hosts lots of yodeling and folk dancing. Concerts are presented from Saturday to Thursday, mid-May through September, in the park bandstand in Garmisch, and on Friday in the Partenkirchen park. Tickets are available at **Garmisch-Partenkirchen-Ticket** (✉ Richard-Strauss-Pl., ☎ 08821/752–545, FAX 08821/752–547; ⏲ weekdays 9–1 and 2–7, Sat. 9–1 and 7–8).

The **casino** (✉ Am Kurpark 10, ☎ 08821/95990) is open daily 3 PM to 2 AM and Saturday 3 PM–3 AM, with more than 100 slot machines, roulette, blackjack, and poker tables.

Ettal

★ ❷ *16 km (10 mi) north of Garmisch-Partenkirchen, 85 km (53 mi) south of Munich.*

The village of Ettal is totally dominated by the massive bulk of **Kloster Ettal,** the great monastery founded in 1330 by Holy Roman Emperor Ludwig the Bavarian for a group of knights and a community of Benedictine monks. The abbey was replaced with new buildings in the 18th century and now serves as a school. Open to visitors, the original 10-sided church was brilliantly redecorated in 1744–53, becoming one of the foremost examples of Bavarian rococo. The church's chief treasure is its enormous dome fresco (83 ft wide), painted by Jacob Zeiller, circa 1751–52. The mass of swirling clouds and the pink-and-blue vision of heaven are typical of the rococo fondness for elaborate and glowing illusionistic ceiling painting.

Ettaler, a liqueur made from a centuries-old recipe, is still distilled at the monastery. It's made with more than 70 mountain herbs and has legendary health-giving properties. The ad tells it best: "Two monks know how it's made, 2 million Germans know how it tastes." You can buy bottles of the libation from the gift shop and bookstore outside the monastery. This is the largest Benedictine monastery in Germany; approximately 55 monks live here, including one from Compton, Los Angeles. ☎ *08822/740 for guided tour of church.* *Free.* *Daily 8–6.*

Dining and Lodging

$–$$ ✕ **Edelweiss.** This friendly café and restaurant next to the monastery is an ideal spot for a light lunch or coffee and homemade cakes or pastries. ✉ *Kaiser-Ludwig-Pl. 3,* ☎ *08822/4509. No credit cards.*

$–$$ ✕ **Blauer Gams.** This family-run inn is large but well fitted to the landscape around it. A terrace draws diners outside for a breath of fresh air with lunch; at night dinners of Bavarian specialties take place indoors, either in the pleasant "Klause" dining room ($–$$$), or the little "Stübchen" where a tile oven warms the spirit. Some of the rooms have attractive antique furnishing. ✉ *Vogelherdweg 12, D–82488,* ☎ *08822/6449,* FAX *08822/869. 51 rooms. Restaurant, no a/c, cable TV, pets allowed (fee). No credit cards.*

$–$$ ✕ **Hotel Ludwig der Bayer.** Backed by mountains, this fine old Ettal hotel is run by the Benedictine order. There's nothing monastic about it, except for the exquisite religious carvings and motifs that adorn the walls. Most come from the monastery's own carpentry shop, which also made much of the sturdy furniture in the comfortable bedrooms. The hotel has two excellent restaurants ($–$$) with rustic, Bavarian atmosphere and a vaulted tavern that serves sturdy fare and beer brewed at the monastery. ✉ *Kaiser-Ludwig-Pl. 10, D–82488,* ☎ *08822/9150,* FAX *08822/74480. 70 rooms, 32 apartments. 2 restaurants, 2 bars, no a/c, cable TV, tennis court, pool, gym, sauna, bicycles, bowling, pets allowed (fee). MC, V.*

$–$$ ✕ **Hotel Zur Post.** Families are warmly welcomed at this traditional Gasthof in the center of town. There's a playground in the shady garden, and the Bavarian restaurant, which is covered in warm wood paneling, has a children's menu. ✉ *Kaiser-Ludwig-Pl. 18, D–82488,* ☎ *08822/3596,* FAX *08822/6971. 21 rooms, 4 apartments. Restaurant, no a/c, cable TV, no room phones, gym, sauna, steam room, playground, pets allowed (fee), no-smoking rooms. MC, V. Closed Oct. 26–Dec. 18.*

Schloss Linderhof

❸ *10 km (6 mi) west of Ettal on B–23, 95 km (59 mi) south of Munich.*

Built between 1874 and 1878 on the grounds of his father's hunting lodge, Schloss Linderhof was the only one of Ludwig II's royal residences to have been completed during the monarch's short life and in which he spent much time. Linderhof was the smallest of this ill-fated king's castles and his favorite country retreat. Set in sylvan seclusion, between a reflecting pool and the green slopes of a gentle mountain, the charming, French-style, rococo confection is said to have been inspired by the Petit Trianon at Versailles. From an architectural standpoint it is a quodlibet of conflicting styles, lavish on the outside, somewhat overdecorated on the inside. But the main impetus came from the Sun King of France, Louis XIV, who is referred to in numerous reliefs, mosaics, paintings, and stucco pieces. Ludwig's bedroom is filled with brilliantly colored and gilded ornaments, the Hall of Mirrors is a shimmering dream world, and the dining room has a clever piece of

19th-century engineering—a table that rises from and descends to the kitchens below.

The formal gardens contain still more whimsical touches. There's a Moorish pavilion—bought wholesale from the 1867 Paris Universal Exposition—and a huge artificial grotto in which Ludwig had scenes from Wagner operas performed, with full lighting effects. It took the BASF chemical company much research to develop the proper glass for the blue lighting Ludwig desired. The gilded Neptune in front of the castle spouts a 100-ft water jet. According to hearsay, while staying at Linderhof the eccentric king would dress up as the legendary knight Lohengrin to be rowed in a swan boat on the grotto pond; in winter he took off on midnight sleigh rides behind six plumed horses and a platoon of outriders holding flaring torches (in winter be prepared for an approach road as snowbound as in Ludwig's day—careful driving is called for). ☎ *08822/92030.* *Apr.–Oct. €6, Nov.–Mar. €4.50.* *Fri.–Wed. 9–6, Thurs. 9–8. Pavilion and grotto closed Nov.–Mar.*

Oberammergau

❹ *20 km (12 mi) northwest of Garmisch-Partenkirchen, 4 km (2½ mi) northwest of Ettal, 90 km (56 mi) south of Munich.*

An amateur theatrical production has given this small Bavarian town a fame quite out of proportion to its size. Its location alone, though, in an Alpine valley beneath a sentinel-like peak, makes it a major attraction (allow half an hour for the drive from Garmisch). Its main streets are lined with frescoed houses (such as the 1784 Pilatushaus on Ludwig-Thoma-Strasse), and in summer the village bursts with color as geraniums pour from every window box. Many of these lovely houses are occupied by families whose men are highly skilled wood-carvers, a craft that has flourished here since the depredations of the Thirty Years' War.

Oberammergau, however, is best known for its **Passion Play,** first presented in 1634 as an offering of thanks that the Black Death stopped just short of the village. In faithful accordance with a solemn vow, it will next be performed in the year 2010 as it has every 10 years since 1680. Its 16 acts, which take 5½ hours, depict the final days of Christ, from the Last Supper through the Crucifixion and Resurrection. It is presented daily on a partly open-air stage against a mountain backdrop from late May to late September. The entire village is swept up in the production, with some 1,500 residents directly involved in its preparation and presentation. Men grow beards in the hope of capturing a key role; young women have been known to put off their weddings—the role of Mary went only to unmarried girls until the 1990 performances. In that year tradition was broken when—amid much local controversy—a 31-year-old mother of two was given the part.

You'll find many wood-carvers at work in town, and shop windows are crammed with their creations. From June through October a workshop is open free to the public at the **Pilatushaus** (✉ Ludwig-Thoma-Str. 10); working potters and painters can also be seen. Pilatushaus was completed in 1775, and the frescoes—considered among the most beautiful in town—were done by Franz Seraph Zwinck, one of the greatest *Lüftlmalerei* painters. The house is named for the fresco over the front door depicting Christ before Pilate. Contact the tourist office (☎ 08822/92–310) to sign up for a weeklong course in wood carving (classes are in German), which cost between €310 and €454, depending on whether you are in a bed-and-breakfast or a hotel.

The **Heimatmuseum** (Natural History Museum) has historic examples of the wood craftsman's art and an outstanding collection of Christmas crèches, which date from the mid-18th century. Numerous exhibits also document the wax and wax embossing art, which also flourishes in Oberammergau. ✉ *Dorfstr. 8,* ☎ *08822/94136.* €2. ⏲ *Mid-May–mid-Oct., Tues.–Sun. 2–6; mid-Oct.–mid-May, Sat. 2–6.*

The immense theater in which the Passion Play is performed, the **Oberammergau Passionsspielhaus,** was totally renovated for the performances in 2000 and can be toured during the off-seasons. ✉ *Passionstheater, Passionswiese,* ☎ *08822/32278.* €2. ⏲ *Weekdays 2 PM.*

The 18th-century **St. Peter and St. Paul Church** is regarded as the finest work of rococo architect Josef Schmuzer and has striking frescoes by Matthäus Günther and Franz Seraph Zwinck (in the organ loft). Schmuzer's son Franz Xaver Schmuzer did a lot of the stucco work. ✉ *Pfarrpl. 1,* ☎ *08824/553.* ⏲ *Daily 9 AM–dusk.*

Dining and Lodging

$ ✕ **Ammergauer Stubn.** A homey restaurant with pink tablecloths and a lot of wood, the Stubn has a comprehensive menu that serves both Bavarian specialties and international dishes. You can expect nice roasts and some Swabian dishes, such as Maultaschen, a large meat-filled ravioli. ✉ *Wittelsbach Hotel, Dorfstr. 21,* ☎ *08822/92800. AE, DC, MC. No lunch. Closed Tues. and Nov. 7–Dec. 10.*

$$ ✕🏨 **Hotel Landhaus Feldmeier.** This quiet country-style hotel, idyllically set just outside the village, has mostly spacious rooms with modern pinewood furniture. All have geranium-bedecked balconies, with views of the village and mountains. The rustic restaurant ($$) is one of the region's best. You can dine on the sunny, covered terrace in summer. Only hotel guests can use credit cards in the restaurant. ✉ *Ettalerstr. 29, D–82487,* ☎ *08822/3011,* FAX *08822/6631,* WEB *www.hotel-feldmeier.de. 22 rooms. No a/c, cable TV, Internet, gym, hot tub, sauna, steam room, pets allowed (fee), no-smoking rooms. MC, V. Closed mid-Nov.–mid–Dec.*

$–$$ ✕🏨 **Alte Post.** You can enjoy carefully prepared local cuisine ($–$$) on the original pine tables in this 350-year-old inn. There's a special children's menu, and in summer meals are also served in the beer garden. If it weren't for the steady automobile traffic groaning through Oberammergau, the front terrace of this delightful old building would be something close to paradise. The rooms are simply appointed, with tasteful rustic furniture. ✉ *Dorfstr. 19,* ☎ *08822/9100,* FAX *08822/910–100,* WEB *www.altepost.ogau.de. 31 rooms. Restaurant, no a/c, cable TV, Internet, pets allowed (fee), no-smoking rooms. DC, V. Closed Nov.–mid-Dec.*

$–$$ ★ ✕🏨 **Hotel Turmwirt.** Rich wood paneling reaches from floor to ceiling in this transformed 18th-century inn, set in the shadow of Oberammergau's mountain, the Kofel. The hotel's own band presents regular folk evenings in the restaurant ($–$$$) with its wooden coffered ceiling. The *Ammergauer Pfanne,* a combination of meats and sauces, will take care of the most industrial-sized hunger. Rooms have corner lounge areas, and most come with balconies and sweeping mountain views. ✉ *Ettalerstr. 2, D–82487,* ☎ *08822/92600,* FAX *08822/1437,* WEB *www.turmwirt.de. 22 rooms. Restaurant, no a/c, cable TV, Internet, recreation room, pets allowed (fee), no-smoking rooms. AE, DC, MC, V. Closed most of Jan. and Nov.–mid-Dec.*

$–$$ ✕🏨 **Hotel Wolf.** Americans make up about a third of the guest list at this old hotel, redone in somewhat dubious modern Alpine style. Blue shutters punctuate its white walls, and the steeply gabled upper stories bloom with flowers. The hotel's Hafner Stube is a popular local haunt, with a menu ($–$$) that will satisfy large appetites. ✉ *Dorfstr. 1, D–82487,* ☎ *08822/92330,* FAX *08822/923–333,* WEB *www.hotel-wolf.de. 32 rooms. Restaurant, café, 2 bars, no a/c, cable TV, in-room data ports, pool, sauna, pets allowed, no-smoking rooms. AE, DC, MC, V.*

$ ✕ **Gasthaus zum Stern.** This is a traditional old place (around 500 years old, in fact), with coffered ceiling, thick walls, an old Kachelofen that heats the dining room beyond endurance on cold winter days, and smiling waitresses in dirndls. The food ($–$$) is hearty, traditional Bavarian. For a quieter dinner or lunch, reserve a space in the "Bäckerstube." ✉ *Dorfstr. 33, D–82487,* ☎ *08822/867,* FAX *08822/7027. 17 rooms. No a/c, no telephones, pets allowed. AE, DC, MC, V. Restaurant closed Wed.*

$$ **Parkhotel Sonnenhof.** Away from the sometimes crowded town center, the modern Sonnenhof, in Alpine style but simply too large, provides a balcony with every guest room, so you can sun yourself and soak up the Alpine view. There's also a children's playroom. ✉ *König-Ludwig-Str. 12, D–82487,* ☎ *08822/9130,* FAX *08822/3047,* WEB *www. Parkhotel-Sonnenhof.de. 65 rooms, 2 suites. Restaurant, bar, no a/c, cable TV, some in-room data ports, pool, sauna, billiards, bowling, pets allowed (fee). AE, DC, MC, V.*

Mittenwald

5 *20 km (12 mi) southeast of Garmisch, 105 km (66 mi) south of Munich.*

Many regard Mittenwald as the most beautiful town in the Bavarian Alps. Indeed, it has somehow avoided the architectural sins that have visited other Alpine villages by maintaining a balance between conservation and the needs of tourism. Its medieval prosperity is reflected on its main street, which has splendid houses with ornately carved gables and brilliantly painted facades. Goethe, Germany's greatest author and thinker, called it "a lively picture book," and it still is. The town has even recreated the stream that once flowed through the market square. The main road was detoured around Mittenwald, which markedly raises the quality of life in town.

In the Middle Ages Mittenwald was the staging point for goods shipped from the wealthy city-state of Venice by way of the Brenner Pass and Innsbruck. From there goods were transferred to rafts, which carried them down the Isar River to Munich. In the mid-17th century, however, the international trade route was moved to a different pass, and the fortunes of Mittenwald declined.

In 1684 Matthias Klotz, a farmer's son turned master violin maker, returned from a 20-year stay in Cremona, Italy. There, along with Antonio Stradivari, he had studied under Nicolo Amati, who gave the violin its present form. Klotz taught the art of violin making to his brothers and friends; before long, half the men in the village were crafting the instruments using woods from neighboring forests. Mittenwald became known as "the Village of a Thousand Violins," and stringed instruments—violins, violas, and cellos—were shipped around the world. The violin has made Mittenwald a small cultural oasis in the middle of the Alps. Not only is there an annual violin—and viola, cello, and bow—building contest each year in June, with concerts and lectures, but also an organ festival in the church of St. Peter and St. Paul.

The **Geigenbau und Heimatmuseum** (Violin and Local Museum) describes in fascinating detail the history of the making of the violin in Mittenwald. Ask the museum curator to direct you to the nearest of the several violin makers—they'll be happy to demonstrate the skills handed down to them. ✉ *Ballenhausg. 3,* ☎ *08823/2511.* €2.50. ⏲ *Mid-Dec.–Oct., Tues.–Fri. 10–1 and 3–6, weekends 10–1. Closed Nov.–mid-Dec.*

On the back of the altar in the 18th-century **St. Peter and St. Paul Church** (as in Oberammergau, built by Joseph Schmuzer and decorated by Matthäus Günther) you'll find Matthias Klotz's name, carved there by the violin maker himself. In front of the church, Klotz is memorialized as an artist at work in a vivid bronze sculpted by Ferdinand von Miller (1813–79), creator of the mighty Bavaria monument in Munich. The church, with its elaborate and joyful stuccowork coiling and curling its way around the interior, is one of the most important rococo structures in Bavaria. Note its Gothic choir loft, added in the 18th century. The bold frescoes on its exterior are characteristic of *Lüftlmalerei*, a style that reached its height in Mittenwald. Images, usually religious motifs, were painted on the wet stucco exteriors of houses and churches. On nearby streets you can see other fine examples on the facades of three famous houses: the Goethehaus, the Pilgerhaus, and the Pichlerhaus. Among the artists working here, was the great Franz Seraph Zwinck. ✉ *Ballenhausg., next to Geigenbau und Heimatmuseum.*

Dining and Lodging

$$$–$$$$ ✕ **Arnspitze.** Get a table at the large picture window and soak in the towering Karwendel Mountain range as you ponder a menu that combines the best traditional ingredients with international touches. Chef and owner Herbert Wipfelder looks beyond the edge of his plate all the way to Asia, if need be, to find inspiration. The fish pot-au-feu is Mediterranean in flavor and appearance; the jugged hare in red wine is truly Bavarian. Reservations are a good idea, as gourmands come here from far and wide. ✉ *Innsbrucker Str. 68,* ☎ *08823/2425. AE. Closed Tues. and Nov.–mid-Dec. No lunch Wed.*

$$ ✕ **Post.** Stagecoaches carrying travelers and mail across the Alps stopped here as far back as the 17th century. The hotel has changed a lot since then, but it still retains much of its historic charm. If you're having dinner, pause by the open fire in the cozy lounge-bar while you choose between the wine tavern and the low-beamed Postklause ($–$$). The food in each is excellent, with the emphasis on Bavarian fare such as roasts and great *Semmelknödel* (bread dumplings). ✉ *Obermarkt 9, D–82481,* ☎ *08823/938–2333,* FAX *08823/938–2999,* WEB *www.posthotel-mittenwald.de. 74 rooms, 7 suites. 2 restaurants, bar, no a/c, cable TV, in-room data ports, pool, sauna, Ping-Pong, pets allowed (fee), no-smoking rooms. MC, V.*

$–$$ ✕ **Alpenrose.** Once part of a monastery and later given a baroque facade, the Alpenrose is one of the area's handsomest hotels. The typical Bavarian bedrooms and public rooms have lots of wood paneling, farmhouse cupboards, and finely woven fabrics. The restaurant ($$–$$$$) devotes the entire month of October to venison dishes, for which it has become renowned. In winter the hotel organizes sleigh rides for its guests. A zither player strums away most evenings in the Josefi wine cellar. ✉ *Obermarkt 1, D–82481,* ☎ *08823/92700,* FAX *08823/3720. 16 rooms, 2 apartments. Restaurant, bar, no a/c, cable TV, Internet, sauna, pets allowed (fee). AE, DC, MC, V.*

$–$$ **Bichlerhof.** Carved oak furniture gives the rooms of this Alpine-style hotel a solid, German feel. Late-starters are catered to with a breakfast buffet, which is served until 11 AM and will keep the hardiest hiker going all day. Although the restaurant serves only breakfast, there's no shortage of taverns in the area. Most guest rooms have mountain views. ✉ *Adolf-Baader-Str. 5, D–82481,* ☎ *08823/9190,* FAX *08823/4584. 23 rooms, 2 suites. No a/c, cable TV, in-room data ports, pool,* *gym, sauna, steam room, pets allowed (fee), no-smoking rooms. AE, DC, MC, V.*

$ **Gasthof Stern.** The house is white, the shutters brilliant blue, the painted furniture is not antique, but reminiscent of old peasant Bavaria, the featherbeds are soft. The dining room serves very Bavarian dishes, and the beer garden is a pleasant, familial place to while away the hours and learn Bavarian with the locals. It's all in the middle of town. ✉ *Fritz-Plössl-Pl. 2, D–82481,* ☎ *08823/8358,* FAX *08823/94322. 5 rooms. Restaurant, beer garden, no a/c, no room phones, pets allowed. No credit cards.*

Outdoor Activities and Sports

Mittenwald lies literally in the shadow of the mighty **Karwendel** Alpine range, which rises to a height of nearly 8,000 ft. The **Dammkar** run is nearly 5 mi long, and offers some of the best free-riding skiing, telemarking, or snowboarding in the German Alps. A **cable car** (☎ 08823/8480; ⏲ Dec.–Oct., daily, 8:30–5) carries hikers and skiers to a height of 2,244 meters (7,180 ft), the beginning of numerous trails down, or further up into the Karwendel range (€11.50 one-way, €18 round-trip). You can book a guide with **Bergerlebnis und Wanderschule Oberes Isartal** (☎ 08651/5835). At least a half dozen operators offer countryside sleigh rides. Try **Reisebüro Artz** (✉ Bahnhofstr. 6, ☎ 08651/5070) or inquire at your hotel's reception desk.

Shopping

It's not the kind of gift every visitor wants to take home, but just in case you'd like a violin, cello, or even a double bass, the Alpine resort of Mittenwald can oblige. There are more than 30 craftsmen whose work is coveted by musicians throughout the world. If you're buying or even just curious, call on **Anton Maller** (✉ Professor-Schreyögg-Pl., ☎ 08823/5865). He's been making violins and other stringed instruments for more than 25 years. The **Geigenbau Leonhardt** (✉ Mühlenweg 53a, ☎ 08823/8010) is another good place to purchase one of the town's famous stringed instruments. For traditional Bavarian costumes—dirndls, embroidered shirts and blouses, and lederhosen—try **Trachten Werner** (✉ Hochstr. 1, ☎ 08823/3785). **Trachten Werner-Leichtl** (✉ Dekan-Karl-Pl. 1, ☎ 08823/8282) has a large selection of dirndls and other traditional wear for women.

En Route One of the most beautiful stretches of the Deutsche Alpenstrasse follows the course of the fast-flowing Isar River and is lined by fir-clad slopes and rocky peaks. The first 15 km (9 mi) of this stretch from Wallgau (7 km [4½ mi] north of Mittenwald at the junction of the road north to Benediktbeuren) to Vorderiss is a toll road (€2 per vehicle). Vorderiss is at the western end of the Sylvenstein dam-lake, a mysterious sliver of water whose dark surface covers a submerged village. Ghosts seem to linger in the cool air. Halfway along the lake the road divides, east to the Achen Pass and on to Tegernsee and north to the Alpine resort of Lenggries and Bad Tölz.

Walchensee

20 km (12 mi) north of Mittenwald, on the B–11 85 km (53 mi) south of Munich.

The first of the truly Alpine lakes the traveler encounters north of Mittenwald and Garmisch is the beautiful Walchensee, whose deep, blue waters are ringed by fir-clad mountains and the twin peaks of the Benediktenwand and Herzogstand. Many VIPs were attracted to the lake's shores, from the painter Lovis Corinth, to King Ludwig II of Bavaria. Hiking trails lead off from the town of Walchensee, and the rapidly changing winds of the Walchensee make this stretch of water a surfer's paradise. A chairlift climbs to the summit of the 5,300-ft-high **Herzogstand** (€11 round-trip).

Dining and Lodging

$ ✕ **Karwendelblick.** This large and friendly 1884 edifice stands on a promontory with a magnificent, sunny view of the Karwendel range and the lake. History buffs may be interested to know the place was built by Sir Georg Vollmar, one of the founding fathers of Social Democracy in Bavaria, and its walls saw such grand and radical figures as Karl Liebknecht and Rosa Luxemburg. The restaurant ($–$$) serves excellent Bavarian specialties and fish from the lake. ✉ *Urfeld 15, D–82432,* ☎ *08851/410,* FAX *08851/615–514. 3 rooms. Restaurant, no a/c, cable TV, in-room data ports, pets allowed. Restaurant closed Mon. No credit cards.*

Kochel

6 *35 km (22 mi) north of Mittenwald, on the B–11 60 km (37 mi) south of Munich.*

The serpentine mountain road leading to the spectacular **Kochelsee** was hammered out of the original path in 1492, when Mittenwald picked up the Venetian market. Duke Albrecht VI decided that the rest of the region should have access to the goods and benefits. The hero of the attractive little lakeside town of Kochel is the Schmied von Kochel, or Blacksmith of Kochel, one Balthasar Mayer. His fame stems from his role—and eventual death—in the 1705 peasants' uprising against the Austrians, who had occupied Bavaria in the wake of the Spanish War of Succession (1701–1704). You can see his statue in the town center. The lake is a longtime favorite for summer water sports and mountain walks.

The Kochelsee and the nearby, gentler, and less dramatic Staffelsee provided the inspiration for the bohemian artists who called themselves the *Blauer Reiter* (Blue Rider). Russian painters Wassily Kandinsky and Alfred Kubin and French artist Franz Marc founded the group in 1911 and were later joined by artists such as Paul Klee and August Macke. The best collection of Blauer Reiter works are in Munich, at the Städtische Galerie im Lenbachhaus. After living in various villages in Upper Bavaria, Marc, in 1914, purchased a house in Ried, north of Kochel. He had little time to enjoy it: In 1916 he became one of the millions to die in World War I. Kochel's **Museum Franz Marc** has a small but fine collection of more than 150 of his works. ✉ *Herzogstandweg 43,* ☎ *08851/7114.* *€3.* ⏲ *Apr.–Oct. and Dec. 25–mid-Jan., Tues.–Sun. 2–6.*

OFF THE BEATEN PATH

FREILICHTMUSEUM AN DER GLENTLEITEN – This open-air museum functions just as a Bavarian village did centuries ago, complete with cobbler, blacksmith, and other craftsmen who would have kept such a community self-sufficient. The houses were collected from around Bavaria and rebuilt here. Various items and foodstuffs are for sale in the original shops, but best of all, architectural purists can find all the elements that make up the authentic Alpine style. The museum is over a mile to the south of Grossweil, a little village known for its potters. ✉ *Grossweil, near Kochelsee, off Munich-Garmisch Autobahn,* ☎ *08851/1850,* WEB *www.glentleiten.de.* *€4.50.* ⏲ *Apr.–Oct., Tues.–Sun. 9–6.*

Dining and Lodging

$–$$ ✕🏨 **Seehotel Grauer Bär.** The friendly atmosphere at this hotel on the shore of the Kochelsee has much to do with the family that has owned and managed it since 1905. Ask for one of the spacious rooms overlooking the lake, where the hotel also has its own stretch of private beach. Lake fish entrées often appear on the extensive menu of the airy pavilion-style restaurant ($–$$), where you should try to book a table with a water view. ✉ *Mittenwalderstr. 82–86, D–82431,* ☎ *08851/92500,* FAX *08851/925–015,* WEB *www.grauer-baer.de. 26 rooms, 3 apartments. Restaurant, café, no a/c, cable TV, some in-room data ports, beach, boating, bicycles, pets allowed (fee). AE, DC, MC, V.*

$ ✕🏨 **Alpenhotel Schmied von Kochel.** Under the eaves of a steep roof, flower-box-hung balconies are framed by brightly painted frescoes. The state's blue-and-white-check banner hangs in the tree-shaded beer garden. Farmhouse furniture and antiques complete the scene, which is given a final musical touch by the zither player who strums away regularly in the snug tavern ($). ✉ *Schlehdorferstr. 6, D–82431,* ☎ *08851/9010,* FAX *08851/7331,* WEB *www.schmied-von-kochel.de. 30 rooms. Restaurant, café, beer garden, taproom, no a/c, cable TV, Internet, pets allowed (fee), no-smoking rooms. MC, V. Restaurant closed Mon.*

Outdoor Activities and Sports

Solid hiking boots, a parka of sorts, water, sunscreen, a walking stick, and about six–eight hours time is all you need to explore some of the local mountains. The Herzogstand and Jochberg hikes have refuges to duck into. Take the cable car up the **Herzogstand** (5,539 ft) and follow signs back to Walchensee on the path marked AV 441. The **Jochberg** (5,014 ft) can be accessed by bus from the Blacksmith statue in Kochel. You can get close to the Kesselberg pass, and hike along path number AV 451 to get back down to Kochel. The **Hirschhörndlkopf** (4,848 ft, AV 451 and 483a), and the Rabenkopf (4,677 ft, AV 452, then 451 and 454) hikes begin in Kochel at the Zimmermoos Bridge. The 5,400-ft-high **Benediktenwand,** east of Kochel, is a challenge for mountaineers.

On the shores of Kochelsee, the lido **Trimini** is one of the largest and most spectacular in Bavaria, with a collection of indoor and outdoor pools, water slides, and enough other amusements to keep a family busy the whole day. ✉ *Trimini,* ☎ *08851/5300.* 🎟 *3-hr ticket €6.50, all-day family ticket €21.50.* ⏲ *Daily 9–8:30.*

Murnau

16 km (10 mi) west of Kochel, following unmarked country road skirting northern shore of Staffelsee.

This pretty market town on the shore of Staffelsee is well worth a detour especially since traffic was at least partially banned from the center. Murnau attracted an artistic crowd early in the 20th century. Blauer Reiter group members Wassily Kandinsky and his German wife, Gabriele Münter, lived in Murnau for five years, and playwright Ödön von Horváth (1901–1938) also spent time here. The house Münter and Kandinsky inhabited drew artists from the painter Franz Marc to composer Arnold Schönberg. The **Münter Haus–das "Russenhaus"** (Russian House) provides an insight into the lives of the artist couple—including furniture that they decorated to their own highly individual, colorful tastes, and of course paintings. ✉ *Kottmüllerallee 6,* ☎ *08841/628–880.* 🎟 *€2.50.* ⏲ *Tues.–Sun. 2–5.*

The permanent collection at the **Schlossmuseum** (Castle Museum) is devoted to Münter, von Horváth, and reverse glass painting, which is used as decoration in many restaurants and hotels. ✉ *Schlosshof 4–5,* ☎ *08841/476–207,* WEB *www.schlossmuseum-murnau.de.* €3.50. ⏲ *Oct.–June, Tues.–Sun. 10–5; July–Sept., Tues.–Fri. 10–5, weekends 10–6.*

Dining and Lodging

$$$–$$$$ ✕🏨 **Alpenhof Murnau.** All the luxurious rooms at this handsome, Bavarian-style hotel enjoy views over meadows to the Alps beyond. They're furnished in rich dark woods and matching colors such as wine red and forest green. The elegant, softly lit restaurant ($$$–$$$$), with two rustically furnished rooms, boasts a Michelin star, and rightly claims to be one of the area's best. Window tables have sweeping Alpine views. ✉ *Ramsachstr. 8, D–82418 Murnau,* ☎ *08841/4910,* FAX *08841/5438,* WEB *www.alpenhof-murnau.com. 60 rooms, 17 suites. Restaurant, wine bar, no a/c in some rooms, cable TV, in-room data ports, pool, gym, sauna, steam room, pets allowed (fee), no-smoking rooms. AE, MC, V.*

Benediktbeuren

❼ *45 km (28 mi) north of Mittenwald, 52 km (32 mi) south of Munich.*

The village of Benediktbeuren has a great mid-8th-century **monastery** thought to be the oldest Benedictine institution north of the Alps. It was a flourishing cultural center in the Middle Ages; paradoxically, it also kept record of the most profane poems and songs of those times, the *carmina burana* (also known as the Goliardic songs). During the summer these songs are performed, using Bavarian composer Carl Orff's 1937 orchestration, in the monastery, where the original work was compiled in the 12th century. The frescoes of the monastery's 17th-century church were painted by the father of the Asam brothers, whose church building and artistic decoration made them famous far beyond the borders of Bavaria. Cosmas Damian Asam, the eldest son, was born in Benediktbeuren. The monastery has a delightful beer garden that fills to the brim with hikers and daytrippers in summer. ☎ *08857/880 for concert information.* €3. ⏲ *Monastery church daily 8–6; guided tour of monastery July–Sept., daily at 2:30; Oct.–mid-May, weekends at 2:30; mid-May–June, Wed. and Sat. at 2:30, Sun. at 10:30 and 2:30.*

Bad Tölz

❽ *16 km (10 mi) northeast of Benediktbeuren, 48 km (30 mi) south of Munich.*

If you can, visit Bad Tölz on a Wednesday morning—market day—when stalls stretch along the main street to the Isar River, the dividing line between the old and new towns. The latter, dating from the mid-19th century, sprang up with the discovery of iodine-laden springs, which allowed the locals to call their town *Bad* (bath or spa) Tölz. You can take the waters, either by drinking a cupful from the local springs or going all the way with a full course of health treatments at a specially equipped hotel.

Bad Tölz clings to its ancient customs more tightly than does any other Bavarian community. Folk costumes, for example, are worn regularly. The town is also famous for its painted furniture, particularly farmhouse cupboards and chests. Several local shops specialize in this *Bauernmöbel* (farmhouse furniture, usually hand-carved from pine) and will usually handle export formalities.

If you're in Bad Tölz on November 6, you'll witness one of the most colorful traditions of the Bavarian Alpine area: the Leonhardiritt equestrian procession, which marks the feast day of St. Leonhard, the patron saint of horses. The procession ends north of the town at an 18th-century chapel on the Kalvarienberg, above the Isar River.

★ The **Alpamare,** Bad Tölz's very attractive lido, pumps spa water into its pools, one of which is disguised as a South Sea beach, complete with surf. Its five water slides include a 1,082-ft-long adventure run. Another—the Alpa-Canyon—has 90° drops, and only the hardiest swimmers are advised to try it. A nightmarish dark tunnel is aptly named the Thriller. ✉ *Ludwigstr. 13,* ☎ *08041/509–334,* WEB *www.alpamare.de.* 🎫 *4-hr ticket €14 weekdays, €20 weekends and school holidays; between 9 AM and 11 AM and after 5 PM price drops by up to €7.* ⏲ *Mon.–Thurs. 9–9, Fri.–Sun. 9 AM–10 PM.*

The **Heimatmuseum,** in the Altes Rathaus (Old Town Hall), has many fine examples of Bauernmöbel, as well as a fascinating exhibit on the history of the town and its environs. ✉ *Marktstr. 48,* ☎ *08041/504–688.* 🎫 *€2.50.* ⏲ *Tues., Wed., and Fri. 10–noon and 2–4, Thurs. 10–noon and 2–6, Sat. 10–4, Sun. 10–6.*

Bad Tölz's local mountain, the **Blomberg,** 3 km (2 mi) west of town, has moderately difficult ski runs, and can also be tackled on a toboggan in winter and in summer. The winter run of 5 km (3 mi) is the longest in Bavaria, although the artificial, concrete channel used in summer snakes 3,938 ft down the mountain. A ski-lift ride to the start of the run and toboggan rental are included in the price. ☎ *08041/3726.* 🎫 *€7 per tobaggan ride.* ⏲ *Jan.–Nov., daily 9–4; Nov.–Dec., hrs depend on weather conditions.*

Dining and Lodging

$$$–$$$$ ★ ✕🏨 **Hotel Jodquellenhof-Alpamare.** The *Jodquellen* are the iodine springs that have made Bad Tölz wealthy. You can take advantage of these revitalizing waters at this luxurious spa, where the emphasis is on fitness. Vegetarian and low-calorie entrées are served in the restaurant ($$$–$$$$). The imposing 19th-century building, with private access to the Alpamare Lido, contains stylish rooms, with granite and marble bathrooms. The room price includes full use of the spa facilities. ✉ *Ludwigstr. 13–15, D–83646,* ☎ *08041/5090,* FAX *08041/509–441. 81 rooms. Restaurant, no a/c, cable TV, in-room data ports, pool, hot tubs, sauna, spa, steam room. AE, DC, MC, V.*

$$ 🏨 **Hotel Bellaria.** This beautifully restored 19th-century villa with baroque furnishings is just the place for romance. Its young owners will reserve the basement sauna and hot tub for evenings à deux, with a candelabra and bottle of champagne as part of the service. The spa park and pedestrian mall are right outside the door. ✉ *Ludwigstr. 22, D–83646,* ☎ *08041/80080,* FAX *08041/800–844,* WEB *www.villa-bellaria.de. 23 rooms. No a/c, cable TV, Internet, gym, hot tub, sauna, spa, pets allowed, no-smoking rooms. DC, MC, V.*

Nightlife and the Arts

Bad Tölz is world renowned for its outstanding **boys choir.** When it's not on tour, the choir gives regular concerts in the Kurhaus (program details available from the Städtische Kurverwaltung, ☎ 08041/78670). The town has four discos; **Arena** (✉ Demmeljochstr. 42) is considered the best.

Shopping

Looking for a typical piece of Bavarian farmhouse furniture to ship home? Bad Tölz and the surrounding villages provide a rich hunting ground. Try the **Scheune** (✉ Miesbacherstr. 33, ☎ 09041/83240), an old barn stacked high with pine and oaken cupboards, tables, chairs, and carved bedsteads.

Lenggries

❾ *10 km (6 mi) south of Bad Tölz, 12 km (7 mi) north of Sylvenstein Lake, 55 km (34 mi) south of Munich.*

Lenggries is a small but popular ski resort, wedged into a narrow valley between the towering Benediktenwand Mountain and the peaks of the Tegernsee Alps. There are fine walks into the Brauneck mountain range and along the Isar River, and the skiing is the best in the region.

Dining and Lodging

$$ ✕🏨 **Four Points by Sheraton Brauneck.** This leading Bavarian Alpine hotel does not disappoint. Many rooms have views of the mountains that ring Lenggries, and the lifts are a short walk from the hotel. Relax après-ski in the Isargrotte sauna-whirlpool. Good international cuisine is served in the stylish restaurant ($). ✉ *Münchner Str. 25, D–83661,* ☎ *08042/5020,* FAX *08042/4224,* WEB *www.sheraton.com. 102 rooms, 5 apartments. Restaurant, bar, no a/c, cable TV, some in-room data ports, room service, hot tub, sauna, steam room, bicycles, bowling, concierge, pets allowed (fee), no-smoking rooms. AE, DC, MC, V. Closed Easter and mid-July–mid-Aug.*

$ ✕🏨 **Altwirt.** The history of this former coaching inn stretches back to the 15th century. The house is under preservation order and is one of the sights to see in Lenggries. Its restaurant ($–$$) serves such regional specialties as venison with cranberry sauce and dumplings. Its rooms are neat and plain. ✉ *Marktstr. 13, D–83661,* ☎ *08042/8085,* FAX *08042/5357. 20 rooms. Restaurant, no a/c, cable TV, Internet, sauna, pets allowed (fee), no-smoking rooms. MC, V. Restaurant closed Mon.*

Tegernsee

★ ❿ *16 km (10 mi) east of Bad Tölz, 50 km (31 mi) south of Munich.*

The beautiful shores of the Tegernsee are among the most expensive properties in all Germany. So many wealthy Germans have their homes here that the locals dubbed it the Lago di Bonzo (*bonze* means "big shot," and the Italian word *lago* suggests an expensive Italian lake resort where the wealthy and well-connected rub elbows). Although many houses qualify as small palaces, most hotels have sensible rates. Tegernsee's wooded shores, rising gently to scalable mountain peaks of no more than 6,300 ft, invite hikers, walkers, and picnicking families (the tourist office in the town of Tegernsee has hiking maps). The lake itself draws swimmers and yachters. In fall the russet-clad trees provide a colorful contrast to the snowcapped mountains.

On the eastern shore of the lake, the town of Tegernsee is home to a medieval **Benedictine monastery** (✉ Schlosspl.). Founded in the 8th century, this was one of the most productive cultural centers in southern Germany; the Minnesänger (musician and poet) Walther von der Vogelweide (1170–1230) was a welcome guest. Not so welcome were Hungarian invaders, who laid waste to the monastery in the 10th century. Fire caused further damage in following centuries, and secularization sealed the monastery's fate at the beginning of the 19th, when Bavarian king Maximilian I bought the surviving buildings for use as a summer retreat.

The late-Gothic **church** was refurbished in Italian baroque style in the 18th century. The frescoes are by Hans Georg Asam, whose work also graces the Benediktbeuren monastery. The property houses a beer tavern, a brewery, a restaurant, and a high school. Students in what was the monastery write their exams beneath inspiring baroque frescoes.

Maximilian showed off this corner of his kingdom to Czar Alexander of Russia and Emperor Franz Josef of Austria during their journey to the Congress of Verona in October 1822, and you can follow their steps through the woods to one of the loveliest lookout points in Bavaria, the **Grosses Paraplui.** A plaque marks the spot where they admired the open expanse of the Tegernsee and the mountains beyond. The path starts opposite Schlossplatz and is well marked.

Rottach-Egern is the fashionable and upscale resort at the southern end of the lake. Its classy shops, chic restaurants, and expensive boutiques are as well stocked and interesting as many in Munich; its leading hotels are world-class. Rottach-Egern's church, **St. Laurentius,** has baroque influences.

Dining and Lodging

$–$$$$ ✕ **Freihaus Brenner.** Proprietor Josef Brenner has brought a taste of nouvelle cuisine to the Tegernsee and to the otherwise robust regional specialties. His attractive restaurant commands fine views from high above Bad Wiessee. Try any of his suggested dishes, ranging from wild rabbit in elderberry sauce to fresh lake fish. ✉ *Freihaushöhe 4, Bad Wiessee,* ☎ *08022/82004. MC, V.*

$–$$$ ✕ **Weinhaus Moschner.** You're pretty much expected to drink wine in this dark, old tavern on the edge of ritzy Rottach-Egern, though beer from the monastery brewery is also served. The menu is heavy on the sausage, but nobody comes here just to eat. Join the locals at a rough wooden table in the log-wall tavern taproom, order a plate of smoked pork and a glass of ale or Franconian wine, and leave the fine dining until tomorrow—it's the camaraderie and atmosphere here that counts. ✉ *Kisslingerstr. 2, Rottach-Egern,* ☎ *08022/5522. AE, MC, DC, V. Closed Mon.–Tues.*

$ ✕ **Herzogliches Bräustüberl.** Once part of Tegernsee's Benedictine monastery, then a royal retreat, the Bräustüberl is now an immensely popular beer hall and brewery. Only basic Bavarian snacks (sausages, pretzels, all the way up to steak tartare) are served in this crowded place, but hearty meals can be ordered in the adjoining Keller. In summer quaff your beer beneath the huge chestnuts and admire the scenery over the rim of your glass. ✉ *Schlosspl. 1, Tegernsee,* ☎ *08022/4141. Reservations not accepted. No credit cards. Closed Nov.*

$$$–$$$$ ✕🏨 **Bischoff am See.** The Leeberghof has reincarnated itself in a brand new hotel, right on the lake with its own pier. This top-of-the-line hideaway has eight suites, two of which have their own sauna, two with a steam shower, two with hot tubs and two with open fireplaces. The restaurant ($$$–$$$$; closed Monday, Tuesday) prepares international specialties and has 700 wines on its wine list. ✉ *Schweighofstr. 53, D–83684 Tegernsee,* ☎ *08022/3966,* FAX *08022/1720,* WEB *www.bischoff-am-see.de. 3 rooms, 8 suites. Restaurant, bar, cable TV with movies, no a/c in some rooms, pets allowed (fee), no-smoking rooms. MC, V.*

$$–$$$ ✕🏨 **Hotel Bayern.** The elegant, turreted Bayern and its two spacious annexes sit high above the Tegernsee, backed by the wooded slopes of Neureuth Mountain. Rooms overlooking the lake are in big demand despite their relatively high cost, so book early. All guests can enjoy panoramic views of the lake and mountains from the extensive terrace fronting the main building. You can dine in the hotel's stylish little restaurant ($$$–$$$$) or the cozy tavern. ✉ *Neureuthstr. 23, D–83684 Tegernsee,* ☎ *08022/1820,* FAX *08022/3775,* WEB *www.hotel-bayern.de.*

83 rooms, 4 suites. 2 restaurants, bar, no a/c, cable TV, in-room data ports, pool, hair salon, spa, bowling, pets allowed (fee), no-smoking rooms. AE, MC, V.

$$ ✕ **Seegarten.** This lakeside hotel, with pinewood wall paneling and matching furniture, has cheerful rooms in the bright primary colors typical of Bavarian country-farmhouse style. Ask for a room with a balcony overlooking the Tegernsee. The Seegarten's kitchen ($–$$) is famous for its cakes, made by the in-house pastry chef. In winter a log fire and hot, spiced wine welcome you in the cozy vestibule. ✉ *Adrian-Stoop-Str. 4, D–83707 Bad Wiessee,* ☎ *08022/98490,* FAX *08022/85087. 18 rooms. Restaurant, no a/c, cable TV, Internet, pets allowed. AE, MC, V.*

$–$$ ✕ **Seehotel Zur Post.** The lake views from most rooms are somewhat compromised by the main road outside, but a central location and a winter garden and terrace are pluses. The restaurant ($–$$), with a panoramic view of the mountains and the lake, serves fresh fish, but there are also special venison weeks, worthy of a long detour. ✉ *Seestr. 3, D–83684 Tegernsee,* ☎ *08022/3951,* FAX *08022/1699,* WEB *www.seehotel-zur-post.de. 43 rooms, 39 with bath or shower. Restaurant, no a/c, cable TV, pets allowed (fee), no-smoking rooms. DC, MC, V.*

$$$–$$$$ **Hotel Bachmair am See.** Set in parklike grounds between the lakeside and a mountain range, this luxurious complex of five hotels and guest houses is the place for a splurge. Prices are high, but the range and quality of the amenities are unmatched in this part of Bavaria. The hotel's nightclub attracts international entertainers. Teatime in the main building's elegant lounge, overlooking the lake, is a Savoy-style experience. Prices include a lunch or dinner at the hotel. ✉ *Seestr. 47, D–83700 Rottach-Egern,* ☎ *08022/2720,* FAX *08022/272–790,* WEB *www.bachmair.de. 100 rooms, 10 apartments. 4 restaurants, no a/c, cable TV, Internet, 2 tennis courts, pool, gym, hair salon, sauna, bicycles, squash, 2 bars, nightclub, pets allowed (fee). AE, DC, MC, V.*

Nightlife and the Arts

Every resort has its **spa orchestra**—in the summer they play daily in the music box–style bandstands that dot the lakeside promenades. A strong Tegernsee tradition is the summer-long program of **festivals,** some set deep in the forest. Tegernsee's lake festival in August, when sailing clubs deck their boats with garlands and lanterns, is an unforgettable experience.

Bad Wiessee has a lakeside **casino** (☎ 08022/82028) that's open daily 3 PM–2 AM and sets the tone for a surprisingly lively after-dark scene around the Tegernsee. The **Leeberghof** (✉ Schweighoferstr. 53, ☎ 08022/3966), on the lake shore in Tegernsee, has a sensational terrace bar with prices to match one of Bavaria's finest views.

Shopping

Bad Tölz and nearby villages are famous for the beauty and variety of their traditional dress. In Bad Tölz, follow the lovely Marktstrasse up from the river and watch for the outsize top hat at the corner of Hindenburgstrasse, at No. 61a Marktstrasse. Here you'll find all the region can offer—in the shop of Gregor and Maria Schöttl. **Trachten Brendl** (✉ Hauptstr. 8, Tegernsee, ☎ 08022/3322) has a colorful selection of Bavarian traditional costumes and other handwoven fabrics. At her workshop just outside Gmund, **Marianne Winter-Andres** (✉ Miesbacherstr. 88, Gmund, ☎ 08022/74643) creates a wide and attractive range of high-quality pottery at sensible prices.

OFF THE BEATEN PATH

WALLBERG – For the best vista in the area, climb this 5,700-ft mountain at the south end of the Tegernsee. It's a hard four-hour hike, though anyone in good shape should be able to make it since it involves no rock climbing. A cable car makes the ascent in just 15 minutes and costs €7.50 one-way, €13 round-trip. At the summit are a restaurant and sun terrace and several trailheads; in winter the skiing is excellent.

Schliersee

11 *20 km (12 mi) east of Tegernsee, 55 km (34 mi) southeast of Munich.*

Schliersee is smaller, quieter, and less fashionable than Tegernsee, but hardly less beautiful. The different histories of the two lakes is made clear in the names local people have long given them: the Tegernsee is *Herrensee* (Masters' Lake), while the Schliersee *Bauernsee* (Peasants' Lake), although today Schliersee is seen as being more for the well-heeled. There are walking and ski trails on the mountain slopes that ring its placid waters. The lake is shallow and often freezes over in winter, when the tiny island in its center is a favorite hiking destination.

Schliersee was the site of a monastery, built in the 8th century by a group of noblemen. It subsequently became a choral academy, which eventually moved to Munich. Today only the restored 17th-century **Schliersee church** in the middle of town recalls this piece of local history. The church has some frescoes and stuccowork by Johann Baptist Zimmermann.

Dining and Lodging

$–$$ ✕ **Zum Hofhaus am See.** What better place to enjoy a meal than in a small beer garden on the shore? The Hofhaus radiates a kind of friendly intimacy—even if the waitress doesn't crack a smile. Down-to-earth food is the order of the day, such as the hocks, or fresh forest mushrooms in cream with an herbed dumpling served in a stoneware bowl. Be aware: the fish is not from the lake. ✉ *Mesnerg. 2,* ☎ *08026/94499. No credit cards.*

$–$$ ✕🏨 **Hotel Gasthof Terofal.** This handsome, steep-eaved, flower-filled inn is in the center of Schliersee town. In the coziest rooms, carved and painted four-poster beds are part of the traditional Bavarian furnishings. The beamed tavern-restaurant ($–$$) serves excellent Bavarian fare, and there's nightly zither playing. Comedy performances take place regularly at the inn's own theater. ✉ *Xaver-Terofal-Pl. 2, D–83727,* ☎ *08026/4045,* FAX *08026/2676. 23 rooms. Restaurant, beer garden, no-smoking rooms, cable TV with movies, in-room data ports, no a/c, pets allowed (fee), theater. Closed mid-Jan.–mid-Feb. No credit cards.*

Shopping

If at the end of your Upper Bavarian tour you're still looking for *something,* stop at the busy market town of Miesbach (north of Schliersee) and climb the stairs to **Cilly's Gschirrladn** (✉ Stadtpl. 10, Miesbach, ☎ 08025/1705). A warren of rooms is stocked ceiling high with every variety of item for the home, from embroidered tablecloths to fine German porcelain.

Spitzingsee

12 *10 km (6 mi) south of Schliersee, 65 km (40 mi) southeast of Munich.*

Arguably the most beautiful of this group of Bavarian lakes, the Spitzingsee is cradled 3,500 ft up between the Taubenstein, Rosskopf, and Stumpfling peaks, and the drive there is spectacular. The lake is usually frozen over in winter and almost buried in snow. In summer the lake is warm enough for a swim. Walking in this area is breathtaking during every season and in every sense. The skiing is very good, too. The only downside is the overrun town of Spitzingsee, whose modern architecture violates almost every Golden Rule of aesthetics.

Dining and Lodging

$$$–$$$$ ✕🏨 **Arabella-Sheraton Alpenhotel.** For an out-of-the-way break in the mountains, head for this luxurious hotel on the shore of the Spitzingsee—even though its architecture is an eyesore. Rooms meet the high standards of comfort expected from the hotel chains that run the establishment. If you can't stay overnight, come for a leisurely lunch ($$–$$$) of lake fish or in-season venison. ✉ *Seeweg 7, D–83727,* ☎ *08026/7980,* FAX *08026/798–879,* WEB *www.arabellasheraton.de. 109 rooms, 13 suites. 2 restaurants, bar, no a/c, cable TV, some in-room data ports, pool, gym, sauna, steam room, 2 tennis courts, boating, bowling, library, pets allowed (fee), no-smoking rooms. AE, DC, MC, V.*

Bayrischzell

⓭ *10 km (6 mi) east of Schliersee, 65 km (40 mi) southeast of Munich.*

Bayrischzell is in an attractive family-resort area, where many a Bavarian first learned to ski. The wide-open slopes of the Sudelfeld Mountain are ideal for undemanding skiing; in summer and fall you can explore innumerable upland walking trails. Access to the Sudelfeld area costs €1.50 per car.

The town sits at the end of a wide valley overlooked by the 6,000-ft **Wendelstein** mountain, which draws expert skiers. At its summit is a tiny stone-and-slate-roof chapel that's much in demand for wedding ceremonies. The cross above the entrance was carried up the mountain by Max Kleiber, who designed the 19th-century church. An instructive **geopark** laid out beneath the summit explains the 250-million-year geological history of the area on 36 graphic signboards. You can reach the summit from two directions: by cable car,which sets out from Osterhofen on the Bayrischzell-Munich road and costs €16.50 round-trip, €9.50 one-way and by historic cog railway; catch it at Brannenburg, on the north side of the mountain, between Bayrischzell and the Inn Valley autobahn; a round-trip costs €22,50; it's closed November and the first three weeks of December. The cable car's last descent is at 4 PM, the cog railway closes for two weeks in mid-April.

Dining and Lodging

$–$$$$ ✕🏨 **Hotel Feuriger Tatzelwurm.** This archetypal old Bavarian inn (with a modern wing) is named after the nearby Tatzelwurm Gorge and is ideally placed for hikes or ski trips. The inn sits in isolated splendor above a forest pond, some 980 ft from the main Oberaudorf-Bayrischzell road. Bavarian dishes (also vegetarian) are served in the warren of paneled dining rooms ($–$$$$), one of which is dominated by a historic tile stove. The two-person *Jadgherrenplatte Brünnstein* will let you sample the game of the area (both people need to be ravenous to finish off this plate). ✉ *Am Tatzelwurm, D–82080 Oberaudorf/Bayrischzell,* ☎ *08034/30080,* FAX *08034/7170. 44 rooms. Restaurant, no a/c, cable TV, spa, bicycles, Ping-Pong, pets allowed (fee), no-smoking rooms. DC, MC, V.*

$–$$$ ✕🏨 **Wendelstein.** This large restaurant ($) in the middle of Bayrischzell fills up quickly on winter evenings. For warm summer days, there is always the beer garden. The generous portions come at reasonable prices. If you are not into slabs of meat, however, you can try some of the vegetarian dishes such as a schnitzel of celery. Rooms here are simple, but comfortable. ✉ *Ursprungstr. 1,* ☎ *08023/80890,* FAX *08023/808–969. 18 rooms. Restaurant, beer garden, no a/c, cable TV, Internet, pets allowed (fee), no-smoking rooms. AE, MC, V. Closed Nov.–mid-Dec. and Mon.*

En Route A few miles east of Bayrischzell on the Sudelfeld Road is the **Tatzelwurm** gorge and waterfall, named for a winged dragon who supposedly inhabits these parts. Dragon or no, this can be an eerie place to drive at dusk. A hiking trail is signposted. From the gorge the road drops sharply to the valley of the Inn River, leading to the busy ski resort of Oberaudorf.

The Inn River valley, an ancient trade route, carries the most important road link between Germany and Italy. The wide, green Inn gushes here, and in the parish church of St. Bartholomew, at **Rossholzen** (16 km [10 mi] north of Oberaudorf), you can see memorials and naively painted tributes to the local people who have lost their lives in its chilly waters. The church has a baroque altar incorporating vivid Gothic elements. A simple tavern adjacent to the church offers an ideal opportunity for a break on the Alpine Road.

Rosenheim

14 *34 km (21 mi) north of Bayrischzell, 55 km (34 mi) east of Munich.*

Bustling Rosenheim is a medieval market town that has kept much of its character despite the onslaught of industrial development. The arcaded streets of low-eaved houses are characteristic of Inn Valley towns. The lake Chiemsee is nearby, and the area has a handful of rural lakes of its own (Simssee, Hofstättersee, and Rinssee). Leisure activities and culture at lower prices than Munich have made the area very popular. The old restored locomotive shed, the **Lokschuppen** (⊠ Rathausstr. 24, ☎ 08031/365–9036) attracts crowds from as far away as Salzburg and Munich to its special exhibitions (mostly of art).

The Inn River was a major trade artery that bestowed a fair amount of wealth onto Rosenheim, especially in the Middle Ages. It not only served the purpose of transportation, but also created jobs thanks to fishing, shipping, bridge-building, shipbuilding, and the like. The **Inn Museum** tells the story of the river in many displays, covering geology to business. ⊠ *Innstr. 74,* ☎ *08031/31511.* €2. *May–Oct., Fri. 9–noon, weekends 10–4.*

Wood is the other big business around Rosenheim. **Das Holztechnische Museum** documents how it is grown and how it is used, for example in interior decoration, transportation, architecture, and art. ⊠ *Max-Josephs-Pl. 4,* ☎ *08031/16900.* €2. *Tues.–Sat. 9–1 and 2–5.*

Lodging

$$ **Panorama Cityhotel.** Rosenheim is not known for it's hotels, but it is a fairly important town that attracts a good deal of businesspeople. The Panorama is a modern, convenient hotel in the middle of town offering comfortable rooms that promise a pleasant, no-risk stay. It even has two nicely furnished apartments at reasonable rates. Note that prices rise during Oktoberfest (Rosenheim is only 45 minutes by train from Munich). ⊠ *Brixstr. 3, D–83022,* ☎ *08031/3060,* FAX *08031/306–415,* WEB *www.panoramacityhotel.de. 89 rooms, Bar, no a/c, cable TV with movies, in-room data ports, minibars, parking (fee), pets allowed, no-smoking rooms. AE, DC, MC, V.*

Chiemsee

15 *20 km (12 mi) east of Rosenheim, 80 km (50 mi) east of Munich.*

Chiemsee is north of the Deutsche Alpenstrasse, but it demands a detour, if only to visit King Ludwig's huge palace on one of its idyllic islands. It's the largest Bavarian lake, and although it's surrounded by reedy flatlands, the nearby mountains provide a majestic backdrop. The town of **Prien** is the lake's principal resort. The tourist offices of Prien and Aschau have a €18 transportation package covering a boat trip, a round-trip rail ticket between the two resorts, and a round-trip ride by cable car to the top of Kampen Mountain, above Aschau.

Despite its distance from Munich, the beautiful Chiemsee drew Bavarian royalty to its shores. Its dreamlike, melancholy air caught the imagination of King Ludwig II, and it was on one of the lake's three islands that he built his third and last castle, sumptuous **Schloss Herrenchiemsee.** The palace took after Louis XIV's great one at Versailles, but this was due to more than simple admiration: Ludwig, whose name was the German equivalent of Louis, was keen to establish that he, too, possessed the absolute authority of his namesake, the Sun King. As with most of Ludwig's projects, the building was never completed, and Ludwig only spent nine days in the castle. Moreover, Herrenchiemsee broke the state coffers and Ludwig's private ones as well. The gold leaf that seems to cover over half of the rooms is especially thin. Nonetheless, what remains is impressive—and ostentatious. Regular ferries out to the island depart from Stock, Prien's harbor. If you want to make the journey in style, board the original 1887 steam train from Prien to Stock to pick up the ferry. A horse-drawn carriage takes you to the palace itself.

Most spectacular is the Hall of Mirrors, a dazzling gallery where candlelighted concerts are held in summer. Also of interest are the ornate bedrooms Ludwig planned, the "self-rising" table that ascended set from the kitchen quarters, the elaborately painted bathroom with a small pool for a tub, and the formal gardens. The south wing houses a **museum** containing Ludwig's christening robe and death mask, as well as other artifacts of his life. While the palace was being built, Ludwig stayed in a royal suite of apartments in a former monastery building on the island, the Altes Schloss. Germany's postwar constitution was drawn up here in 1948, and this episode of the country's history is the centerpiece of the museum housed in the ancient building, the **Museum im Alten Schloss** (🎫 €1.50). ☎ *Palace 08051/68870.* 🎫 *Palace €4, museum €2, combined ticket with Museum im Alten Schloss €5.50 (Apr.–Sept.) or €5 (Oct.–Mar.).* ⏲ *Apr.–Sept., daily 9–6; Oct.–Mar., daily 10–4; English-language palace tours, daily 11:45 and 2:25.*

Boats on the way between Stock and Herrenchiemsee Island also call at the small retreat of **Fraueninsel** (Ladies' Island). The **Benedictine convent** there, founded 1,200 years ago, now serves as a school. One of its earliest abbesses, Irmengard, daughter of King Ludwig der Deutsche, died here in the 9th century. Her grave in the convent chapel was discovered in 1961, the same year that early frescoes there were brought to light. The chapel is open daily from dawn to dusk. Otherwise, the island has just a few private houses, a couple of shops, and a hotel.

OFF THE BEATEN PATH

AMERANG – Just north of Bad Endorf, Amerang has two interesting museums. In the **Museum für Deutsche Automobilgeschichte** (Museum of German Automobile History), 220 automobiles begin with an 1886 Benz and culminate in contemporary models. The world's largest small-gauge model railway panorama is spread out over nearly 6,000 square ft. ✉ *Wasserburger Str. 38,* ☎ *08075/8141,* WEB *www.efa-automuseum.de.* 🎫 *€6.50.* ⏲ *Tues.–Sun. 10–6.*

The **Bauernhofmuseum** (Farm Museum) consists of four beautiful farm houses with a bakery, bee hives, saw mill, and blacksmith's workshop. It's worth seeing to find out more about everyday life in the Chiemgau. Every Sunday afternoon an 85-year-old roper shows off his craft, as does a lacemaker. On alternate Sundays, spinning and feltmaking, and blacksmithing are demonstrated. You can take in the idyllic surroundings from the beer garden. ✉ *Im Hopfengarten,* ☎ *08075/915–090.* 🎫 *€3.* ⏲ *Mid-Mar.–mid-Nov., Tues.–Sun. 9–6, last admission at 5.*

Dining and Lodging

$–$$$ ✕ **Wirth von Amerang.** Theme restaurants are an up and coming business in Bavaria and the Wirth is at the spearhead. The interior design comes very close to medieval, with brick stoves of handmade bricks, dripping candles, and a floor resembling packed clay. The food is definitely Bavarian, with *Knödels* (dumplings) and pork roast, hocks and a top-notch potato soup. Reservations are recommended. You may want to purchase the pumpkinseed oil or a home-made schnapps. ✉ *Postweg 4, Amerang,* ☎ *08075/185–918. No credit cards. No lunch Nov.–Mar.*

$$ ✕🏨 **Inselhotel zur Linde.** Catch a boat to this enchanting inn on the car-free Fraueninsel: but remember, if you miss the last connection to the mainland (at 9 PM), you'll have to stay the night. The island is by and large a credit-card-free zone, so be sure to bring cash. Rooms are simply furnished and decorated with brightly colored fabrics. The Linde is one of Bavaria's oldest hotels, founded 600 years ago as a refuge for pilgrims. Artists have favored the inn for years, and one of the tables in the small Fischerstüberl dining room ($–$$) is reserved for them. ✉ *Fraueninsel im Chiemsee 1, D–83256,* ☎ *08054/90366,* FAX *08054/7299. 14 rooms. Restaurant, bar, no a/c, Internet. MC, V. Closed mid-Jan.–mid-Mar.*

$–$$ ✕🏨 **Hotel Luitpold am See.** Boats to the Chiemsee islands tie up right outside your window at this handsome old Prien hotel, which organizes shipboard disco evenings as part of its entertainment program. Rooms have traditional pinewood furniture, including carved cupboards and bedsteads. Fish from the lake are served at the pleasant restaurant ($–$$). ✉ *Seestr. 110, D–83209 Prien am Chiemsee,* ☎ *08051/609–100,* FAX *08051/609–175,* WEB *www.luitpold-am-see.de. 51 rooms. Restaurant, café, no a/c, cable TV, Internet, pets allowed (fee), no-smoking rooms. AE, DC, MC, V.*

$ ✕🏨 **Schlosshotel Herrenchiemsee.** This handsome mansion on the island of Herrenchiemsee predates King Ludwig's palace, which is a 15-minute walk away through the woods. The rooms aren't palatial but are nonetheless comfortable. A big plus is the pavilionlike restaurant ($–$$), serving fresh fish. If you're here to eat, make sure to catch the last boat to the mainland (9 PM)—otherwise you'll get a good night's sleep on this traffic-free island. ✉ *Herrenchiemsee, D–83209,* ☎ *08051/1509,* FAX *08051/1509. 12 rooms, 6 with bath or shower. Restaurant, no a/c, no room phones, pets allowed. AE, DC, MC, V. Hotel closed Oct.–Easter.*

Outdoor Activities and Sports

There are boatyards all around the lake and several windsurfing schools. The **Mistral-Windsurfing-Center,** at Gdstadt (✉ Waldstr. 20, ☎ 08054/909–906), has been in operation for decades. From its boatyard the average windsurfer can make it with ease to the next island. The gentle hills of the region are ideal for golf. **Golfanlage Bauernberg** (☎ 08051/62215) in Prien has a year-round, 9-hole course.

Aschau

16 *10 km (6 mi) south of Chiemsee, 75 km (46 mi) east of Munich.*

Aschau is an enchanting red-roof village nestling in a wide valley of the Chiemgauer Alps. Its **Schloss Hohenaschau** is one of the few medieval castles in southern Germany to have been restored in the 17th century in baroque style. Chamber-music concerts are presented regularly in the Rittersaal (Knights Hall) during the summer. Parts of the castle can be visited—the rest of the rooms are used as a vacation home for Germany's federal tax officials! The **Prientalmuseum** (Museum of the Prien Valley) with historical documents on the region is in the former deacon's house. ☎ *08052/904–937.* 🎫 *Castle €3; museum €2.* ⏲ *May–Sept., Tues.–Fri. tours at 9:30, 10:30, and 11:30; Apr. and Oct., Thurs. 9:30, 10:30, and 11:30; museum open during tour times and Sun. 1:30–5.*

Dining and Lodging

$$$–$$$$ ★ ✕🏨 **Residenz Heinz Winkler.** Star chef Heinz Winkler has turned a sturdy village inn into one of Germany's most extraordinary hotel-restaurant complexes. Rooms in the main house are noble in proportions and furnishings, and the maisonette-style suites in the annexes are cozily romantic. All have views of the mountains. The restaurant ($$$$) has kept with ease the three Michelin stars that Winkler won when in charge of Munich's Tantris. A grand piano and a harp add their own notes of harmony to this deliciously sophisticated scene. ✉ *Kirchpl. 1,* ☎ *08052/17990,* FAX *08052/179–966,* WEB *www.residenz-heinz-winkler.de. 22 rooms. Restaurant, bar, no a/c, cable TV, in-room data ports, pool, sauna, spa, steam room, pets allowed (fee). AE, DC, MC, V.*

$–$$ 🏨 **Hotel Bonnschlössl.** This turreted country palace is set in its own park studded with centuries-old trees. In good weather breakfast is served on the balustraded terrace. The hotel is 6 km (4 mi) north of Aschau, and has a similarly enchanting sister property in the nearby village of Bernau, the Gasthof Alter Wirt, and apartments for rent. Both the Schloss and the Gasthof are protected by preservation orders. Emperor Maximilian I stayed overnight at the Gasthof in 1504 on his way to besiege the castle of Marquartstein. ✉ *Kirchpl. 9, D–83233 Bernau,* ☎ *08051/89011,* FAX *08051/89103,* WEB *www.alter-wirt-bernau.de. 41 rooms. Restaurant, Weinstube, beer garden, no a/c, cable TV, sauna, spa, pets allowed, no-smoking rooms. MC, V. Closed Mon.*

En Route At Aschau you'll join the most scenic section of the Deutsche Alpenstrasse as it passes through a string of villages—Bernau, Rottau, Grassau, Marquartstein, and Oberwössen. In summer the farmhouses of Rottau nearly disappear behind facades of flowers. The houses of Grassau shrink beside the bulk of the 15th-century Church of the Ascension, worth visiting for its rich 17th-century stuccowork. For those interested in technical things, stop at the **Klaushäusl** (☎ 08641/5467; ⏲ May–Oct., Tues.–Sat 2–5, Sun. 10–5; 🎫 €2), between Rottau and Grassau. The little stone house is home to one of the many pumps that used to carry brine from Berchtesgaden and Bad Reichenhall all the way to Rosenheim. It operated from 1810 to 1957.

Reit im Winkl

17 *16 km (10 mi) south of Chiemsee, 100 km (62 mi) east of Munich.*

Reit im Winkl has produced at least two German ski champions, who trained on the demanding runs high above the village. The intensity of the tourism here means crowds and the usual automobile traffic. Many of the quickly built houses are often disproportionately large and though meant to be "Alpine," they somehow don't quite cut it. A nice way to tour town is by **horse-drawn cart** (☎ 08641/5657 or 0171/698–0504) or sled in winter. The ski area **Winklmoosalm Mountain** can be reached by bus or chairlift, and it's a great place for bracing upland walks in summer and fall.

The **Heimatmuseum** (Museum of Local History, also called *Hausenhäusl*) is one of Reit im Winkl's last intact "small houses" in which people lived and worked in the mountains. It exhibits a weaver's and a shoemaker's workshop, and has reconstructed the living space of a typical family of so-called *Kleinhäusler* (literally, small house residents). ✉ *Weitseestr. 10,* ☎ *08640/80020.* 🎫 *€1.50.* ⏲ *June–Sept. 2–4.*

Dining and Lodging

$–$$ ✕ **Kupferkanne.** Outside, a garden surrounds the building; inside, you could be in an Alpine farmstead. The food is good country fare enhanced by Austrian specialties and spicy concoctions from the Balkans. Try the *Salzburger Brez'n,* a thick, creamy bread-based soup. ✉ *Weitseestr. 18,* ☎ *08640/1450. No credit cards. Closed Sat. and Nov.*

$–$$ ✕🏨 **Landgasthof Rosi Mittermaier.** Rosi Mittermaier, skiing star of the 1976 Innsbruck Olympics, owns this charming Gasthof with her husband, Christian Neureuther, a champion skier himself. On their frequent visits to the inn, they're always ready with advice about the ski runs or mountain trails. It's essential to book in advance. In the rustic Café Olympia or cozy, pine-paneled tavern-restaurant ($–$$) duck dishes are the specialty, and the *Käsekuchen* (cheesecake) is legendary. ✉ *Chiemseestr. 2a, D–83242,* ☎ *08640/1011,* FAX *08640/1013. 8 rooms. Restaurant, café, cable TV, some in-room data ports, sauna, pets allowed (fee), no-smoking rooms. No credit cards.*

En Route Between Reit im Winkl and Ruhpolding is the **Holzknechtmuseum** (Forester Museum), devoted to the sylvan lives and tribulations of the forest workers. The parklike grounds show how skilled these fellows were with their axes and saws, and how they arranged their working lives outdoors: the huge hand-built waterwheel that drove a pump is particularly impressive. ✉ *Laubau,* ☎ *08663/639.* 🎫 *€3.* ⏲ *Tues.–Sat. 1–5.*

Ruhpolding

⓲ *24 km (15 mi) east of Reit im Winkl, 125 km (77 mi) east of Munich.*

The Bavarian tourist boom began in this resort back in the 1930s. In those days tourists were greeted at the train station by a brass band. In the 16th century the Bavarian rulers journeyed to Ruhpolding to hunt, and the Renaissance-style hunting lodge of Prince Wilhelm V still stands (it's now used as the offices of the local forestry service). The hilltop 18th-century **Pfarrkirche St. Georg** (Parish Church of St. George) is one of the finest baroque and rococo churches in the Bavarian Alps and has a magnificent view of the town. In one of its side altars stands a rare 13th-century carving, the Ruhpoldinger Madonna. Note also the crypt chapel in the quiet churchyard.

Youngsters are encouraged to play with many of the fine exhibits at the **Ruhpoldinger Modellbahnschau** (Model Railway Museum), which has a small-gauge track. There's a high-tech Märklin panorama with nearly 200 ft of track and roads with moving cars and trucks. This is the model railway raised to high art. The most recent exhibit is the 20-ft "winter mountains" landscape. ✉ *Schulg. 4,* ☎ *08663/5613.* 🎫 *€4.* ⏲ *Weekends 9:30–5:30.*

OFF THE BEATEN PATH **BRAND** – In this village just north of Ruhpolding, you can visit a 300-year-old bell foundry, now a fascinating museum of the ancient crafts of the foundry man and blacksmith. In the Middle Ages, thanks to local iron ore and water power, no fewer than 40 smithies plied their trade here, making everything from church bells to goat bells. Tyrenia Ullrich, who watches over the museum, is the daughter of the last smith to work here. The museum is signposted from the main road. A half-hour hike through the forest is needed to reach the place. ☎ *08663/2309.* 🎫 *€3.* ⏲ *Mid-May–June and mid-Sept.–mid-Oct., weekdays 10–noon and 2–4; July–mid-Sept., weekdays 10–4.*

Dining and Lodging

$–$$$$ ✕🏨 **Hotel zur Post.** A Zur Post sign in any Bavarian town or village indicates where you'll find good local fare ($–$$). In business for more than 650 years, Ruhpolding's inn has been in the hands of the same family for 150 years. Call in advance for room reservations. Off-season, the hotel has excellent deals that include discounts on greens fees for the local golf course, entrance to the wellness spa, a ride on the cable car, and a meal a day in addition to breakfast. ✉ *Hauptstr. 35, D–83324,* ☎ *08663/5430,* FAX *08663/1483. 56 rooms, 19 apartments. Restaurant, no a/c, cable TV, pets allowed (fee). MC, V. Closed Wed.*

Bad Reichenhall

⑲ *30 km (19 mi) east of Ruhpolding, 20 km (12 mi) west of Salzburg.*

Bad Reichenhall shares a remote corner of Bavaria, almost surrounded by the Austrian border, with another prominent resort, Berchtesgaden. Although the latter is more famous, Bad Reichenhall is older, with saline springs that made the town rich. Salt is so much a part of the town that you can practically taste it in the air. Europe's largest source of brine was first tapped in pre-Christian times; salt mining during the Middle Ages supported the economies of cities as far away as Munich and Passau. Tourism gave the local economy an additional boost and another use for the salt, namely as medication for the lungs and to help general well-being. Beauty, wellness, health, rest and recovery . . . just some of the topics associated with this small but effective town. In the early 19th century King Ludwig I built an elaborate saltworks and spa house—the **Alte Saline and Quellenhaus**—in vaulted, pseudomedieval style. Their pump installations are astonishing examples of 19th-century engineering. A "saline" **chapel** is part of the spa's facilities and was built in exotic Byzantine style. An interesting museum in the same complex looks at the history of the salt trade. The Alte Saline also houses a **glass foundry** (☎ 08651/69738, WEB www.glashuettebgl; 🎫 free; ⏲ weekdays 9:30–6, Sat. 9–1) run by the famous company Riedl, makers of fine tableware. Glassblowers and engravers display their art, and children can try their mouths, so to speak, at glassblowing. The showroom has many articles for sale. ✉ *Salinen Str.,* ☎ *08651/700–2146,* WEB *www.suedsalz.de.* 🎫 *€5; combined ticket with Berchtesgaden salt mine €13.50.* ⏲ *May–Oct., daily 10–11:30 and 2–4; Nov.–Apr., Tues. and Thurs. 2–4.*

Hotels here base spa treatments on the health-giving properties of the saline springs and the black mud from the area's waterlogged moors. Breathing salt-laden air is a remedy for various lung conditions. The waters can also be taken in the elegant, pillared **Wandelhalle** pavilion of the attractive spa gardens throughout the year. ✉ *Salzburgerstr..* ⏲ *Mon.–Sat. 8–12:30 and 3–5, Sun. 10–12:30.*

The ancient church **St. Zeno** is dedicated to the patron saint of those imperiled by floods and the dangers of the deep, an ironic note in a town that flourishes on the riches of its underground springs. This 12th-century basilica, one of the largest in Bavaria, was remodeled in the 16th and 17th centuries, but some of the original Romanesque cloisters remain, although these can only be seen during services and from 11 to noon on Sunday and holidays. ✉ *Kirchpl. 1,* ☎ *08651/4889.*

Dining and Lodging

$$–$$$$ ✕🏨 **Steigenberger-Hotel Axelmannstein.** Ludwig would have enjoyed the palatial air that pervades this hotel—and he would have been able to afford the price, which rivals that of top hotels in Germany's most expensive cities but does include a meal. Luxurious comfort is found in rooms ranging in style from Bavarian rustic to Laura Ashley demure. The fine restaurant ($$$) attracts discerning Austrian visitors from across the nearby border. Outside is a manicured park and the town center. ✉ *Salzburgerstr. 2–6, D–83435,* ☎ *08651/7770,* FAX *08651/5932,* WEB *www.bad-reichenhall.steigenberger.de. 143 rooms, 8 suites. 2 restaurants, bar, no a/c, cable TV, tennis court, pool, gym, hair salon, sauna, spa, bowling, baby-sitting, pets allowed (fee), no-smoking rooms. AE, DC, MC, V.*

$$–$$$ ★ ✕🏨 **Parkhotel Luisenbad.** If you fancy spoiling yourself in a typical German fin-de-siècle spa hotel, this is *the* place—a fine porticoed and pillared building whose imposing pastel-pink facade holds the promise of luxury. Rooms are large, furnished in deep-cushioned, dark-wood comfort, most with flower-filled balconies or loggias. The elegant restaurant ($$–$$$) serves international and traditional Bavarian cuisines, and a pine-paneled tavern, Die Holzstubn'n, pours excellent local brew. ✉ *Ludwigstr. 33, D–83435,* ☎ *08651/6040,* FAX *08651/62928,* WEB *www.parkhotel.de. 75 rooms, 8 suites. Restaurant, bar, beer garden, no a/c, cable TV, Internet, pool, gym, hot tub, sauna, bicycles, recreation room, pets allowed (fee). DC, MC, V.*

$–$$ ★ 🏨 **Pension Hubertus.** This delightfully traditional family-run lodging stands on the shore of the tiny Thumsee, 5 km (3 mi) from the town center. The Hubertus's private grounds lead down to the lake, where guests can swim or boat (the water is bracingly cool). Rooms are Bavarian rustic in style and furnished with hand-carved beds and cupboards. Ask for one with a balcony overlooking the lake. You can also breakfast in the glassed-in winter garden. There are special rates in the off-season (October–April). ✉ *Am Thumsee 5, D–83435,* ☎ *08651/2252,* FAX *08651/63845. 18 rooms. No a/c, cable TV, no phones in some rooms, gym, boating, paddle tennis, some pets allowed (fee), no-smoking rooms. AE, MC, V, DC.*

$–$$ 🏨 **Villa Erika.** This four-story villa painted a staid red, has been family-run since 1898, and it shows in the best sense. Everything radiates comfort, from the light-filled dining room to the generous garden that supplies the kitchen. Owner Anton Oberarzbacher cooks the dinner menus (€12) himself, tapping from a repertoire that includes French and Italian cuisine. ✉ *Adolf-Schmid-Str. 3, D–83435 Bad Reichenhall,* ☎ *08651/95360,* FAX *08651/953–6200,* WEB *www.bad-reichenhall.de/hotels/erika. 33 rooms. Restaurant, no a/c, cable TV, in-room data ports, pets allowed. AE, MC, V. Closed Nov.–Feb. Restaurant closed Sun.*

Nightlife and the Arts

Bad Reichenhall is proud of its long musical tradition and of its orchestra, founded more than a century ago. It performs six days a week throughout the year in the chandelier-hung Kurgastzentrum Theater or, when weather permits, in the open-air pavilion, and at a special Mozart Week in March. Call the **Orchesterbüro** (☎ 08651/8661) for program details. As a spa town and winter resort, Bad Reichenhall is a natural for night haunts. The big draw is the elegant **casino** (✉ Wittelsbacherstr. 17, ☎ 08651/95800), open daily 3 PM–1 or 2 AM depending on business.

Shopping

Using flowers and herbs grown in the Bavarian Alps, the **Josef Mack** company (✉ Ludwigstr. 36., ☎ 08651/78280) has made medicinal herbal preparations since 1856. **Leuthenmayr** (✉ Ludwigstr. 27, ☎ 08651/2869) is a youngster in the business, selling its "cure-all" dwarf-pine oil since 1908. Candle-making is a local specialty, and the **Kerzenwelt Donabauer** (✉ Reichenhaller Str. 15, Piding, ☎ 08651/8143), just outside Bad Reichenhall, has a selection of more than 1,000 decorative items in wax. It has also a free wax museum depicting fairy-tale characters.

Berchtesgaden

⓴ *18 km (11 mi) south of Bad Reichenhall, 20 km (12 mi) south of Salzburg.*

Berchtesgaden's reputation is unjustly rooted in its brief association with Adolf Hitler, who dreamed besottedly of his "1,000-year Reich" from the mountaintop where millions of tourists before and after him drank in only the superb beauty of the Alpine panorama. Below those giddy heights of his retreat is a historic old market town and mountain resort of great charm. Although as a high-altitude ski station it may not have quite the cachet of Garmisch-Partenkirchen, in summer it serves as one of the region's most popular (and crowded) resorts, where an ornate palace and working salt mine make up some of the diversions in this heavenly setting.

Salt—or "white gold," as it was known in medieval times—was the basis of Berchtesgaden's wealth. In the 12th century Emperor Barbarossa gave mining rights to a Benedictine abbey that had been founded here a century earlier. The abbey was secularized early in the 19th century, when it was taken over by the Wittelsbach rulers, who began coming here in 1810.

The last royal resident of the Berchtesgaden abbey, Crown Prince Rupprecht, died here in 1955, and furnished it with rare family treasures that now form the basis of a permanent collection—the **Königliches Schloss Berchtesgaden Museum.** Fine Renaissance rooms exhibit the prince's sacred art, which is particularly rich in wood sculptures by such great late-Gothic artists as Tilman Riemenschneider and Veit Stoss. You can also visit the abbey's original, cavernous 13th-century dormitory and cool cloisters. ✉ *Schlosspl. 2,* ☎ *08652/2085,* WEB *www.haus-bayern.com.* 🎫 *€7 with tour.* ⏲ *Easter–Sept., Sun.–Fri. 10–1 and 2–5; Oct.–Easter, weekdays 10–1 and 2–5; last admission and tour at 4.*

The **Heimatmuseum,** in the Schloss Adelsheim, displays examples of wood carving and other local crafts. Wood carving in Berchtesgaden dates to long before Oberammergau established itself as the premier wood-carving center of the Alps. ✉ *Schroffenbergallee 6,* ☎ *08652/4410.* 🎫 *€2.* ⏲ *Tues.–Sun. 10–6, guided tours at 3.*

★ The **Salzbergwerk** (salt mine) is one of the chief attractions of the entire region. In the days when the mine was owned by Berchtesgaden's princely rulers, only select guests were allowed to see how the source of the city's wealth was extracted from the earth. Today, during a 90-minute tour, you can sit astride a miniature train that transports you nearly 1 km (½ mi) into the mountain to an enormous chamber where the salt is mined. Included in the tour are rides down the wooden chutes used by miners to get from one level to another, and a boat ride on an underground saline lake the size of a football field. ✉ *2 km (1 mi) from center of Berchtesgaden on B–305 Salzburg Rd.,* ☎ *08652/60020,* WEB *www.salzbergwerk-berchtesgaden.de.* 🎟 *€12; combined ticket with Bad Reichenhall's saline museum: €14.* ⏲ *May–mid-Oct., daily 9–5; mid-Oct.–Apr., Mon.–Sat. 12:30–3:30.*

21 The **Obersalzberg,** site of Hitler's luxurious mountain retreat, is part of the north slope of the Hoher Goll, high above Berchtesgaden. It was a remote mountain community of farmers and foresters before Hitler's deputy, Martin Bormann, selected the site for a complex of Alpine homes for top Nazi leaders. Hitler's chalet, the Berghof, and all the others were destroyed in 1945, with the exception of a hotel that had been taken over by the Nazis, the Hotel zum Türken. Beneath the hotel is a section of the labyrinth of tunnels built as a last retreat for Hitler and his cronies, and the macabre, murky **bunkers** can be visited (🎟 €2.50; ⏲ May–Oct., Tues.–Sun. 9–5; Nov.–Apr., Tues.–Sun. 10–3). Nearby, a **museum** (✉ Dokumentation Obersalzberg, Salzbergstr. 41, ☎ 08652/947–960, WEB www.obersalzberg.de; 🎟 €2.50; ⏲ Apr.–Oct., Tues.–Sun. 9–5; Nov.–Mar., Tues.–Sun. 10–3) documents the Third Reich's history in the region. Beyond Obersalzberg, the hairpin bends of Germany's highest road come to the base of the 6,000-ft peak on which sits the **Kehlsteinhaus** (☎ 08652/2969), the erstwhile Adlerhorst (Eagle's Nest), Hitler's personal retreat and his official guest house. It was a Martin Bormann's gift to the führer on Hitler's 50th birthday. The road leading to it, built in 1937–39, climbs more than 2,000 dizzying ft in less than 6 km (4 mi). A tunnel in the mountain will bring you to an elevator that whisks you up to what appears to be the top of the world (you can walk up in about half an hour). There are refreshment rooms and a restaurant. The round-trip from Berchtesgaden's post office by bus and elevator costs €12 per person. The bus runs mid-May through September, daily from 9 to 4:50. By car you can travel only as far as the Obersalzberg bus station. From there the round-trip fare is €10. The full round-trip takes one hour. From July through September the tourist office organizes Eagle's Nest by Night tours, including a cocktail and three-course dinner accompanied by live Bavarian music.

Dining and Lodging

$–$$ ✕ **Fischer.** You can pop into this farmhouse-style eatery for Apfelstrudel and coffee or for a simple meal from a menu that includes local specialties, such as sausage or cheese platters, salads, or more substantial dishes with dumplings, and light Mediterranean fare, mostly fish or noodles. It's a short walk across the bridge from the railway station. ✉ *Königseerstr. 51,* ☎ *08652/9550. MC, V. Closed Nov.–mid-Dec. and several wks after Easter*

$–$$ ✕ **Hotel Post.** This central and reliable hostelry offers for the most part fine Bavarian food, with some lighter Italian fare—pastas, salmon, flounder—for anyone needing a break from the hocks and pork roast. If trout from the nearby Königsee is available, order it. In summer you can eat in the beer garden. ✉ *Maximilianstr. 2,* ☎ *08652/5067. MC, V.*

$$ ✕🏨 **Alpenhotel Denninglehen.** Nonsmokers appreciate the special dining room set aside just for them in this mountain hotel's restaurant. The house was built in 1981 in Alpine style, with lots of wood paneling, heavy beams, wide balconies with cascades of geraniums in summer. Skiers enjoy the fact that the slopes are about 200 yards away. The restaurant's menu is regional (the usual schnitzels and roasts) with a few items from the French repertoire (a fine steak in pepper sauce, for example). ✉ *Am Priesterstein 7, Berchtesgaden-Oberau,* ☎ *08652/97890,* FAX *08652/64710,* WEB *www.deninglehen.de. Restaurant, no a/c, pool, sauna, pets allowed (fee), no-smoking rooms. MC. Closed last 2 wks in Jan.*

$$ **Hotel Grünberger.** Only a few strides from the train station, in the town center, the Grünberger overlooks the River Ache, beside which you can relax on a private terrace. The cozy rooms have farmhouse-style furnishings and some antiques. A buffet breakfast is included in the rate. ✉ *Hansererweg 1, D–83471,* ☎ *08652/4560,* FAX *08652/62254,* WEB *www.hotel-gruenberger.de. 65 rooms. No a/c, cable TV, no TV in some rooms, no room phones, Internet, pool, sauna, beer garden, no-smoking rooms. MC, V. Closed Nov.–mid-Dec.*

$$ **Hotel Watzmann.** American army personnel provided the Hotel Watzmann plenty of business when there was a station in the area, and the cozy Bavarian style and good restaurant still attract Americans. Rooms are solidly furnished in oak, with such Bavarian touches as chamois hides on the walls. The hotel offers remarkable value for your money, especially in the off-season. ✉ *Franziskanerpl. 2, D–83471,* ☎ *08652/2055,* FAX *08652/5174. 30 rooms, 23 with bath or shower; 2 suites. No a/c, cable TV, pets allowed, no-smoking rooms. AE, MC, V. Closed early Nov.–mid-Dec.*

$$ **Hotel Wittelsbach.** This is one of the oldest (built in 1892) and most traditional lodgings in the area. The small rooms have dark pinewood furnishings and deep-red-and-green drapes and carpets. Ask for one with a balcony. ✉ *Maximilianstr. 16, D–83471,* ☎ *08652/96380,* FAX *08652/66304,* WEB *www.urlaubstip.de. 26 rooms, 3 apartments. No a/c, cable TV, Internet, pets allowed. AE, DC, MC, V.*

$$ **Hotel zum Türken.** The view alone is worth the 10-minute journey from Berchtesgaden to this hotel. Confiscated during World War II by the Nazis, it's at the foot of the road to Hitler's mountaintop retreat. Beneath it are remains of Nazi wartime bunkers. There's no restaurant, although evening meals can be ordered in advance. A TV is available in the common room. ✉ *Hintereck 2, D–83471 Obersalzberg-Berchtesgaden,* ☎ *08652/2428,* FAX *08652/4710. 17 rooms, 12 with bath or shower. No a/c, no phones in some rooms, pets allowed, no-smoking rooms. AE, DC, MC, V. Closed Nov.–Dec. 20.*

$$ **Stolls Hotel Alpina.** Set above the Königsee in the delightful little village of Schönau, the Alpina offers rural solitude and easy access to Berchtesgaden. Families are catered to with apartments, a resident doctor, and a playroom. ✉ *Ulmenweg 14, D–83471 Schönau,* ☎ *08652/65090,* FAX *08652/61608. 44 rooms, 6 apartments. No a/c, cable TV, some in-room data ports, pool, hair salon, sauna, pets allowed (fee). AE, DC, MC, V. Closed early Nov.–mid-Dec.*

OFF THE BEATEN PATH

SCHELLENBERG EISHÖHLEN – Germany's largest ice caves lie 10 km (6 mi) north of Berchtesgaden. By car take the B–305, or take the bus (€4) from the Berchtesgaden post office to the village of Marktschellenberg. From there you can reach the caves on foot by walking 2½ hours along the clearly marked route. A guided tour of the caves takes one hour. On the way to Marktschellenberg watch for the **Almbachklamm,** a narrow valley good for hikes. At its entrance is an old (1683) mill for making and polishing marble balls. *€4,* ☎ *08650/352.* *Mid-June–mid-Oct., daily 10–5.*

Outdoor Activities and Sports

Germany's highest course, the **Berchtesgaden Golf Club** (✉ Salzbergstr. 33, ☎ 08652/2100), is on a 3,300-ft plateau of the Obersalzberg. Only fit players should attempt the demanding 9-hole course. Seven Berchtesgaden hotels offer their guests a 30% reduction on the €25 greens fee—contact the tourist office or the club for details.

At the sleek, glassy, and classy **Watzmann Therme** you'll find fragrant steamrooms, saunas with infrared cabins for sore muscles, an elegant pool, whirlpools, and more. If you happen to be staying a few days, you might catch a Tai Chi course, enjoy a bio-release facial massage, or an evening of relaxing underwater exercises. ✉ *Bergwerkstr.,* ☎ *08652/94640.* 💵 *€12.80 for 4 hrs, €14.30 for a day including sauna.* ⏲ *Daily 10–10.*

Berchtesgaden National Park

5 km (3 mi) south of Berchtesgaden.

The deep, mysterious, and fabled Königsee is the most photographed panorama in Germany, adorning millions of calendars. Together with its much smaller sister, the Obersee, it is nestled within the Berchtesgaden National Park, 210 square km (82 square mi) of wild mountain country where flora and fauna have been left to develop as nature intended. No roads penetrate the area, and even the mountain paths are difficult to follow. The park administration organizes guided tours of the area from June through September (contact the Nationalparkhaus, ✉ Franziskanerpl. 7, D–83471 Berchtesgaden, ☎ 08652/64343, WEB www.nationalpark-berchtesgaden.de).

One less strenuous way into the Berchtesgaden National Park is by boat. A fleet of 21 excursion boats, electrically driven so that no noise disturbs the peace, operates on the ★ **Königsee** (King Lake). Only the skipper of the boat is allowed to shatter the silence—his trumpet fanfare demonstrates a remarkable echo as notes reverberate between the almost vertical cliffs that plunge into the dark green water. A cross on a rocky promontory marks the spot where a boatload of pilgrims hit the cliffs and sank more than 100 years ago. The voyagers were on their way to the tiny, twin-tower baroque chapel of St. Bartholomä, built in the 17th century on a peninsula where an early Gothic church once stood. The princely rulers of Berchtesgaden built a hunting lodge at the side of the chapel; a tavern and a restaurant now occupy its rooms.

Smaller than the Königsee but equally beautiful, the **Obersee** can be reached by a 15-minute walk from the second stop (Salet) on the boat tour. The lake's backdrop of jagged mountains and precipitous cliffs is broken by a waterfall, the Rothbachfall, that plunges more than 1,000 ft to the valley floor.

Boat service (☎ 08652/963–618, WEB www.seenschifffahrt.de) on the Königsee runs year-round, except when the lake freezes. Round-trips stop at St. Bartholomä and at Salet, the landing stage for the Obersee. Boat trips stop only at St. Bartholomä October–April. A round-trip to the Königsee and Obersee lasts almost two hours, without stops, and costs €12.50. The shorter trip to St. Bartholomä and back costs €10. In summer the Berchtesgaden tourist office organizes evening cruises on the Königsee, which includes a concert in St. Bartholomä Church and a four-course dinner in the neighboring hunting lodge.

THE BAVARIAN ALPS A TO Z

To research prices, get advice from other travelers, and book travel arrangements, visit www.fodors.com.

AIRPORTS

Munich, 95 km (59 mi) northwest of Garmisch-Partenkirchen, is the gateway to the Bavarian Alps. If you're staying in Berchtesgaden, consider the closer airport in Salzburg, Austria, although it has fewer international flights.

BOAT TRAVEL

Passenger boats operate on all the major Bavarian lakes. They're mostly excursion boats, and many run only in summer. However, there's year-round service on the Chiemsee. Eight boats operate year-round on the Tegernsee, connecting the towns of Tegernsee, Rottach-Egern, Bad Wiessee, and Gmund.

BUS TRAVEL

The Alpine region is not well served by long-distance buses. There is a fairly good network of local buses, but they tend to run at commuter times. Inquire either at any local train station or travel agent, at your hotel, or log onto the German railways' itinerary planning site, www.bahn.hafas.de. Larger resorts operate buses to outlying areas. The Wendelstein region, for example, is serviced by the Wendelstein Ringlinie, offering fares from a simple €7 per day to more complex ones involving skiing tickets. It connects the skiing areas of Sudelfeld with Bayrischzell, the Tatzelwurm Gorge, Bad Aibling near Rosenheim, and other towns and areas.

CAR RENTALS

➤ LOCAL AGENCIES: **Avis** (✉ Königseerstr. 47, Berchtesgaden, ☎ 08652/69107; ✉ St.-Martin-Str. 17, Garmisch-Partenkirchen, ☎ 08821/934–242). **Hertz** (✉ Isarstr. 1d, Rosenheim, ☎ 08031/609–666). **Sixt** (✉ Bahnhofstr. 31, Garmisch-Partenkirchen; ✉ Hauptbahnhof [main railway station], Rosenheim, ☎ 08031/43004; 01805/252–525 for national reservations).

CAR TRAVEL

Three autobahns reach into the Bavarian Alps: A–7 comes in from the northwest (Frankfurt, Stuttgart, Ulm) and ends near Füssen in the western Bavarian Alps; A–95 runs from Munich to Garmisch-Partenkirchen; take A–8 from Munich for Tegernsee, Schliersee, and Chiemsee, and for Berchtesgaden. All provide speedy access to a network of well-paved country roads that penetrate high into the mountains. (Germany's highest road runs above Berchtesgaden at more than 5,000 ft.) Note that on weekends and at the start and end of national holidays, the A–8 can become a long parking lot either heading toward Austria or toward Munich. The two major climbs around the Irschenberg and Bernau are particularly affected. Weekend traffic also jams up the end of the A–95 near Garmisch-Partenkirchen.

HOLIDAY ROUTES

The Deutsche Alpenstrasse (German Alpine Road) is not a continuous highway but a series of roads that run between Lindau (on the Bodensee) and Berchtesgaden, and add up to about 485 km (300 mi). The spectacular journey skirts the northern edge of the Alps for most of the way before heading deep into the mountains on the final stretch between Inzell and Berchtesgaden. The dramatic stretch between Garmisch-Partenkirchen and Berchtesgaden runs about 300 km (186 mi) and affords wonderful views.

The *Blaue Route* (Blue Route) follows the valleys of the Inn and Salzach rivers along the German-Austrian border above Salzburg. This off-the-beaten-track territory includes three quiet lakes: the Tachingersee, the Wagingersee, and the Abstdorfersee. They are the warmest bodies of water in Upper Bavaria, ideal for family vacations. At Wasserburg, east of Munich, you can join the final section of the *Deutsche Ferienstrasse* (German Holiday Road), another combination of roads that run on to Traunstein, east of Chiemsee, and then into the Alps.

EMERGENCIES

➤ CONTACTS: **Police and ambulance** (☎ 110). **Fire and emergency medical aid** (☎ 112).

TOURS

BERCHTESGADEN

In Berchtesgaden the Schwaiger bus company runs tours of the area and across the Austrian border as far as Salzburg. An American couple runs Berchtesgaden Mini-bus Tours out of the local tourist office, opposite the railroad station.

➤ LOCAL OPERATORS: **Schwaiger** (☎ 08652/2525). **Berchtesgaden Mini-bus Tours** (☎ 08652/64971).

GARMISCH-PARTENKIRCHEN

Bus tours to King Ludwig II's castles at Neuschwanstein and Linderhof and to the Ettal Monastery, near Oberammergau, are offered by DER travel agencies. Local agencies in Garmisch also run tours to Neuschwanstein, Linderhof, Ettal, and into the neighboring Austrian Tyrol.

The Garmisch mountain railway company, the Bayerische Zugspitzbahn, offers special excursions to the top of the Zugspitze, Germany's highest mountain, by cog rail and/or cable car.

➤ LOCAL OPERATORS: **Bayerische Zugspitzbahn** (☎ 08821/7970). **DER** (✉ Garmisch-Partenkirchen, ☎ 08821/55125). **Dominikus Kümmerle** (☎ 08821/4955). **Hans Biersack** (☎ 08821/4920). **Hilmar Röser** (☎ 08821/2926). **Weiss-Blau-Reisen** (☎ 08821/3766).

TRAIN TRAVEL

Most Alpine resorts are connected with Munich by regular express and slower services. Trains to Garmisch-Partenkirchen depart hourly from Munich's Hauptbahnhof. Garmisch-Partenkirchen and Mittenwald are on the InterCity Express network, which has regular direct service to all regions of the country. (Klais, just outside Garmisch, is Germany's highest InterCity train station.) A train from Munich also connects to Gmund on Tegernsee. Bad Reichenhall, Berchtesgaden, Prien, and Rosenheim are linked directly to north German cities by long-distance express service. If you're making a day trip to the Zugspitze from Munich, Augsburg, or any other southern Bavarian center, take advantage of an unbeatable deal offered by Deutsche Bahn that includes rail fare and a day's pass to all the Garmisch-Partenkirchen mountains, including the the Zugspitze.

VISITOR INFORMATION

The Bavarian regional tourist office in Munich, Tourismusverband München Oberbayern, provides general information about Upper Bavaria and the Bavarian Alps.

➤ CONTACTS: **Aschau** (✉ Verkehrsamt, Kampenwandstr. 38, D–83229, ☎ 08052/904–937, WEB www.aschau.de). **Bad Reichenhall** (✉ Kur-und-Verkehrsverein, im Kurgastzentrum, Wittelsbacherstr. 15, D–83424, ☎ 08651/606–303, WEB www.bad-reichenhall.de). **Bad Tölz** (✉ Kurverwaltung, Ludwigstr. 11, D–83646, ☎ 08041/78670, WEB www.bad-toelz.de). **Bad Wiessee** (✉ Kuramt, Adrian-Stoop-Str. 20, D–837004, ☎ 08022/86030, WEB www.Bad–Wiessee.de). **Bayrischzell** (✉ Kurverwaltung, Kirchpl. 2, [mailing address: Postfach 2, Kurverwaltung D–83735], ☎ 08023/1034, WEB www.bayrischzell.de). **Berchtesgaden** (✉ Kurdirektion, D–83471, ☎ 08652/9670, WEB www.berchtesgadener-land.com). **Chiemsee** (✉ Tourismusverband Chiemsee, Kurverwaltung, Alte Rathausstr. 11, D–83209 Prien, ☎ 08051/69050, WEB www.chiemsee.de). **Ettal** (✉ Verkehrsamt, Kaiser-Ludwig-Pl., D–82488, ☎ 08822/3534).

Garmisch-Partenkirchen (✉ Verkehrsamt der Kurverwaltung, Richard-Strauss-Pl. 2, D–82467, ☎ 08821/180–420, WEB www.garmisch-partenkirchen.de). **Kochel am See** (✉ Kalmbachstr. 11, D–82431, ☎ 08851/338, WEB www.kochel.de). **Mittenwald** (✉ Kurverwaltung, Dammkarstr. 3, D–82481, ☎ 08823/33981, WEB www.mittenwald.de). **Oberammergau** (✉ Verkehrsamt, Eugen-Papst-Str. 9a, D–82487, ☎ 08822/92310, FAX 08822/923–190, WEB oberammergau.de). **Prien am Chiemsee** (✉ Alter Rathausstr. 11, D–83209, ☎ 08051/69050, WEB www.prien.chiemsee.de). **Reit im Winkl** (✉ Verkehrsamt, Rathauspl. 1, D–83242, ☎ 08640/80020, WEB www.reit-im-winkl.de). **Rottach-Egern/Tegernsee** (✉ Kuramt, Hauptstr. 2, D–83684, ☎ 08022/180–149, WEB www.tegernsee.de). **Tourismusverband München Oberbayern** (✉ Bodenseestr. 113, D–81243 Munich, ☎ 089/829–2180).

4 THE BAVARIAN FOREST

Low-key, understated, and affordable, the Bavarian Forest is a welcome alternative to Germany's hyped-up, overcrowded tourist regions. Farming and forestry are mainstay industries, tourism is growing, and glassblowing shouldn't be missed. At its northwestern periphery on the Danube River lies medieval Regensburg and in the southeast, where the Danube meets the rivers Inn and Ilz, is Passau, a 2,000-year-old town, as beautiful as it is historic.

Updated by Inez Sharp

FOR YEARS THIS PICTURESQUE, WOODED REGION of Lower Bavaria (Niederbayern) was an isolated part of western Europe, with its eastern boundary flanked by the Iron Curtain and the impenetrable, dark density of the Bohemian Forest. The flavor of Lower Bavaria is vastly different from the popular concept of Bavaria (that world supposedly populated by men in lederhosen and funny feathered green hats and buxom women in flowing dirndls, who sing along with oompah bands and knock back great steins of beer). Instead, people here are reserved; even their accent is gentler than that of their southern countrymen. Farming and forestry is the chief economic base of this rural land, where the flat grainfields south of the Danube rise to wooded heights. Bordering the Bavarian Forest at its northern edge is the Oberpfalz (Upper Palatinate) district of Bavaria. The ancient capital Regensburg is an excellent base for excursions into the forest.

Together the uninterrupted expanses of the Bavarian and Bohemian forests are the largest in Europe. Villages of jumbled red roofs and onion-dome churches pepper the vast forest, which has largely buffered communities from further development. Cut off for centuries from the outside world, the small towns of the *Bayerischer Wald* (Bavarian Forest) developed a tough self-sufficiency, which is evident today in a kind of cultural independence. Ancient, even heathen traditions are kept alive and each community boasts its own natural history museum or collections of local curiosities (snuffboxes, for instance). The centuries-old glassmaking industry, which was once a source of considerable wealth, is carried on as much for the tourist trade as for the wider, international market. One of the region's official tourist routes, the *Glasstrasse* (the Glass Road), is constantly being extended to accommodate the small foundries whose furnaces are literally being fanned into life by the promise of tourism.

The collapse of Communism in Czechoslovakia and the formation of the Czech Republic made possible the renewal of old contacts between Germans and Bohemian Czechs. The ancient trading route between Deggendorf and Prague—the Böhmweg—has been revived for hikers. No visit to the Bavarian Forest would be complete without at least a day trip across the border; bus trips into Bohemia, as far as Prague and Plsen, are organized by every local tourist office.

The Bavarian Forest has long been a secret with Germans in search of relaxing, affordable holidays at mountainside lodges or country inns, and tourism is growing. In some parts of the forest the concentration of small hotels, pensions, and holiday apartments is the highest in Germany, but their presence doesn't overwhelm the natural surroundings, since that's what people are coming to explore. All those in search of peace and quiet—hikers, nature lovers, anglers, horseback riders, skiers looking for uncrowded slopes, and golfers distressed by steep greens fees at more fashionable courses—will find their niche here.

Pleasures and Pastimes

Dining

The region has given Germany one of its most popular dishes, the *Pichelsteiner Eintopf*, a delicious broth of vegetables and pork. Sausages come in all varieties—the best are *Regensburger* (short, thick, spicy sausages, rather like the bratwurst of Nürnberg) and *Bauernseufzer* (literally, "farmer's sigh") sausage. Dumplings, made out of anything and everything, appear on practically every menu. Try *Deggendorfer Knödel* (bread dumplings) if you fancy something really local. The Danube provides a number of excellent types of fish, particularly *Donauwaller* (Danube catfish), from Passau, served *blau* (poached) or *gebacken* (breaded and fried). Radishes are a specialty, especially *Weichser Retticbe* (a large white radish), and are a good accompaniment to the many local beers. Passau alone has four breweries—at the Hacklberg, one of the most photogenic in Germany, you can sample excellent beer at its tavern.

CATEGORY	COST*
$$$$	over €20
$$$	€15–€20
$$	€10–€15
$	under €10

**per person for a main course at dinner*

Lodging

Prices here are among the lowest in Germany. Many hotels offer special 14-day packages for the price of a 10-day stay, and 10 days for the price of seven. There are also numerous sports packages. All local tourist offices can supply lists of accommodations; most can help with reservations.

CATEGORY	COST*
$$$$	over €225
$$$	€150–€225
$$	€75–€150
$	under €75

**All prices are for two people in a double room, including tax and service.*

Outdoor Activities and Sports

GOLF

In addition to attractive courses on rolling, wooded hills, golfers can enjoy at least two important local advantages: lower greens fees (sometimes a fraction of what's charged in Upper Bavaria) and clubs that welcome visitors. One comfortable hotel near Passau, the Golf-Hotel Anetseder, is on a 21-hole golf course and has special golfing-holiday packages.

HIKING AND BIKING

The Bavarian Forest is prime hiking country, crisscrossed with trails of varied difficulty, including three officially recognized and marked hiking trails. The longest, the *Pandurensteig,* runs nearly 167 km (104 mi), from Waldmünchen, in the northwest, to Passau, in the southeast, and across the heights of the Bavarian Forest National Park. It follows an old trading route and the towns of Schönberg, Regen, and Bayerisch-Eisenstein have close access to the trail. The Pandurensteig can be covered in stages with the aid of a tourist package that transfers hikers' luggage from one overnight stop to the next.

Resorts between Deggendorf and Bayerisch-Eisenstein on the Czech border have remapped the centuries-old *Böhmweg* trading route, which connected the Danube and Moldau rivers. It can be comfortably covered in three or four days, with accommodations at village taverns on the way. Cyclists can also cover this route or attempt to do others through the forest, with special deals that often include luggage transport. Like the Böhmweg, the *Gunterweg* strikes deep into the Czech Republic, following the 1,000-year-old wanderings of the missionary St. Gunter. Passau is the starting point of several bike paths following the three rivers converging on the city. One of the bike paths leads along the Danube River as far as Vienna.

SKIING

Advanced downhill skiers make for the World Cup slopes of the Grosser Arber. The summit is reached by chairlifts from Bayerisch-Eisenstein and from just outside Bodenmais. Other ski areas in the Bavarian Forest are not as demanding, and many resorts are ideal for families. St. Englmar, Frauenau, Furth im Wald, Waldmünchen, and the villages around the Brotjackelriegel, near Deggendorf, are the best.

Cross-country skiing trails are everywhere; a map of 22 of the finest and a separate list of resorts offering all-inclusive ski holidays can be obtained free of charge from the Tourismusverband Ostbayern.

Exploring the Bavarian Forest

The Bavarian Forest is a compact area between the Danube River and the borders of Austria and the Czech Republic. The region has three major towns, Regensburg, Deggendorf, and Passau, all good bases for day trips into the forest or for longer outings. Many of the larger country hotels are ideal for a family vacation, as they usually offer a very wide range of leisure and sports facilities. You could spend a week or two at such a resort and enjoy everything the Bavarian Forest has to offer without venturing beyond the village boundaries.

Numbers in the text correspond to numbers in the margin and on the Bavarian Forest, Regensburg, and Passau maps.

Great Itineraries

IF YOU HAVE 3 DAYS

Spend a day exploring historic **Regensburg** ①–⑬, then on the second day take a leisurely two-hour drive to **Bodenmais** ⑱ and the nearby silvermine at **Silberberg.** On your third day, head out to Grafenau and the **Bavarian Forest National Park** ㉕. Alternatively, base yourself in Deggendorf or Passau. From **Deggendorf** ㉒ it's only 7 km (4½ mi) along the Danube to the spectacular Benedictine abbey of **Metten** ㉓, founded in the 9th century by Charlemagne. It's a full day's trip north of Deggendorf to the **Grosser Arber** Mountain, the highest in both the Bavarian and the Bohemian forests, the latter on the other side of the nearby Czech frontier.After a day exploring **Passau** ㉗–㊲, take a boat trip down the Danube into neighboring Austria. Spend your third day exploring the **Bavarian Forest National Park** ㉕, 50 km (31 mi) north of the city. If you're driving, take the B–85 along the valley of the River Ilz.

IF YOU HAVE 5 DAYS

Spend one day touring **Regensburg** ①–⑬ before traveling down to **Deggendorf** ㉒ and the nearby abbey in **Metten** ㉓. On day three head north to the **Grosser Arber,** overnighting in **Bodenmais** ⑱, **Zwiesel** ⑳, or **Viechtach** ⑰, all famous for fine glass. From Zwiesel follow the course of the Regen River as far as Frauenau and head into the **Bavarian Forest National Park** ㉕ to stay in the resort town of Grafenau. From Grafenau follow the Ilz River down to **Passau** ㉗–㊲.

IF YOU HAVE 7 DAYS

Spend a day and a half exploring the delights of medieval **Regensburg** ①–⑬ before taking the B–8 up to the little town of **Cham** ⑯, where you can admire the remains of its medieval wall. Head southeast on B–85, watching for the ruins of a medieval castle on the summit of the 2,500-ft-high **Haidstein Peak.** Farther on, between the villages of Prackenbach and Viechtach, you'll view the **Pfahl,** a ridge of glistening white quartz. Overnight in **Viechtach** ⑰, and don't miss a visit to the Gläserne Scheune, a glassmaker's studio. On your third day continue on B–85, turn left at the next village, Patersdorf, and head through the depths of the forest for **Bodenmais** ⑱. The pretty resort is overlooked by the region's highest mountain, the **Grosser Arber.** The Czech border cuts through the forest on the mountain's northern

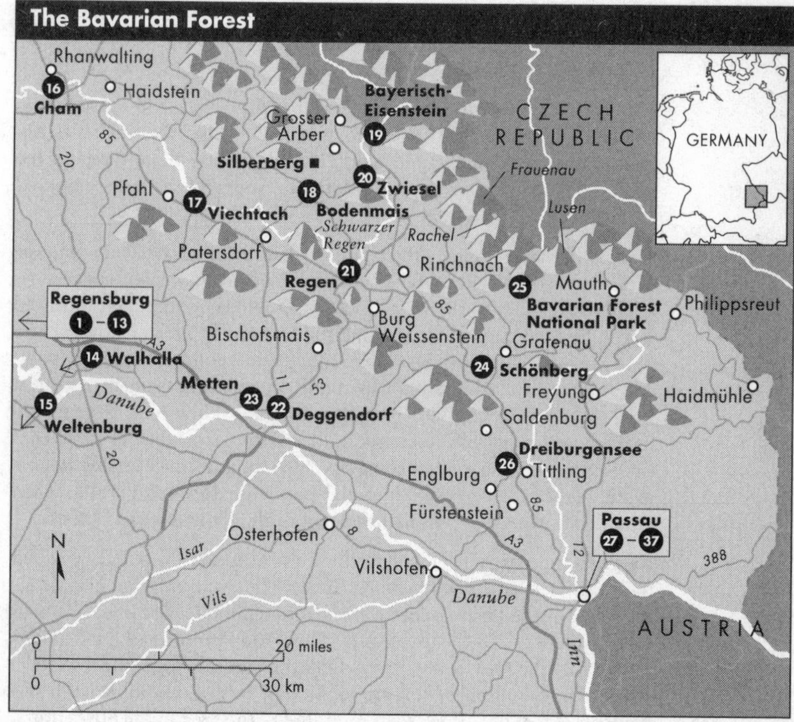

slopes, dividing the train station of **Bayerisch-Eisenstein** ⑲ in half. Spend the third night in the center of the Bavarian Forest's glass industry, **Zwiesel** ⑳, 15 km (9 mi) south of Bayerisch-Eisenstein. The road continues south to **Regen** ㉑, a busy market town that's a good lunch stop, and then snakes through wooded uplands before dropping into Deggendorf, in the wide valley of the Danube. Allow a day for **Deggendorf** ㉒, including a side trip to the Benedictine abbey of **Metten** ㉓. Next, cross the Danube River to visit the beautiful baroque church of St. Margaretha in **Osterhofen,** follow the south bank of the river to Vilshofen, and cross the bridge over the Danube there to head north again into the forest. Spend your fifth night in Grafenau and explore the **Bavarian Forest National Park** ㉕ the next day. On the road south to **Passau** ㉗–㊲ you'll pass through the Dreiburgenland, named for the three famous castles that mark the route. Plan a stop at the **Dreiburgensee** ㉖, in Tittling, to see the open-air museum of reconstructed Bavarian Forest houses. From there it's an easy 20 km (12 mi) to Passau for a final night and day.

When to Tour the Bavarian Forest

Summer is the time to visit Regensburg and the Bavarian Forest. Although local tourist offices do their best to publicize events spread throughout the calendar year, only winter-sports fans and hardy types venture deep into the forest in the months between late fall and early spring. November is so unpleasant—shrouding the whole region in cold, damp fog for days on end—that many hotels put up the shutters until the December vacation season begins. The cold continues through February, and snow lies deep in the ski resorts from December through March. When the wintery delights of the forest start to pall head out to Regensburg or Passau for a day of shopping and sightseeing.

REGENSBURG

120 km (74 mi) northwest of Munich.

Few visitors to Bavaria venture this far off the well-trod tourist trails and even Germans are surprised when they discover medieval Regensburg. Because it escaped World War II with no major damage, the capital of the Oberfalz (Upper Palatinate) is one of the best-preserved medieval cities in Germany.

The key to Regensburg is the Danube. Before the Rhine-Main-Danube Canal was completed in the 1990s, the great river was no longer navigable a few miles to the west, and this simple geographic fact allowed Regensburg to control trade along the Danube between Germany and central Europe for centuries. The Danube was a conduit of ideas as well. It was from Regensburg that Christianity spread across much of central Europe in the 7th and 8th centuries. By the Middle Ages Regensburg had become a political, economic, and intellectual center. For many centuries it was the most important city in southeastern Germany, serving as the seat of the Perpetual Imperial Diet from 1663 until 1806, when Napoléon ordered the dismemberment of the Holy Roman Empire.

Regensburg's story begins with the Celts around 500 BC. They called their little settlement Radasbona. In AD 179, as an original marble inscription in the Historisches Museum proclaims, it became a Roman military post called Castra Regina. The Porta Praetoria of the Romans remains in the Old Town, and whenever you see huge ashlars incorporated into buildings, you are looking at bits of the old Roman settlement. When Bavarian tribes migrated to the area in the 6th century, they occupied what remained of the Roman town and, apparently on the basis of its Latin name, called it Regensburg. Anglo-Saxon missionaries led by St. Boniface in 739 made the town a bishopric before heading down the Danube to convert the heathen in even more far-flung lands. Charlemagne, first of the Holy Roman Emperors, arrived at the end of the 8th century and incorporated Regensburg into his burgeoning domain.

The spirit of Regensburg is very special: on the one hand are the ancient and hallowed walls; on the other is a crowd of lively students from the university (founded in 1967), who are reminders that this city is not a museum. The inner city is still used by people for their everyday needs, and international consumer chains haven't taken over individually owned shops. Any serious tour of Regensburg includes an unusually large number of places of worship. If your spirits wilt at the thought of inspecting them all, you should at least see the Dom (cathedral), famous for its Domspatzen (boys' choir—the literal translation is "cathedral sparrows").

A Good Walk

Begin your walk in the very center of Regensburg, on medieval Rathausplatz. At the tourist office you can book a tour of the adjacent **Altes Rathaus** ① and pick up maps and brochures. Head east along Goliathstrasse, making a short detour halfway down to the bank of the Danube and the **Steinerne Brücke** ②, which was key to the city's rise to medieval trading power. Walk to this bridge's center for an unforgettable view of Regensburg's old town center, with the ancient tower, now the **Brückturm Museum** ③, acting as a gate leading to the jumble of cobblestone streets and steeply eaved houses. From the tower follow Residenzstrasse south, and within a few minutes you'll reach Domplatz, dominated by Regensburg's soaring cathedral, **Dom St. Peter** ④. Behind the cathedral square is the quieter Alter Kornmarkt, bor-

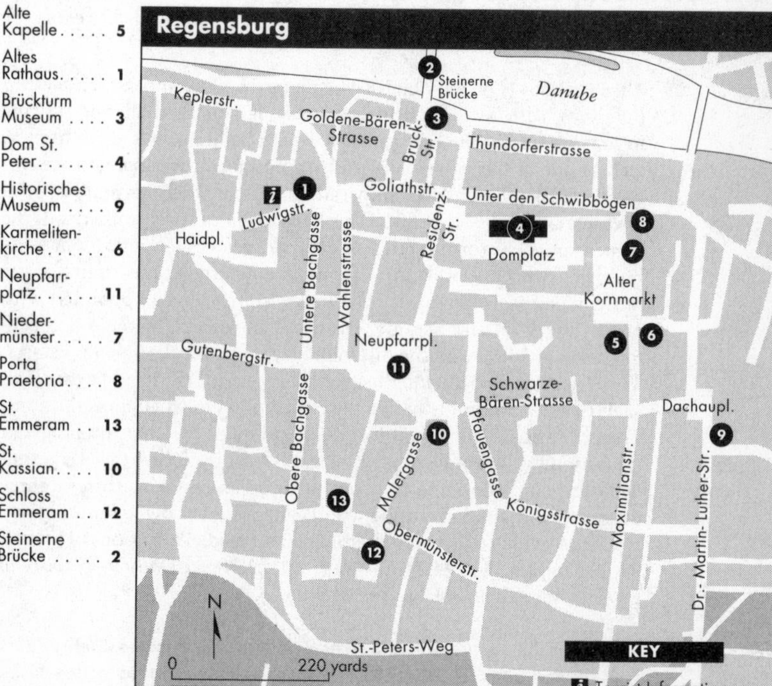

dered on three sides by historic churches: the **Alte Kapelle** ⑤, the adjoining **Karmelitenkirche** ⑥, and the **Niedermünster** ⑦. At the northern exit of Alter Kornmarkt is a reminder of Regensburg's Roman past, the **Porta Praetoria** ⑧, a former gateway to the Roman camp. Other Roman remains can be viewed in Regensburg's highly interesting city museum, the **Historisches Museum** ⑨, on Dachauplatz, just south of the Alter Kornmarkt. Regensburg's oldest church, **St. Kassian** ⑩, is 200 yards west of Dachauplatz and Alter Kornmarkt, at the southern edge of another ancient city square, **Neupfarrplatz** ⑪, where you'll also find the city's first Protestant church, the Neupfarrkirche. Leave Neupfarrplatz at its southern edge and a short stroll brings you to the great bulk of Regensburg's extraordinary palace, **Schloss Emmeram** ⑫. Adjoining the palace is the church of **St. Emmeram** ⑬. To complete your walk, continue westward along Obermünsterstrasse, turning right into Obere Bachgasse. This street eventually becomes Untere Bachgasse, which will take you back within minutes to your starting point, Rathausplatz.

TIMING

Regensburg is compact; its old town center is just over 1 square mi. All of its attractions lie on the south side of the Danube, so you won't have to cross it more than once—and then only to admire the city from the north bank. Try to time your tour so that you arrive at lunchtime at the ancient Historische Wurstküche, a tavern nestling between the river and the bridge. You'll need about two hours or more to explore Schloss Emmeram and the neighboring St. Emmeram Church. Schedule at least another hour to visit the cathedral.

Sights to See

5 **Alte Kapelle** (Old Chapel). The Carolingian structure was erected in the 9th century. Its dowdy exterior gives little hint of the joyous rococo treasures within—extravagant concoctions of sinuous gilt stucco, rich marble, and giddy frescoes, the whole illuminated by light pour-

ing in from the upper windows. ✉ *Alter Kornmarkt 8.* ⏲ *Daily 9–dusk.*

❶ **Altes Rathaus** (Old City Hall). The picture-book complex of medieval buildings, with half-timbering, windows large and small, and flowers in tubs, is among the best-preserved such buildings in the country, as well as one of the most historically important. It was here, in the imposing Gothic **Reichssaal** (Imperial Hall), that the Perpetual Imperial Diet met from 1663 to 1806. This parliament of sorts consisted of the emperor, the electors (seven or eight), the princes (about 50), and the burghers, who assembled to discuss and determine the affairs of the far-reaching German lands. The hall is sumptuously appointed with tapestries, flags, and heraldic designs. Note especially the wood ceiling, built in 1408, and the different elevations for the various estates. The Reichssaal is occasionally used for concerts. The neighboring **Ratsaal** (Council Room) is where the electors met for their consultations. The cellar holds the actual torture chamber of the city; the **Fragstatt** (Questioning Room); and the execution room, called the **Armesünderstübchen** (Poor Sinners' Room). Any prisoner who withstood three degrees of questioning without confessing was considered innocent and released—which tells you something about medieval notions of justice. ✉ *Rathauspl.,* ☎ *0941/507–4411.* 🎫 *€2.50.* ⏲ *Daily 9–4; tours in English May–Sept., Mon.–Sat. at 3:15.*

NEED A BREAK? Just across the square from the Altes Rathaus is the **Prinzess Confiserie Café** (✉ Rathauspl. 2, ☎ 0941/57671), Germany's oldest coffeehouse, which first opened its doors to the general public in 1686. The home-made chocolates are especially recommendable, after the rich cakes, of course.

❸ **Brückturm Museum** (Bridge Tower Museum). All tiny windows, weathered tiles, and pink plaster, this 17th-century tower stands at the south end of the Steinerne Brücke. The tower displays a host of items relating to the construction and history of the old bridge. It also offers a gorgeous view of the Regensburg roof landscape. The brooding building with a massive roof to the left of the Brückturm is an old salt warehouse that now houses the Salzstadel Wirtshaus, where you can try your first Regensburger sausage. ✉ *Steinerne Brücke,* ☎ *0941/21283. Call ahead to inquire about English tours.* 🎫 *€2.* ⏲ *Apr.–Oct., daily 10–5.*

★ ❹ **Dom St. Peter** (St. Peter's Cathedral). Regensburg's transcendent cathedral, modeled on the airy, vertical lines of French Gothic architecture, is something of a rarity this far south in Germany. Begun in the 13th century, it stands on the site of a much earlier Carolingian church. A remarkable feature of the cathedral is that it can hold 6,000 people, three times the population of Regensburg when building began. Construction dragged on for almost 600 years until Ludwig I of Bavaria, then ruler of Regensburg, finally had the towers built. These had to be replaced in the mid-1950s. Behind the Dom is a little workshop where a team of 15 stonecutters are busy full-time during the summer recutting and restoring parts of the cathedral.

Before heading into the Dom, admire the intricate and frothy carvings of its facade. Inside, the glowing 14th-century stained glass in the choir and the exquisitely detailed statues of the archangel Gabriel and the Virgin in the crossing (the intersection of the nave and the transepts) are among the church's outstanding features. ✉ *Dompl.,* ☎ *0941/597–1002.* 🎫 *Tour (only in German, for tours in English call ahead) €2.50.* ⏲ *Cathedral tour May–Oct., weekdays at 10, 11, and 2, Sun. at noon and 2; Nov.–Apr., weekdays at 11, Sun. at noon.*

Be sure to visit the **Kreuzgang** (Cloisters), reached via the garden. There you'll find a small octagonal chapel, the Allerheiligenkapelle (All Saints Chapel), a Romanesque building that is all sturdy grace and massive walls, a work by Italian masons from the mid 12th century. You can barely make out the faded remains of stylized 11th-century frescoes on its ancient walls. The equally ancient shell of St. Stephan's Church, the Alter Dom (Old Cathedral), can also be visited. The cloisters, chapel, and Alter Dom can be seen only on a guided one-hour tour. €2.50. *Tour mid-May–Oct., daily at 10, 11, and 2; Nov.–Mar., weekdays at 11, Sun. at noon; Apr.–mid-May, daily at 11 and 2.*

The **Domschatzmuseum** (Cathedral Museum), contains valuable treasures going back to the 11th century. Some of the vestments and the monstrances, which are fine examples of eight centuries worth of the goldsmith's trade, are still used during special services. The entrance is in the nave. ✉ *Dompl.,* ☎ *0941/57645.* €1.50. *Apr.–Oct., Tues.–Sat. 10–5, Sun. noon–5; Dec.–Mar., Fri. and Sat. 10–4, Sun. noon–4. Closed Nov.*

NEED A BREAK?

The restaurant **Haus Heuport** (✉ Dompl. 7, ☎ 0941/599–9297), opposite the entrance of the Dom, is in one of the old and grand private ballrooms of the city. The service is excellent, all dishes taste good, and the tables at the windows have a wonderful view of the Dom.

★ 9 **Historisches Museum** (Historical Museum). The municipal museum vividly relates the cultural history of Regensburg. It is one of the highlights of the city, both for its unusual and beautiful setting—a former Gothic monastery—and for its wide-ranging collections, from Roman artifacts to Renaissance tapestries and remains from Regensburg's 16th-century Jewish ghetto. The most significant exhibits are the paintings by Albrecht Altdorfer (1480–1538), a native of Regensburg and, along with Cranach, Grünewald, and Dürer, one of the leading painters of the German Renaissance. His work has the same sense of heightened reality found in that of his contemporaries, in which the lessons of Italian painting are used to produce an emotional rather than a rational effect. His paintings would not have seemed out of place among those of 19th-century Romantics. Far from seeing the world around him as essentially hostile, or at least alien, he saw it as something intrinsically beautiful, whether wild or domesticated. Altdorfer made two drawings of the old Synagogue of Regensburg, priceless documents that are on exhibit here. ✉ *Dachaupl. 2–4,* ☎ *0941/507–1442.* €2. *Tues.–Sun. 10–4.*

6 **Karmelitenkirche** (Church of the Carmelites). This lovely church, styled in baroque from crypt to cupola, stands next to the Alte Kapelle. It has a finely decorated facade designed by the 17th-century Italian master Carlo Lurago. ✉ *Alter Kornmarkt.*

11 **Neupfarrplatz.** This oversize open square's history as a Jewish ghetto has come to light in recent years. The Regensburg Jews had lived in fair harmony with the town's citizens, but hard economic times and superstition led to their eviction by decree in 1519. While the synagogue was being torn down, one worker survived a very bad fall. A church was promptly built to celebrate the miracle and before long a pilgrimage began, and the **Neupfarrkirche** (New Parish Church) was built as well to accommodate the flow of pilgrims. During the Reformation, the Parish Church was given to the Protestants, hence its bare-bones interior. In the late 1990s, excavation work (for the power company) on the square uncovered well-kept cellars, and to the west of the church, the old synagogue, including the foundations of its Romanesque pre-

decessor. Archaeologists salvaged the few items they could from the old stones (including a stash of 684 gold coins) and not knowing what to do with the sea of foundations, ultimately carefully reburied them. Recovered items were carefully restored and are on exhibit in the Historisches Museum. Only one small underground area to the south of the church, the **Document,** accommodates viewing of the foundations. In a former cellar, surrounded by the original walls, visitors can watch a short video reconstructing life in the old Jewish ghetto. Over the old synagogue, the Israeli artist Dani Karavan designed a stylized groundplan where people can sit and meet. Call the educational institution VHS for a tour of the Document (reservations are requested). For spontaneous visits, tickets are available at Tabak Götz on the western side of the square, at Neupfarrplatz 3. ✉ *Neupfarrpl.,* ☎ *0941/507–2433 for tours led by VHS,* WEB *www.vhs-regensburg.de.* ⏲ *Church daily 9–dusk. Document open Thurs.–Sat. for 2:30 tour.* 🎫 *Document €2.50.*

NEED A BREAK? The Dampfnudel is a kind of sweet yeast dough dumpling that is tasty and filling. The best in Bavaria can be had at **Dampfnudel Uli** (✉ Watmarkt 4), a little establishment in a former chapel. The decoration is incredibly eclectic, from Bavarian crafts to a portrait of Ronald Reagan inscribed: "To Uli Deutzer, with best wishes, Ronald Reagan." The owner also has a picture of President Bush, Sr. It's open Tuesday–Friday 10–6 and Saturday 10–3.

7 **Niedermünster.** This 12th-century building with a baroque interior was originally the church of a community of nuns, all of them from noble families. For a quarter hour beginning at 12:05 PM daily, concerts are given by students of the church music school. ✉ *Alter Kornmarkt 5,* ☎ *0941/597–1002.*

8 **Porta Praetoria.** The rough-hewn former gate to the old Roman camp is one of the most interesting relics of Roman times in Regensburg. Look through the grille on its east side to see a section of the original Roman street, about 10 ft below today's street level. ✉ *North side of Alter Kornmarkt.*

13 **St. Emmeram.** The Thurn und Taxis family church stands across from Schloss Emmeram. The foundations of the church date to the 7th and 8th centuries. A richly decorated baroque interior was added in 1730 by the Asam brothers. St. Emmeram contains the graves of the 7th-century martyred Regensburg bishop Emmeram and the 10th-century St. Wolfgang. ✉ *Emmeramspl. 3,* ☎ *0941/53853.* ⏲ *Mon.–Thurs., Sat. 10–4:30, Fri. 1–4:30, Sun. noon–4:30.*

10 **St. Kassian.** Regensburg's oldest church was founded in the 8th century. Don't be fooled by its dour exterior; inside, it is filled with delicate rococo decoration. ✉ *St. Kassianpl. 1.* ⏲ *Daily 9–5:30.*

12 **Schloss Emmeram** (Emmeram Palace). Formerly a Benedictine monastery, this is the ancestral home of the princely Thurn und Taxis family, which made its fame and fortune after being granted the right to carry official and private mail throughout the empire and Spain by Emperor Maximilian I (1493–1519) and by Philip I, king of Spain, who ruled during the same period. Their business extended over the centuries into the Low Countries (Holland, Belgium, and Luxembourg), Hungary, and Italy. The little horn that still symbolizes the post office in several European countries comes from the Thurn und Taxis coat of arms. For a while Schloss Emmeram was heavily featured in the gossip columns thanks to the wild parties and somewhat extravagant lifestyle of the young dowager Princess Gloria von Thurn und Taxis. After the death of her husband, Prince Johannes, in 1990, she had to auction off be-

longings in order to pay inheritance taxes. Ultimately a deal was cut, allowing her to keep many of the palace's treasures as long they were put on display.

The **Thurn und Taxis Palace,** with its splendid ballroom and throne room, is an eloquent witness to courtly life in the 19th century. A visit usually includes the fine **Kreuzgang** (cloister) of the former Benedictine abbey of St. Emmeram. The items in the **Thurn und Taxis Museum,** which is part of the Bavarian National Museum in Munich, have been carefully selected for their fine craftsmanship—be it dueling pistols, a plain marshal's staff, a boudoir, or a snuffbox. The palace's **Marstallmuseum** (the former royal stables) holds the family's coaches and carriages as well as related items. ☎ *0941/50480.* *Palace and cloisters €8; Marstallmuseum €4.50; Marstall plus Thurn und Taxis Museum €4.50; Thurn und Taxis Museum alone €3.50.* ⏲ *Weekdays 11–5, weekends 10–5. Marstallmuseum closed Nov.–Mar.*

★ ❷ **Steinerne Brücke** (Stone Bridge). This impressive old bridge resting on massive pontoons is Regensburg's most celebrated sight. It was completed in 1146 and was rightfully considered a miraculous piece of engineering at the time. As the only crossing point over the Danube for miles, it effectively cemented Regensburg's control over trade. The significance of the little statue on the bridge is a mystery, but the figure seems to be a witness to the legendary rivalry between the master builders of the bridge and those of the Dom.

Dining and Lodging

$–$$ ✕ **Leerer Beutel.** Excellent international cuisine—from antipasti to solid pork roast—is served in the pleasant atmosphere of a vaulted room supported by massive rough-hewn beams. The huge old warehouse it's lodged in is also a venue for concerts, exhibitions, and film screenings, so it's the ideal place to spend the evening. ✉ *Bertoldstr. 9,* ☎ *0941/58997. AE, DC, MC, V. No lunch Mon.*

$ ✕ **Historische Wurstküche.** Succulent Regensburger sausages—the best in town—are prepared right before your eyes here on an open beechwood charcoal grill in the tiny kitchen, and if you eat them inside in the tiny dining room, you'll have to squeeze past the cook. Inside are plaques recording the levels the river reached in the various floods that have doused the restaurant's kitchen in the past 100 years. ✉ *Thundorferstr. 3,* ☎ *0941/59098. No credit cards.*

$ ✕ **Lokanta.** Although Regensburg seems so typically German, it is a dynamic and international town. This lively restaurant with a mixed crowd at the tables and a pastel orange color scheme serves simple and excellent Kurdish-Turkish dishes. A few plates of the *amuses-gueules* (mixed appetizers) will be just the thing before or after a concert. ✉ *Wollwirkerg.,* ☎ *0941/53321. No credit cards.*

$$–$$$ ✕🏨 **Hotel-Restaurant Bischofshof am Dom.** This is one of Germany's most historic hostelries, a former bishop's palace where you can sleep in an apartment that includes part of a Roman gateway. Other chambers are only slightly less historic, and some have seen emperors and princes as guests. If your room overlooks the central cobblestone courtyard, you'll awaken to a neighboring church's carillon playing a German hymn, and you'll retire to the strains of the Bavarian national anthem. The hotel's restaurant ($) serves fine regional cuisine (including the famous Regensburg sausages, of course) at reasonable prices. The beer comes from a brewery founded in 1649. ✉ *Krautermarkt 3, D–93047,* ☎ *0941/58460,* FAX *0941/53508,* WEB *bischofshof-am-dom.de. 51 rooms, 3 suites. Restaurant, bar, beer garden, no a/c, cable TV, pets allowed (fee). AE, DC, MC, V.*

$$ ✕ 🏨 **Hôtel Orphée.** This protected monument hotel offers a special experience with theme rooms: the first floor is devoted to the upcoming bourgeoisie of the 19th century (the Sigmund Freud room, for example), the second floor gives you a feel of how the aristocracy lived. If you would like a TV in your room, ask upon making a reservation. The reception and breakfast room are in the dark wood-paneled Orphée Restaurant in the next street. The menu is mostly French ($$) with a selection of crepes, salads, and heavier meaty dishes. ✉ *Untere Bachgasse, D–93047,* ☎ *0941/596–020,* FAX *0941/5960–2222,* WEB *www.hotel-orphee.de. 15 rooms. Restaurant, bar, no a/c, no TV in some rooms, pets allowed (fee). MC, V.*

$$ 🏨 **Hotel Münchner Hof.** In this little hotel nestled in the block near the Neupfarrkirche, the rooms are generous and tastefully decorated. In some, the original arches of the ancient building are visible. The restaurant is quiet and comfortable, serving Bavarian specialties and good Munich beer. The bottom line: you get top service at a good price, and Regensburg is at your feet. ✉ *Tändlerg. 9, D–93047,* ☎ *0941/58440,* FAX *0941/561–709,* WEB *www.muenchner-hof.de. 53 rooms. Restaurant, no a/c, cable TV, some in-room data ports, pets allowed (fee), no-smoking rooms. AE, MC, DC, V.*

$$ 🏨 **Kaiserhof am Dom.** Renaissance windows punctuate the green facade of this historic city mansion. The rooms are 20th-century modern, with perks such as underfloor heating and cable TV. Try for one with a view of the cathedral, which stands directly across the street. Breakfast is served beneath the high-vaulted ceiling of the former 14th-century chapel, and there's also a smart brasserie. ✉ *Kramg. 10–12, D–93047,* ☎ *0941/585–350,* FAX *0941/585–3595,* WEB *www.kaiserhof.germany.de. 30 rooms. Café, no a/c, cable TV, Internet, pets allowed (fee). AE, DC, MC, V.*

$$ 🏨 **Parkhotel Maximilian.** A handsome 18th-century palace between the railway station and the Old Town is home to the most elegant and sophisticated hotel in Regensburg. Rooms are well appointed, generous in size, and luxurious. Breakfast, meals, or drinks can be had on a pretty terrace in the back of the hotel. ✉ *Maximilianstr. 28, D–93047,* ☎ *0941/56850,* FAX *0941/52942,* WEB *www.maximilian-hotel.de. 47 rooms, 3 suites. Café, 2 bars, no a/c, cable TV with movies, in-room data ports, hair salon, recreation room, pets allowed (fee), no-smoking rooms. AE, DC, MC, V. Closed Mon.*

Shopping

Tucked away at the Untere Bachgasse (✉ Untere Bachgasse 11) is the colorful **Bear's & Friends,** where you can tank up on your gummi bears. They come in all shapes and sizes and colors, in organic and inorganic versions, with and without cow-based gelatin.

Nightlife and the Arts

Regensburg offers a range of musical experiences, though none so moving as a performance by the famous boys' choir at the cathedral. The best-sung mass is held on Sunday at 9 AM. It can be a remarkable experience, and it's worth scheduling your visit to the city to hear the choir. A three-week program of music and theater is presented during the **Regensburger Kultursommer,** a partly open-air festival from the end of July to the beginning of August.

The kind of happy-go-lucky, friendly, mixed nightlife that is hardly extant in Munich is alive and well in this small university city in the many *Kneipen,* bar-cum-pub-cum-bistro or restaurants, such as the Leerer Beutel. It's good to ask around for what happens to be jumping at any given time. The **Jenseits** (✉ Keplerstr. 15, ☎ 094/54944) puts on a mix of jazz and classical music, and even exhibitions.

Regensburg A to Z

CAR RENTAL

Regensburg is 120 km (74 mi) from Munich and 332 km (206 mi) from Frankfurt.

➤ CONTACTS: **Avis** (✉ Prüfeningerstr. 98, Regensburg, ☎ 0941/396–090). **Sixt** (✉ Im Gewerbepark C38, Regensburg, ☎ 0941/401–035).

BOAT TRAVEL

The most popular excursions are boat trips on the Danube River from Regensburg to Ludwig I's imposing Greek-style Doric temple of Walhalla or to the monastery at Weltenburg. There are daily sailings to Walhalla from Easter through October. The round-trip costs €6 and takes three hours. To reach Weltenburg from Regensburg, change boats at Kelheim. The Regensburg–Kelheim ride takes 2½ hours; Kelheim to Weltenburg takes 30 minutes (the fare is €5.50). Daylong upstream cruises from Regensburg, which take in Weltenburg via the valley of Altmühltal, are also possible. Regensburg boats depart from the Steinerne Brücke.

➤ TOUR-OPERATOR RECOMMENDATIONS: **Regensburg departures** (☎ 0941/55359). **Kelheim departures** (☎ 09441/3402 or 09441/8290, WEB www.renate.de).

TRAIN TRAVEL

Regular InterCity services connect Nürnberg and Regensburg with Frankfurt and other major German cities. There are hourly trains from Munich direct to Regensburg.

VISITOR INFORMATION

English-language guided walking tours of Regensburg are conducted May–September, Wednesday and Saturday at 1:30. They cost €6 and begin at the tourist office. Eichstätt offers walking tours of the city for €3, Saturday and Wednesday at 1:30 at the tourist information office.

➤ TOURIST INFORMATION: **Tourist-Information** (✉ Altes Rathaus, D–93047, ☎ 0941/507–4410, WEB www.regensburg.de).

Walhalla

★ ⓮ *11 km (7 mi) east of Regensburg.*

Walhalla is an excursion from Regensburg you won't want to miss, especially if you have an interest in the wilder expressions of 19th-century German nationalism. Danube river cruises stop here for the town's incongruous Greek-style Doric temple. To get to the temple from the river, you'll have to climb 358 marble steps. There is, however, a parking lot near the top. To drive to it, take the Danube Valley country road (unnumbered) east from Regensburg 8 km (5 mi) to Donaustauf. The Walhalla temple is 1 km (½ mi) outside the village and well signposted. Walhalla—a name resonant with Nordic mythology—was where the god Odin received the souls of dead heroes. This monumental temple was erected in 1840 for Ludwig I to honor important German personages through the ages. In the neoclassic style then prevailing, it's actually a copy of the Parthenon, in Athens. Even if you consider the building more a monument to kitsch, it remains a supremely well-built structure and its expanses of costly marble are evidence of both the financial resources and the craftsmanship at Ludwig's command.

Weltenburg

★ ⓯ *25 km (15 mi) southwest of Regensburg.*

In Weltenburg you'll find the great **Stiftskirche Sts. Georg und Martin** (Abbey Church of St. George and St. Martin), on the bank of the Danube River. The most dramatic approach to the abbey is by boat from Kelheim, 10 km (6 mi) downstream. On the stunning ride the boat winds between towering limestone cliffs that rise straight up from the tree-lined riverbanks. The abbey, constructed between 1716 and 1718, is commonly regarded as the masterpiece of the brothers Cosmas Damian and Egid Quirin Asam, two leading baroque architects and decorators of Bavaria. Their extraordinary composition of painted figures whirling on the ceiling, lavish and brilliantly polished marble, highly wrought statuary, and stucco dancing in rhythmic arabesques across the curving walls, is the epitome of Bavarian baroque. Note especially the bronze equestrian statue of St. George above the high altar, reaching down imperiously with his flamelike, twisted gilt sword to dispatch the winged dragon at his feet. ⏲ *Daily 9–dusk.*

THE WESTERN BAVARIAN FOREST

Although the Bavarian Forest has no recognized boundaries, it can be said to end in the west where the upland, wooded slopes drop to the Franconian flatlands north of Regensburg.

Cham

⓰ *58 km (36 mi) northeast of Regensburg via A–3 and B–20; 58 km (36 mi) northwest of Deggendorf.*

Beautifully set on the Regen River, Cham regards itself as the gateway to the forest and is further distinguished by its intact sections of 14th-century town walls, including the massive Straubinger Turm (tower) and the Biertor (gate). Every day at five minutes past noon a glockenspiel in the 15th-century **Rathaus** (city hall) tower plays the French national anthem, the "Marseillaise." It's a municipal commemoration of the town's most famous son, Count Nikolaus von Luckner, who rose through the ranks of various armies to become a French marshal to whom French troops dedicated their most famous song.

Dining and Lodging

$–$$ ✕ **Bürgerstuben.** The Stuben is in Cham's central Stadthalle (city hall), where card-playing, beer-swilling regulars add some local color to the evening. Tasty local dishes and an appealingly simple atmosphere round out the authentic Bavarian experience. ✉ *Fürtherstr. 11,* ☎ *09971/1707. No credit cards. Closed Mon.*

$ 🏨 **Hotel am Stadtpark.** This popular lodging is an unbeatable value, with comfortable rooms costing as little as €46—including a forest view and a large breakfast. The house stands on the edge of Cham's resort park. Families are especially welcome, and the hotel has three large apartments and a huge suite that can accommodate up to eight people. There's no restaurant, but Cham has no shortage of cheap and cheerful inns. ✉ *Tilsiterstr. 3, D–93413,* ☎ *09971/2253,* FAX *09971/79253,* WEB *www.hotel-am-stadtpark-cham.de. 10 rooms, 1 suite, 3 apartments. No a/c, no room TVs. No credit cards.*

$ 🏨 **Randsbergerhof.** Generations of German knights lived here before the house was converted into a comfortable hotel. A suit of armor from the noble Randsberg family in the beamed restaurant recalls the hotel's romantic history. Its variety of keep-fit facilities make the hotel ideal for sports enthusiasts and once you've exhausted yourself playing squash you can retire to the in-house cinema, which shows at least four different films a day. ✉ *Randsbergerhofstr. 15–17, D–93413,* ☎ *09971/85770,* FAX *09971/20299,* WEB *www.randsbergerhof.de. 88 rooms, 4 suites. 2 restaurants, no a/c, Internet, pool, sauna, bowling, squash, meeting rooms. AE, DC, MC, V.*

Nightlife and the Arts

Germany's oldest street **folk festival** (☎ 09973/50980 or 09973/19433), dating from medieval times, takes place in Furth im Wald (20 km [12 mi] north of Cham). Dressed in period costume, townsfolk participate in the ritual slaying of a fire-breathing "dragon" that stalks the main street. The week-long festival takes place between the second and third Sunday of August.

Outdoor Activities and Sports

Cyclists can explore the countryside by choosing from the bike excursions offered by **Travel agents Baumgartner** (✉ Schwanenestr. 8, Cham, ☎ 09971/858–080, FAX 09971/858–088, WEB www.baumgartner-reisen.de). One-day trips start from €30.

Golf Club Furth im Wald ev. (✉ Voithenberg 3, Furth, ☎ 09973/2089) has an attractive and challenging 18-hole course.

En Route As you head southeast of Cham on B–85, watch on the left for the ruins of a medieval castle perched on the 2,500-ft-high **Haidstein Peak.** Around the year 1200 it was home to the German poet Wolfram von Eschenbach, author of the metrical romance *Parzival.* On the mountain slopes is a 1,000-year-old linden tree known as Wolframslinde (Wolfram's Lime Tree). With a circumference of more than 50 ft, its hollow trunk could easily shelter 50 people. Continuing on B–85, you'll pass villages with trim streets and gardens and see two sinuous lakes created by the dammed Regen River. From here the Weisser (white) Regen soon becomes the Schwarzer (black) Regen.

Between the village of Prackenbach and the little town of Viechtach you'll see a dramatic section of the **Pfahl,** one of Europe's most extraordinary geological phenomena. The ridge of glistening white quartz juts out of the ground in an arrow-straight spur that extends more than 100 km (62 mi) through the Bavarian Forest. Here the quartz rises in folds to heights of 100 ft or more.

Viechtach

17 *30 km (19 mi) southeast of Cham, 29 km (18 mi) north of Deggendorf.*

This little market town nestled in the folds of the Bavarian Forest won a major government prize for its environmental protection programs, and the award includes a special seal of approval (a fir tree) designating hotels and guest houses deemed "ecologically friendly." The little fir is now proudly displayed on most Viechtach houses. The town is also a center of glassmaking. The spectacularly decorated rococo church of **St. Augustin** dominates Viechtach's central market square, its severe white-and-yellow west front contrasting colorfully with the surrounding high-gable Renaissance and baroque buildings.

The unusual **Gläserne Scheune** (Glazed Barn), decorated on the outside with colorful paintings, houses a variety of exhibitions in glass, including glass walls painted with historic local scenes. ✉ *Raubühl 3,* ☎ *09942/8147,* WEB *www.glaeserne-scheune.de.* 🎫 *€3.50.* 🕙 *Apr.–Sept., daily 10–5; Oct., daily 10–4.*

Four centuries of glassmaking are documented in Viechtach's **Kristallmuseum** (Crystal Museum), which also has a vivid exhibition on the

Pfahl, together with samples of more than 1,000 crystals and minerals and replicas of the world's most famous diamonds. ✉ *Linprunstr. 4,* ☎ *09942/5497.* 🎫 *€2.* ⏲ *Mon.–Sat. 9–6, Sun. 10–4. Closed Sun. in Feb. and Nov.*

Candle-making is another ancient craft still practiced in the Bavarian Forest. Discover how beeswax is turned into candles at Viechtach's **Wachszieher & Lebzelter Museum** (Lebzelter Wax Museum). ✉ *Ringstr. 7,* ☎ *09942/8812.* 🎫 *€1.50.* ⏲ *Sun.–Fri. 8–6.*

★ Among the most unusual museums of the Bavarian Forest is the **Ägayrischen Gewölbe** (Ägarian Vaults, 1432), a collection of 400 replicas of Egyptian antiquities spanning 4,000 years. The originals are in some of the world's leading museums. Owner and artist Reinhard Schimd uses the adjacent chapel (1580) to exhibit his own art, currently a project on Tarot cards, which probably originated in Eygpt. ✉ *Spitalg. 5,* ☎ *09942/801–638,* WEB *www.ge-woelbe.de.* 🎫 *€2.50.* ⏲ *Apr.–June and Sept.–Oct., Tues.–Sun. 10–4; July–Aug., daily 10–4.*

Dining and Lodging

$$ ✕🏨 **Hotel Schmaus.** Run by the same family for 13 generations, this former stagecoach inn is for the energetic. The kitchen ($–$$$) turns out meals on the assumption that every guest has just finished a 40-km (25-mi) hike through the forest, although the all-weather sports facilities could make you equally hungry. In summer dine in the grill garden. Ask to stay in the older section—some of the modern rooms are somewhat plain. ✉ *Stadtpl. 5, D–94234,* ☎ *09942/94160,* FAX *09942/941–630.* WEB *www.Hotel-Schmaus.de. 40 rooms. Restaurant, Weinstube, no a/c, Internet, 2 tennis courts, pool, sauna, meeting rooms. AE, DC, MC, V. Closed last 3 wks of Jan.*

$$ 🏨 **Am Pfahl.** It's hard to imagine any wish that isn't met by this large but refreshingly personal hotel on the edge of Viechtach, right next to the famous Pfahl. Sports enthusiasts are well catered to with tennis, squash, and badminton courts; mountain bikes; and expert information about other activities in the area. The staff can arrange day trips though a local bus company. ✉ *Waldfrieden 1, D–94234,* ☎ *09942/95700,* FAX *09942/957–150,* WEB *www.bayern.touristic.de/hotelampfahl. 98 rooms. Restaurant, bar, no a/c, cable TV, 2 tennis courts, pool, sauna, steam room, mountain bikes, archery, badminton. AE, MC, V.*

Nightlife and the Arts

A **theater festival** with roots in the Middle Ages is held from mid-July to early August in Neunussberg Castle, just outside Viechtach. Call the Viechtach tourist office for details.

Shopping

For glass objects and other arts and crafts, try the **Viechtacher Kunststube,** in the Altes Rathaus (✉ Stadtpl. 1, ☎ 09942/2441). **Glas Rötzer** (✉ Hafnerhöhe, ☎ 09942/1340) sells handicrafts such as glass and pottery. Günther Götte's **Pegasus-Studio** (✉ Kandlbach 3, ☎ 09942/2729) has a wide range of local pottery.

Bodenmais

18 *24 km (15 mi) east of Viechtach, 34 km (21 mi) north of Deggendorf.*

This resort is in a valley below the Bavarian Forest's highest mountain, the Grosser Arber. A nearby silver mine helped Bodenmais prosper before tourism reached this isolated part of the country. Bodenmais's long tradition of glassmaking includes Bavaria's largest glassworks, the **Joska Waldglashütte,** which welcomes visitors at its foundry and showrooms in the Am Moosbach industrial zone. The foundry also has a restaurant. ✉ *Am Moosbach 1,* ☎ *09924/7790.* 🎟 *Free.* ⏲ *Weekdays 9–6, Sat. 9–2.*

You can watch glassblowers at the foundry **Austen Glashütte** and buy goods at very reasonable prices. ✉ *Bahnhofstr. 57,* ☎ *09924/905–990.* 🎟 *Free.* ⏲ *Weekdays 10–6, Sat. 10–4.*

OFF THE BEATEN PATH

SILBERBERG – The 600-year-old silver mine closed in 1962, but you can still view its workings near the summit of the 3,000-ft-high Silberberg. The air within the mine is so pure that one of the side shafts is used to treat asthmatics and people with chronic bronchial complaints. You can walk from Bodenmais to the entrance of the mine or take the chairlift from Arbersee Road, about 2 km (1½ mi) north of Bodenmais. ☎ *09924/304 for details on guided tours,* WEB *www.silberberg-online.de.* 🎟 *€5.20.* ⏲ *Apr.–June and Sept.–Oct., daily 10–4; July and Aug. daily 9–4:45; Nov.–Dec. 25, Wed. only for one tour at 1; Dec. 26–Jan. 8, daily 10–3; Jan. 9–Mar., Tues., Wed., Fri., Sat. 1–3.*

Dining and Lodging

$ ✕🏨 **Bodenmaiser Hof.** The maisonette rooms in this expansive and meticulously run hotel are particularly large and luxurious, with galleried sleeping areas and living rooms beneath. Ordinary double rooms are also generous in size, and most have terraces or balconies with forest views. The winter-garden restaurant ($–$$$) and a tavern are warm retreats on cold days, and a glass-roof terrace beckons in summer. The hotel produces its own bread and meat and even has an in-house distillery that creates a fine schnapps. ✉ *Risslochweg 4, D–94249,* ☎ *09924/9540,* FAX *09924/95440,* WEB *www.Bodenmaiser-Hof.de. 20 rooms, 10 suites. Restaurant, café, no a/c, gym, sauna, hair salon. No credit cards.*

$$ 🏨 **Feriengut-Hotel Böhmhof.** The Böhmhof estate on the edge of the forest has been owned by the Geiger family for more than three centuries. Their long tradition of hospitality can be felt from the friendly reception to the comfortable, spacious rooms, several of which are "country-house suites" with separate living areas. One estate building provides farmhouse-style accommodations, ideal for families. The outdoor and indoor pools allow for year-round swimming; walking and cross-country ski trails start at the front door. ✉ *Böhmhof 1, D–94249,* ☎ *09924/94300,* FAX *09924/943–013,* WEB *www.feriengut-boemhof.de. 22 rooms, 15 suites. Restaurant, café, no a/c, cable TV, Internet, 1 indoor and 1 outdoor pool, gym, hot tub, sauna, recreation room. No credit cards. Closed mid-Nov.–mid-Dec.*

Outdoor Activities and Sports

Bodenmais is 13 km (8 mi) south of the **Grosser Arber,** the highest mountain (4,800 ft) of both the Bavarian Forest and the Czech Republic's Bohemian Forest. Several hiking trails lead to the summit; in winter it offers challenging skiing and in 2000 was an International Skiing Federation World Cup venue. A bus service runs from Bodenmais to the base of the mountain, where a chairlift (€8) makes the 10-minute trip to the summit. There's a great view of the central European stretch of woodland from here. Short walks from the bottom of the lift lead to two woodland lakes, the **Grosser Arbersee** and the smaller **Kleiner Arbersee,** both ideal for summer swimming and boating. Beside the Grosser Arbersee, children can wander through the **Märchenwald** (Fairytale Wood), which has a collection of colorful model scenes from famous stories. You can rent boats from the Gaststätte Arbersee across from the Märchenwald entrance. ✉ *Arberseestr. 42.* 🎟 *Marchenwald €2.* ⏲ *Marchenwald May–Oct., daily 10–5.*

Bayerisch-Eisenstein

19 *17 km (11 mi) north of Bodenmais, 7 km (4½ mi) east of the Grosser Arber.*

Travelers who can't resist quirky sights should detour to this little town on the Czech Republic border. The frontier actually cuts the local train station in half. More than 20 **historic old steam locomotives** are housed in one of the ancient engine sheds, and some of them regularly roll back into service for outings into the Czech Republic. ✉ *Bahnhofstr. 44,* ☎ *09925/1376.* *Half-day excursion €10.* *Apr.–Nov. and Dec. 26–early Jan., Tues.–Sat. 10–12:30 and 2–5; Nov.–Dec. 25 and early Jan.–Mar., weekends 10–2.*

You can see glassblowers at work at the **Alwe Kristallglashütte,** in the village of Regenhütte, just outside Bayerisch-Eisenstein. ✉ *Arberseestr.,* ☎ *09925/1231.* *Free.* *Foundry weekdays 9–3, Sat. 9–noon; showroom and shop weekdays 9–5, weekends 9–4.*

Dining and Lodging

$ ✕ **Waldwinkel Hotel.** This hotel comprises three separate buildings—the Ferienhotel Waldspitze and two apartment houses close by. The forest setting and range of facilities make this large, friendly complex an ideal vacation base. Bohemian specialties such as *Böhmische Knödel* (bread dumplings) are included on the restaurant menu ($–$$). Rooms are spacious and have solid Bavarian-style furniture. ✉ *Hauptstr. 4, D–94252,* ☎ *09925/94100,* FAX *09925/941–0199.* WEB *www.waldwinkelhotel.com. 55 rooms. Restaurant, café, no a/c, cable TV, pool, gym, sauna, steam room, billiards, Ping-Pong. No credit cards.*

Zwiesel

20 *15 km (9 mi) south of Bayerisch-Eisenstein, 40 km (25 mi) northeast of Deggendorf, 70 km (43 mi) northwest of Passau.*

As the region's glass-making center, Zwiesel has 18 firms and more than 2,000 townspeople involved in shaping, engraving, or painting glass. Most open their foundries to visitors. At **Kunstglasbläserei Seemann** (Seemann Artistic Glass Foundry; ✉ Stormbergerstr. 36, ☎ 09922/1091), in the village of Rabenstein, you can try your own skill at blowing glass on Thursday from 10 to noon and often on Friday from 9 AM to 11 AM (but please call in advance). Take home the result of your efforts for a €5 fee.

Just 2 km (1 mi) north of Zwiesel, in the village of Theresienthal, the **Glasmuseum zum Schlössl** (Castle Glass Museum) is one of the biggest of its kind in the Bavarian Forest. Here you'll see how glassblowing developed through the centuries. The museum is part of a glass park that includes two of Europe's oldest glass foundries, as well as showrooms, shops, and a restaurant. ✉ *Glaspark Theresienthal,* ☎ *09922/1030.* *€3, including guided tour.* *Weekdays 10–2.*

The **Waldmuseum Zwiesel** (Zwiesel Forest Museum) has displays dedicated to the centuries-old customs and heritage of the entire forest region. ✉ *Stadtpl. 29,* ☎ *09922/60888.* *€2.* *Mid-May–mid-Oct., weekdays 9–5, weekends 10–noon and 2–4; mid-Oct.–mid-May, weekdays 10–noon and 2–5, weekends 10–noon. Closed Nov.*

The Bavarian Forest has a long toy-making tradition, and the **Zwiesel Spielzeugmuseum** (Zwiesel Toy Museum) has one of the region's largest collections of playthings ancient and modern. ✉ *Prälat-Neun-Str. 4,* ☎ *09922/5526.* *€2.50.* *Daily 10–5. Closed Nov.–Christmas.*

Zwiesel produces a variety of beers and a notorious schnapps, Bärwurz. You can sample the house-brewed bitter Janka Pils or a malty, dark wheat brew at most of the town's taverns. The distillery **Bayerwald Bärwurzerei** has added to its products a liqueur, Hieke Bärwurz, which at 40 proof rivals the schnapps for pure head-spinning effect. ✉ *Frauenauerstr. 80–82,* ☎ *09922/84330.* ⏲ *June–Oct., weekdays 8–6, Sat. 9–4, Sun. and holidays 9:30–4; Nov.–May weekdays 8–6, Sat. 9–4.*

Lodging

$$ **Hotel Sonnenhof.** This large, friendly pension is set in rolling countryside on the edge of Zwiesel, with panoramic views of the Bavarian Forest. It's an ideal base for exploring the area, and special rates apply for stays of a week or more. Families are warmly welcomed. ✉ *Ahornweg 10, D–94227,* ☎ *09922/9005,* FAX *09922/60521,* WEB *www.sonnenhof-zwiesel.de. 23 rooms. Restaurant, pool, sauna, bicycles, paddle tennis, no a/c, cable TV. AE, DC, MC, V. Closed mid-Nov.–Dec. 24.*

$–$$ **Hotel zur Waldbahn.** The great-grandfather of the current owner, assisted by 13 children, built the Hotel zur Waldbahn more than 100 years ago to accommodate train passengers traveling to Bohemia. Today the emphasis is still on making the traveler feel at home within the hotel's wood-paneled walls. After dining at the restaurant, lay your weary head on snowy white pillows in rooms furnished in a blend of modern and traditional styles. ✉ *Bahnhofpl. 2, D–94227,* ☎ *09922/8570,* FAX *09922/857–222,* WEB *www.zurwaldbahn.de. 28 rooms. Restaurant, no a/c, indoor pool, gym, hot tub, sauna. V. Closed mid-Mar.–mid-Apr.*

Golf

There's a beautifully landscaped 18-hole course at **Golf Park Oberzwieselau** (✉ Lindberg, ☎ 09922/2367; 9922/80113 in summer) about 1½ miles from Zwiesel. The club president is an affable German baron.

Regen

21 *10 km (6 mi) southwest of Zwiesel, 28 km (17 mi) northeast of Deggendorf, 60 km (37 mi) northwest of Passau.*

Regen, a busy market town with 16th-century houses around its large central square, is famous for its annual bash during the last weekend in July. A great party commemorates the 17th-century creation of *Pichelsteiner Eintopf* (pork-and-vegetable stew), a filling dish that has become a staple throughout Germany. The stylish celebrations include sports events on the Regen River, so pack a swimsuit. Regen's other claim to fame is an extraordinary display of Christmas crèches.

Frau Maria-Elisabeth Pscheidl, a Regen resident who has been crafting Nativity scenes herself for more than 30 years, has amassed an inordinate number of these Christmas crèches. The local tourist office claims her collection is the largest and best in the world—it even has the Vatican seal of approval. Many of her creations are displayed in the **Pscheidl Bayerwald-Krippe Museum,** run by the town council in Frau Pscheidl's home. ✉ *Ludwigsbrücke 3,* ☎ *09921/2893.* 🎫 *€1.* ⏲ *Weekdays 9–11:30 and 2–4.*

OFF THE BEATEN PATH

BURG WEISSENSTEIN – The world's largest snuffbox collection can be viewed in one of the outhouses of Weissenstein Castle, near Regen. The 1,300 snuffboxes were collected over a period of 46 years by Regen's former mayor, Alois Reitbauer. His reward was an entry in the *Guinness Book of Records.* ✉ *Weissenstein 32,* ☎ *09921/5106.* 🎫 *€1.50.* ⏲ *Late May–mid-Sept., daily 10–noon and 1–5.*

RINCHNACH – This village, 8 km (5 mi) east of Regen, has an impressive monastery that began as an 11th-century monk's lonely retreat. Built in the 15th century, the church was renovated in baroque style by Johann Michael Fischer in the 1720s. Visit its expansive interior to see his masterly wrought-iron work and some typically heroic frescoes. Two early 18th-century altar paintings by Cosmas Damian Asam are also on view. ⏲ *Daily 9–dusk.*

Dining

$–$$ ✕ **Restaurant am Rathaus.** If you're anywhere in the Regen area on a Sunday, head for this Bavarian restaurant for a great lunch or dinner deal—a quarter of a roast duck complete with red cabbage and dumplings for less than €5! If duck's not your favorite, there are other dishes of similar value on the menu, much of it cooked in traditional fashion on a hot-stone oven. ✉ *Stadtpl. 3,* ☎ *09921/2220. Reservations not accepted. No credit cards. Closed Wed.*

THE EASTERN BAVARIAN FOREST

East of Deggendorf the countryside falls in hilly folds to the Danube and the beautiful border city of Passau. North of Passau the forest climbs again to the remote Dreiländereck, the spot where Germany, Austria, and the Czech Republic meet.

Deggendorf

22 *28 km (17 mi) southwest of Regen, 140 km (87 mi) northeast of Munich.*

Between the Danube and the forested hills that rise in tiers to the Czech border, Deggendorf justifiably regards itself as the Bavarian Forest's southern gateway. The town was once on the banks of the Danube, but repeated flooding forced its inhabitants to higher ground in the 13th century. You can still see a 30-yard stretch of the protective wall built around the medieval town.

Deggendorf is unique in Lower Bavaria for its specially developed "cultural quarter," created from a section of the Old Town. Lining the leafy, traffic-free square are the city museum; a public library; a handicrafts museum—the only one of its kind in the Bavarian Forest; and the Kapuzinerstadl, a warehouse converted into a concert hall and theater venue.

The 16th-century **Rathaus,** in the center of the wide main street, the Marktstrasse, has a central tower with a tiny apartment that traditionally housed the town watchman and lookout. From its windows you can get a fine view. The rooms haven't changed over the centuries. ✉ *Oberer Stadtpl.,* ☎ *0991/296–0169.* 🎫 *€20.* ⏲ *Tower can only be visited as part of guided tour of the town, June–Sept., daily at 9:30.*

★ The **Heilig Grabkirche** (Church of the Holy Sepulchre) was originally built as a Gothic basilica in the 14th century. Its lofty tower—regarded as the finest baroque church tower in southern Germany—was added 400 years later by the Munich master builder Johann Michael Fischer. ✉ *Michael-Fischer-Pl.* ⏲ *Daily 9–dusk.*

Exhibits at the **Handwerksmuseum** (Museum of Trades and Crafts) focus on typical regional handicrafts such as glassmaking and wood carving. ✉ *Maria-Ward-Pl. 1,* ☎ *0991/296–0555.* 🎫 *€2, also valid for admission to the Stadtmuseum.* ⏲ *Tues.–Sat. 10–4, Sun. 10–5.*

The **Stadtmuseum** (City Museum) traces the history of the Danubian people. ✉ *Östlicher Stadtgraben 28,* ☎ *0991/296–0555.* 🎫 *€2, also valid for admission to Handwerksmuseum.* ⏲ *Tues.–Sat. 10–4, Sun. 10–5.*

OFF THE BEATEN PATH **ST. MARGARETHA KIRCHE** – This church contains important work by baroque artists, including a series of large, ornate frescoes and altar paintings by Cosmas Damian Asam, as well as elaborate sculptures of angels and cherubs, entwined on the church pillars, by Egid Quirin Asam and Johann Michael Fischer. The three worked here in a rare partnership between 1728 and 1741. Cosmas Damian's self-portrait is amid the extravagant decor. To get here, cross the Danube just outside Deggendorf or take the ferry at Winzer,and then the Passau road (B–15) to the village of Osterhofen. ✉ *Osterhofen.* ⏲ *Daily 9–7, except during Sun. services. Free guided tours Tues. and Thurs. at 3 (meet at main church door).*

Dining and Lodging

$–$$ ✕ **Ratskeller.** In the vaulted rooms of the Rathaus, you could easily find yourself sharing a table with a town councillor, perhaps even the mayor. The menu includes both Bavarian and modern German cuisine; the beer flows freely. ✉ *Oberer Stadtpl. 1,* ☎ *0991/6737. No credit cards.*

$–$$ ✕ **Zum Grafenwirt.** In winter ask the host for a table near the fine old tile stove that sits in the dining room. Try such filling dishes as roast pork and Bavarian dumplings. In summer watch for Danube fish on the menu. ✉ *Bahnhofstr. 7,* ☎ *0991/8729. AE, MC, V. Closed Tues.*

$$ ✕🏨 **Astron Parkhotel.** A monumental mural by Elvira Bach welcomes you in the reception area of this spacious luxury hotel, and the artistic touch is continued in the large and airy guest rooms, all with original paintings on the walls. The Tassilo restaurant ($$) and adjoining winter garden serve diverse items such as pork medallions with a feta cheese and a pimento sauce, or lamb ragout with potato and spinach gratin. In summer a shady beer garden beckons; in winter a log fire burns invitingly in the lounge. The Danube promenade and the Old Town center are both nearby. ✉ *Edlmairstr. 4, D–94469,* ☎ *0991/34460,* FAX *0991/344–6423,* WEB *www.astron-hotels.de. 112 rooms, 13 suites. Restaurant, no a/c, cable TV, gym, hot tub, sauna, bicycles, bar, beer garden. AE, DC, MC, V.*

$$ ✕🏨 **Schlosshotel Egg.** The "Egg" doesn't stand for something you might eat in this castle-hotel's excellent restaurant ($–$$$); it's derived from Ekke, the name of the 12th-century owner. Today the hotel, 13 km (8 mi) northwest of Deggendorf, is a memorable place in which to lay your head. A vaulted dining room, the Burgstall, and a paved courtyard garden maintain the medieval mood of the ivy-covered old building. There are just a few comfortable apartment-size suites, so it's essential to book ahead. ✉ *94505 Schloss Egg-Bernried, D–94505,* ☎ *09905/289,* FAX *09905/741–022,* WEB *www.schlosshotel-egg.de. 8 suites. Restaurant, beer garden, no a/c, cable TV. V. Closed Jan. and Feb.*

$ ★ ✕🏨 **Donauhof.** This lovely 19th-century stone warehouse has spotless rooms with modern Scandinavian furniture. The Wintergarten Café ($–$$) is a local favorite for its delicious cakes and coffee. ✉ *Hafenstr. 1, D–94469,* ☎ *0991/38990,* FAX *0991/389–966,* WEB *www.hotel-donauhof.de. 85 rooms, 3 suites. Restaurant, café, no a/c, cable TV, sauna, solarium, meeting rooms. AE, DC, MC, V.*

Outdoor Activities and Sports

In Schaufling, **Deggenorfer Golfclub ev.** (✉ Rusel 123, ☎ 09920/8911) is a challenging course high above Deggendorf, and offers views of the Bavarian Forest and the Danube Plain.

Metten

㉓ *7 km (4½ mi) west of Deggendorf.*

This village along the Danube holds two outstanding examples of baroque art within the white walls and quiet cloisters of its **Benedictine monastery,** founded in the 9th century by Charlemagne. The

18th-century **library** has a collection of 160,000 books whose gilt leather spines are complemented by the heroic splendor of their surroundings—Herculean figures support the frescoed, vaulted ceiling, and allegorical paintings and fine stuccowork identify different categories of books. In the **church** is Cosmas Damian Asam's altarpiece *Lucifer Destroyed by St. Michael*; created around 1720, its vivid coloring and swirling composition is typical of the time. ☎ *0991/91080.* €2. *Guided tours daily 10 and 3.*

Schönberg

24 *40 km (25 mi) northeast of Deggendorf.*

In little Schönberg's **Marktplatz** (market square), arcaded shops and houses present an almost Italian air. As you head farther south down the Inn Valley, this Italian influence—the so-called Inn Valley style—becomes more pronounced.

Lodging

$–$$ **Landhaus zur Ohe.** A *Landhaus* is a country house, but this description doesn't do justice to this large holiday hotel with its huge range of amenities. The hotel backs directly onto the forest and commands a view of open, rolling countryside. Rooms are light and airy, with pale pinewood furniture. Most have balconies with panoramic views. Children are particularly well catered to, with play areas inside and out and a small zoo with domestic and farm animals. ✉ *Maukenreuth 1, Schönberg D–94513,* ☎ *08554/96070,* FAX *08554/556,* WEB *www.landhaus-zur-ohe.de. 41 rooms, 6 suites. Restaurant, pool, no a/c, cable TV, gym, hair salon, sauna, spa, billiards, paddle tennis, bar, playground. MC, V. Closed Nov.*

Bavarian Forest National Park

★ 25 *15 km (9 mi) northeast of Schönberg, main entrance at Neuschönau, 50 km (31 mi) north of Passau.*

The Bavarian Forest National Park is a 32,000-acre stretch of protected dense forest. Substantial efforts have been made to reintroduce bears, wolves, lynx, and other animals to the park, though today the animals are restricted to large enclosures. Well-marked paths lead to points where wildlife can best be seen. Bracing walks also take you through the thickly wooded terrain to the two highest peaks of the park, the 4,350-ft **Rachel** and the 4,116-ft **Lusen.** Specially marked educational trails trace the geology and botany of the area, and picnic spots and playgrounds abound. In winter park wardens will lead you through the snow to where wild deer from the mountains feed. A visitor center—the **Hans-Eisenmann-Haus** (☎ 08558/96150; daily 9–5)—is at the main entrance to the park, on the edge of the village of Neuschönau. Slide shows and English-language brochures provide introductions to the area. There is no entrance fee to the park, but expect to pay €1 per hour for parking.

Tours of the national park are organized by the **Grafenau Verkehrsamt** (tourist office; ✉ Rathausg. 1, ☎ 08552/96230). For as little as €135, the Verkehrsamt offers a winter week's B&B package, including a visit to the national park, two tours on cross-country skis, and two on snowshoes.

There are several glass foundries in the villages bordering the national park. You can watch glassblowers at work and buy products at their source at the **Kristallglasfabrik** (✉ Hauptstr. 2–4, Spiegelau, ☎ 08553/2400; shop weekdays 9:30–6, Sat. 9:30–4, May–Oct. also Sun. 11–4; workshop demonstrations weekdays 9:15–1:45). At the **Glasmacherhof** (✉ Birkenweg 21, Mauth, ☎ 08557/96140, WEB www.glassmacherhof-mauth.

com; ⏲ weekdays 9–5, Sat. 9–noon) you can not only shop but are also encouraged to try glassblowing yourself.

The town of **Grafenau** has two unusual and interesting museums. The **Bauernhausmuseum** (☎ 08552/3318), in the resort's spa-park, consists of two restored Lower Bavarian farmhouses containing furnishings and implements from the 18th and 19th centuries. The **Schnupftabak-Museum** (Snuff Museum; ✉ Spitalstr.), in a historic almshouse, depicts (and attempts to explain) the habit of sniffing snuff. Snuffboxes from several countries disprove the theory that only Bavarians are addicted. Both museums are open mid-December–October, daily 2–5 and cost €1.50 each.

Dining and Lodging

$–$$$ ✕ **Adalbert Stifter.** Named after a popular 19th-century novelist, this friendly country hotel-restaurant at the foot of the Dreisessel Mountain is at its best turning out the sort of time-honored dishes Stifter knew. Try one of the Bohemian-style roasts, served with fresh dumplings. ✉ *Frauenberg 32, Frauenberg,* ☎ *08556/355. No credit cards. Closed Nov.*

$$ ★ ✕🏨 **Säumerhof.** The Bavarian Forest isn't known for haute cuisine, but here in Grafenau, one of its prettiest resorts, is a restaurant that bears comparison with Germany's best. It's part of a small country hotel run by the Endl family. Gebhard Endl's territory is the kitchen, where he produces original dishes ($$–$$$$) using local ingredients. Try the pheasant on champagne cabbage or the roast rabbit in herb-cream sauce. ✉ *Steinberg 32, D–94481 Grafenau,* ☎ *08552/408–990,* FAX *08552/408–9950,* WEB *www.saeumerhof.de. 10 rooms. Restaurant, no a/c, cable TV, sauna. AE, DC, MC, V.*

$ ✕🏨 **Gasthof-Restaurant Barnriegel.** On the edge of the Bavarian Forest National Park, this family-run restaurant ($–$$$) caters to those made hungry by a day's walking. Sauerbraten is one of the best dishes on the menu; local lake fish is also a specialty. Fresh vegetables and herbs come from the Barnriegel's own garden. The weary will also be provided for here with a stay in one of the inexpensive but comfortable pinewood-furnished rooms. ✉ *Halbwaldstr. 32, D–94151 Finsterau,* ☎ *08557/96020,* FAX *08557/960–249.* WEB *www.baernriegel.de. 24 rooms. No a/c, cable TV, hot tub, gym. No credit cards. Closed Nov. 15–Dec. 15.*

$$ 🏨 **Mercure Hotel Sonnenhof.** If you are traveling with children, this is the hotel for you: during vacation time the staff includes a *Spieltante* (playtime auntie) who keeps youngsters amused. The ultramodern hotel is set on extensive grounds, and there's lots to do—even horse-drawn sleigh rides in winter. You can choose between two room styles: country house, with light woods and pastel tones, or rustic, with dark furnishings and brightly colored fabrics. ✉ *Sonnenstr. 12, D–94481 Grafenau,* ☎ *08552/4480,* FAX *08552/4680,* WEB *www.mercure.de. 144 rooms, 3 suites. 2 restaurants, bar, no a/c, cable TV, miniature golf, 6 tennis courts, pool, gym, hair salon, sauna, bowling. AE, DC, MC, V.*

$$ 🏨 **Romantik Hotel Die Bierhütte.** The name means "beer hut," and it was once a royal brewery. Now a member of the select Romantik hotel group, the elegant 18th-century building has its own quiet grounds beside a lake, near the village of Hohenau. The rooms are furnished with rustic pine wood beds and flowered fabrics. ✉ *Bierhütte 10, D–94545 Hohenau,* ☎ *08558/96120,* FAX *08558/961–270,* WEB *www.romantikhotels.com. 37 rooms, 6 suites, 4 apartments. Restaurant, no a/c, cable TV, hair salon, sauna. AE, DC, MC, V.*

Dreiburgenland

On the Ostmarkstrasse (B–85) between Schönberg and Passau.

Fürstenstein, Englburg, and Saldenburg are the three castle-rich villages that make up Dreiburgenland, or Land of the Three Castles. Unfortunately none of the castles are open to visitors, but the area is wonderful for hiking and local shops sell maps called *Wanderkarten* that suggest walking tours.

26 On the shore of the **Dreiburgensee** in Tittling, you'll find the **Museumsdorf Bayerischer Wald** (Open-Air Museum), which consists of 50 reconstructed Bavarian Forest houses. You can sit on the benches of a 17th-century schoolhouse, drink schnapps in an 18th-century tavern, or see how grain was ground in a 15th-century mill. Although the buildings are closed in winter, guests can still take a stroll through the grounds for the price of €1. ✉ *Next to Hotel Dreiburgensee, Tittling,* ☎ *08504/8482.* €2.50. ⏲ *Mid-Mar.–Oct., daily 8–5; Nov.–mid-Mar., daily 9–4.*

Dining and Lodging

$ ✕ **Hotel Dreiburgensee.** The hotel primarily books extended vacations, but it's also convenient for an overnight stop if you're visiting the nearby open-air museum. All the hotel's rooms have balconies with views of the Dreiburgensee or the forest. Some have Bavarian-style four-poster beds with painted headboards and large, fluffy goose-down covers. Children love the sturdy bunk beds in the spacious family rooms. ✉ *Am Dreiburgensee, D–94100 Tittling/Passau,* ☎ *08504/2092,* FAX *08504/4926. 100 rooms. Restaurant, café, no a/c, miniature golf, pool, gym, sauna, boating, bicycles, playground. No credit cards. Closed Nov.–Mar.*

Passau

33 km (20 mi) southeast of Schönberg, 66 km (41 mi) southeast of Deggendorf, 179 km (111 mi) northeast of Munich.

The city perches on a narrow point of land where the Inn and the Danube rivers meet, with wooded heights rising on the far sides of both rivers; the much smaller River Ilz also joins the Danube nearby. Most of the finest and oldest homes face the busy waterfront, where freighters and barges load and unload during journeys to and from the Black Sea and the Rhine. Narrow streets of peculiarly varying levels rise to a hill in the center of the old city. These harmonious proportions are complemented by the typical Inn Valley houses that line the streets, joined to each other by picturesque archways. Passau's Mediterranean air is due in part to the many Italian architects who worked here, and to a special quality of light that painters through the centuries have tried to capture in their work.

Passau is a remote yet important embarkation point for the traffic that has plied its way along the Danube for centuries. Settled more than 2,000 years ago by the Celts, then by the Romans, Passau later passed into the possession of prince-bishops whose domains stretched into present-day Hungary. At its height, the Passau episcopate was the largest in the entire Holy Roman Empire. The influence wielded by the prince-bishops over nearly six centuries has left its traces in the town's Residenz (bishop's palace), the Veste Oberhaus (the bishop's summer castle), and the magnificent Dom (cathedral).

For 45 postwar years Passau was a backwater in a "lost" corner of West Germany until the collapse of the Iron Curtain opened nearby frontiers, putting the historic city back on the central European map. Despite its small size, Passau has a stately, grand-dame atmosphere.

A Good Walk

Sandwiched as it is between the Danube and Inn rivers, Passau is a very snug city. Begin your walk at the tourist office on the west side of

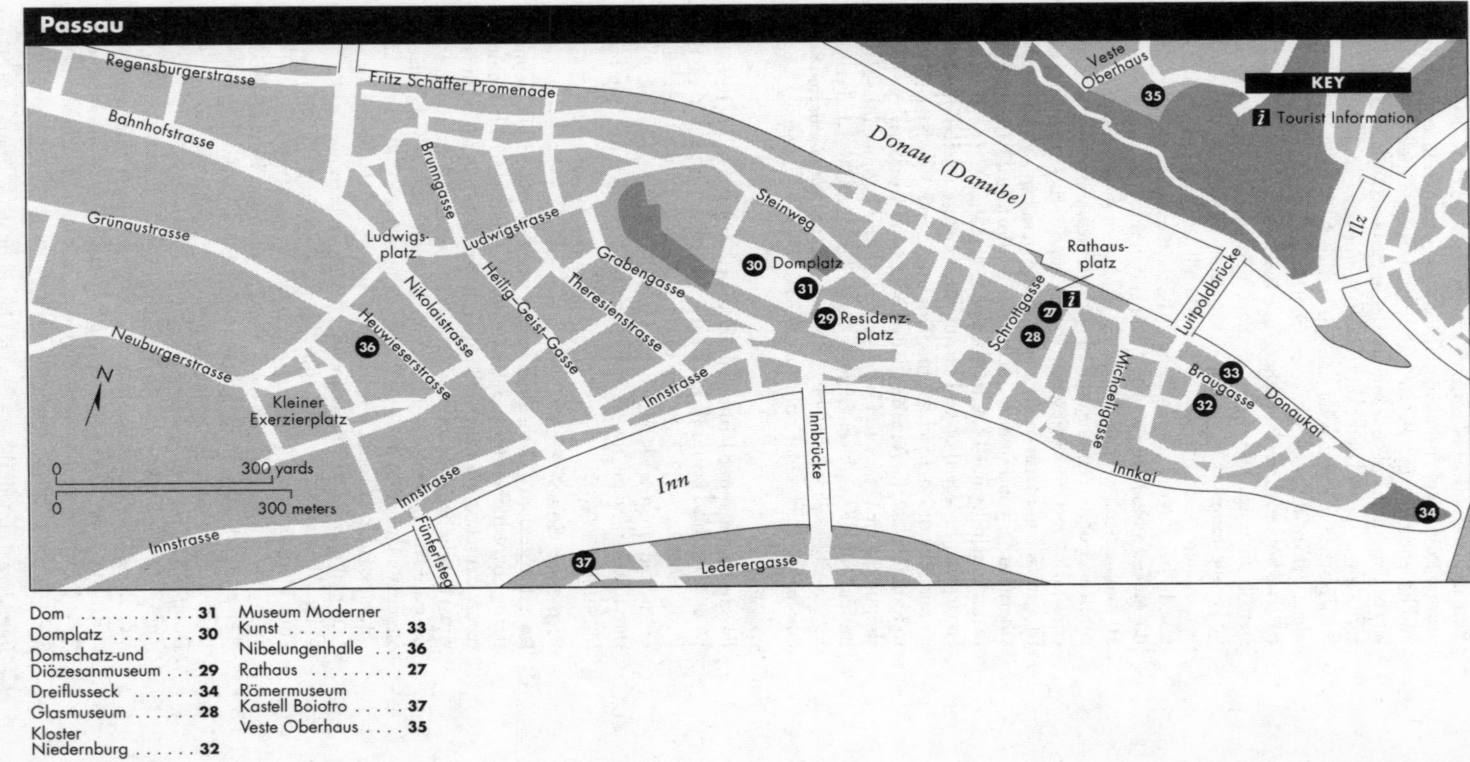

Dom **31**	Museum Moderner Kunst **33**
Domplatz **30**	Nibelungenhalle . . . **36**
Domschatz-und Diözesanmuseum . . . **29**	Rathaus **27**
Dreiflusseck **34**	Römermuseum Kastell Boiotro **37**
Glasmuseum **28**	Veste Oberhaus **35**
Kloster Niedernburg **32**	

Rathausplatz, where you can pick up brochures and maps. Passau's 14th-century **Rathaus** ㉗ forms one side of the square and faces the Danube and its landing stages. Before leaving the square in the direction of the city center, stop by the **Glasmuseum** ㉘, in the Hotel Wilder Mann. Next, turn right at the end of the short street, Schrottgasse, and you're on Residenzplatz, dominated by the baroque bulk of the Neue Bischöfliche Residenz, where religious treasures from the city's illustrious episcopal past are housed in the **Domschatz- und Diözesanmuseum** ㉙. A flight of steps leading up from the Domschatz- und Diözesan Museum brings you to the **Domplatz** ㉚ and Passau's towering **Dom** ㉛. Descend the steps in the square's southwest corner, and you'll arrive at the Inn River. Follow the bank to the east, and you'll pass the **Kloster Niedernburg** ㉜ and the **Museum Moderner Kunst** ㉝, which is in the same street. A further 10-minute stroll will take you to the gardens of the **Dreiflusseck** ㉞, the confluence of the Danube, Inn, and Ilz rivers. Continue along the southern bank of the Danube upstream to the Luitpoldbrücke; cross this bridge to reach the northern bank, where a steep path leads you to the **Veste Oberhaus** ㉟; you can also catch a bus to this fortress from Rathausplatz. Catch the bus back to the city center, alighting at Kleiner Exerzierplatz, bordered on one side by the immense **Nibelungenhalle** ㊱, a remainder of Nazi architecture. Now make your way back eastward to Rathausplatz, finding time to explore Passau's attractive pedestrian shopping zone (an area of eight streets). If time permits and you're in museum mode, walk south along the Heilig Geist Gasse and cross the Inn River by its pedestrian bridge to the outstanding **Römermuseum Kastell Boiotro** ㊲, which holds remnants of Passau's Roman past.

TIMING

Passau can be toured leisurely in the course of one day. Try to visit the Dom at noon to hear a recital on its great organ, the world's largest. Early morning is the best time to catch the light falling from the east on the old town walls and the confluence of the three rivers. Passau shrouded in the dank river fogs of winter rivals even Venice for its brooding atmosphere.

Sights to See

31 **Dom** (St. Stephan's Cathedral). Passau's mighty cathedral rises majestically on the highest point of the earliest-settled part of the city. A baptismal church stood here in the 6th century. Two hundred years later, when Passau became a bishop's seat, the first basilica was built. It was dedicated to St. Stephan and became the original mother church of St. Stephan's Cathedral in Vienna. A fire reduced the medieval basilica to smoking ruins in 1662; it was then rebuilt by Italian master architect Carlo Lurago. What you see today is the largest baroque basilica north of the Alps, complete with an octagonal dome and flanking towers. Little in its marble- and stucco-encrusted interior reminds you of Germany, and much proclaims the exuberance of Rome. Beneath the dome is an enormous **organ.** Built between 1924 and 1928 and enlarged in 1979–80, it claims no fewer than 17,774 pipes and 233 stops. ✉ *Dompl.* 🎟 *Free. Concerts midday €3, evening €5.* ⏲ *May–Oct., daily 8–11 and 12:30–6; Nov.–Apr., daily 8–dusk. Tours May–Oct. and Dec. 20–25 weekdays 12:30 (assemble at cathedral's front right-hand aisle); Nov.–Dec. 19 and Dec. 26–Apr., Mon.–Sat. noon (assemble under the cathedral organ); concerts May–Oct. and Dec. 20–25, Mon.–Wed. and Fri. noon, Thurs. noon and 7:30* PM.

30 **Domplatz** (Cathedral Square). This large square in front of the Dom is bordered by sturdy 17th- and 18th-century buildings, including the **Alte Residenz,** the former bishop's palace and now a courthouse. The fine statue depicts Bavarian king Maximilian Joseph I.

29 **Domschatz- und Diözesanmuseum** (Cathedral Treasury and Diocesan Museum). The cathedral museum houses one of Bavaria's largest collections of religious treasures, the legacy of Passau's rich episcopal history. The museum is part of the **Neue Residenz** (New Residence), which has a stately baroque entrance opening onto a magnificent staircase—a scintillating study in marble, fresco, and stucco. ✉ *Residenzpl.* 🎫 *€1.50.* ⏲ *Apr.–Oct., Mon.–Sat. 10–4.*

34 **Dreiflusseck** (Junction of the Three Rivers). At this tongue of land at the eastern extremity of Passau, the Danube, Inn, and tiny Ilz rivers join together in an embrace that, thanks to a phenomenon of nature, leaves each of them with a distinct identity until they all flow out of Passau's grip and into Austria, where their waters merge into the Danube, bound for the Black Sea. For the best perspective climb to the Veste Oberhaus to see how the Inn's green water, typical of a mountain river, slowly gives way to the darker hues of the Danube and how the brownish Ilz adds its small contribution. It's the end of the journey for the Inn—which flows here from the mountains of Switzerland and through Austria—and the much shorter Ilz, which rises in the Bavarian Forest.

28 **Glasmuseum** (Glass Museum). The Bavarian Forest's most comprehensive exhibit of glass is in the lovely Hotel Wilder Mann. The history of central Europe's glassmaking is captured in 30,000 items, from baroque to art deco. ✉ *Am Rathauspl.,* ☎ *0851/35071.* 🎫 *€4.* ⏲ *Oct.–May, daily 1–4; June–Sept., daily 10–4.*

32 **Kloster Niedernburg** (Niedernburg Abbey). Founded in the 8th century as a convent, the abbey was destroyed by fire and rebuilt in the last century in a clumsy neo-Romanesque style. Today it's a girls' school. In its church you can see the 11th-century tomb of a queen who was once abbess here—Gisela, sister of Emperor Heinrich II and widow of Hungary's first and subsequently sainted king, Stephan, who became the patron of the Passau Cathedral. ✉ *Bräug.* ⏲ *Daily 9–dusk.*

36 **Nibelungenhalle** (Nibelungen Hall). This huge Nazi-era hall is on Passau's windswept **Kleiner Exerzierplatz** (Small Drill Square), once a Benedictine monastery garden but now an ugly parking lot. The hall's name is taken from the *Nibelungenlied,* the epic poem, written in Passau in the 12th century, that inspired Richard Wagner's immense operatic cycle *Der Ring des Nibelungen.* Later Hitler distorted the same legendary material in an attempt to legitimize the Nazi creed. His obsession with Wagner—almost surpassing that of Ludwig II—was part of his sense of himself as the preserver of a heroic Teutonic tradition. The hall is used for political rallies and trade shows and was also the reception center for the first refugees who fled East Germany in late summer 1989. ✉ *Kleiner Exerzierpl.*

27 **Rathaus** (City Hall). Passau's 14th-century city hall sits like a Venetian merchant's house on a small square fronting the Danube. It was the home of a wealthy German merchant before being declared the seat of city government after a 1298 uprising. Two assembly rooms have wall paintings depicting scenes from local history and lore, including the (fictional) arrival in the city of Siegfried's fair Kriemhild, from the Nibelungen fable. The Rathaus tower has Bavaria's largest glockenspiel, which plays daily at 10:30, 2, and 7:25, with an additional performance at 3:30 on Saturday. ✉ *Rathauspl.,* ☎ *0851/3960.* 🎫 *€1.50.* ⏲ *Apr.–Oct. and Dec. 24–Jan. 1, daily 10–4.*

37 **Römermuseum Kastell Boiotro** (Roman Museum). A stout fortress with five defense towers and walls more than 12-ft thick came to light as archaeologists excavated the site of a 17th-century pilgrimage church

on a hill known as Mariahilfberg, on the south bank of the Inn. The Roman citadel Boiotro was discovered along with a Roman well, its water still plentiful and fresh. Pottery, lead figures, and other artifacts from the area are housed in this museum at the edge of the site. ✉ *Ledererg. 43,* ☎ *0851/34769.* 🎫 *€2.* ⏲ *Mar.–May and Sept.–Nov., Tues.–Sun. 10–noon and 2–4; June–Aug., Tues.–Sun. 10–noon and 1–4.*

33 **Museum Moderner Kunst** (Museum of Modern Art). Changing exhibitions of 20th- and 21st-century art include works by artists such as Otto Dix, Keith Haring, and Gustav Klimt. The museum is housed in a fascinating jumble of buildings, incorporating so many architectural styles that this alone makes a visit worthwhile. ✉ *Bräug. 17,* ☎ *0851/383–8790,* WEB *www.mmk-passau.de.* 🎫 *€5.* ⏲ *Tues.–Sun. 10–6.*

35 **Veste Oberhaus** (Upper House Stronghold). The powerful fortress and summer castle commissioned by Bishop Ulrich II in 1219 looks over Passau from an impregnable site on the other side of the river, opposite the Rathaus. Today the Veste Oberhaus is Passau's most important museum, containing exhibits that illustrate the city's 2,000-year history. From the terrace of its café-restaurant (open Easter–October), there's a magnificent view of Passau and the convergence of the three rivers. ✉ *Oberhausleitenstiege,* ☎ *0851/493–3512.* 🎫 *Museum €4.* ⏲ *Mar.–Oct., weekdays 9–5, weekends 10–6. Bus from Rathauspl. to museum Apr.–Oct. every ½ hr 10:30–5.*

Dining and Lodging

$$–$$$ ✕ **Passauer Wolf.** The owner of this hotel, Richard Kerscher, is also master of his own kitchen, and restaurant guides crown his efforts with the highest praise. Kerscher's stylish restaurant, which commands views of the Danube from its snug window seats, is considered Passau's best. His delicacies, all based on traditional German recipes, are also served in the vaulted 16th-century wine bar. ✉ *Rindermarkt 6–8,* ☎ *0851/931–5110. AE, DC, MC, V. Closed Sun. No lunch Sat.*

$–$$$ ✕ **Blauer Bock.** This is one of Passau's oldest houses (first mentioned in city records in 1257) and has been welcoming travelers since 1875. The Danube flows by the tavern windows, and in summer you can watch the river traffic from a beer garden. The food is as traditional as you'll find, with pork and potatoes in every variety. ✉ *Höllg. 20,* ☎ *0851/34637. MC, V.*

$–$$$ ✕ **Heilig-Geist-Stiftsschänke.** For atmospheric dining this 14th-century monastery–turned–wine cellar is a must. In summer eat beneath chestnut trees; in winter seek out the warmth of the vaulted, dark-paneled dining rooms. The wines—made in Austria from grapes from the Spitalkirche Heiliger Geist vineyards—are excellent and suit all seasons. The fish comes from the Stift's own ponds. ✉ *Heilig-Geist-G. 4,* ☎ *0851/2607. MC, V. Closed Wed. and Jan. 10–Feb. 1.*

$–$$$ ✕ **Peschl Terrasse.** The beer you sip on the high, sunny terrace overlooking the Danube is brought fresh from the Old Town brewery below, which, along with this traditional Bavarian restaurant, has been in the same family since 1855. ✉ *Rosstränke 4,* ☎ *0851/2489. AE, DC, MC, V. Closed Mon.*

$–$$ ✕ **Hacklberger Bräustüberl.** Shaded by magnificent old trees, locals sit in this famous brewery's enormous beer garden (seating more than 1,000), sipping a Hacklberger and tucking into a plate of sausages. In the winter they simply move to the wood paneled interior where beer has been on tap from the brewery next door since 1618. ✉ *Bräuhauspl. 7,* ☎ *0851/58382. MC, V.*

$$$ 🏨 **Hotel Weisser Hase.** The "White Rabbit" began accommodating travelers in the early 16th century but is thoroughly modernized. Rooms are decorated with cherrywood and mahogany veneers and soft matching colors. The large bathrooms are finished in Italian marble. The hotel stands sturdily in the town center, at the start of the pedestrian shopping zone, a short walk from all the major sights. ✉ *Heilig-Geist-G. 1, D–94032,* ☎ *0851/92110,* FAX *0851/921–1100,* WEB *www.weisser-hase.de. 108 rooms, 1 suite. Restaurant, cable TV, in-room data ports, sauna, bar, no a/c, parking (fee). AE, DC, MC, V. Closed Jan.–mid-Feb.*

$$–$$$ ★ **Hotel Wilder Mann.** Passau's most historic hotel dates from the 11th century and shares prominence with the ancient city hall on the waterfront market square. Empress Elizabeth of Austria and American astronaut Neil Armstrong have been among its guests. On beds of carved oak you'll sleep beneath chandeliers and richly stuccoed ceilings. The esteemed Glasmuseum is within the hotel. ✉ *Am Rathauspl. 1, D–94032,* ☎ *0851/35071,* FAX *0851/31712,* WEB *www.rotel-tours.de. 48 rooms, 5 suites. Restaurant, no a/c, cable TV. AE, DC, MC, V.*

$$ **Hotel König.** Though built in 1984, the König blends successfully with the graceful Italian-style buildings alongside the elegant Danube waterfront. Rooms are large and airy; most have a fine view of the river. ✉ *Untere Donaulände 1, D–94032,* ☎ *0851/3850,* FAX *0851/385–460,* WEB *www.hotel-koenig.de. 41 rooms. No a/c, cable TV, in-room data ports, sauna, steam room, bar, meeting room. AE, DC, MC, V.*

$$ **Schloss Ort.** This 13th-century castle's large rooms have views of the Inn River, which flows beneath the hotel's stout walls. The rooms are decorated in a variety of styles with old-fashioned four-poster beds or modern wrought iron details. The restaurant is closed in winter, but the kitchen will always oblige hungry hotel guests. In summer the garden terrace is a delightful place on which to eat and to watch the river roll by. ✉ *Ort 11, D–94032.* ☎ *0851/34072,* FAX *0851/31817,* WEB *www.schlosshotel-passau.de. 18 rooms. Restaurant, no a/c, cable TV. MC, V.*

$ **Golf-Hotel Anetseder.** You don't have to be a golfer to enjoy a stay at this lodge-style hotel 7 km (4½ mi) north of Passau, although there are enticing offers that include use of the 21-hole course, which is overlooked by most of the 14 apartments. The apartments, all with kitchen facilities, are furnished in a casual, sporty style, with lots of pine wood furniture. The Bavarian Forest begins outside the hotel entrance. ✉ *Rassbach 8, Thyrnau D–94136,* ☎ *08501/91313,* FAX *08501/91314,* WEB *www.rassbach.de. 14 apartments. Restaurant, no a/c, cable TV, kitchenettes. AE, V. Closed Nov.–Feb.*

$ **Rotel Inn.** "Rotels" are usually hotels on wheels, an idea developed by a local entrepreneur to accommodate tour groups in North Africa and Asia. The first permanent Rotel Inn is on the banks of the Danube in central Passau and resembles an ocean liner. Its rooms are small and cabinlike, but they're clean, decorated in a pop-art style, and amazingly cheap. The building's unique design—a red, white, and blue facade and flowing roof lines—has actually been patented. It's definitely for young travelers, but also fun for families. ✉ *Am Hauptbahnhof/Donauufer, D–94032,* ☎ *0851/95160,* FAX *0851/951–6100,* WEB *www.rotel-tours.de. 100 rooms. No a/c. No credit cards. Closed Oct.–Mar.*

Golf

Europe's most extensive golf course (21 holes) is at **Golf-Hotel Anetseder** (✉ 7 km [4½ mi] northeast of Passau in Thyrnau, ☎ 08501/91313).

Nightlife and the Arts

Passau is the cultural center of Lower Bavaria. Its **Europäische Wochen** (European Weeks) festival—featuring everything from opera to pantomime—is a major event on the European music calendar. The festival runs from June to early August. For program details and reservations, write the Kartenzentrale der Europäischen Wochen Passau (✉ Dr.-Hans-Kapfinger-Str. 22, D–94032 Passau, ☎ 0851/560–960).

Passau's thriving theater company, the **Stadttheater Passau** (✉ Gottfried-Schäffer-Str. 2–4, ☎ 0851/929–1913) has its home in the beautiful little baroque opera house of Passau's prince-bishops, the Fürstbischöfliches Opernhaus. The theater also hosts opera, operetta, and occasionally ballet.

Live jazz programs are regularly presented at **Theater im Scharfrichterhaus** (✉ Milchg. 2, ☎ 0851/35900), home of the city's nationally famous cabaret company. The company hosts a cabaret festival every fall from October through December.

Passau's **Christmas fair**—the Christkindlmarkt—is the biggest and most spectacular of the Bavarian Forest. It's held in and around the Nibelungenhalle from late November until just before Christmas.

OFF THE BEATEN PATH

MT. DREISESSEL – You can't get much more off the beaten track than in the remote corner of the country north of Passau, where the German frontier bobs and weaves along the Czech Republic and Austria. Where the border cuts across the summit of Mt. Dreisessel, west of Altreichenau, it's possible to walk in and out of a virtually forgotten corner of the Czech Republic—a feat that was possible even when the border was guarded everywhere else by heavily armed soldiers. *Dreisessel* means "three armchairs," an apt description of the summit and its boulders, which are shaped like the furniture of a giant's castle. If you're driving to the Dreisessel, take B–12 to Philippsreut, just before the frontier, and then follow the well-marked country road. The mountain is about 67 km (42 mi) from Passau. Several bus operators in Passau and surrounding villages offer tours. There are no visitor facilities within the forest.

THE BAVARIAN FOREST A TO Z

To research prices, get advice from other travelers, and book travel arrangements, visit www.fodors.com.

AIRPORTS

The nearest airports are in Munich and Nürnberg. Each is about 160 km (100 mi) from the western edge of the Bavarian Forest.

BOAT AND FERRY TRAVEL

Cruises on Passau's three rivers begin and end at the Danube jetties on Fritz-Schäffer Promenade. Ludwig Wurm has a range of small cruise-ship services upriver between Passau and Regensburg, taking in Deggendorf, Metten, Straubing, and Walhalla. Wurm & Köck runs 45-minute trips daily on the Danube, Inn, and Ilz from March through October, in the last week of December, and on weekends from mid-November to Christmas Eve. Prices begin at €8.50. A two-hour Danube cruise aboard the *Sissi* costs €9; cruises run daily at 11:15 and 2:45 from early May to the end of October. There is also a trip to Linz, Austria (it's possible to stay overnight in Linz, but you can return on the same day), for €72. If it's luxury you're looking for, you can take the 225-ft day-cruise vessel, *Regina Danubia,* which travels between Passau and Engelhartszell, Austria every Sunday and which serves a buffet lunch.

DDSG offers two-day cruises to Vienna for around €130 per person one-way and Danube cruise connections via Budapest all the way to the Black Sea.

An Austrian shipping operator, M. Schaurecker, runs a daily service on the Inn River from Tuesday through Sunday, mid-March through October, between Passau and the enchanting Austrian river town of Schärding. The round-trip fare is €8.

➤ BOAT AND FERRY INFORMATION: **DDSG** (✉ Im Ort 14a, D–94032 Passau, ☎ 0851/33035, WEB www.ddsg-blue-danube.at). **Ludwig Wurm** (✉ Donaustr. 71, D–94342 Irlbach, ☎ 09424/1341). **M. Schaurecker** (✉ A.-Stifterstr. 34, A–4780 Schärding, ☎ 0043/7712–3231). **Wurm & Köck** (✉ Höllg. 26, D–94032 Passau, ☎ 0851/929–292, WEB www.donauschiffahrt.com).

BUS TRAVEL

Villages not on the railway line are well served by postbus. In winter a network of special ski buses links most of the region's resorts. Resorts on the edge of the Bavarian Forest National Park and below the Rachel and Lusen mountains are linked May–October by bus. A fleet of Igel (Hedgehog) minibuses penetrates deep into the forest on roads barred to other motor traffic. Passau has a municipal bus service that reaches into the hinterland.

CAR TRAVEL

The principal autobahns that link to the Bavarian Forest are the A–3 from Regensburg and the A–92 from Munich. Traffic on both roads is always relatively light. Regensburg is 120 km (74 miles) from Munich and 77 km (47 miles) from Deggendorf. Passau is 120 km (75 mi) from Regensberg and 179 km (111 mi) from Munich.

The B–85 runs the length of the Bavarian Forest from Passau to Cham, and its designation as a scenic route (the Ostmarkstrasse) extends northward to Bayreuth.

EMERGENCIES

➤ CONTACTS: **Police and ambulance** (☎ 110). **Fire and emergency medical aid** (☎ 112).

TOURS

Many town tourist offices (including Freyung, Furth im Wald, Grafenau, and Tittling) organize bus tours of the region and day trips to the Czech Republic. The Freyung tourist office has weekly half-day trips to the Bavarian Forest National Park and to Dreisessel Mountain. In Tittling the Hötl bus company has daily forest excursions in summer. From Zwiesel, Lambürger operates regional bus tours, as well as a tour three times a week to Prague, with a supper stop on the way home in the Plsen brewery tavern. There's a weekly tour to the Czech spas Marienbad and Karlsbad (Karlovy Vary) and another to the original home of Budweiser beer, Budweis.

The Passau tourist office leads tours of Passau from April through October. There are two tours (at 10:30 and 2:30) on weekdays and one (at 2:30) on weekends. Tours start at the Maximilian Joseph statue in the Domplatz (cathedral square) and last one hour. Day tours of the Bavarian Forest (€7.50) are offered every Monday by the Verkehrsamt Lalling, the tourist office of a town near Passau. The Wolff Ost-Reisen bus company, in Furth im Wald, runs one- and two-day excursions to Prague twice a week May–October, as well as trips to the Czech spa town of Karlsbad.

The major visitor information offices all have details on hiking packages. Typical is a €115 five-day tour along the Böhmweg, which includes overnight accommodations, full breakfasts, and a schnapps reception by one of the tourist offices en route. Luggage is transported for you. Deutsche Bahn, the German railway, sends hikers out on its three-day tour of the Bavarian Forest National Park with a bottle of Bärwurz schnapps. The €97 cost of the tour includes three nights' accommodations in a pension, breakfast, and luggage transfer.

➤ TOUR-OPERATORS: **Deutsche Bahn** (✉ Bahnhofspl., Zwiesel D–94227, ☎ 01805/996–633). **Hötl** (☎ 08504/4040). **Lambürger** (✉ Stadtpl. 37, Zwiesel, ☎ 09922/84120). **Passau tourist office** (☎ 08551/955–980). **Verkehrsamt Lalling** (☎ 09904/374). **Wolff Ost-Reisen** (☎ 09973/5080).

TRAIN TRAVEL

Two main rail lines cross the region: one runs west–east via Nürnberg, Regensburg, Passau, and Vienna; the other runs south–north via Munich, Landshut, and Straubing. This latter route slices right through the heart of the Bavarian Forest, making stops in Deggendorf, Plattling, and Bayerischer Eisenstein on its way to the Czech Republic (if you're going on to Prague, this is the train to take). Deutsche Bahn runs a special holiday express daily from Hamburg to Bavarian Forest resorts, with Zwiesel as its final destination. The express links up with train services from Berlin and Frankfurt International Airport. Plattling, just south of Deggendorf, and Cham are the main rail junctions for the area. Passau is the principal rail gateway between southeast Germany and Austria.

VISITOR INFORMATION

For information on the whole region, contact Tourismusverband Ostbayern.

➤ TOURIST INFORMATION: **Bayerisch-Eisenstein** (✉ Verkehrsamt Bayerisch-Eisenstein, Schulbergstr. 1, D–94252, ☎ 09925/327, WEB www.bayerisch-eisenstein.de). **Bodenmais** (✉ Kur-Verkehrsamt, Bahnhofstr. 56, D–94249, ☎ 09924/778–135, WEB www.bodenmais.de). **Cham** (✉ Fremdenverkehrsverein Cham, Propsteistr. 46, D–93413, ☎ 09971/803–493). **Deggendorf** (✉ Kultur- und Verkehrsamt, Oberer Stadtpl. 4, D–94469, ☎ 0991/296–0169, WEB www.deggendorf.de). **Freyung** (✉ Touristinformation/Kurverwaltung, Rathauspl. 2, D–94078, ☎ 08551/588–150, WEB www.freyung.de). **Furth im Wald** (✉ Tourist-Information Furth im Wald, Schlosspl. 1, D–93437, ☎ 09973/50980, WEB www.furth.de). **Grafenau** (✉ Verkehrsamt Grafenau, Rathausg. 1, D–94481, ☎ 08552/962–343, WEB www.grafenau.de). **Passau** (✉ Tourist-Information Passau, Rathauspl. 3, D–94032, ☎ 0851/955–980, WEB www.passau.de). **Regen** (✉ Verkehramt Haus des Gastes, Stadtpl., D–94209, ☎ 09921/2929, WEB www.regen.de). **Regensburg** (✉ Altes Rathaus, D–93047, ☎ 0941/507–3410, WEB www.regensburg.de). **Schönberg** (✉ Verkehsamt, Marktpl. 16, D–94513, ☎ 08554/960–441). **Spiegelau** (✉ Touristinformation Spiegelau, Konrad-Wilsdorf-Str. 5, D–94518, ☎ 08553/960–017, WEB www.tourismus-bayern.com). **St. Englmar** (✉ Kurverwaltung St. Englmar, Rathausstr. 6, D–94379, ☎ 09965/840–320). **Tittling** (✉ Verkehrsamt Tittling, Marktpl. 10, D–94104, ☎ 08504/40114, WEB www.btl.de/tittling). **Tourismusverband Ostbayern** (✉ Luitpoldstr. 20, D–93047 Regensburg, ☎ 0941/585–390, WEB www.ostbayern-tourismus.de). **Viechtach** (✉ Tourismusverband, Rathaus, Stadtpl. 1, D–94234, ☎ 09942/1661, WEB www.viechtach.de). **Waldkirchen** (✉ Fremdenverkehrsamt Waldkirchen, Ringmauerstr. 14, D–94065, ☎ 08581/20250, WEB www.waldkirchen.de). **Zwiesel** (✉ Kurverwaltung, Stadtpl. 27, D–94227, ☎ 09922/1308, WEB www.zwiesel.de).

5 THE ROMANTIC ROAD

Within the massive gates of fortified settlements, half-timber houses lean against one another along narrow cobble lanes. Fountains and flowers adorn ancient squares, and formidable walls are punctuated by watchtowers built to keep a lookout for marauding enemies. The sights along this tour route add up to a pageant of history, art, and architecture, providing an essence of Germany at its most picturesque and romantic.

Updated by Inez Sharp

OF ALL THE TOURIST ROUTES that crisscross Germany, none rivals the aptly named Romantische Strasse, or Romantic Road. The scenery is more pastoral than spectacular, but the route is memorable for the medieval towns, villages, castles, and churches that anchor its 355-km (220-mi) length. Many of these are tucked away beyond low hills, their spires and towers just visible through the greenery.

The road runs south from Würzburg, in northern Bavaria, to Füssen, on the border with Austria. You can, of course, follow it in the opposite direction, as a number of bus tours do. Either way, among the major sights you'll see are one of Europe's most scintillating baroque palaces, in Würzburg, and perhaps the best-preserved medieval town on the Continent, Rothenburg-ob-der-Tauber. Ulm, a short trip off the Romantic Road, is included here because of its magnificent cathedral. Then there's the handsome Renaissance city of Augsburg. Finally the fantastical highlight will be Ludwig II's castle, Neuschwanstein.

The Romantic Road concept developed as West Germany rebuilt its tourist industry after World War II. A public-relations wizard coined the catchy title for a historic passage through Bavaria and Baden-Württemberg that could be advertised as a unit. In 1950 the Romantic Road was born. The name itself isn't meant to attract lovebirds, but refers to a variation of the word *romance* that means wonderful, fabulous, and imaginative. And, of course, the Romantic Road started as a road on which the Romans traveled.

On its way the road crosses centuries-old battlefields. The most cataclysmic conflict, the Thirty Years' War, destroyed the region's economic base in the 17th century. The depletion of resources prevented improvements that would have modernized the area—thereby assuring the survival of the historic towns' now charmingly quaint infrastructures.

As you travel the Romantic Road, two names crop up repeatedly: Walther von der Vogelweide and Tilman Riemenschneider. Walther von der Vogelweide, who died in Würzburg in 1230, was the most famous of the German *Minnesänger,* poet-musicians who wrote and sang of courtly love in the age of chivalry. Knights and other nobles would hire them to help win the favors of fair ladies. Von der Vogelweide broke with this tradition by writing love songs to maidens of less-than-noble rank. He also accepted commissions of a political nature, producing what amounted to medieval political manifestos. His work was romantic, lyrical, witty, and filled with a sighing wistfulness and philosophical questioning. Medieval sculptor Tilman Riemenschneider spent his most creative and esteemed years in Würzburg, where he also ended his life a pauper and outcast due to his support of farmers and guildsmen during the 1524–25 Peasants' War.

Pleasures and Pastimes

Dining

The best Franconian and Swabian food combines hearty regional specialties with nouvelle elements. Various forms of pasta are common. *Schupfnudeln* (little potato dumplings) are eaten either with a sweet or savory accompaniment, and *Spätzle* (small tagliatellelike ribbons of rolled dough) is often served with *Rinderbraten* (roast beef), the traditional Sunday lunchtime dish. One of the best regional dishes is *Maultaschen,* a Swabian version of ravioli, usually served floating in broth strewn with chives. Würzburg is one of the leading wine-producing areas of Germany, and the many Franconian beers range from Räucherbier (literally, "smoked beer") to the lighter ales of Ulm.

CATEGORY	COST*
$$$$	over €20
$$$	€15–€20
$$	€10–€15
$	under €10

**per person for a main course at dinner*

Golf

The countryside along the Romantic Road is ideal territory for golf; you can tee off in Aschaffenburg, Bad Mergentheim, Würzburg, at Burg Colmberg (east of Rothenburg), Augsburg, at Schloss Igling, just outside Landsberg, and virtually in the shadow of King Ludwig's fairytale castle, Neuschwanstein.

Lodging

With a few exceptions, the Romantic Road hotels are quiet and rustic, and you'll find high standards of comfort and cleanliness. Make reservations as far in advance as possible if you plan to visit in summer. Hotels in Würzburg, Rothenburg, and Füssen are often full year-round. Augsburg hotels are in great demand during trade fairs in nearby Munich. Tourist information offices can usually help with accommodations, especially if you arrive early in the day.

CATEGORY	COST*
$$$$	over €225
$$$	€150–€225
$$	€75–€150
$	under €75

**All prices are for two people in a standard double room, including tax and service charge.*

Exploring the Romantic Road

The Romantic Road runs from the vineyard-hung slopes of the Main River valley at Würzburg to the snow-covered mountains overlooking Füssen in the Allgäuer Alps. For much of its route it follows two enchanting rivers, the Tauber and the Lech, and at one point crosses the great Danube, still a surprisingly narrow river this far from the Black Sea end of its journey. The city of Augsburg, because of its proximity to the hub of Munich, marks the natural halfway point of the Romantic Road. South of Augsburg, the road climbs gradually into the Alpine foothills and the landscape changes from the lush green of Franconian river valleys to mountain-backed meadows and forests.

Great Itineraries

Although a long-distance bus covers the Romantic Road daily during summer in less than 12 hours, each town tugs insistently at the visitor, and it's difficult to resist an overnight stay when one is sent to bed by a night watchman's bell (as in Rothenburg or Dinkelsbühl). Würzburg or Augsburg are each worth two or three days of exploration, and such attractions as the minster of Ulm are time consuming but rewarding diversions from the recognized Romantic Road.

Numbers in the text correspond to numbers in the margin and on the Romantic Road, Würzburg, Rothenburg-ob-der-Tauber, and Augsburg maps.

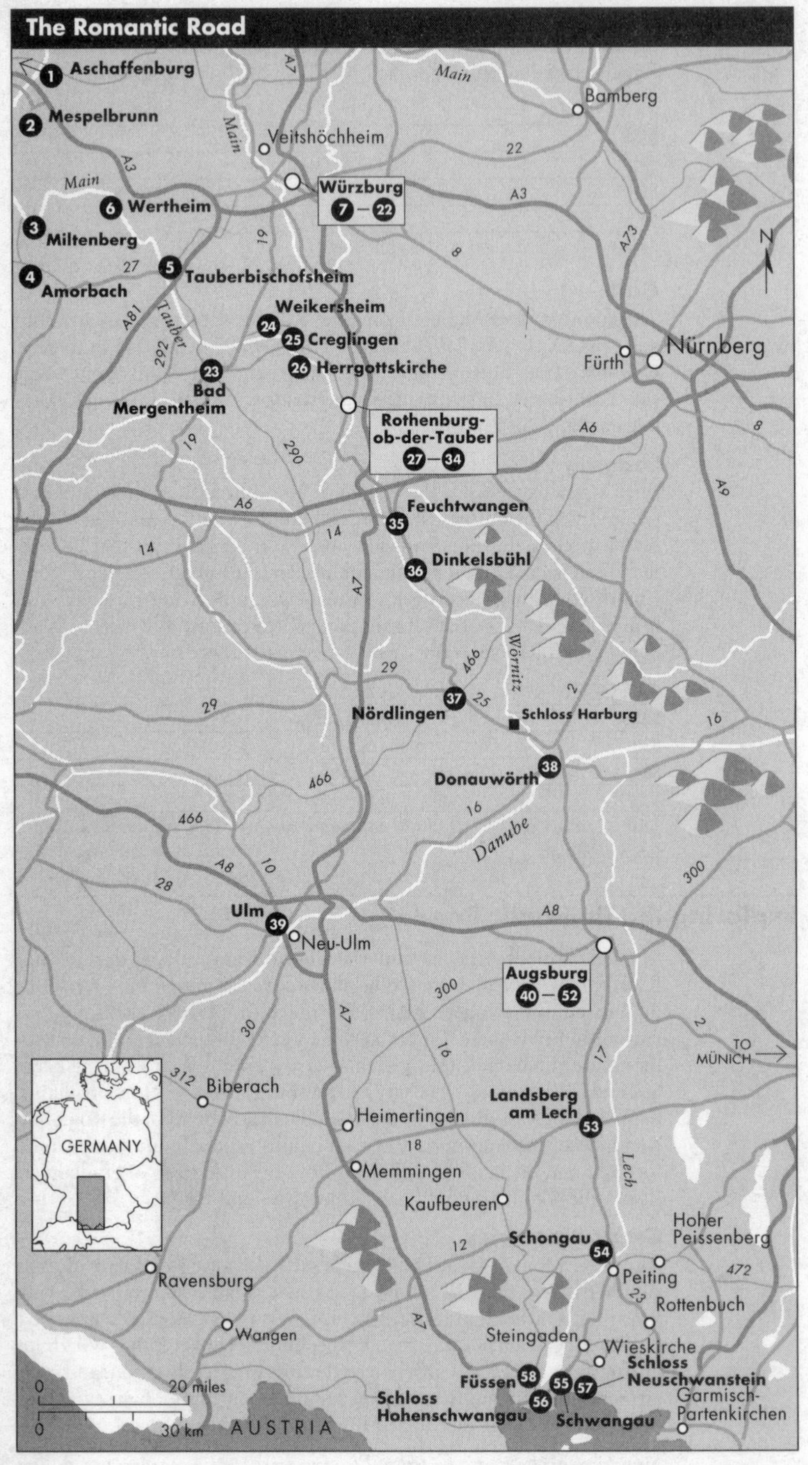
The Romantic Road
1 Aschaffenburg
2 Mespelbrunn
3 Miltenberg
4 Amorbach
5 Tauberbischofsheim
6 Wertheim
Würzburg 7–22
23 Bad Mergentheim
24 Weikersheim
25 Creglingen
26 Herrgottskirche
Rothenburg-ob-der-Tauber 27–34
35 Feuchtwangen
36 Dinkelsbühl
37 Nördlingen
Schloss Harburg
38 Donauwörth
39 Ulm
Neu-Ulm
Augsburg 40–52
53 Landsberg am Lech
54 Schongau
Schloss Neuschwanstein
55
56
57
58 Füssen
Schloss Hohenschwangau
Schwangau
Main
Bamberg
Veitshöchheim
Nürnberg
Fürth
Tauber
Wörnitz
Danube
Lech
Biberach
Heimertingen
Memmingen
Kaufbeuren
Ravensburg
Wangen
Hoher Peissenberg
Peiting
Rottenbuch
Steingaden
Wieskirche
Garmisch-Partenkirchen
TO MÜNICH
AUSTRIA
GERMANY
N
0
20 miles
0
30 km

IF YOU HAVE 3 DAYS

Join the Romantic Road at **Augsburg** ㊵–(52) and spend your first day and night immersing yourself in the Fugger family history. On the second day head north, making stops at **Donauwörth** ㊳ (lingering for a lunchtime view of the Danube), **Nördlingen** ㊲, **Dinkelsbühl** ㊱, and **Feuchtwangen** ㉟; stay overnight within the ancient walls of **Rothenburg-ob-der-Tauber** ㉗–㉞. On the third day continue on to **Creglingen** ㉕ to admire the Tilman Riemenschneider altar in the **Herrgottskirche** ㉖, just outside the village, and then travel through the lovely Tauber River valley, visiting **Weikersheim** ㉔, **Bad Mergentheim** ㉓, and **Tauberbischofsheim** ⑤, until you reach your final destination, **Würzburg** ⑦–㉒.

IF YOU HAVE 5 DAYS

Tackle the entire length of the Romantic Road, starting with a day and night in **Würzburg** ⑦–㉒. From Würzburg follow the three-day itinerary described above in reverse order to **Rothenburg** ㉗–㉞, where you'll spend the night. Continue to **Dinkelsbühl** ㊱ and **Nördlingen** ㊲ and rest after the third day in **Augsburg** ㊵–(52). Explore the rich city before joining the Lech River valley at **Landsberg am Lech** (53) (where Hitler wrote *Mein Kampf* while in the town prison). Continue on to **Schongau** (54), where you'll see the Alps rising up ahead; they're the signal to watch for one of the most glorious sights of the Romantic Road, the rococo **Wieskirche,** which stands in a heavenly Alpine meadow (Wiese). As it heads into the Alps, the Romantic Road has even more spectacular sights, particularly the most eccentric of "Mad" King Ludwig's castles, **Schloss Neuschwanstein** (57). Finally, spend the day in **Füssen** (58) (the end of the Romantic Road).

IF YOU HAVE 7 DAYS

Begin at **Aschaffenburg** ①, 50 km (31 mi) east of Frankfurt, with its magnificent Renaissance castle, the Schloss Johannisburg. Next visit a smaller but no less impressive castle, **Mespelbrunn** ②, in the Spessart uplands. Continue through the Main Valley and explore the lovely old medieval towns of **Miltenberg** ③ and **Wertheim** ⑥. Devote two days to **Würzburg** ⑦–㉒ before heading south. Take day four to investigate **Rothenburg-ob-der-Tauber** ㉗–㉞ (overnighting within its medieval walls), and spend the fifth day of your tour visiting two other exquisitely preserved medieval towns, **Dinkelsbühl** ㊱ and **Nördlingen** ㊲. Rest your fifth night in **Augsburg** ㊵–(52). On the sixth day continue to **Füssen** (58), which provides a good base for day trips to **Schloss Neuschwanstein** (57) and the lovely **Wieskirche.**

When to Tour the Romantic Road

Late summer and early autumn are the best times to travel the Romantic Road, when the grapes ripen on the vines around Würzburg and the geraniums run riot on the medieval walls of towns such as Rothenburg and Dinkelsbühl. You'll also miss the high-season summer crush of tourists. Otherwise, consider visiting the region in the depths of December, when Christmas markets pack the ancient squares of the Romantic Road towns and snow gives turreted Schloss Neuschwanstein its final magic touch.

NORTHERN ROMANTIC ROAD

The northern section of the Romantic Road skirts the wild open countryside of the Spessart uplands, following the sinuous course of the Main River eastward as far as Würzburg, before heading south through the plains of Swabia and along the lovely Tauber and Lech rivers.

Aschaffenburg

❶ *50 km (31 mi) east of Frankfurt.*

Strictly speaking, Aschaffenburg isn't on the Romantic Road; it's one of the highlights of another German holiday route, the Strasse der Residenzen, which features palaces of electors and bishops. The town bears mention for its imposing Renaissance palace, **Schloss Johannisburg.** The prince-electors of Mainz, hereditary rulers of Aschaffenburg in the 17th and 18th centuries, lived here. The exterior of the doughty sandstone palace harks back to the Middle Ages, and four massive corner towers guard the inner courtyard. The **Schloss Museum** (Palace Museum) charts the history of the town and contains a representative collection of German glass. A small section of the **Staatsgalerie** (City Art Gallery; ✉ Schlosspl. 4; ⏲ Apr.–Oct., Tues.–Sun. 9–6; Nov.–Mar., Tues.–Sun. 10–4) is devoted to Lucas Cranach the Elder (1472–1553), a leading painter of the German Renaissance, known for his enigmatic nudes and haunting landscapes. The palace grounds contain a striking copy of the temple of Castor and Pollux in Pompeii, the **Pompejanum** (🎟 €2.50; ⏲ Apr.–Sept., Tues.–Sun. 9–5:30), constructed for Ludwig I of Bavaria in 1840–50. A wine cellar–restaurant, the Schlossweinstuben, is an ideal setting for Franconian wines and food. ✉ *Schlosspl. 1,* ☎ *06021/12440.* 🎟 *€2.50 for all but Pompejanum.* ⏲ *Apr.–Oct., Tues.–Sun. 9–noon and 1–5; Nov.–Mar., Tues.–Sun. 11–4.*

The **Stiftskirche** (Collegiate Church) of Sts. Peter and Alexander has a gaunt and haunting painting by Matthias Grünewald (circa 1475–1528), *The Lamentation of Christ.* It was part of a much larger and now lost altarpiece. See how, in spite of the lessons of Italian Renaissance painting, naturalism and perspective still produce an essentially Gothic image, attenuated and otherworldly. Little remains of the original Romanesque building here, save the cloisters; most of what you see dates from the 16th and 17th centuries. ✉ *Lanlingstr.* ⏲ *Daily 9–dusk.*

Germany's oldest chessboard, a 14th-century treasure, can be seen in the **Stiftsmuseum** (Collegiate Church Museum), in the former chapter house of the Stiftskirche. The museum also contains ecclesiastical treasures and medieval carvings. ✉ *Stiftspl. 1a,* ☎ *06021/386–7414.* 🎟 *€2.50.* ⏲ *Wed.–Mon. 10–1 and 2–5.*

The **Automuseum Rosso Bianco** (Rosso Bianco Automobile Museum) claims to have the largest collection of historic sports cars in the world. ✉ *Obernauer Str. 125,* ☎ *06021/21358.* 🎟 *€6.* ⏲ *Apr.–Oct., Tues.–Sun. 10–6; Nov.–Mar., Sun. 10–6.*

Dining and Lodging

$–$$ ✕🏨 **Hotel-Gasthof Zum Goldenen Ochsen.** The half-timber, lantern-hung exterior of the Golden Bull is colorful testimony to this ancient lodging, which was sheltering travelers in Renaissance times. It's been in the present family for one of its four centuries. Many of the cozy rooms have views over Schloss Johannisburg, the park, and the river valley. Wholesome Franconian fare is served in a reconstructed 200-year-old Tyrolean farm tavern ($$). ✉ *Karlstr. 16, D–63739,* ☎ *06021/23132,* FAX *06021/25785. 38 rooms. Restaurant, café, no a/c, cable TV. AE, DC, MC, V. Restaurant closed 3 wks in Aug., hotel and restaurant 1 wk in Jan. or Feb.*

Outdoor Activities and Sports

BALLOONING

British and American pilots fly a fleet of hot-air balloons for **Discover Ballooning** (☎ 06106/79641), based near Aschaffenburg.

GOLF

There are two attractive courses in the Aschaffenburg area. **The Golf and Country Club Erftal** (☎ 09378/789), southeast of Miltenberg is run by British golf-pro Andrew Payne and his wife Penny. The club has two 9-hole courses with spectacular views. The 18-hole **Main-Spessart Club** (☎ 09391/8435) at Marktheidenfeld extends a warm welcome for foreign guests, and has a 6-hole practice course for those with no handicap.

Mespelbrunn

❷ *14 km (9 mi) southeast of Aschaffenburg.*

The main attraction of Mespelbrunn is a **castle,** surrounded by a moat and dominated by a massive round tower dating from the mid-16th century. The **Rittersaal** (Knights' Room), on the first floor, displays suits of armor, assorted weapons, and massive dark furniture. A more delicate note is struck by the 18th-century **Chinesischer Salon** (Chinese Room), upstairs. *☎ 06092/269. €3.50 including guided tour. ⏲ Mid-Mar.–mid-Nov., Mon.–Sat. 9–noon and 1–5, Sun. 9–5.*

En Route The road south cuts through the still sparsely populated forest area of the **Spessart,** a walker's paradise that used to be the hunting grounds of the archbishops of Mainz and the haunt of Robin Hood–type outlaws. The road meets up with the River Main at the village of **Grossheubach** and then follows it on a serpentine route to Würzburg.

Miltenberg

❸ *30 km (18 mi) south of Mespelbrunn, 70 km (43 mi) west of Würzburg.*

If you love the charm of Rothenburg-ob-der-Tauber but shrink from crowds, Miltenberg—a sleepy riverside town on the southern slopes of the forested Spessart—provides the ideal antidote. The steeply sloping **Marktplatz** is the standout attraction. A 16th-century fountain, bordered by geraniums, splashes in its center; tall half-timber houses—some six stories high, with crooked windows balancing yet more flowers—stand guard all around. One of them is the town museum. To see more of these appealing buildings, stroll down Hauptstrasse, site of the **Rathaus** (town hall) and the 15th-century **Haus zum Riesen** (Giant's House). The town takes its name from its castle, whose entrance is on the Marktplatz.

Dining and Lodging

$–$$ ✕🏨 **Haus zum Riesen.** Built in 1590, the "giant's house" is one of the oldest inns in Germany—the origins of its strange name are lost. The individually furnished rooms range from charmingly old-fashioned to simply rustic to Biedermeier. In the restaurant ($$–$$$) great roasts and fat sausages are served with excellent local beer and wines. *✉ Hauptstr. 97, ☎ 09371/3644. 14 rooms. Restaurant, no a/c, no room TVs. MC, V. Closed Jan. and Feb.*

En Route From Miltenberg you can choose one of two scenic routes to Würzburg. One road, B–426, follows the meanderings of the Main River. Taking the southern loop of B–469 to B–47 to B–27 leads you first to historic towns such as Tauberbischofsheim and Amorbach.

Amorbach

❹ *12 km (7 mi) south of Miltenberg.*

The little town of Amorbach, in the beautiful Odenwald Forest, has an impressive onetime **Benedictine** abbey church. From the 8th through the 18th centuries, one architectural style is superimposed upon the next. The facade of the church seems a standard baroque structure, with twin dome towers flanking a lively and well-proportioned central section; in fact, it is a rare example of the baroque grafted directly onto a Romanesque building. Look closely and you'll notice the characteristic round arches of the Romanesque marching up the muscular towers. It's the onion-shape domes and the colored stucco applied in the 18th century that make them seem baroque. There are no such stylistic confusions in the interior, however; all is baroque power and ornamentation. The mighty organ, built by the esteemed Stumm family, is recognized as one of the finest in Europe. Brief organ recitals (☎ 09373/971–545) are given during church tours from mid-March through the beginning of November, Monday through Saturday at 11 and 3, and Sunday at noon. ✉ *Schlosspl.,* ☎ *09373/971–545.* 🎫 *€3 for tour of church and monastery (not including organ recital).* ⏲ *Mid-Mar.–early Nov., Mon.–Sat. 9:30–5:45, Sun. 11–5:45; early Nov.–Dec. 26, daily 10:30–12:30 and 1:30–4; Dec. 27–mid-Mar., weekends 10:30–12:30 and 1:30–4.*

Amorbach has several rustic half-timber houses; the **Templerhaus** was built in 1291 by a local nobleman. ✉ *Bederweg.* 🎫 *€1.* ⏲ *May–Oct., Wed. 4:30–5:30, Sat. 11–noon.*

The **Sammlung Berger** (Berger Collection) has a collection of 17,000 teapots, mostly from Britain and the United States. An unusual exhibit traces the story of Pepsi-Cola, thanks to Herr Berger's personal obsession with the company. The gift shop sells a wide range of teapots made by a local firm. ✉ *Wolkmannstr. 2,* ☎ *09373/618.* 🎫 *Free.* ⏲ *Apr.–Oct., Tues.–Sun. 11–6.*

OFF THE BEATEN PATH

BURG WILDENBERG – Minnesinger Wolfram von Eschenbach (1170–1220) may have written part of his Parzival tale in this 1,000-year-old fortress. The metrical epic of the Holy Grail inspired Richard Wagner's libretto for *Parsifal.* The ruins are 5 km (3 mi) southeast of Amorbach. The castle keep is still standing, and on a clear day affords a fine view of the Odenwald Forest. 🎫 *€1.50.* ⏲ *Sun. 10–5.*

Dining

$ ✕ **Cafe Schlossmühle.** This charming café is in the former mill of the abbey, and on warm days you can enjoy their delicious pastries sitting outside beside the mill stream. ✉ *Schlosspl. 4,* ☎ *09373/1254. No credit cards. Closed Jan. and 2 wks in Aug.*

Tauberbischofsheim

❺ *40 km (25 mi) east of Amorbach, 36 km (22 mi) southwest of Würzburg.*

The bustling little Tauber River town of Tauberbischofsheim has a parish church, open daily 9–dusk, with a side altar richly carved by a follower of Tilman Riemenschneider. The 13th-century **Kurmainzisches Schloss** (Main Electors' Castle) has a collection of historical furnishings, tools, and costumes of commoners. ✉ *Schlosspl. 7,* ☎ *09341/3760.* 🎫 *€2.* ⏲ *Easter–Oct.; Tues.–Sat. 2:30–4:30, Sun. 10–noon and 2–4:30.*

Wertheim

❻ *30 km (19 mi) east of Miltenberg.*

Wertheim is the chief town on the northern Main Valley road to Würzburg and has a beautiful location at the confluence of the Main and Tauber rivers. The town was founded in 1306 and proclaims its medieval origins through a jumble of half-timber houses with jutting gables. Those in the central Marktplatz are the most attractive. The romantic ruins of **Burg Wertheim,** a 12th-century fortress built for the counts of Wertheim, have a restaurant and a memorable view of the Main Valley.

Würzburg

40 km (25 mi) east of Wertheim, 115 km (71 mi) east of Frankfurt.

The basically baroque city of Würzburg, the pearl of the Romantic Road, is a heady example of what happens when great genius teams up with great wealth. Beginning in the 10th century, Würzburg was ruled by powerful (and rich) prince-bishops, who created the city with all the remarkable attributes you see today.

The city is at the junction of two age-old trade routes in a calm valley backed by vineyard-covered hills. Festung Marienberg, a fortified castle on the steep hill across the Main River, overlooks the compact town. Constructed between 1200 and 1600, the fortress was the residence of the prince-bishops for 450 years.

Present-day Würzburg is by no means completely original. On March 16, 1945, seven weeks before Germany capitulated, Würzburg was all but obliterated by Allied saturation bombing. The 20-minute raid destroyed 87% of the city and killed at least 4,000 people. Reconstruction has returned most of the city's famous sights to their former splendor. Except for a new pedestrian zone, it remains a largely authentic restoration.

A Good Walk

No two sights are more than 2 km (1 mi) from each other. Begin your tour on Marktplatz (Market Square) at the city tourist office, in the mansion **Haus zum Falken** ⑦. Collect the handy English-language tour map with a route marked out. Red signs throughout the city point the way between major sights. Next door to the Haus zum Falken is one of the city's loveliest churches, the delicate **Marienkapelle** ⑧. Leave the square at its eastern exit, and you'll find yourself on Würzburg's traffic-free shopping street, **Schönbornstrasse** ⑨, named after the city's greatest patron, the prince-bishop Johann Philipp Franz von Schönborn. Head north, passing the **Augustinerkirche** ⑩, a former Dominican church, and you'll arrive within a few minutes at the broad Juliuspromenade, dominated by the impressive baroque **Juliusspital** ⑪, an infirmary. Follow Juliuspromenade eastward, and you'll come to the first baroque church built in Franconia, the **Stift Haug** ⑫. Next, follow the street opposite the church, Textorstrasse, to Theaterstrasse, passing the Gothic **Bürgerspital** ⑬, another charitable institution. At the end of Theaterstrasse stands the mighty **Residenz** ⑭ of the Würzburg prince-bishops, built for Schönborn by the great baroque-era architect Balthasar Neumann.

From the Residenz walk down Domerschulstrasse and turn left onto Schönthalstrasse for the **Alte Universität** ⑮. The southern section of the building is taken up by the Neubaukirche, a fine Renaissance church. Next, head north on Schönthalstrasse to Plattnerstrasse; where this street becomes Schönbornstrasse you'll find Würzburg's cathedral, the **Dom St. Kilian** ⑯, and the nearby **Neumünster** ⑰ church. From the cathedral take Domstrasse westward, and you'll see the high tower of the 14th-century **Rathaus** ⑱; beyond this the **Alte Mainbrücke** ⑲ crosses the Main River. Stroll north along the riverbank to one of Würzburg's familiar landmarks, the **Alter Kranen** ⑳, a wharf crane. To conclude your walk, cross the river on the bridge and climb the vineyard-covered hill to the great brooding fortress, the **Festung Marienberg** ㉑. Within its massive walls are two very interesting museums. You can ride back

Alte Mainbrücke . 19
Alte Universität . . 15
Alter Kranen 20
Augustinerkirche 10
Bürgerspital . 13
Dom St. Kilian 16
Festung Marienburg . 21
Haus zum Falken. 7
Juliusspital . . 11
Marienkapelle 8
Neumünster 17
Rathaus 18
Residenz . . . 14
Schloss Veitshöchheim 22
Schönbornstrasse. 9
Stift Haug . . 12

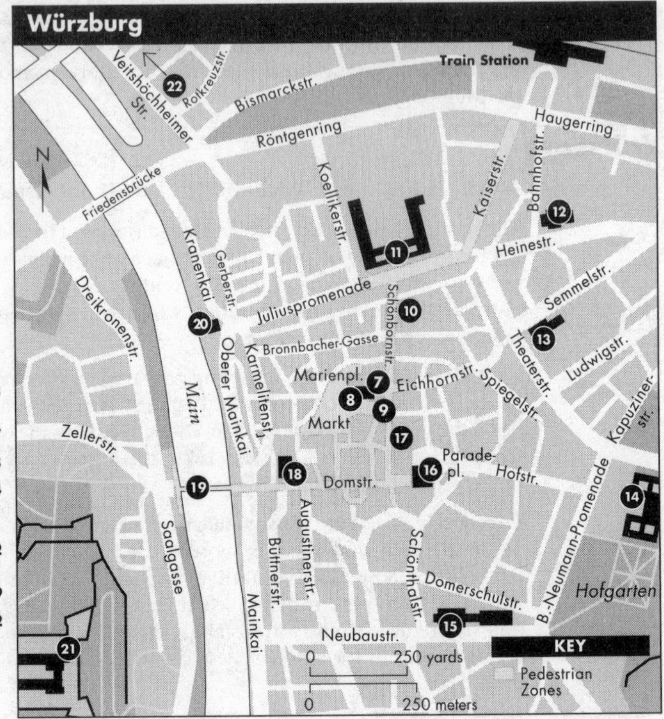

into central Würzburg on the bus that stops in front of the main entrance.

TIMING

You need two days to do full justice to Würzburg. The Residenz alone demands several hours' attention. But if time is short, head for the Residenz as the doors open in the morning, before the first crowds assemble. Aim to complete your tour of the Residenz by lunchtime; then continue to the nearby Juliusspital Weinstuben or one of the many traditional taverns in the area for lunch. In the afternoon explore central Würzburg and cross the Main River to visit the Festung Marienberg and the Mainfränkisches Museum.

Sights to See

19 **Alte Mainbrücke** (Old Main Bridge). This ancient structure crossing the Main River began construction toward its present form in 1473. Twin rows of infinitely graceful statues of saints line the bridge. They were placed there in 1730, at the height of Würzburg's baroque period. Note particularly the *Patronna Franconiae* (commonly known as the Weeping Madonna). There's also a beautiful view of the Marienberg Fortress from the bridge—statues in the foreground, Marienberg and its vineyards as the focal point—which makes a perfect photograph to treasure as a souvenir of this historic city.

15 **Alte Universität** (Old University). Founded by Prince-Bishop Julius Echter and built in 1582, this rambling institution is one of Würzburg's most interesting Renaissance structures. ✉ *Neubaustr. 1–9.*

20 **Alter Kranen** (Old Crane). Near the Main River and north of the Old Main Bridge, the crane was erected in 1772–73 by Balthasar Neumann's son, Franz Ignaz Michael.

10 **Augustinerkirche** (Church of St. Augustine). This baroque church, another work by Neumann, was a 13th-century Dominican chapel; Neu-

mann retained the soaring, graceful choir and commissioned Antonio Bossi to add colorful stuccowork to the rest of the church. ✉ *Dominikanerpl. 2,* ☎ *0931/30970.* ⏲ *Daily 7–6.*

15 **Bürgerspital** (Almshouse). Wealthy burghers founded this refuge for the city's poor and needy in 1319; it now sells wine. The arcade courtyard is baroque in style. From mid-March through October there is a weekly tour (Saturday at 2), which includes a glass of wine. ✉ *Theaterstr. 19,* ☎ *0931/35030.* 🎟 *Tour €5.*

16 **Dom St. Kilian.** St. Kilian Basilica, Würzburg's Romanesque cathedral and the fourth largest of its kind in Germany, was begun in 1045. Step inside and you'll find yourself, somewhat disconcertingly, in a shimmering rococo treasure house. This is only fitting: Prince-Bishop von Schönborn is buried here, and it's hard to imagine him slumbering amid the dour weightiness of a Romanesque edifice. His tomb is the work of his architect and builder Balthasar Neumann; Würzburg's master sculptor Tilman Riemenschneider carved the tombstones of two other bishops at the cathedral. ✉ *Paradepl., south end of Schönbornstr.,* ☎ *0931/321–1830.* 🎟 *Tour €2.* ⏲ *Easter–Oct., daily 8–6; Nov.–Easter, daily 8–noon and 2–6; guided tours May–Oct., Mon.–Sat. 12:20, Sun. 12:30.*

21 **Festung Marienberg** (Marienberg Fortress). Beginning in the 13th century, this complex was the original home of the prince-bishops. The oldest buildings—note especially the **Marienkirche** (Church of the Virgin Mary), the core of the residence—date from around 700, although excavations have disclosed evidence that there was a already a settlement here in the Iron Age, 3,000 years ago. In addition to the roughhewn medieval fortifications, there are a number of Renaissance and baroque apartments. To reach the hilltop Marienberg, you can make the fairly stiff climb on foot through vineyards, or take the bus from the Residenz. It runs every 40 minutes from February to October, starting at 9:45 AM.

★ The highlight is the remarkable collection of art treasures in the **Mainfränkisches Museum** (Main-Franconian Museum; ☎ 0931/205–940; 🎟 €3; ⏲ Apr.–Oct., Tues.–Sun. 10–5; Nov.–Mar., Tues.–Sun. 10–4), which traces the city's rich and varied history. The standout is the gallery devoted to Würzburg-born sculptor Tilman Riemenschneider, who lived from the late 15th to the early 16th centuries; the collection includes the originals of the great Adam and Eve statues, copies of which adorn the portal of the Marienkapelle. Two previously unknown works by Riemenschneider—a Madonna and child and a Crucifixion—were discovered in 1994–95. Both had been in private collections, where they had remained for decades without anyone realizing they were by Riemenschneider. They were added to the collection in 1996, together with two other works discovered in private possession and thought to be by pupils of the master. Paintings by Tiepolo and Cranach the Elder and exhibits of porcelain, firearms, antique toys, and ancient Greek and Roman art are also on view. Other exhibits include enormous old winepresses and the history of Franconian wine making. In the summer months there are also tours around the fortress starting from the Scherenberg Tor. ☎ *0931/373–6510.* 🎟 *Tour €2.* ⏲ *Apr.–Oct., Tues.–Fri. 11, 2, and 3, weekends 10, 11, 1, 2, 3, and 4.*

The Marienberg collections are so vast that they spill over into another outstanding museum that is part of the fortress, the **Fürstenbaumuseum** (Princes' Quarters Museum), which traces the 1,200 years of Würzburg's history. There are some breathtaking exhibits of local goldsmiths' art. ☎ *0931/43838.* 🎟 *€ 2.50. Combined ticket for Mainfränkisches and*

Close-Up

TILMAN RIEMENSCHNEIDER

TILMAN RIEMENSCHNEIDER, Germany's master of late-Gothic sculpture (1460–1531), lived an extraordinary life. His skill with wood and stone was recognized at an early age, and he soon presided over a major Würzburg workshop. Riemenschneider worked alone, however, on the life-size figures that dominate his sculptures. Details such as the folds of a robe or wrinkles upon a face highlight his grace and harmony of line.

At the height of his career Riemenschneider was appointed city councillor; later he became mayor of Würzburg. In 1523, however, he made the fateful error of siding with the small farmers and guild members in the Peasants' War. He was arrested and held for eight weeks in the dungeons of the Marienberg Fortress, above Würzburg, where he was frequently tortured. Most of his wealth was confiscated, and he returned home a broken man. He died in 1531.

For nearly three centuries he and his sculptures were all but forgotten. Only in 1822, when ditchdiggers uncovered the site of his grave, was Riemenschneider once again included among Germany's greatest artists. Today Riemenschneider is recognized as the giant of German sculpture. The richest collection of his works is in Würzburg, although other masterpieces are on view in churches and museums along the Romantic Road as well as in other parts of Germany; for example, the renowned *Windsheim Altar of the Twelve Apostles* is in the Palatine Museum in Heidelberg.

Fürstenbau museums €4. ⏲ Apr.–Sept., Tues.–Sun. 9–5; Oct.–Mar., Tues.–Sun. 10–4.

7 **Haus zum Falken.** The city's most splendid baroque mansion, formerly a humble inn, now houses the city tourist office. Its colorful rococo facade was added in 1751. ✉ *Am Marktpl. 9,* ☎ *0931/373–398 or 0931/372–398.* ⏲ *Nov.–Mar., weekdays 10–6 and Sat. 10–2; Apr.–Oct., weekdays 10–6, weekends 10–2.*

11 **Juliusspital.** Founded in 1576 by Prince-Bishop Julius Echter as a home for the poor, the elderly, and the sick, this enormous edifice now houses an impressive restaurant serving wine from the institution's own vineyards. It also sells wineglasses. All profits from the restaurant are used to run the adjacent home for the elderly. A glass of wine is included in a weekly tour of the wine cellars. ✉ *Juliuspromenade 19,* ☎ *0931/393–1400.* *Tours €5.* ⏲ *Daily, 10 AM–midnight. Tours Apr.–Oct., Fri. at 3.*

8 **Marienkapelle** (St. Mary's Chapel). This tranquil Gothic church (1377–1480) tucked modestly away at one end of Würzburg's market square is almost lost amid the historic old facades. Balthasar Neumann lies buried in the church. Pause beneath the finely carved portal and inspect the striking figures of Adam and Eve; you shouldn't have great difficulty recognizing the style of Tilman Riemenschneider. These are copies; the original statues are in Würzburg's Mainfränkisches Museum. ✉ *Marktpl.,* ☎ *0931/321–1830.* ⏲ *Daily 8–6:30.*

17 **Neumünster** (New Minster). Next to the Dom St. Kilian, this 11th-century Romanesque basilica was completed in 1716. The original church was built above the grave of the early Irish martyr St. Kilian, who brought Christianity to Würzburg and, with two companions, was put to death here in 689. Their missionary zeal bore fruit, however—17 years after their death a church was consecrated in their memory. By 742 Würzburg had become a diocese, and over the following centuries 39 flourishing churches were established throughout the city. The Neumünster's former cloistered churchyard contains the grave of Walther von der Vogelweide, one of the most famous German minstrels. ✉ *Schönbornstr.,* ☎ *0931/321–1830.* ⏲ *Daily 7–6.*

18 **Rathaus.** The Gothic town hall, once headquarters of the bishop's administrator, has been the center of municipal government since 1316. A permanent exhibition in the tower documents Würzburg's destruction by Allied bombs, some examples of which are on display. ✉ *Marktpl.,* ☎ *0931/370.* 🎫 *Free.* ⏲ *Weekdays 9–5; tours May–Oct., Sat. at 10.*

★ 14 **Residenz** (Residence). The line of Würzburg's prince-bishops lived in this glorious baroque palace after moving down from the hilltop Festung Marienberg. Construction started in 1719 under the brilliant direction of Balthasar Neumann. Most of the interior decoration was entrusted to the Italian stuccoist Antonio Bossi and the Venetian painter Giovanni Battista Tiepolo. But the man whose spirit infuses the Residenz was the pleasure-loving prince-bishop Johann Phillip Franz von Schönborn, who financed the venture but did not live to see the completion of what is now considered one of Europe's most sumptuous buildings, known as the "Palace of Palaces." This dazzling structure is a 10-minute walk from the railway station, along pedestrians-only Kaiserstrasse and then Theaterstrasse.

From the moment you enter the building, the splendor of the Residenz is evident as the largest baroque staircase in the country, the **Treppenhaus,** stretches away from you. Halfway up, the stairway splits and peels away 180 degrees to the left and to the right. Soaring above on the vaulting is Tiepolo's giant fresco *The Four Continents,* a gorgeous exercise in blue and pink, with allegorical figures at the corners representing the four continents known at the time (take a careful look at the elephant's trunk). Tiepolo immortalized himself and Balthasar Neumann as two of the figures—they're not too difficult to spot. The fresco, which survived a devastating wartime bombing raid, is being restored bit by bit, so don't be surprised to find a small section covered by scaffolding.

Next, make your way to the **Weissersaal** (White Room) and then beyond to the grandest of the state rooms, the **Kaisersaal** (Throne Room). The baroque ideal of the *Gesamtkunstwerk*—fusion of all the arts—is perfectly illustrated here. Architecture melts into stucco; stucco invades the frescoes; the frescoes extend the real space of the room into their illusionary world. Nothing is quite what it seems, and no expense was spared to make it so. Tiepolo's frescoes show the 12th-century visit of Emperor Frederick Barbarossa to Würzburg to claim his bride. That the characters all wear 16th-century Venetian dress hardly seems to matter. Few interiors use such startling opulence to similar effect. If you take part in the guided tour, you'll also see private chambers of the various former residents.

The **Hofkirche** (chapel; ⏲ Apr.–Oct., daily 9–5; Nov.–Mar., daily 10–4) demonstrates the prince-bishops' love of ostentation. Among the lavish marble, rich gilding, and delicate stuccowork, note the Tiepolo altarpieces, ethereal visions of *The Fall of the Angels* and *The Assumption* *of the Virgin.* Finally, tour the **Hofgarten**; the entrance is next to the chapel. The 18th-century formal garden has stately gushing fountains and trim ankle-high shrubs outlining geometric flower beds and gravel walks. *Residenzpl., ☎ 0931/355–1712. €4 including guided tour. Apr.–Oct., daily 9–5:30; Nov.–Mar., daily 10–4.*

22 **Schloss Veitshöchheim.** This first summer palace of the prince-bishops is 8 km (5 mi) north of Würzburg, at Veitshöchheim. After extensive renovations, it will probably re-open to the public in the summer 2003, but the gardens remain open. A bus service to the palace runs from Würzburg's Kirchplatz. From mid-April to mid-October a boat service operates between Würzburg and the palace daily from 10 to 4. The 40-minute trip costs €7.50 round-trip. *☎ 0931/91582. Gardens free. Garden daily 7–dusk.*

9 **Schönbornstrasse.** Würzburg's main pedestrian mall is chock-full of upscale boutiques and not-so-posh eateries. The cafés are great for people-watching.

12 **Stift Haug.** Franconia's first baroque church was designed by the Italian architect Antonio Petrini and built between 1670 and 1691. Its elegant twin spires and central cupola make an impressive exterior; unfortunately the once-exuberant interior was destroyed in the March 1945 bombing of the city. The altarpiece is a 1583 Crucifixion scene by Tintoretto. *⊠ Bahnhofstr. at Heinestr., ☎ 0931/54102. Daily 8–6:30.*

Dining and Lodging

$–$$$$ ★ ✕ **Ratskeller.** The vaulted cellars of Würzburg's Rathaus shelter one of the city's most popular restaurants. Beer is served, but Franconian wine is what the regulars drink. The food is staunch Franconian fare. *⊠ Beim Grafeneckart, Langg. 1, ☎ 0931/13021 AE, DC, MC, V.*

$$–$$$ ✕ **Altstadt Hotel, Gianni's Bistro** If you're tired of hearty German fare head to this wonderful little Italian restaurant. The charismatic owner, Gianni Marchiorello, will give you a warm welcome and you can sample some freshly made pasta washed down with an excellent wine from south of the Alps. *⊠ Theaterstr. 7, ☎ 0931/321–640. AE, DC, MC, V.*

$–$$$ ✕ **Backöfele.** More than 400 years of tradition are sustained by this old tavern. Hidden away behind huge wooden doors in a back street, the Backöfele's cavelike interior is a popular meeting place for students, pensioners, and families alike. The menu includes plenty of local favorites such as suckling pig and marinated potroast. *⊠ Ursulinerg. 2, ☎ 0931/59059. AE, MC, V.*

$–$$$ ✕ **Juliusspital Weinstuben.** This recently renovated tavern serves wine from its own vineyard; the food—predominantly large portions of basic Franconian fare—takes second billing. *⊠ Juliuspromenade 19, ☎ 0931/393–1400. No credit cards.*

$–$$$ ★ ✕ **Wein- und Speisehaus zum Stachel.** On a warm spring or summer day take a bench in the ancient courtyard of the Stachel, which is shaded by a canopy of vine leaves and girded by high walls of creeper-hung stone. The entrées are satisfyingly Franconian, from lightly baked onion cake to hearty roast pork. But the real reason to come here is to sample the wine, made from the tavern's own grapes. *⊠ Gresseng. 1, ☎ 0931/52770. No credit cards. Closed Sun.*

$$–$$$ ✕ **Hotel Greifensteiner Hof.** The modern Greifensteiner offers comfortable, individually furnished rooms in a quiet corner of the city, just off the market square. The cheaper doubles are small but lack no comforts or facilities. The hotel restaurant, the Fränkische Stuben ($–$$), has very good cuisine—mostly Franconian specialties. *⊠ Dettelbacherg. 2, D–97070, ☎ 0931/35170, FAX 0931/57057, WEB www.greifensteiner-hof.de. 42 rooms. Restaurant, cable TV, meeting room. AE, DC, MC, V.*

$$ ✕🏨 **Fränkischer Hotelgasthof zur Stadt Mainz.** This traditional Franconian inn, dating from the early 15th century, is among the country's best. Its frescoed facade is a favored motif for photographers. Within, the friendly old hostelry provides comfort and a cuisine ($–$$$) based on its own historic recipe book. Eel from the Main River, prepared in a dill sauce, and locally caught carp and pike are specialties. Homemade apple strudel is served with afternoon coffee and also finds its way onto the dinner dessert menu. The breakfast buffet is enormous. Rooms are comfortably furnished, with old-fashioned touches such as gilt mirrors and heavy drapes. ✉ *Semmelstr. 39, D–97070,* ☎ *0931/53155,* FAX *0931/58510,* WEB *www.hotel-stadtmainz.de. 15 rooms. Restaurant, no a/c. AE, MC, V. Closed 2 wks in Jan.*

$$ ✕🏨 **Hotel Walfisch.** Guest rooms are furnished in solid Franconian style with farmhouse cupboards, bright fabrics, and heavy drapes. You'll breakfast in a dining room on the banks of the Main with views of the vineyard-covered Marienberg. For lunch and dinner try the hotel's cozy Walfisch-Stube restaurant ($$–$$$). ✉ *Am Pleidenturm 5, D–97070,* ☎ *0931/35200,* FAX *0931/352–0500,* WEB *www.hotel-walfisch.com. 40 rooms. Restaurant, cable TV, meeting room. AE, DC, MC, V.*

$$ ✕🏨 **Ringhotel Wittelsbacher Höh.** From most of the cozy rooms under the steep eaves of this historic redbrick mansion, you'll have a view of Würzburg and the vineyards. The restaurant's wine list embraces most of the leading local vintages, and Franconian and international dishes ($$–$$$) pack the menu. In summer take a table on the terrace and soak in the view. ✉ *Hexenbruchweg 10, D–97082,* ☎ *0931/42085,* FAX *0931/415–458,* WEB *www.ringhotels.de. 73 rooms, 1 suite. Restaurant, sauna, no a/c, cable TV. AE, DC, MC, V.*

$$$$ ★ 🏨 **Hotel Rebstock zu Würzburg.** This hotel's rococo facade has welcomed guests for centuries. The spacious lobby, with its open fireplace and beckoning bar, sets the tone, and there's an attractive winter garden where the foot-weary traveler can drink a cup of coffee and write postcards home. All rooms are individually decorated and furnished in English country-house style, with Laura Ashley fabrics. ✉ *Neubaustr. 7, D–97070,* ☎ *0931/30930,* FAX *0931/309–3100,* WEB *www.rebstock.com. 63 rooms, 9 suites. Restaurant, bar, no a/c in some rooms, meeting rooms, no-smoking rooms, cable TV. AE, DC, MC, V.*

$–$$ 🏨 **Strauss.** Close to the river and the pedestrians-only center, the pink-stucco Strauss has been in the same family for more than 100 years. Rooms are simply furnished in light woods; those on the top floor are particularly cozy, some with exposed beams. The beamed Würzburg restaurant serves Franconian cuisine, as well as international dishes, complemented by excellent Franconian wines. ✉ *Juliuspromenade 5, D–97070,* ☎ *0931/30570,* FAX *0931/305–7555,* WEB *www.hotel-strauss.de. 75 rooms, 3 suites. Restaurant, bicycles, no a/c, cable TV. AE, DC, MC, V. Closed Dec. 20–mid-Jan.*

Nightlife and the Arts

Würzburg's cultural year starts with a Classical Music Days Festival in April and May and ends with a Johann Sebastian Bach Festival in November. Its annual Mozart Festival, between May and June, attracts visitors from all over the world. Most concerts are held in the magnificent setting of the Residenz. The annual jazz festival is in November. The town hosts a series of wine festivals, climaxing in the Vintners' Festival, in September.

Outdoor Activities and Sports

Visitors are welcome to play at the 9-hole course of **Würzburg Golf Club** (✉ Am Golf Pl. 2, ☎ 0931/67890). Take the B–19 out of town in the direction of Bad Mergentheim. The exit for the golf club is signposted on the right.

Wine lovers and hikers should visit the **Stein-Wein-Pfad,** a (signposted) trail through the vineyards that rise up from the north west edge of Würzburg. A two-hour round-trip affords visitors stunning views of the city as well as the chance to try the excellent local wines directly at the source. The starting point for the walk is the vineyard of **Weingut am Stein, Ludwig Knoll** (✉ Mittlere Steinbergweg 5, ☎ 0931/25808), 10 minutes on foot from the main railway station.

Shopping

Würzburg is the true wine center of the Romantic Road. Visit any of the vineyards that rise from the Main River and choose a *Bocksbeutel,* the distinctive green, flagon-shape wine bottle of Franconia. It's claimed that the shape came about because wine-guzzling monks found it the easiest to hide under their robes. The old **Bürgerspital** and **Juliusspital** both sell fine wines. You'll want to linger on **Schönbornstrasse** and the adjacent marketplace. Wine and Franconia's distinctive goblets are sold in many of the shops here. Homemade chocolates and other local delicacies share shelf space with the best Franconian wine and schnapps at the **Bayerisches Schokoladenhaus** (✉ Eichhornstr. 2, ☎ 0931/18080).

The **Haus des Frankenweins** (House of Franconian Wine; ✉ Kranenkai 1, ☎ 0931/390–110) has wine tastings for individual visitors. Some 100 Franconian wines and a wide range of wine accessories are sold.

En Route From Würzburg follow the Romantic Road through Bavarian Franconia and Swabia and into the mountains of Upper Bavaria. For the first stretch, to Bad Mergentheim, take either the B–27 to Tauberbischofsheim and then the B–290, or the more direct B–19. Both routes take you through the open countryside of the Hohenloher Plain.

Bad Mergentheim

23 *44 km (28 mi) south of Würzburg.*

Between 1525 and 1809, Bad Mergentheim was the home of the Teutonic Knights, one of the most successful medieval orders of chivalry. Their greatest glories came in the 15th century, when they were one of the dominant powers of the Baltic, ruling large areas of present-day eastern Germany, Poland, and Lithuania. The following centuries saw a steady decline in the order's commercial success. In 1809 Napoléon expelled the Teutonic Knights from Bad Mergentheim as he marched toward his ultimately disastrous Russian campaign. The French emperor had little time for what he considered the medieval superstition of such orders. The expulsion seemed to sound the death knell of the little town. But in 1826 a shepherd discovered mineral springs on the north bank of the river. They proved to be the strongest sodium sulfate and bitter-salt waters in Europe, with health-giving properties that ensured the town's future prosperity.

The **Deutschordensschloss,** the Teutonic knights' former castle, at the eastern end of the town, has a museum that follows the history of the order. ✉ *Schloss 16,* ☎ *07931/52212.* *€3.50; guided tours €1.50.* *Tues.–Sun. 10–5. Tours Thurs. and Sun. at 3.*

The **Wildpark Bad Mergentheim,** just outside Bad Mergentheim, is a wildlife park with Europe's largest selection of European species, including wolves and bears. ✉ *B–290,* ☎ *07931/41344,* WEB *www.wildtierpark.de.* *€7.* *Mid-Mar.–Oct., daily 9–6; Nov.–mid-Mar., weekends 10:30–5.*

OFF THE BEATEN PATH **STUPPACH** – This village, 11 km (7 mi) southeast of Bad Mergentheim, has a chapel guarding one of the great Renaissance German paintings, the *Stuppacher Madonna,* by Matthias Grünewald (circa 1475–1528). It was only in 1908 that experts finally recognized it as the work of Grünewald; repainting in the 17th century had turned it into an unexceptional work. Though Grünewald was familiar with the developments in perspective and natural lighting of Italian Renaissance painting, his work remained resolutely anti-Renaissance in spirit: tortured, emotional, dark. While his contemporary Dürer used the lessons of Italian painting to reproduce its clarity and rationalism, Grünewald used them for expressionistic purposes to heighten his essentially Gothic imagery. ⏲ *Chapel Mar.–Apr., daily 10–5; May–Oct., daily 9–5:30; Nov.–Feb., daily 11–4.*

Dining and Lodging

$ ✕ **Kettler's Altfränkische Weinstube.** You'll want to come here to try the *Nürnberger Bratwürste*—finger-size spicy sausages—and to enjoy the atmosphere of a snug 180-year-old Franconian tavern. The wine list is enormous. ✉ *Krumme G. 12,* ☎ *07931/7308. No credit cards.*

$$–$$$ ✕🏨 **Victoria.** This is one of the area's finest spa hotels, combining cosmopolitan flair with rural solitude. Rooms are large, luxurious, and furnished in the style of a country mansion, with king-size beds, well-cushioned armchairs, subdued lighting, and prints on the textile-hung walls. The lounge is scarcely less opulent, with an open fireplace and a library. The restaurant ($$$$) is Michelin-starred, but most visitors eat at the excellent wine bar ($$), where a magnificent tile oven takes pride of place. ✉ *Poststr. 2–4, D–97980,* ☎ *07931/5930,* FAX *07931/593–500,* WEB *www.victoria-hotel.de. 75 rooms, 3 suites. Restaurant, bar, pub, no a/c, cable TV, hair salon, sauna, steam room, massage. AE, DC, MC, V.*

Weikersheim

24 *10 km (6 mi) east of Bad Mergentheim, 40 km (25 mi) south of Würzburg.*

The Tauber River town of Weikersheim is dominated by the **castle** of the counts of Hohenlohe. Its great hall is the scene each summer of an international youth music festival, and the **Rittersaal** (Knights' Hall) contains life-size stucco wall sculptures of animals, reflecting the counts' love of hunting. In the cellars you can drink a glass of cool wine drawn from the huge casks that seem to prop up the building. Outside again, stroll through the enchanting gardens and enjoy the view of the Tauber River and its leafy valley. ☎ *07934/8364.* 🎟 *€4; €1.50 for gardens only.* ⏲ *Apr.–Oct., daily 9–6; Nov.–Mar., daily 10–noon and 1:30–4:30.*

Dining and Lodging

$–$$ ✕🏨 **Flair Hotel Laurentius.** This traditional old hotel on Weikersheim's market square is an ideal stopover on the Romantic Road. You can avoid the crowds and the relatively high prices of nearby Rothenburg and still be within an hour's drive of most sights on the northern route. Rooms are very comfortable and individually furnished, some with German antiques. The vaulted ground floor has a wine tavern, a very good restaurant ($$–$$$$) named, like the hotel, after the patron saint of cooks, and a brasserie. ✉ *Marktpl. 5, D–97990,* ☎ *07934/91080,* FAX *07934/910–818,* WEB *www.hotel-laurentius.de. 13 rooms. Restaurant, café, Weinstube, no a/c, cable TV. AE, DC, MC, V.*

Creglingen

25 *20 km (12 mi) east of Weikersheim, 40 km (25 mi) south of Würzburg.*

The village of Creglingen has been an important pilgrimage site since the 14th century, when a farmer had a vision of a heavenly host plow-
26 ing his field. The **Herrgottskirche** (Chapel of Our Lord) is in the Herrgottstal (Valley of the Lord), 3 km (2 mi) south of Creglingen; the way there is well signposted. The chapel was built by the counts of Hohenlohe, and in the early 16th century Tilman Riemenschneider carved an altarpiece for it. This enormous work, 33 ft high, depicts in minute detail the life and ascension of the Virgin Mary. Riemenschneider entrusted much of the background detail to the craftsmen of his Würzburg workshop, but he allowed no one but himself to attempt its life-size figures. Its intricate detail and attenuated figures are a high point of late-Gothic sculpture. *☎ 07933/338. 🎟 €1.50. ⏲ Apr.–Oct., daily 9:15–5:30; Nov.–Mar., Tues.–Sun. 10–noon and 1–4, closed Jan. 7–31.*

The **Fingerhutmuseum** (Thimble Museum) is opposite the Herrgottskirche. *Fingerhut* is German for "thimble," and this delightful, privately run museum has thousands of them, some dating from Roman times. *☎ 07933/370. 🎟 €1.50. ⏲ Apr.–Oct., daily 9–6; Nov.–Mar., daily 1–4.*

The fascinating **Feuerwehrmuseum** (Firefighting Museum), with an impressive collection of old fire engines, lies 8 km (5 mi) north of Creglingen, within the stout castle walls of Schloss Waldmannshofen. *⊠ Waldmannshofen, ☎ 09335/8166 🎟 €2.50. ⏲ Daily 10–noon and 2–5.*

Lodging

$ **Heuhotel Ferienbauernhof.** For a truly off-the-beaten-track experience, book a space in the hayloft of the Stahl family's farm at Creglingen. Guests bed down in freshly turned hay in the farmhouse granary. Bed linen and blankets are provided. The overnight rate of €16 includes a cold supper and breakfast. For €21 more you can swap the granary for one of three comparatively luxurious double rooms or even an apartment. Children are particularly well catered to, with tours of the farmyard and their own playground. *⊠ Weidenhof 1, D–97993, ☎ 07933/378, FAX 07933/7515, WEB www.ferienbauernhof-heuhotel.de. Bicycles, no a/c no room TVs. No credit cards.*

Rothenburg-ob-der-Tauber

★ *20 km (12 mi) southeast of Creglingen, 75 km (47 mi) west of Nürnberg.*

Rothenburg-ob-der-Tauber (literally, "red castle on the Tauber") is the kind of medieval town that even Walt Disney might have thought too picturesque to be true, with half-timber architecture galore and a wealth of fountains and flowers against a backdrop of towers and turrets. As late as the 17th century it was a small but thriving market town that had grown up around the ruins of two 12th-century churches destroyed by an earthquake. Then it was laid low economically by the havoc of the Thirty Years' War, and with its economic base devastated, it slumbered until modern tourism rediscovered it. It milks its best-preserved-medieval-town-in-Europe image to the fullest, undoubtedly something of a tourist trap but genuine enough for all the hype. There really is no place quite like it. Whether Rothenburg is at its most appealing in summer, when the balconies of its ancient houses are festooned with flowers, or in winter, when snow lies on its steep gables, is a matter of taste. Few people are likely to find this extraordinary little survivor from another age anything short of remarkable.

A Good Walk

Sights are dotted around town, and the streets don't lend themselves to a particular route. However, the **Rathaus** ㉗, on Rathausplatz, is a logical place to begin a tour. The **Herterlichbrunnen** ㉘ is just steps away, on Marktplatz, and a bit farther north is the **Stadtpfarrkirche St. Jakob** ㉙, where you'll find a magnificent Riemenschneider altar. From the church follow Klingengasse north to the church of **St. Wolfgang** ㉚, built into the defenses of the town. On the outside it blends into the forbidding **Stadtmauern** ㉛. Through an underground passage you can reach the sentry walk above and follow the western stretch of the city wall to the **Reichsstadtmuseum** ㉜. Farther along the wall you'll reach the **Mittelalterliches Kriminalmuseum** ㉝. In nearby Hofbronnengasse, the **Puppen und Spielzeugmuseum** ㉞ is within a 15th-century building.

TIMING

Crowds will affect the pace at which you can tour the town. Early morning is the only time to appreciate the place in relative calm. The best times to see the mechanical figures on the Rathaus wall are in the evening, at 8, 9, or 10.

Sights to See

28 **Herterlichbrunnen** (Herterlich Fountain). A *Schäfertanz* (Shepherds' Dance) was performed around the ornate Renaissance fountain on the central Marktplatz whenever Rothenburg celebrated a major event. The dance is still done, though nowadays for the benefit of tourists. It takes place in front of the Rathaus several times a year, chiefly at Easter, in late May, and regularly in June and July. ✉ *Marktpl.*

33 **Mittelalterliches Kriminalmuseum** (Medieval Criminal Museum). The gruesome medieval implements of torture on display here are not for the fainthearted. The museum, the largest of its kind in Europe, also soberly documents the history of German legal processes in the Middle Ages. ✉ *Burgg. 3,* ☎ *09861/5359.* *€3.50.* *Apr.–Oct., daily 9:30–6; Nov. and Jan.–Mar., daily 2–4; Dec., daily 10–4.*

34 **Puppen und Spielzeugmuseum** (Doll and Toy Museum). This complex of medieval and baroque buildings houses more than 1,000 dolls, the oldest dating from 1780, the newest from 1940, as well as a collection of dollhouses, and model shops and theaters guaranteed to charm every youngster. ✉ *Hofbronneng. 13,* ☎ *09861/7330.* *€4.* *Jan.–Feb., daily 11–5; Mar.–Dec., daily 9:30–6.*

27 **Rathaus.** Half of the city hall is Gothic, begun in 1240; the other half is neoclassical, started in 1572. Below the building are the **Historiengewölbe** (Historical Vaults; €2; Apr.–Oct., daily 9:30–5:30; Dec. Christmas market season, daily 1–4), a museum that concentrates on the Thirty Years' War. Great prominence is given to an account of the Meistertrunk (Master Drink), an event that will follow you around Rothenburg. It came about when the Protestant town was captured by Catholic forces. During the victory celebrations, the conquering general was embarrassed to find himself unable to drink a great tankard of wine in one go, as his manhood demanded. He volunteered to spare the town further destruction if any of the city councillors could drain the mighty six-pint draught. The mayor took up the challenge and succeeded, and Rothenburg was preserved. The tankard itself is on display at the Reichsstadtmuseum. On the north side of the main square is a fine clock, placed there 50 years after the mayor's feat. A mechanical figure acts out the epic Master Drink daily on the hour from 11 to 3 and in the evening at 8, 9, and 10. The feat is also celebrated at two

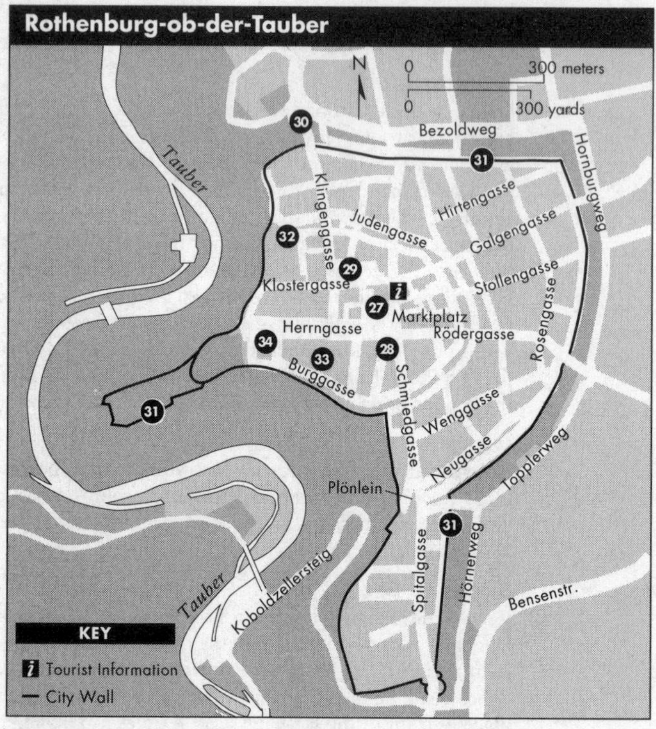

annual pageants, when townsfolk parade through the streets in 17th-century garb. The Rathaus tower, which normally offers a good view of the town, is closed for renovations. ✉ *Rathauspl.*

32 **Reichsstadtmuseum** (Imperial City Museum). This city museum is two attractions in one. Its artifacts illustrate Rothenburg and its history. Among them is the great tankard, or *Pokal,* of the Meistertrunk. The setting of the museum is the other attraction; it's in a former Dominican convent, the oldest parts of which date from the 13th century. Tour the building to see the cloisters, the kitchens, and the dormitory; then see the collections. ✉ *Klosterhof 5,* ☎ *09861/939–043.* *€3.* *Apr.–Oct., daily 10–5; Nov.–Mar., daily 1–4.*

30 **St. Wolfgang.** A historic parish church of Gothic origins with a baroque interior, St. Wolfgang's is most notable for how it blends into the forbidding city wall. ✉ *Klingeng.,* ☎ *09861/40492.* *€1.* *Mid-Mar.–Oct., daily 10–1 and 2–5.*

31 **Stadtmauern** (City Walls). Rothenburg's city walls are more than 2 km (1 mi) long and provide an excellent way of circumnavigating the town from above. The walls' wooden walkway is covered by eaves. Stairs every 200 or 300 yards provide ready access. There are superb views of the tangle of pointed and tiled red roofs and of the rolling country beyond.

29 **Stadtpfarrkirche St. Jakob** (Parish Church of St. James). The church has some notable Riemenschneider sculptures, including the famous *Heiliges Blut* (Holy Blood) altar. Above the altar a crystal capsule is said to contain drops of Christ's blood. There are three 14th- and 15th-century stained-glass windows in the choir, and the Herlin-Altar is famous for its 15th-century painted panels. ✉ *Klosterg. 15,* ☎ *09861/700–620.* *€1.50.* *Jan.–Mar. and Nov., daily 10–noon and 2–4; Apr.–Oct., daily 9–5:30; Dec., daily 10–5.*

Dining and Lodging

$–$$$ ★ ✕ **Baumeisterhaus.** In summer you can dine in one of Rothenburg's loveliest courtyards, a half-timber oasis of peace that's part of a magnificent Renaissance house. If the weather's cooler, move inside to the paneled dining room. The menu, changed daily, features Bavarian and Franconian specialties. The Franconian sauerbraten or the Bavarian *Schweinsbraten* (a crusty hunk of roast pork in a beer-reduced sauce) are especially good. ✉ *Obere Schmiedg. 3,* ☎ *09861/94700. AE, DC, MC, V.*

$$$ ★ ✕🏨 **Hotel Eisenhut.** It's fitting that the prettiest small town in Germany should have one of the prettiest small hotels. It stands in the center of town and occupies what were originally four separate town houses, the oldest dating from the 12th century, the newest from the 16th. Inside there are enough oil paintings, antiques, and heavy beams to make any Teutonic knight feel at home. Its restaurant ($$$–$$$$) is among the region's best. ✉ *Herrng. 3–5, D–91541,* ☎ *09861/7050,* FAX *09861/70545,* WEB *www.eisenhut.com. 77 rooms, 2 suites. Restaurant, café, beer garden, piano bar, no a/c, cable TV. AE, DC, MC, V.*

$$ ✕🏨 **Hotel Goldener Hirsch.** This lantern-hung, green-shuttered 15th-century patrician house is an inextricable part of Rothenburg's history. The Meistertrunk play was first performed here. Baroque antiques are everywhere, from the lobby to the uppermost, bay-window bedroom. The view of the Tauber Valley from the windows of the elegant, pillared restaurant ($$–$$$$) *Die Blaue Terrasse* almost rivals its nouvelle cuisine, prepared with regional touches. Snails and asparagus (in season) are perennial favorites. ✉ *Untere Schmiedg. 16–25, D–91541,* ☎ *09861/7080,* FAX *09861/708–100,* WEB *www.goldenerhirsch.rothenburg.de. 72 rooms. No a/c. AE, DC, MC, V.*

$–$$ ✕🏨 **Hotel-Restaurant Burg Colmberg.** This wonderfully atmospheric castle lies on the Burgenstrasse (Castle Road), where you can escape the tourist bustle of Rothenburg. The 13th-century fortress was converted some 30 years ago into a hotel that combines a high standard of comfort with most of the original medieval features. Many bedrooms have historic mullioned windows, and most have dark wood furniture that complements the setting. The beamed restaurant Zur Remise ($$–$$$) serves venison from the castle's own hunting grounds. The golf course is next to the hotel grounds, but can only be reached by driving a circuitous route. ✉ *Burg 1–3, D–91598 Colmberg, 18 km (11 mi) southeast of Rothenburg,* ☎ *09803/91920,* FAX *09803/262,* WEB *www.germany-castles-hotels.com. 24 rooms, 2 suites. Restaurant, Weinstube, 9-hole golf course, bicycles, playground, no-smoking rooms, no a/c, cable TV. AE, MC, V. Closed Jan.*

$ ✕🏨 **Hotel Zapf An der Wörnitzquelle.** An American, Thomas Roe, runs the highly regarded restaurant ($–$$) in this pleasant country inn in the village of Schillingfurst, 20 km (12 mi) from Rothenburg and 5 km (3 mi) from the Romantic Road. Try the local speciality *Schillingsfürster Zigeuner Eintopf,* a delicious vegetable hotpot served with neck of pork. Ask for a room in the main house, a striking building with a stepped-gable Renaissance facade. Most rooms are in the less lovely modern extension; they are nevertheless comfortable and well furnished, with balconies. ✉ *Dombühlerstr. 9, D–91583 Schillingfurst,* ☎ *09868/989–390 hotel; 09868/5029 restaurant,* FAX *09868/5464,* WEB *www.hotelzapf.de. 17 rooms, 4 apartments. Restaurant, café, beer garden, sauna, bicycles, no a/c, cable TV. AE, DC, MC, V.*

$$–$$$ 🏨 **Burg-Hotel Relais de Silence.** This exquisite little hotel abuts the town wall and was once part of a Rothenburg monastery. Most rooms have a view of the Tauber Valley. All have plush furnishings, with antiques or fine reproductions. Breakfast is served in good weather on a terrace adjoining the wall. ✉ *Klosterg. 1–3, D–91541,* ☎ *09861/94890,* FAX

09861/948–940. 17 rooms. No a/c, cable TV, Internet, laundry facilities. AE, DC, MC, V.

$$–$$$ **Romantik-Hotel Markusturm.** The Markusturm began as a 13th-century custom house, an integral part of the city defense wall, and has since developed over the centuries into an inn and staging post and finally into a luxurious small hotel. Some rooms are beamed, others have Laura Ashley decor or gaily painted bedsteads, and some have valuable antiques from as far back as medieval times. ✉ *Röderg. 1, D–91541,* ☏ *09861/94280,* FAX *09861/2692,* WEB *www.markusturm.de. 23 rooms, 2 suites. Restaurant, sauna, no-smoking rooms, no a/c, cable TV. AE, DC, MC, V.*

$$ **Hotel Reichs-Küchenmeister.** Master chefs in the service of the Holy Roman Emperor were the inspiration for the name of this historic hotel-restaurant, one of the oldest trader's houses in Rothenburg. For five generations it has been run by the same energetic family. Rooms are furnished in a stylish mixture of old and new; light veneer pieces share space with heavy oak bedsteads and painted cupboards. ✉ *Kirchpl. 8–10, D–91541,* ☏ *09861/9700,* FAX *09861/970–409. 45 rooms, 2 suites, 3 apartments. Restaurant, pub, hot tub, sauna, no-smoking rooms, no a/c, cable TV. AE, MC, V.*

$–$$ **Hotel-Gasthof Zum Rappen.** Close to the Würzburger Tor (a town gate) and first mentioned in town records in 1603, this tavern offers a surprisingly high standard of comfort behind its stout, yellow-stucco, geranium-smothered facade. Guest rooms have a colorful, airy touch, with light woods and floral fabrics. Those in the modern annex have balconies overlooking a quiet courtyard. Friday and Saturday are dance nights in the Rappenschmiede Weinstube. ✉ *Würzburger Tor 6 and 10, D–91541,* ☏ *09861/95710,* FAX *09861/6076. 131 rooms. Restaurant, beer garden, Weinstube, no a/c. AE, DC, MC, V.*

$ **Gasthof Klingentor.** This sturdy old staging post is outside the city walls but still within a 10-minute walk of Rothenburg's Old Town center. Rooms are spacious and furnished in the local rustic style. Its inexpensive restaurant serves substantial Franconian fare. A well-marked cycle and hiking path starts outside the front door. ✉ *Mergentheimerstr. 14, D–91541,* ☏ *09861/3468,* FAX *09861/3492. 20 rooms, 16 with bath. Restaurant, beer garden, no-smoking rooms, no a/c, cable TV, no TV in some rooms. MC, V.*

$ **Hotel-Gasthof Post.** This small family-run hotel, just two minutes on foot from the eastern city gate, must be one of the friendliest in town. The rooms are simple but clean, and all have their own shower or bath. The Dreyer family is happy to help with questions about sights in and around Rothenburg. ✉ *Ansbacherstr. 27, D–91541,* ☏ *09861/6058,* FAX *09861/7896. 18 rooms. Restaurant, no a/c, cable TV. DC, MC, V.*

Nightlife and the Arts

Highlights of Rothenburg's annual calendar are the **Meistertrunk Festival,** over the Whitsun weekend, celebrating the famous wager that is said to have saved the town from destruction in the Thirty Years' War, and the **Reichstadt-Festtage,** on the first weekend of September, commemorating Rothenburg's attainment of Free Imperial City status in 1274. Both are spectacular festivals, when thousands of townspeople and local horsemen reenact the events in period costume.

Outdoor Activities and Sports

For scenery and a mild challenge, try the 9-hole golf course at **Burg Colmberg** (✉ Rothenburgerstr. 35, ☏ 09803/600), 18 km (11 mi) east of Rothenburg.

Happy Ballooning (☏ 09861/87888, WEB www.happy-ballooning.de) conducts daily trips over Rothenburg and the countryside for €180.

Shopping

On the old and atmospheric premises of the **Kunstwerke Friese** (✉ Grüner Markt 7–8, near the Rathaus, ☎ 09861/7166) you'll find all those items that will remind you of your trip, everything from cuckoo clocks and beer tankards to porcelain and glassware. If you are looking specifically for Hummel articles, try **Haus der Tausend Geschenke** (✉ Obere Schmiedeg. 13, ☎ 09861/4801).

Käthe Wohlfahrt (✉ Herrng. 1, ☎ 09861/4090) carries children's toys and seasonal decorations. The Christmas Village part of the store is a wonderland of mostly German-made toys and decorations.

Teddyland (✉ Herrng. 10, ☎ 09861/8904) has Germany's largest teddy bear population. More than 5,000 of them pack this extraordinary store, all awaiting new homes. Children adore the place, but be warned: these are pedigree teddies, and they don't come cheap.

Feuchtwangen

35 *30 km (19 mi) south of Rothenburg-ob-der-Tauber.*

Feuchtwangen has a central market square with a splashing fountain and an ideal ensemble of half-timber houses. Summer is the time to visit, when, from mid-June to mid-August, open-air theater productions are staged in the low, graceful cloisters next to the **Stiftskirche** (Collegiate Church; ✉ Kirchpl.). Inside the church is a 15th-century altar carved by Albrecht Dürer's teacher, Michael Wohlgemut.

The **Fränkisches Museum** has an excellent collection of Franconian folk arts and crafts, including more than 600 ceramics. ✉ *Museumstr. 19,* ☎ *09852/2575.* €2. *Mar.–Dec., Tues.–Sun. 10–noon and 2–5.*

A state-run **casino** (✉ Am Casino 1, ☎ 09852/90060) has 12 roulette tables plus four tables for blackjack and two for poker. Admission is €2.50.

Dining and Lodging

$ ✕ **Ursel's Kleine Wirtschaft.** Ursel's "little tavern" is a typical Franconian establishment, cheap and cheerful, with a simple menu and a good selection of regional beers and wines. Friday, by the way, is set aside for tripe dishes. ✉ *Herrenstr. 12,* ☎ *09852/615–191. No credit cards.*

$$ ★ ✕ **Romantik Hotel Greifen Post.** The solid exterior of this historic house (formerly a staging post on the medieval route between Paris and Prague) gives little hint of the luxuries within. Ask for the 17th-century room with the four-poster bed. If that's taken, settle for the romantic Louis XVI–style room, the Biedermeier-style room, or the room designed in Laura Ashley English country-house style. The indoor pool is within the original Renaissance walls of this ancient house. Frescoes of Feuchtwangen's past decorate the restaurant ($$–$$$), where you can eat specialities such as stuffed quail or fresh trout. ✉ *Marktpl. 8, D–91555,* ☎ *09852/6800,* FAX *09852/68068,* WEB *www.romantik.de/greifen. 35 rooms. Restaurant, bar, pool, sauna, bicycles, meeting rooms, no-smoking rooms, no a/c, cable TV. AE, DC, MC, V.*

Dinkelsbühl

★ 36 *12 km (7 mi) south of Feuchtwangen.*

Within the walls of Dinkelsbühl, a beautifully preserved medieval town, the rush of traffic seems a lifetime away. There's less to see here than in Rothenburg, and the mood is much less tourist-oriented. Like Rothenburg, Dinkelsbühl was caught up in the Thirty Years' War, and it also preserves a fanciful episode from those bloody times. Local lore says that when Dinkelsbühl was under siege by Swedish forces and in imminent danger of destruction, a young girl led the children of the town to the enemy commander and implored him in their name for mercy. The commander of the Swedish army is said to have been so moved by the plea that he spared the town. Whether or not it's true, the story is retold every year during the Kinderzech Festival, a pageant by the children of Dinkelsbühl during a 10-day festival in July. An annual open-air-theater festival takes place from mid-June until mid-August.

The **Stadtpfarrkirche St. Georg** (St. George's Parish Church) is the standout sight in town. At 235 ft in length it's large enough to be a cathedral, and it is among the best examples in Bavaria of the late-Gothic style. Note especially the complex fan vaulting that spreads sinuously across the ceiling. If you can face the climb, head up the 200-ft tower for amazing views over the jumble of rooftops. ✉ *Marktpl.*, ☎ *09851/2245.* *Tower €1.50.* ⏲ *Church daily 9–noon and 2–6; tower May–Sept., Sat. 10–6, Sun. 1–6.*

The **Museum 3 Dimension** is the world's first museum of three-dimensional technology. Exhibits describe how its lifelike effects are achieved in photography, the cinema, and other art forms. Children enjoy the 3-D film run at various times during the day, as well as the 3-D art on display. ✉ *Nördlinger Tor/Stadtmühle*, ☎ *09851/6336.* *€7; family ticket €22.* ⏲ *Apr.–Oct., daily 10–6; Nov.–Mar., weekends 11–4 (except Dec. 26–Jan. 5, daily 11–4).*

Dining and Lodging

$$–$$$ ✕ **Hotel Deutsches Haus.** This picture-postcard medieval inn, with a facade of half-timber gables and flower boxes, has many rooms fitted with antique furniture. One of them has a romantic four-poster bed. Dine beneath heavy oak beams in the restaurant ($–$$), where you can try the local specialty, which is a type of grain called Dinkel. It's very nutritious and often served roasted with potatoes and salmon. ✉ *Weinmarkt 3, D–91550*, ☎ *09851/6058 or 09851/6059*, FAX *09851/7911*, WEB *www.deutsches-haus-dkb.de. 8 rooms, 2 suites. Restaurant, Internet, meeting rooms, no-smoking rooms, no a/c, cable TV. AE, DC, MC, V. Closed Jan. 8–31.*

$–$$ ✕ **Hotel Goldene Kanne.** This central hotel, built in 1690, offers a high standard of comfort. Rooms are furnished with solid German oak; many have sitting-room corners with desks. The rooms even have fax connections—a rarity in this part of Germany. It's particularly recommended for families (seven of the rooms have children's beds), although lovers are also catered to with a special honeymoon suite. The cozy restaurant ($$–$$$) serves both local and international cuisine and has regular offbeat specialty weeks, featuring exotic pancake preparations and potato recipes. ✉ *Segringerstr. 8, D–91550*, ☎ *09851/572–910*, FAX *09851/572–929*, WEB *www.hotel-goldene-kanne.de. 22 rooms, 2 suites. Restaurant, café, Internet, no a/c, cable TV. AE, DC, MC, V.*

$–$$ ✕ **Hotel-Restaurant Blauer Hecht.** A brewery tavern in the 18th century (beer is still brewed in the backyard), this Ring hotel is furnished with the sleek, dark-veneer and pastel-shade contrasts favored by the group's interior designers. It's central but quiet. The restaurant ($$–$$$) serves fish from the hotel's own ponds. ✉ *Schweinemarkt 1, D–91550*, ☎ *09851/5810*, FAX *09851/581–170*, WEB *www.ringhotels.de. 43 rooms, 1 suite. Restaurant, bar, pool, sauna, steam room, no-smoking rooms, no a/c, cable TV. AE, DC, MC, V.*

Shopping

Deleika (✉ Waldeck 33, ☎ 09857/97990) makes barrel organs to order, although it won't deliver the monkey! The firm also has a museum of barrel organs and other mechanical instruments. It's just outside Dinkelsbühl. Call ahead. If you're looking for a very special present to take home, visit the **Dinkelsbüler Kunst-Stuben** (✉ Segringer Str. 52, ☎ 08951/6750). The owner, Mr. Appelberg, sells his own drawings, paintings, and etchings of the town. **Jürgen Pleikies** (✉ Segringerstr. 53–55, ☎ 09851/7596) is doing his part to restore his town's former reputation for fine earthenware; he also offers courses at the potter's wheel. At **Weschcke und Ries** (✉ Segringerstr. 20, ☎ 09851/9439) Hummel porcelain figures share window space with other German porcelain and glassware.

Nördlingen

37 *32 km (20 mi) southeast of Dinkelsbühl, 70 km (43 mi) northwest of Augsburg.*

In Nördlingen the cry of *"So G'sell so"*—"All's well"—still rings out every night across the ancient walls and turrets. Sentries sound out the traditional message from the 300-ft tower of the central parish church of **St. Georg** at half-hour intervals between 10 PM and midnight. The tradition goes back to an incident during the Thirty Years' War, when an enemy attempt to slip into the town was detected by a resident. You can climb the 365 steps up the tower—known locally as the Daniel—for an unsurpassed view of the town and countryside, including, on clear days, 99 villages. The ground plan of the town is two concentric circles. The inner circle of streets, whose central point is St. Georg, marks the earliest medieval boundary. A few hundred yards beyond it is the outer boundary, a wall built to accommodate expansion. Fortified with 11 towers and punctuated by five massive gates, it's one of the best-preserved town walls in Germany. ✉ *Marktpl.* 🎫 *Tower €1.50.* ⏲ *Daily 9–dusk.*

Nördlingen lies in the center of a huge, basinlike depression, the **Ries,** that until the beginning of this century was believed to be the remains of an extinct volcano. In 1960 it was proven by two Americans that the 24-km-wide (15-mi-wide) crater was caused by a meteorite at least 1 km (½ mi) in diameter that hit the ground at more than 100,000 mph. It turned the surface rock and subsoil upside down, hurling debris as far as Slovakia and wiping out virtually all plant and animal life within a radius of more than 100 mi. The compressed rock, or *Suevit,* formed by the explosive impact of the meteorite was used to construct many of the town's buildings, including St. Georg's tower. The **Rieskrater Museum** (Ries Crater Museum), housed in a converted 15th-century barn, tells the story of the Ries crater. ✉ *Eugene-Schoemaker-Pl. 1,* ☎ *09081/273–8220.* 🎫 *€3.* ⏲ *Nov.–Apr., Tues.–Sun. 10–noon and 1:30–4:30; May–Oct., Tues.–Sun. 10–4:30.*

Nördlingen possesses one of Germany's largest steam railway engine museums, the **Bayerisches Eisenbahnmuseum,** adjacent to the railroad station. About a dozen times a year some of the old locomotives puff away on outings to Harburg. Call for a timetable. ✉ *Am Hohen Weg,* ☎ *09083/340.* 🎫 *€4.* ⏲ *Mar.–June and Sept.–Oct., Sun. 10–5; July–Aug., Tues.–Sat. noon–4 and Sun. 10–5.*

Dining and Lodging

$$–$$$$ ✕ **Meyer's-Keller.** Choose between a table in the beer Stube or in the fancier restaurant; in summer take a place under chestnut and plane trees in the beer garden. Prices in the excellent restaurant are higher, and the menu is suitably diverse and imaginative. The Rieser Surprise Menu, for €23, features only fresh products from local farms, while a gourmet menu for about double the price includes a glass of carefully selected wine with each of the four courses. Fish dishes include freshly delivered Atlantic specialties. ✉ *Marienhöhe 8,* ☎ *09081/4493. AE, MC, V. Closed Mon. No lunch Tues.*

$$ ✕🏨 **Astron Hotel Klösterle.** Where barefoot monks once went about their ascetic daily routine, you can dine amid ancient stonework ($–$$$). The comfortable, well-appointed guest rooms are anything but monastic. The hotel's striking white-and-yellow facade, with its Renaissance windows and steeply stepped gables, fits snugly into the Old Town center. You can admire the town's jumble of roofs from the top-floor fitness center and sauna–steam bath. ✉ *Beim Klösterle 1, D–86720,* ☎ *09081/88054,* FAX *09081/22740,* WEB *www.astron.hotels.de. 92 rooms, 6 suites. Restaurant, Weinstube, gym, sauna, steam room, bicycles, no a/c, cable TV. AE, DC, MC, V.*

$$ 🏨 **Kaiserhof-Hotel-Sonne.** The great German poet Goethe stayed here, only one in a long line of distinguished guests led off by Emperor Friedrich III in 1487. The vaulted-cellar wine tavern is a reminder of those days. The three honeymoon suites are furnished in 18th-century style, with hand-painted four-poster beds. ✉ *Marktpl. 3, D–86720,* ☎ *09081/5067,* FAX *09081/23999. 40 rooms. Restaurant, Weinstube, no a/c, cable TV. AE, MC, V.*

$ 🏨 **Hotel Zur Goldenen Rose.** This small, modern hotel is in the heart of town, ideal for those who wish to explore Nördlingen on foot. The in-house restaurant serves wholesome, inexpensive dishes. ✉ *Baldingerstr. 42, D–86720,* ☎ *09081/86019,* FAX *09081/24591. 17 rooms, 1 apartment. Restaurant, no-smoking rooms, no a/c, cable TV. MC, V.*

Nightlife and the Arts

An annual open-air **theater festival** takes place in front of the ancient walls of Nördlingen's Alter Bastei (Old Bastion). It's held from the end of June through July.

Outdoor Activities and Sports

Ever cycled around a huge meteor crater? You can do just that in the **Nördlingen Ries,** the basinlike depression left behind by the meteor that hit the area in prehistoric times. The Nördlingen tourist office (☎ 09081/84116) has a list of 10 recommended bike routes, including one 47-km (29-mi) trail around the northern part of the meteor crater. **Radsport Boeckle** (✉ Reimlingerstr. 19, ☎ 09081/801–040) rents bikes. For a spectacular view of the town and Ries crater, contact the local flying club, the **Rieser Flugsportverein** (☎ 09081/21050), for a ride in a light aircraft.

A traditional **horse race,** the Scharlachrennen, with medieval origins, is held annually in August. It's the central focus of an international show-jumping festival.

Shopping

Nördlingen has a **market** in the pedestrian shopping zone on Wednesday and Saturday. **Otto Wolf** (✉ Marktpl., ☎ 09081/4606) stocks a wide selection of Hummel figures at competitive prices.

En Route At the point where the little Wörnitz River breaks through the Franconian Jura Mountains, 20 km (12 mi) southeast of Nördlingen, you'll find one of southern Germany's best-preserved medieval castles. **Schloss Harburg** was already old when it passed into the possession of the counts of Oettingen in 1295; before that time it belonged to the Hohenstaufen emperors. The ancient and noble house of Oettingen still owns the castle, and inside you can view treasures collected by the family. Among them are works by Tilman Riemenschneider, along with illuminated manuscripts dating as far back as the 8th century and an exquisite 12th-century ivory crucifix. The castle is literally on the B–25, which runs under it through a tunnel in the rock. ✉ *Harburg*, ☎ *09080/96990*, WEB *www.fuerst-wallerstein.de*. *€4, including guided tour*. *Apr.–Oct., Tues.–Sun. 10–5; Nov.–Mar., Tues.–Sun. 10–4.*

Donauwörth

38 *11 km (7 mi) south of Harburg, 41 km (25 mi) north of Augsburg.*

At the old walled town of Donauwörth, the Wörnitz River meets the Danube. If you're driving, pull off into the clearly marked lot on B–25, just north of town. Below you sprawls a striking natural relief map of Donauwörth and its two rivers. The oldest part of town is on an island. A wood bridge connects it to the north bank and the single surviving town gate, the Riederstor. North of the gate is one of the finest avenues of the Romantic Road: Reichsstrasse (Empire Street), so named because it was once a vital link in the Road of the Holy Roman Empire between Nürnberg and Augsburg. The Fuggers, a famous family of traders and bankers from Augsburg, acquired a palatial home here in the 16th century; its fine Renaissance-style facade under a steeply gabled roof stands proudly at the upper end of Reichsstrasse.

Donauwörth is the home of the famous Käthe Kruse dolls, beloved for their sweet looks and frilly, floral outfits. You can buy them at several outlets in town, and they have their own museum, where more than 130 examples dating from 1912 are displayed in a specially renovated monastery building, the **Käthe-Kruse-Puppen-Museum.** ✉ *Pflegstr. 21a*, ☎ *0906/789–185*. *€2.* *May–Sept., Tues.–Sun. 11–5; Apr. and Oct., Tues.–Sun. 2–5; Nov.–Mar., Wed. and weekends 2–5.*

Dining and Lodging

$–$$ ✕ **Posthotel Traube.** The restaurant of the hotel Traube is the place to try some good solid German fare. Tuck into a steak smothered in onions or a juicy schnitzel. ✉ *Kapellstr. 14–16*, ☎ *0906/706–440. AE, DC, MC, V.*

$$ ★ **Parkhotel.** Members of the Landidyll chain of hotels have one feature in common: an idyllic location. This one qualifies with its position high above Donauwörth. Most rooms have floor-to-ceiling windows with panoramic views. All are decorated in bright pastel tones and with wicker chairs and sofas. ✉ *Sternschanzenstr. 1, D–86609*, ☎ *0906/706–510*, FAX *0906/706–5180*, WEB *www.parkhotel-donauwoerth.de. 45 rooms. Weinstube, in-room data ports, pool, bowling, no-smoking rooms, no a/c, cable TV. AE, DC, MC, V.*

Outdoor Activities and Sports

There's challenging canoeing on the four rivers (including the Danube) in and around Donauwörth. The **Kanu-Laden in Donauwörth** (✉ Alte Augsburger Str. 12, ☎ 0906/8086) rents canoes and can provide professional advice and suggested routes.

Ulm

39 *70 km (43 mi) southwest of Donauwörth, 65 km (40 mi) west of Augsburg.*

Ulm isn't strictly on the Romantic Road, but it's definitely worth visiting, if only for one reason: its mighty minster, with the world's tallest church tower (536 ft). The town's other claim to fame is that Albert Einstein was born here in 1879. To get to Ulm from Donauwörth, take the B–16 highway west, connecting with the B–28. For a prettier ride head back to Nördlingen and take the Schwäbische Albstrasse (the B–466) south to Ulm. From Nördlingen it's about 60 km (37 mi).

Ulm grew as a medieval trading city thanks to its location on the Danube River and, like so many other towns in the area, declined as a result of the Thirty Years' War. It was transferred between the neighboring states of Bavaria and Baden-Württemberg, becoming part of the latter in 1810. In response, Bavaria built Neu-Ulm in its territory, on the southern shore of the Danube. Today Ulm's Old Town presses against the river. In the Fisherman and Tanner quarters the cobblestone alleys and stone-and-wood bridges over the Blau (a small Danube tributary) are especially picturesque. A ticket covering entry to Ulm's two museums and other attractions costs €5.

Ulm's **Münster** (minster), the largest church in southern Germany, was unscathed by wartime bombing. It stands over the huddled medieval gables of Old Ulm, visible long before you hit the ugly suburbs encroaching on the Swabian countryside. Its single, filigree tower challenges the physically fit to plod 536 ft up the 768 steps of a giddily twisting spiral stone staircase to a spectacular observation point below the spire. On clear days the highest steeple in the world will reward you with views of the Swiss and Bavarian Alps, 160 km (100 mi) to the south. The Münster was begun in the late-Gothic age (1377) and took five centuries to build, with completion in the neo-Gothic years of the late 19th century. It contains some notable treasures, including late-Gothic choir stalls and a Renaissance altar. ✉ *Münsterpl.* 🎫 *Tower €3, organ recitals €1.50.* ⏲ *Daily 9–5. Organ recitals May–Oct., daily 11:30.*

The central **Marktplatz** is bordered by handsome medieval houses with stepped gables. A market is held here on Wednesday and Saturday mornings. A reproduction of local tailor Ludwig Berblinger's flying machine hangs inside the elaborately painted **Rathaus.** In 1811 Berblinger, a tailor and local eccentric, cobbled together a pair of wings and made a big splash by trying to fly across the river. He didn't make it, but he grabbed a place in German history books. ✉ *Marktpl. 1.*

The **Ulmer Museum** (Ulm Museum), on the south side of Marktplatz, is an excellent natural history and art museum. Exhibits illustrate centuries of development in this part of the Danube Valley, and a modern art section has works by Kandinsky, Klee, Léger, and Lichtenstein. ✉ *Marktpl. 9,* ☎ *0731/161–4330.* 🎫 *€2.50.* ⏲ *Tues.–Sun. 11–5, Thurs. 11–8; guided tour on Thurs. at 6.*

Einstein's home was a casualty of an Allied raid and was never rebuilt. The **Einstein Denkmal** (Einstein Monument; ✉ Friedrich-Ebert-Str.), erected in 1979, marks the site opposite the main railway station.

German bread is world renowned, so it's not surprising that a national museum is devoted to bread making. The **Deutsches Brotmuseum** (German Bread Museum) is housed in a former salt warehouse, just north of the Münster. It's by no means as crusty or dry as some might fear, with some often-amusing tableaux illustrating how bread has been baked over the centuries. ✉ *Salzstadelg. 10,* ☎ *0731/69955.* 🎫 *€2.50.* ⏲ *Daily 10–5, Wed. until 8:30, guided tours Wed. at 7.*

Complete your visit to Ulm with a walk down to the banks of the Danube, where you'll find long sections of the **old city wall** and fortifications intact.

Dining and Lodging

$–$$ ✕ **Zunfthaus der Schiffleute.** The sturdy half-timber Zunfthaus (Guildhall) has stood here for more than 500 years, first as a fishermen's pub and now as a charming tavern-restaurant. Ulm's fishermen had their guild headquarters here, and when the nearby Danube flooded, the fish swam right up to the door. Today they land on the menu. One of the "foreign" intruders on the menu is Bavarian white sausage, *Weisswurst*. The local beer is an excellent accompaniment. The minimum amount for credit cards is €25. ✉ *Fischerg. 31,* ☎ *0731/64411. AE, DC, MC, V.*

$ ✕ **Barfüsser.** Ulm's leading brewery has two taverns, one just around the corner from the central Münsterplatz and the other across the river in Neu-Ulm (with a beer garden overlooking the Danube). The brewery's own Swabian pretzels are served in both taverns. ✉ *Lautenberg 1,* ☎ *0731/602–1110;* ✉ *Paulstr. 4,* ☎ *0731/974–480. AE, MC, V.*

$–$$ ✕ **Hotel-Landgasthof Hirsch.** Five generations of the same Swabian family have run this century-old country tavern. In winter a fire burns in the large fireplace of the rustic lounge, and the excellent restaurant ($–$$) is a draw throughout the year. *Hirschbraten* (venison steaks) are the house speciality. The rooms are done in a country-house style. The hotel is 3 km (2 mi) from Ulm, in the Finningen district, and bus stops are nearby. ✉ *Dorfstr. 4, D–89233 Finningen,* ☎ *0731/970–744,* FAX *0731/724–131,* WEB *www.hirsch-nu.de. 22 rooms. Restaurant, lobby lounge, bowling, no a/c, cable TV. AE, DC, MC, V.*

$–$$ ✕ **Inter-City Hotel.** This is one of smartest of the German Inter-City hotels you'll find at many main railway stations. The hotel is in the city center, and although Ulm is a busy rail junction, you won't hear a thing from your soundproof room. Special work corners (with small desks and fax-modem data ports) are handy for business travelers. It has a busy restaurant and a French-style bistro. ✉ *Bahnhofpl. 1, D–89073,* ☎ *0731/96550,* FAX *0731/965–5999. 135 rooms. 2 restaurants, bar, in-room data ports, no a/c, cable TV. AE, DC, MC, V.*

$ **Hotel Ulmer Stuben.** You won't be able to miss the eye-catching white-gable exterior of this hotel. It may look old-fashioned from the outside, but the rooms are modern and comfortable and the city center is just a few minutes walk away. ✉ *Zinglerstr. 11, D–89073,* ☎ *0731/962–200,* FAX *0731/962–2055. 24 rooms. Restaurant, bowling, no a/c, cable TV. No credit cards.*

Nightlife and the Arts

The mighty organ of the **Münster** can be heard in special recitals every Sunday at 11:15 from Easter until November.

Ulm has a lively after-hours scene. The piano bar in the **Hotel Maritim** (✉ Basteistr. 40, ☎ 0731/9230) has nightly music. Jazz fans make for the **Jazzkeller** (✉ Prittwitzstr. 10, ☎ 0731/601–210).

Augsburg

65 km (40 mi) east of Ulm, 41 km (25 mi) south of Donauwörth, 60 km (37 mi) west of Munich.

Augsburg is Bavaria's third-largest city, after Munich and Nürnberg. It dates to 15 years before the birth of Christ, when a son of the Roman emperor Augustus set up a military camp here on the banks of the Lech River. The settlement that grew up around it was known as Augusta, a name Italian visitors to the city still call it. It was granted city rights in 1156, and 200 years later was first mentioned in municipal records of the Fugger family, who were to Augsburg what the Medici family was to Florence. Although less than an hour from the capital of Bavaria, you are now firmly in Swabia, once such a powerful dukedom under the Hohenstaufens that its territory covered virtually all of present-day Switzerland. Today Swabia is an administrative district of

Bavaria, and Augsburg has yielded the position it once held to the younger city of Munich.

A Good Walk

A walking tour of Augsburg is easy because signs on almost every street corner point the way to the chief sights. The signs are integrated into three color-charted tours devised by the tourist office. There's an office at Bahnhofstrasse 7, near the Hauptbahnhof, and on the south side of the central Rathausplatz. Pick up tour maps and begin your walk at Rathausplatz; the walk described below covers several of the sights described in the "green" tour.

On the eastern side of Rathausplatz rises the impressive bulk of the city's 17th-century town hall, the **Rathaus** ⑩. Even taller than the two onion domes of the Rathaus is the nearby **Perlachturm** ㊶. Follow the green signs north along Schlachthausgasse to the **Brecht Haus** ㊷, where the playwright was born; it's now a museum. Cross the nearby brook via the small bridge leading to Auf dem Rain and turn left into Barfüsserstrasse, leading to Jakoberstrasse. After 300 ft you'll find on the right the **Fuggerei** ㊸, a 16th-century housing project. Following the green signs, recross the brook (which follows the route of a Roman-built canal) and pass the small alley Hinterer Lech and turn left down Mittlerer Lech. This will lead you to the **Holbein Haus** ㊹, the home of painter Hans Holbein the Elder (at Vorderer Lech).

Continue farther south, recrossing the brook onto Oberer Graben, and head south through the Vogeltor, a Gothic city gate, to the southern extremities of the medieval defense wall. The gate here, the **Rotes Tor** ㊺, was the main entrance to Augsburg in earlier centuries. Now follow the green route north through a small park enclosed by the remains of the ancient bastion and continue northward; you'll soon see the soaring tower of the Gothic church of **Sts. Ulrich and Afra** ㊻, on Ulrichsplatz. Ulrichsplatz leads directly north into **Maximilianstrasse,** Augsburg's main thoroughfare. At No. 46 stands the **Schaezler Palais** ㊼, home of two impressive art collections. The Herkulesbrunnen, the fountain in the center of the street outside the palace, is a symbolic work by the Renaissance sculptor Adrian de Vries. You can see a second de Vries fountain farther north on the same street. Just steps away on Maximilianstrasse 36 is the sturdy **Fuggerhäuser** ㊽, former home of Jakob Fugger, founder of the Fuggerei.

Wend your way across Zeugplatz, Bürgermeister-Fischer-Strasse, and Martin-Luther-Platz, to Anna-Strasse. If you have time and energy, stop at the **Maximilian-Museum** ㊾, on Phillipine-Welser-Strasse. The exquisite **St. Annakirche** ㊿ is on Anna-Strasse. Head north from here, cross busy Karlstrasse, and through the Kesselmarkt and across Johannisgasse to the gardens of the city cathedral, **Dom St. Maria** (51). A short walk north along Frauentorstrasse takes you to the **Mozart-Haus** (52), birthplace of Mozart's father, Leopold. By retracing your steps to the cathedral, into Hoher Weg and then Karolinenstrasse, you'll arrive within a few minutes back at Rathausplatz.

TIMING

You'll need a complete day if you linger in any of the museums. Set aside at least two hours for the Schaezler Palais, and a half hour each for the churches of Sts. Ulrich and Afra and the Dom St. Maria. There are plenty of opportunities en route for lunch or a coffee break.

Sights to See

㊷ **Brecht Haus.** This modest artisan's house was the birthplace of the renowned playwright Bertolt Brecht (1898–1956), author of *Mother Courage* and *The Three-Penny Opera*. He lived here until he moved

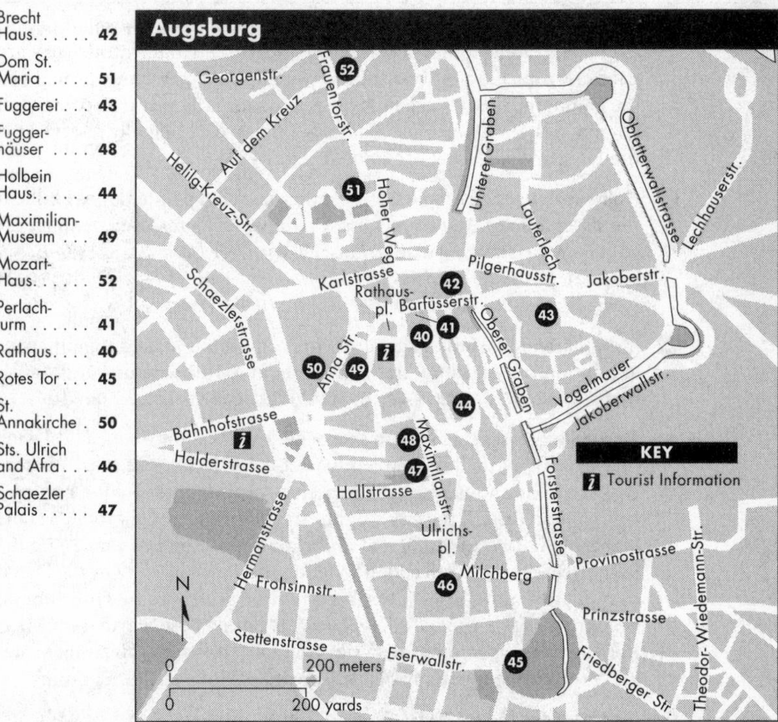

to Munich in 1917 and then, during Hitler's reign, to Scandinavia and later the United States. After the war he settled in East Berlin to direct the Berliner Ensemble. Today the house serves as a memorial to Brecht's life and work. ✉ *Auf dem Rain 7.* 🎫 *€1.50.* ⏲ *Tues.–Sun. 10–5.*

51 **Dom St. Maria** (Cathedral of the Virgin Mary). Augsburg's cathedral stands out within the city's panorama because of its square Gothic towers, which were built in the 9th century. A 10th-century Romanesque crypt, built in the time of Bishop Ulrich, also remains from the cathedral's early years. The heavy bronze doors on the south portal represent 11th-century craftsmanship; 11th-century windows on the south side of the nave, depicting the prophets Jonah, Daniel, Hosea, Moses, and David, form the oldest cycle of stained glass in central Europe. Five important paintings by Hans Holbein the Elder adorn the altar.

The cathedral's treasures are on display at the **Diözesan Museum St. Afra** (✉ Kornhausg. 3-5, ☎ 0821/316–6330; 🎫 €2.50; ⏲ Tues.–Sat., 10–5; Sun., 2–5). A short walk from the cathedral will take you to the quiet courtyards and small raised garden of the former episcopal residence, a series of 18th-century buildings in baroque and rococo styles that now serve as the Swabian regional government offices. ✉ *Dompl.* ⏲ *Daily 9–dusk.*

43 **Fuggerei.** This neat little settlement is the world's oldest social housing project, established by the Fugger family in 1516 to accommodate the city's deserving poor. The 104 homes still serve the same purpose; the annual rent of "one Rhenish guilder" (€1) hasn't changed, either. Residents must be Augsburg citizens, Catholic, and destitute through no fault of their own—and they must pray daily for their original benefactors, the Fugger family. ✉ *Jacoberstr.*

48 **Fuggerhäuser.** The 16th-century former home and business quarters of the Fugger family now houses a restaurant in its cellar and offices

on the upper floors. In the ground-floor entrance are busts of two of Augsburg's most industrious Fuggers, Raymund and Anton. They are tributes from a grateful city to the wealth these merchants brought to the community. Beyond a modern glass door is a quiet courtyard with colonnades, the **Damenhof** (Ladies' Courtyard), originally reserved for the Fugger women. ✉ *Maximilianstr. 36–38.*

44 **Holbein Haus.** The rebuilt 16th-century home of painter Hans Holbein the Elder, one of Augsburg's most famous residents, is now a city art gallery, with changing exhibitions. ✉ *Vorderer Lech 20.* *Admission varies.* *May–Oct., Tues.–Wed., and Fri.–Sun. 10–5, Thurs. 10–8; Nov.–Apr., Tues.–Wed., and Fri.–Sun. 10–4, Thurs. 10–8.*

49 **Maximilian-Museum.** Augsburg's main museum houses a permanent exhibition of Augsburg arts and crafts in a 16th-century merchant's mansion. ✉ *Philippine-Welser-Str. 24.* *€4.* *Tues.–Sun. 10–5.*

Maximilianstrasse. This main shopping street was once a medieval wine market. Today the high-gabled, pastel-color facades of the 16th-century merchant houses assert themselves against encroaching modernized shops. Most of the city's sights are on this thoroughfare or a short walk away. Two monumental and elaborate fountains punctuate the long street. At the north end the **Merkur,** designed in 1599 by the Dutch master Adrian de Vries (after a Florentine sculpture by Giovanni da Bologna), shows winged Mercury in his classic pose. Farther up Maximilianstrasse is another de Vries fountain: a bronze **Hercules** struggling to subdue the many-headed Hydra.

52 **Mozart-Haus** (Mozart House). Leopold Mozart, the father of Wolfgang Amadeus Mozart, was born in this bourgeois 17th-century residence; he was an accomplished composer and musician in his own right. The house now serves as a Mozart memorial and museum, with some fascinating contemporary documents on the Mozart family. ✉ *Frauentorstr. 30,* ☎ *0821/324–3894.* *€1.50.* *Tues.–Sun. 10–5.*

41 **Perlachturm** (Perlach Tower). This 258-ft-high plastered brick bell tower has foundations dating to the 11th century. Although it's a long climb to the top of the tower, the view over Augsburg and the countryside is worth the effort. ✉ *Rathauspl.* *€1.* *May–mid-Oct., daily 10–6; Dec., weekends noon–7.*

40 **Rathaus.** Augsburg's city hall was Germany's largest when it was built in the early 17th century; it is now regarded as the finest Renaissance secular structure north of the Alps. Its **Goldenener Saal** (Golden Hall) was given its name because of its rich decoration—a gold-based harmony of wall frescoes, carved pillars, and coffered ceiling. ✉ *Rathauspl.,* ☎ *0821/5020.* *€1.50.* *10–6 on days when no official functions take place.*

45 **Rotes Tor** (Red Gate). The city's most important medieval entrance gate once straddled the main trading road to Italy. It provides the backdrop to an open-air opera and operetta festival in June and July. ✉ *Eserwallstr.*

50 **St. Annakirche** (St. Anna's Church). This site was formerly part of a Carmelite monastery, where Martin Luther stayed in 1518 during his meetings with Cardinal Cajetanus, the papal legate sent from Rome to persuade the reformer to renounce his heretical views. Luther refused, and the place where he publicly declared his rejection of papal pressure is marked with a plaque on Maximilianstrasse. You can wander through the quiet cloisters, dating from the 14th century, and view the chapel used by the Fugger family until the Reformation. ✉ *Anna-Str., west of Rathauspl.,* *Tues.–Sat. 10–12.30 and 3–6, Sun. noon–6.*

46 **Sts. Ulrich and Afra.** Standing at the highest point of the city, this basilica was built on the site of a Roman cemetery where St. Afra was martyred in AD 304. The original structure was begun in the late-Gothic style in 1467; a baroque preaching hall was added in 1710 as the Protestant church of St. Ulrich. St. Afra is buried in the crypt, near the tomb of St. Ulrich, a 10th-century bishop who helped stop a Hungarian army at the gates of Augsburg in the Battle of the Lech River. The remains of a third patron of the church, St. Simpert, are preserved in one of the church's most elaborate side chapels. From the steps of the magnificent altar, look back along the high nave to the finely carved baroque wrought-iron and wood railing that borders the entrance. As you leave, look into the separate but adjacent church of St. Ulrich, the former chapter house that was reconstructed by the Lutherans after the Reformation. ✉ *Ulrichspl.* ⏲ *Daily 9–dusk.*

47 **Schaezler Palais.** This elegant 18th-century city palace was built by the von Liebenhofens, a family of wealthy bankers. Schaezler was the name of a baron who married into the family. The von Liebenhofens wanted to outdo the Fuggers—but not at any price. To save money, in an age when property was taxed according to the length of its frontage on the street, they commissioned a long, narrow building running far back from Maximilianstrasse. The palace is composed of a series of interconnecting rooms leading back to a green-and-white rococo ballroom: an extravagant two-story hall heavily decorated with mirrors, chandeliers, and wall sconces. While on her way from Vienna to Paris to marry Louis XVI, in 1770, Marie Antoinette was the guest of honor at the inauguration ball.

Today the palace rooms contain the **Deutsche Barockgalerie** (German Baroque Gallery), a major art collection that features works of the 17th and 18th centuries. The palace adjoins the former church of a Dominican monastery. A steel door behind the palace's banquet hall leads into another world of high-vaulted ceilings, where the **Staatsgalerie Altdeutsche Meister**, a Bavarian state collection, highlights old-master paintings, among them a Dürer portrait of one of the Fuggers. ✉ *Maximilianstr. 46.* 🎫 *€2.* ⏲ *Tues.–Sun. 10–5.*

Dining and Lodging

$$$$ ★ ✕ **Welser Kuche.** You can practically hear the great oak tables groan under the array of Swabian specialties offered at this special place. There is a reservations-only policy, so you must book in advance and there are only two set menus to choose from. Be sure to try the Spätzle. ✉ *Maximilianstr. 83,* ☎ *0821/33930; 08231/96110 for reservations. Reservations essential. AE, DC, MC, V. No lunch.*

$$–$$$$ ✕ **Die Ecke.** This attractive and popular restaurant is tucked away in an *Ecke* (corner) behind Augsburg's city hall. The Ecke is valued for the imaginative variety of its cuisine and the scope of its wine list. In season the venison dishes are among Bavaria's best. Fish—in particular, locally caught trout (the *truit meunière*, sautéed in butter and lightly dressed with herbs and lemon, is magnificent)—is another specialty. ✉ *Elias-Holl-Pl. 2,* ☎ *0821/510–600. Reservations essential. AE, DC, MC, V.*

$–$$$$ ✕ **Restaurant Oblinger.** The intimate restaurant of respected chef Albert Oblinger is within his Oblinger Hotel. Some of the specialties with which he achieved national prominence include Augsburg-style herb soup (rich vegetable broth spiced with rosemary and other herbs). The Swabian dumplings and regional accompaniments such as raviolilike Maultaschen are as good as ever. ✉ *Pfärrle 16,* ☎ *0821/345–8392. AE, DC, MC, V.*

$$$ ✕🏨 **Steigenberger Drei Mohren Hotel.** Kings and princes, Napoléon and the duke of Wellington, who defeated him at Waterloo, have all slept here. The historic hotel takes its name from three very early guests of lesser renown: Abyssinian bishops who sought shelter in this worldly German city. Except the modern fourth- and fifth-floor rooms, all the rooms maintain a luxurious, traditional style. Dining options are the Mediterranean-style restaurant ($$$), the well-loved, traditional Maximilian's, and the busy bistro. ✉ *Maximilianstr. 40, D–86150,* ☎ *0821/50360,* FAX *0821/157–864,* WEB *www.steigenberger.com. 106 rooms, 5 suites. 2 restaurants, bar, meeting rooms, no-smoking rooms, no a/c, cable TV. AE, DC, MC, V.*

$$–$$$ ✕🏨 **Romantikhotel Augsburger Hof.** A preservation order protects the beautiful Renaissance facade of this charming old Augsburg mansion, but rather than recreating an old-world atmosphere inside, the owners opted for a cheerful, but classic look with natural wood finishes and flowered curtains. The restaurant ($$–$$$$) serves excellent Maultaschen. The cathedral is around the corner; the town center is a five-minute stroll. ✉ *Auf dem Kreuz 2, D–86152,* ☎ *0821/343–050,* FAX *0821/343–0555,* WEB *www.augsburger-hof.de. 36 rooms. Restaurant, sauna, no-smoking rooms, no a/c, cable TV. AE, DC, MC, V.*

$$ ✕🏨 **Privat Hotel Riegele.** The tavern-restaurant ($$–$$$), the Bräustüble, is a local favorite. The hotel itself is a worthy successor to the Schmid family's previous house, the Hotel am Rathaus (still in the shadow of the Perlachturm and recommended as an alternative lodging). All the comforts there are found in the new hotel—and, of course, the friendly service is unchanged. Public rooms and some bedrooms have plush armchairs, deep-pile rugs, and heavy drapes. ✉ *Viktoriastr. 4, D–86150,* ☎ *0821/509–000,* FAX *0821/517–746,* WEB *www.hotel-riegele.de. 27 rooms, 1 apartment. Restaurant, meeting rooms, no a/c, cable TV. AE, DC, MC, V.*

$$ 🏨 **Dom Hotel.** Just across the street from Augsburg's cathedral, this snug establishment has personality. Ask for one of the attic rooms, where you'll sleep under beam ceilings and wake to a rooftop view of the city. Even if you have to settle for a room in the apartment-house extension, you'll lack no comforts. A garden terrace borders the old city walls, and there's also an indoor pool, sauna, and solarium. ✉ *Frauentorstr. 8, D–86152,* ☎ *0821/343–930,* FAX *0821/3439–3200. 44 rooms, 8 suites. Pool, sauna, no a/c, cable TV. AE, DC, MC, V.*

$ 🏨 **Hotel-Garni Schlössle.** This family-run and very friendly little bed-and-breakfast is on the western outskirts of Augsburg, in the Stadtbergen district. A 10-minute tram ride brings you to the city center. The location offers fresh country air, walks, and sporting facilities (a golf course is within a good tee-shot's range)—and unbeatable value. Rooms under the steep eaves are particularly cozy. ✉ *Bauernstr. 37, D–86391 Stadtbergen,* ☎ *0821/243–930,* FAX *0821/437–451. 14 rooms. No a/c, cable TV, no smoking. MC, V.*

Nightlife and the Arts

Augsburg has chamber and symphony orchestras, as well as ballet and opera companies. The city stages a Mozart Festival of international stature in September. The **Kongresshalle** (✉ Göggingerstr. 10, ☎ 0821/324–2348) presents music and dance performances from September through July. For **information** about programs, call 0931/58686.

Augsburg's annual open-air **opera and operetta** season takes place in June and July. Productions move to the romantic inner courtyard of the **Fugger Palace** for part of July and August. Phone the city tourist office for details (☎ 0821/502–070).

Children love the city's excellent **Augsburger Puppenkiste** (puppet theater; ✉ Spitalg. 15, next to Rotes Tor, ☎ 0821/434–440).

Outdoor Activities and Sports

Augsburg Golf Club (✉ Engelshoferstr. 2, Augsburg-Bobingen, ☎ 08234/5621) welcomes visiting members of overseas golf clubs.

Shopping

Viktoria Passage, an arcade of diverse shops and boutiques opposite the main railway station, has some of Augsburg's best wares. **Maximilianstrasse,** the city's broad main street, is also a good shopping area.

En Route Leaving Augsburg southward on B–17—the southern stretch of the Romantic Road—you'll drive across the Lech battlefield, where Hungarian invaders were stopped in 955. Rich Bavarian pastures extend as far as the Lech River, which the Romantic Road meets at the historic town of Landsberg.

TOWARD THE ALPS

South of Augsburg, the Romantic Road climbs gradually into the foothills of the Bavarian Alps, which burst into view between Landsberg and Schongau. The route ends dramatically at the northern wall of the Alps at Füssen, on the Austrian border.

Landsberg am Lech

53 *35 km (22 mi) south of Augsburg, 58 km (36 mi) west of Munich.*

Although Landsberg has a colorful history, it is most famous today because of one notorious guest—Adolf Hitler, who wrote much of *Mein Kampf* while in prison there. The town was founded by the Bavarian ruler Heinrich der Löwe (Henry the Lion) in the 12th century and grew wealthy from the salt trade. You'll see impressive evidence of Landsberg's early wealth among the solid old houses packed within its turreted walls; the early 18th-century **Historisches Rathaus** (Old Town Hall) is one of the finest in the region.

The artist Sir Hubert von Herkomer (1847–1914) was born in the small village of Waal, just outside Landsberg. Within Landsberg's town walls is an unusual monument he built for his mother, Josefine. It's a romantic, medieval-style tower, bristling with turrets and galleries. He called it his Mutterturm, or "mother tower." The young Hubert moved with his parents to the United States and, later, to England. He died in Devon in 1914. The **Herkomer Museum** within the tower's rough-stone walls is a permanent exhibition on the artist's life and work. ✉ *Von-Kühlmann-Str., 2,* ☎ *08191/942–328.* *€2.50.* *Tues.–Sun. 2–5.*

The **Historisches Schuhmuseum** (Shoe History Museum) is devoted to the humble shoe. The exhibits—from all over the world and spanning five centuries—include slippers worn by King Ludwig II and a pair of delicate boots that once graced the feet of his beloved cousin Sisi, Empress Elisabeth of Austria. The museum is privately run, and you must call beforehand to arrange a guided tour. ✉ *Vorderer Anger 274,* ☎ *08191/42296.* *€1.50.* *By appointment.*

Outdoor Activities and Sports

You can play nine holes of golf in the beautifully landscaped grounds of a castle just outside Landsberg, at **Schloss Igling** (☎ 08248/1003).

Schongau

54 *28 km (17 mi) south of Landsberg, 70 km (43 mi) southwest of Munich.*

Schongau, founded in the 11th century at about the same time as Landsberg, has virtually intact wall fortifications, complete with towers and gates. In medieval and Renaissance times, the town was an important trading post on the route from Italy to Augsburg. The steeply gabled 16th-century Ballenhaus was a warehouse before it was elevated to the rank of Rathaus.

A popular **Märchenwald** (fairy-tale forest) lies 1½ km (1 mi) outside Schongau, suitably set in a clearing in the woods. It comes complete with mechanical models of fairy-tale scenes, deer enclosures, and an old-time miniature railway. ✉ *Diessenerstr. 6,* ☎ *08861/7527,* WEB *www.schongauer-maerchenwald.de.* *€3.50.* *Apr. and Oct., daily 9–6; May–Sept., daily 9–7.*

Dining and Lodging

$–$$ **Alte Post.** Fancy a flight over the Bavarian Alps? You're at the right address, because Franz Lutzenberger, the host at the Alte Post, is a spare-time pilot. If he's too busy in the hotel to take guests for a joyride, he'll gladly organize flights from a nearby airfield. Costs range upward from €77. His hotel in the center of Schongau is a typically Bavarian hostelry—a sturdy, yellow-fronted inn, with comfortable accommodations and a tavern-restaurant ($–$$$) serving hearty portions of local fare (the roast pork and dumplings are thoroughly recommended). ✉ *Marienpl. 19, D–86956,* ☎ *08861/23200,* FAX *08861/232–080. 34 rooms. Restaurant, no a/c, cable TV. MC, V.*

$ **Hotel Holl.** The Alpine-style hotel on wooded slopes is a 10-minute stroll from the town center, with great views from most rooms. It's ideal for travelers seeking peace and quiet. The restaurant ($–$$) under the steep eaves features regional specialities including fish dishes using the catch from local rivers and lakes. ✉ *Altenstädterstr. 39, D–86956,* ☎ *08861/23310,* FAX *08861/233–112. 21 rooms, 1 suite. Restaurant, meeting rooms, no-smoking rooms, no a/c, cable TV. AE, DC, MC, V.*

Outdoor Activities and Sports

The rolling meadowlands that form the foothills of the Bavarian Alps are ideal for hikers and cyclists. Tour operators focus on five main routes, providing luggage transport and arranging for accommodations. The **Schongau Verkehrsamt** (☎ 08861/7216) has details.

OFF THE BEATEN PATH

HOHER PEISSENBERG – The Bavarian Alps rise up above lush meadowland and signal the approaching end of the Romantic Road. Some 15 km (9 mi) east of Schongau (on the B–472) is the first real peak of the Alpine chain, the 3,000-ft-high Hoher Peissenberg. A pilgrimage chapel was consecrated on the mountain in the 16th century; a century later a larger church was added, with a fine ceiling fresco and delicate carvings by local Bavarian masters.

ROTTENBUCH – The small country road B–23 (watch for the turn just before the village of Peissenberg) leads to this town, 13 km (8 mi) south of Schongau. In the 11th century the Augustinian order built an impressive monastery on the Ammer River here. The Gothic church was redecorated in rococo style in the 18th century, and the lavish interior of cream, gold, and rose stuccowork and statuary is stunning.

WIESKIRCHE – This church—a glorious example of German rococo architecture—stands in an Alpine meadow just off the Romantic Road near the village of Steingaden, 9 km (5½ mi) east of Rottenbuch, on the Steingaden road. Its yellow-and-white walls and steep red roof are set off by the dark backdrop of the Trauchgauer Mountains. The architect Dominicus Zimmermann, former mayor of Landsberg and creator of much of that town's rococo architecture, built the church in 1745 on the spot where six years earlier a local woman claimed to have seen tears running down the face of a picture of Christ. Although the church was dedicated as the Pilgrimage Church of the Scourged Christ, it is now known simply as the Wieskirche (Church of the Meadow). Visit it on a bright day if you can, when light streaming through its high windows displays the full glory of the glittering interior. Together with the pilgrimage church of Vierzehnheiligen in Franconia, the Wieskirche represents the culmination of German rococo ecclesiastical architecture. As at Vierzehnheiligen, the simple exterior gives little hint of the ravishing interior. A complex oval plan is animated by brilliantly colored stuccowork, statues, and gilt. A luminous ceiling fresco completes the decoration. Note the beautifully detailed choir and organ loft. Concerts are presented in the church from the end of June through the beginning of August. Contact the **Verkehrsamt** (☎ 08861/7216) in Schongau for details. *Free.* *Daily 8–dusk.*

Schwangau

55 *18 km (11 mi) south of Steingaden, 105 km (65 mi) southwest of Munich.*

The lakeside resort town of Schwangau is an ideal center from which to explore the surrounding mountains. Here you'll encounter the heritage of Bavaria's famous 19th-century King Ludwig II. Ludwig spent much of his youth at Schloss Hohenschwangau; it is said that its neo-Gothic atmosphere provided the primary influences that shaped his wildly romantic Schloss Neuschwanstein, the fairy-tale castle he built across the valley after he became king.

The two castles are 1 km (½ mi) from each other and about 2 km (1 mi) from the center of Schwangau. Road signs to the castles read KONIGSCHLÖSSER. Cars and buses are barred from the approach roads, but the mile journey to Neuschwanstein can be made in horse-drawn carriages, which stop in the tiny village of Hohenschwangau. A bus from the village (the stop is outside the Schlosshotel Lisl, Neuschwansteinstrasse 1–3) takes a back route to an outlook called Aussichtspunkt Jugend; from there it's only a 10-minute walk to the castle. Schloss Hohenschwangau is a 15-minute walk from the village, and Neuschwanstein is a 25-minute, pleasant uphill walk. There are three convenient parking areas for visitors arriving by car: at Colomannstrasse, Schwangauerstrasse, and Parkstrasse, all on the western edge of Hohenschwangau. There are four paths leading from the parking lots to Schloss Neuschwanstein and Schloss Hohenschwangau, all clearly marked.

56 **Schloss Hohenschwangau** was built by the knights of Schwangau in the 12th century. Later it was remodeled by Ludwig's father, the Bavarian crown prince (and later king) Maximilian, between 1832 and 1836. Unlike Ludwig's more famous castle across the valley, Neuschwanstein, the somewhat garishly yellow Schloss Hohenschwangau has the feeling of a noble home, where comforts would be valued as much as outward splendor. It was here that the young Ludwig met the composer Richard Wagner. Their friendship shaped and deepened the future king's interest in theater, music, and German mythology—the mythology Wagner drew upon for his *Ring* cycle of operas. *€7, including guided tour.* *Daily 10–4.*

Close-Up

THE FAIRY-TALE KING

KING LUDWIG II (1845–1886), the enigmatic presence indelibly associated with Bavaria, was one of the last rulers of the Wittelsbach dynasty, which ruled Bavaria from 1180 to 1918. Though his family had created grandiose architecture in Munich, Ludwig II disliked the city and preferred isolation in the countryside. In it he constructed monumental edifices born of fanciful imagination and spent most of the royal purse on his endeavors. Although he was also a great lover of literature, theater, and opera (he was Richard Wagner's great patron), it is his fairy-tale-like castles that are his legacy.

Ludwig II reigned from 1864 to 1886, all the while avoiding political duties whenever possible. By 1878 he had completed his Schloss Linderhof retreat and immediately began Schloss Herrenchiemsee, a tribute to Versailles and Louis XIV (☞ Chapter 3). The grandest of his extravagant projects is Neuschwanstein, one of Germany's top attractions and concrete proof of the king's eccentricity. In 1886, before Neuschwanstein was finished, members of the government became convinced that Ludwig had taken leave of his senses. A medical commission declared the king insane and forced him to abdicate. Within two days of incarceration in the Berg Castle, on Starnbergersee (☞ Side Trips from Munich *in* Chapter 2), Ludwig and his doctor were found drowned in the lake's shallow waters. Their deaths are still a mystery. A poor leader, but still a visionary, Ludwig II is memorialized in a musical based in Füssen, *Ludwig II—Longing for Paradise.*

★ 57 **Schloss Neuschwanstein** was conceived by a set designer instead of an architect, thanks to Ludwig's deep love of the theater. The castle soars from its mountainside like a stage creation—it should hardly come as a surprise that Walt Disney took it as the model for his castle in the movie *Sleeping Beauty* and later for the Disneyland castle itself.

The life of the proprietor of this spectacular castle reads like one of the great Gothic mysteries of the 19th century, and the castle well symbolizes that life. Yet during the 17 years from the start of Schloss Neuschwanstein's construction until his death, the king spent less than six months in the country residence, and the interior was never finished. The Byzantine-style throne room is without a throne; Ludwig died before one could be installed. The walls of the rooms leading to Ludwig's bedroom are painted with murals depicting characters from Wagner's operas—Siegfried and the Nibelungen, Lohengrin, Tristan, and others. Ludwig's bed and its canopy are made of intricately carved oak. A small corridor behind the bedroom was made as a ghostly grotto, reminiscent of Wagner's *Tannhäuser.* Chamber concerts are held in September in the gaily decorated minstrels' hall—one room, at least, that was completed as Ludwig conceived it (program details are available from the Verkehrsamt, Schwangau, ☎ 08362/81980). On the walls outside the castle's gift shop are plans and photos of the castle's construction. There are some spectacular walks around the castle. The delicate **Marienbrücke** (Mary's Bridge) is spun like a medieval maiden's hair across a deep, narrow gorge. From this vantage point there are giddy views of the castle and the great Upper Bavarian Plain beyond. *€7, including guided tour.* ⏲ *Daily 10–4.*

If you plan to visit Hohenschwangau or Neuschwanstein, bear in mind that more than 1 million people pass through the two castles every year. If you visit in the summer, get there early. The best time to see either castle without waiting a long time is a weekday between January and April. The prettiest time, however, is in the fall. Get your ticket at the center near the parking lot before going up to the castle. The average wait between buying a ticket and entering the castle is one hour. With a deposit or credit card number you can book your tickets in advance through **Verwaltung Hohenschwangau** (✉ Alpseestr. 12, D–87645 Hohenschwangau, ☎ 08362/930–830, FAX 0832/930–8320). There is a €1.50 processing fee per ticket; a written confirmation will follow. You can cancel or change entrance times up to two hours before the confirmed entrance time.

Dining and Lodging

$$$ ✕🏨 **König Ludwig.** This handsome Alpine hotel-restaurant, smothered in flowers in summer and in snow in deep winter, is named for the king who felt so at home in this area. The wood-paneled restaurant serves Bavarian fare with an international touch, and venison is a seasonal specialty. Rooms are furnished in rustic Bavarian style. Room rates include a substantial breakfast buffet. ✉ *Kreuzweg 11–15, D–87645,* ☎ *08362/8890,* FAX *08362/81779. 102 rooms, 36 apartments. Restaurant, bar, pool, hair salon, massage, sauna, steam room, no a/c, cable TV. No credit cards.*

$$–$$$ ✕🏨 **Schlosshotel Lisl und Jägerhaus.** These jointly run 19th-century properties are across the street from one another, and both share views of the nearby castles. The intimate Jägerhaus has five suites and six double rooms, all decorated with floral wallpaper and drapery. The bathrooms have swan-motif fixtures. The Lisl's rooms have bright blue carpeting and fabrics. Lisl's restaurant, Salon Wittelsbacher, provides a view of Neuschwanstein, as well as a tasty dish of *Tafelspitz* (boiled beef with horseradish). ✉ *Neuschwansteinstr. 1–3, D–87643,* ☎ *08362/8870,* FAX *08362/81107,* WEB *www.lisl.de. 42 rooms, 5 suites. 2 restaurants, bar, lobby lounge, no a/c, cable TV. AE, MC, V.*

$$ ✕🏨 **Hotel Müller.** Between the two Schwangau castles, the Müller fits beautifully into the stunning landscape, its creamy Bavarian baroque facade complemented by the green mountain forest. Inside, the baroque influence is everywhere, from the finely furnished bedrooms to the chandelier-hung public rooms and restaurant ($–$$). The mahogany-paneled, glazed veranda (with open fireplace) provides a magnificent view of Hohenschwangau Castle. Round your day off with a local specialty such as the *Allgäuer Lendentopf* (sirloin) served with Spätzle. ✉ *Alpseestr. 16, D–87643 Hohenschwangau,* ☎ *08362/81990,* FAX *08362/819–913,* WEB *www.hotel-mueller.de. 39 rooms, 4 suites. 2 restaurants, bar, no a/c, cable TV. AE, DC, MC, V.*

Outdoor Activities and Sports

Schwangau's mountain, the Tegelberg, offers challenging upland hiking in spring, summer, and fall and good skiing in winter. There's a cable car (€14 round-trip) and six ski lifts. A summer sledge-run snakes for 1 km (½ mi) down the lower slopes (six rides for €9.50). At the bottom of the run is a children's playground and beer garden. Hikers can combine a stiff mountain walk with a tour of the geographic, geological, zoological, and historical landscape of this region by following the **Kulturpfad Schutzengelweg,** a trail marked by placards explaining points of interest. The trail climbs to 5,670 ft and takes about 2½ hours to complete.

Füssen

58 *5 km (3 mi) southwest of Schwangau, 110 km (68 mi) south of Munich.*

Füssen has a beautiful location at the foot of the mountains that separate Bavaria from the Austrian Tyrol. The Lech River, which accompanies much of the final section of the Romantic Road, embraces the town as it rushes northward. The town's **Hohes Schloss** (High Castle) is one of the best-preserved late-Gothic castles in Germany. It was built on the site of the Roman fortress that once guarded this Alpine section of the Via Claudia, the trade route from Rome to the Danube. Evidence of Roman occupation of the area has been uncovered at the foot of the nearby Tegelberg Mountain, and the **excavations** next to the Tegelberg cable-car station can be visited daily. The Hohes Schloss was the seat of Bavarian rulers before Emperor Heinrich VII mortgaged it and the rest of the town to the bishop of Augsburg for 400 pieces of silver. The mortgage was never redeemed, and Füssen remained the property of the Augsburg episcopate until secularization in the early 19th century. The bishops of Augsburg used the castle as their summer Alpine residence. It has a spectacular 16th-century **Rittersaal** (Knights' Hall) with a carved ceiling and a princes' chamber with a Gothic tile stove. ✉ *Magnuspl. 10,* ☎ *08362/903–146.* 🎟 *€2.50.* ⏲ *Apr.–Oct., Tues.–Sun. 11–4; Nov.–Mar., Tues.–Sun. 2–4.*

The summer presence of the bishops of Augsburg ensured that Füssen received an impressive number of baroque and rococo churches. Füssen's **Rathaus** (✉ Lechalde 3) was once a Benedictine abbey, built in the 9th century at the site of the grave of St. Magnus, who spent most of his life ministering in the area. A Romanesque crypt beneath the baroque abbey church has a partially preserved 10th-century fresco, the oldest in Bavaria. In summer chamber concerts are held in the high-ceiling baroque splendor of the former abbey's **Fürstensaal** (Princes' Hall). Program details are available from the tourist office.

Füssen's main shopping street, called **Reichenstrasse,** was, like Augsburg's Maximilianstrasse, once part of the Roman Via Claudia. This cobblestone pedestrian walkway is lined with high-gabled medieval houses and backed by the bulwarks of the castle and the easternmost buttresses of the Allgäu Alps.

Dining and Lodging

$–$$ ✕ **Gasthaus zum Schwanen.** This modest establishment serves good regional cooking with no frills. The excellent Swabian Maultaschen are made on the premises. ✉ *Brotmarkt 4,* ☎ *08362/6174. MC, V. Closed Mon. and Nov.*

$$ ✕🏨 **Alpen-Schlössle.** A Schlössle is a small castle, and although this comfortable, rustic hotel and restaurant doesn't quite qualify (apart from a solitary, corner tower), its mountain site, just outside Füssen, might well have appealed to King Ludwig. The elegant little restaurant ($–$$$$; closed Tuesday) is prized for its imaginative cuisine, based on local products such as beef and veal from the Allgäu region. For fine-weather dining there's a very attractive, sunny terrace. The small rooms are richly furnished with Russian pine, larch, and cherrywood. ✉ *Alatseestr. 28, D–87629,* ☎ *08362/4017,* FAX *08362/39847. 11 rooms. Restaurant, no a/c, cable TV. MC, V.*

$$ ✕🏨 **Hotel Hirsch.** A mother and daughter team provide friendly service at this traditional Füssen hotel. Outside the majestic building is its trademark stag (*Hirsch* in German); inside, the decor is pure Bavarian—large closets are brightly painted and old photographs of the hotel hang on the walls. Rooms are simply furnished with comfortable beds. In the popular Bierstüberl, the pub section, guests are greeted

by a painting of King Ludwig II. The brightly lighted restaurant ($) serves good Allgäu specialties such as Maultaschen. ✉ *Kaiser-Maximilian-Pl. 7 D-87629,* ☎ *08362/93980,* FAX *08362/939–877,* WEB *www.hotelhirschfuessen.de. 58 rooms. 2 restaurants, pub, meeting rooms, no-smoking rooms, no a/c, cable TV. AE, DC, MC, V.*

$–$$ ✕🏨 **Altstadthotel Zum Hechten.** Geraniums flower for most of the year on this comfortable inn's balconies. It's one of the town's oldest lodgings, directly below the castle. The inn's own butcher shop provides the meat for its restaurant ($), which has sturdy, round tables and colorfully frescoed walls. Vegetarian meals are served in a separate restaurant. ✉ *Ritterstr. 6, D–87629,* ☎ *08362/91600,* FAX *08362/916–099,* WEB *www.hotel-hechten.com. 36 rooms, 30 with bath or shower. 2 restaurants, no a/c, cable TV, gym, sauna, bowling. AE, MC.*

Nightlife and the Arts

The musical *Ludwig II—Longing for Paradise* premiered in April 2000 in a specially built theater complex on the shore of the Forggensee. Subtitles in English appear above the stage. It's best to tour Neuschwanstein and have some understanding of this lonely king's life before attending a performance. For information on tickets contact **Ludwig Musical AG & Co.** (☎ 01805/583–944; 800/669–8687 in the U.S.) Orders processed in the United States have a mark-up of 25%.

Outdoor Activities and Sports

Pleasure boats cruise Forggensee lake mid-June–early October. Alpine winds ensure good sailing and windsurfing. The **Forgensee-Yachtschule** (✉ Seestr. 10, Dietringen, ☎ 08367/471) offers courses of up to two weeks' duration, with hotel or apartment accommodations. There are also boatyards and jetties with craft for rent at Waltenhofen.

There's good skiing in the mountains above Füssen, and cross-country enthusiasts are catered to with more than 20 km (12 mi) of prepared track. Füssen's highest peak, the Tegelberg, has a ski school, **Skischule Tegelberg A. Geiger** (☎ 08362/8455).

THE ROMANTIC ROAD A TO Z

To research prices, get advice from other travelers, and book travel arrangements, visit www.fodors.com.

AIRPORTS

The major international airports serving the Romantic Road are Frankfurt and Munich. Regional airports include Nürnberg and Augsburg.

BIKE AND TRAVEL

Wertheim is the starting point of a picturesque bike route along the Tauber River valley. The 100-km (62-mi) route follows the course of the river until Rothenburg-ob-der-Tauber. This is the most beautiful stretch of the Romantic Road, rich in ancient villages and flanked by thickly wooded heights crowned by castles and mansions. The bike route crisscrosses the river and at Tauberrettersheim passes over a bridge built by Würzburg's baroque architect Balthasar Neumann, who normally applied his talents to less mundane constructions.

➤ Bike Rental and Tours: **Rad und -freizeittouristik (Michael Skazel)** (✉ Am Stadtschreiber 27, Tauberbischofsheim D–97932, ☎ 09341/5395, FAX 09341/7889, WEB www.skazel.de).

BOAT AND FERRY TRAVEL

Passenger service on the most romantic section of the Main River, between Aschaffenburg and Wertheim, is operated by two local lines, the Wertheimer Personenschifffahrt, and the Reederei Henneberger.

➤ BOAT AND FERRY INFORMATION: **Wertheimer Personenschifffahrt** (✉ Mainpl. 20, D–97877 Wertheim, ☎ 09342/1414). **Reederei Henneberger** (✉ Mainanlagen, D–63897 Miltenberg, ☎ 09371/3330).

BUS TRAVEL

From April through October daily bus service covers the northern stretch of the Romantic Road, leaving Frankfurt at 8 AM and arriving in Munich at 8 PM; daily buses in the opposite direction leave Munich at 9 AM and arrive in Frankfurt at 8:30 PM. A second bus covers the section of the route between Dinkelsbühl and Füssen. Buses leave Dinkelsbühl daily at 4:15 PM and arrive in Füssen at 8 PM. In the other direction, buses leave Füssen daily at 8 AM, arriving in Dinkelsbühl at 12:45 PM. All buses stop at the major sights along the road. A Frankfurt–Füssen ticket costs €69 (€137 round-trip). Deutsche Touring also operates six more extensive tours along the Romantic Road and along the region's other major holiday route, the Burgenstrasse (Castle Road), which ends at Rothenburg. The tours range from two to five days and cost from €256 to €770. Reservations are essential; contact Deutsche Touring. Local buses cover much of the route but are infrequent and slow.

➤ BUS INFORMATION: **Deutsche Touring** (✉ Am Römerhof 17, D–60486 Frankfurt/Main, ☎ 069/79030; WEB touring-germany.com; ✉ Arnulfstr. 3, north wing of Hauptbahnhof, Munich, ☎ 089/8898–9513).

CAR RENTAL

➤ MAJOR AGENCIES: **Avis** (✉ Proviantbachstr. 30, Augsburg, ☎ 0821/38241; ✉ Nürnberger-Str. 90, Würzburg, ☎ 0931/24043). **Europcar** (✉ Pilgerhausstr. 24, Augsburg, ☎ 0821/346–510; ✉ Am Hauptbahnhof, Würzburg, ☎ 0931/12060; ✉ Gattingerstr.5, Würzburg, ☎ 0931/200–480). **Hertz** (✉ Werner-Heisenstr. 11, Königsbrunn [near Augsburg]), ☎ 08231/34930; ✉ Rottendorferstr. 40–42, Würzburg, ☎ 0931/784–6913). **Sixt** (✉ Viktoriastr. 1 [in Hauptbahnhof], Augsburg, ☎ 0821/349–8502; ✉ Bahnhofpl. 4 [in Hauptbahnhof], Würzburg, ☎ 0931/465–1406).

CAR TRAVEL

Würzburg is the northernmost city of the Romantic Road and the natural starting point for a tour. It's on the Frankfurt–Nürnberg Autobahn, the A–3, and is 115 km (71 mi) from Frankfurt. If you are using Munich as a gateway, Augsburg is 60 km (37 mi) from Munich via A–8.

The Romantic Road is most easily traveled by car, starting from Würzburg as outlined above and following the B–27 country highway south to meet Roads B–290, B–19, B–292, and B–25 along the Wörnitz River.

The roads are well-trafficked, two-lane, so figure on covering no more than 70 km (40 mi) each hour, particularly in summer. The 40-km (24-mi) section of the route that's the least "romantic," the A–2 between Augsburg and Donauwörth, is also heavily used by trucks and other large vehicles traveling to northern Bavaria, so expect delays. For route maps, with roads and sights highlighted, contact the Tourist Information Land an der Romantischen Strasse or Touristik-Arbeitsgemeinschaft Romantische Strasse (☞ Visitor Information).

TOURS

All the cities and towns on the Romantic Road offer guided tours, either on foot or by bus. Details are available from the local tourist information offices. Following is a sample of the more typical tours.

AUGSBURG

Augsburg has self-guided walking tours, with routes posted on color-coded signs throughout the downtown area. From mid-May to mid-October a bus tour (€9.50) starts from the Rathaus at 2, Thursday through Sunday, and walking tours (€4.50) set out from the Rathaus daily at 10:30. From mid-October until May a walking tour takes place every Saturday at 2. All tours are conducted in German and English. The tourist office organizes morning and afternoon trips into the countryside north and south of Augsburg.

DINKELSBÜHL

The watchman does a nightly round at 9 from April through October, and though he doesn't give official tours, he's always happy to answer questions (but don't expect a reply in fluent English). Daily guided tours of Dinkelsbühl in horse-drawn carriages (April–October) cost €4.

ROTHENBURG-OB-DER-TAUBER

The costumed nightwatchman conducts a nightly tour of the town, leading the way with a lantern. From April to October and in December, tours in English begin at 8 and 9:30 and cost €3 (a daytime tour begins at 2).

ULM

The tourist office's 90-minute tour includes a visit to the Münster, the Old Town Hall, the Fischerviertel (Fishermen's Quarter), and the Danube riverbank. From May through October there are tours at 10 and 2:30 Monday–Saturday, 11 and 2:30 Sunday; from November through April tours are at 10 on Saturday and 11 on Sunday. The departure point is the tourist office on Münsterplatz; the cost is €5. From May to mid-October you can view Ulm from on board the motor cruiser *Ulmer Spatz*. There are up to five 50-minute cruises daily (€5). The boats tie up at the Metzgerturm, a two-minute walk from the city hall.

WÜRZBURG

Two-hour bus tours of the city start at the main railway station from April through October, Monday–Saturday at 2 and Sunday and holidays at 10:30. The fare is €8.50. Guided walking tours start at the Haus zum Falken tourist office from April through October, daily at 10:30. The two-hour tours cost €5 and include a visit to the Residenz. If you'd rather guide yourself, pick up a map from the same tourist office and follow the extremely helpful directions marked throughout the city by distinctive signposts.

Three shipping companies ply the Main River from Würzburg. The Fränkische Personenschiffahrt (FPS) and the Würzburger Personenschiffahrt Kurth & Schiebe operate excursions to vineyards; wine tasting is included in the price. Fränkische Personenschiffahrt also offers cruises of up to two weeks on the Main, Neckar, and Danube rivers and on the Main–Danube Canal. Kurth & Schiebe and Veitshöchheimer Personenschiffahrt offer daily service to Veitshöchheim, once the summer residence of the bishops of Augsburg. Views of Aschaffenburg and its mighty palace are part of the attraction of Main cruises offered by the Aschaffenburger Personenschiffahrt Sankt Martin.

➤ TOUR-OPERATOR RECOMMENDATIONS: **Aschaffenburger Personenschifffahrt Sankt Martin** (✉ Ruhlandstr. 5, D–63741 Aschaffenburg, ☎ 06021/87288). **Fränkische Personenschifffahrt** (FPS; ✉ Postfach 408, D–97301 Kitzingen, ☎ 09321/91810, WEB www.mainschifffahrt.de). **Veitshöchheimer Personenschiffahrt** (✉ Obere Maing. 8, D–97209 Veitshöchheim, ☎ 0931/91553). **Würzburger Personenschifffahrt Kurth & Schiebe** (✉ St.-Norbert-Str. 9, D–97299 Zell, ☎ 0931/58573).

TRAIN TRAVEL

Infrequent trains link most major towns of the Romantic Road, but both Würzburg and Augsburg are on the InterCity and high-speed InterCity Express routes and have fast, frequent service to and from Berlin, Frankfurt, Munich, Stuttgart, and Hamburg. Deutsche Bahn offers special weekend excursion rates covering travel from most German railroad stations to Würzburg and hotel accommodations for up to four nights. Details are available at any train station.

VISITOR INFORMATION

A central tourist office based in Dinkelsbühl covers the entire Romantic Road: Touristik-Arbeitsgemeinschaft Romantische Strasse. Their color brochure describes all the attractions along the Romantic Road.

➤ TOURIST INFORMATION: **Amorbach** (✉ Verkehrsamt, Altes Rathaus, D–63916, ☎ 09373/20940, WEB www.amorbach.de). **Aschaffenburg** (✉ Dalbergstr. 6, D–63739, ☎ 06021/3940, WEB www.info-aschaffenburg.de). **Augsburg** (✉ Tourist-Information, Bahnhofstr. 7, D–86150, ☎ 0821/502–070, WEB www.regio-augsburg.de). **Bad Mergentheim** (✉ Städtisches Kultur-und Verkehrsamt, Marktpl. 3, D–96980, ☎ 07931/57135, WEB www.bad-mergentheim.de). **Dinkelsbühl** (✉ Tourist-Information, Marktpl., D–91550, ☎ 09851/90240, WEB www.dinkelsbuehl.de). **Donauwörth** (✉ Städtisches Verkehrs-und Kulturamt, Rathausg. 1, D–86609, ☎ 0906/789–151, WEB www.donauwoerth.de). **Feuchtwangen** (✉ Kultur-und Verkehrsamt, Marktpl. 1, D–91555, ☎ 09852/90444). **Füssen** (✉ Kurverwaltung, Kaiser-Maximilian-Pl. 1, D–87629, ☎ 08362/93850, WEB www.fuessen.de). **Harburg** (✉ Fremdenverkehrsverein, Schlossstr. 1, D–86655, ☎ 09080/96990). **Landsberg am Lech** (✉ Kultur-und Fremdenverkehrsamt, Hauptpl. 152, D–89896, ☎ 08191/128–245, WEB www.landsberg.de). **Mespelbrunn** (✉ Fremdenverkehrsverein, Hauptstr. 158, D–63875, ☎ 06092/319). **Miltenberg** (✉ Fremdenverkehrsamt, Rathauspl., D–63897, ☎ 09371/404–119). **Nördlingen** (✉ Städtisches Verkehrsamt, Marktpl. 2, D–86720, ☎ 09081/4380). **Rothenburg-ob-der-Tauber** (✉ Tourist-Information, Rathaus, Marktpl. 2, D–91541, ☎ 09861/40492, WEB www.rothenburg.de). **Schongau** (✉ Tourist-Information, Münzstr. 5, D–86956, ☎ 08861/7216, WEB www.schongau.de). **Schwangau** (✉ Kurverwaltung, Rathaus, Münchenerstr. 2, D–87645, ☎ 08362/81980, WEB www.schwangau.de). **Tauberbischofsheim** (✉ Marktpl. 8, D–97941, ☎ 09341/80313, WEB www.tauberbischofsheim.de). **Tourist Information Land an der Romantischen Strasse** (✉ Kreisverkehrsamt, Crailsheimerstr. 1, D–91522 Ansbach, ☎ 0981/4680). **Touristik-Arbeitsgemeinschaft Romantische Strasse** (✉ Marktpl., D–91550 Dinkelsbühl, ☎ 09851/90271, FAX 09851/90281, WEB www.romantischestrasse.de). **Ulm** (✉ Tourist-Information, Münsterpl. 50 [Stadthaus], D–89073, ☎ 0731/161–2830, WEB www.tourismus.ulm.de). **Weikersheim** (✉ Städtisches Kultur-und Verkehrsamt, im Rathaus, Marktpl., D–97990, ☎ 07934/10255, FAX 07934/10558). **Wertheim** (✉ Am Spitzen Turm, D–97877, ☎ 09342/1066). **Würzburg** (✉ Fremdenverkehrsamt, Am Congress-Centrum, D–97070, ☎ 0931/372–335, WEB www.wuerzburg.de).

6 FRANCONIA

A predominantly rural part of Bavaria, Franconia was most important politically in the days of the Holy Roman Empire. Its beautiful and historic towns include Coburg, Bayreuth, Bamberg, and Nürnberg. Wagner fans especially shouldn't miss Bayreuth, where the great composer settled and built his theater. The annual festival that honors him brings other town functions to a halt every summer.

Updated by Marton Rakai

ALL THAT IS LEFT OF THE HUGE, ANCIENT kingdom of the Franks is the region known today as Franken (Franconia). The Franks were not only tough warriors, but also hard workers, sharp tradespeople, and burghers with a good political nose. The name *frank* means bold, wild, and courageous in the old Frankish tongue. It was only in the early 19th century, following Napoléon's conquest of what is now southern Germany, that the area was incorporated into northern Bavaria. Modern Franconia stretches from the Bohemian Forest on the Czech border to the outskirts of Frankfurt. But its heart—and the focal point of this chapter—is an area known as the Fränkische Schweiz (Franconian Switzerland), bounded by Nürnberg (Nuremberg) in the south, Bamberg in the west, and the cultural center of Bayreuth in the east. Its rural appearance belies a solid economic backbone that is buttressed by the influx of businesses in what's known as the New Economy (electronics, call centers, and software).

Franconia is hardly an overrun tourist destination, yet its long and rich history, its diversified landscapes and leisure activities (including skiing, golf, hiking, cycling), and its gastronomic specialties place it high on the enjoyment scale.

Pleasures and Pastimes

Dining

Franconia is known for its good and filling food and for its simple and atmospheric *Gasthäuser.* Pork is a staple, served either as *Schweinsbraten* (a plain roast) or sauerbraten (marinated). Nürnberg has a unique shoulder cut called *Schäfele* (literally, little shovel), served with *Knödel* (dumplings made from either bread or potatoes). Sausages are also a specialty in Nürnberg, where they are eaten either grilled or heated in a stock of onions and wine (*saurer Zipfel*).

Not to be missed are Franconia's liquid refreshments from both the grape and the grain. Franconian white wines, usually sold in distinctive flagons called *Bocksbeutel,* are renowned for their special bouquet (Silvaner is the traditional grape). The region has the largest concentration of local breweries in the world (Bamberg alone has 10, Bayreuth 7), producing a wide range of brews, the most distinctive of which is the dark, smoky *Rauchbier.*

CATEGORY	COST*
$$$$	over €20
$$$	€15–€20
$$	€10–€15
$	under €10

**per person for a main course at dinner*

Hiking

The wild stretches of forest and numerous nature parks in northern Franconia make this ideal hiking country. There are more than 40,000 km (25,000 mi) of hiking trails, with the greatest concentration in the Altmühltal Nature Park, a wooded gorge, and in the Frankenwald.

Lodging

Make reservations well in advance for hotels in all the larger towns and cities if you plan to visit anytime between June and September. During the Nürnberg Toy Fair at the beginning of February rooms are rare and at a premium. If you're visiting Bayreuth during the annual Wagner Festival, in July and August, consider making reservations up to a year in advance. Remember, too, that during the festival prices can be double the normal rates.

CATEGORY	COST*
$$$$	over €225
$$$	€150–€225
$$	€75–€150
$	under €75

**All prices are for two people in a double room, including tax and service.*

Skiing

The highest peaks of Franconia's upland region, the Fichtelgebirge and Frankenwald, rarely pass the 3,200-ft mark, but their exposed location in central Germany near Bayreuth assures them good snow conditions most winters. Cross-country skiers also head to this region because of its lack of mass tourism.

Exploring Franconia

Although many proud Franconians would dispute it, this historic homeland of the Franks, one of the oldest Germanic peoples, is unmistakably part of Bavaria. Its southern border areas end at the Danube and merge into Lower Bavaria (Niederbayern) and the Bavarian Forest, while its northern border is marked by the Main River, which is seen as the dividing line between northern and southern Germany. Despite its extensive geographic spread, however, Franconia is a homogeneous region of rolling agricultural landscapes and thick forests climbing to the mountains of the Fichtelgebirge. Franconian towns such as Bayreuth, Coburg, and Bamberg are practically places of cultural pilgrimage, while rebuilt Nürnberg is the epitome of German medieval beauty.

Numbers in the text correspond to numbers in the margin and on the Franconia and Nürnberg maps.

Great Itineraries

IF YOU HAVE 3 DAYS

Make **Nürnberg** ⑥–⑳ your base and take day trips on each of the three days to **Bayreuth** ④ (an imperative visit whether or not it's Wagner Festival season); **Bamberg** ⑤, once the seat of the most powerful ruling families in the country; and **Coburg** ①, home of the Saxe-Coburg duchy. Each town is only a 50- to 70-minute drive away.

IF YOU HAVE 5 DAYS

Take a day trip from **Nürnberg** ⑥–⑳ to **Bayreuth** ④, and on your third day settle in **Coburg** ①, visiting **Bamberg** ⑤ on the way. On the fourth day take side trips to **Banz Abbey** and **Vierzehnheiligen,** two mighty churches that stand facing each other across the valley of the River Main. On the fifth day follow the Main upstream from Coburg to **Kulmbach** ③, the beer capital of Germany. Among its several brands is reputedly the world's strongest brew.

When to Tour

Summer is the best time to explore Franconia, though spring and fall are also fine when the weather cooperates. Avoid the cold and wet months of November, January, and February, unless you're coming to ski. If you're in Nürnberg in December, you're in time for one of Germany's largest and loveliest Christmas markets.

Franconia

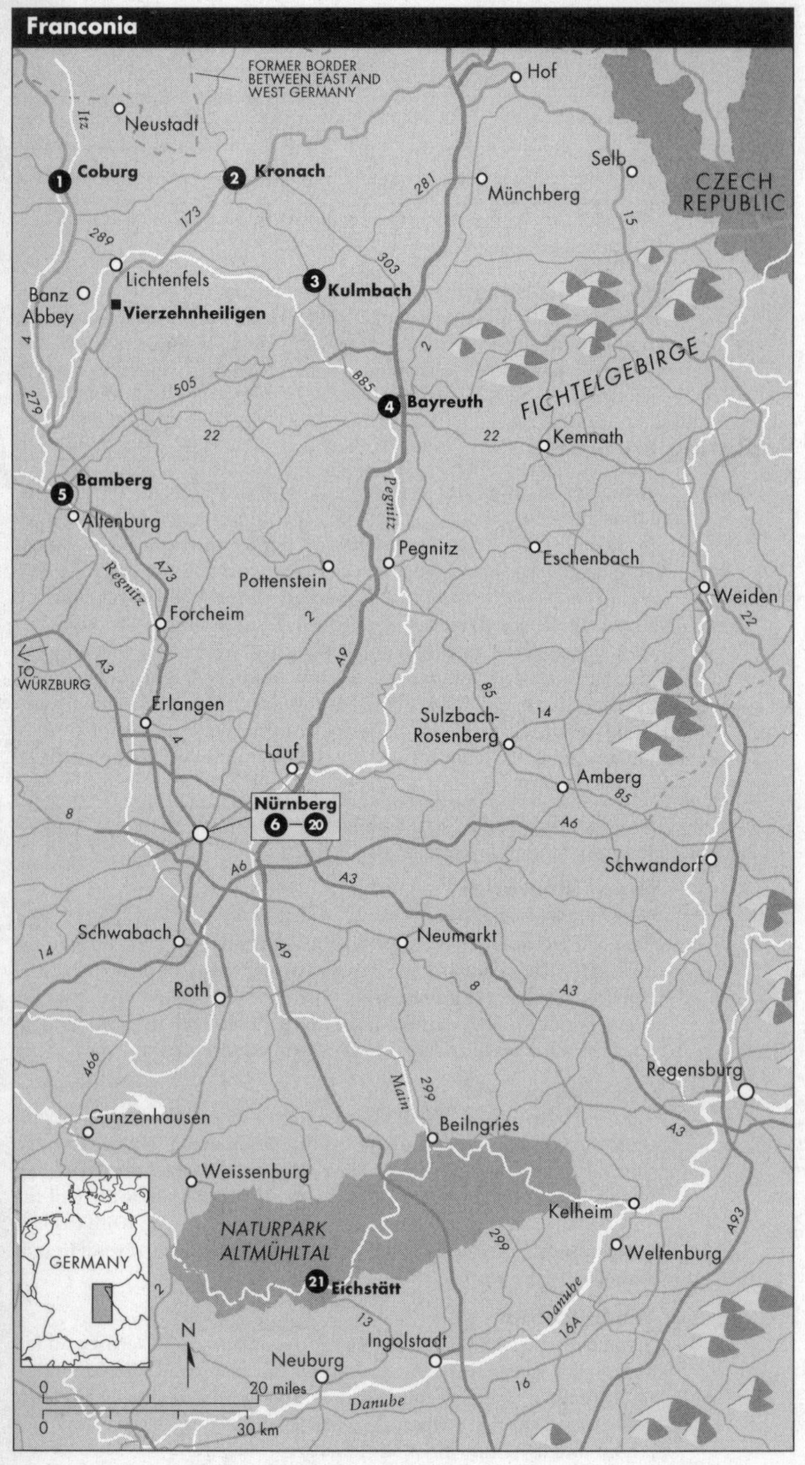

FORMER BORDER BETWEEN EAST AND WEST GERMANY
Hof
Itz
Neustadt
Selb
1 Coburg
2 Kronach
CZECH REPUBLIC
281
Münchberg
173
15
289
303
Lichtenfels
3 Kulmbach
Banz Abbey
Vierzehnheiligen
4
2
FICHTELGEBIRGE
B85
505
279
4 Bayreuth
22
22
Kemnath
5 Bamberg
Pegnitz
Altenburg
Pegnitz
Eschenbach
Regnitz
A73
Pottenstein
Weiden
22
Forcheim
2
TO WÜRZBURG
A3
A9
85
14
Sulzbach-Rosenberg
Erlangen
4
Lauf
Amberg
85
Nürnberg 6—20
8
A6
A6
Schwandorf
A3
Schwabach
Neumarkt
14
A9
8
A3
Roth
466
Main
299
Regensburg
Gunzenhausen
Beilngries
A3
Weissenburg
Kelheim
A93
NATURPARK ALTMÜHLTAL
299
Weltenburg
GERMANY
2
21 Eichstätt
Danube
16A
13
N
Ingolstadt
Neuburg
16
0
20 miles
Danube
0
30 km

NORTHERN FRANCONIA

Three major German cultural centers lie within this region of Franconia: Coburg, a town with blood links to royal dynasties throughout Europe; Bamberg, with its own claim to German royal history and an Old Town on the UNESCO World Heritage list; and Bayreuth, where composer Richard Wagner finally settled and a place of musical pilgrimage for Wagner fans from all over the world.

Coburg

❶ *105 km (65 mi) north of Nürnberg.*

Coburg is a treasure—and a surprisingly little-known one—whether it's glittering under the summer sky or frosted white with the snows of winter. The east–west border once isolated this area, but since Germany's reunification it has experienced a minor economic revolution. It was founded in the 11th century and remained in the possession of the dukes of Saxe-Coburg-Gotha until 1918; the present duke still lives there. The remarkable Saxe-Coburg dynasty established itself as something of a royal stud farm, providing a seemingly inexhaustible supply of blue-blood marriage partners to ruling houses the length and breadth of Europe. The most famous of these royal mates was Prince Albert, who married Queen Victoria, after which she gained special renown in Coburg. Their numerous children, married off to other kings, queens, and emperors, helped to spread the tried-and-tested Saxe-Coburg stock even farther afield. Despite all the old history that sweats from each sandstone ashlar, Coburg is a modern and bustling town.

Coburg's **Marktplatz** (Market Square) has a statue of Prince Albert, the high-minded consort, proudly standing surrounded by gracious Renaissance and baroque buildings. The **Rathaus** (town hall), begun in 1500, is the most imposing structure here. A forest of ornate gables and spires projects from its well-proportioned facade. Look at the statue of the **Bratwurstmännla** on the building (it's actually St. Mauritius in armor); the staff he carries is said to be the official length against which the town's famous bratwursts are measured. If this sounds like guidebook babble to you, convince yourself otherwise by trying a bratwurst from one of the stands in the square.

Prince Albert spent much of his childhood in **Schloss Ehrenburg,** the ducal palace. Built in the mid-16th century, it has been greatly altered over the years, principally following a fire in the early 19th century. The duke Ernst I invited Friedrich Schinkel from Berlin to redo the palace in the then-popular Gothic style. Some of the original Renaissance features were kept. The rooms of the castle are quite special, especially the upstairs, where the ceilings are heavily decorated with stucco and the floors are wonderful patterns of various woods. The Hall of Giants is named for the larger-than-life caryatids that support the ceiling; the favorite sight downstairs is Queen Victoria's flush toilet, which was the first one installed in Germany. Here, too, the ceiling is worth noting for its playful, gentle stucco. The baroque chapel attached to Ehrenburg is often used for weddings. ✉ *Schlosspl.,* ☎ *09561/80880,* WEB *www.schloss-ehrenburg.de.* 🎫 *€3; if you intend to visit Schloss Rosenau, ask for a combined ticket for €4.50.* ⏲ *Tour Tues.–Sun. 10–5 on the hr (additional 4:30 tour Apr.–Sept.).*

Near Schloss Ehrenburg, the **Puppenmuseum** (Doll Museum) contains a collection of more than 900 antique dolls and art dolls, and around 150 carefully furnished dollhouses. The building itself once housed the poet and orientalist Friedrich Rückert. The museum includes a doll and toy shop. ✉ *Rückertstr. 2–3,* ☎ *09561/74047.* 💳 *€2.* ⏲ *Apr.–Oct., Tues.–Sun. 9–5; Nov.–Mar., daily 10–5.*

The **Veste Coburg** fortress, one of the largest and most impressive in the country, is Coburg's main attraction. The brooding bulk of the castle lies on a small hill above the town. Construction began around 1055, but with progressive rebuilding and remodeling, today's predominantly late Gothic–early Renaissance edifice bears little resemblance to the original rude fortress. One part of the castle harbors the **Kunstsammlungen,** a grand set of collections including art, with works by Dürer, Cranach, and Hans Holbein, among others; sculpture from the school of the great Tilman Riemenschneider (1460–1531); furniture and textiles; magnificent weapons, armor, and tournament garb from four centuries; carriages and ornate sleighs; glass; and more. The room where Martin Luther lived for six months in 1530 while he observed the goings-on of the Augsburg Diet has an especially dignified atmosphere. The **Jagdintarsien-Zimmer** (Hunting Marquetry Room), an elaborately decorated room that dates to the early 17th century, has some of the finest woodwork in southern Germany. Inquire at the ticket office for tours and reduced family tickets. ☎ *09561/87948.* 💳 *€3.* ⏲ *Museums Apr.–Oct., Tues.–Sun. 10–5; Nov.–Mar., Tues.–Sun. 1–4; castle Apr.–Oct., Tues.–Sun. 10–5; Nov.–Mar., Tues.–Sun. 2–5; castle grounds 6:30–6.*

The **Naturkundemuseum** (Natural History Museum) is in the castle's former palace garden, the Hofgarten. This is the country's leading museum of its kind, with more than 8,000 exhibits of flora and fauna, geology, human history, and mineralogy divided up into four major categories: Earth, Evolution, the Human Being, and Earth History. ✉ *Veste Coburg,* ☎ *09561/808–120,* WEB *www.naturkunde-museum-coburg.de.* 💳 *€1.50.* ⏲ *Weekdays 9–1 and 1:30–5; weekends 9–5.*

The **Burgschänke,** Veste Coburg's own tavern, allows you to soak up centuries of history while sampling a Coburg beer and one of the traditional dishes from the basic menu. The tavern is closed Monday and January–mid-February. ✉ *Veste Coburg,* ☎ *09561/80980.*

Perched on a hill 5 km (3 mi) to the west of Coburg is **Schloss Callenberg,** until 1231 the main castle of the Knights of Callenberg. In the 16th century it was taken over by the Coburgs. From 1842 on it served as the summer residence of the hereditary Coburg prince and later Duke Ernst II. It holds a number of important collections, including that of the Windsor gallery; art and crafts from Holland, Germany, and Italy from the Renaissance to the 19th century; precious baroque, empire, and Biedermeier furniture; table and standing clocks from three centuries; a selection of weapons; and various handicrafts. The best way to reach the castle is by car via Baiersdorf, or by taking Bus 5 from the Marktplatz. ✉ *Callenberg,* ☎ *09561/55150,* WEB *www.schloss-callenberg.de.* 💳 *€3.* ⏲ *Tour Apr.–Oct., daily at 10, 11, noon, 2, 3, and 4; Nov.–Mar., Tues.–Sun. at 2, 3, and 4; and by appointment; closed last 3 wks of Jan.*

OFF THE BEATEN PATH

AHORN – This town 4 km (2½ mi) southwest of Coburg has a wonderful museum that gives close insight into the life and times of farmers in the region. The houses of the **Grätemuseum des Coburger Landes** (Museum of Farm Appliances of the Coburg Region) date to the early 18th century and are constructed of sandstone with harmonious half-timber superstructures. Exhibits depict estate life, with everything from farm implements to a smithy, while outside farm animals roam about. Snacks and drinks are available at the *Schäferstuben,* the Shepherd's Room. ✉ *On Rte. B–303 before Ahorn,* ☎ *09561/1304.* 💳 *€2.* ⏲ *Apr.–Oct., Tues.–Sun. 2–5; Nov.–Mar., Sun. 2–5 and by appointment.*

WILDPARK SCHLOSS TAMBACH – This old castle a few miles west of Ahorn off B–303 is still in private hands. Its grand collection of wild animals and birds include boar, deer, eagles, condors, owls, falcons, and storks. Flight demos are held March through August at 11, 3, and 5. The **Jagd- und Fischereimuseum** (Museum of Hunting and Fishing), laid out on two floors, displays everything you have ever wanted to know about hunting, from clothing to weapons, stuffed animals, pennants, and tricks of the trade throughout the centuries. ✉ *Schlossallee 1a, Tambach,* ☎ *09567/1861.* 🎫 *€2.50.* ⏲ *Mar.–Oct., Mon.–Sat. 10–5:30, Sun. 10–6; Nov.–early Jan., Sun. 10–5; early Jan.–Feb. open by appointment.*

Dining and Lodging

$–$$$$ ✕ **Künstlerklause.** The atmosphere in this little warren of rooms with dark-wood paneling, a fireplace, and old photos is relaxed, and the comfortable leather seats welcome a mixed crowd from businesspeople to artists. The upscale cuisine gets the occasional exotic touch through spices. You might find a standard turkey schnitzel with dumplings, or venison in aspic with diced and fried sweet potato, celery, and carrots in juniper sauce. There are always some lower-price dishes on the menu. ✉ *Theaterpl. 4a,* ☎ *09561/90705. Reservations essential. No credit cards. Closed Mon.*

$–$$ ✕ **Ratskeller.** The local specialties taste better beneath the old vaults and within earshot of the Coburg marketplace. The decor is a little tacky, but the food is prepared with gusto. Try the sauerbraten, along with a glass of crisp Franconian white wine. Evenings the prices become a little higher and the menu adds a few more dishes. ✉ *Markt 1,* ☎ *09561/92400. No credit cards.*

$–$$ ★ ✕🏨 **Hotel Festungshof.** Duke Carl Eduard had this guest mansion built right outside the Veste in Coburg. This turn-of-the-20th-century building has comfortably (if not very imaginatively) furnished rooms. The restaurant ($–$$$) has solid Franconian cooking, with seasonal dishes as well—fish in the summer, venison in winter; the café has a generous terrace, and the beer garden seats 300. A bus connects to the town center, or you can take a 20-minute walk through the castle garden and the wooded landscape to reach the market square. ✉ *Rosenauerstr. 30, D–96450,* ☎ *09561/80290,* FAX *09561/802–933,* WEB *www.hotel-festungshof.de. 14 rooms. Restaurant, café, beer garden, no a/c, cable TV, Internet, pets allowed (fee). MC, V. No dinner Sun.*

$$–$$$ 🏨 **Romantic Hotel Goldene Traube.** Book a room overlooking the square, and on summer evenings you can fall asleep to the splash of the fountain named after Queen Victoria. The hotel feels such a strong link with Britain's former queen and empress that it even named its bar after her. There's also a sauna complex with solarium. ✉ *Am Viktoriabrunnen 2, D–96450,* ☎ *09561/8760,* FAX *09561/876–222. 69 rooms, 1 suite. Restaurant, no a/c, cable TV, in-room data ports, miniature golf, gym, sauna, steam room, bicycles, bar, pets allowed (fee), no-smoking rooms. AE, DC, MC, V.*

$$ 🏨 **Hotel Mercure Coburg.** What you can expect at the Mercure is modern, clean, well-designed rooms that are airy and functional. In the morning, an excellent breakfast buffet gets you ready for the day's sightseeing. Friendly and very helpful staff round off the offer. The Mercure is about 15 minutes on foot south of the center. ✉ *Ketschendorfer Str. 86, 96450,* ☎ *09561/8210 or 0800/100–0048,* FAX *09561/821–444,* WEB *www.mercure.com. 123 rooms. No a/c, cable TV with movies, in-room data ports, pets allowed, no-smoking rooms. AE, DC, MC, V.*

Nightlife and the Arts

Check the Coburg tourist office's Web site for events. Coburg is home to Europe's only **Brazilian Samba Festival,** a wild bacchanal held in mid-July in the august streets. Though allegedly "just an idea someone had," it seems linked to the fact that the town's patron saint, St. Mauritius, has been represented by the head of a black man since the Middle Ages, an old custom stemming from the fact that the 3rd-century legionnaire was a North African.

Coburg's **Landestheater** (✉ Schlossplatz 6, ☎ 09561/92742) opera season runs from October through mid-July. Call (9 AM–1 PM) for tickets.

Shopping

Coburg is a culinary delight, famous for its *Schmätzen* (gingerbread) and *Elizenkuchen* (almond cake). You'll find home-baked versions in any of the many excellent **patisseries** or at a Grossman store (there are three in Coburg). Rödental, northeast of Coburg, is the home of the world-famous M. I. Hummel figurines, made by the Göbel porcelain manufacturer. There's a **Hummel Museum** (✉ Coburgerstr. 7, Rödental, ☎ 09563/92303, WEB www.goebel.de) devoted to them, open Monday–Saturday, 9–5. Besides the museum's store, there are several retail outlets in the village.

En Route Near the village of Rödental, 9 km (5½ mi) northeast of Coburg, the 550-year-old **Schloss Rosenau** sits in all its neo-Gothic glory in the midst of an English-style park. Prince Albert was born here in 1819 and one room is devoted entirely to Albert and his Queen, Victoria. Much of the castle furniture was made especially for the Saxe-Coburg family by noted Viennese craftsmen. In the garden's Orangerie is the **Museum für Modernes Glas** (Museum for Modern Glass), which displays nearly 40 years' worth of glass sculptures. ☎ *09563/4747 castle; 09563/1606 museum.* 💳 *Castle: €2.50; museum: €1 (free with entrance ticket to the Veste in Coburg).* ⏲ *Tour Apr.–Oct., daily at 10, 11, noon, 2, 3, and 4; Nov.–Mar., Tues.–Sun. at 3 and 4; and by appointment. Closed last 3 wks of Jan.*

Neustadt

15 km (10 mi) northeast of Coburg.

★ The **Museum der Deutschen Spielzeugindustrie** (Museum of the German Toymaking Industry) in Neustadt is a must. All manner of toys and dolls, from wooden to plasticine are included. Dolls model traditional German costumes in one room, and in another, the craft of doll- and toy-making is revealed. Christmas decorations and production is also on display. In short, everything you ever wanted to know about toys and never dared ask is right here in a modern, barnlike building. A bevy of very sooty-looking teddy bears makes up part of the antiques collection, and then there's your modern action figures, various ethnic dolls, and Barbie, still defying the encroachment of more than 40 years. ✉ *Hindenburgpl. 1,* ☎ *09568/5600.* 💳 *€3.* ⏲ *Mon.–Sun. 10–5; last admission 4:15.*

Lichtenfels

21 km (13 mi) southeast of Coburg.

Rather than speeding from Coburg to Bayreuth on the autobahn, take a detour along the small road (B–289) to Lichtenfels, just across the Main River. You might call the little town a basket case—it's known for its basket-weaving tradition. The basketwork market (☎ 09571/18283), on the third weekend in September, is one of a kind. All sorts of baskets are sold and a German basket queen is also chosen and revered. To get a little closer to the tradition, climb up to the town's hallmark tower, the **Oberer Torturm** and inspect the basketmaker's workshop there.

Just south of Lichtenfels off the main road (B–173) to Bamberg are two religious gems, a church and an abbey, each proudly crowning the heights along the banks of the Main River. On the east side of the Main is ★ **Vierzehnheiligen,** a tall, elegant yellow-sandstone edifice, whose interior represents one of the great examples of rococo decoration. The church was built by Balthasar Neumann (architect of the Residenz at Würzburg) between 1743 and 1772 to commemorate a vision of Christ and 14 saints—*vierzehn Heiligen*—that appeared to a shepherd in 1445. The interior, known as "God's ballroom," is supported by 14 columns. In the middle of the church is the Mercy Altar (Gnadenaltar) featuring the 14 saints. Thanks to clever play with light, light colors, and playful gold and blue trimmings, the interior seems to be in perpetual motion. Guided tours of the church are given on request; a donation is expected. ☎ *09571/95080.* ⏲ *Oct.–May, daily 8–4; June–Sept., daily 7–7.*

On the west bank of the Main is **Kloster Banz** (Banz Abbey), standing on what some call the "holy mountain of Bavaria." There had been a monastery here since 1069, but the present buildings—now a political-seminar center and think tank—date from the end of the 17th century. The highlight of the complex is the **Klosterkirche** (Abbey Church), the work of architect Leonard Dientzenhofen and his brother the stuccoist Johann Dientzenhofer (1663–1726). Balthasar Neumann later contributed a good deal of work. To get to Banz from Vierzehnheiligen, drive south to Unnersdorf, where you can cross the river. From Lichtenfels take the road via Seubelsdorf and Reuendorf. ☎ *09573/7311 or 09573/5092.* ⏲ *Guided tour of church May–Oct., daily 9–noon and 2–5; Nov.–Apr., daily 9–noon.*

A delightful basket museum, the **Deutsches Korb Museum Michelau,** in nearby Michelau, displays everything from furniture to decoration and household items. ✉ *Bismarckstr. 4, Michelau,* ☎ *09571/83548.* 🎫 *€2.* ⏲ *Apr.–Oct., Tues.–Sun. 10–4:30; Nov.–Mar., Mon.–Thurs. 10–4:30, Fri. 9–noon.*

Kronach

❷ *24 km (15 mi) northeast of Lichtenfels, 120 km (74 mi) north of Nürnberg.*

Kronach is a charming little gateway to the natural splendor of the Frankenwald region. In its old medieval section, the **Obere Stadt** (Upper Town), harmonious sandstone houses are surrounded by old walls and surmounted by a majestic fortress. Kronach is best known as the birthplace of Renaissance painter Lucas Cranach the Elder (1472–1553), but there is a running argument as to which house he was born in—Am Marktplatz 1 or in the house called Am Scharfen Eck, at Lucas-Cranach-Strasse 38, which is now an Italian restaurant.

Festung Rosenberg (Rosenberg Fortress) is a few minutes' walk from the town center. Standing below its mighty walls, it is easy to see why it was never taken by enemy forces. During World War I it served as a POW camp with no less a figure than Charles de Gaulle as a "guest." Today Rosenberg houses a youth hostel and, more important, the **Fränkische Galerie** (the Franconian Gallery), an extension of the Bavarian National Museum in Munich featuring paintings and sculpted works from the Middle Ages and the Renaissance. Lucas Cranach the Elder and Tilman Riemenschneider are represented, as well as artists from the Dürer School and the Bamberg School. In July and August the central courtyard is an atmospheric backdrop for performances of Goethe's *Faust.* The grounds of the fortress are also used by wood sculptors in the summer. Some of the finished works can still be seen such as the *Neuer Wächter* (New Guard) standing sentinel near the entrance portal. ☎ *09261/60410,* WEB *www.kronach.de.* *€3.50.* ⏲ *Fortress tours Apr.–Oct., Tues.–Sun. at 10, 11, 2, and 3:30; Nov.–Mar., Tues.–Sun. at 11 and 2; Galerie Apr.–Oct., Tues.–Sun. 9–6; Nov.–Mar., Tues.–Sun. 10–4.*

Kulmbach

❸ *19 km (12 mi) southeast of Kronach, 32 km (20 mi) east of Lichtenfels.*

Kulmbach has a claim to fame that belies its size. In a country in which the brewing and beer drinking break all records, this town produces more beer per capita than anywhere else: 9,000 pints for each man, woman, and child. A quarter of Kulmbachers earn their living directly or indirectly from beer. A special local brew only available in winter and during the Lenten season is *Eisbock,* a dark beer that is frozen as part of the brewing process to make it stronger. The locals claim it's the sparkling clear springwater from the nearby Fichtelgebirge hills that makes their beer so special.

Kulmbach celebrates its beer every year in a nine-day festival that starts on the last Saturday in July. The main festival site, a mammoth tent, is called the Festspulhaus—literally, "festival swill house"—a none-too-subtle dig at nearby Bayreuth and its tony Festspielhaus, where Wagner's operas are performed.

The **Erste Kulmbacher Union Brewery** (✉ Lichtenfelserstr., ☎ 09221/705–113), one of Kulmbach's six breweries, produces the strongest beer in the world—the *Doppelbock* Kulminator 28—which takes nine months to brew and has an alcohol content of more than 11%. The brewery runs the **Bayerisches Brauereimuseum Kulmbach** (the Kulmbach Brewery Museum) jointly with the nearby Mönchshof-Bräu brewery and inn. ✉ *Hoferstr. 20,* ☎ *09221/4264.* *Tour €2.50; €1.50 if you spend €5 in the brewery tavern.*

The **Plassenburg,** the town's castle and symbol, is the most important Renaissance castle in the country. It stands on a rise overlooking Kulmbach, a 20-minute hike from the Old Town. The first building here, begun in the mid-12th century, was torched by marauding Bavarians who were anxious to put a stop to the ambitions of Duke Albrecht Alcibiades—a man who spent several years murdering, plundering, and pillaging his way through Franconia. His successors built today's castle, starting in about 1560. Externally there's little to suggest the graceful Renaissance interior, but as you enter the main courtyard, the scene changes abruptly. The tiered space of the courtyard is covered with precisely carved figures, medallions, and other intricate ornaments, the whole comprising one of the most remarkable and delicate architectural ensembles in Europe. Inside, the **Deutsches Zinnfigurenmuseum** (Tin Figures Museum), with more than 300,000 miniature statuettes and tin soldiers, holds the largest collection of its kind in the world. The figures are arranged in scenes from all periods of history. From April to October casting of the tin figures is demonstrated daily 2–5. The **Landschaftsmuseum Obermain** (Obermain Landscape Museum) here documents the history and culture of this region. ☎ *09221/5550.* €2. ⏲ *Daily 10–5.*

OFF THE BEATEN PATH **NEUENMARKT** – In this "railway village" near Kulmbach more than 25 beautifully preserved, gleaming locomotives huff and puff in a living railroad museum. Every now and then a nostalgic train will take you to the Brewery Museum in Kulmbach. The museum also has model trains set up in incredibly detailed landscape replicas. ✉ *Birkenstr. 5,* ☎ *09227/5700,* WEB *www.dampflokmuseum.de.* €3. ⏲ *Tues.–Sun. 10–5.*

Dining and Lodging

$–$$ ✕🏨 **Hotel zur Gondel.** It's well worth driving the few miles to Altenkunstadt, between Kulmbach and Lichtenfels, for a few nights at these two elaborate half-timber houses right on the main square. The restaurant serves an excellent candlelit meal of Franconian and international specialties in a stylized rustic setting or in the delightful inner courtyard. The Jahn family has made sure that solidly appointed rooms will then welcome you for a well-deserved rest. ✉ *Marktpl. 7, D–96264 Altenkunstadt,* ☎ *09572/3661,* FAX *09572/4596. 36 rooms. Restaurant, cable TV, pets allowed. MC, V. No lunch Sat.*

$$ 🏨 **Hotel Kronprinz.** This old hotel tucked away in the middle of Kulmbach's old town, right in the shadow of Plassenburg Castle, covers all basic needs. The furnishings are somewhat bland. The café serves simple, small meals (hot dogs, sandwiches, etc.), and perhaps better, substantial portions of cake and coffee. ✉ *Fischerg. 4–6, D–95326,* ☎ *09221/92180,* FAX *09221/921–836,* WEB *www.kronprinz-kulmbach.de. 19 rooms. Café, bar, no a/c, cable TV, in-room data ports. AE, DC, MC, V.*

Bayreuth

❹ *24 km (15 mi) south of Kulmbach, 80 km (50 mi) northeast of Nürnberg.*

Bayreuth is pronounced Bye-*roit,* though it might as well be called Wagner. This small Franconian town was where 19th-century composer and musical revolutionary Richard Wagner (1813–83) finally settled after a lifetime of rootless shifting through Europe, and here he built his great theater, the Festspielhaus, as a suitable setting for his grand operas on mythological Germanic themes. The annual Wagner Festival, first held in 1876, brings hordes of Wagner lovers who push prices sky high, fill hotels to bursting, and earn themselves much-sought-after social kudos in the process (to some, it's one of *the* places to be seen). The festival is held from late July until late August, so unless you plan to visit the town specifically for it, this is the time to stay away. But Wagner and late-Romantic is not all there is to the town. You will find buskers of all kinds playing in the sun-drenched streets, rock concerts, the occasional sports event, museums and galleries, and one of the most luxurious havens of wellness south of the Main River, the Lohengrin Therme. The Bayreuth tourist office on Luitpoldplatz offers the Bayreuth Card for €9, giving you free use of the bus system, a free tour of the town, free entrance to nine museums and a daily paper, the *Nordbayrischer Kurier.*

Built by Wagner, Wahnfried, now the **Richard-Wagner-Museum,** was the only house he ever owned. It's a simple, austere neoclassic building built in 1874, whose name, "peace from madness," was well earned. The war left only the facade; the rest was carefully rebuilt. Wagner lived here with his wife, Cosima, daughter of pianist Franz Liszt; and here they are buried. King Ludwig II of Bavaria, the young and impressionable "fairy-tale king," who gave Wagner so much financial support, is remembered in a bust before the entrance. The exhibits, arranged along a well-marked itinerary through the house, require a great deal of German-language reading. The thrill is in seeing Wagner's handwriting and the original scores of such masterpieces as *Parsifal, Tristan und Isolde, Lohengrin, Der Fliegende Holländer,* and *Götter-*

dämmerung. You can also see designs for productions of his operas, as well as his piano and huge library. At 10, noon, and 2, excerpts from his operas are played in the living room, and a video on his life is shown at 11 and 3. The little house where Franz Liszt also lived and died is right next door and can be visited on the Wagner ticket, but be sure to express your interest in advance. It, too, is heavy on the paper, but the last rooms—with pictures, photos, and silhouettes of the master, his students, acolytes, and friends—is well worth the detour. ✉ *Richard-Wagner-Str. 48,* ☎ *0921/757–2816,* WEB *www.wagnermuseum.de.* 🎫 *€4; €4.50 during the festival.* ⏲ *Fri.–Mon. and Wed. 9–5; Tues. and Thurs. 9–8.*

Conspiracy theorists take note: right around the corner from the Richard-Wagner-Museum is the remarkable little **Deutsches Freimaurer-Museum** (German Freemasons Museum), founded in 1902, which explains the origins of the Freemasons and the ins and outs of the fraternal organization. Everyday items on exhibit bear the famous symbols of the order. Though the placards are not in English, the exhibits do in most cases speak for themselves. The library, with more than 16,000 volumes, is a center for research into freemasonry in Germany. ✉ *Im Hofgarten 1,* ☎ *0921/69824.* 🎫 *€1.* ⏲ *Tues.–Fri. 10–noon and 2–4, Sat. 10–noon, 10–4 during the festival period.*

The **Festspielhaus** (Festival Theater) is by no means beautiful. In fact, this high temple of the Wagner cult is surprisingly plain. The spartan look is explained partly by Wagner's desire to achieve perfect acoustics. The wood seats have no upholstering, for example, and the walls are bare of all ornament. The stage is enormous, capable of holding the huge casts required for Wagner's largest operas. Performances take place only during the annual Wagner Festival, still masterminded by descendants of the composer. ✉ *Festspielhügel 1,* ☎ *0921/78780.* 🎫 *€2.50.* ⏲ *Tour Tues.–Sun. at 10, 10:45, 2:15, and 3. Closed Nov., during rehearsals, and afternoons during the festival.*

The **Neues Schloss** (New Palace) is a glamorous 18th-century palace built by the Margravine Wilhelmine, sister of Frederick the Great of Prussia and a woman of enormous energy and decided tastes. Though Wagner is the man most closely associated with Bayreuth, his choice of this setting is largely due to the work of a woman who lived 100 years before him. Wilhelmine devoured books, wrote plays and operas (which she directed and, of course, acted in), and had buildings constructed, transforming much of the town and bringing it near bankruptcy. Her distinctive touch is much in evidence at the palace, built when a mysterious fire conveniently destroyed parts of the original palace. Anyone with a taste for the wilder flights of rococo decoration will love it. Some rooms also have been given over to one of Europe's finest collections of faience ware. ✉ *Ludwigstr. 21,* ☎ *0921/759–6921.* 🎫 *€2.50.* ⏲ *Apr.–Sept., Mon.–Sun. 9–6, Thurs. 9–8; Oct.–Mar., Mon.–Sun. 10–4; call for English-language tour times.*

Another great architectural legacy of Wilhelmine is the **Markgräfliches Opernhaus** (Margravial Opera House). Built between 1745 and 1748, it is a rococo jewel, sumptuously decorated in red, gold, and blue. Apollo and the nine Muses cavort across the frescoed ceiling. It was this delicate 500-seat theater that originally drew Wagner to Bayreuth, since he felt that it might prove a suitable setting for his own operas. In fact, although it may be a perfect place to hear Mozart, it's hard to imagine a less suitable setting for Wagner's epic works. Visitors are treated to a light and sound show. ✉ *Opernstr.,* ☎ *0921/759–6922.* 🎫 *€4.* ⏲ *Apr.–Sept., Tues.–Sun. 9–6 (last admission at 5:30), Thurs. until 8, last admission at 7:30; Oct.–Mar., Tues.–Sun. 10–noon and 1:30–*

3:30. Light and sound shows Apr.–Oct. begin at 9:15, last admission at 3:30 (Thurs., last admission 6:15; Nov.–Mar., last admission 2:45). Closed Mon., during performances, and on rehearsal days.

It is wise to remember that Bayreuth is a solid little industrious Franconian town, and that there is a lot more to it than opera and Wagner. A visit to the **Historisches Museum Bayreuth** (Bayreuth Historical Museum) is like poking around a miraculous attic with 34 rooms. It's no wonder the museum won the Bavarian Museum Award. A wonderfully eclectic collection includes items from the life of the town, be they royal remnants, faience items from the 18th-century manufacturer, clothes, or odd sports appliances. ✉ *Kirchpl. 6,* ☎ *0921/764–0123.* 🎫 *€1.50.* ⏲ *Tues.–Sun. 10–5 (also Mon. 10–5 during the festival), Thurs. until 8.*

Bayreuth's newest and proudest cultural attraction, the **Kunstmuseum** (Art Museum) houses several permanent collections donated or lent by private collectors. Works by Lyonel Feininger, Max Beckmann (lithographs from his *Berlin Journeys*), and woodcuts by Emil Schuhmacher are highlights. An unusual collection donated by the BAT tobacco company features paintings, sculptures, and ephemera relating to tobacco, the culture of smoking, and the processing of the leaf. The museum lies within the generous rooms of the old Town Hall and shares space with an upscale restaurant called Oskar. ✉ *Maximilianstr. 33,* ☎ *0921/764–5310.* 🎫 *€1.53.* ⏲ *Tues.–Sun. 10–5, Thurs. until 8; open Mon. during the festival.*

Near the center of town in the old, 1887 Maisel Brewery building, the **Brauerei und Büttnerei-Museum** (Brewery and Coopers Museum) reveals the tradition of the brewing trade over the past two centuries with a focus on the Maisel's trade, of course. The brewery operated until 1981, when its much bigger home was completed next door. After the 90-minute tour in this museum that earned an accolade from the Guinness Book of Records for being the largest of its kind, you can quaff a cool, freshly tapped beer in the museum's own pub, which has traditional Bavarian Weissbier. ✉ *Kulmbacherstr. 40,* ☎ *0921/401–234,* WEB *www.maisel.com.* 🎫 *€2.50.* ⏲ *Tour Mon.–Thurs. at 10 AM; individual tours by prior arrangement.*

The **Altes Schloss Eremitage** (Old Palace and Hermitage), 5 km (3 mi) north of Bayreuth on B–85, makes an appealing departure from the sonorous and austere Wagnerian mood of much of the town. It's an early 18th-century palace, built as a summer palace and remodeled in 1740 by the Margravine Wilhelmine. Although her taste is not much in evidence in the drab exterior, the interior, alive with light and color, displays her guiding hand in every elegant line. The extraordinary **Japanischer Saal** (Japanese Room), filled with Asian treasures and chinoiserie furniture, is the finest room. The park and gardens, partly formal, partly natural, are enjoyable for idle strolling. Fountain displays take place at the two fake grottoes at the top of the hour 10–5 daily. ☎ *0921/759–6937.* 🎫 *Schloss (including guided tour every ½ hr) €2.50; park free.* ⏲ *Apr.–Sept., daily 9–6, Thurs. until 8, closed Oct.–Mar.; park open year-round.*

The **Lohengrin Therme** (Lohengrin Spa), on the way to Seulbitz, is a modern and exciting center of wellness and the ideal place to take a break from the travel schedule. The program includes a pool, hot tubs, Jacuzzis, a beautiful sauna area (including a hot rock steam room, a snow room, and gentle saunas), massages, light therapy, and more. Tickets for entrance and services can range from €8 for the pool and Jacuzzi area to €20 for a full Turkish massage. ✉ *Kurpromenade 5,*

☎ *0921/792–400.* WEB *www.lohengrin-therme.de.* ⊙ *Daily 8–10; sauna and wellness Sun.–Thurs. 10–10, Fri. and Sat. 10–11.*

Dining and Lodging

$–$$ ✕ **Brauereischänke am Markt.** The bratwurst is homemade at this boisterous Old Town inn. Another local specialty is *Bierrippchen* (pork ribs braised in a dark beer sauce). The inn's yeasty Zwickel beer is the ideal accompaniment to a meal. On sunny summer days you can people-watch from the sun-drenched beer garden on the pedestrian street. ✉ *Maximilianstr. 56,* ☎ *0921/64919. AE, MC. Closed Sun.*

$–$$ ✕ **Weihenstephan.** Long wooden tables, hearty regional specialties, and beer straight from the barrel (from the oldest brewery in Germany) make this hotel tavern a perennial favorite. How old is old? The famous Weihenstephan in Freising, near Munich, dates to 1040. In summer the crowded, flower-strewn terrace is the place to be. ✉ *Bahnhofstr. 5,* ☎ *0921/82288. DC, MC, V.*

$ ✕ **Brauhaus-Gaststätte Hopfengwölb.** Don't let being in a commercial zone bother you—just sit back and watch beer being brewed at this family-run tavern. Hearty Franconian-style *Frühschoppen* (midmorning meal) with lots of wurst are the specialty, and there's a daily-changing lunch menu. Thursday evening is set aside for the real blowouts, when the oak tables groan under the weight of food. ✉ *Bindlacherstr. 10,* ☎ *0921/95950. No credit cards. Closed weekends. No dinner Mon.–Wed. and Fri.–Sun.*

$$–$$$ ★ ✕🏨 **Goldener Anker.** No question about it, this is *the* place to stay in Bayreuth. The hotel is right next to the Markgräfliches Opernhaus and has been entertaining composers, singers, conductors, and players for more than 100 years, as the signed photographs in the lobby and the signatures in the guest book attest. The establishment has been run by the same family since 1753. Rooms are small but individually decorated; many have antique pieces. The restaurant ($$$–$$$$) is justly popular. Book your room far in advance. ✉ *Opernstr. 6, D–95444,* ☎ *0921/65051,* FAX *0921/65500,* WEB *www.anker-bayreuth.de. 40 rooms. Restaurant, no a/c, cable TV, some in-room data ports, pets allowed. AE, DC, MC, V. Restaurant closed Mon., Tues. and Dec. 20–Jan. 10.*

$$–$$$ ✕🏨 **Jagdschloss Thiergarten.** Make reservations well in advance for this small, top-notch hotel in a 250-year-old former hunting lodge. Staying here is like being a guest of your favorite aunt if she were an elderly millionaire. Rooms are furnished either in elegant white Venetian style or heavy German baroque, and all have a plush, lived-in character. The intimate Kaminhalle, with an ornate fireplace, and the Venezianischer Salon, dominated by a glittering 300-year-old Venetian chandelier, offer regional and nouvelle cuisine ($$–$$$$). Reservations and a jacket and tie are essential at the restaurants. The hotel is 6½ km (4 mi) from Bayreuth in the Thiergarten suburb. ✉ *Oberthiergärtenerstr. 36, D–95448,* ☎ *09209/9840,* FAX *09209/98429.* WEB *www.schlosshotel-thiergarten.de. 8 rooms, 1 suite. 2 restaurants, no a/c, cable TV, pool, sauna, bar, pets allowed (fee). AE, DC, MC, V. Restaurants closed Mon.*

$$ ✕🏨 **Hotel Lohmühle.** The old part of this hotel is in Bayreuth's only old half-timber house, a former saw mill by a stream. It's just a two-minute walk to the town center. The rooms are done up rustically with visible beams and such; the newer, neighboring building has correspondingly modern rooms. Between the two is a gallery with a bar in which you can enjoy a small aperitif before trying some of the restaurant's traditional, hearty cooking ($$–$$$), such as Schüfele or carp. ✉ *Badstr. 37, D–95445,* ☎ *0921/53060,* FAX *0921/530–6469. 42 rooms. Restaurant, bar, no a/c, cable TV, in-room data ports, pets allowed (fee), no-smoking rooms. AE, DC, MC, V. No dinner Sun.*

Outdoor Activities and Sports

At **Golfanlagen Bayreuth** (☎ 0921/970–704), just outside Bayreuth, there's an 18-hole championship course, a pitch-and-putt 9-holer, and a driving range. Clubs can be rented, and for those too young to swing one there's a playground.

Nightlife and the Arts

Opera lovers swear that there are few more intense operatic experiences than those offered by the annual **Wagner Festival** in Bayreuth, held July–August. For tickets write to the Bayreuther Festspiele Kartenbüro (✉ Postfach 100262, D–95402 Bayreuth, ☎ 0921/78780), but be warned: the waiting list is years long! You'll do best if you plan your visit a couple of years in advance. Rooms can be nearly impossible to find during the festival, too. If you don't get Wagner tickets, console yourself with visits to the exquisite 18th-century **Markgräfliches Opernhaus** (✉ Opernstr., ☎ 0921/251–416); performances are given most nights from May through September. Check with the tourist office for details.

Shopping

The **Hofgarten Passage,** off Richard-Wagner-Strasse, is one of the fanciest shopping arcades in the region; it's crammed with smart boutiques selling anything from high German fashion to simple local artifacts.

En Route The B–22 highway west to Bamberg is part of the officially designated **Strasse der Residenzen** (Road of Residences), named for the many episcopal and princely palaces along its way—including Bamberg's stunning Neue Residenz. The road cuts through the Fränkische Schweiz—or Franconian Switzerland—which got its name from its fir-clad upland landscape. Just north of Hollfeld, 23 km (14 mi) west of Bayreuth, the Jurassic rock of the region breaks through the surface in a bizarre, craggy formation known as the Felsgarten (Rock Garden).

Bamberg

5 *65 km (40 mi) west of Bayreuth, 80 km (50 mi) north of Nürnberg.*

Few towns in Germany survived the war with as little damage as Bamberg, which is on the Regnitz River. This former residence of one of Germany's most powerful imperial dynasties is on UNESCO's World Heritage site list. Bamberg, originally nothing more than a fortress in the hands of the Babenberg dynasty—later contracted to Bamberg—rose to prominence in the 11th century thanks to the political and economic drive of its most famous offspring, Holy Roman Emperor Heinrich II. He transformed the imperial residence into a flourishing episcopal city. His cathedral, consecrated in 1237, still dominates the historic area. For a short period Heinrich II proclaimed Bamberg the capital of the Holy Roman Empire of the German nation. Moreover, Bamberg earned fame as the second city to introduce book printing, in 1460.

The simplest pleasure here is to stroll through the narrow, sinuous streets of Old Bamberg, past half-timber and gabled houses and formal 18th-century mansions. Peek into flower-filled cobblestone courtyards or take time out in a waterside café in "little Venice," watching the small steamers as they chug past the colorful row of fishermen's houses. Bamberg's historic core is tucked snugly on a small island in the Regnitz; to the west is the so-called Bishops Town; to the east, Burghers Town. Connecting them is a bridge on which stands the **Altes Rathaus** (Old Town Hall), a rickety Gothic building dressed extravagantly in rococo. It was built in this unusual place so that the burghers of Bamberg could avoid paying real estate taxes to their bishops and archbishops. It's best seen from the next bridge upstream; from there it seems a wonder it isn't swept off by the river. The excellent collection of porcelain here is on permanent loan from the Ludwig estate. It contains a vast sampling of many 18th-century styles, from almost sober Meissens with bucolic Watteau scenes, to simple but rare Haguenau pieces from Alsace and voluble Strasbourg faiences. ✉ *Obere Brücke 1,* ☎ *0951/871–871.* 🎫 *€3.10,* ⏲ *Tues.–Sun. 9:30–4:30.*

The **Neue Residenz** (New Residence), Bamberg's contribution to the Road of Residences, is a glittering baroque palace that was once the home of the prince-electors. Their plans to extend the immense palace even further is evident at the corner on Obere Karolinenstrasse, where the ashlar bonding was left open to accept another wing. The most memorable room in the palace is the **Kaisersaal** (Throne Room), complete with impressive ceiling frescoes and elaborate stuccowork. Among the thousands of books and illuminated manuscripts in the **Staatsbibliothek** (State Library) are the original prayer books belonging to Heinrich and his wife, a 5th-century codex of the Roman historian Livy, and manuscripts by the 16th-century painters Dürer and Cranach. The rose garden behind the Neue Residenz offers an aromatic and romantic space to stroll in addition to a view of Bamberg's roof landscape. ✉ *Dompl. 8,* ☎ *0951/519–390 Staatsbibliothek.* 🎫 *Neue Residenz €3, Staatsbibliothek free.* ⏲ *Neue Residenz by tour only, Apr.–Sept., daily 9–noon and 1:30–5; Oct.–Mar., daily 9–noon and 1:30–4; Staatsbibliothek, weekdays 9–5, Sat. 9–noon. Closed Sat. in Aug.*

★ Bamberg's great **Dom** (cathedral) is one of the country's most important, a building that tells not only the town's story but that of much of Germany as well. The first building here was begun by Heinrich II in 1003, and it was in this partially completed cathedral that he was crowned Holy Roman Emperor in 1012. In 1237 it was mostly destroyed by fire, and the present late Romanesque–early Gothic building was begun. The dominant features are the massive towers at each corner. Heading into the dark interior, you'll find one of the most striking collections of monuments and art treasures of any European church. The most famous piece is the **Bamberger Reiter** (Bamberg Rider), an equestrian statue carved—no one knows by whom—around 1230 and thought to be an allegory of chivalrous virtue or a representation of King Stephen of Hungary. The larger-than-life figure is an extraordinarily realistic work for the period, more like a poised Renaissance statue than a stylized Gothic piece. Compare it with the mass of carved figures huddled in the tympana above the church portals. In the center of the nave you'll find another masterpiece, the massive tomb of Heinrich and his wife, Kunigunde. It's the work of Tilman Riemenschneider, Germany's greatest Renaissance sculptor. Pope Clement II is also buried in the cathedral, in an imposing tomb beneath the high altar; he is the only pope to be buried north of the Alps. ✉ *Dompl.,* ☎ *0951/502–330.* ⏲ *Nov.–Apr., Sun.–Fri. 9:30–5, Sat. 9:30–11:45 and 12:35–5; May–Oct., daily 9:30–6.*

The **Diözesanmuseum** (Cathedral Museum), directly next to the cathedral, contains one of many nails and splinters of wood reputed to be from the cross of Jesus. The "star-spangled" cloak stitched with gold that was given to Emperor Heinrich II by an Italian prince is among the finest items displayed. More macabre exhibits in this rich ecclesiastical collection are the elaborately mounted skulls of Heinrich and Kunigunde. The building itself was designed by Balthasar Neumann (1687–1753), the architect of Vierzehnheiligen, and constructed between 1730 and 1733. ✉ *Dompl. 5,* ☎ *0951/502–325.* 🎫 *€2, tour free.* ⏲ *Tues.–Sun. 10–5; tour in English by prior arrangement.*

On the north side of the Dom is the **Alte Hofhaltung,** the former imperial and episcopal palace. It's a sturdy and weatherworn half-timber Gothic building with a large, unruly Renaissance courtyard that is used for various events, notably theater in summer. Today it contains the **Historisches Museum** (Historical Museum), with a collection of documents and maps that will appeal most to history buffs who read German well. Over the next few years restoration work will increase the size of the museum and more exhibits will be on display. ✉ *Dompl. 8,* ☎ *0951/519–0746.* 🎫 *€2.10.* ⏲ *May–Oct., Tues.–Sun. 9–5.*

Bamberg's wealthy burghers built no fewer than 50 churches. Among the very special ones is the Church of Our Lady, known simply as **Obere Pfarre** (Upper Parish), whose history goes back to around 1325. It is unusual in that it is still entirely Gothic from the outside. Secondly, the grand choir, which was added at a later period, is lacking windows. And then there is the odd squarish box perched atop the tower. This watchman's abode served to end the tower before it grew taller than the neighboring cathedral. The interior is heavily baroque. Note the slanted floor, which allowed crowds of pilgrims to see the object of their veneration, a 14th-century Madonna. Don't miss the *Ascension of Mary* by Tintoretto at the rear of the church. Around Christmas, the Obere Pfarre is the site of the city's greatest nativity scene. Avoid the church during services, unless you are worshipping. ✉ *Untere Seelg.* ⏲ *Daily 7–7.*

St. Michael, a former Benedictine monastery, has been gazing over Bamberg since about 1015. After being overwhelmed by so much baroque elsewhere, entering this haven of simplicity is quite an experience. The entire choir is intricately carved, but the ceiling is gently decorated with very exact depictions of 578 flowers and healing herbs. The tomb of St. Otto is in a little chapel off the transept and the stained-glass windows hold symbols of death and transfiguration. The monastery is now used as a home for the aged. One tract, however, was taken over by the **Franconian Brewery Museum,** which exhibits everything that has to do with beer, from the making of malt, to recipes. ✉ *Michelsberg 10f,* ☎ *0951/53016.* 🎫 *Museum €2.* ⏲ *Apr.–Oct., Wed.–Sun. 1–5.*

In an 18th-century university building, the **Naturkunde Museum** (Museum of Natural History) exhibits cover a wide range of subjects, from fossils to volcanoes. The pride of the place is the collection of 800 stuffed birds in a magnificent room that also has a whale's jawbone casually lying on the floor. ☎ *0951/863–1248,* WEB *www.uni-bamberg.de/NatMus.* 🎫 *€ 1.50.* ⏲ *Apr.–Sept., daily 9–5; Oct.–Mar., daily 10–4.*

Dining and Lodging

$ ✕ **Café Abseits.** Abseits means off the beaten path, but that's not truly the case here. This quietly chic eatery has a merry and mixed crowd of burghers and students, light-colored walls with large prints (for sale), a steady flow of thirty types of beer, well-made, tasty dishes (specials every day for the business crowd), and à la carte breakfast that can be ordered until 3 PM (5 PM on Sundays and holidays). ✉ *Pödeldorferstr. 39,* ☎ *0951/303–422. No credit cards.*

$ ✕ **Klosterbräu.** The massive old stone and half-timber house has been standing since 1533, and some of the customers nursing their dark, smoky beer near the big stove seem as if they were just a few generations away from the original patrons. The cuisine is basic, robust, filling, and tasty, with such items as a bowl of beans with a slab of smoked pork, or marinated pork kidneys with boiled potatoes. ✉ *Obere Mühlbrücke,* ☎ *0951/52265. No credit cards. Closed Wed.*

$$ ✕🏨 **Hotel-Restaurant St. Nepomuk.** This very timbery half-timber house seems to float over the Regnitz. Sitting in the dining room, with its podium fireplace, discrete lights, serene atmosphere, and direct view of the river, you do get the feeling of being on board a ship. The Grüner family makes a special effort to bring in not only high quality food to the restaurant ($$$), but a world of excellent wines as well. The rooms are comfortable, and of course have quite a view. Each is furnished individually in elegant style. ✉ *Obere Mühlbrücke 9, D–96047,* ☎ *0951/98420,* FAX *0951/984–2100,* WEB *www.hotel-nepomuk.de. 47 rooms. Restaurant, no a/c, cable TV, pets allowed (fee), no-smoking rooms. DC, MC, V.*

$$ ✕🏨 **Romantik Hotel Weinhaus Messerschmitt.** Willy Messerschmitt of aviation fame grew up in this beautiful late-baroque house with a steep-eaved, green-shutter, stucco exterior. The very comfortable hotel has spacious and luxurious rooms, some with exposed beams and many of them lighted by chandeliers. You'll dine under beams and a coffered ceiling in the excellent Messerschmitt restaurant ($$–$$$), one of Bamberg's most popular culinary havens. The hotel is fitted for guests with disabilities. ✉ *Langestr. 41, D–96047,* ☎ *0951/27866,* FAX *0951/26141. 17 rooms. Restaurant, bar, no a/c, cable TV, no-smoking rooms. AE, DC, MC, V.*

Nightlife and the Arts

The **Sinfonie an der Regnitz** (✉ Muss-Str. 20, ☎ 0951/964–7200), a fine riverside concert hall, is home to Bamberg's world-class resident symphony orchestra. The **Hoffmann Theater** (✉ Schillerpl. 5, ☎ 0951/871–433) has opera and operetta from September through July. In June and July open-air performances are given at the **Alte Hofhaltung** (✉ Dompl. 8, ☎ 0951/519–0746). The city's first-class choir, **Capella Antiqua Bambergensis,** concentrates on ancient music. Throughout the summer organ concerts are given in the **Dom.** For program details and tickets to all cultural events call ☎ ☎ 0951/871–161. If you happen to be traveling around Christmastime, make sure you keep an eye out for crèches, a Bamberg specialty.

En Route From Bamberg you can either take the fast autobahn (A–73) south to Nürnberg or a parallel country road that follows the Main-Danube Canal (running parallel to the Regnitz River at this point) and joins the A–73 just under 25 km (15 mi) later at Forchheim-Nord. The canal, a mighty feat of engineering first envisioned by Charlemagne but only completed in the 1990s, connects the North Sea and the Black Sea by linking the Rhine and the Danube rivers via the Main River. There's no tangible division between northern and southern Franconia. You do, however, leave the thickly wooded heights of the Fichtelgebirge and the Fränkische Schweiz behind, and the countryside opens up as if to announce the imminent arrival of a more populated region. Eighteen kilometers (11 miles) south of Bamberg in the village of Buttenheim is a little blue-and-white half-timber house where Löb Strauss was born—in egregious poverty—in 1826. Take the tape-recorded tour of the **Levi-Strauss-Museum** (✉ Marktstr. 33, ☎ 09545/442–602, 🎫 €2.60, ⏲ Tues.–Thurs. 2–6, weekends 11–5 and by appointment) and learn how Löb emigrated to the United States and changed his name to Levi, and became the first name in denim. The stone-washed color of the house's beams, by the way, is the original 17th-century color.

NÜRNBERG

Nürnberg (Nuremberg) is the principal city of Franconia and second in size and significance in Bavaria only to Munich. With a recorded history stretching back to 1050, it's among the most historic of Germany's cities; the core of the Old Town, through which the Pegnitz River flows, is still surrounded by its original medieval walls. Nürnberg has always taken a leading role in German affairs. It was here, for example, that the Holy Roman Emperors traditionally held the first Diet, or convention of the estates, of their incumbency. And it was here, too, that Hitler staged the most grandiose Nazi rallies; later, this was the site of the Allies' war trials, where top-ranking Nazis were charged with—and almost without exception convicted of—crimes against humanity. The rebuilding of Nürnberg after the war was virtually a miracle considering the 90 percent destruction of the Old Town. As if putting an end its difficult, violent history, in 2001, Nürnberg became the world's first city to receive the UNESCO prize for Human Rights Education.

As a major intersection on the medieval trade routes, Nürnberg became a wealthy town. With prosperity came a great flowering of the arts and sciences. Albrecht Dürer (1471–1528), the first indisputable genius of the Renaissance in Germany, was born here in 1471. He married in 1509 and bought a house in the city where he lived and worked for the rest of his life. Other leading Nürnberg artists of the Renaissance include painter Michael Wolgemut (a teacher of Dürer), stonecutter Adam Kraft, and the brass founder Peter Vischer. The tradition of the Meistersinger, poets and musicians who turned songwriting into a special craft with a wealth of rules and regulations, also flourished here in the 16th century, thanks to the high standard set by the local cobbler Hans Sachs (1494–1576), celebrated three centuries later by Wagner in his *Meistersinger von Nürnberg*. The Thirty Years' War and the shift to sea routes for transportation led to a long decline, which only ended in the early 19th century when the first railroad opened in Nürnberg. Among a great host of inventions associated with the city, the most significant are the pocket watch, gun casting, the clarinet, and the geographical globe (the first of which was made before Columbus discovered the Americas). Among Nürnberg's famous products are *Lebkuchen* (gingerbread of sorts) and Faber-Castell pencils.

Exploring

Nürnberg is 63 km (39 mi) south of Bamberg and rich in special events and celebrations. By far the most famous is the **Christkindlesmarkt** (Christ-Child Market), an enormous pre-Christmas fair that runs from the Friday before Advent to Christmas Eve. One of the highlights is the candle procession, held every second Thursday of the market season in which thousands of children parade through the city streets.

A Good Walk

Start your walk at the Hauptbahnhof, the main train station, whose tourist office offers maps and brochures. Enter the Old Town through the **Königstor,** the old King's Gate. The old town walls, finished in 1452, come complete with moats, sturdy gateways, and watchtowers. Year-round floodlighting adds to their brooding romance. Take a left on Luitpoldstrasse and note on your left the **Neues Museum** ⑥, Nürnberg's museum for contemporary art. Take a left on Vordere Sterngasse and then a right when you reach the old wall again. Take your second right onto Strasse der Menschenrechte (Human Rights Street), which has an installation of 30 columns inscribed with the articles from the Declaration of Human Rights. On the right is one of Germany's most extraordinary museums, the **Germanisches Nationalmuseum** ⑦. A few hours spent here examining the sections devoted to the city will prepare you for the step back in time you'll make during the rest of your walk through Nürnberg. Follow Kornmarkt east and turn left on Pfannenschmiedsgasse to reach the beautiful **St. Lorenz Kirche** ⑧.

Continue north on Königstrasse and cross the bridge over the Pegnitz River at its most photogenic point, where the former hospital **Heilig-Geist-Spital** ⑨ broods over the waters, and soon you'll reach the city's

- Albrecht-Dürer-Haus 18
- Altes Rathaus 14
- Frauenkirche 11
- Gänsemännchenbrunnen 15
- Germanisches Nationalmuseum 7
- Hauptmarkt . 10
- Heilig-Geist-Spital 9
- Kaiserburg . . 17
- Museum für Kommunikation 20
- Neues Museum 6
- St. Lorenz Kirche 8
- St. Sebaldus Kirche 13
- Schöner Brunnen 12
- Spielzeugmuseum 19
- Stadtmuseum 16

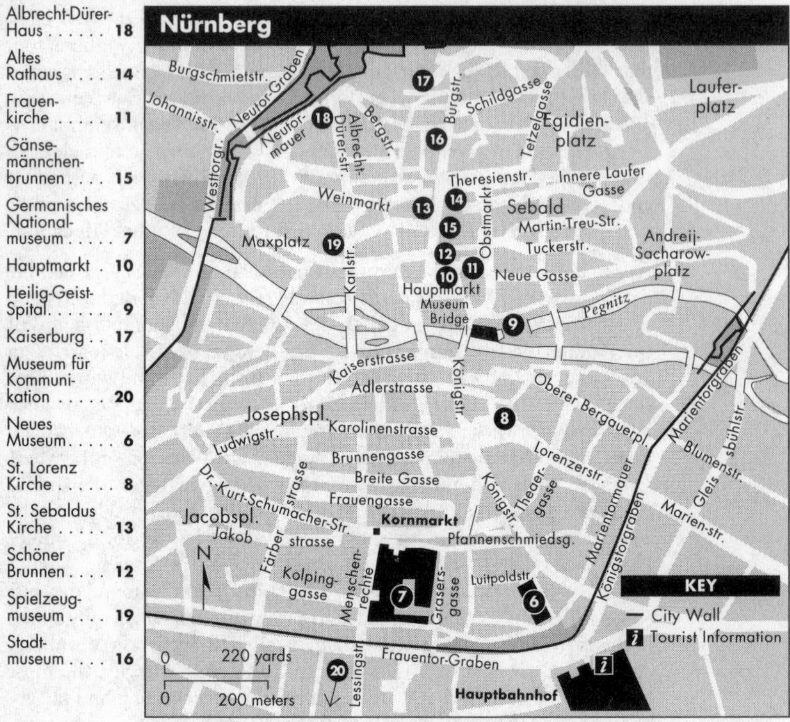

central market square, the **Hauptmarkt** ⑩, with the delicate late-Gothic **Frauenkirche** ⑪ standing modestly on the east side and the handsome **Schöner Brunnen** ⑫ (fountain), in the northwestern corner. Just north of the Hauptmarkt is Rathausplatz, site of another Gothic masterpiece of church architecture, **St. Sebaldus Kirche** ⑬. The **Altes Rathaus** ⑭, faces the church; behind the city hall is another pretty fountain, the **Gänsemännchenbrunnen** ⑮. To the north of the Altes Rathaus on Burgstrasse, stands the fine Renaissance Fembohaus, which contains the **Stadtmuseum** ⑯. Save some energy for the climb up Burgstrasse to the great **Kaiserburg** ⑰, whose shadow falls on the **Albrecht-Dürer-Haus** ⑱, at the top of Albrecht-Dürer-Strasse, just below the castle. Follow this street southward, and you'll come to a delightful toy museum, the **Spielzeugmuseum** ⑲, on Karlstrasse. If you still have time or energy, it's about a 15-minute walk to the trains and stamps of the **Museum für Kommunikation** ⑳, on Lessingstrasse, just south of the Germanisches Nationalmuseum. You can then return to your starting point for that much-needed refreshment. The train station has an extensive mall of restaurants and bars.

TIMING

You'll need a full day to walk around Nürnberg, two if you wish to take more time at its fascinating museums. Most of the major sights are within a few minutes' walk of each other. Begin or end your day at the Kaiserburg, whose ramparts offer a spectacular view over this medieval gem of a town.

Sights to See

★ ⑱ **Albrecht-Dürer-Haus** (Albrecht Dürer House). The great painter Albrecht Dürer lived here from 1509 until his death in 1528. This beautifully preserved late-medieval house is typical of the prosperous merchants' homes that once filled Nürnberg. Dürer, who enriched German art with Italianate elements, was more than a painter. He raised the woodcut, a notoriously difficult medium, to new heights of technical sophistication, combining great skill with a haunting, immensely detailed drawing style and complex, allegorical subject matter, while earning a good living at the same time. A number of original prints adorn the walls, and printing techniques are demonstrated in the old studio. An excellent opportunity to find out about life in the house is to take the Saturday 11 AM tour with a guide role-playing "Agnes Dürer," Dürer's wife. ✉ *Albrecht-Dürer-Str. 39,* ☎ *0911/231–2568.* 💳 *€4, with tour €6.50.* ⏲ *Mar.–Oct. and during Christkindlesmarkt, Tues.–Wed. and Fri.–Sun. 10–5, Thurs. 10–8; Nov.–Feb., Tues.–Fri. 1–5, weekends 10–5.*

⓮ **Altes Rathaus** (Old Town Hall). This ancient building on Rathausplatz abuts the rear of St. Sebaldus Kirche; it was erected in 1332, destroyed in World War II, and subsequently restored. Its intact medieval dungeons, consisting of 12 small rooms and one large torture chamber called the Chapel, provide insight into the gruesome applications of medieval law. ✉ *Rathauspl.,* ☎ *0911/23360.* 💳 *€2.* ⏲ *Tues.–Sun. 10–5:30; Christkindlesmarkt daily 10–5:30.*

⓴ **Museum für Kommunikation** (Communication Museum). Two museums have been amalgamated under a single roof here, the German Railway Museum and the Museum of Communication, in short, museums about how people get in touch. The first train to run in Germany did so on December 7, 1835, from Nürnberg to nearby Fürth. A model of the epochal train is here, along with a series of original 19th- and early 20th-century trains and stagecoaches. Philatelists will want to check out some of the 40,000-odd stamps in the extensive exhibits on the German postal system. You can also find out about the history of sending messages, from the old coaches to optical fiber networks here. ✉ *Lessingstr. 6,* ☎ *0911/219–2428.* 💳 *€3.* ⏲ *Tues.–Sun. 9–5.*

⓫ **Frauenkirche** (Church of Our Lady). The fine late-Gothic Frauenkirche was built in 1350, with the approval of Holy Roman Emperor Charles IV, on the site of a synagogue that was burned down during a 1349 pogrom. The modern tabernacle beneath the main altar was designed to look like a Torah scroll as a kind of memorial to that despicable act. The church's real attraction is the **Männleinlaufen,** a clock dating from 1509, which is set in its facade. It's one of those colorful mechanical marvels at which Germans have long excelled. Every day at noon the seven electors of the Holy Roman Empire glide out of the clock to bow to Emperor Charles IV before sliding back under cover. It's worth scheduling your morning to catch the display. ✉ *Hauptmarkt.* ⏲ *Mon.–Sat. 9–6, Sun. 12:30–6.*

⓯ **Gänsemännchenbrunnen** (Gooseman's Fountain). A work of rare elegance and great technical sophistication, this lovely Renaissance bronze fountain facing the Altes Rathaus was cast in 1550. ✉ *Rathauspl.*

★ ❼ **Germanisches Nationalmuseum** (German National Museum). You could spend days visiting this vast museum showcasing the country's cultural and scientific achievements, ethnic background, and history. It is the largest of its kind in Germany and perhaps the best arranged. The museum is in what was once a Carthusian monastery, complete with cloisters and monastic outbuildings. The exhibition begins outside, with the tall, sleek pillars of the Way of Human Rights designed by Israeli artist Dani Karavan. There are few aspects of German culture, from the Stone Age to the 19th century, that are not covered by the museum, and quantity and quality are evenly matched. One highlight is the superb collection of Renaissance German paintings (with Dürer, Cranach, and Altdorfer well represented). Others may prefer the exquisite medieval ecclesiastical exhibits—manuscripts, altarpieces, statuary, stained glass, jewel-encrusted reliquaries—the collections of arms and armor, the scientific instruments, or the toys. Few will be disappointed. ✉ *Kartäuserg. 1,* ☎ *0911/13310,* WEB *www.gnm.de.* 🎫 €4. ⏲ *Tues. and Thurs.–Sun. 10–6, Wed. 10–9.*

NEED A BREAK? Opposite the Germanisches Nationalmuseum is a minimalist, Italian-oriented restaurant named **Vivere** (✉ Kartäuserg. 12, ☎ 0911/133–1286), which is a branch of Arte, located in the museum. Al dente pasta or meat and fish dishes will bring you back to earth after the long hours spent in the museum. Entrées cost around €7–€12.

10 **Hauptmarkt** (Main Market). Nürnberg's central market square was at one time the city's Jewish Quarter. When the people of Nürnberg petitioned their emperor, Charles IV, for a big central market, the emperor happened to be in desperate need of money, and, above all, political support. The Jewish Quarter was the preferred site, but as the official protector of the Jewish people, the emperor could not just openly take away their property. Instead, he instigated a pogrom that left the Jewish Quarter in flames and more than 500 dead. The next step of razing the ruins and resettling the remaining Jews thus appeared perfectly logical.

A market still operates here. Its colorful stands, piled high with produce and shaded by striped awnings, are essential to the life of the city. The market women are a formidable-looking bunch, dispensing flowers, fruit, and abuse in equal measure. It's here that the Christkindlesmarkt is held.

9 **Heilig-Geist-Spital** (Holy Ghost Hospital). This ancient edifice dating from 1339 is set on graceful arches over the Pegnitz River, south of the Hauptmarkt. It has a charming courtyard, with elegant wood balconies and spacious arcades, and a restaurant. ✉ *Spitalg. 16,* ☎ *0911/221–761.*

17 **Kaiserburg** (Imperial Castle). The city's main attraction is a grand yet playful collection of buildings standing just inside the city walls; it was once the residence of the Holy Roman Emperors. The complex comprises three separate groups. The oldest, dating from around 1050, is the **Burggrafenburg** (Castellan's Castle), with a craggy old pentagonal tower and the bailiff's house. It stands in the center of the complex. To the east is the **Kaiserstallung** (Imperial Stables), built in the 15th century as a granary and now serving as a youth hostel. The real interest of this vast complex of ancient buildings, however, centers on the westernmost part of the fortress, which begins at the **Sinwell Turm** (Sinwell Tower). The **Kaiserburg Museum** is here, a subsidiary of the Germanisches Nationalmuseum that displays ancient armors and has exhibits relating to horsemanship in the imperial era and to the history of the fortress. This section of the castle also has a wonderful Romanesque **Doppelkappelle** (Double Chapel). The upper part—richer, larger, and more ornate than the lower chapel—was where the emperor and his family worshiped. Also visit the **Rittersaal** (Knights' Hall) and the **Kaisersaal** (Throne Room). Their heavy oak beams, painted ceilings, and sparse interiors have changed little since they were built in the 15th century. ✉ *Burgstr.,* ☎ *0911/225–726.* 🎫 €5.50. ⏲ *Apr.–Sept., daily 9–6, Thurs. until 8; Oct.–Mar., daily 10–4.*

★ 6 **Neues Museum** (New Museum). Anything but medieval, this museum opened in mid-2000 and is devoted to international design since 1945. The remarkable collection, supplemented by changing exhibitions, is in a new edifice that achieves the perfect synthesis between the old and the new. It is mostly built of traditional pink-sandstone ashlars, while the facade is a flowing, transparent composition of glass. The interior is a work of art in itself—cool stone, with a ramp that slowly spirals you up to the gallery. Extraordinary things await, including a Beuys installation (*Ausfegen,* or Sweep-out), or the *Avalanche* by François Morellet, a striking collection of violet, argon gas-filled fluorescent tubes. The café-restaurant adjoining the museum also contains modern art, silver-wrapped candies, and video projections. ✉ *Luitpoldstr. 5,* ☎ *0911/240–2020.* 🎫 *€3.50.* ⏲ *Tues.–Fri. 10–8, weekend 10–6.*

8 **St. Lorenz Kirche** (St. Laurence Church). In a city with several striking churches, St. Lorenz is considered by many to be the most beautiful. It was begun around 1250 and completed in about 1477; it later became a Lutheran church. Two towers flank the main entrance of the sizeable church, which is covered with a forest of carvings. In the lofty interior note the works by sculptors Adam Kraft and Veit Stoss: Kraft's great stone tabernacle, to the left of the altar, and Stoss's *Annunciation,* at the east end of the nave, are their finest works. There are many other carvings throughout the building, testimony to the artistic wealth of late-medieval Nürnberg. ✉ *Lorenzer Pl.,* ☎ *0911/209–287.* ⏲ *Mon.–Sat. 9–5, Sun. noon–4.*

13 **St. Sebaldus Kirche** (St. Sebaldus Church). Although St. Sebaldus lacks the quantity of art treasures found in its rival St. Lorenz, its nave and choir are among the purest examples of Gothic ecclesiastical architecture in Germany: elegant, tall, and airy. Veit Stoss carved the crucifixion group at the east end of the nave, while the elaborate bronze shrine, containing the remains of St. Sebaldus himself, was cast by Peter Vischer and his five sons around 1520. Not to be missed either is the **Sebaldus Chörlein,** an ornate Gothic oriel that was added to the Sebaldus parish house in 1361 (the original is in the Germanisches Nationalmuseum). ✉ *Albrecht-Dürer-Pl. 1,* ☎ *0911/214–2500.* ⏲ *Daily 7–7.*

12 **Schöner Brunnen** (Beautiful Fountain). The elegant 60-ft-high Gothic fountain carved around the year 1400 looks as though it should be on the summit of some lofty Gothic cathedral. It is adorned with 40 figures arranged in tiers—prophets, saints, local noblemen, sundry electors of the Holy Roman Empire, and one or two strays such as Julius Caesar and Alexander the Great. A gold ring is set into the railing surrounding the fountain, reportedly placed there by an apprentice carver. Stroking it is said to bring good luck. ✉ *Hauptmarkt.*

19 **Spielzeugmuseum** (Toy Museum). Both young and old are captivated by this playful museum, which has a few exhibits dating from the Renaissance; most, however, are from the 19th century. Simple dolls vie with mechanical toys of extraordinary complexity, such as a wooden Ferris wheel from the Erz Mountains adorned with little colored lights. The top floor displays Barbies and intricate Lego constructions. ✉ *Karlstr. 13–15,* ☎ *0911/231–3164.* 🎫 *€4.* ⏲ *Tues. and Thurs.–Sun. 10–5, Wed. 10–9.*

16 **Stadtmuseum** (City Museum). This city history museum, the Fembohaus, is a dignified patrician dwelling completed in 1598. It is one of the finest Renaissance mansions in Nürnberg. Each room explores another aspect of Nürnberg history, from crafts to gastronomy. On the first floor, films relating to the city's long history are screened. ✉ *Burgstr. 15,* ☎ *0911/231–2595.* 🎫 *€4.* ⏲ *Tues.–Wed. and Fri.–Sun. 10–5, Thurs. 10–8.*

OFF THE BEATEN PATH

TIERGARTEN NÜRNBERG – The well-stocked Nürnberg Zoo has a dolphinarium that children love; it's worth the extra admission fee. The zoo is on the northwest edge of town; reach it by taking the Number 5 streetcar from the city center. ✉ *Am Tiergarten 30,* ☎ *0911/54546.* 🎟 *€5.20; Dolphinarium €3.* ⏲ *Zoo and dolphinarium Apr.–Sept., daily 8–7:30; Mar. and Oct., daily 8–5:30; Nov.–Feb., daily 9–5; Dolphinarium display daily at 11, 2, and 4.*

ZEPPELINFELD – The enormous parade grounds where Hitler addressed his largest Nazi rallies lie on the eastern edge of the city. Nowadays it sometimes shakes to the amplified beat of pop concerts. The central stand area contains a remarkable museum with the **Ausstellung Faszination und Gewalt** (Fascination and Terror exhibition), which documents the political, social, and architectural history of the Nazi Party in Nürnberg. It's within one section of the gigantic, horseshoe-shape Congressional Hall built by the Nazis to harbor a crowd of 50,000. Austrian architect Günther Domenig added a courageous glass corridor that adds light to the overwhelmingly solid construction. Tours of the grounds are offered by a private association called *Geschichte für Alle* (History for All). ☎ *0911/869–897 for Zeppelinfeld; 0911/332–735 for tour.* 🎟 *€1.50 museum, €5 tour.* ⏲ *Museum mid-May–Oct., Mon.–Sun. 10–6; Nov.–mid-May, by appointment. Tours Dec.–Mar., Sun. at 2; Apr.–Nov., weekends at 2. Meet at Luitpoldhain tram terminus (No. 9).*

JÜDISCHES MUSEUM FRANKEN – The Holocaust is not the focus of the Jewish Museum of Franconia; rather, items pertaining to the everyday life of the Jewish community in Franconia and Fürth are examined: books, Seder plates, coat hangers, old statutes concerning Jews, children's toys. Among the most famous members of the Fürth community was Henry Kissinger, born here in 1923. Changing exhibitions relate to contemporary Jewish life in Germany, and in the basement is the Mikwe, the ritual bath, which was used by the family who lived here centuries ago. To get to the museum from Nürnberg, you can take the U1 U-bahn to the stop "Rathaus." ✉ *Königstr. 89, Fürth, 10 km (6 mi) west of Nürnberg.* ☎ *0911/770–577,* WEB *www.juedisches-museum.org.* 🎟 *€3* ⏲ *Sun.–Mon. and Wed.–Fri. 10–5, Tues. 10–8.*

Dining and Lodging

$$$$ ★ ✕ **Essigbrätlein.** Some rank this the top restaurant in the city and even among the best in Germany. As the oldest restaurant in Nürnberg, built in 1550 and originally used as a meeting place for wine merchants, it is unquestionably one of the most atmospheric. Today its tiny but elegant period interior caters to the distinguishing gourmet with a taste for special spice mixes (owner Andrée Köthe's hobby). The menu changes daily with light and exotic dishes such as *Geschmorter Fenchel mit Bohnencreme* (fennel on creamed beans) or the more substantial *Lamb mit Gewürzlauch* (lamb with spiced leek). ✉ *Weinmarkt 3,* ☎ *0911/225–131. Reservations essential. AE, DC, MC, V. Closed Sun. and Mon.*

$–$$ ★ ✕ **Barfüsser Kleines Brauhaus.** The huge cellar rooms of the old grain customs warehouse houses this minibrewery and restaurant. Locals meet for lunch or dinner to enjoy Franconian specialties or just plain home cooking along with the fine beer brewed on the premises. The vaulted ceiling and thick stone pillars are a simple but elegant backdrop. Try the carp, a regional specialty only available in months with the letter "r." ✉ *Königstr. 60,* ☎ *0911/204–242. AE, MC, V.*

$–$$ ★ ✕ **Heilig-Geist-Spital.** Heavy wood furnishings and a choice of more than 100 wines make this 650-year-old wine tavern a popular spot. The menu includes grilled pork chops, panfried potatoes, and German cheeses. ✉ *Spitalg. 16,* ☎ *0911/221–761. AE, DC, MC, V.*

$ ✕ **Historische Bratwurst-Küche Zum Gulden Stern.** A house built in 1375 holds the oldest bratwurst restaurant in the world and even survived the last war. The famous Nürnberg bratwursts are always freshly roasted on a beechwood fire; the boiled variation is prepared in a tasty stock of Franconian wine and onions. This is where the city council met in 1998 to decide upon the official size and weight of the Nürnberg bratwurst. ✉ *Zirkelschmiedg. 26,* ☎ *0911/205–9288. DC, MC, V.*

$$ ✕🏨 **Hotel-Weinhaus Steichele.** This skillfully converted former 19th-century wine merchant's warehouse is part of the Flair hotel group but is still managed by the family that has been running it for three generations. It's handily close to the main train station yet on a quiet street of the old walled town. The rooms, decorated in Bavarian rustic decor, are cozy. Two wood-paneled, traditionally furnished taverns ($–$$$) serve Franconian fare. ✉ *Knorrstr. 2–8, D–90402,* ☎ *0911/202–280,* FAX *0911/221–914. 56 rooms. Restaurant, Weinstube, no a/c, cable TV, pets allowed. AE, DC, MC, V.*

$$$–$$$$ 🏨 **Maritim.** If you value modern convenience over old-world charm, consider staying in this luxurious hotel, conveniently located between the railway station and the Old Town. Clever interior design has given the sleek decor stylized historic touches, such as coffered ceilings and checkered tiles. Breakfast costs an extra €13, but the range and excellence of the buffet fully warrant the expense. ✉ *Frauentorgraben 11, D–90443,* ☎ *0911/23630,* FAX *0911/236–3836, 306 rooms, 10 suites. 2 restaurants, cable TV with movies, in-room data ports, in-room fax, pool, gym, massage, sauna, steam room, bar, pets allowed (fee), no-smoking rooms. AE, DC, MC, V.*

$$–$$$ 🏨 **Agneshof.** This comfortable hotel is sandwiched north of the Old Town between the fortress and St. Sebaldus Church. Interiors are very modern, tastefully done, and the hotel also has a small wellness section that will be welcome after a long day exploring. ✉ *Agnesg. 10, D–90403,* ☎ *0911/214–440,* FAX *0911/2144–4144,* WEB *www.hotel-net.de/agneshof. 72 rooms. No a/c, cable TV with movies, in-room data ports, hot tub, sauna, pets allowed (fee), no-smoking rooms. AE, DC, MC, V.*

$$–$$$ 🏨 **Hotel Deutscher Kaiser.** This 19th-century sandstone building is typical of its time, when majestic medieval styles were imitated in Nürnberg. It's location couldn't be better, right near the train station, but within the walls of the city, a few steps away from most major sights. The furnishings range from antique to hotel-generic, and the owners are renovating room by room, so if you happen to have one of the "older rooms," chalk the slight wear up to comfortable patina. ✉ *Königststr. 55, D–90402,* ☎ *0911/203–341,* FAX *0911/241–8982,* WEB *www.deutscher-kaiser-hotel.de. 52 rooms. No a/c, cable TV, in-room data ports, gym, pets allowed (fee), no-smoking rooms. AE, DC, MC, V.*

$$ 🏨 **Albrecht Dürer Hotel Garni.** If all you're looking for is a place to sleep, this tiny hotel above a little bar near the Kaiserburg is a bargain and is still in a good location. Light pine cash-and-carry furniture, comfortable beds, a shower, and eight kinds of beer in the bar is what you can expect. Some of the rooms can open up to a suite for families. ✉ *Bergstr. 25, D–90403,* ☎ *0911/204–592,* FAX *0911/204–104. 9 rooms. Bar, no a/c, cable TV, Internet, pets allowed (fee), no-smoking rooms. AE, DC, MC, V.*

$$ 🏨 **Burghotel Stammhaus.** Accommodations are small but cozy, and the service is familial and friendly here. The breakfast room with its balcony overlooking the houses of the Old Town has a charm all its own. A pool is in the basement. ✉ *Schildg. 14, D–90403,* ☎ *0911/203–040,* FAX *0911/226–503,* WEB *www.burghotel-stamm.de. 22 rooms. No a/c, cable TV, in-room data ports, pool, pets allowed. AE, DC, MC, V.*

$$ 🏨 **Hotel Fackelmann.** This compact, convenient hotel near the Old Town is designed for giving quiet comfort to either the leisure traveler or the business person in town for one of the big trade fairs. Clean, light rooms, a breakfast buffet, and a fitness area are all included. ✉ *Essenwein-*

str. 10, D–90443, ☎ 0911/206–840, FAX 0911/206–86460, WEB www.hotel-fackelmann.de. 34 rooms. No a/c, cable TV, in-room data ports, sauna, gym, pets allowed (fee), no-smoking rooms. AE, MC, V.

Nightlife and the Arts

Nürnberg has an annual summer festival, **Sommer in Nürnberg,** from May through September, with more than 200 events. Its international organ festival in June and July is regarded as Europe's finest. From May through August classical music concerts are given in the Rittersaal of the **Kaiserburg,** while regular pop and rock shows are staged in the dry moat of the castle. In June and July open-air concerts are given in the Kaiserburg's Serenadenhof. For reservations and program details call ☎ 0911/225–726.

Shopping

Step into the **Handwerkerhof,** in the tower at the Old Town gate (Am Königstor) opposite the main railway station, and you'll think you're back in the Middle Ages. Craftspeople are busy at work in a "medieval mall," turning out the kind of handiwork that has been produced in Nürnberg for centuries: pewter; glassware; basketwork; wood carvings; and, of course, toys. The Lebkuchen specialist **Lebkuchen-Schmidt** has a shop here as well. The mall is open mid-March–December 24, weekdays 10–6:30, Saturday 10–4. December 1–24 the mall is also open on Sunday 10–6:30.

The **Scherenschnittstudio** (✉ Albrecht-Dürer-Str. 13, ☎ 0911/244–7483) specializes in scissor-cut silhouettes. You can come and pose for owner Karin Dütz, send a picture (profile, do not smile), or just browse to pick up some items of this old and skilled craft.

ALTMÜHLTAL

The winding river valley Altmühltal stretches from Gunzenhausen in the west to Kelheim in the east, where the gentle Altmühl river flows into the Danube River. It's ideal for a quiet holiday, since the valley hasn't really been discovered by the larger tourist crowds. A relaxing getaway for canoe paddlers (the river flows at times through gorge-like landscapes), the Altmühltal first drew attention with its geology. In 1789, one Alois Senefelder discovered that the limestone from the region around Solnhofen had special ink-retaining properties for lithography, which actually revolutionized the printing industry. The limestone, too, is a treasure-trove of fossils, which are liberally exhibited in the region's museums. The park area Naturpark Altmühltal encompasses towns near the river's path—Weissenburg, Eichstätt, Beilngries, Dietfurt, and Riedenburg—and extends south to Ingolstadt and Neuburg on the Danube.

Eichstätt

21 *80 km (50 mi) south of Nürnberg via A–73 and A–9, exit Altmühltal, follow signs, 20 km (13 mi) to Eichstätt.*

The center of the Altmühltal is, perhaps, Eichstätt, a market town and bishopric with some impressive monuments. The Marktplatz's 1695 fountain features the local patron holy man, St. Willibald. While all the facades here are baroque, they are in fact built onto medieval structures. Only the tower of the Town Hall still reveals its ancient origins. The old fortress **Willibaldsburg** dominates Eichstätt, but in palace garb. It was used first to defend the town and then, from the 14th to the 18th century, to represent it. Now it serves as the town hallmark and cultural center. The **Jura-Museum** here displays all sorts of items relating to local geology, geography, and topology, including many fossils. ☎ *08421/4730.* 🎫 *€3.* ⏲ *Apr.–Sept., Tues.–Sun. 9–6, Oct.–Mar., Tues.–Sun. 10–4.*

The **Dom** (✉ Dompl.), a two-tower structure dating back to the 11th century, underwent a baroque facelift in the early 18th century by Gabriel de Gabrieli, one of a fine school of masters hailing from the canton of Graubünden in Switzerland. Among the cathedral's treasures are the 16th-century stained-glass windows by Hans Holbein the Elder. The **Diocesan Museum** (☎ 08421/50279; 🎫 €2.50; ⏲ Apr.–Oct., Tues.–Sat 9.30–1, 2–5; Nov.–Mar. by appointment only), accessible from the cathedral cloister, has wealth of instructive exhibits documenting the construction of the cathedral, local people's religious customs, and the lives of the bishop-princes of Eichstätt as well as their vestments and monstrances.

The former prince-bishop's residence, also a work by de Gabrieli, is part of the cathedral complex and now used by the local administration. The **Spiegelsaal** (Hall of Mirrors) is one of the splendid rooms here that can be seen on tours. The former chapel of the residence is now a small gallery devoted to the local painter Christian Otto Müller (1901–70), whose landscapes of the Eichstätt area led to his nickname "Cézanne of the Altmühltal." ✉ *Residenzpl. 1,* ☎ *08421/70220.* ⏲ *Tours Easter–Oct., Mon.–Thurs. 11 and 3, Fri. 11, weekends 10–11:30 and 2–3:30 every half hr.*

Dining and Lodging

$–$$$ ✕ **Krone am Dom.** On a warm day, this is the spot to sit outside and watch the goings-on on the square in front of the cathedral. The Krone's traditional Bavarian cooking includes very tasty venison dishes. ✉ *Dompl.,* ☎ *08421/4406. MC, V.*

$$ 🏨 **Hotel Adler.** White with pink trimmings, the centuries-old hostelry on the market square was recently restored and earned itself the Bavarian Environmental Award in the process. Rooms are comfortable and spacious, especially the eight studio rooms, which are almost suite size. ✉ *Marktpl. 22–24, D–85072,* ☎ *08421/6767,* FAX *08421/8283,* WEB *www.ei.online.de/adler. 28 rooms. No a/c, cable TV, sauna, pets allowed (fee), no-smoking rooms. AE, DC, MC, V.*

FRANCONIA A TO Z

To research prices, get advice from other travelers, and book travel arrangements, visit www.fodors.com.

AIRPORTS

The international airports near Franconia are at Frankfurt and Munich. Nürnberg and Bayreuth have regional airports; there are frequent flights between Frankfurt and Nürnberg. If there's fog in Munich, the Nürnberg airport serves as backup.

BIKE TRAVEL

The scenic Altmühltal Valley is particularly suitable for biking and is especially known for its rock formations. Otherwise the area consists of hills and landscapes dotted with pretty and sleepy villages. The tourist board for the Naturpark Altmühltal issues leaflets with suggested cycling tours and lists of rental outlets. Bicycles can also be rented from most major train stations. Cycling along the Danube is another favorite. Ships let you take a bicycle along for a small fee (usually €1), so you can enjoy the scenery one way and get exercise on the other.

BOAT TRAVEL

A total of 15 different lines operate cruises on the Altmühl and Main rivers and the Main-Donau Canal from April through October. Contact the Franconia tourist board and ask for details on the Weisse Flotte cruises.

Several boats follow the Main River from Aschaffenburg to Würzburg and from Würzburg to Bamberg. These are worth considering if you plan to spend a lot of time in Franconia. For information contact Fränkische Personen-Schiffahrt or the Würzburg tourist office.

From March through October Personenschiffahrt Kropf boats leave Bamberg daily beginning at 11 AM for short cruises on the Regnitz River and the Main-Danube Canal; the cost is €6.50.
➤ TOUR-OPERATOR RECOMMENDATIONS: **Fränkische Personen-Schiffahrt** (☎ 09321/91810). **Personenschiffahrt Kropf** (✉ Kapuzinerstr. 5, Bamberg, ☎ 0951/26679). **Würzburg tourist office** (✉ Marktpl., Würzburg, ☎ 0931/37398).

BUS TRAVEL

The only major bus line in Franconia runs between Rothenburg-ob-der-Tauber and Nürnberg, but it takes long and is not nearly as comfortable as the train. Local buses run from most train stations to smaller towns and villages, though the service isn't frequent. Buses for the Fichtelgebirge in northern Franconia leave from Bayreuth's post office, near the train station.

CAR RENTAL

➤ MAJOR AGENCIES: **Avis** (✉ Markgrafenallee 6, Bayreuth, ☎ 0921/789–550; ✉ Lossaustr. 6 [main railway station bldg.], Coburg, ☎ 09561/73075; ✉ Allersbergerstr. 139, Nürnberg, ☎ 0911/49696). **Bavaria Autovermietung** (✉ Leiblstr. 23, Nürnberg, ☎ 0911/311–718). **Europcar** (✉ Nürnberg Airport off A–3, Nürnberg, ☎ 0911/528–484). **Hertz** (✉ Wasserg. 15, Coburg, ☎ 09561/24135; ✉ Nürnberg Airport, Nürnberg, ☎ 0911/527–719). **Sixt** (✉ Gleissbühlstr. 12–14, Nürnberg, ☎ 0911/438–710).

CAR TRAVEL

Franconia is served by five main autobahns: A–7 from Hamburg, A–3 from Köln and Frankfurt, A–81 from Stuttgart, A–6 from Heilbronn, and A–9 from Munich. Nürnberg is 167 km (104 mi) from Munich and 222 km (138 mi) from Frankfurt. The Altmühltal can be accessed from the A–9 (exit Beilngries north of Ingolstadt), or from Donauwörth on the Romantic Road (41 km [25 mi] to Treuchtlingen).

Some nearby scenic driving includes the eastern section of the Burgenstrasse (Castle Road), running from Heidelberg to Nürnberg; the Bocksbeutel Strasse (Franconian Wine Road), which follows the course of the Main River from Zeil am Main along the wine-growing slopes of the valley to Aschaffenburg; and the Strasse der Kaiser und Könige (Emperors' and Kings' Road), leading from Frankfurt to Vienna through Franconia via Aschaffenburg, Würzburg, and Nürnberg.

EMERGENCIES

➤ CONTACTS: **Police and ambulance** (☎ 110). **Fire and emergency medical aid** (☎ 112).

TOURS

In Bamberg guided walking tours set out from the tourist information office April–October, Monday–Saturday at 10:30 and 2, and Sunday at 11; November–December, Monday–Saturday at 2, and Sunday at 11; and January–March, Monday–Saturday at 2. The cost is €5.50.

Bayreuth also offers walking tours beginning at Leopoldplatz at 10.30 daily from May to October. They cost €4.50. Guided walking tours of the historical center of Coburg depart at 3 every Saturday from the Albert statue in the market square. The cost is €2. Eichstätt offers walking tours of the city for €3, Saturday and Wednesday at 1:30 at the tourist information office.

In Nürnberg English-language bus tours of the city are conducted May–October and December, daily at 9:30, starting at the Mauthalle, Hallplatz 2. The 2½-hour tour costs €10. An English-language tour on foot through the Old Town is conducted daily at 2:30; it departs from the tourist information office. The tour costs €4. City tours are also conducted in gaily painted trolley buses April–October, daily at 45-minute intervals beginning at 10; November–March, weekends only, starting at 10 at the *Schöner Brunnen.* Tours are in German unless at least five of the participants request English. The cost is €4. For more information, call ☎ 0911/202–2910.

TRAIN TRAVEL

Regular InterCity services connect Nürnberg with Frankfurt and other major German cities. Trains run hourly from Frankfurt to Munich, with a stop at Nürnberg. The trip takes about three hours to Munich, two hours to Nürnberg. Nürnberg is a stop on the high-speed InterCity Express north–south routes, and there are hourly trains from Munich direct to Nürnberg.

Some InterCity trains stop in Bamberg, which is most speedily reached from Munich. Local trains from Nürnberg connect with Bayreuth and areas of southern Franconia. In the Altmühltal, Treuchtlingen is on the Munich–Nürnberg line.

VISITOR INFORMATION

The principal regional tourist office for Franconia is Fremdenverkehrsverband Franken e.V. For information on resorts and snow conditions, call the Tourist Information Fichtelgebirge.

➤ TOURIST INFORMATION: **Bamberg** (✉ Fremdenverkehrsamt, Geyerswörthstr. 3, D–96047, ☎ 0951/871–161, WEB www.bamberg.de/tourismus). **Bayreuth** (✉ Fremdenverkehrsverein, Luitpoldpl. 9, D–95444, ☎ 0921/88588, FAX 0921/88555, WEB www.bayreuth.de). **Coburg** (✉ Fremdenverkehrs- und Kongressbetrieb, Herrng. 4, D–96450, ☎ 09561/74180, WEB www.coburg-tourist.de). **Eichstätt** (✉ Dompl. 8, D–85072, ☎ 08421/98800, FAX 08421/988–030, WEB www.eichstaett.de). **Fichtelgebirge Tourist Information** (☎ 09272/969–030). **Franconia Tourist Board** (Fremdenverkehrsverband Franken e.V.; ✉ Fürtherstr. 21, D–90429 Nürnberg, ☎ 0911/264–202). **Kronach** (✉ Marktpl., D–96317, ☎ 09261/97236). **Kulmbach** (✉ Fremdenverkehrsbüro, Stadthalle, Sutte 2, D–95326, ☎ 09221/95880). **Lichtenfels** (✉ Am Marktpl. 1, D–96215, ☎ 09571/7950). **Naturpark Altmühltal Tourist Office** (Fremdenverkehrsamt; ✉ Notre Dame 1, D–85072 Eichstätt, ☎ 08421/98760). **Nürnberg** (✉ Congress- und Tourismus-Zentrale Frauentorgraben 3, D–90443, ☎ 0911/23360, WEB www.nuernberg.de). **Weissenburg** (✉ Martin-Luther-Pl. 3, D–91781, ☎ 09141/907–124).

7 THE BODENSEE

Charming villages are strung along the Bodensee (Lake Constance) like pearls on a string. Behind the towns rise vineyards and orchards and on a clear day the snow-covered Swiss alps are visible far off in the distance. To fully appreciate the gentle landscape and local culture, leave your car and take it all in by bicycle.

Updated by
Uli Ehrhardt

LAPPING THE SHORES OF Germany, Switzerland, and Austria, the Bodensee (Lake Constance), at 65 km (40 mi) long and 15 km (9 mi) wide, is the largest lake in the German-speaking world. Though called a lake, it's actually a vast swelling of the Rhine, gouged out by a massive glacier in the Ice Age and flooded by the river as the ice receded. The Rhine flows into its southeast corner, where Switzerland and Austria meet, and flows out at its west end. On the German side, the Bodensee is bordered almost entirely by the state of Baden-Württemberg (a small portion of the eastern tip, from Lindau to Nonnenhorn, belongs to Bavaria).

A natural summer playground, the Bodensee is ringed with little towns and busy resorts. It's one of the warmest areas of the country, and not just because of its southern latitude, but also due to the warming influence of the water, which gathers heat in the summer and releases it in the winter like a massive radiator. The lake itself practically never freezes over—it has done so only once during the last two centuries.

The lake's natural attractions, not least of which are its abundance of fresh fish and its fertile soil, were as compelling several thousand years ago as they are today, making this one of the oldest continually inhabited areas of Germany. Highlights include the medieval island town of Lindau; Friedrichshafen, birthplace of the zeppelin; the rococo Wallfahrtskirche in Birnau; and the town of Konstanz, on the Swiss-German border. A day trip to Austria and Switzerland (and to little Liechtenstein) is easy to make, and border formalities are few.

Pleasures and Pastimes

Biking

Spring through autumn, Germans pack their wheels and head for the scenic bike path that circles the entire lake. You can rent a bike as a guest at many hotels, at some tourist offices, from sports shops, and from bicycle tour operators. You can always save yourself some pumping by cutting across the lake on a ferry. Biking maps are available from newspaper stands, book shops, and tourist offices, and you can leave your baggage in the long-term storage available at the train stations in Konstanz, Überlingen, Friedrichshafen, and Lindau.

Dining

Fish specialties predominate around the Bodensee. There are 35 types of fish in the lake, with *Felchen* (a meaty white fish) the most highly prized. Felchen belongs to the salmon family and is best eaten *blau* (poached in a mixture of water and vinegar with spices called *Essigsud*) or *Müllerin* (baked in almonds). Wash it down with a top-quality Meersburg white wine. If you venture north to Upper Swabia, *Pfannkuchen* and *Spätzle,* both flour-and-egg dishes, are the most common specialties. Pfannkuchen (pancakes) are generally filled with meat, cheese, jam, or sultanas, or chopped into fine strips and scattered in a clear consommé known as *Flädlesuppe.* Spätzle are roughly chopped, golden-color fried egg noodles that are the usual accompaniment to the Swabian Sunday roast-beef lunch of *Rinderbraten.* One of the best-known Swabian dishes is *Maultaschen,* a kind of ravioli, usually served floating in a broth strewn with chives.

In this area, international dishes are not only on the menu, but on the map—you only have to drive a few miles to try the Swiss or Austrian dish you're craving in its own land. *Seeweine* (lake wines) from area vineyards include Müller-Thurgau, Spätburgunder, Ruländer, and Kerner.

CATEGORY	COST*
$$$$	over €20
$$$	€15–€20
$$	€10–€15
$	under €10

**per person for a main course at dinner*

Lodging

The towns and resorts around the lake have a wide range of hotels, from venerable wedding-cake-style, fin-de-siècle palaces to more modest *Gasthöfe*. If you're visiting in July and August, make reservations in advance. For lower rates and a more rural atmosphere, consider staying a few miles away from the lake.

CATEGORY	COST*
$$$$	over €225
$$$	€150–€225
$$	€75–€150
$	under €75

**All prices are for two people in a double room, including tax and service.*

Shopping

The Bodensee is artists' territory, and shopping means combing the many small galleries for watercolors, engravings, and prints. Local potters sell their wares directly from their shops. International goods are available in abundance. In Konstanz, if you must have Swiss chocolate or a Swiss watch, walk a few feet across the border into Kreuzlingen, the Swiss part of the twin-city. To do some serious shopping there are two cities within an hour's drive—St. Gallen, known for its textiles and embroidery, and Zurich, with its famous Bahnhofstrasse, Switzerland's most elegant and expensive shopping street. Just across the bay from Lindau is the Austrian city of Bregenz with some reputable Loden shops that carry fashionable alpine apparel.

Exploring the Bodensee

You can travel the entire length of the German shore of the Bodensee easily in a day—by car, train, or boat—but the enchanting towns along the way will deter any plan to rush through. Lindau is a pretty and unusual resort, close to Austria, Liechtenstein, and the mountains of the German Allgäu. Friedrichshafen is busier and sits at the head of a road inland to Ravensburg, Weingarten, and the extraordinary churches of the Baroque Road. Meersburg, built on a slope that slides down to the lakeside, is arguably the loveliest Bodensee town and is just a short ferry ride from the area's largest city, Konstanz, the regional gateway to Switzerland.

Great Itineraries

Numbers in the text correspond to numbers in the margin and on the Bodensee (Lake Constance) map.

IF YOU HAVE 3 DAYS

Stroll around **Lindau** ①, and then make for the next "town in the lake," **Wasserburg** ②. Reserve a couple of hours for the Zeppelin Museum in **Friedrichshafen** ④, which celebrates the airships once built there. Overnight in lovely **Meersburg** ⑤, rising early to catch the sunrise over the lake and the ferry to **Konstanz** ⑩, on the opposite shore. From here there's a difficult choice—a day trip either to the Swiss Alps or to two Bodensee islands, **Mainau** ⑪ and **Reichenau** ⑫. After an overnight stay in Konstanz, go west to **Radolfzell** ⑬, rent a bike, and explore the **Höri** ⑭ peninsula.

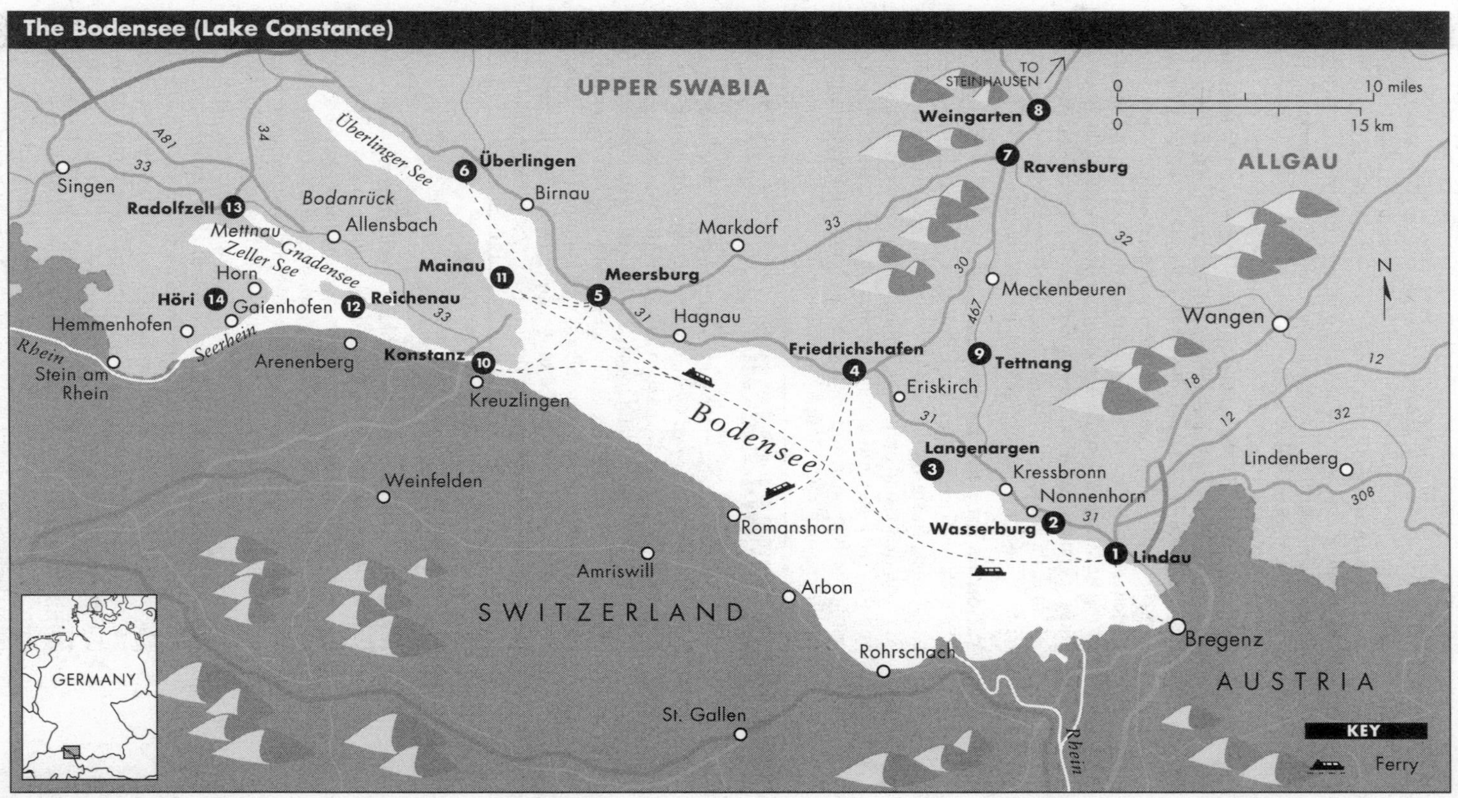
The Bodensee (Lake Constance)
UPPER SWABIA
TO STEINHAUSEN
0 10 miles
0 15 km
ALLGAU
N
Singen
Radolfzell 13
Bodanrück
Allensbach
Überlinger See
6 Überlingen
Birnau
Markdorf
8 Weingarten
7 Ravensburg
Meckenbeuren
Wangen
Mettnau
Gnadensee
Zeller See
Horn
Höri 14
Gaienhofen
Hemmenhofen
12 Reichenau
Mainau 11
5 Meersburg
Hagnau
Friedrichshafen 4
9 Tettnang
Eriskirch
Rhein
Seerhein
Stein am Rhein
Arenenberg
Konstanz 10
Kreuzlingen
Bodensee
Langenargen 3
Kressbronn
Nonnenhorn
Wasserburg 2
1 Lindau
Lindenberg
Weinfelden
Romanshorn
Amriswil
Arbon
SWITZERLAND
Rohrschach
Bregenz
AUSTRIA
St. Gallen
Rhein
GERMANY
KEY
Ferry

IF YOU HAVE 5 DAYS

Start your itinerary at **Lindau** ①, continuing to **Wasserburg** ②, **Langenargen** ③ (for a panoramic view of the lake from Montfort Castle), and **Friedrichshafen** ④; then head inland via the B–30 to medieval **Ravensburg** ⑦, where you can find a number of historic hostelries. Although the great baroque pilgrimage church of **Weingarten** ⑧ is only 5 km (3 mi) north of Ravensburg, allow a morning or an afternoon to do the magnificent structure justice. Return south to the lake and an overnight stay in **Meersburg** ⑤. Catch the ferry to **Konstanz** ⑩, on the opposite shore, and allow a full day and night to get to know this fascinating city. Devote the next day to the islands of **Mainau** ⑪ and sup in one of the ancient taverns of **Reichenau** ⑫; then head for **Radolfzell** ⑬, at the end of the peninsula that juts into the western end of the Bodensee. From there it's a short drive around the head of the lake to **Überlingen** ⑥, where you can easily relax in its balmy clime. A visit to the nearby pilgrimage church **Wallfahrtskirche**—a rococo masterpiece—is a marvelous finale to any Bodensee tour.

When to Tour the Bodensee

The Bodensee's temperate climate makes for pleasant weather from April to October. In spring orchard blossoms explode everywhere, and on Mainau, the "island of flowers," more than a million tulips, hyacinths, and narcissi burst into bloom. Holiday crowds come in summer, and autumn can be long and mellow. Some hotels and restaurants in the smaller resort towns close for the winter.

THE NORTHERN SHORE

There's a feeling here, in the midst of a peaceful Alpine landscape, that the Bodensee is a part of Germany and yet separated from it—which is literally the case in towns such as Lindau and Wasserburg, which sit in the lake tethered to land by causeways. At the northwestern finger of the lake, Überlingen, a beauty of a resort beached on a small inlet of water, attracts many vacationers as well as those restoring their health at spas. Clear days reveal the snowcapped mountains of Switzerland to the south and the peaks of the Austrian Vorarlberg to the east.

Lindau

❶ *180 km (112 mi) southwest of Munich.*

If not for its narrow causeway linking it with the mainland, ancient Lindau would be an island. On a hazy summer's day, the walls and roofs of Old Lindau seem to float on the shimmering lake. Little Lindau was made a Free Imperial City within the Holy Roman Empire in 1275. It had developed as a fishing settlement and then spent hundreds of years as a trading center along the route between the rich lands of Swabia and Italy. The *Lindauer Bote,* an important stagecoach service between Germany and Italy in the 18th and 19th centuries, was based here; Goethe traveled via this service on his first visit to Italy in 1786. The stagecoach was revived a few years ago and every June it sets off on its 10-day journey to Italy. You can book a seat through the Lindau tourist office.

As the German empire crumbled toward the end of the 18th century, battered by Napoléon's revolutionary armies, Lindau fell victim to competing political groups. It was ruled by the Austrian Empire before passing into Bavarian control in 1805. One of Lindau's striking landmarks on the inner harbor walls is a **seated lion,** the proud symbol of Bavaria. Carved from Bavarian marble and standing 20 ft high, the lion stares out across the lake from a massive plinth. Standing sentinel with the

Close-Up

THREE-DAY BIKE TOUR

THE BEST WAY to experience the Bodensee area is by bike. In three days you can cross the borders of three nations, and the only burn your thighs will suffer on the flat landscape is from the sun. You could start anywhere, but this tour will begin in Lindau at the southeastern corner of the lake. Book a room in Lindau for your third night, in Meersburg or Konstanz for the first night, and in Romanshorn, Switzerland for the second. Leave your baggage at the Lindau hotel or in a train station locker, bringing with you only what you can comfortably carry on your back (don't forget your bathing suit). A sign displaying a bicyclist with a blue back wheel will be your guide for the bike paths through all three countries. Even without the signs or map, the water is an easy point of reference.

Once out of Lindau, turn left on the mainland and in 4 km (2½ mi) take a spin around Wasserburg. After, continue onward through meadows and marshland. You'll pass the charming villages of Nonnenhorn, Kressbronn, Langenargen, and Eriskirch.

After Langenargen, which is 8 km (5 mi) from Wasserburg, Friedrichshafen is another 18 km to the northwest. Once in town, reserve an hour or two for the Zeppelin Museum. After Friedrichshafen the bicycle path runs along the main road for a few kilometers. Follow the sign to Immenstaad to get away from the traffic. Pass through the village and continue towards the village of Hagnau. After another 17 km (10½ mi) stay overnight in lovely Meersburg, rising early to catch the sunrise over the lake and the ferry to Konstanz.

When you come off the ferry, after approximately 110 yards, take a right turn into a small street that leads you along the shore to the flower island of Mainau. Return the same way past the ferry dock and continue straight ahead into a street parallel to the lake. This way brings you into Konstanz through the scenic "back entrance." Basically keep as close to the water as you can—you'll cross a bridge over the Rhine, go through the old part of town, and head back to the harbor. If you spend some time in Konstanz, set out south in the early afternoon again. In two minutes you'll be in the Swiss city of Kreuzlingen.

After 23 km (14 mi) you'll arrive in Romanshorn to spend the night. It's not a tourist destination, but try one of its two nice hotels, the Inseli (www.inseli.ch) or the Schloss Hotel Garni (www.hotelschloss-romanshorn.ch). If you need to return quickly to Lindau, take the ferry—the last one leaves Romanshorn at about 7:30 PM—to Friedrichshafen where you can board a train for Lindau. The whole journey from Romanshorn to Lindau will take two to three hours. Assuming you're still game for biking, however, leave Romanshorn as early in the morning as possible. After 9 km (5½ mi) you'll pass Arbon, another 7 km (4½ mi) and you'll cycle through Rorschach, 9 km (5½ mi) more and you come to the small town of Rheineck on the border of Austria. After the border there are several paths to follow—keep as close to the lake as possible. After a while you'll cross the Rhine again.

Bregenz, the capital city of Vorarlberg, is 20 km (12 mi) from the border. There are plenty of attractions here, such as the cable car that ascends 1,064 meters (3,870 ft) to a marvelous view of the lake and the broad Rhine Valley. If you're too pooped to bike the 9 km (5½ mi) back to Lindau, you can board a train with your bicycle in Bregenz. Trains depart every half hour until about 7 PM; the last one leaves around 9 PM. You can also ferry across the bay—the last one departs at 6:30 PM—which is the nicest way to arrive in Lindau.

seated lion is the **Neuer Leuchtturm** (New Lighthouse), across the inner harbor's passageway. At the harbor's edge is the **Alter Leuchtturm** (Old Lighthouse), firmly based on the weathered remains of the 13th-century city walls.

A maze of ancient streets leading from the harbor makes up the **Altstadt** (Old Town). Old half-timber and gable houses line its main street, pedestrians-only Maximilianstrasse. The **Altes Rathaus** (Old Town Hall; ✉ Maximilianstr.) is the finest of Lindau's handsome historical buildings. It was constructed between 1422 and 1436 in the midst of a vineyard and given a Renaissance face-lift 150 years later, though the original stepped gables remain. Emperor Maximilian I held an imperial diet here in 1496; a fresco on the south facade depicts a scene from this high point of local history. A part of the building that served as the town prison is identified by an ancient inscription enjoining the townsfolk "to turn aside from evil and learn to do good."

The **Barfüsserkirche** (Church of the Barefoot Pilgrims; ✉ Fischerg.), built from 1241 to 1270, is now Lindau's principal theater and the Gothic choir is a memorable setting for concerts. Ludwigstrasse and Fischergasse lead to a watchtower, once part of the original city walls. Pause in the little park behind it, the **Stadtgarten** (City Park). If it's early evening, you'll see the first gamblers of the night making for the neighboring casino.

The **Peterskirche** (St. Peter's Church; ✉ Schrannenpl.) is a solid Romanesque building, constructed in the 10th century and reputedly the oldest church in the Bodensee region. Step inside to see the frescoes by Hans Holbein the Elder (1465–1524), some of which depict scenes from the life of St. Peter, the patron saint of fishermen.

Lindau's **Marktplatz** (Market Square) is lined by a series of sturdy and attractive old buildings. The Gothic **Stephanskirche** (St. Stephen's Church) is simple and sparely decorated; the **Marienkirche** (St. Mary's Church) is exuberantly baroque.

The **Haus zum Cavazzen** home dates from the 18th century and is richly decorated with stucco and frescoes. Today it's the municipal art gallery and local history museum. ✉ *Am Marktpl. 6.* ☎ *08382/944–073.* 🎫 *€2.50.* ⏲ *Apr.–Oct., Tues.–Fri. and Sun. 11–5, Sat. 2–5.*

Dining and Lodging

$$$$ ★ ✕ **Restaurant Hoyerberg Schlössle.** A commanding terrace view across the lake to Bregenz and the Alps combined with elegant nouvelle cuisine makes this one of the best dining experiences in Lindau. The specialties are fish and game, which change seasonally, and there are prix-fixe menus of four and six courses; one offers lobster, noodles with white truffles and goose liver, and roast breast of squab. The decor features brick-trim arched windows, fresh flowers, and elegant high-back chairs. ✉ *Hoyerbergstr. 64,* ☎ *08382/25295. Reservations essential. AE, DC, MC, V. Closed Mon. and Feb. No lunch Tues.*

$$$$ ✕ **Restaurant Lanz.** Locals know the cuisine served in Anton Lanz's unpretentious house is top quality. Chef Lanz has received many awards for his regional and French recipes—one of his specialties is a four-course meal with self-raised crabs from his own stream. The rooms of the restaurant are spacious and elegant. Restaurant Lanz is in the little Allgäu village of Stockenweiler, 10 km (6 mi) from Lindau on B–12. ✉ *Hergensweiler-Stockenweiler 32,* ☎ *08388/99035. AE, MC, V. Closed Wed. and Thurs.; 2 wks after Pentecost.*

$–$$ ✕ **Gasthaus zum Sünfzen.** In the heart of the Old Town, the Gasthaus is an appealing old inn with small lead-glass windows and a simple wood-paneled interior. Entrées include venison from deer shot on forest hunts led by landlord Hans Grättinger, as well as fish caught locally and sausage from the restaurant's own butcher shop. Try either the spinach Spätzle or the Felchen fillet. The menu changes daily and seasonally. ✉ *Maximilianstr. 1,* ☎ *08382/5865. AE, MC, V. Closed Feb.*

$$–$$$$ ✕🏨 **Hotel Bayerischer Hof/Hotel Reutemann.** This is *the* address in town, a stately hotel directly on the edge of the lake, with a terrace lush with semitropical, long-flowering plants, trees, and shrubs. Most of the luxuriously appointed rooms have views of the lake and the Austrian and Swiss mountains beyond. Freshly caught pike perch is a highlight of the extensive menus in the stylish restaurants ($$–$$$$). If the hotel is full or can't provide the room you want, you'll be directed to the adjacent, slightly less expensive Hotel Reutemann, which has been under the same management and ownership for three generations. ✉ *Seepromenade, D–88131,* ☎ *08382/9150,* FAX *08382/915–591,* WEB *www.bayerischerhof-lindau.de. 98 rooms, 2 suites. Restaurant, bar, café, no a/c, pool, boating, bicycles, massage, sauna, meeting rooms. DC, MC, V.*

$$ 🏨 **Gasthof Engel.** Claiming to be the oldest inn in Lindau, the Engel traces its pedigree back to 1390. Tucked into one of the Old Town's ancient, narrow streets, the property creaks with history. Twisted oak beams are exposed inside and outside the terraced house. The bedrooms are simply furnished but comfortable. ✉ *Schafg. 4, D–88131,* ☎ *08382/5240,* FAX *08382/5644. 9 rooms, 7 with shower. Restaurant, no a/c, no room TVs. No credit cards. Closed Nov.*

$ 🏨 **Jugendherberge.** This well-run youth hostel is open to travelers up to 26 years old and families with at least one child under 18. Rooms have anywhere from one to six beds and a shower and toilet. There are also special family rooms. ✉ *Herbergsweg 11, D–88131,* ☎ *08382/96710,* FAX *08382/967–150,* WEB *www.djh.de. 65 rooms. Café, cafeteria, no a/c, no room phones, no room TVs, recreation room, laundry facilities. No credit cards.*

Nightlife and the Arts

You can play American and French roulette, black jack, and poker at Lindau's elegant **casino** (✉ Chelles Alle 1, ☎ 08382/27740), which was built in 1999. It's open weekdays 3 PM–2 AM, weekends 3 PM–3 AM. A dramatic floating stage supports orchestras and opera stars during the famous **Bregenzer Festspiele** (Bregenz Music Festival; ✉ Bregenz, ☎ 0043/5574–4076, WEB www.bregenzerfestspiele.com) from mid-July to the end of August. Make reservations well in advance. Bregenz is 8 mi from Lindau, on the other side of the bay.

Outdoor Activities and Sports

BIKING

You can rent bikes at **Fahrradstation** (✉ Im Hauptbahnhof, ☎ 08382/21261). Bikes cost €10 per day, and four days cost €30.

BOATING AND WINDSURFING

The best way to see Lindau is from the lake. Take one of the pleasure boats of the **Weisse Flotte** that leave Lindau's harbor five or six times a day for the 20-minute ride to Bregenz in Austria. These large boats carry up to 800 people on three decks. The round-trip costs €7.

The **Bodensee Yachtschule** (✉ Christoph Eychmüller Schiffswerfte 3, ☎ 08382/944–588), in Lindau, charters yachts and has one-week camp sessions for children. You can rent windsurfing boards at **Windsurfschule Kreitmeir** (✉ Strandbad Eichwald, ☎ 08382/23346, WEB www.bodensee-yachtschule.de).

Shopping

Biedermann (✉ Maximilianstr. 2, ☎ 08382/944–913) carries the expensive menswear and women's wear Collections Femmes et Hommes from Italy, as well as custom-made clothing, cashmere sweaters, and Italian shoes. A find for interior decorators, **Böhm** (✉ Maximilianstr. 21 and Krummg. 6, ☎ 08382/94880) consists of three old houses full of lamps, mirrors, precious porcelain, and elegant furniture. Böhm will deliver worldwide. Michael Zeller's reputable shop, **The Colony** (✉ Binderg. 7, ☎ 08382/93020, WEB www.zeller.de), sells watercolors, engravings, prints, silver, and furniture. Michael Zeller also organizes the celebrated, twice-yearly Internationale Bodensee-Kunstauktion (art auction) in May and October. Smaller auctions are held during the Christmas season and in February and June.

Wasserburg

❷ *6 km (4 mi) west of Lindau.*

Wasserburg means "water castle," which describes exactly what this enchanting island town once was—a fortress, built by the St. Gallen Monastery in 924. The later owners, the counts of Montfort zu Tettnang, sold the fortress to the Fugger family of Augsburg to pay off mounting debts. The Fuggers in turn became so impoverished they couldn't even afford to maintain the drawbridge that connected the castle with the shore. Instead they built a causeway. In the 18th century the castle passed into the hands of the Habsburgs, and in 1805 the Bavarian government took it over.

Wasserburg has some of the most photographed sights of the Bodensee: the yellow, stair-gabled presbytery; the fishermen's St. Georg Kirche, with its onion dome; and the little Malhaus museum, with the castle, Schloss Wasserburg, in the background.

Lodging

$$ **Hotel Lipprandt.** This modern hotel has a long, lush lawn, which leads to the water's edge. Lay out on a recliner or enjoy the view from a room with a balcony. Meals are served only in the evening and only for house guests. ✉ *Halbinselstr. 63–67, D–88142,* ☎ *08382/98760,* FAX *08382/887–245,* WEB *www.hotel-lipprandt.de. 36 rooms. Restaurant, no a/c, pool, hot tub, beach. MC, V. Closed Nov.*

$$ **Hotel zum Lieben Augustin am See.** On the edge of the lake and just before the peninsula, five buildings make up this hotel. You can choose not only between lake or garden views, but also between rooms, suites, or apartments. The hotel has a private beach and bicycles for rent. ✉ *Halbinselstr. 70, D–88142,* ☎ *08382/9800,* FAX *08382/887–082. 40 rooms, 4 apartments, 4 suites. Restaurant, no a/c, pool, hot tub, beach, bicycles, meeting rooms. DC, MC, V. Closed Jan., Feb.*

Langenargen

❸ *8 km (5 mi) west of Wasserburg.*

The small, pretty town of Langenargen is a typical Bodensee summer resort, but because it's not as spectacular as nearby Wasserburg, there are practically no day-trippers in sight. If you walk along the shore, you'll come across the region's most unusual castle, Schloss Montfort.

Schloss Montfort (Montfort Castle)—named for the original owners, the counts of Montfort-Werdenberg—was a conventional enough medieval fortification until the 19th century, when it was rebuilt in pseudo-Moorish style by its new owner, King Wilhelm I of Württemberg. If you can, see it from a passenger ship on the lake; the castle is especially memorable in the early morning or late afternoon, when the softened, watery light gives additional mystery to its outline. These days the castle houses a café, restaurant, and disco. Its tower can be climbed. ✉ *Untere Seestr. 5.* 🎫 *Tower €1.* ⏲ *Easter–Oct., daily 9–5.*

The parish church of **St. Martin** (✉ Marktpl. 1) was built in 1718 by Anton III of Montfort and belongs to the great churches of the Barockstrasse. The painting above the organ is presumed to be the work of the baroque painter Franz Anton Maulbertsch, born in Langenargen, who had his great successes in Vienna.

Friedrichshafen

❹ *10 km (6 mi) west of Langenargen.*

Named for its founder, King Friedrich I of Württemberg, Friedrichshafen is a young town (dating to 1811). In an area otherwise given over to resort towns and agriculture, Friedrichshafen played a central role in Germany's aeronautic tradition, which saw the development of the zeppelin airship before World War I and the Dornier seaplanes in the 1920s and '30s. The zeppelins were once launched from a floating hangar on the lake and the Dornier water planes were tested here. The city was almost wiped off the map by World War II air raids on its factories. It was rebuilt after the war and today is home to international firms such as EADS (airplanes, rockets) and ZF (gearshifts).

Graf Zeppelin (Ferdinand Graf von Zeppelin) was born across the lake in Konstanz, but Friedrichshafen was where on July 2, 1900, his first "airship"—the LZ 1—was launched. The fascinating story of the zeppelin airships is told in the ★ **Zeppelin Museum,** which holds the world's most significant collection of artifacts pertaining to airship history in its 43,000 square ft of exhibition space. In a wing of the restored Bauhaus **Friedrichshafen Hafenbahnhof** (Harbor railway station), the main attraction is the reconstruction of an 108-ft-long section of the legendary *Hindenburg,* the LZ 129. Here you can get a passenger's perspective on one of the great zeppelins. Climb aboard the airship via a retractable stairway and stroll past the authentically furnished passenger rooms, the lounges, and the dining room. The illusion of traveling in a zeppelin is followed by exhibits on the history and technology of airship aviation. Take a moment to visit the museum shop. ✉ *Seestr. 22,* ☎ *07541/38010,* WEB *www.zeppelin-museum.de.* 🎫 *€6.50.* ⏲ *May–Oct., Tues.–Sun. 10–6; Nov.–Apr., Tues.–Sun. 10–5.*

Since 1999, **Zeppelin Luftschifftechnik** has been operating new zeppelins in Friedrichshafen. You can board the Zeppelin NT (New Technology—smaller and not inflammable) for either an air journey or on its mooring mast at the airport. ✉ *Allmannsweilerstr. 132,* ☎ *07541/202–516,* WEB *www.zeppelin-nt.com.*

Schloss Hofen (Hofen Castle), a short walk from town along the lakeside promenade, is a small palace that served as the summer residence of Württemberg kings until 1918. Today Duke Friedrich von Württemberg lives here with his family. The palace was formerly a priory—its foundations date from the 11th century. You can visit the adjoining priory **church,** a splendid example of regional baroque architecture. The swirling white stucco of the interior was executed by the Schmuzer family from Wessobrunn whose master craftsman, Franz Schmuzer, also created the priory church's magnificent marble altar.

From Friedrichshafen you can go directly to Romanshorn in Switzerland on a car ferry that leaves every hour from the harbor. The 40-minute trip offers an impressive view from the upper passenger deck:

Swiss mountains ahead; Austrian mountains on your left; and the rolling green hills of Germany behind you. If you take your car, go one way by boat, and then return by driving from Romanshorn to Bregenz in Austria, then past Lindau, and back to Friedrichshafen. Car and driver one-way costs €18; an extra person costs €5.40. Romanshorn, by the way, has a grassy public beach.

Dining and Lodging

$–$$ ✕ **Lukullum.** Students, businesspeople, and guests from the nearby top hotels rub elbows at this lively, novel restaurant. The friendly service keeps up with the pace of the socializing. If you're by yourself grab a seat at the bar that stretches nearly the length of the room. Partitioned areas named after tourist regions allow privacy for groups or families, and another room has a more traditional setup of tables. The dishes are good and basic, with surprising international touches. ✉ *Friedrichstr. 21,* ☎ *07541/6818. AE, DC, MC, V. No lunch.*

$$ ★ ✕🏨 **Ringhotel Buchhorner Hof.** This traditional hotel near the train station, now part of the Ring group, has been run by the same family since it opened in 1870. Hunting trophies on the walls, leather armchairs, and Turkish rugs decorate the public areas; bedrooms are large and comfortable. The restaurant ($$$) is plush and subdued, with delicately carved chairs and mahogany-panel walls. It offers a choice of menus with dishes such as pork medallions, perch fillet, and lamb chops. ✉ *Friedrichstr. 33, D–88045,* ☎ *07541/2050,* FAX *07541/32663.* WEB *www.buchhorn.de. 87 rooms, 4 suites, 2 apartments. Restaurant, bar, no a/c in some rooms, some in-room data ports, some in-room faxes, cable TV, miniature golf, gym, massage, sauna, bicycles, meeting rooms, some pets allowed. AE, DC, MC, V.*

$$ ✕🏨 **Ringhotel Krone.** This Bavarian-theme hotel made up of four buildings is in the Schnetzenhausen district's semirural surroundings, 4 mi from the center of town. You can roam the area on a bike rented from the hotel. All rooms have balconies. The restaurant ($$) specializes in game dishes and fish. ✉ *Untere Mühlbachstr. 1, D–88045,* ☎ *07541/4080,* FAX *07541/43601,* WEB *www.ringhotel-krone.de. 115 rooms. Restaurant, bar, no a/c in some rooms, some in-room data ports, 4 tennis courts, pool, gym, hot tub, sauna, bicycles, bowling, pets allowed, meeting rooms. AE, DC, MC, V.*

$ 🏨 **Hotel Wohlwender.** If a hotel is simply a place for you to sleep, choose this small, clean, inexpensive one. You simply get the basics here. There is a restaurant, but you're better off somewhere with more atmosphere. ✉ *Olgastr. 64, D–88046,* ☎ *07541/70780,* FAX *07540/707-828. 14 rooms. Restaurant, no a/c, some pets allowed. AE, MC, V.*

Nightlife and the Arts

College students and a mostly young crowd raise their glasses and voices above the din at **Cafebar Belushi** (✉ Montfortstr. 3, ☎ 07541/32531).

Friedrichhafen's **Graf-Zeppelin-Haus** (✉ Olgastr. 20, ☎ 07541/72071) is a modern convention center on the lakeside promenade, a seven-minute walk from the train station. It is also a cultural center, where musicals, light opera, and classical as well as pop-rock concerts take place several times a week.

Shopping

Most of the town's shops line the pedestrian zone near the harbor. **Christina Teske** (✉ Seestr. 1, ☎ 07541/75356) carries women's and men's clothing. The gift shop **Ebe** (✉ Buchhornpl., ☎ 07541/26036) sells handmade candles, dolls, and postcards.

Meersburg

5 *18 km (11 mi) west of Friedrichshafen.*

The most romantic way to approach Meersburg is from the lake. Seen from the water on a summer afternoon with the sun slanting low, the steeply terraced town can seem floodlighted, like an elaborate stage setting. (Meersburg is well aware of its too-good-to-be-true charm—some may find the gusto with which it has embraced tourism crass, and the town can get crowded on weekends.) If you arrive by ferry from Lindau, Konstanz, Überlingen, or Mainau, you'll step ashore in the Unterstadt (Lower Town). It's about a 150-ft climb to the Oberstadt (Upper Town), but the walk between the two halves is not arduous as you head up Steigstrasse, a street lined with shops and restaurants. The market square is ringed by such historic half-timber structures as the medieval Rathaus, and with no cars allowed, a sense of timelessness is preserved.

★ Watching majestically over the town and the lake far below is the **Altes Schloss** (Old Castle), Germany's oldest inhabited castle and one of the most impressive. Meersburg is said to have been founded in 628 by Dagobert, king of the Franks, who supposedly laid the castle's first stone. The massive central tower, with walls 10-ft thick, is named after him. In 1526 the Catholic bishop of Konstanz moved into the castle after he was thrown out by newly converted Protestant Konstanz. Bishops remained here until the middle of the 18th century, when they built themselves what they felt to be a more suitable residence—the baroque Neues Schloss. Plans to tear down the Altes Schloss in the early 19th century were shelved when it was taken over by Baron Joseph von Lassberg, a man much intrigued by the castle's medieval romance. He turned it into a home for like-minded poets and artists, among them his sister-in-law, Annette von Droste-Hülshoff (1797–1848), one of Germany's finest poets. The Altes Schloss is still private property, but much of it can be visited, including the richly furnished rooms where Droste-Hülshoff lived and the chamber where she died, as well as the imposing knights' hall, the minstrels' gallery, and the sinister dungeons. The **Altes Schloss Museum** (Old Castle Museum) contains a fascinating collection of weapons and armor, including a rare set of medieval jousting equipment. ☎ *07532/80000.* 🎫 *€5.* ⏲ *Mar.–Oct., daily 9–6:30; Nov.–Feb., daily 10–6.*

The spacious and elegant **Neues Schloss** (New Castle) is directly across from its predecessor. It was built partly by Balthasar Neumann, the leading German architect of the 18th century, and partly by an Italian, Franz Anton Bagnato. Neumann's work is most obvious in the stately sweep of the grand double staircase, with its intricate grillwork and heroic statues. The interior's other standout is the glittering **Spiegelsaal** (Hall of Mirrors). In an unlikely combination of 18th-century grace and 20th-century technology, the first floor of the palace houses the **Dornier Museum,** which traces the history of the German aircraft and aerospace industries. ☎ *07532/414–071; 07532/431–110 for tours in English.* 🎫 *€3.* ⏲ *Apr.–Oct., daily 10–1 and 2–6.*

Sunbathed, south-facing Meersburg and the neighboring towns have been the center of the Bodensee wine trade for centuries. You can pay your respects to the noble profession in the **Weinbau Museum** (Vineyard Museum). A barrel capable of holding 50,000 liters (about the same number of quarts) and an immense wine press dating from 1607 are highlights of the collection. ✉ *Vorburg. 11,* ☎ *07532/431–110.* 🎫 *€1.50.* ⏲ *Apr.–Oct., Tues., Fri., and Sun. 2–6.*

An idyllic retreat almost hidden among the vineyards, the Fürstenhäusle was built in 1640 by a local vintner and later used as a holiday home by poet Annette von Droste-Hülshoff. It's now the **Droste Museum,** containing many of her personal possessions and giving a vivid sense of Meersburg in her time. ✉ *Stettenerstr. 9, east of Obertor, the town's north gate,* ☎ *07532/6088.* 🎫 *€2.50.* ⏲ *Easter–mid-Oct., Mon.–Sat. 10–12:30 and 2–5, Sun. 2–5.*

Dining and Lodging

$$–$$$$ ✕ **Winzerstube zum Becher.** This traditional restaurant near the new castle has been in the Benz family for three generations. If you want to try regional dishes and especially fresh fish from the lake, this is the place. A popular meat entrée is *canard a l'orange.* Do try the white wine from the restaurant's own vineyard. Booking ahead is advisable, as the three wood-panel rooms have only a few tables each. ✉ *Höllg. 4,* ☎ *07532/9009. AE, DC, V. Closed Jan. and Mon.*

$ ✕ **Café da Bruno.** After walking about half-way up the steep Steigstrasse between the lower and upper parts of town, you can take a short break at this self-serve pizzeria. Besides pizza, there's also inexpensive German fare. A glass of Lambrusco, an Italian wine, goes well with a slice. ✉ *Höllstr. 27,* ☎ *07532/414–578. MC, V. Closed Nov.–Apr.*

$ ✕ **Cafe Podium.** Most people take in the beautiful lake view over a quick snack of coffee and cake, or an omelette or sandwich. A large parking lot across the street makes the café both a scenic and convenient stop for those coming or going to the car ferry. ✉ *Unteruhldingerstr. 3,* ☎ *no phone. Closed Nov.–Mar.*

$$–$$$ ✕🏨 **Romantik Hotel Residenz am See.** This tastefully modern hotel was completely rebuilt and reopened in May 2001. Most of the elegant rooms face the lake, but the most quiet ones look out onto a vineyard. The restaurant has a warm atmosphere with earthy, terra-cotta tone walls and floor to ceiling windows. Fish is the specialty—try the pike perch in season. The vegetarian menu is a pleasant surprise. Any guilt you feel at disturbing the form of your artfully composed desert will quickly dissipate once you start tasting it. ✉ *Uferpromenade 11, D–88709,* ☎ *07532/80040,* FAX *07532/800–470,* WEB *www.romantikhotels.com. 23 rooms. Restaurant, bar, no a/c, meeting rooms. AE, DC, MC, V.*

$$ ✕🏨 **Löwen.** This centuries-old, ivy-clad tavern on Meersburg's market square is a local landmark. Its welcoming restaurant ($$–$$$$) serves such regional specialties as Spätzle and Maultaschen, and, in season, venison and *Spargel* (asparagus) find their way onto the menu. Guest rooms are cozily furnished and have their own sitting corners, and some have genuine Biedermeier furniture. ✉ *Marktpl. 2, D–88709,* ☎ *07532/43040,* FAX *07532/430–410,* WEB *www.hotel-loewen-meersburg.de. 21 rooms. Restaurant, Weinstube, no a/c, bicycles, meeting rooms, some pets allowed, no-smoking rooms. AE, DC, MC, V.*

$$ 🏨 **Drei Stuben.** The interior decorators have seen to every imaginable detail in this restored 17th-century town house. If you have a choice, take a look at the rooms before booking as they are all done in different styles. Some have antique furniture; others are modern with paintings to match. ✉ *Kirchstr. 7, D-88709,* ☎ *07532/80090,* FAX *07532/1367. 25 rooms. Restaurant, bar, no a/c, in-room data ports, meeting rooms, some pets allowed. MC, V. Closed Dec. and Jan.*

$–$$ 🏨 **Zum Bären.** Built in 1605 and incorporating 13th-century Gothic foundations, the Bären was an important staging point for Germany's first postal service. The ivy-smothered facade, with its characteristic steeple, hasn't changed much over the centuries, but interior comforts certainly have. Some rooms are furnished with Bodensee antiques and brightly painted rustic wardrobes. If you have the chance, book Room 23 or 13. Both have semicircular alcoves with two overstuffed armchairs and six windows overlooking the market place. ✉ *Marktpl. 11, D–88709,* ☎ *07532/43220,* FAX *07532/432–244. 17 rooms. Restaurant, no a/c, some pets allowed. No credit cards. Closed Dec.–Feb.*

$ **Gästehaus am Hafen.** This family-run, half-timber pension is in the middle of the Old Town, near the harbor. The rooms are small, but do have refrigerators, and still room for a child's bed, if needed. There's a place to store bikes as well. ✉ *Spitalg. 3,* ☎ *07532/7069,* FAX *07532/7789. 7 rooms. No a/c, refrigerators, no room phones. No credit cards.*

Nightlife and the Arts

The Spiegelsaal (Hall of Mirrors) of the Neues Schloss is the magnificent setting for the annual **international chamber music festival** (☎ 07532/431–112).

Outdoor Activities and Sports

You can rent rowboats and paddle boats in the harbor, and just west of town are rocky beaches for swimming and sunbathing. The heavenly, hot spring–heated **Beheiztes Freibad** (heated outdoor pool) east of the harbor has lots of grass, a little sand, three pools, a thermal bath (33°C [91.4°F]), a sauna, minigolf, and a volleyball court. ✉ *Uferpromenade,* ☎ *07532/414–060.* €3. ⏲ *Mar.–Oct., daily 9–8.*

Shopping

Just at the entrance to Schlossplatz—the square in front of the Neues Schloss—are a few nice shops. **Ulmer** (✉ Schlosspl. 3, ☎ 07532/5788) has well-selected gifts. Their specialty is children's clothes, including charming lederhosen for kids. **Benz** (✉ Höllg. 2, ☎ 07532/9965) sells handmade pottery.

En Route As you proceed northwest along the lake's shore, a settlement of **Pfahlbauten** (Pile Dwellings) sticks out of the lake—a reconstructed village of Stone Age and Bronze Age dwellings built on stilts. This is how the original lake dwellers lived, surviving off the fish that swam outside their humble huts. The nearby **Pfahlbauten Freilichtmuseum** (Open-Air Museum of German Prehistory) contains actual finds excavated in the area. ✉ *Strandpromenade 6, Unteruhldingen,* ☎ *07556/8543.* €5. ⏲ *Apr.–Oct., daily 8–6; Nov.–Mar., daily 9–5.*

★ Just northwest of Unteruhldingen the **Wallfahrtskirche Birnau** (Pilgrimage Church) overlooks the lake from a small hill. The church was built by the masterful architect Peter Thumb between 1746 and 1750. Its simple exterior consists of plain gray-and-white plaster and a tapering clock-tower spire above the main entrance; the interior, by contrast, is overwhelmingly rich, full of movement, light, and color. It's hard to single out highlights from such a profusion of ornament, but seek out the *Honigschlecker* (Honey Sucker), a gold-and-white cherub beside the altar, dedicated to St. Bernard of Clairvaux, "whose words are sweet as honey" (it's the last altar on the right as you face the high altar). The cherub is sucking honey from his finger, which he's just pulled out of a beehive. The fanciful spirit of this dainty punning is continued in the small squares of glass set into the pink screen that rises high above the main altar; the gilt dripping from the walls; the swaying, swooning statues; and the swooping figures on the ceiling. ✉ *Birnau.* ⏲ *Daily 7–7.*

Überlingen

❻ *13 km (8 mi) west of Meersburg, 24 km (15 mi) west of Friedrichshafen.*

This Bodensee resort has an attractive waterfront and an almost Mediterranean flair. It's midway along the north shore of the Überlingersee, a narrow finger of the Bodensee that points to the northwest.

Überlingen is ancient, a Free Imperial City since the 13th century, with no fewer than seven of its original city gates and towers left, as well as substantial portions of the old city walls. What was once the moat is now a grassy walkway, with the walls of the Old Town towering on one side and the Stadtpark stretching away on the other. The **Stadtpark** (city park) cultivates rare plants and has a famous collection of cacti. The heart of the city is the Münsterplatz.

★ The huge **Nikolausmünster** (Church of St. Nicholas) is disproportionate to the town's small size. It was built between 1512 and 1563 on the site of at least two previous churches. The interior is all Gothic solemnity and massiveness, with a lofty stone-vaulted ceiling and high, pointed arches lining the nave. The single most remarkable feature is not Gothic at all but opulently Renaissance—the massive high altar, carved from lime wood that looks almost like ivory. Statues, curlicues, and columns jostle for space on it. ✉ *Münsterpl.*

Inside the late-Gothic **Altes Rathaus** (Old Town Hall) is a high point of Gothic decoration, the **Rathaussaal**, or council chamber. Its most striking feature amid the riot of carving is the series of figures representing the states of the Holy Roman Empire. There's a naïveté to the figures—their beautifully carved heads are all just a little too large, their legs a little too spindly—that makes them easy to love. ✉ *Münsterpl.* 🎫 *Free.* ⏲ *Apr.–mid-Oct., weekdays 9–noon and 2:30–5, Sat. 9–noon.*

The **Städtische Museen** (City Museum) houses exhibits tracing Bodensee history and a vast collection of dollhouses. ✉ *Krummebergstr. 30,* ☎ *07531/991–079.* 🎫 *€2.* ⏲ *Apr.–Oct., Tues.–Sat. 9–12:30 and 2–5, Sun. 10–3.*

Dining and Lodging

$$ ✕🏨 **Romantik Hotel Johanniter Kreuz.** The setting is a small village 3 km (2 mi) to the north of Überlingen. The old part of the hotel dates from the 17th century and is truly romantic—half-timber, with a huge fireplace in the center of the restaurant ($–$$$). In the modern annex you can relax on your room's balcony. An 18-hole golf course overlooking the lake is just a 1½ km (1mi) away. ✉ *Johanniterweg 11, Andelshofen D–88662,* ☎ *07551/61091,* FAX *07551/67336,* WEB *www.romantikhotels.com. 25 rooms. Restaurant, bar, no a/c, some in-room data ports, hot tub, sauna, massage, meeting rooms. DC, MC, V.*

$$ ✕🏨 **Schäpfle.** This ivy-covered hotel is in the center of town, hardly 65 yards from the lake. The charm of the old house has been preserved and supplemented through time. In the hallways are quaint furniture and even an old Singer sewing machine painted with flowers. The rooms are not old-looking at all, and feel all the more welcoming due to the light, Danish-style farm furniture. Guests and Überlingen residents congregate in the comfortable taproom, where the regional and international dishes are reasonably priced ($–$$$). If you order the Felchen, try it with Müller-Thurgau, Überlingen's dry, white wine. ✉ *Jakob-Kessenringstr. 14,* ☎ *07551/63494,* FAX *07551/67695. 17 rooms. Restaurant, no a/c, some pets allowed, no-smoking floor. No credit cards.*

$–$$ ✕🏨 **Landgasthof zum Adler.** You'll appreciate the unpretentiousness of this rustic country inn in a small village a few miles north of Überlingen. It has a blue-and-white half-timber facade, scrubbed wooden floors, and thick down comforters on the beds. The food ($–$$$) is simple and delicious; trout is a specialty. ✉ *Hauptstr. 44, D–88662 Üb–Lippertsreute,* ☎ *07553/82550,* FAX *07553/825–570. 17 rooms. Restaurant, no a/c, meeting rooms, some pets allowed. No credit cards. Closed 2 wks in Nov.*

$$ 🏨 **Bad Hotel mit Villa Seeburg.** This stately hotel has the double advantage of being both on the lake and in the center of town. The spare, modern rooms are done in crisp whites and creams. Try to get a room looking toward the park and the lake, even if they are a bit more expensive. ✉ *Christophstr. 2,* ☎ *07551/8370,* FAX *07551/837–100,* WEB *www.bad-hotel-ueberlingen.de. 62 rooms. Restaurant, bar, no a/c, meeting rooms. AE, MC, V. Restaurant closed Jan.–Mar. 14.*

Nightlife and the Arts

At the end of August organ concerts in the Nikolausmünster make up the **Überlinger Orgelsommer.**

Shopping

It must be the atmosphere of Überlingen that makes artists come, work, and live here—there are more than 20 ateliers and artist shops in town—the tourist office has a brochure that lists them. **Galerie Tschirschky** (✉ Turmg. 9, ☎ 07551/308797) has a fine selection of exquisite china ware, all handpainted by the proprietor at reasonable prices. **Holzer** (✉ Turmg. 8, ☎ 07551/61525) is the studio of a master craftsman of gold jewelry.

THE UPPER SWABIAN BAROQUE ROAD

From Friedrichshafen Highway B–30 leads north along the valley of the little River Schussen and links up with one of Germany's less-known but most attractive scenic routes. The *Oberschwäbische Barockstrasse* (Upper Swabian Baroque Road) follows a rich series of baroque churches and abbeys, including Germany's largest baroque church, in Weingarten.

Ravensburg

❼ *20 km (12 mi) north of Friedrichshafen.*

Ravensburg once competed with Augsburg and Nürnberg for economic supremacy in southern Germany. The Thirty Years' War put an end to the city's hopes by reducing it to little more than a medieval backwater. The city's loss proved fortuitous only in that many of its original features have remained much as they were when built. Fourteen of the town gates and towers survive, for example, and the Altstadt is among the best-preserved in Germany.

That ecclesiastical and commercial life were never entirely separate in medieval towns is evident in the former **Karmeliterklosterkirche** (Carmelite Monastery Church), once part of a 14th-century monastery and now a Protestant church. The stairs on the west side of the church's chancel lead to the meeting room of the Ravensburger Gesellschaft (the Ravensburg Society), an organization of linen merchants established in 1400. The linen trade was largely responsible for the town's rapid economic growth.

Marienplatz, the central square, has many old buildings that recall Ravensburg's wealthy years: the late-Gothic **Rathaus,** with a Renaissance bay window; the 14th-century **Kornhaus** (Granary), once the corn exchange for all of Upper Swabia; the 15th-century **Waaghaus** (Weighing House), the town's weighing station and central warehouse, incorporating a tower where the watchman had his lookout; and the colorfully frescoed **Lederhaus,** once the headquarters of the city's leather workers.

One of Ravensburg's **defensive towers** is visible from Marienplatz, the **Grüner Turm** (Green Tower), so called for its green tiles; many are the 14th-century originals. Another stout defense tower is the massive

Obertor (Upper Tower), the oldest gate in the city walls. From it you can see one of the most curious of the city's towers, the **Mehlsack**, or Flour Sack Tower (because of its bulk and the original whitewash exterior), 170 ft high and standing on the highest point of the city.

Ravensburg's true parish church, the **Liebfrauenkirche** (Church of Our Lady), is a 14th-century structure, elegantly simple on the outside but almost entirely rebuilt inside. Some of the original stained glass remains, however, as does the heavily gilt altar. In a side altar is a copy of a carved Madonna, the *Schutzmantelfrau*; the late 14th-century original is in Berlin's Dahlem Museum. ✉ *Kirchstr. 18.* ⊙ *Daily 7–7.*

Ravensburg is a familiar name to all jigsaw-puzzle fans, because its eponymous Ravensburg publishing house produces the world's largest selection of puzzles, in addition to many other children's games. The history of the jigsaw puzzle gets put together in the company's **puzzle museum.** ✉ *Markstr. 26,* ☎ *0751/860.* *Free.* ⊙ *Thurs. 2–6.*

Ravensburger Spieleland is an amusement park designed for small children located 10 km (6 mi) from Ravensburg, in the direction of Lindau. Entrance is free to children on their birthday. ✉ *Liebenau–Am Hangenwald 1, Meckenbeuren,* ☎ *07542/4000 or 07542/400–101,* WEB *www.spieleland.com.* *€17.* ⊙ *Apr.–May, Sept.–early Nov., daily 10–5; June–Aug. 10–6.*

Dining and Lodging

$–$$ ✕ **Cafe-Restaurant Central.** The ground-floor café serves good pastries, as well as snacks and wines by the glass. If you want more variety, climb the stairs for Italian cuisine at the restaurant on the second floor. ✉ *Marienpl. 48,* ☎ *0751/32533. MC, V.*

$$ ★ ✕ **Romantikhotel Waldhorn.** This historic hostelry has been in the Dressel/Bouley family for more than 150 years. Suites and rooms in the main building overlook the square. Rooms in the annex have views into the quiet gardens. The menu ($$–$$$$) is prepared by Albert Bouley, fifth-generation proprietor and chef. In the dark-wood–paneled dining room you can enjoy the seven-course Waldhorn menu. Albert Bouley also minds the kitchen of Rebleute, around the corner on Schulgasse 15. The setting, an old guild hall with a beautiful *Tonnendecke* (barrel ceiling), serves more regional (and less expensive) specialties. ✉ *Marienpl. 15, D–88212,* ☎ *0751/36120,* FAX *0751/361–2100,* WEB *www.waldhorn.de. 30 rooms, 3 suites, 7 apartments. Restaurant, bar, no a/c, in-room data ports, meeting rooms, some pets allowed. AE, DC, MC, V. Restaurant closed Sun. and Mon.*

$ ✕ **Gasthof Ochsen.** The Ochsen is a typical, family-owned Swabian inn, and the personable Kimpfler family extends a warm welcome. If you have a choice, choose room number 2, which has three windows overlooking the lively scene (in summer, especially) of the Marktplatz. When checking in, reserve a table for dinner, as the restaurant ($–$$) can often book up. This is the place to try Maultaschen and *Zwiebelrostbraten* (well-done steak with lots of onions). If you know some German and yet don't understand a word of what the locals are saying at the next table, its Swabian, the regional dialect. ✉ *Eichelstr. 17, just off Marienpl.,* ☎ *0751/25480,* FAX *0751/352–5350. 15 rooms. Restaurant, no room phones, meeting rooms, some pets allowed. MC.*

Weingarten

8 *5 km (3 mi) north of Ravensburg.*

Weingarten is famous Germany-wide for its huge and hugely impressive pilgrimage church, which you see up on a hill from miles away, long before you get to the town.

At 220 ft high and more than 300 ft long, **Weingarten Basilica** is the largest baroque church in Germany, the basilica of one of the oldest and most venerable convents in the country, founded in 1056 by the wife of Guelph II. The Guelph dynasty ruled large areas of Upper Swabia, and generations of family members lie buried in the church. The majestic edifice was renowned because of the little vial it possesses, said to contain drops of Christ's blood. First mentioned by Charlemagne, the vial passed to the convent in 1094, entrusted to its safekeeping by the Guelph queen Juditha, sister-in-law of William the Conqueror. At a stroke Weingarten became one of Germany's foremost pilgrimage sites. On the Friday after Ascension, the anniversary of the day the relic was entrusted to the convent, a huge procession of pilgrims headed by 2,000 horsemen (many local farmers breed horses just for this occasion) wends its way to the basilica. It was decorated by leading early 18th-century German and Austrian artists: stucco by Franz Schmuzer, ceiling frescoes by Cosmas Damian Asam, and a Donato Frisoni altar—one of the most breathtakingly ornate in Europe, with nearly 80-ft-high towers on either side. The organ, installed by Josef Gabler between 1737 and 1750, is among the largest in the country. ⏲ *Daily 8–6.*

If you want to learn about early Germans—residents from the 6th, 7th, and 8th centuries whose graves are just outside town—visit the **Alamannenmuseum** in the Kornhaus, at one time a granary. Archaeologists discovered the hundreds of Alamanni graves in the 1950s. ✉ *Karlstr. 28.* 🎟 *Free.* ⏲ *Mar.–Oct. and Dec.–Jan., Wed. and weekends 3–5.*

Steinhausen

33 km (19 mi) north of Weingarten on the B–30.

Follow a visit to the Weingarten pilgrimage basilica with a detour to Steinhausen. As you drive toward Bad Schussenried through forests and fields, a white, light baroque-rococo church will come into view in the distance. Only as you come closer can you see that the church is surrounded by half a dozen houses, mostly farms, all of them less than half the size of the church. Dominikus Zimmermann built the charming late-baroque church in 1728–33. The interior forms an oval, bordered by 10 slender pillars. The walls are simply white, but the vaulted ceilings foam over with color and decoration. The frescoes glorify the life of the Virgin. If you look closely, you can see that the artist included some birds and animals of the area in his sculptures and paintings.

A local brewery in nearby Bad Schussenried runs the **Schussenried Bierkrugmuseum** (Beer-Mug Museum), with more than 1,000 exhibits of mugs spanning five centuries. On the second floor is a souvenir shop with the right gift for the beer drinker back home. ✉ *Wilhelm-Schussen-Str. 12,* ☎ *07583/40411.* 🎟 *€2.50.*

Tettnang

❾ *13 km (8 mi) south of Ravensburg on the B–467.*

Looking at Tettnang from the south, one sees practically nothing of the small town but the Neues Schloss, former ancestral home of the counts of Montfort zu Tettnang. By 1780 the dynasty had fallen on such hard times that it ceded the town to the Habsburgs for hard cash, and 25 years later it passed to the Bavarian Wittelsbachs.

The **Neues Schloss** (New Castle) is an extravagant baroque palace that was built in the early 18th century, burned down in 1753, and then partially rebuilt before the Montfort finances ran dry. Enough remains, however, to give some idea of the rulers' former wealth and ostentatious lifestyle. The palace is open only for tours. Call ahead to arrange for an English-speaking guide. ☏ *07542/953–839.* 🎫 €2. ⏲ *Tours in German Apr.–Oct., daily 10:30, 2:30, and 4.*

OFF THE BEATEN PATH **HOPFENMUSEUM TETTNANG** (Tettnang Hops Museum) – If you're a beer drinker, you've probably already tasted a product of the Tettnang area, because Tettnang is the second-biggest hops-growing area in Germany and exports most of its hops to the United States. This museum dedicated to brewing is in the tiny village of Siggenweiler. ✉ *Siggenweiler,* ☏ *07542/952–206.* ⏲ *May–Oct., Tues.–Sun. 2–5.*

Dining

$–$$$ ✕ **Gasthof Krone.** This traditional German Gaststube has wood paneling, a *Stammtisch* (where the regulars sit), and good, solid German food. If it's hunting season, try the game. Owned by the Tauscher family, the Gasthof only serves beer from their own brewery, behind the restaurant. To visit the brewery and get explanations in English of how a small German brewery operates, English speakers at the tourist office may be able to oblige you. Call 07542/953–839 in advance. ✉ *Bärenpl. 7,* ☏ *07542/7452. No credit cards.*

AROUND THE BODANRÜCK PENINSULA

The immense Bodensee owes its name to a small, insignificant town, Bodman, on the Bodanrück Peninsula, which is at the northwestern edge of the lake. The area's most popular destinations, Konstanz and Mainau, are reachable by ferry from Meersburg. That's by far the most romantic way to cross the lake, although a main road (the B–31, then the B–34, and finally the B–33) skirts the eastern side of the Bodensee and ends its German journey at Konstanz.

Konstanz

⑩ *A ½-hr ferry ride from Meersburg.*

The university town of Konstanz is the largest on the Bodensee; it straddles the Rhine as it flows out of the lake, placing itself both on the Bodanrück Peninsula and the Swiss side of the lake. Because of its location, Konstanz suffered no wartime bombing—the Allies were unwilling to risk the inadvertent bombing of neutral Switzerland—and so Konstanz is among the best-preserved major medieval towns in Germany. On the peninsula side of the town, east of the main bridge connecting Konstanz's two halves, runs **Seestrasse,** where the wealthy wander and the young try their new in-line skates on a stately promenade of neoclassical mansions with views of the Bodensee.

It's claimed that Konstanz was founded in the 3rd century by Emperor Constantine Chlorus, father of Constantine the Great. The story is probably untrue, though it's certain there was a Roman garrison here. By the 6th century Konstanz had become a bishopric; in 1192 it became a Free Imperial City. What really put it on the map was the Council of Constance, held between 1414 and 1418 to settle the Great Schism (1378–1417), the rift in the church caused by two separate lines of popes, one leading from Rome, the other from Avignon. The council resolved the problem in 1417 by electing Martin V as the true, and only, pope. The church had also agreed to restore the German Holy Roman Emperor's (Sigismund's) role in electing the pope, but only if Sigismund silenced the rebel theologian Jan Hus (1372–1415) of Bohemia. Even though Sigismund had allowed Hus safe passage to Konstanz for the

Council, he won the church's favor by having Hus burned at the stake in July 1415.

For all its vivid history, most people enjoy Konstanz for its more worldly pleasures—the elegant Altstadt, trips on the lake, walks along the promenade, the classy shops, the restaurants, the views. The heart of the city is the **Marktstätte** (Market Place), near the harbor, with the simple bulk of the Konzilgebäude looming behind it. Erected in 1388 as a warehouse, the **Konzilgebäude** (Council Hall) is now a concert hall. Beside the Konzilgebäude are statues of Jan Hus and native son Graf Zeppelin (1838–1917). The Dominican monastery where Hus was held before his execution is still here, doing duty as a luxurious hotel, the Steigenberger Insel-Hotel.

The huge aquarium **Sealife** has gathered all the fish species that inhabit the Rhine and Lake Constance, from the river's beginnings in the Swiss Alps to its end in Rotterdam and the North Sea. If you're pressed for time or the aquarium is crowded with school children, visit the **nature museum** at the side entrance, which has excellent exhibits on area fauna and flora. ✉ *Hafenstr. 9,* ☎ *07531/128–270,* WEB *www.sealife.de.* 🎫 *€10.* ⏲ *July–Aug., daily 10–7; May, June, Sept., daily 10–6; Nov.–Apr., daily 10–5.*

The **Altes Rathaus** (Old Town Hall) was built during the Renaissance and painted with vivid frescoes—swags of flowers and fruits, shields, architectural details, and sturdy knights wielding immense swords. Walk into the courtyard to admire its Renaissance restraint. Within the medieval guild house of the city's butchers, the **Rosgartenmuseum** (Rose Garden Museum) has a rich collection of art and artifacts from the Bodensee region. Highlights include exhibits of the pile-dwelling people who inhabited the lake during the Bronze Age and sculpture and altar paintings from the Middle Ages. ✉ *Rosgartenstr. 3–5,* ☎ *07531/900–246.* 🎫 *€1.50.* ⏲ *Tues.–Thurs. 10–5, Fri.–Sun. 10–4.*

Konstanz's cathedral, the **Münster,** was built on the site of the original Roman fortress. Construction on the cathedral continued from the 10th through the 19th centuries, resulting in today's odd architectural contrasts. The twin-tower facade is sturdily Romanesque. However, the elegant and airy chapels along the aisles are full-blown 15th-century Gothic, the complex nave vaulting is Renaissance, and the choir is severely neoclassic. The Mauritius Chapel behind the altar is a richly worked 13th-century Gothic structure, 12 ft high, with some of its original vivid coloring and gilding. It's studded with statues of the Apostles and figures from the childhood of Jesus. ✉ *Münsterpl.*

The **Niederburg,** the oldest part of Konstanz, is a tangle of old, twisting streets leading to the Rhine. At the river take a look at the two city towers here: the Rheintor (Rhine Tower), the one nearer the lake, and the aptly named Pulverturm (Powder Tower), the former city arsenal.

Dining and Lodging

$–$$$ ✕ **Barbarossa.** The murals on the facade of this Old Town building depict some of its history, and inside are huge old wooden support beams. The stained-glass windows and dark wood paneling give the restaurant a cozy, warm atmosphere. Fish and game in season are the specialties. ✉ *Obermarkt 8,* ☎ *07531/22021. AE, D, MC, V.*

$ ✕ **Brauhaus J. Albrecht.** This small brewery with shiny copper cauldrons has a large dining room serving homey dishes such as fried eggs with homefries and *Kasseler* (smoked pork chops) with potato salad. For those in a hurry, there are stand-up tables. ✉ *Konradig. 2,* ☎ *07531/25045. No credit cards.*

$ ✕ **Hafenhalle.** You don't have to cross the Swiss border for Swiss Rosti and Bauernbratwurst. This warm-weather spot on the harbor serves it up as well. If you need to catch a train, the station is nearby and service is quick. The best thing about this "harbor hall" is that you can sit outside on the terrace and watch the busy harbor traffic, while either having drinks or small snacks. ✉ *Hafenstr. 10,* ☎ *07531/21126. No credit cards.*

$ ✕ **Radieschen.** Choose between excellent vegetarian or meat dishes at this Turkish restaurant. The inexpensive salad buffet belies its high quality. You might have to wait a bit before a table is available, but it's possible to join diners at a table where chairs are free—no one usually minds if you ask. ✉ *Hohenhausg. 1,* ☎ *07531/22887. No credit cards.*

$ ✕ **Zum Guten Hirten.** A traditional atmosphere is kept at this late-15th-century wine tavern, whose name means "good shepherd." In the particularly authentic Bauernstube, Swiss specialties such as *Rösti*—panfried potatoes and onions mixed with chopped smoked ham—are served. Try the dish accompanied by a crisp white wine from a Bodensee vineyard. ✉ *Zollernstr. 8,* ☎ *07531/27344. No credit cards.*

$$$–$$$$ ★ ✕🏨 **Seehotel Siber.** The major attraction in this small turn-of-the-20th-century villa is its restaurant—the most elegant in the region ($$$$; reservations essential; jacket and tie). Prepared by Bertold Siber, one of Germany's leading chefs, the food is classical with regional touches. Try the lobster salad or bouillabaisse with local lake fish. The restaurant is divided into three rooms: one resembles a library and the center room is airy and spacious, with bold modern paintings. In summer you can eat on a terrace overlooking the lake. Bedrooms 3 and 7 have balconies affording similar views. The hotel is a member of the Relais & Chateau group. ✉ *Seestr. 25, D–78464,* ☎ *07531/996–6990,* FAX *07531/9966–9933,* WEB *www.seehotel-siber.de. 11 rooms, 1 suite. Restaurant, café, some rooms with a/c, in-room data ports, Internet, dance club, pets allowed, no-smoking rooms. DC, MC, V. Hotel and restaurant closed 2 wks in Feb.*

$$$–$$$$ ★ ✕🏨 **Steigenberger Insel-Hotel.** This former 16th-century monastery, with its original cloisters, offers the most luxurious lodging in town. It's linked to historic figures as the site where Jan Hus was held before his execution and where, centuries later, Graf Zeppelin was born. Bedrooms are spacious and stylish, more like those of a private home than a hotel, and many have lake views. The formal terrace restaurant has superb views across the lake. The Dominikanerstube is the more intimate restaurant. Both restaurants ($$$–$$$$) feature regional specialties, and there's the clubby, relaxed Zeppelin Bar. Flower gardens surround the hotel, keeping the bustle of Konstanz at bay. ✉ *Auf der Insel 1, D–78462,* ☎ *07531/1250,* FAX *07531/26402,* WEB *www.steigenberger.com. 100 rooms, 2 suites. 2 restaurants, bar, no a/c, in-room data ports, beach, recreation room, baby-sitting, meeting rooms, some pets allowed. AE, DC, MC, V.*

$$ ✕🏨 **Stadthotel.** This friendly hotel is a five-minute walk from the lake. Some rooms have a bath, others just a shower, and all have a TV. The Poseidon restaurant ($), on site, draws locals and guests with its Greek cuisine. ✉ *Bruderturmg. 12, D–78462,* ☎ *07531/90460,* FAX *07531/904–646,* WEB *www.stadthotel-konstanz.com. 24 rooms. Restaurant, no a/c, in-room data ports, some pets allowed. AE, DC, MC, V.*

Nightlife and the Arts

The season of the **Bodensee Symphony Orchestra,** based in Konstanz, runs from October through April. Konstanz's international **summer music festival** runs from mid-June to mid-July, including celebrated organ concerts in the cathedral. Performances are held in the picturesque

Renaissancehof (courtyard) of the town hall. For all schedule information and tickets, contact the Konstanz tourist office (☎ 07531/133–030).

The **Stadttheater** (✉ Konzilstr., ☎ 07531/130–050 for festival office), Germany's oldest active theater, has staged plays since 1609 and has its own repertory company. The local season runs from September through June. From July through August the company moves to its summer theater in Meersburg. For **program details** contact the theater (✉ Konzilstr. 11, D–78462, ☎ 07531/20070). For the **Meersburg** program call ☎ 07532/82383.

The Bodensee nightlife scene is concentrated in Konstanz. The **casino** (✉ Seestr. 2, ☎ 07531/81570) is open 3 PM–3 AM. **Disco in Seehotel Siber** (✉ Seestr. 25, ☎ 07531/63044) is open Wednesday–Monday from 10 PM to 4 AM. **K 9** (✉ Obere Laube 71, ☎ 07531/16713) draws all ages with its dance club, theater, and cabaret in the former Church of St. Paul. Concerts and variously themed DJ nights are held at **Kulturladen** (✉ Joseph Belli Weg 5, ☎ 07531/52954).

An absolute must is the cozy and crowded **Seekuh** (✉ Konzilstr. 1, ☎ 07531/27232), which features the occasional live jazz night. The very popular **Theatercafé** (✉ Konzilstr. 3, ☎ 07531/20243) draws a stylish crowd that's not too hip to dance when the mood strikes.

Shopping

Konstanz is a very good city for shopping, drawing even the Swiss from St. Gallen and Zurich, which have plenty of shops of their own. It's worthwhile to roam the streets of the old part of town, where there are several gold- and silversmiths and jewelers. Elegant **Modehaus Jacqueline** (✉ Hussenstr. 29, ☎ 07531/22990) has enough style for a city 10 times the size of Konstanz. The store gets most of its business from wealthy Swiss who come to Konstanz for what they consider bargain prices. Jacqueline deals in well-known names such as Rena Lange and Celine, and has some unusual Italian lines such as Cavalli. Accessories from Moschino include handbags and exquisite shoes. **Oexle–China and Glassware** (✉ Marktstätte 26, ☎ 07531/21307) carries not only famous china brands such as Meissen, Rosenthal, and Arzberg, but also beautiful china and glasses of lesser-known names such as Theresienthal and Royal Copenhagen. Among their quality gift items are Hummel figures, Kristallglass, and Swiss army knives.

As soon as you step into **Parfümerie-Drogerie Gradmann** (✉ Hussenstr. 10, ☎ 07531/23088), a large perfumery, you'll be enveloped in enchanting scents: Lancome, Chanel, Sisley, Canta, and many other names compete for your nose's attention. Beyond the designer labels are a great choice of practical items for daily use, such as toiletries and even writing tools.

The small, but fine and not too expensive **pierre-moden** (✉ Hussenstr. 3, ☎ 07531/22150) carries somewhat bold but always stylish men's fashions. You'll find well known Carlo Colucci's imaginative knitwear, Signum shirts, Joker jeans, and items from Lacoste.

Outdoor Activities and Sports

BIKING

Bike rentals generally cost €10 per day. You can book bicycle tours and rent bikes at **velotours** (✉ Fritz Arnold-Str. 2d, ☎ 07531/98280, WEB www.velotours.de). **Kulturrädle** (✉ Hauptbahnhof, ☎ 07531/27310) rents bikes at the main train station. The longer you rent the bike for, the cheaper the daily rate.

BOATING

Sail yachts as well as motor yachts are available at **Engert Yachtcharter** (✉ Hafenstr. 8, ☎ 07531/16537, WEB www.bodensee-yachtzentrum.de). Their shop right on the harbor is every sailor's delight. Small sailboats can be chartered from the **Bodensee Segelschule Konstanz/Wallhausen** (✉ Zum Wittmoosstr. 10, Wallhausen, ☎ 07533/4780).

Mainau

11 *7 km (4½ mi) north of Konstanz by road; by ferry, 50 min from Konstanz, 20 min from Meersburg.*

One of the most unusual sights in Germany, Mainau is a tiny island given over to the cultivation of rare plants and splashy displays of more than a million tulips, hyacinths, and narcissi. Rhododendrons and roses bloom from May to July, dahlias dominate the late summer. A greenhouse nurtures palms and tropical plants.

The island was originally the property of the Teutonic knights, who settled here during the 13th century. In the 19th century Mainau passed to Grand Duke Friedrich I of Baden, a man with a passion for botany. He laid out most of the gardens and introduced many of the island's more exotic specimens. His daughter Victoria, later queen of Sweden, gave the island to her son, Prince Wilhelm, and it has remained Swedish ever since. Today it's owned by Prince Wilhelm's son, Count Lennart Bernadotte, who lives in the castle. In the former main reception hall are changing art exhibitions during the year.

Beyond the flora, the island's other colorful extravagance is **Das Schmetterlinghaus**, Germany's largest butterfly conservatory. On a circular walk through a semitropical landscape with water cascading through rare vegetation, you'll see hundreds of butterflies at close quarters flying, feeding, and mating. The exhibition in the foyer explains the butterflies' life cycle, habitats, and ecological connections. Like the park, this oasis is open year-round.

At the island's information center, **Nature and Culture on Lake Constance,** you can view a multimedia show in which 14 projectors create a three-dimensional effect, capturing the beauty of the countryside around Lake Constance. The show also addresses environmental issues and how to observe ecologically sound behavior on vacation and at home.

Ferries to the island from Meersburg and Konstanz depart approximately every 1½ hours between 9 and 5. The entrance fee to the island is €9.50.

Dining

There are three restaurants on the island but no lodgings.

$$$ ✕ **Schwedenschenke.** The lunchtime crowd gets what it needs here—fast and good service. At dinnertime (reservations essential) the atmosphere downshifts and candlelight draws attention to the restaurant's stylishness. Given that the resident Bernadotte family is Swedish, the specialties of the chef are Swedish dishes. Have your hotel reserve a table for you. In the evening your reservation will be checked at the gate, and you can drive onto the island without having to pay the admission. ✉ *Insel Mainau,* ☎ *07531/3030. AE, D, MC, V.*

Reichenau

12 *10 km (6 mi) northwest of Konstanz, 50 min by ferry from Konstanz.*

Reichenau is an island rich in vegetation, but unlike Mainau, it's less glamorous vegetables, not flowers, that prevail. In fact, 15% of its area covered by greenhouses and crops of one kind or another. Though it seems unlikely amid the cabbage, cauliflower, lettuce, and potatoes, the island has three of Europe's most beautiful Romanesque churches. Little Reichenau, 5 km (3 mi) long and 1½ km (1 mi) wide, connected to the Bodanrück Peninsula by just a narrow causeway, was a great monastic center of the early Middle Ages. Secure from marauding tribesmen on its fertile island, the monastic community blossomed from the 8th through the 12th centuries, in the process developing into a major center of learning and the arts. The churches are in each of the island's villages—**Oberzell, Mittelzell, Niederzell,** which are only separated by 1 km (½ mi). Along the shore are pleasant pathways for walking or biking.

The **Stiftskirche St. Georg** (Collegiate Church of St. George), in Oberzell, was built around 900; now cabbages grow in ranks up to its rough plaster walls. Small round-head windows, a simple tower, and russet-color tiles provide the only exterior decoration. Inside, look for the wall paintings along the nave; they date from around 1000 and show the miracles of Christ. Their simple colors and unsteady outlines have an innocent, almost childlike charm. The striped backgrounds are typical of Romanesque frescoes.

Begun in 816, the **Münster of St. Maria and St. Markus,** the monastery's church, is the largest and most important of the island's trio of Romanesque churches. The monastery was founded in 725 by St. Pirmin and became one of the most important cultural centers of the Carolingian Empire. It reached its zenith around 1000, when 700 monks lived here. It was then probably the most important center of book illumination in Germany. The building is simple, but by no means crude. Visit the Schatzkammer (treasury) to see some of its more important treasures. They include a 5th-century ivory goblet with two carefully incised scenes of Christ's miracles and some priceless stained glass that is almost 1,000 years old. *Münsterpl. 3, Mittelzell,* ☎ *07534/92070 for guided tours.* ⏲ *May–Sept., daily 11–noon and 3–4.*

A **local-history museum** in the Old Town Hall of Mittelzell lends interesting insights into life on the island over the centuries. ✉ *Mittelzell.* 🎫 *€1.* ⏲ *May–Sept., Tues.–Sun. 3–5.*

The **Stiftskirche St. Peter and St. Paul** (St. Peter and Paul Parish Church), at Niederzell, contains some Romanesque frescoes in the apse.

OFF THE BEATEN PATH

WOLLMATINGER RIED – Just north of Konstanz on the Bodanrück Peninsula is the 1,000-acre Wollmatinger Ried, a moorland bird sanctuary. There are three-hour guided tours of the moor April through mid-October (Wednesday and Saturday at 4 PM) as well as other nature walks. Native breeding birds include the marsh harrier, the hobby falcon, the black kite, great reed warbler, and black-necked grebe. There are also remains of prehistoric pile houses. Bring sturdy, comfortable shoes and mosquito repellent. Binoculars can be rented. ✉ *Kindlebildstr. 87, Reichenau,* ☎ *07531/78870.* 🎫 *Free, donation.* ⏲ *Apr.–Sept., weekdays 9–noon and 2–5, weekends 1–5; Oct.–Mar., weekdays 9–noon and 2–5.*

Dining and Lodging

$$ ✕🏨 **Strandhotel Löchnerhaus.** The Strand (beach) Hotel stands commandingly on the water's edge, a stone's throw from the lake and about 80 yards from its own boat pier. Freshly caught lake fish figure prominently on the menu of the restaurant ($–$$$). Most rooms have lake views; those that don't look out over a quiet, shady garden. ✉ *An der Schiffslände 12, D–78479,* ☎ *07534/8030,* FAX *07534/582. 44 rooms.*

Restaurant, no a/c, beach, boating, meeting rooms, some pets allowed. MC, V.

Radolfzell

13 *22 km (14 mi) northwest of Konstanz.*

Radolfzell originally belonged to the Abbey of Reichenau, just a few miles away across the lake, until it became part of the Habsburg empire in the 15th century. In the old part of town are shops in half-timber houses and on the shore a long promenade with cafés, a boat rental place, and a small harbor for sailboats and the ships of the *Weisse Flotte* (White Fleet). In honor of the three local saints, the *Hausherrenfest* is celebrated every third Sunday in July, with a water procession of decorated boats. The center of town is dominated by the Gothic **Münster unserer Lieben Frau** (Minster of our Dear Lady). A farmers' market sets up every Wednesday and Saturday morning in the shadow of the cathedral.

Just east of Radolfzell is the small **Mettnau Peninsula,** which separates two fingers of the Bodensee, the Gnadensee from the Zeller See. The nature reserve, **Naturschutzgebiet Mettnau,** has free entry and guided tours of the reedy vegetation as well as bird-watching opportunities. You can spot many species of ducks, songbirds, curlews, lapwings, and cormorants. Tours depart from the **nature center,** which also has exhibits. ✉ *Floerickeweg 2a,* ☎ *07732/12339.* 🎫 *Free.* ⏲ *Daily. Nature center and tours Mar.–Oct., weekends and holidays 2–6.*

Höri

14 *4 km (2½ mi) south of Radolfzell.*

Höri is a rural peninsula, settled with small villages, between the Zeller See and Seerhein portions of Bodensee. In the village of Horn, the beautiful setting of the church **St. Johannes and Veit of Horn** inspired a king of Württemberg to admit, "If I weren't king, I'd like to be the priest of Horn." From here you have a view of the reedy landscape; the Zeller See and the island of Reichenau; the silhouette of Konstanz; and, on a clear day, the snowcapped Alps.

In the early 1900s members of Dresden's artist group Die Brücke discovered the area. The most expressive paintings of the Bodensee landscape were created by Erich Heckel (1883–1970) and Otto Dix (1891–1969). Dix lived in the village of Hemmenhofen from 1936 until his death. You can see some of his landscapes in the **Otto Dix Haus.** ✉ *Hemmenhofen,* ☎ *07735/3151.* 🎫 *€2.50.* ⏲ *Apr.–Oct., Wed.–Sat. 2–5, Sun. and public holidays 11–4.*

The Nobel laureate novelist and poet Hermann Hesse (1877–1962) lived in Gaienhofen from 1904 to 1912, before he emigrated to Switzerland. The **Hesse Haus** museum has biographical displays, books for sale, and occasional art exhibits. ✉ *Gaienhofen,* ☎ *07735/81832.* 🎫 *€2.50.* ⏲ *Apr.–Oct., Tues.–Sat. 2–5, Sun. 11–5.*

THE BODENSEE A TO Z

To research prices, get advice from other travelers, and book travel arrangements, visit www.fodors.com.

AIRPORTS

The closest international airport to the Bodensee is in Zurich, Switzerland, 60 km (37 mi) from Konstanz, connected by the autobahn. There are also direct trains from the Zurich airport to Konstanz. From Frankfurt there are several flights a day to the regional airport at Friedrichshafen.

BOAT AND FERRY TRAVEL

Note that the English pronunciation of "ferry" sounds a lot like the German word "fähre," which means car ferry. "Schiffe" is the term used for passenger ferries, which have different docking points from the car ferries in the various towns.

The Weisse Flotte line of boats links most of the larger towns and resorts. One of the nicest trips is from Konstanz to Meersburg and then on to the island of Mainau. The round-trip cost is €8.80. A Bodensee-Pass is helpful only if you plan to use the boats frequently: €30 grants you one free day of travel plus six days of half-price travel. Excursions around the lake last from one hour to a full day. Many cross to Austria and Switzerland; some head west along the Rhine to the Schaffhausen Falls, the largest waterfall in Europe. Information on lake excursions is available from all local tourist offices and travel agencies.
➤ PASSES AND EXCURSIONS: **Bodensee-Schiffsbetriebe** (✉ Hafenstr. 6, D–78462 Konstanz, ☎ 07531/281–389, WEB www.bsb-online.com; ✉ Friedrichshafen, ☎ 07541/92380; ✉ Lindau, ☎ 08382/944–416).

BUS TRAVEL

Buses serve most smaller communities that have no train links, but service is infrequent. Along the shore there are buses that run every half hour during the day from Überlingen to Friedrichshafen, stopping in towns such as Meersburg, Hagnau, and Immenstaad (which have no train connections).

CAR RENTALS

➤ LOCAL AGENTS: **Avis** (✉ Friedrichshafen Airport, ☎ 07541/930–705; ✉ Macairestr. 10, Konstanz, ☎ 07531/99000; ✉ Kemptenerstr. 25, Lindau, ☎ 08382/966–333). **Europcar** (✉ Eugenstr. 47, Friedrichshafen, ☎ 07541/23053; ✉ Von Emmerichstr. 3, Konstanz, ☎ 07531/52833). **Sixt** (✉ Zeppelinstr. 66, Friedrichshafen, ☎ 07541/33066; ✉ Karl-Benz-Str. 14, Konstanz, ☎ 07531/690–044).

CAR TRAVEL

Construction on the A–96 autobahn that runs from Munich to Lindau is ongoing. For a more scenic route, take the B–12 via Landsberg and Kempten. For a scenic, but slower route from Frankfurt, take the B–311 at Ulm and follow the Oberschwäbische Barockstrasse (Upper Swabian Baroque Road) to Friedrichshafen. Lindau is also a terminus of the Deutsche Alpenstrasse (German Alpine Road). It runs east–west from Salzburg to Lindau.

Lakeside roads in the Bodensee area are scenic, but experience occasional heavy traffic in summer. Formalities at border-crossing points are few. However, in addition to your passport, you'll need insurance and registration papers for your car. For rental cars check with the rental company to verify it imposes no restrictions on crossing frontiers. Car ferries link Romanshorn, in Switzerland, with Friedrichshafen, as well as Konstanz with Meersburg. Taking either ferry saves substantial mileage. The fare depends on the size of the car; a one-way fare for a medium-size car costs €7.

TOURS

Most of the larger tourist centers have city tours with English-speaking guides, but call ahead to confirm availability.

AIRPLANE TOURS

A fascinating way to view the lake is from a three-passenger Cessna operated by Slansky/Dussmann from Friedrichshafen's airport. They will also take you into the Alps, following your wishes.

➤ CONTACT INFORMATION: **Slansky/Dussmann** (☏ 07532/808–866 or 08388/1269).

BIKING TOURS

Konstanz-based Velotours arranges bicycling tours with accommodations and baggage transport around the Bodensee. Velotours also rents out bikes at €10 per day.

➤ CONTACT INFORMATION: **Velotours** (✉ Fritz-Arnold-Str. 2d, Konstanz, ☏ 07531/98280, WEB www.velotours.de).

WINE TOURS

Wine-tasting tours are available in Überlingen, in the atmospheric Spitalweingut zum Heiligen Geist as well as in Konstanz and Meersburg. Call the local tourist offices for information.

➤ CONTACT INFORMATION: **Spitalweingut zum Heiligen Geist** (✉ Mühlbachstr. 115, ☏ 07551/65855).

TRAIN TRAVEL

From Frankfurt to Friedrichshafen and Lindau, take the ICE (Inter City Express) to Ulm and then transfer (total time 3½ hours). There are direct trains to Konstanz every two hours from Frankfurt (4½ hours), which pass through the beautiful scenery of the Black Forest. From Munich to Lindau, the EC (Europe Express) train takes 2½ hours. From Zurich to Konstanz, the trip lasts 1½ hours. Local trains encircle the Bodensee, stopping at most towns and villages.

VISITOR INFORMATION

Information on the entire Bodensee region is available from the Internationaler Bodensee Tourismus.

➤ TOURIST INFORMATION: **Bad Schussenried** (✉ Kultur- und Verkehrsamt, Georg-Kaess-Str. 10, D–88427, ☏ 07583/940–171, WEB www.bad-schussenried.de). **Friedrichshafen** (✉ Tourist-Information, Bahnhofpl. 2, D–88045, ☏ 07541/30010, WEB www.friedrichshaven.de). **Internationaler Bodensee Tourismus** (✉ Insel Mainau, D–78465 Konstanz, ☏ 07531/90940, FAX 07531/909–494, WEB www.bodensee-tourismus.com). **Konstanz** (✉ Tourist-Information, Konstanz, Fischmarkt 2, D–78462, ☏ 07531/133–030, WEB www.konstanz.de). **Langenargen** (✉ Langenargen Verkehrsamt, Obere Seestr. 2/2, D–88085, ☏ 07543/933–092, WEB www.langenargen.de). **Lindau** (✉ Verkehrsverein Lindau, Ludwigstr. 68, D–88103, ☏ 08382/260–030, WEB www.lindau.de). **Meersburg** (✉ Verkehrsverwaltung, Kirchstr. 4, D–88709, ☏ 07532/431–110, WEB www.meersburg.de). **Radolfzell** (✉ Tourist Information im Bahnhof, D–78315, ☏ 07732/81500, WEB www.radolfzell.de). **Ravensburg** (✉ Städtisches Verkehrsamt, Kirchstr. 16, D–88212, ☏ 0751/82324, WEB www.ravensburg.de). **Reichenau** (✉ Verkehrsbüro, Ergat 5, D–78479, ☏ 07534/92070, WEB www.reichenau.de). **Romanshorn Tourist-Information** (✉ Im Bahnhof, 8590 Romanshorn, Switzerland, ☏ 071/463–3232, FAX 071/461–1980). **Tettnang** (✉ Verkehrsamt, Montfortpl. 1, D–88069, ☏ 07542/953–839, WEB www.tettnang.de). **Überlingen** (✉ Kurverwaltung, Landungspl. 14, D–88662, ☏ 07551/991–122, WEB www.ueberlingen.de). **Weingarten** (✉ Kultur- und Verkehrsamt, Münsterpl. 1, D–88250, ☏ 0751/405–125, WEB www.weingarten-info.de).

8 THE BLACK FOREST

Cake and smoked ham aren't the only reasons to visit the Black Forest, but they are good ones. Spa and casino resorts, outdoor activities, and cuckoo clocks are other draws. The Romans were the first to take advantage of the area's healing waters, 19 centuries ago, and royalty and the cultural elite paraded about the region in the 1800s. Here you can splurge in high-fashion, high-cost towns such as Baden-Baden one day and relax in a down-home German country village the next.

Updated by Marton Radkai

THE NAME CONJURES UP IMAGES OF A WILD, isolated place where time passes slowly. The dense woodland of the Black Forest—*Schwarzwald* in German—stretches away to the horizon, but this southwest corner of Baden-Württemberg (in the larger region known as Swabia) is neither inaccessible nor a backwater. The first travelers checked in here 19 centuries ago, when the Roman emperor Caracalla and his army rested and soothed their battle wounds in the natural-spring waters at what later became Baden-Baden.

Europe's upper-crust society discovered Baden-Baden when it convened nearby for the Congress of Rastatt from 1797 to 1799, which attempted to end the wars of the French Revolution. In the 19th century, kings, queens, emperors, princes, princesses, members of Napoléon's family, and the Russian nobility, along with actors, writers, and composers, flocked to the little spa town. Turgenev, Dostoyevsky, and Tolstoy were among the Russian contingent. Victor Hugo was a frequent visitor. Brahms composed lilting melodies in this calm setting. Queen Victoria spent her vacations here, and Mark Twain waxed poetic on the forest's beauty in his 1880 book *A Tramp Abroad,* putting the Black Forest on the map for Americans.

Today it's a favorite getaway for movie stars and millionaires, and you too can "take the waters," as the Romans first did, at thermal resorts large or small. The Black Forest sporting scene caters particularly to the German enthusiasm for hiking, with virtually limitless trails wending their way in and out of the woods. In winter the terrain is ideally suited for cross-country skiing.

The Black Forest's enviable great outdoors is blessed by dependable snow in winter and warming sun in summer. Freudenstadt, at the center of the Black Forest, claims the greatest number of annual hours of sunshine of any town in Germany. You can play tennis, swim, or bike at most resorts, and some have golf courses of international standard.

The summer's warmth also benefits the vineyards of the Badische Weinstrasse (Baden Wine Road), which often aligns with the B–3 near the French border. Gutedel and Muskateller, two of the world's oldest grape varieties, are grown here. Baden cooperatives produce mostly dry wines that go well with the region's fine traditional food.

The Black Forest also happens to be the home of the cuckoo clock, despite Orson Welles's claim in *The Third Man* that all Switzerland managed to create in 500 years of peace and prosperity was this trivial timepiece. Cuckoo clocks are still made (and sold) here, as they have been for centuries, along with hand-carved wood items and exquisite examples of glassblowing. Clock-making gave rise to a precision mechanics industry that is a guarantor of prosperity and employment throughout the region.

Despite its fame and the wealth of some of its visitors, the Black Forest doesn't have to be an expensive place to visit. It's possible to stay at a modest family-run country inn or farmhouse where the enormous breakfast will keep you going for the better part of the day—all for not much more than the price of a meal in a city restaurant.

Pleasures and Pastimes

Biking

Bicycles can be rented in nearly all towns and many villages. The Deutsche Bahn, Germany's national railway, has excellent deals on bicycle rentals at train stations. Several regional tourist offices sponsor tours on which the biker's luggage is transported separately from one overnight stop to the next. Six- to 10-day tours are available at reasonable rates, including bed-and-breakfast and bike rental.

Dining

Restaurants in the Black Forest range from the well-upholstered luxury of Baden-Baden's chic eating spots to simple country inns. Old *Kachelöfen* (tile heating stoves) are still in use in many area restaurants; try to sit by one if it's cold outside. Some specialties here betray the influence of neighboring France, but if you really want to go native, try *z'Nini* (dialect for *neun*, nine), the local farmers' second breakfast, generally eaten around 9 AM. It consists of smoked bacon, called *Schwarzwaldgeräuchertes*—the most authentic is smoked over fir cones—a hunk of bread, and a glass of chilled white wine. Swabian dishes include *Zwiebelrostbraten* (fried beefsteak with onions), *Maultaschen* (a kind of large ravioli), and *Spätzle* (small, chewy noodles). Don't pass up the chance to try *Schwarzwälder Schinken* (pinecone-smoked ham) and *Schwarzwälder Kirschtorte* (kirsch-soaked layers of chocolate cake with sour cherry and whipped cream filling). *Kirschwasser,* locally called *Chriesewässerle* (from the French *cerise*, meaning "cherry"), is cherry brandy, the most famous of the region's excellent schnapps varieties.

If traveling in May or June, keep an eye out for asparagus. The "asparagus road" begins in Schwetzingen and passes through Bruchsal, Karlsruhe, and Rastatt. Special gourmet tours center on the enjoyment of this king of vegetables and vegetable of kings, as it was once called.

CATEGORY	COST*
$$$$	over €20
$$$	€15–€20
$$	€10–€15
$	under €10

**per person for a main course at dinner*

Fishing

Innumerable mountain rivers and streams make this area a fisherman's paradise. Native trout are abundant in many rivers, including the Nagold, Elz, Alb, and Wildgutach, and in mountain lakes such as the Schluchsee and Titisee. Licenses are available from most local tourist offices, which usually also provide maps and rental equipment.

Hiking and Walking

The Black Forest is ideal country for walkers. The three principal trails are well marked and cross the region from north to south, the longest stretching from Pforzheim to the Swiss city of Basel, 280 km (174 mi) away. Walks vary in length from a few hours to a week. As in many other German regions, the tourist office has gotten together with local inns to create *Wandern ohne Gepäck* (Hike Without Luggage) tours along the old clock carriers' route. Your bags are transported ahead by car to meet you each evening at that day's destination.

Lodging

Accommodations in the Black Forest are varied and numerous, from simple rooms in farmhouses to five-star luxury. Some properties have been passed down in the same family for generations. *Gasthöfe* offer low prices and as much local color as you'll ever want.

CATEGORY	COST*
$$$$	over €225
$$$	€150–€225
$$	€75–€150
$	under €75

**All prices are for two people in a double room, including tax and service.*

Spas and Health Resorts

There's an amazing variety of places to have a relaxing soak, from expensive spa towns to rustic places deep in the woods. Baden-Baden is stately and elegant. Bad Dürrheim has Europe's highest-brine spa. For a garden setting, head for Bad Herrenalb. Bad Liebenzell has an Olympic-size pool, and the spa towns of Feldberg and Hinterzarten also provide opportunities to hike. Many of the spas offer special rates for stays lasting several days or even weeks.

Winter Sports

Despite Swiss claims to the contrary, the Black Forest is the true home of downhill skiing. In 1891 a French diplomat was sighted sliding down the slopes of the Feldberg, the Black Forest's highest mountain, on what are thought to be the world's first downhill skis. The idea caught on among the locals, and a few months later Germany's first ski club was formed. The world's first ski lift opened at Schollach in 1907. There are now more than 200 ski lifts in the Black Forest, but the slopes of the Feldberg are still the top ski area.

Exploring the Black Forest

The northern Black Forest is known for its broad ridges and thickly forested slopes; it contains the largest number of spas. The central region, Triberg in particular, is especially popular for its associations with folklore, cuckoo clocks, and the *Schwarzwaldbahn* (Black Forest Railway). The southern portion of the Black Forest has the most dramatic scenery and the most frequented recreation areas. Two main attractions are the Titisee and the Schluchsee, two beautiful lakes created by glaciers.

Numbers in the text correspond to numbers in the margin and on the Black Forest map.

Great Itineraries

Many first-time visitors to the Black Forest literally can't see the forest for the trees (although they have suffered in recent years from the effects of acid rain and a fierce 1999 windstorm). Take time to stray from the beaten path and inhale the cool, mysterious air of the darker recesses. Walk or ride through its shadowy corridors or across its open upland; paddle a canoe down the rippling currents of the Nagold and Wolf rivers. Then take time out to relax in a spa, order a dry Baden wine enlivened by a dash of local mineral water, and seek out the nearest restaurant that devotes itself to local specialties. If you have money to spare at the end of your trip, try your luck at Baden-Baden's gaming tables.

IF YOU HAVE 3 DAYS

Start your first day at the confluence of three rivers in **Pforzheim** ①. Envy the glittering jewelry collection at the famous Schmuckmuseum, and then visit nearby Maulbronn's beautiful 12th-century Cistercian abbey. Spend a night in quaint **Bad Liebenzell** ②, and on the second day soak in one of the Black Forest's oldest spas. After a visit to the ruined abbey in **Hirsau,** near **Calw** ③, head south to **Triberg** ⑭, site of Germany's highest waterfall and the Schwarzwaldmuseum, with regional folklore exhibits. On the last day go north to look at the farm-

The Black Forest

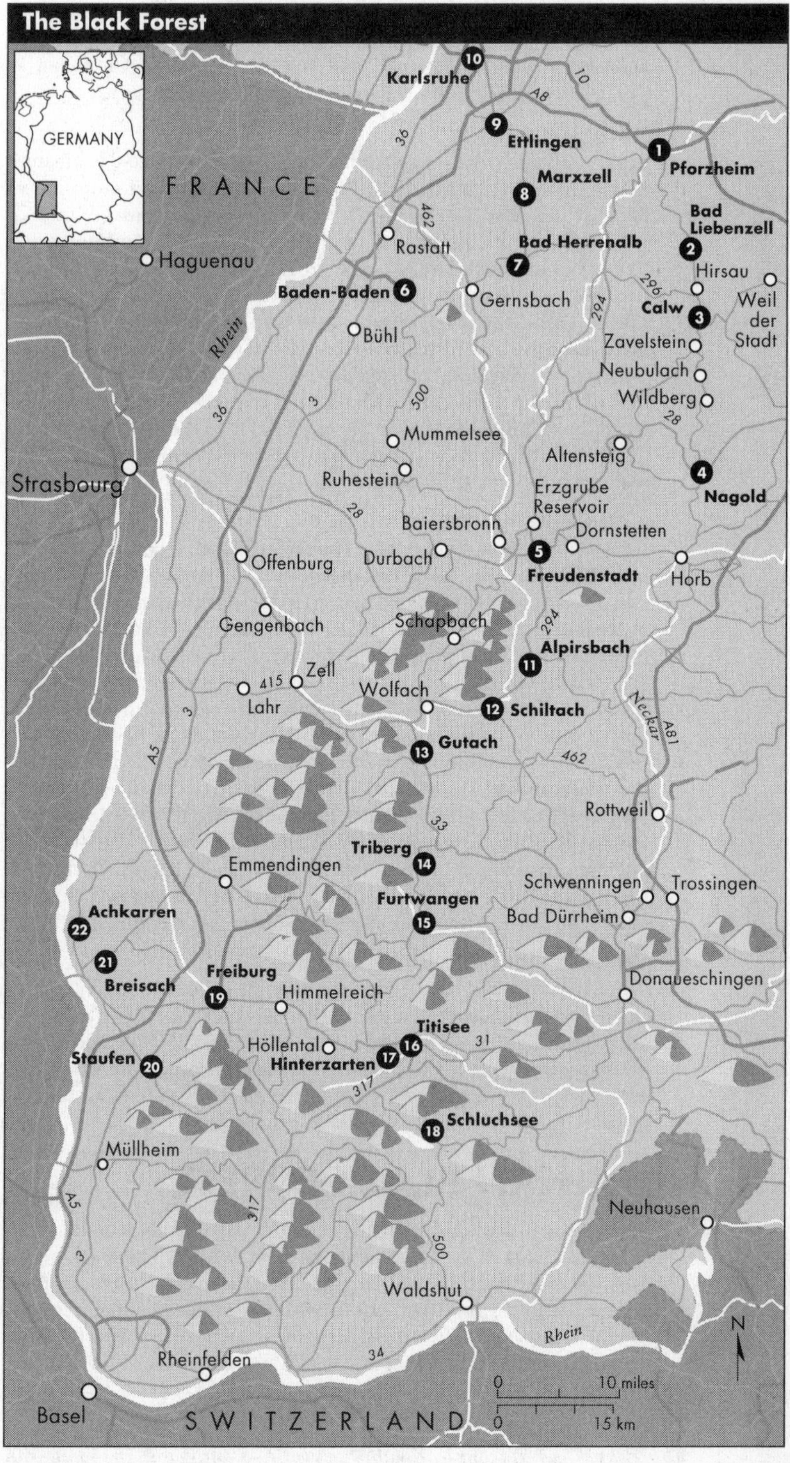

houses at the Open-Air Museum Vogtsbauernhof, near **Wolfach,** before driving along the *Schwarzwald-Hochstrasse* (Black Forest Highway) from Mummelsee (with a stop at the lake) to **Baden-Baden** ⑥. Save plenty of time for a walk around the fashionable spa.

IF YOU HAVE 5 DAYS

Begin your trip by following the first two days of the three-day itinerary described above, starting at **Pforzheim** ①, and then stopping at Maulbronn, **Bad Liebenzell** ②, **Calw** ③, **Freudenstadt** ⑤, and **Triberg** ⑭. On the third day continue directly south to **Furtwangen** ⑮ to survey Germany's largest clock museum. The **Titisee** ⑯, the jewel of the Black Forest lakes, is a good place to spend the third night. After taking some time to enjoy Titisee and the mountain-enclosed **Schluchsee** ⑱, you're ready to brave the winding road northwest through the **Höllental.** End your day at **Freiburg** ⑲, which lies at the foot of the Black Forest; its Münster, or cathedral, has the most perfect spire of any German Gothic church. Drive north from Freiburg on B–3 through the Baden vineyards to elegant **Baden-Baden** ⑥, where you can relax on the fifth day.

IF YOU HAVE 10 DAYS

After visiting the attractions near **Pforzheim** ①, spend the first two nights in **Bad Liebenzell** ②. **Freudenstadt** ⑤ is a good base for the next two days; from here make excursions to the source of the Kinzig River in **Lossburg**; to the Schwarzwälder Freilichtmuseum Vogtsbauernhof in **Gutach** ⑬; the **Alpirsbach** ⑪ brewery; and Glasswald Lake, near Schapbach. On the fifth day continue on to **Triberg** ⑭ to explore its waterfall and cuckoo clock museums and then to **Furtwangen** ⑮. Spend the fifth and sixth nights near the shores of the **Titisee** ⑯. From the lake visit the Feldberg, the Black Forest's highest mountain, and the **Schluchsee** ⑱. Spend the following two days and nights in **Freiburg** ⑲, allowing time for Schauinsland Mountain; the town of **Staufen** ⑳, where the legendary Dr. Faustus made his pact with the devil; and the vineyards on the slopes of the Kaiserstuhl. Finally, drive north through the Rhine Valley for two nights in **Baden-Baden** ⑥. Indulge in the city's attractions and take a trip to nearby Merkur Mountain.

When to Tour the Black Forest

The Black Forest is one of the most heavily visited mountain regions in Europe, so make reservations well in advance for the better-known spas and hotels. In summer the areas around Schluchsee and Titisee are particularly crowded. In early fall and late spring, the Black Forest scenery is less crowded (except during the Easter holidays) but just as beautiful. Some spa hotels close for the winter.

THE NORTHERN BLACK FOREST

This region is crossed by broad ridges that are densely wooded, with little lakes such as the Mummelsee and the Wildsee. The Black Forest Spa Route (270 km [167 mi]) links many of the spas in the region, from Baden-Baden (the best known) to Wildbad. Other regional treasures are the lovely Nagold River; ancient towns such as Bad Herrenalb and Hirsau; and the magnificent abbey at Maulbronn, near Pforzheim.

Pforzheim

❶ *35 km (22 mi) from Karlsruhe, just off A–8 autobahn, the main Munich–Karlsruhe route.*

The Romans founded Pforzheim at the meeting place of three rivers, the Nagold, the Enz, and the Würm. Known today as the "gateway to the Black Forest," Pforzheim was at one time the home of one of the great early 16th-century Humanists, Johannes Reuchlin. The city was almost totally destroyed in World War II, which accounts for its not-so-attractive blocky postwar architectural style. Pforzheim owes its prosperity to its role in Europe's jewelry trade and its wristwatch industry. To get a sense of the "Gold City," explore the jewelry shops on streets around Leopoldplatz and the pedestrian area. The restored church of **St. Michael** (✉ Schlossberg 10), near the train station, is the final resting place of the Baden princes. The original mixture of 13th- and 15th-century styles has been faithfully reproduced; compare the airy Gothic choir with the church's sturdy Romanesque entrance.

The Reuchlinhaus, the city cultural center, houses the **Schmuckmuseum** (Jewelry Museum). Its collection of jewelry from five millenia is one of the finest in the world. ✉ *Jahnstr. 42,* ☎ *07231/392–126.* 🎫 *Free.* ⏲ *Tues.–Sun. 10–5.*

Pforzheim has long been known as a center of the German clock-making industry. In the **Technisches Museum** (Technical Museum), one of the country's leading museums devoted to the craft, you can see watch- and clock makers at work; there's also a reconstructed 18th-century clock factory. ✉ *Bleichstr. 81,* ☎ *07231/392–869.* 🎫 *Free.* ⏲ *Wed. 9–noon and 3–6, and every 2nd and 4th Sun. of month 10–5.*

★ **Kloster Maulbronn** (Maulbronn Monastery), in the little town of Maulbronn, 18 km (11 mi) northeast of Pforzheim, is the best-preserved medieval monastery north of the Alps, with an entire complex of 30 buildings on UNESCO's World Heritage List. The main buildings were constructed between the 12th and 14th centuries. The monastery's church was built in a time of architectural transition from the Romanesque to the Gothic style and would influence Gothic architecture throughout northern and central Europe. Next to the church is the cloister, with a fountain house and refectories for the monks and lay brothers. The monastery's fortified walls still stand and its medieval water-management system, with its elaborate network of drains, irrigation canals, and reservoirs, remains intact. ✉ *Off B–35,* ☎ *07043/926–610,* WEB *www.schloesser-magazin.de.* 🎫 *€4.* ⏲ *Mar.–Oct., daily 9–5:30; Nov.–Feb., Tues.–Sun. 9:30–5; guided tour at 11:15 and 3.*

Dining

$$$$ ✕ **Silberburg.** The Alsatian owners of this cozy restaurant outside the city center serve classic French cuisine. Try the duck in one of chef Gilbert Noesser's exquisite sauces. ✉ *Dietlingerstr. 27,* ☎ *07231/441–159. AE, DC, MC, V. Closed Mon. and Aug. No lunch Tues.*

En Route The road south of Pforzheim, B–463, follows the twists and turns of the pretty little Nagold River. Gardening enthusiasts should follow the signs to the **Alpine Garden** (on the left as you leave the city limits). The garden, on the banks of the Würm River, stocks more than 100,000 varieties of plants, including the rarest Alpine flowers. ☎ *07231/70590.* 🎫 *€2.50.* ⏲ *Mid-Apr.–Oct., daily 8–7.*

Bad Liebenzell

❷ *31 km (19 mi) south of Pforzheim on Highway 463.*

Bathhouses were built in Bad Liebenzell as early as 1403. Nearly six centuries later the same hot springs feed the more modern spas. Apart from medicinal baths (highly recommended for the treatment of circulatory problems), the town has the **Paracelsusbad lido complex,** with outdoor and indoor hot-water pools, and a steam grotto. There's also mixed nude bathing at the Sauna Pinea, whose little park complex outside affords beautiful panoramic views of wooded slopes. The park has an interesting installation—a solar system model that lights up at night and lets you wander around the cosmos, so to speak. ✉ *Reuchlinweg 1,* ☎ *07052/408–250.* 🎫 *€15 for 3 hrs in bath; €12 for 3½ hrs in sauna.* ⏲ *Bath: Apr.–Oct., Mon.–Sat. 8 AM–9 PM, Sun. 8–8; Nov.–Mar., Mon.–Thurs. and Sat. 8:30 AM–9 PM, Fri. and Sun. 8:30–8. Sauna: year-round, Mon.–Thurs. 1–10, Fri. 1–11, Sat. 9 AM–11 PM, Sun. 9–8, Thurs. for women only in the sauna.*

A principal pastime in and around Bad Liebenzell is walking along the Nagold River valley. A path winding through the thick woods around the little town leads to the 13th-century castle of **Liebenzell.** Climb the red sandstone tower for an even more spectacular view of the region. The castle is a favorite place for outings, and the restaurant there serves meals and snacks. The rest of the fortress is home to a seminar house.

Dining and Lodging

$$–$$$ ★ ✕🏨 **Kronen Hotel.** Most of the functional rooms at this comfortable hotel are in a large, rather bland modern wing. The Black Forest landscape is very close, however, and the Nagold River flows right in front of the hotel. One kitchen serves the hotel's three restaurants ($–$$$$), one of which is non-smoking. The cuisine is so-called *Vitalkost,* meaning light, with plenty of fresh vegetables and herbs, good salads, and fruit. ✉ *Badweg 7, D–75378,* ☎ *07052/4090,* FAX *07052/409–420,* WEB *www.kronenhotel-de. 42 rooms. 3 restaurants, café, no a/c, cable TV, Internet, pool, sauna, some pets allowed (fee), no-smoking rooms. AE, DC, V, MC.*

En Route **Weil der Stadt,** a former imperial city, is in the hills 13 km (8 mi) west of Bad Liebenzell. This small, sleepy town of turrets and gables has only its well-preserved city walls and fortifications to remind you of its onetime importance. The astronomer Johannes Kepler, born here in 1571, was the first man to track and accurately explain the orbits of the planets. The little half-timber house in which he was born is now haven to the **Kepler Museum,** in the town center. It is devoted to his writings and discoveries. ✉ *Keplerg. 2,* ☎ *07033/6586.* 🎫 *€2, a tour costs €10.* ⏲ *June–Sept., Tues.–Fri. 10–noon and 2–4, Sat. 11–noon and 2–4, Sun. 11–noon and 2–5; Oct.–May, 1st and 3rd Sun. of month 11–noon and 2–5.*

Calw

❸ *8 km (5 mi) south of Bad Liebenzell on B–463.*

Calw, one of the Black Forest's prettiest towns, was the birthplace of Nobel Prize–winning novelist Hermann Hesse (1877–1962). He was born at Marktplatz 6, now a private home inhabited by a gentleman who designs carpets. Pause on the town's 15th-century bridge over the Nagold River; you might see a local tanner spreading hides on the river wall to dry as his ancestors have done for centuries. The town's market square, with its two sparkling fountains surrounded by 18th-century half-timber houses whose sharp gables pierce the sky, is an ideal spot for relaxing, picnicking, or people-watching, especially when it's market time. Calw has been investing heavily in restoring more of its old buildings, and it is paying off.

The **Hermann Hesse Museum** recounts the life of the great author and philosopher, and genuine cosmopolite, in personal belongings, photographs, manuscripts, and documents (English translation). The lower floor of the museum houses the Calw municipal gallery, with changing exhibitions and permanent display of the works of painters Richard

Ziegler, Rudolf Schlichter, and others. ✉ *Marktpl. 30,* ☎ *07051/7522.* 🎫 *€2.50.* ⏲ *Tues.–Sun. 11–5, Thurs. 11–7.*

Hirsau, 3 km (2 mi) north of Calw, has ruins of a 9th-century monastery, now the setting for the Klosterspiele Hirsau (open-air theater performances) in July and August. Buy advance tickets at the tourist office in Calw (✉ Marktbrücke 1, ☎ 07051/968–844).

Dining and Lodging

$$ ★ ✕🏨 **Kloster Hirsau–Klosterschenke.** The hotel, a model of comfort and gracious hospitality, is just outside Calw in Calw-Hirsau, near the ruins of the monastery. The restaurant ($$–$$$) serves such regional specialties as *Schneckensuppe* (snail soup) and *Schwäbischer Rostbraten* (panfried beefsteak topped with sautéed onions). ✉ *Wildbaderstr. 2, D–75365,* ☎ *07051/96740,* FAX *07051/51795. 42 rooms. Restaurant, no a/c, cable TV, some in-room data ports, bowling, some pets allowed (fee), no-smoking rooms. AE, MC, V.*

$–$$ ✕🏨 **Ratsstube.** Most of the original features, including 16th-century beams and brickwork, are preserved at this historic house in the center of Calw. Rooms are small, but they are brightly decorated with pastel colors. The restaurant ($–$$) serves such sturdy fare as Zwiebelrostbraten, or the finer wild duck in orange sauce. A salad buffet will take care of smaller appetites, and lunchtime always has a special dish. ✉ *Marktpl. 12, D–75365,* ☎ *07051/92050,* FAX *07051/70826. 13 rooms. Restaurant, no a/c, cable TV, some pets allowed. MC, V.*

OFF THE BEATEN PATH **ZAVELSTEIN** – On the road south, watch for a sign to this tiny town 5 km (3 mi) out of Calw. The short detour up a side valley to this spot is well worth taking, particularly in spring, when surrounding meadows are carpeted with wild crocuses.

En Route Back on the main road going south, you'll come next to a turnoff marked TALMÜHLE/SEITZENTAL. A winding road leads to **Neubulach,** a town that was home to one of the oldest and, until it closed in 1924, most productive **silver mines** of the Black Forest. Since then doctors have discovered that the dust-free interior of the mine helps in the treatment of asthma patients. Today a therapy center is in the mine. The ancient shafts can also be visited. ☎ *07053/969–510.* 🎫 *Guided tour of mine €3.* ⏲ *Apr.–Nov., weekdays 10–4 and weekend 10–5.*

The small, fortified town of **Wildberg,** 8 km (5 mi) farther south, has a 15th-century wood town hall and the remains of a medieval castle.

Nagold

❹ *10 km (6 mi) south of Wildberg.*

The town of half-timber buildings lies at the confluence of two gentle-flowing rivers, the Nagold and the Waldach. The town's elliptical street plan was designed some 750 years ago when Nagold was first established. The Romanesque **Remigiuskirche** (Remigius Church), and the modest hilltop remains of a medieval castle are its historic highlights.

Dining and Lodging

$$ ✕🏨 **Pfrondorfermühle.** This old mill with half-timber houses and modern annexes is on the road between Nagold and Wildberg. It offers family-style Black Forest comfort and hospitality. The quietly appointed restaurant has a delightful range of cuisine, from simple Maultaschen to fine salmon in basil sauce. There are two luxurious suites for special occasions and a dance bar, in case you feel the need to live it up. ✉ *Badstr. 1, D-72202 Nagold,* ☎ *07452/84000,* FAX

07452/840–048, WEB www.pfrondorfermuehle.de. 19 rooms. Restaurant, bar, no a/c, cable TV, some pets allowed (fee). AE.

En Route Head west toward Freudenstadt on local highway B–28. The road skirts another gem of the Black Forest, the ancient town of **Altensteig,** which is on a sunny terracelike slope above the Nagold River. A steep, marked route up the hill through the narrow medieval streets brings you (huffing and puffing) into an unspoiled Old Town with half-timber houses and a 13th-century fort with a well-preserved tower housing an exceptionally nice **museum** (☎ 07453/1360; free, except for special exhibitions; ⏲ May–Sept., Wed. 2–4, Sun. 11–noon and 2–5; Oct.–Apr., Sun. 11–noon and 2–5). It contains various displays relating to life and work in the Black Forest, including the castle's own fully equipped old kitchen and wood exhibitions.

In summer pause at the man-made reservoir near **Erzgrube,** 12 km (7 mi) from Altensteig (follow signs to Erzgrube), for a swim, a picnic, or a hike through one of the densest parts of the Black Forest, where 200-year-old trees tower 150 ft or more.

B–28 continues, passing the oldest town of the northern Black Forest, **Dornstetten.** If you fancy another dip into the past, stop to see the 17th-century town hall, flanked by equally venerable buildings, the low eaves of their red roofs frame magnificent half-timber facades. The fountain dates from the 16th century.

Freudenstadt

5 *40 km (25 mi) south of Nagold, 22 km (14 mi) southwest of Altensteig.*

At 2,415 ft high, Freudenstadt claims to be the sunniest German resort. The country's largest nature preserve, the Parkwald, with miles of walking trails, abuts it. The tourist office organizes bike tours of the countryside.

The town was flattened by the French in April of 1945 because the Nazis had declared it a stronghold—and has since been rebuilt with painstaking care. It was founded in 1599 to house both silver miners and refugees from religious persecution in what is now the Austrian province of Carinthia (*Freudenstadt* means "city of joy"). You'll find the streets still laid out in the checkerboard formation decreed by the original planners. The vast central square, more than 650 ft long, and edged with arcaded shops, is Germany's largest marketplace. It still awaits the palace that was to have been built there for the city's founder, Prince Frederick I of Württemberg, who died before work could begin. When the fountains all spout on this vast expanse, it can be quite a sight, and refreshing as well. Don't miss Freudenstadt's Protestant **parish church,** just off the square. Its lofty nave is L-shape, a rare architectural liberty in the early 17th century. It was constructed in this way so the sexes would be separated and unable to see each other during services. Though the church seems bare, there are several fine sculptures of angels visible along the edge of the ceiling.

OFF THE BEATEN PATH

SCHAPBACH – From this town 22 km (14 mi) southwest of Freudenstadt, in the enchanting Wolfach River valley, head up into the hills to **Glaswaldsee.** The tree-fringed lake will probably be all yours. Parts of the neighboring Poppel Valley are so wild that carnivorous flowers number among the rare plants carpeting the countryside. In July and August the bug-eating *Sonnentau* is in full bloom in the **Hohlohsee** (Hohloh Lake) nature reserve, near Enzklösterle. Farther north, just off B–500 near Hornisgrinde Mountain, a path to the remote **Wildsee** passes through a nature reserve, where rare wildflowers bloom in spring.

Dining and Lodging

$$–$$$$ ★ ✕ **Warteck.** Flowers fill this house, even in the nooks and crannies between the lead-pane windows. The menu strikes a delicious balance between local and extraregional cuisine. Choices include succulent lamb in wild herbs, or *Leipziger Allerlei,* a vegetable stew with river crabs. In season the *Spargel* (asparagus) is dressed in an aromatic hazelnut vinaigrette. ✉ *Stuttgarterstr. 14,* ☎ *07441/91920. DC, MC, V. Closed Tues.*

$–$$ ✕ **Ratskeller.** If it's cold outside, ask for a place near the Kachelofen, a large, traditional tile stove. Swabian dishes usually on the menu are Zwiebelrostbraten, served with sauerkraut, and pork fillet with mushroom gravy. In season there's venison, and a specialty is the homemade trout roulade with crab sauce. ✉ *Marktpl. 8,* ☎ *07441/952–805. V. Closed Wed.*

$$–$$$$ ★ ✕🏨 **Schwarzwaldhotel Birkenhof.** A woodland setting and a wide range of sports facilities are principal attractions of this motel-like hostelry above town. The two restaurants ($$–$$$) offer hearty Black Forest fare. ✉ *Wildbaderstr. 95, D–72250,* ☎ *07441/8920,* FAX *07441/4763. 62 rooms. Restaurant, café, no a/c, cable TV, in-room data ports, pool, sauna, bowling, squash, bar, some pets allowed (fee), no-smoking rooms. AE, MC, V.*

$$ ✕🏨 **Bären.** The Montigels have owned the sturdy old Gasthof Bären since 1878, and they strive to maintain tradition and personal service. Rooms are modern but contain such homey touches as farmhouse-style bedsteads and cupboards. The beamed restaurant ($–$$) is a favorite with the locals. Its menu includes Swabian dishes (roasts in heavy sauces, fried Maultaschen) and lighter international fare. The trout is caught locally. ✉ *Langestr. 33, D–72250,* ☎ *07441/2729,* FAX *07441/2887. 33 rooms. Restaurant, cable TV, some in-room data ports, no-smoking rooms. Restaurant closed Mon., Fri., and for lunch, except on Sun. DC, MC, V.*

$ ✕🏨 **Hotel Adler.** It's a simple hotel just off the main square, but that does not mean uncomfortable. Some of the very affordable rooms even have a balcony that lets you enjoy a view of behind-the-scenes Freudenstadt. The restaurant ($–$$) provides a square meal with local specialties. Some evenings are devoted to pancakes in all shapes and sizes and with all kinds of filling. ✉ *Forststr. 6, D–72250,* ☎ *07441/91520,* FAX *07441/915–252,* WEB *www.adler.fds.de. 13 rooms. Restaurant, no a/c, cable TV. MC, V.*

$ ✕🏨 **Zum Schwanen.** After all the pink sandstone and dark beams, this bright, white building just a few steps from the main square has an especially uplifting quality to it. Many locals come to enjoy fine regional specialties ($–$$) in the restaurant with light wood paneling. The cakes, by the way, are also excellent in the company of an afternoon coffee on the warm terrace. ✉ *Forststr. 6, D–72250,* ☎ *07441/91550,* FAX *07441/915–544. 16 rooms. Restaurant, no a/c, cable TV, some in-room data ports, some pets allowed (fee), no-smoking rooms. MC, V.*

Shopping

Germans prize Black Forest ham as an aromatic souvenir. You can buy one at any butcher shop in the region, but it's more fun to visit a *Schinkenräucherei* (smokehouse), where the ham is actually cured. **Hermann Wein's** (☎ 07443/2450) Schinkenräucherein, in the village of Musbach, near Freudenstadt, is one of the leading smokehouses in the area. If you have a group of people, call ahead to find out if the staff can show you around.

Baiersbronn

7 km (4½ mi) northwest of Freudenstadt.

The mountain resort of Baiersbronn has an incredible collection of hotels and bed-and-breakfasts providing rest and relaxation in the beautiful surroundings. Economic life here, however, was not always so bright, and in the 1830s and 1850s many of the locals headed for the United States and Canada. Nowadays Haists and Finkbeiners from the New World return to look for distant relatives in Baiersbronn. Most people come here to walk, ski, golf, and ride horseback. An interesting walk leads from restaurant to restaurant. Near the town hall and church in the upper part of town is the little **Hauff's Märchenmuseum** (Fairy-tale Museum), devoted to the crafts and life around Baiersbronn and the fairy-tale author Wilhelm Hauff (1802–1827), who once lived here. ✉ *Rosenpl. 3,* ☎ *07442/841–414.* 🎫 *€1.50.* ⏲ *Wed. and weekends 2–5.*

Dining and Lodging

$$$–$$$$ ★ ✕🏨 **Traube Tonbach.** The luxurious Traube Tonbach hotel has three outstanding restaurants ($$$$). If the classic French cuisine of the fabulous Schwarzwaldstube (closed Monday and Tuesday) is too expensive (menus begin at €74), try either the international fare of the Köhlerstube or eat at the Bauernstube, renowned for its Swabian dishes. In the latter two you dine beneath beam ceilings at tables bright with fine silver and glassware. The hotel is a harmonious blend of old and new, and each room presents sweeping views of the Black Forest. A small army of extremely helpful and friendly staff nearly outnumbers the guests. You can write folks back home from the Internet café. ✉ *Tonbachstr. 237, D–72270 Tonbach/Baiersbronn,* ☎ *07442/4920,* FAX *07442/492–692,* WEB *www.traube.tonbach.de. 108 rooms, 55 apartments, 12 suites. 3 restaurants, café, cafeteria, no a/c, cable TV, Internet, tennis court, 3 pools, gym, hair salon, sauna, bowling, some pets allowed (fee). AE, DC, MC, V.*

$$$ ★ ✕🏨 **Bareiss.** This modern resort resembles a cruise ship moored on a hilltop above Baiersbronn. Inside, some guest rooms have dark-wood furniture and tapestry-papered walls, while others have a light and airy Laura Ashley decor. Its elegant Restaurant Bareiss ($$$$; closed Monday and Tuesday) serves imaginative cuisine and carefully selected wines (30 brands of champagne alone). In its rustic Dorfstuben, homemade sausage and smoked pork loin are ever popular. By the open fire in its Kaminstube, international dishes are served. The hotel itself is among the most lavish and best equipped in the Black Forest. Some suites (€382 and up in season) have their own saunas, solariums, and whirlpool baths. ✉ *Gärtenbühlweg 14, D–07442 Mitteltal/Baiersbronn,* ☎ *07442/470,* FAX *07442/47320,* WEB *www.relaischateaux.fr/bareiss. 53 rooms, 37 apartments, 10 suites. 3 restaurants, no a/c in some rooms, cable TV, some in-room data ports, 6 tennis courts, 6 pools, gym, hair salon, sauna, bicycles, billiards, bowling, bar, some pets allowed (fee), no-smoking rooms. AE, DC, MC, V.*

$$ ✕🏨 **Hotel Lamm.** The half-timber exterior of this 200-year-old building presents a clear picture of the traditional Black Forest hotel within. Rooms are furnished with heavy oak fittings and some fine antiques. In winter the lounge's fireplace is a welcome sight when returning from the slopes (the ski lift is nearby). In its beamed restaurant ($$–$$$) you can order fish fresh from the hotel's trout pools. ✉ *Ellbacherstr. 4, D–72270 Mitteltal/Baiersbronn,* ☎ *07442/4980,* FAX *07442/49878,* WEB *www.lamm-mitteltal.de. 48 rooms, 6 apartments. Restaurant, no a/c, cable TV, Internet, pool, sauna, billiards, some pets allowed (fee). DC, MC, V.*

En Route Return to the Schwarzwald-Hochstrasse now, winding through a land of myth and fable. At the little village of Ruhestein, the side road on the left leads to the **Allerheiligen** (All Saints) ruins. This 12th-century monastery was secularized in 1803, when plans were drawn up to turn it into a prison. Two days later lightning started a fire that burned the monastery to the ground. The locals claim it was divine intervention.

Five kilometers (3 mi) north of Ruhestein is the **Mummelsee,** a small, almost circular lake. Unfortunately, a plethora of souvenir shops, a hotel, and an enormous parking lot detract from what was once a tranquil spot. Because of the lake's high mineral content, there are no fish in it. According to folklore, water nymphs surface after nightfall to dance until they are called back by the king of the lake. Throwing stones into the lake is said to tempt a monster out of its depths. If you can, visit during the mist-laden days of spring. The lake is a popular destination in the summer (for boating, not swimming), and if the path around the lake is too crowded, you can rent a pedal boat and head for the middle.

Bühlerhöhe

On B–500, 3 km (2 mi) after the turnoff to the town of Bühl, which is 17 km (11 mi) north of Ruhestein, 16 km (10 mi) south of Baden-Baden.

Several of the finest hotels and restaurants in the Black Forest are on Bühlerhöhe, the thickly wooded heights above the town of Bühl. The Bühl Valley and the surrounding area have spas, ruins, quaint villages, and a legendary velvety red wine called *Affenthaler.*

Dining and Lodging

$$$$ ★ ✕🏨 **Schlosshotel Bühlerhöhe.** This premiere "castle-hotel" stands majestically on its own extensive grounds 15 km (9 mi) above Baden-Baden, with spectacular views over the heights of the Black Forest. Walking trails start virtually at the hotel door. Its restaurant, the Imperial ($$$$; closed Monday–Tuesday and January–mid-February), features French fare with international touches, such as lamb in feta cheese crust with ratatouille and gnocchi. In its Schlossrestaurant, overlooking the Rhine Valley, the food is both more regional and international. ✉ *Schwarzwaldhochstr. 1, D–77815 Bühl/Baden-Baden,* ☎ *07226/550,* FAX *07226/55777,* WEB *www.buehlerhoehe.com. 73 rooms, 17 suites. 2 restaurants, no a/c in some rooms, cable TV with movies, Internet, tennis court, pool, health club, sauna, bar, some pets allowed (fee), no-smoking rooms. AE, DC, MC, V.*

$$ ✕🏨 **Die Grüne Bettlad.** Hand-painted furniture, bright with flowers, adds great charm to the rooms of this 300-year-old half-timber hotel down in the town of Bühl. In its cozy, old-fashioned restaurant ($$$–$$$$) the dishes are regional but with modern updates. Roast lamb with herbs and a ragout of prawns are among popular items. ✉ *Blumenstr. 4, D–77815 Bühl,* ☎ *07223/93130,* FAX *07223/931–310. 6 rooms. Restaurant, no a/c, cable TV, some pets allowed (fee). MC, V. Closed Sun., Mon. and Dec. 25–mid-Jan. and 2 wks in late July.*

$–$$ 🏨 **Cafe-Pension Jägersteig.** Magnificent views of the wide Rhine Valley as far as the French Vosges Mountains are included in the room rate at this spectacularly situated pension, high above the town of Bühl and its vineyards. ✉ *Kappelwindeckstr. 95a, D–77815 Bühl/Baden-Baden,* ☎ *07223/98590,* FAX *07223/985–998. 14 rooms. Restaurant, no a/c, cable TV, in-room data ports, some pets allowed (fee). MC, V.*

Baden-Baden

★ ❻ *51 km (32 mi) north of Freudenstadt, 24 km (15 mi) north of Mummelsee.*

Baden-Baden, the famous and fashionable spa, is downhill all the way north on B–500 from the Mummelsee. The town rests in a wooded valley and is atop the extensive underground hot springs that gave the city its name. Roman legions of the emperor Caracalla discovered the springs and named the area Aquae. The leisure classes of the 19th century rediscovered the bubbling waters, establishing Baden-Baden as the unofficial summer residence of many European royal families. Their palatial homes and stately villas still grace its tree-lined avenues. Relaxing Baden-Baden seems to have become a favorite place for high-powered negotiations in the political and business world. The location, many say, is conducive to harmony.

As Germany's ultimate high-fashion resort, the small city basks unabashedly in wealth and pleasure. In fact, Baden-Baden boasts Germany's highest concentration of millionaires. Baden-Baden's image as a soft-music-and-champagne-in-a-silver-bucket kind of place is being rejuvenated to a certain extent. The spa concept is focusing more on wellness these days, and the shops and eateries in town are gearing up for a younger crowd. The pop music scene is well established as well, cheek-by-jowl with ballet, plays, concerts (by the excellent Southwest German Radio Symphony Orchestra). There's horse racing at the Iffezheim racetrack to the west of town and high-stakes action at Baden-Baden's renowned casino.

The main preoccupation here is ambling about to wherever your whim takes you. Sophienstrasse is a superb old-fashioned alley lined with trees that leads into the heart of town. The **Lichtentaler Allee,** right in the middle of town, is an extensive park with carefully groomed paths; occasional sculptures; and an extensive rose garden, the **Gönneranlage,** with more than 300 types of roses. Close by is the **Russian church** (🎫 €.50; ⏲ Feb.–Nov. 10–6), identifiable by its golden onion dome. At the other end of the park the paths climb up the **Michaelsberg,** where the Black Forest brooks have been arranged into pretty waterfalls.

The Lichtentaler Allee ends at **Kloster Lichtenthal,** a medieval Cistercian abbey surrounded by thick defensive walls. The small royal chapel next to the church was built in 1288 and was used from the late 14th century onward as a final resting place for the Baden dynasty princes. The abbey is still inhabited by nuns (around 30) who tend the garden, run a school, and have a fine touch with religious artwork. ✉ *Hauptstr. 40,* ☎ *07221/504–910.* 🎫 *Tours in groups of 7 and more €2.* ⏲ *Tours Tues.–Sun. 3* PM.

Baden-Baden is quite proud of its **casino,** Germany's largest and oldest, and some say most beautiful. It is part of the entire spa complex that includes a manicured park along the Oos river, the Kurhaus, the *Trinkhalle* (Drinking Hall), a theater, shops, hotels, and restaurants. A Parisian, Jacques Bénazet, persuaded the sleepy little Black Forest spa to build gambling rooms to enliven its evenings. In 1853 his son Edouard Bénazet commissioned Charles Séchan, a stage designer associated with the Paris opera house, to create a design along the lines of the greatest French imperial palaces. The result was a series of richly decorated gaming rooms in which even an emperor could feel at home—and did. Kaiser Wilhelm I was a regular visitor, as was his chancellor, Bismarck. The Russian novelist Dostoyevsky, the Aga Khan, and Marlene Dietrich all patronized the place. Visitors are required to sign a declaration that they enter with sufficient funds to settle subsequent debts (minimum stake is €2.50 weekdays, €5 weekends; maximum €10,000). Passports are necessary as proof of identity and jacket and tie are required. Guided tours are offered. ✉ *Kaiserallee 1,* ☎ *07221/*

21060. €3. Tours €4. Mon.–Thurs. 2 PM–2 AM, Fri.–Sun. 2 PM–3 AM. Tours Apr.–Sept., daily 9–noon, Oct.–Mar., daily 10–11:45 AM.

If you've come to take the waters, be sure to have a look in the casino and perhaps take a swim in the palatial **Caracalla-Therme,** a vast modern complex that adjoins the casino with no fewer than seven pools. Strolling around this supremely elegant resort, you can sample the gracious atmosphere that, more than almost anywhere else in Germany, retains the feeling of a more unhurried, leisured age.

Dining and Lodging

$$–$$$$ ✕ **Le Jardin de France.** This clean, crisp little French restaurant, whose owners are Alsatian, emphasizes elegant, imaginative dining in a simple setting. The duck might be roasted with raisins, figs, and nuts at Christmastime; the crayfish might be prepared with chanterelles. ✉ *Rotenbachtalstr. 10,* ☎ *07221/300–7860. AE, DC, MC, V. Closed Mon. No lunch Tues. and Fri.*

$–$$$ ✕ **Klosterschänke.** This rustic restaurant is a 10-minute drive from the center of Baden-Baden, and the food is well worth the trip, particularly on a summer evening, when you can dine outside on a tree-covered terrace. You'll probably share a rough oak table with locals; the Baden wine and locally brewed beer ensure conviviality. The menu is surprisingly imaginative, with Black Forest trout prepared in a local meunière variation. This is the best place for venison when it's in season. ✉ *Landstr. 84,* ☎ *07221/25854. V. Closed Mon. and 1 wk in summer. No lunch Tues.*

$–$$ ✕ **Weinstube Zum Engel.** The Frölich family has been in charge of the Angel (in the suburb of Neuweier) for four generations. Eduard Frölich is responsible for the wine, Gerti Frölich for the kitchen. It is an ideal place for traditional German food such as sauerbraten or Wiener schnitzel. The selection of wines, served by the glass, does supreme justice to the fine local vintages. ✉ *Mauerbergstr. 62,* ☎ *07223/57243. No credit cards. Closed Mon., Tues., and 2 wks in Mar.*

$$$–$$$$ ★ ✕ **Der Kleine Prinz.** Delicately rendered murals depicting scenes from St. Exupéry's *The Little Prince* give a lively touch to this antique-filled hotel. Owners Norbert Rademacher, a veteran of the New York Hilton and Waldorf Astoria, and his interior-designer wife, Edeltraud, have skillfully combined two elegant city mansions into a unique lodging. Guest rooms are individually decorated in diverse styles. The sprawling penthouse suite has an open fireplace. Two other rooms have fireplaces, and many include double bathtubs with whirlpool baths. In the excellent restaurant ($$$–$$$$), Chef Berthold Krieg has been in charge of the kitchen for more than a decade. His nouvelle cuisine combined with unmistakable German thoroughness has won the restaurant highest acclaim in demanding Baden-Baden. Try the excellent essence of turbot for a heavenly fish experience. ✉ *Lichtentalerstr. 36, D–76530,* ☎ *07221/346–600,* FAX *07221/346–6059,* WEB *www.derkleineprinz.de. 25 rooms, 13 suites. Restaurant, bar, no a/c in some rooms, cable TV with movies, in-room data ports, Internet, laundry service, parking (fee), some pets allowed (fee). AE, MC, V.*

$$$$ ★ **Brenner's Park Hotel & Spa.** With some justification, this stately hotel set in a private park claims to be one of the best in the world. Behind it passes leafy Lichtentaler Allee, where Queen Victoria and Czar Alexander II, among others, strolled in their day. Luxury abounds in the hotel, and all the rooms and suites (the latter costing up to €670 a day) are sumptuously furnished and appointed. ✉ *Schillerstr. 6, D–76530,* ☎ *07221/9000,* FAX *07221/38772,* WEB *www.brenners-park.de. 68 rooms, 18 suites, 12 apartments. 2 restaurants, no a/c in some rooms,* *cable TV, some in-room data ports, pool, gym, hair salon, sauna, spa, bar, some pets allowed (fee). AE, DC, MC, V.*

$$$–$$$$ **Belle Epoque.** This spacious two-story 1870s house, in its own garden behind wrought-iron gates, is the the sister hotel to Der Kleine Prinz. The entire building is under monument protection. Each of its rooms is furnished in a separate style, ranging from Henri II to art nouveau. Under the eaves are the Brahms or Mozart rooms, garrets of sheer luxury. In the garden is Baden-Baden's only sequoia. ✉ *Maria-Victoria-Str. 2b, D–76530,* ☎ *07221/300–660,* FAX *07221/300–666,* WEB *www.hotelbelleepoque.de. 16 rooms. Cable TV, in-room data ports. AE, D, MC, V.*

$$ **Deutscher Kaiser.** In an expensive town this central, established hotel provides homey and individually styled rooms at comfortable prices. All the double rooms have balconies on a quiet street. The hotel is a few minutes' stroll from the casino. ✉ *Merkurstr. 9, D–76530,* ☎ *07221/2700,* FAX *07221/270–270,* WEB *www.deutscher-kaiser-baden-baden.de. 28 rooms, 1 apartment. No a/c, cable TV, in-room data ports, some pets allowed (fee). AE, DC, MC, V.*

$$ **Merkur.** The Merkur's large, comfortable rooms typify the high standards that German hospitality upholds. A solid breakfast is served in the pleasant breakfast room. Though in the middle of Baden-Baden, the hotel's setting is quiet. Ask for the special arrangements for stays lasting several days. ✉ *Merkurstr. 8,* ☎ *07221/3030,* FAX *07221/303–333,* WEB *www.hotel-merkur.com. 36 rooms. Restaurant, bar, no a/c, cable TV with movies, in-room data ports, some pets allowed (fee), no-smoking rooms. AE, D, MC, V.*

$ **Am Markt.** This 250-plus-year-old building houses a modest inn run (for more than 30 years) by the Bogner family. In the oldest part of town—a traffic-free zone—it's close to such major attractions as the Roman baths. Some rooms overlook the city. ✉ *Marktpl. 17–18, D–76530,* ☎ *07221/27040,* FAX *07221/27044. 27 rooms, 12 with bath. Restaurant, no a/c, some pets allowed. AE, DC, MC, V.*

Nightlife and the Arts

Nightlife revolves around Baden-Baden's elegant **casino,** but there are more cultural attractions as well. Baden-Baden has one of Germany's most beautiful performance halls, the **Theater** (✉ Am Goethepl., ☎ 07221/932–700), a late-baroque jewel built in 1860–62 in the style of the Paris Opera. It opened with the world premiere of Berlioz's opera *Beatrice et Benedict*. Today the theater presents a regular series of dramas, operas, and ballets.

The **Festspielhaus** (✉ Lange-Str. at Robert-Schumann-Pl., ☎ 07221/301–3101) is a state-of-the-art concert hall superbly fitted onto the old train station. Each summer Baden-Baden holds a two-week **Philharmonischer Sommer Festival** (✉ Schloss Solms, Solmsstr., ☎ 07221/932–791). Venues include the Kurhaus, the Kurgarten, St. Jacob's, and the Brenner's Park Hotel. The **Kurhaus** (✉ Kaiserallee 1, ☎ 07221/932–700) hosts concerts year-round.

Baden-Baden tends to be a quiet place, but there is a nightclub in the Kurhaus, **Equipage.** The Hotel Merkur has a small nightclub called the **Living Room** (✉ Merkurstr. 8). For a subdued evening stop by the **Oleander Bar,** in Baden-Baden's top hotel, the Brenner's Park (✉ Schillerstr. 6, ☎ 07221/9000).

Outdoor Activities and Sports

GOLF

The 18-hole Baden-Baden course is considered one of Europe's finest. Contact the **Golf Club** (✉ Fremersbergstr. 127, ☎ 07221/23579).

HORSEBACK RIDING

Riding facilities in Baden-Baden include an **equestrian hall** (✉ Gunzenbachstr. 4a, ☎ 07221/949–625), a special area for riding instructions, and a sand track 1-km (½-mi) long. Annual international meets take place in late May, early June, late August, and early September.

SWIMMING

The **Caracalla-Therme** complex is the most lavish swimming pool in the Black Forest region. Built in the 1980s, it has five indoor and two outdoor pools; a sauna, a solarium, and Jacuzzis; state-of-the-art fitness areas; as well as courses of thermal water-therapy treatment. ✉ *Römerpl. 11,* ☎ *07221/275–940.* 🎟 *2 hrs €11; 3 hrs €13; 4 hrs €15.* ⏲ *Daily 8 AM–10 PM.*

The **Friedrichsbad** is a 19th-century bathing paradise. The sexes have different entrances, but meet in the middle, so to speak. The swimming pool allows mixed nude bathing every day except before 4 PM on Monday, Tuesday, and Thursday; people who feel modest about such things should cross the Römerplatz to the Caracalla Pool. ✉ *Römerpl. 1,* ☎ *07221/275–920.* 🎟 *3 hrs €21; 3½ hrs, including massage, €29. Children under 18 not admitted.* ⏲ *Mon.–Sat. 9 AM–10 PM, Sun. noon–8.*

Shopping

Like everything else in Baden-Baden, the shops lean toward elegance. High-end antiques shops have great appeal for both collectors and browsers, but you will need a well-stuffed wallet.

The region's wines, especially the dry Baden whites and delicate reds, are highly valued in Germany. Buy them directly from any vintner on the Baden Wine Road. At Yburg, outside Baden-Baden, the 400-year-old **Nägelsförster Hof** (✉ Nägelssörstr. 1, ☎ 07221/35550) wine tavern and shop has panoramic views of the town and wine tastings (weekdays 8–6).

En Route The road to Gernsbach, a couple of miles east of Baden-Baden, skirts the 2,000-ft-high mountain peak **Merkur,** named after a Roman monument to the god Mercury, which still stands just below the mountain summit. You can take the cable car to the summit, but it's not a trip for the fainthearted—the incline of more than 50% is one of Europe's steepest. 🎟 *Round-trip €3.50.* ⏲ *Mid-Feb.–mid-Dec., daily 10–6.*

Bad Herrenalb

7 *28 km (17 mi) northeast of Baden-Baden, 8 km (5 mi) south of Marxzell.*

The woodlands of the Alb River valley fold around the popular spa of Bad Herrenalb. The town has all the amenities for relaxation, from an extensive park, to shops; cafés; and, of course, the spa facilities, which address even cardiovascular and respiratory illnesses, rheumatism, and convalescing. The hills are crisscrossed with well-kept hiking paths. Neighboring Frauenalb (the "Frauen," women, is the counterpart to "Herren," men) has the ruins of a former cloister.

Dining and Lodging

$$$ ★ ✕🏨 **Mönchs Posthotel.** This half-timber building with an ornate turret is surrounded by beautiful gardens that include the ruins of an old monastery. The Locanda restaurant ($$$–$$$$; closed Monday, Tuesday, and Christmas–February), in the park, offers Mediterranean fare, and the Kloster Schänke serves local dishes year-round. Guest rooms are comfortable and elegantly furnished, and no two are the same. ✉ *Doblerstr. 2, D–76332,* ☎ *07083/7440,* FAX *07083/74422. 24 rooms,*

1 suite, 6 apartments. 2 restaurants, no a/c, cable TV, pool, hair salon, massage, some pets allowed (fee). AE, DC, MC, V.

Marxzell

8 *8 km (5 mi) north of Bad Herrenalb on road to Karlsruhe.*

In the village of Marxzell a group of ancient locomotives and other old machines at the side of the road lure you into the **Fahrzeugmuseum** (Transport Museum). It looks more like a junkyard, with geese and ducks waddling freely about, but every kind of early engine is represented in this museum dedicated to the German automobile pioneer Karl Benz (1844–1929). Germans say it was he who built the first practical automobile, in 1888, a claim hotly disputed by the French. They assert a Frenchman constructed a steam-powered tricycle in 1769 that seated four and traveled for 20 minutes at 3.6 kph (2.25 mph). On display are motorcycles, Rolls Royces, Mercedes, Alfa Romeos, and Jaguars. ✉ *Albtalstr. 2,* ☎ *07248/6262.* €2.50. ⏲ *Daily 2–5.*

Ettlingen

9 *12 km (7 mi) north of Marxzell.*

Ettlingen is a 1,200-year-old town that's now practically a suburb of its newer and much larger neighbor, Karlsruhe, just a streetcar ride away. Bordered by the Alb River, Ettlingen's ancient center is a maze of auto-free cobblestone streets. Come in the summer for the annual Schlossberg theater and music festival in the beautiful baroque **Schloss.** The palace was built in the mid-18th century, and its striking domed chapel—today a concert hall—was designed by Cosmas Damian Asam, a leading architect of the south German baroque. Its ornate, swirling ceiling fresco is typical of the heroic, large-scale, illusionistic decoration of the period. ✉ *Schlosspl. 3,* ☎ *07243/101–273.* *Free.* ⏲ *Tues.–Sun. 10–5; tour weekends at 2.*

Dining and Lodging

$–$$ ✕ **Ratsstuben.** Originally used to store salt, these 16th-century cellars by the fast-flowing Alb River now serve international fare and Teutonic food. ✉ *Kirchenpl. 1–3,* ☎ *07243/76130. DC, MC, V.*

$$$–$$$$ ★ ✕ **Hotel-Restaurant Erbprinz.** This is one of the most historic hotels in Ettlingen, and it even has its own streetcar stop. For many, the real reason for staying here is the top-rated restaurant's magnificent nouvelle German cuisine ($$$–$$$$)—though the rooms are also very comfortable. In summer dine in the charming garden, hidden away behind the hotel's green-and-gilt fencing. You might want to try pine-honey ice cream in an almond basket for dessert. ✉ *Rheinstr. 1, D–76275,* ☎ *07243/3220,* FAX *07243/16471,* WEB *www.hotel-erbprinz.de. 41 rooms, 7 suites. Restaurant, no a/c in some rooms, cable TV, in-room data ports, some pets allowed (fee). AE, DC, MC, V.*

Rastatt

20 km (12 mi) southwest of Ettlingen.

The pink-sandstone, three-wing **Schloss** that is the centerpiece of Rastatt was built at the end of the 17th century by Margrave Ludwig Wilhelm of Baden (known as Ludwig the Turk for his exploits in the Turkish wars). It was the first baroque palace of such enormous proportions to be built in Germany. Its highlights include its chapel, gardens, and a pagoda. Inside the palace itself are museums of German history. ✉ *Schlossstr.* *Free.* ⏲ *Guided tours Nov.–Mar., Tues.–Sun. 10–4; Apr.–Oct., Tues.–Sun. 10–5.*

Five kilometers (3 mi) south of Rastatt, in Förch, Ludwig the Turk's Bohemian-born wife, Sibylle Augusta, constructed her own charming little summer palace, **Schloss Favorite** (Favorite Castle), after his death. Inside, in an exotic, imaginative baroque interior of mirrors, tiles, and marble, her collection of miniatures, mosaics, and porcelain is strikingly displayed. ✉ *Off B–462,* ☎ *07222/41207.* 🎫 *€4.* ⏲ *Mid-Mar.–Sept., Tues.–Sun. 9–5.*

Karlsruhe

10 *10 km (6 mi) north of Ettlingen.*

Karlsruhe, founded at the beginning of the 18th century, is a young upstart, but what it lacks in years it makes up for in industrial and administrative importance, sitting as it does astride a vital autobahn and railroad crossroads. It is best known as the seat of the German Supreme Court, and has a high concentration of legal practitioners. The town quite literally grew up around the former **Schloss** of the margrave Karl Wilhelm, which was begun in 1715. Thirty-two avenues radiate from the palace, 23 leading into the extensive grounds, and the remaining nine forming the grid of the Old Town. It's said that the margrave fell asleep under a great oak while searching for a fan lost by his wife and dreamed that his new city should be laid out in the shape of a fan. All but one of the principal streets lead directly to the palace. The exception is Kaiserstrasse, constructed in 1800. In the palace, the **Badisches Landesmuseum** (Baden State Museum) has a large number of Greek and Roman antiquities and trophies Ludwig the Turk brought back from campaigns in Turkey in the 17th century. Most of the other exhibits are devoted to local history. ✉ *Schloss,* ☎ *0721/92665.* 🎫 *€2.50.* ⏲ *Tues. and Thurs.–Sun. 10–5, Wed. 10–8.*

Despite wartime bomb damage, much of the **Old Town** retains its elegant 18th-century appearance thanks to faithful restoration. Walk to the **Marktplatz,** the central square, to see the austere stone pyramid that marks the **margrave's tomb** and the severe neoclassic **Stephanskirche** (St. Stephen's Church), modeled on the Pantheon in Rome and built around 1810. The interior, rebuilt after the war, is incongruously modern.

★ One of the most important collections of paintings in the Black Forest region hangs in the **Staatliche Kunsthalle** (State Art Gallery). Look for masterpieces by Grünewald, Holbein, Rembrandt, and Monet, and also for work by the Black Forest painter Hans Thoma. In the **Kunsthalle Orangerie,** next door, is work by such modern artists as Braque and Beckmann. ✉ *Hans-Thoma-Str. 2,* ☎ *0721/926–3355,* WEB *www.kuntshallekarlsruhe.de.* 🎫 *€6; €12 for both museums.* ⏲ *Tues.–Fri. 10–5, weekends 10–6.*

★ In a former munitions factory, the vast **Zentrum für Kunst und Medientechnologie** (Center for Art and Media Technology), or simply ZKM, is an all-day adventure consisting of two separate museums. At the **Medienmuseum** (Media Museum) you can watch movies, listen to music, try out video games, flirt with a virtual partner, or sit on a real bicycle and pedal through a virtual New York City. The **Museum für Neue Kunst** (Museum of Modern Art; ☎ 01721/8100–1325; 🎫 €4) is a topnotch collection of media art in all genres from the end of the 20th century. Take Bus 55 to Brauerstrasse to get here. ✉ *Lorenzstr. 19,* ☎ *0721/8100–1200,* WEB *www.zkm.de.* 🎫 *€5.10; combined ticket €7.50.* ⏲ *Wed.–Sat. noon–8, Sun. 10–6.*

Nightlife and the Arts

One of the best opera houses in the region is Karlsruhe's **Badisches Staatstheater** (✉ Baumeisterstr. 11, ☎ 0721/35570). The culinary delights of Karlsruhe are especially well displayed during the **Brigandefeschd** during the second half of May—or into June, depending on how weekends fall. Anyone in the gastronomical business in Karlsruhe has a stand out in the center of town. Street theater is prominent in the annual summer **Museum Fest,** which is centered at the Badisches Landesmuseum. For more information, call the Karlsruhe tourist office.

THE CENTRAL BLACK FOREST

The Central Black Forest takes in the Simonswald, Elz, and Glotter valleys as well as Triberg and Furtwangen, with their cuckoo clock museums. The area around the Triberg Falls—the highest falls in Germany—is also renowned for pom-pom hats, thatch-roof farmhouses, and mountain railways. The Schwarzwaldbahn (Black Forest Railway; Offenburg–Villingen line), which passes through Triberg, is one of the most scenic in all of Europe.

Alpirsbach

11 *16 km (10 mi) south of Freudenstadt.*

The Kloster Alpirsbach monastery was built in flamboyant Gothic style and has had several restorations. The **Brauerei** (brewery) was once part of the monastery and has brewed beer since the Middle Ages. The unusually soft water gives the beer a flavor that is widely acclaimed. Call ahead before visiting. ✉ *Marktpl. 1,* ☎ *07444/670.* €3. ⏲ *Thurs. 10–noon for individual tourists; Mon.–Wed. 10–noon for groups.*

The Protestant Romanesque **Stiftskirche** (Abbey Church), also on the monastery grounds, is one of the best preserved in the region. Inside it is virtually empty, except for some faded 12th-century frescoes in the nave and a 20-ft Romanesque wooden bench decorated with small lathed wooden beads. In summer concerts are held regularly in the church.

Dining and Lodging

$–$$ ✕ **Zwickel Kaps.** Sit down at one of the massive wooden tables—next to the porcelain-tile stove if it's a cold day—and order a bowl of *Flädelsuppe* (broth with pancake strips) and beef stewed in local wine. ✉ *Marktstr. 3,* ☎ *07444/51727. MC, V. Closed Mon., 2 wks after Carnival, and 1st wk in Nov.*

$$ ✕ **Gasthof Waldhorn.** Just off the main road, the Waldhorn is where the locals come to enjoy a beer or to discuss some soccer or politics in a congenial atmosphere. The robust meals ($$–$$$$), in portions fit for two, are served at family-size tables. The old half-timber hotel is remarkably large owing to a modern annex that is not visible from the outside. Rooms are clean and comfortable. ✉ *Kreuzg. 4, D–72275 Alpirsbach,* ☎ *07444/95110,* FAX *07444/951–155. 24 rooms. Pub, no a/c, cable TV, Internet, some pets allowed. AE, DC, MC, V.*

Schiltach

12 *10 km (6 mi) south of Alpirsbach.*

Stop at Schiltach to admire the outer **frescoes** on the 16th-century Rathaus, which tell the town's vivid history; specifically, when witchcraft was suspected in the town's three big fires—1510, 1533, and 1590—and when the raftsmen held sway. The Rathaus itself stands among one of the most delightful ensembles of half-timber houses on this route. Schiltach has four well-stocked and highly instructive museums. Opposite the Rathaus is the **Apothekenmuseum,** Germany's largest pharmacy museum, with an alchemist's office and everything relating to the past preparation, storage, and sale of medicine. ✉ *Marktpl. 5,* ☎ *07836/360.* 🎫 *€1.50.* ⏲ *Apr.–Oct., Tues.–Fri. and Sun. 10:30–noon and 2:30–5, Sat. 2:30–4:30.*

The **Museum am Markt** is devoted to town history (including the business with the suspected witchcraft), its guilds, crafts, and citizenry. ✉ *Marktpl. 13,* ☎ *07836/5875.* 🎫 *Free.* ⏲ *Apr.–Oct., Mon.–Sun. 11–4; from the 4th advent to Jan. 6, 2–4 only.*

On the main street, you'll find the **Schüttesägmuseum,** whose name refers to the water-powered saw used before the steam engine and even into modern times. The museum specializes in saws and the lumber industry. The machines are demonstrated on Friday at 3 PM. ✉ *Hauptstr. 1,* ☎ *07836/5875.* 🎫 *Free.* ⏲ *Apr.–Oct., Tues.–Sun. 11–5.*

Schiltach's big industry is bath furnishings made by the Hansgrohe company, founded in 1901. The factory also has a **museum** showing everything relating to bathing and kitchens from the last 150 years on nearly 35,000 square ft. ✉ *Auestr. 10,* ☎ *07836/511–208.* 🎫 *€1.* ⏲ *Daily 11–4.*

Wolfach

14 km (9 mi) south of Schiltach.

This cobblestone town is known for its 600-year-old castle, the colorful facade of its town hall, and its market square edged with turreted and half-timber houses. The Wolfach and Kinzig rivers meet here, and a loggers' rafting festival is held each July.

En Route The **Dorotheenhütte** (Dorothea Blast Furnace) is one of the few remaining Black Forest factories where glass is blown using centuries-old techniques. You can watch the teams at work making vases or blowing and etching drinking glasses. The large sales room includes a Christmas display and has all kinds of items that make excellent souvenirs. ✉ *Glashüttenweg 4,* ☎ *07834/751.* 🎫 *€3.* ⏲ *Daily 9–4:30; shop is open until 5:30. Closed Sun. and holidays Jan. 1–Apr. 30.*

Dining and Lodging

$ ✕🏨 **Gasthof Hecht.** There's a crisp, modern look to the rooms in this 300-year-old half-timber guest house on Wolfach's main street and a kitchen ($–$$) that serves such hearty fare as *Gamsbraten mit Steinpilzen* (chamois roast with cèpe mushrooms). ✉ *Hauptstr. 51, D–77709 Wolfach,* ☎ *07834/538,* FAX *07834/47223,* WEB *www.hecht-wolfach.de. 17 rooms. Restaurant, no a/c, cable TV, in-room data ports, some pets allowed. AE, D, MC, V. Restaurant closed Tues., 3 wks in Jan. No dinner Mon.*

Gutach

⓭ *8 km (5 mi) south of Wolfach, 17 km (11 mi) north of Triberg.*

Gutach lies in Gutachtal, a valley famous for the traditional costume, complete with pom-pom hats, worn by the women on feast days and holidays. Married women wear black ones, unmarried women red ones. The village is one of the few places in the Black Forest where you can still see thatch roofs. However, escalating costs caused by a decline in skilled thatchers, and the ever-present risk of fire, make for fewer thatch roofs than there were 20 years ago.

Near Gutach is one of the most appealing museums in the Black Forest, the **Schwarzwälder Freilichtmuseum Vogtsbauernhof** (Black Forest Open-Air Museum). Farmhouses and other rural buildings from all parts of the region have been transported here from their original locations and reassembled, complete with traditional furniture, to create a living museum of Black Forest building types through the centuries. Demonstrations ranging from traditional dances to woodworking capture life as it was in centuries past. ✉ *B–33,* ☎ *07831/93560.* 🎫 *€4.50.* ⏲ *Apr.–Oct., daily 9–6.*

OFF THE BEATEN PATH

SCHWARZWALDER TRACHTENMUSEUM (Black Forest Traditional Costume Museum) – This museum in a former Capuchin monastery in the village of Haslach, 10 km (6 mi) northwest of Gutach, is rich in pom-pom-topped straw hats, bejeweled headdresses, embroidered velvet vests, and *Fasnet* (Carnival) regalia of all parts of the forest. The town, being off the beaten path somewhat, still has an original and unpolished look and feel to it. ✉ *Altes Kapuziner Kloster,* ☎ *07832/706–170.* 🎫 *€2.* ⏲ *Apr.–Oct., Tues.–Fri. 9–5, Sun. 10–5; Nov.–Mar., Tues.–Fri. 9–noon and 1–5; in Jan. by appointment.*

Gengenbach

27 km (17 mi) north of Gutach, 52 km (33 mi) west of Freudenstadt.

Walled, half-timber Gengenbach, with its splendidly restored marketplace, is a very special place both at Carnival time and at Advent. On the first day of the pre-Lenten Carnival, townspeople awaken "Schalk," the horned symbol of the festival, from his resting place in the marketplace's Niggelturm, and on the last day he is escorted back. At Advent the 24 windows on the front of the town hall are opened one by one each day in the way of an Advent calendar to reveal pictures. Sometimes called the Rothenburg of Baden, because of its wall and the brightly colored medieval houses on its narrow streets, Gengenbach, in any season, is a charming sight to see. A farmer's market is held around the town hall.

The three-nave abbey church **St. Marien,** which adjoins the huge baroque Benedictine monastery behind the town hall, dates from the early 12th century. The Romanesque frescoes have been covered up by rather remarkable late 19th-century paintings by one Carl Philipp Schilling. Note, especially, the coffered ceilings. ⏲ *Daily 9–7.*

Dining and Lodging

$ ✕🏨 **Pfeffermühle.** Only few restaurants situated in ancient buildings truly succeed in modernizing while maintaining an authentic ambience within their ancient walls. The Pfeffermühle ($–$$) does, and it's easy to imagine the chalky officials from Gengenbach's beautiful Rathaus meeting here for the tasty *Pfeffersack,* a filet mignon steak drowned in pepper sauce. The Pfeffermühle maintains a separate hotel just outside the Old Town, but all reservations are made through the restaurant. ✉ *Viktor-Kretzstr. 17, D–77723 Gengenbach,* ☎ *07803/93350,* FAX *07803/6628,* WEB *www.pfeffermuehle-gengenbach.de. 24 rooms. Restaurant, no a/c, cable TV, in-room data ports, some pets allowed (fee), no-smoking rooms. AE, D, MC, V. Closed Thurs.*

Triberg

★ ⓮ *16 km (10 mi) south of Gutach.*

Though known for its waterfall, its museum, clocks, and other quaint man-made or natural sights, Triberg also has a small literary connection. In 1922 Ernest Hemingway spent time in town and in the Black Forest as a journalist for the *Toronto Star.* During the Triberg Hemingway days held at the end of July, fishing, readings, and special Hemingway menus at the Wehrle celebrate the great writer.

At the head of the Gutach Valley, the Gutach River plunges nearly 500 ft over seven huge granite steps at Triberg's **waterfall.** The pleasant 45-minute walk from the center of town to the top of the spectacular falls is well signposted. You can also take a longer walk that goes by a small pilgrimage church and the old Mesnerhäschen, the sacristan's house. *Waterfall €1.25; may be waived in winter.*

Triberg and Furtwangen are the towns in which to see original cuckoo clocks before buying a modern version. Black Forest culture is the focus of Triberg's famous **Schwarzwaldmuseum** (Black Forest Museum). All the cottage industries of the Black Forest, many deriving from woodwork, are exhibited here, some in neatly reconstructed workshops. The impressive collection of cuckoo clocks includes one from circa 1750 with a simple wooden mechanism. Barrel organs and fairground organs from Berlin are newcomers to the collection. ✉ *Wallfahrtstr. 4,* ☎ *07722/4434.* *€3.50.* ⏲ *May–Oct., daily 9–6; mid-Nov.–mid-Dec. only weekends 10–5, mid-Dec.–Apr., daily 10–5.*

The place to purchase a cuckoo clock is **Haus der 1000 Uhren** (House of 1,000 Clocks). The shop lives up to its name: its in-town branches are two old houses bursting with all manner of clocks; the main branch, just out of town, is distinguished by a huge cuckoo clock on the roof and a special section devoted exclusively to *Standuhren,* or grandfather clocks. The staff is multilingual and very friendly. ✉ *Branches on Triberg's main street below entrance to waterfall and off B–33 toward Offenburg,* ☎ *07722/96300.* ⏲ *Mon.–Sat. 9–5, Sun. 10–4:30.*

The **Schwarzwaldbahn** (Black Forest Railway; €13) links Offenburg and Singen (Hohentwiel) in a 149-km (93-mi) stretch. The Horberg–Triberg–St. Georgen segment is one of Germany's most scenic train rides and a remarkable example of 19th-century engineering. The track winds in near circles and plunges through a total of 39 tunnels, one of which is over a mile long. For tickets and information contact the **Tourist-Information Triberg im Kurhaus** (☎ 07722/953–230).

Dining and Lodging

$$–$$$ ✕🏨 **Romantik Parkhotel Wehrle.** This large mansion has been in the Wehrle family's possession since 1707; its steep-eaved, wisteria-covered facade dominates the town center between the marketplace and the municipal park. The service is impeccable. Rooms are individually furnished in a variety of woods with such pleasant touches as fresh flowers. The main restaurant ($$$–$$$$) has international haute cuisine; the Ochsenstube ($–$$) tends towards specialties from Baden, for example trout done a dozen different ways, all delicious. Try it grilled over coals with fennel. The Roter Salon, a dining room in a red scheme, is the non-smoking section of the Ochsenstube. ✉ *Gartenstr. 24, D–78098 Triberg im Schwarzwald,* ☎ *07722/86020,* FAX *07722/860–290,* WEB *www.romantikhotels.com/triberg. 50 rooms, 1 apartment, 1 suite. 2 restaurants, no a/c, cable TV, in-room data ports, pool, gym, sauna, parking (fee), some pets allowed (fee), no-smoking rooms. AE, DC, MC, V.*

$ ★ ✕🏨 **Hotel-Restaurant-Pfaff.** This old post-and-beam restaurant ($$), with its blue-tile Kachelofen attracts people of all types with affordable regional specialties. Try the fresh *Forelle* (trout), either steamed or *Gasthof* (in the pan), garnished with mushrooms. The Pfaff family has owned the inn since 1882. It stands right at the gateway to the famous cascade of Triberg. ✉ *Hauptstr. 85, D–78098 Triberg,* ☎ *07722/4479,* FAX *07722/7879,* WEB *www.hotel-pfaff.com. 23 rooms. Restau-*

rant, no a/c, cable TV, Internet, some pets allowed (fee), no-smoking rooms. AE, D, MC, V.

Furtwangen

15 *16 km (10 mi) south of Triberg.*

The somewhat nondescript Furtwangen is on a tourist route dubbed "the German Clock Road." You don't have to be a clock enthusiast, however, to drop in on the **Uhren Museum** (Clock Museum), the largest such museum in Germany. In a huge, ingeniously designed space, the museum charts the development of Black Forest clocks, and exhibits all types of timepieces, from church clock mechanisms, kinetic wristwatches, and old decorative desktop clocks, to punch clocks and digital blinking objects. The oddest piece is the "art clock" by local artisan August Noll, which was built from 1880 to 1885, and features the time in Calcutta, New York, Melbourne, and London, among other places. It emits the sound of a crowing of a rooster in the morning, among other chimes marking yearly events. It is occasionally demonstrated during tours. You can set your own watch to the sun dial built into the concrete of the square in front of the museum. In fact, this remarkable creation even nearly ticks off the seconds. ✉ *Robert-Gerwig-Pl. 11,* ☎ *07723/920–117.* 🎫 *€3.* ⏲ *Apr.–Oct., daily 9–6; Nov.–Mar., daily 10–5.*

The **Uhrenkabinett Wehrle** (Wehrle's Clock Gallery; ✉ Lindenstr. 2, ☎ 07223/53240) has an extensive selection of antique and modern clocks in all shapes and sizes.

THE SOUTHERN BLACK FOREST

In the south you'll find the most spectacular mountain scenery in the area, culminating in the Feldberg—at 4,899 ft, the highest mountain in the Black Forest. The region also has two large lakes, the Titisee and the Schluchsee. Freiburg is a romantic university city that incorporates vineyards, a superb Gothic cathedral, and Schauinsland Mountain.

Titisee

16 *37 km (23 mi) south of Furtwangen.*

The Titisee, carved by a glacier in the last ice age, is the most scenic lake in the Black Forest. The 2½-km-long (1½-mi-long) lake is invariably crowded in summer with boats and windsurfers, which can be rented at several points along the shore. The landscape is heavily wooded and ideal for long bike tours, which can be organized through the Titisee tourist office.

At the cuckoo clock workshop **Drubba,** (✉ Seestr. 37, ☎ 07651/981–200) clock making is demonstrated, and high-quality clocks are sold.

Dining and Lodging

$$ ✕🏨 **Hotel Adler Post.** This solid, old building is in the middle of Neustadt, a township to the east of Titisee, about 5 km (3 mi) from the lake. All the rooms are comfortably and traditionally furnished, some with hand-painted furniture and exposed beams. The reception room is full of Biedermeier antiques. The restaurant ($$–$$$$) cooks up excellent local specialties. ✉ *Hauptstr. 16, D–79822 Neustadt,* ☎ *07651/5066,* FAX *07651/3729. 30 rooms. Restaurant, no a/c, cable TV, in-room data ports, pool, massage, sauna, some pets allowed, no-smoking rooms. MC, V.*

Hinterzarten

17 *5 km (3 mi) west of Titisee, 32 km (20 mi) east of Freiburg.*

The lovely 800-year-old town of Hinterzarten is the most important resort in the southern Black Forest. Some buildings date from the 12th century, among them the church St. Oswaldskirche, built in 1146. Hinterzarten's oldest inn, the Weisses Rossle, has been in business since 1347. The Park Hotel Adler was established in 1446, although the original building was burned down during the Thirty Years' War. Hinterzarten is known throughout Germany for its summer ski jump, the **Adlerschanze** (✉ off Winterhaldenweg, to the south of town), which is used for competitions and for training purposes. Several smaller jumps for "beginners" are currently being built. The town's small **Schwarzwälder Ski Museum** recounts in photographs, paintings, costumes, and equipment the history of Black Forest skiing, which began in the 1890s on the nearby Feldberg. ✉ *Erlenbruchstr. 35,* ☎ *no phone.* €3. ⏲ *Wed. and Fri. 3–6; weekends noon–6.*

Dining and Lodging

$$$–$$$$ ★ ✕ **Park Hotel Adler.** This hotel with sumptuously appointed rooms stands on nearly 2 acres of grounds. The paneled Wirtshus restaurant ($$$–$$$$) lives up to its "inn" image with reasonable prices for the excellent regional fare. The whitefish fillets in almond-apricot butter is a delicacy worth trying. You can also choose from a large selection of cakes. By the way, Marie Antoinette once ate here. ✉ *Adlerpl. 3, D–79856,* ☎ *07652/1270,* FAX *07652/127–717,* WEB *www.parkhoteladler.de. 46 rooms, 32 suites. 2 restaurants, bar, no a/c, cable TV, in-room data ports, driving range, tennis court, pool, sauna, paddle tennis, some pets allowed (fee), no-smoking rooms. AE, DC, MC, V.*

$$ **Sassenhof.** Traditional Black Forest style reigns supreme here, from the steep-eaved wood exterior to the elegant sitting areas and guest rooms furnished with rustic, brightly painted pieces, many of them decoratively carved. Breakfast, tea, and small meals are served, but no hot dinners. ✉ *Adlerweg 17, D–79854,* ☎ *07652/1515,* FAX *07652/484,* WEB *www.sbo.de/sassenhof. 30 rooms, 10 suites. No a/c, cable TV, Internet, pool, hair salon, massage, sauna, bicycles, some pets allowed (fee). AE, DC, MC, V. Closed mid-Oct.–mid-Nov.*

Outdoor Activities and Sports

Hinterzarten is at the highest point along the Freiburg–Donaueschingen road; from it a network of far-ranging trails fans out into the forest, making it one of Germany's most popular centers for *Langlauf* (cross-country skiing) in winter and hiking in summer. Cycling is another favorite sport up in these hills and dales. The topology offers something for everyone, gentle excursions or tough mountain bike expeditions. For more information contact Feldberg's tourist office (☎ 07652/12060).

Schluchsee

18 *25 km (16 mi) from Hinterzarten (take Highway B–317, then pick up B–500).*

The largest of the Black Forest lakes, mountain-enclosed Schluchsee is near Feldberg Mountain. Schluchsee is a diverse resort, where sports enthusiasts revel in swimming, windsurfing, fishing, and, in winter, skiing. For details on outfitters contact the tourist office.

Dining

$$ **Kur- und Sporthotel Feldberger Hof.** This is the biggest and best-appointed hotel in the area. Amid the woods and meadows of the Feld-

Close-Up

DRIVEN TO WANDERLUST

YOU'RE ON THE AUTOBAHN, not zipping through the countryside at illegal state-side speeds but crawling along at 25 mph. Far from *Fahrvergnügen* ("the pleasure of driving"—remember the Volkswagen commercial?), this is *Stau*: complete gridlock.

The facilitators of today's wanderlust, that German passion for hiking and traveling, are cars, complete with heatable upholstery and that roll of toilet paper perched on the rear window shelf, often covered by a little knitted hat. Wanderlust gains momentum when BMWs and Mercedes accelerate to a staggering 180 mph. Herein lies the true idea of wanderlust: to move freely through the countryside rather than to arrive somewhere.

Wanderlust has been a cultural leitmotiv for centuries. Living conditions were fairly harsh in Germany until the mid-1800s, and the political system and tightly organized society usually repressive. In an empire strongly defined by provincial regions, wanderlust came to represent a rebellious departure from one's homeland. In the 19th century romantic literature and art idealized the image of independent travelers. Back then, it was mostly young and confused men, such as the famous *Taugenichts* (ne'er-do-wells) of Joseph von Eichendorff's novel, who traveled the world with the navel-gazing intent of finding their inner selves. To those who did not belong to the affluent noble class, wanderlust was a means to practical training. Even today apprentices of many professions, most notably carpenters, might need to travel the country for several years, offering their services along the way, before they are considered qualified to settle down and start their own business.

The aspiring middle class in the early 19th century coined the phrase *Reisen bildet* (travel educates)—a saying many German teenagers today, dragged through museums while on vacation, cringe to hear. Goethe, the Humboldt brothers, and their ilk set a precedent by earnestly exploring wherever they traveled. Based on the number of Germans chasing tans along beaches around the globe, it appears that wanderlust as cultural exploration may have dropped off. Still, you'll encounter organized groups of Germans at any sightseeing spot in the country. They might even be on a *Bildungsurlaub* (educational vacation), a uniquely German social institution. It's a paid "vacation" an employer is obligated to grant employees so they can travel and "improve" themselves.

But wanderlust also stands in sharp juxtaposition to that other German passion, a longing for being settled. The best part about traveling, Germans love to say, is the return home. Wanderlust is a brief departure from that well-kept little house tucked away snugly behind that wall or fence. German companies (and the German state) encourage forays by forking out up to six weeks of vacation a year *and* a month's extra pay to be spent during wanderlust season—even if it's spent on the autobahn, for that matter.

— Jürgen Scheunemann

berg, and a pleasant walk from the Schluchsee, it has everything for sports lovers—from a large pool to ski lifts, which are right outside the hotel. ✉ *Am Seebuck, D–79859,* ☎ *07676/180,* FAX *07676/1220,* WEB *www.feldberger-hof.de. 140 rooms. 3 restaurants, café, 2 bars, no a/c, cable TV, pool, hair salon, health club, sauna, steam room, theater, children's programs, some pets allowed (fee). AE, DC, MC, V.*

$ **Hotel Waldeck.** Geraniums smother the sun-drenched balconies of the Waldeck, and in winter the decorative equivalent is the snow piling up on the slopes outside. Walking trails begin practically at the front door, and the local forest creeps up to the hotel terrace. Some rooms have traditional furnishings; others carry a generic, modern look. ✉ *Feldberg Altglashütten, D–79859,* ☎ *07655/364 or 07655/91030,* FAX *07655/231,* WEB *www.hotel-waldeck-feldberg.de. 23 rooms. Restaurant, bar, no a/c, cable TV, Internet, free parking, some pets allowed (fee), no-smoking rooms. DC, MC, V. Closed Wed.*

Hiking and Skiing

The best Alpine skiing in the Black Forest is on the slopes of the Feldberg. The Seebuck, Grafenmatt, and Fahl Alpin area offers 12 lifts and 25 km (15 mi) of pistes (all accessible with a single ski pass). For more information contact Feldberg's tourist office.

En Route To get to Freiburg, the largest city in the southern Black Forest, you have to brave the curves of the winding road through the **Höllental** (Hell Valley). (In 1770 Empress Maria Theresa's 15-year-old daughter—the future queen Marie Antoinette—made her way along what was then a coach road on her way from Vienna to Paris. She traveled with an entourage of 250 officials and servants in some 50 horse-drawn carriages.) The first stop at the end of the valley is a little village called **Himmelreich,** or Kingdom of Heaven. Railroad engineers are said to have given the village its name in the 19th century, grateful as they were to finally have laid a line through Hell Valley. At the entrance to Höllental is a deep gorge, the **Ravennaschlucht.** It's worth scrambling through to reach the tiny 12th-century chapel of **St. Oswald,** the oldest parish church in the Black Forest (there are parking spots off the road). Look for a bronze statue of a deer high on a roadside cliff, 5 km (3 mi) farther on. It commemorates the legend of a deer that amazed hunters by leaping the deep gorge at this point. Another 16 km (10 mi) will bring you to Freiburg.

Freiburg

⓳ *Via B–31, 23 km (14 mi) from turnoff (317) to Schluchsee.*

Freiburg, or Freiburg im Breisgau (to distinguish it from the Freiberg in Saxony), was founded in the 12th century. After extensive wartime bomb damage, skillful restoration has helped re-create the original and compelling medieval atmosphere of one of the loveliest historic towns in Germany. The 16th-century geographer Martin Waldseemüller was born here; in 1507 he was the first to put the name *America* on a map. Freiburg has had its share of misadventures through the years. In 1632 and 1638 Protestant Swedish troops in the Thirty Years' War captured the city; in 1644 it was taken by Catholic Bavarian soldiers; and in 1677, 1713, and 1744 French troops captured it.

For an intimate view of Freiburg, wander through the streets around the Münster or follow the main shopping artery of Kaiser-Joseph-Strasse. The courageous decision by the municipal government to keep cars off the streets has made the inner city very pleasant to stroll. After you pass a city gate (Martinstor), follow Fischerau off to the left. River fishermen used to live on this little alley. You'll come to quaint shops

along the bank of one of the city's larger canals, which continues past the former Augustinian cloister to the equally picturesque area around the *Insel* (island). This canal is a larger version of the *Bächle* (brooklets) running through many streets in Freiburg's Old Town. The *Bächle* were created in the 13th century to bring fresh water into the town, but nowadays they serve to cool the air a little on hot summer days. Tradition has it that anyone who steps into one is sure to return to Freiburg. The tourist office sponsors English walking tours April 15 through October 31, on Monday and Friday at 2:30, Wednesday–Thursday and weekends at 10:30. The two-hour tours cost €5.

★ The **Münster unserer Lieben Frau** (Cathedral), Freiburg's most famous landmark, towers over the medieval streets. The pioneering 19th-century Swiss art historian Jacob Burckhardt described its delicately perforated 380-ft spire as the finest in Europe. The cathedral took three centuries to build, from around 1200 to 1515, and only suffered minor bruises during the massive bombardment of November 27th, 1944. The people of Freiburg actually financed the nearly three centuries of buildings themselves, and to this day they still refer to it as their own Minaster, not as a cathedral. You can easily trace the progress of generations of builders through the changing architectural styles, from the fat columns and solid, rounded arches of the Romanesque period to the lofty Gothic windows and airy interior of the choir. Of particular interest are the luminous 13th-century stained-glass windows, which tell stories of healings and were sponsored by wealthy town burghers or the guilds (accounting for the depiction of boots, a scissor, a hammer and tongs, etc.). Masterpieces include a 16th-century triptych by Hans Baldung Grien, and paintings by Holbein the Younger and Lucas Cranach the Elder. If you can summon the energy, climb the tower. In addition to a magnificent view of the city and the Black Forest beyond, you'll get a closer look at the 16 Minster bells including the over 3-ton 1258 "Hosanna," one of Germany's oldest functioning bells. ✉ *Münsterpl.,* ☎ *0761/31099; 0761/388–101 tours,* WEB *www.freiburg-online.com.* 🎫 *Bell tower €1.50.* ⏲ *Mon.–Sat. 10–6, Sun. 1–6.*

The **Münsterplatz,** the square around Freiburg's cathedral, which once served as a cemetery, holds a market (Monday–Saturday) in front of the Renaissance **Kaufhaus** (Market House). You can stock up on local specialties for the road, from wood-oven baked bread, to hams, wines, vinegars, fruits, and Kirschwasser. The square is also lined with traditional taverns. The big iron door at number 12 houses the **Foltermuseum** (Torture Museum), whose explicatory texts do not fail to point out the gruesomeness and often sheer stupidity of Christian jurisprudence for over 600 years. ✉ *Münsterpl. 12,* ☎ *0761/292–1900.* 🎫 *€4.10.* ⏲ *Daily 11–6.*

Freiburg's famous **Rathaus** is constructed from two 16th-century patrician houses joined together. Among its attractive Renaissance features is an oriel, or bay window, clinging to a corner and bearing a bas-relief of the romantic medieval legend of the Maiden and the Unicorn. ✉ *Rathauspl. 2–4.* ⏲ *Weekdays 8–noon.*

The former house of painter, sculptor, and architect Johann Christian Wentzinger (1710–1797), the **Wentzingerhaus,** contains fascinating exhibits on the history of the city, from a 1:50 scale model of the Minster as a construction site and the poignant remains of a typewriter recovered from a bombed-out bank. The ceiling fresco painted by Wentzinger himself in the stairway is the museum's pride and joy. ✉ *Münsterpl. 30,* ☎ *0761/201–2515,* WEB *www.msg-freiburg.de.* 🎟 *€3.* ⏲ *Tues.–Fri. 9:30–5, weekends 10:30–5.*

A visit to Freiburg's cathedral is not really complete without also exploring the **Augustinermuseum,** at the former Augustinian cloister. Original sculpture from the cathedral is on display, as well as gold and silver reliquaries. The collection of stained-glass windows, dating from the Middle Ages to today, is one of the most important in Germany. ✉ *Am Augustinerpl. (Salzstr. 32),* ☎ *0761/201–2531.* 🎟 *€2.* ⏲ *Tues.–Sun. 10–5.*

Dining and Lodging

$$$ ✕ **Alte Weinstube zur Traube.** The fruit of the vine is not the only item on the menu at this cozy old wine tavern, which offers a rich and varied selection of classic French and Swabian dishes. *Zander* (pike) roulade with crab sauce and braised pork with lentils are especially recommended. ✉ *Schusterstr. 17,* ☎ *0761/32190. AE, V. Closed Sun. and 3 wks mid-Aug. No lunch Mon.*

$$$–$$$$ ★ ✕ **Markgräfler Hof.** The imaginative Mediterranean and Swabian fare in this restaurant ranges from such dishes as braised tomatoes and artichokes with lukewarm vegetables to fricassé calf liver with fresh herbs and *brägele* (pan-fried potatoes). It's hard to go wrong with the wide variety of choices. A small but fine wine list complements the menu. ✉ *Gerberau 22,* ☎ *0761/32540. AE, D, MC, V. Closed Sun., Mon.*

$–$$$$ ✕ **Kühler Krug.** Wild game and goose liver terrine are among the specialties at this restaurant, which has even given its name to a distinctive saddle-of-venison dish. Those who prefer fish shouldn't despair—there's an imaginative range of freshwater varieties available. ✉ *Torpl. 1, Günterstal,* ☎ *0761/29103. MC, V. Closed Wed.*

$ ✕ **Freiburger Salatstuben.** Come here for healthy vegetarian food prepared in creative ways—try the homemade whole-wheat noodles with cauliflower in a pepper cream sauce, or just pick and choose from the huge salad bar. Service is cafeteria style, but all that nutrition and fiber costs no more than a meal at the McDonald's around the corner—food is priced by the gram. University students crowd the place at peak hours. ✉ *Am Martinstor-Löwenstr. 1,* ☎ *0761/35155. No credit cards. Closed Sun.*

$ ✕ **Karchers Weinstube.** This Weinstube is full of locals and is just like the ones described in romantic novels—with an old, shoe-scrubbed floor, well-worn tables, wood furnishings and paneling, a large and diverse wine list, excellent and basic dishes served with *Rösti* (fried potatoes) or *Schupfnudel* (oblong potato-based dumplings) and—in season—*Feldsalat* (lamb's lettuce). You can also try potato soup in about a dozen variations. ✉ *Eisenbahnstr. 29,* ☎ *0761/22773. No credit cards.*

$$$$ ★ ✕🏨 **Colombi.** Freiburg's most luxurious hotel also has two esteemed restaurants ($$–$$$$). The Hans Thoma Stube is the most originally designed, namely in two reconstructed 18th-century farmhouse rooms, lavishly furnished and decorated with Black Forest antiques. It serves local dishes such as lentil soup and venison. The second restaurant is divided into two rooms, the Zirbelstube and the Falkenstube. It's fine cuisine is urbane rather than rustic, and the menu pairs innovative sauces with traditional meat and fish dishes. Restaurant reservations are essential. The hotel is centrally located but very quiet. ✉ *Am Colombi Park/Rotteckring 16, D–79098,* ☎ *0761/21060,* FAX *0761/31410,* WEB *www.colombi.de. 80 rooms, 48 suites. 2 restaurants, cable TV, in-room data ports, patisserie, room service, indoor pool, sauna, spa, steam room, piano bar, baby-sitting, parking (fee), some pets allowed (fee), no-smoking rooms. AE, DC, MC, V.*

$$–$$$ ✕🏨 **Victoria.** In keeping with their ecological concerns, owners Astrid and Bertram Späth have gone to great lengths to make their elegant 1870s hotel eco-friendly: hardwood floors are wet-vacuumed to prevent dust, beds have special mattresses and covers, special cleaning products are used, no extra packaging and wraps pile up waste, and the electricity is supplied by solar cells and a windmill. The unique "rock experience room," with a waterbed designed by artist Willi Jung, is a must for a special stay. The hotel can arrange for free travel on local transit with your €25 deposit. At night, a mixed crowd fills the Café Colonial Hemingway. ✉ *Eisenbahnstr. 54, D–79098,* ☎ *0761/207–340,* FAX *0761/2073–4444,* WEB *www.Hotel-Victoria.de. 63 rooms. Bar, no a/c, cable TV, in-room data ports, free parking, some pets allowed (fee), no-smoking rooms. AE, DC, MC, V.*

$$–$$$ ★ ✕🏨 **Zum Roten Bären.** This Ring Group inn, which dates from 1311, retains its individual character, with very comfortable lodging and excellent dining in a warren of restaurants and taverns ($$–$$$$). If it's a chilly evening, order a table next to the large Kachelofen, which dominates the main, beamed restaurant. Take a tour of the two basement floors, composed of cellars dating from the original 12th-century foundation of Freiburg and now well stocked with fine wines. ✉ *Oberlinden 12, D–79098 Freiburg im Breisgau,* ☎ *0761/387–870,* FAX *0761/387–8717,* WEB *www.roter-baeren.de. 25 rooms, 3 apartments. 3 restaurants, no a/c, cable TV, in-room data ports, sauna, Weinstube, parking (fee), some pets allowed (fee), no-smoking rooms. AE, DC, MC, V. Closed Mon.*

$$ ✕🏨 **Rappen.** This hotel's brightly painted rooms overlook the cathedral square and marketplace with all its lively chatter. Three rooms are designated as "anti-allergy." The restaurant ($) hosts the market people and locals coming in for a glass of wine in the morning (there are about 40 wines, German and French) and serves fresh vegetables, game, and fish. ✉ *Münsterpl. 13, D–79098,* ☎ *0761/31353,* FAX *0761/382–252,* WEB *www.hotelrappen.de. 24 rooms. Restaurant, no a/c, cable TV, some pets allowed (fee). AE, DC, MC, V. Closed Sun., Jan., and Feb.*

$$ ✕🏨 **Oberkirchs Weinstuben.** Across from the cathedral and next to the Kaufhaus, this wine cellar is a bastion of tradition and Gemütlichkeit (comfort and conviviality). The proprietor personally bags some of the game that ends up in the kitchen. Fresh trout is another specialty. In summer the dark-oak dining tables spill onto a garden terrace. Approximately 20 Baden wines are served by the glass, from white Gutedel to red Spätburgunder, many supplied from the restaurant's own vineyards. Twenty-six charming guest rooms are in the Weinstuben and in a neighboring centuries-old house. ✉ *Münsterpl. 22, D–79098,* ☎ *0761/31011. 26 rooms. Restaurant, no a/c, cable TV, in-room data ports, some pets allowed (fee). AE, MC, V. Restaurant closed Sun. and late Dec.–Feb.*

$$–$$$ 🏨 **Park Hotel Post Meier.** Near the train station, the Post has been a hotel since the turn of the 20th century, with good, old-fashioned service to prove it. The art nouveau facade with stone balconies and central copper-dome tower has earned the building protected status. A large breakfast buffet is included in the room price. ✉ *Eisenbahnstr. 35, D–79098,* ☎ *0761/385–480,* FAX *0761/31680. 43 rooms. No a/c, cable TV, in-room data ports, no-smoking rooms AE, MC, V.*

Nightlife and the Arts

Performances in Freiburg's annual summer theater festival are centered in the city's theater complex, spilling out into the streets and squares. The music scene really comes alive in summer. The annual ***Zeltmusik*** (BZ-Kartenservice; ✉ Bertoldstr. 7, ☎ 0800/222–4224) festival is a jamboree held under huge tents in June and July. The emphasis is on jazz, but most types of music can be heard. There are summer chamber music concerts in the courtyard of the Kaufhaus, opposite the Münster, and the Münster itself hosts an annual summer program of organ recitals. Freiburg has a multistage complex, the **Konzerthaus** (✉ Städtische Bühne, Bertoldstr. 46, ☎ 0761/34874), near the train station.

Nightlife in Freiburg takes place in the city's *Kneipen* (pubs), wine bars, and wine cellars, which are plentiful on the streets around the cathedral. For student pubs, wander around **Stühlinger,** the neighborhood immediately south of the train station. The **Agar** (✉ Löwenstr. 8, ☎ 0761/380–650) is a good dance club with a fairly young crowd. Plenty of people take their nightcap at the **Cocktailbar Hemingway** (✉ Eisenbahnstr. 54, ☎ 0761/207–340), which stays open until 3 AM on weekends and features live music on Thursday. **Funpark** (✉ Hans-Bunte-Str. 16, near the autobahn access road for the Freiburg Nord exit, ☎ 0761/556–5757), the large-scale, cool night place for the young, is in the northern industrial zone of Freiburg. The wild decor includes an airplane. **Jazzhaus** (✉ Schnewlinstr. 1, ☎ 0761/34973) has live music nightly and draws big acts and serious up-and-coming artists to its brick cellar. A very mixed crowd meets daily and nightly at **Kagan café bar club lounge** (✉ Bismarckallee 9, ☎ 0761/767–2766; 🎫 on weekends €8) in the skyscraper over the train station. It opens for breakfast at 10 and dancing on weekends (cover charge €7.50) goes until 5 AM, with dinner served until around 1 AM and snacks until 4 AM. The view of the Old Town is incomparable.

Staufen

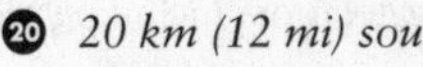

20 *20 km (12 mi) south of Freiburg via B–31.*

Once you've braved Hell Valley to get to Freiburg, a visit to the nearby town of Staufen, where Dr. Faustus is reputed to have made his pact with the devil, should hold no horrors. The Faustus legend is remembered today chiefly because of Goethe's *Faust,* the finest drama written on the subject of a man selling his soul to the devil in return for eternal youth and knowledge. The original Faustus was a 16th-century alchemist and scientist. His pact was not with the devil but with a local baron who was convinced that Faustus could make his fortune by converting base metal into gold. While attempting to do so, Dr. Faustus caused an explosion that produced such noise and such a sulfurous stink that the townspeople were convinced the devil had carried him off. In fact, he was killed in the accident. You can visit the ancient **Gasthaus zum Löwen** (✉ Hauptstr. 47), where Faustus lived in room number 5, allegedly, and died. The inn is right on the central square of Staufen, a town with a visible inclination toward modern art in ancient settings.

Dining and Lodging

$–$$ ✕ **Kornhaus.** This former granary, with its light, white interior exhibiting modern paintings of local artists almost invades the entire market square on hot summer days. Regional specialities combine with solid German cuisine and a few nods to vegetarians with a cèpe stew on a bed of noodles, for example. The excellent wines come from the nearby vineyard of Wilhelm Zähringer in Heitersheim. ✉ *Marktpl.,* ☎ *07633/5401. May close for 2 wks in Nov. MC, V.*

$$–$$$ ★ ✕🏨 **Romantik Hotel Spielweg.** Half an hour's drive from Freiburg, this family-run inn has everything for an indulgent holiday, with pools, tennis courts, and Karl-Josef Fuchs's regional cooking ($$–$$$$). ✉ *Hauptstr. 61, D–79244 Obermünstertal, 12 km (7 mi) southeast of Staufen,* ☎ *07636/7090,* FAX *07636/70966,* WEB *www.romantikhotels.com. 37 rooms, 2 suites. Restaurant, no a/c, cable TV, some in-room data ports, indoor and outdoor pool, hair salon, massage, sauna, bicycles, pets allowed (fee), no-smoking rooms. AE, DC, MC, V.*

$$ ✕🏨 **Landgasthaus zur Linde.** Guests have been welcomed here for 350 years, but the comforts inside the inns' old walls are contemporary. The kitchen ($$) creates wholesome sustenance out of local ingredients and plays up seasonal specialties, such as asparagus in May and June, and mushrooms from the valley in autumn. The terrace is a favorite for hikers passing through, as are the various snacks (*Vesper*). ✉ *Krumlinden 13, D–79244 Obermünstertal, 14 km (9 mi) southeast of Staufen,* ☎ *07636/7570,* FAX *07636/1632. 16 rooms, 2 suites. Restaurant, no a/c, cable TV, some pets allowed (fee). MC, V. Restaurant closed Mon. and Thurs.*

Breisach

21 *20 km (12 mi) northwest of Freiburg on B–31.*

The town of Breisach stands by the Rhine River; everything you see to the west on the opposite bank is in France. Hotels here have terrace restaurants from which to enjoy the scenery. Towering high above the town and the surrounding vineyards is the **Stephansmünster** (Cathedral of St. Stephen), built between 1200 and 1500 (and almost entirely rebuilt after World War II). North of Breisach rises the **Kaiserstuhl** (Emperor's Chair), a volcanic outcrop clothed in vineyards that produce some of Baden's best wines—reds from the Spätburgunder grape and whites that have an uncanny depth. The especially dry and warm microclimate has given rise to special vegetation, including sequoias and a wide variety of orchids.

Achkarren

22 *5 km (3 mi) north of Breisach.*

Sample high-quality wines—the Weissherbst, in particular—in one of the taverns of Achkarren or take a short hike along a vineyard path. The fine little **Weinmuseum** (Wine Museum) is in a renovated barn in the village center. A small vineyard out front displays the various types of grape used to make wine in the Kaiserstuhl region. 🎫 *€1.50.* ⏲ *Apr.–Oct., Tues.–Fri. 2–5, weekends 11–5.*

Dining and Lodging

$$ ✕🏨 **Hotel Krone.** You could spend an entire afternoon and evening here either on the terrace or in the dining room ($$–$$$$) trying the wines and enjoying, say, a fillet of wild salmon in a horseradish crust, a boar's roast, or some lighter asparagus creation. The house, which also serves as a hotel, has been around since 1561, and the Höfflin-Schüssler family, now in its fourth generation as hoteliers, knows how to make vis-

itors feel welcome. ✉ *Schlossbergstr. 15–17 Vogtsburg-Achkarren,* ☎ *07662/93130,* FAX *7662/931–350,* WEB *www.Hotel-Krone-Achkarren.de. 23 rooms. Restaurant, no a/c, cable TV, in-room data ports, 2 tennis courts, some pets allowed (fee). MC, V. Restaurant closed Wed.*

THE BLACK FOREST A TO Z

To research prices, get advice from other travelers, and book travel arrangements, visit www.fodors.com.

AIRPORTS

The closest international airports are at Stuttgart, Strasbourg, in neighboring French Alsace, and the Swiss border city of Basel, the latter just 70 km (43 mi) from Freiburg. In Germany Frankfurt's airport is the next closest after Stuttgart's.

BUS TRAVEL

The bus system works closely together with the German railways to reach every corner of the Black Forest. At the train stations you will find either a bus station right near the entrance or you can follow signs to the central bus stations (ZOB). For more information, contact the Regionalbusverkehr Südwest (Regional Bus Lines) in Karlsruhe.

➤ BUS INFORMATION: **Regionalbusverkehr Südwest** (Regional Bus Lines: ☎ 0721/84060 in Karlsruhe).

CAR RENTAL

➤ MAJOR AGENCIES: **Avis** (✉ Kazenmaier GmbH & Co. KG, Maximilianstr. 54, Baden-Baden, ☎ 07221/504–190; ✉ St-Georgenerstr. 7, Freiburg, ☎ 0761/19719; ✉ Westliche Karl-Friedrich-Str. 141, Pforzheim, ☎ 07231/440–828). **Europcar** (✉ Rheinstr. 29, Baden-Baden, ☎ 07221/50660 or 0180/580–0000; ✉ Zähringerstr. 42, Freiburg, ☎ 0761/515–100). **Hertz** (✉ Lörracherstr. 49, Freiburg, ☎ 0761/478–090).

CAR TRAVEL

Good two-lane highways crisscross the entire region. The main highways are the A–5 (Frankfurt–Karlsruhe–Basel), running through the Rhine Valley along the western length of the Black Forest the A–81 (Stuttgart–Bodensee), in the east; and the A–8 (Karlsruhe–Stuttgart), in the north. The B–3 runs parallel to the A–5 and follows the Baden Wine Road. Traffic jams on weekends and holidays are not uncommon. Taking the side roads might not save time, but they are a lot more interesting. The Schwarzwald-Hochstrasse is one of the area's most scenic (but also most trafficked) routes, running from Freudenstadt to Baden-Baden. The region's tourist office has mapped out thematic driving routes: the High Road, the Low Road, the Spa Road, the Baden Wine Road, and the Clock Road. Most points along these routes can also be reached by train or bus.

Freiburg, the region's major city, is 275 km (170 mi) from Frankfurt and 410 km (254 mi) from Munich.

OUTDOORS AND SPORTS

BIKING

Much of the Black Forest is a biker's paradise (provided the rider is stalwart since there are so many ups and downs). There are many bike rental shops throughout the region, and cycling maps are available at most tourist offices. For information on biking in Germany, contact the National German Cycling Association. To facilitate your bike traveling, you may want to cover certain distances by VeloBus or train. Reservations are advisable. For train travel can call the Deutsche Bahn's special line for bicyclists. Deutsche Bahn also rents bikes.

➤ Biking Info: **Deutsche Bahn** (☎ 08105/151–415 bike hot line). **National German Cycling Association** (✉ Augustenstr. 29, D–70197 Stuttgart, ☎ 0711/628–999). **VeloBus** (☎ 0721/966–8610).

FISHING

Licenses cost €4–€6 a day and are available from most local tourist offices, which can also usually provide maps and rental equipment. Contact the Black Forest tourist information offices for details.

HIKING AND WALKING

The regional tourist office offers *Wandern ohne Gepäck* (Hike Without Luggage) tours along the old clock-carriers' route. The participating hotels are connected by one-day hikes in a circular route, each section ranging from 16 km to 27 km (10 mi to 17 mi). Your bags are transported ahead by car to meet you each evening at that day's destination. Prices are reasonable: three nights with hotel and breakfast start at €175. For reservations and information contact Wandern Ohne Gepäck at the Uhrenträgergemeinschaft in Triberg.

Along the Baden Wine Road spring and summer weekend hikes will take you through vineyard country to five wineries for wine tasting. The package includes two overnights and two meals typical of the region. Information and reservations can be obtained from Tourist-Information Durbach.

➤ Contacts: **Tourist-Information Durbach** (✉ Tal 36, D–7770 Durbach, ☎ 0781/42153, FAX 0781/43989, WEB www.durbach.de). **Wandern Ohne Gepäck** (Uhrenträgergemeinschaft, ✉ Hauptstr. 51, D–78094 Triberg, ☎ 07722/860–2111, FAX 07722/860–2190, WEB www.uhrentraeger.de).

HORSEBACK RIDING

Farms throughout the Black Forest offer riding vacations; addresses are available from local tourist offices and the Schwarzwald Turismusverband in Freiburg.

TOURS

Bus tours (some in English) of the Black Forest and parts of neighboring France and Switzerland, as well as walking tours of Freiburg, are available in Freiburg from Freiburg Kultur.

➤ Fees and Schedules: **Freiburg Kultur** (✉ Rotteckring 14, ☎ 0761/290–7447, FAX 0761/290–7449).

TRAIN TRAVEL

The main rail route through the Black Forest runs north–south, following the Rhine Valley from Karlsruhe to Basel. There are fast and frequent trains to Freiburg and Baden-Baden from most major German cities (you generally have to change at Karlsruhe).

Local lines connect most of the smaller towns. Two east–west routes—the Schwarzwaldbahn (Black Forest Railway) and the Höllental Railway—are among the most spectacular in the country. Details are available from Deutsche Bahn.

VISITOR INFORMATION

For information on the northern Black Forest, contact Touristik Nördlicher Schwarzwald; for the central area, contact Schwarzwald Tourismus GmbH—Mittlerer Schwarzwald; for the southern area, contact Tourismus Südlicher Schwarzwald.

➤ Tourist Information: **Baden-Baden** (✉ Baden-Baden Marketing GmbH, Solmsstrasse 1, D–76530, ☎ 07221/275–2001, FAX 07221/275–202, WEB www.baden-baden.de). **Bad Herrenalb** (✉ Kurverwaltung, D–76332, ☎ 07083/500–555, WEB www.badherrenalb.de). **Bad Lieben-**

zell (✉ Kurverwaltung, Kurhausdamm 4, D–75378, ☎ 07052/4080, WEB www.bad-liebenzell.de). **Freiburg** (✉ Information, Rotteckring 14, D–79098, ☎ 0761/388–1880, WEB www.freiburg.de). **Freudenstadt** (✉ Kongresse–Touristik–Kur, Promenadenpl. 1, D–72250, ☎ 07441/8640). **Hinterzarten** (✉ Verkehrsamt, Freiburgerstr. 1, D–79854, ☎ 07652/12060, WEB www.hinterzarten.de). **Karlsruhe** (✉ Karlsruher Tagungs-und Touristik Service, Bahnhofpl. 6, D–76137, ☎ 0721/35530, WEB www.karlsruhe.de/Tourismus). **Pforzheim** (✉ Stadtinformation, Rathaus, Marktpl. 1, D–75175, ☎ 07231/145–4560, WEB www.pforzheim.de). **Schluchsee** (✉ Kurverwaltung, Fischbacherstr. 7, D–79859, ☎ 07656/7732, WEB www.schluchsee.de). **Schwarzwald Tourismus GmbH-Mittlerer Schwarzwald** (✉ Gerberstr. 8, D–77652 Offenburg, ☎ 07721/923–7777, FAX 0781/923–7770, WEB www.schwarzwald-tourismus.com). **Titisee-Neustadt** (✉ Tourist-Information, Strandbadstr., D–79822, ☎ 07651/98040, WEB www.titisee.de). **Tourismus Südlicher Schwarzwald** (✉ Stadtstr. 2, D–79104 Freiburg, ☎ 0761/296–2260 or 0761/218–7304, FAX 0761/218–7534, WEB www.schwarzwald-sued.de). **Touristik Nördlicher Schwarzwald** (✉ Am Weisenhauspl. 26, D–75172 Pforzheim, ☎ 07231/147–380, FAX 07231/147–3820, WEB www.noerdlicher-schwarzwald.de). **Triberg** (✉ Kurverwaltung im Kurhaus, Luisenstr. 10, D–78098, ☎ 07722/953–230, FAX 07722/953–236, WEB www.triberg.de).

9 HEIDELBERG AND THE NECKAR VALLEY

This area bounces between vineyard-lined cities and quaint university towns—Stuttgart among the former, Heidelberg and Tübingen among the latter—with castles, small villages, and the Neckar River throughout. Along the scenic Burgenstrasse (Castle Road), each medieval town is guarded by a castle.

Updated by Kerry Brady Stewart

THE NECKAR RIVER UNITES BEAUTY and historic resonance as it flows toward the Rhine through the state of Baden-Württemberg, eventually reaching Heidelberg's graceful baroque towers and the majestic ruins of its red sandstone castle. Much of this route follows the west–east course of the Burgenstrasse (Castle Road), which stretches nearly one 1,000 km (621 mi) from Mannheim to Prague, taking in some 70 castles and palaces along the way. Every town or bend in the river seems to have its guardian castle, sometimes in ruins but often revived as a museum or hotel. Off the main road, quiet side valleys and little towns slumber in leafy peace.

Pleasures and Pastimes

Dining

Fish and *Wild* (game) from the streams and woods lining the Neckar Valley, as well as seasonal favorites, such as *Spargel* (asparagus) and *Pilze* (mushrooms)—*Morcheln* (morels), *Pfifferlinge* (chanterelles), and *Steinpilze* (cèpes)—are regulars on menus in this area. Pfälzer specialties (☞ Chapter 10) are also common, but the penchant for potatoes yields to *Knödel* (dumplings) and pasta farther south. The latter includes the Swabian and Baden staples *Maultaschen* (stuffed "pockets" of pasta) and *Spätzle* (roundish egg noodles), as well as *Schupfnudeln* (finger-size noodles of potato dough), also called *Bube-* or *Buwespitzle*. Look for *Linsen* (lentils) and sauerkraut in soups or as sides. *Schwäbischer Rostbraten* (beefsteaks topped with fried onions) and *Schäufele* (pickled and slightly smoked pork shoulder) are popular meat dishes.

Considerable quantities of red wine are produced along the Neckar Valley. Crisp, light Trollinger is often served in the traditional *Viertele,* a round, quarter-liter (8-ounce) glass with a handle. Deeper-colored, more substantial reds include Spatburgunder (pinot noir) and its mutation Schwarzriesling (pinot meunier), Lemberger, and Dornfelder. Riesling, Kerner, and Müller-Thurgau (synonymous with Rivaner), as well as Grauburgunder (pinot gris) and Weissburgunder (pinot blanc) are the typical white wines. A birch-broom or wreath over the doorway of a vintner's home signifies a *Besenwirtschaft* (broomstick inn), a rustic pub where you can enjoy wines with snacks and simple fare. Many vintners offer economical bed-and-breakfasts.

CATEGORY	COST*
$$$$	over €20
$$$	€15–€20
$$	€10–€15
$	under €10

**per person for a main course at dinner*

Festivals

Important cultural festivals for music, opera, and theater include the **Schlossfestspiele** on the castle grounds in Schwetzingen (May), Heidelberg (July and August), Zwingenberg (late August), and Ludwigsburg (mid-June to September). Since 1818 thousands have flocked to the Stuttgart suburb of Cannstatt in early October for the annual **Volksfest** (folk festival). Two wine festivals of particular note are the **Stuttgarter Weindorf** from late August to early September and the **Heilbronner Weindorf** in early September. Last but not least are the fabulous **fireworks** and castle illuminations in Heidelberg (with an arts-and-crafts market on the riverbank) on the first Saturday of June and September, and the second Saturday of July.

Lodging

This area is full of castle-hotels and charming country inns that range in comfort from upscale rustic to luxurious. For a riverside view ask for a *Zimmer* (room) or *Tisch* (table) *mit Neckarblick*. The Neckar Valley offers idyllic alternatives to the cost and crowds of Heidelberg. Driving time from Eberbach, for example, is half an hour; from Bad Wimpfen, about an hour.

CATEGORY	COST*
$$$$	over €225
$$$	€150–€225
$$	€75–€150
$	under €75

**All prices are for two people in a double room, including tax and service.*

Exploring Heidelberg and the Neckar Valley

Heidelberg is a destination unto itself, but it can also be seen as the major stop on the Burgenstrasse, which makes its way through the narrower parts of the Neckar Valley. The route in this chapter follows the Neckar River upstream (east, then south) from Heidelberg. The road snakes between the river and the wooded slopes of the Odenwald forest before reaching the rolling, vine-covered countryside around Heilbronn. From there it's a 50-km (31-mi) drive, partly along the Neckar, to Stuttgart. About 40 km (25 mi) farther you rejoin the river at the charming university town of Tübingen.

Great Itineraries

Numbers in the text correspond to numbers in the margin and on the Neckar Valley and Heidelberg maps.

IF YOU HAVE 3 DAYS

Spend a full day and night exploring the university town **Heidelberg** ①–⑰. On the second day take a trip up the Neckar to the castles of **Hirschhorn** ⑳ and **Burg Hornberg** ㉓ (both have hotels for an overnight stay, with excellent restaurants). On the third day visit the **Staatsgalerie** (State Gallery) in **Stuttgart** ㉗.

IF YOU HAVE 5 DAYS

Spend your first two days and nights in **Heidelberg** ①–⑰. On the third day continue up the Neckar to **Burg Guttenberg** (with its aviary of birds of prey) and the castles of **Hirschhorn** ⑳ and **Burg Hornberg** ㉓. Stay overnight at one of the many castle hotels in the area. Investigate the remains of the imperial palace and other sights in **Bad Wimpfen** ㉔ on the fourth day and end the trip in the medieval streets of **Tübingen** ㉙.

IF YOU HAVE 7 DAYS

Spend your first two days and nights in **Heidelberg** ①–⑰. On the third day head up the Neckar to **Burg Guttenberg** and the **Hirschhorn** ⑳ castle, staying there or in **Eberbach** ㉑ for two nights. Continue on to explore **Mosbach** ㉒ and the castle at **Burg Hornberg** ㉓, with time out for a river cruise. Spend the fifth day and night in **Bad Wimpfen** ㉔, with a possible side trip to the museum of bicycle and motorcycle technology at **Neckarsulm** ㉕. On the sixth day and night visit the sights and enjoy the nightlife of **Stuttgart** ㉗. On day seven stop in **Bebenhausen** ㉗ en route to **Tübingen** ㉙, where the journey ends.

When to Tour Heidelberg and the Neckar Valley

If you plan to visit Heidelberg in summer, make reservations well in advance and expect to pay top rates. To get away from the crowds,

The Neckar Valley

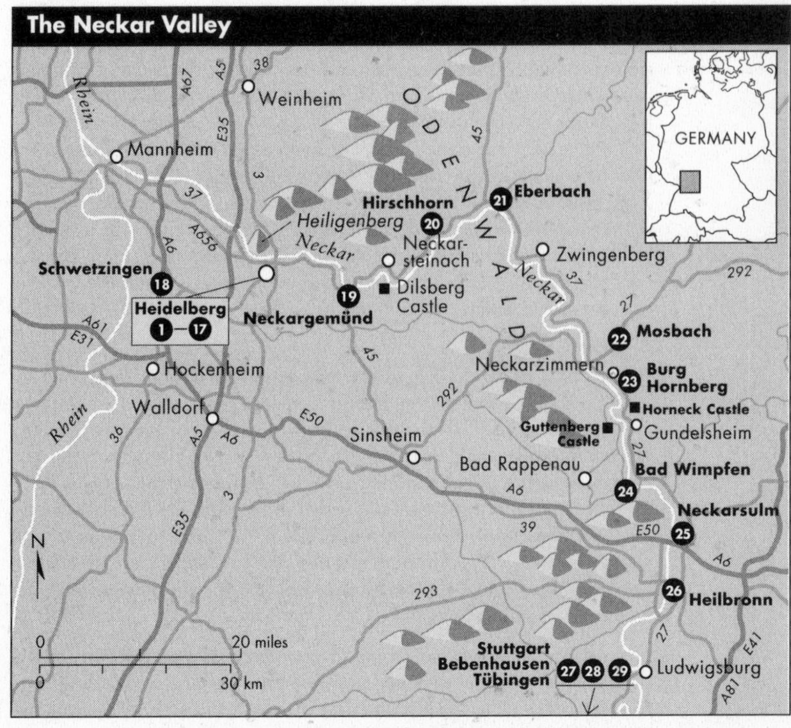

consider staying out of town and driving or taking the bus into the city. Hotels and restaurants are much cheaper just a little upriver. A visit in late fall, when the vines turn a faded gold, or early spring, with the first green shoots of the year, can be captivating. In the depths of winter, river mists creep through narrow streets of Heidelberg's Old Town and awaken the ghosts of a romantic past.

THE NECKAR-RHINE TRIANGLE

The natural beauty of Heidelberg is created by the embrace of mountains, forests, vineyards, and the Neckar River, crowned by its ruined castle. The Neckar and the Rhine meet at nearby Mannheim, a major industrial center and the second-largest river port in Europe. Schwetzingen, known as Germany's "asparagus" capital, lies in the triangle's center.

Heidelberg

57 km (35 mi) northeast of Karlsruhe.

If any city in Germany encapsulates the spirit of the country, it is Heidelberg. Scores of poets and composers—virtually the entire 19th-century German Romantic movement—have sung its praises. Goethe and Mark Twain both fell in love here: the German writer with a beautiful young woman, the American author with the city itself. Sigmund Romberg set his operetta *The Student Prince* in the city; Carl Maria von Weber wrote his lushly Romantic opera *Der Freischütz* here. Composer Robert Schumann was a student at the university. The campaign these artists waged on behalf of the town has been astoundingly successful. Heidelberg's fame is out of all proportion to its size (population 140,000); more than 3½ million visitors crowd its streets every year.

Heidelberg was the political center of the Rhineland Palatinate. At the end of the Thirty Years' War (1618–48), the elector Carl Ludwig married his daughter to the brother of Louis XIV in the hope of bringing peace to the Rhineland. But when the elector's son died without an heir, Louis XIV used the marriage alliance as an excuse to claim Heidelberg, and in 1689 the town was sacked and laid waste. Four years later he sacked the town again. From its ashes arose what you see today: a baroque town built on Gothic foundations, with narrow, twisting streets and alleyways. Modern Heidelberg changed under the influence of U.S. army barracks and industrial development stretching into the suburbs, but the old heart of the city remains intact, exuding the spirit of romantic Germany.

A Good Walk

Begin a tour of Heidelberg at the **Königstuhl Bergbahn** (funicular) ①, which will take you up to the famous **Schloss** ②, one of Germany's most memorable sights. It was already in ruins when 19th-century Romantics fell under its spell, drawn by the mystery of its Gothic turrets, Renaissance walls, and abandoned gardens. (You can also choose to hike up the winding Burgweg [castle walk] to the complex.) The fascinating **Deutsches Apotheken-Museum** (German Apothecary Museum) is within the castle walls. The funicular can take you higher from the Schloss to **Molkenkur** ③, the site of another castle ruin, and **Königstuhl** ④, a high hill with fine views.

From the Schloss ramparts take the Burgweg down to the city's Altstadt (Old Town), sandwiched between the Neckar River and the surrounding hills. The steep path from the castle ends abruptly near the **Kornmarkt** (Grain Market). Cross the square north to Hauptstrasse, an elegant pedestrian street that runs straight through the city. Bear right, and you will immediately enter Karlsplatz; on the far side are two traditional pubs, Zum Sepp'l and Zum Roten Ochsen, where fraternity students have engaged in beer-drinking contests for the last 200-some years. The pub walls are lined with swords, trophies, faded photos, and dueling and drinking paraphernalia. Going left from Kornmarkt, it is only a few steps to the ***Marktplatz,*** the city's main square. The **Rathaus** ⑤ is a stately baroque building dating from 1701 that fronts the market square. From the center of the square, the late-Gothic **Heiliggeistkirche** ⑥ towers over the city. Just as in medieval times, there are shopping stalls between its buttresses. **Hotel zum Ritter** ⑦, with an elaborate Renaissance facade of curlicues, columns, and gables, stands opposite Heiliggeistkirche. Walking farther down Hauptstrasse west of Marktplatz, you reach Universitätsplatz and the **Alte Universität** ⑧, which was founded in 1386 and rebuilt in the early 18th century. It is one of four separate university complexes in the town. Go behind the Old University and down tiny Augustinerstrasse to find the **Studentenkarzer** ⑨, or student prison. Tradition once dictated that the university rather than the police should deal with unruly students. To the south, the **Neue Universität** ⑩ is on the southeast corner of Universitätsplatz. Just off Universitätsplatz, on the street called Plöck, stands the **Universitätsbibliothek** ⑪ (University Library). The Gothic **Peterskirche** ⑫, the city's oldest parish church, is opposite the library.

Next, return to Hauptstrasse and walk west a couple of blocks to visit the **Kurpfälzisches Museum** ⑬, Heidelberg's leading museum, housed in a former baroque palace. Six blocks west of the Kurpfälzisches Museum, on the south side of Hauptstrasse, is an alley leading to a courtyard and the entrance to Europe's only museum devoted to the history of industrial packaging, the **Deutsches Verpackungs-Museum** ⑭. Walk back toward Marktplatz and turn left at Dreikönigstrasse; a short

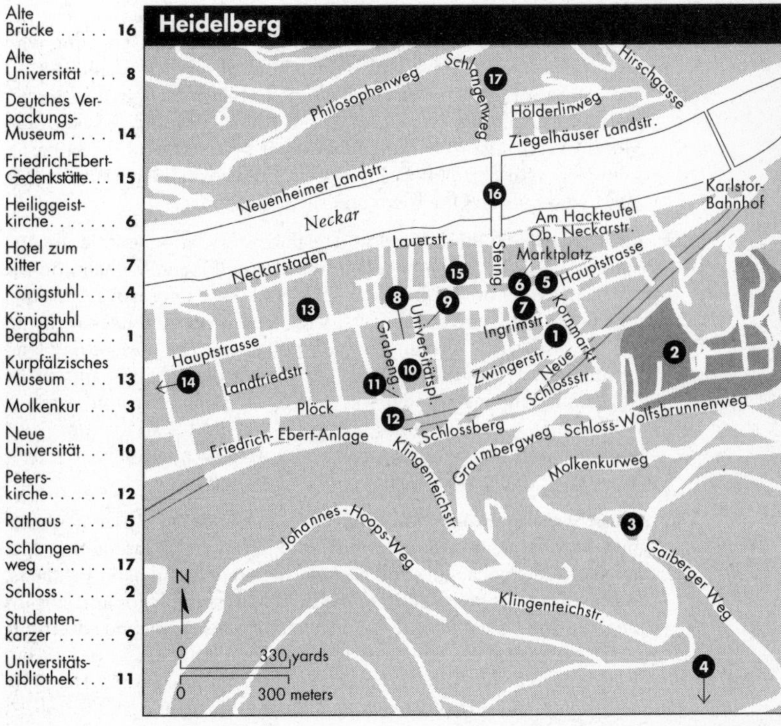

block brings you to Untere Strasse, where you go right, then immediately left at the first street, called Pfaffengasse. Halfway down the street on the left-hand side (No. 18) is the **Friedrich-Ebert-Gedenkstätte** ⑮, the birthplace the president of the ill-fated Weimar Republic. Continue on to the end of the street and turn right along the river to reach the twin turrets of the **Alte Brücke** ⑯. From the bridge you'll have views of the Old Town and the castle above. For the most inspiring view of Heidelberg, climb up the steep, winding **Schlangenweg** ⑰ through the vineyards to the Philosophenweg (Philosophers' Path); then go right and continue through the woods above the river to the Hölderlin Memorial, a grove traditionally frequented by poets and scholars. Try to arrive there as the sun sets and watch the red sandstone castle turn to gold.

TIMING

Allow at least two hours to tour the Schloss—and expect long lines in summer (up to 30 minutes). For the rest of the tour, add another two hours, four if you plan on seeing the collection of the Kurpfälzisches Museum, the manuscript exhibition at the University Library, and the inside of the Student Prison.

Sights to See

16 **Alte Brücke** (Old Bridge). Walk onto the bridge from the Old Town under a portcullis spanned by two *Spitzhelm* towers (so called for their resemblance to old-time German helmets). The twin towers were part of medieval Heidelberg's fortifications. In the west tower are three dank dungeons that once held common criminals. Between the towers, above the gate, are more salubrious lockups, with views of the river and the castle; these were reserved for debtors. Above the portcullis you'll see a memorial plaque that pays warm tribute to the Austrian forces who helped Heidelberg beat back a French attempt to capture the bridge

in 1799. The bridge itself is the ninth to be built on this spot; ice floes and floods destroyed its predecessors. The elector Carl Theodor, who built it in 1786–88, must have been confident this one would last: he had a statue of himself erected on it, upon a plinth decorated with river gods and goddesses (symbolic of the Rhine, Danube, Neckar, and Mosel rivers). Just to be safe, he also put up a statue of the saint, St. John Nepomuk. From the center of the bridge you'll have some of the finest views of the Old Town and the castle above.

8 **Alte Universität** (Old University). The three-story baroque structure was built in 1712–18 at the behest of the elector Johann Wilhelm on the site of an earlier university building. It houses the impressive Alta Aula (old auditorium) and the University Museum with exhibits that chronicle the history of Germany's oldest university. The present-day Universitätsplatz (University Square) was built over the remains of an Augustinian monastery that was destroyed by the French in 1693. ⊠ *Grabeng. 1–3,* ☎ *Museum 06221/542–152.* 🎫 *€2.50 for Alta Aula, museum, and the Studentenkarzer.* ⏲ *Apr.–Oct., Mon.–Sat. 10–4; Nov.–Mar., Tues.–Fri. 10–4.*

14 **Deutsches Verpackungs-Museum** (German Packaging Museum). A former church was innovatively converted to house this fascinating documentation of packaging and package design of brand name products. Representing the years 1800 to the present, historic logos and slogans are a trip down memory lane—not only for graphic artists and advertising or PR professionals. The entrance is not on Hauptstrasse per se, but in the courtyard behind the street, reached via an alley. ⊠ *Hauptstr. 22,* ☎ *06221/21361,* WEB *www.Verpackungsmuseum.de.* 🎫 *€3.50.* ⏲ *Wed.–Fri. 1–6, weekends 11–6.*

15 **Friedrich-Ebert-Gedenkstätte** (Friedrich Ebert Memorial). The humble rooms of a tiny back-street apartment were the birthplace of Friedrich Ebert, Germany's first democratically elected president (in 1920) and leader of the ill-fated Weimar Republic. Display cases have documents that tell the story of the tailor's son who took charge of a nation accustomed to being ruled by a kaiser. ⊠ *Pfaffeng. 18,* ☎ *06221/91070,* WEB *www.ebert-gedenkstaette.de.* 🎫 *Free.* ⏲ *Tues., Wed., and Fri.–Sun. 10–6, Thurs. 10–8.*

6 **Heiliggeistkirche** (Church of the Holy Ghost). The foundation stone of the building was laid in 1398, but it was not actually finished until 1544. Unlike that of most other Gothic churches, the facade of the Heiliggeistkirche is uniform—you cannot discern the choir or naves from the outside. The gargoyles looking down on the south side (where Hauptstrasse crosses Marktplatz) are remarkable for their sheer ugliness. The church fell victim to the plundering General Tilly, leader of the Catholic League during the Thirty Years' War. Tilly loaded the church's greatest treasure—the *Bibliotheca Palatina,* at the time the largest library in Germany—onto 500 carts and trundled it off to Rome, where he presented it to the pope. Few volumes found their way back to Heidelberg. At the end of the 17th century, French troops plundered the church again, destroying the family tombs of the Palatinate electors; only the 15th-century tomb of Elector Ruprecht III and his wife, Elisabeth von Hohenzollern, remains today. ⊠ *Marktpl.* ⏲ *Apr.–Oct., Mon.–Sat. 11–5, Sun. 12:30–5; Nov.–Mar., Fri. and Sat. 11–3, Sun. 12:30–3.*

7 **Hotel zum Ritter.** The hotel's name refers to the statue of a Roman knight ("Ritter") atop one of the many gables. Its French builder, Charles Bélier, had the Latin inscription *Persta Invicta Venus* added to the facade in gold letters—"Venus, Remain Unconquerable." It appears this in-

junction was effective, as this was the city's only Renaissance building to be spared the attentions of the invading French in 1689 and 1693. Between 1695 and 1705 it was used as Heidelberg's town hall; later it became an inn, and it is still a hotel today. ✉ *Hauptstr. 178,* ☎ *06221/1350.*

★ ❹ **Königstuhl** (King's Throne). The second-highest hill in the Odenwald range—1,700 ft above Heidelberg—is only a hop, skip, and funicular ride from Heidelberg. On a clear day you can see south as far as the Black Forest and west to the Vosges Mountains of France. The hill is at the center of a close-knit network of hiking trails. Signs and colored arrows from the top lead hikers through the woods of the Odenwald.

❶ **Königstuhl Bergbahn** (funicular). The funicular hoists visitors in 17 minutes to the summit of Königstuhl. On the way it stops at the ruined Heidelberg Schloss and Molkenkur. The funicular leaves every 10 minutes in summer and every 20 minutes in winter. ✉ *Kornmarkt.* 🎫 *Round-trip to Schloss €3, round-trip to Königstuhl heights €5.10.*

Kornmarkt (Grain Market). A baroque statue of the Virgin Mary is in the center of this old Heidelberg square, which has a view of the castle ruins.

⓭ **Kurpfälzisches Museum** (Palatinate Museum). The baroque palace that houses the museum was built as a residence for a university professor in 1712. It's a pleasure just to wander around, which is more or less unavoidable, since the museum's layout is so confusing. The collections chart the history of the city and its region. Among the exhibits are two standouts. One is a replica of the jaw of Heidelberg Man, a key link in the evolutionary chain thought to date from a half-million years ago; the original was unearthed near the city in 1907. The larger attraction is the **Windsheimer Zwölfbotenaltar** (Twelve Apostles Altarpiece), one of the largest and finest works of early Renaissance sculptor Tilman Riemenschneider. Its exquisite detailing and technical sophistication are evident in the simple faith that radiates from the faces of the apostles. On the top floor of the museum there's a rich range of 19th-century German paintings and drawings, many depicting Heidelberg. The restaurant in the Museum's quiet, shady courtyard is a good place for a break. ✉ *Hauptstr. 97,* ☎ *06221/583–402.* 🎫 *€2.50.* ⏲ *Tues. and Thurs.–Sun. 10–5, Wed. 10–9.*

Marktplatz (Market Square). Heidelberg's main square, with the Rathaus on one side and the Heiliggeistkirche on the other, has been its focal point since the Middle Ages. Public courts of justice were held here in earlier centuries, and people accused of witchcraft and heresy were burned at the stake. The baroque fountain in the middle, the Herkulesbrunnen (Hercules Fountain), is the work of 18th-century artist H. Charrasky. Until 1740 a rotating, hanging cage stood next to it. For minor crimes, people were imprisoned in it and exposed to the laughter, insults, and abuse of their fellow citizens. The square is surrounded by narrow side streets that should be explored.

❸ **Molkenkur.** The next stop after the castle on the Königstuhl funicular, Molkenkur was the site of Heidelberg's second castle. Lightning struck it in 1527, and it was never rebuilt. Today it is occupied by a restaurant with magnificent views of the Odenwald and the Rhine plain.

❿ **Neue Universität** (New University). The plain building on the south side of Universitätsplatz was erected between 1930 and 1932 through funds raised by the U.S. ambassador to Germany, J. G. Schurman, who had been a student at the university. The only decoration on the building's three wings is a statue of Athena, the Greek goddess of wisdom, above the entrance. The inner courtyard contains a medieval tower (1380) incorporated into the newer building—the **Hexenturm** (Witches Tower)—which is all that is left of the old city walls. Suspected witches were locked up there in the Middle Ages. It later became a memorial to former students killed in World War I. ✉ *Grabeng.*

OFF THE BEATEN PATH **NEUENHEIM** – To escape the crowds of Heidelberg, walk across the Theodor Heuss Bridge to the suburb of Neuenheim. At the turn of the 20th century this old fishing village developed into a residential area full of posh art nouveau villas. North of the Brückenkopf (bridgehead) you'll find antiques and designer shops, boutiques, and cafés on Brückenstrasse, Bergstrasse (one block east), and Ladenburger Strasse (parallel to the river). To savor the neighborhood spirit, visit the charming farmers' market on Wednesday or Saturday mornings at the corner of Ladenburger and Luther streets. The beer pubs Vetter's and o'reilly's (once voted best Irish pub in Germany) draw a young crowd; the chic bistros Le Coq and Bar d'Aix cater to a more mature set; and Marktstübel and Dorfschänke serve good food in a casual, cozy atmosphere. All are within a five-minute walk from one another on the streets named above.

⓬ **Peterskirche** (St. Peter's Church). The city's oldest parish church has a graveyard including the final resting places, some more than 500 years old, of many famous Heidelberg citizens. The church itself is not open. ✉ *Plöck 62.*

❺ **Rathaus** (Town Hall). Work began on the town hall in 1701, a few years after the French destroyed the city. The massive coat of arms above the balcony is the work of sculptor Charrasky, who also created the statue of Hercules atop the fountain in the middle of the square. ✉ *Marktpl.*

⓱ **Schlangenweg** (Snake Path). This walkway starts just above the Alte Brücke opposite the Old Town and cuts steeply through terraced vineyards until it reaches the woods, where it crosses the **Philosophenweg** (Philosophers' Path).

★ ❷ **Schloss** (Castle). What's most striking is the architectural variety of this great complex. The oldest parts still standing date from the 15th century, though most of the castle was built in the Renaissance and baroque styles of the 16th and 17th centuries, when the castle was the seat of the Palatinate electors. There's even an "English wing," built in 1612 by the elector Friedrich V for his teenage Scottish bride, Elizabeth Stuart; its plain, square-window facade is positively foreign compared to the more opulent styles of the castle. (The enamored Friedrich also had a charming garden laid out for his young bride; its imposing arched entryway, the Elisabethentor, was put up overnight as a surprise for her 19th birthday.) The architectural highlight remains the Renaissance courtyard—harmonious, graceful, and ornate.

The castle includes the **Deutsches Apotheken–Museum** (German Apothecary Museum; ☎ 06221/25880; ⏲ daily 10–5:30). This museum, on the lower floor of the Ottheinrichsbau (Otto Heinrich Building), is filled with ancient carboys and other flagons and receptacles (each with a carefully painted enamel label), beautifully made scales, little drawers, shelves, a marvelous reconstruction of an 18th-century apothecary shop, dried beetles and toads, and a mummy with a full head of hair.

Even if you have to wait, you should make a point of seeing the **Grosses Fass** (Great Cask), an enormous wine barrel in the cellar, made from 130 oak trees and capable of holding 58,500 gallons. It was used to hold wines paid as taxes by wine growers in the Palatinate. During the rule of the elector Carl Philip, the barrel was guarded by the court jester, a Tyrolean dwarf called Perkeo—when offered wine, he always answered, "*Perche no?*" ("Why not?"), hence his nickname. Legend has it that he could consume frighteningly large quantities of wine and that he died when he drank a glass of water by mistake. A statue of Perkeo stands next to the two-story-high barrel.

The castle may be reached by taking the Königstuhl Bergbahn. Generations of earlier visitors hiked up to it on the Burgweg, a winding road. Of course, it is easier to walk down. In summer there are fireworks displays from the castle terrace (on the first Saturday in June and September and the second Saturday in July). In July and August the castle hosts an open-air theater festival. Performances of *The Student Prince* figure prominently. *Castle info: ☎ 06221/538–431 (ticket booth), 06221/53840 (office). Courtyard, Great Cask, and Apotheken–Museum €2; tours of the interior, an additional €3. Daily 8–5:30; tours in English Easter–Sept., daily at quarter past the hr 10:15–4:15; Oct.–Easter, daily 11:15–2:15 and 3:45.*

9 **Studentenkarzer** (Student Prison). University officials locked students up here from 1778 to 1914—mostly for minor offenses. They could be held for up to 14 days and were left to subsist on bread and water for the first three days; thereafter, they were allowed to attend lectures, receive guests, and have food brought in from the outside. A stay in the jail became as coveted as a scar inflicted in the university's fencing clubs. There's bravado, even poetic flair, to be deciphered from two centuries of graffiti that cover the walls and ceilings of the narrow cells. *✉ Augustinerg., ☎ 06221/543–554. €2.50. Apr.–Oct., Mon.–Sat. 10–4; Nov.–Mar., Tues.–Fri. 10–2.*

11 **Universitätsbibliothek** (University Library). Its 2½ million volumes include the 14th-century *Manesse Codex*, a unique collection of medieval songs and poetry once performed in the courts of Germany by the *Minnesänger* (singers). The original is too fragile to be exhibited, so a copy is on display. *✉ Plöck 107–109, ☎ 06221/542–380. Free. Mon.–Sat. 10–6.*

Dining and Lodging

$$$$ ✕ **Schlossweinstube.** This spacious baroque dining room specializes in *Ente von Heidelberg* (roast duck with dumplings) and offers refuge from the castle crowds. Apart from two beautiful tile ovens, the setting is modern and minimalist. Bistro Backhaus ($; closed Nov.–Mar.) is more rustic, with wooden tables, sandstone floors, and a nearly 50-ft-high *Backkamin* (baking oven). Regional specialties as well as coffee and cake are served here (daily 12–5). You can sample rare wines (Eiswein, Beerenauslese) by the glass in the Fasskeller, or pick up a bottle with a designer label depicting Heidelberg (a nice souvenir). Reservations are essential for terrace seating. *✉ Schlosshof (on the castle grounds), ☎ 06221/97970. AE, DC, MC, V. Schlossweinstube closed Jan. and Wed. Lunch on Sun. only, with advance reservation.*

$$$$ ★ ✕ **Simplicissimus.** Olive oil, garlic, and herbs of Provence accentuate many of chef Johann Lummer's culinary delights. Saddle of lamb is a specialty; the *Dessertteller,* a sampler, is a crowning finish to any meal here. The wine list focuses on old-world estates, particularly clarets. The elegant art nouveau interior is done in shades of red with darkwood accents. In the summer, dine alfresco in the courtyard. *✉ Ingrimstr. 16, ☎ 06221/183–336. AE, MC, V. Closed Tues., 2 wks in Feb. or Mar., 2 wks in Sept. No lunch.*

$$$$ ★ ✕ **Zur Herrenmühle.** Ursula and Günter Ueberle's gourmet cuisine is served in a 17th-century grain mill that's been transformed into a ro-

mantic, cozy restaurant with an idyllic courtyard. Fish is a specialty. Try the *Variation von Edelfischen* (medley of fine fish), served with homemade noodles. The prix-fixe menus offer good value. ✉ *Hauptstr. 239 (near Karlstor),* ☎ *06221/602–909. AE, DC, MC, V. Closed Sun. and 1st half of Jan. No lunch.*

$–$$ ✕ **Schnitzelbank.** A hole-in-the-wall where tourists rarely venture, this former cooper's workshop is now a cozy, candlelit pub filled with locals seated at long wooden tables. It's hard not to fall into conversation with the people at your elbow. The menu features wines and specialties from Baden and the Pfalz, such as Schäufele or a hearty *Pfälzer Teller,* a platter of bratwurst, *Leberknödel* (liver dumplings), and slices of *Saumagen* (a spicy meat-and-potato mixture encased in a "sow's stomach"). ✉ *Bauamtsg. 7,* ☎ *06221/21189. MC, V. No lunch weekdays.*

$–$$ ✕ **Zum Roten Ochsen.** Many of the rough-hewn oak tables here have initials carved into them, a legacy of the thousands who have visited Heidelberg's most famous old tavern. Bismarck, Mark Twain, and John Foster Dulles may have left their mark—they all ate here. You can wash down simple fare, such as goulash soup and bratwurst, or heartier dishes, such as *Tellerfleisch* (boiled beef) and sauerbraten, with German wines or Heidelberg beer—evenings, to the tune of live piano music. The "Red Ox" has been run by the Spengel family for 164 years. ✉ *Hauptstr. 217,* ☎ *06221/20977,* FAX *06221/164–383. Reservations essential. No credit cards. Closed Sun. and mid-Dec.–mid-Jan. No lunch Nov.–Mar.*

$ ✕ **Café Journal.** Come to this old-world paradise for coffee and cake, tasty bistro fare, and people-watching. The pedestrians strutting on the Hauptstrasse provide local theater, as do the people indoors. As in its sister cafés in Mannheim and Schwetzingen, newspapers from around the world, hung on hooks, line the walls. It closes after midnight. ✉ *Hauptstr. 162,* ☎ *06221/161–712. AE, MC, V.*

$ ✕ **Café Knösel.** Heidelberg's oldest (1863) coffeehouse has always been a popular meeting place for students and professors. It's still producing café founder Fridolin Knösel's *Heidelberger Studentenkuss* (student kiss, a chocolate wrapped in paper showing two students touching lips), an acceptable way for 19th-century students to "exchange kisses" in public. ✉ *Haspelg. 20,* ☎ *06221/22345. No credit cards. Closed Mon.*

$ ✕ **Havana Cocktailbar–Restaurant.** Palm trees and salsa music add Latin zest to the handsome interior of the neoclassical Kongresshaus (convention center) and its broad terrace. It's a perfect backdrop for sipping one of the more than 100 cocktails or the hearty house wine (a Spanish red) with the freshly prepared tapas, *Rollos* (stuffed tortillas), or pasta and vegetarian dishes. There's live piano music some evenings and on Saturday at 6 PM beginners can take a salsa class. ✉ *Neckarstaden 24,* ☎ *06221/389–3430. DC, MC, V. No lunch Oct.–Mar. weekdays.*

$$$$ ✕🏨 **Der Europäische Hof–Hotel Europa.** This is the most luxurious of Heidelberg's hotels, centrally located, and offering a wide range of facilities. Public rooms are sumptuously furnished, and bedrooms are spacious and tasteful; all suites have whirlpools. In the elegant Kurfürstenstube rich shades of yellow and blue are offset by the original woodwork of 1865. In the summer meals are served on the fountain-lined terrace ($$$$). There are great views of the castle from the glass-lined fitness and wellness centers. ✉ *Friedrich-Ebert-Anlage 1, D–69117,* ☎ *06221/5150,* FAX *06221/515–506,* WEB *www.europaeischerhof.com. 102 rooms, 16 suites. Restaurant, coffee shop, no a/c in some rooms, in-room data ports, minibars, pool, gym, hair salon, sauna, steam room, bar, some pets allowed, no-smoking rooms. AE, DC, MC, V.*

$$$–$$$$ ★ ✕🏨 **Hotel Hirschgasse.** This historical hotel (1472) is across the river opposite Karlstor, yet only a 15-minute walk to the center of Old

Town. The Mensurstube ($$$) was once a tavern where university students indulged their fencing duels, and Mark Twain mentions it in *A Tramp Abroad*. Today Ernest Kraft and his British wife Alison serve regional fare from Baden and the Pfalz, and wines from the vineyard next door. Le Gourmet ($$$$) is the more elegant of the two restaurants, serving cuisine with Mediterranean accents. Its beamed ceiling and stone walls are quite cozy, as are the rooms, all richly decorated in Laura Ashley style. ✉ *Hirschg. 3, D–69120,* ☎ *06221/4540,* FAX *06221/454–111,* WEB *www.hirschgasse.de. 20 suites. 2 restaurants, no a/c, in-room data ports, minibars, some pets allowed (fee), no-smoking rooms. DC, MC, V. Le Gourmet closed 2 wks in early Jan. and 2 wks in early Aug. Both restaurants closed Sun.–Mon. No lunch.*

$$$ ★ ✕🏨 **Romantik Hotel zum Ritter St. Georg.** If this is your first visit to Germany, try to stay here. It's the only Renaissance building in Heidelberg, and its historical ambience is unique. Some rooms are more modern and spacious than others, but all are comfortable. You can enjoy German and international favorites in the restaurant Belier or in the Ritterstube ($–$$$). Both are wood paneled and offer old-world charm. ✉ *Hauptstr. 178, D–69117,* ☎ *06221/1350,* FAX *06221/135–230,* WEB *www.ritter-heidelberg.de. 39 rooms, 36 with bath, 1 suite. 2 restaurants, no a/c, in-room data ports, minibars, some pets allowed, no-smoking rooms. AE, DC, MC, V.*

$$ ✕🏨 **Gasthaus Backmulde.** This traditional tavern in the heart of Heidelberg has a surprising range of items on its menu ($$–$$), from delicately marinated fresh vegetables that accompany the excellent meat dishes to imaginative soups that add modern twists to ancient recipes (a Franconian potato broth, for instance, rich with garden herbs). Guest rooms are small but comfortable. ✉ *Schiffg. 11, D–69117,* ☎ *06221/53660,* FAX *06221/536–660.* WEB *www.gasthaus-backmulde-hotel.de. 13 rooms. Restaurant, no a/c, some pets allowed (fee). No credit cards. Restaurant closed Sun. No lunch Mon.*

$$ ✕🏨 **KulturBrauerei Heidelberg.** Rooms with warm, sunny colors and modern decor are brilliantly incorporated into this old malt factory in the heart of Old Town. Smoking is not allowed in any guest room. The restaurant ($–$$$) is lively until well past midnight. House-brewed Scheffel's beer is the beverage of choice (although there are two wines from the excellent Baden estate Dr. Heger). Try the *Kohlrouladen* (homemade stuffed cabbage rolls) or *Spannferkel* (roast suckling pig). The cellar houses the brewery and a weekend jazz club. ✉ *Leyerg. 6, D–69117,* ☎ *06221/502–980,* FAX *06221/502–9879,* WEB *www.heidelberger-kulturbrauerei.de. 20 rooms, 1 suite. Restaurant, in-room data ports, minibars, some pets allowed, no a/c, no-smoking rooms. MC, V.*

$$ ✕🏨 **Schnookeloch.** This lively old tavern ($–$$$) dates from 1703 and is inextricably linked with Heidelberg's history and its university. Look for men both old and young with scars on their cheeks. There are still a handful of students who duel with swords, crazy as it might sound. A piano player plays Wednesday through Sunday. Upstairs there are modern, pleasantly furnished guest rooms. ✉ *Haspelg. 8, D–69117,* ☎ *06221/138–080,* FAX *06221/138–0813. 11 rooms. Restaurant, minibars, beer garden, no a/c, some pets allowed. AE, DC, MC, V.*

$$ ✕🏨 **Weisser Bock.** Exposed beams and stucco ceilings are part of this hotel's charm. Rooms are individually decorated with warm wood furnishings and offer modern comfort. Art deco fans will be charmed by the restaurant ($$$–$$$$) decor and pretty table settings. Fresh fish is a highlight of the creative cuisine. The homemade smoked salmon and an unusual cream of Jerusalem artichoke soup with crayfish are recommended. The proprietor is a great wine fan and the extensive wine list reflects it. Smoking is permitted only in the restaurant. ✉ *Grosse Mantelg. 24, D–69117,* ☎ *06221/90000,* FAX *06221/900–099.* WEB

www.weisserbock.de. 21 rooms, 2 suites. Restaurant, minibars, bar, no a/c, no smoking. DC, MC, V.

$$ **Holländer Hof.** The pink-and-white-painted facade of this ornate 19th-century building opposite the Alte Brücke stands out in its row fronting the Neckar River. Many of its rooms overlook the busy waterway and the forested hillside of the opposite shore. The rooms are modern and pleasant. ✉ *Neckarstaden 66, D–69117,* ☎ *06221/60500,* FAX *06221/605–060,* WEB *www.hollaender-hof.de. 38 rooms, 1 suite. No a/c, in-room data ports, minibars, some pets allowed (fee), no-smoking floor. AE, DC, MC, V.*

$–$$ **Hotel Kohler.** It's a little bit of a walk to the city's Old Town but only a couple of minutes by bus. Rooms are impeccably clean, well lighted, and equipped with solid hardwood furniture and double-glazed windows. The staff is very friendly and helpful. ✉ *Goethestr. 2, D–69115,* ☎ *06221/970–097,* FAX *06221/970–096,* WEB *www.hotel-kohler.de. 41 rooms. No a/c, in-room data ports, bicycles, no-smoking rooms. MC, V. Closed mid-Dec.–mid-Jan.*

$ **Jugendherberge Tiergartenstrasse.** Here's a clean, cheap youth hostel that can provide you with a good night's sleep. A new wing with four-bed rooms and private baths opened in 2002. Check on the curfew and, if necessary, get a key if you plan to stay out later. From the Hauptbahnhof, take Bus 33 to Jugendherberge (last bus shortly after midnight on weekdays, weekends around 3 AM)—ask the reception desk for precise times; reception is open 7:30 AM–9 AM and 1 PM–11:30 PM. A bed with breakfast costs €17.90 if you're over 27 years old. ✉ *Tiergartenstr. 5,* ☎ *06221/412–066,* FAX *06221/402–559. 530 beds. Laundry facilities. No credit cards.*

Nightlife and the Arts

Information on all upcoming events is given in the monthly *Heidelberg aktuell,* free and available from the tourist office or on the Internet (www.heidelberg-aktuell.de). Theater tickets may be purchased at the **Theaterkasse** (✉ Theaterstr. 4, ☎ 06221/582–000).

THE ARTS

Heidelberg has a thriving theater scene. The **Kulturzentrum Karlstorbahnhof** (✉ Am Karlstor 1, ☎ 06221/978–911) is a 19th-century train station reincarnated as a theater, cinema, and café. The **Theater der Stadt** (✉ Theaterstr. 4, ☎ 06221/582–000) is the best-known theater in town. Avant-garde productions take place at the **Zimmer theater** (✉ Hauptstr. 118, ☎ 06221/21069). For information on performances at the castle during the annual **Schlossfestspiele,** call ☎ 06221/582–000.

NIGHTLIFE

Heidelberg nightlife is concentrated in the area around the Heiliggeistkirche (Church of the Holy Ghost), in the Old Town. Don't miss a visit to one of the old student taverns that have been in business for ages and have the atmosphere to prove it. Today's students, however, are more likely to hang out in one of the dozen or more bars on **Untere Strasse,** which runs parallel to and between Hauptstrasse and the Neckar River, starting from Market Square. Begin at one end of the street and work your way down; you'll find bars that specialize in all sorts of tastes. The fanciest bars and yuppie cafés are along **Hauptstrasse.**

Mark Twain rubbed elbows with students at **Zum Roten Ochsen** (✉ Hauptstr. 217, ☎ 06221/20977). **Zum Sepp'l** (✉ Hauptstr. 213, ☎ 06221/23085) is another traditional, always-packed pub. **Schnookeloch** (✉ Haspelg. 8, ☎ 06221/138–080) has long been patronized by dueling frats.

Billy Blues (im Ziegler) (✉ Bergheimer Str. 1b, ☎ 06221/25333) is a restaurant, bar, and disco, with "after-work parties" and live music Tuesday. The "54" in **Cave 54** (✉ Krämerg. 2, ☎ 06221/27840) refers to the year the Cave opened, making it one of the oldest jazz cellars in Germany. It's a favorite with serious jazz fans and the small, smoky chamber has a way of suddenly filling up after midnight. There's dancing after sets. Covers are around €5.

The hot sounds of salsa fill the cellar of the **Havana Club** (✉ Neckarstaden 24, ☎ 06221/389–3430) Friday and Saturday after 9 PM. Before the crowds arrive you can practice the steps at a salsa class Saturday at 6 PM. The cover charge includes a drink voucher.

Nachtschicht (Night Shift) in the Landfried factory (f4:Bergheimer Str. 147, ☎ 06221/164–404) is a popular meeting point, not least for the after-work crowd on Wednesday.

Smoky, loud, and always crowded after 10 PM, the old beer hall **Reichsapfel/Lager** (✉ Untere Str. 35, ☎ 06221/485–542) has taken on a sleek, contemporary look after renovations. Seated, or standing around high tables, you can enjoy drinks and light fare, often with live music and/or DJs. Check out the reduced drinks prices during the "lounge hour" (7–9 PM) and "midnight express" (midnight–1 AM).

The **Schwimmbad Musik Club** (✉ Tiergartenstr. 13, near the zoo, ☎ 06221/470–201) is a multiculti fixture of Heidelberg nightlife, with its ambitious concert program (Nirvana used to play here), DJs, disco, videos, and movies. Theme evenings and parties round out the offerings. It's closed Sunday–Tuesday.

It's worth elbowing your way into **Vetters Alt-Heidelberger Brauhaus** (✉ Steing. 9, ☎ 06221/165–850) for the brewed-on-the-premises beer. There is also a branch in Neuenheim (across the river) with a butcher shop, where the homemade sausage is produced for both pubs.

Outdoor Activities and Sports

Heidelberg has a pool fed by thermal water at Vangerowstrasse 4 and pools at the extensive Tiergartenschwimmbad, next to the zoo.

Most tennis clubs along the Neckar accept visitors. In Heidelberg you can play at the **Tennis-Inn** (✉ Harbigweg 1, ☎ 06221/602–106). **Tennis & Squash Treff** (✉ Harbigweg 8, ☎ 06221/602–693) is also open to the public.

Shopping

Heidelberg's **Hauptstrasse,** or Main Street, is a pedestrian zone lined with shops, sights, and restaurants that stretches more than 1 km (½ mi) through the heart of town. But don't spend your money before exploring the shops on such side streets as **Plöck, Ingrimstrasse,** and **Untere Strasse,** where there are candy stores, bookstores, and antiques shops on the ground floors of baroque buildings. If your budget allows, the city can be a good place to find reasonably priced German antiques, and the Neckar Valley region produces fine glass and crystal. Heidelberg has open-air **markets** on Wednesday and Saturday mornings in Marktplatz, the central market square, between the town hall and Holy Ghost Church, and on Friedrich-Ebert-Platz on Tuesday and Friday mornings.

In **Aurum & Argentum** (✉ Brückenstr. 22, ☎ 06221/473–453) you'll find a local gold- and silversmith with impeccable craftsmanship; the finely executed pieces start at €150. Its hours are Tuesday–Friday 2:30–6:30 and Saturday 10–2.

The old glass display cases at **Heidelberger Zuckerladen** (✉ Plöck 52, ☎ 06221/24365) contain lollipops, as well as flower bouquets made out of chocolate, and wonderful apple tarts. This is the sort of place your grandparents came to for "penny" candy.

Tischler Casserole & Tabula (✉ Hauptstr. 73. ☎ 06221/14800) is a paradise for kitchen accessories, *e.g.*, pots, pans, nifty kitchen utensils, knives, glassware, and everything to help you set a beautiful table. It's closed Monday morning.

Buy your cutlery and tableware at **Unholtz** (✉ Hauptstr. 160, ☎ 06221/20964) and keep it for life—it's made by famous German manufacturers of some of the world's best knives.

Schwetzingen

18 *10 km (6 mi) west of Heidelberg.*

Schwetzingen is famous for its **Schloss,** a formal 18th-century palace constructed as a summer residence by the Palatinate electors. It's a noble, rose-color building, imposing and harmonious; a highlight is the rococo theater in one wing. The extensive park blends formal French and informal English styles, with neatly bordered gravel walks trailing off into the dark woodland. The 18th-century planners of this delightful oasis had fun adding such touches as an exotic mosque, complete with minarets and a shimmering pool (although they got a little confused and gave the building a very baroque portal), and the "classical ruin" that was *de rigueur* in this period. ☎ *06202/128–828.* WEB *www.schloesser-und-gaerten.de.* *Palace (including tour and gardens), Apr.–Oct. €5.50; Nov.–Mar. €5; gardens only, Apr.–Oct. €3; Nov.–Mar. €2.50.* *Palace tours (on the hr): Apr.–Oct., Tues.–Fri. 10–4, weekends 10–5; Nov.–Mar., Fri. tour at 2 PM, weekends 11–3. Gardens: Apr.–Sept., daily 8–8; Oct., daily 9–6; Nov.–Feb., daily 9–5; Mar., daily 9–6.*

Dining and Lodging

A rare pleasure awaits you if you're in Schwetzingen in April, May, or June: the town is Germany's asparagus center, and nearly every local restaurant has a *Spargelkarte* (a special menu featuring fresh asparagus dishes).

$$–$$$ **Romantik Hotel Goldener Löwe.** The Golden Lion has been a favorite staging stop for travelers for two centuries. The attractive old house, with its steep, dormer-windowed roof, was originally a butcher shop and wine tavern. Now it's a very welcoming hotel and a restaurant ($$$–$$$$) that serves modern cuisine with an Italian accent. There are comfortable rooms, some with exposed beams, all individually furnished. ✉ *Schloss Str. 4, D–68723,* ☎ *06202/28090,* FAX *06202/10726. 15 rooms, 1 suite, 3 apartments. Restaurant, no a/c, in-room data ports, minibars, some pets allowed (fee), no-smoking rooms. AE, DC, MC, V. Restaurant closed 2 wks in Aug., Sun. eve., and Thurs.*

The Arts

The annual **Schwetzinger Festspiele,** from late April to early June, features operas and concerts by international artists in the lovely rococo theater of Schwetzingen Palace. The period rooms of the palace are also the venue for the **Mozartfest,** the last half of September. The local tourist office (☎ 06202/945–875 tourist office) has details on both performing arts festivals.

THE BURGENSTRASSE (CASTLE ROAD)

Upstream from Heidelberg, the Neckar Valley narrows, presenting a landscape of orchards, vineyards, and wooded hills crowned with castles rising above the gently flowing stream. It's one of the most impressive stretches of the Burgenstrasse. The small valleys along the Neckar Valley road (B–37)—the locals call them *Klingen*—that cut north into the Odenwald are off-the-beaten-track territory. One of the most atmospheric is the Wolfsschlucht, which starts below the castle at Zwingenberg. The dank, shadowy little gorge inspired Carl Maria von Weber's opera *Der Freischütz* (The Marksman).

Neckargemünd

⓳ *11 km (7 mi) upstream from Heidelberg.*

The first hamlet on the Burgenstrasse is Neckargemünd, once a bustling river town. Today it's a sleepy sort of place, although it can make a good base from which to see Heidelberg.

Dining and Lodging

$$–$$$ ✕ **Landgasthof Die Rainbach.** This long-popular country inn 2 km (1 mi) east of Neckargemünd, in the Rainbach district, prepares traditional fare as well as fine dishes using international ingredients. If the weather's good, take a table on the terrace, which commands a view of the river. In winter warm up in the paneled restaurant with a dish of freshly prepared soup and roasted game served with rich, fruity sauces. There is parking on the riverbank. ✉ *Ortstr. 9,* ☎ *06223/2455. MC, V.*

$$ ★ ✕ **Hotel zum Schwanen.** At this family-run inn on the northern bank of the Neckar, opposite the village of Neckargemünd, you can dine in a garden by the river or in the glassed-in dining room. The kitchen ($$) serves regional specialties and a good number of fish dishes. The owners and staff are courteous and the rooms have modern furnishings and river views. ✉ *Uferstr. 16, D–69151 Neckargemünd–Kleingemünd,* ☎ *06223/92400,* FAX *06223/2413,* WEB *www.hotel-schwanen.com. 20 rooms, 1 suite. Restaurant, no a/c, in-room data ports, minibars, bicycles, some pets allowed (fee), no-smoking rooms. AE, DC, MC, V.*

En Route Eight kilometers (5 mi) past Neckargemünd on the Neckar Valley road is the impregnable **Burg Dilsberg** (€1.50; Apr.–Oct., Tues.–Sun. 10–5:30), one of the few castles hereabouts to have withstood General Tilly's otherwise all-conquering forces in the Thirty Years' War. Until the student prison in Heidelberg was built, the castle's dungeons were used to accommodate the university's more unruly dissidents. The view from its battlements, over the valley and the green expanse of the Odenwald beyond, is worth the climb.

Opposite Dilsberg is **Neckarsteinach,** known as the *Vierburgenstadt* (Town of the Four Castles). What remains of the castles is largely ruins. The sections that are still intact make up the baronial residence of an aristocratic German family.

Hirschhorn

⓴ *8 km (5 mi) east of Neckarsteinach, 23 km (14 mi) east of Heidelberg.*

Hirsch (stag) and *Horn* (antlers) make up the name of the Knights of Hirschhorn, the medieval ruling family which gave its name to both their 12th-century castle complex and the village it presided over. The town's coat of arms depicts a leaping stag. Ensconced into the hillside halfway between the castle and the river is a former Carmelite monastery and its beautiful 15th-century Gothic church with remarkable frescoes (open for visits). Hirschhorn's position on a hairpin loop of the Neckar can best be savored from the castle terrace, over a glass of wine, coffee and cake, or a fine meal.

The past comes to life the first weekend of September at the annual, two-day **Ritterfest,** a colorful "Knights' Festival" complete with a medieval arts and crafts market.

Dining and Lodging

$$ ★ ✕🏨 **Schlosshotel auf der Burg Hirschhorn.** This very pleasant hotel and restaurant is set in historic Hirschhorn Castle, perched high over the medieval village and the Neckar. The terrace offers splendid views (ask for table No. 30 in the corner). The rooms are modern and well furnished. Eight are in the castle and 17 in the old stables. *Wildschwein* (wild boar), *Hirsch* (venison), and fresh fish are the house specialties ($$–$$$). The friendly proprietors, the Oberrauners, bake a delicious, warm Apfelstrudel based on a recipe from their home in Vienna. A good selection of wines is available. ✉ *D–69434 Hirschhorn/Neckar,* ☎ *06272/92090,* FAX *06272/3267,* WEB *www.castle-hotel.de. 21 rooms, 4 suites. Restaurant, café, no a/c, in-room data ports, minibars, some pets allowed (fee). AE, MC, V. Hotel and restaurant closed Dec. 15–end of Jan. Restaurant closed Mon. in Feb.–Easter and Nov.–mid-Dec.*

Eberbach

21 *11 km (7 mi) east of Hirschhorn.*

The Neckar makes a wide bend to the south here. The landscape around romantic Eberbach is punctuated by four square towers from the medieval town fortifications and three castle ruins. Historic houses abound, and on **Alter Markt** (old market square) there is a particularly fine sgraffito facade to admire, the Hotel Karpfen. Stop by the **Naturpark-Informationszentrum** (Natural Park Info Center) for details about the extensive hiking trails through the Odenwald forest.

Dining and Lodging

$–$$$ ✕ **Pleutersbacher Weinstube.** Jürgen and Martina Klier's cozy wine restaurant in the suburb of Pleutersbach (on the south side of the Neckar, opposite Eberbach proper) is a favorite with locals. Amid exposed beams and rustic wood furnishings you can enjoy tasty regional fare, such as *Käs'Spätzle* (a cheese gratin version of these wonderful noodles), as well as daily specials and theme menus based on seasonal ingredients, such as matjes herring, kale, or *Bärlauch,* a cousin of garlic and onion. A good selection of by-the-glass, half bottles and older vintage German and international wines are served. ✉ *Eberbacherstr. 5,* ☎ *06271/5705. No credit cards. Closed Mon. Lunch on Sun. only.*

$–$$ ✕🏨 **Hotel Karpfen.** Behind the beautiful painted facade of this traditional hotel and restaurant awaits a warm welcome from the Rohrlapper and Jung families. The wooden furnishings and floors lend the rooms warmth and a rustic charm. The restaurant ($–$$$) has wallpapered walls and antique rose accents, a nice setting for fresh *Forelle* (trout) from the streams of the Odenwald forest, game, and regional specialties, including local wines. ✉ *Am Alten Markt 1, D–69412,* ☎ *06271/71015,* FAX *06271/71010,* WEB *www.hotel-karpfen.com. 47 rooms, 2 suites, 1 apartment. Restaurant, no a/c, some in-room data ports, some pets allowed (fee). AE, MC, V. Restaurant closed Tues., 4 wks in Feb.*

En Route Eight kilometers (5 miles) beyond Eberbach, a castle stands above the village of **Zwingenberg,** its medieval towers thrusting through the dark woodland. Some say it's the most romantic of all the castles along the Neckar (the one at Heidelberg excepted). The annual Schlossfestspiele

(☎ 06268/927–720, WEB www.festspiel.de), with performances of *Der Freischutz,* take place within its ancient walls in August.

Mosbach

22 *25 km (16 mi) southeast of Eberbach.*

The little town of Mosbach is one of the most charming towns on the Neckar, and its ancient market square contains one of Germany's most exquisite half-timber buildings—the early 17th-century **Palm'sches Haus** (Palm House), its upper stories laced with intricate timbering. The **Rathaus,** built 50 years earlier, is a modest affair by comparison.

Dining and Lodging

$$–$$$$ ★ ✕ **Zum Ochsen.** Chef Achim Münch and his charming American wife, Heyley, run this country inn in Nüstenbach, a suburb north of Mosbach. The decor is stylish—one room elegant, the other more rustic. The interesting display of antique silver is also for sale. Fresh, seasonal cuisine and fish are always featured, as well as such creative dishes as baked fondue or venison in a pistachio crust. There is a good selection of wines at very fair prices. You can spend the night in their antiques-filled cottage next door ($, sleeps four, no smoking). ✉ *Im Weiler 6,* ☎ *06261/15428,* FAX *06261/893–645. MC, V. Closed 2 wks in Feb. or Mar., 2 wks in Aug. or Sept., and Tues. No lunch Mon.–Sat.*

$ ✕🏨 **Zum Lamm.** The half-timber Lamb on Mosbach's main street is one of the town's prettiest houses. Its cozy rooms are individually furnished, with flowers filling the window boxes. The restaurant ($–$$), complete with requisite exposed beams, serves local and international dishes, incorporating meat from the hotel's own butcher shop. ✉ *Hauptstr. 59, D–74821,* ☎ *06261/89020,* FAX *06261/890–291. 50 rooms. Restaurant, no a/c, some minibars, some pets allowed, no-smoking rooms. AE, MC, V.*

Outdoor Activities and Sports

Ebullient Irene Bering offers hot-air-balloon tours of the Neckar Valley and countryside for €205 per person. Flights last 1½ hours, but with prep time and return trip to starting point—and the ceremonial Champagne toast and certificate in honor of your flight—allow four–five hours. Contact **Ballon Tour** (☎ 06261/18477, FAX 06261/37277) at the *Flugplatz* (airfield) in Mosbach-Lohrbach.

Neckarzimmern

5 km (3 mi) south of Mosbach.

23 The massive circular bulk of **Burg Hornberg** rises above the woods that drop to the riverbank and the town of Neckarzimmern. The road to the castle leads through vineyards that have been providing excellent dry white wines for centuries. Today the castle is part hotel-restaurant and part museum. In the 16th century it was home to the larger-than-life knight Götz von Berlichingen (1480–1562). When he lost his right arm fighting in a petty dynastic squabble he had a blacksmith fashion an iron replacement for him. The original designs for this fearsome artificial limb are on view in the castle, as is a suit of armor that belonged to him. Scenes from his life are also represented. For most Germans, the rambunctious knight is best remembered for a remark he delivered to the Palatinate elector that was faithfully reproduced in Goethe's play, *Götz von Berlichingen.* Responding to a reprimand, von Berlichingen told the elector, more or less, to "kiss my ass" (the original German is substantially more earthy). To this day the polite version of this insult is known as a "Götz von Berlichingen." Ask the hotel receptionist where the entrance to the castle is. 🎫 *€2.80.*

Dining and Lodging

$$ ★ ✕🏨 **Burg Hornberg.** Your host is the present baron of the castle. From the heights of the terrace and glassed-in restaurant ($$$)—housed in the former *Marstall,* or royal stables—there are stunning views. Fresh fish and game are specialties as are its own estate-bottled wines. They have excellent Riesling wines and the rarities Traminer and Muskateller. The hotel's rooms are comfortable and modern in style. ✉ *D–74865 Neckarzimmern,* ☎ *06261/92460,* FAX *06261/924–644,* WEB *www.castle-hotel-hornberg.com. 22 rooms, 2 suites. Restaurant, no a/c, cable TV, in-room data ports, some minibars, some pets allowed (fee), no -smoking rooms. MC, V. Closed late Dec.–late Jan.*

Shopping

The factory **Franz Kaspar** (✉ Hauptstr. 11, ☎ 06261/923–014; 06261/92400 for tour reservations), known for its fine crystal, gives free tours weekdays 9–4, Saturday 10–6, Sunday 10:30–6 that demonstrate the manufacturing process. Its outlet shop is open daily. Near the factory, and at the foot of the hill leading to Burg Hornberg, the **Schlosskellerei** (☎ 06261/5001) sells wine weekdays 10–5. Within Burg Hornberg's courtyard, the **wine shop** (☎ 06261/5001) is open April–October, daily 10–5, November–March, weekends 10–5.

En Route The fine medieval **Schloss Horneck** was destroyed during the Peasants' War (1525) by Götz von Berlichingen and his troops. It was subsequently rebuilt and stands in all its medieval glory. Once it was owned by the Teutonic Knights; today it houses a home for the elderly and a local history museum. ✉ *5 km (3 mi) south of Burg Hornburg,* ☎ *06269/421–2160.* 🎫 *€2.* ⏲ *Tues.–Sun. 11–5.*

A few bends of the river south of Schloss Horneck bring you to one of the best preserved of the Neckar castles, the 15th-century **Burg Guttenberg.** Within its stout stone walls is a restaurant (closed Monday) with views of the river valley. The castle is also home to Europe's leading center for the study and protection of birds of prey, and some are released on demonstration flights (€8) from the castle walls from March through mid-November, daily at 11 and 3. ☎ *06266/388,* WEB *www.burg-guttenberg.de.* 🎫 *Castle €4; combined admission €11.* ⏲ *Mar.–mid-Nov., daily 9–6.*

Bad Wimpfen

★ 24 *8 km (5 mi) south of Neckarzimmern.*

At the confluence of the Neckar and Jagst rivers, Bad Wimpfen is one of the most stunning towns of the Neckar Valley. On the riverbank site of an ancient Celtic settlement, the Romans built a fortress and a bridge here in the 1st century AD. Wimpfen im Tal (Wimpfen in the Valley), the oldest part of town, is home to the Benedictine monastery Gruessau and its church, **Ritterstiftskirche St. Peter** (✉ Lindenpl.), which dates from the 10th and 13th centuries. The cloisters are delightful, an example of German Gothic at its most uncluttered.

On the hilltop, Wimpfen am Berg, the Staufen emperor Barbarossa built his largest **Pfalz** (residence) in 1182. The town not only thrived, but also enjoyed the status of a Free Imperial City from 1300 to 1803. Since then, its fortune has been tied to the local saltworks that enabled it to develop medicinal saline baths and its reputation as a spa—hence the town was renamed Bad Wimpfen in 1930.

A walking tour marked by signs bearing the town arms begins at the Rathaus on market square, adjacent to the Burgviertel (palace quarter) and the buildings of the former imperial residence. These are nestled along the town wall between the turreted **Blauer Turm** (Blue Tower) and the massive stone **Roter Turm** (Red Tower), the western and eastern strongholds of the palace, respectively. Ascend either for a grand view. The **Steinhaus,** Germany's largest Romanesque living quarters and once the imperial apartments reserved for women, is now a history museum (closed Monday). Next to the Steinhaus are the remains of the northern facade of the palace, an arcade of superbly carved Romanesque pillars that flanked the imperial hall in its heyday. The imperial chapel, next to the Red Tower, holds a collection of ecclesiastical artworks (closed Monday). Other historical houses in the quarter are on Schwibbogengasse (Nos. 5 and 16). ✉ *Kaiserpl.,* ☎ *07063/97200.* ⏲ *Palace tours daily; reserve in advance.*

Among Bad Wimpfen's finest 15- and 16th-century half-timber houses are those on Badgasse (Nos. 8 and 10), Hauptstrasse (Nos. 69 and 83), and Klostergasse (Nos. 4, 6, 8, and 9). The 13th-century stained glass, wall paintings, medieval altars, and the stone pieta in the Gothic **Stadtkirche** (city church) are worth seeing, as are the crucifixion sculptures (1515) by the Rhenish master Hans Backoffen on Kirchplatz, behind the church.

In Germany, pigs are a symbol of good luck. At the **Schweine-Museum** (Pig Museum), you'll see them in every form imaginable—depicted on posters and porcelain, modeled into household items, and as toys, including Porky Pig. In all, it's a mixture of historically valuable items and kitsch. ✉ *Kronengässchen 2,* ☎ *07063/6689,* WEB *www.schweinemuseum.de.* *€2.60.* ⏲ *Daily 10–5.*

Dining and Lodging

$$ ✕ **Tafelhaus Perkeo.** The interior and decor of this lovingly restored historical house is warm and inviting. Alfresco dining is also possible. Beate Stiefel oversees service and Heiko Habelt is in the kitchen, preparing well-made regional dishes, seasonal cuisine (the menu changes frequently), and fresh fish. The ambience, food, and wine offered here set this restaurant well apart from the town's many group-oriented eateries. ✉ *Hauptstr. 82,* ☎ *07063/932–354. MC, V. Closed Wed.*

$$ ★ ✕ **Hotel Schloss Heinsheim.** This baroque castle in a beautiful park has been in the von Racknitz family since 1721. The rooms are individually furnished—some with antiques, others are more rustic in style. You can dine on the terrace or in the country manor–like restaurant ($$–$$$$). Start with a Swabian *Hochzeitssuppe* (wedding soup), followed by breast of duck with pink peppercorns or Dover sole in champagne sauce. Most wines on the list are French or German (Baden, Württemberg). ✉ *Gundelsheimer Str. 36, D–74906 Bad Rappenau,* ☎ *07264/95030,* FAX *07264/4208,* WEB *www.schloss-heinsheim.de. 40 rooms, 1 suite. Restaurant, no a/c, some in-room data ports, minibars, pool, bicycles, bar, some pets allowed (fee). AE, DC, MC, V. Closed Jan. Restaurant closed Mon.–Tues.*

$$ ✕ **Hotel Sonne und Weinstube Feyerabend.** This family-run hotel right in the center of town has rooms in two medieval half-timber buildings. The atmosphere is cozy throughout, with upholstered antique furniture, low ceilings, and thick down comforters. The tavern serves local specialties ($$$–$$$$)—Spätzle, fish, and game in season. ✉ *Hauptstr. 87 and Langg. 3, D–74206,* ☎ *07063/245,* FAX *07063/6591,* WEB *www.sonne-wimpfen.de. 18 rooms. Restaurant, café, Weinstube, no a/c, some in-room data ports, some pets allowed. MC, V. Closed late Dec.–mid-Jan. Restaurant also closed Sun. dinner and Thurs.*

$$ **Hotel Neckarblick.** The Salier family extends the warmest of welcomes to its guests. There's a peaceful terrace, where you can sit in summer and contemplate the Neckar River. Many rooms have a view and

flower boxes in the windows. The furniture is comfortable and modern, like the hotel building. For medieval atmosphere, the heart of Bad Wimpfen is only a few blocks away. Although there is no restaurant, the Saliers serve platters of cold cuts and cheese upon request, and offer free shuttle service to and from the train station. ✉ *Erich-Salier-Str. 48, D–74206,* ☎ *07063/961–620.* FAX *07063/8548,* WEB *www.neckarblick.de. 14 rooms. No a/c, minibars, bicycles, lounge, some pets allowed (fee), no-smoking rooms. AE, MC, V.*

Neckarsulm

25 *10 km (6 mi) south of Bad Wimpfen.*

Motorbike fans won't want to miss the town of Neckarsulm. It's a busy little industrial center, home of the German automobile manufacturer Audi and the **Deutsches-Zweirad Museum** (German Motorcycle Museum). It's close to the factory where motorbikes were first manufactured in Germany. Among its 300 exhibits are the world's first mass-produced motorcycles (the Hildebrand and Wolfmüller); a number of famous racing machines; and a rare Daimler machine, the first made by that legendary name. The museum also has an exhibit of early bicycles, dating from 1816, as well as early automobiles. All are arranged over five floors in a handsome 400-year-old castle that belonged to the Teutonic Knights until 1806. ✉ *Urbanstr. 11,* ☎ *07132/35271,* WEB *www.zweirad-museum.de.* 🎫 *€4.* ⏲ *Tues.–Wed. and Fri.–Sun. 9–5, Thurs. 9–7.*

SWABIAN CITIES

Heilbronn, Stuttgart, and Tübingen are all part of the ancient province of Swabia, a region strongly influenced by Protestantism and Calvinism. The inhabitants speak the Swabian dialect of German. Heilbronn lies on both sides of the Neckar. Stuttgart, the capital of the state of Baden-Würtemberg and one of Germany's leading industrial cities, is surrounded by hills on three sides, with the fourth side opening up toward its river harbor. The medieval town of Tübingen clings to steep slopes and hilltops above the Neckar.

Heilbronn

26 *6 km (4 mi) south of Neckarsulm, 50 km (31 mi) north of Stuttgart.*

Most of the leading sights in Heilbronn are grouped in and around the ★ Marktplatz, which is dominated by the sturdy **Rathaus,** built in the Gothic style in 1417 and remodeled during the Renaissance. Set into the Rathaus's clean-lined facade and beneath the steep red roof is a magnificently ornate 16th-century clock. It's divided into four distinct parts. The lowest is an astronomical clock, showing the day of the week, the month, and the year. Above it is the main clock—note how its hour hand is larger than the minute hand, a convention common in the 16th century. Above this there's a smaller dial that shows the phases of the sun and the moon. The final clock is a bell at the topmost level. Suspended from a delicate stone surround, it's struck alternately by the two angels on either side. The entire elaborate mechanism swings into action at noon. As the hour strikes, an angel at the base of the clock sounds a trumpet; another turns an hourglass and counts the hours with a scepter. Simultaneously, the twin golden rams between them charge each other and lock horns while a cockerel spreads its wings and crows. Behind the market square is the **Kilianskirche** (Church of St. Kilian), Heilbronn's most famous church, dedicated to the Irish monk who brought Christianity to the Rhineland in the Dark Ages and who lies buried in Würzburg. Its lofty Gothic tower was capped in the early 16th century with a fussy, lanternlike structure that ranks as the first major Renaissance work north of the Alps. At its summit there's a soldier carrying a banner decorated with the city arms. Walk around the church to the south side (the side opposite the main entrance) to see the well that gave the city its name.

Dining and Lodging

$–$$$ ✕ **Ratskeller.** Both the handsome table settings in the vaulted cellar and the seats on the spacious terrace in front of the town hall are pleasant settings for the Mosthaf brothers' tasty food, excellent wines, and cheerful service. Try the braised rabbit in mustard sauce or a salmon trout fillet in a whipped lemon sauce. The *Tagesessen* (daily special) is a good value. ✉ *Marktpl. 7,* ☎ *07131/84628. AE. Closed Sun.*

$–$$ ✕ **Restaurant-Café Am Stadtgarten Harmonie.** Eat on the terrace in summer to enjoy the view of the city park. Inside, the decor is traditional with a modern twist, as is the menu. Traditional German dishes and Swabian specialties, such as Rostbraten and *sauere Kutteln* (tripe), are served. ✉ *Allee 28,* ☎ *07131/87954. AE, DC, MC, V. Closed Tues. and Aug. No dinner Sun.*

$ ✕ **Vinum.** Whether you want coffee and a croissant, fresh tapas, or a beefsteak with onions, it's all available here from 9 AM 'til midnight, seven days of the week. As the name implies, Vinum is also a wine bar—with 140 German and international wines from which to choose. ✉ *Marktplatz 1,* ☎ *07131/642–7220. No credit cards.*

$$ ✕🏨 **Hotel und Gutsgaststätte Rappenhof.** This cheerful country inn is on a hill in the midst of the vineyards of Weinsberg (6 km [4 mi] northeast of Heilbronn), where you can take in the fresh air and panoramic views from the terrace or on a scenic walk along the signposted Wine Panorama Path. The restaurant ($$–$$$) features hearty country cooking, such as sauerbraten with *Semmelknödel* (bread dumplings), and regional wines. ✉ *D–74189 Weinsberg,* ☎ *07134/5190,* FAX *07134/51955,* WEB *www.rappenhof.de. 39 rooms. Restaurant, no a/c, some in-room data ports, minibars, bicycles, some pets allowed (fee), no-smoking rooms. AE, DC, MC, V. Closed mid-Dec.–mid-Jan.*

$$ ✕🏨 **Insel-Hotel.** *Insel* means "island," and that's where the luxurious Insel-Hotel is—on a river island tethered to the city by the busy Friedrich Ebert Bridge. The Mayer family combines a personal touch with polished service and facilities. Enjoy alfresco dining in the summer, when chefs fire up the charcoal grill on the Mediterranean-like terrace of the Schwäbisches Restaurant ($$$–$$$$). The roof garden affords great views. ✉ *Friedrich-Ebert-Brücke, D–74072,* ☎ *07131/6300,* FAX *07131/626–060,* WEB *www.insel-hotel.de. 120 rooms, 4 suites. Restaurant, no a/c, some in-room data ports, pool, gym, sauna, bar, free parking, some pets allowed, no-smoking rooms. AE, DC, MC, V.*

$$ ★ ✕🏨 **Schlosshotel Liebenstein.** Nestled in the hills above the village of Neckarwestheim, south of Heilbronn, is one of the area's most beautiful castles, Schloss Liebenstein. Within the 3-ft-thick, whitewashed castle walls, the peaceful hush of centuries reigns over a setting of comfort and noble elegance. Guest rooms have views of forests, vineyards, and a golf course. The restaurant Lazuli ($$$$) has gourmet cuisine (3- to 7-course menus only); Kurfürst ($–$$) serves regional fare; and light meals are available in the beer garden. ✉ *Schloss Liebenstein, D–74382 Neckarwestheim,* ☎ *07133/98990,* FAX *07133/6045,* WEB *www.liebenstein.com. 22 rooms, 2 suites. 3 restaurants, bar, beer garden, no a/c, 2 golf courses, bicycles, some pets allowed, no-smoking rooms. AE, MC, V. Hotel and Lazuli closed last wk Dec.–1st wk Jan.* ⊙ *Lazuli open weekdays for dinner only.*

Nightlife and the Arts

The Festhalle Harmonie and Stadttheater are the major (but not the only) venues for theater, dance, opera, musicals, and concerts. The city has two resident orchestras: **Württemberg Chamber Orchestra** and **Heilbronn Symphony Orchestra.** The **Heilbronn tourist office** distributes a monthly *Veranstaltungskalender* (calendar of events) and also sells tickets to cultural events (☎ 07131/562–270).

Shopping

The city's internationally renowned **Weindorf** wine festival, during mid-September, showcases more than 200 wines from the Heilbronn region alone. Outside festival time, you'll find numerous shops stocking wine along Heilbronn's central pedestrian shopping zone, and you can also sample and purchase directly from private wine estates or a *Weingärtner genossenschaft* (vintners' cooperative winery). One of Württemberg's finest producers, the **Staatsweingut Weinsberg** (State Wine Domain; ✉ Traubenpl. 5, Weinsberg, ☎ 07134/504–167) has an architecturally striking wine shop with 70 wines and 30 other products of the grape on offer. It's open weekdays 9–5.

En Route ★ Ludwigsburg, a scant 15 km (9 mi) north of Stuttgart, merits a stop to visit Germany's largest baroque palace, **Residenzschloss Ludwigsburg.** The "Versailles of Swabia" is surrounded by the fragrant, colorful 74-acre park **Blühendes Barock** (Blooming Baroque; €6.50; WEB www.blueba.de), replete with splendid gardens, fountains, aviaries, a Märchengarten (fairy-tale garden) and a "water playground" that delight visitors of all ages. Concerts and theatrical performances are held here during the annual **Schlossfestspiele** (June–mid-September). The palace is also home to the **Porzellan-Manufaktur Ludwigsburg,** where you can watch the artists hand-paint the manufactory's exquisite porcelain (Wednesday and Thursday, 2–4 PM). A five-minute walk north of the palace (across Marbacher Strasse) brings you to the **Jagdschloss Favorite** (€2), a "small" summer residence and hunting lodge of the Dukes of Württemberg. ✉ *Schloss Str. 30,* ☎ *07141/186–440,* WEB *www.schloesser-und-gaerten.de. Residenzschloss €3.50; Barocke Erlebniskarte (combined admission to all sights) €10. Residenzschloss mid-Mar.–Oct., daily 9–noon, 1–5; Nov.–mid-Mar., daily 10–noon, 1–4. Jagdschloss mid-Mar.–mid-Oct., daily 9–noon, 1:30–5; mid-Oct.–mid-Mar., Tues.–Sun. 10–noon, 1:30–4. Blühendes Barock mid-Mar.–Oct., daily 7:30 AM–8:30 PM; winter hrs are shorter. Porcelain shop weekdays 9:30–12:30, 1:30–5:30, Sat. 10–1.*

Stuttgart

27 *50 km (31 mi) south on B–27 from Heilbronn.*

Stuttgart is a place of fairly extreme contradictions. It has been called, among other things, "Germany's biggest small town" and "the city where work is a pleasure." For centuries Stuttgart, whose name derives from *Stutengarten,* or "stud farm," remained a pastoral backwater along the Neckar. Then the Industrial Revolution propelled the city into the machine age, after which it was leveled in World War II. Since then Stuttgart has regained its position as one of Germany's top industrial centers.

Here, *Schaffen*—"doing, achieving"—is all. This is Germany's can-do city, whose natives have turned out Mercedes-Benz and Porsche cars, Bosch electrical equipment, and a host of other products exported worldwide. Yet Stuttgart is also a city of culture and the arts, with world-class museums and a famous ballet company. Moreover, it's the domain of fine local wines; the vineyards actually approach the city center in a rim of green hills. Forests, vineyards, meadows, and orchards compose more than half the city, which is enclosed on three sides by woods.

An ideal introduction to the contrasts of Stuttgart is a guided city bus tour. Included is a visit to the needle-nose TV tower, high on a mountaintop above the city, affording stupendous views. Built in 1956, it was the first of its kind in the world. On your own, the best place to begin exploring Stuttgart is the Hauptbahnhof (main train station); from there walk down the pedestrian street Königstrasse to Schillerplatz, a small, charming square named after the 18th-century poet and playwright Friedrich Schiller, who was born in nearby Marbach. It is surrounded by historic buildings, many of them rebuilt after the war.

Just off Schillerplatz, the **Stiftskirche** (Collegiate Church of the Holy Cross; ✉ Stiftstr. 12, Mitte.) is Stuttgart's most familiar sight, with its two oddly matched towers. Built in the 12th century and then substantially rebuilt in a late-Gothic style (1433–1531), the church became Protestant in 1534. It was reconsecrated in 1958 after being badly damaged in a 1944 bombing raid. The choir has a famous series of Renaissance figures of the counts of Württemberg sculpted by Simon Schlör (1576–1608). The church is scheduled to reopen in late 2002 after a renovation.

Schlossplatz (Palace Square) is a huge area enclosed by royal palaces, with elegant arcades branching off to other stately plazas. The magnificent baroque **Neues Schloss** (New Castle), now occupied by Baden-Württemberg state government offices, dominates the square. The **Kunstgebäude** (House of Art), the building with a golden stag on its cupola, houses the **Galerie der Stadt Stuttgart** (Stuttgart City Gallery) and the **Württembergischer Kunstverein** (Württemberg Art Society), which feature artworks of the 19th and 20th centuries, the world's largest Otto Dix collection (including the *Grossstadt* [*Metropolis*] triptych, which distills the essence of 1920s Germany on canvas), and changing shows of contemporary German artists' works. ✉ *Schlosspl. 2, Mitte,* ☎ *0711/216–2188.* 🎫 *Free; special exhibitions €3–6.* ⏲ *City Gallery and Art Society: Tues.–Sun. 11–6, Wed. until 8.*

The **Schlossgarten** (Palace Garden) borders the Schlossplatz and extends northeast across Schillerstrasse all the way to Bad Cannstatt on the Neckar River. The park is graced by an exhibition hall, planetarium, lakes, sculptures, and the hot spring–mineral baths Leuze and Berg. Adjacent to the Schlossgarten is Rosenstein Park with the city's two natural history museums and the **Wilhelma** zoological and botanical gardens. From here it is but a brief walk along the riverbank to the pier for Neckar-Käpt'n boat trips on the Neckar. ✉ *Neckartalstr., Wilhelma,* ☎ *0711/54020.* 🎫 *€8. Nov.–Feb. and in summer after 4 PM, €5.* ⏲ *May–Aug., daily 8:15–6; Sept.–Apr., daily 8:15–4. The greenhouses and animal halls are open 30 mins and 45 mins longer, respectively, than the box office hrs.*

Across the street from the Neues Schloss stands the **Altes Schloss** (Old Castle), the former residence of the counts and dukes of Württemberg. Built as a moated castle around 1320, wings were added in the mid-15th century to turn this into a Renaissance palace. The palace now houses the **Württember gisches Landesmuseum** (Württemberg State Museum), with imaginative exhibits tracing the development of the area from the Stone Age to modern times. The displays of medieval life are especially noteworthy. ✉ *Schillerpl. 6, Mitte,* ☎ *0711/279–3400.* 🎫 *€2.60.* ⏲ *Tues. 10–1, Wed.–Sun. 10–5.*

★ The **Staatsgalerie** (State Gallery) possesses one of the finest art collections in Germany. The old part of the complex, dating from 1842, has paintings from the Middle Ages through the 19th century, including works by Cranach, Holbein, Hals, Memling, Rubens, Rembrandt, Cézanne, Courbet, and Manet. Connected to the original building is the **New State Gallery**, designed by British architect James Stirling in 1984 as a melding of classical and modern, sometimes jarring, elements (such as chartreuse window mullions). Considered one of the most successful postmodern buildings, it houses works by such 20th-century artists as Braque, Chagall, de Chirico, Dali, Kandinsky, Klee, Mondrian, and Picasso. The gallery is staging a major Impressionist exhibition through February 2003. ✉ *Konrad-Adenauer-Str. 30–32, Mitte,* ☎ *0711/212–4050,* WEB *www.staatsgalerie.de.* 🎫 *€4.50 (free on Wed.).* ⏲ *Tues.–Wed. and Fri.–Sun. 10–6, Thurs. 10–9, 1st Sat. of month 10–midnight.*

In late 2002, Stuttgart's "cultural mile" was enriched with yet another post-modern architectural masterpiece by James Stirling, the **Haus der Geschichte Baden-Württemberg** (Museum of the History of Baden-Württemberg). It chronicles the state's history during the 19th and 20th centuries. Theme parks and multimedia presentations enable you to interact with the thousands of fascinating objects on display. ✉ *Konrad-Adenauer-Str. 16, Mitte,* ☎ *0711/212–3950,* WEB *www.hdgbw.de.* 🎫 *€ 3.* ⏲ *Tues.–Sun. 10–6.*

An extraordinary urban planning project underway is "Stuttgart 21." An area comprising about 250 acres—now covered with train tracks north of the main station—is being converted into a new neighborhood and the tracks are being moved underground. The **Bahnhofsturm** (train station tower), crowned by the Mercedes star, has an information center with three floors of exhibitions on the project as well as a great viewing platform. ✉ *Arnulf-Klett-Pl., Mitte,* ☎ *0711/2092–37230.* 🎫 *Free.* ⏲ *Tues.–Sun. 10–7.*

OFF THE BEATEN PATH

GOTTLIEB DAIMLER MEMORIAL WORKSHOP – The first successful internal combustion engine was perfected here in 1883, and you can see the tools, blueprints, and models of early cars that helped pave the way for the Mercedes line. ✉ *Taubenheimstr. 13, Stuttgart-Bad Cannstatt,* ☎ *0711/569–399.* 🎫 *Free.* ⏲ *Tues.–Sun. 10–4.*

MERCEDES-BENZ MUSEUM – The oldest car factory in the world shows off a collection of about 100 historic racing and luxury cars here. Follow signs to the soccer stadium. ✉ *Mercedesstr. 137, Stuttgart-Untertürkheim,* ☎ *0711/172–2578.* 🎫 *Free.* ⏲ *Tues.–Sun. 9–5.*

PORSCHE MUSEUM – This Porsche factory in the northern suburb of Zuffenhausen has a small but significant collection of legendary Porsche racing cars. ✉ *Porschepl. 1, Stuttgart-Zuffenhausen,* ☎ *0711/911–5685.* 🎫 *Free.* ⏲ *Weekdays 9–4, weekends 9–5.*

WEISSENHOFSIEDLUNG – The Weissenhof Colony was a minicity created for a 1927 exhibition of the "New Home." Sixteen leading architects from five countries—among them Mies van der Rohe, Le Corbusier, and Walter Gropius—created residences that offered optimal living conditions at affordable prices. The still-functioning colony is on a hillside overlooking Friedrich-Ebert-Strasse. To get there from the city center, take Tram 10 toward Killesberg to the Kunstakadamie stop. The i-Punkt Weissenhof issues a brochure indicating which architects designed the various homes and is the meeting point for guided tours (Saturday 11 AM). ✉ *Am Weissenhof 15, Stuttgart-Killesberg,* ☎ *0711/854–641.*

Dining and Lodging

$$$$ ★ ✕ **Wielandshöhe.** Stuttgart's culinary skyline is sprinkled with many star chefs, including Vincent Klink, whose temple is set high above the

city in the suburb of Degerloch. Although he is one of Germany's top chefs, he and his wife, Elisabeth, are very down-to-earth, cordial hosts. Her floral arrangements add a baroque touch to the otherwise quiet decor, but your vision—and palate—will ultimately focus on the artfully presented cuisine. To the extent possible, all products are sourced locally or are homemade, from the duck salami, to pasta, to the blend of spices for curry. The wine list is exemplary. ✉ *Alte Weinsteige 71, Degerloch,* ☎ *0711/640–8848,* WEB *www.wielandshoehe.com. Reservations essential. AE, DC, MC, V. Closed Sun. and Mon.*

$$$$ ★ ✕🏨 **Am Schlossgarten.** Stuttgart's top accommodation is a modern structure set in spacious gardens, a stone's throw from sights, shops, and the train station. Pretty floral prints and plush chairs add a homey feeling to the elegant rooms. Luxurious baths and business amenities add to the overall comfort. In addition to receiving first-class service, you can wine and dine in the French restaurant Zirbelstube ($$$$), the less expensive Schlossgarten restaurant that serves upscale regional favorites, in the bistro Vinothek, or the café overlooking the garden. ✉ *Schillerstr. 23, Mitte D–70173,* ☎ *0711/20260,* FAX *0711/202–6888,* WEB *www.schlossgartenhotel.com. 112 rooms, 4 suites. 3 restaurants, café, in-room data ports, minibars, bicycles, bar, dry cleaning, laundry service, concierge, some pets allowed (fee), no-smoking rooms. AE, DC, MC, V. Zirbelstube is closed four wks Aug.–Sept. and Sun.–Mon. Vinothek is closed Sun.*

$$$–$$$$ ✕🏨 **Der Zauberlehrling.** The Sorcerer's Apprentice is aptly named. In addition to their popular restaurant, Z-Bistro ($$$)—with magical entertainment on *Tischzauberei* evenings—Karen and Axel Heldmann have conjured up a small luxury hotel. Each room's decor is based on a theme (Asian, Mediterranean, Country Manor), and four have a private whirlpool. Innovative menus, a 3-course menu of organic products, and regional favorites are all part of the culinary lineup, enhanced by a very good wine list. Enjoy the terrace in summer and end the evening with cigars and single malts. ✉ *Rosenstr. 38, Bohnenviertel,* ☎ *0711/237–7770,* FAX *0711/237–7775,* WEB *www.zauberlehrling.de. 9 rooms. Restaurant, no a/c, in-room data ports, minibars. AE, MC, V. Restaurant closed Sun. No lunch Sat.*

$$ ★ ✕🏨 **Alter Fritz.** Katrin Fritsche describes her small country mansion as a "hotel for individualists." With only 10 rooms, she is able to cater to guests with a personal touch. The picturesque house with its steep eaves and shuttered windows, high up on the wooded Killesberg Hill, is ideally located for visitors to trade fairs and is a 15-minute bus ride from the main railway station. **Der kleine Fritz** serves good food at reasonable prices ($$$). House guests can opt to dine in the pretty breakfast room and select from a smaller menu ($). ✉ *Feuerbacher Weg 101, Killesberg D–70192,* ☎ *0711/135–650,* FAX *0711/135–6565. 10 rooms. Restaurant, no a/c, some in-room data ports, minibars, free parking. No credit cards. Closed 2 wks in Aug. and 2 wks in Dec. Restaurant closed Mon. No lunch.*

$$$ 🏨 **Hotel Mercure Stuttgart Airport.** This hotel has a light and airy design, with large windows throughout the spacious lobby, restaurant, public rooms, and comfortable bedrooms; everything is decorated in tasteful, pastel colors. It offers shuttle service to the airport (6 km [4 mi]), and downtown Stuttgart (11 km [7 mi]) can be reached by public transportation or by car in less than half an hour. It is but a 3-minute drive to the shops, casino, and musicals at the SI-Erlebnis-Centrum. ✉ *Eichwiesenring 1, Fasanenhof D–70567,* ☎ *0711/72660,* FAX *0711/726–6444,* WEB *www.mercure.de. 148 rooms. Restaurant, cable TV, in-room data ports, minibars, health club, sauna, bar, free parking, some pets allowed (fee), no-smoking rooms. AE, DC, MC, V.*

Nightlife and the Arts

The **i-Punkt tourist office** (✉ Königstr. 1A, Mitte, ☎ 0711/222–8243) keeps a current calendar of events and sells tickets via phone, and half-price, same day tickets at the office (weekdays after 4, Sat. 9:30–4).

THE ARTS

Stuttgart's internationally renowned ballet company performs in the **Staatstheater** (✉ Oberer Schlossgarten 6, Mitte, ☎ 0711/202–090). The ballet season runs from September through June and alternates with the highly respected State Opera. For program details contact the Stuttgart tourist office. The box office is open weekdays 10–6, Saturday 10–2.

The **SI-Centrum** is an entire entertainment complex (hotels, bars, restaurants, gambling casino, wellness center, cinemas, shops, theaters) built in 1994 to showcase musicals, particularly blockbuster hits from England. *Tanz der Vampire* (*Dance of the Vampire*), a musical version of Roman Polanski's parody, *The Fearless Vampire Killers,* and *Das Phantom der Oper (Phantom of the Opera)* will be playing in 2003. ✉ *Plieninger Str. 100, Stuttgart-Möhringen,* WEB *www.si-centrum.de.*

NIGHTLIFE

There is no dearth of rustic beer gardens and wine pubs or sophisticated cocktail bars in and around Stuttgart. Night owls should head for the **Schwabenzentrum** on Eberhardstrasse, the **Bohnenviertel,** or "Bean Quarter" (Charlotten-, Olga-, and Pfarrstrasse), and **Calwer Strasse.**

Outdoor Activities and Sports

BOAT TRIPS

From the pier opposite the zoo entrance, **Neckar-Käpt'n** (☎ 0711/5499–7060, WEB www.neckar-kaeptn.de) offers a wide range of boat trips, as far north as scenic Besigheim and Lauffen.

HIKING

Stuttgart has a 53-km (33-mi) network of marked hiking trails in the nearby hills; follow the signs with the city's emblem: a horse set in a yellow ring.

TENNIS

Stuttgart is the true tennis center of the region, and the city has several clubs that welcome visitors. The largest is **Jens Weinberger's Tennis and Sports School** (✉ Emerholzweg 73, ☎ 0711/801–025) in the suburb of Stammheim.

Shopping

Calwer Strasse is home to the glitzy arcade **Calwer Passage,** full of chrome and glass. Shops here carry everything from local women's fashion (Beate Mössinger) to furniture. Don't miss the beautiful art nouveau **Markthalle** on Dorotheenstrasse. One of Germany's finest market halls, it is an architectural gem brimming with exotic fruits and spices, meats, and flowers.

Two of Germany's top men's fashion designers—Hugo Boss and Ulli Knecht—are based in Stuttgart. **Holy's** (✉ Königstr. 54/A, Mitte, ☎ 0711/222–9444) is an exclusive boutique, which carries clothes (for men and women) by all the most sought-after designers.

Günter Krauss's glittering shop (✉ Kronprinzstr. 21, Mitte, ☎ 0711/297–395) specializes in designer jewelry. The shop itself—walls of white Italian marble with gilt fixtures and mirrors—has won many design awards.

Breuninger (✉ Marktstr. 1–3, Mitte, ☎ 0711/2110), a leading regional department-store chain, has glass elevators that rise and fall under the dome of the central arcade.

Bebenhausen

28 *6 km (4 mi) north of Tübingen, on the west side of B–27/464.*

If you blink, you'll miss the turnoff for the little settlement of Bebenhausen, and that would be a shame because it is really worth a visit. ★ The **Zisterzienzerkloster** (Cistercian Monastery) is a rare example of an almost perfectly preserved medieval monastery dating from the late 12th century. Due to the secularization of 1806, the abbot's abode was rebuilt as a hunting castle for King Frederick of Württemberg. Expansion and restoration went on as the castle and monastery continued to be a royal residence into this century. Even after the monarchy was dissolved in 1918, the last Württembergs were given lifetime rights here; this came to an end in 1946 with the death of Charlotte, wife of Wilhelm II. For a few years after the war the state senate convened in the castle; today both castle and monastery are open to the public, although the castle is open for guided tours only. ☎ *07071/602–802.* *Monastery €2.50, castle €3, combined admission €5.* *Monastery Apr.–Oct., Mon. 9–noon and 1–6, Tues.–Sun. 9–6; Nov.–Mar., Tues.–Sun. 9–noon and 1–5. Castle tours (hourly) Apr.–Oct., Tues.–Fri. 9–noon and 2–5, weekends 10–noon and 2–5; Nov.–Mar., Tues.–Fri. 9–noon and 2–4, weekends 10–noon and 2–4.*

Dining

$$$–$$$$ ★ ✕ **Waldhorn.** Chef Ulrich Schilling and his wife, Jutta, offer extraordinary meals and hospitality. "Variations of foie gras" and "essence of rose hip parfait" are classics, as are the masterfully prepared four- or seven-course menus. Lobster and an Asian appetizer platter are new on the menu. The wine list features a well-chosen selection of international wines and top Baden and Württemberg estates. Garden tables have a castle view. A meal here would be a perfect start or finale to the concerts held on the monastery/castle grounds in the summer. ✉ *Schönbuchstr. 49 (on B–27/464),* ☎ *07071/61270. Reservations essential. AE. Closed Mon. and Tues.*

Tübingen

29 *40 km (25 mi) south of Stuttgart on B–27 on the Neckar River.*

With its half-timber houses, winding alleyways, and hilltop setting overlooking the Neckar, Tübingen provides the quintessential German experience. The medieval flavor is quite authentic, as the town was untouched by wartime bombings. Dating to the 11th century, Tübingen flourished as a trade center; its weights and measures and currency were the standard through much of the area. The town declined in importance after the 14th century, when it was taken over by the counts of Württemberg. Between the 14th and the 19th centuries, its size hardly changed as it became a university and residential town, its castle the only symbol of ruling power.

Yet Tübingen hasn't been sheltered from the world. It resonates with a youthful air. Even more than Heidelberg, Tübingen is virtually synonymous with its university, a leading center of learning since it was founded in 1477. Illustrious students of yesteryear include the astronomer Johannes Kepler and the philosopher G. W. F. Hegel. The latter studied at the Protestant theological seminary, still a cornerstone of the university's international reputation. One of Hegel's roommates was Friedrich Hölderlin, a visionary poet who succumbed to madness in his early thirties. Tübingen's population is around 83,000, of which at least 20,000 are students. During term time it can be hard to find a seat in pubs and cafés; during vacations the town sometimes seems deserted. The best way to see and appreciate Tübingen is simply to stroll around, soaking up its age-old atmosphere of quiet erudition.

A Good Walk

Tübingen's modest size makes it ideal for a walk. Begin at the Eberhards-Brücke, which crosses an island with a magnificent planting of trees—most of them at least 200 years old—known as the Platanenallee. If time permits, stroll up and down the island. If not, go to the north end of the bridge, take a sharp left down a steep staircase to reach the shore of the Neckar, and follow it to a yellow tower, the **Hölderlinturm.** The poet Friedrich Hölderlin was housed in the tower after he lost his sanity, and it is now a small museum commemorating his life and work. Next, walk away from the river up the steps of Hölderlinsteg and continue left up the Bursagasse to pass by the **Bursa,** a former student dormitory that dates from the Middle Ages. Facing the Bursa, turn left up the street called Klosterberg and then turn left again into the courtyard of the **Evangelisches Stift.** Richer in history than in immediate visual interest, this site was a center of European intellectual thought for centuries. Proceed up Klosterberg to the narrow steps and cobblestones of Burgsteige, one of the oldest thoroughfares in the town and lined with houses dating from the Middle Ages. You might be a little breathless when you finally arrive at the top and enter the portal of the **Schloss Hohentübingen.** The portal is fitted as a Roman-style triumphal arch in true Renaissance spirit.

Cross the Schloss's courtyard and enter the tunnel-like passage directly in front of you; it leads to the other side of the castle. Take a moment to enjoy the view of the river from the ruined ramparts and then descend to your right through tree-shaded Kapitansweg—looking at the remains of the original city walls on your way—to Haaggasse and then left into the narrow Judengasse (Jewish Alley). Jewish citizens lived in this neighborhood until 1477, when they were driven out of the city. Next, stop at the intersection of Judengasse and Ammergasse; all around you are old half-timber buildings. The little stream that runs through Ammergasse was part of the medieval sewage system.

Across the square, Jakobsgasse leads to Jakobuskirche (Jacob's Church), in medieval times a station on the famous pilgrims' route to Santiago di Compostella in Spain. Go to the other side of the church, make a right into Madergasse, and then turn left at Schmiedtorstrasse, where you will find the Fruchtschranne on the right-hand side—a massive half-timber house built to store fruit and grain in the 15th century. Continue down the street to Bachgasse; turn right, then right again onto the street called Bei der Fruchtschranne and follow it a short distance to a courtyard on the left just before the intersection with Kornhausstrasse. The courtyard leads to the entrance of the 15th-century **Kornhaus,** now a city museum. Continue to Kornstrasse and go left and immediately right into Marktgasse, which takes you uphill to the **Marktplatz,** a sloping, uneven cobblestone parallelogram that dominates the heart of Tübingen's Altstadt (Old City). Its **Neptune Fountain** is graced with a statue of the sea god. The square is bounded on one side by the amazing **Rathaus.**

From the square turn into Wienergasse and then left into Münzgasse; No. 20 is the site of the former **Studentenkarzer.** The large yellow baroque building just beyond is the **Alte Aula,** for many centuries the university's most important building. The well-preserved late-Gothic **Stiftskirche** now rises before you. Climbing the hundred-odd steps up the bell tower will allow you to take a second, faraway look at almost everything you've seen en route.

TIMING

The walk around town takes about 1½ hours. If you go inside the Hölderlinturm, Stadtsmuseum, and Stiftskirche, add half an hour for each sight.

Sights to See

Alte Aula (Old Auditorium). Erected in 1547, the half-timber university building was reconstructed in 1777, when it acquired an Italian roof, a symmetrical facade, and a balcony decorated with two crossed scepters symbolizing the town's center of learning. In earlier times grain was stored under the roof as part of the professors' salaries. The libraries and lecture halls were on the lower floors. ✉ *Münzg.*

OFF THE BEATEN PATH

BOTANISCHER GARTEN – The botanical garden, north of the Neckar River above the city, is one of Tübingen's favorite modern attractions. To get there, take Bus 5 or 17 from the train station. ✉ *Hartmeyerstr. 123,* ☎ *07071/297–8822,* WEB *www.botgarden.uni-tuebingen.de.* 🎫 *Free.* ⏲ *Park daily 8–4:45. Greenhouses daily 10–noon and 1:30–4:30.*

Bursa (Student Dormitory). The word *bursa* meant "purse" in the Middle Ages and later came to refer to student lodgings such as this former student dormitory. Despite its classical facade, which it acquired in the early 19th century, the building actually dates back to 1477. Medieval students had to master a broad curriculum that included the *septem artes liberales* (seven liberal arts) of Grammar, Dialectic, Rhetoric, Arithmetic, Geometry, Astronomy, and Music, in addition to praying several times a day, fasting regularly, and speaking only Latin within the confines of the building. ✉ *Bursag. 4.*

Evangelisches Stift (Protestant Seminary). From the outside you can't tell that this site has served for centuries as a center of European intellectual thought. It was founded in 1534, partly as a political move during the Reformation; the Protestant duke of Württemberg, Ulrich, wanted facilities to train Protestant clerics so that Protestantism could retain its foothold in the region (he would have been disappointed to know a major Catholic seminary arrived here in 1817). Since that time philosophical rather than political considerations have prevailed within these walls. Hegel, Hölderlin, and the philosopher Schelling all shared a room as students here—even in a university town this seems an unusually high concentration of brain power. ✉ *Klosterg.*

Hölderlinturm (Hölderlin's Tower). "Mad" Friedrich Hölderlin lived here for 36 years, until his death in 1843, in the care of the master cabinetmaker Zimmer and his daughter. If you don't speak German, you may want to arrange for an English tour to get the most out of the exhibits. You can also acquaint yourself with a couple of Hölderlin poems in translation to get a sense of the writer's imagery and notably "modern" style. ✉ *Bursag. 6,* ☎ *07071/22040.* 🎫 *€1.50.* ⏲ *Tues.–Fri. 10–noon and 3–5, weekends 2–5. Tours weekends and holidays at 5 PM; English-language tours available by arrangement.*

Kornhaus (Grain House). During the Middle Ages, townspeople stored and sold grain on the first floor of this structure (built in 1453); social events took place on the second floor. Among the Kornhaus's occupants through the centuries were duelists, medieval apprentices, traveling players, 18th-century schoolchildren, an academy for young ladies, the Nazi Women's League, a driving school, and the city's restoration department. It now houses the City Museum. ✉ *Kornhausstr.*

10, ☏ 07071/945–460, WEB www.tuebingen.de. Admission varies. ⏲ Tues.–Fri. 3–6, weekends 11–6.

OFF THE BEATEN PATH

KUNSTHALLE (ART GALLERY) – Situated north of the Neckar, the art gallery has become a leading exhibition venue and generates a special kind of "art tourism," making it difficult to find lodging if a popular show is on. The exhibition scheduled for January–March 2003 will focus on the German expressionist painter August Macke (1887–1914), a member of *Der Blaue Reiter* group. ✉ *Philosophenweg 76, ☏ 07071/96910, WEB www.kunst-halle-tuebingen.de. Admission varies: €6–€8. ⏲ Tues.–Sun. 10–6.*

★ **Marktplatz** (Market Square). Houses of prominent burghers of centuries gone by surround the square. At the open-air market on Monday, Wednesday, and Friday, you can buy flowers, bread, pastries, poultry, sausage, and cheese.

★ **Rathaus** (Town Hall). Begun in 1433, the Rathaus expanded over the next 150 years or so. Its ornate Renaissance facade is bright with colorful murals and a marvelous astronomical clock dating from 1511. The halls and reception rooms are adorned with half-timbering and paintings from the late 19th century. ✉ *Marktpl.*

★ **Schloss Hohentübingen.** This impressive castle was built on top of 11th-century fortifications. The Renaissance portal has the look of a Roman triumphal arch with a lot of decorative scrollwork thrown in—fruits, garlands, and, at the top, the coat of arms of the Württemberg ducal family, which includes the famous Order of the Garter. A roster of deities occupies the base: Poseidon; the sea goddess Amphitrite; Nike, goddess of victory; and Athena, goddess of wisdom and war. Enter the double-doored opening and immediately notice that one-half of the courtyard is painted and the other half isn't—the result of a difference of opinion among the art historians who tried to restore the castle to its original appearance. The castle was a bone of contention during the Thirty Years' War, and the French blew up one of its towers in 1647. Now it serves an altogether more peaceable function: housing classical archaeology and several other university departments. One of the castle cellars contains an 84,000-liter wine barrel and the largest bat colony in southern Germany. The **Museum** occupies one wing and a tower with exhibits about the history of the city and the castle and a small collection of Greek and Roman artifacts. But the castle's main attraction is its magnificent view over river and town.

★ **Stiftskirche** (Collegiate Church). The late-Gothic church is in an excellent state of preservation; its original features include the stained-glass windows, the choir stalls, the ornate baptismal font, and the elaborate stone pulpit. The windows are famous for their colors and were much admired by Goethe. The dukes of Württemberg from the 15th through the 17th centuries are interred beneath them in the choir. ✉ *Holzmarkt., Bell tower €1. ⏲ Church Feb.–Oct., daily 9–5; Nov.–Jan., daily 9–4; bell tower Fri.–Sun. 11:30–5.*

Studentenkarzer (Student Prison). The oldest surviving university prison in Germany consists of just two small rooms. For more than three centuries (1515–1845) students were locked up here for such offenses as swearing, failing to attend sermons, wearing clothing considered lewd, or playing dice. The figures on the walls are not graffiti but scenes from biblical history that were supposed to contribute to the moral improvement of the incarcerated students. You can enter the prison only on a guided tour organized by the Tübingen Tourist Board. ✉ *Münzg. 20, ☏ 07071/91360 for tour. €1. ⏲ Tour Apr.–Oct., weekends 2 PM.*

Dining and Lodging

$–$$$ ✕ **Forelle.** Beautiful ceilings painted with vine motifs, exposed beams, and an old tile oven make for a gemütlich atmosphere. This small restaurant fills up fast, not least because the Swabian cooking is excellent. All products (and the wines) are sourced locally, including the inn's namesake, trout. Splurge on the saddle of venison in *Wacholdersahnesosse* (juniper berry cream sauce) with mushroom-filled Maultauschen. ✉ *Kronenstr. 8,* ☎ *07071/24094. MC, V.*

$–$$ ✕ **Neckarmüller.** This shady, riverside beer garden and restaurant near the Eberhards-Brücke serves house-brewed beer with snacks, salads, and *Vesper* (sausage and cheese). For bigger appetites, the Schwabenteller, a platter of Swabian specialties (Maultaschen, Spätzle, sauerkraut, and beefsteaks in cream sauce), is more than ample. Don't wait to be served. The sign that reads SELBSTABHOLUNG means you fetch it yourself. ✉ *Gartenstr. 4,* ☎ *07071/27848. DC, MC, V.*

$ ✕ **Neckarbistror.** The café has light and airy 1960s decor and a beautiful view up and down the Neckar. Hölderlin's Tower is just a few houses upriver. The eclectic menu includes such dishes as cassoulet, lasagna, and Maultaschen. The pastries are irresistible. ✉ *Neckarg. 22,* ☎ *07071/22122. AE, DC, MC, V.*

$$ ✕🏨 **Hotel Am Schloss.** The climb is steep from the Altstadt to this hotel, next to the castle that towers over the town, but the reward is lovely views from the geranium-bedecked windows and terrace. Proprietor Herbert Rösch has written several books about regional cuisine, including one devoted to Maultaschen. In his restaurant ($–$$), 28 versions of "Swabian tortellini" are on the menu, together with other regional dishes and wines from Württemberg. Let the hotel help you with parking. ✉ *Burgsteige 18, D–72070,* ☎ *07071/92940,* FAX *07071/929–410,* WEB *www.hotelamschloss.de. 37 rooms. Restaurant, no a/c, some minibars, bicycles, some pets allowed (fee), no-smoking rooms. AE, MC, V. Restaurant closed Tues. Oct.–Mar.*

$$ 🏨 **Hotel Hospiz.** This modern, family-run hotel provides friendly service, comfort, and a convenient Altstadt location near the castle. Parking is difficult, so take advantage of the hotel's offer to park the car for you. ✉ *Neckarhalde 2, at corner of Burgsteige, D–72070,* ☎ *07071/9240,* FAX *07071/924–200,* WEB *www.hotel-hospiz.de. 50 rooms, 45 with bath or shower. No a/c, minibars, lobby lounge, some pets allowed, no-smoking rooms. AE, MC, V.*

Nightlife and the Arts

As a student town, Tübingen has an active small theater scene. Check with the tourist office for a listing of what is going on—the more eclectic offerings are likely to be the better ones. In addition to dozens of Old Town student pubs, there's a lively crowd after 9 at the **Jazzkeller** (✉ Haagg. 15/2, ☎ 07071/550–906). **Die Kelter** (✉ Schmiedtorstr. 17, ☎ 07071/254–675) is good for jazz, music, and light fare, and it has a wine shop. The upstairs cocktail bar at **Café Nass** (✉ Kirchg. 19, ☎ 07071/551–250) opens at 5 PM. From 9 AM until well past midnight there's action at **Tangente-Jour** (✉ Münzg. 17, ☎ 07071/24572), a bistro next to the Stiftskirche. **Zentrum Zoo** (✉ Schleifmühleweg 86, ☎ 07071/94480) has live music, a dance club, and a huge beer garden that is immensely popular with all ages. It's about a 20-minute walk from the town center.

Outdoor Activities and Sports

The Tübingen tourist office has maps with hiking routes around the town, including historic and geologic *Lehrpfade,* or **educational walks.** A classic Tübingen walk goes from the castle down to the little chapel called the **Wurmlinger Kapelle,** taking about two hours. On the way it's customary to stop off at the restaurant Schwärzlocher Hof to sample the good food and great views.

OFF THE BEATEN PATH ★ **BURG HOHENZOLLERN** – The Hohenzollern House of Prussia was the most powerful family in German history. It lost its throne when Kaiser William II abdicated after Germany's defeat in World War I. The Swabian branch of the family owns one-third of the castle, the Prussian branch two-thirds. Today's neo-Gothic structure is a successor of a castle dating from the 11th century. Perched high on a conical wooded hill, its majestic silhouette is visible from miles away. On the fascinating castle tour you'll see the Prussian royal crown and beautiful period rooms—splendid from floor to ceiling, with playful details, such as door handles carved to resemble peacocks and dogs. The royal tombs, once housed in the Christ Chapel, were returned to Potsdam in 1991 after German reunification. The castle restaurant, Burgschänke (closed January and Monday in February and March), is catered by the talented chefs of Hotel Brielhof at the foot of the hill, where the ascent from the B–27 begins. You can enjoy a first-class meal at the Brielhof, then make the one-hour hike up to the castle. ✉ *Hechingen, 25 km (15 mi) south of Tübingen on the B–27,* ☎ *07471/2428,* WEB *www.burg-hohenzollern.com.* *€5.* *Mid-Mar.–mid-Oct., daily 9–5:30; mid-Oct.–mid-Mar., daily 9–4:30.*

HEIDELBERG AND THE NECKAR VALLEY A TO Z

To research prices, get advice from other travelers, and book travel arrangements, visit www.fodors.com.

AIRPORTS

From the Frankfurt and Stuttgart airports, there's fast and easy access, by car and train, to all major centers along the Neckar.

With advance reservations you can get to Heidelberg from the Frankfurt airport via the shuttle service TLS. The trip takes about an hour and costs €27 per person; with four people, €20.75 each.

➤ AIRPORT TRANSFER: **TLS** (☎ 06221/770–077, FAX 06221/770–070, WEB www.tls-heidelberg.de).

BUS TRAVEL

Europabus 189 runs the length of the Burgenstrasse daily from mid-May through September, making stops all along the Neckar. For information contact Deutsche Touring (☞ Bus Travel *in* Smart Travel Tips A to Z). Local buses run from Mannheim, Heidelberg, Heilbronn, and Stuttgart to most places along the river.

CAR RENTALS

Avis, Europcar, Hertz, and Sixt all have rental offices at the Frankfurt and Stuttgart airports and main train stations.

➤ LOCAL AGENCIES: **Avis** (✉ Karlsruherstr. 43, Heidelberg, ☎ 06221/22215; ✉ Salzstr. 112, Heilbronn, ☎ 07131/172–077; ✉ Katharinenstr. 18, Stuttgart, ☎ 0711/239–320; ✉ Reutlinger Str. 72–74, Tübingen, ☎ 07071/37625). **Europcar** (✉ Bergheimerstr. 159, Heidelberg, ☎ 06221/53990; ✉ Wilhelmstr. 27, Heilbronn, ☎ 07131/62110; ✉ Frankenstr. 3, Stuttgart-Zuffenhausen, ☎ 0711/987–9390; ✉ Eisenbahnstr. 21, Tübingen, ☎ 07071/13370). **Hertz** (✉ Crowne Plaza, Kurfürstenanlage 1, Heidelberg, ☎ 06221/23434; ✉ Weiberstr. 17, Heilbronn, ☎ 07131/724–100; ✉ Hauptbahnhof Arnulf-Klett-Pl. 2,

Track 16, Stuttgart, ☎ 0711/226–2921). **Sixt** (✉ Eppelheimer Str. 50C, Heidelberg, ☎ 06221/138–990; ✉ Salzstr. 186, Heilbronn, ☎ 07131/580–026; ✉ Leonhardpl. 17, Stuttgart, ☎ 0711/243–952).

CAR TRAVEL

Heidelberg is a 15-minute drive (10 km [6 mi]) on A–656 from Mannheim, a major junction of the autobahn system. Heilbronn stands beside the east–west A–6 and the north–south A–81. The route followed in this chapter, the Burgenstrasse, Route B–37, follows the north bank of the Neckar River from Heidelberg to Mosbach, from which it continues south to Heilbronn as B–27, the road parallel to and predating the autobahn (A–81). B–27 still leads to Stuttgart and Tübingen.

TOURS

BOAT TOURS

From Easter through October there are regular boat trips on the Neckar from Heidelberg, Heilbronn, and Stuttgart. If time is short, take a *Rundfahrt* (round-trip excursion). The Tübingen tourist office organizes punting on the Neckar.

CITY TOURS

Medieval Bad Wimpfen offers a town walk year-round, Sunday at 2 (€1.80) and free guided tours in English for visitors who spend at least one night. Upon arrival, ask the hotel to arrange a town tour and ask for the free pass *Bad Wimpfen à la card* for reduced or free admission to historic sights and museums.

From April through October there are daily walking tours of Heidelberg in German (Thursday through Sunday in English) at 10:30 AM; tours November through March are in German only, Saturday at 10:30; the cost is €6. They depart from the Lion's Fountain on Universitätsplatz. Bilingual bus tours run April–October on Thursday and Friday at 2:30, on Saturday at 10:30 and 2:30, on Sunday at 10:30. From November through March bus tours depart Saturday at 2:30. They cost €12 and depart from Universitätsplatz. The *HeidelbergCard* costs €12 (two days) and includes free or reduced admission to most tourist attractions as well as free use of all public transportation (including the Bergbahn to the castle) and other extras, such as free guided walking tours, discounts on bus tours, and a city guidebook. It can be purchased at the tourist information office at the main train station and many local hotels.

Walking tours (in German) of Heilbronn, Hirschhorn, and Mosbach depart from the respective tourist offices. Heilbronn's year-round tours are Saturday at 11:30, for €2.10. There is also a tour April–September, Tuesday evening at 6:15 (€4.50) that concludes with a Viertele glass of wine in a Heilbronn wine pub. In June–September there are free tours of Hirschhorn on Saturday at 2:00. Free tours of Mosbach take place May–September, Wednesday at 2:30.

The visitor-friendly (three-day) STUTTCARD *plus* (€14) and STUTTCARD (€8.50), with or without access to free public transportation, are available from the Stuttgart tourist office opposite the main train station. This is also where to book tours and the meeting point for city walking tours in German (year-round, Saturday at 10; April–October, also Wednesday at 5) for €7.50. Bilingual bus tours depart from the bus stop around the corner from the tourist office, in front of Hotel am Schlossgarten (April–October, daily at 2 PM and November–March, Friday, Saturday, and Sunday at 2 PM) for €17. All tours last 2½ hours. A bilingual Saturday-evening walking tour (7 PM–after midnight) includes a visit to a nightclub (with a show), a pub crawl, and dinner.

From February through October the Tübingen tourist office runs guided city tours Wednesday at 10 AM and weekends at 2:30, for €3.10, from the Rathaus on Market Square. Overnight guests receive a free *Tourist-Regio-Card* from their hotel (ask for it) for reduced admission fees to museums, concerts, theaters, and sports facilities.

TRAIN TRAVEL

Western Germany's most important rail junction is in nearby Mannheim, with hourly InterCity trains from all major German cities. Heidelberg is equally easy to get to. The super-high-speed InterCityExpress service, which reaches 280 km (174 mi) per hour, is Germany's fastest. Travel time between Frankfurt and Stuttgart is less than 1½ hours; between Heidelberg and Stuttgart 26 minutes. There are express trains to Heilbronn from Heidelberg and Stuttgart and direct trains from Stuttgart to Tübingen. Local services link many of the smaller towns.

VISITOR INFORMATION

For information on the entire Burgenstrasse, contact "Die Burgenstrasse." For information on the hilly area south of Stuttgart and Tübingen, contact the Touristik-Gemeinschaft Schwäbische Alb.

➤ REGIONAL TOURIST OFFICES: **Die Burgenstrasse** (✉ Marktpl. 11, D–74072 Heilbronn, ☎ 07131/562–283, FAX 07131/563–349, WEB www burgenstrasse.de). **Touristik-Gemeinschaft Schwäbische Alb** (✉ Marktpl. 1, D–72574 Bad Urach, ☎ 07125/948–106, FAX 07125/948–108, WEB www.schwaebischealb.de).

➤ TOURIST OFFICES: **Bad Wimpfen** (✉ Tourist-Information, Gästezentrum Alter Bahnhof, D–74206, ☎ 07063/97200, FAX 07063/972–020, WEB www.badwimpfen.de). **Heidelberg** (✉ Tourist Information am Hauptbahnhof, Willy-Brandt-Pl. 1, D–69115, ☎ 06221/19433, FAX 06221/138–8111, WEB www.cvb-heidelberg.de). **Heilbronn** (✉ Tourist-Information, Kaiserstr. 17, D–74072, ☎ 07131/562–270, FAX 07131/563–349, WEB www.heilbronn-marketing.de). **Hirschhorn** (✉ Tourist-Information, Alleeweg 2, D–69434, ☎ 06272/1742, FAX 06272/912–351, WEB www.hirschhorn.de). **Mosbach** (✉ Städtisches Verkehrsamt, Am Marktplatz 4, D–74821, ☎ 06261/91880, FAX 06261/918–815, WEB www.mosbach.de). **Schwetzingen** (✉ Stadtinformation, Dreikönigstr. 3, D–68723, ☎ 06202/945–875, FAX 06202/945–877, WEB www. schwetzingen.de). **Stuttgart** (✉ Touristik-Information i-Punkt, Königstr. 1A, D–70173, ☎ 0711/222–8240, FAX 0711/222–8253, WEB www. stuttgart-tourist.de). **Tübingen** (✉ Verkehrsverein Tübingen, An der Neckarbrücke, D–72072, ☎ 07071/91360, FAX 07071/35070, WEB www.tuebingen-info.de).

WINE INFORMATION

The regional wine promotion boards can provide information on the local wines and where to sample them. Ask for details about wine-growers who also run economical bed-and-breakfasts. In Baden, which includes Heidelberg, contact Weinwerbezentrale badischer Winzergenossenschaften. The vineyards of Württemberg line the Neckar Valley. Contact Werbegemeinschaft Württembergischer Weingärtnergenossenschaften.

➤ CONTACTS: **Weinwerbezentrale badischer Winzergenossenschaften** (✉ Kesslerstr. 5, D–76185 Karlsruhe, ☎ 0721/557–028, FAX 0721/557–020, WEB www.badischerwein.com). **Werbegemeinschaft Württembergischer Weingärtnergenossenschaften** (✉ Raiffeisenstr. 6, D–71696 Möglingen, ☎ 07141/24460, FAX 07141/244–620, WEB www.wwg.de).

10 FRANKFURT

Frankfurt is the gateway by air to Germany—and to the rest of the Continent. Many German banks are headquartered here, and the Frankfurt Börse is Germany's leading stock exchange. The city's New York–style skyline would stun the 30 Holy Roman emperors who were once elected and crowned here. But Frankfurt is not just a commercial metropolis; it's a cultural center as well.

Updated by Ted Shoemaker

UNLIKE GERMAN CITIES THAT RECLAIMED much of their prewar appearance after World War II, Frankfurt looked to the future and erected skyscrapers to house its many banking institutions. The city cheekily nicknamed itself Mainhattan, using the name of the Main River that flows through it to suggest that other famous metropolis across the Atlantic. Although modest in size (fifth among German cities, with a population of 652,000), Frankfurt is Germany's financial powerhouse. Not only is the German Central Bank (Bundesbank) here but also the European Central Bank (ECB), which manages the euro. Some 370 credit institutions (more than half of them foreign banks) have offices in Frankfurt, including the headquarters of five of Germany's largest banks. You can see how the city acquired its other nickname: "Bankfurt am Main."

According to legend, a deer is said to have revealed the ford in the Main River to the Frankish emperor Charlemagne. A stone ridge, now blasted away, made the shallow river a great conduit for trade and by the early 13th century Frankfurt (*furt* means "ford") had emerged as a major trading center. Frankfurt's first international Autumn Fair was held in 1240; in 1330 it added a Spring Fair. Today these and other trade shows showcase the latest in books, cars, consumer goods, and technology. The city's stock exchange, one of the half dozen most important in the world, was established in 1585 and the Rothschild family opened their first bank here in 1798. The long history of trade might help explain the Frankfurters' temperament—competitive but open-minded.

So why come to Frankfurt if not on business? Partly for its history, which spans more than 1,200 years. It was one of the joint capitals of Charlemagne's empire, the city where Holy Roman emperors were elected and crowned, the site of Gutenberg's print shop, the birthplace of Goethe (1749–1832), Germany's greatest poet, and the city where the first German parliament met.

Because of all its commercialism Frankfurt has a reputation of being crass, cold, and boring. But people who know the city think this characterization is unfair. The district of Sachsenhausen is as *Gemütlich* (fun, friendly, and cozy) as you will find anywhere. The city has world-class ballet, opera, theater, and art exhibitions; an important piece of Germany's publishing industry; a large university (38,000 students) famous for such modern thinkers as Adorno and Habermas; and two of the three most important daily newspapers in Germany, the *Frankfurter Allgemeine* and the *Frankfurter Rundschau*. In Frankfurt you find yourself in the heart of a powerful, sophisticated, and cosmopolitan nation. There may not be that much here to remind you of the Old World, but there's a great deal that explains the success story of postwar Germany.

Pleasures and Pastimes

Dining

Many international cuisines are represented in the financial hub of Europe. For vegetarians there's usually at least one meatless dish on a German menu, and substantial salads are popular, too (though often served with bacon). Frankfurt's local cuisine comes from the region's farm tradition. Pork ribs and chops, stewed beef, blood sausage, potato soup, and pancakes with bacon fulfill such proverbs as "better once full than twice hungry" and "you work the way you eat." The city's most famous contribution to the world's diet is the *Frankfurter Würstchen*—

a thin smoked pork sausage—better known to Americans as the hot dog. *Grüne Sosse* is a thin cream sauce of herbs served with potatoes and hard-boiled eggs. The oddly named *Handkäs mit Musik* (hand cheese with music) consists of slices of cheese covered with raw onions, oil, and vinegar, served with bread and butter (an acquired taste for many). All these things are served in Sachsenhausen *Apfelwein* (apple wine, or hard cider) taverns. Apfelwein is poured from a distinctive gray stoneware pitcher, called a *Bembel,* into an equally distinctive, ribbed tumbler.

Jazz and Techno

Frankfurt was a real pioneer in the German jazz scene, and also has done much for the development of techno music. Jazz musicians make the rounds from smoky backstreet cafés all the way to the Old Opera House, and the local broadcaster, Hessischer Rundfunk, sponsors the German Jazz Festival in the fall. The Frankfurter Jazzkeller has been the most noted venue for German jazz fans for decades.

Museums

Frankfurt is full of museums, and 13 of them were newly built or renovated during the 1980s. Interesting for their architecture as well as for their content, the exhibition halls are Frankfurt's tourist draw. Sachsenhausen, which is largely residential, is home to seven of these museums. They line the side of the Main, on Schaumainkai, known locally as the Museumsufer (Museum Riverbank).

EXPLORING FRANKFURT

The Hauptbahnhof (main train station) area and adjoining Westend district are mostly devoted to business, and banks tower overhead. You'll find the department stores of the Hauptwache and Zeil only a few blocks east of the station, but avoid the drug-ridden red-light district, also near the station. The city's past can be found in the Old Town's restored medieval quarter and in Sachsenhausen, across the river, where pubs and museums greatly outnumber banks.

Numbers in the text correspond to numbers in the margin and on the Frankfurt map.

Great Itineraries

IF YOU HAVE 1 DAY

Begin at the Goethehaus und Goethemuseum, the home of Germany's greatest poet. The house is within a 5- to 10-minute walk of either the Hauptwache or Willy Brandt Platz subway stations. Next, follow Bethmannstrasse as it turns into Braubachstrasse to reach the Museum für Moderne Kunst, one of Frankfurt's modern architectural monuments. Walk a few blocks and several centuries back in time south to the Kaiserdom. The cathedral is next to the heart of the city, the Römerberg. The medieval square holds the Römer, or city hall. After lunch cross over the Main on the Eiserner Steg to reach the Städelsches Kunstinstitut und Städtische Galerie, with its important collection of old masters and impressionists, and the Städtische Galerie Liebieghaus, which contains sculpture from the third millennium BC up to the modern age. In the evening, relax in one of Sachsenhausen's apple-cider taverns.

IF YOU HAVE 2 DAYS

Spend your first morning at the Goethehaus and Goethemuseum and Römerberg Square, where the Römer, Nikolaikirche, Historisches Museum, Paulskirche, and the Kaiserdom are all nearby. After viewing the cathedral, continue up Domstrasse to the Museum für Moderne Kunst. Take a midday break before continuing northward to Germany's shop-

Alte Oper 21
Börse 9
Deutsches Architekturmuseum 27
Deutsches Filmmuseum 28
Eiserner Steg 15
Fressgasse 20
Goethehaus und Goethemuseum 19
Hauptwache 7
Historisches Museum 4
Jüdisches Museum 17
Kaiserdom 13
Karmeliterkloster . . . 18
Katherinenkirche 8
Kuhhirtenturm 31
Leonhardskirche . . . 16
Liebfrauenkirche 6
Museum für Kommunication 26
Museum für Angewandte Kunst 30
Museum für Moderne Kunst 12
Museum für Volkerkunde 29
Naturkundemuseum Senckenberg 23
Nikolaikirche 3
Palmengarten und Botanischer Garten 22
Paulskirche 5
Römer 2
Römerberg 1
Schirn Kunsthalle . . . 14
Städelsches Kunstinstitut und Städtische Galerie . . 25
Städtische Galerie Liebieghaus 24
Staufenmauer 11
Zoologischer Garten 10

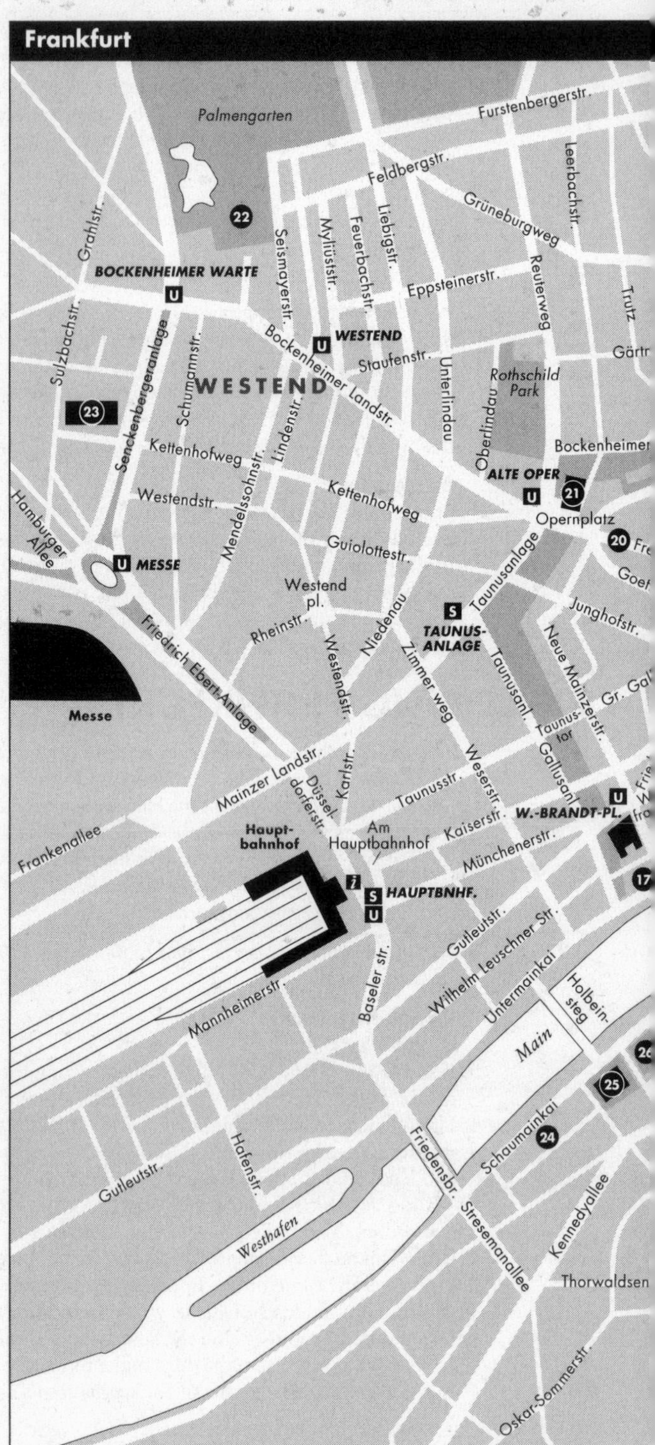

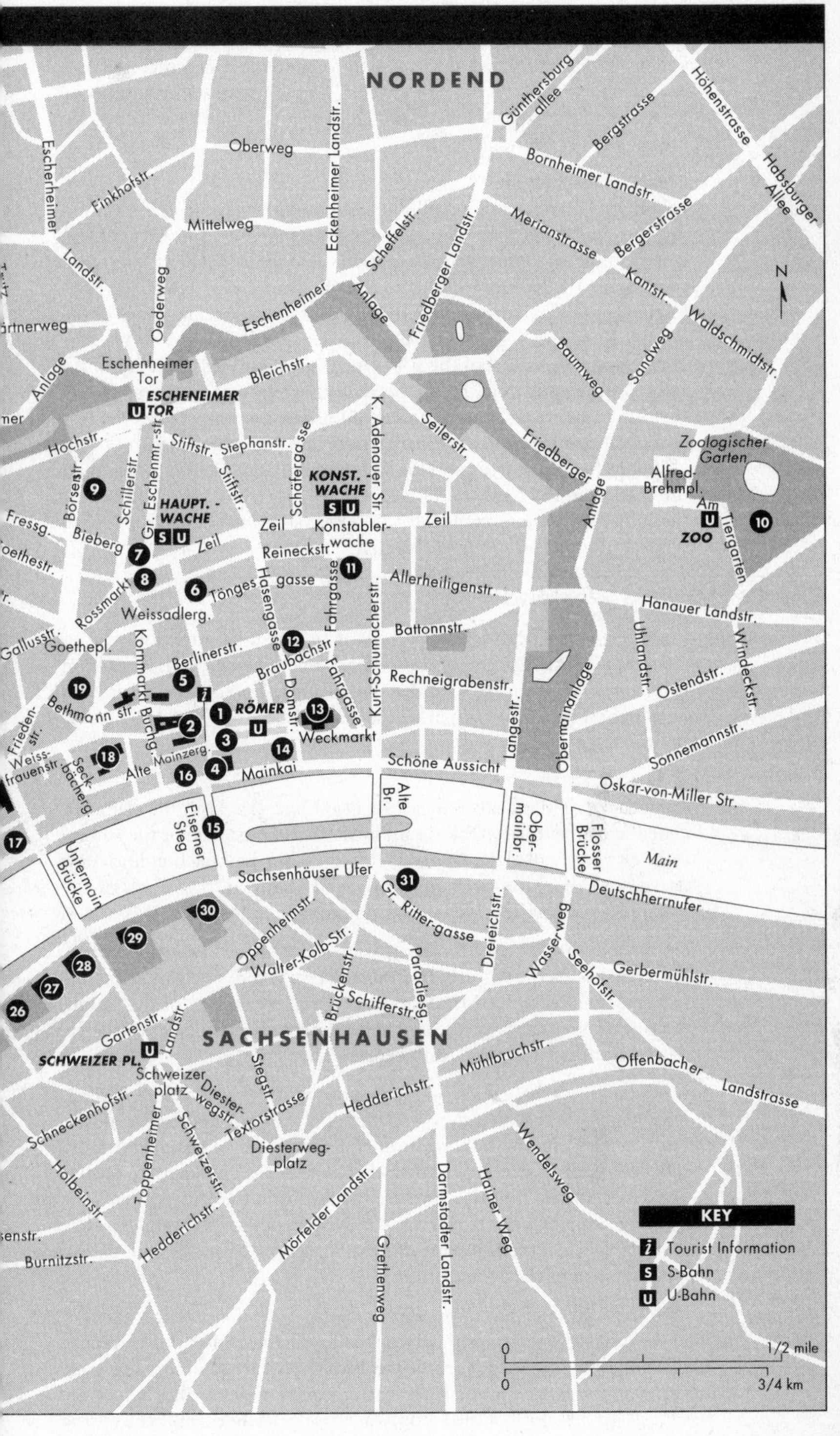
NORDEND
SACHSENHAUSEN
ESCHENEIMER TOR
HAUPT. - WACHE
KONST. - WACHE
RÖMER
ZOO
SCHWEIZER PL.
Main
KEY
Tourist Information
S-Bahn
U-Bahn
1/2 mile
3/4 km

'til-you-drop Zeil district and the Zoologischer Garten, one of Europe's best zoos. End the evening listening to music in the Frankfurter Jazzkeller. The entire second day can be devoted to the Sachsenhausen museums, starting with the Städelsches Kunstinstitut und Städtische Galerie and the Städtische Galerie Liebieghaus. Finally, explore Sachsenhausen's nightlife.

IF YOU HAVE 3 DAYS

Spend your first two days following the itinerary outlined above. On the morning of the third day, see the Naturkundemuseum Senckenberg; it has a famous collection of dinosaurs and giant whales. Afterward visit the nearby Palmengarten und Botanischer Garten, which have climatic zones from tropical to sub-Antarctic and a dazzling range of orchids. Take the U-bahn to Opernplatz, and emerge before the 19th-century splendor of the Alte Oper: lunch on Fressgasse is not far away. In the afternoon, go to the visitors' gallery of the Börse to feel the pulse of Europe's banking capital. Then continue on to the less worldly Karmeliterkloster. Secularized in 1803, the monastery and buildings house the Museum für Vor- und Frühgeschichte. Just around the corner on the bank of the Main, in the former Rothschild Palais, the Jüdisches Museum tells the 1,000-year story of Frankfurt's Jewish quarter and its end in the Holocaust.

City Center and Westend

Frankfurt was rebuilt after World War II with little attention paid to the past. Nevertheless, important historical monuments can still be found between the modern architecture. The city is very walkable; its growth hasn't encroached on its parks, gardens, pedestrian arcades, or outdoor cafés.

A Good Tour

Römerberg ①, the historic heart of Frankfurt, has been the center of civic life for centuries. Taking up most of the west side of the square is the city hall, called the **Römer** ②. It's a modest-looking building compared with many of Germany's other city halls. In the center of the square stands the fine 16th-century Fountain of Justitia.

On the south side of the Römerberg is the red sandstone **Nikolaikirche** ③. Beside it stands the **Historisches Museum** ④, where you can see a perfect scale model of historic Frankfurt. On the east side of the square is a row of painstakingly restored half-timber houses called the Ostzeile, dating from the 15th and 16th centuries.

From the Römerberg walk up the pedestrian street called Neue Kräme. Looming up on the left is the circular bulk of the **Paulskirche** ⑤, a mostly 18th-century church building, more interesting for its political than its religious significance. It was here that the short-lived German parliament met for the first time in May 1848. From the Paulskirche keep heading along the Neue Kräme, which becomes Liebfrauenstrasse, and you'll reach the **Liebfrauenkirche** ⑥, a late-Gothic church dating from the end of the 14th century.

Liebfrauenstrasse ends at the **Hauptwache** ⑦, a square that is the hub of the city's transportation network, and is named after the 18th-century building that stands on it. The building's café can attend to your appetite if you need a break. A vast shopping mall also lies below the square. To the south of the Hauptwache is the **Katharinenkirche** ⑧, the most important Protestant church in the city. North of the Hauptwache, Schillerstrasse leads to the Börsenplatz and Frankfurt's leading stock exchange, the **Börse** ⑨.

The Hauptwache is at the west end of the **Zeil,** Frankfurt's largest pedestrian zone and main shopping street. Its department stores sell every conceivable type of consumer goods and can get very crowded. A 15- to 20-minute walk all the way down the Zeil brings you to Alfred-Brehm-Platz and the entrance to the **Zoologischer Garten** ⑩. This is one of Frankfurt's chief attractions, ranking among the best zoos in Europe. If you don't want to walk the Zeil's full length, turn right at the square Konstabler Wache onto Fahrgasse. Follow the signs reading AN DER STAUFENMAUER to the **Staufenmauer** ⑪, which is one of the few surviving stretches of the old city wall.

Continue down Fahrgasse, and turn right onto Battonstrasse. At the corner of Battonstrasse and Domstrasse you'll see the striking wedge-shape outline of the **Museum für Moderne Kunst** ⑫. Walk south down Domstrasse a few steps and another silhouette appears, that of the grand, Gothic cathedral, **Kaiserdom** ⑬. There is an archaeological site next to the cathedral containing remains of Roman baths; from there walk through the pedestrian zone alongside the modern edifice of the **Schirn Kunsthalle** ⑭, a major venue for art exhibitions.

Continue back to the Römerberg and turn left to get to the Mainkai, the busy street that runs parallel to the tree-lined Main River. On your left you will see the Rententurm, one of the city's medieval gates, with its pinnacled towers at the base of the main spire extending out over the walls. To your right and in front is the **Eiserner Steg** ⑮, an iron footbridge connecting central Frankfurt with the old district of Sachsenhausen. River trips, boat excursions, and the old steam train leave from here.

Past the Eiserner Steg is the **Leonhardskirche** ⑯, which has one of the few 15th-century stained-glass windows to have survived World War II. Continue down the river and just past the Untermainbrücke is the **Jüdisches Museum** ⑰, No. 14–15 in the former Rothschild Palais, which focuses on the history of Frankfurt's Jewish community.

Backtrack a short way, and turn left into the narrow Karmelitergasse, which will take you to the **Karmeliterkloster** ⑱. The monastery and its buildings house an early history museum and the largest religious fresco north of the Alps. Exit onto Münzgasse, turn left, and go to the junction of Bethmannstrasse and Berlinerstrasse. Use the pedestrian walkway and cross over to the north side of Berlinerstrasse; then turn left again onto Grosser Hirschgraben. At No. 23 there will probably be a small crowd outside the **Goethehaus und Goethemuseum** ⑲, where writer Johann Wolfgang von Goethe was born in 1749.

On leaving the Goethehaus, go to Goetheplatz and continue past the Gutenberg Memorial into the pedestrian zone to Rathenau-Platz. At the end of the square turn left again, this time onto Grosse Bockenheimer Strasse, known locally as **Fressgasse** ⑳ because of its many delicatessens, bakeries, and cafés.

Fressgasse ends at Opernplatz and the **Alte Oper** ㉑, a prime venue for classical concerts as well as conferences and, every now and then, an opera. You can get a good look at Frankfurt's skyline from the opera house steps, or from the street Taunusanlage, opposite. Looking down Taunusanlage, you'll see the twin towers of the Deutsche Bank (the two towers are known as *zoll und haben,* or "debit and credit"). The very tall building to the left, topped by an antenna, is the 849-ft Commerzbank, the tallest building in Europe. Between them is the Maintower, headquarters of the Hessischer Landesbank.

Take the U-bahn two stops from Alte Oper to Bockenheimer Warte, walk down Bockenheimer Landstrasse and turn left on Palmengartenstrasse to reach the delightful **Palmengarten und Botanischer Garten** ㉒. Also close to the Bockenheimer Warte stop is the **Naturkundemuseum Senckenberg** ㉓, with fun hands-on exhibits.

TIMING

Count on spending a full day on this tour. It is impossible to see all the museums on one trip. You should block out 45 minutes for the Goethehaus und Goethemuseum, an hour and 15 minutes for the Städelsches Kunstinstitut und Städtische Galerie, and an hour for the Städtische Galerie Liebieghaus. For the remaining museums it is a question of time and preference. Take your pick from the following and allow at least 45 minutes for each: the Historisches Museum, the Deutsches Filmmuseum, the Museum für Kunsthandwerk, the Deutsches Architekturmuseum, and the Jüdisches Museum. If you intend to visit the Zoologischer Garten, expect to spend 1½ hours there.

Sights to See

㉑ **Alte Oper** (Old Opera House). Kaiser Wilhelm I traveled from Berlin for the gala opening of the opera house in 1880. Gutted in World War II, the house remained a hollow shell for 40 years while controversy raged over its reconstruction. The exterior and lobby are faithful to the original, though the remainder of the building is more like a modern multi-purpose hall. Even if you don't go to a performance, it's worth having a look at the ponderous and ornate lobby, an example of 19th-century neoclassicism at its most self-confident. ✉ *Opernpl., City Center,* ☎ *069/134–0400,* WEB *www.alte-oper-frankfurt.de.*

OFF THE BEATEN PATH

ALTER JÜDISCHER FRIEDHOF (Old Jewish Cemetery) – The old Jewish quarter is east of Börneplatz, a short walk south of the Konstablerwache, or east of the Römer, U-bahn station. Partly vandalized in the Nazi era, the cemetery was in use between the 13th and 19th centuries and is one of the few reminders of prewar Jewish life in Frankfurt. A newer Jewish cemetery is part of the cemetery at Eckenheimer Landstrasse 238 (about 1½ mi north). Quite a few Americans have ancestors buried there. ✉ *Kurt-Schumacher-Str. and Battonstr., City Center,* ☎ *069/561–826.* *Free.* *Daily 8:30–4:30.*

❾ **Börse** (Stock Exchange). This is the center of Germany's stock and money market. The Börse was founded by Frankfurt merchants in 1585 to establish some order in their often chaotic dealings, but the present building dates from the 1870s. These days computerized networks and international telephone systems have removed some of the drama from the dealers' floor, but it is still an exciting scene to watch from the visitors' gallery. ✉ *Börsepl., City Center,* ☎ *069/21010,* WEB *www.deutsche-boerse.com.* *Free.* *Visitors' gallery weekdays 10:30–6.*

⓯ **Eiserner Steg** (Iron Bridge). A pedestrian walkway and the first suspension bridge in Europe, the bridge connects the city center with Sachsenhausen.

Eschenheimer Turm (Eschenheim Tower). Built in the early 15th century, this tower, a block north of the Hauptwache, remains the finest example of the city's original 42 towers. ✉ *Eschenheimer Tor, City Center.*

⓴ **Fressgasse** ("Pig-Out Alley"). Grosse Bockenheimer Strasse is the proper name of this pedestrian street, one of the city's liveliest thoroughfares, but Frankfurters have given it this sobriquet because of its amazing choice of delicatessens, wine merchants, cafés, and restaurants. Food shops offer fresh or smoked fish, cheeses, and a wide range of local specialties, including frankfurters. In the summer you can sit at tables on the sidewalk and dine alfresco.

★ 19 **Goethehaus und Goethemuseum** (Goethe's House and Museum). The house where Germany's most famous poet was born in 1749 is furnished with many original pieces that belonged to his family, including manuscripts in his own hand. Though Goethe is most associated with Weimar, where he lived most of his life, Frankfurters are proud to claim him as a native son. The original house was destroyed by Allied bombing and has been carefully rebuilt and restored in every detail as the young Goethe would have known it. Goethe studied law and became a member of the bar in Frankfurt but preferred the life of a writer and published his first best-seller, the drama *Götz von Berlichingen,* at the age of 20. He sealed his fame a few years later with the tragic love story *Die Leiden des jungen Werthers (The Sorrows of Young Werther).* Goethe also wrote the first version of his masterpiece, *Faust,* in Frankfurt. The adjoining museum contains works of art that inspired Goethe (he was an amateur painter) and works associated with his literary contemporaries who were members of the Sturm und Drang movement. This circle of writers and artists abandoned neoclassical ideals for the darker world of human subjectivity, and helped create the romantic cult of the youthful genius in rebellion against society. ✉ *Grosser Hirschgraben 23–25, Altstadt,* ☎ *069/138–800,* WEB *www.goethehaus-frankfurt.de.* 🎫 *€5.* ⏲ *Apr.–Sept., weekdays 9–6, weekends 10–4; Oct.–Mar., weekdays 9–4, weekends 10–4.*

7 **Hauptwache.** This square is where Grosse Bockeheimer Strasse (Fressgasse) runs into the Zeil, a main shopping street; a vast underground shopping mall stretches below it. The attractive baroque building with a steeply sloping roof is the actual Hauptwache (Main Guardhouse). Built in 1729, it had been tastelessly added to over the years and was demolished to permit the excavation for the mall and subway station beneath it. The occasion was used to restore it to its original appearance. Today it houses a café.

4 **Historisches Museum** (Historical Museum). This fascinating museum encompasses all aspects of the city's history over the past eight centuries. It contains a scale model of historic Frankfurt, complete with every street, house, and church. There is also an astonishing display of silver and a children's museum with interactive exhibits. ✉ *Saalg. 19, Altstadt,* ☎ *069/2123–5599,* WEB *www.historisches-museum.frankfurt.de.* 🎫 *€4; free Wed.* ⏲ *Tues. and Thurs.–Sun. 10–5, Wed. 10–8.*

17 **Jüdisches Museum** (Jewish Museum). The story of Frankfurt's Jewish quarter is told in the former Rothschild Palais. Prior to the Holocaust, the community was the second largest in Germany. The museum contains extensive archives of Jewish history and culture, including a library of 5,000 books, a large photographic collection, and a documentation center. A branch of the museum, **Museum Judengasse** (✉ Kurt-Schumacher-Str. 10, City Center, ☎ 069/297–7419, 🎫 €1.50, ⏲ Tues. and Thurs.–Sun. 10–5, Wed. 10–8), is built around the foundations of mostly 18th-century buildings in what once was the ghetto. The branch is also near the Old Jewish Cemetery (Alter Jüdischer Friedhof). ✉ *Untermainkai 14–15, Altstadt,* ☎ *069/212–35000,* WEB *www.juedischesmuseum.de.* 🎫 *€2.60.* ⏲ *Tues. and Thurs.–Sun. 10–5, Wed. 10–8.*

13 **Kaiserdom.** Because the Holy Roman emperors were chosen and crowned here from the 16th to the 18th centuries, the church is known as the Kaiserdom (Imperial Cathedral), even though it isn't the seat of a bishop. Officially the Church of St. Bartholomew, it was built largely

between the 13th and 15th centuries and survived World War II with most of its treasures intact. It replaced a church established by Charlemagne's son, Ludwig the Pious, on the present site of the Römerberg. The many magnificent, original Gothic carvings include a life-size crucifixion group and the fine 15th-century *Maria-Schlaf* (Altar of Mary Sleeping). The most impressive exterior feature is the tall, red sandstone tower (almost 300 ft high), which was added between 1415 and 1514. It was the tallest structure in Frankfurt before the skyscrapers, and the view from the top remains an exciting panorama. In 1953 excavations in front of the main entrance revealed the remains of a Roman settlement and the foundations of a Carolingian imperial palace. The **Dommuseum** (Cathedral Museum) occupies the former Gothic cloister. ✉ *Dompl. 1, Altstadt,* ☎ *069/1337–6184.* 🎫 *Dommuseum €2.* ⏲ *Church Mon.–Thurs. and Sat. 9–noon and 2:30–6, Fri. and Sun. 2:30–6 (closes at 5 in winter). Dommuseum Tues.–Fri. 10–5, weekends 11–5.*

18 **Karmeliterkloster** (Carmelite Monastery). Secularized in 1803, the church and adjacent buildings contain the **Museum für Vor- und Frühgeschichte** (Museum of Prehistory and Early History). The **main cloister** (🎫 free) displays the largest religious fresco north of the Alps, a 16th-century representation of Christ's birth and death by Jörg Ratgeb. ✉ *Karmeliterg. 1, Altstadt,* ☎ *069/2123–5896.* 🎫 *Museum €4; free Wed.* ⏲ *Museum and cloister Tues. and Thurs.–Sun. 10–5, Wed. 10–8.*

8 **Katharinenkirche** (St. Catherine's Church). This house of worship, the first independent Protestant church in Gothic style, was originally built between 1678 and 1681. The church it replaced on this site, dating from 1343, was the setting of the first Protestant sermon preached in Frankfurt, in 1522. Goethe was confirmed here. ✉ *An der Hauptwache, City Center.* ⏲ *Weekdays 2–6.*

16 **Leonhardskirche** (St. Leonard's Church). Begun in the Romanesque style and continued in the late-Gothic style, this beautifully preserved Catholic church contains five naves, two 13th-century Romanesque arches, and 15th-century stained glass. The "pendant," or hanging vaulting, was already a major Frankfurt tourist attraction during the 17th century. Masses are held in English Saturdays at 5 and Sundays at 10. ✉ *Am Leonhardstor and Untermainkai, Altstadt.* ⏲ *Tues.–Sun. 10–noon and 3–6.*

6 **Liebfrauenkirche** (Church of Our Lady). The peaceful, concealed courtyard of this Catholic church makes it hard to believe you're in the swirl of the shopping district. Dating from the 14th century, the late-Gothic church still has a fine tympanum relief over the south door and ornate rococo wood carvings inside. ✉ *Liebfrauenberg 3, City Center.* ⏲ *Daily 7–7, except during services.*

Messegelände (Fairgrounds). Also called the congress center, this huge complex is Europe's busiest trade fair center and is full of congresses, conferences, and seminars. Important international trade fairs showcase the latest books, cars, fashion, medical and high technology, and consumer goods. In addition to the two major fairs in spring and fall, there is an automobile show in September of odd-number years, the Fur Fair at Easter, and the International Book Fair in the fall. ✉ *Ludwig-Erhard-Anlage 1, Messe,* ☎ *069/75750,* WEB *www.messe-frankfurt.de.*

12 **Museum für Moderne Kunst** (Museum of Modern Art). Austrian architect Hans Hollein designed this distinctive triangular building, shaped like a wedge of cake. The collection features American pop art and works by such German artists as Gerhard Richter and Joseph Beuys. ✉ *Dom-*

str. 10, City Center, ☎ *069/2123–0447,* WEB *www.frankfurt-business.de/mmk.* €5. ⏲ *Tues. and Thurs.–Sun. 10–5, Wed. 10–8.*

23 **Naturkundemuseum Senckenberg** (Natural History Museum). An important collection of fossils, animals, plants, and geological exhibits is upstaged by the famous diplodocus dinosaur, imported from New York—the only complete specimen of its kind in Europe. Many of the exhibits on prehistoric animals have been designed with children in mind, and there is a whole series of dioramas in which stuffed animals are presented. ✉ *Senckenberganlage 25, Bockenheim,* ☎ *069/75420,* WEB *www.senckenberg.uni-frankfurt.de.* €5. ⏲ *Mon., Tues., Thurs., and Fri. 9–5, Wed. 9–8, weekends 9–6.*

3 **Nikolaikirche** (St. Nicholas Church). This small red sandstone church was built in the late 13th century as the court chapel for emperors of the Holy Roman Empire. Try to time your visit to coincide with the chimes of the carillon, which rings out three times a day, at 9, noon, and 5. ✉ *South side of Römerberg, Altstadt.* ⏲ *Oct.–Mar., daily 10–6; Apr.–Sept., daily 10–8.*

22 **Palmengarten und Botanischer Garten** (Tropical Garden and Botanical Gardens). A splendid cluster of tropical and semitropical greenhouses contains a wide variety of flora, including cacti, orchids, and palms. The surrounding park, which can be surveyed from a miniature train, has many recreational facilities such as a little lake where you can rent rowboats, a play area for children, and a wading pool. Between the Palmengarten and the adjoining Grüneburgpark, the botanical gardens have a wide assortment of wild, ornamental, and rare plants from around the world. Special collections include a 2½-acre rock garden as well as rose and rhododendron gardens. During most of the year there are flower shows and exhibitions; in summer concerts are held in an outdoor music pavilion. ✉ *Siesmayerstr. 63, Westend,* ☎ *069/2123–3939,* WEB *www.stadt-frankfurt.de/palmengarten.* €3.50. ⏲ *Feb.–Oct., daily 9–6; Nov.–Jan., daily 9–4.*

5 **Paulskirche** (St. Paul's Church). This church was the site of the first all-German parliament in 1848. The parliament lasted only a year, having achieved little more than offering the Prussian king the crown of Germany. Today the church, which has been secularized and not very tastefully restored, remains a symbol of German democracy and is used mainly for ceremonies. The German Book Dealers' annual Peace Prize is awarded in the hall, as is the Goethe Prize. ✉ *Paulspl., Altstadt.* ⏲ *Daily 10–5.*

2 **Römer** (City Hall). Three individual patrician buildings make up the Römer. From left to right, they are the Alt-Limpurg, the Zum Römer (from which the entire structure takes its name), and the Löwenstein. The mercantile-minded Frankfurt burghers used the complex not only for political and ceremonial purposes but also for trade fairs and other commercial ventures. Its gabled Gothic facade with an ornate balcony is widely known as the city's official emblem.

The most important events to take place in the Römer were the festivities celebrating the coronations of the Holy Roman emperors. These were mounted starting in 1562 in the glittering **Kaisersaal** (Imperial Hall), last used in 1792 to celebrate the election of the emperor Francis II, who would later be forced to abdicate by Napoléon. It is said that 16-year-old Goethe posed as a waiter to get a firsthand impression of the banquet celebrating the coronation of Emperor Joseph II. The most vivid description of the ceremony is told in his book *Dichtung und Wahrheit* (*Poetry and Truth*). When no official business is being conducted, you can see the impressive, full-length 19th-century portraits of the 52 emperors of the Holy Roman Empire, which line the walls of the reconstructed banquet hall. ✉ *West side of Römerberg, Altstadt,* ☎ *069/2123–4814.* 💶 *€1.50.* ⏲ *Daily 10–1 and 2–5. Closed during official functions.*

❶ **Römerberg.** This square north of the Main River, lovingly restored after wartime bomb damage, is the historical focal point of the city. The Römer, the Nikolaikirche, the Historiches Museum, and the half-timber Ostzeile houses are all found here. The 16th-century Fountain of Justitia (Justice) stands in the center of the Römerberg. At the coronation of Emperor Matthias in 1612, wine flowed from the fountain instead of water. This practice has been revived by the city fathers on special occasions. ✉ *Between Braubachstr. and the Main River, Altstadt.*

⓮ **Schirn Kunsthalle** (Schirn Art Gallery). One of Frankfurt's most modern museums is devoted exclusively to changing exhibits of modern art and photography. Past shows include "Audio-Visual Spaces," Mercedes posters, and Polish landscapes of the 19th and 20th centuries. It stands opposite the Kaiserdom. ✉ *Am Römerberg 6a, Altstadt,* ☎ *069/299–8820,* WEB *www.schirn-kunsthalle.de.* 💶 *€5–€7, depending on exhibition.* ⏲ *Tues. and Sun. 11–7, Wed.–Sat. 11–10.*

⓫ **Staufenmauer** (Staufen Wall). The Staufenmauer is one of the few remaining sections of the old city's fortifications and dates from the 12th century. ✉ *Fahrg., Altstadt.*

Struwwelpeter-Museum (Slovenly Peter Museum). This museum contains a collection of letters, sketches, and manuscripts by Dr. Heinrich Hoffmann, a Frankfurt physician and creator of the children's book hero Struwwelpeter, or "Slovenly Peter," the character you see as a puppet or doll in Frankfurt's shops. ✉ *Benderg. 1, Altstadt,* ☎ *069/281–333.* 💶 *Free.* ⏲ *Tues. and Thurs.–Sun. 11–5, Wed. 11–8.*

Zeil. The heart of Frankfurt's shopping district is this ritzy pedestrian street, running east from Hauptwache Square. City officials claim it's the country's busiest shopping street. The Zeil is also known as "the Golden Mile."

★ ❿ **Zoologischer Garten** (Zoo). Founded in 1858, this is one of the most important and attractive zoos in Europe, with many of the animals and birds living in a natural environment. Its remarkable collection includes some 5,000 animals of 600 different species, a bears' castle, an exotarium (aquarium plus reptiles), and an aviary, reputedly the largest in Europe. Nocturnal creatures move about in a special section. The zoo has a restaurant and a café, along with afternoon concerts in summer. ✉ *Alfred-Brehm Pl. 16, Ostend,* ☎ *069/2123–3727,* WEB *www.zoo-frankfurt.de.* 💶 *€5.50.* ⏲ *Nov.–Mar., daily 9–5; Apr.–Oct., daily 9–7.*

Sachsenhausen

★ The old quarter of Sachsenhausen, on the south bank of the Main River, has been sensitively preserved and its cobblestone streets, half-timber houses, and beer gardens make it a very popular area to stroll. Sachsenhausen's two big attractions are the Museumufer (Museum Riverbank), which has seven museums almost next door to one another, and the famous *Apfelwein* (apple-wine or cider) taverns around the Rittergasse pedestrian area. A green pine wreath above a tavern's entrance tells passersby that a freshly pressed—and alcoholic—apple cider is on tap. You can eat well in these small inns, too. Formerly a separate village, Sachsenhausen is said to have been established by Charlemagne, who settled the Main's banks with a group of Saxon families in the

8th century. It was an important bridgehead for the crusader Knights of the Teutonic Order and in 1318 officially became part of Frankfurt.

A Good Walk

The best place to begin is at the charming 17th-century villa housing the **Städtische Galerie Liebieghaus** ㉔, the westernmost of the museums. It has an internationally famous collection of classical, medieval, and Renaissance sculpture. From it you need only turn to your right and follow the riverside road, Schaumainkai, for about 2 km (1 mi), passing all of the museums and winding up around the Rittergasse.

The **Städelsches Kunstinstitut und Städtische Galerie** ㉕ houses one of the most significant art collections in Germany, and the **Museum für Kommunikation** ㉖ displays postal coaches, ancient telephones that work, and a huge stamp collection. The **Deutsches Architekturmuseum** ㉗ traces man's structures from Stone Age huts to high-rises. Film artifacts and classic film videos are featured at the **Deutsches Filmmuseum** ㉘. After this museum, you could take a break at an Apfelwein tavern on Schweizer Strasse. The next museum after the bridge is the **Museum für Völkerkunde** ㉙, which holds ethnological artifacts from the Pacific, Indonesia, Africa, and America. A stunning collection of European and Asian applied art in the **Museum für Angewandte Kunst** ㉚ comes next. Continue down the river road (the name changes from Schaumainkai to Sachsenhäuser Ufer). Just beyond the first bridge carrying car traffic, follow Grosse Rittergasse to the right. A bit down this street, on your left, is the **Kuhhirtenturm** ㉛, the only remaining part of Sachsenhausen's original fortifications.

A few steps farther and you will be in the heart of the Apfelwein district, which is especially lively on summer evenings when it becomes one big outdoor festival. Some of the apple-wine taverns and other watering places are also open weekday afternoons. The area has a distinctly medieval air, with narrow back alleys, quaint little inns, and quiet squares that escaped the modern developer, yet it's also full of shops, cafés, and bars thronging with people.

TIMING

Allow an hour and 15 minutes for the Städelsches Kunstinstitut und Städtische Galerie, and an hour for the Städtische Galerie Liebieghaus. You could spend at least 45 minutes in each of the other museums along the walk. At the end of the day relax in an apple-wine tavern.

Sights to See

㉗ **Deutsches Architekturmuseum** (German Architecture Museum). Created by German architect Oswald Mathias Ungers, this 19th-century villa contains an entirely modern interior. There are five floors of drawings, models, and audiovisual displays that chart the progress of architecture through the ages, as well as many special exhibits. ✉ *Schaumainkai 43, Sachsenhausen,* ☎ *069/2123–8844,* WEB *www.dam-online.de.* 🎫 *€4.* ⏲ *Tues. and Thurs.–Sun. 10–5, Wed. 10–8.*

㉘ **Deutsches Filmmuseum** (German Film Museum). Germany's first museum of cinematography houses an exciting collection of film artifacts. Visitors can view its collection of classic film videos, and a theater in the basement has regular evening screenings of every sort of film from avant-garde to Hungarian to silent-era flicks. ✉ *Schaumainkai 41, Sachsenhausen,* ☎ *069/2123–8830,* WEB *www.deutsches-filmmuseum.de.* 🎫 *€2.50.* ⏲ *Tues., Thurs., Fri., and Sun. 10–5, Wed. 10–8, Sat. 2–8.*

NEED A BREAK?

Two of Sachsenhausen's livliest Apfelwein taverns are well removed from the Rittergasse and handy to the Museumufer. You'll find them adjacent to one another if you turn down on Schweizer Strasse, just next to the Deutsches Filmmuseum, and walk five minutes. **Zum Gemalten Haus** (✉ Schweizer Str. 67, Sachsenhausen, ☎ 069/614–559) will provide all the hard cider and Gemütlichkeit you could want. **Zum Wagner** (✉ Schweizer Str. 71, Sachsenhausen, ☎ 069/612–565) reeks so with "old Sachsenhausen" schmaltz that it's downright corny.

31 **Kuhhirtenturm** (Shepherd's Tower). This is the last of nine towers, built in the 15th century, that formed part of Sachsenhausen's fortifications. The composer Paul Hindemith lived in the tower from 1923 to 1927, while working at the Frankfurt Opera. ✉ *Grosser Ritterg., Sachsenhausen.*

26 **Museum für Kommunikation** (Museum for Communication). This is the place for getting in on the electronic age. You can surf the Internet, talk to one another on picture telephones, and learn of glass fiber technology. Exhibitions on historic communication methods include mail coaches, stamps, ancient dial telephones with their clunky switching equipment, and a reconstructed 19th-century post office. ✉ *Schaumainkai 53, Sachsenhausen,* ☎ *069/60600,* WEB *www.museumsstiftung.de/frankfurt.* *Free.* ⏲ *Tues.–Fri. 9–5, weekends 11–7.*

30 **Museum für Angewandte Kunst** (Museum of Applied Arts). More than 30,000 objects representing European and Asian decorative arts are exhibited in this museum designed by American architect Richard Meier. The collection of furniture, glassware, and porcelain has expanded to include Web sites, computers, and graphic design. ✉ *Schaumainkai 17, Sachsenhausen,* ☎ *069/2123–4037.* *€5; free Wed.* ⏲ *Tues. and Thurs.–Sun. 10–5, Wed. 10–8.*

29 **Museum für Völkerkunde** (Ethnological Museum). The lifestyles and customs of aboriginal societies from around the world are examined through items such as masks, ritual objects, and jewelry here. ✉ *Schaumainkai 29, Sachsenhausen,* ☎ *069/2123–1510.* *€3.50; free Wed.* ⏲ *Tues. and Thurs.–Sun. 10–5, Wed. 10–8.*

★ 25 **Städelsches Kunstinstitut und Städtische Galerie** (Städel Art Institute and Municipal Gallery). Here you will find one of Germany's most important art collections, with paintings by Dürer, Vermeer, Rembrandt, Rubens, Monet, Renoir, and other masters. The section on German expressionism is particularly strong, with representative works by Frankfurt artist Max Beckmann. ✉ *Schaumainkai 63, Sachsenhausen,* ☎ *069/605–0980,* WEB *www.staedelmuseum.de.* *€5; free Wed.* ⏲ *Tues., Thurs., Fri., and Sun. 10–5, Wed. 10–8, Sat. 2–8.*

★ 24 **Städtische Galerie Liebieghaus** (Liebieg Municipal Museum of Sculpture). The sculpture collection here from 5,000 years of civilizations and epochs is considered one of the most important in Europe. From antiquity the collection includes a statue of a Sumarian functionary and a relief from the temple of Egyptian king Sahure (2455 BC–2443 BC). From the Middle Ages there is an 11th-century throned Madonna with child from Trier, and from the Renaissance an altar relief by the noted Florentine sculptor Lucca della Robbia (1399–1482). Works such as the *Immaculata*, by Matthias Steinl (1688), represent the baroque era. Some pieces are exhibited in the lovely gardens surrounding the house. ✉ *Schaumainkai 71, Sachsenhausen,* ☎ *069/2123–8617.* *€4.* ⏲ *Tues. and Thurs.–Sun. 10–5, Wed. 10–8.*

DINING

Business travelers keep the nicer restaurants busy, so be sure to make advance reservations for lunch or dinner whenever possible. Several upscale restaurants serve bargain lunch menus. For example, Erno's Bistro and Gargantua have midday menus for €25. At the apple-wine taverns there's always room for a couple more at the long tables, and patrons are very accommodating when it comes to squeezing together.

CATEGORY	COST*
$$$$	over €20
$$$	€15–€20
$$	€10–€15
$	under €10

per person for a main course at dinner

City Center

$$$$ ✕ **Restaurant Français.** Frankfurt's oldest hotel restaurant, in the Steigenberger Frankfurter Hof, offers sophisticated international fare with a French accent. The ornate green-and-gold dining room with Louis XIV furnishings and well-spaced tables is a perfect place for a business meal or to enjoy the seven-course tasting menu, including breast of quail in lentil soup, followed by duck supreme or baked turbo fillets in a mango-and-ginger sauce. ✉ *Bethmannstr. 33, City Center,* ☎ *069/215–138. Reservations essential. Jacket and tie. AE, DC, MC, V. Closed Sun., Mon. and 6 wks in July or Aug. No lunch Sat.*

$$–$$$ ✕ **Kangaroo's.** The main dining room of this very popular, Australia-theme restaurant in the Schillerpassage is glass-roofed and lush with greenery. Highway signs warn of kangaroos ahead. The adventurous will try the "Australia Platter" with kangaroo, crocodile, and emu meat (but Aussies, too, eat beef, chicken, and salads.) Most people patronize this downtown restaurant for the food, but it's also a friendly place to gather for a Foster's beer and a chat. ✉ *Rahmhofstr. 2–4, City Center,* ☎ *069/282–100. AE, DC, MC, V.*

$–$$$ ✕ **Mikuni.** A few paper lanterns and wall posters don't do much to offset the German furnishings, but the many Japanese patrons here vouch for the authentic Japanese fare. The menu is in Japanese as well as German, each arriving guest receives a hot towel, soup is drunk from the bowl, and even Germans seldom ask for a knife and fork to replace their chopsticks. Prices are more reasonable here than at other sushi bars. ✉ *Fahrg. 91–95, City Center,* ☎ *069/283–627. AE, MC. Closed Sun.*

$$ ★ ✕ **Maintower.** Atop the skyscraper that houses Hessischer Landesbank, this popular restaurant-cum-café-cum-bar captures an unbeatable view. Through 25-ft floor to ceiling windows, all of "Mainhattan" is at your feet. Prices are surprisingly reasonable, though you will have to pay €4.50 per person just to take the elevator up. The cuisine is part global, part regional. It's hard to get a table for supper, though it's less of a problem for afternoon coffee, or for spending an evening in the clouds at the bar. ✉ *Neue Mainzer Str. 52–58, City Center,* ☎ *069/3650–4770. AE, V.*

$$ ✕ **Steinernes Haus.** Diners share long wooden tables beneath prints of old Frankfurt and traditional clothing mounted on the walls. The house specialty is a rump steak brought to the table uncooked with a heated rock tablet on which it is prepared. The beef broth is the perfect antidote to cold weather. The menu has other old German standards along with daily specials. Traditional fare popular with locals includes *Rippchen* (smoked pork) and *Zigeunerhackbraten* (spicy meat loaf). If you don't specify a *Kleines,* or small glass of beer, you'll automatically get a liter mug. ✉ *Braubachstr. 35, Altstadt,* ☎ *069/283–491. Reservations essential. MC, V.*

Dining

Altes Zollhaus 25
Arche Nova 2
Bistrot 77 22
Café Karin 13
Café Laumer 6
Chicago Meatpackers 12
Dr. Flotte 1
Edelweiss 23
Erno's Bistro 5
Fichtekränzi 19
Gargantua 4
Grossenwahn 28
Harvey's 27
Historix 14
Jewel of India 7
Kangaroo's 16
Maingau Stuben . . . 20
Maintower 10
Mikuni 17
Momberger 26
Omonia 8
Pizzeria Romanella 9
Restaurant Français 11
Steinernes Haus . . . 15
Tandure 18
Wäldches 3
Zum Rad 24
Zum Wagner 21

Lodging

An der Messe 5
Art Hotel Robert Mayer 2
Dorint Hotel 9
Hessischer Hof 7
Hilton Frankfurt 6
Hotel Nizza 16
Hotel Westend 4
Hotel-Pension West 1
InterCity Hotel 8
Maingau 14
Palmenhof 3
Pension Aller 10
Pension Stella 13
Sheraton Frankfurt 15
Steigenberger Hotel Frankfurter Hof 12
Steigenberger Maxx 18
Terminus 11
Waldhotel Hensels Felsenkeller 17

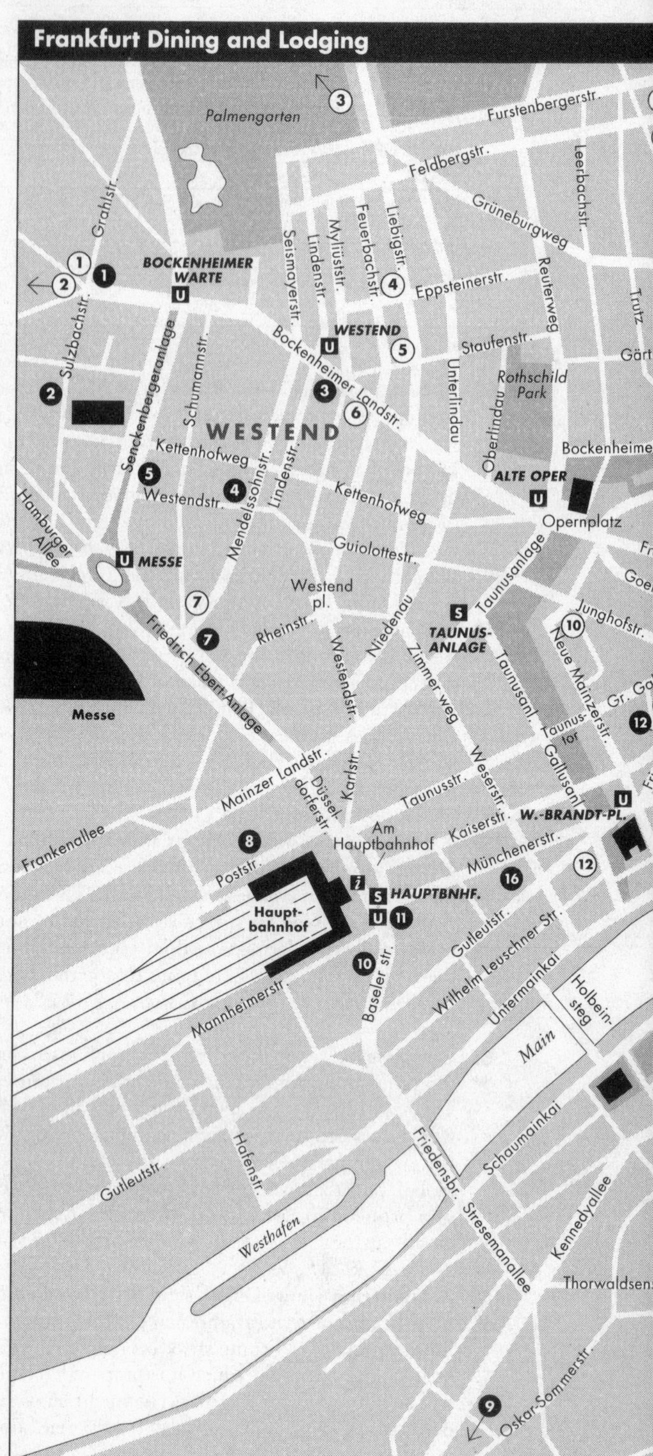

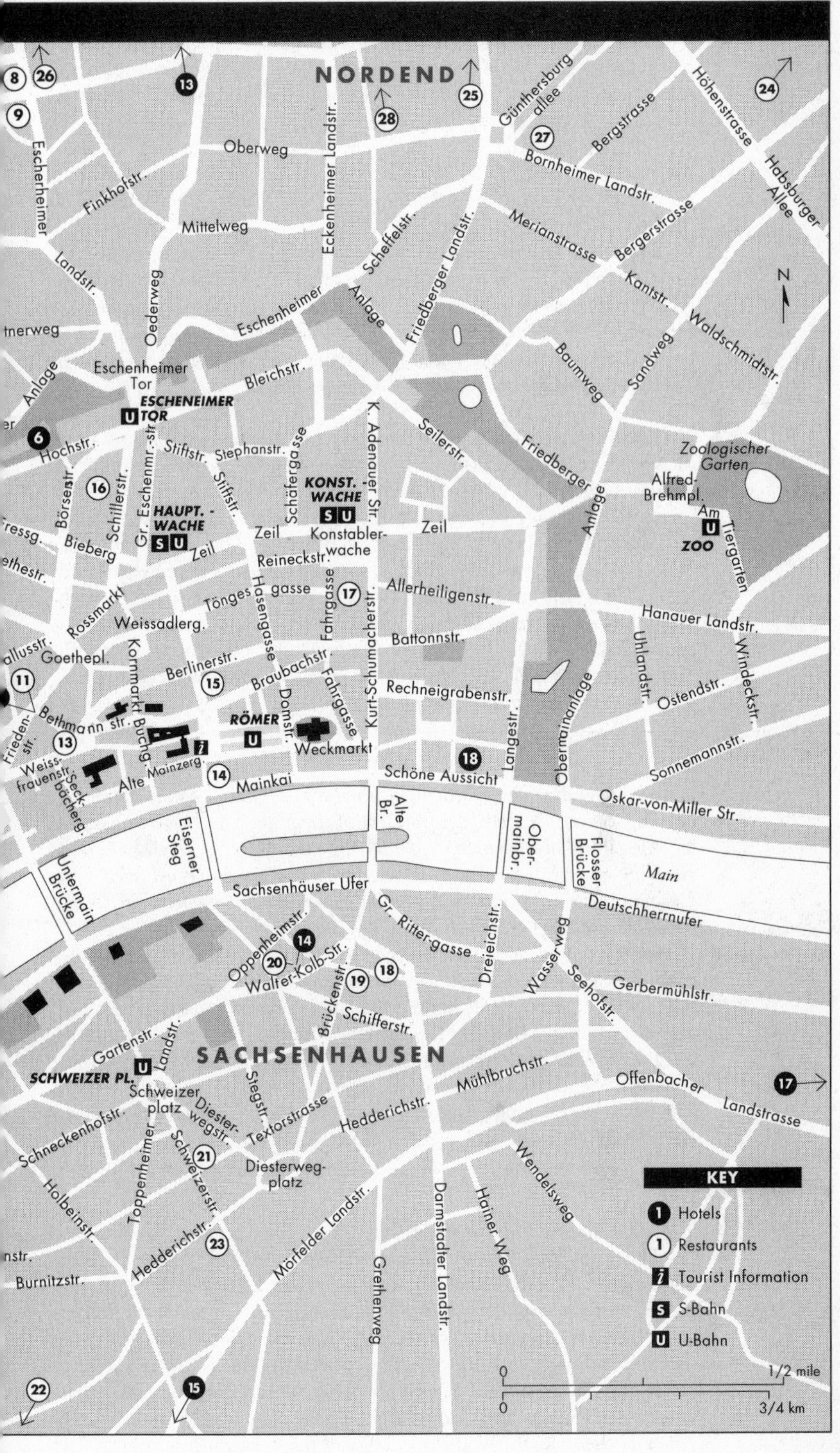

NORDEND
SACHSENHAUSEN
Oberweg
Mittelweg
Finkhofstr.
Eschersheimer Landstr.
Eckenheimer Landstr.
Oederweg
Eschenheimer Anlage
Scheffelstr.
Friedberger Landstr.
Günthersburg allee
Bergstrasse
Höhenstrasse
Habsburger Allee
Bornheimer Landstr.
Merianstrasse
Bergerstrasse
Kantstr.
Waldschmidtstr.
Sandweg
Baumweg
Friedberger Anlage
Seilerstr.
Bleichstr.
Eschenheimer Tor
ESCHENEIMER TOR
Hochstr.
Stiftstr.
Stephanstr.
Schäfergasse
K. Adenauer Str.
KONST. - WACHE
HAUPT. - WACHE
Börsenstr.
Schillerstr.
Gr. Eschenm.-str.
Zeil
Konstablerwache
Reineckstr.
Töngesgasse
Hasengasse
Fahrgasse
Kurt-Schumacherstr.
Allerheiligenstr.
Battonnstr.
Braubachstr.
Berlinerstr.
Weissadlerg.
Rossmarkt
Bieberg
Goethepl.
Kornmarkt
Buchg.
Bethmann str.
RÖMER
Domstr.
Weckmarkt
Recheneigrabenstr.
Langestr.
Obermainanlage
Schöne Aussicht
Mainkai
Alte Mainzerg.
Weissfrauenstr.
Seckbächerg.
Friedenstr.
Zoologischer Garten
Alfred-Brehmpl.
Am Tiergarten
ZOO
Hanauer Landstr.
Uhlandstr.
Windeckstr.
Ostendstr.
Sonnemannstr.
Oskar-von-Miller Str.
Eiserner Steg
Alte Br.
Obermainbr.
Flosser Brücke
Untermain Brücke
Main
Sachsenhäuser Ufer
Deutschherrnufer
Gr. Ritter-gasse
Oppenheimstr.
Walter-Kolb-Str.
Brückenstr.
Schifferstr.
Dreieichstr.
Wasserweg
Seehofstr.
Gerbermühlstr.
Gartenstr.
Landstr.
SCHWEIZER PL.
Schweizer platz
Diesterwegstr.
Stegstr.
Textorstrasse
Hedderichstr.
Mühlbruchstr.
Offenbacher Landstrasse
Schneckenhofstr.
Holbeinstr.
Toppenheimer
Schweizerstr.
Diesterwegplatz
Heddrichstr.
Burnitzstr.
Mörfelder Landstr.
Grethenweg
Darmstadter Landstr.
Hainer Weg
Wendelsweg
KEY
Hotels
Restaurants
Tourist Information
S-Bahn
U-Bahn
0
1/2 mile
3/4 km

$–$$ ✕ **Chicago Meatpackers.** Americans who wonder if this place is what it claims to be should be glad to hear that it is the "official restaurant" of the Frankfurt Galaxy American football team, the members of which are, with few exceptions, American gridiron types. They dine here every Wednesday evening. If that doesn't convince you, the pitchers of beer, cocktails, all-you-can-eat spare ribs, huge hamburgers, rock music blaring from loudspeakers, and a model train running around the ceiling will. ✉ *Untermainanlage 8, City Center,* ☎ *069/231–659. AE, DC, MC, V.*

$ ✕ **Café Karin.** An understated café that attracts an interesting cross section of patrons, this is a great place to breakfast (only a few euros), to recover from a shopping spree, or to eat something healthy in preparation for a night out. Sample the goat cheese salad or whole-grain ratatouille crepes. Cakes and baked goods come from a whole-grain bakery. There is a no-smoking section. ✉ *Grosser Hirschgraben 28, Altstadt,* ☎ *069/295–217. No credit cards.*

$ ✕ **Historix.** It goes without saying that Apfelwein is an important part of Frankfurt, and it's fitting that apple wine gets its own permanent exhibit in the Historisches Museum. Inside the museum, the Historix serves the beverage in Bembel pitchers and with all the typical food and accoutrements of the hard-cider business. The wall facing the street is one big plate-glass window, something you're not likely to find in a real tavern, but every inch of wall space has been covered with schmaltzy old pictures of the apple-wine scene, and historic Bembels are on display. The tables are overshadowed by a fake apple tree with huge fruit. ✉ *Saalg. 19, Altstadt,* ☎ *069/294–400. No credit cards. Closed Mon. No dinner weekends.*

Nordend

$$ ✕ **Grossenwahn.** The Nordend is noted for its "scene" establishments, and this corner locale is the funkiest of them all. The name translates as "Megalomania," which says it all. One whiff of the air tells you that smoking is tolerated without restriction, and the menu is esoteric with German, Greek, Italian, and French elements. ✉ *Lenaustr. 97, Nordend,* ☎ *069/599–356. AE, MC, V.*

$$ ✕ **Harvey's.** This is very much the "in" place in Frankfurt today, the place to see and be seen. It first achieved notoriety as a gay and lesbian hangout, deriving its name from San Francisco's martyred gay supervisor Harvey Milk. But the straight community is more and more attracted by the imaginative menu, the good music, the friendly atmosphere, and the chameleon-like changes in design, several times a year. The menu, too, is changeable. Breakfast is served until 4 PM. ✉ *Nordend,* ☎ *069/497–3032. No credit cards.*

Westend

$$$$ ★ ✕ **Erno's Bistro.** This tiny, unpretentious place in a quiet Westend neighborhood looks like an unlikely candidate for "the best restaurant in Germany." Yet that is what one French critic has called it, but that's just patriotism for you—after all, the French bistro's specialty, fish, is often flown in daily from France itself. Any critic will agree, however, that this oldtimer with fresh, nouvelle preparations is one of the best restaurants in Frankfurt. It's closed weekends, during the Christmas and Easter seasons and during much of the summer; in other words, when its clientele, the well-heeled elite of the business community, are unlikely to be in town. ✉ *Liebigstr. 15, Westend,* ☎ *069/721–997. Reservations essential. AE, DC, MC, V. Closed weekends and July–early Aug.*

$$$$ ✕ **Gargantua.** One of Frankfurt's most creative chefs, Klaus Trebes, who doubles as a food columnist, serves up new versions of German classics and French-accented dishes in a laid-back dining room decorated with contemporary art. His menu features such dishes as artichoke risotto with goose liver, lentil salad with stewed beef, and grilled dorade served on pureed white beans and pesto. One corner of the restaurant is reserved for those who only want to sample the outstanding wine list. ✉ *Liebigstr. 47, Westend,* ☏ *069/720–718. AE, MC, V. Closed Sun. No lunch Sat.*

$$–$$$ ✕ **Pizzeria Romanella.** Don't let the name and simple exterior fool you. This is a true *ristorante* with a very extensive menu of Italian fare. All the tables are full at supper time, when diners enjoy pastas and veal dishes. The pizzas are good, but no better than elsewhere. ✉ *Wolfsgangstr. 84, Westend,* ☏ *069/596–1117. No credit cards. Closed Sat.*

$$ ✕ **Jewel of India.** The elegant decor, gracious service, and delicious Indian-Pakistani food make the Jewel a good choice for lunch (it's just a couple of blocks from the Messe trade-fair grounds). It's a lot calmer and quieter than the neighborhood's popular Italian restaurants. The chicken tandoori in saffron-yogurt marinade and lamb dishes such as *rogan josh* harmoniously blend spices and flavors without being overpowering. ✉ *Wilhelm-Hauff-Str. 5, Messe,* ☏ *069/752–375. AE, DC, MC, V. No lunch weekends.*

$$ ✕ **Omonia.** This cozy cellar locale offers the best Greek cuisine in town. Those with a good appetite should try the Omonia Platter, with lamb in several forms, plus Greek-style pasta and vegetables. The place is popular and the tables few, so make a reservation. ✉ *Vogtstr. 43, Westend,* ☏ *069/593–314. AE, DC MC, V. No lunch weekends.*

$ ✕ **Café Laumer.** The ambience of an old-time Viennese café, with a subdued decor and rear garden, is well preserved here. It owes its literary tradition to Theodor Adorno, a philosopher and sociologist of the "Frankfurt School," who drank his daily coffee here. For fear of attracting more patrons than the often crowded café can handle, it isn't even listed in the phone book. In a compromise with the café tradition, meals are also served, but open hours don't permit you to linger over a dinner. It's open for breakfast, lunch, and afternoon coffee, but closes at 7 PM. ✉ *Bockenheimer Landstr. 67, Westend,* ☏ *069/727–912. DC, MC, V. No dinner.*

Sachsenhausen

$$$$ ✕ **Bistrot 77.** The Mosbach brothers, sons of an Alsatian vintner whose wines they serve, offer outstanding food in a spare bistro with plain walls and a tile floor. The menu is predominantly Alsatian with an accent on fresh vegetables and fine cuts of meat, such as lamb rib. An extravagant delicacy is grilled tuna fish with lobster medallions on white beans. The cheese wagon is rolled around at the end, and a calvados or cognac tops things off nicely. ✉ *Ziegelhüttenweg 1–3, Sachsenhausen,* ☏ *069/614–040. AE, MC, V. Closed Sun. No lunch Sat.*

$$$$ ★ ✕ **Maingau Stuben.** Chef Werner Döpfner himself greets you and lights your candle at this very "in" restaurant. A polished clientele are drawn by the linen tablecloths, subdued lighting, and such nearly forgotten practices as carving the meat tableside. Chef Döpfner is one of Frankfurt's best, serving contemporary dishes such as seafood salad with scallops and lobster mousse, and rack of venison in a walnut crust. He also has a cellar full of rare German wines. ✉ *Schifferstr. 38–40, Sachsenhausen,* ☏ *069/610–752. AE, MC, V. Closed Mon. No lunch Sat. No dinner Sun.*

$–$$ ✕ **Edelweiss.** This place is full of homesick Austrians enjoying their native cuisine, including the genuine Wiener schnitzel, and Kaiser Franz Josef's favorite, *Tafelspitze,* made of boiled beef with a chive sauce. Then there is the roast chicken with a salad made of "earth apples" (potatoes) and the beloved *Kaiserschmarrn* (egg pancakes with raisins, apples, cinnamon, and jam). The interior is rustically wooden within, and there is a pleasant terrace. ✉ *Schweizer Str. 96, Sachsenhausen,* ☎ *069/619–696. AE, DC, MC, V. No lunch weekends.*

$–$$ ✕ **Fichtekränzi.** This is the real thing—a traditional apple-cider tavern in the heart of Sachsenhausen. In summer the courtyard is the place to be; in winter you sit in the noisy tavern proper at long tables with benches. It's often crowded, so if there isn't room when you arrive, order a glass of apple cider and hang around until someone leaves. Traditional cider-tavern dishes include Rippchen (smoked pork). ✉ *Wallstr. 5, Sachsenhausen,* ☎ *069/612–778. No credit cards. No lunch.*

$–$$ ✕ **Tandure.** The aroma of the clay oven—called a *tandure*—wafts through the dining room in this small Turkish restaurant decorated with Turkish carpeting and Anatolian handicrafts. As an appetizer you might want to try the *sigara böregi* (phyllo pastry stuffed with sheep's cheese) or *imam bayildi* (stewed eggplant). Lamb, marinated and cooked in the tandure, is the house specialty. It's open until midnight. ✉ *Wallstr. 10, Sachsenhausen,* ☎ *069/612–543. AE, MC, V.*

$–$$ ★ ✕ **Zum Wagner.** The kitchen produces the same hearty German dishes as other apple-wine taverns, only better. Try the *Tafelspitz mit Frankfurter Grüner Sosse* (stewed beef with a sauce of green herbs), or come on Friday for fresh fish. Beer and wine are served as well as cider. This Sachsenhausen classic, with sepia-tone murals of merrymaking, succeeds in being touristy and traditional all at once. ✉ *Schweizer Str. 71, Sachsenhausen,* ☎ *069/612–565. No credit cards.*

Outer Frankfurt

$$$ ✕ **Altes Zollhaus.** Very good versions of traditional German specialties are served in this beautiful, 200-year-old half-timber house on the edge of town. Try a game dish. In summer you can eat in the beautiful garden. To get here, take Bus 30 from Konstablerwache to Heiligenstock, or drive out on Bundestrasse 521 in the direction of Bad Vilbel. ✉ *Friedberger Landstr. 531, Seckbach,* ☎ *069/472–707. AE, DC, MC, V. Closed Mon. No lunch, except Sun.*

$$–$$$ ✕ **Arche Nova.** This sunny establishment is a feature of Frankfurt's Ökohaus, which was built according to environmental principles (solar panels, catching rainwater, etc.). In keeping with the character of the place, it's more or less vegetarian with such dishes as a vegetable platter with feta cheese or a curry soup with grated coconut and banana. Much of what's served, even some of the beers, is organic. ✉ *Kasselerstr. 1a, Bockenheim,* ☎ *069/707–5859. No credit cards.*

$–$$ ✕ **Momberger.** This merry spot in the outlying district of Heddernheim is one of the many typical apple wine locales that are not located in Sachsenhausen. It's a picturebook place with apple wine from wooden vats, generous platters of smoked meats, and centuries-old tradition. Portions and prices, too, are a bit reminiscent of the old days. ✉ *Alt Heddernheim 13, Heddernheim,* ☎ *069/576–666. No credit cards. Closed Sat.*

$–$$ ★ ✕ **Wäldches.** This is Frankfurt's busiest brewpub, in a countrified location nevertheless handy to a transit station, and a favorite stop for bikers and hikers. By noon on pleasant summer Sundays, the big beer garden can be standing room only. The home-brewed light and dark beers go nicely with the largely German cuisine, which is substantial but not stodgy. If you like the beer you can take some of it with you in an old-fashioned bottle with a wired porcelain stopper. ✉ *Am Ginnheimer Wäldchen 8, Ginnheim,* ☎ *069/520–522. No credit cards. No lunch Oct.–Mar.*

$–$$ ✕ **Zum Rad.** Named for the huge *Rad* (wagon wheel) that decorates it, this Apfelwein tavern is in the small, villagelike district of Seckbach, off the northeastern edge of the city. Outside tables are shaded by chestnut trees in an extensive courtyard. The typically Hessian cuisine includes such dishes as *Ochsenbrust* (brisket of beef) and Handkäs mit Musik. ✉ *Leonhardsg. 2, Seckbach,* ☎ *069/479–128. No credit cards. Closed Tues., also Mon. during Nov.–Apr.*

$ ✕ **Dr. Flotte.** This smoky tavern is right out of another era, with high ceilings, arched windows, and a collection of early appliances, including radios and sewing machines. It's in the middle of the university district, and students join the 80-year-old ladies quaffing beer. The varied, largely German cuisine is quite affordable. ✉ *Gräfstr. 87, Bockenheim,* ☎ *069/704–595. No credit cards.*

LODGING

Businesspeople descend on Frankfurt year-round, so most hotels in the city are expensive (though many also offer significant reductions on weekends) and are frequently booked up well in advance. Many hotels add as much as a 50% surcharge during trade fairs (*Messen*), of which there are about 30 a year. You can contact the German National Tourist Office for the trade fair schedule. The majority of the larger hotels are close to the main train station, fairgrounds, and business district (*Bankenviertel*) and are a 20-minute walk from the Old Town. Lower prices and—for some, anyway—more atmosphere are found at smaller hotels and pensions in the suburbs; the efficient public transportation network makes them easy to reach.

CATEGORY	COST*
$$$$	over €225
$$$	€150–€225
$$	€75–€150
$	under €75

**All prices are for two people in a double room, including tax and service.*

City Center

$$$$ 🏨 **Hilton Frankfurt.** This respected chain's downtown Frankfurt location has all the perks the business traveler wants, from fax and modem lines to voice mail and video on command. Its Pacific Colors Restaurant has a large terrace overlooking a park. The Vista Bar & Lounge is just below the hotel's airy and transparent atrium. ✉ *Hochstr. 4, City Center, D–60313,* ☎ *069/133–8000,* FAX *069/1338–1338,* WEB *www.frankfurt.hilton.com. 342 rooms. Restaurant, 2 bars, room service, in-room data ports, in-room safes, minibars, cable TV with movies and video games, indoor pool, health club, hair salon, hot tub, massage, sauna, steam room, meeting room, parking (fee), some pets allowed, no-smoking floors. AE, DC, MC, V.*

$$$$ ★ 🏨 **Steigenberger Maxx.** The Maxx may be on a busy, noisy street, but the area is about as lovely as an inner-city location can be. It's right at the point where the Anlage, the long, narrow park that was once the city wall, meets the landscaped bank of the Main River. You can rent a hotel bike and pedal for miles along either. The hotel models itself after a vision of casual Hollywood glamour from the '30s through '50s, tipping its hat to *Casablanca* style in the public areas. It's also air-conditioned, a rarity in Germany. ✉ *Langestr 5–9, City Center, D–60311,*

☎ *069/219–300,* FAX *069/2193–0599,* WEB *www.frankfurt-city.maxx-hotels.de. 150 rooms, 4 suites. Restaurant, bar, room service, in-room data ports, in-room safes, minibars, cable TV with movies, Internet, bicycles, business services, meeting rooms, some pets allowed (fee), no-smoking rooms. AE, DC, MC, V.*

$$$–$$$$ **Hessischer Hof.** This is the choice of many businesspeople, not just because it's near the fairgrounds but also for the air of class that pervades its handsome and imposing interior (the exterior is nondescript). Many of the public room furnishings are antiques owned by the family of the Princes of Hessen. Rooms are today done in either a British or Biedermeyer style. The Sèvres Restaurant, so called for the fine display of that porcelain arranged along the walls, features excellent contemporary cuisine. Jimmy's is one of the cult bars in town. ✉ *Friedrich-Ebert-Anlage 40, Messe, D–60325,* ☎ *069/75400,* FAX *069/7540–2924,* WEB *www.hessischer-hof.de. 106 rooms, 11 suites. Restaurant, bar, room service, in-room data ports, minibar, cable TV, meeting rooms, parking (fee), some pets allowed, no-smoking rooms. AE, DC, MC, V.*

$$$–$$$$ ★ **Steigenberger Hotel Frankfurter Hof.** The Victorian Frankfurter Hof is one of the city's oldest hotels but its modern services earn it kudos from business publications around the world. The atmosphere throughout is one of old-fashioned, formal elegance, with burnished woods, fresh flowers, and thick-carpeted hush. Kaiser Wilhelm once slept here and so have modern heads of state. Although it fronts on a courtyard you must enter it through a modest side entrance. ✉ *Am Kaiserpl., City Center, D-60311,* ☎ *069/21502,* FAX *069/215–900,* WEB *www.frankfurter-hof.steigenberger.com. 286 rooms, 46 suites. 3 restaurants, bar, room service, in-room data ports, minibars, cable TV with movies, Internet, sauna, concierge, meeting rooms, parking (fee), some pets allowed (fee). AE, DC, MC, V.*

$$ **Hotel Nizza.** This beautiful Victorian building is furnished with antiques, and the proprietor added a modern touch in three bathrooms with her own artistic murals. There is a pleasant roof garden with lots of potted shrubbery where you can have breakfast with views of rooftops and the skyline. ✉ *Elbestr. 10, City Center, D–60329,* ☎ *069/242–5380,* FAX *069/2425–3830. 24 rooms, 21 with bath or shower. Bar, no a/c, in-room data ports, cable TV, some pets allowed. MC, V.*

$$ ★ **InterCityHotel.** InterCity hotels were set up by the Steigenberger chain with the business traveler in mind, and if there ever was a hotel at the vortex of arrivals and departures, it's this centrally located hostelry in an elegant old-world building. It's right across the street from the main train station, and guests get a pass good for unlimited travel on the local public transportation. The station's underground garage is also at your disposal. ✉ *Poststr. 8, Bahnhof, D–60329,* ☎ *069/273–910,* FAX *069/2739–1999,* WEB *www.intercityhotel.at/. 384 rooms, 3 suites. Restaurant, bar, no a/c, in-room data ports, minibars, cable TV with movies, business services, meeting rooms, some pets allowed (fee), no-smoking floor. AE, DC, MC, V.*

$$ **Terminus.** Across the street from the main train station, this modern, sparkling clean hotel has its own underground garage. It somehow also manages to keep a quiet summer garden despite its location. The rooms are some of the least expensive in town, but include a bath, TV, and phone. ✉ *Münchener Str. 59, City Center, D–60329,* ☎ *069/242–320,* FAX *069/237–411. 107 rooms. Restaurant, bar, no a/c, in-room data ports, cable TV with movies, meeting rooms, some pets allowed, parking (fee). AE, DC, MC, V.*

$–$$ **Pension Aller.** Quiet, solid comforts for a modest price and a friendly welcome are right near the train station. The third floor of a sociologist's private home offers cozy, well-lighted rooms in the back of the building. Reserve in advance because it gets a lot of return guests. ✉ *Gutleutstr. 94, City Center, D–60329,* ☎ *069/252–596,* FAX *069/232–330. 10 rooms with shower. No a/c, no phones in some rooms, no TV in some rooms, meeting room, some pets allowed. No credit cards.*

Westend

$$–$$$$ **An der Messe.** This little place a couple of blocks from the fairgrounds provides a pleasant alternative to the giant hotels of the city. It's stylish, with a pink marble lobby and chicly appointed bedrooms. The staff is courteously efficient. The only drawback is the lack of a restaurant. ✉ *Westendstr. 104, Messe, D–60325,* ☎ *069/747–979,* FAX *069/748–349. 46 rooms, 2 suites. No a/c, in-room data ports, cable TV, some pets allowed (fee). AE, DC, MC, V.*

$$$ ★ **Palmenhof.** Near the botanical garden, this luxuriously modern hotel occupies a renovated art nouveau building. The high-ceiling rooms have up-to-date comfort but retain the elegance of the old building. In the basement is a cozy restaurant, L'Artechoc, with a Mediterranean menu. ✉ *Bockenheimer Landstr. 89–91, Westend, D–60325,* ☎ *069/753–0060,* FAX *069/7530–0666. 46 rooms, 37 apartments, 2 suites. Restaurant, no a/c, in-room data ports, some microwaves, cable TV with movies, some pets allowed. AE, DC, MC, V.*

$$–$$$ **Hotel Westend.** "*Klein aber fein*" ("small but nice") is what Germans say about a place like this. Everywhere you turn in the stylish, family-run establishment, you'll trip over antiques. The hotel itself has no restaurant, but the classy neighborhood has plenty. ✉ *Westendstr. 15, Westend, D–60325,* ☎ *069/7898–8180,* FAX *069/745–396. 20 rooms, 15 with bath or shower. No a/c, in-room data ports, cable TV, meeting rooms, some pets allowed. AE, DC, MC, V.*

Sachsenhausen

$–$$ **Maingau.** You'll find this pleasant hotel-restaurant in the middle of the lively Sachsenhausen quarter. Rooms are modest but spotless, comfortable, and equipped with TVs; the room rate includes a substantial breakfast buffet. Chef Werner Döpfner has made the restaurant, Maingau-Stuben, one of Frankfurt's best. (Caution: though the hotel is inexpensive, the restaurant is anything but!) ✉ *Schifferstr. 38–40, Sachsenhausen, D–60594,* ☎ *069/609–140,* FAX *069/620–790. 100 rooms. Restaurant, room service, no a/c, in-room data ports, minibars, cable TV with video games, meeting rooms, some pets allowed. AE, MC, V.*

Outer Frankfurt

$$$–$$$$ **Dorint Hotel.** The Frankfurt member of the Dorint chain is a modern, well-appointed hotel with all the comforts and facilities expected from this well-run group, including an indoor pool. The hotel is south of the river in the Niederrad district, but there are good bus and subway connections with the city center and Sachsenhausen. ✉ *Hahnstr. 9, Niederrad, D–60528,* ☎ *069/663–060,* FAX *069/6630–6600,* WEB *www.dorint.de/frankfurt. 191 rooms, 8 suites. 2 restaurants, bar, no a/c in some rooms, in-room data ports, cable TV with movies, indoor pool, sauna, meeting rooms, parking (fee), no-smoking rooms. AE, DC, MC, V.*

$$$–$$$$ **Sheraton Frankfurt.** This huge hotel is immediately accessible to one of Frankfurt Airport's terminals. It, like the airport, is also adjacent to the Frankfurter Kreuz, the major autobahn intersection, with superhighway connections to all of Europe. No need to worry about noise though—the rooms are all soundproof. In addition to the usual comforts, each room is equipped with an answering machine and a modem. Forty-four of the rooms have ISDN connections that permit a fax machine, printer, and copier. ✉ *Hugo-Eckener-Ring 15, Flughafen Terminal 1, Airport, D–60549,* ☎ *069/69770,* FAX *069/6977–2209,* WEB *www.sheraton.com/frankfurt. 1,006 rooms, 28 suites. 2 restaurants, 2 bars, in-room data ports, minibars, cable TV with movies, gym, massage, sauna, steam room, concierge, meeting rooms, parking (fee), some pets allowed, no-smoking rooms. AE, DC, MC, V.*

$$ ★ **Art Hotel Robert Mayer.** For creative types who shun the sterile decor of hotel chains, this elegant villa dating from 1905 offers an alternative: 11 rooms, each decorated by a different Frankfurt artist, with furniture designs by the likes of Rietveld and Frank Lloyd Wright. The room designed by Therese Traube contrasts abstract newspaper collage with a replica Louis XIV armchair. The art tradition is stressed in a special weekend arrangement that includes an individual guided tour of an art museum. It has no restaurant, but a large breakfast buffet is included in the price of the room. ✉ *Robert-Mayer-Str. 44, Bockenheim, D–60486,* ☎ *069/970–9100,* FAX *069/9709–1010,* WEB *www. art–hotel–robert–mayer.de. 11 rooms, 1 suite. No a/c, in-room data ports, cable TV, some pets allowed (fee). AE, DC, MC, V.*

$$ **Hotel-Pension West.** For home comforts, a handy location (near the university and U-bahn), and good value, try this family-run pension. It's in an older building and scores high for old-fashioned appeal. The rooms are more than adequate for a night or two. ✉ *Gräfstr. 81, Bockenheim, D–60486,* ☎ *069/247–9020,* FAX *069/707–5309. 15 rooms. No a/c, in-room data ports, cable TV with movies and video games, meeting rooms, some pets allowed. AE, DC, MC, V.*

$ **Pension Stella.** This little hostelry is located in one of the most pleasant old neighborhoods in town, an area of villas between a park with a water castle and the studios of Hessischer Rundfunk. The five rooms, each with bath or shower, are comfortable and the price is right. ✉ *Frauensteinstr. 8, Nordend, D–60322,* ☎ FAX *069/554–026. 5 rooms. No a/c, no room phones, cable TV, parking (free), no-smoking rooms. No credit cards.*

$ **Waldhotel Hensels Felsenkeller.** It's a considerable walk from public transportation, especially if you're carrying luggage, but it's clean, very inexpensive, and in a beautiful location right on the edge of the city forest. Rooms are basic; the less expensive ones have shared showers. The nearest stop is Buchrainstrasse on tram lines 15 and 16. ✉ *Buchrainstr. 95, Oberrad, D–60599,* ☎ *069/652–086,* FAX *069/658–379. 16 rooms, 7 with bath. Restaurant, no a/c, no room phones, cable TV, some pets allowed. MC, V.*

NIGHTLIFE AND THE ARTS

The Arts

Frankfurt has the largest budget for cultural affairs of any city in the country. The Städtische Bühnen—municipal theaters, including the city's opera company—are the prime venues. Frankfurt has what is probably the most lavish theater in the country, the Alte Oper, a magnificently ornate 19th-century opera house. The building is no longer used for opera, but as a multipurpose hall for pop and classical concerts and dances.

Theater tickets can be purchased from the tourist office at Römerberg 27 and from theater box offices. **Frankfurt Ticket GmbH** (✉ Hauptwache Passage, City Center, ☎ 069/134–0400) is one of the best ticket agencies. **Best Tickets GmbH** (✉ Zeil 112–114, City Center, ☎ 069/9139–

7621) is right downtown in the Zeilgalerie. The **Karstadt department store** (✉ Zeil 90, City Center, ☎ 069/294–848) doubles as a ticket office.

Ballet, Concerts, and Opera

Telephone ticket sales for the Alte Oper, Frankfurt Opera, and Frankfurt Ballet all are handled through **Frankfurt Ticket** (☎ 069/134–0400). The most glamorous venue for classical music concerts is the **Alte Oper** (✉ Opernpl., City Center); tickets to performances can range from €10 to nearly €150. The **Frankfurt Opera** (✉ Städtische Bühnen, Untermainanlage 11, City Center) has made a name for itself as a company for dramatic artistry. Sharing the same venue as the Frankfurt Opera, the world-renowned **Frankfurt Ballet** (✉ Städtische Bühnen, Untermainanlage 11, City Center) is under the modern-thinking direction of American William Forsythe.

The **Festhalle** (✉ Ludwig-Erhard-Anlage 1, Messe, ☎ 069/7575–6404), on the fairgrounds, is the scene of many rock concerts, horse shows, ice shows, sporting events, and other large-scale spectaculars.

The city is also the home of the Radio-Sinfonie-Orchester Frankfurt, part of Hessischer Rundfunk. It performs regularly in the 850-seat **Kammermusiksaal** (✉ Bertramstr. 8, Dornbusch, ☎ 069/550–123), part of that broadcasting operation's campuslike facilities.

Theater

Theatrical productions in Frankfurt are nearly always in German, and in the case of the alternative Die Schmiere, in a German dialect. For English-language productions, try the **English Theater** (✉ Kaiserstr. 52, City Center, ☎ 069/2423–1620), which offers an array of musicals, thrillers, dramas, and comedy with British or American casts. The **Künstlerhaus Mouson Turm** (✉ Waldschmidtstr. 4, Nordend, ☎ 069/4058–9520) is a cultural center that hosts a regular series of concerts of all kinds, as well as plays and exhibits. The municipally owned **Schauspielhaus** (✉ Willy-Brandt-Pl., City Center, ☎ 069/134–0400) has a repertoire including works by Sophocles, Goethe, Shakespeare, Brecht, and Beckett. For a zany theatrical experience, try **Die Schmiere** (✉ Seckbächerg. 2, City Center, ☎ 069/281–066), which offers trenchant satire and also disarmingly calls itself "the worst theater in the world." Renowned for international experimental productions, including dance theater and other forms of nonverbal drama, is **Theater am Turm** (TAT; ✉ Bockenheimer Warte, Bockenheim, ☎ 069/134–0400), in the Bockenheimer Depot, a former trolley barn.

Nightlife

Frankfurt at night is a city of stark contrasts. Old hippies and baby-faced counterculturalists, Turkish and Greek guest workers, people on pensions, chess players, exhibitionists, and loners all have their piece of the action. People from the banking world seek different amusements than the city's 38,000 students, but their paths cross in such places as the cider taverns in Sachsenhausen and the gay bars of the Nordend. Sachsenhausen (Frankfurt's "Left Bank") is a good place to start for bars, clubs, and Apfelwein taverns. The ever-more-fashionable Nordend has an almost equal number of bars and clubs but fewer tourists. Frankfurt is one of Europe's leading cities for Techno, the computer-generated music of ultrafast beats that's the anthem of German youth culture. Most bars close between 2 AM and 4 AM.

Bars and Live Music Venues

A major trend in the night spots is the "After Work" or "After Hours" happy hour with half-price drinks, lasting usually from 5 or 6 PM to 9 or 10 PM one weekday per week. You can go to Jimmy's every week night, the Opium on Tuesday, Monza and the Studio Bar on Wednesday, and the Galerie on Thursday.

Wagons and pushcarts decorate the cellar Irish pub **An Sibin** (✉ Wallstr. 9, Sachsenhausen, ☎ 069/603–2159), presumably to remind you of the Emerald Isle's folksy character. Serious elbow lifting and heartfelt conversations take place in English, Gaelic, Hessian dialect, and German. There is live music most nights along with Guinness right out of the keg and some good pub grub.

The tiny, cozy **Balalaika** (✉ Dreikönigstr. 30, Sachsenhausen ☎ 069/612–226) provides intimacy and live music without charging the high prices you'd expect at such a place. The secret is proprietress Anita Honis, a professional American singer from Harlem, who usually gets out her acoustic guitar several times during an evening.

If you're seeking something soothing, sit down at **Casablanca Bar** (✉ Parkhotel, Wiesenhüttenpl. 28, City Center, ☎ 069/26970) and listen to the tinkling of the ivories. For a strong elixir, ask the bartender to shake up a Mai Tai or their prizewinning "Challenger."

Like much of the Marriott Hotel it's in, the **Champion's Bar** (✉ Hamburger Allee 2-10, Messe, ☎ 069/7955–2540) is designed to make Americans feel at home. The wall is lined with jerseys, and autographed helmets and photographs of American athletes. The TV is tuned to baseball, football, and basketball broadcasts, and the food leans to buffalo wings, potato skins, and hamburgers. Parties take place on American holidays like Halloween, Thanksgiving, and Valentine's Day.

Cooky's (✉ Am Salzhaus 4, City Center, ☎ 069/287–662) is open into the wee hours and is one of the most popular local haunts for rock music; live bands perform on Monday night. You can also dance and have a meal.

Frankfurt teems with Irish pubs, but **Fox and Hound** (✉ Niedenau 2, Westend, ☎ 069/9720–2009) is the only *English* pub in town. The patrons, mainly British, come to watch constant satellite transmissions of the latest football (soccer to Americans), rugby, and cricket matches, to enjoy the authentic pub grub (try the basket of chips), and to participate in the Sunday-night quiz for free drinks and cash prizes. It's a noisy bunch.

Jimmy's Bar (✉ Friedrich-Ebert-Anlage 40, Messe, ☎ 069/7540–2961) is classy and expensive—like the Hessischer Hof Hotel in which it's located. It's been the meeting place of the business elite since 1951, and what every other bar in town would like to be. The ladies are more chic, the gentlemen more charming, the pianist, who plays from 10 PM onward, more winning. The bar stools and lounge chairs are of red leather, the bar of mahogany. There is hot food from the hotel kitchen 'til 3 AM. You must ring the doorbell to get in, although regulars have a key.

The **Luna Bar** (✉ Stiftstr. 6, City Center, ☎ 069/294–774) is a cocktail-lovers paradise, with good drinks at reasonable prices by Frankfurt standards. Dress is smart but casual, and there is live music twice a month.

Dance and Nightclubs

The Brotfabrik (✉ Bachmannstr. 2-4, Hausen, ☎ 069/9784–5512), a former industrial bakery, is in a desolate part of town, but all is lively inside. Most of the live dance music has a Latin beat; there's salsa every

Wednesday. Its impressive main hall is the venue for live jazz concerts and an extensive program of ethnic music from all the world.

Beneath the heating pipes of a former brewery, **King Kamehameha** (✉ Hanauer Landstr. 192, Ostend, ☎ 069/4800–3701) is designed to suit every type of night owl. You can relax in the quiet cocktail bar, dance to a house band, or see one of the many live concerts, cabarets, comedy acts, or fashion shows that take place on stage. It's closed Monday.

Trendy **Living XXL** (✉ Kaiserstr. 29, City Center, ☎ 069/242–9370) is one of the biggest bar-restaurants in Germany and is as hyped as the Eurotower in which it's located, the headquarters of the newly established European Central Bank. On Friday and Saturday it offers a "subdued" disco, geared to the easy-listening preferences of the banking community, but it's not so prudish as to exclude regular gay entertainment. Its spacious, terraced interior has drawn architectural praise.

There's not much that doesn't take place at the **Tigerpalast** (✉ Heiligkreuzg. 16–20, City Center, ☎ 069/9200–2250). The best variety shows and circus performances entertain guests, who dine elegantly and get some dancing in themselves. Shows often sell out, so book tickets as far in advance as possible. It's closed Monday.

Jazz

The oldest jazz cellar in Germany, **Der Frankfurter Jazzkeller** (✉ Kleine Bockenheimer Str. 18a, City Center, ☎ 069/288–537) was founded by legendary trumpeter Carlo Bohländer, and has hosted the likes of Louis Armstrong. It offers hot, modern jazz, often free (otherwise the cover is around €20). It's closed Monday.

Anything can happen at **Dreikönigskeller** (✉ Färberstr. 71, Sachsenhausen, ☎ 069/629–273): you might hear 1940s or '50s jazz, blues, funk, rock-wave, or indie-punk. It's patronized mostly by students, as well as a sprinkling of older, hip people, all smoking as voraciously as the musicians.

Sinkkasten (✉ Brönnerstr. 5–9, City Center, ☎ 069/280–385), a Frankfurt musical institution, is a class act—a great place for jazz, rock, pop, and African music, often by unknown or hardly-known groups. It's sometimes hard to get in but worth the effort. There's live music Monday through Wednesday and Saturday.

Wine Cellars

Popular with crowds before and after performances at the nearby Old Opera, **Vinum** (✉ Kleine Hochstr. 9, City Center, ☎ 069/293–037) is in an arched cellar lined with wine kegs. The food, unlike the wine, is overpriced.

OUTDOOR ACTIVITIES AND SPORTS

Despite the ever-present smog in summer, Frankfurt is full of parks and other green oases where you can breathe easier. South of the city, the huge, 4,000-acre **Stadtwald** makes Frankfurt one of Germany's most forested metropolises. The forest has innumerable paths and trails, bird sanctuaries, impressive sports stadiums, and a number of good restaurants. The Waldlehrpfad trail there leads past a series of rare trees, each identified by a small sign. The Oberschweinstiege stop on streetcar Line 14 is right in the middle of the park. Alternately, you can take Bus 36 from Konstablerwache to Hainerweg.

The **Taunus Hills** are also a great getaway for Frankfurters, and public transportation gets you there without hassle. Take U-bahn 3 to Hohemark. In the Seckbach district, northeast of the city, Frankfurters hike the 590-ft **Lohrberg Hill.** The climb yields a fabulous view of the town and the Taunus, Spessart, and Odenwald hills. Along the way you'll also see the last remaining vineyard within the Frankfurt city limits, the Seckbach Vineyard. Take the U-4 subway to Seckbacher Landstrasse, then Bus 43 to Draisbornstrasse.

Biking

Even within the city limits there are inviting places for recreational biking. The big Stadtwald in the southern part of the city is criss-crossed with well-tended paths that are nice and flat. The river banks are, for the most part, lined with paths bikers can use. There are not only both sides of the Main, but also the banks of the little Nidda River, which flows through Heddernheim, Eschersheim, Hausen, and Rödelheim before joining the Main at Höchst. Some bikers also like the Taunus Hills but note that word "hills."

Theo Intra's shop (✉ Westerbachstr. 273, Sossenheim, ☎ 069/342–780) has a large selection of bikes, from tandems to racing models. It's located on the city's northern edge, convenient to the inviting trails of the Taunus. Take the U–6 or U–7 to Bockenheimer Warte, then Bus 50 to Carl-Sonnenschein-Strasse. Also on the edge of the city is **Fahrradverlieh Werkstatt** (✉ Am Burghof 55, Bonames, ☎ 069/9504–1716), reachable by taking the U–2 suburban train from the Hauptwache to Kalbach. Bike rentals will cost you €6 to €9 per day.

Fitness Centers

Near the central Hauptwache, the **Fitness Company** (✉ Zeil 109, City Center, ☎ 069/9637–3100) has everything anyone needs to work out. There are more than 60 aerobics and other classes and 150 different fitness machines, from Nautilus to StairMaster. English is spoken. A day's training costs €18. **CityFitness** (✉ Trakehnerstr. 5, Hausen, ☎ 069/703–788) has an extensive program of bodybuilding, aerobics, and stretching, mainly after hours and on weekends. An hour's course costs €10.

Golf

There's an 18-hole course in the city, **Frankfurter Golfclub** (✉ Golfstr. 41, Niederrad, ☎ 069/666–2317).

Jogging

The banks of the Main River are a good place to jog, and to avoid retracing your steps, you can always cross a bridge and return down the opposite side. In the Westend, **Grüneberg Park** is 2 km (1 mi) around, with a *Trimm Dich* (get fit) exercise facility in the northeast corner. The **Anlagenring,** a park following the line of the old city walls around the city, is also a popular route. For a vigorous forest run, go to the Stadtwald or the Taunus Hills.

Swimming

Incredible as it may seem, people used to swim along the banks of the Main. Pictures from the 1930s show happy crowds splashing in a roped-off area. That day is long gone (you'd probably dissolve), but there are a number of indoor and outdoor pools. The often-crowded **Brentanobad** (✉ Rödelheimer Parkweg, Rödelheim, ☎ 069/2123–9020) is an outdoor pool surrounded by lawns and old trees. The **Rebstockbad** (✉ August-Euler-Str. 7, Rebstock, ☎ 069/708–078) leisure center has an indoor pool, a pool with a wave machine and palm-fringed beach, and an outdoor pool with giant water chutes. The **Stadionbad** (✉ Morfelder Landstr. 362, Niederrad, ☎ 069/678–041) has an outdoor pool, a giant water chute, and exercise lawns. For everything from "adventure pools" and bowling to a sauna and fitness center, head to the **Titus Therme** (✉ Walter-Möller-Pl. 2, Nordweststadt, ☎ 069/958–050) pool complex.

Tennis

Europa Tennis & Squash Park (✉ Ginheimer Landstr. 49, Ginnheim, ☎ 069/532–040) has three indoor and five outdoor courts. **Tennishalle Nordwest** (✉ Oberschelderweg 8, Heddernheim, ☎ 069/572–077) has three indoor courts and one outdoor. Book in advance.

SHOPPING

Shopping Districts

The tree-shaded pedestrian zone of the **Zeil** is claimed to be the richest shop-'til-you-drop mile in Germany. Other cities ask where Frankfurt gets the figures to prove the boast, but there is no doubt that the Zeil, between Hauptwache and Konstablerwache, is incredible for its variety of department and specialty stores. The Zeil is only the centerpiece of the downtown shopping area. The subway station below the Hauptwache also doubles as a vast underground mall. West of the Hauptwache are two parallel streets highly regarded by shoppers. One is the luxurious **Goethestrasse,** lined with boutiques, art galleries, jewelry stores, and antiques shops. The other is **Grosse Bockenheimer Strasse,** better known as the Fressgasse ("Pig Out Alley"). Cafés, restaurants, a shopping arcade, and, especially, pricey food stores line the street, tempting gourmands with everything from crumbly cheeses and smoked fish to vintage wines and chocolate creams. Heading southward toward the cathedral and the river you'll find an area of art and antiques shops on **Braubachstrasse, Fahrgasse,** and **Weckmarkt.**

The Zeil area abounds in arcades. The moderately priced **Zeilgallerie** (✉ Zeil 112–114, City Center, ☎ 069/9207–3414) has 56 shops and an IMAX theater. The **Schillerpassage** (✉ Rahmhofstr. 2, City Center) is strong on men's and women's fashion boutiques.

Clothing Stores

All of the top women's labels are represented in Inge Winterberg's collection at **Class-X** (✉ Börsenstr. 7-11, City Center, ☎ 069/131–0853). There are bags from Coccinelle, shoes from Free Lance, Jewelry from Rio Berlin. Tailors can provide an item in another color or fabric if the lady likes, but the styles can't be altered.

Peek & Cloppenburg (✉ Zeil 71–75, City Center, ☎ 069/298–950) is a huge, nicely departmentalized clothing store where men and women can find what they need for the office, gym, and nightclub. Clothes range from easily affordable items to pricy labels.

Pfüller Modehaus (✉ Goethestr. 15–17, City Center, ☎ 069/1337–8070) offers a wide range of choices on three floors for women, from classic to trendy, from lingerie to overcoats, from hats to stockings. Gavinci and Hugo Boss are just a few of the many labels sold.

Prenatal (✉ An der Hauptwache 7, City Center, ☎ 069/288–001) sells a comprehensive collection of baby and maternity clothes.

Department Stores

There are two department stores on the Zeil, offering much in the way of clothing, furnishings, electronics, food and other items. The **Galerie Kaufhof** (✉ Zeil 116–126, City Center, ☎ 060/21910) has an array of up-to-date retailing practices including touch screens that describe products. (One tells you what wines at what temperature go with what food.) The Dinea Restaurant on the top floor has a striking view. The Hertie department store, having been acquired by another chain, has changed its name to **Karstadt** (✉ Zeil 90, City Center, ☎ 069/929–050). It's otherwise the same old store, the equal of Galerie Kaufhof in variety, with the best gourmet food department in town.

Flea Markets

Sachsenhausen's weekend flea market takes place on Saturday from 8 to 2 on the river bank, between **Dürerstrasse** and the **Eiserner Steg.** Purveyors of the cheap have taken over. Get there early for the bargains as the better-quality stuff gets snapped up quickly. Shopping success or no, the market can be fun for browsing.

Gift Ideas

Cold, hard cash is what springs to mind when in the financial capital of Germany, not souvenirs. Frankfurt does produce fine porcelain, though, and it can be bought at the **Höchster Porzellan Manufaktur,** in the suburb of Höchst.

One thing typical of Frankfurt is the Äpfelwein (hard cider). You can get a bottle of it at any grocery store, but more enduring souvenirs would be Bembel pitchers and glasses that are equally a part of the Apfelwein tradition. The blue-stoneware Bembels have a fat belly, and the glasses, usually with a crest, are ribbed to give them "traction" (in the old days this was good for preventing the glass from slipping from greasy hands). You can get the Bembels and glasses at just about any gift shop, but **Frankfurter Dippemarkt** (✉ Fahrg. 80, Altstadt, ☎ 069/282–559) has a selection that will overwhelm you.

A famous children's book in Germany, *Struwwelpeter* (Slovenly Peter), was the work of a Frankfurt doctor, Heinrich Hoffmann. He wrote the poems and drew the rather amateurish pictures in 1844 just to warn his own children of the dire consequences of being naughty. He did not originally intend to publish the book, but the reaction of his children and his friends convinced him he had a gem on his hands. The book has several English translations; one by Mark Twain no less! The **Struwwelpeter-Museum** (✉ Benderg. 1, Altstadt, ☎ 069/281–333) has copies of some of them, including one with the German version on one page and the Mark Twain version facing. The museum's gift shop also has coffee cups and playing cards with Struwwelpeter illustrations.

An edible gift you can take home is the Frankfurter sausage, which gave America one of its favorite snacks. The hot dog, on a long roll, made its first appearance at Chicago's World's Columbian Exhibition in 1893, and this sausage, sent over in cans from Frankfurt, was the basic ingredient. It's still available in cans. Try **Plöger** (✉ Grosse Bockenheimer Str. 30, City Center, ☎ 069/138–7110) on the Fressgasse. One taste of this high-quality smoked sausage will convince you that American imitations resemble the true frankfurter only in size and shape.

Food and Drink

The pastry shop **Konditorei Lochner** (✉ Kalbächerg. 10, City Center, ☎ 069/920–7320) has local delicacies such as *Bethmännchen und Brenten* (marzipan cookies) or *Frankfurter Kranz* (a kind of creamy cake). All types of sweets and pastries are found at the café **Laumer** (✉ Bockenheimer Landstr. 67, Westend, ☎ 069/727–912).

Weinhandlung Dr. Teufel (✉ Kleiner Hirschgraben 4, City Center, ☎ 069/283–236) is as good a place as any for the popular wines, and the best place in town for diversity. There's also a complete line of glasses, carafes, corkscrews and other accessories, and books on all aspects of viticulture.

Home Furnishings

Drapes and bed linen, antique-looking wardrobes, and Japanese-style paper lanterns are part of the selection at **Cri-Cri** (✉ Rossmarkt 13, ☎ 069/131–0606), with three floors dedicated to furniture and the decorative arts. There's also a selection of teas, coffees, and Italian wines, replete with samples.

SIDE TRIPS FROM FRANKFURT

Frankfurt is so centrally located in Germany that the list of possible excursions—day trips and longer treks—is nearly endless. It's the ideal starting point for journeys to the Rhineland, to the west; Heidelberg and the Neckar Valley, to the south; and Würzburg and Franconia, to the southeast.

Destinations reachable by the local transportation system include Höchst, Neu-Isenburg, and the Taunus Hills, which includes Bad Homburg and Kronberg. Just to the northwest and west of Frankfurt, the Taunus Hills is an area of mixed pine and hardwood forest, medieval castles, and photogenic towns that many Frankfurters regard as their own backyard. It's home to Frankfurt's wealthy bankers and businesspeople, and on weekends you can see them enjoying their playground: hiking through the hills, climbing the Grosse Feldberg, taking the waters at Bad Homburg's health-enhancing mineral springs, or just lazing in elegant stretches of parkland.

Bad Homburg

The Taunus Hills area has many royal associations. Emperor Wilhelm II, the infamous "kaiser" of World War I, spent a month each year at Bad Homburg, the area's principal city. And it was the kaiser's mother, the daughter of Britain's Queen Victoria, who built the magnificent palace, now a luxurious hotel, in the Taunus town of Kronberg. Another frequent visitor to Bad Homburg was Britain's Prince of Wales, later King Edward VII, who made the name *Homburg* world famous by attaching it to a hat.

Bad Homburg's greatest attraction has been the **Kurpark** (spa), in the heart of the Old Town, with more than 31 fountains. Romans first used the springs, which were rediscovered and made famous in the 19th century. In the park you'll find not only the popular, highly saline Elisabethenbrunnen Spring but also a Siamese temple and a Russian chapel, mementos left by more royal guests—King Chulalongkorn of Siam and Czar Nicholas II. The Kurpark is a good place to begin a walking tour of the town; Bad Homburg's **tourist office** (✉ Louisenstr. 58, ☎ 06172/1780) is in the nearby Kurhaus. ✉ *Between Paul-Ehrlich-Weg and Kaiser-Friedrich-Promenade.*

Adjacent to the Kurpark, the **casino** boasts with some justice that it is the "Mother of Monte Carlo." The first casino in Bad Homburg, one of the first in the world, was established in 1841, but closed down in 1866 because Prussian law forbade gambling. The proprietor, François Blanc, then moved his operation to the French Riviera and the Bad Homburg casino wasn't reopened until 1949. A bus runs between the casino and Frankfurt's Hauptbahnhof (south side). It leaves Frankfurt every hour on the hour between 2 PM and 10 PM and then hourly from 10:25 PM to 1:25 AM. Buses back to Frankfurt run every hour on the hour, from 4 PM to the casino's closing. The €6 fare will be refunded after the casino's full entry fee has been deducted. ✉ *Im Kurpark,* ☎ *06172/17010.* 🎫 *€2.50 for the full gaming area, €1 for the slot machines only.* ⏲ *Slot machines, 2 PM–1:30 AM, remainder 3 PM–3 AM.*

The most historically noteworthy sight in Bad Homburg is the 17th-century **Schloss,** where the kaiser stayed when he was in residence. The 172-ft Weisser Turm (White Tower) is all that remains of the medieval castle that once stood here. The Schloss was built between 1680 and 1685 by Friedrich II of Hesse-Homburg, and a few alterations were made during the 19th century. The state apartments are exquisitely furnished, and the Spiegelkabinett (Hall of Mirrors) is especially worthy of a visit. In the surrounding park look for two venerable cedars from Lebanon, both now about 200 years old. ✉ *Herrng.*, ☎ *06172/926–2147.* 🎫 *€3.50.* ⏲ *Mar.–Oct., Tues.–Sun. 10–5; Nov.–Feb., Tues.–Sun. 10–4.*

The **Hutmuseum** (Hat Museum), a part of the Museum im Gotisches Haus, is a shrine to headgear. Its collection includes everything from 18th-century three-corner hats to silk toppers, from simple bonnets to the massive, feathered creation of 19th-century milliners. But mainly it's a shrine to the distinguished hat that was developed in Bad Homburg and bears its name. The Homburg hat was made around the turn of the 20th century for Britain's Prince of Wales, later King Edward VII, a frequent visitor. He liked the shape of the Tyrolean hunting hat, but found its green color and decorative feather a bit undignified. So, for him, the Homburg hatters removed the feather, turned the felt gray, and established a fashion item once worn by diplomats, state dignitaries, and other distinguished gentlemen worldwide. ✉ *Tannenwaldweg 102,* ☎ *06172/37618.* ⏲ *Tues. and Thurs.–Sat. 2–5, Wed. 2–7, Sun. noon–6.*

Just a short, convenient bus ride from Bad Homburg is the highest mountain in the Taunus, the 2,850-ft, eminently hikeable **Grosse Feldberg.**

Only 6½ km (4 mi) from Bad Homburg, and accessible by direct bus service, is the **Römerkastell-Saalburg** (Saalburg Roman Fort). Built in AD 120, the fort could accommodate a cohort (500 men) and was part of the fortifications along the Limes Wall, which ran from the Danube River to the Rhine River and was meant to protect the Roman Empire from barbarian invasion. On the initiative of Kaiser Wilhelm II the fort was rebuilt as the Romans originally left it—with wells, armories, parade grounds, and catapults, as well as shops, houses, baths, and temples. All of these are for viewing only. You can't take a bath or buy a souvenir in the shops, though there is a contemporary restaurant on the grounds. There is also a **museum** with Roman exhibits. The Saalburg is north of Bad Homburg on Route 456 in the direction of Usingen. ✉ *Saalburg-Kastell,* ☎ *06175/93740.* 🎫 *€2.50.* ⏲ *Fort and museum Mar.–Oct., daily 9–6; Nov.–Feb., daily 9–4.*

About a 45-minute walk through the woods along a well-marked path from the Römerkastell-Saalburg is an open-air museum at **Hessenpark,** near Neu Anspach. The museum presents a clear picture of the world in which 18th- and 19th-century Hessians lived, using 135 acres of rebuilt villages with houses, schools, and farms typical of the time. The park, 15 km (9 mi) outside Bad Homburg in the direction of Usingen, can also be reached by public transportation. Take the Taunusbahn from the Frankfurt main station to Wehrheim, then transfer to Bus 514. ✉ *Laubweg, Neu-Anspach,* ☎ *06081/5880.* 🎫 *€4.* ⏲ *Mar.–Apr. and Sept.–Oct., daily 9–6; May–Aug., daily 9–8.*

Dining and Lodging

Although most of the well-known spas in Bad Homburg have expensive restaurants, there are still enough affordable places to eat.

$$$$ ✕ **Sänger's Restaurant.** You get a quintessential spa experience here: fine dining at high prices. But service is friendly, and their specialties, calf's head–lobster salad or stuffed oxtail, may make you forget the bill. ✉ *Kaiser-Friedrich-Promenade 85,* ☎ *06172/928–839. AE, MC, V. Closed Sun. No lunch.*

$–$$$$ ★ ✕ **Zum Wasserweibchen.** Chef Inge Kuper is a local culinary legend. Although prices are high for some items on the menu, the portions are large. The clientele sometimes includes celebrities, and the service is friendly and unpretentious. You can't go wrong with the potato cakes with salmon mousse, the brisket of beef, or any of the desserts. ✉ *Am Mühlberg 57,* ☎ *06172/29878. AE, MC, V. Closed Sat.*

$–$$ ✕ **Kartoffelküche.** This simple restaurant serves traditional dishes accompanied by potatoes cooked every way imaginable. The potato and broccoli gratin and the potato pizza are excellent, and for dessert try potato strudel with vanilla sauce. ✉ *Audenstr. 4,* ☎ *06172/21500. AE, DC, MC, V.*

$$$ ✕🏨 **Maritim Kurhaus Hotel.** Standing in a quiet location on the edge of the spa park but near the city center, the hotel offers large, richly furnished rooms with king-size beds and deep armchairs. Some rooms have balconies. The cozy Bürgerstube ($$) serves both solid German cuisine and international dishes. For late-night gamblers and those with early planes to catch, the hotel offers "early bird breakfasts" from 11 PM to 6:30 AM. ✉ *Ludwigstr. 3 D–61348,* ☎ *06172/6600,* FAX *06172/660–100,* WEB *www.maritim.de. 148 rooms, 10 suites. Restaurant, café, bar, no a/c, in-room data ports, cable TV with movies, meeting rooms, some pets allowed (fee), no-smoking rooms. AE, DC, MC, V.*

$$$ ★ 🏨 **Steigenberger Bad Homburg.** Renown for catering to Europe's royalty in its pre–World War I heyday, this hotel began as the Ritters Parkhotel in 1883 after Conrad Ritter combined a row of villas opposite Kurpark. Though the Steigenberger group has since dropped the historic and prominent name, it knows perfectly well how to cater to the still well-heeled clientele. Rooms are furnished in art deco style and Charley's Bistro evokes the spirit of Gay Paree with literary dinners and jazz brunches. The nearby park is ideal for jogging. ✉ *Kaiser-Friedrich-Promenade 69–75, D–61348,* ☎ *06172/1810,* FAX *06172/181–630,* WEB *www.bad-homburg.steigenberger.com. 196 rooms, 17 suites. Restaurant, bar, cable TV, room service, in-room data ports, in-room safes, minibars, Internet, sauna, steam room, gym, laundry service, concierge, meeting rooms, no-smoking floor. AE, DC, MC, V.*

Kronberg

The Taunus town of Kronberg, 15 km (9 mi) northwest of Frankfurt, has a magnificent castle-hotel originally built by the daughter of Queen Victoria, and an open-air zoo. Kronberg's half-timber houses and crooked, winding streets, all on a steep hillside, were so picturesque that a whole 19th-century art movement, the Kronberger Malerkolonie, was inspired by them.

★ 🐥 Established by a very wealthy heir of the man who created the Opel automobile, the large **Opel Zoo** has more than 1,000 native and exotic animals, plus a petting zoo and an "adventure" playground with more than 100 rides and amusements. There are also a nature path, a geological garden, and a picnic area with grills that can be reserved. Camel and pony rides are offered in the summer. ✉ *Königsteiner Str. 35,* ☎ *06173/79749.* 🎫 *€6.* ⏲ *Apr.–Sept., daily 8:30–6; Oct.–Mar., daily 9–5.*

Lodging

$$$$ 🏨 **Schlosshotel Kronberg.** This magnificent palace was built for Kaiserin Victoria, daughter of the British queen of the same name and mother of Wilhelm II, the infamous kaiser of World War I. She lived here after she was widowed and until her death in 1901. It's richly endowed with furnishings and works of art and is surrounded by a park with old trees, a grotto, a rose garden, and an 18-hole golf course. It's one of the few ho-

tels left where you can leave your shoes outside your door for cleaning. Jimmy's Bar, with pianist, is a local rendezvous. There is free transfer to a nearby fitness center. ✉ *Hainstr. 25, D–61476 Kronberg im Taunus,* ☎ *06173/70101,* FAX *06173/701–267,* WEB *www.schlosshotel-kronberg.de. 51 rooms and 7 suites. Restaurant, bar, room service, no a/c, in-room data ports, cable TV with movies, minibars, concierge, meeting rooms, some pets allowed (fee), no-smoking rooms. AE, DC, MC, V.*

Bad Homburg and Kronberg A to Z

CAR TRAVEL

Bad Homburg is about a 30- to 45-minute drive north of Frankfurt on the A–5. You can get to Kronberg in about the same time by taking the A–66 (Frankfurt–Wiesbaden) to the Nordwestkreuz interchange and following the signs to Eschborn and Kronberg.

BUS AND TRAIN TRAVEL

Bad Homburg and Kronberg are easily reached by the S-bahn from Hauptwache, the main station, and other points in downtown Frankfurt. The S–5 goes to Bad Homburg, the S–4 to Kronberg. There is also a Taunusbahn (from the main station only) that stops in Bad Homburg and then continues into the far Taunus, including the Römerkastell-Saalburg and Wehrheim, with bus connections to Hessenpark.

VISITOR INFORMATION

The Bad Homburg tourist office keeps late hours weekdays and is closed on Sunday. Kronberg's office closes at noon on weekdays and is closed the entire weekend.

➤ CONTACT: **Kur- und Kongress GmbH Bad Homburg** (✉ Louisenstr. 58,D–61348 Bad Homburg, ☎ 06172/1780, WEB www.bad-homburg.de). **Verkehrs- und Kulturamt Kronberg** (✉ Katharinenstr. 7, D–61476 Kronberg, ☎ 06173/703–220, WEB www.kronberg.de).

Höchst

Take S-1 or S-2 suburban train from Frankfurt's main train station, Hauptwache, or Konstablerwache.

Höchst, a town with a castle and an Altstadt (Old Town) right out of a picture book, was not devastated by wartime bombing, so its castle and the market square, with its half-timber houses, are well preserved. The name *Höchst* is synonymous with chemicals because of the huge firm that has been here for more than a century. The historic part of town is well removed from the industrial area, and, indeed, the company Höchst has made major contributions to the Altstadt's fine state of repair. For a week in July the whole Alstadt is hung with lanterns for the Schlossfest, one of Frankfurt's more popular outdoor festivals.

The **Höchster Schloss,** first built in 1360, houses two **museums,** one about company history and one about Höchst history, the latter with an excellent collection of porcelain. (The castle and a nearby villa were used for decades following the war by the American military broadcaster AFN.) ✉ *Museums: Am Burggraben 3,* ☎ *069/305–6988.* 🎫 *Free.* ⏲ *Daily 10–4.*

Höchst was once a porcelain-manufacturing town to rival Dresden and Vienna. Production ceased in the late 18th century but was revived by an enterprising businessman in 1965. Of special interest in town is the **Höchster Porzellan Manufaktur,** where you can watch the whole porcelain manufacturing process in the attractive "Porzellanhof." The store sells everything from figurines to dinner services, as well as a selection of glassware and silver. ✉ *Palleskestr. 32,* ☎ *069/300–9020.* 🎫 *€10 (€5 off any purchase).* ⏲ *Weekdays 9–6, Sat. 9–1.*

Not far from the Höchster Schloss, you can also see a fine exhibit of porcelain at the **Bolongaropalast** (Bolongaro Palace), a magnificent residence facing the river. It was built in the late 18th century by an Italian snuff manufacturer. Its facade—almost the length of a football field—is nothing to sneeze at. ✉ *Bolongaro Str. at Königsteinerstr.,* ☎ *069/3106–5520.* 🎫 *Free.* ⏲ *Daily 9–4.*

Höchst's most interesting attraction is the **Justiniuskirche** (Justinius Church), Frankfurt's oldest building. Dating from the 7th century, the church is part early Romanesque and part 15th-century Gothic. The view from the top of the hill is well worth the walk. ✉ *Justiniuspl. at Bolongaro Str.*

Lodging

$ **Hotel-Schiff *Peter Schlott*.** The hotel ship is moored on the Main River, a 15-minute train or tram ride from the city center. Guest cabins are on the small side, but the river views more than compensate, and there is a common room with a television. It's not for you if you're subject to seasickness, but ideal if you like to be rocked to sleep. ✉ *Bolongerostr. 25, D–65929,* ☎ *069/300–4643,* FAX *069/307–671,* WEB *hotel-schiff-schlott.de. 19 rooms, 10 with shower. Restaurant, no a/c, no room phones, no room TVs, some pets allowed. AE, MC, V.*

Neu-Isenburg

Take S–3 or S–4 from the main station or Hauptwache.

Though an extensive forested area to the south of Frankfurt was leveled in the mid-1930s to make room for the airport, a considerable stretch remains, and Neu-Isenburg is the center of it. At the time of the airport's construction, Germans believed the future of air travel lay in the lighter-than-air zeppelin (the 1937 *Hindenburg* disaster put such notions to rest). **Zeppelinheim,** a once-independent town, now a part of Neu-Isenburg, was constructed to provide hangar space and housing for zeppelin flight and maintenance crews.

Just beyond the airport runway, the **Zeppelin Museum** is dedicated to the history of airships in Germany. Exhibits include big, 1:100 scale models of some of the zeppelins, videos of the zeppelin era and its fiery end at Lakehurst, New Jersey, and a reconstruction of the *Hindenburg*'s promenade deck, with a "view" of Rio de Janeiro. The domed construction gives you impression you're actually aboard one of the airships. ✉ *Kapitän-Lehmann-Str. 2, Neu-Isenburg,* ☎ *069/694–390.* 🎫 *Free.* ⏲ *Fri. 1–5, weekends 10–5.*

Lodging

$$$–$$$$ ★ **Kempinski Hotel Gravenbruch.** At a parkland site in leafy Neu Isenburg (a 15-minute drive south of Frankfurt), this sophisticated hotel maintains the atmosphere of the 16th-century manor around which it was built. Some of the luxuriously appointed rooms and suites are arranged as duplex penthouse apartments. Ask for a room overlooking the lake. ✉ *An der Bundestr. 459, D–63263 Neu-Isenburg,* ☎ *06102/5050,* FAX *06102/505–900,* WEB *www.rma.de/hotels/hotels/kempinski-frankfurt.htm. 282 rooms, 28 suites. 2 restaurants, bar, room service, in-room data ports, minibars, cable TV with movies, indoor pool, hair salon, sauna, business services, meeting rooms, some pets allowed, no-smoking rooms. AE, DC, MC, V.*

FRANKFURT A TO Z

To research prices, get advice from other travelers, and book travel arrangements, visit www.fodors.com.

AIRPORTS AND TRANSFERS

Flughafen Frankfurt Main is the biggest airport on the Continent, second in Europe only to London's Heathrow. There are direct flights to Frankfurt from many U.S. cities and from all major European cities.

The airport is 10 km (6 mi) southwest of the downtown area by the A–5 Autobahn, and has its own railway station for the high-speed InterCity (IC) and InterCity Express (ICE) trains. Getting into Frankfurt from the airport is easy. The S-bahn 8 (suburban train) runs from the airport to downtown. Most travelers get off at the Hauptbahnhof (main train station) or at Hauptwache, in the heart of Frankfurt. Trains run at least every 15 minutes, and the trip takes about 15 minutes. The one-way fare is €3.05. A taxi from the airport into the city center normally takes around 20 minutes; allow double that during rush hours. The fare is around €15. If driving a rental car from the airport, take the main road out of the airport and follow the signs reading STADTMITTE (downtown).

➤ AIRPORT INFORMATION: **Flughafen Frankfurt Main** (☎ 069/6900, WEB www.frankfurt-airport.de).

BUS TRAVEL TO AND FROM FRANKFURT

Some 100 European cities have bus links with Frankfurt. Buses arrive and depart from the south side of the Hauptbahnhof.

➤ INFORMATION: **Deutsche Touring** (✉ Am Römerhof 17, Rebstock, ☎ 069/79030).

CAR RENTAL

➤ AGENCIES: **Avis** (✉ Schmidtstr. 39, Rebstock, ☎ 069/730–111). **Europcar** (✉ Lyonerstr. 68, Niederrad, ☎ 069/6772–0291; ✉ Frankfurt Airport Hall A, arrival level, ☎ 069/697–970). **Hertz** (✉ Hanauer Landstr. 117, Ostend, ☎ 069/449–090; ✉ Cambergerstr. 21, Gallus, ☎ 069/2425–2627).

CAR TRAVEL

Frankfurt is the meeting point of a number of major autobahns. The most important are A–3, running south from Köln and then west on to Würzburg and Nürnberg, and A–5, running south from Giessen and then on toward Mannheim and Heidelberg. A complex series of beltways surrounds the city. If you're driving to Frankfurt on A–5 from either north or south, exit at Nordwestkreuz and follow A–66 to the Nordend district, just north of downtown. Driving south on A–3, exit onto A–66 and follow the signs to Frankfurt-Höchst and then the Nordwestkreuz. Driving west on A–3, exit at the Offenbacher Kreuz onto A–661 and follow the signs for Frankfurt-Stadtmitte.

Traffic, accidents, and construction can make driving in Frankfurt aggravating. Speeders are caught with hidden cameras and tow trucks cruise the streets in search of illegal parkers. On the positive side, there are many reasonably priced parking garages around the downtown area, and a well-developed "park and ride" system with the suburban train lines. The transit map shows nearly a hundred outlying stations with a "P" symbol beside them, meaning there is convenient parking there.

CONSULATES

➤ AUSTRALIA: ✉ Grüneburgweg 58–62, Westend, D–60322, ☎ 069/905–580.

➤ UNITED KINGDOM: ✉ Bockenheimer Landstr. 42, Westend, D–60323, ☎ 069/170–0020.

➤ UNITED STATES: ✉ Siesmayerstr. 21, Westend, D–60323, ☎ 069/75350.

EMERGENCIES

➤ AMBULANCE AND FIRE SERVICES: ☎ 112.
➤ DENTISTS: ☎ 069/660–7271.
➤ DOCTORS: ☎ 069/19292.
➤ POLICE: ☎ 110.

ENGLISH-LANGUAGE MEDIA

➤ BOOKS: **British Bookshop** (✉ Börsenstr. 17, City Center, ☎ 069/280–492).

TELEVISION AND RADIO

Though the U.S. military has moved out of Frankfurt, the news, sports, and music of the American Forces Network, the celebrated soldier radio station, is still easy to receive. Its AM broadcast (primarily talk) is at 87.3; the FM signal (primarily music) is at 98.7.

TAXIS

Cabs are not always easy to hail from the sidewalk; some stop, while others will pick up only from the city's numerous taxi stands or outside hotels or the train station. You can always order a cab. Fares start at €2.05 (€2.55 in the wee hours) and increase by a per-km (½ mi) charge of €1.48 for the first three, €1.33 thereafter. Count on paying €6.50 for a short city ride.
➤ TAXI COMPANIES: ☎ 069/250–001 or 069/230–001.

TOURS

BOAT TOURS

Day trips on the Main River and Rhine excursions run from March through October and leave from the Frankfurt Mainkai am Eiserner Steg, just south of the Römer complex.
➤ FEES AND SCHEDULES: **Frankfurt Personenschiffahrt GmbH** (✉ Mainkai 36, Altstadt, ☎ 069/281–884).

BUS TOURS

Two-and-a-half-hour city bus tours with English-speaking guides are offered throughout the year. From April through October tours leave from outside the main tourist information office at Römerberg 27 daily at 10 AM and 2 PM; you can also pick up these tours 15 minutes later from the south side of the train station. The tour includes the price of admission to the Goethehaus and the top of the Maintower. November through March, tours leave daily at 2, stopping at 2:15 at the south side of the train station. The cost is €22.50. Gray Line offers two-hour city tours by bus four times a day for €28.50. They leave from the line's office at Wiesenhüttenplatz 39, or they will pick you up at an inner-city hotel.

The City Transit Authority runs a brightly painted old-time streetcar—the *Ebbelwoi Express* (Cider Express)—on weekend and holiday afternoons. Departures are from the Heide Strasse tram stop in Bornheim, and the fare, €5, includes a glass of Apfelwein and a salt stick.
➤ FEES AND SCHEDULES: **Tourist Office** (✉ Römerberg 27, Altstadt, ☎ 069/2123–8708). **Verkehrsgesellschaft Frankfurt am Main** (City Transit Authority ☎ 069/2132–22425). **Gray Line** (✉ Wiesenhüttenpl. 39, City Center, ☎ 069/230–492).

EXCURSION TOURS

The Historische Eisenbahn Frankfurt runs a vintage steam train with a buffet car along the banks of the Main River on weekends. The train runs from the Eiserner Steg bridge west to Frankfurt-Griesham and east to Frankfurt-Mainkur. The fare is €4.

Deutsche Touring will take you to Rothenburg, Heidelberg, and the Black Forest. Gray Line has trips to the Rhine, the Black Forest, and the Romantic Road.

➤ FEES AND SCHEDULES: **Deutsche Touring** (✉ Am Römerhof 17, Rebstock, ☎ 069/79030). **Gray Line** (✉ Wiesenhüttenpl. 39, City Center, ☎ 069/230–492). **Historische Eisenbahn Frankfurt** (✉ Eisener Steg, Altstadt, ☎ 069/436–093).

WALKING TOURS

The tourist office's walking tours cover a variety of topics, including Goethe, Jewish history, literature, transportation, architecture, and business. Tours can also be tailored to your interests. For an English-speaking guide, the cost is €119 for up to two hours, and €59 per hour after that.

➤ FEES AND SCHEDULES: **Tourist office** (✉ Römerberg 27, Altstadt, ☎ 069/2123–8800).

TRAIN TRAVEL

EuroCity, InterCity, and InterCity Express trains connect Frankfurt with all German cities and many major European ones. The InterCity Express line links Frankfurt with Berlin, Hamburg, Munich, and a number of other major hubs. All long-distance trains arrive at and depart from the Hauptbahnhof, and many also stop at the long-distance train station at the airport. Be aware that the red-light district is just northeast of the train station.

➤ TRAIN INFORMATION: **Deutsche Bahn** (German Railways; ☎ 01805/996–633).

TRANSPORTATION AROUND FRANKFURT

Frankfurt's smooth-running, well-integrated public transportation system (called RMV) consists of the U-Bahn (subway), S-Bahn (suburban railway), Strassenbahn (streetcars), and buses. Fares for the entire system, which includes a very extensive surrounding area, are uniform, though they are based on a complex zone system. Within the time that your ticket is valid (one hour for most inner-city destinations), you can transfer from one part of the system to another.

A basic one-way ticket for a ride in the inner zone costs €1.90 during the peak hours of 6 AM–9 AM and 4 PM–6:30 PM weekdays. (€1.60 the rest of the time.) There is also a reduced *Kurzstrecke* ("short stretch") fare of €1.50 (€1.05 off-peak). A day ticket for unlimited travel in the inner zones costs €4.35.

DISCOUNT FARES

The Frankfurt tourist office offers a one- or two-day ticket—the Frankfurt Card—allowing unlimited travel in the inner zone (and to the airport) and a 50% reduction on admission to 15 museums (€6.15 for one day, €9.75 for two days). If you are attending a conference in Frankfurt, go to the tourist office and ask for a Congress Ticket (€2.60), a one-day ticket valid for unlimited travel in the city and to the airport.

PAYING

Tickets may be purchased from automatic vending machines, which are at all U-Bahn and S-Bahn stations. Each station has a list of short-stretch destinations that can be reached from it, and if you're going to one of them, press the *Kurzstrecke* button on the vending machine. There is a second vertical row of buttons for the lower children's fares. Vending machines also have an extensive list of what might be called "long-stretch" destinations; those beyond the city limits. Each has a number beside it. Press the appropriate buttons for this destination, and then for either the adult or child fare, and the proper fare will appear. If your destination isn't on either list, it's a standard fare. Machines accept coins and notes and make change. If you are caught without a ticket, there's a fine of €30.

Bus drivers also sell tickets, but only if you boarded at a stop that does not have a vending machine. Weekly and monthly tickets are sold at central ticket offices and newsstands.

TRAVEL AGENCIES

➤ CONTACTS: **American Express International** (✉ Theodor Heuss Allee 112, Bockenheim, ☎ 069/97970). **Hapag-Lloyd Reisebüro** (✉ Kaiserstr. 14, City Center, ☎ 069/216–216).

VISITOR INFORMATION

For advance information write to the Tourismus und Congress GmbH Frankfurt/Main. The main tourist office is at Römerberg 27 in the heart of the Old Town. It's open weekdays 9:30–5:30, weekends 10–4. There are two other information offices. One is in the main hall of the railroad station. The other, at Zeil 94a, is open weekdays 10–6, Saturday 10–4. All three offices can help you find accommodations.

Two airport information offices can also help with accommodations. The airport's Flughafen-Information, on the first floor of Arrivals Hall B, is open daily 6 AM–10 PM. The DER Deutsches Reisebüro, in Terminal 1 Arrivals Hall B, is open weekdays 6 AM–8 PM, weekends 7 AM–1 PM.

➤ TOURIST INFORMATION: **Tourismus und Congress GmbH Frankfurt/Main** (✉ Kaiserstr. 56, City Center, D–60329 Frankfurt am Main, ☎ 069/2123–8800, WEB www.frankfurt.de). **Main tourist office** (✉ Römerberg 27, Altstadt, ☎ 069/2123–8708).

11 THE PFALZ AND THE RHINE TERRACE

The Romans planted the first Rhineland vineyards 2,000 years ago. By the Middle Ages viticulture was flourishing at the hands of the church and the state, and a bustling wine trade had developed in Speyer, Worms, and Mainz. The vineyard area that once supplied these imperial residences is now Germany's two largest wine regions, Rheinhessen and the Pfalz.

Updated by Kerry Brady Stewart

THE STATE OF RHEINLAND-PFALZ (Rhineland Palatinate) is home to six of Germany's 13 wine-growing regions, including the two largest, Rheinhessen and the Pfalz. Bordered on the east by the Rhine and stretching from the French border north to Mainz, these two regions were the "wine cellar of the Holy Roman Empire." Thriving viticulture and splendid Romanesque cathedrals are the legacies of the bishops and emperors of Speyer, Worms, and Mainz. Two routes parallel to the Rhine link dozens of wine villages. In the Pfalz follow the Deutsche Weinstrasse (German Wine Road); in eastern Rheinhessen (the Rhine Terrace), the home of the mild wine Liebfraumilch, the Liebfrauenstrasse guides you from Worms to Mainz.

The Pfalz has a mild, sunny climate and an ambience to match. Vines carpet the foothills of the thickly forested Haardt Mountains, an extension of the Alsatian Vosges. The Pfälzerwald (Palatinate Forest) with its pine and chestnut trees is the region's other natural attraction. Hiking and cycling trails lead through the vineyards, the woods, and up to castles on the heights. As the Wine Road winds its way north from the French border, idyllic wine villages beckon with flower-draped facades and courtyards full of palms, oleanders, and fig trees. WEINVERKAUF (wine for sale) or WEINPROBE (wine tasting) signs are posted everywhere, each one an invitation to stop in to sample the wines.

The border between the Pfalz and Rheinhessen is invisible. Yet a few miles into the hinterland, a profile takes shape. Rheinhessen is a region of gentle, rolling hills and expansive farmland, where vines are but one of many crops and vineyards are often scattered miles apart. The slopes overlooking the Rhine between Worms and Mainz—the so-called Rhine Terrace—are a notable exception. This is a nearly uninterrupted ribbon of vines culminating with the famous vineyards of Oppenheim, Nierstein, and Nackenheim on the outskirts of Mainz.

Pleasures and Pastimes

Biking

Country roads and traffic-free vineyard paths are a cyclist's paradise. There are also well-marked cycling trails, such as the *Radwanderweg Deutsche Weinstrasse,* which runs parallel to its namesake from the French border to Bockenheim, and the *Radweg* (cycling trail) along the Rhine between Worms and Mainz. The Palatinate Forest, Germany's largest single tract of woods, has more than 10,000 km (6,200 mi) of paths.

Dining

The best introduction to regional country cooking is the *Pfälzer Teller,* a platter of bratwurst (grilled sausage), *Leberknödel* (liver dumplings), and slices of *Saumagen* (a spicy meat-and-potato mixture encased in a "sow's stomach"), with *Weinkraut* (sauerkraut braised in wine) and *Kartoffelpüree* (mashed potatoes) on the side. Rheinhessen is known for the hearty casseroles *Dippe-Has* (hare and pork baked in red wine) and *Backes Grumbeere* (scalloped potatoes cooked with bacon, sour cream, white wine, and a layer of pork). *Spargel* (asparagus); *Wild* (game); chestnuts; and mushrooms, particularly *Pfifferlinge* (chanterelles), are seasonal favorites. During the grape harvest, from September through November, try *Federweisser* (fermenting grape juice) and *Zwiebelkuchen* (onion quiche)—specialties unique to the wine country.

Above all, savor the local wines. Those from Rheinhessen are often sleeker and less voluminous than their Pfälzer counterparts. Many are sold as *offene Weine* (wines by the glass) and are *trocken* (dry) or *halb-*

trocken (semidry). The classic white varieties are Riesling, Silvaner, Müller-Thurgau (also called Rivaner), Grauburgunder (pinot gris), and Weissburgunder (pinot blanc); Spätburgunder (pinot noir), Dornfelder, and Portugieser are the most popular red wines. The word *Weissherbst* after the grape variety signals a rosé wine.

CATEGORY	COST*
$$$$	over €20
$$$	€15–€20
$$	€10–€15
$	under €10

**per person for a main course at dinner*

Festivals

Wine and *Sekt* (sparkling wine) flow freely from March through October at festivals that include parades, fireworks, and rides. The Pfalz is home to the world's largest wine festival in mid-September, the Dürkheimer Wurstmarkt (sausage market, so named because of the 400,000 pounds of sausage consumed during eight days of merrymaking). In Neustadt, the German Wine Queen is crowned during the 10-day Deutsches Weinlesefest (German wine harvest festival) in October. The Mainzer Johannisnacht (in honor of Johannes Gutenberg) in late June, the Wormser Backfischfest (fried-fish festival) in late August, and the Brezelfest (pretzel festival) in Speyer on the second weekend in July are the major wine and folk festivals along this part of the Rhine.

Hiking

The Wanderweg Deutsche Weinstrasse, a walking route that traverses vineyards, woods, and wine villages, covers the length of the Pfalz. It connects with many trails in the Palatinate Forest that lead to Celtic and Roman landmarks and dozens of castles dating primarily from the Salian and Hohenstaufen periods (11th–13th centuries). South of Annweiler, between the Wine Road and Daun, are the fascinating geological formations and sandstone cliffs of the Wasgau. In Rheinhessen you can hike along two marked trails parallel to the Rhine: the Rheinterrassenwanderweg and the Rheinhöhenweg along the heights. Both regions have many *Lehrpfade* (educational paths) signposted at intervals with information about the flora and fauna.

Lodging

Accommodations in all price categories are plentiful, but book in advance if your visit coincides with a large festival. Bed-and-breakfasts abound. Look for signs reading FREMDENZIMMER or ZIMMER FREI (rooms available). A *Ferienwohnung* (holiday apartment), abbreviated FeWo in tourist brochures, is an economical alternative if you plan to stay in one location for several nights.

CATEGORY	COST*
$$$$	over €225
$$$	€150–€225
$$	€75–€150
$	under €75

**All prices are for two people in a double room, including tax and service.*

Shopping

There is no dearth of places to sample and purchase wine and Sekt. Rarities, such as the dessert wines Beerenauslese, Eiswein, and Trockenbeerenauslese, are good souvenirs. *Trester* (German grappa), often sold in stunning designer bottles; *Weinessig* (wine vinegar); *Weingelee* (wine jelly); or wine-related accessories, such as table linens and coasters with grape motifs, or unusual corkscrews and bottle-stoppers, make lovely gifts. Some local tourist offices as well as many wine estates and *Winzergenossenschaften* (wine growers' cooperatives) have good shops.

Throughout the region there are many *offene Ateliers* (artist workshops open to the public) selling everything from sculptures to paintings; *Töpferei* signs indicate a pottery.

Exploring the Pfalz and Rhine Terrace

The Pfalz and Rheinhessen wine regions lie west of the Rhine in the central and southern part of the state of Rheinland-Pfalz. The area between Schweigen-Rechtenbach, on the French border, and Neustadt is known as the Südliche Weinstrasse (Southern Wine Road, abbreviated SÜW) and is the most romantic and serpentine part of the Wine Road. The scene farther north is more spacious and the vineyards fan out onto the vast Rhine Plain. The 45-km (28-mi) stretch between Worms and Mainz along the Rhine takes in Rheinhessen's most prestigious vineyards. From here you are poised to explore the northern portion of the Rhineland.

Great Itineraries

If time is short, it is best to explore the Pfalz and Rheinhessen by car. There are, however, many scenic paths for hikers and cyclists, and public transportation is excellent.

Numbers in the text correspond to numbers in the margin and on the Pfalz and the Rhine Terrace and Worms maps.

IF YOU HAVE 3 DAYS

Start at the French border in **Schweigen-Rechtenbach** ①, then visit two sites west of the Wine Road: enchanting Dörrenbach and the legendary **Burg Trifels,** near **Annweiler** ④. For a contrast, tour the Pompeian-style palace **Schloss Villa Ludwigshöhe,** overlooking Edenkoben on the Wine Road, then continue uphill via chairlift to the vantage point at the **Rietburg castle.** Stay overnight in **St. Martin** ⑥. The next day travel via **Neustadt** ⑦ to **Speyer** ⑧ to see the Romanesque imperial cathedral, the **Kaiserdom,** and the world's oldest bottle of wine in the **Historisches Museum der Pfalz.** Backtrack to the Wine Road to overnight in either **Deidesheim** ⑨ or **Bad Dürkheim** ⑩. Begin your third day with a visit to the magnificent **Limburg Monastery** ruins above Bad Dürkheim. Continue north on the Wine Road, with detours to the romantic medieval towns of **Freinsheim** ⑪ and Neuleiningen. Your journey and the Wine Road end in **Bockenheim.**

IF YOU HAVE 5 DAYS

From **Schweigen-Rechtenbach** ① visit **Dörrenbach** before exploring the cliffs and castles of the **Wasgau** area west of **Bad Bergzabern** ②. Overnight in **Gleiszellen** or **Herxheim-Hayna.** Devote the second day to the sights between **Klingenmünster** and **Edenkoben,** with an excursion to **Burg Trifels.** After staying in **St. Martin** ⑥, see the **Kalmit,** the region's highest peak, before heading for **Speyer** ⑧. Back on the Wine Road, visit **Deidesheim** ⑨ en route to **Bad Dürkheim** ⑩, home base for two nights. In the morning visit **Limburg Monastery** or **Hardenburg Fortress**; then relax at the spa, hike or bike through the Palatinate Forest, or tour a wine estate. The final day take in the northern end of the Wine Road via **Freinsheim** ⑪ and Neuleiningen, before turning east to **Worms** ⑫–⑳ for a look at the amazing **Wormser Dom** and the **Judenfriedhof,** Europe's oldest and largest Jewish cemetery.

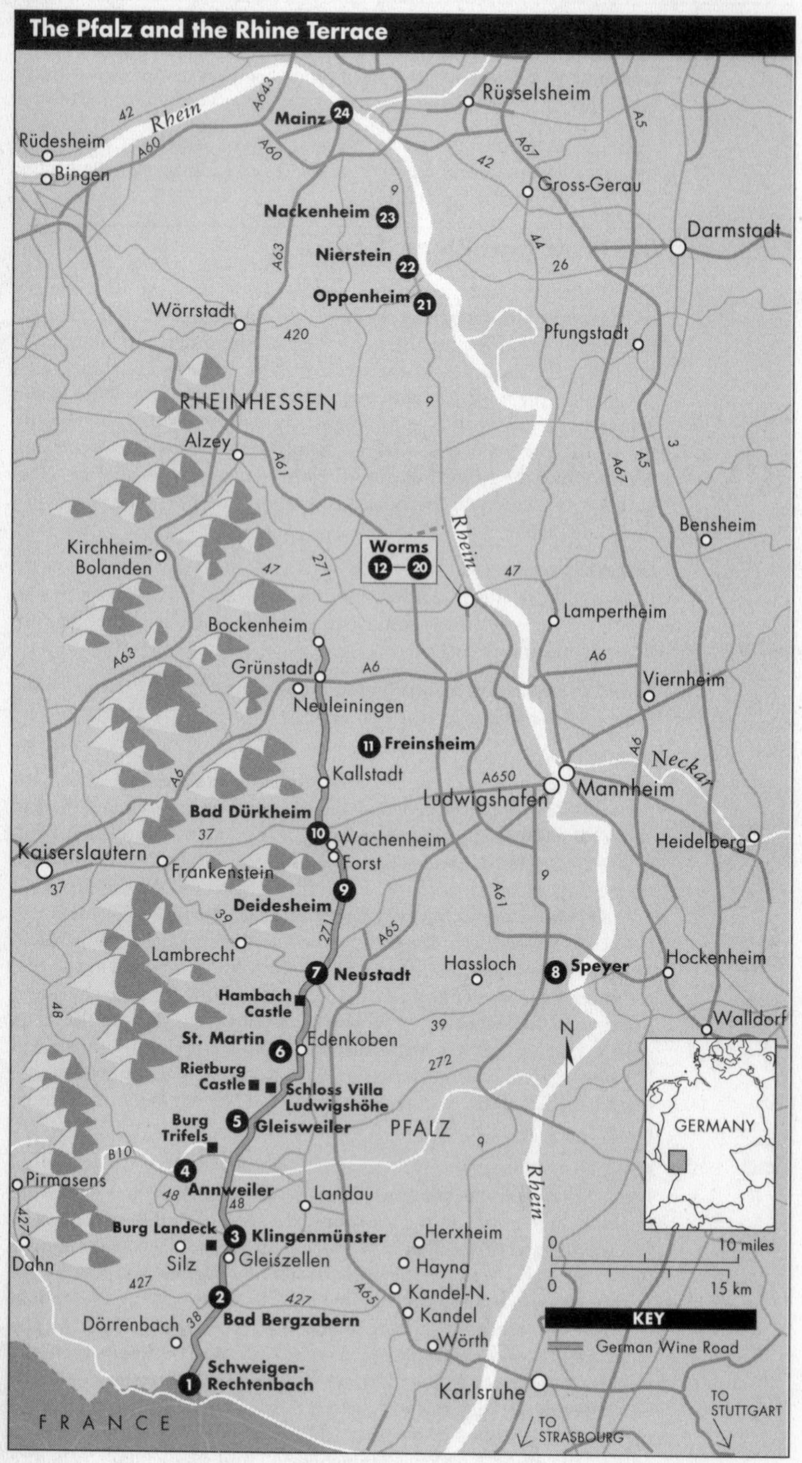
The Pfalz and the Rhine Terrace
Rhein
Rüdesheim
Bingen
Mainz 24
Rüsselsheim
Gross-Gerau
Darmstadt
Nackenheim 23
Nierstein 22
Oppenheim 21
Wörrstadt
Pfungstadt
RHEINHESSEN
Alzey
Bensheim
Worms 12—20
Kirchheim-Bolanden
Lampertheim
Bockenheim
Grünstadt
Neuleiningen
Viernheim
11 Freinsheim
Kallstadt
Neckar
Ludwigshafen
Mannheim
Bad Dürkheim
10 Wachenheim
Heidelberg
Kaiserslautern
Frankenstein
Forst
9 Deidesheim
Lambrecht
7 Neustadt
Hassloch
8 Speyer
Hockenheim
Hambach Castle
Walldorf
St. Martin 6
Edenkoben
Rietburg Castle
Schloss Villa Ludwigshöhe
Burg Trifels
5 Gleisweiler
PFALZ
GERMANY
Pirmasens
4 Annweiler
Landau
Burg Landeck
3 Klingenmünster
Herxheim
Dahn
Silz
Gleiszellen
Hayna
2 Bad Bergzabern
Kandel-N.
Kandel
Dörrenbach
Wörth
1 Schweigen-Rechtenbach
Karlsruhe
FRANCE
TO STRASBOURG
TO STUTTGART
0 10 miles
0 15 km
KEY
German Wine Road

IF YOU HAVE 7 DAYS

Follow the five-day itinerary above, overnighting in **Worms** ⑫–⑳ the fifth night. Proceed north on B–9 to see Rheinhessen's most famous wine villages. In **Oppenheim** ㉑ visit the **Katharinenkirche,** a beautiful Gothic church, and in **Nierstein** ㉒ enjoy a Rhine panorama. Spend a peaceful night in **Nackenheim** ㉓ or end the day in **Mainz** ㉔ with a pub crawl. On the seventh day see the **Mainzer Dom** and the **Gutenberg Museum,** devoted to the history of printing. Visit the **Kupferberg Sekt Cellars** for a sparkling finale to your trip.

When to Tour the Pfalz and Rhinehessen

The wine festival season begins in March with the *Mandelblüten* (blossoming of the almond trees) along the Wine Road and continues through October. By May the vines' tender shoots and leaves appear. As the wine harvest progresses in September and October, foliage takes on reddish-golden hues.

THE GERMAN WINE ROAD

The Wine Road spans the length of the Pfalz wine region. You can travel from north to south or vice versa. Given its central location, the Pfalz is convenient to visit before or after a trip to the Black Forest, Heidelberg, or the northern Rhineland.

Schweigen-Rechtenbach

❶ *21 km (13 mi) southwest of Landau on B–38.*

The southernmost wine village of the Pfalz lies on the French border. During the economically depressed 1930s, local vintners established a route through the vineyards to promote tourism. The German Wine Road was inaugurated in 1935; a year later the massive stone **Deutsches Weintor** (German Wine Gate) was erected to add visual impact to the marketing concept. Halfway up the gateway is a platform that offers a fine view of the vineyards—to the south, French; to the north, German. Schweigen's 1-km (½-mi) **Weinlehrpfad** (educational wine path) wanders through the vineyards, and, with signs and exhibits, explains the history of viticulture from Roman times to the present.

En Route Drive north on B–38 toward Bad Bergzabern. Two kilometers (one mile) before you reach the town, turn left to see the enchanting village of **Dörrenbach.** It has an uncommon Gothic *Wehrkirche* (fortified church) that overlooks the Renaissance town hall, considered the most beautiful half-timber building in the Pfalz.

Bad Bergzabern

❷ *10 km (6 mi) north of Schweigen-Rechtenbach on B–38.*

The landmark of this little spa town is the baroque **Schloss** (palace) of the dukes of Zweibrücken. Walk into the courtyard to see the elaborate portals of earlier residences on the site. The town's other gem is an impressive stone building with scrolled gables and decorative oriels. Built about 1600, it houses the wine restaurant **Zum Engel.** There are many historic facades to admire along Marktstrasse. Stop at No. 48, **Café Herzog,** to sample *Weinperlen* (wine pearls), unusual wine-filled chocolates, or the ice cream version, *Weinperleneis.* It's closed on Monday.

Dining and Lodging

$–$$$ ✕ **Zum Engel.** Enjoy fish, game, or Palatinate specialties in the prettiest Renaissance house of the Pfalz. The wines are from local producers and very reasonably priced. ✉ *Königstr. 45, Bad Bergzabern,* ☎ *06343/4933. No credit cards. No dinner Sun. Closed Mon.*

$$ ★ ✕🏨 **Hotel Zur Krone.** The simple facade belies the upscale inn that offers modern facilities; tasteful decor; and above all, a warm welcome from the Kuntz family. Reservations are essential at the main restaurant ($$$$). Start with chef Karl-Emil Kuntz's *Gruss aus der Küche* (greetings from the kitchen), a medley of appetizers. Terrines and parfaits are specialties as is the homemade goat cheese. The same kitchen team cooks for the Pfälzer Stube (closed Tuesday). The wine list is excellent. Hayna, an idyllic suburb of Herxheim, lies between the Rhine and the Wine Road, 20 km (12 mi) east of Bad Bergzabern via the B–427. ✉ *Hauptstr. 62–64, D–76863 Herxheim-Hayna,* ☎ *07276/5080,* FAX *07276/50814,* WEB *www.hotelkrone.de. 50 rooms, 3 suites. 2 restaurants, minibars, no a/c, in-room data ports, 2 tennis courts, indoor pool, sauna, steam room, bicycles, bar, pub, some pets allowed (fee), no-smoking rooms. AE, MC, V. No lunch. Restaurant closed Mon. and Tues., 1st 2 wks in Jan., and 2 wks in July–Aug.*

$–$$ ✕🏨 **Gasthof Zum Lam.** Flowers cascade from the windowsills of this half-timber inn in the heart of Gleiszellen (to the north of Bad Bergzabern). Exposed beams add rustic charm to the airy rooms; the bathrooms are bright and very modern. The restaurant ($–$$$) is no less inviting with its dome-shape tile stove, natural stone walls, and wooden beams everywhere. In summer you can dine on the vine-shaded terrace. ✉ *Winzerg. 37, D–76889 Gleiszellen,* ☎ *06343/939–212,* FAX *06343/939–213,* WEB *www.zum-lam.de. 11 rooms, 1 suite. Restaurant, beer garden, no a/c, some pets allowed (fee). No credit cards. Hotel and restaurant closed 3 wks in Jan. Restaurant closed Wed. No lunch Nov.–Apr., except weekends.*

En Route Continue north on the Wine Road—now B–48 (B–38 leads to Landau)—toward Klingenmünster. Four kilometers (2½ miles) north of Bad Bergzabern turn left and drive to **Gleiszellen** to see the Winzergasse (Vintners' Lane). This little vine-canopied street is lined with a beautiful ensemble of half-timber houses. Try a glass of the town's specialty: spicy, aromatic Muskateller wine, a rarity seldom found elsewhere in Germany.

Klingenmünster

❸ *8 km (5 mi) north of Bad Bergzabern on B–48.*

The village grew out of the **Benedictine monastery** founded here by the Merovingian king Dagobart in the 7th century. The monastery church is still in use. Despite its baroque appearance, parts of it date from the 12th century, as do the remains of the cloister. On the hillside are the ruins of **Burg Landeck,** built around 1200 to protect the monastery. The keep and inner walls are accessible via a drawbridge that spans a 33-ft-deep moat. You can walk through the chestnut forest from the monastery to the castle in about half an hour. Your reward will be a magnificent view over the Rhine Valley and south as far as the Black Forest.

OFF THE BEATEN PATH **Wild- und Wanderpark Südliche Weinstrasse** (Game and Hiking Park of the Southern Wine Road) – Deer, Scottish Highland cattle, rare wild sheep, mountain goats, and eagles and snowy owls roam freely here. Allow one hour for the *kleiner Rundgang* (short circuit) and half an hour more for the longer trail. A petting zoo, playground, and restaurant are on the grounds. ✉ *Silz, 6 km (4 mi) west of Klingenmünster; 10 km (6 mi) south of Annweiler,* ☎ *06346/5588,* WEB *www.wildpark-silz.de.* 🎫 *€4.* ⏲ *Mid-Mar.–mid-Nov., daily 9–dusk; mid-Nov.–mid-Mar., daily 10–dusk.*

Annweiler

❹ *11 km (7 mi) northwest of Klingenmünster at the junction of B–48 and B–10.*

In 1219 Annweiler was declared a Free Imperial City by Emperor Friedrich II. Stroll along Wassergasse, Gerbergasse (Tanners' Lane), and Quodgasse to see the half-timber houses and the waterwheels on the Queich River, which is more like a creek. Annweiler is a gateway to the **Wasgau,** the romantic southern portion of the Palatinate Forest, marked by sandstone cliffs and ancient castles. The fruits of the forest are celebrated in early October, when local chefs present chestnut-themed menus during the *Kastanienfest* (chestnut festival).

★ **Burg Trifels,** one of Germany's most imposing castles, is perched on the highest of three sandstone bluffs overlooking Annweiler. Celts, Romans, and Salians all had settlements on this site, but it was under the Hohenstaufen emperors (12th and 13th centuries) that Trifels was built on a grand scale. It housed the crown jewels from 1125 to 1274 (replicas are on display today). It was also an imperial prison, perhaps where Richard the Lion-Hearted was held captive in 1193–94.

Although it was never conquered, the fortress was severely damaged by lightning in 1602. Reconstruction began in 1938, shaped by visions of grandeur to create a national shrine of the imperial past. Accordingly, the monumental proportions of some parts of today's castle bear no resemblance to those of the original Romanesque structure. The imperial hall is a grand setting for the *Serenaden* (concerts) held in summer. ☎ *06346/8470,* WEB *www.burgen-rlp.de.* 🎫 *€2.60.* ⏲ *Apr.–Sept., daily 9–6; Oct.–Nov. and Jan.–Mar., daily 9–5. Closed Dec.*

OFF THE BEATEN PATH

MUSEUM "DIE SCHUHFABRIK" (Shoe Factory Museum) – In this former shoe factory in Hauenstein, 12 km (7½ mi) west of Annweiler on B–10, you can learn about the history of shoe making, once an important industry in this part of Germany. Demonstrations on historical machinery and 14 factory outlet stores nearby make this a worthwhile excursion. ✉ *Turnstr. 5,* ☎ *06392/915–165.* 🎫 *€3.20.* ⏲ *Dec.–Feb., weekdays 1–4, weekends 10–4; Mar.–Nov., daily 10–5.*

Dining and Lodging

$–$$ ✕ **Restaurant s' Reiwerle.** Within the cozy stone walls of their 300-year-old half-timber house the Neumann family serves Pfälzer cuisine; chestnut-based dishes, such as *Keschtebrieh* (chestnut soup); the specialty *Heidschnuckenbraten* (lamb from the Lüneberger Heide, the heath south of Hamburg); and local Pfalz wines. *Reiwerle* (RYE vair leh) is dialect for a spigot to tap wine from a cask. ✉ *Flitschberg 7,* ☎ *06346/929–362. No credit cards. Closed Thurs. and 1 wk in winter.*

$–$$ ✕ **Zur alten Gerberei.** An open fireplace, exposed beams, and sandstone walls give this old *Gerberei* (tannery) a cozy feel. The Queich flows right past the outdoor seats. In addition to Pfälzer specialties and vegetarian dishes, you can try Alsatian *Flammkuchen,* similar to pizza, but baked on a wafer-thin crust. There are 15 Pfälzer wines by the glass. ✉ *Am Prangertshof 11, at Gerberg.,* ☎ *06346/3566. No credit cards. Closed Mon. and 4 wks in winter. No lunch Tues.–Sat.*

$$ ✕🏨 **Landhaus Herrenberg.** A flower-filled courtyard welcomes guests to this country inn. The rooms are modern and spacious, with blond-wood furnishings. The suite comes with a whirlpool. The Lergenmüllers are vintners known for award-winning red wines. In the restaurant ($$–$$$$) they showcase their wines with fine regional cuisine using many homegrown ingredients. Try a *Degustationsmenü,* a three- or four-course menu with wines preselected to accompany each

course. You can pick up some good souvenirs here, such as pickled pumpkin, marinated nuts, and excellent still and sparkling wines. ✉ *Lindenbergstr. 72, D–76829 Landau-Nussdorf,* ☎ *06341/60205,* FAX *06341/60709,* WEB *www.landhaus-herrenberg.de. 8 rooms, 1 suite. Restaurant, Weinstube, no a/c, minibars, some pets allowed (fee), no-smoking rooms. AE, MC, V. Restaurant closed Thurs. No lunch.*

Outdoor Activities and Sports

BIKING, CLIMBING, AND HIKING

Dozens of marked trails guide you to the Wasgau's striking geological formations, sandstone cliffs, and castles carved into the cliffs. From Annweiler you can access many of these trails via a circular tour by car (55½ km [35 mi]). Proceed west on B–10 to Hinterweidenthal (16½ km [10 mi]), then south on B–427 to Dahn (7 km [4 mi]), and continue southeast to Erlenbach (9 km [5½ mi]). Return to Annweiler via Vorderweidenthal (1 km [½ mi]) and Silz (7 km [4 mi]). Each town is a good starting point for a scenic ride, climb, or hike.

GOLF

The **Golfanlage Landgut Dreihof** (☎ 06348/615–0237), between Essingen and Offenbach, 5 km (3 mi) east of Landau, has an 18-hole championship course, a 9-hole course, pitch-and-putt greens, and a driving range.

HORSEBACK RIDING

Experienced riders can gallop through the Wasgau with Jutta Weiland, equestrian expert and owner of **Schönbacherhof** (✉ Am Silzerberg 1, ☎ 06346/5875, WEB www.silz.de). Castle-to-castle tours are her specialty. The stables are near Silz, less than 10 km (6 mi) south of Annweiler or 6 km (4 mi) west of Klingenmünster. The **Ferien- und Reiterhof Munz** (✉ Auf dem Berg 2, Gossersweiler-Stein, ☎ 06346/5272), a complex of stables and holiday cottages, is less than 3 km (2 mi) north of Silz. The trails in this vicinity are not suited for beginners. Near Essingen advanced riders can go riding in the vine-filled Hainbach Valley from Bützler's riding stables, **Gut Dreihof** (☎ 06348/7971).

SWIMMING

Erlebnis means "adventure" or "experience," and this is what Landau's **Erlebnisbad La Ola** promises with its 330-ft-long slide (partly in a tunnel with special lighting effects), six pools, outdoor thermal baths, simulated ocean waves, whirlpools, and saunas. ✉ *Horstring 2, Landau,* ☎ *06341/55115,* WEB *www.la-ola.de.* 💶 *€3.50 (1½ hrs), €7.50 (all day); €1.50 supplement weekends and holidays; €6.50 supplement for sauna.* ⏲ *Sun. 10–9, Mon. 2–11, Tues.–Thurs. and Sat. 10* AM*–11* PM*, Fri. 10–midnight.*

SHOPPING

The **süw Shop** (✉ An der Kreuzmühle 2, ☎ 06341/940–407), in Landau's Südliche Weinstrasse regional tourist office, sells gift items, products of the grape, wine-related accessories, and detailed maps of cycling and hiking trails. The shop is closed Friday afternoon and weekends.

Gleisweiler

❺ *16 km (10 mi) north of Klingenmünster on the Wine Road; 11 km (7 mi) northeast of Annweiler.*

The little town of Gleisweiler is reputedly the warmest spot in Germany. The **Park der Privatklinik Bad Gleisweiler** (✉ Badstr. 28), a flourishing subtropical park on the grounds of a sanatorium, supports the claim with its camellias in spring, bananas and lemons in summer, and exotic trees (cedars, ginkgos, and a 130-ft-high sequoia) year-round.

Cool off in the *Waldddusche* (forest shower), an unusual waterfall and wading pond. These were set up circa 1850 as cold-water therapeutic baths by the founder of the sanatorium. It's a 20-minute walk from town via Hainbachtal Strasse.

En Route Venerable old chestnut trees line **Theresienstrasse** in **Rhodt,** halfway between Gleisweiler and Edenkoben. It rivals Gleiszellen's Winzergasse as one of the most picturesque lanes of the Pfalz. Fragrant, spicy Traminer (or Gewürztraminer) is a specialty here, and on the eastern outskirts of town, opposite the cooperative winery on Edesheimer Strasse, you can see a plot of 350-year-old Traminer grapes, Germany's oldest producing vines.

Schloss Villa Ludwigshöhe

★ *8 km (5 mi) north of Gleisweiler, slightly west of Edenkoben on the Wine Road.*

Bavaria's King Ludwig I built a summer residence on the slopes overlooking Edenkoben, in what he called "the most beautiful square mile of my realm." You can reach the neoclassical Schloss Villa Ludwigshöhe by car or bus from Edenkoben or take a scenic 45-minute walk through the vineyards along the Weinlehrpfad. Historical wine presses and vintners' tools are displayed at intervals along the path. It starts at the corner of Landauer Strasse and Villa Strasse in Edenkoben.

The layout and decor—Pompeian-style murals, splendid parquet floors, and Biedermeier and Empire furnishings—of the palace provide quite a contrast to medieval castles elsewhere in the Pfalz. It also houses an extensive collection of paintings and prints by the leading German impressionist Max Slevogt (1868–1932). ☎ *06323/93016,* WEB *www.burgen-rlp.de.* €2.60. *Apr.–Sept., Tues.–Sun. 9–6; Oct.–Nov. and Jan.–Mar., Tues.–Sun. 9–5. Closed Dec.*

From Schloss Villa Ludwigshöhe you can hike (30 minutes) or ride the ★ Rietburgbahn chairlift (10 minutes) up to the **Rietburg** castle ruins for a sweeping view of the Pfalz. A restaurant, game park, and playground are on the grounds. *€4.50 round-trip, €3.50 one-way. Mar., Sun. 9–5; Apr.–Oct., weekdays 9–5:30, weekends 9–6.*

St. Martin

6 *10 km (6 mi) north of Gleisweiler, slightly west of the Wine Road. Turn left at the northern edge of Edenkoben.*

This is one of the most charming wine villages of the Pfalz. The entire ★ **Altstadt** (Old Town) is under historical preservation protection. For 350 years the Knights of Dalberg lived in the castle **Kropsburg,** the romantic ruins of which overlook the town. The Renaissance tombstones are among the many artworks in the late-Gothic Church of **St. Martin.** The town's namesake is honored with a parade and wine festival on November 11.

Dining and Lodging

$$ ★ **St. Martiner Castell.** The Mücke family transformed a simple vintner's house into a fine hotel and restaurant, retaining many of the original features, such as exposed beams and an old wine press. Although in the heart of town, the hotel is an oasis of peace, particularly the rooms with balconies overlooking the garden. A native of the Loire Valley, Frau Mücke adds French flair to the menu ($$–$$$), including a six-course *Schlemmer-Menü* (gourmet menu). The wine list offers a good selection of bottles from a neighboring wine estate. ✉ *Maikammerer Str. 2, D–67487,* ☎ *06323/9510,* FAX *06323/951–200,* WEB *www.hotelcastell.de.*

26 rooms. Restaurant, Weinstube, no a/c, some in-room data ports, sauna, some pets allowed (fee), no-smoking rooms. MC, V. Closed Feb. Restaurant closed Tues. and in Feb.

$ ✕🏨 **Landhaus Christmann.** This bright, modern house in the midst of the vineyards has stylish rooms decorated with both antiques and modern furnishings. Some rooms have balconies with a view of the Hambacher Schloss. Vintners and distillers, the Christmanns offer 20 wines by the glass in their restaurant Gutsausschank Kabinett ($–$$), as well as culinary wine tastings. ✉ *Riedweg 1, D–67487,* ☎ *06323/94270,* FAX *06323/942–727,* WEB *www.landhaus-christmann.de. 6 rooms, 3 apartments. Restaurant, no a/c, no room phones, some pets allowed (fee), no-smoking rooms. No credit cards. Hotel and restaurant closed 2 wks in Jan.–Feb. and 2 wks in July–Aug. Restaurant closed Mon.–Wed. No lunch.*

Nightlife and the Arts

Schloss Villa Ludwigshöhe, Kloster Heilsbruck (a former Cistercian convent near Edenkoben), and **Schloss Edesheim** are backdrops for concerts and theater in summer. For a calendar of events contact the Südliche Weinstrasse regional tourist office in Landau.

Shopping

Artist Georg Wiedemann is responsible for both content and design of the exquisite products of Germany's premier wine vinegar estate, **Doktorenhof** (✉ Raiffeisenstr. 5, ☎ 06323/5505) in Venningen, 2 km (1 mi) east of Edenkoben. Make an appointment for a unique vinegar tasting and tour of the cellars or pick up a gift at his shop. He's open weekdays 8–4, Wednesday until 6, and Saturday 9–2 (no credit cards).

En Route Depart St. Martin via the Totenkopf-Höhenstrasse, a very scenic road through the forest. Turn right at the intersection with Kalmitstrasse and proceed to the vantage point atop the **Kalmit,** the region's highest peak (2,200 ft). The view is second to none. Return to the Kalmitstrasse, drive toward Maikammer, and stop at the chapel **Mariä-Schmerzen-Kapelle** (Our Lady of Sorrows Chapel) in Alsterweiler. It houses the work of an unknown master, a remarkable Gothic triptych depicting the crucifixion. Maikammer has half-timber houses, patrician manors, and a baroque church, and is the last (or first) wine village in the Südliche Weinstrasse district.

Back on the Wine Road it's a brief drive to the Neustadt suburb of Hambach. The sturdy block of **Hambacher Schloss** is considered the "cradle of German democracy." It was here, on May 27, 1832, that 30,000 patriots demonstrated for German unity, raising the German colors for the first time. Inside, there are exhibits about the uprising and the history of the castle. The French destroyed the 11th-century imperial fortress in 1688. It has been largely rebuilt during the past 50 years in neo-Gothic style. It is an impressive setting for theater and concerts. On a clear day you can see the spire of Strasbourg Cathedral and the northern fringe of the Black Forest from the terrace restaurant. ✉ *Hambach,* ☎ *06321/30881,* WEB *www.hambacher-schloss.de.* 🎫 *€4.50.* ⏲ *Mar.–Nov., daily 10–6.*

Neustadt

❼ *8 km (5 mi) north of St. Martin; 5 km (3 mi) north of Hambach on the Wine Road.*

Neustadt and its nine wine suburbs are at the midpoint of the Wine Road and the edge of the district known as Deutsche Weinstrasse–Mittelhaardt. With around 5,000 acres of vines, they jointly comprise Germany's largest wine-growing community. The German Wine Harvest

Festival culminates every October with the coronation of the German Wine Queen and a parade with more than 100 floats. You can sample some 100 Neustadt wines year-round at the **Haus des Weines** (House of Wine), which is opposite the town hall. The Gothic house from 1276 is bordered by a splendid Renaissance courtyard. ✉ *Rathausstr. 6,* ☎ *06321/355–871. Closed Sun. and Mon.*

The **Marktplatz** (market square) is the focal point of the Old Town and a beehive of activity on Tuesday, Thursday, and Saturday, when farmers come to sell their wares. The square itself is ringed by baroque and Renaissance buildings (Nos. 1, 4, 8, and 11) and the Gothic **Stiftskirche** (Collegiate Church), built as a burial church for the counts Palatine. In summer concerts take place in the church (Saturday 11:30–noon), after which you can ascend the southern tower (187 ft) for a bird's-eye view of the town. The world's largest cast-iron bell—weighing more than 17 tons—hangs in the northern tower. Indoors, see the elaborate tombstones near the choir and the fanciful grotesque figures carved into the baldachins and corbels.

The Pfalz is home to the legendary, elusive *Elwetritschen,* part bird and part human, said to roam the forest and vineyards at night. "Hunting Elwetritschen" is both a sport and an alibi. Local sculptor Gernot Rumpf has immortalized them in a **fountain** on Marstallplatz. No two are alike. Near the market square, hunt for the one that "escaped" from its misty home. End a walking tour of the Old Town on the medieval lanes Metzgergasse, Mittelgasse, and Hintergasse to see beautifully restored half-timber houses, many of which are now pubs, cafés, and boutiques.

Thirty historical train engines and railway cars are on display at the **Eisenbahn Museum,** behind the main train station. Take a ride through the Palatinate Forest on one of the museum's historical steam trains, the *Kuckucksbähnel* (€12), which departs around 10:30 AM every other Sunday between Easter and mid-October. It takes an hour and a half to cover the 13-km (8-mi) stretch from Neustadt to Elmstein. ✉ *Neustadt train station, Schillerstr. entrance,* ☎ *06325/8626.* *€3.* *Weekends and holidays 10–4.*

Dining and Lodging

$–$$$$ ✕ **Altstadtkeller.** Tucked behind a wooden portal, this vaulted sandstone "cellar" (it's actually on the ground floor) is a cozy setting for very tasty food. The regular menu includes a number of salads and a good selection of fish and steaks, and the daily specials are geared to what's in season. Owner Jürgen Reis is a wine enthusiast and his well-chosen list shows it. ✉ *Kunigundenstr. 2,* ☎ *06321/32320,* WEB *www.altstadtkeller-neustadt.de. AE, DC, MC, V. Closed 3 wks in July–Aug. and Mon. No dinner Sun.*

$$–$$$ ✕ **Brezel.** The gilded *Brezel* (pretzel) hanging in front of the 17th-century half-timber house (once a bakery) is the namesake of Helga and Stefan Braun's classy, yet comfortable, wine restaurant. White walls, softened by light wooden floors and beams, are hung with paintings by the late Impressionist Otto Dill. In the back, dine beneath the vaulted ceiling of a former wine cellar. Fish is the specialty, but the entire menu is based on fresh, seasonal ingredients. The luncheon special is a good value and the excellent wines are reasonably priced. ✉ *Rathausstr. 32, between Ludwigstr. and Sauter Str.,* ☎ *06321/481–971,* WEB *www.brezel-restaurant.de. MC. Closed 1 wk in Feb., 2 wks in late July, and Tues. No lunch Wed.*

$–$$ ★ ✕ **Weinstube Eselsburg.** The *Esel* (donkey) lends its name to Mussbach's best-known vineyard, Eselshaut (donkey's hide); this wine pub; and one of its specialties, *Eselsuppe,* a hearty soup of pork, beef, and vegetables. Always packed with regulars, this pub is decorated with original artwork by the owner, Peter Wiedemann, and his late father, Fritz, the pub's founder. Enjoy top Pfälzer wines in the flower-filled courtyard in summer or in the warmth of an open hearth in winter. From October to May, try the *Schlachtfest* (meat and sausages from freshly slaughtered pigs) the first Tuesday of the month. ✉ *Kurpfalzstr. 62, Neustadt-Mussbach,* ☎ *06321/66984. MC, V. Closed Sun.–Tues. and mid-Dec.–mid-Jan. No lunch.*

$ ✕🏨 **Burgschänke Rittersberg.** From the terrace of the Rusche family's restaurant ($–$$$), you have a view of the Hambacher Schloss towering above and the vineyards below. The menu has something for every taste, such as homemade *Wildschinken* (ham made from boar) or fresh trout or salmon in a sorrel sauce. The rooms are very simple and the surroundings peaceful. ✉ *Hambacher Schloss 19, D–67434 Neustadt-Hambach,* ☎ *06321/39900,* FAX *06321/32799,* WEB *www.hotel-rittersberg.de. 5 rooms. Restaurant, Weinstube, no a/c, no room TVs, in-room data ports. MC, V. Restaurant and hotel closed 2 wks in Jan. and 2 wks in summer. Restaurant closed Thurs.*

$ ★ ✕🏨 **Mithras-Stuben/Weinstube Kommerzienrat.** Convivial proprietor and wine devotee Bernd Hagedorn named his four spacious apartments after Mithras, the ancient Persian god of light and deity of a religious cult embraced by Roman legionnaires. The contemporary furnishings, Oriental rugs, and modern baths are a far cry from what the Romans had in the Pfalz 2,000 years ago. An incredible 300 Pfälzer and 250 imported wines can be sampled by the glass in the restaurant ($–$$$). *Rumpsteak* (beef steak), served with tasty *Bratkartoffeln* (home-fried potatoes) or *Rösti* (potato pancakes), and Pfälzer Gyros (a unique meat-and-cheese dish) are favorites. ✉ *Kurpfalzstr. 161/Loblocherstr. 34, 67435 Neustadt-Gimmeldingen,* ☎ *06321/679–0335 or 06321/68200,* FAX *06321/679–0331,* WEB *www.weinstube-kommerzienrat.de. 4 apartments. Restaurant, no a/c, some in-room data ports, kitchenettes, shop, some pets allowed (fee), no-smoking rooms. MC, V. Restaurant closed Thurs. No lunch.*

$ 🏨 **Gästehaus Reber.** This little 18th-century stone vintner's house has been renovated to offer modern comfort but not at the expense of its charm. Every room has a balcony or terrace, and there's breakfast in the cozy vaulted cellar. Close to the Palatinate Forest and on the Wanderweg Deutsche Weinstrasse, it is ideal for hikers. ✉ *Heidenburgstr. 12, D–67435 Neustadt-Gimmeldingen,* ☎ *06321/96360,* FAX *06321/963–620. 4 rooms. Lounge, no a/c, some pets allowed (fee). No credit cards.*

Nightlife and the Arts

The **Saalbau** (✉ Hetzelpl. 1, ☎ 06321/926–892), opposite the train station, is Neustadt's convention center and main venue for concerts, theater, and events. In summer there is open-air theater at **Villa Böhm** (✉ Maximilianstr. 25), which also houses the city's history museum. Concerts, art exhibits, and wine festivals are held at the **Herrenhof** (✉ An der Eselshaut 18) in the suburb of Mussbach. Owned by the Johanniter-Orden (Order of the Knights of St. John) from the 13th to 18th centuries, it is the oldest wine estate of the Pfalz. Contact the Neustadt tourist office for program details and tickets.

Outdoor Activities and Sports

The Neustadt tourist office has brochures and maps that outline circular biking and hiking routes, including the educational wine paths in Gimmeldingen and Haardt.

En Route The **Holiday Park,** in Hassloch, 10 km (6 mi) east of Neustadt, is one of Europe's largest amusement parks. The admission fee (free on your birthday) covers all attractions, from shows to giant-screen cinema, and special activities for children. The free-fall tower, hell barrels, and Thunder River rafting are just a few of many fun rides. ☎ *06324/599–3900,* WEB *www.holidaypark.de.* 🎫 *€20.* ⏲ *Early Apr.–early Nov., daily 10–6.*

Speyer

8 *25 km (15 mi) east of Neustadt via B–39, 22 km (14) mi south of Mannheim via B–9 and B–44.*

Speyer was one of the great cities of the Holy Roman Empire, founded in pre-Celtic times, taken over by the Romans, and expanded in the 11th century by the Salian emperors. Between 1294, when it was declared a Free Imperial City, and 1570, no fewer than 50 imperial diets ★ were convened here. Ascend the **Altpörtel,** the impressive town gate, for a grand view of Maximilianstrasse, the street that led kings and emperors straight to the cathedral. 🎫 *€1.* ⏲ *Apr.–Oct., weekdays 10–noon and 2–4, weekends 10–5.*

★ The **Kaiserdom** (Imperial Cathedral), one of the finest Romanesque cathedrals in the world, conveys the pomp and majesty of the early Holy Roman emperors. It was built in about 30 years, between 1030 and 1061, by the emperors Konrad II, Henry III, and Henry IV. The latter replaced the flat ceiling with groined vaults in the late 11th century, an innovative feat in its day. A restoration program in the 1950s returned the building to almost exactly its original condition.

See the exterior before venturing inside. You can walk most of the way around it, and there's a fine view of the east end from the park by the Rhine. Much of the architectural detail, including the dwarf galleries and ornamental capitals, was inspired and executed by stone masons from Lombardy, which belonged to the German Empire at the time. The four towers symbolize the four seasons and that the power of the empire extends in all four directions. Look up as you enter the nearly 100-ft-high portal. It is richly carved with mythical creatures. In contrast to Gothic cathedrals, whose walls are supported externally by flying buttresses, allowing for a minimum of masonry and a maximum of light, at Speyer the columns supporting the roof are massive. The **Krypta** (crypt) lies beneath the chancel. The largest in Germany and strikingly beautiful in its simplicity, it is the burial site of four emperors, four kings, and three empresses. ✉ *Dompl.* 🎫 *Donation requested.* ⏲ *Apr.–Oct., daily 9–7; Nov.–Mar., daily 9–5. Closed during services.*

★ Opposite the cathedral, the **Historisches Museum der Pfalz** (Palatinate Historical Museum) houses the **Domschatz** (Cathedral Treasury). Other collections chronicle the art and cultural history of Speyer and the Pfalz from the Stone Age to modern times. Try to see the precious "Golden Hat of Schifferstadt," a golden, cone-shape object used for religious purposes during the Bronze Age. The **Wine Museum** exhibits artifacts from Roman times to the present, including the world's oldest bottle of wine, from circa AD 300. A major exhibition on "Knights and Castles" will run from late March to early October in 2003. ✉ *Dompl. 4,* ☎ *06232/132–514,* FAX *06232/132–519,* WEB *www.museum.speyer.de.* 🎫 *€4.50; free Tues. 4–6.* ⏲ *Tues.–Sun. 10–6.*

Speyer was an important medieval Jewish cultural center. In the **Jewish quarter,** behind the Palatinate Historical Museum, you can see synagogue remains from 1104 and Germany's oldest (pre-1128) ritual baths, the 33-ft-deep ***Mikwe.*** ✉ *Judenbadg,* ☎ *06232/291–971.* 🎫 *€1.* ⏲ *Apr.–Oct., weekdays 10–1 and 2–5, weekends 10–5.*

A turn-of-the-20th-century factory hall houses the **Technik-Museum** (Technology Museum), a large collection of locomotives, aircraft, old automobiles, fire engines, and automatic musical instruments. Highlights here are the 420-ton U-boat (you can go inside) and the massive 3-D IMAX cinemas. ✉ *Geibstr. 2,* ☎ *06232/67080,* WEB *www.technik-museum.de.* 🎟 *Museum or IMAX €9, combination ticket €14.* ⏲ *Daily 9–6.*

Dining and Lodging

$$$–$$$$ ★ ✕ **Backmulde.** Bread is still baked daily in this historic bakery, now a friendly, comfortable, and upscale wine restaurant. Homemade bread, homegrown fruits and vegetables, and local products are all part of chef and proprietor Gunter Schmidt's requirements of freshness. The aromas and flavors of his fare often have a Mediterranean accent and the menu changes according to season. The wine list features an array of Champagnes, and more than 600 wines—half from the Pfalz and a well-chosen selection from abroad—spanning decades of vintages. Schmidt's own wines are from the Heiligenstein vineyard on the outskirts of Speyer. ✉ *Karmeliterstr. 11–13,* ☎ *06232/71577. AE, DC, MC, V. Closed Sun., Mon., and mid-Aug.–early Sept.*

$–$$$ ✕ **Wirtschaft Zum Alten Engel.** This 200-year-old vaulted brick cellar, with its rustic wood furnishings and cozy niches, is an intimate setting for a hearty meal. Seasonal dishes supplement the large selection of Pfälzer and Alsatian specialties, such as *Ochsenfetzen* (slices of beef), coq au vin, or *Choucroute* (similar to a Pfälzer Teller). The wine list features about 100 Pfälzer wines. ✉ *Mühlturmstr. 7,* ☎ *06232/70914. No credit cards. Closed 2 wks in Aug. and Sun.*

$ ★ ✕🏨 **Kutscherhaus.** Charming rustic decor and a profusion of flowers have replaced the *Kutschen* (coaches) in this turn-of-the-20th-century coachman's house. The menu ($–$$) offers regional cuisine as well as creative vegetarian and pasta dishes. In summer you can sit beneath the old plane trees in the beer garden and select from a sumptuous buffet. Three modern, comfortable suites can sleep up to four persons each. ✉ *Am Fischmarkt 5a, D–67346,* ☎ *06232/70592,* FAX *06232/620–922,* WEB *www.kutscherhaus-speyer.de. 3 suites. Restaurant, beer garden, no a/c, minibars, bicycles, some pets allowed. AE, MC, V. Restaurant closed Wed, Thurs.*

$$ 🏨 **Hotel Goldener Engel.** A scant two blocks west of the Altpörtel is the "Golden Angel," a friendly, family-run hotel furnished with antiques and innovative, metal-and-wood designer furniture. Paintings by contemporary artists and striking photos of Namibia and the Yukon line the walls—the latter a tribute to proprietor Paul Schaefer's wanderlust. The restaurant Wirtschaft Zum Alten Engel is in the cellar. ✉ *Mühlturmstr. 5–7, D–67346,* ☎ *06232/13260,* FAX *06232/132–695. 44 rooms, 2 suites. Restaurant, no a/c in some rooms, bicycles, some pets allowed (fee). MC, V. Closed 2 wks late Dec.–early Jan.*

Nightlife and the Arts

Highlights for music lovers are **Orgelfrühling,** the organ concerts in the Gedächtniskirche (Memorial Church) in spring, and the concerts in the cathedral during September's **Internationale Musiktage.** Call the Speyer tourist office for program details and tickets. Walk into the town hall courtyard to enter the **Kulturhof Flachsgasse,** home of the city's art collection and special exhibitions. ✉ *Flachsgasse.* 🎟 *Free admission.* ⏲ *Tues.–Sun. 11–6.*

The music, dancing, acrobatics, magic, and comedy of the 3½-hour shows at **Variete-Palast Speyer** make for lively entertainment. A four- or five-course dinner is served during evening performances. Showtime is 3 PM Sunday and 7 PM every night of the week. ✉ *Untere Langgasse 6,* ☎ *06232/676–767,* FAX *06232/676–768,* WEB *www.varietepalast.cqr.de.* 🎟 *Weeknights €69, weekends €79.*

Deidesheim

9 *8 km (5 mi) north of Neustadt via the Wine Road, now B–271.*

Deidesheim is the first of a trio of villages on the Wine Road renowned for their vineyards and the wine estates known as the "three Bs of the Pfalz"—Bassermann, Buhl, and Bürklin.

The half-timber houses and historical facades framing Deidesheim's **Marktplatz** form a picturesque group, including the Church of St. Ulrich, a Gothic gem inside and out, and the old **Rathaus**, whose doorway is crowned by a baldachin and baroque dome. The attractive open staircase leading up to the entrance is the site of the festive *Geissbock-Versteigerung* (billy-goat auction) every Pentecost Tuesday, followed by a parade and folk dancing. The goat is the tribute neighboring Lambrecht has paid Deidesheim since 1404 for grazing rights. Inside see the richly appointed **Ratssaal** (council chamber) and the museum of wine culture. ✉ *Marktpl.* 🎫 *€2.* ⏲ *Mar.–Dec., Wed.–Sun. 4–6.*

Vines, flowers, and *Feigen* (fig trees) cloak the houses behind St. Ulrich on Heumarktstrasse and its extension, Deichelgasse (nicknamed Feigengasse). Cross the Wine Road to reach the grounds of **Schloss Deidesheim,** now a wine estate and pub (closed Wednesday and Thursday). The bishops of Speyer built a moated castle on the site in the 13th century. Twice destroyed and rebuilt, the present castle dates from 1810 and the moats have been converted into gardens.

Dining and Lodging

$$–$$$$ ✕ **Weinstube St. Urban.** St. Urban is the vintners' patron saint and considered responsible for the outcome of the harvest between his name day on May 25 until the harvest in autumn. This is not a "typical" Weinstube, but rather an upscale wine restaurant offering very good regional cuisine and wines in several beautiful rooms. It's in the Hotel Deidesheimer Hof. ✉ *Am Marktpl. 1,* ☎ *06326/96870. AE, DC, MC, V. Closed 1st wk in Jan.*

$$–$$$ ★ ✕ **Weinschmecker.** The restaurant and Vinothek of Herbert Nikola, an expert on Pfälzer wines and festivals, is on the eastern edge of town. Italian tiles and whitewashed walls give it a light, airy Mediterranean look—the menu reflects the same. The focus, however, is on top-quality Pfälzer wines, 200 of which (from about 40 estates) are featured; 120 are available by the glass. ✉ *Steing. 2,* ☎ *06326/980–460. No credit cards. Closed Sun. and Mon. No lunch.*

$$–$$$$ ★ ✕🏨 **Hotel Deidesheimer Hof.** If your timing's right, you could rub elbows with the heads of state, entertainers, or sports stars who frequent this house. Despite the aura of the guest book, the hotel retains its country charm and friendly service. Rooms are luxurious, and several have baths with round tubs or whirlpools. The restaurant Schwarzer Hahn ($$$$) is for serious wining and dining. The set menus, from three to seven courses, are an excellent choice. À la carte you can sample Pfälzer specialties, including sophisticated renditions of the region's famous dish, Saumagen. More than 600 wines grace the wine list. ✉ *Am Marktpl. 1, D–67146,* ☎ *06326/96870,* FAX *06326/7685,* WEB *www.deidesheimerhof.de. 24 rooms, 4 suites. Restaurant, Weinstube, no a/c in some rooms, some in-room data ports, minibars, bicycles, bar, lounge, library, some pets allowed (fee), no-smoking rooms. AE, DC, MC, V. Hotel and restaurant closed 1st wk in Jan. Restaurant closed Sun. and Mon. and 4 wks in July and Aug. No lunch.*

$$ ★ ✕🏨 **Hatterer's Hotel-Restaurant Le Jardin d'Hiver.** Clément Hatterer, the hospitable Alsatian owner and chef, has anticipated all the comforts you could ask for in his stylish hotel. Whether you dine in the winter garden, decorated in soothing shades of lilac, or in the sunny courtyard garden filled with exotic plants, the food and wine are exceptional. Like the menu ($$$–$$$$), the wine list features Pfälzer and Alsatian specialties. First floor guest rooms have a contemporary look; those on the second floor are more spacious and are outfitted in a country style with wood furniture. ✉ *Weinstr. 12, D–67146,* ☎ *06326/6011,* FAX *06326/7539,* WEB *www.hotel-hatterer.com. 57 rooms. Restaurant, no a/c, some in-room data ports, minibars, bicycles, bar, some pets allowed (fee). AE, DC, MC, V.*

$ **Gästehaus Johanna.** Expect a warm welcome from the Doll family. Their guest rooms are completely modern and no less cheerful. Ask for a room with a balcony facing the Haardt Mountains. ✉ *Kathrinenstr. 1, D–67146,* ☎ *06326/96700,* FAX *06326/7668,* WEB *www.ghaus-johanna.de. 9 rooms. No a/c, minibars, gym, some pets allowed (fee), no-smoking rooms. No credit cards.*

$ **Landhotel Lucashof.** Klaus and Christine Lucas are well known for their wines and hospitality. Their beautifully decorated, modern guest rooms are named after famous vineyards in Forst, and four have balconies—"Pechstein" is particularly nice. You can enjoy their award-winning wines in the tasting room, beneath a shady pergola in the courtyard, or in the privacy of your room (the refrigerator in the breakfast room is stocked for guests). Delicious food and wine at pubs in Forst's Old Town are a 3-minute walk away. ✉ *Wiesenweg 1a, D–67147 Forst,* ☎ *06326/336,* FAX *06326/5794,* WEB *www.lucashof.de. 7 rooms. No a/c, some pets allowed (fee), no-smoking rooms. No credit cards. Closed mid-Dec.–Jan.*

Shopping

The Biffar family not only runs a first-class **wine estate** (✉ Niederkircher Str. 13–15, ☎ 06326/5028) but also manufactures very exclusive candied fruits and ginger (delicious souvenirs).

En Route **Forst** and **Wachenheim,** both a few minutes' drive north of Deidesheim, complete the trio of famous wine villages. As you approach Forst, depart briefly from B–271 (take the left fork in the road) to see the Old Town with its vine- and ivy-clad sandstone and half-timber vintners' mansions. Peek through the large portals to see the lush courtyards. Many estates on this lane have pubs, as does the town's *Winzerverein* (cooperative winery). Wachenheim is another 2 km (1 mi) down the road. Its cooperative, Wachtenburg Winzer (with a good restaurant), is on the left at the entrance to town. Head for the Wachtenburg (castle) ruins up on the hill for a glass of wine. The Burgschänke (castle pub) is open if the flag is flying.

A couple of miles east of the Wine Road, between Wachenheim and ★ Friedelsheim, is the **Villa Rustica,** a fascinating open-air museum showing the foundations of a Roman farm dating from circa AD 20.

Bad Dürkheim

❿ *6 km (4 mi) north of Deidesheim on B–271.*

This pretty spa is nestled into the hills at the edge of the Palatinate Forest and ringed by vineyards on the other three sides. The saline springs discovered here in 1338 are the source of today's drinking and bathing cures, and at harvest time there's also a detoxifying *Traubenkur* (grape juice cure). A trip to the neoclassical **Kurhaus** and its beautiful gardens might be just the ticket if you've overindulged at the Dürkheimer Wurstmarkt, the world's largest wine festival. Legendary quantities of *Weck, Worscht, un Woi* (dialect for rolls, sausage, and wine) are consumed at the fair, including half a million *Schoppen,* the region's traditional pint-size glasses of wine. The festival grounds are also the site of the world's largest wine cask, the **Dürkheimer Riesenfass,** with a capacity of 1.7 million liters. Built in 1934 by an ambitious cooper, the cask is a restaurant that can seat well over 450 people.

Northwest of town is the **Heidenmauer** (heathen wall), the remains of an ancient Celtic ring wall more than 2 km (1 mi) in circumference and up to 20 ft thick in parts, and nearby are the rock drawings at **Krimhildenstuhl,** an old Roman quarry where the legionnaires of Mainz excavated sandstone.

Overlooking the suburb of Grethen are the ruins of **Kloster Limburg** (Limburg Monastery). Emperor Konrad II laid the cornerstone in 1030, supposedly on the same day as he laid the cornerstone of the Kaiserdom in Speyer. The monastery was never completely rebuilt after a fire in 1504, but it is a majestic backdrop for open-air performances in summer. The massive ruins of 13th-century **Hardenburg** Fortress lies 3 km (2 mi) farther west (via B–37) of the Kloster Limburg. In its heyday it was inhabited by more than 200 people. It succumbed to fire in 1794. ✉ *B–37.* €2.10. ⏲ *Apr.–Sept., Tues.–Sun. 9–6; Jan.–Mar. and Oct.–Nov., Tues.–Sun. 9–5. Closed Dec.*

Dining and Lodging

$$–$$$$ ✕ **Dürkheimer Riesenfass.** The two-story "giant cask" is divided into various rooms and niches with rustic wood furnishings. Ask to see the impressive *Festsaal mit Empore* (banquet hall with gallery) upstairs. Regional wines, Pfälzer specialties, and international dishes are served year-round and specialties in season. The terrace seats 300. ✉ *St. Michael Allee 1,* ☎ *06322/2143,* WEB *www.duerkheimer-fass.de. AE, MC, V.*

$–$$$ ★ ✕ **Weinstube Bach-Mayer.** From the warmth of the tile stove to the polished wooden tables and benches, this small wine pub appeals with its down-home atmosphere, tasty country cooking, and hearty Pfälzer wines. It's a local favorite. ✉ *Gerberstr. 13,* ☎ *06322/92120,* WEB *www.weinstube-bach-mayer.de. MC, V. Closed Sun. and 2 wks in mid-Jan. and during Wurstmarkt. No lunch.*

$$–$$$ ★ ✕🏨 **Kurparkhotel.** Part of the Kurhaus complex, the Kurparkhotel is the place to be pampered from head to toe. Haus A has the most elegant rooms, several with balconies. Haus B, also modern and comfortable, is less exclusive. This is a typical, elegant spa hotel, with extensive health and beauty facilities, thermal baths, a casino, and concerts in the garden. The flower-lined terrace at the restaurant Graf zu Leiningen ($$–$$$$) is a beautiful setting for coffee or tea with delicious, homemade pastries in the afternoon or an elegant *Feinschmecker-Menü* (five-course, gourmet menu) in the evening. ✉ *Schlosspl. 1–4, D–67098,* ☎ *06322/7970,* FAX *06322/797–158,* WEB *www.kurpark-hotel.de. 113 rooms. Restaurant, no a/c, in-room data ports, minibars, pool, sauna, spa, steam room, Turkish baths, bicycles, bowling, bar, casino, laundry service, some pets allowed (fee), no-smoking floors. AE, DC, MC, V.*

$ ✕🏨 **Weingut und Gästehaus Ernst Karst und Sohn.** This cheerful guest house is adjacent to the Karst family's wine estate, in the midst of the vineyards. Rooms are light and airy, furnished mostly in pine; all of them have splendid views of the countryside—which you are invited to explore on the bikes the Karsts loan. Tastings and cellar tours are possible, or sample the wines with regional dishes at the nearby restaurant, Weinrefugium ($–$$), at Schlachthausstrasse 1a (closed Monday, and two weeks in September; no lunch Tuesday). ✉ *In den Almen 15, D–67098,* ☎ *06322/2862,* FAX *06322/65965,* WEB *www.weingut-karst.de. 3 rooms, 6 apartments. Restaurant, no a/c, minibars, bicycles, no-smoking rooms. No credit cards. Closed Nov.–Jan.*

$$$ ★ **Weingut Fitz-Ritter.** Konrad Fitz and his American wife, Alice, have a centuries-old stone cottage that sleeps up to four people on the park-like grounds of their 218-year-old wine estate. You'll have a pool all to yourselves and there are concerts and festivals in the garden, courtyard, and vaulted cellars (request a calendar of events). Tastings and tours of the cellars, vineyards, and garden are possible. The minimum stay is seven nights. ✉ *Weinstr. Nord 51, D–67098,* ☎ *06322/5389,* FAX *06322/66005,* WEB *www.fitz-ritter.com. 1 cottage. No a/c, kitchen, pool, some pets allowed, no smoking. MC, V.*

Nightlife and the Arts

The **Spielbank** (casino) in the Kurparkhotel is a daily diversion after 2 PM (€2.50); jacket and tie are required. Concerts and theater take place at the **Limburg Monastery.** Contact the local tourist office for program details.

Outdoor Activities and Sports

GOLF

Tee up amid the vineyards at an 18-hole course with a driving range and pitch-and-putt greens. The **Golfgarten Deutsche Weinstrasse** is in Dackenheim, 8 km (5 mi) north of Bad Dürkheim. ✉ *Im Bitzgrund,* ☎ *06353/989–212,* WEB *www.golfgarten.de.*

SWIMMING

The **Kurhaus Staatsbad** (✉ Kurbrunnenstr. 14, ☎ 06322/9640) houses all kinds of bathing facilities for leisure and wellness, including thermal baths, herbal steam baths, a sauna, and the Turkish bath Hamam. It's open weekdays 9–9 and weekends 9–5.

En Route When the vineyards of Ungstein, a suburb north of Bad Dürkheim, were modernized in 1981, a **Roman wine estate** was discovered. Among the finds was an ancient *Kelterhaus* (pressing house). Watch for signs to Villa Weilberg, to the left of the Wine Road (B–271).

Around Freinsheim

11 *7 km (4½ mi) northeast of Bad Dürkheim, via Kallstadt (the right turn to Freinsheim is signposted midway through Kallstadt).*

The next village on the Wine Road north of Bad Dürkheim is **Kallstadt,** where you can enjoy Saumagen in your glass and on your plate—for this is the home of the excellent **Saumagen Vineyard.** Both its wine and the specialty dish are served with pride everywhere in town, not just at the *Saumagenkerwe* (wine festival) the first weekend in September.

Off the Wine Road to the east, **Freinsheim's** *Stadtmauer* (town wall), probably built between 1400 and 1540, is one of the best-preserved fortifications in the Pfalz. Walk along it to see the massive town gates (Eisentor and Haintor) and the numerous towers, two of which can be rented as holiday apartments. Many of the town's historical houses are baroque, including the **Rathaus** (1737), with its covered stairway and sandstone balustrade. Next to it is a **Protestant church,** a Gothic structure to which Renaissance and baroque elements were added over the years. No fewer than five large festivals are celebrated here between April and September—quite a showing for a town this small.

Drive 5 km (3 mi) west to Weisenheim am Berg (you'll cross over the Wine Road at Herxheim) and watch for signs toward Bobenheim and Kleinkarlbach. This road, which runs parallel to the Wine Road and along the vineyard heights, affords a wonderful panorama of the expansive vineyards stretching onto the Rhine Plain. Follow the signs to **Neuleiningen,** then wind your way uphill to reach the romantic Old

Town, ringed by a medieval wall. The ruins of the 13th-century castle are a good start for a town walk.

Dining and Lodging

$$–$$$ ✕ **Alt Freinsheim.** Cordial chef Axel Steffl's domain is tucked away on a narrow lane between Hauptstrasse and Freinsheim's town wall (northern edge). Old stone walls, exposed beams, and the tiny size of the restaurant make for a cozy dining experience. Whether you opt for his country cooking, such as *Kartoffelstrudel* (potato strudel with liverwurst and blood sausage), or a refined entrée with one of his creative sauces, everything is homemade. The good selection of local wines is as reasonably priced as the food. ✉ *Korngasse 5, Freinsheim,* ☏ *06353/2582. No credit cards. Closed Wed. and 3 wks in summer. No lunch.*

$$ ★ ✕ **Weinhaus Henninger.** Walter Henninger numbers among the elite of Pfälzer vintners, but there's nothing pretentious about the atmosphere or cooking at his wood-paneled wine pub. It's a jovial place, frequented by locals who come for the delicious, hearty fare and excellent wines. The soups and *Eintopf* dishes (stews), Rumpsteak with sautéed onions, and daily specials are recommended. ✉ *Weinstr. 93, Kallstadt,* ☏ *06322/2277. No credit cards. Closed Mon. and 2 wks in Jan. No lunch in Feb.*

$$ ★ ✕🏨 **Hotel-Restaurant Alte Pfarrey.** The Old Rectory is on the hilltop above the Old Town of Neuleiningen. The comfortable inn with modern facilities is made up of several Gothic houses. Rooms are distinctive for their antique furnishings. Susanne and Utz Ueberschaer tend to the personal service and first-rate culinary delights ($$–$$$$). The focus is on light international favorites prepared with fresh, local ingredients. The wine list is very good, with offerings from the New and Old World. Jewelry fans: don't miss the vitrine showcasing son Tobias's designer jewelry. ✉ *Unterg. 54, D–67271 Neuleiningen,* ☏ *06359/86066,* FAX *06359/86060. 9 rooms. Restaurant, no a/c, no room TVs, some pets allowed (fee). DC, MC, V. Closed Mon., Tues., and 3 wks in Aug.*

$$ ★ ✕🏨 **Hotel-Restaurant Luther.** This elegant country inn is set in a baroque manor next to Freinsheim's town wall. The rooms provide modern comfort amid refined decor, with fresh flowers throughout the house. Gisela Luther's handsome table settings and Dieter Luther's artistic food presentations make dining here ($$$$) a joy for all the senses. One of Germany's leading chefs, Dieter is known for his imaginative combinations, such as lobster with fennel or venison with kumquats. Save room for a chocolate creation or the crème brûlée quintet. Spanish, Bordeaux, and top Pfälzer wines are focal points of the wine list. ✉ *Hauptstr. 29, D–67251 Freinsheim,* ☏ *06353/93480,* FAX *06353/934–845,* WEB *www.luther-freinsheim.de. 23 rooms. Restaurant, no a/c, some in-room data ports, minibars, no-smoking rooms. AE, MC, V. Hotel closed Jan. Restaurant closed Sun. and Jan. No lunch.*

$$ ★ ✕🏨 **Hotel-Restaurant Weinkastell Zum Weissen Ross.** Behind the cheerful facade of this half-timber house, with its wrought-iron sign depicting a *weisser Ross* (white stallion), you can experience Pfälzer hospitality at its best. Rooms have warm colors, solid oak furnishings, and modern baths, and several have romantic alcove or four-poster beds. Jutta and Norbert Kohnke offer service and cuisine ($$$$) that are top-notch. The superb wines come from her brother's wine estate next door, Weingut Koehler-Rupprecht, and there's a well-chosen selection of international red wines. This is the best place in the Pfalz to sample "Saumagen twice." ✉ *Weinstr. 80–82, D–67169 Kallstadt,* ☏ *06322/5033,* FAX *06322/66091. 13 rooms, 1 apartment. Restaurant, no a/c, bicycles, some pets allowed. AE, MC, V. Hotel closed Jan. to mid-Feb. Restaurant closed Mon., Tues., Jan. to mid-Feb., and 1 wk in late July or early Aug.*

$ **Town Wall Tower.** For a room with a view in a highly original setting, overnight in a medieval *Turm* (tower). The Hahnenturm sleeps two; the Herzogturm can accommodate a family. Contact the Freinsheim tourist office for reservations. ✉ *Hauptstr. 2, D–67251 Freinsheim,* ☎ *06353/989–294,* FAX *06353/989–904,* WEB *http://stadt.freinsheim.de. 2 rooms. No a/c, no room phones, no room TVs, kitchenettes. No credit cards.*

En Route Neuleiningen is 4 km (2½ mi) west of the Wine Road–town Kirchheim. **Bockenheim,** 10 km (6 mi) north, is dominated by an imposing gateway. Like its counterpart in Schweigen-Rechtenbach, the **Haus der Deutschen Weinstrasse** marks the end (or start) of its namesake, the German Wine Road.

THE RHINE TERRACE

Like Speyer, the cities of Worms and Mainz were Free Imperial Cities and major centers of Christian and Jewish culture. Germany's first synagogue and Europe's oldest surviving Jewish cemetery, both from the 11th century, are in Worms. The imperial diets of Worms and Speyer in 1521 and 1529 stormed around Martin Luther (1483–1546) and the rise of Protestantism. In 1455 Johannes Gutenberg (1400–68), the inventor of movable type, printed the Gutenberg Bible in Mainz.

Worms

15 km (9 mi) east of Bockenheim via B–47 from Monsheim, 45 km (28 mi) south of Mainz on B–9.

Although devastated in World War II, Worms (pronounced *vawrms*) is among the most ancient cities of Germany with a history going back some 6,000 years. Once settled by the Romans, Worms later became one of the imperial cities of the Holy Roman Empire. More than 100 imperial diets were held here, including the 1521 meeting where Martin Luther pleaded his cause. In addition to having a great Romanesque cathedral, Worms is a center of the wine trade.

Worms developed into an important garrison town under the Romans, but it is better known for its greatest legend, the *Nibelungenlied,* derived from the short-lived kingdom established by Gunther and his Burgundian tribe in the early 5th century. The complex and sprawling story was given its final shape in the 12th century and tells of love, betrayal, greed, war, and death. It ends when Attila the Hun defeats the Nibelungen (Burgundians), who find their court destroyed, their treasure lost, and their heroes dead. One of the most famous incidents tells how Hagen, treacherous and scheming, hurls the court riches into the Rhine. Near the Nibelungen Bridge there's a bronze statue of him caught in the act. The *Nibelungenlied* may be legend, but the story is based on fact. A Queen Brunhilda, for example, is said to have lived here. It's also known that a Burgundian tribe was defeated in 436 by Attila the Hun in what is present-day Hungary.

Not until Charlemagne resettled Worms almost 400 years later, making it one of the major cities of his empire, did the city prosper again. Worms was more than an administrative and commercial center, it was a great ecclesiastical city as well. The first expression of this religious importance was the original cathedral, consecrated in 1018. Between 1130 and and 1181 it was rebuilt in three phases into the church you see today.

★ 12 The *Nibelungenlied* comes to life in the **Nibelungen Museum,** a stunning sight-and-sound exhibition cleverly installed in two medieval towers and the portion of the old town wall between them. The structure itself is architecturally fascinating inside and out, and the rampart affords a wonderful view of the town. Language is no problem: the tour script (via headphones and printed matter) is in excellent English. Allow 1½ hours for a thorough visit. ✉ *Fischerpförtchen 10,* ☎ *06241/202–120,* WEB *www.nibelungen-museum.de.* 🎫 €*5.50.* ⏲ *Tues.–Sun. 10–5.*

★ 13 If you've seen Speyer Cathedral, you'll quickly realize that the **Wormser Dom St. Peter** (Cathedral of St. Peter), by contrast, contains many Gothic elements. In part this is simply a matter of chronology. Speyer Cathedral was completed nearly 70 years before the one in Worms was even begun, long before the lighter, more vertical lines of the Gothic style evolved. Furthermore, once built, Speyer Cathedral was left largely untouched in later periods; the Worms Cathedral was remodeled frequently as new architectural styles and new values developed. The Gothic influence can be seen both inside and out, from the elaborate tympanum with biblical scenes over the southern portal (today's entrance), to the great rose window in the west choir, to the five sculptures recounting the life of Christ in the north aisle. The cathedral was completely gutted by fire in 1689 in the War of the Palatinate Succession. For this reason many of the furnishings are baroque, including the magnificent gilt high altar from 1742, designed by the master architect Balthasar Neumann (1687–1753). The choir stalls are no less decorative. They were built between 1755 and 1759 in rococo style. Walk around the building to see the artistic detail of the exterior. ✉ *Dompl.,* ☎ *06241/6115.* 🎫 *Donation requested.* ⏲ *Apr.–Oct., daily 9–5:45; Nov.–Mar., daily 9–4:45. Closed during services.*

An imperial palace once stood in what is now the **Heylshofgarten,** a park just north of the cathedral. This was the site of the fateful meeting between Luther and Emperor Charles V in April 1521 that ultimately led to the Reformation. Luther refused to recant his theses demanding Church reforms and went into exile in Eisenach, where he
★ 14 translated the New Testament in 1521 and 1522. The **Kunsthaus Heylshof** (Heylshof Art Gallery) in the Heylshofgarten is one of the leading art museums of the region. It has an exquisite collection of German, Dutch, and French paintings as well as stained glass, glassware, porcelain, and ceramics from the 15th to 19th centuries. ✉ *Stephansg. 9,* ☎ *06241/22000.* 🎫 €*2.50.* ⏲ *May–Sept., Tues.–Sun. 11–5; Oct.–Dec. and mid-Feb.–Apr., Tues.–Sat. 2–5, Sun. 11–5.*

15 The Lutheran **Dreifaltigkeitskirche** (Church of the Holy Trinity) is just across the square from the Heylshofgarten. Remodeling during the 19th and 20th centuries produced today's austere interior, although the facade and tower are still joyfully baroque. ✉ *Marktpl.* ⏲ *Apr.–Sept., daily 9–5; Oct.–Mar., daily 9–4.*

16 The **Lutherdenkmal** (Luther Monument) commemorates Luther's appearance at the Diet of Worms. He ended his speech with the words: "Here I stand. I have no choice. God help me. Amen." The 19th-century monument includes a large statue of Luther ringed by other figures from the Reformation. It is set in a small park on the street named Lutherring.

The Jewish quarter is along the town wall between Martinspforte and Friesenspitze and between Judengasse and Hintere Judengasse. The first
★ 17 **Synagoge** (synagogue) was built in 1034, rebuilt in 1175, and expanded in 1212 with a building for women. Destroyed in 1938, it was rebuilt in 1961 using as much of the original masonry as had survived. ✉ *Hin-*

Dreifaltigkeitskirche 15
Judenfriedhof Heiliger Sand 18
Kunsthaus Heylshof . . . 14
Liebfrauenkirche 20
Lutherdenkmal . . . 16
Nibelungen Museum . . . 12
Städtisches Museum . . . 19
Synagoge . . 17
Wormser Dom St. Peter . . . 13

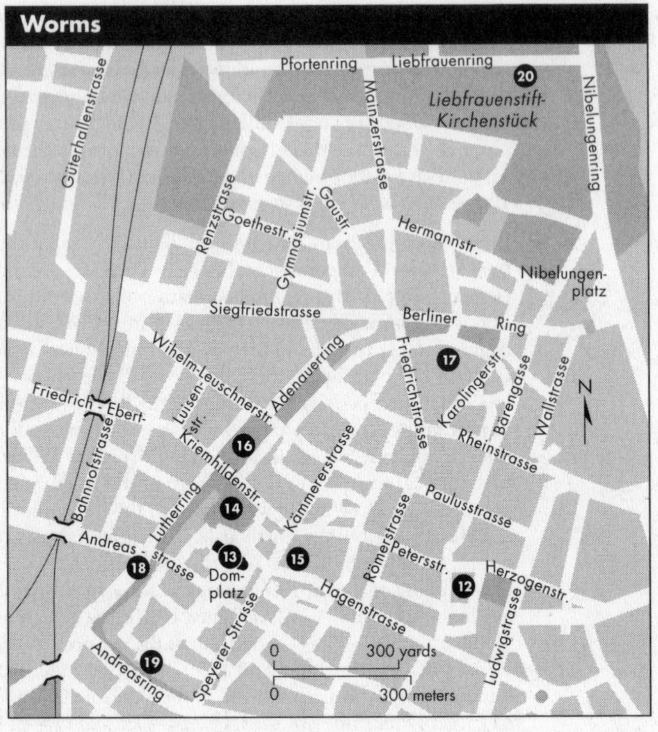

tere Judeng. ⏲ Apr.–Oct., daily 10–12:30 and 1:30–5; Nov.–Mar., daily 10–noon and 2–4. Closed during services.

The **Raschi-Haus,** the former study hall, dance hall, and Jewish hospital, is next door to the synagogue. It houses the city archives and the **Jewish Museum.** ✉ *Hintere Judeng. 6,* ☎ *06241/853–4707.* 🎫 *€1.50.* ⏲ *Apr.–Oct., Tues.–Sun. 10–12:30 and 1:30–5; Nov.–Mar., Tues.–Sun. 10–12:30 and 1:30–4:30.*

18 The **Judenfriedhof Heiliger Sand** (Holy Sand Jewish Cemetery) is the oldest Jewish cemetery in Europe. The oldest of some 2,000 tombstones date from 1076. ✉ *Andreasstr. and Willy-Brandt-Ring.* ⏲ *Daily.*

19 To bone up on the history of Worms, visit the **Städtisches Museum** (Municipal Museum), housed in the cloisters of a Romanesque church in the Andreasstift. ✉ *Weckerlingpl. 7,* ☎ *06241/946–390.* 🎫 *€3.* ⏲ *Tues.–Sun. 10–5.*

On the northern outskirts of Worms, the twin-tower Gothic
20 **Liebfrauenkirche** (Church of Our Lady) is set amid vineyards. The church is the namesake of the mild white wine named Liebfraumilch, literally, the "Milk of Our Lady." Today this popular wine can be made from grapes grown throughout Rheinhessen, the Pfalz, the Nahe, and the Rheingau wine regions, since the original, small vineyard surrounding the church could not possibly meet demand.

Dining and Lodging

$$$–$$$$ ★ ✕ **Rôtisserie Dubs.** A pioneer of the Rheinhessen restaurant scene, Wolfgang Dubs focused on creative regional cuisine and seasonal specialties long before it was in vogue. Fish or fowl, meat or game are all expertly prepared and garnished. For a more casual meal, try his cozy dépendance next door, Gasthaus Zum Schiff ($). The daily specials are a very good value. Wine enthusiast Dubs offers his own wines, top Ger-

man and French estates, and a few New World wines, such as Opus One. Rheindürkheim is 9 km (5½ mi) north of Worms via B–9. ✉ *Kirchstr. 6 (near the Rhine), Worms-Rheindürkheim,* ☎ *06242/2023. MC. Closed Tues., 2 wks in Jan., and 2 wks in summer. No lunch Sat.*

$–$$$ ★ ✕ **Bistro Léger.** Barbara and Jorg Seider's bistro caters to baby boomers who appreciate the casual, friendly atmosphere and fresh, well-prepared food. The salads are outstanding, as is the homemade fish soup. Very popular are the menus with variations on a theme during "fish weeks" and "fowl weeks." There's a good selection of regional wines. ✉ *Siegfriedstr. 2,* ☎ *06241/46277. MC, V. Closed Sun.*

$$ ✕ **Dom-Hotel.** The appeal of this hotel with modern, comfortable rooms lies in its friendly staff and its terrific location in the heart of the pedestrian zone (a parking garage is available). At the hotel's upscale restaurant ($$–$$$$) you can watch the happenings on the square below. The focus is on international and regional cuisine and wines. ✉ *Obermarkt 10, D–67547,* ☎ *06241/9070,* FAX *06241/23515,* WEB *www.dom-hotel.de. 60 rooms, 1 apartment. Restaurant, no a/c, in-room data ports, minibars, bicycles, laundry service, some pets allowed (fee), no-smoking rooms. AE, DC, MC, V. Restaurant closed Sun. and 2 wks in July. No lunch Sat.*

$$ ✕ **Landhotel Zum Schwanen.** Guido Schmetzer and his wife are the ebullient hosts of this lovingly restored country inn in Osthofen (10 km [6 mi] northwest of Worms). The 18th-century estate is grouped around a nicely landscaped courtyard which fills up with alfresco diners on warm evenings. Like the rooms, Restaurant Weinstube ($$–$$$) is light, airy, and furnished with sleek, contemporary furniture. The Mediterranean flair of the inn is also reflected in the ingredients and seasoning of several dishes on the menu, but regional favorites, such as Saumagen or Tafelspitz, are also served. Schmetzer's lineup of fine, local wines is exemplary. ✉ *Friedrich-Ebert-Str. 40, 67574 Osthofen (west of B–9),* ☎ *06242/9140,* FAX *06242/914–299,* WEB *www.zum-schwanen-osthofen.de. 30 rooms. Restaurant, beer garden, no a/c, some in-room data ports, minibars, bicycles, some pets allowed (fee), no-smoking rooms. AE, MC, V. Restaurant closed first 2 wks in Jan. and 2 wks late July–early Aug. No lunch Sat.*

$ ✕ **Land- und Winzerhotel Bechtel.** The friendly Bechtel family, winegrowers and proud parents of a former German Wine Queen, offer very pleasant accommodations on the grounds of their wine estate in the suburb of Heppenheim, about 10 km (6 mi) west of Worms (depart Worms on Speyerer Strasse, an extension of Valckenbergstrasse, which runs parallel to the east side of the Dom). The rooms are modern, and all have balconies. You can enjoy hearty country cooking (daily specials) as well as more refined fare in the restaurant ($$–$$$$) or on its terrace with the estate's wines. Wine tastings in the vaulted cellars are also possible. ✉ *Pfälzer Waldstr. 100, D–67551 Worms-Heppenheim,* ☎ *06241/36536,* FAX *06241/34745. 15 rooms. Restaurant, no a/c, minibars, sauna, bicycles, some pets allowed (fee), no-smoking rooms. AE, MC, V.*

$ **Haus Kalisch am Dom.** For more than 30 years the Kalisch family has welcomed guests to its little inn opposite the cathedral. There are no frills, but the rooms are comfortable and have private baths and TVs. ✉ *Neumarkt 9, D–67547,* ☎ *06241/27666,* FAX *06241/25073. 13 rooms. No a/c, no room phones, some pets allowed. No credit cards. Closed 3 wks in Dec. and Jan.*

Nightlife and the Arts

Worms's nine-day wine and folk festival, the **Backfischfest** (Fried-Fish Festival), begins the last weekend of August. It evolved from the thanksgiving celebrations held by the once-powerful fishers' guild. There are rides, entertainment, a parade, fireworks, and *Fischerstechen* (jousting in the harbor).

The **Städtisches Spiel- und Festhaus** (✉ Rathenaustr., ☎ 06241/22525) is the cultural hub of Worms, presenting theater, concerts, ballet, and special events. Concerts are also held in the Municipal Museum, in the Andreasstift, and at the 19th-century palace Schloss Herrnsheim, in the northern suburb of Herrnsheim. The annual **jazz festival** (late June or early July) is staged primarily around Weckerlingplatz and the cathedral. Contact the tourist office for program details.

Shopping

For tasteful wine accessories and excellent wines drop by P. J. Valckenberg's wine shop, **Der Weinladen** (✉ Weckerlingpl. 1, ☎ 06241/911–180) near the Municipal Museum. The winery owns nearly all of the Liebfrauenstift-Kirchenstuck vineyard surrounding the Liebfrauenkirche. The store is closed Sunday and Monday and does not accept credit cards.

Oppenheim

21 *26 km (16 mi) north of Worms and 23 km (16 mi) south of Mainz on B–9.*

En route to Oppenheim, the vine-covered hills parallel to the Rhine gradually steepen. Then, unexpectedly, the spires of the Gothic ★ **St. Katharine's Church** come into view. The contrast of its pink sandstone facade against a bright blue sky is striking. Built between 1220 and 1439, it is the most important Gothic church between Strasbourg and Köln. The interior affords a rare opportunity to admire original 14th-century stained-glass windows and two magnificent rose windows, the Lily Window and the Rose of Oppenheim. The church houses masterfully carved tombstones, while the chapel behind it has a *Beinhaus* (charnel house) that contains the bones of 20,000 citizens and soldiers from the 15th to 18th centuries. ✉ *Katharinenstr. and Merianstr., just north of the market square.* ⊙ *Apr.–Oct., daily 8–6; Nov.–Mar., daily 9–5.*

Oppenheim and its neighbors to the north, Nierstein and Nackenheim, are home to Rheinhessen's finest vineyards. The **Deutsches Weinbaumuseum** (German Viticultural Museum) has wine-related artifacts that chronicle the region's 2,000-year-old wine-making tradition and the world's largest collection of mousetraps. ✉ *Wormser Str. 49,* ☎ *06133/2544.* 🎫 *€2.10.* ⊙ *Apr.–Oct., Tues.–Fri. 2–5, weekends 10–noon and 2–5.*

Nightlife and the Arts

Concerts are held in St. Katharine's, and open-air theater takes place in the **Burgruine Landskrone,** the 12th-century imperial fortress ruins a few minutes' walk northwest of the church. From here there is a wonderful view of the town and the vineyards, extending all the way to Worms on a clear day. For more jovial entertainment, accompanied by *Blasmusik* (brass-band oompah music), attend the **wine festival** in mid-August on the market square, which is ringed by half-timber houses and the 16th-century Rathaus.

Nierstein

22 *3 km (2 mi) north of Oppenheim on B–9.*

Surrounded by 2,700 acres of vines, Nierstein is the largest wine-growing community on the Rhine and boasts Germany's oldest documented **vineyard** (AD 742), the "Glöck," surrounding St. Kilian's Church. You can sample wines at the **Winzergenossenschaft** (cooperative winery; ✉ Karolingerstr. 6), which is the starting point of an easy hike or drive to the vineyard heights and the vantage point at the *Wartturm* (watch tower). Tasting stands are set up along the route, providing delightful wine presentations in the vineyards *am roten Hang* (referring to the steep sites of red soils of slate, clay, and sand) in mid-June. Early August brings the wine festival, with stands throughout the town and a festive parade in medieval costumes.

Nackenheim

23 *5 km (3 mi) north of Nierstein on B–9.*

This wine village lies slightly to the west of B–9; from the south, turn left and cross the railroad tracks (opposite the tip of the island in the Rhine) to reach the town center, 2 km (1 mi) down the country road. The writer Carl Zuckmayer (1896–1977) was born here and immortalized the town in his farce *Der fröhliche Weinberg* (*The Merry Vineyard*) in 1925. He described Rheinhessen wine as "the wine of laughter . . . charming and appealing." You can put his words to the test the last weekend of July, when wine festival booths are set up between the half-timber town hall on Carl-Zuckmayer-Platz and the baroque **Church of St. Gereon.** The church's scrolled gables, belfry, and elaborate altars are worth seeing.

Dining and Lodging

$$–$$$ ✕ **Zum alten Zollhaus.** Walk through the arched gateway to reach the beautiful garden and the entrance to this historical house. Cozy niches, fresh flowers, and handsome antiques provide a very pleasant setting for very good food and wine. Ilse Hees, the friendly proprietor, offers daily specials as well as standards, such as roast breast of duck. The *Trilogie vom Lachs* (cold salmon) served with a mustard sauce is excellent. The wine list focuses on Rheinhessen wines, and a good number are available by the glass. ✉ *Wormser Str. 7, next to Carl-Gunderloch-Pl.,* ☎ *06135/8726. No credit cards. Closed Sun., Mon., 2 wks late Feb., and 2 wks late Sept. No lunch.*

$–$$ ★ ✕🏨 **Landhotel und Weinstube St. Gereon.** The Jordan family's charming, half-timber country inn has modern rooms that feature pale shades of yellow, blond-wood floors, and light-color furnishings. Stone walls and light pine furniture on terra-cotta tiles give the restaurant ($$$) a warm, rustic look, too. Try a *Winzerauflauf* (vintner's soufflé) of pasta, potatoes, onions, wine, and cheese or ask if the hearty regional specialties Dippe-Has or Backes Grumbeere are available. All 20 wines served come from Rheinhessen. ✉ *Carl-Zuckmayer-Pl. 3, D–55299,* ☎ *06135/92990,* FAX *06135/929–992. 15 rooms. Restaurant, no a/c, in-room data ports, bicycles, laundry service, some pets allowed (fee), no-smoking rooms. MC, V. Restaurant closed Tues. and Wed.*

Outdoor Activities and Sports

BIKING

The old towpath along the riverbank is an ideal cycling trail to Mainz or Worms, and the vineyard paths are well suited for exploring the countryside.

GOLF

Seven kilometers (4½ miles) southwest of Nackenheim, the **Golfanlage Domtal Mommenheim** (✉ Am Golfpl., Mommenheim, ☎ 06138/92020) is in the midst of and named after the Nierstein vineyard site Domtal. It's a beautiful setting to play 18 holes or to just unwind at the driving range.

HIKING

Enjoy the views from the vineyard heights on the **Rheinhöhenweg** trail. Allow three hours to hike the 10-km (6-mi) stretch between

Nackenheim, Nierstein, and Oppenheim. Start at the corner of Weinbergstrasse and Johann-Winkler-Strasse. The educational wine path through the St. Alban vineyard is a pleasant walk in Bodenheim (4 km [2½ mi] northwest of Nackenheim).

Mainz

24 *14 km (9 mi) north of Nackenheim, 45 km (28 mi) north of Worms on B–9, and 42 km (26 mi) west of Frankfurt on A–3.*

Mainz is the capital of the state of Rheinland-Pfalz. Today's city was built on the site of a Roman citadel from 38 BC, though some of the local artifacts in its Landesmuseum date from 300,000 BC. Given its central location at the confluence of the Main and Rhine rivers, it's not surprising that Mainz has always been an important trading center, rebuilt time and time again in the wake of wars. The city's fine museums and historical buildings bear witness to a splendid past.

To see the sights, head for the Touristik Centrale (tourist office) to pick up a *Mainz Card,* a terrific one-day pass for €6 that includes a basic walking tour, unlimited use of public transportation, and free entry to museums and the casino, as well as a reduction in price on some hotel rooms, KD cruises, and theater tickets.

The **Marktplatz** and *Höfchen* (little courtyard) around the cathedral, the focal points of the town, are especially colorful on Tuesday, Friday, and Saturday, when farmers set up their stands to sell produce and flowers. This is also the site of the *Sektfest* (sparkling wine festival) in early June and the *Johannismarkt,* a huge wine festival with fireworks, a few weeks later.

★ The entrance to the **Dom** (Cathedral of St. Martin and St. Stephan) is on the south side of the market square, midway between the eastern and western chancels that symbolize the worldly empire and the sacerdotal realm, respectively. Emperor Otto II began building the oldest of the Rhineland's trio of grand Romanesque cathedrals in 975, the year in which he named Willigis archbishop and chancellor of the empire. Henry II, the last Saxon emperor of the Holy Roman Empire, was crowned here in 1002, as was his successor, Konrad II, the first Salian emperor, in 1024. In 1009, on the very day of its consecration, the cathedral burned to the ground. It was the first of seven fires the Dom has endured in the course of its millennium. Today's cathedral dates mostly from the 11th to 13th centuries. During the Gothic period, remodeling diluted the Romanesque identity of the original; an imposing baroque spire was added in the 18th century. Nevertheless, the building remains essentially Romanesque and its floor plan demonstrates a clear link to the cathedrals in Speyer and Worms. The interior is a virtual sculpture gallery of elaborate monuments and tombstones of archbishops, bishops, and canons, many of which are significant artworks from the 13th to 19th centuries. ✉ *Domstr. 3 (Markt),* ☎ *06131/253–412.* 🎫 *Donations requested.* ⏲ *Mar.–Oct., weekdays 9–6:30, Sat. 9–4, Sun. 12:45–2:45 and 4–5; Nov.–Feb., weekdays 9–5, Sat. 9–4, Sun. 12:45–2:45 and 4–6:30. Closed during services.*

From the Middle Ages until secularization in the early 19th century, the archbishops of Mainz, who numbered among the imperial electors, were extremely influential politicians and property owners. The wealth of religious art treasures they left behind can be viewed in the **Dom und Diözesanmuseum,** in the cathedral cloisters. ✉ *Domstr. 3,* ☎ *06131/253–344.* 🎫 *Free.* ⏲ *Tues.–Sun. 10–5.*

★ Opposite the east end of the cathedral (closest to the Rhine) is the **Gutenberg Museum,** devoted to the history of writing and printing from Babylonian and Egyptian times to the present. Exhibits include historical printing presses, incunabula, and medieval manuscripts with illuminated letters, as well as a precious 42-line Gutenberg Bible printed in circa 1455. A replica workshop demonstrates how Gutenberg implemented his invention of movable type. ✉ *Liebfrauenpl. 5,* ☎ *06131/122–640,* WEB *www.gutenberg-museum.de.* 🎫 *€3.* ⏲ *Tues.–Sat. 9–5, Sun. 11–3.*

★ The Kurfürstliches Schloss (Electoral Palace) houses the **Römisch-Germanisches Zentralmuseum,** a wonderful collection of original artifacts and copies of items that chronicle cultural developments in the area up to the early Middle Ages. ✉ *Ernst-Ludwig-Pl. on Grosse Bleiche,* ☎ *06131/91240.* 🎫 *Free.* ⏲ *Tues.–Sun. 10–6.*

The remains of five 4th-century wooden Roman warships and two full-size replicas are on display at the **Museum für Antike Schiffahrt** (Museum of Ancient Navigation). These were unearthed in 1981 when the foundation for the Hilton's new wing was dug. For more than a decade the wood was injected with a water-and-paraffin mixture to restore hardness. ✉ *Neutorstr. 2b,* ☎ *06131/286–630.* 🎫 *Free.* ⏲ *Tues.–Sun. 10–6.*

★ The various collections of the **Landesmuseum** (Museum of the State of Rheinland-Pfalz) are in the former electors' stables, easily recognized by the statue of a golden stallion over the entrance. Exhibits range from the Stone Age to the 20th century. Among the highlights are a tiny Celtic glass dog from the 1st or 2nd century BC, Roman masonry, paintings by Dutch masters, artworks from the baroque to art nouveau periods, and collections of porcelain and faience. ✉ *Grosse Bleiche 49–51,* ☎ *06131/28570.* 🎫 *€3.* ⏲ *Tues. 10–8, Wed.–Sun. 10–5.*

The animals in Mainz's **Naturhistorisches Museum** (Natural History Museum) may all be stuffed and mounted, but these lifelike groups can demonstrate the relationships among various families of fauna better than any zoo. Fossils and geological exhibits show the evolution of the region's plants, animals, and soils. ✉ *Reichklarastr. 1,* ☎ *06131/122–646.* 🎫 *€1.50.* ⏲ *Wed. and Fri.–Sun. 10–5, Tues. and Thurs. 10–8.*

Schillerplatz, ringed by beautiful baroque palaces, is the site of the ebullient Fastnachtbrunnen (Carnival Fountain), with 200 figures related to Mainz's "fifth season" of the year. From Shillerplatz it is but a short ★ walk up Gaustrasse to **St. Stephanskirche** (St. Steven's Church), which affords a hilltop view of the city. In 990 Willigis built a basilica on the site; today's Gothic hall church dates from the late 13th and early 14th centuries. Postwar restoration included the installation of six vividly blue, stained-glass windows depicting scenes from the Bible, designed in the 1970s by the Russian-born painter Marc Chagall. ✉ *Kleine Weissg. 12 (via Gaustr.),* ☎ *06131/231–640.* ⏲ *Feb.–Nov., Mon.–Sat. 10–noon and 2–5; Dec.–Jan., Mon.–Sat. 10–noon and 2–4:30; year-round, afternoon only on Sun.*

The hillside **Kupferberg Sektkellerei** (sparkling wine cellars) were built in 1850 on a site where the Romans cultivated vines and built cellars. The Kupferberg family expanded the cellars into 60 seven-story deep vaulted cellars—the deepest in the world. The winery has a splendid collection of glassware; posters from the Belle Epoque period (1898–1914); richly carved casks from the 18th and 19th centuries; and the Traubensaal (Grape Hall), a tremendous example of the art nouveau style. Two-hour tours include a tasting of five sparkling wines; one-hour tours include one glass of Sekt. Reservations are required. ✉ *Kupferbergterrasse 17–19,* ☎ *06131/9230,* WEB *www.kupferberg.de.* 🎫 *€11 or €6.50.* ⏲ *Shop weekdays 10–6. MC, V.*

Dining and Lodging

$-$$$$ ✕ **Fischrestaurant Jackob.** Fresh fish (the fish shop next door belongs to the restaurant) is served at reasonable prices in a setting of old foghorns and ship photographs. *Muscheln* (mussels) are available in season. ✉ *Fischtor 7,* ☏ *06131/229–299. V. Closed Sun. Dinner only on Fri., Oct.–May.*

$-$$$$ ★ ✕ **Gebert's Weinstuben.** Gebert's traditional wine restaurant serves refined versions of regional favorites in a very personal atmosphere. Try the *Handkäs-Suppe* (cheese soup) or Saumagen made not of pork, but rather *Wildschwein* (wild boar). *Gans mit Schmoräpfel und Klöse* (goose with braised apples and dumplings) is served from 11 November until Christmas. The seasonal specialties, homemade noodles, and handmade chocolate pralines are always delicious. German wines (especially Rheinhessen) dominate the excellent wine list. Summer dining alfresco is possible in the smartly renovated courtyard. ✉ *Frauenlobstr. 94 (near the Rhine),* ☏ *06131/611–619.* WEB *www.geberts-weinstuben.de. AE, DC, MC, V. Closed Sat. and 3 wks in summer. No lunch Sun.*

$$-$$$ ✕ **Heiliggeist.** Meals are served until after midnight at this lively café-bistro-bar. Modern, minimal decor provides an interesting contrast to the historical vaulted ceilings. The compact menu includes elaborate salad platters as well as creatively spiced and sauced fish and meat dishes. One house specialty worth trying is the *Croustarte,* an upscale version of pizza. There is an extensive beverage list that you'd expect at a bar. Wines by the glass are pricey, but bottles are fairly reasonable. ✉ *Mailandsg. 11,* ☏ *06131/225–757.* WEB *www.heiliggeist-online.de. No credit cards. No lunch.*

$-$$$ ✕ **Mollers.** In the final phase of the state theater renovation, a chic glass-lined café-restaurant was opened on the top floor. It affords a fabulous view of Mainz and surroundings, whether you opt for afternoon coffee and cake, an evening meal (served until midnight), or weekend brunch. Many of the vegetarian, fish and meat dishes and numerous salads can be ordered as a *kleine Portion* (small serving). From the main entrance to the theater, walk straight ahead and past the ground-floor bistro to reach the elevators for the ascent. ✉ *Gutenbergplatz 7,* ☏ *06131/627–9215. MC, V. Closed Wed. No lunch weekdays.*

$-$$ ✕ **Eisgrub-Bräu.** It's loud, it's lively, and the beer is brewed in the vaulted cellars on site. An Eisgrub brew is just the ticket to wash down a hearty plate of *Haxen* (pork hocks) or *Meterwurst* (yard-long, rolled bratwurst), *Bratkartoffeln* (home fries), and sauerkraut. Breakfast (daily) and a buffet lunch (weekdays) are also served. Brewery tours are free, but make a reservation in advance. It's open daily 9 AM–1 AM. ✉ *Weisslilieng. 1a,* ☏ *06131/221–104. MC, V.*

$-$$ ★ ✕ **Haus des Weines.** In addition to the pleasant ambience, tasty food, and a great selection of wines, the late hours are customer-friendly. The luncheon specials (€5.20) and huge salads are a very good value and the menu covers a broad range, from snacks to full-course meals. Enjoy a glass of wine with the Mainz specialties *Spundekäs* (cheese whipped with cream and onions) or *Handkäse mit Musik* (pungent, semihard cheese served with diced onions in vinaigrette). ✉ *Gutenbergpl. 3,* ☏ *06131/221–300. AE, MC, V.*

$$$-$$$$ 🏨 **Hyatt Regency Mainz.** The blend of contemporary art and architecture with the old stone walls of historical Fort Malakoff on the Rhine is a visually stunning success. From the spacious atrium lobby to the luxurious rooms, everything is sleek, modern, and designed for comfort. Niches in a vaulted cellar and live music attract a lively crowd of locals and travelers to the trendy Malakoff Bar, and tables in the garden courtyard are always at a premium in the summer. The boutiques and pubs of the Old Town are but a five- to ten-minute walk away. ✉ *Malakoff-Terrasse 1, 55116,* ☏ *06131/731–234,* FAX *06131/731–235,*

WEB *www.mainz.hyatt.com. 265 rooms, 3 suites. Restaurant, in-room data ports, minibars, indoor pool, gym, massage, sauna, steam room, bicycles, bar, lobby lounge, laundry service, concierge, concierge floor, some pets allowed (fee), no-smoking rooms. AE, DC, MC, V.*

$–$$ **Hotel Ibis.** Modern, functional rooms and a great location on the edge of the Old Town are what the Ibis offers. Ask about the various discount rates that are available (except during trade fairs and major events). ✉ *Holzhofstr. 2, at Rheinstr., D–55116,* ☎ *06131/2470,* FAX *06131/234–126,* WEB *www.ibishotel.com. 144 rooms. In-room data ports, bar, laundry service, some pets allowed (fee), no-smoking rooms. AE, DC, MC, V.*

$–$$ **Hotel Weinhaus Rebstock.** This 15th-century house is tucked away in the Old Town's pedestrian zone. A family-run operation, it offers friendly service and comfortable rooms, seven with a view of the cathedral. Park at the garage of the Karstadt department store (entrance on Weissliliengasse), a minute's walk. ✉ *Heiliggrabg. 6, near Bischofspl. D–55116,* ☎ *06131/230–317,* FAX *06131/230–318. 11 rooms, 5 with bath. No a/c, no room phones, some pets allowed. MC, V.*

Nightlife and the Arts

Mainz supports a broad spectrum of cultural events, music from classical to avant-garde, as well as dance, opera, and theater performances, at many venues throughout the city. Music lovers can attend concerts in venues ranging from the cathedral, the Kurfürstliches Schloss, and the Kupferberg sparkling wine cellars, to the Rathaus, market square, and historic churches. The home stage of the Staatstheater Mainz is the **Grosses Haus** (✉ Gutenbergpl., ☎ 06131/28510 or 06131/285–1222). A smaller stage, the Kleines Haus, is also on the premises. **TiC** is a sister stage of the Grosses Haus (✉ Spritzeng. 2, ☎ 06131/28510) that features works of contemporary artists. **Mainzer Kammerspiele** (✉ Rheinstr. 4, Fort Malakoff Park, ☎ 06131/225–002) is a multiarts venue. The Mainzer Forum-Theater (cabaret) performs in the **Unterhaus** (✉ Münsterstr. 7, ☎ 06131/232–121).

The **Frankfurter Hof** (✉ Augustinerstr. 55) hosts many (often contemporary) musical events and lively dance parties. A traditional setting for concerts is the **Villa Musica** (✉ Auf der Bastei 3), with a repertoire ranging from classical to modern.

Nightlife is centered in the numerous wine pubs. Rustic and cozy, they're packed with locals who come to enjoy a meal or snack with a glass (or more) of local wine. Most are on the Old Town's main street, **Augustinerstrasse,** and its side streets (Grebenstrasse, Kirschgarten, Kartäuserstrasse, Jakobsbergstrasse) and around the Gutenberg Museum, on Liebfrauenplatz. The wood-paneled pub **Wilhelmi** (✉ Rheinstr. 51, ☎ 06131/224–949) is a favorite with the post-student crowd. **Schreiner** (✉ Rheinstr. 38, ☎ 06131/225–720) attracts a mature clientele and is an old, traditional Mainz favorite.

Carnival season runs from November 11 at 11:11 AM to Ash Wednesday. There are dozens of costume balls, parties, political cabaret sessions—culminating with a huge parade of colorful floats and marching bands through downtown on the Monday before Lent.

Shopping

The Old Town is full of boutiques, and the major department stores (Karstadt and Kaufhof-Galeria) sell everything imaginable, including gourmet foods in their lower levels. The shopping district lies basically between the Grosse Bleiche and the Old Town and includes the **Am Brand** Zentrum, an ancient marketplace that is now a pedestrian zone brimming with shops.

The excellent **Weincabinet** (✉ Leichhofstr. 10, behind the cathedral, ☎ 06131/228–858) sells an array of the region's best wines and accessories. The flea market **Krempelmarkt** is on the bank of the Rhine between the Hilton Hotel and Kaiserstrasse. It takes place from 7 to 1 the first and third Saturday of the month from April to October and the first Saturday from November to March.

THE PFALZ AND THE RHINE TERRACE A TO Z

To research prices, get advice from other travelers, and book travel arrangements, visit www.fodors.com.

AIRPORTS

Frankfurt is the closest major international airport for the entire Rhineland. International airports in Stuttgart and France's Strasbourg are closer to the southern end of the German Wine Road.

BIKE TRAVEL

There is no charge for transporting bicycles on local trains throughout Rheinland-Pfalz weekdays after 9 AM and anytime weekends and holidays. The train stations in the towns of this chapter, however, do not rent bicycles. For maps, suggested routes, bike rental locations, and details on *Pauschal-Angebote* (package deals) or *Gepäcktransport* (luggage-forwarding service), contact Pfalz-Touristik or Rheinhessen-Information.

CAR RENTAL

Avis, Europcar, Hertz, and Sixt have rental offices at Frankfurt's airport and main train station.

➤ LOCAL AGENCIES: **Avis** (✉ Rheinallee 183, Mainz, ☎ 06131/625–523; ✉ Wormser Landstr. 22, Speyer, ☎ 06232/31680; ✉ Alzeyerstr. 44, Worms, ☎ 06241/591–081). **Europcar** (✉ Am Mombacher Kreisel 1, Mainz, ☎ 06131/913–500; ✉ Gutleutstr. 8, Worms, ☎ 06241/45767). **Hertz** (✉ Alte Mainzer Str. 127, Mainz, ☎ 06131/985–644; ✉ Klosterstr. 45, Worms, ☎ 06241/411–462). **Sixt** (✉ Bingerstr. 19, Mainz, ☎ 06131/270–710).

CAR TRAVEL

It's 162 km (100 mi) between Schweigen-Rechtenbach and Mainz, the southernmost and northernmost points of this itinerary. The main route is the Deutsche Weinstrasse, which is a *Bundesstrasse* (two-lane highway), abbreviated "B," as in B–38, B–48, and B–271. The route from Worms to Mainz is B–9. The autobahn, abbreviated "A," parallel to the Wine Road in the Pfalz is A–65 from Kandel to Kreuz Mutterstadt (the junction with A–61, south of Ludwigshafen), and in Rheinhessen, A–61 to Alzey, and, finally, A–63 to Mainz. The A–6 runs west to east through the Pfalz from Kaiserslautern to Kreuz Frankenthal (the junction with A–61, north of Ludwigshafen).

Autobahn access to Mainz, the northernmost point of the itinerary, is fast and easy. A–63, A–61, and A–65 run through the area roughly north–south, and A–8 approaches the southern part of the German Wine Road via Karlsruhe.

TOURS

Town walking tours usually begin at the tourist information office. Annweiler tours are at 10 AM on Wednesday from May to October, free of charge. Bad Dürkheim has free tours March to mid-November, departing Monday at 10:30 from the fountain in front of the train station. Deidesheim conducts tours from May to October on Saturday at 10 (€3). Mainz has year-round tours departing Saturday at 2 (€5) from the Touristik Centrale. The office is one story above street level on the footbridge over Rheinstrasse. There are additional tours from May to October, Wednesday and Friday at 2.

Tours of Landau are at 10 AM on the second Saturday of the month from May to October (€3). Neustadt tours cost €3 and take place April through mid-November, Wednesday and Saturday at 10:30. Speyer tours are at 11 on weekends between April and October; the cost is €2.50. Wachenheim tours are in September and October, Thursday at 4, and cost €1. Worms begins its tours at the southern portal (main entrance) of the cathedral on Saturday at 10:30 and Sunday at 2, between March and October. The cost is €3.

The Köln-Düsseldorfer Deutsche Rheinschiffahrt (KD Rhine Line; ☞ Cruise Travel *in* Smart Travel Tips A to Z) travels down the Rhine from Mainz to Köln.

TRAIN TRAVEL

Mainz and Mannheim are hubs for IC (InterCity) and ICE (InterCity Express) trains.

TRANSPORTATION AROUND THE PFALZ AND THE RHINE TERRACE

An excellent network of public transportation called *Rheinland-Pfalz-Takt* operates throughout the region with well-coordinated *RegioLinie* (buses) and *Nahverkehrszüge* (local trains). The travel service of the Deutsche Bahn (German Railway) provides information on schedules, connections, prices, and so on, 24 hours daily from anywhere in Germany.

VISITOR INFORMATION

The KulturCard (€5) entitles you to a 50% discount at many cultural events, museums, and sights in Rhineland–Pfalz. The card is sold at the newspaper offices of the *RheinPfalz* and *Rhein Zeitung*, and by mail through SWR. For discounts in Mainz, buy the MainzCard (€6) at the tourist office or at a hotel.

The regional and local tourist and wine information offices in the southern Pfalz, the northern Pfalz, and Rheinhessen can help you make the most of your visit. The German Wine Information Bureau (☞ Wine, Beer & Spirits *in* Smart Travel Tips A to Z) promotes the wines of all the wine regions.

➤ KULTURCARD: **SWR** (✉ Stichwort KulturCard, Postfach 3740, 55027 Mainz).

➤ PFALZ REGION: **Pfalz-Touristik** (✉ Landauer Str. 66, D–67434 Neustadt a.d. Weinstrasse, ☎ 06321/39160, FAX 06321/391–619, WEB www.pfalz-touristik.de). **Pfalzwein** (✉ Chemnitzer Str. 3, D–67433 Neustadt a.d. Weinstrasse, ☎ 06321/912–328, FAX 06321/12881, WEB www.zum-wohl-die-pfalz.de).

➤ NORTHERN PFALZ: **Deutsche Weinstrasse** (✉ Chemnitzer Str. 3, D–67433 Neustadt a.d. Weinstrasse, ☎ 06321/912–333, FAX 06321/912–330, WEB www.deutsche-weinstrasse.de).

➤ SOUTHERN PFALZ: **Südliche Weinstrasse** (✉ An der Kreuzmühle 2, D–76829 Landau, ☎ 06341/940–407, FAX 06341/940–502, WEB www.suedlicheweinstrasse.de).

➤ RHEINHESSEN AREA: **Rheinhessen-Information** (✉ Wilhelm-Leuschner-Str. 44, D–55218 Ingelheim, ☎ 06132/44170, FAX 06132/441–744, WEB www.rheinhessen-info.de). **Rheinhessenwein** (✉ An der Brunnenstube 33–35, D–55120 Mainz-Mombach, ☎ 06131/99680, FAX 06131/682–701, WEB www.rheinhessenwein.de).

➤ TOURIST INFORMATION: **Annweiler** (✉ Büro für Tourismus, Hauptstr. 20, D–76855, ☎ 06346/2200, FAX 06346/7917, WEB www.trifelsland.de). **Bad Dürkheim** (✉ Tourist-Information, Kurbrunnenstr. 14, D–67098, ☎ 06322/956–6250, FAX 06322/956—6259, WEB www.bad-duerkheim.de). **Deidesheim** (✉ Tourist Service, Bahnhofstr. 5, D–67146, ☎ 06326/96770, FAX 06326/967–718, WEB www.deidesheim.de). **Landau** (✉ Büro für Tourismus, Marktstr. 50, D–76829, ☎ 06341/13182, FAX 06341/13195, WEB www.landau.de). **Mainz** (Touristik Centrale; ✉ Brückenturm am Rathaus, D–55116, ☎ 06131/286–210, FAX 06131/286–2155, WEB www.info-mainz.de). **Neustadt-an-der-Weinstrasse** (✉ Tourist-Information, Hetzelpl. 1, D–67433, ☎ 06321/926–892, FAX 06321/926–891, WEB www.neustadt.pfalz.com). **Speyer** (✉ Tourist-Information, Maximilianstr. 13, D–67346, ☎ 06232/142–392, FAX 06232/142–332, WEB www.speyer.de). **Wachenheim** (✉ Tourist-Information, Weinstr. 16, D–67157, ☎ 06322/958–032, FAX 06322/958–059, WEB www.wachenheim.de). **Worms** (✉ Tourist-Information, Neumarkt 14, D–67547, ☎ 06241/25045, FAX 06241/26328, WEB www.worms-touristinfo.de).

12 THE RHINELAND

Vater Rhein, or "Father Rhine," is Germany's historic lifeline, and the region from Mainz to Koblenz is its heart. Its banks are crowned by magnificent castle after castle and by breathtaking, vine-terraced hills that provide the livelihood for many of the villages hugging the shores. In the words of French poet Victor Hugo, "The Rhine combines everything. The Rhine is swift as the Rhône, wide as the Loire, winding as the Seine . . . royal as the Danube and covered with fables and phantoms like a river in Asia . . ."

THE IMPORTANCE OF THE RHINE CAN HARDLY BE OVERESTIMATED. Although not the longest river in Europe (the Danube is more than twice its length), the Rhine has been the main river-trade artery between the heart of the Continent and the North Sea (and Atlantic Ocean) throughout recorded history. The Rhine runs 1,320 km (820 mi) from the Bodensee (Lake Constance) west to Basel, then north through Germany, and, finally, west through the Netherlands to Rotterdam.

Vineyards, a legacy of the Romans, are an inherent part of the Rhine landscape from Wiesbaden to Bonn. The Rhine tempers the climate sufficiently for grapes to ripen this far north. Indeed, the wine regions along the Rhine, such as the Rheingau, and its most important tributary, the Mosel, are synonymous with the world's finest Riesling wines. Thanks to the river, these wines were shipped far beyond the borders of Germany, which in turn gave rise to the wine trade that shaped the fortune of many a riverside town. Rüdesheim, Bingen, Koblenz, and Köln (Cologne) remain important commercial wine centers to this day.

The Rhine became Germany's top tourist site 200 years ago. Around 1790 a spearhead of adventurous travelers from throughout Europe arrived by horse-drawn carriages to explore the stretch of the river between Bingen and Koblenz, now known as the Rhine gorge or Mittelrhein (Middle Rhine). The Prussian-Rhine Steamship Co. (forerunner of the Köln-Düsseldorfer) started passenger service between Mainz and Köln in 1827. Shortly thereafter, the railroad opened the region to an early form of mass tourism.

The river is steeped in legend and myth. The Loreley, a steep jutting slate cliff, was once believed to be the home of a beautiful and bewitching maiden who lured boatmen to a watery end in the swift currents. Heinrich Heine's poem *Song of Loreley* (1827), inspired by Clemens Brentano's *Legend of Loreley* (1812) and set to music in 1837 by Friedrich Silcher, has been the theme song of the landmark ever since. The Nibelungen, a Burgundian race said to have lived on its banks, serve as subjects for Wagner's epic opera cycle *Der Ring des Nibelungen* (1852–72).

William Turner captured misty Rhine sunsets on canvas. Famous literary counterparts, such as Goethe's *The Feast of St. Roch* (1814), Lord Byron's *Childe Harold's Pilgrimage* (1816), or Mark Twain's *A Tramp Abroad* (1880), captured the spirit of Rhine Romanticism on paper, encouraging others to follow in their footsteps.

No less romantic is the dreamy landscape of the Mosel Valley. Vines and forests still carpet the steep, slate slopes lining the river from Trier, the former capital of the western Roman Empire, to its confluence with the Rhine at Koblenz. En route there is a wealth of Roman artifacts, medieval churches, and castle ruins to admire.

Pleasures and Pastimes

Dining

Regional cuisine features fresh fish and *Wild* (game), as well as sauces and soups based on the local Riesling and Spätburgunder (pinot noir) wines. *Tafelspitz* (boiled beef) and *Rheinischer Sauerbraten* (Rhenish marinated pot roast in a sweet-and-sour raisin gravy) are traditional favorites. The *Kartoffel* (potato) is prominent in soups, in *Reibekuchen* and *Rösti* (potato pancakes), and in *Dibbe- or Dippekuchen* (dialect: *Döppekoche*), a casserole baked in a cast-iron pot and served with apple compote. *Himmel und Erde,* literally, "Heaven and Earth," is a mixture of mashed potatoes and chunky applesauce, topped with panfried slices of blood sausage and onions.

Although Düsseldorf, Köln, and Wiesbaden are home to many talented chefs, some of Germany's most creative classic and contemporary cooking is also found in smaller towns or country inns.

CATEGORY	COST*
$$$$	over €20
$$$	€15–€20
$$	€10–€15
$	under €10

**per person for a main course at dinner*

Festivals

The Rhineland is a stronghold of Germany's **Fastnacht** (Carnival festivities), which takes place from 11:11 AM on November 11 to Ash Wednesday, culminating with huge parades in Düsseldorf, Köln, and Mainz on the Monday before Lent. Some attractions close for the five days leading up to Ash Wednesday.

Festivals lasting well over a week at venues throughout the Rheingau are the **Gourmet Festival** (mid-March) and **Glorreiche Tage** (mid-November); the **Rheingau Musik Festival** (mid-June through August), with more than 100 concerts, often held at Kloster Eberbach, Schloss Johannisberg, or Wiesbaden's Kurhaus; and theater and concerts during the **Burghof Spiele** in and near Eltville (late June to late August). Wiesbaden hosts the region's largest wine festival, the **Rheingauer Weinwoche** (mid-August), and the **Internationale Maifestspiele** (throughout May), featuring performances by world-renowned artists. Bonn is home to the **International Beethoven Festival** (mid-September).

The spectacular fireworks display "**Rhine in Flames**" takes place the first Saturday evening in May (Linz–Bonn), July (Bingen–Rüdesheim), and August (Andernach); the second Saturday evening in August (Koblenz) and September (Oberwesel); and the third Saturday evening in September (St. Goar).

Lodging

The most romantic places to lay your head are the old riverside inns and castle hotels. Ask for a *Rheinblick* (Rhine view) room. Hotels are often booked well in advance, especially for festivals and when there are trade fairs in Köln, Düsseldorf, or Frankfurt, making rooms in Wiesbaden and the Rheingau scarce and expensive. Many hotels close for the winter.

CATEGORY	COST*
$$$$	over €225
$$$	€150–€225
$$	€75–€150
$	under €75

**All prices are for two people in a double room, including tax and service.*

Music

Few regions in Europe rival the quality of classical music performances and venues on the Rhine. Beethoven was born in Bonn, and the city hosts a Beethoven festival every year in mid- to late September. Düsseldorf, once home to Mendelssohn, Schumann, and Brahms, has the finest concert hall in Germany after Berlin's Philharmonie: the Tonhalle, in a former planetarium. Köln also has one of Germany's best concert halls, and its opera company is known for exciting classical

The Rhineland

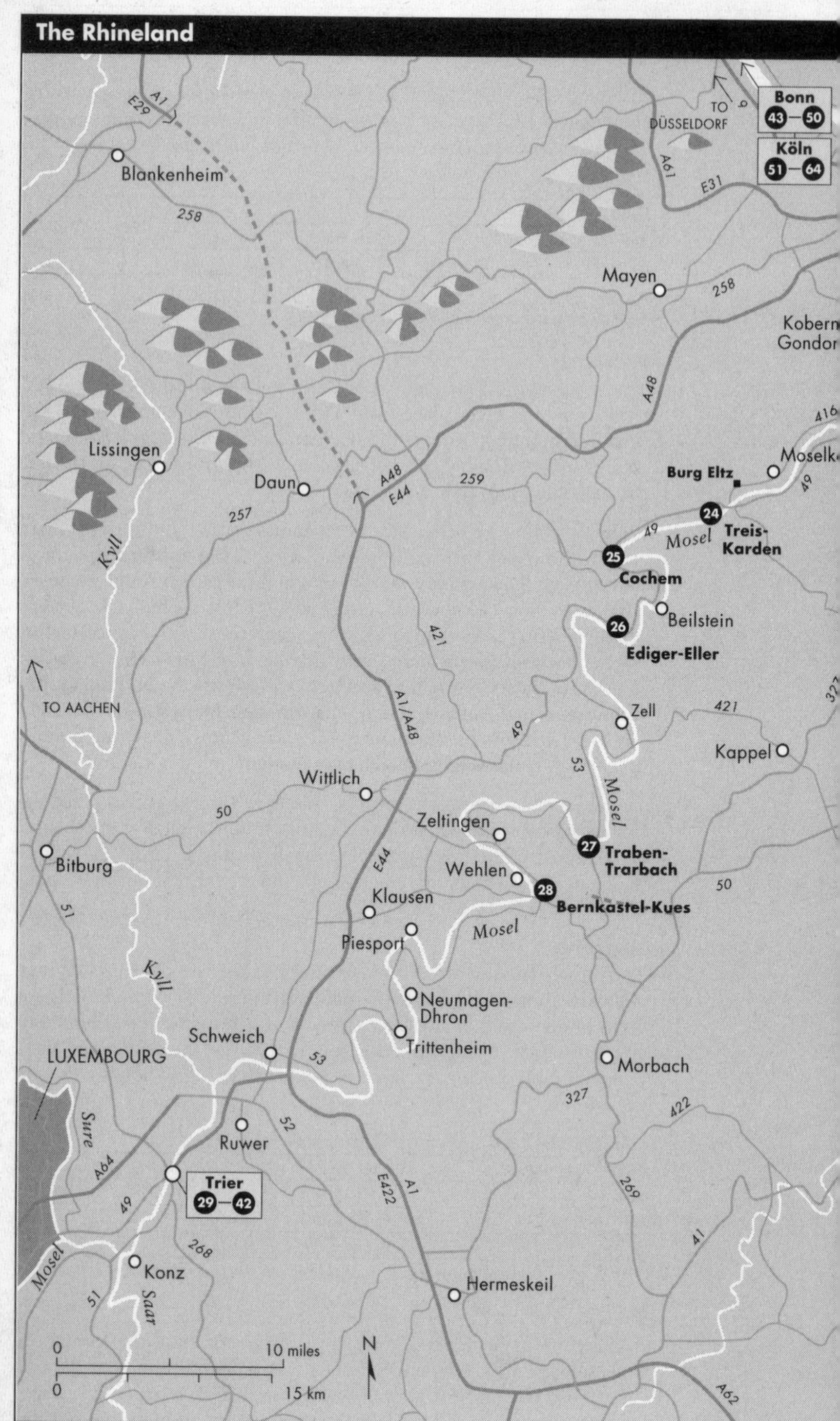

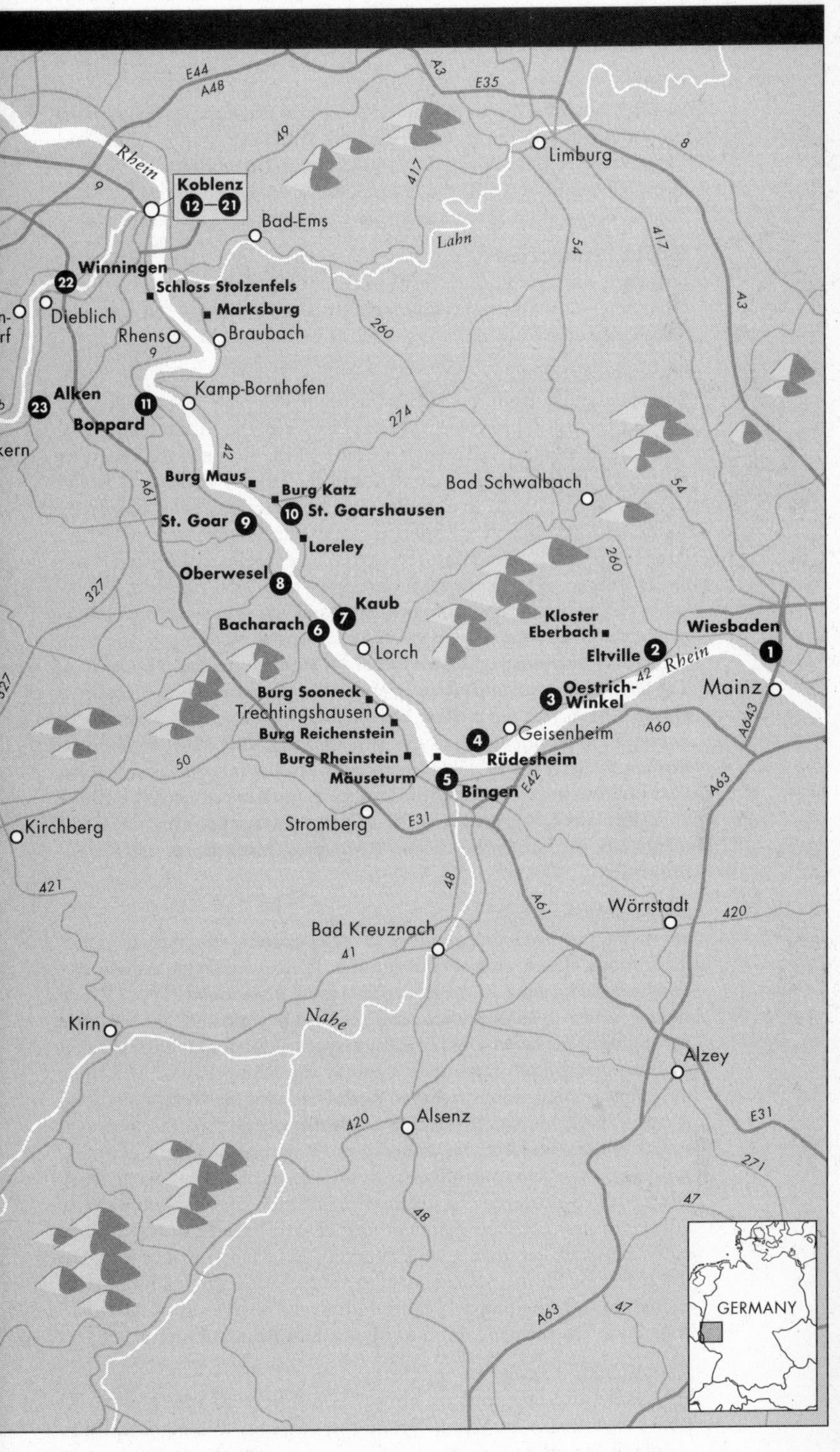

Koblenz 12—21
Bad-Ems
Limburg
Lahn
Rhein
Winningen 22
Schloss Stolzenfels
Marksburg
Dieblich
Rhens
Braubach
Kamp-Bornhofen
Alken 23
Boppard 11
Burg Maus
Burg Katz
St. Goar 9
10 St. Goarshausen
Loreley
Bad Schwalbach
Oberwesel 8
Kaub 7
Bacharach 6
Lorch
Kloster Eberbach
Wiesbaden 1
Eltville 2
Mainz
Oestrich-Winkel 3
Burg Sooneck
Trechtingshausen
Burg Reichenstein
Burg Rheinstein
Mäuseturm
4
Geisenheim
Rüdesheim
5 Bingen
Kirchberg
Stromberg
Wörrstadt
Bad Kreuznach
Kirn
Nahe
Alzey
Alsenz
GERMANY
E44
A48
A3
E35
49
417
8
9
54
A3
260
274
42
A61
327
50
E42
A60
A643
A63
E31
421
48
420
41
271
47

and contemporary productions. The cathedrals of Aachen, Köln, and Trier are magnificent settings for concerts and organ recitals.

Wine

Riesling is the predominant white grape and Spätburgunder (pinot noir) the most important red variety in the Rheingau, Mittelrhein, and Mosel wine regions covered in this chapter. Three abutting wine regions—Rheinhessen and the Nahe, near Bingen, and the Ahr, southwest of Bonn—add to the variety of wines available along this route.

Great Itineraries

Driving is the ideal way to travel—up one side of the Rhine and down the other—with time out for a cruise. But even the train route between Wiesbaden and Koblenz offers thrilling views.

IF YOU HAVE 3 DAYS

Travel down the Rhine toward Rüdesheim, stopping near **Eltville** ② to visit the historical monastery **Kloster Eberbach,** the cultural wine center of the Rheingau. Take in the beauty of the Rhine Gorge, with its steep vineyards, legendary castles, and the **Loreley** rock, on a Rhine steamer cruise from **Rüdesheim** ④ to **St. Goarshausen** ⑩. Return by train and overnight in a Rheingau wine village between Eltville and Rüdesheim. The second day, ferry from Rüdesheim to **Bingen** ⑤ for a closer look at the romantic Mittelrhein. The period rooms in Rheinstein, Reichenstein, and Sooneck castles evoke the region's medieval past, as do the town walls, towers, and historic buildings in the wine villages of **Bacharach** ⑥, **Oberwesel** ⑧, **St. Goar** ⑨, and **Boppard** ⑪. The latter also has significant relics from Roman times. From there drive about 20 km (12 mi) to the Mosel Valley (toward Brodenbach) to overnight in a wine village such as Dieblich, **Alken** ㉓, or **Treis-Karden** ㉔. Start the third day with a visit to the fairy-tale castle **Burg Eltz.** Follow the Mosel downstream to its confluence with the Rhine at **Koblenz** ⑫–㉑, spending the rest of the day exploring the sights of the city or the nearby castles **Stolzenfels, Marksburg,** and **Ehrenbreitstein.**

IF YOU HAVE 5 DAYS

Spend an afternoon and night in **Wiesbaden** ① to enjoy the thermal springs, elegant shops, and nightlife. The next morning visit **Kloster Eberbach** and a wine estate, or proceed to **Rüdesheim** ④ for a Rhine steamer cruise to **St. Goarshausen** ⑩. Return by train and take the cable car to the Niederwald-Denkmal (monument) overlooking Rüdesheim for an outstanding panoramic view of the Rhine Valley. The third morning continue downstream to **Kaub** ⑦ to visit the **Pfalz,** a medieval fortress. Ferry across the Rhine to **Bacharach** ⑥. See the medieval towns of **Oberwesel** ⑧, **St. Goar** ⑨, and **Boppard** ⑪. Overnight in **Koblenz** ⑫–㉑. The fourth day travel along the Mosel River to **Burg Eltz,** followed by stops in **Cochem** ㉕ and a few of the charming wine villages upstream. Overnight in or near **Bernkastel-Kues** ㉘, with its picturesque market square, wine museum, and wine-tasting centers. On day five enjoy the natural beauty of the Mosel during an hour-long boat excursion from Bernkastel before following the river upstream to **Trier** ㉙–㊷, the former capital of the western Roman Empire.

IF YOU HAVE 7 DAYS

Follow the five-day itinerary above. Travel from **Trier** ㉙–㊷ to **Köln** ㊿–64 via the autobahn. Spend the sixth day and night in Köln, visiting the Dom, a masterpiece of Gothic architecture, and one or more of the Romanesque churches and excellent museums. Devote the last day to **Aachen,** an elegant spa and the single greatest storehouse of Carolingian architecture in Europe.

When to Tour the Rhineland

The peak season for cultural, food, and wine festivals is March–mid-November, followed by colorful Christmas markets in December. The season for many hotels, restaurants, riverboats, cable cars, and sights is from Easter through October, particularly in smaller towns. Opening hours at castles, churches, and small museums are shorter during winter. Orchards blossom in March and the vineyards are verdant from May until mid-September, when the vines turn a shimmering gold.

THE RHEINGAU

Updated by Kerry Brady Stewart

The heart of the region begins in Wiesbaden, where the Rhine makes a sharp bend and flows east to west for some 30 km (19 mi) before resuming its south–north course at Rüdesheim. Wiesbaden is a good starting point to follow any of the well-marked cycling, hiking, and driving routes through the Rheingau's villages and vineyards. The cycling and hiking trails extend to Kaub in the Mittelrhein. Nearly every Rheingau village has an outdoor *Weinprobierstand* (wine-tasting stand), usually near the riverbank. They are staffed and stocked by a different wine estate every weekend in the summer.

Wiesbaden

❶ *40 km (25 mi) west of Frankfurt via A–66.*

Wiesbaden, the capital of the state of Hesse, is a small city of tree-lined avenues with elegant shops and handsome facades. Its hot mineral springs have been a drawing card since the days when it was known as Aquis Mattiacis (the waters of the Mattiaci)—the words boldly inscribed on the portal of the Kurhaus—and Wisibada (the bath in the meadow). In the first century AD the Romans built thermal baths here, a site then inhabited by a Germanic tribe, the Mattiaci. Modern Wiesbaden dates from the 19th century, when the dukes of Nassau and, later, the Prussian aristocracy commissioned the grand public buildings and parks that shape the city's profile today. Wiesbaden developed into a fashionable spa that attracted the rich and the famous. Their ornate villas on the Neroberg and turn-of-the-20th-century town houses are part of the city's flair.

★ Built in 1907, the neoclassical **Kurhaus** (✉ Kurhauspl.) is the social-cultural center of town. It houses the casino and the Thiersch-Saal, a splendid setting for concerts. The Staatstheater (1894), opulently appointed in baroque and rococo revival style, and two beautifully landscaped parks flank the Kurhaus. Today you can "take the waters" in an ambience reminiscent of Roman times in the **Irisch-Römisches Bad** (Irish-Roman bath; ✉ Langg. 38–40) at the Kaiser-Friedrich-Therme, a superb art nouveau bathhouse from 1913. On Kranzplatz, 15 of Wiesbaden's 26 springs converge at the steaming **Kochbrunnen** Fountain, where the healthful waters are there for the tasting.

Historical buildings ring the Schlossplatz (Palace Square) and the adjoining **Marktplatz** (Market Square), site of the farmers' market (Wednesday and Saturday). Behind the neo-Gothic brick Marktkirche (Market Church) food and wine vendors also ply their wares in the vaulted cellars of the Marktkeller. The **Altstadt** (Old Town) is just behind the Schloss (now the seat of parliament, the Hessischer Landtag) on Grabenstrasse, Wagemannstrasse, and Goldgasse. The **Museum Wiesbaden** is known for its collection of expressionist paintings, particularly the works of the Russian artist Alexej Jawlensky. ✉ *Friedrich-Ebert-Allee 2,* ☎

0611/335–2250, WEB www.museum-wiesbaden.de. €2.50. Tues. 10–8, Wed.–Sun. 10–5.

Dining and Lodging

$$–$$$$ ✕ **Käfer's.** This popular Kurhaus bistro with striking art nouveau decor, a grand piano (live music nightly), and a good-size bar attracts an upscale clientele. Book a table for two in one of the window alcoves (Nos. 7, 12, 25, and 29) for some privacy among the otherwise close-set tables. *Lachs-Bescheidenheit* (smoked salmon on a potato pancake, garnished with arugula) is a favorite and the Wiener schnitzel is excellent. There is a good international selection of wines, and a bottle of Veuve Clicquot Brut Champagne at €45.60 is an excellent value. Käfer's also caters the beer garden behind the Kurhaus. ✉ *Kurhauspl. 1,* ☎ *0611/536–200. AE, MC, V.*

$–$$ ✕ **Sherry & Port.** Gerd Royko's friendly neighborhood bistro-pub hosts live music Friday and Saturday from September to March. During warm months dining is at outdoor tables that ring a huge fountain on tree-lined Adolfsallee. In addition to the fantastic number of sherries (32), ports (17), and malt whiskeys (20) by the glass, there's a good selection of beers (Guinness on tap) and wines to accompany everything from tapas, salads, and pasta to steaks. ✉ *Adolfsallee 11,* ☎ *0611/373–632. No credit cards. Closed Sun.*

$$$$ ✕🏨 **Nassauer Hof.** Wiesbaden's premiere address for well over a century, this elegant hotel opposite the Kurhaus lies on the site of a Roman fortress that was converted into a spa and, ultimately, a guest house. It is internationally renowned for its luxuriously appointed rooms; top-flight service; and restaurants, Ente ($$$$, closed one week in January) and Orangerie ($$–$$$)—both open daily for lunch and dinner. ✉ *Kaiser-Friedrich-Pl. 3–4, D–65183,* ☎ *0611/1330,* FAX *0611/133–632,* WEB *www.nassauer-hof.de. 160 rooms, 26 suites. 2 restaurants, in-room data ports, minibars, pool, massage, sauna, lobby lounge, piano bar, concierge, no-smoking rooms. AE, DC, MC, V.*

$$$ ✕🏨 **Trüffel.** For years truffle lovers have indulged in the "diamonds of the kitchen"—or the sumptuous chocolate versions—at Cristina and Dr. Manuel Stirn's first-rate delicatessen and bistro. When the Stirns moved into larger quarters near the Kurhaus in 2002, they added a classy hotel and restaurant to their operations. Personal service, stylish decor, and luxury baths make for a very pleasant stay. Truffles are still on the menu at the bistro and the restaurant. The chocolates (and superb foods and beverages) merit a detour to the delicatessen. ✉ *Weberg. 6–8, D–65183,* ☎ *0611/990–550,* FAX *0611/990–5555,* WEB *www.trueffel.net. 24 rooms, 4 suites. 2 restaurants, café, patisserie, 2 bars, in-room data ports, minibars, shop, no-smoking rooms. AE, DC, MC, V.*

$$–$$$ 🏨 **Best Western Hotel Hansa.** This very comfortable, modern hotel in an art nouveau house is centrally located between the main train station and the Old Town. ✉ *Bahnhofstr. 23, D–65185,* ☎ *0611/901–240,* FAX *0611/9012–4666,* WEB *www.hansa.bestwestern.de. 81 rooms, 1 suite. No a/c, no-smoking rooms. AE, DC, MC, V.*

$ 🏨 **Ibis.** The two modern Ibis hotels in town offer excellent value and locations within walking distance of all sights: the first is on the edge of the Old Town, opposite the Kochbrunnen; the second is in the heart of the shop-filled pedestrian zone. ✉ *Kranzpl. 10, D–65183,* ☎ *0611/36140,* FAX *0611/361–4499,* WEB *www.ibishotel.com. 131 rooms;* ✉ *Mauritiusstr. 5–7, D–65183,* ☎ *0611/16710,* FAX *0611/167–1750. 149 rooms. In-room data ports, bar, some pets allowed (fee), no a/c, no-smoking rooms. AE, DC, MC, V.*

Nightlife and the Arts

In addition to the casino, restaurants, bars, and beer garden at the Kurhaus, nightlife is centered in the many bistros and pubs on

Taunusstrasse and in the Old Town. The tourist office provides schedules and sells tickets for most venues listed below.

The **Hessisches Staatstheater** (⊠ Chr.-Zais-Str. 3, ☎ 0611/132–325) presents classical and contemporary opera, theater, ballet, and musicals on three stages: Grosses Haus, Kleines Haus, and Studio. Great classics and avant-garde films, as well as dance and small theatrical productions, are specialties of the **Caligari Filmbühne** (⊠ Marktpl. 9, behind Marktkirche, ☎ 0611/333–947). Smaller dramatic productions and cabaret are performed at the intimate **Pariser Hoftheater** (⊠ Spiegelg. 9, ☎ 0611/300–607). **Thalhaus** (⊠ Nerotal 18, ☎ 0611/185–1267) is a lively, multiarts venue.

The Hessian State Orchestra performs in the **Kurhaus** (⊠ Kurhauspl. 1, ☎ 0611/17290). Concerts and musicals are staged at the **Rhein-Main-Hallen** (⊠ Rheinstr. 20, ☎ 0611/1440). The **Villa Clementine** (⊠ Frankfurter Str. 1, ☎ 0611/313–642) is a regular concert venue. The sparkling wine cellars of **Henkell & Söhnlein** (⊠ Biebricher Allee 142, ☎ 0611/630) host a series of concerts in their splendid foyer. Many churches offer concerts, including the free organ concerts Saturday at 11:30 in the **Marktkirche.**

The **Spielbank** (casino) with the Grosses Spiel (roulette, blackjack) in the Kurhaus and the Kleines Spiel (slots) in the neighboring Kolonnade is lively from 3 PM to 3 AM and 2 PM–3 AM, respectively. The former is one of Europe's grand casinos, where jacket and tie are required. Minimum age is 18 (bring your passport). ⊠ *Kurhauspl. 1,* ☎ *0611/536–100,* WEB *www.spielbank-wiesbaden.de.* 🎫 *Grosses Spiel €2.50, Kleines Spiel €1. Closed Christmas and some holidays.*

Outdoor Activities and Sports

SWIMMING

Pamper yourself with the **Kaiser-Friedrich-Therme**'s thermal spring and cold-water pools, various steam baths and saunas, two solaria, massage, and a score of health and wellness treatments in elegant art nouveau surroundings. Towels and robes can be rented on site, but come prepared for "textile-free" bathing. Children under 16 are not admitted. ⊠ *Langg. 38–40 (the entrance faces Webergasse),* ☎ *0611/172–9660.* 🎫 *4 hrs €17.50, for pools, steam baths, and saunas.* ⏲ *Sat.–Thurs. 10–10, Fri. 10–midnight; Tues. women only.*

The **Opelbad,** a large outdoor swimming pool on the Neroberg, is idyllically set on the edge of the city forest, overlooking Wiesbaden and the Rheingau. ⊠ *Neroberg,* ☎ *0611/172–9885.* 🎫 *€6.* ⏲ *mid-Apr.–Sept., daily 7 AM–8 PM.*

Shopping

Broad, tree-lined Wilhelmstrasse, with designer boutiques housed in its fin-de-siècle buildings, is one of Germany's most elegant shopping streets. Wiesbaden is also known as one of the best places in the country to find antiques; Taunusstrasse has excellent antiques shops. The Altstadt is full of upscale boutiques; Kirchgasse and its extension, Langgasse, are the heart of the shop-filled pedestrian zone.

Near the market square, the wood-paneled **Linnenkohl** (⊠ Ellenbogeng. 15, ☎ 0611/304–886) is filled with the aromas of freshly ground coffee and exotic teas from around the world (150 on offer). In addition, the shop stocks more than 300 single malt whiskies and other noble spirits, as well as exquisite chocolates, cookies, jams, honeys, and porcelain accessories from China, Japan, and Great Britain.

Eltville

❷ *14 km (9 mi) west of Wiesbaden via A–66 and B–42.*

Eltville, Alta Villa in Roman times, was first in the Rheingau to receive town rights (1332). Eltville flourished as a favorite residence of the archbishops of Mainz in the 14th and 15th centuries, and it was during this time that the **Kurfürstliche Burg** (electors' castle) was built. The castle has an exhibition commemorating Johannes Gutenberg (1400–68), the inventor of movable type. He lived in Eltville on and off and it was here that he was named a courtier by elector Adolf II of Nassau in 1465. ✉ *Burgstr. 1,* ☎ *no phone.* 🎫 *€2.50.* ⏲ *Apr.–Oct., 1st Sun. every month, tours at 3 PM; rose garden (free) May–Sept., daily 9:30–7.*

The parish church of **Sts. Peter and Paul** has late-Gothic frescoes, Renaissance tombstones, and a carved baptismal by the Rhenish sculptor Hans Backoffen (or his studio). Worth seeing are Burg Crass on the riverbank and the half-timber houses and aristocratic **manors** on the lanes between the river and Rheingauer Strasse (B–42), notably the Bechtermünzer Hof (Kirchgasse 6), Stockheimer Hof (Ellenbogengasse 6), and Eltzer Hof (at the Martinstor gateway).

Sekt production in the Rheingau is concentrated in Eltville, Wiesbaden, and Rüdesheim. The tree-lined Rhine promenade here hosts the annual *Sekt* (sparkling wine) festival during the first weekend of July. The administrative headquarters and main cellars of the **Hessian State Wine Domains** are in town. Germany's largest wine estate, it owns nearly 500 acres of vineyards throughout the Rheingau and in the Hessische Bergstrasse wine region south of Frankfurt. Its shops in the art nouveau press house built in 1911 and at nearby Kloster Eberbach offer a comprehensive regional selection. ✉ *Schwalbacher Str. 56–62,* ☎ *06123/92300,* WEB *www.StaatsweingueterHessen.de. AE, MC, V.* ⏲ *Weekdays 9–6, Sat. 10–4.*

For a good look at the central Rheingau, make a brief circular tour from Eltville. Drive 3 km (2 mi) north via the Kiedricher Strasse to the Gothic village of **Kiedrich.** In the distance you'll see the tower of Scharfenstein castle (1215) and the spires of **St. Valentine's Church** and St. Michael's Chapel, both from the 15th century. Try to visit the church on a Sunday for the 9:30 mass to admire the splendid Gothic furnishings and star vaulting amid the sounds of one of Germany's oldest organs and Gregorian chants. The chapel next door, once a charnel house, has a unique chandelier sculpted around a nearly life-size, two-sided Madonna.

These Gothic gems have survived intact thanks to 19th-century restorations patronized by the English baronet John Sutton. Today Sutton's beautiful villa south of the church is home to one of Germany's leading wine estates, **Weingut Robert Weil.** Its famed Kiedricher Gräfenberg Riesling wines can be sampled in the ultramodern *Vinothek* (tasting room and wineshop). ✉ *Mühlberg 5,* ☎ *06123/2308,* WEB *www.weingut-robert-weil.com.* ⏲ *Weekdays 8–5:30, Sat. 10–4, Sun. 11–5.*

★ The former Cistercian monastery **Kloster Eberbach** is idyllically set in a secluded forest clearing 3 km (2 mi) west of Kiedrich. Its Romanesque and Gothic buildings (12th–14th centuries) look untouched by time—one reason why Umberto Eco's medieval murder mystery *The Name of the Rose,* starring Sean Connery, was partially filmed here. The monastery's impressive collection of old wine presses and the historical Cabinet Cellar, once reserved for the best barrels, bear witness to a viticultural tradition that spans nearly nine centuries. The wines can be sampled year-round in the **wineshop** or restaurants on the grounds. The church, with its excellent acoustics, and the large medieval dormitories are the settings for concerts, wine auctions, and festive wine events. ✉ *Stiftung Kloster Eberbach, Postfach 1453, D–65334 Eltville,* ☎ *06723/91780,* WEB *www.klostereberbach.de.* 🎫 *€3.* ⏲ *Apr.–Oct., daily 10–6; Nov.–Mar., weekdays 10–4, weekends 11–4.*

From Eberbach take the road toward Hattenheim, stopping at the first right-hand turnoff to admire the monastery's premier vineyard, **Steinberg.** It is encircled by a 3-km-long (2-mi-long) stone wall (13th–18th centuries). The vineyard has an outdoor pub, *Brot und Wein* (bread and wine). ⏲ *May–Sept., weekends 11–7.*

The *Brunnen* (springs) beneath the vineyards of Hattenheim and Erbach, both on the Rhine, lend their name to three excellent **vineyards**: Nussbrunnen, Wisselbrunnen, and Marcobrunnen—on the boundary between the two towns. As you return to Eltville (2 km [1 mi] east of Erbach on B–42) you will pass the elegant 19th-century palace Schloss Reinhartshausen.

Dining and Lodging

$–$$ ✕ **Gutsausschank im Baiken.** Andrea and Stefan Seyffardt's cozy wine restaurant is set on a hilltop amid the famed Rauenthaler Baiken vineyard. The magnificent panorama, the fresh country cooking, and superb wines—from the Hessian State Wine Domains—make for a "Rheingau Riesling" experience par excellence. Try for a seat on the vine-canopied terrace, ringed with lush flowers and potted palms, to savor the view. ✉ *Auf dem Acker 1 (via Schwalbacher Str. and Wiesweg in Eltville),* ☎ *06123/900–345. No credit cards. Closed Mon. and Nov.–mid-Apr. No lunch except Sun.*

$$$–$$$$ ✕🏨 **Schloss Reinhartshausen.** A palace in every sense of the word, this hotel and wine estate majestically overlooks the Rhine and beautifully landscaped gardens. Antiques and artworks fill the house and some rooms have fireplaces and whirlpools. The restaurant Marcobrunn ($$$$), named after the famed vineyard site, is known for superb classical cuisine with Mediterranean accents. Lighter fare is served in the airy Wintergarten ($$$$), and regional dishes in Balzers Schlosskeller. Approximately 1,000 wines, with emphasis on top Rheingau growths, are on the wine list. The estate's wines are also sold in the Vinothek. ✉ *Hauptstr. 43, D–65346 Eltville-Erbach,* ☎ *06123/6760,* FAX *06123/676–400,* WEB *www.schloss-hotel.de. 39 rooms, 15 suites, 1 apartment. 3 restaurants, Weinstube, in-room data ports, minibars, indoor pool, sauna, bicycles, bar, lobby lounge, shop, some pets allowed (fee), no-smoking rooms. AE, DC, MC, V. Marcobrunn closed Mon. and 3 wks in Jan., 3 wks in July. No lunch Tues. No lunch in the Schlosskeller.*

$$$ ✕🏨 **Kronenschlösschen.** The atmosphere of this stylish art nouveau house (1894) is intimate, and the individually designed rooms have antique furnishings and marble baths. Chef Patrik Kimpel oversees both the gourmet restaurant Kronenschlösschen ($$–$$$$) and the more casual Bistro ($–$$$). Fish, poultry, beef, and lamb are always beautifully presented with very flavorful sauces. You can also dine in the parklike garden. The wine list focuses on the finest Rheingau estates for whites and Old and New World estates for reds. ✉ *Rheinallee, D–65347 Eltville-Hattenheim,* ☎ *06723/640,* FAX *06723/7663,* WEB *www.kronenschloesschen.de. 8 rooms, 10 suites. 2 restaurants, bar, no a/c, in-room data ports, minibars, laundry service, some pets allowed, no-smoking rooms. AE, DC, MC, V. No lunch weekdays or Sat. at Kronenschlösschen. Both restaurants closed 3 wks in Jan.*

$$ ✕🏨 **Burg Crass.** The riverfront side of this ancient castle (1076) has been fitted with floor-to-ceiling windows that open onto a magnificent terrace in the summer. High ceilings, tall plants, chic dark wood furnishings, and many works of art are a stunning setting for contemporary cuisine and excellent wines and sparkling wines at the Vinothek 510.8 ($). The *flottes Teller*—a small-size entrée—is a good value. Posh Vaux–Das Sektrestaurant serves set menus ($$$$) only. Rooms are modern, with the charming decor you would expect in a country inn. ✉ *Freygässchen 1 (from B–42, on the eastern edge of town), D–65343 Eltville,* ☎ *06123/69060,* FAX *06123/690–669,* WEB *www.kellerundkunst.de. 7 rooms, 1 apartment. 2 restaurants, wine bar, no a/c, in-room data ports, shop, some pets allowed (fee). MC, V. Restaurant Vaux closed Mon. and 1st half of Jan.; no dinner Sun.*

$$ ✕🏨 **Klosterschänke und Gästehaus Kloster Eberbach.** The monks never had it this good: the Marschollek family's light, modern, and comfortable rooms are a far cry from the unheated, stone dormitories of the past. Beneath the vaulted ceiling of the Klosterschänke ($–$$) you can sample the wines of the Hessian State Wine Domains with regional cuisine. Try the *Weinfleisch* (pork goulash in Riesling sauce) or *Zisterzienser Brot,* "Cistercian bread," minced meat in a plum-and-bacon dressing with boiled potatoes. ✉ *Kloster Eberbach, D–65346 Eltville, via Kiedrich or Hattenheim,* ☎ *06723/9930,* FAX *06723/993–100,* WEB *www.klostereberbach.com. 30 rooms. Restaurant, no a/c, in-room data ports, some pets allowed, no smoking rooms. AE, MC, V.*

$$ ✕🏨 **Maximilianshof.** For generations the von Oetinger family has shared its home, its wines, and its simple, hearty cooking ($) with guests from near and far. In winter, the warmth of the art nouveau parlor beckons with its plush sofas, while in summer, tables are set out on the pretty terrace. Across the courtyard, they've built a cheerful, modern guesthouse with nine rooms, each named after a local vineyard site. "Honigberg" has a private sauna; "Hohenrain" has a nifty little kitchen and can be booked as a holiday flat for up to five persons. ✉ *Rheinallee 2, D–65346 Eltville–Erbach,* ☎ *06123/92240,* FAX *06123/922–425,* WEB *www.maximilianshof.de. 9 rooms. Restaurant, no a/c, in-room data ports, some pets allowed (fee). DC, MC, V. Restaurant closed Mon. and mid-Jan. to mid-Feb. Lunch on weekends, Apr.–Oct.; on Sun., Nov.–Mar.*

$$ ✕🏨 **Zum Krug.** Winegrower Josef Laufer more than lives up to the hospitality promised by the wreath and *Krug* (earthenware pitcher) hanging above the front door. The rooms have modern baths and dark wood furnishings. Equally cozy is the wood-paneled restaurant ($$–$$$$), with its old tiled oven. The German fare includes wild duck, goose, game, or sauerbraten served in rich, flavorful gravies. The wine list is legendary for its scope (600 Rheingau wines) and large selection of older vintages. ✉ *Hauptstr. 34, D–65347 Eltville–Hattenheim,* ☎ *06723/99680,* FAX *06723/996–825,* WEB *www.hotel-zum-krug.de. 10 rooms. Restaurant, minibars, no a/c, some pets allowed, no-smoking rooms. AE, DC, MC, V. Closed 1st half of Jan. and 2nd half of July. Restaurant also closed Mon.; no dinner Sun.*

Oestrich-Winkel

❸ *21 km (13 mi) west of Wiesbaden, 7 km (4½ mi) west of Eltville on B–42.*

Oestrich's vineyard area is the largest in the Rheingau. Lenchen and Doosberg are the most important vineyards. You can sample the wines opposite the 18th-century crane at the outdoor wine tasting stand.

The village of Winkel (pronounced *vin*-kle) lies west of Oestrich. A Winkeler Hasensprung wine from the fabulous 1811 vintage was Goethe's wine of choice during his stay here in 1814 with the Brentano family, who still welcome visitors to the restaurant at their home. The oldest (1211) of Germany's great private wine estates, **Schloss Vollrads,** lies 3 km (2 mi) north of town. The moated tower (1330) was the Greiffenclau residence for 350 years until the present palace was built in the 17th century. The period rooms are open during concerts, festivals, and wine tastings. *North on Schillerstr.; turn right on Greiffenclaustr.,* ☎ *06723/660,* WEB *www.schlossvollrads.com.* ⏲ *Vinothek weekdays. 8:30–noon and 1–5; weekends 11–6.*

★ The origins of this grand wine estate **Schloss Johannisberg** date from 1100, when Benedictine monks built a monastery and planted vines on the slopes below. The palace and remarkable cellars (visits by appointment only) were built in the early 18th century by the prince-abbots of Fulda. Every autumn a courier was sent from Johannisberg to Fulda to obtain permission to harvest the grapes. In 1775 he returned after considerable delay. Although the harvest was later and the grapes far riper than usual, the wines were exceptionally rich and fruity. *Spätlese* (literally, "late harvest," pronounced *shpate*-lay-zeh) wines have been highly esteemed ever since. A statue in the courtyard commemorates the "late rider." There are tastings at the Vinothek and the *Gutsauschank* (estate's restaurant). To get here from Winkel's main street, drive north on Schillerstrasse and proceed all the way uphill (there is a fine view at the top). After the road curves to the left, watch for the left turn to the castle. ✉ *Weinbaudomäne Schloss Johannisberg, Geisenheim-Johannisberg,* ☎ *06722/70090 or 06722/700–935,* WEB *www.schloss-johannisberg.de.* ⏲ *Vinothek: Mar.–Oct., weekdays 10–1 and 2–6, weekends 11–6; Nov.–Feb., weekdays 10–1 and 2–6, weekends 11–5.*

Dining and Lodging

$$–$$$ ✕ **Gutsausschank Brentano Haus.** Part of the Brentano family's home and lovely garden, once a favorite meeting place of the Rhine Romanticists, has been converted into a cozy wine pub that serves regional cuisine with Baron von Brentano's estate-bottled wines. Tischbein's famous portrait of Goethe adorns the house wine label. The Goethe Zimmer (Goethe Room), with mementos and furnishings from Goethe's time, may be visited by appointment only. ✉ *Am Lindenpl. 2, Winkel,* ☎ *06723/7426 pub; 06723/2068 estate. No credit cards. Apr.–Sept., closed Thurs.; Oct.–Mar., closed Wed., Thurs. and no lunch weekdays.*

$$–$$$ ✕ **Gutsausschank Schloss Johannisberg.** The glassed-in terrace affords a spectacular view of the Rhine and the vineyards from which the wine in your glass originated. Rheingau Riesling soup and *Bauernente* (farmer's duck) are house specialties. ✉ *Schloss Johannisberg,* ☎ *06722/96090. AE, MC, V.*

$–$$$ ✕ **Gutsrestaurant Schloss Vollrads.** Chef Matthias Böhler's "farmers' specialties" and creative seasonal menus are served with the estate's wines in the cavalier house (1650) or on the flower-lined terrace facing the garden. Check the Schloss Vollrads Web site (www.schlossvollrads.com) for a calendar of the many food-and-wine events throughout the year. ✉ *Schloss Vollrads, north of Winkel,* ☎ *06723/5270. MC, V. Closed Wed., Apr.–Oct.; Tues.–Thurs., Nov.–Mar.; 2 wks in Jan. and 2 wks in Nov.*

$$$ 🏨 **Hotel Schwan.** This green-and-white half-timber inn has been in the Wenckstern family since it was built in 1628. All rooms offer modern comfort; the decor in the guest house is simpler than in the historical main building. Many rooms afford a Rhine view, as does the beautiful terrace. The staff is friendly and helpful, and you can sample and purchase the family's wines on site. ✉ *Rheinallee 5 (in Oestrich), D–65375 Oestrich-Winkel,* ☎ *06723/8090,* FAX *06723/7820.* WEB *www.hotel-schwan.de. 56 rooms. Restaurant, no a/c, some in-room data ports, minibars, bar, some pets allowed, no-smoking rooms. AE, DC, MC, V. Hotel and restaurant closed late Dec.–early Jan.*

Rüdesheim

4 *30 km (19 mi) west of Wiesbaden, 9 km (5½ mi) west of Oestrich-Winkel on B–42.*

Tourism and wine are the heart and soul of Rüdesheim and best epitomized by the **Drosselgasse** (Thrush Alley). Less than 500 ft long, this narrow, pub-lined lane is abuzz with music and merrymaking from noon until well past midnight every day from Easter through October.

The **Asbach Weinbrennerei** (wine distillery) has produced Asbach, one of Germany's most popular brands of *Weinbrand* (wine brandy, the equivalent of Cognac) here since 1892. It is a key ingredient in its brandy-filled *Pralinen* (chocolates) and in the local version of Irish coffee, Rüdesheimer Kaffee. A tour of the distillery operations concludes with a tasting. ✉ *Asbach Besucher Center, Ingelheimer Str. 4, on the eastern edge of town,* ☏ *06722/497–345,* WEB *www.asbach.de.* 🎫 *€2.50.* ⏲ *Year-round, Mon.–Thurs. 9–6, Fri. 9–1; Apr.–Oct. and Dec., Sat. 9–6, Sun. 9–3.*

The **Weinmuseum Brömserburg** (Brömserburg wine museum), housed in one of the oldest castles on the Rhine (circa 1000 AD), displays wine-related artifacts and drinking vessels dating from Roman times. There are great views from the roof and the terrace, where you can sample local wines from mid-March to October. ✉ *Rheinstr. 2,* ☏ *06722/2348,* WEB *www.rheingauer-weinmuseum.de.* 🎫 *€3.* ⏲ *Mid-Mar.–mid-Nov., daily 9–6.*

The 15th-century **Brömserhof** (Brömser Manor) holds Germany's largest collection of mechanical music instruments. Tours are educational and entertaining. ✉ *Siegfried's Mechanisches Musikkabinett, Oberstr. 29,* ☏ *06722/49217.* 🎫 *€5.* ⏲ *Mar.–Dec., daily 10–6.*

High above Rüdesheim and visible for miles stands "Germania," a colossal female statue crowning the **Niederwald-Denkmal** (Niederwald Monument). It was built from 1877 to 1883 to commemorate the rebirth of the German Empire after the Franco-Prussian War (1870–71). There are splendid panoramic views from the monument and from other vantage points on the edge of the forested plateau. You can reach the monument on foot, by car (via Grabenstrasse), or by sweeping over the vineyards in the *Seilbahn* (cable car). There is also a *Sessellift* (chairlift) to and from Assmannshausen, a red wine enclave, on the west side of the hill. ✉ *Oberstr. 37,* ☏ *06722/2402,* WEB *www.seilbahn-ruedesheim.de.* 🎫 *One-way €4, round-trip or combi-ticket for cable car and chairlift €6.* ⏲ *Mid-Mar.–Oct., daily 9:30–4 (June–Sept. until 6:30).*

With the wings of a glider you can silently soar over the Rhine Valley. At the **Luftsport-Club Rheingau** you can catch a 30- to 60-minute *Segelflug* (glider flight) on a glider plane between Rüdesheim and the Loreley; allow 1½ hours for pre- and postflight preparations. ✉ *3 km (2 mi) north of the Niederwald-Denkmal and Landgut Ebenthal,* ☏ *06722/2979,* WEB *www.rheingau-media.com/lcr.* 🎫 *€10 (10 mins) and € 0.50 (each additional min).* ⏲ *Apr.–Oct., weekends 10–7.*

Dining and Lodging

$–$$$ ✕ **Rüdesheimer Schloss.** In a tithe house built in 1729, this wine tavern specializes in Hessian cuisine and Rheingauer Riesling and Spätburgunder wines from the Breuer family's own estate and those of its illustrious neighbors. The selection of older vintages is remarkable. Start with the delectable *Sauerkrautsuppe* (sauerkraut soup). Benedictine-style "*Schloss Ente*" (duck with dates and figs), *Ochsenbrust* (boiled breast of beef), and *Woihinkel* (chicken in Riesling sauce) are all excellent. Typical Drosselgasse music and dancing are an entertaining backdrop indoors and in the tree-shaded courtyard. ✉ *Drosselg.,* ☎ *06722/ 90500. AE, DC, MC, V. Closed Jan.–Feb., except on request.*

$$–$$$ ✕🏨 **Hotel Krone Assmannshausen.** This elegant, antique-filled hotel and restaurant ($$$$) offers first-class service and fine wining and dining. Classic cuisine prepared by chef Willi Mittler and a superb collection of wines including those from the family's own vineyards make for very memorable meals indoors or on the terrace overlooking the Rhine. Two of the suites have their own sauna. ✉ *Rheinuferstr. 10, D–65385 Rüdesheim-Assmannshausen,* ☎ *06722/4030,* FAX *06722/3049,* WEB *www.hotel-krone.com. 52 rooms, 13 suites. Restaurant, bar, in-room data ports, minibars, pool, some pets allowed (fee), no a/c, no-smoking rooms. AE, DC, MC, V.*

$$ 🏨 **Breuer's Rüdesheimer Schloss.** Gracious hosts Susanne and Heinrich Breuer have beautifully integrated modern designer decor into the historic walls of this stylish hotel. The Constantinescu Suite (No. 20) and the Rhine Suite (No. 14), with its large terrace, are especially popular; most rooms offer a vineyard view. Cellar or vineyard tours and wine tastings can be arranged. Wines from the family's renowned Rheingau estate, Weingut Georg Breuer, and tasteful wine accessories are available at the Vinothek (on Grabenstrasse 8). ✉ *Steing. 10, D–65385 Rüdesheim,* ☎ *06722/90500,* FAX *06722/47960,* WEB *www.ruedesheimer-schloss.com. 18 rooms, 3 suites. Restaurant, no a/c, in-room data ports, minibars, bicycles, bar, shop, some pets allowed, no-smoking rooms. AE, DC, MC, V. Closed late Dec.–early Jan.*

THE MITTELRHEIN

Updated by Kerry Brady Stewart

Bingen, like Rüdesheim, is a gateway to the Mittelrhein. From here to Koblenz is the greatest concentration of Rhine castles. Most date from the 12th and 13th centuries but were destroyed in 1689 when French troops systematically blew them up and burned them down during the war of Palatinate succession. It is primarily thanks to the Prussian royal family and its penchant for historical preservation that numerous Rhine castles were rebuilt or restored in the 19th and early 20th centuries.

Two roads run parallel to the Rhine: B–42 (east side) and B–9 (west side). The spectacular views from the heights can best be enjoyed via the routes known as the Loreley-Burgenstrasse (east side), from Kaub to the Loreley to Kamp-Bornhofen, or the Rheingoldstrasse (west side), from Rheindiebach to Rhens. The Rheinhöhenweg (Rhine Heights Path) affords hikers the same splendid views, including descents into the villages en route. These marked trails run between Oppenheim on the Rhine Terrace and Bonn for 240 km (149 mi) and between Wiesbaden and Bonn-Beuel for 272 km (169 mi). The traffic-free paths through the vineyards and along the riverbanks are wonderful routes for hikers and cyclists alike.

Bingen

❺ *35 km (22 mi) west of Wiesbaden via Mainz and A–60; ferry from the wharf opposite Rüdesheim's train station.*

Bingen overlooks the Nahe-Rhine conflux near a treacherous stretch of shallows and rapids known as the Binger Loch (Bingen Hole). Early on, Bingen developed into an important commercial center, for it was here—as in Rüdesheim on the opposite shore—that goods were moved from ship to shore to circumvent the unnavigable waters. Bingen was also the crossroad of Roman trade routes between Mainz, Koblenz, and Trier. Thanks to this central location, it grew into a major center of the wine trade and remains so today. Wine is celebrated during 11 days of merrymaking in early September at the annual **Winzerfest.**

Bingen was destroyed repeatedly by wars and fires, thus there are many ancient foundations but few visible architectural remains of the past. Since Celtic times the Kloppberg (Klopp Hill), in the center of town, has been the site of a succession of citadels, all named **Burg Klopp** since 1282. The terrace has good views of the Rhine, the Nahe, and the surrounding hills.

Not far from the millennium-old Drususbrücke, a stone bridge over the Nahe, is the late Gothic **Basilica of St. Martin.** It was originally built in 793 on the site of a Roman temple. The 11th-century crypt and Gothic and baroque furnishings merit a visit.

★ The **Historisches Museum am Strom** (History Museum) is housed in a former power station (1898) on the riverbank. Here you can see an intact set of Roman surgical tools (2nd century), period rooms from the Rhine Romantic era, and displays about the Abbess St. Hildegard von Bingen (1098–1179), one of the most remarkable women of the Middle Ages. An outspoken critic of papal and imperial machinations, she was a highly respected scholar, naturopath, and artist whose mystic writings and music are much in vogue today. ✉ *Museumsstr. 3,* ☎ *06721/990–654,* WEB *www.bingen.de.* 🎫 *€3.* ⏲ *Tues.–Sun. 10–5.*

The forested plateau of the *Rochusberg* (St. Roch Hill) is the pretty setting of the **Rochuskapelle** (St. Roch Chapel). Originally built in 1666 to celebrate the end of the plague, it has been rebuilt twice. Goethe attended the consecration festivities on August 16, 1814, the forerunner of today's Rochusfest, a weeklong folk festival in mid-August. The chapel (open during Sunday services at 8 and 10) contains an altar dedicated to St. Hildegard and relics and furnishings from the convents she founded on the Ruppertsberg (in the suburb of Bingerbrück) and in Eibingen (east of Rüdesheim). The **Hildegard Forum** (☎ 06721/181–000, ⏲ Tues.–Fri. 2–6, weekends 11–6), near the chapel, has exhibits related to St. Hildegard, a medieval herb garden, and a restaurant serving tasty, wholesome foods (*Dinkel,* or spelt, is a main ingredient) based on Hildegard's nutritional teachings.

Dining and Lodging

$$ ✕ **Schlösschen am Mäuseturm.** Dining on the terrace of this Schlösschen (little castle) with its view of the Mäuseturm and the Rhine makes for a very pleasant evening. The Steiningers serve fresh, seasonal cuisine as well as Pfälzer specialties (☞ Chapter 10). The wine list offers 24 wines by the glass, including Trockenbeerenauslese, a rare, liqueur-like wine. ✉ *Stromberger Str. 28A, (in suburb of Bingerbrück),* ☎ *06721/36699. MC. Closed Sun. and 1 wk in Aug. No lunch.*

$ ✕ **Weinstube Kruger-Rumpf.** It is well worth the 10-minute drive from Bingen (just across the Nahe River) to enjoy Cornelia Rumpf's refined country cooking with Stefan Rumpf's exquisite Nahe wines (Riesling, Weissburgunder [pinot blanc], and Silvaner are especially fine). House specialties are a rich potato soup with slices of fried blood sausage, boiled beef with green herb sauce, and *Winzerschmaus* (casserole of potatoes, sauerkraut, bacon, cheese, and herbs). The house dates from 1790; the wisteria-draped garden beckons in the summer. ✉ *Rheinstr. 47, Münster-Sarmsheim, 4 km (2½ mi) southwest of Bingen,* ☎ *06721/43859. Reservations essential. MC. Closed Mon.; 2 wks in late Dec.–early Jan. and Mon. No lunch.*

$$$ ✕🏨 **Johann Lafer's Stromburg.** It's a pretty 15-minute drive through the *Binger Wald* (Bingen Forest) to this luxurious castle hotel and restaurant overlooking Stromberg. Johann Lafer is a starred chef who pioneered cooking shows in Germany. In the elegant Le Val d'Or (reservations essential), the medley of Asian seafood with Singapore noodles and the *Dessert–Impressionen* are standing favorites. The less formal Turmstube ($$$$) offers tasty regional dishes. The wine list features 200 top Nahe wines and several hundred Old and New World wines, with a particularly fine collection from Bordeaux and Burgundy. ✉ *Am Schlossberg 1, D–55442 Stromberg, 12 km (7½ mi) west of Bingerbrück via Weiler and Waldalgesheim,* ☎ *06724/93100,* FAX *06724/931–090,* WEB *www.johannlafer.de. 13 rooms, 1 suite. 2 restaurants, bar, lobby lounge, no a/c, in-room data ports, minibars, some pets allowed (fee). AE, DC, MC, V.*

Outdoor Activities and Sports

HIKING AND WALKING

There are excellent signposted wine and nature trails in the park on the heights of the **Höhenpark Rochusberg.** In the **Binger Wald** (near Bingerbrück), information panels along the *Erlebnispfad* ("experience path") detail the forest's flora and inhabitants. The tourist office has brochures outlining circular walks.

En Route On the 5-km (3-mi) drive on B–9 to Trechtingshausen, you will pass by Bingen's landmark, the "**Mäuseturm**" (mice tower), perched on a rocky island near the Binger Loch. The name derives from a gruesome legend. One version tells that during a famine in 969, the miserly Archbishop Hatto hoarded grain and sought refuge in the tower to escape the peasants' pleas for food. The stockpile attracted scads of mice to the tower, where they devoured everything in sight, including Hatto. In fact, the tower was built by the archbishops of Mainz in the 13th–14th centuries as a *Mautturm* (watch tower and toll station) for their fortress Ehrenfels on the opposite shore (now a ruin). It was restored in neo-Gothic style by the king of Prussia in 1855, who also rebuilt Burg Sooneck.

The three castles open for visits near Trechtingshausen (turnoffs are signposted on B–9) will fascinate lovers of history and art. As you enter each castle's gateway, you can't help but marvel at what a feat of engineering it was to have built such a massive *Burg* (fortress or castle) on the stony cliffs overlooking the Rhine. They have all lain in ruin once or more during their turbulent histories. Their outer walls and period rooms still evoke memories of Germany's medieval past as well as the 19th-century era of Rhine Romanticism. You can enjoy superb Rhine vistas from the castles' terraces, where coffee, cake, and local wines are served, except Monday. Reichenstein also serves meals.

★ **Burg Rheinstein** was the home of Rudolf von Habsburg from 1282 to 1286. To establish law and order on the Rhine, he destroyed the neighboring castles of Burg Reichenstein and Burg Sooneck and hanged their notorious robber barons from the oak trees around the Clemens Church, a late-Romanesque basilica near Trechtingshausen. The Gobelin tapestries, 15th-century stained glass, wall and ceiling frescoes, and antique furniture—including a rare "giraffe spinet" upon which Kaiser Wilhelm I is said to have tickled the ivories—are well worth seeing. Rheinstein was the first of many a Rhine ruin to be rebuilt by a royal Prussian family in the 19th century. ☎ *06721/6348,* WEB *www.burg-rheinstein.de.* *€3.50.* *Mid-Mar.–mid-Nov., daily 9:30–5:30; mid-Nov.–mid-Mar., Mon.–Thurs. 2–5, Sun. 10–5.*

Burg Reichenstein has collections of decorative cast-iron slabs (from ovens and historical room-heating devices), hunting weapons and armor, period rooms, and paintings. ☎ *06721/6117.* *€3.40.* *Easter–Oct., Tues.–Sun. 10–6.*

Burg Sooneck, on the edge of the Soon (pronounced zone) Forest, houses a valuable collection of Empire, Biedermeier, and neo-Gothic furnishings, medieval weapons, and paintings from the Rhine Romantic era. ✉ *Niederheimbach,* ☎ *06743/6064,* WEB *www.burgen-rlp.de.* €2.60. ⊙ *Easter–Sept., Tues.–Sun. 10–6; Oct.–Nov. and Jan.–Easter, Tues.–Sun. 10–5.*

Bacharach

❻ *16 km (10 mi) north of Bingen; ferry 3 km (2 mi) north of town, to Kaub.*

Bacharach, a derivative of the Latin *Bacchi ara* (altar of Bacchus), has long been associated with wine. Like Rüdesheim, Bingen, and Kaub, it was a shipping station where barrels would interrupt their Rhine journey for land transport. Wine from the town's most famous vineyard, the Bacharacher Hahn, is served on the KD Rhine steamers. In late June you can sample wines at the *Weinblütenfest* (vine blossom festival) in the side valley suburb of Steeg, and in early October, at the *Winzerfest* (wine festival) in Bacharach proper.

Park on the riverbank and enter the town through one of its medieval gateways. You can ascend the 14th-century town wall for a walk along the ramparts facing the Rhine, then stroll along the main street (one street, but three names: Koblenzer Strasse, Oberstrasse, and Mainzer Strasse) for a look at patrician manors, typically built around a *Hof* (courtyard), and half-timber houses. Haus Sickingen, Posthof, Zollhof, Rathaus (town hall), and Altes Haus are fine examples. The massive tower in the center of town belongs to the parish church of **St. Peter.** A good example of the transition from Romanesque to Gothic styles, it has an impressive four-story nave. From the parish church a set of stone steps (signposted) leads to Bacharach's landmark, the sandstone ruins of the Gothic **Werner Kapelle,** highly admired for its filigree tracery. The chapel's roof succumbed to falling rocks in 1689, when the French blew up Burg Stahleck. Originally a Staufen fortress (11th century), the castle lay dormant until 1925, when a youth hostel was built on the foundations. The sweeping views it affords are worth the 10-minute walk.

Dining and Lodging

$–$$$ ✕ **Weinhaus Altes Haus.** Charming inside and out, this medieval half-timber house is a favorite setting for films and photos. The cheerful proprietor, Irina Weber, uses the freshest ingredients possible and buys her meat and game from local butchers and hunters. *Rieslingrahmsuppe* (Riesling cream soup), *Reibekuchen* (potato pancakes), and the hearty *Hunsrücker Teller* (boiled beef with horseradish sauce) are favorites, in addition to the seasonal specialties. She offers a good selection of wines from the family's vineyards. ✉ *Oberstr. 61,* ☎ *06743/1209. AE, MC, V. Closed Wed. and mid-Dec.–Easter.*

$ ✕ **Gutsausschank Zum Grünen Baum.** Winegrower Fritz Bastian runs this cozy tavern in a half-timber house from 1579. He is the sole owner of the vineyard Insel Heyles'en Werth, on the island opposite Bacharach. The "wine carousel" is a great way to sample a full range of flavors and styles (15 wines), at its best under the tutelage of the congenial host. Snacks are served (from 1 PM), including delicious homemade, air-dried *Schinken* (ham), as well as sausages and cheese. ✉ *Oberstr. 63,* ☎ *06743/1208. No credit cards. Closed Thurs. and Feb.*

$–$$ ✕🏨 **RheinHotel Andreas Stüber.** This friendly family operation offers modern rooms (each named after a vineyard) with Rhine or castle views. The restaurant ($–$$) has an excellent selection of Bacharacher wines to help wash down hearty regional specialties, such as *Hinkelsdreck* (chicken liver pâté), *Stichpfeffer* (peppery pork ragout), or *Rieslingbraten* (beef marinated in wine). ✉ *Langstr. 50 (on the town wall), D–55422 Bacharach,* ☎ *06743/1243,* FAX *06743/1413,* WEB *www.rhein-hotel-bacharach.de. 14 rooms, 1 apartment. Restaurant, fans, minibars, bicycles, pub, some pets allowed (fee), no-smoking rooms. MC, V. Closed Nov.–mid-Mar. Restaurant closed Tues.*

$–$$$ **Altkölnischer Hof.** Flowers line the windows of the Scherschlicht family's pretty, half-timber hotel near market square. The rooms are simply but attractively furnished in country style and some have balconies. ✉ *Blücherstr. 2, D–55422 Bacharach,* ☎ *06743/1339,* FAX *06743/2793,* WEB *www.hotel-bacharach-rhein.de. 20 rooms, 2 suites. Restaurant, no a/c, some minibars, bicycles, pub, some pets allowed (fee), no-smoking rooms. AE, MC, V. Closed Nov.–Mar.*

Kaub

7 *19 km (12 mi) north of Rüdesheim; ferry from Bacharach.*

The village of Kaub (pronounced cowp), once a major customs post, has profited from its slate quarries and wine for centuries. On New Year's Eve 1813–14, General Blücher led his troops from here across the Rhine on a pontoon bridge of barges to expel Napoléon's troops from the Rhineland. The small **Blüchermuseum** with furnishings and militaria from that time is housed in his former headquarters. ✉ *Metzgerg. 6,* ☎ *06774/400.* *€2.* *Apr.–Oct., daily 11–4, Nov.–Mar., daily 2–5. Closed Mon.*

Pfalzgrafenstein Castle—known locally as the "Pfalz"—is built on a rock in the middle of the Rhine. Originally a five-sided tower, it was later enclosed by a six-sided defense wall that makes it look like a stone ship anchored in the Rhine. It was never destroyed. Unlike the elaborate period rooms of many Rhine castles, the Pfalz provides a good look at sparse medieval living quarters and has an interesting collection of ordinary household goods. ☎ *0172/262–2800.* WEB *www.burgen-rlp.de.* *€4.10, including boat ride to and from Kaub.* *Apr.–Sept., daily 9–1 and 2–6; Oct.–Mar., Tues.–Sun. 9–1 and 2–5. Closed Dec.*

Dining and Lodging

$$ **Zum Turm.** Set next to a medieval *Turm* (tower) near the Rhine, this little inn offers spacious guest rooms on the floors above its cozy restaurant ($$–$$$$) and terrace. Any fish, game, and produce chef Harald Kutsche can't source from local farms are imported from the market halls of Paris. For a starter try the home-smoked salmon or splurge on anglerfish on lobster ragout. The daily set menus are excellent options. The Mittelrhein and Rheingau are the focus of the wine list. ✉ *Zollstr. 50, D–56349,* ☎ *06774/92200,* FAX *06774/922–011,* WEB *www.rhein-hotel-turm.com. 6 rooms. Restaurant, no a/c, minibars, bicycles, some pets allowed (fee). DC, MC, V. Closed 2 wks in Feb., 2 wks in Nov. Restaurant closed Tues.; weekday lunch on request only Nov.–Mar.*

Oberwesel

8 *8 km (5 mi) north of Bacharach.*

Oberwesel retains its medieval silhouette. Sixteen of the original 21 towers and much of the town wall still stand in the shadow of Schönburg Castle. The "town of towers" is also renowned for its Riesling wines, celebrated at two lively wine festivals, the *Weinmarkt,* in early and mid-September. Both Gothic churches on opposite ends of town are worth visiting. The **Liebfrauenkirche** (Church of Our Lady), popularly known as the "red church" because of its brightly colored exterior, has a superb rood screen, masterful sculptures, tombstones and paintings, and one of Germany's oldest altars (1331). Set on a hill, **St. Martin**—the so-called white church—with a fortresslike tower, has beautifully painted vaulting, and a magnificent baroque altar.

Dining and Lodging

$–$$ ✕ **Historische Weinwirtschaft.** Tables in the flower-laden garden in front of this lovingly restored stone house are at a premium in the summer, yet seats in the nooks and crannies indoors are just as inviting. Dark beams, exposed stone walls, and antique furniture set the mood on the ground and first floors, and the vaulted cellar houses contemporary art exhibitions. Ask Iris Marx, the ebullient proprietor, to translate the menu (it's in local dialect) of regional dishes. She offers country cooking at its best. The wine list is excellent and features 32 wines by the glass. ✉ *Liebfrauenstr. 17,* ☎ *06744/8186,* WEB *www.historische-weinwirtschaft.de. AE, MC, V. Closed Tues. and Jan. No lunch except Sun. May–Sept.*

$$–$$$ ★ ✕🏨 **Burghotel Auf Schönburg.** Part of the Schönburg Castle complex (12th century) has been lovingly restored as a romantic hotel and restaurant ($$–$$$$; closed Monday), with terraces in the courtyard and overlooking the Rhine. Antique furnishings and historical rooms (library, chapel, prison tower) make for an unforgettable ambience, enhanced by the extraordinarily friendly, personal service of your hosts, the Hüttls, and staff. If you have only a night or two in the area, go for this hotel's first-rate lodging, food, and wine. Luggage transfer from the parking lot below the entrance is easily arranged at the front desk. ✉ *D–55430,* ☎ *06744/93930,* FAX *06744/1613,* WEB *www.hotel-schoenburg.com. 20 rooms, 2 suites. Restaurant, no a/c, some in-room data ports, minibars, library, some pets allowed. DC, MC, V. Closed Jan.–Mar.*

$$ ✕🏨 **Römerkrug.** Rooms with exposed beams, pretty floral prints, and historic furnishings are tucked within the half-timber facades (1458) of Elke Matzner's small inn on the market square. Fish and game are house specialties ($$–$$$), but there's light cuisine with Asian accents as well as Rhine specialties, such as Himmel und Erde. There is a well-chosen selection of Mittelrhein wines. ✉ *Marktpl. 1, D–55430,* ☎ *06744/7091,* FAX *06744/1677. 6 rooms, 1 apartment. Restaurant, no a/c, some pets allowed. AE, MC, V. Hotel closed Jan. Restaurant closed Wed. and Jan.*

St. Goar

9 *7 km (4½ mi) north of Oberwesel; ferry to St. Goarshausen.*

St. Goar and its counterpoint on the opposite shore, St. Goarshausen, are named after a Celtic missionary who settled here in the 6th century. He became the patron saint of innkeepers—an auspicious sign for both towns that now live from tourism and wine. September is especially busy, with *Weinforum Mittelrhein* (a major wine-and-food presentation in Burg Rheinfels) on the first weekend, and on both sides of the Rhine, wine festivals and the splendid fireworks display "Rhine in Flames" on the third weekend.

St. Goar's tomb once rested in the 15th-century collegiate church, the **Stiftskirche,** built over a Romanesque crypt reminiscent of those of churches in Speyer and Köln. ✉ *Kirchpl.,.* ⏲ *Apr.–Oct., daily 11–5.*

The extensive castle ruins of **Burg Rheinfels** overlooking the town bear witness to the fact that St. Goar was once the best-fortified town in the Mittelrhein. From its beginnings in 1245, it was repeatedly enlarged by the counts of Katzenelnbogen, a powerful local dynasty, and their successors, the landgraves of Hesse. Although it repelled Louis IV's troops in 1689, Rheinfels was blasted by the French in 1797. Take time for a walk through the impressive ruins and the museum, which has an exquisite model of how the fortress looked in its heyday. To avoid the steep ascent on foot, buy a round-trip ticket (€3) for the *Burgexpress*, which departs from the bus stop on Heerstrasse, opposite the riverside parking lot for tour buses. ✉ *Off Schlossberg Str.*, ☎ *06741/383.* 🎫 *€4.* ⏲ *Apr.–Oct., daily 9–6; Nov.–Mar., weekends (weather permitting) 10–4.*

Dining and Lodging

$$ ✕🏨 **Schloss-Hotel & Villa Rheinfels.** Directly opposite Burg Rheinfels, this hotel offers modern comfort in very pleasant surroundings. The expansive views from the restaurant's terrace ($$–$$$) or a table in one of the window alcoves (Nos. 51, 52, 61, and 62) make a meal or glass of wine especially memorable. Regional and seasonal specialties are served in the main restaurant, Auf Scharfeneck, and evenings, also in the Burgschänke in the cellar. Highly recommended is the *Wispertal Forelle* (trout from the Wisper Valley). ✉ *Schlossberg 47, D–56329,* ☎ *06741/8020,* FAX *06741/802–802,* WEB *www.schlosshotel-rheinfels.de. 54 rooms, 2 suites. 2 restaurants, no a/c, some in-room data ports, minibars, pool, sauna, bicycles, bar, some pets allowed (fee). AE, DC, MC, V.*

$–$$ ✕🏨 **Hotel Landsknecht.** The Nickenig family makes everyone feel at home in their riverside restaurant and hotel north of St. Goar. Daughter Martina, a former wine queen, and Joachim Lorenz, a wine maker, operate the Vinothek, where you can sample his prize-winning Bopparder Hamm wines. These go well with the restaurant's hearty local dishes. Friday evenings in the summer there is a barbecue on the splendid Rhine terrace. Rooms are individually furnished and quite comfortable; some offer a Rhine view (Nos. 4, 5, and 8 are especially nice). ✉ *Rheinuferstr. (B–9), D–56329 St. Goar-Fellen,* ☎ *06741/2011,* FAX *06741/7499,* WEB *www.hotel-landsknecht.de. 14 rooms, 1 suite. Restaurant, no a/c, in-room data ports, minibars, bicycles, shop, some pets allowed (fee), no-smoking rooms. AE, DC, MC, V. Closed mid-Dec.–Feb.*

St. Goarshausen

⑩ *29 km (18 mi) north of Rüdesheim; ferry from St. Goar.*

St. Goarshausen lies at the foot of two 14th-century castles whose names, Katz (cat) and Maus (mouse), reflect but one of the many power plays on the Rhine in the Middle Ages. Territorial supremacy and the concomitant privilege of collecting tolls fueled the fires of rivalry. In response to the construction of Burg Rheinfels, the archbishop of Trier erected a small castle north of St. Goarshausen to protect his interests. In turn, the masters of Rheinfels, the counts of Katzenelnbogen, built a bigger castle directly above the town. Its name was shortened to "Katz," and its smaller neighbor was scornfully referred to as "Maus." Katz is not open to the public. **Maus** has a terrace café (great views) and demonstrations featuring eagles and falcons in flight. ☎ *06771/7669,* WEB *www.burg-maus.de.* 🎫 *€6.50.* ⏲ *Mid-Mar.–Sept., daily at 11 and 2:30. Sun. also at 4:30.*

Some 10 km (6 mi) north of the Maus castle, near Kamp-Bornhofen, is a castle duo separated by a "quarrel wall": **Liebenstein and Sterrenberg,** known as the *Feindliche Brüder* (rival brothers). Both impressive ruins have terrace cafés that afford good views.

One of the Rhineland's main attractions lies 4 km (2½ mi) south of St. Goarshausen: the steep (430 ft-high) slate cliff named after the beautiful blond nymph **Loreley.** Here she sat, singing songs so lovely that sailors and fishermen were lured to the treacherous rapids—and their demise. The legend stems from a tale by Clemens Brentano, retold as a ballad by Heinrich Heine and set to music by Friedrich Silcher at the height of Rhine Romanticism in the 19th century. The summit is a great vantage point.

OFF THE BEATEN PATH

BESUCHERZENTRUM LORELEY – The 10-minute film and hands-on exhibits at this visitor center are entertaining ways to learn about the region's flora and fauna, geology, wine, shipping, and above all, the myth of the Loreley. You can sample and purchase wines at the vinothek, stock up on souvenirs in the shop (and euros at the ATM), and have a snack at the bistro before heading for the nearby vantage point at the cliff's summit. Hiking trails are signposted in the landscaped park. ✉ *Auf der Loreley,* ☎ *06771/599–093,* WEB *www.besucherzentrum-loreley.de.* € *1.* ⏲ *Apr.–Oct., daily 10–6; Nov.–Mar., daily 11–5.*

Boppard

⓫ *17 km (11 mi) north of St. Goar; ferry to Filsen.*

Boppard is a pleasant little resort that evolved from a Celtic settlement into a Roman fortress, Frankish royal court, and Free Imperial City. The Roman garrison Bodobrica, established here in the 4th century, was enclosed by a 26-ft-high rectangular wall (1,010 by 505 ft) with 28 defense towers. You can see portions of these in the fascinating open-air **archaeological park** (✉ Angertstr., near the B–9 and railroad tracks). The **Stadtmuseum** (town museum), housed in the 14th-century Kurfürstliche Burg (elector's castle) built by the archbishop of Trier, has exhibits on Boppard's Roman and medieval past, as well as an extensive collection of bentwood furniture designed by the town's favorite son, Michael Thonet (1796–1871). The cane-bottom *Stuhl Nr. 14* (chair No. 14) is the famous classic found in coffeehouses around the world since 1859. ✉ *Burgstr.,* ☎ *06742/10369.* *Free.* ⏲ *Apr.–Oct., Tues.–Sun. 10–noon and 2–5.*

Excavations in the 1960s revealed ancient Roman baths beneath the twin-tower, Romanesque **Church of St. Severus** (1236) on the market square. The large triumphal crucifix over the main altar and a lovely statue of a smiling Madonna date from the 13th century. Two baroque altars dominate the interior of the Gothic **Carmelite Church** on Karmeliterstrasse, near the Rhine. It houses intricately carved choir stalls and tombstones, and several beautiful Madonnas. Winegrowers still observe the old custom of laying the first-picked *Trauben* (grapes) at the foot of the Traubenmadonna (1330) to ensure a good harvest. The annual wine festival takes place in late September, just before the Riesling harvest.

On the northern edge of Boppard the Rhine makes its largest loop, skirting the majestic, vine-covered hill known as the **Bopparder Hamm.** From the Mühltal station let the *Sessellbahn* (chairlift) whisk you 1,300 ft uphill to the **Vierseenblick** (four-lake vista), a vantage point from which the Rhine looks like a chain of lakes. *€6.20 round-trip, €4.20 one-way.* ⏲ *Apr.–Oct., daily 10–5 (summer 9:30–6:30).*

Dining and Lodging

$$ ✕ **Best Western Hotel Bellevue.** You can enjoy a Rhine view from many of the rooms in this traditional hotel or from the terrace next to the pretty Rhine promenade. Afternoon tea, dinner, and Sunday lunch are accompanied by piano music (Easter–December, except Wednesday) in the main restaurant ($$$–$$$$). Try the hearty *Reblaus-Teller* of pork medallions in a grape sauce. The other restaurant also offers sumptuous luncheon buffets. ✉ *Rheinallee 41, D–56154,* ☎ *06742/1020,* FAX *06742/102–602,* WEB *www.bellevue.boppard.de. 92 rooms,*

1 suite. 2 restaurants, bar, no a/c in some rooms, some in-room data ports, minibars, pool, gym, sauna, some pets allowed (fee), no-smoking rooms. AE, DC, MC, V.

$ **Weinhaus Heilig Grab.** This wine estate's tavern ($), Boppard's oldest, is full of smiling faces: the wines are excellent, the fare is simple but hearty, and the welcome is warm. Old chestnut trees shade tables in the courtyard. Rooms are furnished with rustic pine furniture. If you'd like to visit the cellars or vineyards, ask your friendly hosts, Rudolf and Susanne Schoeneberger. They also arrange wine tastings. ✉ *Zelkesg. 12, D–56154,* ☎ *06742/2371,* FAX *06742/81220,* WEB *www.heiliggrab.de. 5 rooms. Restaurant, no a/c, no room phones, no smoking room. MC, V. Hotel closed Nov.–Easter. Restaurant closed Tues. No lunch.*

Outdoor Activities and Sports

GOLF

The **Jakobsberg** (✉ Im Tal der Loreley, Boppard/Rhens, ☎ 06742/808–491), 10 km (6 mi) north of Boppard via Spay and Siebenborn, is one of the most magnificent settings in Germany to play a challenging round of 18 holes. The views are superb.

HIKING

The 10-km (6-mi) **Weinwanderweg** (wine hiking trail) through the Bopparder Hamm, from Boppard to Spay, begins north of town on Peternacher Weg. Many other marked trails in the vicinity are outlined in maps and brochures available from the tourist office.

En Route On the outskirts of Koblenz the neo-Gothic towers of **Schloss Stolzenfels** come into view. The castle's origins date from the mid-13th century, when the archbishop of Trier sought to counter the influence (and toll rights) of the archbishop of Mainz, who had just built Burg Lahneck, a castle at the confluence of the Lahn and Rhine rivers. Its superbly furnished period rooms and beautiful gardens are well worth a visit. It is a wonderful setting for concerts. From the B–9 (curbside parking) it's about a 15-minute walk to the castle entrance. ☎ *0261/51656,* WEB *www.burgen-rlp.de.* *€2.60.* *Apr.–Sept., Tues.–Sun. 9–5; Oct., Nov., and Jan.–Mar., Tues.–Sun. 9–4. Closed Dec.*

On the eastern shore, overlooking the town of Braubach, is the **Marksburg.** Built in the 12th century to protect the silver and lead mines in the area, it is the only land-based castle on the Rhine to have survived the centuries intact. Within its massive walls are a collection of weapons and manuscripts, a medieval botanical garden, and a restaurant. ☎ *02627/206,* WEB *www.deutsche-burgen.org.* *€4.50.* *Easter–Oct., daily 10–5; Nov.–Easter, daily 11–4. Closed last wk Dec. Restaurant closed mid-Dec.–mid-Feb.*

Koblenz

20 km (12 mi) north of Boppard.

The ancient city of Koblenz is at a geographic nexus known as the **Deutsches Eck** (German Corner) in the heart of the Mittelrhein region. Rivers and mountains converge here: the Mosel flows into the Rhine on one side; the Lahn flows in on the other a few miles south; and three mountain ridges intersect. Koblenz is one of the Rhineland-Palatinate's cultural, administrative, and business centers.

Founded by the Romans in AD 9, the city's first name was Castrum ad Confluentes (Fort at the Confluence). It became a powerful city in the Middle Ages, when it controlled trade on both the Rhine and the Mosel. Air raids during World War II destroyed 85% of the city, but extensive restoration has done much to re-create its former atmosphere. English-speaking walking tours of the Old Town can be arranged by the tourist office on request.

Koblenz is centered on the west bank of the Rhine. On the east bank
12 stands Europe's largest fortress, **Festung Ehrenbreitstein,** offering a commanding view from 400 ft above the river. The earliest buildings date from about 1100, but the bulk of the fortress was constructed in the 16th century. In 1801 it was partially destroyed by Napoléon and the French occupied Koblenz for the next 18 years. As for the fortress's 16th-century **Vogel Greif cannon,** the French absconded with it in 1794, the Germans took it back in 1940, and the French commandeered it again in 1945. The 15-ton cannon was peaceably returned by French president François Mitterrand in 1984 and is now part of the exhibit on the history of local technologies, from wine growing to industry, in the fortress's **Landesmuseum** (State Museum; ☎ 0261/97030; €3.10, including admission to fortress grounds; Mid-Mar.–mid-Nov., daily 9:15–5).

To reach the east bank of the Rhine take bus 9 from the train station or the **ferry** (☎ 0261/72783; €1.60 round-trip; Mar.–Apr., daily 9–5, May–Sept., daily 8–7) from the Pegelhaus on the Koblenz riverbank (near Rheinstrasse). Take the **Sesselbahn** (cable car) to ascend to the fortress (€6.70 round-trip, including admission to the fortress grounds; Apr., May, and Oct., daily 10–4:50; June–Aug., daily 9–5:50; Sept., daily 10–5:50). For the best value, purchase the combination ticket that includes the grounds, museum, and a 45-minute tour. ☎ *0261/974–2440.* *Grounds €1.10; combo ticket and tour €4.20.* *Mid-Mar.–mid-Nov., daily 9–5.*

13 The **Pfaffendorfer Brücke** (Pfaffendorf Bridge) marks the beginning of
the Old Town. Just off the Pfaffendorf Bridge, between the modern blocks
14 of the Rhein-Mosel-Halle and the Hotel Mercure, is the **Weindorf** (WEB
www.weindorf-koblenz.de), a wine "village" constructed for a mammoth exhibition of German wines in 1925.

15 The **Rheinanlagen** (Rhine Gardens), a 10-km (6-mi) promenade, runs
along the riverbank past the Weindorf. Strolling along the promenade
16 toward town, you'll pass the gracious **Kurfürstliches Schloss,** the prince-elector's palace. It was built in 1786 by Prince-Elector Clemens Wenzeslaus as an elegant escape from the grim Ehrenbreitstein fortress. He lived here for only three years, however; in 1791 he was forced to flee to Augsburg when the French stormed the city. The palace is used for city offices and is closed to visitors.

17 The squat form of the **Rheinkran** (Rhine Crane), built in 1611, is one of Koblenz's landmarks. Marks on the side of the building indicate the heights reached by floodwaters of bygone years. In the mid-19th century a pontoon bridge consisting of a row of barges spanned the Rhine here; when ships approached, two or three barges were simply towed out of the way to let them through.

18 The **Deutsches Eck** (German Corner) is at the sharp intersection of the Rhine and Mosel, a pointed bit of land jutting into the river like the prow of some early ironclad warship. One of the more effusive manifestations of German nationalism—an 1897 statue of Kaiser Wilhelm I, first emperor of the newly united Germany—was erected here. It was destroyed at the end of World War II and replaced in 1953 with a ponderous, altarlike monument to Germany's unity. After German reunification a new statue of Wilhelm was placed atop this monument in 1993. Pieces of the Berlin Wall stand on the Mosel side—a memorial to those who died as a result of the partitioning of the country.

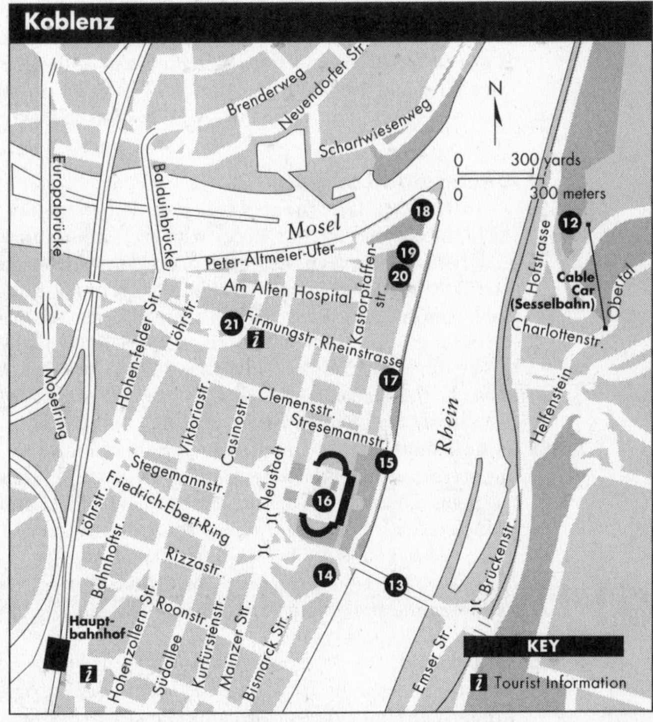

From the Deutsches Eck, the Moselanlagen (Mosel Promenade) leads to Koblenz's oldest restaurant, the Deutscher Kaiser, which marks the start of the Old Town.

19 The **Ludwig Museum** stands just behind the Deutsches Eck, housed in the spic-and-span *Deutschherrenhaus*, a restored 13th-century building. Industrialist Peter Ludwig, one of Germany's leading contemporary art collectors, has founded museums in many Rhineland cities; he's filled this one with part of his huge collection. ✉ *Danziger Freiheit 1,* ☎ *0261/304–040.* €2.50. ⏲ *Tues.–Sat. 10:30–5, Sun. 11–6.*

20 The **St. Kastor Kirche** (St. Castor Church) is a sturdy Romanesque basilica consecrated in 836. It was here in 842 that plans were drawn for the contract signed as the Treaty of Verdun, formalizing the division of Charlemagne's great empire and leading to the creation of Germany and France as separate states. Inside, compare the squat Romanesque columns in the nave with the intricate fan vaulting of the Gothic sections. **The St. Kastor Fountain** outside the church is an intriguing piece of historical one-upmanship. It was built by the occupying French to mark the beginning of Napoléon's ultimately disastrous Russian campaign of 1812. When the Russians reached Koblenz after having roundly defeated the French, they added an ironic SEEN AND APPROVED to the fountain's inscription. ✉ *Kastorhof.* ⏲ *Daily 9–6 except during services.*

The **Mittelrhein Museum** houses the city's art collection in a lovely 16th-century building near Old Town's central square, Am Plan. ✉ *Florinsmarkt 15,* ☎ *0261/129–2520,* WEB *www.mittelrhein-museum.de.* *€2.50.* ⏲ *Tues.–Sat. 10:30–5, Sun. 11–6.*

War damage is evidenced by the blend of old buildings and modern
21 store blocks on and around Am Plan. The **Liebfrauenkirche** (Church

of Our Lady) stands on Roman foundations at the Old Town's highest point. The bulk of the church is of Romanesque design, but its choir is one of the Rhineland's finest examples of 15th-century Gothic architecture, and the west front is graced with two 17th-century baroque towers. ✉ *Am Plan.* ⏲ *Mon.–Sat. 8–6, Sun. 9–8 except during services.*

Dining and Lodging

$$$–$$$$ ✕ **Löffel's Keller.** Tucked away on a little alley between the Liebfrauenkirche and the Mosel in a cozy, 13th-century vaulted cellar Günther Löffel serves upscale regional cuisine with top-flight wines (primarily Mosel whites, and German reds from the Ahr and Baden, as well as Bordeaux). Every month there is a new set menu based on a theme and a new fish menu, both offered with wines by the glass suggested for each course. ✉ *Mehlg. 14–16,* ☎ *0261/100–4715.* WEB *www.loeffels-keller.de. AE, MC, V. Closed Sun., Mon., 2 wks late Dec.–early Jan., and mid-June–mid-Aug. No lunch.*

$–$$$ ✕ **Café Balthazar.** The multistory atrium of a historic house (once a furniture store) has been turned into a very classy, yet comfortable, meeting point. Three meals a day are served amid fabulous art nouveau decor, complete with huge palm trees. You can also come for coffee and cake, or snacks and drinks late into the night. Weekends, the lower level is a disco. The huge terrace on Görres Square is perfect spot for people-watching and soaking up the sun. ✉ *Firmungstr. 2, Am Görrespl.,* ☎ *0261/100–5833. MC, V.*

$–$$$ ✕ **Weindorf.** The Bastian family has upgraded the food-and-wine selection on offer at this reconstructed "wine village" of half-timber houses grouped around a tree-shaded courtyard. The fresh renditions of traditional Rhine and Mosel specialties and a good selection of reasonably priced local wines are popular with locals and visitors alike. Occasionally, there's live music on Sunday mornings. ✉ *Julius-Wegeler-Str. 2,* ☎ *0261/133–7150. AE, DC, MC, V.* ⏲ *Open daily Apr.–Oct. Nov.–Mar. closed Mon., no lunch Tues.–Fri.*

$–$$ ✕ **Weinhaus Hubertus.** Hunting scenes and trophies line the wood-paneled walls of this cozy wine restaurant named after the patron saint of hunters. Karin and Dieter Spahl serve hearty portions of traditional fare, such as Himmel und Erde, and local wines. Try their dessert specialty: *Feigenmus* (fig puree) and Tête de Moine cheese served with a glass of the rare dessert wine Beerenauslese. ✉ *Florinsmarkt 6,* ☎ *0261/31177. AE, DC, MC, V. Closed Tues. No lunch except Sun. June–Oct.*

$ ✕ **Circus Maximus.** Here's a laid-back setting for breakfast, lunch, dinner, or drinks with music (sometimes live) at night. Weekdays, the *Mittagstisch* (luncheon special) at €4.80 or hearty soup-of-the-day made from organically grown ingredients at €2.80 are excellent value. The menu offers everything from sandwiches to salads, baked potatoes or potato gratins, steaks, and pizza. ✉ *Stegemannstr. 30, at Viktoriastr.,* ☎ *0261/300–2357. No credit cards. No lunch weekends.*

$$ ✕🏨 **Zum weissen Schwanen.** Guests have found a warm welcome in this half-timber inn and mill since 1693, a tradition carried on by the Kunz family today. Next to a 13th-century town gateway, it is a thoroughly charming place to overnight or enjoy well-prepared regional specialties ($$–$$$$), contemporary German cuisine, and an excellent selection of local wines. Rooms are individually decorated with period furniture ranging from Biedermeier to Belle Epoque. ✉ *Brunnenstr. 4, D–56338 Braubach, 12 km (7½ mi) south of Koblenz via B–42,* ☎ *02627/9820,* FAX *02627/8802,* WEB *www.zum-weissen-schwanen.de. 16 rooms, 1 suite. Restaurant, no a/c, some in-room data ports, bicycles, bar, some pets allowed, no-smoking rooms. AE, DC, MC, V. Restaurant closed Wed. No lunch Mon.–Sat.*

$$$ **Hotel Mercure.** This modern high-rise on the Rhine is next to the city's conference and events center, the Rhein-Mosel-Halle, and within a short walk of all major sights. Rooms are modern and well appointed; some have fabulous views. ✉ *Julius-Wegeler-Str. 6, D–56068,* ☎ *0261/1360,* FAX *0261/136–1199,* WEB *www.mercure.com. 167 rooms, 1 suite. 2 restaurants, bar, minibars, gym, hot tub, sauna, bicycles, some pets allowed (fee), no-smoking rooms. AE, DC, MC, V.*

$$ **Contel Koblenz.** The Hundertwasser-inspired look of this hotel is unique. Behind the colorful facade there are pleasant, modern rooms (some with waterbeds). You can dine on a terrace surrounded by artificial pools and eclectic "works of art." ✉ *Pastor-Klein-Str. 11, D–56073 Koblenz-Rauental, 2 km (1 mi) from the Deutsches Eck,* ☎ *0261/40650,* FAX *0261/406–5188,* WEB *www.contel-koblenz.de. 185 rooms, 7 apartments. Restaurant, bar, no a/c, in-room data ports, some minibars, massage, sauna, some pets allowed (fee), no-smoking rooms. AE, DC, MC, V.*

Nightlife and the Arts

The courtyard of the Festung Ehrenbreitstein is the site of the **Festspiele** (open-air theater) in late June or early July. *Aida* is scheduled for 2003. The **Staatsorchester Rheinische Philharmonie** (Rhenish Philharmonic Orchestra; ✉ Julius-Wegeler-Str., ☎ 0261/301–2272) plays regularly in the Rhein-Mosel-Halle. The gracious neoclassic **Theater der Stadt Koblenz** (☎ 0261/129–2840), built in 1787, is still in regular use.

Night owls frequent the bar and Abaco Club (a disco Thursday–Saturday) at **Café Balthazar** (✉ Firmungstr. 2, Am Görrespl., ☎ 0261/100–5833) and the many pubs on Florinsmarkt. **Circus Maximus**(✉ Stegemannstr. 30, at Viktoriastr.) offers disco sounds, live music, and theme parties. The **Blaue Biwel** (✉ Entenpfuhl 9, ☎ 0261/35577) and its sister club in the suburb of Güls, Café Hahn (✉ Neustr. 15, ☎ 0261/42302), feature everything from cabaret and stand-up comedians to popular musicians and bands.

Shopping

Koblenz's most pleasant shopping is in the Old City streets around the market square Am Plan. **Löhr Center** (✉ Hohenfelder Str., at Am Wöllershof), a modern, American-style, windowless mall, has some 130 shops and restaurants and will give you an authentic German shopping experience.

En Route Take a fascinating walk through the **Garten der Schmetterlinge Schloss Sayn** (Garden of Butterflies), where butterflies from South America, Asia, and Africa flit back and forth over your head between the branches of banana trees and palms. The palace proper houses a small local history museum, a restaurant, and a café. It is located 15 km (9 mi) north of Koblenz (Bendorf exit off the B–42). ✉ *Im Fürstlichen Schlosspark, D–56170 Bendorf-Sayn,* ☎ *02622/15478,* WEB *www.sayn.de.* *Butterfly garden and museum €6.* ⏲ *Mar.–Oct., daily 9–6; Nov., daily 10–4.*

THE MOSEL VALLEY

Updated by Kerry Brady Stewart

The Mosel is one of the most hauntingly beautiful river valleys on earth. Here, as in the Rhine Valley, forests and vines carpet steep hillsides; castles and church spires dot the landscape; and medieval wine villages line the riverbanks. The Mosel landscape is no less majestic, but it is less narrow and more peaceful than that of the Rhine Gorge; the river's countless bends and loops slow its pace and lend the region a special charm.

From Koblenz to Treis-Karden, two roads run parallel to the Mosel: B–416 (west side) and B–49 (east side). Thereafter, only one road continues upstream, occasionally traversing the river as it winds toward Trier: until Alf, it is B–49; afterwards, B–53.

The signposted routes between Koblenz and Trier include the Mosel Weinstrasse (Mosel Wine Road) along the riverbank and, on the heights, the hiking trails on both sides of the river known as the Moselhöhenweg. The latter extends 224 km (140 mi) on the Hunsrück (eastern) side and 164 km (102 mi) on the Eifel (western) side of the river. Driving time for the river route is at least three hours. On the autobahn (A–1) the distance between Koblenz and Trier can be covered in about an hour.

Winningen

22 *11 km (7 mi) southwest of Koblenz on B–416.*

Winningen is a gateway to the *Terrassenmosel* (terraced Mosel), the portion of the river characterized by steep, terraced vineyards. Monorails and winches help winegrowers, and their tools make the ascent, but tending and harvesting the vines is all done by hand. For a bird's-eye view of the valley drive up Fährstrasse to Am Rosenhang, the start of a pleasant walk along the *Weinlehrpfad* (educational wine path).

The renowned vineyard site Uhlen lies upstream between Winningen and Kobern-Gondorf. Kobern's Oberburg (upper castle) and the St. Matthias Kapelle, a 12th-century chapel, are good vantage points. Near the market square in the village below, you can see an old half-timber house (1321), now quarters for Kobern's tourist office.

Dining and Lodging

$$–$$$$ ✕ **Alte Mühle.** Tucked away in a valley beneath Kobern's castle ruins is Thomas and Gudrun Höreth's lovingly restored "old mill" (1026)—a labyrinth of little rooms and cellars grouped around romantic, oleander- and flower-lined courtyards. Wine presses are on display, along with many wine-related artifacts. The menu offers something for every taste but the absolute hits are the homemade cheeses, terrines, and pâtés, and *Entensülze* (goose in aspic), served with home-fried potatoes. Mature Bordeaux wines supplement the Höreths' own estate-bottled wines. ✉ *Mühlental 17 (via B–416), Kobern,* ☎ *02607/6474. MC, V. Closed Feb. No lunch weekdays.*

$–$$ ✕🏨 **Halferschenke.** This *Schenke* (inn) was once an overnight stop for "Halfer" who, with their horses, towed cargo-laden boats upstream. Today the stone house inn (1832) is run by a friendly young couple, Thomas and Eva Balmes. Light walls, dark wood, and lots of candles and flowers are a lovely setting for his artfully prepared food ($$$–$$$$). An excellent selection of Terrassenmosel wines is available. The rooms, each named after an artist, are modern, airy, and bright. ✉ *Hauptstr. 36, D–56332 Dieblich, via B–49, opposite Kobern,* ☎ *02607/1008,* FAX *02607/960–294,* WEB *www.Halferschenke.de. 4 rooms. Restaurant; no a/c, no room phones, some pets allowed. AE, MC, V. Closed Mon. and 2 wks in autumn. No lunch Tues.–Sat.*

Alken

23 *22 km (13½ mi) southwest of Koblenz.*

The 12th-century castle **Burg Thurant** towers over the village and the Burgberg (castle hill) vineyard. Wine and snacks are served in the courtyard; castle tours take in the chapel, cellar, tower, and a weapons display. Allow a good half hour for the climb from the riverbank. ☎

02605/2004. ✉ €3. ⊙ Mar.–Nov., daily 10–5; Dec.–Feb., weekends 10–4.

Dining and Lodging

$–$$ ✕▣ **Burg Thurant.** The Kopowski's stylish restaurant ($$–$$$) and guest house lie at the foot of the castle, next to a venerable stone tower on the riverbank (B–49). They serve tasty renditions of *Mosel Aal* (Mosel eel), *Bachforelle* (fresh stream trout) in almond butter, and *Entenbrust mit Brombeerjus* (breast of duck in blackberry sauce), accompanied by wines from the region's finest producers. The guest rooms are outfitted with a mixture of antiques and country-style furnishings. ✉ *Moselstr. 16, D–56332, ☎ 02605/3581,* FAX *02605/2152,* WEB *www.terrassenmosel.de. 5 rooms, 1 suite. Restaurant, no a/c, bicycles, some pets allowed (fee), no-smoking rooms. MC. Closed Mon. and Feb. No lunch weekdays.*

En Route ★ **Burg Eltz** (Eltz Castle) is one of Germany's most picturesque, genuinely medieval castles (12th–16th centuries) and merits as much attention as King Ludwig's trio of castles in Bavaria. Nestled deep within the forested Eltz River Valley, the approach to the castle is a downhill walk. The 40-minute tour, with excellent commentary on the castle's history and furnishings, guides you through the period rooms and massive kitchen, but does not include the treasure chamber, a collection of fascinating artworks displayed in five historical rooms. In the summer the lines are long, so bring some water, particularly if you are traveling with children. To get here, exit B–416 at Hatzenport (opposite and southwest of Alken), proceed to Münstermaifeld, and follow signs to the parking lot near the Antoniuskapelle. From here it is a 15-minute walk or take the shuttle bus (€1.50). Hikers can reach the castle from Moselkern in 40 minutes. ✉ *Burg Eltz/Münstermaifeld, ☎ 02672/950–500,* WEB *www.burg-eltz.de.* ✉ *Castle tour €5, treasure chamber €2. ⊙ Apr.–Oct., daily 9:30–5:30.*

Treis-Karden

24 *39 km (24 mi) southwest of Koblenz; Karden is on B–416; Treis is on B–49.*

Treis-Karden are two towns joined for administrative purposes. The richly furnished Romanesque and Gothic **Church of St. Castor,** named after the saint who introduced Christianity to the area in the middle of the 4th century, is well worth a visit, as is the **Stiftsmuseum** in the historical tithe house (1238) behind the church. Exhibits illustrate Karden's history as a religious center, starting with the Celtic and Roman eras. The two stars on the weather vane symbolize the star of Bethlehem and allude to the church's precious "altar of the three kings," Europe's only remaining terra-cotta altar shrine (1420). Attend Sunday service to hear the magnificent baroque organ (1728) built by Johann Michael Stumm, founder of one of the world's greatest organ-building dynasties. ✉ *St.-Castor-Str. 1, Karden, ☎ 02672/6137.* ✉ *Museum €3. ⊙ Easter and May–Oct., Wed.–Fri. 2–5, weekends 10–noon and 2–5.*

Dining and Lodging

$–$$ ✕▣ **Schloss-Hotel Petry.** From a simple guest house a century ago, this family-run hotel has developed into a complex of buildings with very attractive, comfortably furnished rooms and modern facilities. House specialties (Restaurant $$$$, Weinstube $–$$) are *Aal Grün* (green eel), cooked eel served cold with a green herb sauce, and rib roast of lamb. The wine list has a good selection of Mosel wines. ✉ *St.-Castor-Str. 80 (B–416), D–56253, ☎ 02672/9340,* FAX *02672/934–440,* WEB *www.schlosshotel-petry.de. 55 rooms, 19 suites. 2 restaurants, no a/c, some* *in-room data ports, minibars, gym, hot tub, sauna, billiards, bowling, Ping-Pong, bar, some pets allowed (fee), no-smoking rooms. AE, DC, MC, V (restaurant only). Restaurant closed Tues. and Wed.*

Cochem

25 *51 km (31½ mi) southwest of Koblenz on B–49, approximately 93 km (58 mi) from Trier.*

Cochem is one of the most attractive towns of the Mosel Valley, with a riverside promenade to rival any along the Rhine. It is especially lively during the wine festivals in June and late August. If time permits, savor the landscape from the deck of a boat—many excursions are available, lasting from one hour to an entire day. The tourist office on Endertplatz has an excellent English-language outline for a walking tour of the town. From the **Enderttor** (Endert Town Gate) you can see the entrance to Germany's longest railway tunnel, the Kaiser-Wilhelm, an astonishing example of 19th-century engineering. The 4-km-long (2½-mi-long) tunnel saves travelers a 21-km (13-mi) detour along one of the Mosel's great loops.

The 15-minute walk to the **Reichsburg** (Imperial Fortress), the 1,000-year-old castle overlooking the town, will reward you with great views of the area. ☎ *02671/255.* *€4, including 40-min tour.* *Mid-Mar.–mid-Nov., daily 9–5.*

A ride on the **cable car** to the Pinner Kreuz provides great vistas. ✉ *Endertstr.,* ☎ *02671/989–063.* *€5.50 round-trip.* *Late Mar.–mid-Nov., daily 10–6.*

Dining and Lodging

$$ ✕ **Alte Thorschenke.** Next to the Enderttor near the river, this inn dates from 1332. Winding staircases, ancient wooden beams, and historical decor set the mood. Many of the rooms have period furniture (some with four-poster beds). Hunting trophies and portraits of prince electors adorn the wood-paneled walls of the restaurant ($$–$$$$). There is also a cozy Weinstube and a patio for alfresco dining. Highly recommended are the fresh trout or the *Wildplatte* (game platter). The parent firm, Weingut Freiherr von Landenberg, supplies the excellent Mosel wine and welcomes visitors to tour the estate. ✉ *Brückenstr. 3, D–56812,* ☎ *02671/7059,* FAX *02671/4202,* WEB *www.castle-thorschenke.com. 33 rooms, 3 suites. Restaurant, Weinstube, no a/c, minibars, bicycles, shop, some pets allowed (fee), no-smoking rooms. AE, DC, MC, V. Hotel and restaurant closed Jan.–mid-Mar. Restaurant closed Wed. Nov.–mid-Dec.*

$$ ✕ **Lohspeicher–l'Auberge du Vin.** In times past, oak bark for leather tanners was dried and stored in this house (1834) near the market square. Today it is a charming inn with a pretty terrace, run by a vivacious young couple, Ingo and Birgit Beth. His delicacies ($–$$$) are a pleasure for the palate and the eye. At least one saltwater and one freshwater fish are featured daily. Some 20 French and Italian wines supplement the family's own estate-bottled wines. The rooms are pleasant and modern. ✉ *Oberg. 1, Am Marktpl., D–56812,* ☎ *02671/3976,* FAX *02671/1772. 9 rooms. Restaurant, some pets allowed, no a/c. AE, MC, V. Closed Wed. and Feb.*

$$ ✕ **Weissmühle.** This century-old mill is set amid the forested hills of the Enderttal (Endert Valley). It's an oasis from traffic and crowds yet only 2½ km (1½ mi) from Cochem. The rooms are individually decorated—some in an elegant country-manor style; others have rustic, farmhouse furnishings. Beneath the exposed beams and painted ceiling of the restaurant ($$$–$$$$), food from the hotel's own bakery, butcher shop, and trout farm will grace your table. German and French wines are served. ✉ *Im Enderttal, D–56812, via Endertstr., toward Greimersburg; from A–48 exit Kaisersesch,* ☎ *02671/8955,* FAX *02671/8207,* WEB *www.weissmuehle.de. 36 rooms. Restaurant, bar, lounge, no a/c, some in-room data ports, minibars, sauna, steam room, bowling, some pets allowed (fee). DC, MC, V.*

En Route Ten kilometers (six mi) south of Cochem, on the opposite shore, the ruins of Metternich Castle crown the Schlossberg (Castle Hill) vineyard next to the romantic village of **Beilstein.** Take in the stunning Mosel loop panorama from the castle's terrace café before heading for the market square below. Then ascend the *Klostertreppe* (monastery steps) leading to the baroque monastery church for views of the winding streets lined with half-timber houses.

Ediger-Eller

26 *61 km (38 mi) southwest of Koblenz on B–49.*

Ediger is another photogenic wine village with well-preserved houses and remnants of the medieval town wall. The **Martinskirche** (St. Martin's Church; ✉ Kirchstr.) is a remarkable amalgamation of art and architectural styles, inside and out. Take a moment to admire the 117 carved bosses in the star-vaulted ceiling of the nave. Among the many fine sculptures throughout the church and the chapel is the town's treasure: a Renaissance stone relief of "Christ in the Wine Press."

Dining and Lodging

$–$$ ✕🏨 **Zum Löwen.** The drawing cards of this hotel and wine estate run by Saffenreuther family are the friendly service and the excellent cuisine ($$–$$$$). The house specialties are game (from their own preserve) and fine, fruity Rieslings (a mature Riesling with a balance of acidity and naturally ripe sweetness is superb with venison and boar). The rooms have simple decor. In addition to wine tastings, fishing or hunting trips can be arranged. ✉ *Moselweinstr. 23, D–56814 Ediger-Eller,* ☎ *02675/208,* FAX *02675/214. 21 rooms. Restaurant, no a/c, no room phones, bicycles, some pets allowed (fee). AE, MC, V. Closed Christmas and Jan. Restaurant closed Wed. Feb.–Apr.*

En Route As you continue along the winding course of the Mosel, you'll pass Europe's steepest vineyard site, Calmont, opposite the romantic ruins of a 12th-century Augustinian convent before the loop at Bremm. **Zell** is a popular village full of pubs and wineshops plying the crowds with Zeller Schwarze Katz, "black cat" wine, a commercially successful product and the focal point of a large wine festival in late June. Some 6 million vines hug the slopes around Zell, making it one of Germany's largest wine-growing communities. The area between Zell and Schweich (near Trier), known as the Middle Mosel, is the home of some of the world's finest Riesling wines.

Traben-Trarbach

27 *30 km (19 mi) south of Cochem.*

The Mosel divides Traben-Trarbach, which has pleasant promenades on both sides of the river. Its wine festivals are held the second and last weekends in July. Traben's art nouveau buildings are worth seeing (Hotel Bellevue, the gateway on the Mosel bridge, the post office, the train station, and town hall). For a look at fine period rooms and exhibits on the historical development of the area, visit the **Mittelmosel Museum** in Haus Böcking (1750). ✉ *Casino Str. 2,* ☎ *06541/9480.* 🎫 *€2.50.* ⏲ *Mid-Apr.–Oct., Tues.–Fri. 9:30–noon and 1:30–5, weekends 10–1.*

En Route During the next 24 km (15 mi) you'll pass by world-famous vineyards, such as Erdener Treppchen, Ürziger Würzgarten, the *Sonnenuhr* (sundial) sites of Zeltingen and Wehlen, and Graacher Himmelreich, before reaching Bernkastel-Kues.

Bernkastel-Kues

★ 28 *22 km (14 mi) southwest of Traben-Trarbach, 100 km (62 mi) southwest of Koblenz on B–53.*

Bernkastel and Kues straddle the Mosel, on the east and west banks, respectively. Elaborately carved half-timber houses (16th–17th centuries) and a Renaissance town hall (1608) frame St. Michael's Fountain (1606), on Bernkastel's photogenic **market square.** In early September the square and riverbank are lined with wine stands for one of the region's largest wine festivals, the Weinfest der Mittelmosel. From the hilltop ruins of the 13th-century castle **Burg Landshut** there are splendid views. It was here that Trier's Archbishop Boemund II is said to have recovered from an illness after drinking the local wine, henceforth known as the "Doctor." This legendary vineyard soars up from Hinterm Graben street near the town gate Graacher Tor. You can purchase these exquisite wines from Weingut J. Lauerburg (one of the three original owners of the tiny site) at the estate's tasteful wineshop. ✉ *Am Markt 27.* ☎ *06531/2481.* ⏲ *Apr.–Oct., weekdays 10–5, Sat. 11–5.*

The philosopher and theologian Nikolaus Cusanus (1401–64) was born in Kues. The **St.-Nikolaus-Hospital** is a charitable *Stiftung* (foundation) he established in 1458, and it still operates a home for the elderly and a wine estate. Within it is the **Mosel-Weinmuseum** (wine museum; 🎫 €2; ⏲ mid-Apr.–Oct., daily 10–5; Nov.–mid-Apr., daily 2–5), as well as a bistro and a wineshop. You can sample more than 100 wines from the entire Mosel-Saar-Ruwer region in the **Vinothek** (🎫 €9; ⏲ mid-Apr.–Oct., daily 10–5; Nov.–mid-Apr., daily 2–5) in the vaulted cellar. The hospital's famous library, with precious manuscripts, cloister, and Gothic chapel, may be visited only on tours. ✉ *Cusanus-Str. 2,* ☎ *06531/4141.* 🎫 *Historical rooms (tours): €4.* ⏲ *Mid-Apr.–Oct., Tues. 10:30, Fri. 3, or by appointment.*

Some 3,500 winegrowers throughout the region deliver their grapes to the **Moselland Winzergenossenschaft** (cooperative winery), where the wines are produced, bottled, and marketed. It is an impressive operation, and the large wine shop is excellent. ✉ *Bornwiese 6, in the industrial park,* ☎ *06531/570.* 🎫 *Tours with wine tasting €3.50.* ⏲ *Tues. and Thurs. 3, or by appointment.* ⏲ *Jan.–Mar., weekdays 9–noon and 1–5; Apr.–Dec., weekdays 9–noon and 1–6; year-round, Sat. 9–12:30.*

Dining and Lodging

$$–$$$ ★ ✕🏨 **Waldhotel Sonnora.** Helmut and Ulrike Thieltges offer guests one of Germany's absolute finest dining ($$$$, reservations essential) and wining experiences in their elegant country inn set within the forested Eifel Hills. Mr. Thieltges is a multistarred chef, renowned for transforming exclusive ingredients (foie gras, truffles, Persian caviar) into culinary masterpieces. The wine list is equally superb. The dining room, with gilded and white-wood furnishings and plush red carpets, has a Parisian look. Attractive guest rooms and pretty gardens add to a memorable visit. ✉ *Auf dem Eichelfeld, D–54518 Dreis, 8 km (5 mi) southwest of Wittlich, which is 18 km (11 mi) west of Kues via B–50; from A–1, exit Salmtal,* ☎ *06578/98220,* FAX *06578/1402,* WEB *www.hotel-sonnora.de. 20 rooms. Restaurant, no a/c, minibars. AE, MC, V. Closed Mon., Tues., and Jan. and 3 wks in summer.*

$$ ✕🏨 **Gutshotel Reichsgraf von Kesselstatt.** This is a lovely country inn, stylishly decorated with light wood furnishings. The rooms, restaurant ($$–$$$$), and terrace are peaceful and very pleasant. Chef Dieter Braun has a fondness for fresh Mosel fish, such as *Hecht* (pike), *Zander* (pike-perch), and *Aal* (eel); lamb; and game. The inn is affiliated with the prestigious wine estate Reichsgraf von Kesselstatt, whose prize-winning Rieslings are on the wine list. ✉ *Balduinstr. 1, D–54347 Neumagen-Dhron, 20 km (12½ mi) southwest of Bernkastel via B–53,* ☎ *06507/2035,* FAX *06507/5644,* WEB *www.gutshotel-kesselstatt.de. 15 rooms, 5 suites. Restaurant, no a/c, minibars, pool, sauna, bicycles, some pets allowed (fee). AE, MC, V. Closed mid-Jan.–mid-Feb. Restaurant closed Mon. No lunch Tues.–Fri.*

$$ ✕🏨 **Zur Post.** The Rössling family will make you feel welcome in their house (1827) with its comfortable guest rooms and cozy restaurant ($$–$$$) and Weinstube. It's near the riverbank, and the market square is just around the corner. Try the Mosel trout *nach Müllerin Art* (dredged in flour and fried). The wine list is devoted exclusively to Mosel Rieslings. ✉ *Gestade 17, D–54470 Bernkastel-Kues,* ☎ *06531/96700,* FAX *06531/967–050,* WEB *www.hotel-zur-post-bernkastel.de. 42 rooms, 1 suite. Restaurant, Weinstube, no a/c, minibars, sauna, some pets allowed (fee), no-smoking rooms. DC, MC, V. Closed Jan.*

$–$$ 🏨 **Gästehaus E. Prüm.** The traditional wine estate S.A. Prüm has state-of-the-art cellars, a tastefully designed Vinothek, and a beautiful guest house with an idyllic patio facing the Mosel. The spacious rooms and baths are individually decorated in a winning mixture of contemporary and antique furnishings. In all, the ambience is warm and Mediterranean-like. Erika Prüm is a charming hostess; husband Raimund (the redhead) an excellent wine maker, who is happy to organize wine tastings and cellar tours. ✉ *Uferallee 25, D–54470 Bernkastel-Wehlen, north of Kues,* ☎ *06531/3110,* FAX *06531/8555,* WEB *www.sapruem.com. 8 rooms. No a/c, in-room data ports, bicycles, some pets allowed (fee). MC, V. Closed mid-Dec.–Jan.*

En Route The 55-km (34-mi) drive from Bernkastel to Trier takes in another series of outstanding hillside vineyards, including those 6 km (4 mi) upstream at **Brauneberg,** where Thomas Jefferson was enchanted by a 1783 Brauneberger Kammer Auslese during his visit here in 1788. Today, the vineyard is solely owned by Weingut Paulinshof (✉ Paulinsstr. 14, Kesten, ☎ 06535/544, WEB www.paulinshof.de; ⏲ weekdays 8–6, Sat. 9–5). On a magnificent loop 12 km (7½ mi) southwest of Brauneberg is the famous village of **Piesport.** Wines from its 35 vineyards are collectively known as Piesporter Michelsberg; however, the finest individual site, and one of Germany's very best, is the Goldtröpfchen (little droplets of gold). On the western edge of the town, the largest Roman press house (4th century) north of the Alps is on display.

Dhrontal

If the heat of the Mosel's slate slopes becomes oppressive in the summer, revitalize body and soul with a scenic drive through the cool, fragrant forest of the Dhrontal (Dhron Valley) south of Trittenheim, and a stop at an oasis for food-and-wine lovers.

Dining and Lodging

$$ ✕🏨 **Landhaus St. Urban.** Starred chef Harald Rüssel, his charming wife Ruth, and their friendly staff see to it that guests enjoy first-class food, wine, and service in very comfortable surroundings. Aromatic, visually stunning food presentations are served with wines from Germany's leading producers, including the family's Weingut St. Urbans-Hof in Leiwen, where visitors are welcome for tours and tastings. The house decor is stylish, and like the food, it reflects Mediterranean flair. ✉ *Büdlicherbrück 1, D–54426 Naurath/Wald, 8 km (5 mi) south of Trittenheim, toward Hermeskeil; from A–1, exit Mehring,* ☎ *06509/91400,* FAX *06509/914–040,* WEB *www.landhaus-st-urban.de. 14 rooms, 2 suites. Restaurant, no a/c, some in-room data ports, minibars, some pets allowed (fee). AE, MC, V. Closed 2 wks in Jan. Restaurant also closed Tues. and Wed.*

Trier

55 km (34 mi) southwest of Bernkastel-Kues via B–53, 150 km (93 mi) southwest of Koblenz; 30 mins by car to Luxemburg airport.

By 400 BC a Celtic tribe, the Treveri, had settled the Trier Valley. Eventually Julius Caesar's legions arrived at this strategic point on the river and Augusta Treverorum (the town of Emperor Augustus in the land of the Treveri) was founded in 16 BC. It was described as a most opulent city, as beautiful as any outside Rome.

Around AD 275 an Alemannic tribe stormed Augusta Treverorum and reduced it to rubble. But it was rebuilt in even grander style and renamed Treveris. Eventually it evolved into one of the leading cities of the empire and was promoted to "Roma secunda" (a second Rome) north of the Alps. As a powerful administrative capital it was adorned with all the noble civic buildings of a major Roman settlement, as well as public baths, palaces, barracks, an amphitheater, and temples. The Roman emperors Diocletian (who made it one of the four joint capitals of the empire) and Constantine both lived in Trier for years at a time.

Trier survived the collapse of Rome and became an important center of Christianity and, ultimately, one of the most powerful archbishoprics in the Holy Roman Empire. The city thrived throughout the Renaissance and baroque periods, taking full advantage of its location at the meeting point of major east–west and north–south trade routes and growing fat on the commerce that passed through. It also became one of Germany's most important wine-exporting centers. A later claim to fame is the city's status as the birthplace of Karl Marx. Trier is a city of wine as well as history, and beneath its streets are cellars capable of storing nearly 8 million gallons. To do justice to Trier, consider staying for at least two full days. The **Trier Card** entitles the holder to free public transportation and discounts on tours and admission fees to Roman sights, museums, and sports and cultural venues. It costs €9 and is valid for three days. There is also a ticket good for all the Roman sights for €6.20.

A Good Walk

Nearly all of Trier's main sights are close together. Begin your walk where Simeonstrasse passes around the city gate of the Roman city—the **Porta Nigra** ㉙—one of the grandest Roman buildings still standing. Climb up inside for a good view of Trier from the tower gallery. **Tourist-Information Trier** ㉚, next to the Porta Nigra, sells various tours, the discount Trier Card, wines, and souvenirs. In a courtyard off the Porta Nigra, the **Städtisches Museum Simeonstift** ㉛ holds remains of the Romanesque church honoring the early medieval hermit Simeon. From here follow Simeonstrasse to the **Hauptmarkt** ㉜, in the center of the Old Town. You'll find yourself surrounded by old gabled houses, with facades from several ages—medieval, baroque, and 19th century. Turn left into Domstrasse and come almost immediately face to face with Trier's **Dom** ㉝, the oldest Christian church north of the Alps. The 13-century Gothic **Liebfrauenkirche** ㉞ stands next door. Just behind the Dom, the **Bischöfliches Museum** ㉟ houses many antiquities unearthed in excavations around the cathedral.

Next, walk south of the cathedral on Liebfrauenstrasse, curving left through a short street (An-der-Meer-Katz) to Konstantinplatz for a look at the **Römische Palastaula** ㊱, the largest surviving single-hall structure of the ancient world. The **Rheinisches Landesmuseum** ㊲, with an extensive collection of Roman antiquities, stands south of the Palastaula, facing the grounds of the prince-elector's palace. The ruins of the **Kaiserthermen** ㊳, or Imperial Baths, are just 200 yards from museum. The smaller **Barbarathermen** ㊴ lie west of the Kaiserthermen on Südallee, while the remains of the **Amphitheater** ㊵ are just east of the Kaiserthermen. Continue from the Barbarathermen toward the town center along Lorenz-Kellner-Strasse to Brückenstrasse to visit the **Karl-Marx-Haus** ㊶. Then proceed to Viehmarkt, east of St. Antonius Church, to visit the **Viehmarktthermen** ㊷, and an excavated Roman bath. From here Brotstrasse will lead you back to the main market square.

TIMING

The walk itself will take a good two hours. It takes extra time to climb the tower of the Porta Nigra, walk through the vast interior of the Dom and its treasury, visit the underground passageways of the Kaiserthermen, and examine the cellars of the Amphitheater. Allow another half hour each for the Städtisches Museum Simeonstift, the Bischöfliches Museum, and Viehmarktthermen, as well as an additional hour for the Rheinisches Landesmuseum.

Sights to See

40 **Amphitheater.** The sheer size of Trier's oldest Roman structure (circa AD 100) is impressive. In its heyday it seated 20,000 spectators; today it is a stage for the Antiquity Festival. You can climb down to the cellars beneath the arena—animals were kept in cells here before being unleashed to do battle with gladiators. ✉ *Olewiger Str. 25.* 🎫 *€2.10.* 🕒 *Apr.–Sept., daily 9–6; Oct.–Mar., daily 9–5.*

39 **Barbarathermen** (Barbara Baths). These Roman baths are much smaller and two centuries older than the Kaiserthermen. ✉ *Südallee 48, near Friedrich-Wilhelm-Str. and the river.* 🎫 *€2.10.* 🕒 *Apr.–Sept., daily 9–6; Oct.–Mar., daily 9–5.*

35 **Bischöfliches Museum** (Bishop's Museum). The collection here focuses on medieval sacred art, but there are also fascinating models of the cathedral as it existed in Roman times and 15 Roman frescoes (AD 326), discovered in 1946, that may have adorned the emperor Constantine's palace. ✉ *Windstr. 6,* ☎ *0651/710–5255.* 🎫 *€2.* 🕒 *Apr.–Oct., Mon.–Sat. 9–5, Sun. 1–5; Nov.–Mar., Tues.–Sat. 9–1 and 2–5, Sun. 1–5.*

33 **Dom** (Cathedral). Practically every period of Trier's past is represented here. The Dom stands on the site of the Palace of Helen, named for the mother of the emperor Constantine, who tore the palace down in AD 330 and put up a large church in its place. The church burned down in 336 and a second, even larger one was built. Parts of the foundations of this third building can be seen in the east end of the present structure (begun in about 1035). The cathedral you see today is a weighty and sturdy edifice with small, round-head windows, rough stonework, and asymmetrical towers, as much a fortress as a church. Inside, Gothic styles predominate—the result of remodeling in the 13th century—although there are also many baroque tombs, altars, and confessionals. ✉ *Domfreihof.* 🎫 *Tours €3.* 🕒 *Apr.–Oct., daily 6:30–6; Nov.–Mar., daily 6:30–5:30; tours daily 2 PM.*

The Domschatzkammer (Cathedral Treasure Chamber; 🎫 €1; 🕒 Apr.–Oct., Mon.–Sat. 10–5, Sun. 1:30–5; Nov.–Mar., Mon.–Sat. 11–4, Sun. 1:30–4) houses many extraordinary objects. The highlight is the 10th-century Andreas Tragaltar (St. Andrew's Portable Altar),

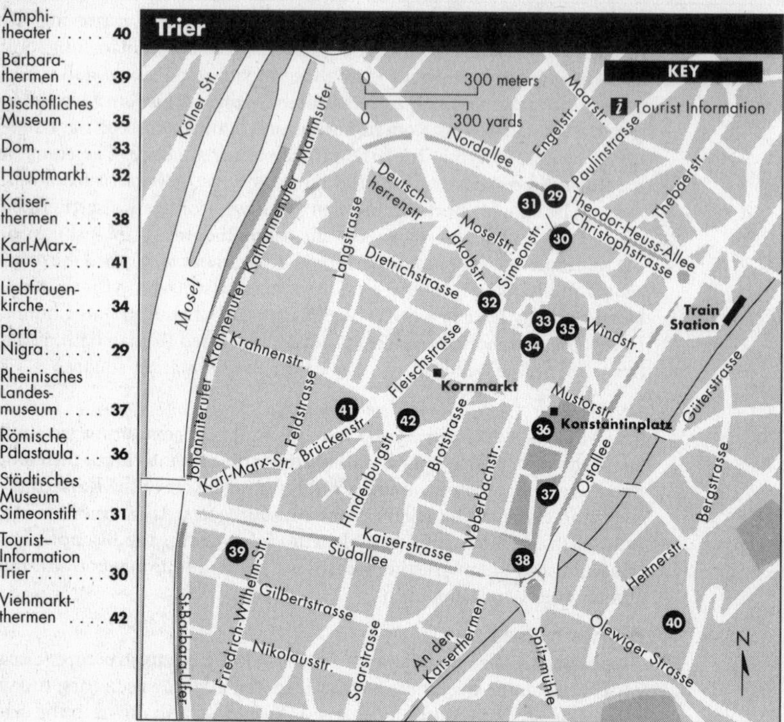

constructed of oak and covered with gold leaf, enamel, and ivory by local craftsmen. It is a reliquary for the soles of St. Andrew's sandals, symbolized by the gilded, life-size foot on the top of the altar.

32 **Hauptmarkt.** The main market square of Old Trier is easily reached via Simeonstrasse. The market cross (958) and richly ornate St. Peter's Fountain (1595), dedicated to the town's patron saint, stand in the square. The farmers' market is open weekdays 7–6 and Saturday 7–1.

38 **Kaiserthermen** (Imperial Baths). This enormous 4th-century bathing palace once housed cold- and hot-water baths and a sports field. Although only the masonry of the **Calderium** (hot baths) and the vast basements remain, they are enough to give a fair idea of the original splendor and size of the complex—it covered an area 270 yards long and 164 yards wide. Originally 98 ft high, the walls you see today are 62 ft high. ⊠ *Corner of Weimarer-Allee and Kaiserstr..* €2.10. ⊙ *Apr.–Sept., daily 9–6; Oct.–Mar., daily 9–5.*

41 **Karl-Marx-Haus.** Marx was born in this solid bourgeois house in 1818. Visitors with a serious interest in social history will be fascinated by its small museum. A signed first edition of *Das Kapital,* the study in which Marx sought to prove the inevitable decline of capitalism, has a place of honor. ⊠ *Brückenstr. 10,* ☎ *0651/970–680.* €2. ⊙ *Apr.–Oct., Mon. 1–6, Tues.–Sun. 10–6; Nov.–Mar., Mon. 2–5, Tues.–Sun. 10–1 and 2–5.*

34 **Liebfrauenkirche** (Church of Our Lady). This is the first Gothic church in Germany, built in the 13th century on the site of a Roman basilica. The original statues from the portal (those that have survived) are in the **Bischöfliches Museum.** Inside, the decoration is austere except for the Canon Karl von Metternich's 17th-century tomb. ⊠ *Liebfrauenstr.* ⊙ *Daily 8–noon and 2–6.*

29 **Porta Nigra** (Black Gate). The best-preserved Roman structure in Trier was originally a city gate, built in the 2nd century (look for holes left by the iron clamps that held the structure together). Its name is misleading, however; the sandstone gate is not black but dark gray. The gate also served as part of Trier's defenses and was proof of the sophistication of Roman military might and its ruthlessness. Attackers were often lured into the two innocent-looking arches of the Porta Nigra, only to find themselves enclosed in a courtyard. In the 11th century the upper stories were converted into a twin church, in use until the 18th century. The tourist office is next door. ✉ *Porta-Nigra-Pl.* 🎫 *€2.* ⏲ *Apr.–Sept., daily 9–6; Oct.–Mar., daily 9–5.*

37 **Rheinisches Landesmuseum** (Rhenish State Museum). The largest collection of Roman antiquities in Germany is housed here. Pride of place goes to the 4th-century stone relief of a Roman ship transporting barrels of wine up the river. This tombstone of a Roman wine merchant was discovered in 1874 when Constantine's citadel in Neumagen was excavated. Have a look at the 108-square-ft model of the city as it looked in the 4th century—it provides a sense of perspective to many of the sights you can still visit today. ✉ *Weimarer-Allee 1,* ☎ *0651/97740,* WEB *www.landesmuseum-trier.de.* 🎫 *€5.50.* ⏲ *May–Oct., weekdays 9:30–5, weekends 10:30–5; Nov.–Apr., Tues.–Fri. 9:30–5, weekends 10:30–5.*

36 **Römische Palastaula** (Roman Basilica). An impressive reminder of Trier's Roman past, this edifice is now Trier's major Protestant church. When first built by the emperor Constantine around AD 310, it was the imperial throne room of the palace. At 239 ft long, 93 ft wide, and 108 ft high, it demonstrates the astounding ambition of its Roman builders and the sophistication of their building techniques. The basilica is one of the two largest Roman interiors in existence (the other is the Pantheon in Rome). Look up at the deeply coffered ceiling; more than any other part of the building, it conveys the opulence of the original structure. ✉ *Konstantinpl.,* ☎ *0651/72468 or 0651/42570.* ⏲ *Apr.–Oct., Mon.–Sat. 9–6, Sun. noon–6; Nov.–Mar., Tues.–Sat. 11–noon and 3–4, Sun. noon–1.*

31 **Städtisches Museum Simeonstift** (Simeon Foundation City Museum). Built around the remains of the Romanesque Simeonskirche, this church is now a museum. It was constructed in the 11th century by Archbishop Poppo in honor of the early medieval hermit Simeon, who for seven years shut himself up in the east tower of the Porta Nigra. Collections include art and artifacts produced in Trier from the Middle Ages to the 19th century. ✉ *An der Porta Nigra,* ☎ *0651/718–1454.* 🎫 *€2.60.* ⏲ *Apr.–Oct., daily 9–5; Nov.–Mar., Tues.–Fri. 9–5, weekends 9–3.*

30 **Tourist-Information Trier.** In addition to dispensing city information, this tourist office sells regional wines and souvenirs. ✉ *An der Porta Nigra,* ☎ *0651/978–080.* ⏲ *Apr. –Oct., Mon.–Sat. 9–6:30, Sun. 9–3:30; Mar., Nov.–Dec., Mon.–Sat. 9–6, Sun. 9–1; Jan.–Feb., Mon.–Sat. 10–5, Sun. 9–1.*

42 **Viehmarktthermen.** Trier's third Roman bath (early 4th century) was discovered beneath Viehmarktplatz when ground was broken for a parking garage. Finds of the excavations from 1987–94 are now beneath a protective glass structure. You can visit the baths and see the cellar of a baroque Capuchin monastery. ✉ *Viehmarktpl.,* ☎ *0651/994–1057.* 🎫 *€2.10.* ⏲ *Daily 9–5.*

Dining and Lodging

$$$–$$$$ ✕ **Schlemmereule.** The name literally means "gourmet owl," and, indeed, chef Peter Schmalen caters to gourmets within the 19th-century Palais Walderdorff complex opposite the cathedral. Lots of windows lend a light, airy look, and there is courtyard seating in the summer. Try the pike-perch in a potato crust and the fabulous crème brûlée. The wine list features 10 wines by the glass and 180 by the bottle, with an emphasis on Mosel wines. ✉ *Palais Walderdorff, Domfreihof 1B,* ☎ *0651/73616. Reservations essential. AE, DC, MC, V. Closed Tues.*

$$$–$$$$ ✕ **Schloss Monaise.** Hubert and Birgit Scheid have infused a breath of fresh air into this 18th-century palace in the suburb of Zewen (southwest of Trier, via B–49 toward Igel and Luxembourg). The decor is modern classic, with Thonet chairs, contemporary art, and pastel colors. The set menus, often themed according to the current art on exhibition, offer excellent value, and there's an extensive wine list. Part of the terrace is reserved for fine dining; the other part is a beer garden, a laid-back venue for spare ribs, salads, and pasta. ✉ *Schloss Monaise 7, Trier-Zewen,* ☎ *0651/828–670. MC, V. Closed 2 wks in Jan. and Tues. from Oct.–mid-Apr.*

$$–$$$$ ✕ **Palais Kesselstatt.** This baroque palace opposite the Liebfrauenkirche is a wonderful setting for fine dining—elegant but not pretentious. There is also seating in the beautiful courtyard in the summer. Katja Weiler is responsible for the efficient, friendly service; Burkhard Weiler reigns in the kitchen. Specialties are rack of lamb or lamb medallions as well as fish dishes. Wines from the Reichsgraf von Kesselstatt estate predominate the wine list, supplemented by Old and New World reds. ✉ *Liebfrauenstr. 10,* ☎ *0651/40204. AE, DC, MC, V. Closed Mon. and mid-Jan.–mid-Feb.*

$$–$$$$ ✕ **Pfeffermühle.** For nearly three decades chef Siegbert Walde has offered guests classic cuisine in elegant surroundings. The 18th-century house on the northern edge of town has two stories of cozy niches, with beautiful table settings in shades of pink; the terrace directly overlooks the Mosel. Foie gras is a favorite ingredient, served in a terrine or sautéed and served in *Ahorn-jus* (maple-flavor juices). White wines from the Mosel's finest producers and top red Bordeaux wines predominate the excellent wine list. ✉ *Zurlaubener Ufer 76,* ☎ *0651/26133. Reservations essential. MC, V. Closed Sun. No lunch Mon.*

$–$$$ ★ ✕ **Zum Domstein.** Whether you opt for cozy dining indoors or outdoor seating in front of or behind this historic house on the market square, don't miss the collection of Roman artifacts displayed in the cellar. Here you can order from menus based on recipes of the Roman gourmet Apicius every evening. Proprietor Rose-Marie Gracher is an expert on the subject. It is a unique experience and highly recommended. ✉ *Am Hauptmarkt 5,* ☎ *0651/74490. MC, V.*

$ ✕ **Walderdorff's Vinothek-Café-Club.** This lively trio has added a lively note into the 19th-century palace opposite Trier cathedral. The café-bistro offers breakfast, sandwiches, salads, pasta, and light fare—prepared by the Schlemmereule team; some 250 local and Old and New World wines are sold in the Vinothek; and the club offers music and dancing in the baroque cellars. ✉ *Palais Walderdorff, Domfreihof 1,* ☎ *0651/9946–9210. DC, MC, V.*

$ ✕ **Weinstube Palais Kesselstatt.** The Hilgers family runs this casual offshoot of Palais Kesselstatt. The interior has exposed beams and polished wood tables; the shady terrace is popular in summer. Two soups daily, light fare, and fresh, regional cuisine are served with wines from the Reichsgraf von Kesselstatt estate. ✉ *Liebfrauenstr. 10,* ☎ *0651/41178. MC, V. Closed Jan.*

$$ ✕🏨 **Weinhaus Becker.** This family-run hotel, gourmet restaurant ($$$$), and wine estate is in the peaceful suburb of Olewig, near the amphitheater. The rooms are individually decorated with light wood furnishings; some have balconies. You can dine in the restaurant's romantic, candlelighted niches or on the terrace. Try the sole stuffed with scallops and Persian caviar sauce. *Geeister Rieslingschaum,* a light parfait, is a delicious finale. Bordeaux and Burgundy wines are available in addition to the estate's own wines—and wine tastings, cellar visits, and guided tours on the wine path can be arranged. ✉ *Olewiger Str. 206, D–54295 Trier-Olewig,* ☎ *0651/938–080,* FAX *0651/938–0888,* WEB *www.weinhaus-becker.de. 19 rooms. Restaurant, no a/c, bicycles, some pets allowed (fee). AE, MC, V. Restaurant closed Mon., 3 wks Jan. and Feb., 1 wk late July. No lunch except Sun.*

$$ **Hotel Petrisberg.** The Pantenburg's friendly, family-run hotel is high on Petrisberg hill overlooking Trier, not far from the amphitheater. You can walk to the Old Town in 20 minutes. The individually decorated rooms have solid pine furnishings; some have balconies with a fabulous view. All rooms are no-smoking. Evenings, you can enjoy snacks and good local wines in the wine pub. ✉ *Sickingenstr. 11–13, D–54296,* ☎ *0651/4640,* FAX *0651/46450,* WEB *www.freenet.de/HotelPetrisberg.de. 26 rooms, 4 apartments. Bicycles, Weinstube, no a/c, some pets allowed (fee), no-smoking. MC, V.*

$$ **Römischer Kaiser.** Centrally located near the Porta Nigra, this handsome patrician manor from 1895 offers well-appointed, attractive, modern rooms. ✉ *Am Porta-Nigra-Pl. 6, D–54292,* ☎ *0651/97700,* FAX *0651/977–099,* WEB *www.hotels-trier.de. 43 rooms. Restaurant, no a/c, some in-room data ports, minibars, some pets allowed (fee). AE, DC, MC, V.*

Festivals

The **Europa-Volksfest** (European Folk Festival), in May or early June, features specialties from several European countries, in addition to rides and entertainment. In late June the entire Old Town is the scene of the **Altstadtfest.** The Kaiserthermen and Amphitheater are impressive stages for the theatrical performances of the **Antikenfestspiele** (Antiquity Festival) from late June to mid-July. The **Moselfest,** with wine, sparkling wine, beer, and fireworks, takes place in July along the riverbank in Zurlauben, followed by a large **Weinfest** (wine festival) in Oelwig in early August, the **Elblingfest** (festival with still and sparkling wines from the grape variety Elbling), in mid-August, and the **Sektgala** (sparkling wine gala), on Viehmarktplatz in late August.

Nightlife and the Arts

Theater Trier (✉ Am Augustinerhof, ☎ 0651/718–1818 box office) offers opera, theater, ballet, and concerts.

Walderdorff's (✉ Domfreihof 1, ☎ 0651/9946–9210) in the Palais Walderdorff has trendy DJ nights, early after-work parties, and occasional live bands. There is music and dancing at **Riverside** (✉ Zurmaiener Str. 173, near traffic circle on northern edge of town, ☎ 0651/21006), a large entertainment center.

BONN AND THE COLOGNE LOWLANDS

Updated by Jennifer Abramsohn

Bonn, the former capital of Germany, is the next major stop after Koblenz on the Rhine. It's close to the legendary Siebengebirge (Seven Hills), a national park and site of Germany's northernmost vineyards. According to German mythology, Siegfried (hero of the Nibelungen saga) killed a dragon here and bathed in its blood to make himself invincible. The lowland, a region of gently rolling hills north of Bonn, lacks the drama of the Rhine gorge upstream but offers the urban pleasures of Köln (Cologne), an ancient cathedral town, and Düsseldorf, an elegant city of art and fashion. Although not geographically in the

Rhineland proper, Aachen is an important side trip for anyone visiting the region. Its stunning cathedral and treasury are the greatest storehouses of Carolingian art and architecture in Europe.

Bonn

44 km (27 mi) north of Koblenz, 28 km (17 mi) south of Köln.

Bonn was the postwar seat of the federal government and parliament until the capital returned to Berlin in 1999. Aptly described by the title of John Le Carré's spy novel *A Small Town in Germany*, the quiet university town was chosen as a stopgap measure to prevent such weightier contenders as Frankfurt from becoming the capital, a move that would have lessened Berlin's chances of regaining its former status. With the exodus of the government from Bonn, the city has lost some of its international flair. Still, other organizations and industries have moved to Bonn to fill the gap, and its status as a UN city has been strengthened. The world-class museums and other cultural institutions that once served the diplomatic elite are still here to be enjoyed. The Museum Mile—a collection of postmodern buildings all opened within three years of the decision to move the government to Berlin, was a sign that Bonn had no intention of shutting down after the Bundestag's departure.

Although Bonn seems to have sprung into existence only after the war, the Romans settled this part of the Rhineland 2,000 years ago, calling it Castra Bonnensia. Life in Bonn's streets, old markets, pedestrian malls, and handsome Sudstadt residential area is unhurried. The town center is a car-free zone; an inner ring road circles it with parking garages on the perimeter. A convenient parking lot is just across from the railway station and within 50 yards of the tourist office. Check with the tourism office for RegioBonnCard packages, which offer free or reduced entry into museums, low-cost transportation, and more.

A Good Tour

After picking up what you need at the tourist office at Windeckstrasse 2, continue to the cathedral **Münster** ㊸, the site where two Roman soldiers were executed in AD 253 for holding Christian beliefs. Across from the cathedral are the **Kurfürstliches Schloss** ㊹, now the main Friedrich-Wilhelm University building, and its gardens (Hofgarten). Walk away from the river and down chestnut-tree-lined Poppelsdorfer Allee to the **Poppelsdorfer Schloss** ㊺, which has a tropical garden. Return toward the Kurfürstliches Schloss along Am Hof, and turn left onto the Markt square to arrive at the lavish, rococo **Rathaus** ㊻. Off the square, Bongasse leads to the modest **Beethoven-Haus** ㊼, the residence of the great composer until he was 22. Backtrack to the Markt, and take Stockenstrasse past the palace gardens to Adenauerallee. Walk south along the Adenauerallee and turn right onto Am Hofgarten. At the corner of Lennstrasse is the glassed-in building of the offbeat **Arithmeum** ㊽. Return via Am Hofgarten to Adenauerallee. About 1km (1 mi) southeast along the Rhine is the Museum Mile. There you'll find the **Haus der Geschichte** ㊾ and the **Kunst- und Ausstellungshalle der Bundesrepublik Deutschland** ㊿, among other museums. To save yourself the walk, catch bus 610 or take U-bahn 16 at the Juridicum subway on Adenauerallee, between Am Hofgarten and Weberstrasse. Get off at the Heussallee/Museumsmeile stop.

For more time to spend inside Bonn's museums, follow the above route, but skip the long walk to the Poppelsdorfer Schloss.

TIMING

Allow a little over two hours for the first walk and 1½ for the shorter version, not including time spent in museums or window shopping.

Sights to See

48 **Arithmeum.** Recommended for technophiles and technophobes alike, the abstract theme of discrete mathematics is made comprehensible and even fun at this university-run museum. Its stated aim is to show "the interface of art and technolgy," and the core of the exhibit is a 1,200-piece collection of historical mechanical calculating machines, which became obsolete with the advent of computers. The art comes in the form of a collection of constructivist paintings that resemble enlarged, colorful computer-chip designs. Put your newly acquired knowledge to work at the end of your visit by creating your own computer chip. ✉ *Lennstrasse 2,* ☎ *0228/738–790,* WEB *www.arithmeum.uni-bonn.de.* 🎫 *€3.* ⏲ *Tues.–Sun. 11–6.*

OFF THE BEATEN PATH

ALTER FRIEDHOF (Old Cemetery) – This ornate, leafy cemetery is the resting place of many of the country's most celebrated sons and daughters. Look for the tomb of composer Robert Schumann (1810–1856) and his wife, Clara, also a composer and accomplished pianist. To reach the cemetery from the main train station, follow Quantiusstrasse north until it becomes Herwarthstrasse; before the street curves, turning into Endenlicherstrasse, take the underpass below the railroad line. You'll then be on Thomastrasse, which borders the cemetery. ✉ *Am Alten Friedhof.* ⏲ *Jan., daily 9–5; Feb., daily 8–6; Mar.–Aug., 7:15 AM–8 PM; Sept., daily 8–8; Oct., daily 8–7; Nov.–Dec., daily 8–5.*

★ 47 **Beethoven-Haus** (Beethoven House). Beethoven was born in Bonn in 1770 and, except for a short stay in Vienna, lived there until the age of 22. The house where he grew up is a museum celebrating his career. You'll find scores, paintings, a grand piano (his last, in fact), and an ear trumpet or two. Perhaps most impressive is the room in which Beethoven was born—empty save for a bust of the composer. The attached museum shop carries everything from kitsch to elegant Beethoven memorabilia. ✉ *Bonng. 20,* ☎ *0228/981–7525.*WEB *www.beethoven-haus-bonn.de.* 🎫 *€4.* ⏲ *Apr.–Sept., Mon.–Sat. 10–6, Sun. 11–4; Oct.–Mar., Mon.–Sat. 10–5, Sun. 11–4.*

49 **Haus der Geschichte** (House of History). German history since World War II is the subject of this museum, which begins with "hour zero," as the Germans call the unconditional surrender of 1945. The museum displays an overwhelming amount of documentary material organized on five levels and engages various types of media. It's not all heavy either—temporary exhibits have featured political cartoonists, "Miss Germany" pageants, and an in-depth examination of the song *Lili Marlene,* sung by troops of every nation during World War II. Check out the historical reconstructions of typical German backyards, behind the museum.✉ *Adenauerallee 250,* ☎ *0228/91650,* WEB *www.hdg.de.* 🎫 *Free.* ⏲ *Tues.–Sun. 9–7. Closed Jan. 1.*

50 **Kunst- und Ausstellungshalle der Bundesrepublik Deutschland** (Art and Exhibition Hall of the German Federal Republic). This is one of the Rhineland's most important venues for major exhibitions about culture and science. Recent exhibits included treasures from Venetian palaces, mythical representations and reality of Troy, art from the Iranian national museum, and works of a graphic artist and photographer. Its modern design, by Viennese architect Gustave Peichl, is as interesting as anything on exhibit in the museum. It employs three enormous blue cones situated on a lawn-like rooftop garden. ✉ *Friedrich-Ebert-Allee 4,* ☎ *0228/917–1200,* WEB *www.bundeskunsthalle.de.* 🎫 *€6.50.* ⏲ *Tues. and Wed. 10–9, Thurs.–Sun. 10–7.*

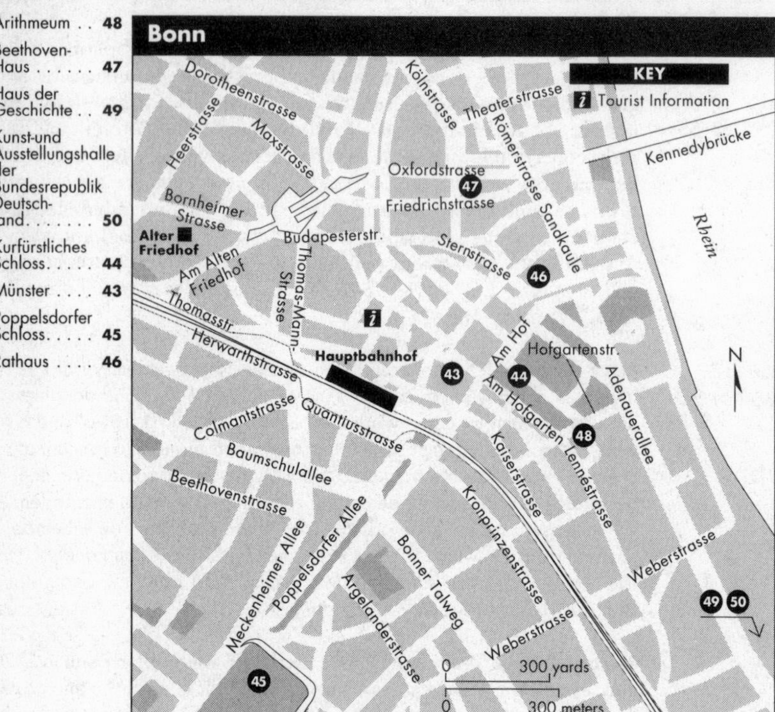

Kunstmuseum (Art Museum). Devoted to contemporary art, this large museum is renowned for the high standard of its collection. The two main focuses are on Rhenish Expressionists and German art since 1945 (Beuys, Baselitz, Kiefer, for example). Changing exhibits are generally excellent, and keep up a link to the international art scene. The museum's airy and inexpensive café is preferable to the stuffier version across the plaza at the Kunst- und Ausstellungshalle. ✉ *Friedrich-Ebert-Allee 2,* ☎ *0228/776–260,* WEB *www.bonn.de/kunstmuseum.* *€5.* ⏲ *Tues.–Sun. 10–6, Wed. until 9.*

44 **Kurfürstliches Schloss** (Prince-Electors' Palace). Built in the 18th century by the prince-electors of Köln, this grand palace now houses a university. If it's a fine day, stroll through the Hofgarten (Palace Gardens). ✉ *Am Hofgarten.*

43 **Münster** (Cathedral). The 900-year-old cathedral is vintage late-Romanesque, with a massive octagonal main tower and a soaring spire. It saw the coronations of two Holy Roman Emperors (in 1314 and 1346) and was one of the Rhineland's most important ecclesiastical centers in the Middle Ages. The 17th-century bronze figure of St. Helen and the ornate rococo pulpit are highlights of the interior. ✉ *Münsterpl.,* ☎ *0228/985–880.* ⏲ *Daily 9* AM*–7* PM.

45 **Poppelsdorfer Schloss** (Poppelsdorf Palace). This former electors' palace was built in the baroque style between 1715 and 1753 and now houses the university's mineralogical collection. Its botanical gardens are open to the public, and have an impressive display of tropical plants. The best exhibit is the mammoth Amazon water lilies, which can support up to 175 lbs. ✉ *Meckenheimer Allee 171,* ☎ *0228/732–259.* *Free.* ⏲ *Apr.–Sept., weekdays 9–6, weekends 9–1; Oct.–Mar., weekdays 9–4.*

46 **Rathaus** (Town Hall). Not very austere, this 18th-century town hall looks more like a pink doll's house. ✉ *Am Markt.*

Dining and Lodging

$$–$$$$ ✕ **Sassella.** When the Bundestag was still in town, this Bonn institution used to be cited in the press as frequently for its back-room political dealings as for its Lombardi-influenced food. But locals, prominent and otherwise, still flock to the restaurant in an 18th-century house outside the town center. The style is pure Italian farmhouse, with stone walls and exposed beams, but the handmade pastas often stray from the typical—note the salmon-filled black-and-white pasta pockets in shrimp sauce. Main dishes run from such classics as lamb with rosemary, to unusual combinations like duck breast with truffle and honey sauce. Reservations are recommended. ✉ *Karthäuserpl. 21,* ☎ *0228/5308–1512. AE, DC, MC, V.*

$–$$$ ✕ **Amadeo.** The popularity of this neighborhood restaurant is due in part to the German affinity for all things Spanish, but also because its food—40 different tapas (€2–€6), inventive salads, and main dishes—rarely misses the mark. The seafood kabobs with Spanish potatoes and spicy tomato sauce are recommended, but if in doubt, try the mixed tapas plate. ✉ *Mozartstr. 1,* ☎ *0228/635–534. No credit cards. No lunch.*

$–$$$ ✕ **Pirandello.** This trattoria with its frescoed brick walls is so cozy that it borders on kitsch. But it is rescued from that fate due to the quality of chef-owner Fausto Langui's Italian regional cooking, and the wines he recommends to go with it. The seasonally changing menu features pizzas, pastas, fish, and meats—all, as a rule, excellently prepared. The colorful and diverse antipasti buffet and market-fresh daily specials such as venison carpaccio or rabbit in chianti sauce keeps guests coming back. Reservations are recommended. ✉ *Brüderg 22,* ☎ *0228/656–606. AE, MC. Closed Sun.*

$–$$ ✕ **Em Höttche.** Travelers and Bonn residents (Beethoven was a regular) have taken sustenance at this tavern since the late 14th century, and today it offers one of the best-value lunches in town. The interior is rustic; the food stout and hearty. Reservations are recommended. ✉ *Markt 4,* ☎ *0228/690–009. No credit cards. Closed Dec. 24 and Dec. 31.*

$$$ 🏨 **Domicil.** A group of buildings around a quiet, central courtyard has been converted into a hotel of great charm and comfort. The rooms are individually furnished and decorated—in styles ranging from fin de siècle romantic to Italian modern. Huge windows give the public rooms a spacious airiness. Breakfast is included with the room rate. There is a limited amount of free parking. ✉ *Thomas-Mann-Str. 24–26, D–53111,* ☎ *0228/729–090,* FAX *0228/691–207,* WEB *www.bestwestern.de. 42 rooms, 3 junior suites, 1 apartment. Bar, no a/c, in-room data ports, cable TV, sauna, Internet, some pets allowed (fee), no-smoking rooms. AE, DC, MC, V.*

$$–$$$ 🏨 **Sternhotel.** For solid comfort and a central location in the Old Town, the Stern is tops. About 80% of the rooms have been renovated in a Danish modern style; the rest are more old-fashioned. A big breakfast buffet comes with the room rate. Weekend rates are a particular bargain. ✉ *Markt 8, D–53111,* ☎ *0228/72670,* FAX *0228/726–7125,* WEB *www.sternhotel-bonn.de. 80 rooms. No a/c, in-room data ports, cable TV, pets allowed (fee), no-smoking rooms. AE, DC, MC, V.*

$$ ★ 🏨 **Haus Hofgarten.** The rooms of this homey town house in Bonn's quiet Sudstadt area each have slightly different amenities, decor, and price. On fine days, take the complimentary breakfast on the patio, or gaze at the display of changing modern art in the breakfast room. ✉ *Fritz-Tillmann-Str. 7, D–53113,* ☎ *0228/223–482 or 0228/223–472,*

FAX *0228/213–902.* WEB *www.cd-hotel.com/d/haus-hofgarten/. 15 rooms. No a/c, in-room data ports, cable TV, some pets allowed (fee). AE, D, MC, V.*

$$ **Mozart.** Elegant on the outside and simple on the inside, this small, attractive hotel is one that Bonn residents recommend to friends. Part of its appeal is its location amid traditional town houses in the romantic, residential "musician's quarter," though it's still just a four-minute walk from the main train station and the city center. Breakfast is included in the room rate. ✉ *Mozartstr. 1, D–53115,* ☎ *0228/659–071 or 0228/659–074,* FAX *0228/659–075,* WEB *www.hotel-mozart-bonn.de. 39 rooms. Parking (fee). AE, D, MC, V.*

Nightlife and the Arts

MUSIC

The Bonn Symphony Orchestra opens its season in grand style every September with a concert on the market square, in front of city hall. Otherwise, concerts are held in the **Beethovenhalle** (✉ Wachsbleiche 17, ☎ 0228/72220). Indoor and outdoor concerts are held at numerous venues during September's **Beethoven Festival** (✉ ☎ 0228/201–0345, WEB www.beethovenfest-bonn.de). In the **Beethoven-Haus** (✉ Bonng. 20, ☎ 0228/981–7525), intimate recitals are sometimes given on an 18th-century grand piano.

Opera productions are staged regularly at the **Oper der Stadt Bonn** (✉ Am Boeselagerhof 1, ☎ 0228/778–000, WEB www.oper.bonn.de), popularly known as "La Scala of the Rhineland." The **Pantheon** theater (✉ Bundeskanzlerpl., ☎ 0228/212–521) is a prime venue for all manner of pop concerts and cabaret. Chamber-music concerts are given regularly at the **Schuman** (✉ Sebastianstr. 182, ☎ 0228/773–656).

THEATER AND DANCE

Musicals and ballet are performed at the **Oper der Stadt Bonn.** From May through October the **Bonner Sommer** festival offers folklore, music, and street theater, much of it outdoors and most of it free. Information is available at the tourist office (✉ Windeckstr. 1, ☎ 0228/775–000).

Shopping

There are plenty of department stores and boutiques in the pedestrian shopping zone around the Markt and the Münster. Bonn's **Wochenmarkt** (Weekly Market) is open daily except Sunday, filling the Markt with vendors of produce and various edibles. Bargain hunters search for secondhand goods and knickknacks at the city's renowned—and huge—**Flohmarkt** (flea market; ✉ Ludwig-Erhard-Allee), held in Rheinaue park under the Konrad-Adenauer-Brücke on the third Saturday of each month from April through October. **Pützchens Markt,** a huge country fair, takes place in the Bonn area the second weekend of September.

Königswinter

12 km (7 mi) northeast of Bonn.

The town of Königswinter has one of the most visited castles on the Rhine, the **Drachenfels.** Its ruins crown one of the highest hills in the Siebengebirge, Germany's oldest nature reserve, with a spectacular view of the Rhine. The reserve has more than 100 km (62 mi) of hiking trails. The castle was built in the 12th century by the archbishop of Köln. Its name commemorates a dragon said to have lived in a nearby cave. As legend has it, the dragon was slain by Siegfried, hero of the epic *Nibelungenlied.*

Dining

$–$$$ ✕ **Gasthaus Sutorius.** Across from the church of St. Margaretha, this wine tavern serves refined variations on German cuisine with an intelligent selection of local wines. In summer, food is served outdoors beneath the linden trees. ✉ *Oelinghovener Str. 7,* ☎ *02244/912–240. MC. Closed Mon. No lunch except Sun.*

Brühl

20 km (12 mi) southwest of Bonn.

In the heart of Brühl you'll discover the Rhineland's most important ★ baroque palace. **Schloss Augustusburg** and the magnificent pleasure park that surrounds it were created in the time of Prince Clemens August, between 1725 and 1768. The palace contains one of the most famous achievements of rococo architecture, a staircase by Balthasar Neumann. The castle can only be visited by guided tours, which leave the reception area every hour or so. An English cassette guide is also available. **Concerts** are held here in summer (☎ 02232/792–640). ✉ *Schloss Str. 6,* ☎ *02232/44000.* WEB *www.schlossbruehl.de.* *€3.* ⏲ *Feb.–Nov., Tues.–Fri. 9–noon and 1:30–4 PM; weekends 10–5 PM.*

The smaller **Jagdschloss Falkenlust,** at the end of an avenue leading straight through Schloss Augustusburg's grounds, was built as a getaway where the prince could indulge his passion for falconry. ✉ *Schloss Str. 6,* ☎ *02232/12111.* *€2.* ⏲ *Feb.–Nov., Tues.–Sun. 9–noon and 2–4:30.*

Köln

28 km (17 mi) north of Bonn, 47 km (29 mi) south of Düsseldorf, 70 km (43 mi) southeast of Aachen.

Köln is the largest city on the Rhine (the fourth largest in Germany) and one of the most interesting. Although not as old as Trier, it has been a dominant power in the Rhineland since Roman times. Known throughout the world for its scented toilet water, eau de cologne (first produced here in 1705 from an Italian formula), Köln is today a major commercial, intellectual, and ecclesiastical center. The city is vibrant and bustling, with something of the same sparkle that makes Munich so memorable. At its heart is tradition, manifested in the abundance of bars and brew houses serving the local Kölsch beer and old Rhine cuisine. These meeting places are the starting place for many a person's night on the town. Köln also puts on a wild carnival every February, with three days of orgiastic revelry, bands, parades, and parties that last all night. Tradition, however, is mixed with the contemporary, found in a host of elegant shops, sophisticated restaurants, modern bars and dance clubs, and an important modern-art scene. The numerous trade fairs held in the two massive convention centers on the east side of the Rhine (in the Deutz district) draw many business travelers.

Köln was first settled by the Romans in 38 BC. For nearly a century it grew slowly, in the shadow of imperial Trier, until a locally born noblewoman, Julia Agrippina, daughter of the Roman general Germanicus, married the Roman emperor Claudius. Her hometown was elevated to the rank of a Roman city and given the name Colonia Claudia Ara Agrippinensium. For the next 300 years Colonia (hence Cologne, or Köln) flourished. Evidence of the Roman city's wealth resides in the Römisch-Germanisches Museum. When the Romans left, Köln was ruled first by the Franks, then by the Merovingians. In the 9th century Charlemagne, the towering figure who united the sprawling German lands (and ruled much of present-day France) as the first

Holy Roman Emperor, restored Köln's fortunes and elevated it to its preeminent role in the Rhineland. Charlemagne also appointed the first archbishop of Köln. The city's ecclesiastical heritage is one of its most striking features; it has a full dozen Romanesque churches and the largest and finest Gothic cathedral in Germany.

Köln eventually became the largest city north of the Alps, and in time evolved into a place of pilgrimage second only to Rome. In the Middle Ages it was a member of the powerful Hanseatic League, occupying a position of greater importance in European commerce than either London or Paris.

Köln was a thriving modern city until World War II, when bombings destroyed 90% of it. Only the cathedral remained relatively unscathed. Almost everything else had to be rebuilt, including all of the glorious Romanesque churches. Early reconstruction was accomplished in a big rush—and it shows. Like many German cities that rebounded during the "Economic Miracle" of the 1950s, Köln is a mishmash of old and new, sometimes awkwardly juxtaposed. A good part of the former Old Town along the Hohe Strasse (old Roman High Road) was turned into a remarkably charmless pedestrian shopping mall. The ensemble is framed by six-lane expressways winding along the rim of the city center—barely yards from the cathedral—perfectly illustrating the problems of postwar reconstruction. However, much of the Altstadt (Old Town), ringed by streets that follow the line of the medieval city walls, is closed to traffic. Most major sights are within this area and are easily reached on foot. Here, too, you'll find the best shops.

At the tourist office, ask about the KölnTourismus card, which offers free or reduced entry into museums and other attractions, combined with free transit in and around the city.

A Good Walk

Any tour of the city should start beneath the towers of the extraordinary Gothic cathedral, the **Dom** ⑤①, comparable to the great French cathedrals and a highlight of a trip to Germany. Spend some time admiring the outside of the building (you can walk almost all the way around it). Notice how there are practically no major horizontal lines—all the accents of the building are vertical. The cathedral's treasures are kept in the Dom Schatzkammer, the cathedral treasury. Behind the Dom toward the river is the **Museum Ludwig** ⑤②, which holds artworks from the early 20th century onward. Sharing the Roncalliplatz plaza with the Museum Ludwig is the **Römisch-Germanisches Museum** ⑤③, which has a large, well-preserved floor mosaic dating from Roman times. From the museum, walk away from the cathedral across Roncalliplatz, go down the steps and turn left on Am Hof Strasse. Walk one block, turn right, and enter Unter Taschenmacher, which, after crossing Kleine Budengasse, becomes Burgerstrasse. Continue down Burgerstrasse to the **Altes Rathaus** ⑤④. To your right as you face the Rathaus, on the other side of Obenmarspforten, is the basalt-and-glass building housing the **Wallraf-Richartz-Museum** ⑤⑤ and its fine and massive collection of 13th- to 19th-century art. Just south of the museum on Martinstrasse is the 15th-century hall of **Gürzenich** ⑤⑥. Crossing back to the Rathaus, enter the small alley beneath the Rathaus tower (to the left as you face it) and walk down a flight of steps to the **Alter Markt** ⑤⑦. Cross the square and enter Lintgasse; after taking a few steps, you will be in the shadow of the outstanding **Gross St. Martin** ⑤⑧, one of Köln's 12 Romanesque churches. You are also near the bank of the Rhine. Turn left and walk north through the Rhein Garten park for a view of the river. Soon you'll reach Heinrich-Böll-Platz, named after the native son who was Germany's greatest postwar novelist. (Five blocks north, along the Rhine,

Köln (Cologne)

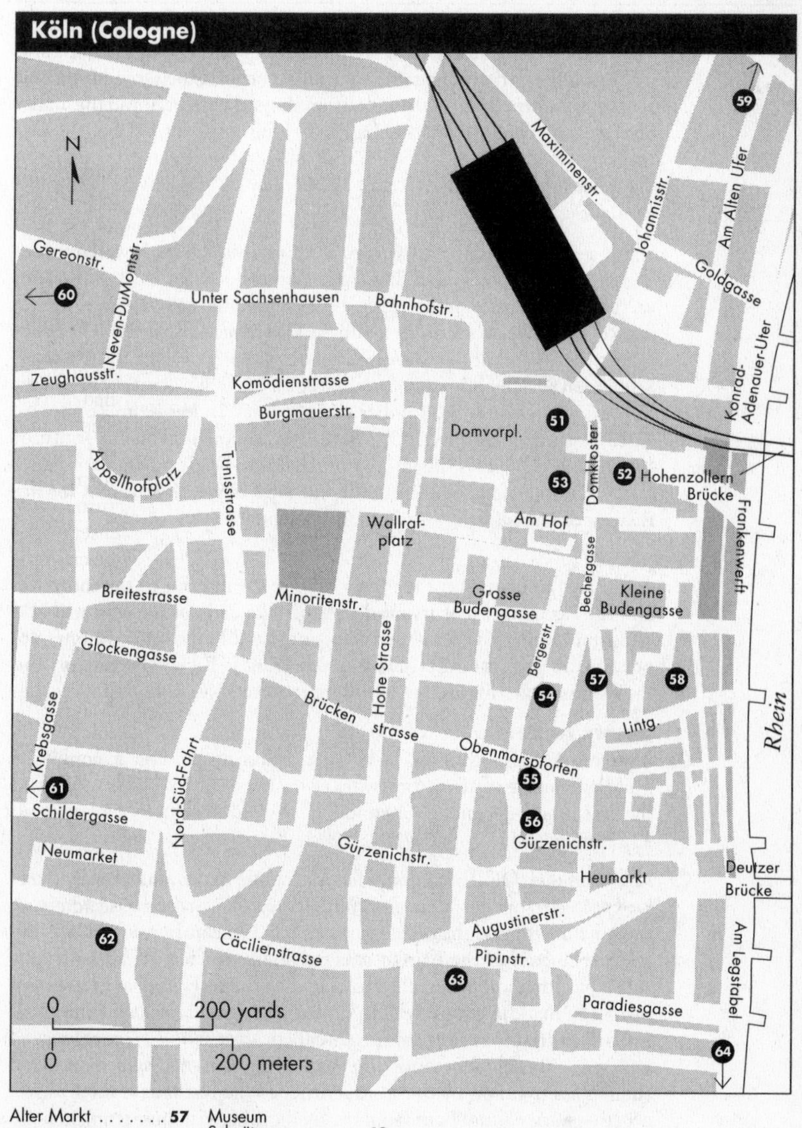

Alter Markt **57**
Altes Rathaus **54**
Dom **51**
Gross St. Martin . . . **58**
Gürzenich **56**
Imhoff-Stollwerck-Museum for the History of Chocolate **64**
Käthe Kollvitz Museum **61**
Museum Ludwig **52**
Museum Schnütgen **62**
Römisch-Germanisches Museum **53**
St. Gereon's **60**
St. Kunibert's **59**
St. Maria im Kapitol **63**
Wallraf–Richartz–Museum **55**

stands **St. Kunibert's** ⑲, the last of Köln's famous Romanesque churches to be built.) Continuing from Heinrich-Böll-Platz, go up the steps and walk past the cathedral again, continuing beyond the Dom Hotel and across Hohe Strasse, an ugly pedestrian shopping street, into Burgmauer Strasse. Follow the waist-high, block-long remnant of the old city walls to Mohrenstrasse. Go right two blocks, then left to a square. On the other side of the square stands **St. Gereon's** ⑳, the jewel of the city's Romanesque churches.

Sights to the south can easily be reached on foot. Head down Mohrenstrasse, which becomes Auf dem Berlich and then Richmodstrasse. Here, on the top floor of a shopping center, is the **Käthe Kollwitz Museum** (61), one of two collections in the country. Cut diagonally across the Neumarkt to Cäcilienstrasse, and continue walking east to the **Museum Schnütgen** (62), which holds a fine collection of medieval art. Further east on Cäcilienstrasse is the somber 11th-century **St. Maria im Kapitol** (63). Need a sugar boost next? On the Rhine, about four blocks south of the Deutzer Bridge, is the impressive building—part postmodern ship, part medieval castle—housing the **Imhoff-Stollwerck-Museum for the History of Chocolate** (64)—free samples available.

TIMING

Allow two hours just for the walk. To see the interior of the cathedral and the cathedral treasury, and to climb the cathedral tower will add almost an hour. The museum collections could take several hours depending on your interests. Visits to the Wallraf-Richartz Museum and the Römisch-Germanisches Museum require at least 45 minutes each.

Sights to See

(57) **Alter Markt** (Old Market). The square has an eclectic assembly of buildings, most of them postwar; two 16th-century houses survived the war intact—Numbers 20 and 22. The oldest structure dates from 1135. ✉ *Altstadt.*

(54) **Altes Rathaus** (Old Town Hall). After a lengthy renovation, the Rathaus is expected to open to visitors in mid-2002. It's worth a look even from the outside, for it is the oldest town hall in Germany, even if it was entirely rebuilt after the war (it was originally erected in the 14th century). Standing on pedestals at one end of the town hall are figures of prophets, made in the early 15th century. Ranging along the south wall are nine additional statues, the so-called *Nine Good Heroes,* carved in 1360. Charlemagne and King Arthur are among them. Beneath a small glass pyramid by the south corner of the Rathaus is the **Mikwe,** a 12th-century ritual bath from the medieval Jewish quarter. When the Rathaus is open, you can request a key from the guard there and descend to the Mikwe's interior. Directly below the Rathaus are the remains of the Roman city governor's headquarters, the Praetorium. ✉ *Rathauspl., Altstadt.* ⏱ *Mon.–Thurs. 7:30–4:45, Fri. 7:30–2.*

★ (51) **Dom** (Cathedral). Köln's landmark embodies one of the purest expressions of the Gothic spirit in Europe. Meant to be a tangible expression of God's kingdom on earth, the cathedral's immense dimensions were so ambitious that construction, begun in 1248, was not completed until 1880, though through the ages builders adhered to the original plans. At 515 ft high, the two west towers of the cathedral were by far the tallest structures in the world when they were finished. The cathedral was built to house what were believed to be the relics of the Magi, the three kings who paid homage to the infant Jesus (the trade in holy mementos was big business in the Middle Ages—and not always scrupulous). Anxious to surpass the great cathedrals then being built in France, the masons set to work. The size of the building was not simply an example of self-aggrandizement on the part of the people of Köln, however; it was a response to the vast numbers of pilgrims who arrived to see the relics. The ambulatory, the passage that curves around the back of the altar, is unusually large, allowing cathedral authorities to funnel large numbers of visitors up to the crossing (where the nave and transepts meet, and where the relics were originally displayed), around the back of the altar, and out again. The cavernous interior is illuminated by light filtering through acres of stained glass.

Today the relics are kept just behind the altar, in the original enormous gold-and-silver **reliquary.** The other great treasure of the cathedral, in the last chapel on the left as you face the altar, is the **Gero Cross,** a monumental oak crucifix dating from 971. The *Adoration of the Kings* (1440), a triptych by Stephan Lochner, Köln's most famous medieval painter, is to the right. The **Dom Schatzkammer** (cathedral treasury, 🎫 €1.50; ⊙ Apr.–Oct., Mon.–Sat. 9–7, Sun. 12:30–7; Nov.–Mar., Mon.–Sat. 9–4, Sun. 1–4) includes the silver shrine of Archbishop Engelbert, who was stabbed to death in 1225. Other highlights are the stained-glass windows, some dating from the 13th century; the 15th-century altarpiece; and the early 14th-century high altar with its glistening white figures and intricate choir screens. Climb to the top of the bell tower to get the complete vertical experience. ⊠ *Dompl., Altstadt,* ☎ *0221/9258–4730,* WEB *www.koelner-dom.de.* 🎫 *Guided tour €3.* ⊙ *Daily 6 AM–7 PM; Dom stairwell daily 9–7; guided tours in English Mon.–Sat. 10:30 and 2:30, Sun. 2:30.*

58 **Gross St. Martin** (Big St. Martin). This remarkable Romanesque parish church was rebuilt after being flattened in World War II. Its massive 13th-century tower, with distinctive corner turrets and an imposing central spire, is another landmark of Köln. The church was built on the site of a Roman granary. ⊠ *An Gross St. Martin 9, Altstadt,* ☎ *0221/257–7924.* ⊙ *Mon.–Sat. 10–6, Sun. 2–4.*

56 **Gürzenich.** At the south end of Martinsviertel, this Gothic structure was all but demolished in World War II but carefully reconstructed afterward. It is named after a medieval knight from whom the city acquired a quantity of valuable real estate in 1437. The official reception and festival hall here has played a central role in civic life through the centuries. At one end of the complex are the remains of the 10th-century Gothic church of **St. Alban,** which were left ruined after the war as a memorial. On what's left of the church floor, you can see a sculpture of a couple kneeling in prayer, *Mourning Parents,* by Käthe Kollwitz, a fitting memorial to the ravages of war. ⊠ *Gürzenichstr., Altstadt.*

64 **Imhoff-Stollwerck-Museum for the History of Chocolate.** This riverside museum recounts 3,000 years of civilization's production and delectation of chocolate, from the Central American Mayans to the colonizing and industrializing Europeans. It is also a real factory with lava flows of chocolate and a conveyer belt jostling thousands of truffles. Visitors get a free tasting. The museum shop, with candy bars stacked to the ceiling, is a great place to pick up interestingly packaged edible gifts. ⊠ *Rheinauhafen 1a, Rheinufer,* ☎ *0221/931–8880,* WEB *www.schokoladenmuseum.de.* 🎫 *€ 5.50.* ⊙ *Tues.–Fri. 10–6, weekends 11–7. Closed Feb. 27–Mar. 5;Dec. 24, 25, and 31, and Jan. 1.*

61 **Käthe Kollwitz Museum.** The works of Käthe Kollwitz (1867–1945), the most important German female artist of the 20th century, focus on social themes like the plight of the poor and the atrocities of war. This is the larger of the country's two Kollwitz collections, and comprises all of her woodcuts, as well as paintings, etchings, lithographs, and sculptures. There are also changing exhibits of other modern

artists. ✉ *Neumarkt 18–24 (in Neumarkt Galerie), Innenstadt,* ☎ *0221/227–2899,* WEB *www.kollwitz.de.* *€ 2.50.* *Tues.–Fri. 10–6, weekends 11–7.*

★ 52 **Museum Ludwig.** This museum is dedicated to art from the beginning of the 20th century to the present day. Its American pop art collection (including Andy Warhol, Jasper Johns, Robert Rauschenberg, Claes Oldenburg, and Roy Lichtenstein) rivals that of New York's Guggenheim Museum. Within the building and at no extra cost is the **Agfa Foto-Historama** (Agfa Photography Museum), which has one of the world's largest collections of historic photographs and cameras. ✉ *Bischofsgartenstr. 1, Innenstadt,* ☎ *0221/2212–6165,* WEB *www.museenkoeln.de.* *€7.70.* *Tues. 10–8, Wed.–Fri. 10–6, weekends 11–6. Closed Feb. 27–Mar. 5;Dec. 24, 25, and 31, and Jan. 1.*

62 **Museum Schnütgen.** A treasure house of medieval art from the Rhine region, the museum has an ideal setting in a 12th-century basilica. Don't miss the crucifix from the St. Georg Church or the original stained-glass windows and carved figures from the Dom. Many of the exhibits—intricately carved ivory book covers, rock crystal reliquaries, illuminated manuscripts—require intense concentration to be fully appreciated. ✉ *Cäcilienstr. 29, Innenstadt,* ☎ *0221/2212–3620,* WEB *www.museenkoeln.de.* *€2.50.* *Tues.–Fri. 10–5 (every 1st Wed. until 8), weekends 11–5. Closed Feb. 27–Mar. 5;Dec. 24, 25, and 31, and Jan. 1.*

NEED A BREAK? Cologne's main pedestrian shopping street is practical but utterly uninspiring—some even say ugly. An airy, artsy oasis is **Cafe Stanton, The Fine Art of Leisure** (✉ Schildergasse 57, behind Antoniterkirche, ☎ 0221/271–0710), with outdoor terrace seating and a view of the Antoniter church's late-Gothic walls. The food is international with an emphasis on the Mediterranean; the selection of cakes is divinely German. Three enormous, surprisingly delicate chandeliers, made entirely of plastic waste, provide lighting.

★ 53 **Römisch-Germanisches Museum** (Roman-Germanic Museum). This cultural landmark was built in the early 1970s around the famous Dionysius mosaic discovered there during the construction of an air-raid shelter in 1941. The huge mosaic, more than 100 yards square, once formed the dining-room floor of a wealthy Roman trader's villa. Its millions of tiny earthenware and glass tiles depict some of the adventures of Dionysius, the Greek god of wine and, to the Romans, the object of a widespread and sinister religious cult. The pillared 1st-century tomb of Lucius Publicius, a prominent Roman officer, some stone Roman coffins, and everyday objects of Roman life are among the museum's other exhibits. Bordering the museum on the south is a restored 90-yard stretch of the old Roman harbor road. ✉ *Roncallipl. 4, Altstadt,* ☎ *0221/2212–4438,* WEB *www.museenkoeln.de.* *€3.60.* *Tues.–Sun. 10–5. Closed Feb. 27–Mar. 5; Dec. 24, 25, and 31, and Jan. 1.*

60 **St. Gereon's.** Experts regard St. Gereon's as one of the most noteworthy medieval structures in existence. This exquisite Romanesque church stands on the site of an old Roman burial ground six blocks west of the train station. An enormous dome rests on walls that were once clad in gold mosaics. Roman masonry forms part of the structure, which is believed to have been built over the grave of its namesake, the 4th-century martyr and patron saint of Köln. ✉ *Gereonsdriesch 2–4, Ringe,* ☎ *0221/134–922.* *Mon.–Sat. 9–12:30 and 1:30–6, Sun. 1:30–6.*

59 **St. Kunibert's.** The most lavish of the churches from the late-Romanesque period is by the Rhine, three blocks north of the train station. Its precious stained-glass windows have filtered the light of day for more than 700 years. Consecrated in 1247, the church contains an unusual room, concealed under the altar, which gives access to a pre-Christian well once believed to promote fertility in women. ⊠ *Kunibertklosterg. 6, Altstadt-Nord,* ☎ *0221/121–214.* ⏲ *Daily 9–noon and 2:30–6:30.*

63 **St. Maria im Kapitol.** Built in the 11th and 12th centuries on the site of a Roman temple, St. Maria's is best known for its two beautifully carved 16-ft-high doors and its enormous crypt, the second largest in Germany after the one in Speyer's cathedral. ⊠ *Marienpl. 19, Altstadt,* ☎ *0221/214–615.* ⏲ *Daily 9:30–6.*

★ 55 **Wallraf-Richartz-Museum.** The Wallraf-Richartz-Museum contains paintings spanning the years 1300 to 1900. The Dutch and Flemish schools are particularly well represented, as is the 15th- to 16th-century Cologne school of German painting. Its two most famous artists are the Master of the Saint Veronica (whose actual name is unknown) and Stefan Lochner, represented by two luminous works, *The Last Judgment* and *The Madonna in the Rose Bower.* Large canvases by Rubens, who spent his youth in Köln, hang prominently on the second floor. There are also outstanding works by Rembrandt, Van Dyck, and Frans Hals. Among the other old masters are Tiepolo, Canaletto, and Boucher. ⊠ *Martinstr. 39, Altstadt,* ☎ *0221/2212–2393,* WEB *www.museenkoeln.de.* 🎟 *€5.10.* ⏲ *Tues. 10–8, Wed.–Fri. 10–6, weekends 11–6. Closed Feb. 27–Mar. 5; Dec. 24, 25, and 31, and Jan. 1.*

Dining and Lodging

The tourist office, across from the cathedral, can make hotel bookings for you for the same night, at a cost of €10 per room.

$$$$ ✕ **Bizim.** The extraordinary chef Enis Akisik has made his Bizim one of the best Turkish restaurants in Germany. Forget shish kebab and prepare yourself for a leisurely, gourmet experience that might include scampi with tarragon sauce, eggplant-coated lamb fillets with a garlic yogurt sauce, or quail grilled on a rosemary spit and served in its own juices. There are four-course tasting menus for lunch (€28) and dinner (€50). ⊠ *Weideng. 47–49, Nordstadt,* ☎ *0221/131–581. Reservations essential. AE, D, MC, V. Closed Sun., Mon. No lunch Sat.*

$$$$ ★ ✕ **Le Moissonnier.** Part of the charm of this restaurant—arguably the best in the city—is its lack of pretension. In contrast to the gray neighborhood, the turn-of-the-20th-century bistro decor radiates warmth from its mirrors, Tiffany lamps, and painted flowers. Owners Vincent and Liliane Moissonnier greet their guests in person, seating them at one of 20 tables and overseeing every detail of their evening. The cuisine is French at its base but intertwines an array of global influences, serving dishes such as warm venison rillettes with porcini and shiitake mushrooms, a fricassee of chestnuts and artichokes, or a bouillabaisse with turbot and calamari and ginger balls. ⊠ *Krefelder Str. 25, Nordstadt,* ☎ *0221/729–479. Reservations essential. No credit cards. Closed Sun. and Mon.*

$$$–$$$$ ✕ **Casa di Biasi.** This romantic eatery serves sophisticated Italian cuisine in a warm, elegant setting. The seasonally changing menu focuses on fish and game, and the wine list is interesting and extensive—although sometimes pricey. Just next door is the Casa's smaller and more casual sister, the Teca di Biasi. This cozy, wood-paneled wine bar serves antipasti, salads, and main dishes up to €13. Reservations are recommended. ⊠ *Eifelpl. 4, Sudstadt,* ☎ *0221/322–433. AE, MC, V. Closed Sun. No lunch on Sat.*

$$–$$$$ ✕ **Fischer's.** If someone were to create a shrine to wine, it would look a lot like this restaurant. Run by one of Germany's star sommeliers (who happens to be a woman), the restaurant offers some 420 wines, 45 of which can be bought by the glass. The kitchen experiments with regional cuisine, with influences from France and the Mediterranean to as far off as Southeast Asia. The dining experience is always elegant, and an expert staff will help you pick the perfect wine for each dish. Reservations are recommended. ✉ *Hohenstaufenring 53, Ringe,* ☎ *0221/310–8470. No credit cards. Closed Sun. No lunch Sat.*

$–$$$$ ✕ **Früh am Dom.** For real down-home German food, there are few places that compare with this time-honored former brewery. Bold frescoes on the vaulted ceilings establish the mood; the authentically Teutonic experience is complete with such dishes as *Hämmchen* (pork knuckle). The beer garden is delightful for summer dining. ✉ *Am Hof 12–14, Altstadt,* ☎ *0221/258–0396. No credit cards.*

$–$$ ✕ **Paeffgen.** There is no better *Brauhaus* in Köln in which to imbibe Kölsch, the city's home brew. You won't sit long in front of an empty glass before a blue-aproned waiter sweeps by and places a full one before you. With its worn wooden decor, colorful clientele, and typical German fare (sauerbraten, Hämmchen, and Reibekuchen), Paeffgen sums up tradition—especially when compared to the trendy nightspots that surround it. ✉ *Friesenstr. 64–66, Friesenviertel,* ☎ *0221/135–461. No credit cards.*

$–$$ ✕ **3-Länder-Eck.** The hearty alpine cuisine of the three *Länder* (countries), Austria, Switzerland, and to a lesser extent Germany, is the specialty of this three-story restaurant in the heart of the Altstadt. The rustic ski-lodge setting goes perfectly with dishes such as roast pork with dumplings, or sautéed duck with red cabbage and spätzle. The food is down-home and portions tend toward the enormous. ✉ *Martinstr. 32, Altstadt,* ☎ *0221/582–265. AE, MC, V.*

$ ✕ **Green Card.** With its high-concept food (Eurasian tapas) and low-budget fare, Green Card hit on a sure-fire recipe for winning over Cologne trendsetters. Its location in an arty neighborhood and its neo-construction-site decor didn't hurt matters either. Baroque combinations such as wontons in curry-arugula sauce, venison teriyaki, scampi in banana-vanilla batter, and green-tea spätzle gratin with Camembert and shiitake mushrooms only sound scary. They actually taste great. ✉ *Maastrichterstr. 2/Brüsseler Pl., Belgisches Viertel,* ☎ *0221/589–3725. No credit cards. No lunch weekends.*

$$$$ ★ ✕🏨 **Excelsior Hotel Ernst.** The Empire-style lobby is striking in sumptuous royal blue, bright yellow, and gold, and a similarly bold grandeur extends to the other public rooms in this 1863 hotel. Old-master paintings (including a Van Dyck) grace the lobby; Gobelins tapestries hang in the ballroom of the same name. Breakfast is served either in the "petit palais" ballroom or in the two-story atrium. The Hansestube restaurant ($$–$$$$) attracts a business crowd with its lunch specials and has a more hushed ambience in the evening, when it serves French haute cuisine with an occasional nod to the health conscious. A much newer restaurant, Taku ($$–$$$$), serves pan-Asian cuisine at slightly less elevated prices. ✉ *Trankg. 1, Altstadt, D–50667,* ☎ *0221/2701,* FAX *0221/135–150,* WEB *www.excelsiorhotelernst.de. 140 rooms, 20 suites. 2 restaurants, bar, no a/c in some rooms, cable TV, Internet, business services, parking (fee), some pets allowed (fee), gym, hair salon, massage, sauna, no-smoking rooms. AE, DC, MC, V.*

$$$–$$$$ ★ ✕🏨 **Hotel im Wasserturm.** What used to be Europe's tallest water tower is now an 11-story luxury hotel-in-the-round. The neoclassic look of the brick exterior remains and few modern architects could create a more unusual setting. The ultramodern interior was the work of the French designer Andrée Putman, known for her minimalist work on the hotel Morgans, in New York. The 11th-floor restaurant-in-the-round ($$$$) has a stunning view of the city. The menu, which changes daily, offers Continental haute-cuisine. ✉ *Kayg. 2, Innenstadt, D–50676,* ☎ *0221/20080,* FAX *0221/200–8888,* WEB *www.hotel-im-wasserturm.de. 48 rooms, 40 suites. Restaurant, bar, room service, cable TV, in-room data ports, laundry service, gym, sauna, parking (fee), some pets allowed. AE, DC, MC, V.*

$$ ★ ✕ **Das Kleine Stapelhäuschen.** One of the few houses along the riverbank to have survived World War II bombings, this is among the oldest buildings in Köln. You can't beat the location, overlooking the river and right by Gross St. Martin; yet the rooms are reasonably priced, making up in age and quaintness for what they lack in luxury. The restaurant ($$–$$$$) is in a slightly higher price bracket and does a respectable enough job with spruced-up versions of German specialties. ✉ *Fischmarkt 1–3, Altstadt, D–50667,* ☎ *0221/257–7862,* FAX *0221/257–4232,* WEB *www.koeln-altstadt.de/stapelhaeuschen. 31 rooms. Restaurant, no a/c, cable TV, in-room data ports, some pets allowed. AE, MC, V.*

$$ ✕ **Chelsea.** This designer hotel has a very strong following among artists and art dealers, as well as the musicians who come to play in the nearby Stadtgarten jazz club. Breakfast is served until noon for these late-risers. The best features of the rooms are the luxuriously large bathrooms and bathtubs. The restaurant-café ($–$$) is great for encounters of an informal kind and for people-watching. It's 20 minutes to the city center on foot, 10 by subway or tram. ✉ *Jülicherstr. 1, Belgisches Viertel, D–50674,* ☎ *0221/207–150,* FAX *0221/239–137,* WEB *www.hotel-chelsea.de. 40 rooms. Restaurant, no a/c, cable TV, parking (fee), some pets allowed. AE, DC, MC, V.*

$$ ✕ **Hopper Hotel et cetera.** The rooms in this chicly renovated monastery are spare but not spartan, although a startlingly realistic sculpture of a bishop, sitting in the reception area, serves as a constant reminder of the building's ecclesiastic origins. The rooms are all decorated with modern works by Cologne artists. A courtyard restaurant, Pomp im Hopper ($$–$$$), serves upscale Mediterranean cuisine and has delightful garden seating. ✉ *Brüsselerstr. 26, Belgisches Viertel, D–50674,* ☎ *0221/924–400,* FAX *0221/924–406,* WEB *www.hopper.de. 48 rooms, 1 suite. Restaurant, café, no a/c, cable TV, in-room data ports, Internet, sauna, gym, business services, parking (fee), some pets allowed (fee), no-smoking rooms. AE, DC, MC, V.*

$ **Hotel Good Sleep.** What it lacks in personality, this hotel makes up for in price and location. A favorite with students and backpackers, Hotel Good Sleep is just steps from the Dom. The small rooms are bland, but bright and clean. Cheaper rooms, with a shower in the hallway, are also available. A copious breakfast buffet is included. ✉ *Komödienstr. 19–21, Altstadt, D–50667,* ☎ *0221/257–2257,* FAX *0221/257–2259,* WEB *www.goodsleep.de. 33 rooms. No a/c, cable TV, some pets allowed. AE, D, MC, V.*

$ **Hotel Im Kupferkessel.** The best things about this small, unassuming hotel are its location (in the shadow St. Gereon's church and a 15-minute walk from the Dom) and the price (single rooms with shared bath can be had for as low as €30). The slightly shabby lobby and breakfast room look like they might have been decorated by someone's grandmother, circa 1950, but the rooms are clean and functional. You can get a dose of aesthetics out at the nearby art galleries. Stair-walking is essential here, as most of the rooms are on the third and fourth floors. Continental breakfast is included in room price. ✉ *Probsteig. 6, Ringe, D–50670,* ☎ *0221/135–338,* WEB *www.im-kupferkessel.de.* FAX *0221/125–121. 13 rooms. No a/c, cable TV, parking (fee). AE, D, MC, V.*

Nightlife and the Arts

THE ARTS

Köln's Westdeutsche Rundfunk Orchestra performs regularly in the city's excellent concert hall, the **Philharmonie** (✉ Bischofsgartenstr. 1, Altstadt, ☎ 0221/280–280, WEB www.koelnticket.de). The Gürzenich Orchestra gives regular concerts in the Philharmonie, but the natural setting for its music is the restored **Gürzenich,** (✉ Martinstr. 29/37, Altstadt, ☎ 0221/925–8990), medieval Köln's official reception mansion. Köln's opera company, the **Oper der Stadt Köln** (✉ Offenbachpl. 1, Innenstadt, ☎ 0221/2212–8400, WEB www.theatergemeinde.de) is known for exciting classical and contemporary productions. Year-round organ recitals in Köln's cathedral are supplemented from June through August with a summer season of organ music. Organ recitals and chamber concerts are also presented in many of the Romanesque churches and in **Antoniterkirche** (✉ Schilderg. 57, Innenstadt, ☎ 0221/257–8674).

Köln's principal theater is the **Schauspielhaus** (✉ Offenbachpl. 1, Innenstadt, ☎ 0221/2212–8252). The Schauspielhaus is also home to the 20 or so private theater companies in the city.

NIGHTLIFE

Köln's nightlife is centered in three distinct areas: between the Alter Markt and Neumarkt in the Old Town; on Zulpicherstrasse; and around the Friesenplatz S-bahn station. Many streets off the Hohenzollernring and Hohenstaufenring, particularly Roonstrasse, also provide a broad range of nightlife.

In summer head straight for the **Stadtgarten** (✉ Venloerstr. 40, Friesenviertel, ☎ 0221/9529–9410) and sit in the Bier Garten for some good outdoor Gemütlichkeit. Any other time of year it is still worth a visit for its excellent jazz club that regularly brings class acts to the city. In summer, the Martinsviertel, a part of the Altstadt around the Gross St. Martin church, which is full of restaurants, brew houses, and *Kneipen* (pubs), is a good place to go around sunset. One particular spot to check out there is **Papa Joe's Biersalon** (✉ Alter Markt 50–52, Altstadt, ☎ 0221/258–2132), which is kind of kitschy but often has classic and Dixieland jazz.

Das Ding (✉ Hohenstaufenring 30–34, Ringe, ☎ 0221/246–348), literally, "the Thing," is a student club that is never empty, even on weeknights. For the last word in the disco experience, make for the **Alter Wartesaal** (✉ Am Hauptbahnhof, Johannisstr. 11, Altstadt, ☎ 0221/912–8850) in the Hauptbahnhof on Friday or Saturday night. The old train-station waiting room has been turned into a concert hall and disco, where dancers swivel on ancient polished parquet and check their style in original mahogany-frame mirrors. In the cellar of a street café by the same name, **Petit Prince** (✉ Hohenzollernring 90, Ringe, ☎ 0221/124–499) plays salsa and other latin music five nights a week. Free dance classes are also frequently given.

Shopping

A good shopping loop begins at the **Neumarkt Galerie** (✉ Richmodstr. 8, Innenstadt), a bright, modern indoor shopping arcade with a web of shops and cafés surrounding an airy atrium. From there, head down the charmless but practical pedestrian shopping zone of the Schildergasse. The big department store **Kaufhof** (✉ Hohestr. 41–53, Innenstadt, ☎ 0221/2230) is off the mall and a center of city life. Its offerings are rich in quantity and quality.

From Schildergasse, go north on Herzogstrasse to arrive at **Glockengasse** (✉ No. 4711, Innenstadt, ☎ 0221/925–0450) and Köln's most celebrated product, eau de cologne. There you can visit the house where the 18th-century Italian chemist Giovanni-Maria Farina first concocted the formula for No. 4711. The shop has extended its selection to include other scents, but the original product remains the centerpiece, available in all sizes from a purse-size bottle to a container that holds a quart or so.

On Breite Strasse, another pedestrian shopping street, **Heubel** (✉ Breite Str. 118, Innenstadt, ☏ 0221/257–6013) carries unusual, beautiful, and often inexpensive imported antiques, housewares, and jewelry. At the end of Breite Strasse is Eherenstrasse, where the young and young-at-heart and can shop for hip fashions and trendy housewares. After a poke around here, explore the small boutiques on Benesisstrasse, which will lead you to Mittelstrasse, best known for high-toned German fashions and luxury goods. Taking Mittelstrasse to the end will return you to the Neumarkt.

Because train stations are exempt from restrictive German laws on store-opening hours, the shopping arcade in the **Hauptbahnhof** (main train station) offers a rare opportunity in Germany: to shop on Sunday, and on weekdays until as late as 10 PM.

Aachen

70 km (43 mi) west of Köln.

At the center of Aachen, the characteristic *drei-Fenster* facades, three windows wide, give way to buildings dating from the days when Charlemagne made Aix-la-Chapelle (as it was then called) one of the great centers of the Holy Roman Empire. Roman legions had been drawn here for the healing properties of the sulfur springs emanating from the nearby Eifel Mountains. Charlemagne's father, Pepin the Short, also settled here to enjoy the waters that gave Bad Aachen—as the town is also known—its name; the waters continue to attract visitors today. But it was certainly Charlemagne who was responsible for the town's architectural wealth. After his coronation in Rome in 800, he spent more and more time in Aachen, building his spectacular palace and ruling his vast empire from within its walls. Aachen is now home to almost 30,000 students, keeping this beautiful old town a bustling center of activity. One-and-a-half hour walking tours depart from the tourist information office weekends at 11, year-round, and weekdays at 2, from April through October. **English tours** can be set up by prior arrangement (☏ 0241/180–2960).

★ The stunning **Dom** (Cathedral) in Aachen, the "Chapelle" of the town's earlier name, remains the single greatest storehouse of Carolingian architecture in Europe. Though it was built over the course of 1,000 years and reflects architectural styles from the Middle Ages to the 19th century, its commanding image is the magnificent octagonal royal chapel, rising up two arched stories to end in the cap of the dome. It was this section, the heart of the church, that Charlemagne saw completed in AD 800. His bones now lie in the Gothic choir, in a golden shrine surrounded by wonderful carvings of saints. Another treasure is his marble throne. Charlemagne had to journey all the way to Rome for his coronation, but the next 32 Holy Roman emperors were crowned here in Aachen, and each marked the occasion by presenting a lavish gift to the cathedral. In the 12th century Barbarossa donated the great chandelier now hanging in the center of the imperial chapel; his grandson, Friedrich II, donated Charlemagne's shrine. Emperor Karl IV journeyed from Prague in the late 14th century for the sole purpose of commissioning a bust of Charlemagne for the cathedral; now on view in the treasury, the bust incorporates a piece of Charlemagne's skull. ✉ *Münsterpl.,* ☎ *0241/4770–9127,* WEB *www.aachendom.de.* ⊙ *Daily 7–7.*

★ The **Domschatzkammer** (Cathedral Treasury) houses sacred art from late antiquity and the Carolingian, Ottonian, and Hohenstaufen eras; highlights include the Cross of Lothair, the Bust of Charlemagne, and the Persephone Sarcophagus. ✉ *Am Domhof, entrance via Klosterg.,* ☎ *0241/4770–9127.* 🎫 *€2.50.* ⊙ *Mon. 10–1, Tues.–Wed. and Fri.–Sun. 10–6, Thurs. 10–9.*

The back of the **Rathaus** (Town Hall) is opposite the cathedral, across Katschhof Square. It was built beginning in the early 14th century on the site of the *Aula,* or "great hall," of Charlemagne's palace. Its first major official function was the coronation banquet of Emperor Karl IV in 1349, held in the great Gothic hall you can still see today (though this was largely rebuilt after the war). On the north wall of the building are statues of 50 emperors of the Holy Roman Empire. The greatest of them all, Charlemagne, stands in bronze atop the Kaiserbrunnen (Imperial Fountain) in the center of the market square. ✉ *Marktpl.,* ☎ *0241/432–7310.* 🎫 *€1.50.* ⊙ *Daily 10–1 and 2–5.*

An old Aachen tradition that continues today is "taking the waters." The arcaded, neoclassical **Elisenbrunnen** (Elisa Fountain), built in 1822, is south of the cathedral and contains two fountains with thermal drinking water. Experts agree that the spa waters here—the hottest north of the Alps—are effective in helping to cure a wide range of ailments. Drinking the sulfurous water in the approved manner can be unpleasant; but as you hold your nose and gulp away, you're emulating the likes of Dürer, Frederick the Great, and Charlemagne.

You can try sitting in the spa waters at **Carolus-Thermen,** a high-tech sauna/spa facility. In Dürer's time there were regular crackdowns on the orgiastic goings-on at the baths. Today, taking the waters is done with a bathing suit on, but beware, the casual German attitude toward nudity takes over in the sauna area, which is declared a "textile-free zone." ✉ *Passstr. 79,* ☎ *0241/182–740,* WEB *www.carolus-thermen.de.* 🎫 *€15–€24.*

Like many German spa towns, Aachen has its **Spielbank** (casino). It's housed in the porticoed former Kurhaus, on the parklike grounds fronting Monheimsallee and facing the Kurbad Quellenhof. Jacket and tie are required. Bring your passport for identification. ✉ *Monheimsallee 44,* ☎ *0241/18080.* 🎫 *€2.50.* ⊙ *Sun.–Fri. 3 PM–3 AM, Sat. 3 PM–4 AM.*

Aachen has its modern side as well—one of the world's most important art collectors, Peter Ludwig, has endowed two museums in his hometown. The **Ludwig Forum für Internationale Kunst** holds a portion of Ludwig's truly enormous collection of contemporary art and hosts traveling exhibits. ✉ *Jülicher Str. 97–109,* ☎ *0241/180–7103 or 7104.* 🎫 *€3.* ⊙ *Tues. and Thurs. 10–5, Wed. and Fri. 10–8, weekends 11–5.*

The **Suermont-Ludwig Museum** is devoted to classical painting up to the beginning of the 20th century. ✉ *Wilhelmstr. 18,* ☎ *0241/479–800.* 🎫 *€3.* ⊙ *Tues., Thurs., and Fri. 11–7, Wed. 11–9, weekends 11–5.*

Dining and Lodging

$$$$ ★ ✕ **Gala.** For the most elegant dining in Aachen, reserve a table at the Gala restaurant adjoining the casino. Dark-paneled walls and original oil paintings make the mood discreetly classy. Chef Maurice de Boer's cooking is international and rich, with nouvelle and creative touches. The four-course set menu (€60) includes wine. ✉ *Monheimsallee 44,* ☎ *0241/153–013. Reservations essential. Jacket and tie. AE, DC, MC, V. Closed Sun. and Mon. No lunch.*

$$$$ ✕ **La Becasse.** Sophisticated French nouvelle cuisine is offered in this modern restaurant just outside the Old Town by the Westpark. Try the distinctively light calves' liver. ✉ *Hanbrucherstr. 1,* ☏ *0241/74444. Reservations essential. D, MC, V. Closed Sun. No lunch Sat. and Mon.*

$$ ✕ **Der Postwagen.** This annex of the more upscale Ratskeller is worth a stop for the building alone, a half-timber medieval edifice at one corner of the old Rathaus. Sitting at one of the low wooden tables, surveying the marketplace through the wavy old glass, you can dine very respectably on solid German fare. If you really want to go local, try *Unser Puttes,* a kind of blood sausage. ✉ *Am Markt,* ☏ *0241/35001. AE, D, MC, V.*

$–$$ ✕ **Am Knipp.** At this historic old Aachen Bierstube, guests dig into their German dishes at low wooden tables next to the tile stove. Pewter pots and beer mugs hang from the rafters. ✉ *Bergdriesch 3,* ☏ *0241/33168. No credit cards. Closed Tues., Dec. 24–Jan. 2.*

$$ ★ ✕🏨 **Hotel Quellenhof.** Built during World War I as a country home for the kaiser, this is one of Europe's grande dames: spacious, elegant, and formal. Rooms have high ceilings; a mix of conservative-style furniture; a walk-in baggage room; and huge, modern bathrooms. Flowers fill the bistro La Brasserie, and the restaurant Lakmé ($$$$) is an oasis of Asian-accented cuisine where diners can create their own three- to five-course menus. Breakfast is included in the room rate. The hotel is part of the Dorint group. ✉ *Monheimsallee 52, D–52062,* ☏ *0241/91320,* FAX *0241/91100,* WEB *www.dorint.de. 175 rooms, 2 suites. 2 restaurants, cable TV, spa. AE, DC, MC, V.*

$$ 🏨 **Hotel Brülls am Dom.** In the historic heart of the city, this family-run hotel offers tradition, convenience, free breakfast, and considerable comfort. It's a short walk to nearly all the major attractions. ✉ *Hühnermarkt, D–52062,* ☏ *0241/31704,* FAX *0241/404–326. 10 rooms. Restaurant. No credit cards.*

$ 🏨 **Hotel Dura.** This small, family-run hotel, just one block from the train station and on a noisy street, is one of the very few low-budget options in the city. There is no restaurant, but you can buy snacks in the kiosk downstairs. ✉ *Lagerhausstr. 5, D–52063,* ☏ *0241/403–135,* FAX *0241/401–8450. 8 rooms, 1 apartment. Bar. D, MC, V.*

Nightlife and the Arts

Most activity in town is concentrated around the market square and Pontstrasse, a pedestrian street that radiates off the square. Start out at Aachen's most popular bar, the **Dom Keller** (✉ Hof 1, ☏ 0241/34265), to mingle with locals of all ages at old wooden tables. The Irish pub **Wild Rover** (✉ Hirschgraben 13, ☏ 0241/35453) serves Guinness on tap to live music every night starting at 9:30. The municipal orchestra gives regular concerts in the **Kongresszentrum Eurogress** (✉ Monheimsallee 48, ☏ 0241/91310).

Shopping

Don't leave Aachen without stocking up on the traditional local gingerbread, *Aachener Printen.* Most bakeries in town offer assortments. Some of the best are at the **Alte Aachener Kaffeestuben** (✉ Büchel 18, ☏ 0241/35724), also known as the *Konditorei van den Daele.* The store-café is worth a visit for its atmosphere and tempting aromas, whether or not you intend to buy anything. It also ships goods.

Düsseldorf

47 km (29 mi) north of Köln.

Düsseldorf may suffer by comparison to Köln's remarkable skyline, but the elegant city has more than enough charm—and money—to boost its confidence. It has a reputation for being the richest city in Germany, with an extravagant lifestyle that epitomizes the economic success of postwar Germany. Although 80% of prewar Düsseldorf was destroyed in World War II, the city has since been more or less rebuilt from the ground up—in part re-creating landmarks of long ago and restoring a medieval riverside quarter.

At the confluence of the Rivers Rhine and Düssel, this dynamic city started as a small fishing town. The name means "village on the Düssel," but obviously this Dorf is a village no more. Raised expressways speed traffic past towering glass-and-steel structures; within them, glass-enclosed shopping malls showcase the fanciest outfits, furs, jewelry, and leather goods that famous designers can create and those with plenty of money can buy.

★ The **Königsallee,** the main shopping avenue, is the epitome of Düsseldorf affluence; it's lined with the crème de la crème of designer boutiques and stores. Known as the Kö, this wide, double boulevard is divided by an ornamental waterway that is actually a part of the River Düssel. Rows of chestnut trees line the Kö, shading a string of sidewalk cafés. Beyond the Triton Fountain, at the street's north end, begins a series of parks and gardens. In these patches of green you can sense a joie de vivre hardly expected in a city devoted to big business.

The lovely **Hofgarten Park,** once the garden of the elector's palace, is reached by heading north to Corneliusplatz. Laid out in 1770 and completed 30 years later, the Hofgarten is an oasis of greenery at the heart of downtown and a focal point for Düsseldorf culture.

The baroque **Schloss Jägerhof,** at the far-east edge of the Hofgarten, is more a combination town house and country lodge than a castle. It houses the **Goethe Museum,** featuring original manuscripts, first editions, personal correspondence, and other memorabilia of Germany's greatest writer. There is also a museum housing a collection of **Meissner Porcelain.** ✉ *Jacobistr. 2,* ☎ *0211/899–6262,* WEB *www.goethe-museum.com.* 🎫 *€2.* ⏲ *Tues.–Fri. and Sun. 11–5, Sat. 1–5.*

The **Stiftung museum kunst palast**(Art Museum Foundation) lies at the northern extremity of the Hofgarten, close to the Rhine. The collection of paintings run the gamut from Rubens, Goya, Tintoretto, and Cranach the Elder to the romantic Düsseldorf School and such modern German expressionists as Beckmann, Kirchner, Nolde, Macke, and Kandinsky. The collection also includes works from Asia and Africa. Changing exhibits include modern photography and installations. ✉ *Ehrenhof 5,* ☎ *0211/899–2460,* WEB *www.museum-kunst-palast.de.* 🎫 *€7.* ⏲ *Tues.–Sun. noon–8.*

The **Kunstsammlung Nordrhein-Westfalen** (North Rhineland–Westphalia Art Collection) displays a dazzling array of 20th-century classic modern paintings, including works by Bonnard, Braque, Matisse, Leger, Johns, and Pollock; there are also many by Paul Klee because the Swiss painter lived in Düsseldorf for a time and taught at the National Academy of Art. The collection is across the street from the city opera house. ✉ *Grabbepl. 5,* ☎ *0211/83810,* WEB *www.kunstsammlung.de.* 🎫 *€ 5.* ⏲ *Tues.–Thurs. and Sun. 10–6, Fri. 10–8.*

The restored **Altstadt** (Old Town) faces the Rhine. Narrow alleys thread their way to some 200 restaurants and taverns offering a wide range of cuisines, all crowded into the 1-square-km (½-square-mi) area between the Rhine and Heine Allee. Traffic is routed away from the river and underneath the **Rhine Promenade,** which is lined by chic shopping arcades and cafés. Joggers, rollerbladers, and folks out for a stroll make much use of the promenade as well. Occasionally you can still see the

Radschläger, young boys who demonstrate their cartwheeling abilities, a Düsseldorf tradition, for the admiration (and tips) of visitors.

A plaque at **Bolkerstrasse 53** indicates where poet Heinrich Heine was born in 1797. The **Heinrich Heine Institute** has a museum and an archive of significant manuscripts. Part of the complex was once the residence of the composer Robert Schumann. ✉ *Bilkerstr. 12–14,* ☎ *0211/899–2902,* WEB *www.duesseldorf.de/kultur/hhinstut.shtml.* 🎫 € *2.* ⏲ *Tues.–Fri. and Sun. 11–5, Sat. 1–5.*

The traffic-free cobblestone streets of the Old Town lead to **Burgplatz** (Castle Square). The 13th-century **Schlossturm** (Castle Tower) is all that remains of the castle built by the de Berg family, which founded Düsseldorf. The tower also houses the **Schiffahrt Museum,** which charts 2,000 years of Rhine boatbuilding and navigation. ✉ *Burgpl. 30,* ☎ *0211/899–4195.* 🎫 *€3.* ⏲ *Tues.–Sun. 11–6.*

The Gothic **St. Lambertus** (St. Lambertus Church: ✉ Stiftspl.) is near the castle tower on Burgplatz. Its spire became distorted because unseasoned wood was used in its construction. The Vatican elevated the 14th-century brick church to a basilica minor (small cathedral) in 1974 in recognition of its role in church history. Built in the 13th century, with additions from 1394, St. Lambertus contains the tomb of William the Rich and a graceful late-Gothic tabernacle.

Dining and Lodging

$$$$ ★ ✕ **Im Schiffchen.** Although it's a bit out of the way, dining in one of Germany's best restaurants makes it worth a trip. This is grande luxe, with cooking that's a fine art. A typical dish might be fried saddle of French milk calf in verveine sauce. The restaurant Aalschokker, on the ground floor, features local specialties created by the same chef but at lower prices. There are 700 wines on the menu. ✉ *Kaiserwerther Markt 9,* ☎ *0211/401–050. Reservations essential. Jacket and tie. AE, DC, MC, V. Closed Sun. and Mon. No lunch.*

$$$–$$$$ ✕ **Weinhaus Tante Anna.** This charming restaurant is furnished with antiques. The cuisine presents modern versions of German classics, demonstrating that there's a lot more to the country's cooking than wurst and sauerkraut. The wine selection is particularly fine. ✉ *Andreasstr. 2,* ☎ *0211/131–163. AE, DC, MC, V. Closed Sun. No lunch.*

$–$$ ✕ **Zum Uerige.** Among beer buffs, Düsseldorf is famous for its *Altbier,* so called because of the old-fashioned brewing method. The mellow and malty copper-color brew is produced by eight breweries in town. This tavern provides the perfect atmosphere for drinking it. The beer is poured straight out of polished oak barrels and served by busy waiters in long blue aprons. ✉ *Bergerstr. 1,* ☎ *0211/866–990. No credit cards.*

$ ✕ **Zur Uel.** A nontraditional brew house, the Uel is the popular hangout for Düsseldorf's students. The basic menu consists of soups, salads, and pastas; the ingredients are fresh and the portions are generous. Every cultural and political event in the city is advertised in the entry hall. ✉ *Ratingerstr. 16,* ☎ *0211/325–369. V.*

$$$$ ★ 🏨 **Steigenberger Parkhotel.** Miraculously quiet despite its central location on the edge of the Hofgarten and at the beginning of the Königsallee, this old hotel is anything but stodgy. The soaring ceilings add to the spaciousness of the guest rooms, each individually decorated in a restrained, elegant style. The pampering continues at the free breakfast buffet, served in the Menuette restaurant, where champagne and smoked salmon are appropriate starters for a shopping expedition on the Kö. ✉ *Corneliuspl. 1, D–40213,* ☎ *0211/13810,* FAX *0211/138–1592,* WEB *www.steigenberger.de. 122 rooms, 12 suites. Restaurant, 2 bars, café, cable TV, no a/c in some rooms, some in-room data ports,* *business services, meeting rooms, free parking, some pets allowed (fee), no-smoking rooms. AE, DC, MC, V.*

$$–$$$ **Carathotel.** Besides bright, well-sized rooms, the true strength of this modern hotel is its location at the southern edge of the Altstadt. After a generous buffet breakfast, you can quickly reach either the Rhine or the Kö with a three-block walk. ✉ *Benratherstr. 7a, D–40213,* ☎ *0211/13050,* FAX *0211/322–214,* WEB *www.horega.de. 73 rooms, 1 suite. Café, cable TV, no a/c in some rooms, some in-room data ports, Internet, business services, sauna, parking (fee), some pets allowed (fee), no-smoking floors. AE, DC, MC, V.*

$$ **Günnewig Hotel Esplanade.** This small, modern hotel has an exceptionally quiet, leafy location still close to the action. From the inviting lobby to the attractive rooms, the ambience here is one of intimacy. Room rates vary depending on the view. Breakfast is included. ✉ *Fürstenpl. 17, D–40215,* ☎ *0211/386–850,* FAX *0211/374–032,* WEB *www.guennewig.de. 80 rooms, 2 suites. Bar, no a/c, cable TV, in-room data ports, pool, sauna, business services, parking (fee), pets allowed (fee), no-smoking floors. AE, DC, MC, V.*

$$ **Hotel Cristallo.** Clearly someone took great pains with the slightly tacky but nonetheless striking decor of this well-located, mid-price hotel. If you like gilt angels in the breakfast room, this is the place for you. The hotel is centrally located near the Kö and has pleasant, eclectically furnished rooms, with comfortable sofas and color TVs even in singles. ✉ *Schadowpl. 7,* ☎ *0211/845–257,* FAX *0211/322–632. 35 rooms. No a/c, cable TV, some pets allowed (fee). AE, DC, MC, V.*

$ **Diana.** If a trade fair hasn't filled this place, it is one of the best bets for a low-priced stay in this high-priced town. The small rooms with adjoining bathrooms are comfortable, if somberly furnished. The Altstadt is a 15-minute walk away. Breakfast is included. ✉ *Jahnstr. 31,* ☎ *0211/375–071,* FAX *0211/364–943. 20 rooms. No a/c, cable TV, some pets allowed (fee). AE, D, MC, V.*

Nightlife and the Arts

The **Altstadt** is a landscape of pubs, dance clubs, ancient brewery houses, and jazz clubs in the vicinity of the Marktplatz and along cobblestone streets named Bolker, Kurze, Flinger, and Mühlen. These places may be crowded, but some are very atmospheric. The local favorite for nightlife is the **Hafen** neighborhood. Its restaurants and bars cater to the hip thirtysomething crowd that works and parties there. **Front Page** (✉ Mannesman Ufer 9, ☎ 0211/323–264) is a slick watering hole. The most popular dance club is **Sam's West** (✉ Königsallee 52, ☎ 0211/328–171).

Düsseldorf, once home to Mendelssohn, Schumann, and Brahms, has the finest concert hall in Germany after Berlin's Philharmonie: the **Tonhalle** (✉ Ehrenhof 41, ☎ 0211/899–6123), a former planetarium on the edge of the Hofgarten. It's the home of the Düsseldorfer Symphoniker, which plays from September to mid-June. **Deutsche Oper am Rhein** (✉ Heinrich Heine Allee 16a, ☎ 0211/890–8211) showcases the city's highly regarded opera company and ballet troupe. The **Robert Schumann Saal** (✉ Ehrenhof 4, ☎ 0211/899–6211, WEB www.museum-kunst-palast.de) has classic and pop concerts, symposia, film, and international theater.

A 30-minute ride outside Düsseldorf by car, train, or S-bahn (from the Hauptbahnhof) will get you to the industrial city of Wuppertal, whose main claim to fame is its transit system of suspended trains, the *Schwebebahn.* It is also home to the **Tanztheater Wuppertal** (✉ Spinnstr. 4, ☎ 0202/569–4444, WEB www.pina-bausch.de), the dance theater company of world-famous choreographer Pina Bausch.

Shopping

The area around Hohe Strasse has antiques. The east side of the **Königsallee** is lined with some of Germany's trendiest boutiques, grandest jewelers, and most extravagant furriers. The shopping arcade **Kö Center** (✉ Königsallee 30) features the most famous names in fashion, from Chanel to Louis Vuitton. **Kö Galerie** (✉ Königsallee 60) has trendy boutiques, and includes a Mövenpick restaurant on its luxurious two-story premises. **Schadow Arcade** (✉ off Schadowpl., at the end of the Kö Galerie) caters to normal budgets, with such stores as Hennes & Mauritz (H & M) and Habitat.

THE RHINELAND A TO Z

To research prices, get advice from other travelers, and book travel arrangements, visit www.fodors.com.

AIRPORTS

The Rhineland is served by three international airports: Frankfurt, Düsseldorf, and Köln-Bonn. Bus and rail lines connect each airport with its respective downtown area and provide rapid access to the rest of the region. The Luxembourg Findel International Airport (a 30-minute drive from Trier) is close to the upper Mosel River Valley.

➤ CONTACT: **Flughafen Düsseldorf** (☎ 0211/421–2223). **Flughafen Köln/Bonn** (✉ Waldstr. 247, Köln, ☎ 02203/404–001).

BIKE TRAVEL

The Mosel Valley, with its small hamlets lining the riverbanks, is an excellent area for biking. The train station in Trier rents bikes; call the Deutsche Bahn bicycle hot line to reserve. Cyclists can follow the marked route of the *Radroute Nahe-Hunsrück-Mosel* from Trier to Bingen, which partially overlaps with the *Moselradwanderweg* from Koblenz to Trier. Both Bonn and Köln have extensive bike paths downtown; these are designated, red-painted or red-brick paths on the edges of roads or sidewalks. (Pedestrians beware: anyone walking on a bike path risks getting mowed down.) Bicyclists are expected to follow the same traffic rules as cars. In Bonn, the Radstation, at the main train station, will not only rent you a bike and provide maps, it will fill your water bottle and check the pressure in your tires for free. In Köln, Rent-a-Bike offers bike rental by the day from April through October, as well as a daily three-hour bike tour of the city.

➤ BIKE RENTALS: **Deutsche Bahn bicycle hot line** (☎ 01805/151–415). **Radstation** (✉ Quantiusstr. 26, Bonn, ☎ 0228/981–4636). **Rent-a-Bike** (✉ Markmannsgasse/under Deutzer Brücke, Köln, ☎ 0171/629–8796).

CAR RENTAL

Each of the companies below has a rental office at the Frankfurt Airport. Avis, Europcar, and Hertz have offices at the Luxembourg Airport as well. Sixt has an office at Wiesbaden's main train station.

➤ MAJOR AGENCIES: **Avis** (✉ Römerstr. 4, Bonn, ☎ 0228/631–433; ✉ Berliner Allee 32, Düsseldorf, ☎ 0211/865–6220; ✉ Andernacher Str. 190–192, Koblenz, ☎ 0261/800–366; ✉ Köln-Bonn Airport, Köln, ☎ 02203/402–343; ✉ Herzogenbuscher Str. 35, Trier, ☎ 0651/270–770; ✉ Dotzheimer Str. 93–95, Wiesbaden, ☎ 0611/449–030). **Europcar** (✉ Potsdammer Pl. 7, Bonn, ☎ 0228/604–340; ✉ Burgunderstr. 35, Düsseldorf, ☎ 0211/950–980; ✉ Andernacher Str. 199, Koblenz, ☎ 0261/889–180; ✉ Köln-Bonn Airport, Köln, ☎ 02203/955–880; ✉ Wasserweg 16, Trier, ☎ 0651/146–540; ✉ Kasteler Str. 42, Wiesbaden, ☎ 0611/186–330). **Hertz** (✉ Juelicherstr. 250, Aachen, ☎ 0241/162–686; ✉ Adenauerallee 216, Bonn, ☎ 0228/201–530; ✉ Immermannstr. 65, Düsseldorf, ☎ 0211/357–025; ✉ Bismarckstr. 19–

21, Köln, ☎ 0221/515–084; ✉ Loeb Str. 4, Trier, ☎ 0651/23137; ✉ Schwalbacher Str. 38, Wiesbaden, ☎ 0611/945–0845). **Sixt** (✉ Tilde-Klose-Weg 6, Düsseldorf, ☎ 0211/471–310; ✉ Friedrich-Mohr-Str. 10A, Koblenz, ☎ 0261/86095; ✉ Aachenerstr. 226–232, Köln, ☎ 0221/887–301; ✉ Bahnhof, Wiesbaden, ☎ 0611/840–300).

CAR TRAVEL

The autobahns and other highways of the Rhineland are busy, so allow plenty of time for driving. Frankfurt is 126 km (78 mi) from Koblenz, 175 km (109 mi) from Bonn, 190 km (118 mi) from Köln, and 230 km (143 mi) from Düsseldorf (the A–3 links Frankfurt with Köln and Düsseldorf and passes near Koblenz and Bonn). The most spectacular stretch of the Rhineland is along the Middle Rhine, between Mainz and Koblenz, which takes in the awesome castles and vineyards of the Rhine Gorge. Highways hug the river on each bank (B–42 on the north/eastern side, and B–9 on the south/western side), and car ferries crisscross the Rhine at many points.

CONSULATES

➤ CANADA: **Canadian Consulate** (✉ Benratherstr. 8, D–40213 Düsseldorf, ☎ 0211/172–170).

➤ UNITED KINGDOM: **British General Consulate** (✉ Yorckstr. 19, D–40476 Düsseldorf, ☎ 0211/94480).

TOURS

BOAT TOURS

No visit to the Rhineland is complete without at least one river cruise, and there are many options from which to choose. Even rowboats and canoes can be rented at most Rhine and Mosel river resorts.

Trips along the Rhine and Mosel range in length from a few hours to days or even a week or more (☞ Cruise Travel *in* Smart Travel Tips A to Z). Viking River Cruises offers various multiday cruises on cabin ships. A major day-trip line is Köln-Düsseldorfer Deutsche Rheinschiffahrt (KD Rhine Line). Its fleet travels the Rhine between Köln and Mainz, daily from Easter to late October, and the Mosel from Koblenz to Cochem, daily from June to September (and reduced service during the spring and fall). There are many special offers, such as free travel on your birthday (bring your passport as proof); half-price for seniors on Monday and Friday; two cyclists travel for the price of one on Tuesday, with no charge for the bikes; family day on Wednesday (three children travel free per paying adult); and economical fares for time-saving round-trip travel—one way by train, return by boat.

Many smaller, family-operated boat companies offer daytime trips and often, nightime dinner-dance cruises. The Koblenz operator Rhein- und Moselschiffahrt Hölzenbein travels between Koblenz and Winningen on the Mosel and between Bonn and Rüdesheim on the Rhine. From Koblenz, Personenschiffahrt Merkelbach makes roundtrip "castle cruises" to Schloss Stolzenfels (one hour) or the Marksburg (two hours), passing by six castles en route. The Hebel-Line has Loreley Valley trips from Boppard. Another important Mittelrhein specialist traveling to the Loreley is the Bingen-Rüdesheimer Fahrgastschiffahrt.

Three shipping companies in Köln leave from the Rhine landing stages near the Hohenzollern Brücke, a short walk from the cathedral.

➤ FEES AND SCHEDULES FOR RHINE TRIPS: **Bingen-Rüdesheimer Fahrgastschiffahrt** (✉ , ☎ 06721/14140, FAX 06721/17398). **Dampfschiffahrt Colonia** (✉ Köln, ☎ 0221/257–4225). **Hebel-Line** (✉ Boppard, ☎ 06742/2420, FAX 06742/4727). **KD Rhine Line** (✉ Köln, ☎

0221/208–8318 or 800/346–6525 in the U.S., WEB www.k-d.com). **KölnTourist Personenschiffahrt am Dom** (✉ Köln, ☎ 0221/121–714). **Personenschiffahrt Merkelbach** (✉ Koblenz, ☎ 0261/76810, FAX 0261/973–3264. **Rhein- und Moselschiffahrt Hölzenbein** (☎ 0261/37744, FAX 0261/16640). **Viking River Cruises** (✉ Köln, ☎ 0221/25860; 877/668–4546 in the U.S., WEB www.vikingkd.com).

➤ FEES AND SCHEDULES FOR MOSEL TRIPS: **Personenschiffahrt Hans Michels** (✉ Bernkastel-Kues, ☎ 06531/8222, FAX 06531/7603). **Personenschiffahrt Kolb** (☎ 02673/1515, FAX 02673/1510). **Rhein- und Moselschiffahrt Hölzenbein** (☎ 0261/37744, FAX 0261/16640).

BUS TOURS

Limousine Travel Service has a daily bus trip from Frankfurt to Rhine wine country. From Rüdesheim travel continues by boat to St. Goarhausen; return to Frankfurt is by bus. The €64 fee includes lunch and a wine tasting.

Bus trips into the Köln countryside (to the Eifel Hills, the Ahr Valley, and the Westerwald) are organized by several city travel agencies. Reisebüro Knipper sells tours to individuals looking for trips outside of the city.

➤ FEES AND SCHEDULES: **Limousine Travel Service** (✉ Wiesenhüttenpl. 39, Frankfurt/Main, ☎ 069/230–492). **Reisebüro Knipper** (✉ Hahnenstr. 41, near Neumarkt, ☎ 0221/205–0820).

CITY TOURS

Tours of Bonn start from the tourist office and are conducted April–October, Tuesday–Sunday, and November–March, Saturday only. Call ahead to check times for tours in English.

Bus tours of Düsseldorf leave year-round at 11 daily and also at 2:30 on Saturday, from the corner of Steinstrasse and Königsallee. From April to October, the 2:30 tour is daily as well. Tickets (€15) can be purchased on the bus, at the information center, or through Adorf Reisebüro.

The Koblenz tourist office has guided tours on Saturday at 2:30, May through October, departing from the Historisches Rathaus on Jesuitenplatz (€2.50). English-language tours are available upon request.

Bus tours of Köln leave from outside the tourist office, opposite the main entrance to the cathedral, hourly 10–3, April–October, and at 11 and 2, November–April. The tour lasts two hours and costs €15; it is conducted in English and German. A two-hour Köln walking tour is available by prior arrangement with the tourist office.

In Trier you can choose to circumnavigate the town with the narrated tours of the Römer-Express trolley, the CityTour doubledecker bus, or a tourist office bus; all cost €6 and depart from Porta Nigra, near the tourist office. You can board the hop-on, hop-off bus TrierTour (€5.60; no narration) at any of its 16 stops in town. The tourist office sells tickets for all tours and also leads various walks. A tour in English (€6) departs daily June through August at 1:30; in May, September, and October, on Saturday at 1:30. The office also provides a Walkman portable tour in English (€6).

Bilingual walking (€5) and bus (€10) tours of Wiesbaden depart from the bus stop in front of the Staatstheater on Kurhausplatz. The walking tour is conducted April through October, Saturday at 10 (November through March, the first and third Saturday). The bus tour is offered year-round, Saturday at 2.

➤ FEES AND SCHEDULES: **Adorf Reisebüro** (✉ Bismarckstr. 45, Düsseldorf, ☎ 0211/418–970).

TRAIN TRAVEL

InterCity and EuroCity expresses connect all the cities and towns of the area. Hourly InterCity routes run between Düsseldorf, Köln, Bonn, and Mainz, with most services extending as far south as Munich and as far north as Hamburg. The Mainz–Bonn route runs beside the Rhine, providing spectacular views all the way. The city transportation networks of Bonn, Köln, and Düsseldorf are linked by S-bahn (for information contact the KVB).

➤ TRAIN INFORMATION: **Deutsche Bahn** (☎ 0180/599–6633). **Kölner Verkehrs-Betriebe** (KVB, ☎ 0221/547–3333).

TRAVEL AGENCIES

➤ LOCAL AGENT REFERRALS: **American Express** (✉ Königs-Allee 98a, D–40215 Düsseldorf, ☎ 0211/385–0019; ✉ Burgmauer 14, D–50667 Köln, ☎ 0221/257–5186).

VISITOR INFORMATION

The Rhineland regional tourist office, Rheinland-Pfalz Tourismus, provides general information on the entire region. The events calendar *Veranstaltungskalender Rheinland-Pfalz*—gives a comprehensive overview of the wine, regional, and folk festivals, as well as concerts, theater, and art exhibitions taking place in many parts of this area.

Many cultural events and museums in the state of Rhineland-Pfalz accept the KulturCard (€5), which grants up to 50% discounts. Buy the card at offices of the *Rhein Zeitung* or by mail through SWR. The Mittelrhein Burgen-Ticket, sold at 10 participating castles in the Mittelrhein area between Rüdesheim and Koblenz offers a tremendous savings on admission fees to 10 castles. The cost is €14 for adults and allows free admission to the castles.

Bonn's tourism office sells the RegioBonnCard package, which offers an array of reductions, plus free entry into most museums, in combination with low- or no-cost transportation for €12.25 per day or €23.50 for two days.

In Köln, most central hotels sell the KölnTourismus Card (€15.50), which entitles you to a sightseeing tour, admission to all the city's museums, free city bus and tram travel, and other reductions.

➤ DISCOUNT TICKETS: **KulturCard** (✉ SWR, Stichwort KulturCard, Postfach 3740, D–55027 Mainz). **Mittelrhein Burgen-Ticket** (WEB www.burgen-am-rhein.de).

➤ TOURIST INFORMATION: **Aachen** (✉ Aachen Tourist Service, Friedrich-Wilhelm-Pl., Postfach 2007, D–52022, ☎ 0241/180–2960, WEB www.aachen-tourist.de). **Bacharach** (✉ Tourist-Information; Oberstr. 45, D–55422, ☎ 06743/919–303, FAX 06743/919–304, WEB www.rhein-nahe-touristik.de). **Bernkastel-Kues** (✉ Tourist-Information; Gestade 6, D–54470, ☎ 06531/402–324, FAX 06531/7953, WEB www.bernkastel-kues.de). **Bingen** (✉ Tourist-Information; Rheinkai 21, D–55411, ☎ 06721/184–205, FAX 06721/16275, WEB www.bingen.de). **Bonn** (✉ Bonn Information; Windeckstr. 2 am Münsterpl., D–53111, ☎ 0228/775–000, WEB www.bonn.de). **Boppard** (✉ Tourist-Information; Marktpl., D–56154, ☎ 06742/3888, FAX 06742/81402, WEB www.boppard.de). **Cochem** (✉ Tourist-Information; Endertpl. 1, D–56812, ☎ 02671/60040, FAX 02671/600–444, WEB www.cochem.de). **Düsseldorf** (✉ Verkehrsverein; Konrad Adenauer Pl. 12, D–40210, ☎ 0211/172–020, WEB www.duesseldorf.de). **Koblenz** (✉ Tourist-Information; Bahnhofpl. 17, D–56068, ☎ 0261/31304, FAX 0261/100–4388, WEB www.koblenz.de). **Köln** (✉ KölnTourismus Office; Unter Fettenhenen 19, D–50667, ☎ 0221/2212–3345, WEB www.koeln.de). **Rheinland-PfalzTourismus** (✉ Löhrstr. 103–105, D–56068 Koblenz, ☎ 0261/915–200, FAX 0261/915–

2040, WEB www.rlp-info.de). **Rüdesheim** (✉ Tourist Information; Geisenheimer Str. 22, D–65385, ☎ 06722/19433, FAX 06722/3485, WEB www.ruedesheim.de). **Trier** (✉ Tourist Information; An der Porta Nigra, D–54290, ☎ 0651/978–080, FAX 0651/44759, WEB www.trier.de/tourismus). **Wiesbaden** (✉ Tourist Information; Marktstr. 6, D–65183, ☎ 0611/17290, FAX 0611/172–9798, WEB www.wiesbaden.de).

WINE INFORMATION

The German Wine Information Bureau (☞ Wine, Beer & Spirits *in* Smart Travel Tips A to Z) provides background information and brochures about all German wine-growing regions. Tips on wine-related events and package offers are available from regional wine information offices.

The tiny red-wine region near Bonn is the Ahr. Mosel-Saar-Ruwer Wein supplies wine information about these three river valleys. Between the Mosel and Rhine valleys lies the Nahe region.

➤ CONTACTS: **Gesellschaft für Rheingauer Weinkultur** (✉ Adam-von-Itzstein-Str. 20, D–65375 Oestrich-Winkel, ☎ 06723/91757, FAX 06723/917–591, WEB www.rheingau.de). **Mittelrhein-Wein** (Am Hafen 2, D–56329 St. Goar, ☎ 06741/7712, FAX 06741/7723). **Mosel-Saar-Ruwer Wein** (✉ Gartenfeldstr. 12a, D–54295 Trier, ☎ 0651/710–280, FAX 0651/45443, WEB www.msr-wein.de). **Touristik-Service Ahr-Rhein-Eifel** (✉ Felix-Rütten-Str. 2, D–53474 Bad Neuenahr-Ahrweiler, ☎ 02641/97730, FAX 02641/977–373, WEB www.ahr-rhein-eifel.de). **Weinland Nahe** (✉ Dessauer Str. 6, D–55545 Bad Kreuznach, ☎ 0671/834–050, FAX 0671/834–0525, WEB www.weinland-nahe.de).

13 THE FAIRY-TALE ROAD

If you're in search of Sleeping Beauty, the Pied Piper, and Rumpelstiltskin, the Fairy-Tale Road is the place to look. One of Germany's special tour routes, it leads through the landscapes that inspired the Brothers Grimm. From its start in Hanau, just east of Frankfurt, to its end in Bremen, 600 km (370 mi) north, it passes dozens of picturesque towns full of half-timber houses and guarded by castles.

Updated by
Ted Shoemaker

THE FAIRY-TALE ROAD, or Märchenstrasse, leads deep into the heart of the country, as well as the German character. It begins just 20 minutes east of Frankfurt in the town of Hanau, and from there wends its way northward some 600 km (about 370 mi), mainly through the states of Hesse and Lower Saxony, following the Fulda and Weser rivers and traversing a countryside as beguiling as any in Europe.

This designated tour route doesn't have the glamour of the Romantic Road, but it also doesn't have the crowds and commercialism. It's perhaps even a route more in tune with romantics. Fairy tales come to life in forgotten villages where black cats snooze in the windows of half-timber houses, in castles surrounded by ancient forests where wild boar snort at timid deer, and in misty valleys where the silence of centuries is broken only by the splash of a ferryman's oar. The meandering, progressive path seems to travel backward in time, into the reaches of childhood, imagination, and the German folk consciousness, to visit old-world settings steeped in legend and fantasy.

This part of Germany shaped the lives and imaginations of the two most famous chroniclers of German folk history and tradition, the Brothers Grimm. From their childhood, the Grimms were enthralled by tales of enchantment, of kings and queens, of golden-haired princesses saved from disaster by stalwart princes—folk tales, myths, epics, and legends that dealt with magic and wicked witches, predatory stepmothers, and a supporting cast of goblins and wizards.

The Grimms did not invent these tales; they were in the public domain long before the brothers began collecting them. The Grimms' devotion to fairy tales could be considered merely a sideline to their main careers. Jacob (1785–1863) was a linguist who formulated Grimm's Law, an explanation of how German, along with Greek and Latin, evolved from an ancestral Indo-European language. Wilhelm (1786–1859) was a literary scholar and critic. Together they spent most of their energies compiling a massive dictionary of the German language. But it is as the authors of the *Kinder und Hausmärchen* (Children's and Household Tales), a work that has been called the best-known book after the Bible, that they are remembered. In 1812 the Grimms introduced the world to some 200 of their favorite stories, with a cast of characters that included Cinderella, Hansel and Gretel, Little Red Riding Hood, Rapunzel, Rumpelstiltskin, Sleeping Beauty, Snow White, and other unforgettable stars of the world of make-believe.

The degree to which the brothers have influenced the world's concept of fairy tales is remarkable, matched only by *The Arabian Nights*. But it would be a mistake to imagine them as kindly, bewhiskered old gents telling stories in their rose-clad cottage for the pleasure of village children. They were serious and successful academics, with interests ranging far beyond what we may think of as amusements for children. Their stories probe deep into the German psyche and deal with far more complex emotions than is suggested by the occasional happily-ever-after endings.

The zigzag course detailed in this chapter follows the spine of Fairy-Tale country and includes a number of side trips and detours. Although the route is best explored by car, most of the attractions along its meandering path can also be reached by train.

Pleasures and Pastimes

Dining

A specialty of Northern Hesse is sausages with *Beulches,* made from potato balls, leeks, and black pudding. *Lauterbacher Strolch* is a special Camembert named after the little fellow who lost his sock in that town. *Weck,* which is local dialect for heavily spiced pork, appears either as *Musterweck,* served on a roll, or as *Weckewerk,* a frying-pan concoction with white bread. Heading north into Lower Saxony you'll encounter the ever-popular *Speckkuchen,* a heavy and filling onion tart. Another favorite main course is *Pfefferpothast,* a sort of heavily browned goulash with lots of pepper. The "hast" at the end of the name is from the old German word *Harst,* meaning "roasting pan." Trout and eels are common in the rivers and streams around Hameln, and by the time you reach Bremen, North German cuisine has taken over the menu. *Aalsuppe grün,* eel soup seasoned with dozens of herbs, is a must in summer, as the hearty *Grünkohl mit Pinkel,* a cabbage dish with sausage, bacon, and cured pork is in winter. And be sure to try the coffee. Fifty percent of the coffee served in Germany comes from beans roasted in Bremen. The city has been producing the stuff since 1673 and knows just how to serve it in *gemütlich* surroundings.

CATEGORY	COST*
$$$$	over €20
$$$	€15–€20
$$	€10–€15
$	under €10

**per person for a main course at dinner*

Golf

There are golf courses at Bad Orb, Bad Pyrmont, Bremen, Göttingen, Hanau, Kassel, Hameln, Hannover, and Celle; guests are welcome at all locations (provided they can produce a handicap from their local clubs). The courses at Hanau (on the former hunting grounds at Wilhelmsbad) and Kassel (high above the city on the edge of Wilhelmshöhe Park) are particularly attractive. At Schloss Schwöbber, near Hameln, golfers tee off on the extensive castle grounds.

Hiking

The hills and forests between Hanau and Hameln are a hiker's paradise. The valleys of the Fulda, Werra, and Weser rivers make enchanting walking country, with ancient waterside inns positioned along the way. Another densely forested route runs from Hannoversch-Münden, in the south, to Porta-Westfalica, where the Weser River breaks through the last range of North German hills and into the plain of Lower Saxony. The tourist offices in the area can give you good tips on where to find nearby trails. A book entitled *Weserbergland. Rother Wanderführer,* by Ulrich Tubbesing, describes 50 selected walks in the area, several of them lasting two or more days. It's available at area bookstores.

Lodging

Make reservations well in advance if you plan to visit during the summer. Though it's one of the less-traveled tourist routes in Germany, the main points of the Fairy-Tale Road are popular. Hannover is particularly busy during trade fair times.

CATEGORY	COST*
$$$$	over €225
$$$	€150–€225
$$	€75–€150
$	under €75

**All prices are for two people in a double room, including tax and service.*

Exploring the Fairy-Tale Road

This isn't a route for travelers in a hurry. The road extends about half the length of Germany, from the banks of the Main River, which marks the border between northern and southern Germany, to the North Sea ports of Bremen and Bremerhaven. The diverse regions have been linked together for the benefit of tourism—to highlight the region's connection with the Grimm brothers and their stories. Some towns on the journey—Bremerhaven and Hanau, for example—are modern, while others, such as Steinau an der Strasse, Hannoversch-Münden, and Hameln, might have stepped right out of a Grimm story.

Numbers in the text correspond to numbers in the margin and on the Fairy-Tale Road map.

Great Itineraries

The itineraries below assume you'll be starting off from Frankfurt, Germany's transportation hub. You could also approach the Fairy-Tale Road from Hamburg in the north.

IF YOU HAVE 3 DAYS

You won't get much farther than the first stretch of the route, but that's enough for an introduction to the influence of the region on the Grimm brothers. Skip downtown **Hanau** ① altogether and begin with **Schloss Philippsruhe,** the oldest French-style baroque palace east of the Rhine, and the spa district of **Wilhelmsbad,** where European royalty and aristocrats once took the waters. Make **Gelnhausen** ② your next stop, for a visit to the remains of Barbarossa's greatest castle. Plan an overnight stay at the **Romantisches Hotel Burg Mühle** or at least dine in its restaurant. Devote your second day to exploring **Steinau an der Strasse** ③, where the Grimm brothers spent much of their childhood, and then continue on to **Fulda** ④, which has an impressive bishop's palace and cathedral.

IF YOU HAVE 5 DAYS

Follow the itinerary described above but include a short stop in **Hanau** ①. On your third day proceed north of Fulda, calling at the medieval towns of **Lauterbach, Alsfeld,** and Marburg, all of which are perfect settings for Grimm tales. Spend the night in **Kassel** ⑥ and try to catch the sunset from the heights of the Wilhelmshöhe. On the fourth day, traverse the valley of the Fulda River to where it meets the Werra to form the Weser, at **Hannoversch-Münden** ⑦, which claimed a place on geographer Alexander von Humboldt's list of the world's most beautiful towns. Follow the lazily winding Weser northward now, making a short detour to **Göttingen** ⑧ for lunch in one of the student taverns in this busy university city. Try to fit in an overnight stay at Sleeping Beauty's Castle in **Sababurg** ⑨, half hidden in the depths of the densely wooded Reinhardswald. On the fifth day return to the Weser River valley road and find time for stops at **Bad Karlshafen** ⑩, **Höxter** ⑪, and **Bodenwerder** ⑫ to explore their streets of half-timber houses, examples of the Weser Renaissance style of building. End your trip at **Hameln** ⑬, the Pied Piper's town.

IF YOU HAVE 7 DAYS

After the five-day itinerary described above, leave the Fairy-Tale Road at Hameln for a detour to **Hannover** ⑭–⑳, which has a magnificent royal park. An overnight stay in Hannover will give you the opportunity to enjoy some nightlife after the tranquillity of much of the Weser Valley route. Or you can postpone that amusement until **Bremen** ㉓, 110 km (68 mi) northwest. Bremen is the northernmost frontier of the Grimm brothers' influence, represented by several statues of the donkey, dog, cat, and rooster of the Bremen town musicians fable.

Fairy-Tale Road

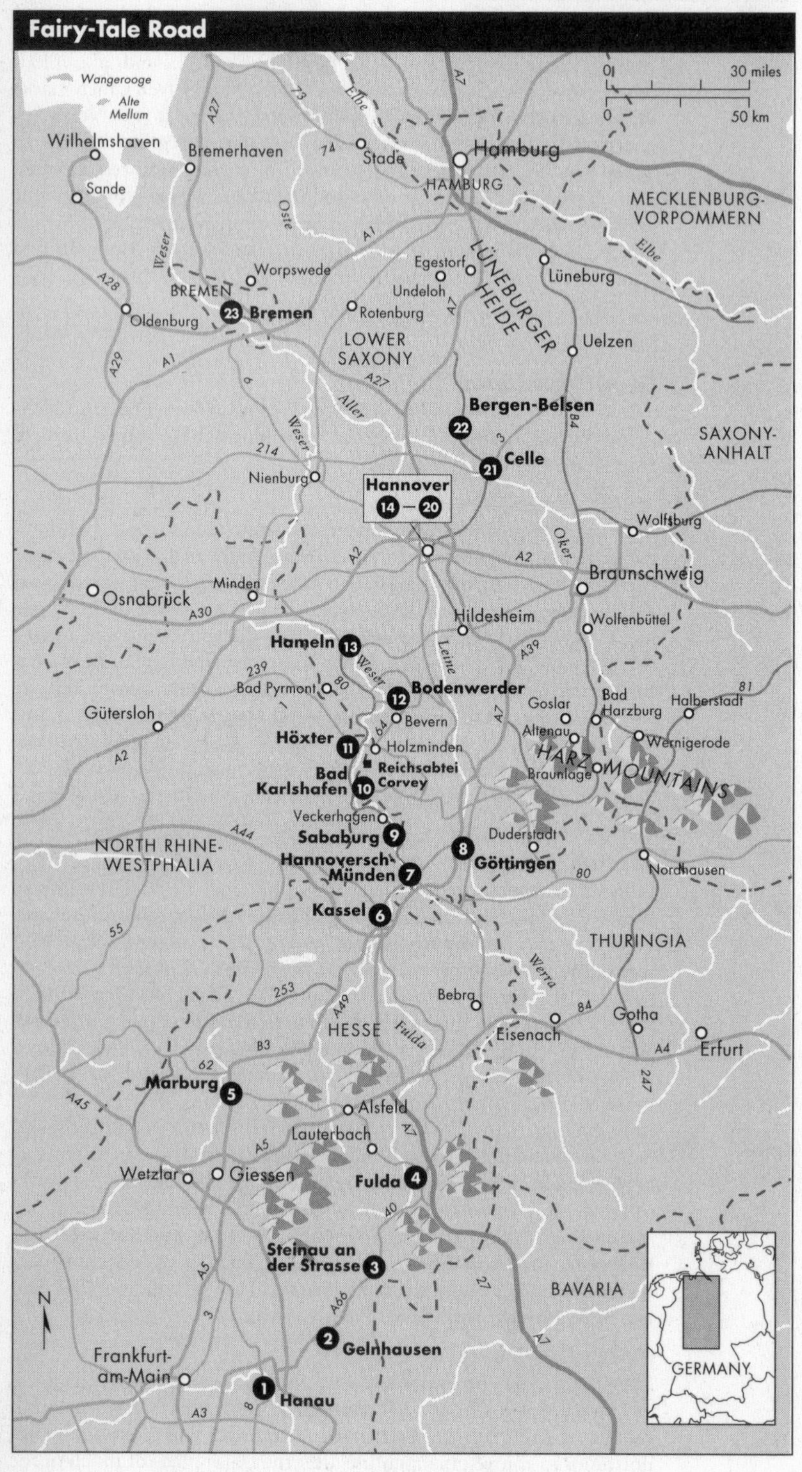

It would be a shame to travel all this way without venturing the final 66 km (40 mi) to the seaport of **Bremerhaven,** which has Germany's largest maritime museum.

When to Tour the Fairy-Tale Road

Summer is the ideal time to travel through this varied landscape, although in spring you'll find the river valleys carpeted in the season's first flowers, while in fall the sleepy current of the Weser is often blanketed in mist; both sights linger in the mind. Travel the Weser Valley road early in the morning or late in the afternoon, when the light has a softening touch on the river.

HESSE

The first portion of the Fairy-Tale Road, from Hanau to Kassel, lies within the state of Hesse. Frankfurt, the gateway to the state, is less than a half hour west of the road's starting point in Hanau.

Hanau

1 *16 km (10 mi) east of Frankfurt.*

The Fairy-Tale Road begins in "once upon a time" fashion at Hanau, the town where the brothers were born: Jacob in 1785, Wilhelm a year later. Although Grimm fans will want to start their pilgrimage here, Hanau is now a traffic-congested suburb of Frankfurt, with post–World War II buildings that are not particularly attractive. Hanau was almost completely obliterated by wartime bombing raids, and there's little of the Altstadt (Old Town) that the Grimm brothers would recognize now.

Hanau's main attraction can be reached only on foot—the **Nationaldenkmal Brüder Grimm** (Brothers Grimm Memorial) in the Neustädter Marktplatz. The bronze memorial, erected in 1898, is a larger-than-life-size statue of the brothers, one seated, the other leaning on his chair, the two of them pondering an open book—a fitting pose for these scholars who unearthed so many medieval myths and legends, earning their reputation as the fathers of the fairy tale.

The solid bulk of Hanau's 18th-century **Rathaus** (town hall) stands behind the Grimm brothers statue. Every day at noon its bells play tribute to another of the city's famous sons, the composer Paul Hindemith (1895–1963), by chiming out one of his canons. On Wednesday and Saturday mornings the Rathaus is the backdrop for the largest street market in the state of Hesse. ✉ *Marktpl. 14.*

The **Altes Rathaus** (Old Town Hall), behind the Rathaus, dominates a corner that has been faithfully reconstructed. This handsome 16th-century Renaissance building has two half-timber upper stories weighted down by a steep slate roof. Today it's a museum. Known as the Deutsches Goldschmiedehaus (German Goldsmiths' House), it has both permanent and temporary exhibitions of the craft, contemporary and historical, of the goldsmith and silversmith. ✉ *Altstädter Markt 6,* ☎ *06181/295–430.* 🎟 *Free.* ⏲ *Tues.–Sun. 10–noon and 2–5.*

The baroque **Schloss Philippsruhe** (Palace of Philipp's Rest) on the bank of the Main River in the suburb of Kesselstadt (Bus 1 will take you there in 10 minutes) has much more than Grimm exhibits. Philippsruhe might remind you of Versailles, although its French-trained architect, Julius Ludwig Rothweil, planned it along the lines of another palace in the Paris area, the much smaller Clagny Palace. Count Philipp Reinhard von Hanau laid the cornerstone in 1701. He didn't enjoy its riverside peace for long, however; he died less than three months after moving in. Historical Hanau treasures, including a priceless collection of faience, are on display in the palace museum, as are exhibits of 17th-century Dutch paintings, silver and cast iron crafts, and cardboard toy theaters popular in the 19th century. A café with a terrace overlooks the Main.

In the early 19th century, following the withdrawal of the French from Hanau, the original formal gardens were replanned as an informal, English-style park. The contrast between the formal palace and informal wooded grounds is striking. Pause to study the entrance gate; its gilding was the work of Parisian masters. ✉ *Phillipsruher Allee 45,* ☎ *06181/20209,* WEB *www.museen-hanau.de/philippsruhe.* €1.50. ⏲ *Tues.–Sun. 11–6.*

A short bus ride west from the center of Hanau is its spa district, **Wilhelmsbad.** It was built at the end of the 18th century by Crown Prince Wilhelm von Hessen-Kassel at the site where two peasant women, out gathering herbs, discovered mineral springs. For a few decades Wilhelmsbad rivaled Baden-Baden as Germany's premier spa and fashionable playground. Then, about 100 years ago, the springs dried up, the casino closed, and Europe's wealthy and titled looked for other amusements. But this is still Grimm fairy-tale land, and Wilhelmsbad, the Sleeping Beauty–like spa, awoke from its slumber in the 1960s to become a rejuvenated resort. Today you'll find baroque buildings and bathhouses; informal, English-style parkland; riding stables; five taverns and restaurants; and one of Germany's loveliest golf courses laid out where the leisure classes once hunted pheasants.

The spa's Arkadenbau (arcade) contains the **Hessisches Puppenmuseum** (Hesse Doll Museum), one of Germany's largest doll museums, with examples dating back 2,000 years. ✉ *Parkpromenade 4,* ☎ *06181/86212.* €2.50. ⏲ *Tues.–Sun. 10–noon and 2–5.*

Dining and Lodging

$$ **Golfhotel.** An occasional "fore" heard from the neighboring golf course or birdsong coming from the backyard woods are the only sounds likely to disturb you at this rural retreat on the edge of the Wilhelmsbad park. Nonsporting types relax at the friendly bar or, in warm weather, on the outside terrace (overlooking the golf links, of course). The hotel's da Enzo restaurant ($$$–$$$$) serves excellent Italian cuisine. There are only seven rooms, so it's essential to book in advance. ✉ *Wilhelmsbader Allee 32, D–63454,* ☎ *06181/99550,* FAX *06181/87722. 7 rooms. Restaurant, café, bar, no a/c, cable TV, meeting rooms, some pets allowed. AE, DC, MC, V.*

Gelnhausen

2 *20 km (12 mi) northeast of Hanau, 35 km (21 mi) northeast of Frankfurt.*

At Gelnhausen you'll find an island in the sleepy little Kinzig River with the remains of **Burg Barbarossa,** a castle that may well have stimulated the imagination of the Grimm brothers. Emperor Friedrich I—known as Barbarossa, or Red Beard—built the castle in this idyllic spot in the 12th century; in 1180 it was the scene of the first all-German Imperial Diet, a gathering of princes and ecclesiastical leaders. Although on an island, the castle was hardly designed as a defensive bastion and was accordingly sacked in the Thirty Years' War. Today only parts of the russet walls and colonnaded entrance remain. Still, stroll beneath the castle's ruined ramparts on its water site, and you'll get a tangible impression of the medieval importance of the court of Barbarossa. ✉ *Burgstr. 14,* ☎ *06051/3805.* €1.80. ⏲ *Mar.–Oct., Tues.–Sun. 10–5; Nov.–Dec. and Feb., Tues.–Sun. 10–4. Closed Jan.*

The **Hexenturm** (Witches Tower), a grim prison, remains from the time when Gelnhausen was the center of a paranoiac witch-hunt in the late 16th century; dozens of women were burned at the stake or thrown—bound hand and foot—into the Kinzig River. Suspects were held in the Hexenturm of the town battlements. Today it houses a bloodcurdling collection of medieval torture instruments. A visit to the tower is only possible as part of a weekly summer season tour of the town, beginning at the Rathaus. The tour, which costs €5, also includes a tour of Burg Barbarossa. ✉ *Am Fretzenstein.* ⏲ *May–Oct., tour Sun. at 2:30.*

Dining and Lodging

$$ ✕🏨 **Romantisches Hotel Burg Mühle.** *Mühle* means "mill," and this hotel was once the tithe mill of the neighboring castle, delivering flour to the community until 1948. In the restaurant ($–$$$) the mill wheel churns away as you eat. Ask for one of the cozy rooms in the oldest part of the hotel. ✉ *Burgstr. 2, D–63571,* ☏ *06051/82050,* FAX *06051/820–554,* WEB *www.burgmuehle.de. 41 rooms. Restaurant, bar, no a/c, cable TV, gym, massage, sauna, no-smoking rooms. DC, MC, V.*

Steinau an der Strasse

❸ *30 km (18 mi) northeast of Gelnhausen, 65 km (40 mi) northeast of Frankfurt.*

For clear evidence of its formative influence on the Brothers Grimm, you need only travel to the little town of Steinau—full name Steinau an der Strasse (Steinau "on the road," referring to an old trade route between Frankfurt and Leipzig). Here Father Grimm served as local magistrate and the Grimm brothers spent much of their childhood. They were preschoolers on arrival and under 12 when they left after their father's untimely death.

Steinau dates from the 13th century and is typical of villages in the region. Marvelously preserved half-timber houses are set along cobblestone streets; imposing castles bristle with towers and turrets. In its woodsy surroundings you can well imagine encountering Little Red Riding Hood, Snow White, or Hansel and Gretel. A major street is named after the brothers; the building where they lived is now known as the "Brothers Grimm House."

★ **Schloss Steinau** (Steinau Castle), straight out of a Grimm fairy tale, stands at the top of the town. Originally an early medieval fortress, it was rebuilt in Renaissance style between 1525 and 1558 and first used by the counts of Hanau as their summer residence, later to guard the increasingly important trade route between Frankfurt and Leipzig. It's not difficult to imagine the young Grimm boys playing in the shadow of its great gray walls or venturing into the encircling dry moat.

The castle houses a **Grimm Museum,** one of two in Steinau. This one exhibits the family's personal effects, including portraits of the Grimm relatives, the family Bible, an original copy of the Grimms' dictionary (the first in the German language), and all sorts of mundane things such as spoons and drinking glasses. Climb the tower for a breathtaking view of Steinau and the countryside. ☏ *06663/6843.* 🎫 *€2, tour of castle and museum €3.25, tower €1.* ⏲ *Mar.–Sept., Tues.–Thurs. and weekends 10–5; Oct.–mid-Dec., Tues.–Thurs. and weekends 10–4.*

The **Steinauer Marionettentheater** (Steinau Marionette Theater) is in the castle's former stables and portrays Grimm fairy tales and other children's classics. Performances are held most weekends at 3. ✉ *Am Kumpen 2,* ☏ *06663/245.* 🎫 *€5.*

★ The carefully restored **Brüder-Grimm-Haus,** where the brothers lived as children and where their father had his office, is the only Grimm residence that's still extant. Other Grimm houses, in Hanau and Kassel, were destroyed during World War II. The house is a few hundred yards from the castle and contains a museum devoted to the Grimms. Among the exhibits are books and pictures, some dating from their time, plus reminders of the Grimms' work as lexicographers. ✉ *Brüder-Grimm-Str. 80,* ☎ *06663/7605.* 🎟 *€2.* ⏲ *Mar.–Dec., daily 2–5.*

The Gothic church of **St. Catherine** (✉ Am Kumpen), where the Grimm brothers' grandfather Friedrich was parson, stands in front of the castle in Steinau's ancient market square. In the square's center, the **Märchenbrunnen** (Fairy-Tale Fountain) dates only from 1985, but its timeless design blends well with the rest of the town.

The 16th-century **Rathaus** has six bronze figures on its white stucco facade; they represent a cross section of 16th-century Steinau's population—from the builder who helped construct the town to the mother and child who continue its traditions. ✉ *Brüder-Grimm-Str. 70,* ☎ *06663/96310.*

Erlebnispark Steinau an der Strasse (Steinau an der Strasse Amusement Park), one of the region's largest leisure parks, is 3 km (2 mi) south of Steinau. It has a small zoo, fairground rides, and a "summer toboggan run." There's a restaurant, too. The very reasonably priced ticket covers all the attractions and as many toboggan rides as kids desire. ✉ *Landstr. 3196,* ☎ *06663/6889.* 🎟 *€7.* ⏲ *Apr.–Oct., daily 9–6.*

A 3-km (2-mi) detour north of Steinau brings you to the **Teufelshöhlen** (Devil's Caves). The caves are 2½ million years old and have two immense chambers, the *Dom* (cathedral) and *Kapelle* (chapel). Weird stalactite formations have accumulated over the millennia, including one in the shape of a giant beehive. ✉ *Landstr. 3179,* ☎ *06663/96310.* 🎟 *€1.50.* ⏲ *Easter–June, Sat. 1–7, Sun. 10–7; July–Oct., weekdays 1–5, Sat. 1–7, Sun. 10–7.*

Dining and Lodging

$ ✕🏨 **Brathähnchenfarm.** All meat here is charcoal-grilled, something your nose will tell you the minute you step into the cheery hotel-restaurant. The name "Roast Chicken Farm" tells you right away what the specialty is, but lamb or pork kebabs, spare ribs, and other grilled delicacies can also be had. Many of the rooms face the surrounding forest. ✉ *Im Ohl, D–36396,* ☎ *06663/961–228,* FAX *06663/1579. 15 rooms. Restaurant, bowling. V.*

$ 🏨 **Weisses Ross.** It may be a simple inn, but you can sleep within its gnarled walls in the knowledge that the Grimm brothers dined and imbibed in its tavern almost 200 years ago. Rooms facing the street have views of ancient buildings but suffer from traffic noise. ✉ *Brüder-Grimm-Str. 48, D–36396,* ☎ *06663/5804. 7 rooms, 5 with shower. No a/c, no room phones, no room TVs, meeting room. No credit cards.*

Shopping

The Steinau area was renowned for centuries as a pottery center, and in the 1880s the town had 40 potteries. Though none remain in business today, **Hans Krüger** (Hans Krüger Kunsttöpferei; ✉ Ringstr. 52, ☎ 06663/6413) set up shop several years ago and carries on the tradition with historical pieces in addition to modern ones. Official records from 1391 mention the tradition in the neighboring village of Marjoss, 12 km (7 mi) south of Steinau, where two potteries still function. Bernhard Breitenberger's **Bauerntöpferei** (✉ Distelbachstr. 24, Marjoss, ☎ 06660/1224) prides itself on traditional Hessian pottery modeled on old pieces. It's especially known for its *Bauerntopf* (farmer's pot) with two handles and a screw top, formerly used to carry soup and coffee to the fields. The **Georg Ruppert family** (✉ Brückenauer Str. 21, Marjoss, ☎ 06660/304) makes traditional Marjoss pottery.

En Route Gelnhausen and Steinau an der Strasse both lie on the German Half-Timber Road (Deutsche Fachwerkstrasse). Towns with historic half-timber buildings make up the route, which stretches from Stade, near Hamburg, to Erbach in the Odenwald and meets the Fairy-Tale Road at several points. A map and brochure can be obtained from the **Deutsche Fachwerkstrasse** (✉ Propstei Johannesberg, D–36041 Fulda, ☎ 0661/43680, FAX 0661/9425–0366, WEB www.fachwerkstrasse.de).

Fulda

❹ *32 km (20 mi) northeast of Steinau an der Strasse, 100 km (62 mi) northeast of Frankfurt.*

The episcopal city of Fulda is a treasure trove of baroque architecture and worth a detour off the Fairy-Tale Road. It also has a half-timber Old Town where the streets are so narrow and twisty that it can be served only by a tiny bus, the Transity, which can be stopped at the wave of a hand. The city's grandest example of baroque design is the immense **Stadtschloss** (City Palace). This great collection of buildings began as a Renaissance palace in the early 17th century and was transformed into its present baroque splendor a century later by Johann Dientzenhofer. Much of the palace is used as municipal offices, but you can visit the apartments of the prince-abbots. The **Fürstensaal** (Princes' Hall), on the second floor, provides a breathtaking display of baroque decorative artistry, with ceiling paintings by the 18th-century Bavarian artist Melchior Steidl and fabric-clad walls. Concerts are regularly held here (contact the city tourist office in the palace for program details, ☎ 0661/102–346). The palace also has permanent displays of the faience for which Fulda was once famous, as well as some fine Fulda porcelain.

Also worth seeing is the **Spiegelsaal** with its many tastefully arranged mirrors. Pause at the windows of the Grünes Zimmer (Green Chamber) to take in the view across the palace park to the **Orangerie,** a large garden with summer-flowering shrubs and plants. If you have time after your palace tour, stroll over for a visit. There's a pleasant café on the first floor. ✉ *Schlossstr.* 🎫 *€2; €2.50 with guided tour.* ⏲ *Mon.–Thurs. 10–6, Fri. 2–6.*

The **Dom** (cathedral), Fulda's 18th-century cathedral with tall twin spires, stands across the broad boulevard that borders the palace park. The cathedral was built by Dientzenhofer on the site of an 8th-century basilica, which at the time was the largest church north of the Alps. The basilica accommodated the ever-growing number of pilgrims who converged on Fulda to pray at the grave of the martyred St. Boniface, the "Apostle of the Germans." A black alabaster bas-relief depicting his death marks the martyr's grave in the crypt. The **Cathedral Museum** (🎫 €2.10; ⏲ Apr.–Oct., Tues.–Sat. 10–5:30, Sun. 12:30–5:30; Nov.–Dec. and Feb.–Mar., Tues.–Sat. 10–12:30 and 1:30–4, Sun. 12:30–4) contains a document bearing St. Boniface's writing, along with several other treasures, including Lucas Cranach the Elder's fine 16th-century painting of Christ and the Adulteress (who looks very comely in her velvet Renaissance costume). ✉ *Dompl.* ⏲ *Apr.–Oct., weekdays 10–6, Sat. 10–3, Sun. 1–6; Nov.–Mar., weekdays 10–5, Sat. 10–3, Sun. 1–6.*

The **Vonderau Museum** is housed in the former Jesuit seminary. Its exhibits chart the cultural and natural history of Fulda and eastern Hesse. A popular section of the museum is its **planetarium,** with a variety of shows, including one for children. Since it has only 35 seats an early reservation is advisable. You get a unique impression of wandering alone through the stars to the sound of music. Performances take place Thursday at 7, Friday at 5 and 8, Saturday at 3 and 8, and Sunday at 3. ✉ *Jesuitenpl. 2,* ☎ *0661/928–3510,* WEB *www.fulda.com/fis/museen.* *Museum €2, planetarium €2.50.* ⏲ *Tues.–Sun. 10–6.*

The **Michaelskirche** (Church of St. Michael) is one of Germany's oldest churches, built in the 9th century along the lines of the Church of the Holy Sepulchre in Jerusalem. It has a harmony and dignity that equal the majesty of the baroque facade of the neighboring Dom. ✉ *Michaelsberg 1.*

The **Rathaus** (city hall) is quite possibly the finest town hall in this part of the country. The particularly delicate half-timbering separates the arcaded first floor from the steep roof and its incongruous but charming battery of small steeples. It can only be viewed from the outside. ✉ *Schlossstr. 1.*

If you need a break from cultural pursuits, head to the **Gokart Bahn** (Go-Cart Track) on the southern outskirts of Fulda. Hop into one of the 5.5 HP Honda machines and navigate the 11 curves of an 1,320-ft-long indoor track. A special "top grip" surface keeps you safely on the piste. It's expensive fun, but where else can you play at being Schumacher for that price? ✉ *Frankfurter Str. 142,* ☎ *0661/402–053.* *€9.50 per ride.* ⏲ *Mon.–Thurs. 3–11, Fri. 3 PM–midnight, Sat. 1 PM–midnight, Sun. 10 AM–11 PM.*

Dining and Lodging

$–$$$ ✕ **Zum Stiftskämmerer.** This former episcopal treasurer's home is now a charming tavern-restaurant, its menu packed with local fare prepared with imagination. A four-course menu priced around €30 is an excellent value, although à la carte dishes can be ordered for as little as €5. Try the *Schlemmertöpfchen,* a delicious (and very filling) combination of pork, chicken breast, and venison steak. ✉ *Kämmerzeller Str. 10,* ☎ *0661/52369. AE, MC, V. Closed Tues.*

$$$–$$$$ ★ **Romantik Hotel Goldener Karpfen.** Fulda is famous for its baroque buildings, and this hotel is a short walk from the finest of them. The hotel, too, dates from the baroque era but has a later facade. Inside it's been renovated to a high standard of comfort. Afternoon coffee in the tapestry-upholstered chairs of the hotel's lounge is one of Fulda's delights, while dining in the elegant restaurant, with linen tablecloths, Persian rugs, and subdued lighting, is another. ✉ *Simpliciusbrunnen 1, D–36037,* ☎ *0661/86800,* FAX *0661/868–0100,* WEB *www.hotel-goldener-karpfen.com. 55 rooms. Restaurant, Weinstube, no a/c in some rooms, in-room data ports, cable TV, gym, sauna, meeting rooms, some pets allowed (fee), no-smoking rooms. AE, DC, MC, V.*

$$$ **Maritim Hotel am Schlossgarten.** This is the luxurious showpiece of the Maritim chain, housed in an 18th-century baroque building overlooking Fulda Palace Park. Chandeliers and oil paintings maintain the historic style, which contrasts with the hotel's modern atrium. The historic atmosphere of the grand old building, however, extends to the basement foundations, where you can dine beneath centuries-old vaulted arches in the Dianakeller restaurant. Many of the rooms have balconies or terraces with views over the park. ✉ *Paulusspromenade 2, D–36037,* ☎ *0661/2820,* FAX *0661/282–499,* WEB *www.maritim.de. 113 rooms, 2 suites. Restaurant, café, bar, no a/c, cable TV, indoor pool, sauna, some pets allowed (fee). AE, DC, MC, V.*

$$ **Hotel Kurfürst.** Behind a baroque facade, this first-class hotel maintains the charm of the original historic house. It's in the heart of the Old Town, within easy walking distance of all attractions. ✉ *Schlossstr. 2, D–36037,* ☎ *0661/83390,* FAX *0661/833–9339,* WEB *www.kurfuerst-fulda.de. 22 rooms. Restaurant, bar, no a/c, in-room data ports, cable TV, meeting rooms, some pets allowed (fee), no-smoking rooms. AE, DC, MC, V.*

$ **Zum Kronhof.** This homey hotel also vies for "funkiest decor" around. There's an array of clashing colors in every room, but it's clean and friendly. You're right behind the Dom so you won't need an alarm clock. A room is usually available, but call ahead just to be safe. ✉ *Am Kronhof 2, D–36037,* ☎ *0661/74147,* FAX *0661/74147. 22 rooms. Restaurant, café, no a/c, no room phones, cable TV, meeting rooms, free parking, some pets allowed, no-smoking rooms. No credit cards.*

Nightlife and the Arts

Chamber-music concerts are held regularly from September through May in the chandelier-hung splendor of the bishop's palace. One wing of the palace is now the city's main theater. Organ recitals are given regularly in Fulda's Dom. Call 0661/102–1814 for details on all of Fulda's **cultural events.**

En Route Kassel is the next major stop on the road north. If you're in a hurry, you can reach Kassel from Fulda in less than an hour via A–7. But the Fairy-Tale Road gives autobahns a wide berth, so if you have time, take B–254 into the Vogelsberg Mountains via Grossenluder to Lauterbach, some 25 km (15 mi) northeast of Fulda.

Lauterbach, a resort town of many medieval half-timber houses, has two castles—the **Riedesel** and the **Eisenbach.** The town is the setting of a well-known folk song in which a little fellow complains of having lost his sock. (The lyrics never crossed the Atlantic, but the tune did, as "Oh Where, Oh Where Has My Little Dog Gone?") Lauterbach's garden gnomes are renowned, and are right up there with beer steins and cuckoo clocks as a beloved, folklorish, German export. These gnomes, made in all shapes and sizes by the firm of Heissner Keramik, stand out on lawns at night with lighted lanterns, direct choruses of birds with batons, or fish in goldfish ponds. There's a selection of the gnomes, including Grimm characters, at **Hagebaumarkt** (✉ Am Sportpl. 2, ☎ 06641/96700) in nearby Angersbach.

The Fairy-Tale Road continues north to **Alsfeld** (34 km [21 mi] northwest of Fulda), notable for its beautifully preserved half-timber houses on narrow, winding cobbled streets. The jewel of Alsfeld—and one of Germany's showpieces—is the **Altes Rathaus** (Old Town Hall), built in 1512. Its facade, combining a ground floor of stone arcades; half-timber upper reaches; and a dizzyingly steep, top-heavy slate roof punctured by two pointed towers shaped like witches' hats—would look right at home in Walt Disney World. To get an unobstructed snapshot of this remarkable building (which is closed to the public), avoid the Marktplatz on Tuesday and Friday, when market stalls clutter the square.

The route next follows the little Schwalm River through a region so inextricably linked with the Grimm fairy tales that it's known as Rotkäppchenland (Little Red Riding Hood Country). **Schwalmstadt** is the capital of the area, and during the town's many festival days, local people deck themselves out in traditional folk costumes. You'll notice that the women's costume includes a little red cap *(Rotkäppchen)* covering a topknot. This is what gave Little Red Riding Hood her name.

Marburg

❺ *60 km (35 mi) northwest of Fulda.*

"I think there are more steps in the streets than in the houses." That is how Jacob Grimm described the half-timber hillside town of Marburg. He and his brother Wilhelm studied at the town's famous university from 1802 to 1805.

Marburg rises steeply from the Lahn River to the spectacular castle that crowns the hill, 335 ft up. Many of the winding, crooked "streets" are indeed stone staircases, and nowadays an elevator can transport you from the level of the river to the marketplace. Several of the hillside houses have a back door five stories above the front door.

And the architecture is stunning. A great deal of money went into restoring the buildings to their original appearance. Half-timbering was out of fashion for most of the centuries since the 1600s, and the building facades had been stuccoed over. Much of the old city is closed to automobile traffic, which is just as well because the cobblestone streets are slippery when wet, especially on a steep hillside. One of the main streets of the old city is named Barfussstrasse (Barefoot Street) because it led to a Franciscan monastery, the residents of which were sworn to humility and poverty.

The university and its students are the main influence on the town's social life, which pulses through the many street cafés, restaurants, and student hangouts around the marketplace. Because so many of the streets are traffic-free, the whole area is filled with outdoor tables when the weather cooperates.

For those who prefer nature to history the Lahn Valley is idyllic. There are paths for biking and hiking, and the river itself can be explored by paddleboat.

Marburg's most important building is the **Elisabethkirche** (St. Elizabeth Church; ✉ Elisabethstr. 3), which marks the burial site of St. Elizabeth (1207–31), the town's favorite daughter. She was a Hungarian princess, betrothed at 4 and married at 12 to the landgrave Ludwig IV of Thuringia. She was widowed in 1228 when her husband fell in one of the Crusades and thereafter gave up all worldly pursuits. She moved to Marburg, founded a hospital, gave her wealth to the poor, and spent the rest of her very short life in poverty, caring for the sick and the aged. She is largely responsible for what Marburg became. Because of her selflessness she was made a saint only four years after her death. The Teutonic Knights built the Elisabethkirche, which quickly became the goal of pilgrimages, enabling the city to prosper. You can visit the shrine in the sacristy that once contained her bones, a masterpiece of the goldsmith's art. The church is a veritable museum of religious art, full of statues and frescoes.

Dining and Lodging

$ ✕ **Cafe Vetter.** This has unquestionably the most spectacular view in a town that's famed for its panoramas. The outdoor terrace is pleasant in good weather, but there's also a glassed-in terrace and two floors of dining rooms with windows facing the valley. It bakes its own cakes and is known for its literary Sundays. ✉ *Reitg. 4,* ☎ *06421/25888. No credit cards. No dinner.*

$$ ✕🏨 **Sorat Hotel Marburg.** This rather unconventional luxury hotel is at the river level, just across the street from the elevator to the marketplace. The color scheme is orange, apricot, and yellow, contrasted with fiery red tables and upholstered furniture. Its Tartagua Restaurant ($–$$$), with bar, terrace, and beer cellar, has become a hip meeting place for those who can afford it. In addition to the usual rolls, eggs, and sausages, the breakfast buffet includes smoked salmon and champagne. ✉ *Pilgrimstein 29, D–35037,* ☎ *06421/9180,* FAX *06421/918–444,* WEB *www.sorat-hotels.com/marburg. 143 rooms, 3 suites. Restaurant, bar, beer garden, in-room data ports, minibars, cable TV,* *exercise equipment, gym, sauna, meeting room, parking (fee), some pets allowed, no-smoking rooms. AE, DC, MC, V.*

Kassel

6 *100 km (62 mi) northeast of Marburg.*

The Brothers Grimm spent time in Kassel as librarians at the court of the king of Westphalia, Jerome Bonaparte (Napoléon's youngest brother), and for the elector of Kassel. In researching stories and legends, their best source was not books but storyteller Dorothea Viehmann, who was born in the Knallhütte tavern, which still is in business in nearby Baunatal.

The **Brüder Grimm Museum,** in the center of Kassel, occupies five rooms of the Palais Bellevue, where the brothers once lived and worked. Exhibits include furniture, memorabilia, letters, manuscripts, and editions of their books, as well as paintings, watercolors, etchings, and drawings by Ludwig Emil Grimm, a third brother and a graphic artist of note. ✉ *Palais Bellevue, Schöne Aussicht 2,* ☎ *0561/777–550.* 🎟 *€3.* ⏲ *Daily 10–4:30.*

The 18th-century **Schloss Wilhelmshöhe** served as a royal residence from 1807 to 1813, when Jerome was king of Westphalia. Later it became the summer residence of the German emperor Wilhelm II. The great palace, with a collection of antique furniture, stands at the end of the 5-km-long (3-mi-long) Wilhelmshöher Allee, an avenue that runs straight as an arrow from one side of the city to the other.

The giant 18th-century **statue of Hercules** that crowns the Wilhelmshöhe heights is an astonishing sight, standing on a massive red-stone octagon. At 2:30 PM on Sunday and Wednesday from mid-May through September, water gushes from a fountain beneath the statue, rushes down a series of cascades to the foot of the hill, and ends its precipitous journey in a 175-ft-high jet of water. It takes so long to accumulate enough water that the sight can be experienced only on those two days, on holidays, and on the first Saturday evening of June, July, August, and September. On those occasions the cascade is also floodlighted and the whole palace is illuminated by candlelight. You can climb the statue from within for a rewarding look over the entire city, spread out over the plain and bisected by the straight line of the Wilhelmshöher Allee. Tramline 1 runs from the city to the Wilhelmshöhe. A café lies a short walk from the statue, and there are several restaurants in the area. ✉ *Schlosspark 3,* ☎ *0561/93570.* 🎟 *€3.50.* ⏲ *Mar.–Oct., Tues.–Sun. 10–5; Nov.–Feb., Tues.–Sun. 10–4.*

The Wilhelmshöhe was laid out as a baroque park—Europe's largest palace grounds—its elegant lawns separating the city from the thick woods of the Habichtswald (Hawk Forest). It comes as something of a surprise to see the turrets of a romantic medieval castle, the **Löwenburg** (Lion Fortress), breaking the harmony. There are more surprises, for this is no true medieval castle but a fanciful, stylized copy of a Scottish castle, built 70 years after the Hercules statue that towers above it. The architect was a Kassel ruler who displayed an early touch of the mania later seen in the castle-building excesses of Bavaria's eccentric Ludwig II. The Löwenburg contains a collection of medieval armor and weapons, tapestries, and furniture. ✉ *Schloss Wilhelmshöhe,* ☎ *0561/935–7200.* 🎟 *€3.50, including tour.* ⏲ *Mar.–Oct., Tues.–Sun. 10–5; Nov.–Feb., Tues.–Sun. 10–4.*

Kassel's leading art gallery and the state art collection lie within the Wilhelmshöhe Palace as part of the **Staatliche Museen.** Its esteemed collection includes 11 Rembrandts as well as outstanding works by Rubens, Hals, Jordaens, Van Dyck, Dürer, Altdorfer, Cranach, and Baldung Grien. ✉ *Schloss Wilhelmshöhe,* ☎ *0561/93777,* WEB *www.museum-kassel.de.* 🎫 *€3.50; free Fri.* ⏲ *Tues.–Sun. 10–5.*

The **Deutsches Tapeten Museum,** (German Wallpaper Museum), the world's most comprehensive museum of wallpaper, has more than 600 exhibits tracing the art through the centuries. ✉ *Brüder-Grimm-Pl. 5,* ☎ *0561/78460,* WEB *www.museum-kassel.de.* 🎫 *€3.50; free Fri.* ⏲ *Tues.–Sun. 10–5.*

To the southeast, outside Hessisch-Lichtenau, is the **Hohe Meissner,** a high hill from which the Grimms' Mother Holle is said to have shaken out her featherbed, causing it to snow. Mother Holle, a good fairy, supposedly lives at the bottom of a pond on the Hohe Meissner.

Dining and Lodging

$$–$$$ ✕ **Autobahnraststätte Knallhütte.** This brewery-cum-inn, established in 1752, was the home of village storyteller Dorothea Viehmann. The Grimms got the best of their stories from her, including Little Red Riding Hood, Hansel and Gretel, and Rumpelstiltskin. Numerous reminders of the tavern's history begin with its name: the crack of a whip (*knall*) sounded the arrival of horse-drawn carriages struggling up the hill. You can sample the brewery's unique beers while enjoying the Knallhütte's menu, which includes a grill night with salad buffet on Thursday. ✉ *Baunatal,* ☎ *0561/492–076. MC, V.*

$–$$$ ✕ **Ratskeller.** Rustic German cuisine is served here within the embracing cellar vaults. The kitchen's North Hessian duck, fresh daily from the oven, is much beloved, as is its *Riesenbratwurst,* a 1½-ft-long coiled roast sausage, served with sauerkraut. ✉ *Obere Konigstr. 8,* ☎ *0561/15928. AE, DC, MC, V.*

$$ ✕🏨 **Hotel Gude.** This modern hotel is 10 minutes by public transportation from the city center. Rooms are spacious and come with marble bathrooms. The Pfeffermühlene ($–$$$$) is one of the region's finest restaurants, with an inventive international menu including German fare. The hotel is ideal for conferences, and has its own underground garage. ✉ *Frankfurter Str. 299, D–34134,* ☎ *0561/48050,* FAX *0561/480–5101,* WEB *www.hotel-gude.de. 84 rooms. Restaurant, café, bar, in-room data ports, in-room safes, minibars, refrigerator, cable TV, indoor pool, gym, massage, meeting room, parking, some pets allowed, no-smoking rooms. AE, DC, MC, V.*

$$–$$$$ 🏨 **City-Hotel.** Just a few minutes from the Rathaus, this city-center hotel is well integrated with its ancient surroundings. Rooms are stylishly decorated and furnished. ✉ *Wilhelmshöher Allee 38–42, D–34119,* ☎ *0561/72810,* FAX *0561/728–1199. 65 rooms. Restaurant, café, bar, no a/c in some rooms, in-room data ports, cable TV, sauna, some pets allowed (fee), no-smoking rooms. AE, DC, MC, V. Closed Christmas wk.*

$$$ 🏨 **Schlosshotel Wilhelmshöhe.** Set in the beautiful baroque Wilhelmshöhe Park, 5 km (3 mi) from town, this is no ancient palace but a contemporary hotel with a sleek gambling casino. Secure a window table in the elegant restaurant for a view of the park grounds. Sports facilities in the immediate vicinity include an 18-hole golf course, tennis courts, and horse stables. The park's palace is a two-minute walk away. ✉ *Schlosspark 8, D–34131,* ☎ *0561/30880,* FAX *0561/308–8428,* WEB *www.schlosshotel.com. 106 rooms, 7 suites. Restaurant, café, bar, no a/c, in-room data ports, cable TV, casino, meeting rooms, some pets allowed (fee), no-smoking rooms. AE, DC, MC, V.*

$ 🏨 **Hotel Lenz.** All rooms have a bath or shower in this clean and quiet hotel, which is somewhat out of the way. To get here take Tram 5 or 9 to Güterbahnhof Niederzwehren, then walk down Frankfurter

Strasse. ✉ *Frankfurter Str. 176, 34134,* ☎ *0561/43373,* FAX *0561/41188. 13 rooms. Restaurant, no a/c, no phones in some rooms, cable TV, bar, some pets allowed, free parking. No credit cards.*

Nightlife and the Arts

THE ARTS

Outdoor concerts are held in Wilhelmshöhe Park on Wednesday, Saturday, and Sunday afternoons from May through September. The Kasseler Musiktage (Kassel Music Days) at the end of October are devoted to music of the 20th century. The municipal orchestra gives classical concerts in the **Stadttheater** (✉ Friedrichspl. 15, ☎ 0561/10940).

Kassel has no fewer than 35 theater companies. The principal venues are the Schauspielhaus, the FRIZZ-Theater, the Stadthalle, and the Stadttheater. Call ☎ 0561/109–4222 for **program details** and tickets for all.

NIGHTLIFE

Kassel's pulsating nightlife is concentrated in the bars and discos of Friedrich-Ebert-Strasse. The **casino** (✉ Schlosspark 8, ☎ 0561/930–850) in the Schlosshotel Wilhelmshöhe provides a note of elegance with its gray-blue-silver decor and windows that afford a spectacular view of the city below. It's open daily 3 PM–3 AM. Admission is €5 for the main area's roulette and card games, and €1 for the slot machines.

Shopping

Kassel's chic **Königsgalerie** (✉ Obere Königstr. 39), a glass-roof atrium, is packed with boutiques, restaurants, and bars.

In the village of Immenhausen, just north of Kassel, a local glass museum, **Glasmuseum Immenhausen** (✉ Am Bahnhof 3, ☎ 05673/2060; 🎫 €2; ⏲ weekdays 9–5, Sat. 10–1, Sun. 10–5; Oct.–Apr., Sun. 1–5), exhibits work by German glassblowers; many of the pieces are for sale. The museum has an extensive collection of modern glass, but its centerpiece is work by the celebrated but now closed Immenhausen glass foundry, the Glashütte Süssmuth.

LOWER SAXONY

Lower Saxony (Niedersachsen), Germany's second-largest state after Bavaria, was formed from an amalgamation of smaller states in 1946. Its landscape is quite diverse, but the focus here is on the Weser River's course from Hannoversch-Münden, in the south, to its end in the North Sea at Bremenhaven. Between Hannoversch-Münden and Hameln is one of Germany's most haunting river roads (B–80 to Bad Karlshafen, B–83 the rest of the way), where the fast-flowing Weser snakes between green banks that hardly show where land ends and water begins. Standing sentinel along the banks are superb little towns, whose half-timber architecture has given rise to the expression "Weser Renaissance."

The states of Lower Saxony and Saxony-Anhalt share the Harz Mountains; *see* Saxony-Anhalt *in* Chapter 17 for more coverage of the region.

Hannoversch-Münden

★ ❼ *24 km (15 mi) north of Kassel, 150 km (93 mi) south of Hannover.*

This delightful town, seemingly untouched by the modern age, shouldn't be missed. In the 18th century the German scientist and explorer Alexander von Humboldt (1769–1859) included it on his short list of the world's most beautiful towns (Passau, in eastern Bavaria, was another choice). You'll have to travel a long way through Germany to find a grouping of half-timber houses (700 of them) as harmonious as these. A 650-year-old bridge over the Weser River leads into the old, walled settlement. The town is surrounded by forests and the Fulda and Werra rivers, which join and flow northward as the Weser River.

Much is made of the fact that the quack doctor to end all quacks died here. Dr. Johann Andreas Eisenbart (1663–1727) would be forgotten today if a ribald 19th-century drinking song hadn't had him shooting out aching teeth with a pistol, anesthetizing with a sledgehammer, and removing boulders from the kidneys. He was, as the song has it, a man who could make "the blind walk and the lame see." But this was libelous: Dr. Eisenbart was as good a doctor as any in his day, which admittedly isn't saying much. The town stages Eisenbart plays each summer and a Glockenspiel on the city hall depicts his feats. There's a statue of the doctor in front of his home at Langestrasse 79, and his grave is outside the St. Ägidien Church. For information on the Dr. Eisenbart plays, contact the **Touristik Naturpark Münden** (✉ Lotzestr. 2, ☎ 05541/75313, FAX 05541/75404, WEB www.hann.muenden.de).

Göttingen

8 *30 km (19 mi) northeast of Hannoversch-Münden, 110 km (68 mi) south of Hannover.*

Although Göttingen is not strictly on the Fairy-Tale Road, it is closely associated with the Brothers Grimm, for they served as professors and librarians at the city's university from 1830 to 1837.

The university dominates life in Göttingen, and most houses more than a century old bear plaques that link them to a famous student or professor. In a house now known as the **Bismarckhäuschen,** beyond the city's old defense wall, Otto von Bismarck, the Iron Chancellor and founder of the 19th-century German Empire, pored over his books as a 17-year-old law student. Bismarck was a reluctant tenant—he was banned from living within the city center because of his "riotous behavior" and fondness for wine. The Bismarckhäschen can be visited only by checking first with the city tourist office (☎ 0551/54000).

Among the delights of Göttingen are the **ancient taverns** where generations of students lifted their steins. Among the best known are the **Kleine Ratskeller** (✉ Judenstr. 30) and the **Zum Altdeutschen** (✉ Prinzenstr. 16). Don't be shy about stepping into either of these taverns or any of the others that catch your eye; the food and drink are inexpensive, and the welcome is invariably warm and friendly. Prinzenstrasse, by the way, is named after three English princes, sons of King George III, who lived on this street while studying in Göttingen from 1786 to 1791.

The statue of **Gänseliesel,** the little Goose Girl of German folklore, stands in the central market square, symbolizing the strong link between the students and their university city. The girl, according to the story, was a princess who was forced to trade places with a peasant, and the statue shows her carrying her geese and smiling shyly into the waters of a fountain. Above her pretty head is a charming wrought-iron art nouveau bower of entwined vines. The students of Göttingen contributed money toward the bronze statue and fountain in 1901 and gave it a ceremonial role: traditionally, graduates who earn a doctorate bestow a kiss of thanks upon Gänseliesel. Göttingen's citizens say she's the most-kissed girl in the world. There was a time, however, when the city fathers were none too pleased with this licentious practice, and in 1926 they banned the tradition. A student challenged the ban before a Berlin court but lost the case. Officially the ban still stands, although neither the city council nor the university takes any notice of it.

Behind the Gänseliesel statue is the **Altes Rathaus** (Old City Hall), begun in the 13th century but basically a part-medieval, part-Renaissance building. The bronze lion's-head knocker on the main door dates from early in the 13th century. Inside, the lobby's striking murals tell the city's story. Beneath the heavily beamed ceiling of the medieval council chamber, the council met, courts sat in judgment, visiting dignitaries were officially received, receptions and festivities were held, and traveling theater groups performed. ✉ *Markt 9,* ☎ *0551/499–800.* 🎫 *Free.* ⏲ *Apr.–Oct., weekdays 9:30–6, weekends 10–4; Nov.–Mar., weekdays 9:30–1, Sat. 10–1, closed Sun.*

In the streets around the Rathaus you'll find magnificent examples of Renaissance architecture. Many of these half-timber, low-gabled buildings house businesses that have been there for centuries. The **Ratsapotheke** (pharmacy) across from the Rathaus is one of the town's oldest buildings; medicines have been doled out there since 1322. ✉ *Weenderstr. 30,* ☎ *0551/57128.*

The 16th-century **Schrödersches Haus** (Schröder House), a short stroll from the Altes Rathaus up Weenderstrasse, is the most appealing storefront—with an ornate, half-timber front—you're likely to find in all Germany. A clothing store called the Camel Shop is inside. ✉ *Weenderstr. 62.*

The **Städtisches Museum** (City Museum) is in Göttingen's only noble home, a 16th-century palace. It charts the history of Göttingen and its university with exhibits of church art, glass objects, and Judaica, and has a valuable collection of antique toys and a reconstructed apothecary's shop. ✉ *Ritterplan 7–8,* ☎ *0551/400–2843.* 🎫 *€1.50.* ⏲ *Tues.–Fri. 10–5, weekends 11–5.*

Just to the east of Göttingen is the **Wilhelm Busch Mühle,** a rustic mill and museum honoring a man who could justifiably be called "the godfather of the comic strip." The mill, with a wheel that still turns, belonged to a friend of Busch's. The admission price includes a tour of the mill, in English if desired. There is a more extensive Busch Museum in Hannover. ✉ *Mühleng. 8, Ebergötzen,* ☎ *05507/7181.* 🎫 *€3.* ⏲ *Mon.–Sat. 9–1 and 2–5, Sun. 10–1 and 2–5. Closed Jan.*

Dining and Lodging

$$–$$$ ✕ **Historischer Rathskeller.** Dine in the vaulted underground chambers of Göttingen's Altes Rathaus and choose from a traditional menu with the friendly assistance of chef Peter Ollhof. ✉ *Altes Rathaus, Markt 9,* ☎ *0551/56433. AE, DC, MC, V.*

$–$$ ★ ✕ **Zum Schwarzen Bären.** The Black Bear is one of Göttingen's oldest tavern-restaurants, a 16th-century half-timber house that breathes history and hospitality. It's specialty is *Bärenpfanne,* a generous mixture of beef, pork, and lamb (but no bear meat), and its wide selection of fried potato dishes. ✉ *Kurzestr. 12,* ☎ *0551/58284. AE, DC, MC, V. Closed Mon. No dinner Sun.*

$$–$$$ 🏨 **Gebhards Hotel.** Though just across a busy road from the train station, this family-run hotel stands aloof and unflurried on its own grounds, a sensitively modernized 18th-century building that's something of a local landmark. Rooms are furnished in dark woods and floral prints highlighted by bowls of fresh flowers. The suites are particularly spacious, with completely separate bedrooms. ✉ *Goethe-Allee 22–23, D–37073,* ☎ *0551/49680,* FAX *0551/496–8110,* WEB *www.hotel-gebhards.de. 53 rooms, 7 suites. Restaurant, no a/c, in-room data ports, cable TV, hot tub, sauna, meeting rooms, some pets allowed, no-smoking rooms. AE, DC, MC, V.*

$ 🏨 **Hotel Beckmann.** The Beckmann family runs this pleasant and homey hotel with friendly efficiency. Rooms are furnished in a spare, modern style, with light woods and pastel shades. The hotel is 5 km (3 mi) out of town, with good bus links to downtown. ✉ *Ulrideshuser-Str. 44, D–37077 Göttingen-Nikolausberg,* ☎ *0551/209–080,* FAX *0551/209–0810,* WEB *www.hotel-beckmann.de. 27 rooms, 21 with bath or shower. No a/c, in-room data ports, cable TV, sauna, meeting rooms, some pets allowed (fee), no-smoking rooms. AE, DC, MC, V.*

$ 🏨 **Landgasthaus Lockemann.** If you like to walk and hike, consider this half-timber lodge at the edge of the Stadtwald (city forest). Locals descend on the friendly, country-style restaurant for hearty German cooking. To get there take Bus 10 from the Busbahnhof, direction Herberhausen, to the last stop, then walk left on Im Beeke. The trip will take 20 minutes. ✉ *Im Beeke 1, D–37075,* ☎ *0551/209–020,* FAX *0551/209–0250. 18 rooms, 7 with bath. Restaurant, bar, beer garden, no a/c, no phones in some rooms, cable TV, some pets allowed. No credit cards.*

Nightlife and the Arts

Göttingen's symphony orchestra presents about 20 concerts a year. In addition, the city has a nationally known boys choir and an annual Handel music festival in June. Call the tourist office for program details and tickets for all three.

Göttingen's elegant **Deutsches Theater** (☎ 0551/496–911), built in 1890, is known throughout Germany. It has four performing areas, including the large Grösse Bühne, with its two tiers of horseshoe-shape balconies, where much experimental theater is performed, and the intimate Keller with its cabaretlike performances. Outdoor performances of Grimm fairy tales are presented on a woodland stage at Bremke (10 km [6 mi] southeast of Göttingen, near Gleichen) on certain summer weekends. Check with the local tourist office for dates.

The old student taverns that crowd the downtown area are the focus of local nightlife, but for something more sophisticated try the **Blue Note** jazz and dance club (✉ Wilhelmspl. 3, ☎ 0551/46907). The **Outpost** dance club (✉ Königsallee 243, ☎ 0551/66251) occasionally has live bands.

En Route To pick up the Fairy-Tale Road where it joins the scenic Weser Valley Road, return to Hannoversch-Münden and head north on B–80. This is a beautiful route served by a local bus between Hannoversch-Münden and Bad Karlshafen. In the village of Veckerhagen take a left turn to the signposted Sababurg.

Sababurg

★ ❾ *10 km (6 mi) north of Göttingen, 100 km (62 mi) south of Hannover.*

Sababurg is home to the **Dornröschenschloss** (Sleeping Beauty's Castle). It stands just as the Grimm fairy tale tells us it did, in the depths of the densely wooded Reinhardswald, still inhabited by deer and wild boar. Sababurg was built in the 14th century by the archbishop of Mainz to protect a nearby pilgrimage chapel. Later it was destroyed and ultimately rebuilt as a turreted hunting lodge for the counts of Hesse. Today it is a fairly fancy hotel. Even if you don't stay the night, a drive to the castle is a highlight of the Fairy-Tale Road. There's a nominal fee to tour the grounds, which include a rose garden and ruins.

The **Tierpark Sababurg** is one of Europe's oldest wildlife refuges. Bison, red deer, wild horses, and all sorts of waterfowl populate the park. There's also a children's zoo. ✉ *Kasinoweg 22,* ☎ *05671/800–*

1251. 🎫 *Apr.–Nov. €4, Dec.–Mar. €3.50.* ⏲ *Apr.–Sept., daily 8–7; Oct. and Mar., daily 9–5; Nov.–Feb., daily 10–4.*

Dining and Lodging

$$–$$$ ★ ✕🏨 **Dornröschenschloss Sababurg.** The medieval fortress thought to have been the inspiration for the Grimm brothers' tale of *The Sleeping Beauty* is now a small luxury hotel snugly set in the castle walls and surrounded by a forest of oaks. Concerts and plays are held on the grounds in summer, and it is a popular place for weddings. The castle was built in 1334, but many of the palatial improvements came during the 17th and 18th centuries. Since 1960 the Koseck family has been enthusiastically welcoming guests to the hotel and showing them the magic of the area. The restaurant ($$–$$$) serves a fine haunch of venison in the autumn, and the fresh trout with a Riesling-based sauce in the spring is equally satisfying. ✉ *D–34369 Hofgeismar,* ☎ *05671/8080,* FAX *05671/808–200. 18 rooms. Restaurant, no a/c, bicycles, meeting rooms, some pets allowed (fee). AE, DC, MC, V.*

En Route A short distance over back roads is another hilltop castle hotel, **Trendelburg.** Legend has it that its tower is the one in which a wicked witch imprisoned Rapunzel. Since it had neither a door nor stairs, the witch, and eventually a handsome prince, could get to Rapunzel only by climbing her long, golden tresses. From Trendelburg follow more back roads to the Weser Valley riverside village of Oberweser. Turn left and take B–80 north.

Bad Karlshafen

❿ *42 km (26 mi) north of Hannoversch-Münden, 55 km (34 mi) northwest of Göttingen, 125 km (77 mi) south of Hannover.*

From the inland harbor of the pretty little spa of Bad Karlshafen, German troops of the state of Waldeck embarked to join the English forces in the American War of Independence. Flat barges took the troops down the Weser to Bremen, where they were shipped across the North Sea for the long voyage west. Many American families can trace their heritage to this small spa and the surrounding countryside.

Viewed from one of the benches overlooking the harbor, there's scarcely a building that's not in the imposing baroque style. The grand **Rathaus** (✉ Hafenpl. 8) behind you is the best example. Bad Karlshafen stands out in solitary splendor amid the simple Weser Renaissance style of other riverside towns.

Dining and Lodging

$$ ✕🏨 **Hotel Menzhausen.** The half-timber exterior of this 16th-century establishment in the small town of Uslar, 12 km (7 mi) east of the Weser River, is matched by the elegant interior of its comfortable restaurant ($–$$$). Ask for a guest room in the Mauerschlösschen, a luxurious extension that incorporates traditional Weser Renaissance design, such as half-timbering and carved beams. ✉ *Langestr. 12, D–37170 Uslar,* ☎ *05571/92230,* FAX *05571/922–330. 41 rooms. Restaurant, Weinstube, no a/c, in-room data ports, cable TV with movies, indoor pool, sauna, meeting room, some pets allowed (fee). V.*

$ ✕🏨 **Gaststätte-Hotel Weserdampfschiff.** You can step right from the deck of a Weser pleasure boat into the welcoming garden of this popular hotel-tavern. Fish from the river land straight into the tavern's frying pan. The rooms are snug; ask for one with a river view. The restaurant ($–$$$) is closed Monday. ✉ *Weserstr. 25, D–34385,* ☎ *05672/2425,* FAX *05672/8119. 14 rooms. Restaurant, no a/c, meeting rooms, some pets allowed. No credit cards.*

$ ✕🏨 **Hessischer Hof.** In the heart of town, this inn started as a tavern for the locals and now includes several comfortably furnished bedrooms. The restaurant ($–$$) serves good, hearty fare. Breakfast is included in the room price, or you may request half-pension. ✉ *Carlstr. 13–15, D–34385,* ☎ *05672/1059,* FAX *05672/2515,* WEB *www.hess-hof.de. 17 rooms. Restaurant, bar, no a/c, no room TVs, meeting rooms, some pets allowed. AE, MC, V.*

Shopping

There are some excellent small, privately run potteries and glassworks in the area. At **Die Glashütte** (✉ Weserstr. 43, ☎ 05672/1414), glass-blowers will fashion and engrave to order.

Höxter

⓫ *24 km (14 mi) north of Bad Karlshafen, 100 km (62 mi) south of Hannover.*

Stop at Höxter to admire its **Rathaus,** a perfect example of the Weser Renaissance style, combining three half-timber stories with a romantically crooked tower. Though it has no better claim than any other town to the story of Hansel and Gretel, Höxter presents a free performance of the Hansel and Gretel story on the first Saturday of each month, May to September.

The **Reichsabtei Corvey** (Imperial Abbey of Corvey) is idyllically set between the wooded heights of the Solling region and the Weser River. The 1,100-year history of the abbey is closely tied with the early development of the German nation. Optimistically described by some as the "Rome of the North," it hosted several sessions of the imperial council in the 12th century and provided lodging for several Holy Roman emperors. In the 16th century the first six volumes of the Roman historian Tacitus's annals were discovered in its vast library. Heinrich Hoffmann von Fallersleben (1798–1874), author of the poem "Deutschland, Deutschland über Alles," worked as librarian here in the 1820s. The poem, set to music by Joseph Haydn, became the German national anthem in 1922. A music festival is held in the church and great hall, the Kaisersaal, in May and June. Corvey, also the name of the village, is reached on an unnumbered road heading east from Höxter (3 km [2 mi]) toward the Weser. There are signposts to the abbey. ☎ *05271/68116.* 🎟 *€3, abbey church €.50.* ⏲ *Apr.–Oct., daily 9–6.*

OFF THE BEATEN PATH

EINBECK – Bock beer originated in this storybook town 20 km (12 mi) east of Höxter. Starting in 1341 the good burghers brewed it in their houses, and the name *Bockbier* is a corruption of the original Einbecker Bier. The **Einbecker Brauhaus** (brewery) still makes the strong brew, and groups can visit it with an advance written request (✉ Papenstr. 4–7, D–37574 Einbeck, ☎ 05561/7970).

Dining and Lodging

$$–$$$$ ★ ✕ **Schloss Bevern.** You'll dine like a baron here, within the honey-color walls of a Renaissance castle in the little town of Bevern, just north of Höxter on the other side of the river. In the enchanting inner courtyard, a solitary dome-top, half-timber tower stands sentinel over a 17th-century fountain. The romance carries into the stylish restaurant, which serves such traditional country dishes as roast pheasant, lamb, or fish at tables with finely cut glassware. ✉ *Am Schloss 1, Bevern,* ☎ *05531/8783. Reservations essential. AE, DC, MC, V. Closed Mon. No lunch Tues.*

$–$$ ★ ✕ **Schlossrestaurant Corvey.** In summer you can dine under centuries-old trees at the Reichsabtei Corvey's excellent restaurant. With advance notice, a *Fürsten-Bankett,* or "princely banquet," can be arranged for groups in the vaulted cellars. ✉ *Reichsabtei Corvey,* ☎ *05271/8323. V.* ⏲ *Apr.–Oct. no dinner, Nov.–Dec. no lunch. Closed Jan.–Mar.*

$$ ✕🏨 **Niedersachsen Ringhotel.** Behind the three-story, half-timber facade of this fine old Höxter house is a hotel with modern comfort and amenities, a member of the respected Ring group. The restaurant ($–$$) has a shady garden terrace and features fresh river fish. ✉ *Grubestr. 3–7, D–37671,* ☎ *05271/6880,* FAX *05271/688–444. 80 rooms. Restaurant, bar, no a/c, in-room data ports, cable TV with movies, indoor pool, sauna, some pets allowed (fee). AE, DC, MC, V.*

Outdoor Activities and Sports

Busch Freizeitservice (✉ Postweg Nord 7, ☎ 05271/921–363) organizes canoe trips on the Fulda, Weser, and Werra rivers, as well as bicycle tours in the surrounding countryside.

Shopping

Germany's oldest **porcelain factory** is at Fürstenberg, 8 km (5 mi) south of Höxter, in a baroque castle high above the Weser River. The crowned Gothic letter *F,* which serves as its trademark, is world famous. You'll find Fürstenberg porcelain in Bad Karlshafen and Höxter, but it's more fun to journey to the 18th-century castle, where production first began in 1747, and buy directly from the manufacturer. Fürstenberg and most dealers will take care of shipping arrangements and any tax refunds. The factory has a sales outlet, a museum, and a café. ✉ *Schloss Fürstenberg,* ☎ *05271/401–161.* 🎫 *Museum €3.50.* ⏲ *Museum: Apr.–Oct., Tues.–Sun. 10–5; Nov.–Mar., weekends 10–5. Shop: Apr.–Oct., Tues.–Sun. 10–6; Nov.–Mar., Tues.–Sat. 10–6.*

Bodenwerder

⓬ *34 km (21 mi) north of Höxter, 70 km (43 mi) south of Hannover.*

The charming Weser town of Bodenwerder plays a central role in German popular literature. It is the home of the Lügenbaron (Lying Baron) von Münchhausen (1720–97), who was known as a teller of whoppers. His reputation was not without foundation, but it was mainly created by a book based in part on the baron's stories and published anonymously by an acquaintance. According to one tale, the baron rode a cannonball toward an enemy fortress but then, having second thoughts, returned to where he started by leaping onto a cannonball heading the other way.

The **Münchhausen-Erinnerungszimmer** (Münchhausen Memorial Room), in the imposing family home in which Baron von Münchhausen grew up (now the Rathaus), is crammed with mementos of his adventurous life, including his cannonball. A fountain in front of the house represents another story. The baron, it seems, was puzzled when his horse kept drinking insatiably at a trough. Investigating, he discovered that the horse had been cut in two by a closing castle gate and that the water ran out as fast as the horse drank. The water in the fountain, of course, flows from the rear of a half-horse. On the first Sunday of the month from May through October, townspeople retell von Münchhausen's life story with performances in front of the Rathaus. ✉ *Münchhausenpl. 1,* ☎ *05533/40547.* 🎫 *Museum €1.20.* ⏲ *Apr.–Oct., daily 10–noon and 2–5.*

Dining and Lodging

$–$$ ✕🏨 **Hotel Deutsches Haus.** The fine half-timber facade of this comfortable country hotel vies for attention with the nearby home of Baron von Münchhausen, now Bodenwerder's town hall. Original wood beams and oak paneling add to the rural feel inside. The hotel's own extensive grounds adjoin the town park, and the Weser River is a short walk away. The restaurant's ($–$$) terrace adjoins the Münchhausen house. A specialty is *Münchhausen Kugeln* (Cannonballs), a dish with turkey, pork, vegetables, and croquettes. ✉ *Münchhausenpl. 4, D–37619,* ☎ *05533/3925,* FAX *05533/4113. 42 rooms. Restaurant, no a/c, in-room data ports, cable TV, bicycles, bowling, some pets allowed, no-smoking rooms. AE, MC, V. Closed Jan.*

$–$$ ✕🏨 **Hotel Goldener Anker.** The Weser boats tie up outside this simple half-timber tavern and hotel, and the sleepy river flows right past your bedroom window. The restaurant ($$–$$$) prepares hearty German fare and sometimes fresh Weser fish; in summer a shady terrace beckons. ✉ *Weserstr. 13, D–37619,* ☎ *05533/400–730,* FAX *05533/400–733. 11 rooms. Restaurant, no a/c, in-room data ports, cable TV, bicycles, meeting room, some pets allowed, no-smoking rooms. MC.*

Hameln

★ ⓭ *24 km (15 mi) north of Bodenwerder, 47 km (29 mi) southwest of Hannover.*

Hameln (or Hamelin, in English) is home to the story of the gaudily attired Pied Piper, who rid the town of rats by playing seductive melodies on his flute. The rodents followed him willingly, waltzing their way right into the Weser. When the town defaulted on its contract and refused to pay the piper, he settled the score by playing his merry tune to lead Hameln's children on the same route. As the children reached the river, the Grimms wrote, "they disappeared forever." The tale is included in the Grimms' book *German Legends*. The origin of the story is lost in the mists of time, but the best guess is that it is associated with the forced resettlement of young people to the sparsely populated eastern territories. Also, during the 13th century, an inordinate number of Hameln's young men were conscripted to fight in an unpopular war in Bohemia and Moravia.

The Pied Piper tale is immortalized in an ultramodern sculpture set above a reflecting pool in the town's pedestrian zone. There are even rat-shape pastries in the windows of Hameln's bakeries. On central Osterstrasse you'll see several beautiful half-timber houses, including the *Rattenfängerhaus* (Rat-Catcher's House) and the **Hochzeitshaus** (Wedding House), a 17th-century, Weser Renaissance building now containing city offices. Between mid-May and mid-September the Hochzeithaus terrace is the scene of two free open-air events commemorating the legend. Local actors and children present a half-hour reenactment each Sunday at noon, and there is now also a 40-minute musical, *Rats*, each Wednesday at 4:30. Get there early to ensure a good place. The carillon of the Hochzeitshaus plays a Pied Piper song every day at 9:35 and 11:35, and mechanical figures enact the story on the west gable of the building at 1:05, 3:35, and 5:35.

Dining and Lodging

$–$$$ ★ ✕ **Rattenfängerhaus.** This brilliant example of Weser Renaissance architecture is Hameln's most famous building, reputedly where the Pied Piper stayed during his rat-extermination assignment (actually, it wasn't built until centuries after his supposed exploits). A plaque in front of it fixes the date of the incident at June 26, 1284. Rats are all over the menu, from the "rat-remover cocktail" to a "rat-tail flambé." But don't be put off: the traditional dishes are excellent, and the restaurant is guaranteed rodent free. ✉ *Osterstr. 28,* ☎ *05151/3888. AE, DC, MC, V.*

$$ **Hotel zur Börse.** This upscale hotel is right on the pedestrian zone in the heart of the old city. It offers comfortable accommodations and friendly service, and its Börsenbistro serves Mediterranean food. ✉ *Osterstr. 41, entrance on Kopmanshof, D–31785, ☎ 05151/7080, FAX 05151/25485. 31 rooms. 2 restaurants, no a/c, in-room data ports, minibars, cable TV with movies, bar, meeting rooms, some pets allowed (fee). AE, DC, MC, V.*

$$ ★ **Hotel zur Krone.** If you fancy a splurge, ask for one of the hotel's elegant suites, with prices starting at €185 a night. It's an expensive but delightful comfort. The building dates from 1645 and is a half-timber marvel. Avoid the modern annex, however; it lacks all charm. ✉ *Osterstr. 30, D–31785, ☎ 05151/9070, FAX 05151/907–217. 32 rooms, 5 suites. Restaurant, no a/c, in-room data ports, cable TV, meeting rooms, some pets allowed, no-smoking rooms. AE, DC, MC, V.*

$ **Pension Ragazzi.** Don't be fooled by the inappropriate Italian name, which it derives from a pizzeria on the ground floor. This very reasonable little hostelry, with simple but modern rooms, is pure Fairy-Tale Road, situated right in the pedestrian zone in the old part of the town. A Continental breakfast is included in the rate. ✉ *Fischpfortenstr. 25, D–31785, ☎ 05151/21513, FAX 05151/923–667. 8 rooms. Pizzeria, no a/c, cable TV, meeting rooms, some pets allowed. No credit cards.*

Nightlife and the Arts

The **Theater Hameln** (✉ Sedanstr. 4, ☎ 0515/916–222) has a top-class, year-round program of dance, drama, opera, and orchestral concerts.

Outdoor Activities and Sports

Schloss Schwöbber (☎ 05154/9870) has two 18-hole golf courses. It's off the unnumbered road between Gross Berkel and Bösingfeld, to the south of Hameln.

Hannover

47 km (29 mi) northeast of Hameln.

Hannover is somewhat off the Fairy-Tale Road, yet its culture and commerce influence the quieter surrounding towns. As a trade-fair center, Hannover competes with such cities as Munich and Leipzig, and it hosted the EXPO world's fair in 2000. It's also an exemplary arts center, with leading museums, an opera house of international repute, and the finest baroque park in the country. Its patronage of the arts is evident in unexpected places: in an international competition, architects and designers created nine unique bus stops for the city. A Hannover Card is available through the tourist office for €8 per day (€12 for three days). It entitles you to free travel on local transportation, free admission to four museums, and discounts on certain sightseeing events and performances. The major sights of Hannover are strung together on a tourist trail marked by red signs. The "Red Thread" is also clearly marked on a map obtainable from the tourist office.

A Good Walk

You can start your tour at the big Kröpke U-bahn station, which is also the place to catch Tramline 5 to the gardens of **Herrenhausen** and the **Wilhelm Busch Museum.** Just a short distance south of the station on Georgstrasse is Hannover's beautiful classical theater, the **Opernhaus** ⑭. From here continue south on Georgstrasse, the city's main shopping street, to Aegidientorplatz, then veer right on Friedrichswall to Willy-Brandt-Allee, beyond which is the Maschpark, containing the vast bulk of the **Neues Rathaus** ⑮. Down Willy-Brandt-Allee you will find the **Niedersächsisches Landesmuseum** ⑯ with its celebrated art collection. At the end of the street is the **Sprengel Museum** ⑰ on Kurt-Schwitters-

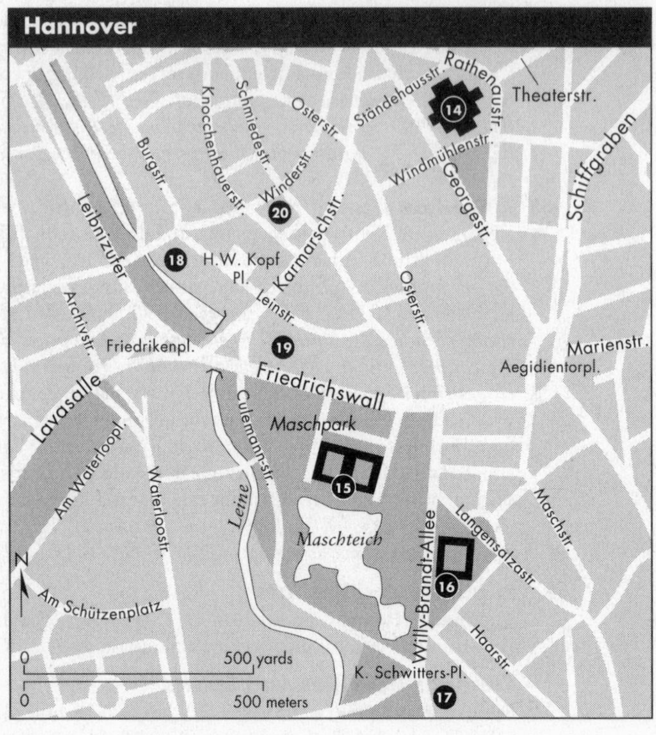

Platz. Stroll through the Maschpark back to Friedrichswall, and just to the west you will come to two royal palaces important in Hannoverian history. The larger one, standing above the River Leine, is the **Leineschloss** ⑱, the seat of the Lower Saxony State Parliament. Facing Leinstrasse is **Wangenheim-Palais** ⑲, a smaller palace where one of the Hannoverian kings resided. Up Karmarschstrasse and two blocks on the left is Hannover's first city hall, the 14th-century **Altes Rathaus** ⑳, a notable example of Hannoverian brick architecture. The central market square behind it is dominated by the Marktkirche, with a splendid Gothic carved altar and fine stained glass inside.

Sights to See

20 **Altes Rathaus.** It took nearly 100 years, starting in 1410, to build this gabled brick edifice, which once contained a merchants hall and an apothecary. In 1844 it was restored to the style of about 1500. The facade's fired clay frieze depicts coats of arms and representation of princes, and a medieval game somewhat comparable to arm wrestling. Inside is a modern interior with boutiques and a restaurant. ⊠ *Köbelingerstr.*

Herrenhausen. The gardens of the former Hannoverian royal summer residence is the city's showpiece (the 17th-century palace was never rebuilt after wartime bombing). The baroque park is unmatched in Germany for its formal precision, with patterned walks, gardens, hedges, chestnut trees, and copses framed by a placid moat. There is a "fig garden" with a collapsible shelter to protect it in the winter and a gastronomy pavilion behind a grotto. From Easter until October fountains play for a few hours daily (weekdays 11–noon and 3–5, weekends 11–noon and 2–5). Herrenhausen is outside the city, a short ride on Tramline 4 or 5. ⊠ *Herrenhauser Str.* €2. *Mar.–Apr., daily 8–6; May–Aug., daily 8–8; Sept., daily 8–7; Oct., daily 8–6; Nov.–Jan., daily 8–4:30.*

An 18th-century residence at the edge of the park is now a museum, the **Fürstenhaus Herrenhausen-Museum,** affording fascinating insight into Hannoverian court life and its links with England. ✉ *Alte Herrenhauser Str. 14,* ☎ *0511/750–947.* 💰 *€3.30.* ⏲ *Tues.–Sun. 10–5.*

18 **Leineschloss.** The former Hannoverian royal palace stands above the River Leine and is now the seat of the Lower Saxony State Parliament. From 1714 until 1837 rulers of the house of Hannover also sat on the British throne as Kings George I–IV. The first of them, George I, spoke no English. George III presided over the loss of the American colonies in the Revolutionary War but sent no Hannoverian troops to help fight, even though he hired troops from other German states for this purpose. The period of joint rule came to an end when Queen Victoria ascended the throne (Hannover didn't allow female monarchs). Tours are conducted weekdays. Brochures in English are available. ✉ *Heinrich-Wilhelm-Kopf-Pl. 1,* ☎ *0511/3030–2041.* 💰 *Free.* ⏲ *Tours, Mon.–Thurs. 10:30 and 1:30, Fri. 10:30.*

15 **Neues Rathaus.** The new city hall was built at the start of the century in Wilhelmine style (for Kaiser Wilhelm), at a time when pomp and circumstance were important ingredients of heavy German bureaucracy. An elevator rises to the dome for a splendid view. ✉ *Trammpl. 2.* 💰 *Dome €2.* ⏲ *Daily 10–6.*

16 **Niedersächsisches Landesmuseum** (Lower Saxony State Museum). The priceless early art collection of this prestigious museum includes works by Tilman Riemenschneider, Veit Stoss, Hans Holbein the Younger, and Lucas Cranach. ✉ *Willy-Brandt-Allee 5,* ☎ *0511/98075.* 💰 *€3.* ⏲ *Tues., Wed., and Fri.–Sun. 10–5, Thurs. 10–7.*

14 **Opernhaus.** Hannover's Late Classical opera house, completed in 1852, has two large wings and a covered, colonnaded portico adorned with statues of great composers and poets. This enabled the finely attired operagoers to disembark from their coaches with dry feet, a function now taken over by an underground garage. The building originally served as the court theater but now is used almost exclusively for opera. It was gutted by fire in a 1943 air raid and restored in 1948. Unless you have tickets to a performance, the only part of the interior you can visit is the foyer with ticket windows. ✉ *Opernpl. 1,* ☎ *0511/9999–1298.*

17 **Sprengel Museum.** An important museum of modern art, the Sprengel holds major works by Max Beckmann, Max Ernst, Paul Klee, Emil Nolde, and Pablo Picasso. The street on which it is located is named after Kurt Schwitters, a native son and prominent dadaist, whose works are also exhibited. ✉ *Kurt-Schwitters-Pl.,* ☎ *0511/1684–3875.* 💰 *€3.50.* ⏲ *Tues. 10–8, Wed.–Sun. 10–6.*

19 **Wangenheim-Palais.** This is one of the more delightful works of the noted architect Georg Friedrich Laves, who also designed the opera and several buildings at Herrenhausen and thoroughly renovated the Leineschloss. After the death of the Count Wangenheim, for whom it was built in 1833, it briefly became the royal palace. Hannoverian king Georg V lived there from 1851 to 1862 before moving to Herrenhausen. It was then the city hall for 50 years and now serves as the offices of the Lower Saxony Economics Ministry. ✉ *Friedrichswall.*

OFF THE BEATEN PATH

WILHELM BUSCH MUSEUM – Many effects and original drawings of the "godfather of the comic strip" are on display in this section of the Georgspalais, which is near the Herrenhausen Gardens. More than a century ago, Wilhelm Busch (1832–1908) wrote and illustrated a very popular children's book, still in print, called *Max und Moritz.* These were very bad boys who mixed gunpowder in the village tailor's pipe tobacco, and with fishing lines down the chimney, filched roasting chickens off the fire. The first American comic strip, *The Katzenjammer Kids* (1897), not only drew on Busch's naughty boys (they even spoke with a German accent) but also on his loose cartoon style. ✉ *Georgengarten 1,* ☎ *0511/1699–9911.* *€4.50.* ⏲ *Tues.–Fri. 10–5, weekends 10–6.*

Dining and Lodging

$$$ ✕ **Basil.** Constructed in 1867 as a riding hall for the Royal Prussian military, this hip restaurant's home is as striking as the menu. Cast-iron pillars support the vaulted brick ceiling, and two-story drapes hang in the huge windows. The menu changes every three weeks, and includes eclectic dishes from the Mediterranean to Asia. Game and white *Spargel* (asparagus) are served in season. ✉ *Dragonerstr. 30A,* ☎ *0511/622–636. AE, MC, V. Closed Sun.*

$ ✕ **Brauhaus Ernst August.** This brewery has so much artificial greenery that you could imagine yourself in a beer garden. Hannoverian pilsner is brewed on the premises, and regional specialties are the menu's focus. There's a souvenir shop where besides beer paraphernalia such as mugs and coasters, you can purchase, empty or full, a huge old-fashioned beer bottle with a porcelain stopper. In the early postwar years American soldiers christened the bottles "snap daddies." Many patrons precede their beer and food with a shot of *Brauerschluck* (Brewer's Gulp), the pub's own potent schnapps. It, too, is sold in a miniature snap daddy. There is live music every evening (no cover charge) and a merry mood prevails with dancing. ✉ *Schmiedstr. 13,* ☎ *0511/365–950. V.*

$ ✕ **Grapenkieker.** An ancient pot steams in the aromatic, farmhouse-style kitchen, and simple, hearty fare prevails. Proprietors Gabriele and Karl-Heinz Wolf are locally famous for their culinary prowess and the warm welcome they give their guests. The half-timber restaurant is 5 km (3 mi) from the city center, in the Isernhagen District, but it's well worth seeking out. ✉ *Hauptstr. 56, Isernhagen,* ☎ *05139/88068. AE, DC, MC, V. Closed Sun. and Mon.*

$$$ ✕🏨 **Kastens Hotel Luisenhof.** This very traditional hotel, both in appearance and service, is a few steps from the main train station. Antiques are everywhere: tapestries on the lobby walls, oil paintings in the foyer, copper engravings in the bar, and an elegant wardrobe on every floor. In-room facilities don't include pay-per-view movies, as most mass market films wouldn't appeal to the taste of the clientele here. The restaurant ($$$$) is international with French touches. ✉ *Luisenstr. 1–3, D–30159,* ☎ *0511/30440,* FAX *0511/304–4807,* WEB *www.kastens-luisenhof.de. 147 rooms, 5 suites. Restaurant, no a/c, in-room data ports, cable TV, bar, meeting rooms, some pets allowed, no-smoking rooms. AE, DC, MC, V.*

$$ ✕🏨 **Hotel Benther Berg.** This large country-house hotel with a modern extension sits amid parkland and woods in Ronneberg-Benthe, a southwest suburb. Rooms are large and furnished mostly in modern dark woods and pastel shades. The restaurant attracts Hannover regulars, who value its international cuisine. ✉ *Vogelsangstr. 18, D–30952 Ronneberg-Benthe,* ☎ *05108/64060,* FAX *05108/640–650,* WEB *www.hotel-benther-berg.de. 70 rooms. Restaurant, café, no a/c, in-room data ports, cable TV, indoor pool, sauna, meeting rooms, some pets allowed (fee), no-smoking rooms. AE, DC, MC, V.*

$$ ✕🏨 **Hotel Körner.** The modern Körner has an almost old-fashioned feel about it, probably created by the friendly and personal service. Rooms are comfortably furnished in light veneers and pastel shades. The small courtyard terrace has a fountain; breakfast is served here in the summer. The Lüzower Jäger restaurant ($–$$$) is decorated with memorabilia from the Hannoverian wars of liberation, and the menu consists of Lower Saxony specialties. ✉ *Körnerstr. 24–25, D–30159,* ☎ *0511/16360,* FAX *0511/18048,* WEB *www.hotel-koerner.de. 77 rooms. Restaurant, no a/c, in-room data ports, cable TV, indoor pool, gym. AE, DC, MC, V.*

Nightlife and the Arts

The **opera company** of Hannover is internationally known, with productions staged in one of Germany's finest 19th-century classical opera houses. Call 0511/9999–1298 for program details and tickets. Hannover's elegant **casino** (✉ Osterstr. 40, ☎ 0511/980–660) is open from 3 PM to 3 AM.

Outdoor Activities

Hannover's inland lake, the **Maschsee,** is a favorite local recreation area. In summer you can swim here or rent a sailboat.

Shopping

Hannover is one of northern Germany's most fashionable cities, and its central pedestrian zone has international shops and boutiques, as well as the very best of German-made articles, from stylish clothes to handmade jewelry. In the glassed-over **Galerie Luise** (✉ Luisenstr. 5) you can spend a couple of hours browsing, with a leisurely lunch or afternoon tea at one of the several restaurants and cafés.

Hannover has what it claims is Germany's oldest **Flohmarkt** (flea market; ✉ Am Hohen Ufer)—certainly one of the largest and most interesting. It's held every Saturday on the bank of the River Leine from 7 to 4. The colorful sculptures by Niki de St. Phalle you'll see on the opposite bank (Am Leibnitzufer) were commissioned by the city, which then had to prevent them from being added to the flea-market junk. Art advocates prevailed, and the sculptures (huge, maternal "nanas") are now an indispensable part of the city landscape.

En Route The Fairy-Tale Road continues north of Hannover as far as Bremen, even though any connection to the Grimm brothers is faint here. You can reach Bremen in less than an hour by taking Autobahn E–45 to the Walsrode interchange and then continuing on Autobahn E–234. An alternative is to return to Hameln and follow the Weser as it breaks free of the Wesergebirge uplands at Porta Westfalica. The meandering route runs through the German plains to the sea and Bremen.

Celle

21 *60 km (35 mi) northeast of Hannover.*

The main street of Celle's Old Town is quite different from the narrow, twisting streets you'd expect to find in a half-timber town. The **Stechbahn** is very broad, and was once used for jousting tournaments. A horseshoe sunk in the pavement in front of the Löwenapotheke supposedly marks where the man who established Celle's present location, Duke Otto the Severe, died in such a tournament.

This charming city, with more than 500 half-timber buildings, is also the southern gateway to the Lüneburg Heath, one of Germany's most pleasant pastoral areas. It's a landscape of bizarrely shaped juniper bushes, of heather that flowers in pinkish purple in the late summer, and of grazing flocks of the heath's own breed of sheep, the cuddly Heidschnucken.

Thanks to a bend in the Aller River and a small tributary, Celle was protected on three sides by streams. To guard the fourth side from invasion by robber barons, Duke Otto built a fortified castle. This became the city's present palace, set in a lush park with the oldest baroque theater in Germany still used for performances. The castle chapel is an important example of North German Renaissance. The city hall (Rathaus) also traces its origins back to Duke Otto's time. It was extended and elaborately decorated in the 14th and 16th centuries.

The **Bomann Museum** is a must for anyone charmed by old furnishings. Its aim is to depict the folk culture of the area along with the history of Celle and of the Kingdom of Hannover. You can see a completely furnished reconstruction of a farmhouse and numerous reconstructed interiors, including a cartwright shop and a smithy. ✉ *Schlosspl. 7,* ☎ *05141/12544.* 🎫 *€2.50.* ⏲ *Tues.–Sun. 10–5.*

The very specialized **Deutsche Stickmuster-Museum** (German Needlework Museum) dedicates itself to needlework and embroidery. The display includes native costumes, shirts, pillows, bedspreads, and the like all adorned with needlework flowers, birds, animals, human figures, and abstract designs. If you want to make your own sampler, you can buy a kit to do just that. ✉ *Palais Im Prinzengarten,* ☎ *05141/382–626.* 🎫 *€3.* ⏲ *Tue.–Thurs. and weekends 10–5.*

Dining and Lodging

$–$$$ ✕ **Ratskeller Celle.** This subterranean establishment with a vaulted stone ceiling lays claim to being the oldest restaurant in Lower Saxony. If you can stand slow service, it's a good place to try the regional specialties, notably dishes from the Heidschnucken lamb. Boar is also a heath specialty, as are seasonal tender white asparagus and chanterelle mushrooms, served with an endless variety of accompaniments. ✉ *Markt 14,* ☎ *05141/29099. AE, V.*

$$$ ✕🏨 **Hotel Fürstenhof.** This baroque hunting château is surrounded by huge chestnut trees in the center of town. The specialty in the Endtenfang ($$$$) restaurant is *le canard du duc,* in which the duck breast is served with a pepper sauce and potatoes au gratin, and the legs, after a sorbet to clear the palate, with a port wine sauce and mushrooms. The grand salon, with its groupings of overstuffed chairs, has a mirror ceiling supported by Grecian columns. Try to book one of the four rooms with antique furnishings in the original lodge. The other rooms are in a modern wing with less character. ✉ *Hannoverische Str. 55, D–29221,* ☎ *05141/201–140,* FAX *05141/201–120,* WEB *www.fuerstenhof.de. 76 rooms. 2 restaurants, bar, no a/c, in-room data ports, cable TV, indoor pool, sauna, meeting rooms, some pets allowed. AE, DC, MC, V.*

$$ 🏨 **Hotel Celler Hof.** This moderately priced hotel is right in the heart of the half-timber old city, just steps from the Rathaus, palace, and Bomann Museum. Since it is owned by the same group as the nearby Hotel Fürstenhof, guests are welcome to use the indoor pool and solarium there. ✉ *Stechbahn 11, D–29221,* ☎ *05141/911–960,* FAX *05141/911–9644,* WEB *www.residenzhotels.de. 49 rooms. Bar, no a/c, cable TV, exercise equipment, sauna, some pets allowed. AE, DC, MC, V.*

Bergen-Belsen

22 *25 km (15 mi) north of Celle.*

Just outside Celle is a sobering contrast to the charm of half-timbering and heather. At the site of the infamous concentration camp on the Lüneburg Heath, the **Gedenkstätte Bergen-Belsen** (Bergen-Belsen Memorial) pays tribute to the victims of the Holocaust. Diarist Anne Frank was among the more than 80,000 persons who died here.

Only the gruesome photographs on display will tell what the camp looked like. There is nothing left of it. The British liberators found thousands and thousands of unburied corpses all over the camp, so as a precaution against disease, all structures were burned to the ground. Volunteer youth groups have unearthed the foundations of the barracks.

Those who venture onto the site of the camp may be surprised at its pleasant, parklike appearance. Reminders of the horrors that once were include numerous burial mounds, mostly overgrown with heather and with stones with such inscriptions as HERE LIE 1,000 DEAD. Anne Frank probably lies in one of them. The SS officers had hoped to have the dead buried and out of sight before the British forces arrived, but the starving prisoners were too weak for the job. Under the direction of the British, the graves you see were dug and filled by the SS officers themselves. The British tried and executed the camp's SS commandant, Josef Kramer, the "Beast of Belsen."

Monuments and shrines include a Jewish memorial dating to 1946, with a commemorative stone dedicated by the Israeli president in 1987; an obelisk and memorial wall erected by the British; a wooden cross dating to only weeks after the liberation, and a commemorative stone from the German government. The main feature of the memorial is a permanent exhibition on the history of the camp and the Nazi persecution system. Though all signs are in German, there are supplementary guides (€2.50) in English and eight other languages. There are also regular showings of a video on the camp in English, German, and French. Children under 12 are not admitted to the showings, and it is said that one of the British photographers who made the footage couldn't bear to look at his work in later years. ✉ *Just off the unnumbered highway connecting Bergen and Winsen,* ☎ *05051/6011.* *Free.* *Daily 9–6.*

Lodging

$ **Hof Averbeck.** This typical heath farm doubling as a bed-and-breakfast proves the Lüneburg Heath is an ideal place for a farm vacation. Well off the main highway, it's great for children, with ponies to ride, animals to feed, and a playground. The farm, which is handy to the Bergen-Belsen Memorial and central for day trips to Hamburg and Hannover, also has cattle, with boar and deer in the surrounding forest and meadows. ✉ *Hassel 3, D–29303 Bergen,* ☎ *05054/249,* FAX *05054/269,* WEB *www.hofaverbeck.de. 14 rooms, 2 apartments. No a/c, no room phones, cable TV, some pets allowed. No credit cards.*

BREMEN

23 Germany's smallest city-state, **Bremen,** is also Germany's oldest port, second in size to Hamburg. Together with Hamburg and Lübeck, Bremen was an early member of the merchant-run Hanseatic League, and its rivalry with the larger port on the Elbe River is still tangible. Though Hamburg may still claim its title as Germany's "door to the world," Bremen likes to boast: "But we have the key."

Bremen is also central to the fable of the Bremer Stadtmusikanten, or Bremen Town Musicians—a rooster, cat, dog, and donkey quartet that came to Bremen to seek its fortune. (Their music and singing was so awful that it caused a band of robbers to flee in terror, thus saving the town.) You'll find statues of this group in various parts of the city. Bremen lies 110 km (68 mi) northwest of Hannover.

Exploring Bremen

Bremen's **Marktplatz** is one of Europe's most impressive market squares. It's bordered by an imposing, 900-year-old Gothic cathedral, an ancient Rathaus, a 16th-century guildhall, and a modern glass-and-steel state parliament building, with gabled town houses finishing the panorama. Alongside the northwest corner of the Rathaus is the famous bronze statue of the four **Bremen Town Musicians,** one atop the other in a sort of pyramid. Their feats are reenacted in a free, open-air play in the courtyard of the Liebfrauenkirche, near the Marktplatz, at noon and 1:30 each Sunday, from May to October. Another well-known figure on the square is the stone statue of the knight in service to Charlemagne, **Roland**, erected in 1404. Three times larger than life, the statue serves as Bremen's good-luck piece and a symbol of freedom and independence.

Construction of the **St. Petri Dom** (St. Peter's Cathedral) began in the mid-11th century. Its two prominent towers are Gothic, but in the late 1800s the cathedral was restored in the Romanesque style. It served as the seat of an archbishop until the Reformation turned the cathedral Protestant. ✉ *Marktpl.* 🎫 *Free.* ⏲ *Weekdays 10–5, Sat. 10–2, Sun. 2–5.*

Charlemagne had established a diocese here in the 9th century, and a 15th-century statue of him, together with seven princes, adorns the Gothic **Rathaus,** which acquired a Weser Renaissance facade during the early 17th century. Tours are given in German. ✉ *Marktpl.* 🎫 *Tour €4.* ⏲ *Tours Mon.–Sat. 11, noon, 3, and 4; Sun. 11 and noon (unless an official function is in progress).*

The **Übersee Museum** (Overseas Museum) has unusual displays on the histories and cultures of the many peoples with whom Bremen traders came into contact. One section is devoted to North America. ✉ *Bahnhofspl. 13,* ☎ *0421/1603–8101.* 🎫 *€5.* ⏲ *Tues.–Sun. 10–6, Thurs. until 9.*

Don't leave Bremen without strolling down **Böttcherstrasse** (Barrel-Maker's Street), at one time inhabited by coopers. Between 1924 and 1931 their houses were torn down and reconstructed in a style at once historically sensitive and modern by Bremen coffee millionaire Ludwig Roselius. (He was the inventor of decaffeinated coffee and held the patent for many years; Sanka was its brand name in the United States.) Many of the restored houses are used as galleries for local artists.

At one end of Böttcherstrasse is the **Roselius-Haus,** a 14th-century building that is now a museum showcasing German and Dutch paintings, as well as wood carvings, furniture, textiles, and decorative arts from the 12th through the 18th centuries. Notice also the arch of Meissen bells at the rooftop. Except when freezing weather makes them dangerously brittle, these chime daily on the hour from noon to 6 (only at noon, 3, and 6, January through April). ✉ *Böttcherstr. 6–10,* ☎ *0421/336–5077.* 🎫 *€6.* ⏲ *Tues.–Sun. 11–6.*

★ Also take a walk through the idyllic **Schnoorviertel** (Schnoor District), a jumble of houses, taverns, and shops once occupied or frequented by fishermen and tradespeople. This is Bremen's oldest district, dating back to the 15th and 16th centuries. The neighborhood is fashionable among artists and craftspeople, who have restored the tiny cottages to serve as galleries and workshops. Other buildings have been converted into popular small cafés and pubs.

OFF THE BEATEN PATH

BREMERHAVEN – This busy port city belongs to Bremen and is 66 km (41 mi) upriver, where the Weser empties into the North Sea. You can take in the enormity of the port from a promenade or from a platform in the North Harbor. The country's largest and most fascinating maritime museum, the **Deutsches Schifffahrtsmuseum** (German Maritime Museum) is a fun place to explore. Part of the museum consists of a harbor with seven old trading ships. A train to Bremerhaven from Bremen takes about one hour. ✉ *Hans-Scharoun-Pl. 1, from Bremen take A–27 to exit for Bremerhaven-Mitte,* ☎ *0471/482–070.* 🎫 *€4.* ⏲ *Tues.–Sun. 10–6. Harbor closed Nov.–Mar.*

Dining and Lodging

$$$$ ★ ✕ **Grashoff's Bistro.** Locals fill the closely packed tables at this popular lunchtime bistro. The menu has a French touch, with an accent on fresh fish from the Bremerhaven market. Old prints and photographs cover the walls. ✉ *Contrescarpe 80,* ☎ *0421/14740. DC, V. Closed Sun. No dinner.*

$$$$ ★ ✕ **Park Restaurant.** Thanks to Chef Henre Precht, the Park is one of the finest dining establishments in Germany. Within the Park Hotel Bremen, it is somewhat small, but the floor-to-ceiling windows and lacquered ceiling open up the room. The stunning dining room is decorated in yellow, black, and cream, with shimmering crystal chandeliers, classical moldings, marble urns, and Louis XVI chairs. Chef Precht introduces a dash of fantasy to his classic French and Italian dishes, which may include air-dried ham and pickled salmon. Reservations are advised. ✉ *Im Bürgerpark,* ☎ *0421/340–8633. Jacket and tie. AE, DC, MC, V.*

$$–$$$ ✕ **Comturei.** The vaults of Bremen's ancient Heiliggeistkirche (Church of the Holy Spirit) were secularized some time ago, becoming a beer cellar and restaurant, where the traditional German cuisine is devilishly good if not exactly heavenly. Special medieval banquet menus are served to groups of more than 10, but there's often a place for a lone diner—and it's a great way to meet the locals. ✉ *Ostertorstr. 30–32,* ☎ *0421/325–050. AE, MC, V.*

$–$$$ ★ ✕ **Ratskeller.** Said to be Germany's oldest and most renowned town-hall restaurant, this one specializes in solid, typical northern German fare, including creatively prepared poultry and fresh seafood. Shortly after the restaurant opened beneath the Rathaus in 1408, the city fathers decreed that only wine could be served there, and the ban on beer still exists. The cellar is lined with wine casks, including an 18th-century barrel that could house a small family. Connoisseurs have more than 600 wine labels from which to choose—and they're all German. ✉ *Am Markt,* ☎ *0421/321–676. AE, DC, MC, V.*

$$ ✕ **Mercure Columbus.** Under the French management of the Accor group, this elegant hotel is adjacent to the train station and only a short stroll from the Old Town. Rooms are spacious; the double-bed rooms actually have two queen-size beds. Breakfast is not included in the room rate, but the enormous buffet is worth the price. ✉ *Bahnhofpl. 5–7, D–28195,* ☎ *0421/30120,* FAX *0421/15369. 148 rooms, 5 suites. Bar, no a/c, in-room data ports, cable TV with movies, sauna, meeting rooms, some pets allowed (fee), no-smoking rooms. AE, DC, MC, V.*

$$$–$$$$ ★ **Park Hotel Bremen.** This palatial lakeside hotel has the atmosphere of an exclusive country mansion. A quiet dignity pervades, from the corridors bathed with natural ceiling light to the beautiful bedrooms, each decorated in an individual style, from opulently Moorish to minimalist Japanese. If you manage to secure a room in the magnificent cupola, you'll awaken to sun streaming through mansard windows. There are views of the surrounding park from all rooms, including many from the exquisite marble bathrooms. The Park Restaurant ($$$$) is the best fine dining around. ✉ *Im Bürgerpark, D–28209,* ☎ *0421/34080,* FAX *0421/340–8602,* WEB *www.parkhotel-bremen.de. 150 rooms, 12 suites. 2 restaurants, café, no a/c, in-room data ports, cable TV with movies and video games, hair salon, massage, bicycles, bar, meeting rooms, some pets allowed (fee), no-smoking rooms. AE, DC, MC, V.*

$–$$ ★ **Hotel Landhaus Louisenthal.** This half-timber country-house hotel on the outskirts of Bremen is 150 years old. Its old-world charm also comes from the caring, family-run management. ✉ *Leher Heerstr. 105, D–28359,* ☎ *0421/232–076,* FAX *0421/236–716. 61 rooms. 2* *restaurants, no a/c, cable TV, sauna, meeting rooms, some pets allowed (fee), no-smoking rooms. AE, DC, MC, V.*

$ **Pension Garni Weidmann.** There are only five rooms in this small and friendly pension in a typical, North German redbrick building so characteristic of Bremen. It does, however, have about the most luxurious bath you'll find (of course, you do have to share it). The rooms even have TV. Rates are €25 per person (€20 excluding breakfast). ✉ *Am Schwarzen Meer 35, D–28205,* ☎ *0421/4984–455,* FAX *0421/4302–894. 5 rooms. No a/c, no room phones, no room TVs, parking (fee), some pets allowed, no-smoking rooms. No credit cards.*

Nightlife and the Arts

Bremen may be Germany's oldest seaport, but it can't match Hamburg for racy nightlife. Nevertheless, the streets around the central Marktplatz and in the historic Schnoor District are filled with all sorts of taverns and bars.

The Bremen and Bremerhaven casinos attract gamblers from as far as Hamburg. Try your luck at American or French roulette and blackjack at the **Bremen casino** (✉ Böttcherstr. 3–5, ☎ 0421/329–000), open daily 3 PM–3 AM. The **Bremerhaven casino** (✉ Theodor-Heuss-Pl. 3, ☎ 0471/413–641), open daily 11 AM until midnight, is strictly for one-armed bandits and machine players.

Music and theater lovers have much to choose from. The **philharmonic orchestra,** which plays regularly at the city's concert hall, Die Glocke (Domsheide 4–5), is of national stature. The **Theater am Goetheplatz** (✉ Goethepl. 1–3) presents operas, operettas, music, and dance programs. The **Concordia** (✉ Schwachhäuser Heerstr. 1) is a multipurpose theater whose stage and audience area can be adjusted to suit the needs of the mostly experimental programs it presents. The **Schauspielhaus** (✉ Ostertorsteinweg 57) presents theater, everything from Goethe to Brecht to Woody Allen, but nearly always in German. Program and ticket information for the philharmonic orchestra, Theater am Goetheplatz, Concordia, and Schauspielhaus is available through a single **box office** (☎ 0421/365–300). Bremen's **Shakespeare Company** (✉ Leibnitzpl. 1, ☎ 0421/365–3333) presents the works of the bard and other plays in German.

Shopping

Bremen's **Schnoorviertel** is the place to go for souvenirs. Its stores are incredibly specialized, selling porcelain dolls, teddy bears, African jewelry, and smoking pipes among many other things. Bremerhaven has one of Germany's oldest established shoemakers, **Leder-Koopmann** (✉ Georgstr. 56, ☎ 0471/302–829), where you can buy first-class footwear and all kinds of leather goods, made with the kind of care that has kept the firm in business since 1898.

THE FAIRY-TALE ROAD A TO Z

To research prices, get advice from other travelers, and book travel arrangements, visit www.fodors.com.

AIRPORTS

Frankfurt, Hannover, and Hamburg have the closest international airports to the area. Frankfurt is less than half an hour from Hanau, and Hamburg is less than an hour from Bremen.

➤ AIRPORT INFORMATION: **Langenhagen Airport** (✉ Petzelstr., Hannover, ☎ 0511/9770).

BIKE AND MOPED TRAVEL

The Fulda and Werra rivers have 190 km (118 mi) of cycle paths, and you can cycle the whole length of the Weser River from Hannoversch-Münden to the outskirts of Bremen without making too many detours from the river valley. The tourist authority, Touristik Naturpark Münden, organizes five- and seven-day cycle tours of the Fulda and Werra River valleys, including bike rentals, overnight accommodations, and luggage transport between stops.

➤ Bike Rentals: **Touristik Naturpark Münden** (✉ Rathaus, Am Lotzestr. 2, D–34346 Hannoversch-Münden, ☎ 05541/75313). **Tourismusverband Weserbergland** (✉ Deisterallee 1, D–31785 Hameln, ☎ 05151/93000).

BOAT AND FERRY TRAVEL

From May through September the Oberweser-Dampfschifffahrt runs its six ships daily on the Weser River between Hameln and Hannoversch-Münden, with stops in Bodenwerder, Höxter, and Bad Karlshafen. Rehbein-Linie Kassel, operates a boat service between Kassel, Hannoversch-Münden, and Bad Karlshafen.

➤ Boat and Ferry Information: **Oberweser-Dampfschifffahrt** (✉ Deisterallee 1, D–31785 Hameln, ☎ 05151/22016). **Rehbein-Linie Kassel** (✉ Weserstr. 5, D–34125 Kassel, ☎ 0561/18505, FAX 0561/102–839).

BUS TRAVEL

Bremen, Kassel, Göttingen, Fulda, and Hanau all are reachable via Europabus (☞ *See* Deutsche Touring in Bus Travel *in* Smart Travel Tips A to Z). Frankfurt, Kassel, Göttingen, and Bremen all have city bus services that extend into the countryside along the Fairy-Tale Road. A local bus serves the scenic Weser Valley Road stretch.

CAR RENTAL

➤ Local Agencies: **Avis** (✉ Kirchbachstr. 200, Bremen, ☎ 0421/201–060; ✉ Am Klagesmarkt 22, Hannover, ☎ 0511/121–740). **Hertz** (✉ Flughafenallee 22, Bremen, ☎ 0421/555–350; ✉ Langenhagen Airport, Hannover, ☎ 0511/779–041). **Sixt** (✉ Flughafenallee 22, Bremen, ☎ 0421/552–081; ✉ Schulenburger Landstr. 66, Hannover, ☎ 0511/352–1213; ✉ Weserstr. 6, Kassel, ☎ 0561/500–880).

CAR TRAVEL

The Fairy-Tale Road incorporates one of Germany's loveliest scenic drives, the Wesertalstrasse, or Weser Valley Road (B–80 and B–83), between Hannoversch-Münden and Hameln; total mileage is approximately 103 km (64 mi). The autobahn network penetrates deep into the area, serving Hanau, Fulda, Kassel, Göttingen, and Bremen directly. Bremen is 60 km (35 mi) northwest of Hannover and 100 km (60 mi) northwest of Celle.

TOURS

BOAT TOURS

Reederei Warrings has two excursions from Bremerhaven: a one-hour trip around the harbor for €7.25 and an all-day round-trip to the fortress North Sea island of Helgoland for €31.50. Book through the Bremerhaven tourist office or through Reederei Warrings. (If you're in a hurry to see the stark, red-cliff island Helgoland, there's a daily round-trip flight for €137 per person with Bremerhaven Airlines.)

Oberweser-Dampfschifffahrt operates summer services on the Weser River between Hameln and Hannoversch Münden and will give you advice on how to combine a boat trip with a tour by bike, bus, or train. It has a five-day round-trip cruise from Bodenwerder to Bad Karlshafen. Included in the price of €325 per person is a daily breakfast buffet, four other meals, and tours to Bodenwerder, the Reichsabtei Corvey, and the Fürstenberg porcelain factory. It also has daily excursions from Hameln, Hannoversch-Münden, Bad Karlshafen, and Bodenwerder.

Rehbein-Linie Kassel (☞ Boat and Ferry Travel) operates a service from Kassel to Bad Karlshafen. It also prides itself on the only "three-river tour" in the area. In a single trip you travel a little on the Fulda and Werra rivers, and also on the river formed when these two meet at the tour's starting point of Hannoversch-Münden, the Weser. One of its three boats, the *Deutschland,* even has a bowling alley aboard. For schedule information and bookings, contact the company at its Kassel headquarters. Another Kassel company, Personenschifffahrt K. & K. Söllner, has two excursion boats plying between Kassel and Hannoversch-Münden.

➤ FEES AND SCHEDULES: **Bremerhaven Airlines** (☏ 0471/971–2100). **Oberweser-Dampfschifffahrt** (☞ Boat and Ferry Travel). **Personenschifffahrt K. & K. Söllner** (✉ Die Schlagd Rondell, D–34125, ☏ 0561/774–670). **Reederei Warrings** (☏ 04464/94950).

BUS TOURS

Year-round tours of the region are offered by a Hameln company, Rattenfänger-Reisen. Guided bus tours of Kassel set off from the Stadttheater Easter–October, every Saturday at 2. Tours are free if you buy a ServiceCard, which costs €7 for 24 hours (the card also entitles you to free travel on all city trams and buses and reduced admission to museums and the casino). Some local authorities—those in Bad Karlshafen, for example—also organize bus tours. Contact individual tourist offices for details.

➤ FEES AND SCHEDULES: **Rattenfänger-Reisen** (✉ Bahnhofstr. 18/20, ☏ 05151/811–414).

WALKING TOURS

Bremen's tours depart daily at 10:30 from the central bus station on Breiteweg. Fulda has a tour of the Old Town, starting at the Stadtschloss, April–October, daily; November–March, weekends and holidays at 11:30. Göttingen shows visitors around April–October, Friday, Saturday, and Sunday at 11:30 (starting from the Old Town Hall).

To sit back and see the sights in comfort, you can hire one of the several Göttingen taxi drivers who double as guides. A city-tour taxi isn't cheap: €28 for one hour. But when were you last shown around by a taxi driver who *really* knew what he or she was talking about?

Hameln offers tours April–October, Monday–Saturday at 3 and Sunday at 10:15 and 3, leaving from the tourist office. The tourist office of Steinau an der Strasse conducts tours at 11:15 on the first Sunday of each month, April–September, departing from the Märchenbrunnen.

➤ FEES AND SCHEDULES: **Göttingen** (☏ 0551/69300). **Hameln** (☏ 05151/202–617). **Steinau an der Strasse** (☏ 06663/963–133).

TRAIN TRAVEL

Hanau, Fulda, Kassel, and Göttingen all are on both the InterCity Express Frankfurt–Hamburg line and the Frankfurt–Berlin line (not all of these trains stop at Hanau). The Frankfurt-Hamburg line also stops in Hannover, and there is additional ICE service to Hannover and to Bremen from Frankfurt and other major cities.

Four cities, though too small for ICE service, are big enough for rail service. They are Hannoversch-Münden, Marburg (change for both at Kassel), Hameln, and Celle (change for both at Hannover).

VISITOR INFORMATION

Information on the entire Fairy-Tale Road can be obtained from the Deutsche Märchenstrasse.

➤ TOURIST INFORMATION: **Alsfeld** (✉ Verkehrsbüro Touristcenter, Am Markt 13, D–36304, ☎ 06631/182–165, WEB www.stadt.alsfeld.de). **Bad Pyrmont** (✉ Touristik Information, Europapl. 1, D–31812, ☎ 05281/940–511, WEB www.badpyrmont.de). **Bodenwerder** (✉ Städtische Verkehrsamt, Weserstr. 3, D–37619, ☎ 05533/40542, WEB www.bodenwerder.de). **Bremen** (✉ Verkehrsverein, Findorffstr. 105, D–28215, ☎ 01805/101–030, WEB www.bremen-tourism.de). **Bremerhaven** (✉ Bremerhaven Touristik, Van-Ronzelen-Str. 2, D–27568, ☎ 0471/946–4610, WEB www.seestadt-bremerhaven.de). **Celle** (✉ Markt 14–16, D–29221, ☎ 05141/1212; 877/862–3553 in the U.S., FAX 05141/12459; 530/937–8787 in the U.S., WEB www.region-celle.de). **Deutsche Märchenstrasse** (✉ Königspl. 53, D–34117 Kassel, ☎ 0561/707–7120, WEB www.deutsche-maerchenstrasse.de). **Fulda** (✉ Städtische Verkehrsbüro, Schlossstr. 1, D–36037, ☎ 0661/102–346, WEB www.fulda.de). **Gelnhausen** (✉ Verkehrsverein, Obermarkt 7, D–63571, ☎ 06051/830–300, WEB www.wfmkk.de). **Göttingen** (✉ Fremdenverkehrsverein, Altes Rathaus, Markt 9, D–37073, ☎ 0551/54000, FAX 0551/499–800, WEB www.goettingen.de). **Hameln** (✉ Hameln Marketing und Tourismus, Deisterallee 1, D–31785, ☎ 05151/202–617, WEB www.hameln.de). **Hanau** (✉ Tourist Information Hanau, Am Markt 14–18, D–63450, ☎ 06181/295–950, WEB www.hanau.de). **Hannover** (✉ Hannover Information, Ernst-August-Pl. 2, D–30159, ☎ 0511/1684–9700, WEB www.hannover.de). **Hannoversch-Münden** (✉ Verkehrsbüro, Lotzstr. 2, D–34346, ☎ 05541/75313, WEB www.hann.muenden.de). **Höxter** (✉ Fremdenverkehrsverein, Historisches Rathaus, Weserstr. 11, D–37671, ☎ 05271/963–431, WEB www.hoexter.de). **Kassel** (✉ Tourist-Information, Obere Königstr. 8, D–34117, ☎ 0561/707–707, WEB www.kassel.de). **Marburg** (✉ Pilgrimstein 26, D–35037 ☎ 06421/99120, WEB www.marburg.de). **Steinau an der Strasse** (✉ Verkehrsamt, Bruder-Grimm-Str. 70, D–36396, ☎ 06663/96310, WEB www.steinau.de).

14 HAMBURG

Water—in the form of the Alster Lakes and the Elbe River—is Hamburg's defining feature and the key to the city's success. The city-state's official title, the Free and Hanseatic City of Hamburg, reflects its kingpin status in the medieval Hanseatic League, a union that dominated trade on the North and the Baltic seas. The seafaring life has given the city some of its most distinctive attractions, from the fish market to the red-light district (the Reeperbahn).

Updated by Jürgen Scheunemann

A HARBOR CITY WITH AN INTERNATIONAL PAST, Hamburg is the most tolerant and open-minded of German cities. The media have made Hamburg their capital by planting some of the leading newspapers, magazines, and television stations here. Add to that the slick world of advertising, show business, and model agencies, and you have a populace of worldly and fashionable professionals. Not surprisingly, the city of movers and shakers is also the city with most of Germany's millionaires.

The *Hanseaten*—members of the distinguished city business and political elite—act with an understatement, modesty, and sincerity that have gained them a formidable reputation throughout Germany. Downtown and in fashionable restaurants, Hanseaten are easily recognizable by their conservative dress code of navy blue and gray. Those accustomed to the warm *Gemütlichkeit* (conviviality) and jolly camaraderie of Munich should be advised that Hamburg initially presents a more somber face, as do most northern German cities. People here are reputed to be notoriously frugal and cool, yet within their own *Kiez* (street and neighborhood) they are generous and hospitable hosts with a penchant for indulging in the most refined delicacies.

For Europeans, the port city invariably triggers thoughts of the gaudy Reeperbahn underworld, that sleazy strip of clip joints, sex shows, and wholesale prostitution that helped earn Hamburg its reputation as "Sin City." Today the infamous red-light district is just as much a hip meeting place for young Hamburgers and tourist crowds, who flirt with the bright lights and chic haunts of the not-so-sinful Reeperbahn, especially on warm summer nights.

Hamburg, or "Hammaburg," was founded in 810 by Charlemagne. For centuries it was a walled city, its gigantic outer fortifications providing a tight little world relatively impervious to outside influences. The city is at the mouth of the Elbe, one of Europe's great rivers and the 97-km (60-mi) umbilical cord that ties the harbor to the North Sea. Its role as a port gained it world renown. It was a powerful member of the Hanseatic League, the medieval union of northern German merchant cities that dominated shipping in the Baltic and North seas, with satellites in Bergen, Visby, Danzig, Riga, Novgorod, and elsewhere.

The Thirty Years' War left Hamburg unscathed, and Napoléon's domination of much of the continent in the early 19th century also failed to affect it. Indeed, it was during the 19th century that Hamburg reached the crest of its power, when the largest shipping fleets on the seas with some of the fastest ships afloat were based here. Its merchants traded with the far corners of the globe. Ties to New York, Buenos Aires, and Rio de Janeiro were stronger than those to Berlin or Frankfurt. During the four decades leading up to World War I, Hamburg became one of the world's richest cities. Its aura of wealth and power continued right up to the outbreak of World War II. Nowadays about 15,000 ships sail up the lower Elbe each year, carrying more than 50 million tons of cargo—from petroleum and locomotives to grain and bananas.

What you see today is the "new" Hamburg. The Great Fire of 1842 all but obliterated the original city; a century later World War II bombing raids destroyed port facilities and leveled more than half of the city proper. In spite of the 1940–44 raids, Hamburg now stands as a remarkably faithful replica of that glittering prewar city—a place of enormous style, verve, and elegance, with considerable architectural diversity, including turn-of-the-20th-century art nouveau buildings. Of particular interest are the 14th-century houses of Deichstrasse—the oldest residential area in Hamburg—and the Kontorhausviertel (Merchant Quarter). The latter contains some unique, north German clinker-brick architecture from the 1920s.

The comparison that Germans like to draw between Hamburg and Venice is somewhat exaggerated. But the city *is* threaded with countless canals and waterways spanned by about 1,000 bridges, even more than you'll find in Venice. Swans glide on the canals. Arcaded passageways run along the waterways. In front of the Renaissance-style Rathaus (city hall) is a square that resembles the Piazza San Marco.

The distinguishing feature of downtown Hamburg is the Alster (Alster Lakes). Once an insignificant waterway, it was dammed in the 18th century to form an artificial lake. Divided at its south end, it is known as the Binnenalster (Inner Alster) and the Aussenalster (Outer Alster)—the two separated by a pair of graceful bridges, the Lombard Brücke and the John F. Kennedy Brücke. The Inner Alster is lined with stately hotels, department stores, fine shops, and cafés; the Outer Alster is framed by parks and gardens against a backdrop of private mansions. From late spring into fall, sailboats and windsurfers skim across the surface of the Outer Alster and white excursion steamers ferry back and forth. The view from these vessels (or from the shore of the Outer Alster) is of the stunning skyline of six spiny spires (five churches and the Rathaus) that is Hamburg's identifying feature. It all creates one of the most distinctive downtown areas of any European city.

Pleasures and Pastimes

Dining

Hamburg is undoubtedly one of the best places in the country to enjoy fresh seafood. The flotilla of fishing boats brings a wide variety of fish to the city—to sophisticated upscale restaurants as well as simple harborside taverns. One of the most celebrated dishes among the robust local specialties is *Aalsuppe* (eel soup), a tangy concoction not entirely unlike Marseilles's famous bouillabaisse. A must in summer is *Aalsuppe grün* (eel soup seasoned with dozens of herbs); *Räucheraal* (smoked eel) is equally good. In the fall try *Bunte oder Gepflückte Finten,* a dish of green and white beans, carrots, and apples. Available anytime of year is *Küken* ragout, a concoction of sweetbreads, spring chicken, tiny veal meatballs, asparagus, clams, and fresh peas cooked in a white sauce. Other northern German specialties include *Stubenküken* (young, male, oven-fried chicken); *Vierländer Mastente* (duck stuffed with apples, onions, and raisins); *Birnen, Bohnen, und Speck* (pears, beans, and bacon); and the sailors' favorite, *Labskaus*—a stew made from pickled meat, potatoes, and (sometimes) herring, garnished with a fried egg, sour pickles, and lots of beets.

The Harbor

A cruise of Germany's gateway to the world is a must. The energy from the continuous ebb and flow of huge cargo vessels and container ships, and the harbor's prosperity and international flavor best symbolize the city's spirit. The narrow cobblestone streets and late-medieval warehouses in the older parts of town testify to Hamburg's powerful Hanseatic past. Bars and nightclubs have transformed some of the harbor area into a hot spot for eyebrow-raising entertainment.

Shopping

Although not as rich or sumptuous on first sight as Düsseldorf or Munich, Hamburg is nevertheless expensive and ranks first among Germany's shopping experiences. Chichi boutiques sell primarily distinguished and somewhat conservative fashion; understatement is the style here. Some of the country's premier designers, such as Karl Lagerfeld, Jil Sander, and Wolfgang Joop, are either native Hamburgers or have worked here for quite some time. Hamburg has the greatest number of shopping malls in the country, mostly small but elegant downtown arcades offering entertainment, fashion, and fine food.

EXPLORING HAMBURG

Hamburg's most important attractions stretch between the Alster Lakes, to the north, and the harbor and the Elbe River, to the south. This area consists of four distinct quarters. St. Georg is the business district around the Hauptbahnhof (main train station). The historic Altstadt (Old City) clusters near the harbor and surrounds the Rathaus (town hall). West of Altstadt is Neustadt (New City). The shabby but thrilling district of St. Pauli includes the Reeperbahn, a strip of sex clubs and bars.

Numbers in the text correspond to numbers in the margin and on the Hamburg map.

Great Itineraries

With more than 1.7 million citizens, Hamburg is Germany's second-largest city, but it's still manageable. Easily traversed on foot, the business district retains its relatively small medieval scale, yet it's dominated by broad boulevards and modern buildings. You can reach the historic quarters near the harbor and St. Pauli in minutes by subway and then explore them on foot.

IF YOU HAVE 2 DAYS

With two days you can see all the major sights in town. Start at the Alster Lakes and head toward the main shopping boulevards of Jungfernstieg and Mönckebergstrasse. A short walk south of Mönckebergstrasse takes you to the majestic Rathaus Square, while a brief walk north on the same street leads to the equally impressive Hauptbahnhof, the largest steel-and-glass construction of its kind in Europe. To the southeast, the Kontorhausviertel is one of the nicest parts of town, a collection of old brick warehouses dating back to the 1920s.

Take a quick tour of the Freihafen Hamburg, Hamburg's port, on your second day. Compare the port's modern warehouses with their antique counterparts on photogenic Deichstrasse in the Altstadt (Old City). You may want to inspect at least one of the city's great churches; a good choice is the city's premier baroque landmark, St. Michaeliskirche. Finally, head over to the Landungsbrücken, the starting point for boat rides in the harbor and along the Elbe River. And don't leave Hamburg without a jaunt down St. Pauli's Reeperbahn.

IF YOU HAVE 3 DAYS

Begin a day watching wild animals roam free at Hagenbecks Tierpark. Equally green are the two parks, Planten un Blomen and the Alter Botanischer Garten, in the business district. After exploring the downtown's other attractions, from the Alster to the Hauptbahnhof, detour to the Kunsthalle and the Museum für Kunst und Gewerbe, both showcasing some of the best paintings and artwork in Germany.

Devote another day to historic Hamburg and the harbor. Take in the docks and don't miss the Speicherstadt's 19th-century warehouses. After a walk among the charming houses on Deichstrasse, continue on to the meticulously restored Krameramtswohnungen, the late-medieval shopkeepers' guild houses. Next, visit the Museum für Hamburgische Geschichte for an excellent overview of the city's dramatic past.

Hamburg

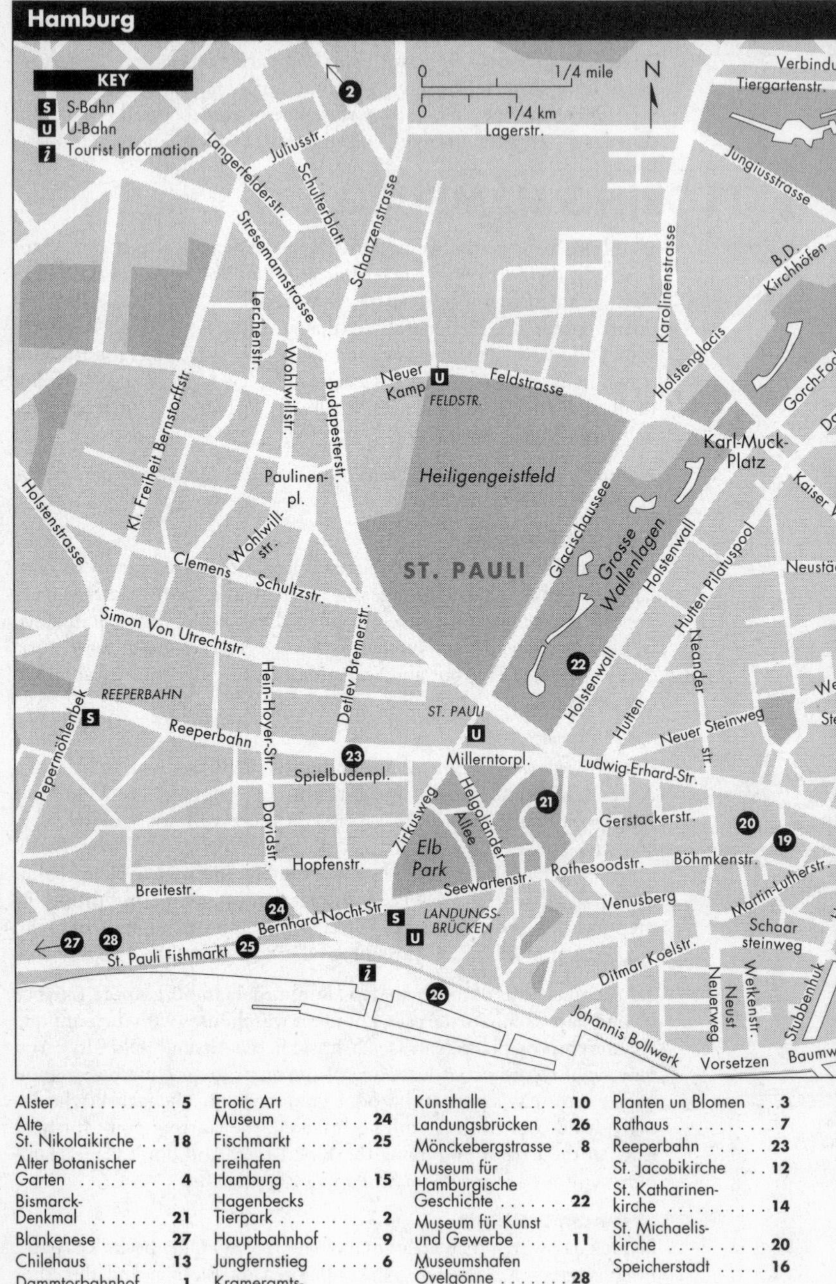

- Alster 5
- Alte St. Nikolaikirche . . . 18
- Alter Botanischer Garten . . . 4
- Bismarck-Denkmal . . . 21
- Blankenese . . . 27
- Chilehaus . . . 13
- Dammtorbahnhof . . . 1
- Deichstrasse . . . 17
- Erotic Art Museum . . . 24
- Fischmarkt . . . 25
- Freihafen Hamburg . . . 15
- Hagenbecks Tierpark . . . 2
- Hauptbahnhof . . . 9
- Jungfernstieg . . . 6
- Krameramts-wohnungen . . . 19
- Kunsthalle . . . 10
- Landungsbrücken . . . 26
- Mönckebergstrasse . . 8
- Museum für Hamburgische Geschichte . . . 22
- Museum für Kunst und Gewerbe . . . 11
- Museumshafen Övelgönne . . . 28
- Planten un Blomen . . 3
- Rathaus . . . 7
- Reeperbahn . . . 23
- St. Jacobikirche . . . 12
- St. Katharinen-kirche . . . 14
- St. Michaelis-kirche . . . 20
- Speicherstadt . . . 16

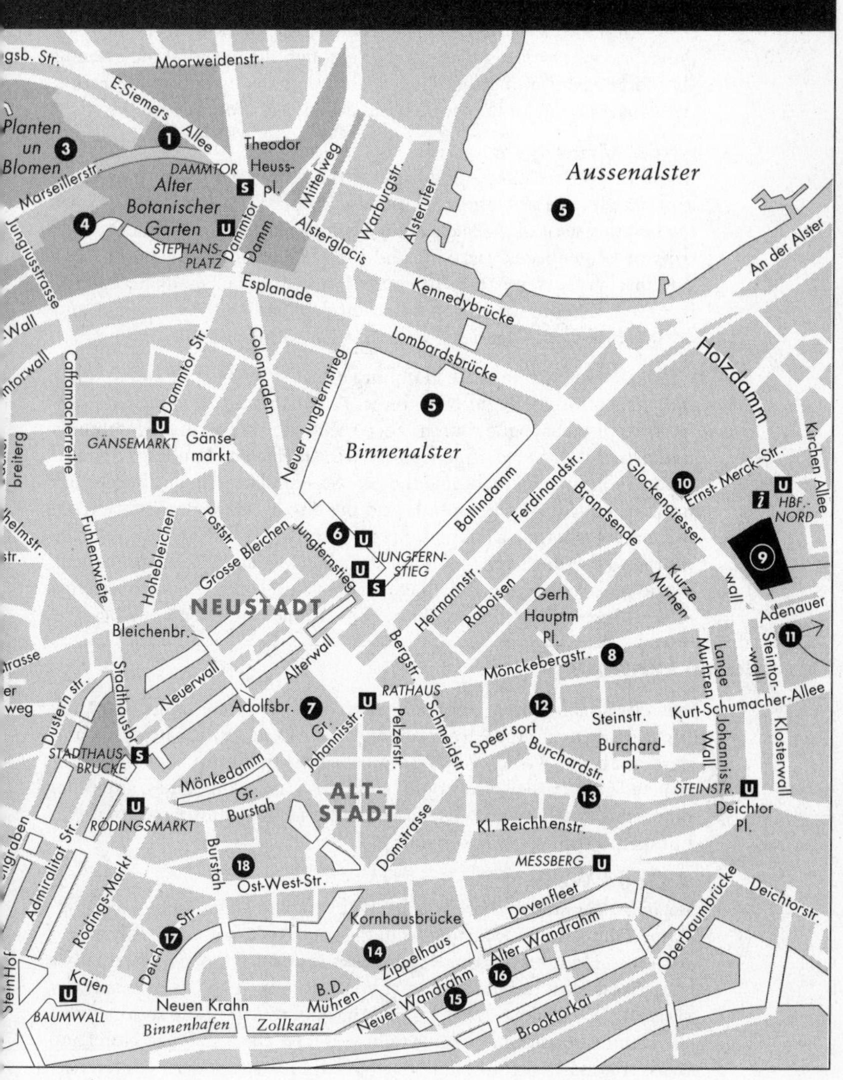

Moorweidenstr.
E.-Siemers Allee
Planten un Blomen
Theodor Heuss-pl.
DAMMTOR
Marseillerstr.
Alter Botanischer Garten
STEPHANS-PLATZ
Dammtor Damm
Mittelweg
Warburgstr.
Alsterufer
Aussenalster
Alsterglacis
Jungiusstrasse
Esplanade
Kennedybrücke
An der Alster
Lombardsbrücke
Holzdamm
Caffamacherreihe
Dammtor Str.
Colonnaden
Neuer Jungfernstieg
Binnenalster
GÄNSEMARKT
Gänse-markt
Fuhlentwiete
Hohebleichen
Poststr.
Grosse Bleichen
Jungfernstieg
JUNGFERN-STIEG
Ballindamm
Ferdinandstr.
Brandsende
Glockengiesser
Ernst-Merck-Str.
Kirchen Allee
HBF.-NORD
NEUSTADT
Bleichenbr.
Hermannstr.
Raboisen
Gerh Hauptm Pl.
Kurze Mühren
Wall
Adenauer
Steintor-wall
Neuerwall
Alterwall
Bergstr.
Mönckebergstr.
Lange Mühren
Stadthausbr.
Adolfsbr.
RATHAUS
Schmiedstr.
Kurt-Schumacher-Allee
Dustern str.
Gr. Johannisstr.
Pelzerstr.
Speer sort
Steinstr.
Johannis Wall
Klosterwall
STADTHAUS-BRÜCKE
Mönkedamm
Burchardstr.
Burchard-pl.
Gr. Burstah
ALT-STADT
STEINSTR.
Deichtor Pl.
RÖDINGSMARKT
Domstrasse
Kl. Reichhenstr.
Admiralitat Str.
Burstah
MESSBERG
Ost-West-Str.
Deichtorstr.
Rödings-Markt
Dovenfleet
Oberbaumbrücke
Kornhausbrücke
Alter Wandrahm
Deich Str.
Zippelhaus
SteinHof
Kajen
B.D. Mühren
Neuer Wandrahm
BAUMWALL
Neuen Krahn
Brooktorkai
Binnenhafen
Zollkanal

Save a day for St. Pauli, too. Early one morning, mingle with locals at the Fischmarkt, a boisterous market. Board one of the boats at the Landungsbrücken for a sightseeing tour through the harbor. One evening should be spent along the Reeperbahn, perhaps including the Erotic Art Museum, one of the few tasteful displays of eroticism on the strip.

IF YOU HAVE 4 DAYS

You'll be able to make some trips off the beaten path with four days. To get a glimpse of Hamburg's playful art nouveau architecture, start the first day west of the lakes at the Dammtorbahnhof and make quick trips to Hagenbecks Tierpark and the Planten un Blomen and Alter Botanischer Garten parks. The inner-city district has many highlights, from the Alster to the Kontorhausviertel, including the Chilehaus and St. Jacobikirche, a medieval church with Gothic altars.

On the second day explore Hamburg's past at the harbor and in other old parts of town. Begin with the St. Katharinenkirche, the city's perfectly restored baroque church. Then spend the afternoon at Hamburg's harbor and its historic attractions, from the Freihafen Hamburg to Krameramtswohnungen, including the Alte St. Nikolaikirche, a church ruin now preserved as a memorial. End the day by viewing the city from the giant Bismarck-Denkmal. Spend a third day in St. Pauli. On the fourth day return to the Landungsbrücken and embark on a boat ride to the terraced, waterside village of Blankenese and the historic ships at the Museumshafen Övelgönne. This is old Hamburg at its best.

Downtown Hamburg

The city's heart (and shops) is centered on two long boulevards, the Jungfernstieg and the Mönckebergstrasse. The area was heavily bombarded during World War II, so most of the buildings here were constructed after it; they now house banks, insurance companies, and other big businesses. Downtown may not be the most beautiful part of town, but its atmosphere is invigorating.

A Good Walk

Begin at **Dammtorbahnhof** ①, a fine example of Hamburg's art nouveau architecture. Departing from the south exit, you can easily take a detour to Hamburg's zoo, **Hagenbecks Tierpark** ②, one of Germany's oldest and most popular urban animal habitats. It has its own subway stop on the U–2 line. After visiting the zoo, return to the south exit of the Dammtor station; on your right you'll see the SAS Plaza Hotel and the Congress Centrum Hamburg (CCH), a vast, modern conference-and-entertainment complex. Continue past the Congress Centrum and bear left in a sweeping arc through the ornamental park **Planten un Blomen** ③. Leave the park at Marseillerstrasse and cross over into the less formal **Alter Botanischer Garten** ④. Both the park and the gardens are in the larger Wallringpark, which encompasses four parks in all. At the garden's southeast exit at Stephansplatz, cross over the Esplanade and walk down Colonnaden to reach the **Alster Lakes** ⑤ and the **Jungfernstieg** ⑥, the most elegant boulevard in downtown Hamburg.

Turn right off the Jungfernstieg onto Reesendamm and make your way to the **Rathaus** ⑦ and its square. Leave by its east side, perhaps pausing to join those relaxing on the steps of the memorial to the poet Heinrich Heine, a great fan of the city.

Beyond the memorial lies **Mönckebergstrasse** ⑧, Hamburg's not-so-elegant but always-bustling shopping boulevard. At its end you'll meet the busy main road of Steintorwall, which was the easternmost link of the defense wall encircling the Old Town in the 17th century. Take the pedestrian underpass to the **Hauptbahnhof** ⑨, Hamburg's impressive central train station. Leave the Hauptbahnhof the way you entered and turn right on Steintorwall, which continues as Glockengiesserwall, until you come to the major art museum, **Kunsthalle** ⑩, on the corner of Ernst-Merck-Strasse.

A quite different but equally fascinating perspective on art is offered by the nearby **Museum für Kunst und Gewerbe** ⑪. To reach it, head in the direction from which you came and turn left on Steintordamm, crossing over the railroad tracks. The large, yellow museum is across the street, its entrance on Brockestrasse.

Turn right when leaving the museum, then right again onto Kurt-Schumacher-Allee. Cross over Steintorwall near the subway and continue west along Steinstrasse to the **St. Jacobikirche** ⑫—you'll recognize it by its needle spire. Cross over Steinstrasse when leaving the church and head down Burchardstrasse, which will bring you to Burchardplatz. This area between Steinstrasse and Messberg is known as the Kontorhausviertel, a restored quarter with redbrick commercial buildings dating to the 1920s. The most famous building is at the south end of Burchardplatz—the **Chilehaus** ⑬ resembles a huge ship.

TIMING

You need half a day for just walking the proposed tour, depending on how much time you devote to the parks, the zoo (both are crowded but most enjoyable on summer weekends), and to shopping (which isn't advisable on Saturday morning because of the crowds). If you add two hours for visits to the museums and the Rathaus and two more hours for the delightful boat tour on the Alster Lakes, you'll end up spending more than a full day downtown.

Sights to See

❺ **Alster** (Alster Lakes). These twin lakes provide downtown Hamburg one of its most memorable vistas. The two lakes meet at the Lombard and Kennedy bridges. In summer the boat landing at the Jungfernstieg, below the Alsterpavillion, is the starting point for the *Alsterdampfer*, the flat-bottom passenger boats that traverse the lakes. Small sailboats and rowboats, hired from yards on the shores of the Alster, are very much a part of the summer scene.

Every Hamburger dreams of living within sight of the Alster, but only the wealthiest can afford it. Some lucky millionaires own the magnificent garden properties around the Alster's perimeter, known as the Millionaire's Coast. But you don't have to be a guest on one of these estates to enjoy the waterfront—the Alster shoreline has 6 km (4 mi) of tree-lined public pathways. Popular among joggers, these trails are a lovely place for a stroll. *U-bahn: Jungfernstieg.*

❹ **Alter Botanischer Garten** (Old Botanical Gardens). This green and open park within Wallringpark cultivates rare and exotic plants. Tropical and subtropical species grow under glass in hothouses, and specialty gardens, including herbal and medicinal plantings, are clustered around the moat. ✉ *Stephanspl., Neustadt,* ☎ *no phone.* 🎫 *Free.* 🕓 *Daily 8–6. U-bahn: Stefanspl.*

⓭ **Chilehaus** (Chile House). This fantastical 10-story structure, which at first looks like a vast landlocked ship, is the standout of the **Kontorhausviertel**, a series of imaginative clinker-brick buildings designed in the New Objectivity style of 1920s civic architect Fritz Schumacher. The building was commissioned by businessman Henry Sloman, who traded in saltpeter from Chile. ✉ *Buchardspl., Altstadt. U-bahn: Messberg.*

❶ **Dammtorbahnhof** (Dammtor Train Station). Built in 1903, this elevated steel-and-glass art nouveau structure is one of Hamburg's finest train stations. It is one of many art nouveau buildings you'll see in the city. You can buy a city map at the newsstand in the station. ✉ *Ernst-Siemers-Allee, Altstadt. U-bahn: Dammtor.*

Deichtorhallen. This complex of warehouses built in 1911–12 is near the Kontorhausviertel and is now one of the country's largest exhibition halls for modern art. Its interior resembles an oversize loft, and its changing exhibits have presenting the works of such artists as Andy Warhol, Roy Lichtenstein, and Miró. ✉ *Deichtorstr. 1–2, Altstadt,* ☎ *040/321–0307.* *Fees vary.* *Tues.–Sun. 11–6. U-bahn: Messberg.*

❷ **Hagenbecks Tierpark** (Hagenbecks Zoo). One of the country's oldest and most popular zoos is family-owned. Founded in 1848, it was the world's first city park to let wild animals such as lions, elephants, chimpanzees, and others roam freely in vast, open-air corrals. Weather permitting, you can even ride an elephant. In the *Troparium,* an artificial habitat creates a rain forest, an African desert, and a tropic sea. The famous walrus *Antje* is North Germany's Television mascot. ✉ *Hagenbeckallee at Hamburg-Stellingen, Niendorf,* ☎ *040/540–0010,* WEB *www.hagenbeck.de.* *€11.50.* *Summer, daily 9–dusk; winter, daily 9–4:30 (last admission at 3:30). U-bahn: Hagenbecks Tierpark.*

❾ **Hauptbahnhof** (Main Train Station). This central train station's cast-iron-and-glass architecture evokes the grandiose self-confidence of imperial Germany. The chief feature of the enormous 394-ft-long structure is its 460-ft-wide glazed roof supported only by pillars at each end. The largest structure of its kind in Europe, it is remarkably spacious and light inside. Though built in 1906 and having gone through many modernizations, it continues to have tremendous architectural impact. Today it sees a heavy volume of international, national, and suburban rail traffic. ✉ *Steintorpl., St. Georg. U-bahn: Hauptbahnhof.*

❻ **Jungfernstieg.** This wide promenade looking out over the Alster Lakes is the city's premier shopping boulevard. Laid out in 1665, it used to be part of a muddy millrace that channeled water into the Elbe. Hidden from view behind the sedate facade of Jungfernstieg is a network of nine covered arcades that together account for almost a mile of shops selling everything from souvenirs to haute couture. Many of these air-conditioned passages have sprung up in the past two decades, but some have been here since the 19th century; the first glass-covered arcade, called Sillem's Bazaar, was built in 1845. *Neustadt. U-bahn: Jungfernstieg.*

NEED A BREAK? Hamburg's best-known and oldest café, the **Alex im Alsterpavillon** (✉ Jungfernstieg 54, Neustadt, ☎ 040/350–1870) is an ideal vantage point from which to observe the constant activity on the Binnenalster.

★ ❿ **Kunsthalle** (Art Gallery). One of the most important art museums in Germany, the Kunsthalle has 3,000 paintings, 400 sculptures, and a coin and medal collection that dates from the 14th century. In the postmodern, cube-shape building designed by Berlin architect O. M. Ungers, the **Galerie der Gegenwart** houses a collection of international modern art created since 1960, including works by Andy Warhol, Joseph Beuys, Georg Baselitz, and David Hockney. Graphic art is well represented, with a special collection of works by Picasso and the late Hamburg artist Horst Janssen, famous for his satirical world view. In the old wing, you can view works by local artists dating from the 16th century. The outstanding collection of German Romantic paintings includes works by Runge, Friedrich, and Spitzweg. Paintings by Holbein, Rembrandt, Van Dyck, Tiepolo, and Canaletto are also on view, while late-19th-century impressionism is represented by works by Leibl, Liebermann, Manet, Monet, and Renoir. ✉ *Glockengiesserwall 1,*

Altstadt, ☎ 040/4285–45765, WEB www.hamburger-kunsthalle.de. €7.50. Tues.–Sun. 10–6, Thurs. 10–9. U-bahn: Hauptbahnhof.

8 **Mönckebergstrasse.** This broad, bustling street of shops—Hamburg's major thoroughfare—cuts through both the historic and new downtown areas. It was laid out in 1908 when this part of the Old Town was redeveloped. The shops here are not as exclusive as those of Jungfernstieg; the stores and shopping precincts on both sides of the street provide a wide selection of goods at more affordable prices. *Altstadt. U-bahn: Jungfernstieg.*

11 **Museum für Kunst und Gewerbe** (Arts and Crafts Museum). The museum houses a wide range of exhibits, from 15th- to 18th-century scientific instruments to an art nouveau interior complete with ornaments and furnishings. It was built in 1876 as a combination museum and school. Its founder, Justus Brinckmann, intended it to be a bastion of the applied arts that would counter what he saw as a decline in taste due to industrial mass production. A keen collector, Brinckmann amassed a wealth of unusual objects, including a collection of ceramics from all over the world. ✉ *Steintorpl. 1, Altstadt, ☎ 040/4285–42630, WEB www.mkg-hamburg.de. €7.20 or €8.20 depending on exhibition. Thurs. after 5 €4.10. Tues., Wed., and Fri.–Sun. 10–6, Thurs. 10–9. U-bahn: Hauptbahnhof.*

3 **Planten un Blomen** (Plants and Flowers Park). Opened in 1935, this huge, tranquil park is renown in Germany for its well-kept gardens. The park lies within the remains of the 17th-century fortified wall that guarded the city during the Thirty Years' War. If you visit on a summer evening, you'll see the Wasserballet, the play of an illuminated fountain set to organ music. Make sure you get to the lake in good time for the show—it begins at 10 PM each evening during the summer (at 9 PM in September). Also during the summer, traditional tea ceremonies are presented in the Japanese Garden, the largest of its kind in Europe.

The Plants and Flowers Park is part of the larger **Wallringpark,** which also includes the Alter Botanischer Garten and the Kleine and Grosse Wallanlagen parks to the south, whose special appeal is their well-equipped leisure facilities, including a children's playground and theater, a model-boat pond, roller- and ice-skating rinks, and outdoor chess. ✉ *Planten un Blomen: Stephanspl., Neustadt, ☎ 040/4283–82327, Free. Mar.–Oct., daily 9–noon, 1–4:45; Nov.–Feb., daily 9–noon, 1–3:45. U-bahn: Stephansplatz.*

★ 7 **Rathaus** (Town Hall). To most Hamburgers this large building is the symbolic heart of the city. As a city-state—an independent city and simultaneously one of the 16 federal states of Germany—Hamburg has a city council and a state government, both of which have their administrative headquarters in the Rathaus. A pompous neo-Renaissance affair, the building dictates political decorum in the city. To this day, the mayor of Hamburg never welcomes VIPs at the foot of its staircase but always awaits them at the very top—whether it's a president or the queen of England.

Both the Rathaus and the **Rathausmarkt** (Town Hall Market) lie on marshy land, a fact vividly brought to mind in 1962, when the entire area was severely flooded. The large square, with its surrounding arcades, was laid out after Hamburg's Great Fire of 1842. The architects set out to create a square with the grandeur of Venice's Piazza San Marco. Building on the Rathaus was begun in 1866, when 4,000 piles were sunk into the moist soil to support the structure. It was completed in 1892, the year a cholera epidemic claimed the lives of 8,605 people in 71 days. A fountain and monument to that unhappy chapter in Hamburg's history is in a rear courtyard of the Rathaus.

The immense building, with its 647 rooms (six more than Buckingham Palace) and imposing central clock tower, is not the most graceful structure in the city, but the sheer opulence of its interior is astonishing. A 45-minute tour begins in the ground-floor Rathausdiele, a vast pillared hall. Although you can only view the state rooms, their tapestries, huge staircases, glittering chandeliers, coffered ceilings, and grand portraits give you a sense of the city's great wealth in the 19th century and its understandable civic pride. ✉ *Rathausmarkt, Altstadt,* ☎ *040/428–310,* WEB *www.hamburg.de.* *English-language tour €1.* ⏲ *Tours Mon.–Thurs., hourly 10–3:15, Fri.–Sun., hourly 10:15–1:15. U-bahn: Mönckebergstr.*

⓬ **St. Jacobikirche** (St. James's Church). This 13th-century church was almost completely destroyed during World War II. Only the furnishings survived and reconstruction was completed in 1962. The interior is not to be missed—it houses such treasures as the vast baroque organ on which Bach played in 1720 and three Gothic altars from the 15th and 16th centuries. ✉ *Jacobikirchhof 22/Steinstr., Altstadt,* ☎ *040/303–7370.* ⏲ *Mon.–Sat. 10–5, Sun. 10–noon. U-bahn: Mönckebergstr.*

The Harbor and Historic Hamburg

Hamburg's historic sections are a fascinating patchwork of time periods where buildings restored to their medieval splendor hold ground next to sleek high-rises. Along the waterfront late-medieval and 19th-century warehouses contrast with the high-tech harbor installations nearby. Narrow cobblestone streets with richly decorated mansions lead to churches of various faiths, reflecting the diverse origins of the sailors and merchants drawn to the city, and to small museums and old restaurants that once served as sailor taverns.

A Good Walk

This tour takes you south to the picturesque quarters around the harbor area (bring your passport as there's a customs point on the walk). Start with a visit to the restored **St. Katharinenkirche** ⑭. To get there from the Messberg U-bahn station, cross the busy Ost-West-Strasse and continue down Dovenfleet, which runs alongside the Zoll Kanal (Customs Canal). On your way, you will pass the Kornhausbrücke, a bridge with a sign on it announcing your entrance to the **Freihafen Hamburg** ⑮ and the **Speicherstadt** ⑯, a complex of 19th-century warehouses. Continue until Dovenfleet turns into Bei den Mühren, and you'll see the church's distinctive green-copper spire.

As you leave the Free Port over the Brooksbrücke (two bridges down from the Kornhausbrücke), you'll pass through a customs control point, at which you may be required to make a customs declaration. Turn left after the bridge, where Bei den Mühren becomes Bei dem Neuen Krahn. Take your second right onto **Deichstrasse** ⑰, the city's 18th-century business district, which runs alongside Nikolaifleet, a former channel of the Alster and one of Hamburg's oldest canals. After exploring this lovely area, take the Cremon Bridge, at the north end of Deichstrasse. This angled pedestrian bridge spans Ost-West-Strasse. You may wish to make a small detour down one of the narrow alleys (Fleetgänge) between the houses to see the fronts of the houses facing the Nikolaifleet.

The Cremon Bridge will take you to Hopfenmarkt Square, just a stone's throw from the ruins of the **Alte St. Nikolaikirche** ⑱. From here head west on Ost-West-Strasse and cross to the other side at the Rödingsmarkt U-bahn station. Continue along Ost-West-Strasse, which turns into Ludwig-Erhard-Strasse, until you reach Krayenkamp, a side street to your left that will take you to the historic **Krameramtswohnungen** ⑲, or shopkeepers' guild houses. The distance from the Nikolaikirche to Krayenkamp is about 1 km (½ mi). Hamburg's best-loved and most famous landmark, the **St. Michaeliskirche** ⑳, is on the other side of the alley Krayenkamp.

From St. Michaeliskirche, walk west on Bömkenstrasse until you reach a park and the enormous **Bismarck-Denkmal** ㉑, rising high above the greenery. From the monument's northeast exit cross Ludwig-Erhard-Strasse and continue on Holstenwall to the **Museum für Hamburgische Geschichte** ㉒, with exhibits depicting the city's past.

TIMING

This can be a rather short walk, manageable in a half day if you only stroll through the historic harbor quarters. You may wish to spend another 1½ hours at the Museum of Hamburg History and still another hour taking a closer look inside the churches.

Sights to See

⓲ **Alte St. Nikolaikirche** (Old St. Nicholas's Church). The tower and outside walls of this 19th-century neo-Gothic church are all that survived World War II. Today these ruins serve as a monument to those killed and persecuted during the war. Next to the tower is a center documenting the church. It is run by a citizens organization that is also spearheading private efforts to partially rebuild the church and redesign the surrounding area. A cellar wine store is open for browsing and wine tasting. ✉ *Ost-West-Str. at Hopfenmarkt, Altstadt,* ☎ *040/220–3200.* ⏲ *Apr.–Sept., weekdays 10–5, weekends 11–4; Oct.–Mar., Thurs. and Fri. 10–5, weekends 11–4. U-bahn: Rödingsmarkt.*

㉑ **Bismarck-Denkmal** (Bismarck Memorial). The colossal 111-ft granite monument, erected between 1903 and 1906, is an equestrian statue of Otto von Bismarck, Prussia's Iron Chancellor, who was the force behind the unification of Germany. The plinth features bas-reliefs of various German tribes. Created by sculptor Hugo Lederer, the statue calls to mind Roland, the famous warrior from the Middle Ages, and symbolizes the German Reich's protection of Hamburg's international trade. ✉ *St. Pauli. U-bahn: St. Pauli.*

⓱ **Deichstrasse.** The oldest residential area in the Old Town of Hamburg, which dates from the 14th century, now consists of lavishly restored houses from the 17th through the 19th centuries. Many of the original houses on Deichstrasse were destroyed in the Great Fire of 1842, which broke out in No. 42 and left approximately 20,000 people homeless; only a few of the early dwellings escaped its ravages. Today Deichstrasse and neighboring Peterstrasse (just south of Ost-West-Strasse) are of great historical interest. At No. 39 Peterstrasse, for example, is the baroque facade of the Beylingstift complex, built in 1700. Farther along, No. 27, constructed as a warehouse in 1780, is the oldest of its kind in Hamburg. All the buildings in the area have been painstakingly restored, thanks largely to the efforts of individuals. ✉ *Altstadt. U-bahn: Rödingsmarkt.*

NEED A BREAK?

There are two good basement restaurants in this area. The **Alt-Hamburger Aalspeicher** (✉ Deichstr. 43, Altstadt, ☎ 040/362–990) serves fresh fish dishes, including Hamburg's famous eel soup with dried fruits. **Das Kontor** (✉ Deichstr. 32, Altstadt, ☎ 040/371–471), an upscale historic Hamburg tavern, offers some of the city's best fried potatoes and delicious, traditional desserts.

15 **Freihafen Hamburg.** Hamburg's Free Port, the city's major attraction, dates to the 12th century, when the city was granted special privileges by Holy Roman Emperor Frederick I (Barbarossa). One of these was freedom from paying duties on goods transported on the Elbe River. The original Free Port was where the Alster meets the Elbe, near Deichstrasse, but it was moved farther south as Hamburg's trade expanded. When Hamburg joined the German Empire's Customs Union in the late 1800s, the Free Port underwent major restructuring to make way for additional storage facilities. An entire residential area was torn down (including many Renaissance and baroque buildings), and the **Speicherstadt** warehouses, the world's largest block of contiguous storage space, came into being between 1885 and 1927. *U-bahn: St. Pauli Landungsbrücken.*

19 **Krameramtswohnungen** (Shopkeepers' Guild Houses). The shopkeepers' guild built this tightly packed group of courtyard houses between 1620 and 1626 for members' widows. The houses became homes for the elderly after 1866. The half-timber, two-story dwellings, with unusual twisted chimneys and decorative brick facades, were restored in the 1970s and are now protected. The house marked "C" is open to the public. A visit inside gives you a sense of what life was like in those 17th-century dwellings. Tour buses stop here, and some of the houses have been converted to shops. ✉ *Historic House "C," Krayenkamp 10, Speicherstadt,* ☎ *040/3750–1988.* 🎫 *€1; Fri. €.50.* ⏲ *Tues.–Sun. 10–5. U-bahn: Rödingsmarkt.*

NEED A BREAK?

Krameramtsstuben (✉ Krayenkamp 10, Speicherstadt, ☎ 040/365–800) is a rustic bar-cum-restaurant where you can sample hearty local dishes, mostly made with fish. It's open daily from 10 AM to midnight.

22 **Museum für Hamburgische Geschichte** (Museum of Hamburg History). The museum's vast and comprehensive collection of artifacts gives you an excellent overview of Hamburg's development, from its origins in the 9th century to the present. Pictures and models portray the history of the port and shipping between 1650 and 1860. One exhibit chronicles pirates in the North Sea during the late Middle Ages. There's also a 16th-century architectural model of Solomon's Temple, measuring 11 square ft. ✉ *Holstenwall 24, Neustadt,* ☎ *040/4284–12380.* 🎫 *€7.50.* ⏲ *Mon. 1–5, Tues.–Sun. 10–6. U-bahn: St. Pauli.*

14 **St. Katharinenkirche** (St. Catherine's Church). Completed in 1660, this house of worship was severely damaged during World War II but has since been carefully reconstructed. Only two 17th-century epitaphs (to Moller and to von der Feehte) remain from the original interior. ✉ *Katharinenkirchhof 1, Altstadt,* ☎ *040/3037–4730.* ⏲ *Apr.–Sept., daily 9–5; Oct.–Mar., weekends 9–2. U-bahn: Messberg.*

★ 20 **St. Michaeliskirche** (St. Michael's Church). The Michel, as it is called locally, is Hamburg's principal church and northern Germany's finest baroque ecclesiastical building. Constructed between 1649 and 1661 (the tower followed in 1669), it was razed after lightning struck almost a century later. It was rebuilt between 1750 and 1786 in the decorative Nordic baroque style but was gutted by a terrible fire in 1906. The replica completed in 1912 was demolished during the Second World War. The present church is a reconstruction.

The distinctive 433-ft brick-and-iron tower bears the largest tower clock in Germany, 26 ft in diameter. Just above the clock is a viewing platform (accessible by elevator or stairs) that affords a magnificent panorama of the city, the Elbe River, and the Alster Lakes. Twice a day, at 10 AM and 9 PM (Sunday at noon), a watchman plays a trumpet solo from the tower platform, and during festivals an entire wind ensemble crowds onto the platform to perform. The **Multivisionsshow** (slide and audio show) recounts Hamburg's history. ✉ *St. Michaeliskirche, Altstadt,* ☎ *040/376–780,* WEB *www.st-michaelis.de.* 🎫 *Tower: €2.50, crypt: €1.25. Ticket for the exhibition Michaelica and show: €2.50.* ⏲ *Apr.–Sept., Mon.–Sat. 9–6, Sun. 11:30–6; Oct.–Mar., Mon.–Sat. 10–5, Sun. 11–5; shows Thurs. and weekends at 12:30, 1:30, 2:30, and 3:30. U-bahn: Landungsbrücken or Rödingsmarkt.*

NEED A BREAK? Just opposite St. Michaeliskirche is one of Hamburg's most traditional restaurants, the **Old Commercial Room** (✉ Englische Planke 10, Speicherstadt, ☎ 040/366–319). Try one of the local specialties, such as Labskaus or Aalsuppe. If you don't make it to the restaurant, you can buy its dishes (precooked and canned) in department stores in both Hamburg and Berlin.

16 **Speicherstadt** (Warehouse District). These imposing warehouses in the Freihafen Hamburg reveal yet another aspect of Hamburg's extraordinary architectural diversity. A Gothic influence is apparent here, with a rich overlay of gables, turrets, and decorative outlines. These massive rust-brown buildings are still used to store and process every conceivable commodity, from coffee and spices to raw silks and handwoven Oriental carpets. Although you won't be able to enter the buildings, the nonstop comings and goings will give you a good sense of a port at work. If you want to learn about the history and architecture of the old warehouses, detour to the **Speicherstadtmuseum.** ✉ *St. Annenufer 2, Block R, Speicherstadt,* ☎ *040/321–191,* WEB *www.speicherstadtmuseum.de.* 🎫 *€2.50.* ⏲ *Tues.–Sun. 10–5. U-bahn: Messberg.*

St. Pauli and the Reeperbahn

The run-down maritime district of St. Pauli is sometimes described as a "Babel of sin," but that's not entirely fair. The Reeperbahn, its major thoroughfare as well as a neighborhood moniker, offers a broad menu of entertainment in addition to the striptease and sex shows. Beyond this strip of pleasure, St. Pauli and Altona are defined by their Elbe waterfront.

A Good Walk

At the St. Pauli U-bahn station, you'll find yourself at the beginning of a long, neon-lighted street stretching nearly 1 km (½ mi). This is the red-light **Reeperbahn** ㉓, full of nightlife entertainment and sex clubs. The best areas to check out are the Grosse Freiheit, Hans-Albers-Platz, and Davidstrasse. Walk down Davidstrasse to reach the not-to-be-missed **Erotic Art Museum** ㉔, exhibiting all aspects of human sexuality. From the museum walk west on Hafenstrasse until you see the first market booths of the **Fischmarkt** ㉕, a shopper's paradise stocked with fresh fish, meat, and produce (only open Sunday).

From the market you can head back on Hafenstrasse to the nearby piers at **Landungsbrücken** ㉖, where ferries depart for short round-trips. Walk through the long limestone building with two towers to reach the ticket booths.

One trip you should try to make is to the riverside village of **Blankenese** ㉗, 14½ km (9 mi) west of Hamburg. From there you can return by ferry, by S-bahn, or on foot. The celebrated Elbe River walk is long, but it's one of Hamburg's prettiest. On the way to Blankenese (or on the return trip), stop by **Museumshafen Övelgönne** ㉘, a quaint little fishing town and a harbor filled with historic vessels.

TIMING

This tour can last a full day and a long night, including a very enjoyable boat trip through the harbor, and a few hours in the theaters and bars along the Reeperbahn. However, you might just want to walk down the red-light strip and check out the Erotic Art Museum and the Landungsbrücken, all in less than three hours. You have to be either an untiring night owl or an early riser to catch the Fischmarkt on Sunday.

Sights to See

27 **Blankenese.** Blankenese is another of Hamburg's surprises—a suburb west of the city with the character of a quaint fishing village. Some Germans like to compare it to the French and Italian rivieras; many consider it the most beautiful part of Hamburg. In the 14th century Blankenese was an important ferry terminal, but it wasn't until the late 18th and 19th centuries that it became a popular residential area. The most picturesque part of town is the steeply graded hillside, where paths and stairs barely separate closely placed homes. The town has a lively fruit and vegetable market, open Tuesday 8–2, Friday 8–6, and Saturday 8–1. Weekday ferries to Blankenese leave from Pier 3 every 10 to 15 minutes and involve two transfers. *Nonstop HADAG ferries depart from Pier 2 for Blankenese late Mar.–Oct., weekends at 10.30 and 2.30. S-bahn: Blankenese.*

NEED A BREAK? A fine view and well-prepared fish await you at **Sagebiel's Fährhaus** (Blankeneser Hauptstr. 107, Blankenese, 040/861–514), a former farmhouse where Kaiser Wilhelm once celebrated his birthday.

24 **Erotic Art Museum.** Sexually provocative art from 1520 to the present—1,800 original works (mostly photographs) in all—is showcased here. The collection is presented with such great taste and decorum that it has won the respect of many who doubted the museum's seriousness. Special exhibits of modern erotic photography and events are staged in a building on Bernhard-Nocht-Strasse. *Nobistor 10a, at Reeperbahn; special exhibits and events at Bernhard-Nocht-Str. 69, St. Pauli, 040/3178–4126,* WEB *www.erotic-art-museum.hamburg.de. Minimum age 16. €8. Sun.–Thurs. 10 AM–midnight, Fri.–Sat. 10 AM–2 AM. U-bahn: St. Pauli.*

25 **Fischmarkt** (Fish Market). The open-air Altona Fischmarkt is worth getting out of bed early for (or just stay up all night). The pitch of fervent dealmaking is unmatched in Germany. Offering real bargains, the market's barkers are famous for their sometimes rude but usually successful bids to shoppers. Sunday fish markets became a tradition in the 18th century, when fishermen sold their catch before church services. Today freshly caught fish are only a part of the scene. You can find almost anything here—from live parrots and palm trees to armloads of flowers and bananas, from valuable antiques to fourth-hand junk. *Between Grosse Elbestr. and St. Pauli Landungsbrücken, St. Pauli. Sun. 5.30 AM–10.30 AM. U-bahn: Landungsbrücken.*

26 **Landungsbrücken** (Piers). A visit to the port is not complete without a tour of one of the most modern and efficient harbors in the world. Hamburg is Germany's largest seaport, with 33 individual docks and 500 berths lying within its 78 square km (30 square mi). Tours of the harbor begin at the main passenger terminal, where a whole range of ferry and barge rides depart. There's usually a breeze, so dress warmly enough for your trip. Don't expect rolling surf and salty air, however, as Hamburg's port is 56 nautical mi from the North Sea. ***Rickmer Rickmers,*** an 1896 sailing ship that once traveled as far as the West Indies, is open to visitors and is docked at Pier 1. *St. Pauli Landungsbrücken*

1, St. Pauli, ☏ *040/319–5959,* WEB *www.rickmer-rickmers.de.* 🎫 *Rickmer Rickmers €3.* ⏲ *Daily 10–6. U-bahn: Landungsbrücken.*

28 **Museumshafen Övelgönne** (Museum Harbor Övelgönne). The glorious days of *Windjammern,* Hamburg's commercial fleet, come alive in this small harbor museum on the Elbe River. Eighteen antique steam and sailing vessels from the late 19th century can be inspected from the pier or boarded on weekends if a crew is around. Behind the harbor, along the quay, are charming little cottages with tidy gardens. ✉ *Anleger Neumühlen, Ottensen,* ☏ *040/397–383,* WEB *www.museumshafen-oevelgoenne.de.* 🎫 *Free.* ⏲ *Daily 24 hrs.*

NEED A BREAK? No Hanseatic Sunday would be complete without a visit to the **Strandperle** (✉ Am Schulberg, Ottensen, ☏ 040/8801–112), a small but stylish kiosk on the river banks near Övelgönne. Join the Hamburg locals and watch the cargo ships pass while downing your beer with lemonade (an *Alsterwasser*) and munching on a bratwurst.

23 **Reeperbahn.** The hottest spots in town are concentrated in the St. Pauli Harbor area, on the Reeperbahn thoroughfare, and on a little side street known as the Grosse Freiheit (Great Liberty—and that's putting it mildly). The striptease shows are expensive and explicit, but a walk through this area is an experience in itself and costs nothing. Saturday night finds St. Pauli pulsating with people determined to have as much fun as possible. It's *not* advisable, however, to travel through this part of the city alone in the wee hours of the morning.

Although some of the sex clubs may be relatively tame, a good many others are pornographic in the extreme. None of them gets going until about 10 PM; all will accommodate you until the early hours. Order your own drinks rather than letting the hostess do it and pay for them as soon as they arrive, double-checking the price list again before handing over the money.

Among the attractions in the St. Pauli area are theaters, clubs, music pubs, discos, and a bowling alley. The Schmidt Theater, on Reeperbahn, has a repertoire of live music, vaudeville, chansons, and cabaret, while the St. Pauli Theater, on Speilbudenplatz, presents popular lowbrow productions in Hamburger dialect. *U-bahn: St. Pauli.*

DINING

Hamburg has plenty of chic restaurants to satisfy the fashion-conscious local professionals, as well as the authentic salty taverns typical of a harbor town.

CATEGORY	COST*
$$$$	over €25
$$$	€20–€25
$$	€15–€20
$	under €15

**per person for a main course at dinner*

Downtown and Historic Hamburg

$–$$$$ ✕ **Ratsweinkeller.** For atmosphere and robust local specialties, there are few more-compelling restaurants than this cavernous, late-19th-century haunt under the city hall. The simple tables are wooden, and ship models hang from the high stone-and-brick arches. You can order surprisingly fancy or no-nonsense meals. Fish specialties predominate,

Hamburg Dining and Lodging

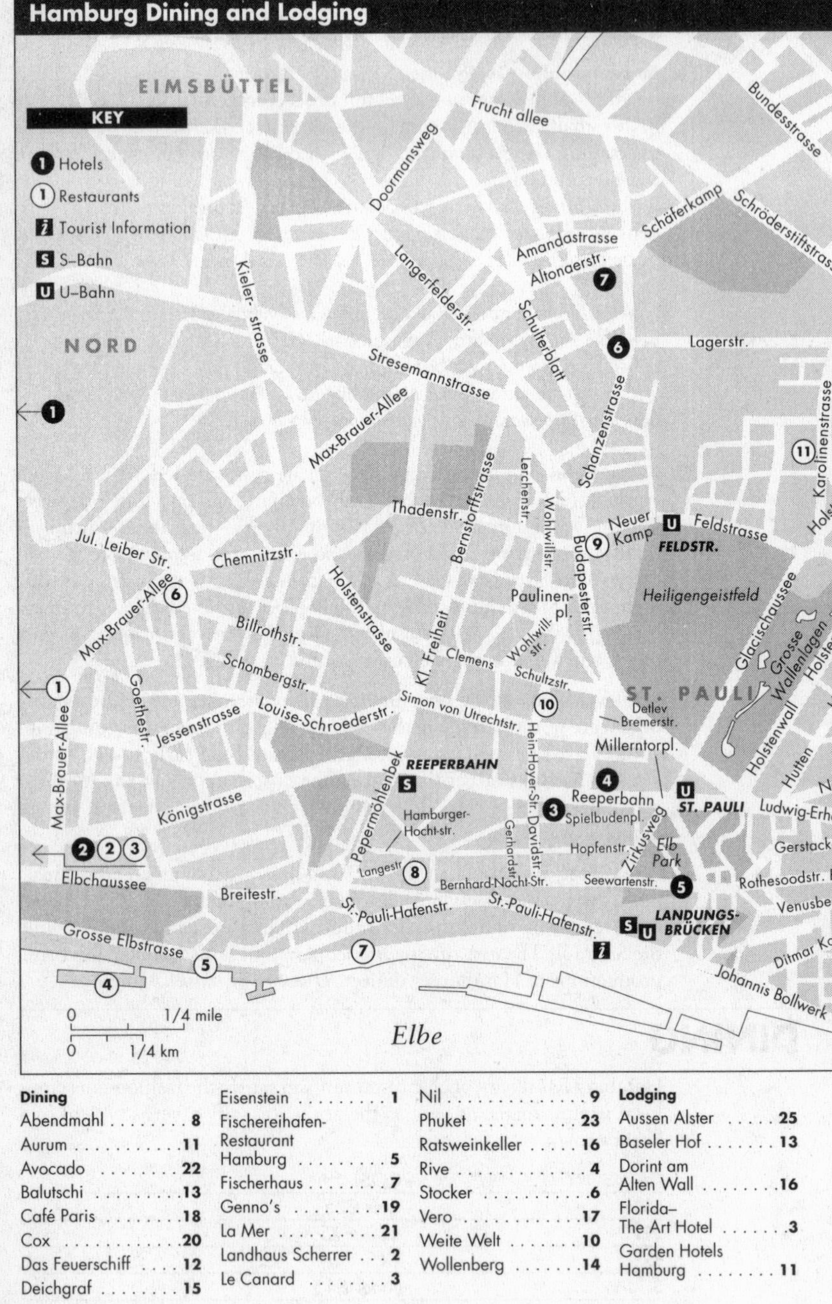

Dining

Abendmahl 8
Aurum 11
Avocado 22
Balutschi 13
Café Paris 18
Cox 20
Das Feuerschiff 12
Deichgraf 15
Eisenstein 1
Fischereihafen-Restaurant Hamburg 5
Fischerhaus 7
Genno's 19
La Mer 21
Landhaus Scherrer . . . 2
Le Canard 3
Nil 9
Phuket 23
Ratsweinkeller 16
Rive 4
Stocker 6
Vero 17
Weite Welt 10
Wollenberg 14

Lodging

Aussen Alster 25
Baseler Hof 13
Dorint am Alten Wall 16
Florida–The Art Hotel 3
Garden Hotels Hamburg 11

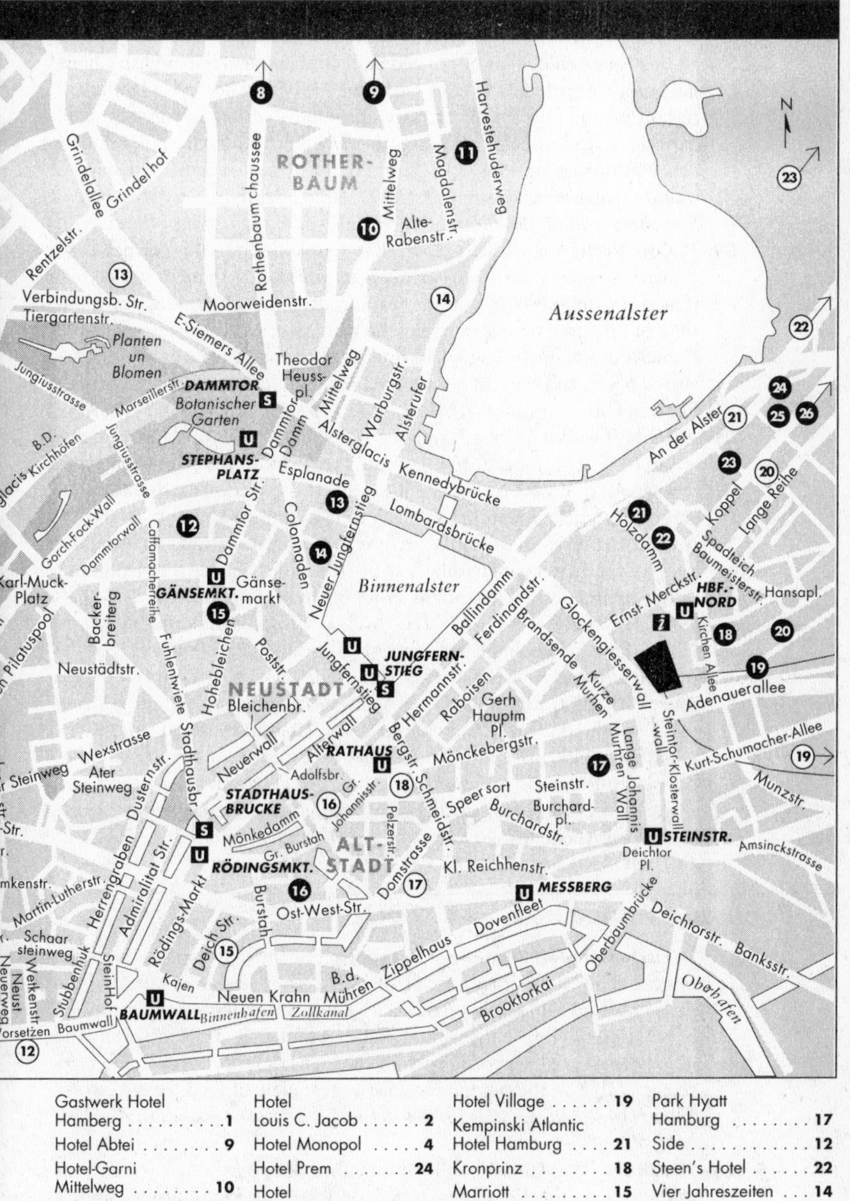

Gastwerk Hotel Hamberg 1
Hotel Abtei 9
Hotel-Garni Mittelweg 10
Hotel Hafen Hamburg/ Hotel Residenz Hafen Hamburg 5
Hotel Louis C. Jacob 2
Hotel Monopol 4
Hotel Prem 24
Hotel Schanzenstern 6
Hotel Sternschanze . . .7
Hotel Terminus Garni 20
Hotel Village 19
Kempinski Atlantic Hotel Hamburg 21
Kronprinz 18
Marriott 15
Mellingburger Schleuse 8
Nippon Hotel 26
Park Hyatt Hamburg 17
Side 12
Steen's Hotel 22
Vier Jahreszeiten . . . 14
Wedina 23

but there's a wide range of choices. ✉ *Grosse Johannisstr. 2, Altstadt,* ☎ *040/364–153. AE, DC, MC, V. No dinner Sun.*

$–$$$ ✕ **Das Feuerschiff.** This bright-red lightship served in the English Channel before it retired to the city harbor in 1989 and became a landmark restaurant and pub. Fresh and tasty German fish dishes are on the menu, as well as traditional seafood entrées from Scandinavia, Poland, and other seafaring nations. On Monday, local bands jam, and once a month a cabaret show is staged. ✉ *Vorsetzen, Hamburg City Sporthafen, Speicherstadt,* ☎ *040/362–553. AE, DC, MC, V. U-bahn: Baumwall.*

$$ ✕ **Café Paris.** Some critics claim that people flock to this former 19th century butchery more to soak up its ambiance than its food, but that's not quite fair. While the restaurant is full of shining porcelain tiles and painted figures covering the vaulted ceiling, it also serves solid French cuisine, including well-known classics such as Boullabaisse, assorted pâtés, and even an occasional German odd-ball like sausage with horseradish. ✉ *Rathausstr. 4, Altstadt,* ☎ *040/3252–7777. AE, MC.*

$$ ✕ **Vero.** If walking along Hamburg's canals reminds you of Venice, this is the perfect restaurant to complete the illusion. An unconventional crossroads of Italian dishes and local flavor, Vero is where to find squid served with mashed potato salad as well as sturgeon ravioli. Its downtown location makes Vero a preferred lunchtime haunt for businesspeople. The better spot to dine here are the tables outside the restaurant, in the atrium of the Zürichhaus shopping mall. ✉ *Domstr. 17–19, Altstadt,* ☎ *040/339–051. AE, DC, MC, V. Closed Mon. and Sun.*

$ ✕ **Deichgraf.** This small and elegant fish restaurant in the heart of the old harbor warehouse district is a Hamburg classic. It's one of the best places to get traditional dishes such as *Hamburger Panfisch* (fried pieces of the day's catch prepared in a wine and mustard sauce) at a very reasonable price of €17.40. The restaurant is in an old merchant house, and historic oil paintings in the dining room depict the hardships of the fisherman of the late 19th century. Reservations are essential on weekends. ✉ *Deichstr. 23, Altstadt,* ☎ *040/364–208. AE, DC, MC, V. Closed Sun.*

St. Pauli and Altona

$$–$$$$ ✕ **Fischereihafen-Restaurant Hamburg.** For the best fish in Hamburg, book a table at this big, upscale restaurant in Altona, just west of the downtown area and right on the Elbe. The menu changes daily according to what's available in the fish market that morning. The restaurant and its oyster bar are a favorite with the city's beau monde. In summer, try to get a table on the sun terrace with a great view of the Elbe. ✉ *Grosse Elbstr. 143, Altona,* ☎ *040/381–816. Reservations essential. AE, DC, MC, V.*

$–$$$ ★ ✕ **Aurum.** The Aurum heralded the move of several other restaurants and cafés to the Karolinenviertel (or Karo, as Hamburgers say), a fashionable but understated nightlife district. In an old city mansion, the Aurum serves fine international cuisine in an almost austere setting—bare, yellowish walls, wooden tables without tablecloths, and simple leather seats. The menu changes weekly, but some favorites returning to the tables are *Lammcaree mit Rosmarinjus* (saddle of lamb in rosemary sauce) or *Merrettichkruste vom Entrecote* (horseradish crust of entrecôte). ✉ *Karolinenstr. 32, Karolinenviertel,* ☎ *040/4318–8432. MC.*

$–$$$ ★ ✕ **Weite Welt.** Weite Welt is an absolute must if you are visiting St. Pauli. The restaurant's name recalls the longing of Hamburg's seafaring folk to see the "great wide world." In an old fish smokehouse on the Reeperbahn's notorious Grosse Freiheit (the live sex shows are just a few steps away), regulars feel right at home thanks to owner Niko

Bornhofen's hospitality. Don't be surprised if he himself tends to your needs and addresses you with the casual *"Du"*. The fish dishes cross the continents of Europe and Asia, and the theme dishes (such as the "Last Supper of the *Titanic*") are a good value. Reservations are essential on weekends. ✉ *Grosse Freiheit 70, St. Pauli,* ☎ *040/319–1214. V. No lunch.*

$$ ★ ✕ **Stocker.** *Nordlichter,* as Northern Germans are affectionately called, love Austrian cuisine and for delicacies including Viennese classics such as schnitzel or boiled beef brisket, Stocker is the city's expert. The restaurant is rather casual and full of Southern charm, a good choice is the *Schmankerlteller,* a hearty sampler with Austrian favorites, or the three-course lunch menu for just €18. In summer, a table in the quaint garden is an absolute must. ✉ *Max-Brauer-Allee 80, Altona,* ☎ *040/3861–5056. AE, DC, MC, V. Closed Mon.*

$–$$$$ ★ ✕ **Rive.** This harborside oyster bar couldn't be a Hamburg establishment without serving at least some local dishes, so take your pick between hearty *Matjes mit drei Saucen* (herring with three sauces), *Dorade in der Salzkruste* (Dorade fried in salt crust), or fancy lobster with aioli. The media clientele come to this shiplike building mostly for the fresh oysters and clams and the spectacular view. ✉ *Van der Smissen Str. 1, Kreuzfahrt-Center, Altona,* ☎ *040/380–5919. Reservations essential. AE.*

$–$$ ★ ✕ **Fischerhaus.** The family-owned fish restaurant may look mediocre, but the food, prepared from family recipes, is outstanding. Most dishes focus on North Sea fish and Hamburg classics such as *Labskaus* (a creamy mix of mashed fish and sausage, served with eggs and pickles), or a plaice dish. A favorite is the *Scholle Finkenwerder Art* (pan-fried plaice with smoked ham and potato salad). When making a reservation, ask for a table upstairs to get a harbor view. ✉ *Fischmarkt 14, St. Pauli,* ☎ *040/314–053. AE, MC, V.*

$–$$ ✕ **Nil.** Media types—the intellectual and cultural elite of Hamburg—gather at this trendy venue for business lunches and prepartying on weekends. The Nil is worth a visit for its interior alone: it's within an old 1950s-style, three-floor shoe shop. The kitchen serves seafood and modern German cuisine, including four different three- to six-course menus, offering fare such as *Zicklein aus dem Ofen mit Bohnen- und Topinamburgemüse* (baked kid, served with beans and Jerusalem artichokes). Reservations are essential for dinner. ✉ *Neuer Pferdemarkt 5, St. Pauli,* ☎ *040/439–7823. No credit cards. Closed Mon. and Tues.*

$ ✕ **Abendmahl.** Off the Reeperbahn, the small Abendmahl is a launching point for the crowds getting ready for the bars and clubs. The fresh dishes on the small menu change daily and focus on French and Italian recipes. But the food plays second fiddle to the inexpensive and inventive drinks and the flirtatious atmosphere. The three-course dinner meal for just €24 is a great deal. ✉ *Hein-Köllisch-Pl. 6, St. Pauli,* ☎ *040/312–758. No credit cards.*

St. Georg

$$–$$$ ✕ **La Mer.** The old-fashioned dining room of the Hotel Prem is perhaps the best hotel restaurant in the city, beautifully set on the Aussenalster, a 10-minute ride from downtown. A host of subtle specialties changes daily, including *Zanderfilet auf Pefferkraut mit gefüllten Waffelkartoffeln* (pike-perch fillet on pepper sauerkraut with stuffed waffle potatoes) or *Brust und Keule vom Perlhuhn auf Schwarzwurzeln mit Kartoffelgratin* (breast and leg of guinea-fowl on black salsify with potato gratin). ✉ *An der Alster 9, St. Georg,* ☎ *040/2483–4040. Jacket and tie. AE, DC, MC, V. No lunch weekends.*

$$ ★ ✕ **Cox.** The Cox has been a reliable and lively restaurant for several years now and simply never goes out of style. It's one of the hippest places around, with waitresses (and patrons, for that matter) who won't give you any attitude. The dishes, mostly German nouvelle cuisine, are known for the careful use of fresh produce and spices from around the globe. The simple and cool interior with red leather banquettes is reminiscent of a French brasserie. The opalescent windows create a timeless atmosphere that seduces some to linger for hours. ✉ *Lange Reihe 68, St. Georg,* ☎ *040/249–422. AE. No lunch weekends.*

Rotherbaum

$$$–$$$$ ★ ✕ **Wollenberg.** There is no better place to catch a glimpse of the picture-perfect "in crowd," star-studded as it is with Hamburg's media personalities. The shiny white villa with a Bauhaus-styled, understated dining hall comes complete with a bar and dance club. You can start your evening with traditional Hamburg fish and game dishes (experimental creations tend to be frowned upon) such as *Zander in Kartoffelkrustwe mit Morcheln* (perch with a potato crust, served with morels), and later dance the night away downstairs. ✉ *Alsterufer 35, Rotherbaum,* ☎ *040/450–1850. Reservations essential. AE, DC, MC, V. Closed Sun.*

$ ✕ **Balutschi.** A favorite among neighborhood students, Balutschi serves affordable and very tasty Pakistani food, prepared with organic products only. The richly decorated restaurant always seems to be crowded, the smell of fresh spices and meat dishes hangs thick in the air. To immerse yourself more profoundly in the distinctively Asian atmosphere, try to get seating in the back room, where guests sit cross-legged around low tables and without shoes. On weekend nights, a reservation is a must. ✉ *Grindelallee 33, Rotherbaum,* ☎ *040/452–479. AE, MC, V.*

Ottensen, Uhlenhorst, and Elsewhere

$$$–$$$$ ✕ **Landhaus Scherrer.** Though this establishment is a ten-minute drive from the downtown area, its parklike setting seems worlds away from the high-rise bustle of the city. Wood-paneled walls and soft lighting create a low-key mood in the building, which was originally a brewery. The food fuses sophisticated specialties with more down-to-earth local dishes. The wine list is exceptional. ✉ *Elbchaussee 130, Ottensen,* ☎ *040/880–1325. AE, DC, MC, V. Closed Sun.*

$$–$$$$ ★ ✕ **Le Canard.** One of Hamburg's top restaurants, Le Canard enjoys a much-coveted location overlooking the harbor and historic vessels at Övelgönne, with enviably elegant decor and cuisine to match. Chef Viehhauser's skills and creativity keep the restaurant's standards high. Fish dishes such as pan-fried turbot predominate, but the roasted duck with red cabbage, traditionally served during the pre-Christmas season, is worth sampling. ✉ *Elbchaussee 139, Ottensen,* ☎ *040/880–5057. Reservations essential. AE, DC, MC, V. Closed Sun.*

$$ ✕ **Eisenstein.** The food is fantastic, considering the low prices, and the crowd bubbly and mostly stylish. A sure bet are the daily menus or the Italian-Mediterranean dishes, including pastas and some excellent pizzas. The Pizza Helsinki (made with sour cream, onions, and fresh gravlax) is truly delicious. The setting, a 19th-century industrial complex with high ceilings and dark redbrick walls, is very rustic. Reservations are essential for dinner. ✉ *Friedensallee 9, Ottensen,* ☎ *040/390–4606. No credit cards.*

$–$$ ★ ✕ **Phuket.** Though it has an unimaginative name and dull facade, Phuket is by far the best Thai, or Asian for that matter, restaurant in town. The place is often jammed with Hamburgers doing pilgrimage from all districts to sample the truly hot fish dishes or the famous chicken in red wine sauce. ✉ *Adolph-Schönfelder-Str. 33–35, Uhlenhorst,* ☎ *040/2982–3380. AE, V.*

$ ✕ **Avocado.** The imaginative vegetarian menu at this popular restaurant is an excellent value. If you're really hungry, try one of the four- or six-course "surprise" dinners (€25–€35 per person). In the pleasant Uhlenhorst District, close to the Aussenalster, this is one of Hamburg's few no-smoking restaurants. ✉ *Kanalstr. 9, Uhlenhorst,* ☎ *040/220–4599. Reservations essential. No credit cards. Closed Mon.*

$ ★ ✕ **Genno's.** Genno's is far from the downtown district in Hamburg-Ham—a run-down residential area where you would hardly expect such a gem of high-quality dining. Owner Eugen Albrecht makes you feel at home with very warm service and equally tasty dishes. The cuisine is a wild mixture of his personal preferences, for example *Lammfilet mit Senfsauce* (fillet of lamb with mustard sauce). The best starter is the *Rote Beete Carpaccio* (beet carpaccio) with white balsamico sauce. The restaurant only has 16 seats, so on weekends especially a reservation is essential. ✉ *Hammer Steindamm 123, Ham,* ☎ *040/202–567. No credit cards. Dinner only. Closed Sun.*

LODGING

Hamburg has a full range of hotels, from five-star, grande-dame luxury enterprises to simple pensions. Nearly year-round conference and convention business keeps most rooms booked well in advance, and the rates are high. But many of the more expensive hotels lower their rates on weekends, when businesspeople have gone home. The tourist office can help with reservations if you arrive with nowhere to stay; ask about the many Happy Hamburg special-accommodation packages.

CATEGORY	COST*
$$$$	over €225
$$$	€150–€225
$$	€75–€150
$	under €75

**All prices are for two people in a double room, including tax and service.*

Downtown and Historic Hamburg

$$$$ ★ **Vier Jahreszeiten.** Some claim that this handsome 19th-century town house on the edge of the Binnenalster is the best hotel in Germany. Antiques—the hotel has a set of near-priceless Gobelin tapestries—fill the public rooms and accentuate the stylish bedrooms; there are fresh flowers in massive vases; rare oil paintings hang on the walls; and all rooms are individually decorated with superb taste. One of the three restaurants, the Jahreszeiten-Grill, has been restored to its 1920s art deco look with dark woods and is worth a visit. If you want a lake-view room, especially one with a balcony, reserve well in advance. ✉ *Neuer Jungfernstieg 9–14, Neustadt D–20354,* ☎ *040/34940,* FAX *040/3494–2600,* WEB *www.hvj.de. 156 rooms, 23 suites. 3 restaurants, room service, in-room data ports, in-room safes, minibars, cable TV with movies, hair salon, health club, massage, sauna, bar, wine shop, baby-sitting, dry cleaning, laundry service, concierge, business services, meeting room, parking (fee), some pets allowed (fee), no-smoking rooms. AE, DC, MC, V.*

$$$–$$$$ ★ **Dorint am Alten Wall.** The flagship hotel of the German hotel chain Dorint is one of the city's finest. Behind the facade of Hamburg's 19th century *Postsparkassenamt* (the German mail service's customer bank) is a sleek decor dominated by gray, white, and dark brown hues. If you

are booking a suite, ask for suite No. 5208 on the fourth floor, whose windows overlook the Fleet canal. All rooms are furnished with timeless design furniture, huge beds (by German standards), and even bigger marble bathrooms. Add to that the central location and the hotel's bistro run by Le Canard chef Josef Viehauser, and a stay at the Dorint is sure to be unforgettable. ✉ *Alter Wall 38–46, Altstadt D–20457,* ☏ *040/369–500,* FAX *040/3695–01000,* WEB *www.dorint.de/hamburg-city. 224 rooms, 18 suites. Restaurant, room service, in-room safes, minibars, cable TV with movies, pool, health club, massage, sauna, bar, baby-sitting, dry cleaning, laundry service, business services, meeting rooms, parking (fee), some pets allowed (fee), no-smoking rooms. AE, DC, MC, V.*

$$$–$$$$ ★ 🏨 **Park Hyatt Hamburg.** This ultramodern hotel is built within the historic walls of the Levantehaus, an old warehouse, not far from the train station. Guest rooms have bright and modern furnishings, somewhat minimalist and Asian in style. Original artwork by local painters adorns the suites. The Club Olympus pool and fitness area is breathtaking, both for its streamlined design and the variety of activities. The Regency Club floor offers such special treats as a free Continental breakfast and a light evening snack. Bagels are smeared in the New York Deli hotel restaurant. ✉ *Bugenhagenstr. 8–10, Neustadt D–20095,* ☏ *040/3332–1234,* FAX *040/3332–1235,* WEB *www.hamburg.hyatt.com. 251 rooms, 31 apartments. 2 restaurants, room service, in-room data ports, minibars, cable TV with movies, indoor pool, hair salon, health club, massage, sauna, bar, baby-sitting, dry cleaning, laundry service, concierge, business services, meeting room, parking (fee), some pets allowed (fee), no-smoking room. AE, DC, MC, V.*

$$$ 🏨 **Marriott.** This was the first Marriott in Germany, and it remains the showpiece—from the extraordinary barrel-roof ceiling of the reception area to the expansive comfort of its guest rooms. The modern green furniture isn't particularly inspired, but you do get amenities such as pay-per-view TV and modem and fax lines. The hotel has a central location—an unbeatable spot on Hamburg's Gänsemarkt, in one of the best shopping areas. The hotel's aptly named American Place is one of the better city-center restaurants. The health club is one of the most modern in northern Germany. ✉ *ABC-Str. 52, Neustadt D–20354,* ☏ *040/35050,* FAX *040/3505–1777,* WEB *www.marriott.com. 277 rooms, 5 suites. Restaurant, room service, in-room data ports, in-room safes, minibars, cable TV with movies, pool, hair salon, health club, hot tub, massage, sauna, bar, piano bar, baby-sitting, dry cleaning, laundry service, concierge, business services, convention center, meeting room, parking (fee), some pets allowed (fee), no-smoking rooms. AE, DC, MC, V.*

$$$ ★ 🏨 **Side.** Deeming itself to be "the luxury hotel of the 21st century," this ambitious newcomer is one of Germany's most architecturally sophisticated hotels. Premiere Milanese designer Mattheo Thun served as the driving force behind the five-star resort in the heart of the city. His vision provided for the stunning lighting arrangement as well as the interior design. Whether soothed by the eggshell-white accents in your room and secluded club atmosphere in the spa, or wowed by the lobby's soaring and stark atrium or the eighth floor lounge, you won't ever want to leave. ✉ *Drehbahn 49, Altstadt D–20304,* ☏ *040/309–990,* FAX *040/3099–9399,* WEB *www.side-hamburg.de. 168 rooms, 10 suites. Restaurant, bar, room service, in-room safes, minibars, cable TV with movies, spa, health club, sauna, dry cleaning, laundry service, meeting rooms, parking (fee), some pets allowed (fee), no-smoking rooms. AE, DC, MC, V.*

$$ 🏨 **Baseler Hof.** It's hard to find a fault in this central hotel near the Binnenalster and the opera house. Service is friendly and efficient, all rooms are neatly furnished, and prices are quite reasonable for this ex-

pensive city. The hotel caters to both individuals and convention groups, so at times the lounge area can become crowded. ✉ *Esplanade 11, Neustadt D–20354,* ☎ *040/359–060,* FAX *040/3590–6918,* WEB *www.baselerhof.de. 151 rooms, 2 suites. Restaurant, no a/c, room service, in-room data ports, bar, baby-sitting, dry cleaning, laundry service, concierge, meeting room, parking (fee), some pets allowed (fee), no-smoking rooms. AE, DC, MC, V.*

$$ **Hotel Village.** Until 1991 the small and charming Hotel Village was a typical brothel near the central train station. Red-and-black carpets and glossy wallpaper in the rooms are a nod to the hotel's past. Some rooms even have their old large beds, replete with baldachin and a revolving mirror on the ceiling. The service (including a 24-hour coffee bar) is extremely friendly and casual. The hotel has gained a reputation as an "in" place where celebrities hide out whenever they want to keep a low profile. ✉ *Steindamm 4, Altstadt D–20099,* ☎ *040/246–137,* FAX *040/486–4949. 19 rooms. No a/c, cable TV, some pets allowed (fee), parking (fee). AE, MC, V.*

$$ **Kronprinz.** For its humble position (on a busy street opposite the railway station) and its moderate price, the Kronprinz is a surprisingly attractive hotel, with a whiff of four-star flair. Rooms are individually styled, modern but homey. ✉ *Kirchenallee 46, Altstadt D–20099,* ☎ *040/243–258,* FAX *040/280–1097. 73 rooms. Restaurant, no a/c, minibars, cable TV, baby-sitting, parking (fee), some pets allowed (fee), no-smoking rooms. AE, DC, MC, V.*

$ ★ **Hotel Terminus Garni.** Unlike its famous namesake in Paris, the Hamburg hotel Terminus is a simple and inexpensive hotel near the central train station. It's popular among British and American budget travelers who appreciate its relaxed atmosphere and reliable service (the hotel is part of the Garni hotel chain). All rooms have a TV. Double rooms share either a bath or shower. ✉ *Steindamm 5, Altstadt D–20,* ☎ *040/280–3144,* FAX *040/241–518. 20 rooms with shared bath. No a/c, no room phones, cable TV. AE, DC, MC, V.*

St. Pauli and Altona

$$–$$$ ★ **Gastwerk Hotel Hamburg.** Proudly dubbing itself Hamburg's first design hotel, the Gastwerk, in a century-old, redbrick gas plant, certainly is the most stylish accommodation in town. Every detail your fingers comes across, from the coffee cups to the doorknobs, has been carefully designed to create an eye-pleasing environment. The simple but incredibly chic furnishings mostly reflect the room's industrial design, but are warmed up by the use of natural materials, various woods (beech, pine), and thick carpets. The loft rooms with large windows, bare walls, and a lot of space are probably the most exciting hotel rooms in Hamburg. You'll wish one were your own apartment. ✉ *Daimlerstr. 67, Altona D–22761,* ☎ *040/890–620,* FAX *040/890–6220,* WEB *www.gastwerk-hotel.de. 90 rooms, 10 suites. Restaurant, room service, in-room safes, minibars, cable TV, health club, sauna, bar, dry cleaning, laundry service, meeting rooms, free parking, some pets allowed (fee), no-smoking rooms. AE, DC, MC, V.*

$$ **Florida–The Art Hotel.** This enchanting, off-beat hotel in the heart of St. Pauli is a treat for the budget traveler. Each room as well as its appliances and gadgets were exclusively designed in painstaking detail by a different artist. Not all of its quarters were intended for the same audience. For instance, in the room entitled "Camera Obscura" street imagery from the red-light district Reeperbahn is projected right before your very eyes. Full baths are at the end of the hall, but the spacious and funky rooms make up for this small drawback. ✉ *Spielbudenpl. 2, St. Pauli D–20359,* ☎ *040/314–393,* FAX *040/3023–7947,* WEB

www.florida-the-art-hotel.de. 14 rooms with shared bath. Bar, no a/c, no room phones, cable TV. AE, DC, MC, V.

$$ **Hotel Hafen Hamburg and Hotel Residenz Hafen Hamburg.** In one building complex just across the famous St. Pauli Landungsbrücken, both hotels are good value considering their three- and four-star status, respectively. The older Hotel Hafen Hamburg, with its smaller but nicely renovated rooms, offers a great view of the harbor, while the larger, ultramodern and upscale Hotel Residenz Hafen annex has less flair but more comfort. A very good deal are the Residenz's double rooms, which come at the price of a single room. The location makes this hotel a perfect starting point for exploring St. Pauli and the Reeperbahn. ✉ *Seewartenstr. 7–9, St. Pauli D–20459,* ☎ *040/3111–3600,* FAX *040/3111–3751,* WEB *www.hotel-hamburg.de. Hotel Hafen: 230 rooms; Hotel Residenz: 125 rooms. Restaurant, no a/c in some rooms, in-room safes, minibars, cable TV with movies, sauna, 3 bars, baby-sitting, dry cleaning, laundry service, meeting room, parking (fee), some pets allowed (fee), no-smoking floor. AE, DC, MC, V.*

$ **Hotel Monopol.** There is no other hotel in the Reeperbahn neighborhood where budget travelers can enjoy a safe and clean stay in the heart of Europe's most bizarre red-light district. The small rooms are old-fashioned, and some look like an odd mixture of 1950s and '80s designs, but the service is warm and has an original touch of Hamburger Kiez. You might run into an artist performing in a Hamburg musical—or in the live sex shows on Reeperbahn, for that matter. ✉ *Reeperbahn 48, St. Pauli D–20359,* ☎ *040/311–770,* FAX *040/3117–7151. 82 rooms. Restaurant, no a/c, room service, cable TV, bar, dry cleaning, laundry service, meeting room, parking (fee), some pets allowed (fee). AE, DC, MC, V.*

$ ★ **Hotel Schanzenstern.** At the heart of the Schanzenviertel, a favorite student quarter, the old Hamburg Mont Blanc-Füller plant houses the alternative Schanzenstern, offering reliable and basic rooms at unbeatable prices. Even though rooms don't have a phone or TV (but are decorated with plants and flowers), and bathrooms have to be shared, this hotel is one of the best in its price range. At €91 for rooms with up to five beds, it's a bargain for families or groups despite the rooms' small size. The restaurant serves organic food. The hotel also offers special deals (ask for Halb- or Vollpension), which include the room and two to three meals a day. ✉ *Bartelsstr. 12, St. Pauli D–20357,* ☎ *040/439–8441,* FAX *040/439–3413,* WEB *www.schanzenstern.de. 19 rooms. Restaurant, no a/c, no room phones or TVs. V.*

$ **Hotel Sternschanze.** One of the last family-run hotels in the Schanzenviertel neighborhood, the small and cozy Hotel Sternschanze, squeezed into an old city apartment complex, has small, but very light and clean rooms. Shared bathrooms are in the hall. Most rooms have a TV. The hotel does not offer breakfast, but shares the relatively quiet street with many bistros and breakfast cafés. ✉ *Schanzenstr. 101, St. Pauli D–20357,* ☎ *040/433–389,* FAX *040/430–5165. 21 rooms with shared bath. No a/c, no room phones, no room TVs. No credit cards.*

St. Georg

$$$$ **Kempinski Atlantic Hotel Hamburg.** There are few hotels in Germany more sumptuous than this gracious Edwardian palace facing the Aussenalster. The stylish mood is achieved with thick-carpeted, marble-inlaid panache, along with sophisticated lighting, and a lobby that is positively baronial. Whether the rooms are traditionally furnished or more modern, they are all typical of Hamburg in their understated luxury. All have spacious sitting areas with a writing desk and easy chairs, as well as large bathrooms, most with two washbasins. Service at the Atlantic is hushed and swift. In fine weather guests can lounge in the

formal outdoor courtyard, where only the gurgling fountain disturbs the peace. ✉ *An der Alster 72–79, St. Georg D–20099,* ☎ *040/28880,* FAX *040/247–129,* WEB *www.kempinski.atlantic.de. 241 rooms, 13 suites. Restaurant, café, room service, in-room data ports, in-room safes, minibars, cable TV with movies, pool, hair salon, health club, massage, sauna, boating, bicycles, bar, shops, baby-sitting, dry cleaning, laundry service, concierge, business services, meeting room, parking (fee), some pets allowed (fee), no-smoking rooms. AE, DC, MC, V.*

$$–$$$$ ★ **Hotel Prem.** Facing the Aussenalster, this extremely personable, quiet, small hotel is Hamburg's gem. Most guests are regulars who have their favorite rooms; no two rooms are the same. The Adenauer Suite (named after the chancellor, who stayed here) is traditionally furnished, including an antique chaise longue and a period writing desk in an alcove with a lake view. Room 102, across the hall, has contemporary furnishings and a platform bed. Suite 2 has two rooms with modern furnishings and a terrace overlooking the lake. The bar is intimate, and the dining at La Mer is superb. ✉ *An der Alster 9, St. Georg D–20099,* ☎ *040/2483–4040,* FAX *040/280–3851,* WEB *www.hotel-prem.de. 51 rooms, 3 suites. Restaurant, no a/c, room service, in-room data ports, in-room safes, minibars, cable TV, massage, sauna, bar, baby-sitting, dry cleaning, laundry service, concierge, business services, meeting room, free parking, some pets allowed (fee). AE, DC, MC, V.*

$$$ **Aussen Alster.** Crisp and contemporary in design, this boutique hotel prides itself on the personal attention it gives its guests. Rooms are compact; most have a full bathroom, but three have a shower only, no bathtub. Stark white walls, white bedspreads, and light-hued carpets create a bright, fresh ambience. A small bar is open in the evening, and a tiny garden is available for summer cocktails. The restaurant serves Italian fare for lunch and dinner. The Aussenalster, where the hotel keeps a sailboat for the use of guests, is at the end of the street. ✉ *Schmilinskystr. 11, St. Georg D–20099,* ☎ *040/241–557,* FAX *040/280–3231,* WEB *www.aussen-alster.de. 27 rooms. Restaurant, no a/c, room service, in-room safes, cable TV, sauna, boating, bicycles, bar, baby-sitting, dry cleaning, laundry service, meeting room, parking (fee), some pets allowed (fee). AE, DC, MC, V.*

$$ **Wedina.** Rooms at this small hotel are neat and compact. When you make a reservation, ask for a room in the Italian-style "Yellow House," with its elegant parquet floor. In the main building the bar and breakfast area face the veranda and a small garden and pool that bring Tuscany to mind. All lodgings are a half block from the Aussenalster and a brisk 10-minute walk from the train station. ✉ *Gurlittstr. 23, St. Georg D–20099,* ☎ *040/243–011,* FAX *040/280–3894. 27 rooms. No a/c, in-room safes, cable TV, bicycles, bar, concierge, business services, parking (fee), some pets allowed (fee), no-smoking rooms. AE, DC, MC, V.*

$ **Steen's Hotel.** This small, family-run hotel in a narrow, four-story town house near the central train station provides modest but very congenial service. The rooms are spacious and clean but lack atmosphere. Bathrooms are tiny. A great plus are the comfortable beds with reclining head and foot rests. The breakfasts amply make up for the uninspired rooms, and the hotel's garage is a great feature since there's never a parking space in this neighborhood. ✉ *Holzdamm 43, St. Georg D–20099,* ☎ *040/244–642,* FAX *040/280–3593. 11 rooms. No a/c, minibars, cable TV, parking (fee). AE, DC, MC, V.*

Elsewhere

$$$$ ★ **Hotel Louis C. Jacob.** Would-be Hanseats frequent this small, yet luxurious hotel nestled amidst the older wharf dwellings along the banks of the Elbe. Far from the hustle-bustle of the city, the intimate Louis C. Jacob, named after the French landscape gardener who founded it in 1791, makes a point of meticulously pampering its guests. Artist Max Liebermann stayed here and painted the terrace with its linden trees. One of the classically furnished suites even bears his name. From a river-view room, you'll be able to watch passing ships and listen as their foghorns bid Hamburg farewell. ✉ *Elbchaussee 401–403, Blankenese D–22609,* ☎ *040/822–550,* FAX *040/8225–5555,* WEB *www.hotel-jacob.de. 66 rooms, 19 suites. 2 restaurants, bar, room service, in-room safes, minibars, cable TV with movies, hot tub, massage, sauna, dry cleaning, laundry service, meeting rooms, parking (fee), some pets allowed (fee), no-smoking rooms. AE, DC, MC, V.*

$$$–$$$$ **Hotel Abtei.** On a quiet, tree-lined street about 2 km (1 mi) north of the downtown area, in Harvestehude, this elegant period hotel offers understated luxury and friendly, personal service. If you want a room with a four-poster bed, ask when making a reservation. One of the nicest rooms in the small hotel is Number 7. All guest rooms have English antique cherrywood and mahogany furniture. The three suites even have their own private conservatories. Breakfast is served in the beautiful garden and afternoon tea takes place in the antique-furnished sitting room. In the evening acclaimed chef Ulrich Heimann oversees the intimate, Michelin-starred restaurant. ✉ *Abteistr. 14, Harvestehude D–20149,* ☎ *040/442–905,* FAX *040/449–820,* WEB *www.abtei-hotel.de. 8 rooms, 3 suites. Restaurant, no a/c, room service, in-room safes, minibars, cable TV, dry cleaning, laundry service, some pets allowed (fee), free parking. AE, MC, V.*

$$$ **Nippon Hotel.** You'll be asked to remove your shoes before entering your room at the Nippon, Germany's second exclusively Japanese hotel (the first is in Düsseldorf). Tatami mats line the floor, futon mattresses are on the beds, and an attentive Japanese staff is at your service. The authenticity might make things a bit *too* spartan and efficient for some, but by cutting some Western-style comforts, the hotel offers a good value in the attractive Uhlenhorst District. The Nippon has a Japanese restaurant and sushi bar. ✉ *Hofweg 75, Uhlenhorst D–22085,* ☎ *040/227–1140,* FAX *040/2271–1490,* WEB *www.nippon-hotel-hh.de. 41 rooms, 1 suite. Restaurant, no a/c, in-room safes, minibars, cable TV, bicycles, dry cleaning, laundry service, concierge, business services, meeting room, parking (fee), some pets allowed (fee), no-smoking rooms. AE, DC, MC, V.*

$$$ **Garden Hotels Hamburg.** The location in chic Pöseldorf, 2 km (1 mi) from the downtown area, may discourage those who want to be in the thick of things, but otherwise this is one of the most appealing hotels in Hamburg, offering outstanding personal service and classy, chic accommodations in three attractive mansions. It's very much the insider's choice. There's no restaurant, but breakfast and light, cold meals are served in the bar and the airy winter garden. ✉ *Magdalenenstr. 60, Pöseldorf D–20148,* ☎ *040/414–040,* FAX *040/414–0420. 57 rooms, 3 suites. No a/c, room service, in-room data ports, minibars, cable TV, massage, bicycles, bar, baby-sitting, dry cleaning, laundry service, concierge, business services, meeting room, parking (fee), some pets allowed (fee), no-smoking rooms. AE, DC, MC, V.*

$$ **Hotel-Garni Mittelweg.** With chintz curtains, flowered wallpaper, old-fashioned dressing tables, and a country-house-style breakfast room, this hotel exudes small-town charm in big-business Hamburg. The converted mansion is in upmarket Pöseldorf, a short walk from the Aussenalster and a quick bus ride from the city center. ✉ *Mittelweg 59, Pöseldorf D–20149,* ☎ *040/414–1010,* FAX *040/4141–0120,* WEB *www.hotel-mittelweg.de. 38 rooms, 1 apartment. No a/c, room service,* *in-room safes, minibars, cable TV, baby-sitting, parking (fee), some pets allowed (fee). No credit cards.*

$$ 🏨 **Mellingburger Schleuse.** If you prefer off-the-beaten-track lodgings, this member of the Ringhotel-Association is a 20-minute drive from the downtown area, idyllically set in a forest. The Alsterwanderweg hiking trail passes right by the doorstep. The hotel is more than 200 years old, with a thatch roof, peasant-style furnishings, and a restaurant that serves traditional northern German dishes. ✉ *Mellingburgredder 1, Sasel D–22395,* ☎ *040/6024–00103,* FAX *040/602–7912. 40 rooms. 2 restaurants, no a/c, cable TV, pool, billiards, bowling, bar, concierge, meeting room, free parking, some pets allowed (fee). AE, DC, MC, V.*

NIGHTLIFE AND THE ARTS

The Arts

The arts flourish in this cosmopolitan metropolis. The city's ballet company is one of the finest in Europe, and the Ballet Festival in July is a cultural high point. Information on events is available in the magazines *Hamburger Vorschau*—pick it up for free in tourist offices and most hotels—and *Szene Hamburg,* sold at newsstands for €2.50.

The best way to order tickets for all major Hamburg theaters, musicals, and most cultural events is the central phone **HAM-Hotline**: ☎ 040/3005–1300. A number of travel agencies also sell tickets for plays, concerts, and the ballet. The tourist office at the **Landungsbrücken** (✉ between Piers 4 and 5, St. Pauli, ☎ 040/3005–1200 or 040/3005–1203) has a ticket office. One of the large downtown ticket agencies is the **Theaterkasse im Alsterhaus** (✉ Jungfernstieg 16, Neustadt, ☎ 040/353–555). The downtown **Theaterkasse Central** (✉ Gerhart-Hauptmann-Pl. 48, Neustadt, ☎ 040/337–124) is at the Landesbank-Galerie.

Ballet and Opera

One of the most beautiful theaters in the country, **Hamburgische Staatsoper** (✉ Grosse Theaterstr. 35, Altstadt, ☎ 040/356–868) is the leading northern German venue for opera and ballet. The Hamburg Ballet is directed by American John Neumeier.

The **Operettenhaus Hamburg** (✉ Spielbudenpl. 1, St. Pauli, ☎ 01805/4444) puts on musicals such as *Fosse.*

Concerts

Both the Hamburg Philharmonic and the Hamburg Symphony Orchestra appear regularly at the **Musikhalle** (✉ Johannes-Brahms-Pl., Neustadt, ☎ 040/346–920). Visiting orchestras from overseas are also presented.

Film

Both independent and mainstream English-language movies are shown at the **Magazin** (✉ Fiefstücken 8a/Efeuweg, Winterhude, ☎ 040/5113–920) and are often subtitled in German. Students audience show up at the **Grindel Kino** (✉ Grindelberg 7a, Harvestehude, ☎ 040/449–333) for blockbuster English-language movies.

Theater

Deutsches Schauspielhaus (✉ Kirchenallee 39, St. Georg, ☎ 040/248–713). One of Germany's leading drama stages is lavishly restored to its full 19th-century opulence and is the most important Hamburg venue for classical and modern theater.

English Theater (✉ Lerchenfeld 14, Hohenfelde, ☎ 040/227–7089). This is the city's only theater presenting English-language drama.

Theater im Hamburger Hafen (✉ Norderelbstr. 6, at Hamburger Hafen, follow signs to Schuppen 70, St. Pauli, ☎ 040/3005–1150). The huge theater is currently staging a German version of the Broadway musical hit *The Lion King.*

Neue Flora Theater (✉ Stresemannstr. 159a, at Alsenstr., Altona, ☎ 0180/54444 or 040/4316–5490). Hamburg is by far Germany's capital for musicals and the Neue Flora offers the best deal. The theater changing productions like the German musical *Mozart–Das Musical.*

Thalia-Theater (✉ Alstertor, St. Georg, ☎ 040/3281–4444). Once one of the country's most controversial theaters, the Thalia's sets and staging of classical drama, from Shakespeare to Schiller, are still perceived as scandalous by many.

Nightlife

The Reeperbahn

Whether you think it sordid or sexy, the Reeperbahn, in the St. Pauli District, is as central to the Hamburg scene as are the classy shops along Jungfernstieg. A walk down **Herbertstrasse** (men only, no women or children permitted), just two blocks south of the Reeperbahn, can be quite an eye-opener. Here prostitutes sit displayed in windows as they await customers. On nearby **Grosse Freiheit** are a number of the better-known sex-show clubs: **Colibri,** at No. 30; **Safari,** at No. 24; and **Salambo,** at No. 11. They cater to the package-tour trade as much as to those on the prowl by themselves. Prices are high. If you order a drink, ask for the price list, which must be displayed by law, and pay as soon as you're served. Not much happens here before 10 PM.

Schmidt Theater and its sister Schmidts Tivoli (✉ Spielbudenpl. 24, 27–28, St. Pauli, ☎ 040/3177–8899 or 040/3005–1400) have become Germany's leading variety theaters. Some of their shows are nationally televised, and the classy repertoire of live music, vaudeville, chansons, and cabaret is quite hilarious and worth the entrance fee. If you don't get a ticket (which is likely to happen), relax in one of their cafés.

A veteran of the age of velvet and plush, **St. Pauli-Theater** (✉ Spielbudenpl. 29, St. Pauli, ☎ 040/314–344) usually serves up a popular brand of low-brow theater in Hamburger dialect, which is even incomprehensible to other northern Germans.

Bars

The Hansestadt has a buzzing and upscale bar scene, with many locations that sometimes also feature live music or DJs and dancing. A real nightlife institution still going strong is the fashionable but cozy **Bar Hamburg** (✉ Rautenbergstr. 6–8, St. Georg, ☎ 040/2805–4880). The **Bereuther** (✉ Klosterallee 100, Hoheluft, ☎ 040/4140–6789) is a sleek bar and disco for thirtysomethings. The rather dull **Tower Bar** (✉ Seewartenstr. 9, St. Pauli, ☎ 040/3111–3524) at the Hotel Hafen Hamburg is worth a visit for the spectacular panorama view of the harbor.

Dance Clubs

One of the hottest clubs in Hamburg, **Gum** (✉ Hamburger Berg 12–13, St. Pauli, ☎ no phone) is packed with young, trendy, and very flirtatious Hamburgers dancing to house music. The **Orange Bar Club** (✉ Grosse Freiheit 26, St. Pauli, ☎ 040/314–236) is a small but always-packed bar and disco in a former brothel, mostly attracting the hip and beautiful thirtysomethings. The mixed crowd dances to European house and American funk music. **Voilà** (✉ Convenstr. 8–10, St. Pauli, ☎ no phone) is a small, somewhat trashy, but fun dance club, where a young techno crowd dances under fake chandeliers. A favorite of the more mature business crowd meets at **Top of Town** (✉ Marseiller Str. 2, Rotherbaum, ☎ 040/3502–3432), on the 26th floor of the SAS Radisson Hotel. It's both elegant and expensive, as most Hamburg clubs are.

Jazz and Live Music Clubs

Birdland (✉ Gärtnerstr. 122, Hoheluft, ☎ 040/405–277) is one of the leading clubs among Hamburg's more than 100 venues, offering everything from traditional New Orleans sounds to avant-garde electronic noise. The **Cotton Club** (✉ Alter Steinweg 10, Neustadt, ☎ 040/343–878), Hamburg's oldest jazz club, books classic New Orleans jazz as well as Swing. **Docks** (✉ Spielbudenplatz 19, St. Pauli, ☎ 040/317–8830) has a stylish bar and is Hamburg's largest venue for live music. It also puts on disco nights.

OUTDOOR ACTIVITIES AND SPORTS

Biking

Most major streets in Hamburg have bicycle lanes. Some of the major hotels will lend their guests bikes. The most central location for renting bikes is at the **Hauptbahnhof** (✉ Entrance Kirchenallee, St. Georg, ☎ 040/3918–50475). Bikes rent for €8 a day. A wide selection of bikes, including racing, mountain, and children's bikes, is rented by Mr. Petersen's **Hamburg anders erfahren** (✉ Insterburger Str. 15, Bramfeld, ☎ 040/640–1800). The bikes cost between €7.50 and €20 a day. There is a discount on multiday rentals. A complete list of bike rentals in Hamburg and the surrounding countryside can be obtained from the **ADFC Hamburg** (✉ Markstr. 18, D–22041, ☎ 040/393–933 or 040/3907–050).

Golf

One of the city's leading golf clubs where members of foreign clubs can visit is the **Hamburger Golf-Club Falkenstein** (✉ In den Bargen 59, Blankenese, ☎ 040/812–177). An alternative for golf players looking for a small and intimate club is the **Golf-Club auf der Wendlohe** (✉ Oldesloerstr. 251, Schnelsen, ☎ 040/552–8966).

Horseback Riding

With many of Germany's premier derbies staged in Hamburg, the city has a traditional affection for horseback riding. One of the best stables is the **Gut Wendlohe** (✉ Oldesloerstr. 236, Schnelsen, ☎ 040/550–4945). The **Reitschule in der Alten Wache** (✉ Bredenbekstr. 63, Wohldorf, ☎ 040/605–0586) has riding classes and lessons for beginners.

Jogging

The best places for jogging are the Planten un Blomen and Alter Botanischer Garten parks and along the leafy promenade around the Alster. The latter route is about 6 km (4 mi) long.

Sailing

You can rent rowboats and sailboats on the Alster in the summer between 10 AM and 9 PM. Rowboats cost around €12 an hour, sailboats around €16 an hour. The largest selection of boats is at the Gurlittinsel pier off An der Alster (on the east bank of the Aussenalster). Another one is at very tip of the Alster, at the street, Fernsicht.

Squash and Tennis

One of the nicest tennis facilities in town is the **Eichenhof-Tennisanlage** (✉ Duvenstedt, Puckaffer Weg 18, Duvenstedt, ☎ 040/4480–2593). It offers seven outdoor and five indoor courts. In downtown Hamburg try the huge **Fit-Fire** (✉ Eilbekerweg 30, Wandsbek, ☎ 040/201–163) with 12 squash courts and a large fitness area. For squash and badminton, the **Sportwerk Hagenbeckstrasse** (✉ Hagenbeckstr. 124a, Stellingen, ☎ 040/546–074) has 8 courts, a swimming pool, a sauna, and a solarium.

Swimming

You can't swim in the Elbe or the Alster—they're health hazards. There are, however, pools—indoor and outdoor—throughout the city. Hands down, the most beautiful swimming pool in town is the 19th-century spa **Bartholomäustherme** (✉ Bartholomäusstr. 95, Uhlenhorst, ☎ 040/221–283). The modern **Alster Schwimmhalle** (✉ Ifflandstr. 21, Hohenfelde, ☎ 040/223–012) lacks atmosphere but is very clean and has a bright main hall.

SHOPPING

Shopping Districts

Hamburg's shopping districts are among the most elegant on the Continent, and the city has Europe's largest expanse of covered shopping arcades, most of them packed with small, exclusive boutiques. The streets **Grosse Bleichen** and **Neuer Wall,** which lead off Jungfernstieg, are a high-price-tag zone. The Grosse Bleichen leads to six of the city's most important covered (or indoor) malls, many of which are connected. The marble-clad **Galleria** is modeled after London's Burlington Arcade. Daylight streams through the immense glass ceilings of the **Hanse-Viertel,** an otherwise ordinary reddish-brown brick building. The **Kaufmannshaus,** also known as the Commercie, and the upscale (and former first-class hotel) **Hamburger Hof** are two of the oldest and most fashionable indoor malls. There are also the **Alte Post** and the **Bleichenhof.**

Hamburg's premier shopping street, **Jungfernstieg,** is just about the most upscale and expensive in the country. It's lined with jewelers' shops—Wempe, Brahmfeld & Guttruf, and Hintze are the top names—and chic clothing boutiques such as Linette, Ursula Aust, Selbach, Windmöller, and Jäger & Koch.

In the fashionable district **Pöseldorf** north of downtown, take a look at Milchstrasse and Mittelweg. Both are filled with small boutiques, restaurants, and cafés.

Running from the main train station to Gerhard-Hauptmann-Platz, the boulevard **Spitalerstrasse** is a pedestrians-only street lined with stores. Prices here are noticeably lower than those on Jungfernstieg.

Antiques

Take a look at the shops in the **St. Georg** district behind the train station, especially those between Lange Reihe and Koppel. You'll find a mixture of genuine antiques (*Antiquitäten*) and junk (*Trödel*). You won't find many bargains, however. ABC-Strasse is another happy hunting ground for antiques lovers.

Antik-Center (✉ Klosterwall 9–21, Altstadt, ☎ 040/326–285). This assortment of 39 shops in the old market hall, close to the main train station, features a wide variety of antiques from all periods.

Department Stores

Alsterhaus (✉ Jungfernstieg 16–20, Neustadt, ☎ 040/359–010). Hamburg's most famous department store is both large and elegant; it's a favorite with locals and a must for visitors. Don't miss its food department. Reward yourself for having braved the crowds by ordering a glass of *Sekt* (German champagne) and fresh seafood.

Karstadt (✉ Mönckebergstr. 16, Altstadt, ☎ 040/30940). Germany's leading department-store chain offers the same goods as the Alsterhaus at similar prices. Hamburg's downtown Karstadt is the city's best place to shop for sports clothing.

Kaufhof (✉ Mönckebergstr. 3, Altstadt, ☎ 040/333–070). Kaufhof offers far more bargains than most other department stores.

Stilwerk (✉ Grosse Elbstr. 68, Altona, ☎ 040/306–210). Hamburg's most fashionable shopping mall resembles a department store and primarily houses furniture and home accessory shops.

Flea and Food Markets

Blankenese. A lively fruit and vegetable market in the heart of this suburb manages to preserve the charm of a small village. ✉ *Bahnhofstr., Blankenese.* ⏲ *Tues. 8–2, Fri. 8–6, Sat. 8–1. S-bahn: Blankenese.*

Fischmarkt (☞ St. Pauli and the Reeperbahn *in* Exploring Hamburg).

Gift Ideas

Binikowski (✉ Lokstedter Weg 68, Eppendorf, ☎ 040/462–852). This shop sells the most famous must-buy *Buddelschiffe* (ships in bottles). There are few better places to shop for one, or for a blue-and-white-stripe sailor's shirt, a sea captain's hat, ship models, or even ship's charts.

Captain's Cabin (✉ St. Pauli Landungsbrücken, St. Pauli, ☎ 040/316–373). This Hamburg institution is an experience not to be missed, the best place for all of the city's specialty maritime goods.

Harry's Hafenbasar (✉ Bernhard-Nocht-Str. 89–91, St. Pauli, ☎ 040/312–482). You can poke through the dusty goods traders and seamen have brought back from the corners of the globe in this eerie, bazaar-like store. It's jam-packed and a bargain-hunter's paradise for anything maritime.

Seifarth and Company (✉ Robert-Koch-Str. 19, Norderstedt, ☎ 040/524–0027). Hamburg is one of the best places in Europe to buy tea. Smoked salmon and caviar are terrific buys here as well. Seifarth and Company also offers lobsters, salmon, and other expensive fish.

Jewelry

Wempe (✉ Jungfernstieg 8, Neustadt, ☎ 040/3344–8824). This is the flagship store (of three Hamburg locations) of Germany's largest and most exclusive jeweler, which also sells watches.

Men's Clothing

The stylish store **Doubleeight. Another Level** (✉ Jungfernstieg 52, Neustadt, ☎ 040/3571–5510) carries both designer and less expensive everyday fashions. A Hamburg classic and a must for the fashion-conscious traveler, **Thomas I-Punkt** (✉ Mönckebergstr. 21, Altstadt, ☎ 040/327–172) sells conservative suits and casual wear of its own label.

Women's Clothing

High-priced fashion, designed by one of Hamburg's newcomers, Petra Rodeck, is found at **balcony** (✉ Fehlandstr. 41, Neustadt, ☎ 040/343–606). The clothing here is daring, cool, and definitely not mainstream. The upscale shopping complex **Kaufrausch** (✉ Isestr. 74, Eppendorf, ☎ 040/477–154) has mostly clothing and accessories stores for women. **Kleidermacher** (✉ Michaelisbrücke 1–3, Neustadt, ☎ 040/3751–8787) carries several young local designers' labels. A small but elegant and very personal store, **Linette** (✉ Eppendorfer Baum 19, Eppendorf, ☎ 040/460–4963) stocks only top names.

SIDE TRIPS FROM HAMBURG

Hamburg is surrounded by the fertile green marshlands of the neighboring states of Schleswig-Holstein and Lower Saxony (Niedersachsen). Two of the most popular side trips are described here.

Altes Land

23 km (14 mi) west of downtown Hamburg (on Finkenwerder Str. and Cranzer Hauptdeich).

The marshy Altes Land extends 30 km (19 mi) west from Hamburg along the south bank of the Elbe River to the town of Stade. This fruit-growing region is dotted with huge half-timber farmhouses and crisscrossed by canals. Hikers come out for walks, especially in spring, when the apple and cherry trees are in blossom. Some of the prettiest trails take you along the dikes running next to the Este and Lühe rivers. Much of the territory is best covered on foot, so wear walking shoes. You may want to bring a picnic lunch as well and spend a long (summer) day here.

From the dock at Cranz, walk south into the suburb of **Neuenfelde.** Here you can visit the **St. Pancratius Kirche** (Church of St. Pancratius), a baroque church with an unusual painted barrel roof, worth a visit for its altar inside. It was built in 1688, and the organ, dating from the same period, was designed by Arp Schnitger, an organ builder and local farmer. ✉ *Am Organistenweg, Altes Land,* ☎ *040/745–9296.* ⏲ *Daily 9–5.*

The 18th-century church and decorative farmhouses of the village of **Jork** lies some 9 km (5½ mi) on foot to the west of Neuenfelde, just beyond the confluence of the Este and Elbe rivers (Bus No. 257 travels to and from Neuenfelde as well). The windmill in **Borstel,** a ten-minute walk from Jork, is worth a short detour.

Stade

60 km (37 mi) west of Hamburg on B–73.

The town of Stade is skirted by marshland, rivers, and small lakes on the western edge of the Altes Land. Thanks to a huge reconstruction program in the 1960s and '70s, the city of 46,000 has regained its late-medieval and baroque appearance. Founded some time before AD 994 and once a thriving member of the Hanseatic League, Stade began losing business to Hamburg, which had the better harbor. Stubborn Stade decided to leave the Hanseatic League in 1601 and was subsequently conquered by the Swedes, who controlled the city for 70 years: and their heritage is still visible.

Close to the **Alter Hafen** (old harbor), which looks rather like a narrow canal, is Stade's most beautiful (and lively) square, the tiny Fischmarkt. Nearby streets, particularly **Wasser West,** have not only many cafés and restaurants but also some of the best-preserved Renaissance and baroque merchants' mansions. The **Schwedenspeicher-Museum** (Swedish Warehouse Museum) once stored food for the Swedish garrison and now traces the city's history from the Stone Age to the present. ✉ *Wasser West 39, Stade,* ☎ *04141/3222.* 🎫 *€1.* ⏲ *Tues.–Fri. 10–5, weekends 10–6.*

A walk through the **Altstadt** (Old City), on an island, gives you a vivid impression of what a northern German city looked like some 300 years ago. Many of the buildings are built in the half-timber or red-brick styles typical of the region. The heart of the Old City is the **Altes**

Rathaus (Old Town Hall), built in 1667, a redbrick blend of Dutch Renaissance and early baroque recalling the city's proud mercantile days. Exhibitions are sometimes held in the historic main hall. ✉ *Hökerstr. 22, Stade,* ☎ *04141/4010.* ⏲ *Weekdays 8:30–5.*

The tower of the baroque **St. Cosmae** (✉ Cosmaekirchhof, off Johannisstr., Stade, ☎ 04141/43042), offers a wonderful view of Stade and the countryside.

HAMBURG A TO Z

To research prices, get advice from other travelers, and book travel arrangements, visit www.fodors.com.

AIR TRAVEL

Hamburg's international airport, Fuhlsbüttel, is 11 km (7 mi) northwest of the city. The Airport-City-Bus (the private Jasper Airport-Shuttle) runs nonstop between the airport and Hamburg's main train station daily at 30-minute intervals between 5 AM and 10:30 PM. Tickets are €4.35. The (public) Airport-Express (Bus 52) runs every 10 minutes between the airport and the Ohlsdorf U- and S-bahn stations, a 17-minute ride from the main train station. The fare is €1.55. A taxi to the downtown area will cost about €16. If you're driving a rental car from the airport, follow the signs to STADTZENTRUM (downtown).

➤ AIRPORT INFORMATION: **Fuhlsbüttel** (☎ 040/50750, WEB www.ham-airport.de).

BOAT AND FERRY TRAVEL

HADAG ferries to Altes Land and Lühe depart from the Landungsbrücken (☞ Tours) twice daily during the week and four times daily on the weekends from mid-April through August and on weekends only in September. Get off at the stop in Lünhe. To reach Neunfelde, take the ferry from Blankenese.

A more exciting way to reach Altes Land or Stade is via a 45-minute ride on a high-speed boat. Elbe-city-jets departs four times a day for Stade from the St. Pauli Landungsbrücken between 9 AM and 6 PM and cost €17 (round-trip). You can also reach the Cranz dock in Altes Land by Elbe-city-jet.

➤ BOAT AND FERRY INFORMATION: **HADAG** (☎ 040/311–7070). **SAL Schiffahrtskontor** (Elbe-city-jet ☎ 04142/81170 or 040/317–7170, WEB www.elbe-city-jet.de).

BUS TRAVEL

Hamburg's bus station, the Zentral-Omnibus-Bahnhof, is right behind the main train station.

➤ BUS INFORMATION: **Zentral-Omnibus-Bahnhof** (✉ ZOB, Adenauerallee 78, St. Georg, ☎ 040/247–575).

CAR TRAVEL

Hamburg is easier to handle by car than many other German cities, and traffic is relatively uncongested. During rush hours, however, there can be as much gridlock as in any other big German city. Several autobahns (A–1, A–7, A–23, A–24, and A–250) connect with Hamburg's three beltways, which then easily take you to the downtown area. Follow the STADTZENTRUM signs. To reach Altes Land and Stade from Hamburg, take B–73 west.

➤ CAR RENTALS: **Avis** (✉ Airport, Fuhlsbüttel, ☎ 040/5075–2314; ✉ Drehbahn 15–25, Neustadt, ☎ 040/341–651; ✉ Herderstr. 52, Winterhude, ☎ 040/220–1188). **Hertz** (✉ Airport, Fuhlsbüttel, ☎ 040/5935–1367; ✉ Kirchenallee 34–36, opposite the Hauptbahnhof,

Altstadt, ☎ 040/280–1201). **Sixt** (✉ Airport, Fuhlsbüttel, ☎ 040/593–9480; ✉ Spaldingstr. 110, Hammerbrook, ☎ 040/232–393).

CONSULATES

➤ CONSULATE INFORMATION: **Ireland** (✉ Feldbrunnenstr. 43, Winterhude, ☎ 040/4418–6213). **New Zealand** (✉ Domstr. 19, Neustadt, ☎ 040/442–5550). **U.S.** (✉ Alsterufer 27, Neustadt, ☎ 040/4117–1100). **U.K.** (✉ Harvestehuder Weg 8a, Harvestehude, ☎ 040/448–0320).

EMERGENCIES

Regarding medical emergencies, welcome to German bureaucracy: 112 is a direct line to the ambulance service operated by the fire department; 110 is the general ambulance service; 040/228–022 is a special city ambulance service providing doctors in an ambulance. The kind of service provided does not differ, only the institution behind it.

Pharmacies offer late-night service on a rotating basis. Every pharmacy displays a notice indicating the schedule. For emergency pharmaceutical assistance, inquire at the nearest police station or call 112.
➤ CONTACTS: **Ambulance and Police** (☎ 110). **Dentist** (☎ 040/11500). **Emergency medical aid and Fire** (☎ 112). **Medical emergencies** (☎ 040/228–022). **Central Poison Center** (☎ 0551/19240 or 030/19240). **Pharmacies** (☎ 112).

ENGLISH-LANGUAGE BOOKSTORE

➤ BOOKSTORE: **Frensche International** (✉ Spitalerstr. 26c, Altstadt, ☎ 040/327–585).

TOURS

BOAT TOURS

There are few better ways to get to know the city than by taking a trip around the massive harbor. The HADAG line and other companies organize round-trips in the port, lasting about one hour (€8.05) and taking in several docks. Between April and late September excursion boats and barges leave every half hour from the Landungsbrücken—Piers 1, 2, 3, and 7—between 10 AM and 6:30 PM. From early October through March departures are every hour. An English-language tour leaves from Pier 1 March–November, daily at 11:15.

Warm-buffet dinner cruises (€45), including as much beer as you dare to drink, depart late April to December, Saturday at 8 PM, from between Piers 6 and 9. Other watery options include renting rowboats on the Stadtpark Lake and surrounding canals, and dancing on "party ships." To make a reservation call the Bordparty-Service cruise line or check for tickets at its visitor information booth.

From April through October, Alster Touristik operates boat trips around the Alster Lakes and through the canals. Tours leave three times a day from the Jungfernstieg promenade in the city center. The Aussenalster 50-minute lake tour ("Fleet Tour") costs €8. Boats for the lake tour leave every ½ hour April–October 3, daily 10–6. From May through September there's also the romantic twilight tour, called Dämmertour, every evening at 8 (€13.30).
➤ BOAT TOUR INFORMATION: **Alster Touristik** (☎ 040/357–4240). **Bordparty-Service** (✉ Landungsbrücken, Pier 9, St. Pauli, ☎ 040/313–687). **HADAG** (☎ 040/311–7070; 040/313–130; 040/313–959; 040/3178–2231 for English-language tour).

ORIENTATION TOURS

Sightseeing bus tours of the city, all with guides who rapidly narrate in both English and German, leave from Kirchenallee by the main train station. A bus tour lasting 1¾ hours sets off daily and costs €13. For €20, one of the bus tours can be combined with two one-hour boat trips on the Alster Lake and the Elbe River. Departure times for tours vary, according to season. City tours aboard the nostalgic *Hummelbahn* (a converted railroad wagon pulled by a tractor) start from the Kirchenallee stop. They run daily April–October. The fare is €13 for 1¾ hours. From May to September, Friday and Saturday at 8 PM, the *Hummelbahn* conducts a three-hour evening tour of the city at a cost of €30 (including a drink).

➤ BUS TOUR INFORMATION: ***Hummelbahn*** (☎ 040/792–8979).

WALKING TOURS

Tours of downtown, the harbor district, and St. Pauli are offered from April to November weekdays at 2:30 by the Tourismus-Zentrale Hamburg. All guided walking tours (€6) are conducted in German, and start at different locations. Downtown tours by Stattreisen Hamburg are held on Saturday (February–November) and are conducted in German only. Tours of the historic Speicherstadt district are conducted by the Speicherstadtmuseum (Sun. at 11, €6).

➤ WALKING TOUR INFORMATION: **Speicherstadtmuseum** (✉ St. Annenufer 2, Block R, Speicherstadt, ☎ 040/321–191, WEB www.speicherstadtmuseum). **StattreisenHamburg** (☎ 040/430–3481). **Tourismus-Zentrale Hamburg** (✉ Steinstr. 7, Altstadt D–20015, ☎ 040/3005–1144).

TAXIS

Taxi meters start at €2, and the fare is €1.53 per km or ½ mi. You can hail taxis on the street or at stands order one by phone.

➤ TAXI INFORMATION: ☎ 040/441–011, 040/686–868, or 040/666–666.

TRAIN TRAVEL

There are two principal stations: the central Hauptbahnhof (main train station) and Hamburg-Altona, west of the downtown area. EuroCity and InterCity trains connect Hamburg with all German cities and many major European ones. Two InterCity Express "supertrain" lines link Hamburg with Berlin, Frankfurt, and Munich, and with Würzburg and Munich. Trains to Stade depart from the Hauptbahnhof.

➤ TRAIN INFORMATION: **Hauptbahnhof** (✉ Steintorpl., Altstadt, ☎ 0180/599–6633).

TRANSPORTATION AROUND HAMBURG

The HVV, Hamburg's public transportation system, includes the U-bahn (subway), the S-bahn (suburban train), and buses. A one-way fare starts at €1.40; €2.20 covers one unlimited ride in the Hamburg city area. Tickets are available on all buses and at automatic machines in all stations and at most bus stops. A *Tageskarte* (all-day ticket), valid from 9 AM to 1 AM, costs €4.25. If you're traveling with family or friends, a *Gruppen-* or *Familienkarte* (group or family ticket) is a good value—a group of up to five can travel for the entire day for only €7.05.

Available from all Hamburg tourist offices, the Hamburg CARD allows unlimited travel on all public transportation within the city, and admission to state museums. The Hamburg CARD is valid for 24 hours (beginning at 6 PM through 6 PM the following day) and costs €6.80 for one adult and up to three children under the age of 12; the family card costs €22.50 for five adults and up to three children under the age of 12. The Hamburg CARD for three days (valid starting at noon the first day) costs €14. The Hamburg CARD light ("light" meaning inexpensive) costs €22.50 for a group of five) and is valid for three days but does not include public transportation.

You must validate your ticket at a machine at the start of your journey. If you are found without a validated ticket, the fine is €32.

In the north of Hamburg the HVV system connects with the A-bahn (Alsternordbahn), a suburban train system that extends into Schleswig-Holstein. Night buses (Nos. 600–640) serve the downtown area all night, leaving the Rathausmarkt and Hauptbahnhof every hour.

➤ TRANSPORTATION INFORMATION: **Hamburg Passenger Transport Board** (Hamburger Verkehrsverbund; ✉ Steinstr. 7, Altstadt, ☎ 040/19449, WEB www.hvv.de) is open daily around the clock.

TRAVEL AGENCIES

➤ AGENCIES: **Reiseland American Express** (✉ Ballindamm 39, Neustadt, ☎ 040/309–080). **Hapag-Lloyd** (✉ Verkehrspavillon Jungfernstieg, Neustadt, ☎ 040/325–8560).

VISITOR INFORMATION

Hamburg has tourist offices around the city. The main branch of the tourist office is in the Hauptbahnhof (main train station) and is open daily 7 AM–11 PM. At the harbor there's an office at the St. Pauli Landungsbrücken, between Piers 4 and 5, open November–February, daily 10–7, and March–October, daily 10–5:30.

In addition to its comprehensive hotel guide, the tourist office also copublishes *Hamburger Vorschau*, a free monthly program of events in the city. The free magazine *Hamburg Tips* is issued quarterly and details major seasonal events.

All tourist offices can help with accommodations, and there's a central call-in booking office for hotel and ticket reservations and general information, the HAM-Hotline. A €4 fee is charged for every room reserved.

➤ VISITOR INFORMATION: **HAM-Hotline** (☎ 040/3005–1300, WEB www.hamburg-tourism.de). **Hamburg Tourist Office** (✉ Hauptbahnhof, Altstadt, ☎ 040/3005–1200; ✉ St. Pauli Landungsbrücken, St. Pauli, ☎ 040/3005–1200 or 040/3005–1203; ✉ Steinstr. 7, Altstadt D–20015, ☎ 040/3005–1144). **Stade Tourismus GmbH** (✉ Schiffertorstr. 6, D–21682 Stade Stade, ☎ 04141/4091–7074, FAX 04141/409–110, WEB www.stade.de).

15 SCHLESWIG-HOLSTEIN AND THE BALTIC COAST

The far north of Germany is a lush, green landscape of marshlands, endless beaches, fishing villages, and lakes—all under a wide open sky. Beachgoers head to the islands of Schleswig-Holstein, which juts out between the often stormy North Sea and the quiet waters of the Baltic. The stretches of limestone cliffs and recondite coves that make up the neighboring Baltic Coast, along eastern Germany's shoreline, beckon those in search of solitude.

By Jürgen Scheunemann

GERMANY'S TRUE NORTH IS A QUIET AND PEACEFUL region that belies its past status as one of the most powerful trading centers in Europe. The salty air and great outdoors is the main pleasure here, not sightseeing. On foggy November evenings or during the hard winter storms that sometimes strand islanders from the mainland, you can well imagine the fairy tales spun by the Vikings who lived here.

The Danish-German heritage in Schleswig-Holstein, Germany's northernmost state, is the result of centuries of land disputes between the two nations—you could call this area southern Scandinavia. Since the early 20th century, its shores and islands have become popular weekend and summer retreats for the well-to-do from Hamburg and Berlin. The island of Sylt, in particular, is known throughout Germany for its rich and beautiful sunbathers.

The rest of Schleswig-Holstein, though equally appealing in its green and mostly serene landscape, is far from rich and worldly. Most people farm or fish and often speak Plattdütsch, or low German, which is difficult for outsiders to understand. Cities such as Flensburg, Husum, Schleswig, the state capital of Kiel, and even Lübeck all exude a laid-back, small-town charm.

The neighboring East German state of Mecklenburg-Vorpommern includes the Baltic Coast and is even more rural. On the resort islands of Hiddensee and Usedom, the clock appears to have stopped before World War II; the architecture, the pace of life, even the old-fashioned trains seem like products of a magical time warp. Though long a popular summer destination for families, few foreign tourists venture here.

This area was not always a restful retreat. Between the 12th and 16th centuries the sea was crucial to the rise of Hanseatic League, a consortium of merchants who monopolized trade across the Baltic. You'll see their wealth invested some of the finest examples of North German Gothic and Renaissance redbrick architecture, with buildings topped by tall, stepped gables. However, the shipbuilding industry in Schleswig-Holstein closed down more than 20 years ago, and the mid-1990s bankruptcy of the industry in Rostock and Stralsund further depressed the economy. The unemployment rate in Mecklenburg-Vorpommern is among the highest in Germany, and a dramatic, westward migration is further depleting this sparsely populated region.

Pleasures and Pastimes

Beaches

Beaches stretch all along the coast of the North Sea and the Baltic. Virtually all these sandy beaches are clean and safe, sloping gently into the water, which is equally gentle and calm. Vacationers pack the seaside resorts during the high season (July–August). Be aware that water temperatures even in August rarely exceed 20°C (65°F). The busiest beaches are at Westerland (Sylt Island), Bansin (Usedom Island), Binz (Rügen Island), Ostseebad Kühlungsborn, and Warnemünde. The most beautiful beaches are at Timmendorf on Poel Island (you can drive there from Wismar or take a White Fleet boat); Kap Arkona (reachable only on foot); and Hiddensee Island, off Rügen. The more remote coves can be found at Kampen on Sylt, at the Ahrenshoop Weststrand, on the Darss Peninsula; at Nienhagen (near Warnemünde); and the Grosser Jasmunder Bodden, on Rügen Island to the west of Lietzow.

There's a *Kurtaxe* (entrance fee) of €1.50–€5 for most beaches; the fees on Sylt average €3 per entry. Some beaches allow nude bathing. In German it's known as *Freikörperkultur* (literally, "free body culture"), or FKK for short. The most popular of these bare-all beaches are on Sylt island, at Nienhagen, and Prerow (on Darss).

Churches

Throughout the region medieval churches with red and white facades are prime examples of the German redbrick Gothic style. In Mecklenburg-Vorpommern even the smallest village proudly boasts a redbrick church, and the cathedrals in cities such as Wismar or Stralsund testify to the region's prosperous past as Hanseatic seaports. Note how many churches are named after the sailors' patron saint, St. Nikolai.

Dining

The restaurants in both coastal states serve mostly seafood such as *Scholle* (flounder) or North Sea *Krabben* (shrimp), often with fried potatoes, eggs, and bacon. Mecklenburg specialties to look for are *Mecklenburger Griebenroller,* a custardy casserole of grated potatoes, eggs, herbs, and chopped bacon; *Mecklenburger Fischsuppe,* a hearty fish soup with vegetables, tomatoes, and sour cream; *Gefüllte Ente* (duck with bread stuffing); and *Pannfisch* (fish patty). A favorite local nightcap since the 17th century is grog, a strong blend of rum, hot water, and local fruits.

CATEGORY	COST*
$$$$	over €20
$$$	€15–€20
$$	€10–€15
$	under €10

**per person for a main course at dinner*

Lodging

In northern Germany you'll find both small *Hotelpensionen* and fully equipped large hotels; along the eastern Baltic Coast, some hotels are renovated high-rises dating from GDR times. Many of the small hotels and pensions in towns such as Kühlungsborn, Binz, or Albeck have been restored to their romantic, quaint splendor of German *Bäderarchitektur* (spa architecture) from the early 20th century. In high season all accommodations, especially on the islands, are in great demand. If you can't book well in advance, inquire at the local tourist office, which will also have information on the 150 campsites along the Baltic coast and on the islands.

CATEGORY	COST*
$$$$	over €225
$$$	€150–€225
$$	€75–€150
$	under €75

**All prices are for two people in a double room, including tax and service.*

Exploring Schleswig-Holstein and the Baltic Coast

Except for such cities as Kiel, Lübeck, Schwerin, and Rostock, both states are essentially rural with a countryside of lakes, meadows, fertile fields, and tree-lined roads. The three major areas of interest are the western coastline of Schleswig-Holstein—primarily Sylt Island—eastern Mecklenburg, and Vorpommern's secluded, tundralike landscape of sandy heath and dunes. In Mecklenburg-Vorpommern any interesting roads that head off to the north are likely to lead to the coast. Vorpommern ends at the Polish border. The coastal region and the islands in particular are ideal for cycling (read: flat). Most large hotels provide bicycles for guests, and many shops rent bikes at modest rates. Some train stations also rent bicycles.

Numbers in the text correspond to numbers in the margin and on the Schleswig-Holstein and Baltic Coast maps.

Great Itineraries

This chapter follows a route through five main ports of the medieval Hanseatic League—Lübeck, Rostock, Stralsund, Flensburg, and Wismar. A standard itinerary will take you from the pleasure island of Sylt, then east along the Baltic coast but slightly inland, and finally to the island of Usedom. Barring summer traffic jams, you could easily drive through the whole region from west to east in less than two days, but that would be the surest way to miss all the hidden treasures in the villages and medieval cities along the way. Instead, try to do it like the natives—at a slow pace. Should you indulge in a weeklong sojourn, you'll certainly perceive the rest of the world as villagers do—as just a faint memory far, far away.

IF YOU HAVE 3 DAYS

Start your trip in **Flensburg** ①, less than two hours from Hamburg, and make **Schleswig** ④ a stop as you head toward **Lübeck** ⑦, western Germany's only Hanseatic town. On the following day visit **Wismar's** ⑧ delightful market square and grand churches and make a side trip south to **Schwerin** ⑨, which is known for its lakes and its magnificent castle, the Schweriner Schloss. Next head to **Rostock** ⑪, once the center of eastern Germany's shipbuilding industry. On the last day pay a visit to **Stralsund** ⑮, a much smaller but more charming medieval town. It serves as a gateway to the most remote and solitary part of the Baltic Coast: the island of **Rügen** ⑯. The **Stubbenkammer** ⑳ and the **Königstuhl** there are outstanding chalk cliffs.

IF YOU HAVE 5 DAYS

Devote a morning to the palace at **Ahrensburg** ⑥, just outside Hamburg, and continue on to the cities of **Schleswig** ④ and **Flensburg** ①. Both still have an abundance of old northern German fishing and farming traditions. When you finish exploring Flensburg the next day, head to medieval **Lübeck** ⑦ to overnight. After seeing Lübeck, visit **Wismar** ⑧ before spending the night in **Schwerin** ⑨. On the fourth day, after a tour of the Schweriner lakes and the Schweriner Schloss, continue your eastward journey via **Bad Doberan** ⑩ and Kühlungsborn, a top beach resort. The little Molli train pulled by a steam locomotive connects the resort and Bad Doberan. Spend the late afternoon and night in **Rostock** ⑪ and the beach resort at **Warnemünde** ⑫. On the fifth day explore the medieval port of **Stralsund** ⑮.

IF YOU HAVE 8 DAYS

Spend your first day and night in **Flensburg** ① and the next in the romantic fishing town of **Husum** ②. On the third morning take the train onto the island of **Sylt** ③. You may find it more economical to leave your car at the Niebüll train embarkment and use bikes, buses, or a rental car on the island. On your fourth day visit **Schleswig** ④ and **Kiel** ⑤ on your way to **Lübeck** ⑦. From Lübeck head east to **Wismar** ⑧ and **Schwerin** ⑨. The sixth day you can sightsee around **Rostock** ⑪ and shop in **Ribnitz-Damgarten** ⑬, the center of Germany's amber industry. If you don't find a souvenir here, you might be luckier in **Ahrenshoop** ⑭, a small coastal village that was once an artists' colony. Spend your sixth night in **Stralsund** ⑮ and your seventh day and night on the island of **Rügen** ⑯. A visit to Vorpommern wouldn't be complete without a trip to **Greifswald** ㉒, the last of the medieval Hanseatic towns on eastern

Germany's coastline. If you still have time on this eighth day, drive to **Wolgast** and over the causeway to **Usedom Island** ㉔.

When to Go

The region's climate is at its best when the two states are also most crowded with vacationers—in July and August. Winter is extremely harsh in this area, and even spring and fall are rather windy, chilly, and rainy. To avoid the crowds, schedule your trip for June or September. But don't expect tolerable water temperatures or hot days on the beach.

SCHLESWIG-HOLSTEIN

This region once thrived, thanks to the Hanseatic League and the Salzstrasse (Salt Route), a merchant route connecting northern Germany's cities. The kings of Denmark warred with the dukes of Schleswig, and, later, the German Empire over the prized northern territory of Schleswig-Holstein. The northernmost strip of land surrounding Flensburg became German in 1864. The state is relatively poor now but is also known for the artists it produced: writers such as Thomas Mann and Theodor Fontane, and painters and sculptors such as Emil Nolde and Ernst Barlach. The quiet, contemplative spirit of the region's people, the marshland's special light, and the ever-changing face of the sea is inspiring. Today the world-famous Schleswig-Holstein-Musikfestival ushers in classical concerts to farmhouses, palaces, and churches.

Flensburg

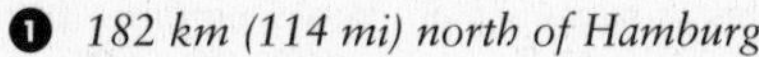

❶ *182 km (114 mi) north of Hamburg.*

Germany's northernmost city is known for its superb beer, Flensburger Pils, and the lovely marshland surrounding it. For centuries people in this border region between Denmark and Germany have lived more or less peacefully, except when distant empires clashed over their land. Locals have a laid-back, dry-humored attitude, and the mixed Danish-German heritage is reflected in the culture and food. The 87,000 residents of the area are nicknamed *Nordlichter* (northern lighters), a reference to the fact that the region is plagued (in fall and winter) by a lack of sunlight due to fog and rain.

Most of Flensburg has retained its special small-town charm, with red-brick warehouses, Gothic churches, half-timber houses, and cobblestone squares. Many of the city's landmarks are off the streets **Holm, Grosse Strasse,** and **Norderstrasse,** which wind their way through the city center to the waterfront. Around the picturesque **Südermarkt,** the Old City's South Market, are several typical commercial warehouses.

The **St. Nikolai-Kirche** (St. Nicholas Church) is named for the patron saint of sailors and was built in 1390. The church's real attraction is hidden inside: one of the most stunning Renaissance organ facades in Germany. ✉ *Nikolaikirchhof,* ☎ *0461/8400–4011.* 🎫 *Free.* ⏲ *Mon.–Sat. 8–7, Sun. 11–5.*

The **Museumsberg Flensburg** (Flensburg Museum Mountain), a unique complex of four museums, reveals the rich diversity of crafts, art, and scientific developments in an otherwise rural area. In addition to a collection of local art-nouveau furniture and tapestries, the **Heinrich-Sauermann-Haus** also exhibits art from the Middle Ages to the present. The museum even houses several original living rooms from North German island farms of the 17th and 18th centuries. Paintings by local artists of the 19th and 20th centuries are hung in the **Hans-Christiansen-Haus.** Some of the more interesting pieces are by Emil Nolde, Ernst

Barlach, and Erich Heckel, all of whom were fascinated by the special and at times mysterious light and atmosphere of North Germany's marshlands. ✉ *Museumsberg,* ☎ *0461/852–956.* 🎫 *€2.60.* ⏲ *Apr.–Oct., Tues.–Sun. 10–5; Nov.–Mar., Tues.–Sun. 10–4.*

The **Nordermarkt** (North Market) is surrounded by old alleyways such as the Rote Strasse, which is lined by redbrick warehouses now converted into galleries, restaurants, and pubs. The marketplace also preserves a reminder of medieval justice: at a small arcade you can see the metal for a neck ring used to publicly humiliate people convicted of certain crimes.

The **Schifffahrtsmuseum**(Maritime Museum) is in the old customs warehouse and can be spotted from far away thanks to the wooden masts of the old sailing vessels lying at anchor in the museum's harbor. The museum itself tells the story of the sea trade that made Flensburg prosperous in the Middle Ages and sent the city's sons as far away as Greenland and the West Indies. A special Rum-Museum explains how the city traded and manufactured some of Germany's finest rum. ✉ *Schiffbrücke 39,* ☎ *0461/852–970.* 🎫 *€2.60.* ⏲ *Apr.–Oct., Tues.–Sun. 10–5; Nov.–Mar., Tues.–Sun. 10–4.*

The chief residence of the dukes of Schleswig-Holstein, **Schloss Glücksburg,** lies 14 km (9 mi) northeast of Flensburg. Built in 1582–87, the bright-white Glücksburg, like many other palaces of the period, was completely surrounded by water. It is also known as the cradle of European high nobility, as the six children of Christian IX, king of Denmark and duke of Schleswig, were married to different European royal families. The palace museum showcases paintings, sculptures, furniture, and porcelain, mostly from the 17th century. ✉ *Glücksburg, off B–199,* ☎ *04631/2213 or 04631/2243,* WEB *www.schloss-gluecksburg.de.* 🎫 *€4.25.* ⏲ *Apr.–Oct., daily 10–6; Nov.–Mar., weekends 10–5; closed Mon. in Oct.*

Dining and Lodging

$ ★ ✕ **Schwarzer Walfisch.** The Black Whale has been cooking up fish since 1751, and its house and dining hall are protected monuments. Especially recommendable is the *Walfischteller* (with salmon, fried cod, North Sea shrimp, an egg sunny-side up, and fried potatoes). Such dishes must be washed down with the dark local beer on tap. ✉ *Angelburgerstr. 44,* ☎ *0461/13525. Reservations essential. No credit cards. Closed Sun.*

$$–$$$ ★ ✕🏨 **Alter Meierhof Vitalhotel.** Outside Flensburg on an inlet of the Baltic Sea, this former dairy farm is now a luxurious hotel that's surprisingly inexpensive for what it offers. Guests come primarily to pamper themselves with massages, mud packs, beauty treatments, and special baths. The fitness and wellness areas—under an artificial star-spangled sky—are all state-of-the-art. Rooms are fairly spacious and have reproduction 19th-century furnishings. When making a reservation, ask for the special wellness or health weekend packages, which include massages, skin treatments, and special meals. You can watch the chefs at work in the restaurant ($$–$$$) that focuses on fresh, international fish dishes. ✉ *Uferstr. 1, D–24960 Glücksburg,* ☎ *04631/61990,* FAX *04631/619–999,* WEB *www.alter-meierhof.de. 43 rooms, 9 suites. 2 restaurants, room service, in-room data ports, in-room safes, minibars, cable TV, pool, hair salon, health club, hot tub, massage, sauna, steam room, Turkish bath, beach, bicycles, bar, baby-sitting, dry cleaning, laundry service, meeting room, free parking, some pets allowed (fee), no-smoking room. No credit cards.*

$$ 🏨 **Mercure Hotel Flensburg.** Part of the upscale German Mercure hotel chain, this modern hotel is a rather somber-looking building whose appeal is its proximity to the harbor. Reserve a room on one of the upper

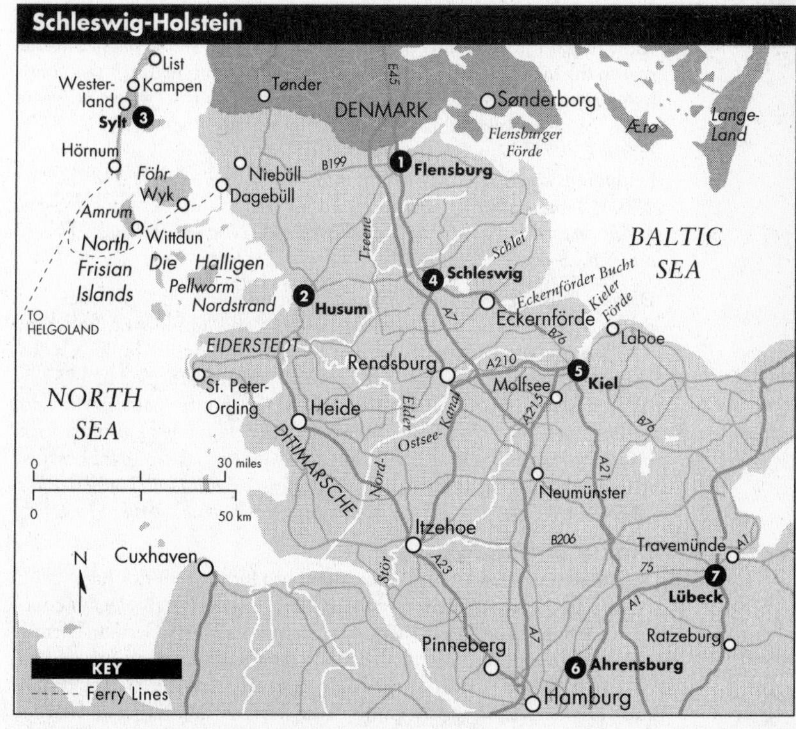

floors, and you'll enjoy a wonderful view. All rooms are fairly spacious. ✉ *Norderhofenden 6–9, D–24937,* ☎ *0461/84110,* FAX *0461/841–1299. 91 rooms, 4 suites. Bar, no a/c, minibars, cable TV, sauna, meeting room, parking (fee), some pets allowed (fee), no-smoking rooms. AE, DC, MC, V.*

Shopping

Holm-Passage (✉ Holm 39, ☎ 0461/21955), the only shopping mall in the city's historic downtown area, has many upscale fashion and specialty stores. A rather exclusive antiques shop, **Borring-Antik** (✉ Speicherlinie 42, ☎ 0461/807–9540), primarily sells 19th-century furniture, fine porcelain, and cutlery.

Husum

2 *45 km (28 mi) southeast of Flensburg, 158 km (98 mi) northeast of Hamburg.*

The town of Husum is the epitome of northern German lifestyle and culture. Immortalized in a poem as the "gray city upon the sea" by its famous son, Theodor Storm, Husum is in fact a popular vacation spot in summer. Its wonderful, deserted beaches and proximity to Sylt and the Danish border make it a perfect place to fully relax.

The central **Marktplatz** (market square) is bordered by 17th- and 18th-century buildings, including the historic Rathaus (town hall), which houses the tourist information office. The best impression of Husum's beginnings in the mid-13th century is found south of the Marktplatz, along **Krämerstrasse,** the **Wasserreihe,** a narrow and tortuous alley, and **Hafenstrasse,** right next to the narrow **Binnenhafen** (city harbor).

The most famous house on Wasserreihe is the **Theodor-Storm-Haus,** where writer Theodor Storm (1817–88) lived between 1866 and 1880.

It is a must if you're interested in German literature as well as if you want to gain insight into the life of the few well-to-do people in this region during the 19th century. The small museum features the poet's living room and a small *Poetenstübchen* (poets' parlor) where he wrote many of his novels, including the famous *Schimmelreiter* (*The Rider on the Gray Horse*). All rooms, the furniture, and many of the writer's belongings showcased are original. ✉ *Wasserreihe 31,* ☏ *04841/666–270,* WEB *www.storm-gesellschaft.de.* *€2.* *Apr.–Oct., Tues.–Fri. 10–noon and 2–5, Mon. and weekends 2–5; Nov.–Mar., Tues., Thurs., and Sat. 2–5.*

Despite Husum's remoteness amid the stormy sea, wide marshes, and dunes, the city used to be a major seaport and administrative center. The **Schloss vor Husum** (Palace of Husum), originally built as a Renaissance castle in the late 16th century, was transformed in 1752 by the dukes of Gottorf into a redbrick baroque country palace. The odd-looking blend of a church-bell tower and bastion is one of its most striking features, as well as the many well-preserved fireplaces whose mantelpieces are richly decorated. ✉ *Professor-Ferdinand-Tönnies-Allee,* ☏ *04841/2545.* *€2.50.* *Mid-Mar.–Oct., Tues.–Sun. 11–5.*

Dining and Lodging

$$$ ★ ✕ **Romantik-Hotel Altes Gymnasium.** In a former redbrick high school behind an orchard of pear trees, you'll find a surprisingly elegant country-style hotel. The Altes Gymnasium combines North German friendly service with English and Italian country-style design. The rooms are spacious with wood-panel floors and modern office amenities. The restaurant Eucken ($$$) serves game (from its own hunter) and German country cooking such as *Rücken vom Salzwiesenlamm mit Kartoffel-Zucchini-Rösti* (salted lamb back with potato and zucchini hash browns). The hotel's huge health and indoor pool area helps you forget the often bad weather in this region. ✉ *Süderstr. 6, D–25813,* ☏ *04841/8330,* FAX *04841/83312,* WEB *www.altes-gymnasium.de. 66 rooms, 6 suites. 2 restaurants, room service, in-room data ports, in-room safes, minibars, cable TV, indoor pool, gym, health club, massage, sauna, bicycles, bar, baby-sitting, dry cleaning, laundry service, free parking, some pets allowed (fee), no-smoking rooms. AE, DC, MC, V.*

Sylt

❸ *44 km (27 mi) northwest of Husum, 196 km (122 mi) northwest of Hamburg.*

Sylt is a long, narrow island (38 km [24 mi] by as little as 222 yards) of unspoiled beaches and marshland off the western coast of Schleswig-Holstein and Denmark. Famous for its clean air and white beaches, Sylt is the hideaway for the jet set of Germany. They come for the secluded beaches, and the exclusiveness provided by the island's inaccessibility. Nature itself, however, eats away at the idyllic habitat: with each winter storm, wind and wave erosion chew off pieces of land, constantly changing the island's shape. The island is a mecca for windsurfers, who rely on constant strong winds.

Wattwanderungen (long walks in the Watt, the shoreline tidelands) is a popular activity here, whether on self-guided or guided tours. The small villages with their thatch-roof houses, the beaches, and the nature conservation areas make Sylt the most enchanting German island, rivaled only by Rügen.

The island's major town is **Westerland,** which is not quite as expensive as Kampen, but more crowded. An ugly assortment of modern hotels lines an undeniably clean and broad beach. Each September windsurfers meet for the Surf Cup competition off the **Brandenburger Strand,** the best surfing spot.

If you are looking for privacy, detour to the villages of **List,** on the northern tip of Sylt, or to **Archsum** or **Hörnum.** The latter is on the southernmost point on the island and, like List, has a little harbor and a lighthouse.

Kampen

9 km (6 mi) from Westerland.

The island's unofficial capital is Kampen, which is the main destination for the wealthier crowd. Their redbrick or shining white thatch-roof houses spread along the coastline. The real draw—apart from the fancy restaurants and chic nightclubs—are the beaches. One of the is-
★ land's best-known features is the **Rotes Kliff** (Red Cliff), a dune cliff on the northern end of the Kampen beaches, which turns an eerie dark red when the sun sets.

The **Naturschutzgebiet Kampener Vogelkoje** (Birds' Nest Nature Conservation Area) once served as a mass trap for wild geese and was built in the mid-17th century. Nowadays it serves as a nature preserve for wild birds. ✉ *Lister Str., Kampen,* ☎ *04651/871–077.* 🎫 *€1.70.* ⏲ *Apr.–Oct., Tues.–Sun. 10–4.*

For a glimpse of the rugged lives of 19th-century fishermen, visit the small village of **Keitum** to the south and drop in on the **Altfriesisches Haus** (Old Frisian House), which preserves an old-world peacefulness in its lush garden setting. The house also documents a time when most seamen thrived on extensive whale hunting. ✉ *Am Kliff 13, Keitum,* ☎ *04651/31101.* 🎫 *€2.20.* ⏲ *Apr.–Oct., daily 10–5.*

The tower of the 800-year-old church **St. Severin,** built on the highest elevation in the region, once served the island's fishermen as a beacon. Strangely enough, the tower also served as a prison until 1806. Today the church is a popular site for weddings. ✉ *Keitum,* ☎ *04651/31713.* 🎫 *Free.* ⏲ *Apr.–Oct., tours Mon. and Thurs. at 5; Nov.–Mar. at 4.*

The small **Sylter Heimatmuseum** (Sylt Island Museum) tells the centuries-long history of the island's seafaring people. It features traditional costumes, tools, and other gear from fishing boats and tells the stories of prominent islanders such as Uwe Jens Lornsen, who fought for Sylt's independence. ✉ *Am Kliff 19, Keitum,* ☎ *04651/31669.* 🎫 *€2.20.* ⏲ *Apr.–Oct., daily 10–5.*

Dining and Lodging

$$–$$$$ ✕ **Dorfkrug Rotes Kliff.** The Dorfkrug has fed the island's seafaring inhabitants since 1876. Enjoy meals such as *Steinbuttfilet* (halibut fillet) or *Gebratener Zander* (fried perch fillet) in a homey setting, where the walls are covered in traditional blue-white Frisian tiles. ✉ *Braderuper Weg 3, Kampen,* ☎ *04651/43500. AE, MC.*

$$–$$$$ ✕ **Sansibar.** Sansibar is one of the island's most popular restaurants.
★ The cuisine includes seafood and fondue with fish or scampi, served with any one of more than 800 wines. To get a table even in the afternoon, you must reserve well in advance. ✉ *Strand, Rantum-Süd, Rantum,* ☎ *04651/964–646. Reservations essential. AE.*

$$$$ ✕🏨 **Dorint Söl'ring Hof.** The latest newcomer to the upscale hotel
★ scene of Sylt is this luxurious resort set in a white, thatch-roofed country house *on* the dunes: the view from most of the rooms is magnificent—with some luck you may even spot frolicking harbor porpoises. The brightly furnished rooms are spacious, covering two floors, and equipped with a fire place. The real attraction here, however, is the restaurant ($$$$) where Michelin-starred chef Johannes King creates deli-

cious German-Mediterranean fish dishes. The hotel is in quiet Rantum, at the southeast of the island. ✉ *Am Sandwall 1, D–25980, Sylt-Rantum,* ☎ *04651/836–200,* FAX *04651/836–2020,* WEB *www.dorint.de. 15 rooms, 8 suites. Restaurant, bar, lounge, no a/c, room service, in-room data ports, in-room safes, minibars, cable TV with movies, health club, massage, sauna, spa, beach, baby-sitting, dry cleaning, laundry service, concierge, meeting room, free parking, some pets allowed (fee), no-smoking rooms. AE, DC, MC, V.*

$$$–$$$$ ✕🏨 **Landhaus Nösse.** Perched on a small elevation in the midst of the Nösse nature conservation area, this excellent hotel and restaurant ($$$$) not only serves Michelin-starred food but also offers secluded accommodations. Most rooms have white-painted wooden walls and ceiling beams, old-style German windows tucked away under the thatch roof, and a beautiful view of the sea and marshes. When making reservations, inquire about the hotel's special weekend and other packages. ✉ *Nösistieg 13, D–25980 Sylt-Ost Morsum,* ☎ *04651/97220,* FAX *04651/891–658,* WEB *www.landhaus-noesse.de. 10 rooms. Restaurant, café, pub, no a/c, cable TV, some pets allowed (fee). AE, MC, V.*

$$$ ★ ✕🏨 **Hotelrestaurant Jörg Müller.** The old thatch-roof farmhouse hotel has a handful of lovely rooms combining Frisian-style designs with classical elegance. The wing added in 2001 has modern rooms. The restaurant Pesel serves local fish dishes, whereas the upscale main restaurant offers a high-quality blend of international and Mediterranean cuisine. The breakfast buffet is an extra €15. ✉ *Süderstr. 8, D–25980 Westerland,* ☎ *04651/27788,* FAX *04651/201–471. 19 rooms, 4 suites. 2 restaurants, room service, in-room safes, minibars, cable TV, hot tub, sauna, steam room, bar, dry cleaning, laundry service, some pets allowed (fee), free parking. AE, DC, MC, V.*

$$–$$$ ★ 🏨 **Ulenhof Wenningstedt.** The Ulenhof, one of Sylt's loveliest old thatch-roof apartment houses, is a quiet alternative to the busier main resorts Kampen and Westerland. The Ulenhof has two buildings 750 yards away from the beach in Wenningstedt. The larger apartments for up to three persons are a good deal. A separate bathing facility offers a huge wellness area with two saunas, a pool, and a *Tecaldarium,* a Roman bathhouse. ✉ *Sachsenring 14, D–25996 Wenningstedt,* ☎ *04651/94540,* FAX *04651/945–431,* WEB *www.ulenhof.de. 35 apartments. No a/c, cable TV, indoor pool, health club, hot tub, massage, sauna, steam room, free parking, no-smoking rooms. No credit cards.*

Nightlife and the Arts

The nightspots in Kampen are generally more upscale and quite expensive compared to the pubs and clubs of Westerland. One of the most classic clubs on Sylt is the **Club Rotes Kliff** (✉ Alte Dorfstr., Kampen, ☎ 04651/43400), a bar and dancing club attracting a hip crowd of all ages. The **Compass** (✉ Friedrichstr. 42, Westerland, ☎ 04651/23513) is not as trendy as the typical Sylt disco. The mostly young patrons, however, create a cheerful party atmosphere on weekend nights.

Schleswig

❹ *37 km (23 mi) south of Flensburg, 114 km (71 mi) north of Hamburg.*

Schleswig-Holstein's oldest city is also one of its best-preserved examples of a typical North German town. Once the seat of the dukes of Schleswig-Holstein, it has not only their palace but also remains of the area's first rulers, the Vikings. Those legendary and fierce warriors from Scandinavia brought terror (but also commerce) to northern Germany between 800 and 1100. Under a wide sky, Schleswig lies on the Schlei River in a landscape of freshwater marshland and lakes, making it a good departure point for bike or canoe tours.

The fishing village comes alive along the **Holm,** an old settlement with tiny and colorful houses. The windblown buildings give a good impression of what villages in northern Germany looked like some 150 years ago. Relax in one of the cafés or further inspect the city's history at the **Städtisches Museum** (Municipal Museum). In a typical noble country palace of the late 17th century, you can explore Schleswig's history from the Stone Age onward. ✉ *Günderothscher Hof, Friedrichstr. 9–11,* ☎ *04621/936–820.* 🎫 *€2.* 🕑 *Tues.–Sun. 10–5.*

The impressive baroque **Schloss Gottorf,** dating from 1703, is the state's largest secular building and once housed the ruling family. It has been transformed into the Schleswig-Holsteinisches Landesmuseum (State Museum of Schleswig-Holstein) and holds a collection of art and handicrafts of northern Germany from the Middle Ages to the present, including paintings by Lucas Cranach the Elder. Among the museum's archaeological exhibits are ancient mummified corpses retrieved from nearby swamps. ✉ *Schloss Gottorf,* ☎ *04621/8130,* WEB *www.schloss-gottorf.de.* 🎫 *€5.* 🕑 *Apr.–Oct., daily 10–6; Nov.–Mar., Tues.–Fri. 10–4, weekends 10–5.*

The most thrilling museum in Schleswig, the **Wikinger-Museum Haithabu** (Haithabu Viking Museum), is at the site of a Viking settlement. This was the Vikings' most important German port and the boats, gold jewelry, and graves they left behind are displayed in the museum. ✉ *Haddeby,* ☎ *04621/8130,* WEB *www.uni-kiel.de/museen/landesmuseum.html.* 🎫 *€3.* 🕑 *Apr.–Oct., daily 9–5; Nov.–Mar., Tues.–Sun. 10–4.*

Dining and Lodging

$–$$$ ✕ **Stadt Flensburg.** This small restaurant in a city mansion that dates to 1699 serves mostly fish from the Schlei River. Fishermen living on the Holm will have caught your dinner. The food is rather solid regional fare such as *Zanderfilet* (perch fillets) or *Gebratene Ente* (baked duck). The familial, warm atmosphere and the local dark tap beers more than make up for the simplicity of the setting. Reservations are advised. ✉ *Lollfuss 102,* ☎ *04621/23984. AE, DC, MC, V. Closed Wed.*

$$ 🏨 **Ringhotel Strandhalle Schleswig.** A modern hotel overlooking the small yacht harbor and the Schlei, this establishment has surprisingly low rates and a good value for its many services. The rooms are furnished in timeless dark furniture, and all have cable television. If you plan to stay a couple of days, ask about the special weekend packages that include nightly four-course meals and other extras. ✉ *Strandweg 2, D–24837,* ☎ *04621/9090,* FAX *04621/909–100. 25 rooms. Restaurant, no a/c, in-room safes, minibars, pool, cable TV, boating, bicycles, meeting room, free parking, some pets allowed (fee), no-smoking rooms. AE, DC, MC, V.*

Shopping

The tiny **Keramik-Stube** (✉ Rathausmarkt, ☎ 04621/24757) offers craft work and beautiful handmade pottery. It's the ideal place to buy a gift. The best place to buy tea is **Teekontor Hansen** (✉ Kornmarkt 3, ☎ 04621/23385). Try their *Schliekieker,* a special and very strong blend of different teas.

Kiel

❺ *53 km (33 mi) southeast of Schleswig, 130 km (81 mi) north of Hamburg.*

The sleepy state capital Kiel is known throughout Europe for its annual *Kieler Woche,* a festival and regatta that attracts hundreds of sailing boats from around the world. Despite the many wharves and industries concentrated in Kiel, the **Kieler Föhrde** (Bay of Kiel) has remained mostly unspoiled. Unfortunately, this cannot be said about the city itself. Because of Kiel's strategic significance during World War II—it served as the German submarine base—the historic city, founded more than 750 years ago, was completely destroyed. Kiel's buildings are mostly modern, and its attraction lies in its outlying beaches, parks, and small towns.

At the **Kieler Hafen** (Kiel Harbor), Germany's largest passenger shipping harbor, you can always catch a glimpse of one of the many ferries leaving for Scandinavia from the **Oslokai** (Oslo Quay). In the background you can spot some of the shipbuilding wharves and—in the Kiel Bay—sometimes even a German submarine charting its way home. In the past, however, it was primarily the fishing industry that built the city.

The **Schifffahrtsmuseum**(Maritime Museum), housed in a hall of the old fish market, includes two antique fishing boats. ✉ *Wall 65,* ☎ *0431/901–3428,* WEB *www.kiel.de/schiffahrtsmuseum.* 🎫 *€1.* ⏲ *Mid-Apr.–mid-Oct., daily 10–6; mid-Oct.–mid-Apr., Tues.–Sun. 10–5.*

A grim reminder of a different marine past is exhibited at the **U-Boot-Museum** (Submarine Museum) in Kiel-Laboe. The vessels of the much-feared German submarine fleet in World War I were mostly built and stationed in Kiel, before leaving for the Atlantic where they attacked American and British supply convoys. Today the submarine U995 serves as a public viewing model of a typical German submarine. The 280-ft-high **Marineehrenmal** (Marine Honor Memorial), in Laboe, was built in 1927–36. All German submarine personnel are required to salute when passing the memorial. You can reach Laboe via ferry from the Kiel harbor or take B–502 north. ✉ *Strandstr. 92, Kiel-Laboe,* ☎ *04343/42700.* 🎫 *Memorial €2.80, museum €2.10.* ⏲ *Mid-Apr.–mid-Oct., daily 9:30–6; mid-Oct.–mid-Apr., daily 9:30–4.*

One of northern Germany's best (though small) collections of modern art can be found at the **Kunsthalle zu Kiel** (Kiel Art Gallery), which specializes in Russian art of the 19th and early 20th centuries, German expressionism, and contemporary international art. The collections include paintings, prints, and sculptures. ✉ *Düsternbrooker Weg 1,* ☎ *0431/880–5756,* WEB *www.kunsthalle.uni-kiel.de.* 🎫 *€3.* ⏲ *Tues., Thurs.–Sun. 10:30–6, Wed. 10:30–8.*

Two attractive beach towns close to Kiel, **Laboe** and **Strande,** are crowded with sun-loving Kielers on summer weekends. Both retain their fishing-village appeal, and you can buy fresh fish directly from the boats in the harbor. Most fishermen here still smoke the fish on board, preparing, for example, the famous *Kieler Sprotten,* a small salty fish somewhat like sardines. Though you can get to Laboe and Strande by car, it's more fun to catch a ferry leaving from Kiel.

Dining and Lodging

$–$$$ ✕ **Feld.** The buzz here is not the food itself, even though the steak, fish, and Asian dishes are formidable, but the stylish crowd, lounging on black leather chairs in the bar or dining at the white-linen covered tables. But don't worry about overblown attitudes—service is considered to be the nicest in town, and Sunday brunch feels like a relaxed get-together of old friends. ✉ *Feldstr. 111,* ☎ *0431/806–0428. Reservations essential. No lunch. AE.*

$$ ★ ✕ **Quam.** Locals who dine out aren't looking for the old-fashioned fish dishes (that's why there isn't a good, traditional fish restaurant in town) but prefer international preparations of fish from all over the world. The stylish Quam, its yellow walls and dimmed lights paying homage to Tuscany, serves international cuisine, including fish specialties from Germany, Italy, France, and Japan, to a mostly young, very chic crowd. The menu changes frequently. ✉ *Düppelstr. 60,* ☎ *0431/85195. Reservations essential. AE.*

$$ ✕🏨 **Hotel Kieler Yachtclub.** This traditional hotel provides standard yet elegant rooms in the main building and completely new, bright accommodations in the *Villentrakt.* The restaurant ($$$) serves mostly local fish dishes; in summer try to get a table on the terrace. The club overlooks the Kieler Föhrde. ✉ *Hindenburgufer 70, D–24105,* ☎ *0431/88130,* FAX *0431/881–3444. 55 rooms, 3 suites. Restaurant, bar, no a/c, room service, minibars, cable TV, dry cleaning, laundry service, meeting room, parking (fee), some pets allowed (fee), no-smoking rooms. AE, DC, MC, V.*

Nightlife and the Arts

Despite its medium size (250,000 inhabitants), the city has a thriving nightlife. One of the many chic and hip bars is the **Hemingway** (✉ Alter Markt, ☎ 0431/96812). The popular bar, the Nachtcafé, has a basement disco, **Velvet** (✉ Eggerstedtstr. 14, ☎ 0431/95550). A college crowd goes to **Traumfabrik** (✉ Grasweg 19, ☎ 0431/548–106) to eat pizza, watch a movie, or dance (Friday is best for dancing).

Ahrensburg

❻ *25 km (16 mi) northeast of Hamburg.*

One of Schleswig-Holstein's major attractions is within a Hamburg suburb. The romantic, 16th-century **Schloss Ahrensburg** (Ahrensburg Castle) lies within lush parkland on the bank of the Hunnau. The whitewashed, brick, moated Renaissance castle stands much as it did when first constructed by Count Peter Rantzau. Its interior has had several remodelings, the first after financier Carl Schimmelmann purchased the estate in 1759.

Furniture and paintings, most dating from the early 19th century, fine porcelain, and exquisite crystal are exhibited on the two museum floors. On the grounds stands a simple 16th-century church; the west tower was a later addition, and baroque alterations were made in the 18th century. The church is nestled between two rows of 12 almshouses, or *Gottesbuden* (God's cottages). ✉ *On bank of the Hunnau,* ☎ *04102/42510,* WEB *www.ahrensburg.de.* 🎫 *€3.50.* ⏲ *Apr.–Sept., Tues.–Sun. 11–5; Oct.–Mar., Tues.–Sun. 11:30.*

Lübeck

★ ❼ *38 km (24 mi) northeast of Ahrensburg, 60 km (37 mi) southeast of Kiel, 56 km (35 mi) northeast of Hamburg.*

The ancient core of Lübeck, one of Europe's largest Old Towns dating from the 12th century, was a chief stronghold of the Hanseatic merchant princes. But it was the roving Heinrich der Löwe (King Henry the Lion) who established the town and, in 1173, laid the foundation stone of the redbrick Gothic cathedral. The town's famous landmark gate, the **Holstentor,** built between 1464 and 1478, is flanked by two round, squat towers and serves as a solid symbol of Lübeck's prosperity as a trading center.

In the **Altstadt** (Old Town), proof of Lübeck's former position as the golden queen of the Hanseatic League is found at every step. More 13th- to 15th-century buildings stand in Lübeck than in all other large northern German cities combined, which has earned the Altstadt a place on UNESCO's register of the world's greatest cultural and natural treasures. The **Rathaus,** dating from 1240, is among the buildings lining the arcaded Marktplatz, one of Europe's most striking medieval market squares. It has been subjected to several architectural face-lifts that have added Romanesque arches, Gothic windows, and a Renaissance roof. ✉ *Breitestr. 64,* ☎ *0451/122–1005.* 🎫 *Guided tour in German €2.56.* ⏲ *Tour weekdays at 11, noon, and 3.*

The impressive redbrick Gothic **Marienkirche** (St. Mary's Church), which has the highest brick nave in the world, looms behind the Rathaus. ✉ *Marienkirchhof,* ☎ *0451/397–700.* ⏲ *Mar. and Oct., daily 10–5; Apr.–Sept., daily 10–6; Nov., weekdays 10–6, weekends 10–5; Dec.–Feb., daily 10–4.*

The **Buddenbrookhaus,** a highly respectable-looking mansion, takes its name from German novelist Thomas Mann's saga *Buddenbrooks.* Mann's family once lived in the house, which is now the **Heinrich and Thomas Mann Zentrum** (Heinrich and Thomas Mann Center). This museum documents the lives and works of two of the most important German writers of the 20th century. A tour and video in English are offered. ✉ *Mengstr. 4,* ☎ *0451/122–4190,* WEB *www.buddenbrockhaus.de.* 🎫 *€4.10.* ⏲ *Apr.–Oct., daily 10–6; Nov.–Mar., daily 10–5.*

Take a look inside the entrance hall of the Gothic **Heiligen-Geist-Hospital** (Hospital of the Holy Ghost). It was built in the 14th century by the town's rich merchants and is still caring for the infirm. ✉ *Am Koberg,* ☎ *0451/122–2040.* ⏲ *Apr.–Sept., Tues.–Sun. 10–5; Oct.–Mar., Tues.–Sun. 10–4.*

Construction of the **Lübecker Dom** (Lübeck Cathedral), the city's oldest building, began in 1173. Both the Dom and the Marienkirche present frequent organ concerts, a real treat in these magnificent redbrick Gothic churches. ✉ *Domkirchhof,* ☎ *0451/74704.* ⏲ *Mar.–Oct., daily 10–6; Nov.–Feb., daily 10–3.*

Dining and Lodging

$$$$ ✕ **Wullenwever.** Culinary critics say this restaurant set a new standard of dining sophistication for Lübeck. It is certainly one of the most attractive establishments in town, with dark furniture, chandeliers, and oil paintings on pale pastel walls. In summer tables fill a quiet flower-strewn courtyard. ✉ *Beckergrube 71,* ☎ *0451/704–333. Reservations essential. AE, V. Closed Sun. and Mon. No lunch.*

$$–$$$$ ★ ✕ **Schiffergesellschaft.** Women weren't allowed in the Schiffergesellschaft (Mariners' Society) from its opening in 1535 until 1870. Today mixed company sits in church-style pews at long 400-year-old oak tables. At each end of the pew is a sculpted coat of arms of a particular city. Shipowners had their set trading routes, and they each had their own pew and table. A good meal here is the *Ostseescholle* (plaice), fried with bacon and served with potatoes and cucumber salad. ✉ *Breitestr. 2,* ☎ *0451/76776. No credit cards.*

$$$ ★ ✕🏨 **SAS Radisson Senator Hotel Lübeck.** Close to the famous Holstentor, the ultramodern hotel's daring architecture still reveals a North German heritage: the redbrick building, with its oversize windows and generous, open lobby, mimics an old Lübeck warehouse. When making a reservation, ask for a (larger) *Business Class* room, whose price includes a breakfast. A big plus are the very comfortable beds, which are large by German standards. The Nautilo restaurant ($$–$$$) serves light Mediterranean cuisine. At the lively bar the local Hanseaten and tourists mingle over beer and aquavit, the strong North German schnapps. ✉ *Willy-Brandt-Allee 6, D–23554,* ☎ *0451/1420,* FAX *0451/142–2222,* WEB *www.radissonSAS.de. 217 rooms, 7 suites. 2 restaurants, room service, in-room data ports, minibars, cable TV with movies, pool, hair salon, health club, massage, sauna, spa, bar, baby-sitting, dry* *cleaning, laundry service, concierge, meeting room, parking (fee), some pets allowed (fee), no-smoking rooms. AE, DC, MC, V.*

$$ ✕🏨 **Ringhotel Jensen.** Only a stone's throw from the Holsten Gate, this hotel is close to all the main attractions and faces the moat surrounding the Old Town. It's family run and very comfortable, with modern rooms, mostly decorated with bright cherrywood furniture. Though small, the guest rooms are big enough for two twin beds and a coffee table and come with either a shower or a bath. The popular Yachtzimmer ($$–$$$) cooks up regional and international dishes. ✉ *An der Obertrave 4–5, D–23552,* ☎ *0451/71646,* FAX *0451/73386,* WEB *www.hotel-jensen.de. 41 rooms, 1 suite. Restaurant, no a/c, cable TV, parking (fee), some pets allowed (fee). AE, DC, MC, V.*

$$ 🏨 **Kaiserhof.** The most comfortable hotel in Lübeck consists of two early 19th-century merchants' houses linked together, retaining many of the original architectural features. It's just a five-minute walk from the cathedral. The spacious bedrooms all have a restful, homey ambience, and the quietest of them overlook the garden at the back. A marvelous breakfast is included in the room cost. ✉ *Kronsforder Allee 11–13, D–23560,* ☎ *0451/703–301,* FAX *0451/795–083,* WEB *www.kaiserhof-luebeck.de. 60 rooms, 6 suites. No a/c, room service, in-room safes, minibars, cable TV, pool, gym, sauna, bar, free parking, some pets allowed (fee). AE, DC, MC, V.*

$$ 🏨 **Klassik Altstadt-Hotel.** Behind the landmark old facade stands a modern hotel. The studios, fitted with small kitchens, are a particularly good value if you plan to stay a few days. There is no restaurant, but breakfast (included in the price) is served in the hotel. ✉ *Fischergrube 52, D–23552,* ☎ *0451/72083,* FAX *0451/73778,* WEB *www.klassik-altstadt-hotel.com. 25 rooms, 2 suites. No a/c, cable TV, meeting room, parking (fee), some pets allowed (fee), no-smoking rooms. AE, DC, MC, V.*

Nightlife and the Arts

Contact the **Musik und Kongresshallen Lübeck** (✉ Willy-Brandt-Allee 10, D–23554, ☎ 0451/790–400) for schedules of the myriad concerts, operas, and theater performances in Lübeck.

In summer try to catch a few performances of the **Schleswig-Holstein Music Festival** (mid-July–late August), which features orchestras composed of young musicians from more than 25 countries. Some concerts are held in the Dom or the Marienkirche; some are staged in barns in small towns and villages. Each year between 1986 and 1989, Leonard Bernstein conducted the festival orchestra on a site where cows and chickens are normally fed. For exact dates and tickets, contact Schleswig-Holstein Konzertorganisation (✉ Kartenzentrale Kiel, Postfach 3840, D–24037 Kiel, ☎ 0431/570–470, FAX 0431/570–4747).

Shopping

The city's largest downtown mall, **Holstentor-Passage** (✉ An der Untertrave 111, ☎ 0451/704–425), is next to the Holstentor and is home to stores selling clothing or home accessories. **Konditorei-Café Niederegger** (✉ Breitestr. 89, ☎ 0451/530–1126) sells the famous Lübeck marzipan molded into a multitude of imaginative forms. It's hard to believe that the almond-paste treat was first introduced during the great medieval Lübeck famine.

WESTERN MECKLENBURG

This long-forgotten Baltic Coast region, pinned between two sprawling urban areas—the state capital of Schwerin, in the west, and Rostock, in the east—is thriving again. Despite its perennial economic woes,

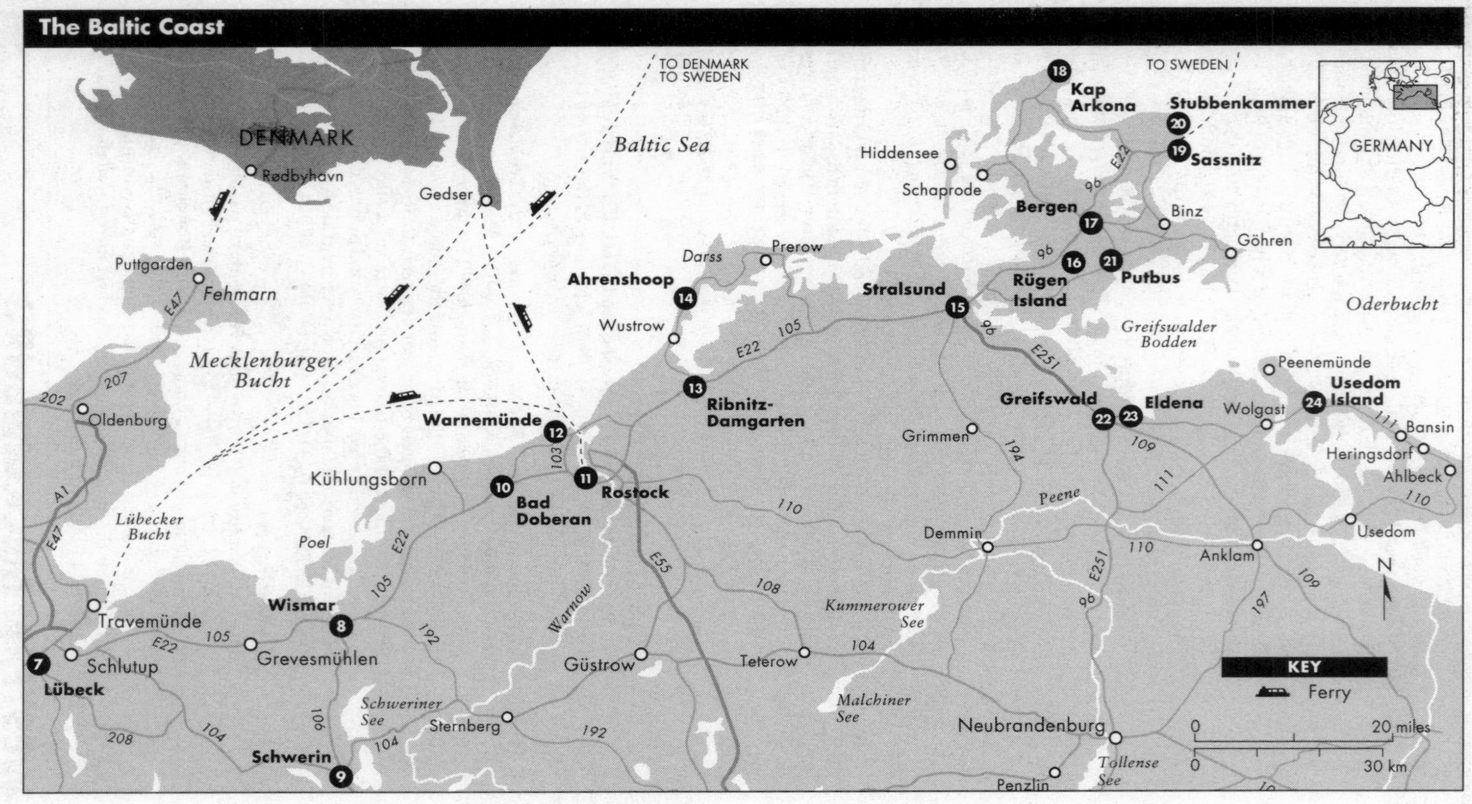
The Baltic Coast
TO DENMARK
TO SWEDEN
TO SWEDEN
DENMARK
Baltic Sea
Rødbyhavn
Gedser
Puttgarden
Fehmarn
Mecklenburger Bucht
Lübecker Bucht
Oderbucht
Greifswalder Bodden
GERMANY
18 Kap Arkona
20 Stubbenkammer
19 Sassnitz
Hiddensee
Schaprode
17 Bergen
Binz
Göhren
16 Rügen Island
21 Putbus
15 Stralsund
14 Ahrenshoop
Darss
Prerow
Wustrow
13 Ribnitz-Damgarten
12 Warnemünde
11 Rostock
10 Bad Doberan
Kühlungsborn
Oldenburg
Poel
Travemünde
Schlutup
7 Lübeck
8 Wismar
Grevesmühlen
9 Schwerin
Schweriner See
Sternberg
Güstrow
Teterow
Warnow
Kummerower See
Malchiner See
Grimmen
Demmin
Peene
22 Greifswald
23 Eldena
Peenemünde
Wolgast
24 Usedom Island
Bansin
Heringsdorf
Ahlbeck
Usedom
Anklam
Neubrandenburg
Penzlin
Tollense See
N
KEY
Ferry
0
20 miles
0
30 km
E47
A1
E22
E55
E251
202
207
208
104
105
106
192
103
108
110
194
96
109
111
197

this part of Germany, and Schwerin in particular, has attracted many new businesses, which suggests a light at the end of the tunnel. Though the region is close to the sea, it is made up largely of seemingly endless fields of wheat and yellow rape and a dozen or so wonderful lakes. "When the Lord made the Earth, He started with Mecklenburg," wrote native novelist Fritz Reuter.

Wismar

★ 8 *60 km (37 mi) east of Lübeck on Rte. 105.*

The old city of Wismar was one of the original three sea-trading towns, along with Lübeck and Rostock, that banded together in 1259 to combat Baltic pirates. From this mutual defense pact grew the great and powerful private trading bloc, the Hanseatic League, which dominated the Baltic for centuries. The Thirty Years' War halved the prewar population—and the power of the Hanseatics was broken. Wismar became the victim of regular military tussles and finally fell to Sweden. In 1803 the town was leased for 100 years to a German Mecklenburg duke, and only when the lease expired did Wismar legally rejoin Germany. The wealth generated by the Hanseatic merchants can still be seen in Wismar's ornate architecture.

★ The **Marktplatz** (Market Square), one of the largest and best preserved in Germany, is framed by patrician gabled houses. Their style ranges from redbrick late Gothic through Dutch Renaissance to 19th-century neoclassical. In 1922 filmmaker Friedrich Wilhelm Murnau used the tortuous streets of Wismar's Old Town in his expressionist horror film classic, *Nosferatu.* The square's **Wasserkunst,** the ornate pumping station done in Dutch Renaissance style, was built between 1580 and 1602 by the Dutch master Philipp Brandin. Not only was it a work of art, it supplied the town with water until the mid-19th century.

The **Alter Schwede** (The Old Swede), a seamen's tavern since 1878, has entertained guests ranging from sailors to the Swedish royal family. Dating from 1380, it's the oldest building on the Marktplatz and is easily identified by its stepped gables and redbrick facade. ✉ *Am Markt 19–22,* ☎ *03841/283–552.*

The ruins of the **Marienkirche** (St. Mary's Church) with its 250-ft tower, bombed in World War II, lie just behind the Marktplatz; the church is still undergoing restoration. At noon, 3, and 5, listen for one of 14 hymns played on its carillon.

The **Fürstenhof** (Princes' Court), home of the former dukes of Mecklenburg, stands next to Marienkirche. It is an early 16th-century Italian Renaissance structure with touches of late Gothic. The facade is a series of fussy friezes depicting scenes from the Trojan War. The **Georgenkirche** (St. George's Church), another victim of the war, is next to the Fürstenhof. Today it's the biggest Gothic religious ruin in Europe.

The late-Gothic **St. Nikolaikirche** (St. Nicholas's Church), with a 120-ft-high nave, was built between 1381 and 1487. A remnant of the town's long domination by Sweden is the additional altar built for Swedish sailors. ✉ *Marktpl.,* ☎ *03841/210–143.* ⏲ *Apr.–May, Mon.–Sat. 10–12:30, 1:30–4; June– Sept., Mon.–Sat. 10–12:30, 1:30–5; Oct.–Mar., Mon.–Sat. 10–noon, 1:30–5.*

If you have an hour to spare, wander among the jetties and quays of the port, a mix of the medieval and the modern. **To'n Zägenkrog,** a seamen's haven decorated with sharks' teeth, stuffed seagulls, and maritime gear, is a good pit stop along the harbor. ✉ *Ziegenmarkt 10,* ☎ *03841/282–716.*

Dining and Lodging

$–$$ ★ ✕ **Alter Schwede.** Regarded as one of the most attractive, authentic taverns on the Baltic—and correspondingly busy—this eatery focuses not onlyon Mecklenburg's game and fish dishes, such as *Rippenbraten mit Backpflaumen* (pork spareribs with baked plums), but also new North German cuisine such as *Lachsfilet im Bierteig gebacken auf Hummersauce, mit Brokkoli und Kartoffelgratin* (salmon baked in bear dough, served with lobster sauce, broccoli, and potato gratin). ✉ *Am Markt 19–22,* ☎ *03841/283–552. AE, MC, V.*

$$ ★ ✕🏨 **Privathotel Alter Speicher.** This small and very personal family-owned hotel is behind the facade of an old merchant house in the downtown area. Some of the rooms may be tiny, but they contribute to the warm and cozy atmosphere. The lobby and restaurants are decorated with wooden beams and panels. The main restaurant ($$$–$$$$) primarily serves game, but it also prepares regional dishes such as *Rauchwarme Räucherfischhappen auf Kräuterrührei und Brot* (smoked fish on scrambled eggs with herbs and bread). ✉ *Bohrstr. 12–12a, D–23966,* ☎ *03841/211–746,* FAX *03841/211–747,* WEB *www.hotel-alter-speicher.de. 70 rooms, 3 suites, 2 apartments. Restaurant, café, bar, no a/c, in-room safes, minibars, cable TV, gym, sauna, meeting room, parking (fee), some pets allowed (fee), no-smoking rooms. DC, MC, V.*

$$ ★ ✕🏨 **Seehotel Nakenstorf.** Set at the dreamy Naun lake, this country hotel is a hidden gem just 15 km east of Wismar. The redbrick farmhouse and old thatched-roof barn make up an upscale yet casual hotel. Each room has a different design (the owners are acclaimed Berlin interior designers), with white walls and terra-cotta tiles. There is a fine restaurant ($$) serving German-Italian seafood on a terrace; a sauna at the lake and a beach invite you to relax. ✉ *Seestr. 1, D–23992 Nakenstorf,* ☎ *038422/25445,* FAX *038422/25630,* WEB *www.seehotel-nakenstorf.de. 11 rooms, 1 suite. Restaurant, no a/c, in-room data ports, cable TV, sauna, beach, boating, bicycles, hiking, horseback riding, free parking, some pets allowed (fee), no-smoking rooms. MC.*

$$ ★ 🏨 **Steigenberger-Hotel Stadt Hamburg.** This first-class hotel hides behind a rigid gray facade dating to the early 19th century. Behind it is an open, airy interior, with skylights and a posh lobby. The rooms have elegant cherrywood art-deco–style furnishings. Downstairs, the Bierkeller, a cavernous 17th-century room with vaulted ceilings, is a trendy nightspot. Ask for special package deals such as the *Joker-Wochenende,* which includes two nights, a four-course dinner, a sightseeing tour or boat trip on the Baltic Sea, and a bottle of champagne—all for €173.50 a person. ✉ *Am Markt 24, D–23966,* ☎ *03841/2390,* FAX *03841/239–239,* WEB *www.wismar.steigenberger.de. 102 rooms, 2 suites. Restaurant, café, no a/c, minibars, cable TV, sauna, meeting room, some pets allowed (fee), no-smoking floor. AE, DC, MC, V.*

Nightlife and the Arts

At the **Niederdeutsche Bühne** (✉ Philipp-Müllerstr. 5, ☎ 03841/705–501), plays in German and operas are performed regularly, and concerts occasionally take place.

Schwerin

★ ❾ *32 km (20 mi) south of Wismar on Rte. 106.*

Schwerin, the second-largest town in the region after Rostock and the capital of the state of Mecklenburg-Vorpommern, is worth a trip just to visit its giant island palace. On the edge of Lake Schwerin, the **Schweriner Schloss** housed the Mecklenburg royal family. When Henry the Lion founded Schwerin in 1160, he enlarged the original palace, which dated from 1018. Surmounted by 15 turrets, large and small, the palace is reminiscent of a French château, and, indeed, portions of it were later modeled on Chambord, in the Loire Valley. The part of it that's neo-Renaissance in style and its many ducal staterooms date from between 1845 and 1857.

North of the main tower is the **Neue Lange Haus** (New Long House), built between 1553 and 1555 and now used as the **Schlossmuseum.** The Communist government restored and maintained the fantastic opulence of this rambling, 80-room reminder of an absolutist monarchy—and then used it to board kindergarten teachers in training. A fifth of the rooms are now used for government offices. Antique furniture, objets d'art, silk tapestries, and paintings are sprinkled throughout the salons (the throne room is particularly extravagant), but of special interest are the ornately patterned and highly burnished inlaid wooden floors and wall panels. The parkland contains many beautiful and rare species of trees. Sandstone replicas of Permoser sculptures adorn the boulevards. ✉ *Lennéstr. 1,* ☎ *0385/565–738,* WEB *www.museum-schwerin.de.* 🎫 *€4.* ⏲ *Mid-Apr.–mid-Oct., Tues.–Sun. 10–6; mid-Oct.–mid-Apr., Tues.–Sun. 10–5.*

The **Alte Garten** (Old Garden), the town's showpiece square, was the setting of military parades during the years of Communist rule. It is dominated by two buildings: the ornate neo-Renaissance state theater, constructed in 1883–86; and the **Staatliches Museum** (State Museum), which houses an interesting collection of paintings by Max Liebermann and Lovis Corinth, plus an exhibition of Meissen porcelain. ✉ *Alter Garten 3,* ☎ *0385/59580,* WEB *www.museum-schwerin.de.* 🎫 *€3.* ⏲ *Mid-Apr.–mid-Oct., Wed.–Sun. 10–6, Tues. 10–8; mid-Oct.–mid-Apr., Wed.–Sun. 10–5, Tues. 10–8.*

The **Dom,** a Gothic cathedral, is the oldest building (built 1222–48) in the city. The bronze baptismal font is from the 14th century; the altar was built in 1440. Religious scenes painted on its walls date from the Middle Ages. Sweeping views of the Old Town and lake await those with the energy to climb the 219 steps to the top of the 320-ft-high cathedral tower. ✉ *Am Dom 4,* ☎ *0385/565–014.* ⏲ *Tower and nave May–mid-Oct., Mon.–Sat. 10–4, Sun. noon–4; mid-Oct.–Apr., weekdays 11–2, Sat. 11–4, Sun. noon–3.*

The **Mecklenburgisches Volkskundemuseum** (Ethnology Museum) is a living-history museum representing traditional work and farm life in Germany. Children and history buffs in particular will enjoy wandering through the 17 preserved buildings, which include a blacksmith's shop dating from 1736, a village school from the 19th century, and a traditional fire station. You can watch demonstrations of the tools. ✉ *Alte Crivitzer Landstr. 13, 6 km (4 mi) south of Schwerin,* ☎ *0385/208–410.* 🎫 *€2.50.* ⏲ *May–Oct., Tues.–Sun. 10–6.*

A visit to Schwerin wouldn't be complete without one of the two-hour **Weisse Flotte** boat tours of the lakes—there are seven in the area. A trip to the island of Kaninchenwerder, a small sanctuary for more than 100 species of water birds, is an unforgettable experience. Boats depart from the pier adjacent to the Schweriner Schloss. ✉ *Anlegestelle Schlosspier,* ☎ *0385/557–770,* WEB *www.weisse-flotte-schwerin.de.* 🎫 *€5.* ⏲ *Late Mar.–Nov., daily 10–5:30.*

Dining and Lodging

$$–$$$ ★ ✕ **Weinhaus Uhle.** One of the most traditional and popular eateries in Schwerin, this restaurant is named after the wine merchant who opened the restaurant back in 1740. The newer *Weinbistro* (wine bistro) offers primarily German wine tasting and a small menu (mostly cheese plates or soups such as lobster cream soup). In the restaurant, regional specialties and international mixed grills are served in a rustic setting,

accompanied by a piano player on Friday and Saturday nights. ✉ *Schusterstr. 13–15,* ☎ *0385/562–956. AE, MC, V.*

$–$$ ★ ✕🏨 **Alt-Schweriner Schankstuben.** A small family-owned restaurant and hotel, the Schankstuben extends standard but very personal service with emphasis on Mecklenburg tradition. The hotel is within three old houses in the historic downtown district. Its restaurant ($–$$) serves local dishes such as *Mecklenburgischer Nackenbraten mit Dörrobst* (Mecklenburg roasted pork with dried fruits). The fish on the menu is equally delicious; ask for the catch of the day. The guest rooms are small but bright and furnished with simple pine furniture. ✉ *Schlachtermarkt 9–13, D–19055,* ☎ *0385/592–530,* FAX *0385/557–4109,* WEB *www.alt-schweriner-schankstuben.de. 16 rooms. Restaurant, café, no a/c, cable TV, meeting room, free parking, some pets allowed (fee), no-smoking rooms. AE, V.*

$$ 🏨 **Ringhotel Arte Schwerin.** This modern hotel in an historic redbrick farmhouse offers intimate and distinguished accommodations. Rooms are decorated in bright, homey colors, and first floor rooms have terraces. The hotel's restaurant Fontane is nothing special, but serves solid North German cuisine. The Arte Schwerin is on peaceful Ostorfer Lake, close to the Schweriner Schloss. ✉ *Dorfstr. 6, D–19061,* ☎ *0385/63450,* FAX *0385/634–5100,* WEB *www.ringhotel-arte.de. 40 rooms. Restaurant, bar, no a/c, room service, in-room safes, minibars, cable TV, hot tub, sauna, dry cleaning, laundry service, meeting room, free parking, some pets allowed (fee), no-smoking rooms. AE, DC, MC, V.*

$$ ★ 🏨 **Sorat-Hotel Speicher am Ziegelsee.** This hotel is one the finest examples of how to give one of Eastern Germany's old and run-down industrial buildings new life. The Speicher am Ziegelsee was built within a deserted, redbrick wheat warehouse dating to 1939, towering high above the old harbor district. It is right next to the Ziegel Lake, north of the historic downtown and the Schweriner Schloss. The hotel's spacious rooms and apartments are decorated with natural materials and earthy tones and have all the amenities of a modern, first-class hotel. ✉ *Speicherstr. 11, D–19055,* ☎ *0385/50030,* FAX *0385/500–3111,* WEB *www.speicher-hotel.de. 59 rooms, 20 apartments. Restaurant, bar, no a/c, room service, kitchenettes, cable TV, gym, hot tub, massage, sauna, steam room, dry cleaning, laundry service, meeting room, free parking, some pets allowed (fee), no-smoking floor. AE, DC, MC, V.*

Nightlife and the Arts

The **Mecklenburgisches Staatstheater** (✉ Am Alten Garten, ☎ 0385/53000) stages German drama and opera. In June check out the **Schlossfestspiele** for open-air drama or comedy performances.

The **Mexxclub** (✉ Klöresgang 2, ☎ no phone) is the city's hottest dance club featuring house and soul DJs, who attract a stylish young crowd every Saturday night.

Shopping

Antiques and bric-a-brac that have languished in cellars and attics since World War II are still surfacing throughout eastern Germany, and the occasional bargain can be found. The best places to look in Schwerin are on and around **Schmiedestrasse, Schlossstrasse,** and **Mecklenburgstrasse.**

Bad Doberan

⑩ *60 km (37 mi) east of Wismar on Rte. 105, 90 km (56 mi) northeast of Schwerin.*

★ Bad Doberan has a meticulously restored redbrick **Klosterkirche** (monastery church), one of the finest of its kind in the region. It was built by Cistercian monks between 1294 and 1368 in the northern German Gothic style, with a central nave and transept. The main altar dates from the early 14th century and features a 45-ft-tall cross. ✉ *Klosterstr. 2,* ☎ *038203/16439.* 🎫 *€1, tours €1.50.* ⏲ *May–Sept., Mon.–Sat. 9–6, Sun. noon–6; Mar., Apr., and Oct., Mon.–Sat. 9–4, Sun. noon–4; Nov.–Feb., Tues.–Fri. 9–noon, 2–4, Sat. 9–4, Sun. noon–4. Tours Apr.–Sept., at 9, 10, and 2; Oct.–Mar., at 2 and 3.*

★ No visit to this part of the country would be complete without a ride on ***Molli,*** a quaint steam train that has been chugging up and down a 16-km (10-mi) narrow-gauge track between Bad Doberan and the nearby beach resorts of **Heiligendamm** and **Kühlungsborn** since 1886. The train was nicknamed after a little local dog that barked its approval every time the smoking iron horse passed by. At the start of the 45-minute journey the engine and its old wooden carriages make their way through the center of Bad Doberan's cobble streets. In summer *Molli* runs 13 times daily between Bad Doberan and Kühlungsborn. ✉ *Mecklenburgische Bäderbahn Molli, Küstenbus GmbH,* ☎ *038203/4150,* WEB *www.molli-bahn.de.* 🎫 *€9 for round-trip on same day.* ⏲ *From Bad Doberan: May–Sept., daily 8:36–6:45; Oct.–Apr., daily 8:35–4:40.*

Dining and Lodging

$ ✕ **Weisser Pavillon.** Here's a mixed setting for you: a 19th-century Chinese pagoda–type structure in an English-style park. Come for lunch or high tea; regional specialties are featured. In summer the café closes at 10 PM. ✉ *Auf dem Kamp,* ☎ *038203/62326. No credit cards.*

$$ ★ ✕🏨 **Romantik-Hotel Friedrich-Franz-Palais.** Built in 1793 for a Mecklenburg duke, this whitewashed member of the Romantik Hotel group has accommodated guests for more than 200 years. Completely restored and renovated, each room exudes old-world elegance with modern comforts. The small restaurant ($$–$$$) mostly serves fresh fish and game in a setting ideal for a candlelight dinner. ✉ *Am Kamp, D–18209,* ☎ *038203/63036,* FAX *038203/62126,* WEB *www.romantikhotels.com. 40 rooms, 2 suites, 3 apartments. Restaurant, café, no a/c, room service, minibars, cable TV, sauna, bicycles, free parking, some pets allowed (fee), no-smoking rooms. AE, DC, MC, V.*

$$ 🏨 **Hotel und Apartments Röntgen.** In the seaside community of Kühlungsborn, just west of Bad Doberan, this white mansion has spacious one- to three-bedroom apartments with kitchenettes, as well as a small bistro specializing in fish dishes. Personalized service is extended by the Röntgen family, which also take pride in their tradition as bakers. You can sample their breads and rolls at breakfast. ✉ *Strandstr. 30a, D–18225 Kühlungsborn,* ☎ *038293/7810,* FAX *038293/78199. 17 apartments. Restaurant, café, no a/c, kitchenettes, cable TV, some pets allowed (fee). AE, MC, V.*

Rostock

⓫ *14 km (9 mi) east of Bad Doberan on Rte. 105.*

Rostock, the biggest port and shipbuilding center of the former East Germany, was founded around 1200. Of all the Hanseatic cities, the once-thriving Rostock suffered the most from the dissolution of the League in 1669. Although Hamburg, Kiel, and Stettin (now part of Poland) became leading port cities, Rostock languished until the late 1950s. The newly formed GDR reestablished Rostock as a major port, but since reunification, port work has been cut in half and, though ferries come from Gedser (Denmark) and Trelleborg (Sweden), there is little traffic. The biggest local annual attraction is Hanse Sail, a week of yacht racing held in August. A sea of blossoms will draw gardeners and photographers to the **Internationale Gartenbauaustellung 2003**

(International Horticultural Exhibition) in a park especially designed for the event. You can find a bee garden, plant sculptures, a historic farm garden, an ecological self-guided trail and much more. In addition, there is an extensive entertainment program. ✉ *Industriestr. 125,* ☎ *0381/782–300,* WEB *www.iga2003.de.* 🎫 *€14.* ⏲ *Apr.–Dec., daily 10–dusk.*

Because it was home to wartime armament factories, the city suffered severe bombings, but much of the Old Town's core has been rebuilt. The main street, the pedestrians-only **Kröpelinerstrasse,** begins at the old western gate, the Kröpeliner Tor. Here you'll find the finest examples of the late-Gothic and Renaissance houses of rich Hanse merchants. The triangular **Universitätsplatz** (University Square), commemorating the founding of northern Europe's first university here in 1419, is home to Rostock University's Italian Renaissance–style main building, finished in 1867.

At the **Neuer Markt** (Town Square) you'll immediately notice the architectural potpourri of the **Rathaus.** Basically 13th-century Gothic with a baroque facade, the building spouts seven slender, decorative towers, looking like candles on a peculiar birthday cake. Historic gabled houses surround the rest of the square.

Four-century-old **St. Marienkirche** (St. Mary's Church), the Gothic architectural prize of Rostock, boasts a bronze baptismal font from 1290 and some interesting baroque features, notably the oak altar (1720) and organ (1770). Unique is the huge astronomical clock dating from 1472; it has a calendar extending to the year 2017. ✉ *Am Ziegenmarkt,* ☎ *0381/492–3396.* ⏲ *Mon.–Sat. 10–5, Sun. 11–noon.*

The **Schifffahrtsmuseum** (Maritime Museum) traces the history of shipping on the Baltic and displays models of ships, which especially intrigue children. It is just beyond the city wall, at the old city gateway, Steintor. ✉ *August-Bebel-Str. 1,* ☎ *0381/252–060.* 🎫 *€3.* ⏲ *Tues.–Sun. 10–6.*

The ***Port Centre*** is a ship that was commandeered and moored alongside the riverbank to become a complex of stores, boutiques, bars, and restaurants. After the collapse of state communism, there weren't enough buildings to house shops, so the ship offered additional space. ✉ *Kapuzenhof.*

The **Zoologischer Garten** (Zoological Garden) has one of the largest collections of exotic animals and birds in northern Germany. This zoo is particularly noted for its polar bears, some of which were bred in Rostock. If you're traveling with children, a visit is a must. ✉ *Rennbahnallee 21,* ☎ *0381/20820,* WEB *www.zoo-rostock.de.* 🎫 *€6.50.* ⏲ *Nov.–Mar., daily 9–5; Apr.–Oct., daily 9–7.*

Dining and Lodging

$$ ✕ **Petrikeller.** Once you've crossed the threshold to the Petrikeller, you'll be in a medieval world of the Hanseatic merchants, seamen, and wild pirates such as Klaus Störtebecker. The restaurant's motto, "*Wer nicht liebt Wein, Weib und Gesang bleibt ein Narr sein Leben lang*" (He who doth not love wine, woman and song, will be a fool his whole life long), a quote from Martin Luther no less, sets the tone for the giddy atmosphere and hearty food. Everything is prepared according to medieval recipes; even the spelling and prices are given in old German. But even here, 50 cents equal one Taler. ✉ *Harte Str. 27,* ☎ *0381/455–855. V. No lunch.*

$–$$ ★ ✕ **Zur Kogge.** Looking like the cabin of some ancient sailing vessel, the oldest sailors' beer tavern in town serves mostly fish. Order the *Meck-*

lenburger Fischsuppe (Baltic Coast fish soup) if it's on the menu; *Grosser Fischteller,* consisting of three kinds of fish—depending on the day's catch—served with vegetables, lobster and shrimp sauce, and potatoes is also a popular choice. ✉ *Wokrenterstr. 27,* ☎ *0381/493–4493. Reservations essential. DC, MC, V.*

$$–$$$ ★ **Steigenberger–Hotel zur Sonne Rostock.** Carrying its over 200 years with great equanimity, the "zur Sonne" is one of the best hotels in town. Within the Old Town, the proud hotel relaxes its guests with a maritime atmosphere, impeccable service, and modern rooms in a Hanseatic mansion. If you don't mind narrow staircases and low ceilings, this is the place to stay. When making a reservation, ask for one of the weekend offers and a top-floor room cozily fitted under the eaves. ✉ *Neuer Markt 2, D–18055,* ☎ *0381/49730,* FAX *0381/497–3351,* WEB *www.rostock.steigenberger.de. 103 rooms, 21 suites. Restaurant, café, bar, no a/c, cable TV, massage, sauna, meeting room, parking (fee), some pets allowed (fee), no-smoking rooms. AE, DC, MC, V.*

$$ **Courtyard by Marriott.** This hotel in a 19th-century mansion is a genuine part of Rostock's historic Old Town. It provides smooth service, and the modern rooms are tastefully decorated. Despite its downtown location, it is a quiet place to stay. A breakfast buffet is included in the room rate. ✉ *Schwaansche/Kröpeliner Str., D–18055,* ☎ *0381/49700,* FAX *0381/497–0700,* WEB *www.marriott.com. 148 rooms, 2 suites. Restaurant, room service, minibars, cable TV with movies, gym, sauna, bar, dry cleaning, laundry service, meeting room, parking (fee), some pets allowed (fee), no-smoking floor. AE, DC, MC, V.*

Nightlife and the Arts

The summer season brings with it a plethora of special concerts, sailing regattas, and parties on the beach. The **Volkstheater** (✉ Doberanerstr. 134/35, ☎ 0381/381–4600) presents plays and concerts.

The bar and café **Kajahn** (✉ Patriotischer Weg 126, ☎ 0381/201–8893) is a stylish nightspot. **Speicher–Discothek** (✉ Am Strande 3a, ☎ 0381/499–7506), a split-level disco, appeals to all ages.

Shopping

Echter Rostocker Doppel-Kümmel und -Korn, a kind of schnapps made from various grains, is a traditional liquor of the area around Rostock. Fishermen have numbed themselves to the cold for centuries with this 80-proof beverage; a 7-liter bottle costs €8–€11.

Warnemünde

⓬ *14 km (9 mi) north of Rostock on Rte. 103.*

Warnemünde is a quaint seaside resort with the best hotels and restaurants in the area, as well as 20 km (12 mi) of beautiful white beach. It has been a popular summer getaway for families in eastern Germany for years. Children enjoy climbing to the top of the town landmark, a 115-ft-high **Leuchtturm** (lighthouse), dating from 1898; on clear days it offers views of the coast and Rostock Harbor. Inland from the lighthouse is the yacht marina known as **Alter Strom** (Old Stream). Once the entry into the port of Warnemünde, it now has bars, cozy restaurants, and specialty shops.

Dining and Lodging

$–$$ ✕ **Fischerklause.** Sailors have stopped in at this restaurant's bar since the turn of the 20th century. The smoked fish sampler served on a lazy Susan is delicious, and the house specialty of fish soup is best washed down with some Rostocker Doppel-Kümmel schnapps. An accordionist entertains the crowd on Friday and Saturday evenings. ✉ *Am Strom 123,* ☎ *0381/52516. Reservations essential. AE, DC, MC, V.*

$$$ **Hotel Neptun.** The 19-story concrete-and-glass Neptun is an eyesore on the outside, but inside it has the redeeming qualities of an upscale hotel. Every one of the neatly decorated rooms has a sea view and a balcony. To go first-class for less money, ask for the hotel's special "Happy Weekend" and "Vacation on the Sea" rates. The hotel's Spa Arkona is one of eastern Germany's finest fitness and sauna clubs. ✉ *Seestr. 19, D–18119,* ☎ *0381/7770,* FAX *0381/54023,* WEB *www.hotel-neptun.de. 340 rooms, 5 suites. 4 restaurants, café, no a/c, room service, in-room safes, minibars, cable TV, saltwater pool, gym, hair salon, sauna, spa, boating, bicycles, 2 bars, dance club, baby-sitting, dry cleaning, laundry service, meeting room, parking (fee), some pets allowed (fee), no-smoking rooms. AE, DC, MC, V.*

$$ **Hotel Germania.** At the harbor entrance and only one block from the beach and the Alter Strom promenade, this small hotel's location alone makes it a good choice. All rooms, which underwent complete renovation in 2001, are tastefully decorated and include a TV. With so many good eateries nearby you won't mind there's no hotel restaurant. ✉ *Am Strom 110–111, D–18119,* ☎ *0381/519–850,* FAX *0381/519–8510. 18 rooms. Bar, no a/c, minibars, cable TV, some pets allowed (fee), parking (fee). AE, DC, MC, V.*

$ **Landhotel Ostseetraum.** This family-owned hotel expertly blends modern style with rural architecture. The farmhouse with a thatch roof is fairly secluded, in an area outside Warnemünde, just 500 yards from the beach. ✉ *Stolteraaweg 34b, D–18119 Warnemünde-Diedrichshagen,* ☎ FAX *0381/51719,* WEB *www.ostseetraum.de. 18 rooms. Restaurant, no a/c, no room TVs, some pets allowed (fee), free parking. AE, MC, V.*

Fishing

Fishing is a rapidly expanding leisure industry in the area. Every port along the coast now has small boats for rent, and some boatmen will lead you to the shoals. For information on equipment, contact the **Rostock tourist office** (☎ 0381/403–0500) for Warnemünder Hafen (Warnemünde Harbor).

Nightlife

In Warnemünde nearly all the seaside hotels and resorts, down to the smallest, have nearly nightly dances during the summer months. Head to the large hotels to search for fun. The pubs in marina **Alter Strom** are gathering places.

The **Skybar,** on the 19th floor of the Neptun Hotel (✉ Seestr. 19, ☎ 0381/7770), is open until 4 AM. Roof access gives you the chance to sit under the stars and watch ship lights twinkle on the sea.

Ribnitz-Damgarten

⓭ *30 km (19 mi) northeast of Warnemünde, 26 km (16 mi) east of Rostock on Rte. 105.*

Ribnitz-Damgarten is the center of the amber (in German, *Bernstein*) business, unique to the Baltic Coast. Amber is a yellow-brown fossil formed from the sap of ancient conifers and is millions of years old. Head for a beach and join the locals in the perennial quest for amber stones washed up among the seaweed. Pebbles with a hole worn through the middle are prevalent on this coast; locals call them *Hühnergötter* (chicken gods) and believe they bring good luck. If you want to test what you find on the beach, know that only true amber will float in a glass of water stirred with 2 teaspoons of salt. In the **Deutsches Bernsteinmuseum** (German Amber Museum), which adjoins the main factory, you can see a fascinating exhibit of how this precious "Baltic gold" is collected from the sea and refined to make jewelry. The museum has examples of amber that are between 35 and 50 million years old. The biggest lump of raw amber ever harvested from the sea weighed more than 23 pounds. ✉ *Im Kloster 1–2,* ☎ *03821/2931.* 🎫 *€3.50.* ⏲ *Apr.–Oct, daily 9:30–5:45; Nov.–Mar., Wed.–Sun. 9:30–5.*

Shopping

You can buy amber jewelry, chess figures, and ornate jewelry boxes in the **Bernsteinmuseum** (✉ Im Kloster 1–2, ☎ 03821/2931). The jewelry, often designed with gold and silver as well as amber, costs from €51 to €513. Fossils are often embedded in the stone—a precious find.

VORPOMMERN

The best description of this region is found in its name, which simply means "before Pommerania." This area, indeed, seems trapped between Mecklenburg and the authentic, old Pommerania farther east, now part of Poland. Although Vorpommern is not the dull, monotonous backwater it is made out to be, its tundralike appearance, pine barrens, heaths, and dunes are not typical tourist draws, either. Its very remoteness and poverty ensure an unforgettable view of unspoiled nature, primarily attracting families and young travelers.

Ahrenshoop

⓮ *75 km (47 mi) north of Ribnitz-Damgarten.*

Ahrenshoop is typical of the seaside villages on the half-island of **Darss.** This curved finger of land was once three islands that became one from centuries of shifting sand. In the late 19th century painters from across Germany and beyond formed an art colony here. After World War II Ahrenshoop again became a mecca of sorts for artists, musicians, and writers of the GDR, but that scene has long dispersed. Continue toward Prerow to get back to the mainland, but be sure to stop at the 17th-century seamen's church on the edge of town.

Since 1966 much of Darss has been a nature reserve, partly to protect the ancient forest of beech, holly, and juniper. The island's best beach is the Weststrand (West Beach), a broad stretch of fine white sand that is free of auto traffic and most development.

Dining

$–$$$$ ★ ✕ **Café Namenlos.** In an old, thatch-roof beach house dating back to 1912, "Cafe Without Name" specializes in local game and fish dishes. Entrées such as *Mecklenburgische Hausente* (Mecklenburg duck filled with apples, raisins, and red cabbage) are served on rustic tables that fit in with the old tile oven and a low ceiling supported by wooden beams. In summer, take a late breakfast or lunch on the terrace overlooking the sea. Ask the waiter to tell you the story of how the restaurant ended up without a proper name. ✉ *Am Schifferberg,* ☎ *038220/6060. AE, MC, V.*

$–$$ ★ ✕🏨 **Elisabeth von Eicken.** The art nouveau villa of the late local painter Elisabeth von Eicken is a popular hotel and restaurant choice for sophisticated travelers. The rooms are small, but individually designed in minimalist, clear styles and adorned with modern art. The airy restaurant ($$–$$$$) is undoubtedly one of the best on the Baltic Sea coast. Dishes combine local fish such as pike, trout, or perch with Asian and Italian ingredients, and the wine list is exquisite. ✉ *Dorfstr. 39, D–18347, Ahrenshoop,* ☎ *038220/6990,* FAX *038220/69924,* WEB *www.elisabeth-von-eicken.de. 6 rooms. Restaurant, no a/c, room service, in-room data ports, minibars, cable TV, baby-sitting, dry cleaning, free parking, some pets allowed (fee), no-smoking rooms. AE, MC, V.*

Stralsund

15 *59 km (37 mi) east of Ahrenshoop, 42 km (26 mi) east of Ribnitz-Damgarten on Rte. 105.*

Although it was rapidly industrialized, this jewel of the Baltic has a historic city center. Following an attack by the Lübeck fleet in 1249, a defensive wall was built around Stralsund, parts of which still stand around the Old Town. In 1815 the Congress of Vienna awarded the city, which had been under Swedish control, to the Prussians.

The **Alter Markt** (Old Market Square) has the best local architecture, ranging from redbrick Gothic through Renaissance to baroque. Most buildings were rich merchants' homes, notably the late-Gothic **Wulflamhaus,** with 17 ornate, steeply stepped gables. Stralsund's architectural masterpiece, however, is the 14th-century **Rathaus,** considered by many to be the finest secular example of redbrick Gothic. Its open corridors reduced wind pressure on the tall facade.

The treasures of the 13th-century Gothic **St. Nikolaikirche** (St. Nicholas's Church) include a 15-ft-high crucifix from the 14th century, an astronomical clock from 1394, and a famous baroque altar. ✉ *Alter Markt,* ☎ *03831/297–199.* ⏲ *Apr.–Sept., Mon.–Sat. 10–5, Sun. 11–noon, 2–4; Oct.–Mar., Mon.–Sat. 10–noon, 2–4, Sun. 11–noon, 2–4.*

The **Katherinenkloster** (St. Catherine's Monastery) is a former cloister; 40 of its rooms now house two museums: the famed Deutsches Meeresmuseum, and the **Kulturhistorisches Museum** (Cultural History Museum), exhibiting diverse artifacts from more than 10,000 years of this coastal region's history. Highlights include a toy collection and 10th-century Viking gold jewelry found on Hiddensee. You'll reach the museums by walking along Ossenreyerstrasse through the Apollonienmarkt on Mönchstrasse. ✉ *Kulturhistorisches Museum, Mönchstr. 25–27,* ☎ *03831/28790.* 🎫 *€3.* ⏲ *Tues.–Sun. 10–5.*

The Stralsund aquarium of Baltic Sea life is part of the three-floor marine museum **Deutsches Meeresmuseum** (German Sea Museum), which also displays the skeletons of a giant whale and a hammerhead shark, and a 25-ft-high chunk of coral. ✉ *Katharinenberg 14–20, entrance on Mönchstr.,* ☎ *03831/26500,* WEB *www.meeresmuseum.de.* 🎫 *€4.50.* ⏲ *Sept.–June, daily 10–5; July–Aug., daily 9–6.*

The monstrous **St. Marienkirche** (St. Mary's Church) is the largest of Stralsund's three redbrick Gothic churches. With 4,000 pipes and intricate decorative figures, the magnificent 17th-century Stellwagen organ (played only during Sunday services) is a delight to see and hear. The view from the church tower of Stralsund's old city center is well worth the 349 steps you must climb to reach the top. ✉ *Neuer Markt, entrance at Bleistr.,* ☎ *03831/293–529.* 🎫 *Tour of church tower €1.* ⏲ *Mon.–Sat. 10–4, Sun. 11:30–4.*

Dining and Lodging

$–$$ ★ ✕ **Wulflamstuben.** This restaurant is on the ground floor of *Wulflamhaus,* a 14th-century gabled house on the old market square. Steaks and fish are the specialty; in late spring or early summer, get the light and tasty *Ostseeflunder* (grilled plaice), fresh from the North Sea. In winter, the hearty *Pommersche Ente* (Pommerian duck), filled with rye bread, apples, and baked plums, is a must. ✉ *Alter Markt 5,* ☎ *03831/291–533. Reservations essential. AE, DC, MC, V.*

$–$$ ✕ **Zum Alten Fritz.** It's worth the trip here just to see the rustic interior and copper brewing equipment. Good, old German beer and ale of all shades are the main focus. In summer the beer garden gets somewhat rambunctious. ✉ *Greifswalder Chaussee 84–85, at B–96a,* ☎ *03831/255–500. MC, V.*

$$ ★ **Hotel zur Post.** This redbrick hotel is a great deal for travelers who want to enjoy a homey yet first-class ambience. It's on the market square near the Old Town. The hotel's interior is a thoughtful mix of traditional North German furnishings and modern design. ✉ *Am Neuen Markt, Tribseerstr. 22, D–18439,* ☎ *03831/200–500,* FAX *03831/200–510,* WEB *www.hotel-zur-post-stralsund.de. 104 rooms, 2 suites, 8 apartments. Restaurant, room service, in-room safes, minibars, cable TV, sauna, bar, dry cleaning, laundry service, meeting room, parking (fee), some pets allowed (fee), no-smoking rooms. AE, MC, V.*

$$ **Norddeutscher Hof.** Don't let the weathered facade fool you; the hotel was completely renovated a few years ago. Unfortunately, the lobby and restaurant were not as tastefully redecorated as the guest rooms. Still, you get the basics at a fair price. ✉ *Neuer Markt 22, D–18439,* ☎ *03831/293–161,* FAX *03831/287–939,* WEB *www.nd-hof.de. 13 rooms. No a/c, cable TV, some pets allowed (fee), free parking. AE, MC, V.*

$ ★ **Schlosspark-Hotel Hohendorf.** Set among the lovely marshlands north of Stralsund and now an elegant country hotel, the historic Schloss Hohendorf was designed by famous Prussian architect Karl Friedrich Schinkel in the late 18th century. Stralsund, the island of Rügen, and all beaches are short drives away. The rooms are on the small side, but their plush carpets, carved beds, and furniture try to recreate the Old World elegance that was typical for this kind of rural palace. ✉ *Hohendorf, D–18445 Hohendorf at Stralsund,* ☎ *038323/2500,* FAX *038323/25061,* WEB *www.schlosspark-hotel-hohendorf.de. 34 rooms, 8 suites. Restaurant, outdoor café, no a/c, room service, cable TV, 2 tennis courts, massage, sauna, bicycles, baby-sitting, dry cleaning, laundry service, meeting rooms, some pets allowed (fee). AE, MC, V.*

Nightlife

Bar Hemingway (✉ Tribseerstr. 22, ☎ 03831/200–500) lures a thirtysomething clientele with the best cocktails in town. A young crowd dances at **Fun und Lollipop** (✉ Grünhofer Bogen 11–14, ☎ 03831/399–039). For a genuine old harbor *Kneipe* (tavern), head to the **Kuttel Daddeldu** (✉ Hafenstr./Hafeninsel, ☎ 03831/299–526).

Shopping

Buddelschiffe (ships in a bottle) are a symbol of the once-magnificent sailing history of this region. They look easy to build, but they aren't, and they're quite delicate. Expect to pay more than €70 for a 1-liter bottle. Also look for **Fischerteppiche** (fisherman's carpets). Eleven square ft of these traditional carpets take 150 hours to create, which explains why they're only meant to be hung on the wall—and why they cost from €260 to €1,200. They're decorated with traditional symbols of the region, such as the mythical griffin.

Rügen Island

⑯ *4 km (2½ mi) northeast of Stralsund on Rte. 96.*

Rügen's diverse and breathtaking landscapes have inspired poets and painters for more than a century. Railways in the mid-19th century brought the first vacationers, and many of the grand mansions and villas on the island date from this period. The island's main route runs between the **Grosser Jasmunder Bodden** (Big Jasmund Inlet), a giant sea inlet, and a smaller expanse of water—the **Kleiner Jasmunder Bodden** (Little Jasmund Inlet Lake)—to the port of Sassnitz. You're best off staying at any of the island's four main vacation centers—Sassnitz, Binz, Sellin, and Göhren.

Bergen

17 *34 km (21 mi) northeast of Stralsund on Rte. 96.*

Bergen, the island's administrative capital, was founded as a Slavic settlement some 900 years ago. The **Marienkircke** (St. Mary's Church) has geometric murals dating back to the late 1100s, and painted brick octagonal pillars. The pulpit and altar are baroque. Outside the front door and built into the church facade is a grave from the 1200s.

OFF THE BEATEN PATH **HIDDENSEE** – Off the northwest corner of Rügen is a smaller island called Hiddensee. The undisturbed solitude of this sticklike island attracted such visitors as Albert Einstein, Thomas Mann, Rainer Maria Rilke, and Sigmund Freud. As Hiddensee is an auto-free zone, leave your car in Schaprode, 21 km (13 mi) west of Bergen, and take a ferry. Vacation cottages and restaurants are on the island.

Kap Arkona

18 *21 km (13 mi) northwest of Stubbenkammer.*

Kap Arkona has a lighthouse marking the northernmost point in eastern Germany, and you can see the Danish island of Moen from a restored watchtower next door. The blustery sand dunes of Kap Arkona are a nature-lover's paradise.

Sassnitz

19 *25 km (16 mi) northeast of Bergen on Rte. 96.*

From Sassnitz, where ferries run to Sweden, walk into **Jasmund Nationalpark** (www.nationalpark-jasmund.de) to stare in awe at the Königstuhl cliffs. For information about the park, contact the Sassnitz tourist office.

Ten kilometers (6 mi) north of Sassnitz are the twin chalk cliffs of Rügen's
20 main attraction, the **Stubbenkammer** headland, on the east coast of the island. From here you can best see the much-photographed chalk cliff called the **Königstuhl,** rising 351 ft from the sea. A steep trail leads down to a beach.

En Route Near the town of Binz is the **Jagdschloss Granitz,** a hunting lodge built in 1836 by Karl Friedrich Schinkel. It stands on the highest point of East Rügen and offers a splendid view in all directions from its lookout tower. It also has an excellent hunting exhibit. ✉ *Binz,* ☎ *038393/2263.* 🎫 *€3.* ⏲ *May–Sept., daily 9–6; Oct.–Apr., Tues.–Sun. 10–4.*

Putbus

21 *59 km (37 mi) southeast of Kap Arkona, 8 km (5 mi) south of Bergen.*

The immaculate white buildings of the **Circus,** a round central plaza gives the city its nickname *Weisse Stadt* ("White City"). It is the heart of the community dating back to the early 19th century, and in the summer the blooming roses in front of the houses (once a requirement by the ruling noble family of Putbus) are truly a great sight.

Lovers of old watches and clocks should not miss the tiny **Uhrenmuseum Putbus,** where watchmaker Franz Sklorz showcases a historic collection of more than 600 clocks, watches, musical gadgets, and more. You might catch him at work as well. ✉ *Alleestr. 13,* ☎ *038301/60988.* 🎫 *€3.* ⏲ *May–Oct., daily 10–6; Nov.–Apr., daily 11–4.*

From Putbus you can take a ride on the 90-year-old miniature steam train, the **Rasender Roland** (Racing Roland), which runs 24 km (16 mi) to Göhren, at the southeast corner of the Rügen. Trains leave hourly; the ride takes 70 minutes one-way. ✉ *Binzer Str. 12,* ☎ *038301/*

8010, WEB www.rasender-roland.de. €8. Apr.–Oct., daily 5:30 AM–10:49 PM from Putbus. Call for winter hrs.

Dining and Lodging

$–$$ ★ **Nautilus.** The quirky maritime interior is reminiscent of Captain Nemo's fantasy-ship, *Nautilus.* An odd mixture of ship and submarine paraphernalia, the Nautilus is jammed with equipment ranging from a deep-diving suit to a periscope. Traditional island food offerings include *Pfefferhering mit Bratkartoffeln* (pepper herring with home fries) and *Gebratener Aal mit Pertisiliensosse* (fried eel served with parsley sauce). ✉ *Neukamp, Putbus,* ☎ *038301/830. AE, MC, V.*

$$ **Hotel Godewind.** Two hundred yards from the beaches of Hiddensee that have so inspired writers, this small hotel offers food and lodging at very reasonable prices. In addition, the hotel rents small cottages and apartments around the island, which are a good value if you intend to stay for more than a few days. Godewind's restaurant ($$) is known on the island for its regional dishes. ✉ *Süderende 53, D–18565 Vitte-Hiddensee,* ☎ *038300/6600,* FAX *038300/660–222.* WEB *www.hotelgodewind.de. 23 rooms, 15 cottages. Restaurant, no a/c, no room TVs, some pets allowed (fee). No credit cards.*

$$ ★ **Hotel Kurhaus Binz.** The grand old lady of the Baltic Sea, the neoclassicist 19th-century Kurhaus Binz, is reviving the splendor of times past, when Binz was called the Nice of the North. The five-star Kurhaus is right on the beach, with a breathtaking sea view in most of the spacious and elegantly furnished rooms. The huge Egyptian-theme spa and wellness area is a real treat. Of the two restaurants, the Kurhaus-Restaurant is the better choice—it serves traditional seafood, but adds exotic touches with special fusion cuisine events. At night, enjoy an evening at the Boddenbarsch variety theater in the Kursaal. ✉ *Strandpromenade 27, D–18609, Binz-Rügen,* ☎ *038393/6650,* FAX *038393/665–555,* WEB *www.tc-hotels.de. 106 rooms, 20 suites. 2 restaurants, room service, in-room data ports, minibars, cable TV with movies, indoor-outdoor pool, health club, massage, sauna, spa, beach, bar, cabaret, baby-sitting, dry cleaning, laundry service, concierge, meeting rooms, parking (fee), some pets allowed (fee), no-smoking floor. AE, DC, MC, V.*

$$ ★ **Hotel Vineta.** This great white building at the promenade in Binz looks very much like a Victorian seaside resort. Its name derives from a local fairy tale that tells of the destruction of the prosperous but sinful city of Vineta in a winter storm. According to the legend, you can still hear the golden bells of the sunken city's towers ringing through the fog. The spacious rooms, however, are quite modern, with darkwood furniture, thick carpets, and a wonderful view of the sea. ✉ *Hauptstr. 20, D–18609 Binz-Rügen,* ☎ *038393/390,* FAX *038393/39444,* WEB *www.hotel-vineta-binz.de. 59 rooms, 18 apartments. 2 restaurants, bar, no a/c, in-room safes, minibars, cable TV, gym, sauna, parking (fee), some pets allowed (fee). AE, MC, V.*

$ ★ **Hotel Villa Granitz.** The little town of Baabe claims to have Rügen Island's most beautiful beach. This mostly wooden mansion, built only seven years ago in the romantic art-nouveau style popular at the turn of the 20th century, is a small and quiet retreat for those who want to avoid the masses in the island's other resorts. All rooms have a large terrace or a balcony; pastel colors (a soft white and yellow) add to the tidy, fairy-tale look of the building. All rooms are spacious; the apartments have small kitchenettes. ✉ *Birkenallee 17, D–18586 Baabe,* ☎ *038303/1410,* FAX *038303/14144,* WEB *www.villa-granitz.de. 44 rooms, 8 suites, 12 apartments. No a/c, refrigerators, cable TV, dry cleaning, laundry service, free parking, some pets allowed (fee), no-smoking room. No credit cards.*

$ 🏨 **Villa Daheim and Villa Elisabeth.** Two of the most striking old city mansions on Rügen, these small hotels both offer a familylike, warm atmosphere in a late-19th-century setting. The houses, just 100 yards apart, have been renovated à la the old glamour of German *Bäderarchitektur,* the style of seaside cottages along the Baltic Coast. The mansions are in the historic heart of Sassnitz yet offer a panoramic view of the sea. ✉ *Rosenstr. 8 and Bergstr. 20, D–18546 Sassnitz,* ☎ *038392/22278,* FAX *038392/35001,* WEB *www.ruegen-urlaub-sassnitz.de. 19 apartments. No a/c, cable TV, bicycles, car rental, free parking. No credit cards.*

Shopping

At the end of the 19th century 16 pieces of 10th-century Viking jewelry were discovered on the Baltic coastline (presently housed in the Kulturhistorisches Museum in Stralsund). Gold and silver replicas of the **Hiddensee Golden Jewelry** are a great souvenir, and their distinctive patterns are found in shops on Rügen Island and on Hiddensee Island.

Water Sports

Equipment for windsurfing, sailing, surfing (although the waves here are modest), and pedal-boat riding is available for hire at the beach resorts. If you have difficulty locating what you want, contact the local tourist offices. The best-protected area along the coast for sailing is **Grosser Jasmunder Bodden,** a huge bay on Rügen Island. Boats for the bay can be hired at Lietzow and Ralswiek.

Greifswald

22 *64 km (40 mi) southeast of Putbus, 32 km (20 mi) southeast of Stralsund on Rte. 96.*

Greifswald is the birthplace of two great German artists—Caspar David Friedrich (1774–1840), the painter of German romanticism, and Wolfgang Koeppen (1906–1996), one of the country's most important postwar novelists. Last in the string of Hanseatic ports on the Baltic Coast, Greifswald became a backwater during the 19th century, when larger ships couldn't negotiate the shallow Ryck River leading to the sea. In 1945 a colonel's surrender of the town to Soviet forces spared its destruction; yet time has taken its toll on some historic buildings. Three churches shape the silhouette of the city. The 13th-century **Dom St. Nikolai** (St. Nicholas's Cathedral), at the start of Martin-Luther-Strasse, is a neo-Gothic and Romantic church with an impressive view from its 300-ft-high tower. ✉ *Domstr.,* ☎ *03834/2627.* ⏲ *May–Oct., Mon.–Sat. 10–4, Sun. 10–1; Nov.–Apr., Mon.–Sat. 11–1, Sun. 10–1.*

The 14th-century **Marienkirche** (St. Mary's Church), the oldest surviving church in Greifswald, has remarkable 60-ft-high arches and a striking four-corner tower. ✉ *Friedrich-Loeffler-Str. 68 at Brüggstr.,* ☎ *03834/2263.* ⏲ *June–Nov., weekdays 10–noon and 2–4.*

Splendid redbrick Gothic houses border the **Marktplatz.** The medieval Rathaus, rebuilt in 1738–50 following a fire, was modified during the 19th century and again in 1936. Its heavy doors bear a quote from Bertolt Brecht. The **Pommersches Landesmuseum** (Pommeranian State Museum) showcases the development of European romantic painters and focuses on works by Caspar David Friedrich such as *Ruine Eldena im Riesengebirge* (Eldene Ruins in the Riesengebirge) and *Greifswalder Marktplatz* (Greifswald Market Square). Other works of art in the gallery include Dutch painters of Friedrich's time. ✉ *Mühlenstr. 15,* ☎ *03834/894–357,* WEB *www.pommersches-landesmuseum.de.* 🎟 *€3.* ⏲ *May–Oct., Tues.–Sun. 10–6; Nov.–Apr., Tues.–Sun. 10–5.*

23 In the suburb of **Eldena** stand the ruins of a 12th-century Zisterzenserkloster (Cistercian monastery). The Gothic monastery was made famous in a painting by Caspar David Friedrich (now at Schloss Charlottenburg's Gallery of Romanticism in Berlin). The monastery, which led to the founding of Greifswald, was plundered by rampaging Swedish soldiers early in the Thirty Years' War. Today it is a protected national monument.

Dining and Lodging

$$ ✕ 🏨 **Alter Speicher.** Its broad selection of delectable grilled items and its wine list have brought this comfortable steak house ($–$$$) regional renown. It also offers small but modern guest rooms; all have private baths. The Alter Speicher is on the edge of the old city center. ✉ *Rossmühlenstr. 25, D–17489,* ☎ *03834/77700,* FAX *03834/777–077,* WEB *www.alter-speicher.de. 14 rooms. Restaurant, no a/c, cable TV, free parking, some pets allowed (fee). AE, DC, MC, V.*

$–$$ 🏨 **Best Western Hotel Greifswald.** The hotel rooms' decor—curtains, bedspreads, and lamp shades covered in stripes and flowers—stands out from the American Southwestern–style palette and patterns common in chain hotels of this region. The hotel's plainly modern design isn't atmospheric, but then, there are modern amenities, a convenient location, and a helpful staff. ✉ *Hans-Beimler-Str. 1–3, D–17491,* ☎ *03834/8010,* FAX *03834/801–100,* WEB *www.bestwestern-hotel-greifswald.de. 51 rooms, 4 apartments. Restaurant, no a/c, room service, minibars, cable TV, gym, hair salon, sauna, bar, meeting room, free parking, some pets allowed (fee), no-smoking rooms. AE, DC, MC, V.*

$ 🏨 **Hotel Maria.** The facilities at this small hotel are clean and modern—and the friendly service is what you'd hope for from a family-owned place. The hotel is right on the harbor; the terrace is the perfect place to linger over a drink while watching the panorama of sailboats. ✉ *Dorfstr. 45, D–17493,* ☎ *03834/841–426,* FAX *03834/840–136,* WEB *www.hotel-maria.de. 10 rooms, 1 suite, 1 apartment. Restaurant, no a/c, cable TV, free parking, some pets allowed. MC, V.*

Usedom Island

24 On its seaboard side, 40-km-long (25-mi-long) **Usedom Island** has almost 32 km (20 mi) of sandy shoreline and a string of resorts. Much of the island's untouched landscape is a nature preserve that provides refuge for a number of rare birds, including the giant sea eagle, which has a wingspan of up to 8 ft. Even in the summer this island is more or less deserted and is ready to be explored by bicycle. Bikes can usually be rented for around €4–€6 a day and about €30 a week.

Wolgast

32 km (20 mi) southeast of Greifswald on Rte. 109, then Rte. 111.

Wolgast is at the causeway that crosses to the island of Usedom. The bridge closes at times to allow boats to pass through, so if you have time to spare, Wolgast has some worthwhile sights. **Rathausplatz** (Town Hall Square) holds a baroque Rathaus and a mid-17th-century half-timber house known as the Kaffeemühle (Coffee Mill). The **Kaffeemühle,** far from just serving coffee, contains a charming local history museum. ✉ *Rathauspl. 6,* ☎ *03836/203–041.* 🎫 *€3.* ⏲ *June–Aug., Tues.–Fri. 10–6, weekends 10–4; Sept.–May, Tues.–Fri. 10–5, Sat. 10–2.*

The massive redbrick Gothic **St. Petri Kirche** (St. Peter's Church) sits on the highest point of the Old Town. The church has copies of Holbein's series of paintings, *Totentanz* (*Dance of Death*). ✉ *Kirchpl. 7,* ☎ *03836/202–269.* 🎫 *Tower €1.50.* ⏲ *Weekdays 10–11:30 and 1:30–5.*

Navigating and parking a car can be tricky on these small streets. You might want to rent a bike at **Fahrrad-Pank** (✉ Bahnhofsstr. 42, ☎ 03836/202–652).

Peenemünde

16 km (10 mi) north of Wolgast.

At the northern end of Usedom Island is Peenemünde, the launch site of the world's first jet rockets, the V1 and V2, developed by Germany toward the end of World War II and mostly fired at London. You can view these rockets as well as models of early airplanes and ships at the extensive **Historisch-Technisches Informationszentrum** (Historical-Technical Information Center), housed in a former army power plant. The ethics of scientific research are also examined. One exhibit covers the secret underground plants where most of the rocket parts were assembled and where thousands of slave laborers died. Explanation of the exhibits in English are available. ✉ *Im Kraftwerk,* ☎ *038371/5050.* *€5.* *Apr.–Oct., Tues.–Sun. 9–6; Nov.–Mar., Tues.–Sun. 10–4.*

Ahlbeck

46 km (29 mi) southeast of Peenemünde on Rte. 111.

Ahlbeck, one of the best resorts on Usedom and the island's main town, features an attractive 19th-century wooden pier with a restaurant. Ahlbeck's promenade is lined with brightly painted turn-of-the-20th-century villas, many of which are now small hotels. If you stroll along the beach to the east you'll arrive at the Polish border—this corner of the island belongs to Poland. Bike along the shaded seaside pathway to the other nearby resorts, Heringsdorf and Bansin. **Fahrradverleih Willerts** (✉ Lindenstr. 89, ☎ 038378/30092) rents bikes year-round. **Fahrradverleih Oberländer** (✉ Am Bahnhof, ☎ 038378/31684) rents bikes at the train station. In Bansin, **Fahrradverleih SG Medizin Bansin** (✉ Waldstr. 5, at Bansin tennis courts, ☎ 038378/22529) rents bikes between April and November.

Dining and Lodging

$–$$ ✕ **Seebrücke.** Perched on pilings over the Baltic, the Sea Bridge is in the historic center of Ahlbeck. The emphasis is on seafood, but the menu has other choices, from *Königsberger Klopse* (spicy meatballs in a thick, creamy sauce) to a tender fillet of lamb. You can also take in the view over coffee and a delectable piece of cake. ✉ *Dünenstr., Ahlbeck,* ☎ *038378/28320. AE, MC, V. Closed Oct.–Apr.*

$ ✕ **Café Asgard.** A visit here is a step back into the 1920s, which is when this restaurant first opened its doors. You'll dine amid silk wallpaper, potted plants, crisp white napery, and fresh flowers. The Asgard is open all day, so if you stop by between mealtimes, settle for a homemade pastry. ✉ *Strandpromenade 15, Bansin,* ☎ *038378/29488. No credit cards.*

$$–$$$$ ★ ✕ **Romantik Seehotel Ahlbecker Hof.** This first-class resort lacks the coziness of Usedom's other hotels but undoubtedly is one of the region's best and has been meticulously restored to imperial glamour. The baths in the guest rooms are luxurious, and there's a fantastic wellness and swimming pool area. A real draw is the hotel's *Kleopatrabad,* a Turkish steam bath. The restaurant ($$$–$$$$) serves some of the finest seafood along the Baltic coastline. ✉ *Dünenstr. 47, D–17419 Ahlbeck,* ☎ *038378/620,* FAX *038378/62100.* WEB *www.seetel.de. 45 rooms, 21 suites. Restaurant, no a/c, room service, in-room safes, minibars, cable TV, 18-hole golf course, pool, gym, hair salon, massage, sauna, Turkish bath, bicycles, bar, dry cleaning, laundry service, meeting room, parking (fee), some pets allowed (fee). AE, MC, V.*

$$ ✕☐ **Ringhotel Ahlbeck Ostseehotel.** Generations of families have stayed at this snug, if slightly dated, hotel in a 19th-century villa on Ahlbeck's promenade. Rooms are airy but modestly furnished, and most have a view of the sea. The restaurant ($$–$$$$) serves mainly hearty, though standard, local dishes. ✉ *Dünenstr. 41, D–17419 Ahlbeck,* ☎ *038378/600,* FAX *038378/60100,* WEB *www.ostseehotel.de. 58 rooms, 12 apartments. Restaurant, no a/c, room service, cable TV, pool, sauna, bicycles, bar, parking (fee), some pets allowed (fee), no-smoking rooms. AE, MC, V.*

$ ✕☐ **Romantik Strandhotel Atlantic.** The small but elegant hotel once served as the intimate summer retreat for Berlin's rich and beautiful. These days, the upscale restaurant ($$–$$$$) and the lavishly decorated guest rooms—all with venerable 19th-century glamour—make this hotel one of the island's best (and most coveted). ✉ *Strandpromenade 18, D–17429 Bansin,* ☎ *038378/605,* FAX *03378/60600,* WEB *www.romantikhotels.com. 24 rooms, 2 suites. Restaurant, room service, in-room safes, minibars, bicycles, bar, pub, dry cleaning, laundry service, meeting room, parking (fee). AE, MC, V.*

SCHLESWIG-HOLSTEIN AND THE BALTIC COAST A TO Z

To research prices, get advice from other travelers, and book travel arrangements, visit www.fodors.com.

AIR TRAVEL

The international airport closest to Schleswig-Holstein is in Hamburg. For an eastern approach to the Baltic Coast tour, use Berlin's Tegel Airport.

BOAT AND FERRY TRAVEL

The Weisse Flotte (White Fleet) line operates ferries linking the Baltic ports, as well as short harbor and coastal cruises. Boats depart from Warnemünde, Zingst (to Hiddensee), Sassnitz, and Stralsund. In addition, ferries run from Stralsund and Sassnitz to destinations in Sweden, Denmark, Poland, and Finland.

Scandlines operates ferries between Sassnitz and the Danish island of Bornholm as well as Sweden.

➤ Boat and Ferry Information: **Scandlines** (✉ ☎ 01805/72263–54637, WEB www.scandlines.de). **Weisse Flotte** (☎ 0180/321–2120 central phone; 03831/268–138 for Warnemünde; 03831/268–138 for Stralsund; 038392/57854 for Sassnitz; 0385/557–770 for Schwerin).

BUS TRAVEL

Local buses link the main train stations with outlying towns and villages, especially the coastal resorts. Buses operate throughout Sylt, Rügen, and Usedom islands.

CAR TRAVEL

The two-lane roads (Bundesstrassen) along the coast can be full of traffic during June, July, and August. The ones leading to Usedom Island can be extremely log-jammed as the causeway bridges have scheduled closings to let ships pass. Using the Bundesstrassen takes more time, but these often tree-lined roads are by far more scenic than the Autobahn.

Sylt island is 196 km (122 mi) from Hamburg via Autobahn A–7 and Bundesstrasse 199 and is ultimately reached via train. The B–199 cuts through some nice countryside, and instead of the A–7 or B–76 between Flensburg, Schleswig, and Kiel, you could take the slow route through the coastal hinterland (B–199, 203, 503). Lübeck, the gateway to Mecklenburg-Vorpommern, is 56 km (35 mi) from Hamburg via the A–1. The B–105 leads to all sightseeing spots in Mecklenburg-Vorpommern. From Stralsund, Route 96 cuts straight across Rügen Island, a distance of 51 km (32 mi). From Berlin take A–11 and head toward Prenzlau for the B–109 all the way to Usedom Island, a distance of 162 km (100 mi). A causeway connects the mainland town of Anklam to the town of Usedom, on Usedom Island.

➤ CAR RENTAL INFORMATION: **Avis** (✉ Willy-Brandt-Allee 6, Lübeck, ☎ 0451/71611; ✉ Am Warnowufer 6, Rostock, ☎ 0381/202–1170; ✉ Wittenburgerstr. 120, Schwerin, ☎ 0385/761–000; ✉ Am Flughafen, Westerland, Sylt, ☎ 04651/23734). **InterrentEuropcar** (✉ Esso-Station am Bahnhof Westerland, Sylt, ☎ 04651/7178). **Hertz** (✉ Willy-Brandt-Allee 1, Lübeck, ☎ 0451/702–250; ✉ Röverzhagener Chaussee 5, Rostock, ☎ 0381/683–065; ✉ Schwerinerstr. 31, Wismar, ☎ 03841/703–259; ✉ Bremsweg 1, Schwerin, ☎ 0385/487–5555).

TOURS

Although tourist offices and museums have worked to improve the quality and amount of English-language literature about this area, English-speaking tours are infrequent and must be requested ahead of time through the local tourist office. Because most tours are designed for groups, there is usually a flat fee of €20.50–€31. Towns currently offering tours are Lübeck, Stralsund, and Rostock. Schwerin has two-hour boat tours of its lakes.

Tours of Old Lübeck depart daily from the tourist offices on the Alter Markt between mid-April and mid-October and on weekends only from mid-October to mid-April. Harbor and coastal cruises also operate from Lübeck; contact the Lübeck tourist office for details.

Many of the former fishermen in these towns give sunset tours of the harbors or shuttle visitors between neighboring towns. This is a unique opportunity to ride on an authentic fishing boat. In Flensburg, Kiel, Rostock, and on Sylt, cruise lines make short trips through the respective bays and/or islands off the coast, sailing even as far as Denmark and Sweden. Inquire at the local tourist office about companies and times, as well as about fishing boat tours.

➤ TOUR CONTACTS: **Lübeck** (☎ 0451/122–8106).

TRAIN TRAVEL

Train travel is much more convenient than bus travel in this area. Sylt, Kiel, Lübeck, Schwerin, and Rostock have InterCity train connections to either Hamburg, Berlin, or both.

A north–south train line links Schwerin and Rostock. An east–west route connects Kiel, Hamburg, Lübeck, and Rostock, and some trains continue through to Stralsund and Sassnitz, on Rügen Island. Train service between the smaller cities of former East Germany is generally much slower than in the west.

Trains are the *only* way to access Sylt, which is connected to the mainland via the train causeway Hindenburgdamm. Deutsche Bahn will transport you and your car from central train stations at Dortmund, Düsseldorf, Hamburg, Stuttgart, and Frankfurt directly onto the island. In addition, a daily shuttle car train leaves Niebüll every 30 minutes from 6 AM to 9 PM. There are no reservations on this train.

Villages and towns on Usedom island are linked by the Usedomer Bäderbahn, whose trains operate between Ahlbeck and Peenemünde as well as between Zinnowitz and Züssow on the mainland. For day excursions, taking the train makes sense to avoid the heavy summertime traffic.

➤ TRAIN INFORMATION: **Niebüll shuttle car train** (☎ 04651/22561). **Usedomer Bäderbahn** (☎ 038378/27132, WEB www.inselusedom.de/ubb.htm).

VISITOR INFORMATION

The regional tourism board for the Baltic Coast is the TOURBU-Zentrale, Landesfremdenverkehrsverband Mecklenburg-Vorpommern. When writing to any information office, address your letter to "Touristeninformation" and then add the city's name.

➤ BALTIC COAST INFORMATION: **Bad Doberan** (✉ Goethestr. 1, D–18209, ☎ 038203/91530, FAX 038203/62154, WEB www.m-vp.de). **Greifswald** (✉ Schuhhagen 22, D–17489, ☎ 03834/521–380, WEB www.greifswald.de). **Lübeck** (✉ Breite Str. 62, [Mailing address: Beckergrube 95, D–23552], ☎ 0451/122–1909; 0451/122–8109 for cruises, FAX 0451/122–1202, WEB www.luebeck.de). **Rostock–Warnemünde** (✉ Neuer Markt 3, D–18055, ☎ 0381/548–000, FAX 0381/381–2601, WEB www.rostock.de). **Rügen Island** (✉ Tourismusverband Rügen, Am Markt 4, D–18528 Bergen, ☎ 03838/80770, FAX 03838/254–440, WEB www.ruegen.de). **Sassnitz** (✉ Seestr. 1, D–18546, ☎ 038392/5160, FAX 038392/51616, WEB www.sassnitz.de). **Schwerin** (✉ Am Markt 10, D–19055, ☎ 0385/592–5212, FAX 0385/555–094, WEB www.schwerin.de). **Stralsund** (✉ Alter Markt 9, D–18439, ☎ 03831/24690, FAX 03831/246–949, WEB www.stralsund.de). **TOURBU-Zentrale, Landesfremdenverkehrsverband Mecklenburg-Vorpommern** (✉ Pl. der Freundschaft 1, D–18059 Rostock, ☎ 0381/403–0500, FAX 0381/403–0555, WEB www.tmv.de). **Usedom Island** (✉ Tourismusverband Insel Usedom e.V., Bäderstr. 4, D–17459 Seebad Ückeritz, ☎ 038375/23410, FAX 038375/23429, WEB www.usedom.de). **Wismar** (✉ Stadthaus, Am Markt 11, D–23966, ☎ 03841/19433, FAX 03841/251–3090, WEB www.wismar.de).

➤ SCHLESWIG-HOLSTEIN INFORMATION: **Flensburg** (✉ Amalie-Lamp-Speicher, Speicherlinie 40, D–24937, ☎ 0461/23090, FAX 0461/17352, WEB www.flensburg.de). **Husum** (✉ Grossstr. 27, D–25813, ☎ 04841/89870, WEB www.husum.de). **Kampen** (✉ Kurverwaltung, Hauptstr. 12, D–25999, ☎ 04651/46980, FAX 04651/469–840, WEB www.kampen.de). **Kiel** (✉ Kiel, Sophienblatt 30, D–24103, ☎ 0431/679–100, FAX 0431/679–1099, WEB www.kiel.de). **Schleswig** (✉ Plessenstr. 7, D–24837, ☎ 04621/24878, FAX 04621/981–619, WEB www.schleswig.de). **Westerland** (✉ Strandstr. 33, [mailing address: Stephanstr. 6, Postfach 1260 D–25969], ☎ 04651/9980, FAX 04651/998–6000, WEB www.westerland.de).

16 BERLIN

In this truly international metropolis the pace of change is staggering. The streets of the eastern downtown centers and of still quaintly shabby neighborhoods are thrilling studies of urban development. As ever, life in Berlin is on the cutting edge.

Updated by Jürgen Scheunemann

BERLIN'S ROLE AS THE FOCAL POINT and touchstone of a reunited Germany began on November 9, 1989, when East Berliners finally breached the infamous Wall. In 1999, 10 years after the wall's demolition, Berlin's capital status returned when the federal parliament moved back to the Reichstag.

Compared to other German cities, Berlin is quite young and, ironically, began as two cities more than 760 years ago. Museum Island, on the Spree River, was once called Cölln, while the mainland city was always known as Berlin. By the 1300s, Berlin was prospering thanks to its location at the intersection of important trade routes. After the ravages of the Thirty Years' War, Berlin rose to power as the seat of the Hohenzollern dynasty. The Great Elector Friedrich Wilhelm, in the almost 50 years of his reign (1640–88), touched off a renaissance by supporting such institutions as the Academy of Arts and the Academy of Sciences. Later, Frederick the Great made Berlin and Potsdam his glorious centers of the enlightened yet autocratic Prussian monarchy.

In the late 19th century, Prussia, ruled by the "Iron Chancellor" Count Otto von Bismarck, proved to be the dominant force in unifying the many independent German states. Berlin maintained its status as Germany's capital for the duration of the German Empire (1871–1918), through the post–World War I Weimar Republic (1919–33), and also through Hitler's so-called Third Reich (1933–45). But the city's golden years were the Roaring '20s, when Berlin, the energetic, modern, and sinful counterpart to Paris, became a center for the cultural avant-garde. World-famous writers, painters, and artists met here while the impoverished bulk of its 4 million inhabitants lived in heavily overpopulated quarters. This "dance on the volcano," as those years of political and economic upheaval have been called, came to a grisly and bloody end after January 1933, when Adolf Hitler became chancellor. The Nazis made Berlin their capital but ultimately failed to remodel the city into a silent monument to their power. During World War II Berlin was bombed to smithereens. By the war's end there was more rubble in Berlin than in all other German cities combined.

Along with the division of Germany after World War II, Berlin was partitioned into American, British, and French zones in the west, and a Soviet zone to the east. By 1947 Berlin had become one of the cold war's first testing grounds. The three western-occupied zones gradually merged, becoming West Berlin, while the Soviet-controlled eastern zone defiantly remained separate. Peace conferences repeatedly failed to resolve the question of Germany's division, and in 1949 the Soviet Union established East Berlin as the capital of its new puppet state, the German Democratic Republic (GDR). The division of the city was cruelly finalized in concrete in August 1961, when the East German government constructed the Berlin Wall, dividing families and friends.

For nearly 30 years Berlin suffered under one of the greatest geographic and political anomalies of all time, a city split in two by a concrete wall—its larger western half an island of capitalist democracy surrounded by an East Germany run by hard-line Communists. With the wall relegated to the souvenir pile of history, visitors can now appreciate the qualities that mark the city as a whole. Its particular charm has always lain in its spaciousness, its trees and greenery, and its racy atmosphere. Moreover, the really stunning parts of the prewar capital are in the historic eastern part of town, which has grand avenues, monumental architecture, and world treasures in its museums. But Berlin's dreams to be a player in the global league of big cities is showing the first cracks: in 2001, the city-owned state bank nearly went bankrupt and forced the city government to resign. A staggering three billion U.S. dollars bank debt incurred by risky real estate deals in East Germany now has to be paid by the state. This could be a mortal blow to a city which has a total debt of 35 billion U.S. dollars already.

The spirit and bounce of the city and its citizens might be able to cope with these dramatic changes. Berliners come off as brash, witty, no-nonsense types who speak German with their own piquant dialect and are considered by their fellow countrymen as a most rude species. The bracing air, the renowned *Berliner Luft,* gets part of the credit for their high-voltage energy. That energy is also attributable to the many residents who have faced adversity all their lives, and have managed to do so with a mordant wit and cynical acceptance of life.

Pleasures and Pastimes

Dining

No longer mocked as a culinary desert, Berlin now sees international and chic restaurants open almost every week, while hearty local specialties are still a favorite among most Berliners. Typical Berlin food includes *Eisbein mit Sauerkraut* (knuckle of pork with pickled cabbage), *Rouladen* (rolled stuffed beef), *Spanferkel* (suckling pig), *Berliner Schüsselsülze* (potted meat in aspic), *Hackepeter* (ground beef), and *Kartoffelpuffer* (fried potato cakes). Spicy *Currywurst* is a chubby frankfurter that's served with thick tomato sauce, curry, and pepper. It's sold at *Bockwurst* stands all over the city. Turkish specialties are also an integral part of the Berlin diet. On almost every street you'll find snack stands selling *Döner kepab* (grilled lamb with salad in a flat-bread pocket).

Museums

Berlin is home to some of the world's finest museums, art galleries, and exhibition halls. Among the jewels of Berlin's more than 100 state and private museums are superb monuments of Greek, Byzantine, and Roman architecture on the renowned Museum Island, and the collections of the two Egyptian museums, which include the famous bust of Queen Nefertiti. Some museums and exhibitions on Museum Island may be closed for periods of time through 2008 as they continue to be reorganized and renovated.

Nightlife

The city has more than 6,000 pubs, music, and dance clubs; clubs pumping techno and European house music particularly thrive. Berlin is the only European city without official closing hours, so you can stretch your drinks until the wee hours of the morning without fear of a last call. Former eastern districts such as Mitte and Prenzlauer Berg have unusual, impromptu venues for parties, bars, and *Kneipen* (pubs). The city presents Germany's leading dramatic and musical productions, as well as lively variety shows.

EXPLORING BERLIN

Berlin is a young and partly planned capital, with streets and boulevards organized in an unusually clear manner. Yet Berlin is also laid out on an epic scale—western Berlin alone is four times the size of the city of Paris. When the city-state of Berlin was incorporated, it swallowed towns and villages far beyond the downtown area. Of its 12 boroughs, the five of most interest to visitors are Charlottenburg-Wilmersdorf in the west, Tiergarten (a district of the Mitte borough) and Kreuzberg in the downtown western area, the historic eastern part of town in Mitte, and Prenzlauer Berg in the northeast. Southwest Berlin has lovely parks, and secluded forests and lakes in the Grunewald area.

Numbers in the text correspond to numbers in the margin and on the Berlin map.

Great Itineraries

Although public transportation makes most sights convenient and inexpensive to reach, the sheer magnitude of the city and its wealth of attractions make it hard for newcomers to see all the important sights.

IF YOU HAVE 2 DAYS

Start in western, downtown Berlin by strolling past the shops and cafés of Kurfürstendamm to the stark shell of the Kaiser-Wilhelm-Gedächtniskirche. Catch the double-decker Bus 100 or 200 (in front of the Zoo railway station), which takes you past the Reichstag and the Government district to the Brandenburger Tor. Exit here to explore historic eastern Berlin, the pre–World War II pride of the city. Shops on Unter den Linden and Friedrichstrasse are recapturing prewar glamour, and there's a wealth of architectural monuments to explore, including those on the Gendarmenmarkt, Berlin's finest square. The real cultural highlights to save time for are the antiquities on Museuminsel on the Spree Canal.

The next day visit the Reichstag and Potsdamer Platz, a study in urban renewal and modern architecture. From here take the U-bahn west to Charlottenburg to explore the palace and nearby museums.

IF YOU HAVE 3 DAYS

Three days allow you a more leisurely pace that will give you time to absorb Berlin's dramatic history and dynamic present. In Charlottenburg tour Schloss Charlottenburg and any of the nearby museums. By taking the U-bahn next to Adenauerplatz, you can browse the most elegant of the Kurfürstendamm boutiques before reaching the grittier scene of Breitscheidplatz, where locals and street performers gather. Stop inside the Kaiser-Wilhelm-Gedächtniskirche, a war memorial, before picking out a gourmet snack at the Kaufhaus des Westens department store just a bit farther down Tauentzienstrasse. You will have had a full day, but you can still visit the unusual Erotik-Museum in the evening, as it's open until midnight.

Start the next morning surveying the city from the dome of the Reichstag, then head south along Ebertstrasse, passing the Brandenburg Gate and leafy Tiergarten on your way to the architectural feast of Potsdamer Platz. Behind the showy corporate and commercial buildings is the Gemäldegalerie, an outstanding fine arts museum. Next head east to Friedrichstrasse for some window-shopping and a look at imperial architecture, which continues on Unter den Linden. Spend the evening around the Hackesche Höfe.

Begin day three at the museums on the Spree canal's Museuminsel, and explore the courtyards and shops around Oranienburger Strasse. Further north, at the Gedenkstätte Berliner Mauer, you can inspect the last original remains of the Berlin Wall.

IF YOU HAVE 5 DAYS

A five-day visit is really the only way to experience the electrifying ambience of the city, and to visit sights off the beaten track. At the end of the three-day itinerary above, ring in the evening at a café near Kollwitzplatz in Prenzlauer Berg, or with evening entertainment at the old Kulturbrauerei.

Berlin

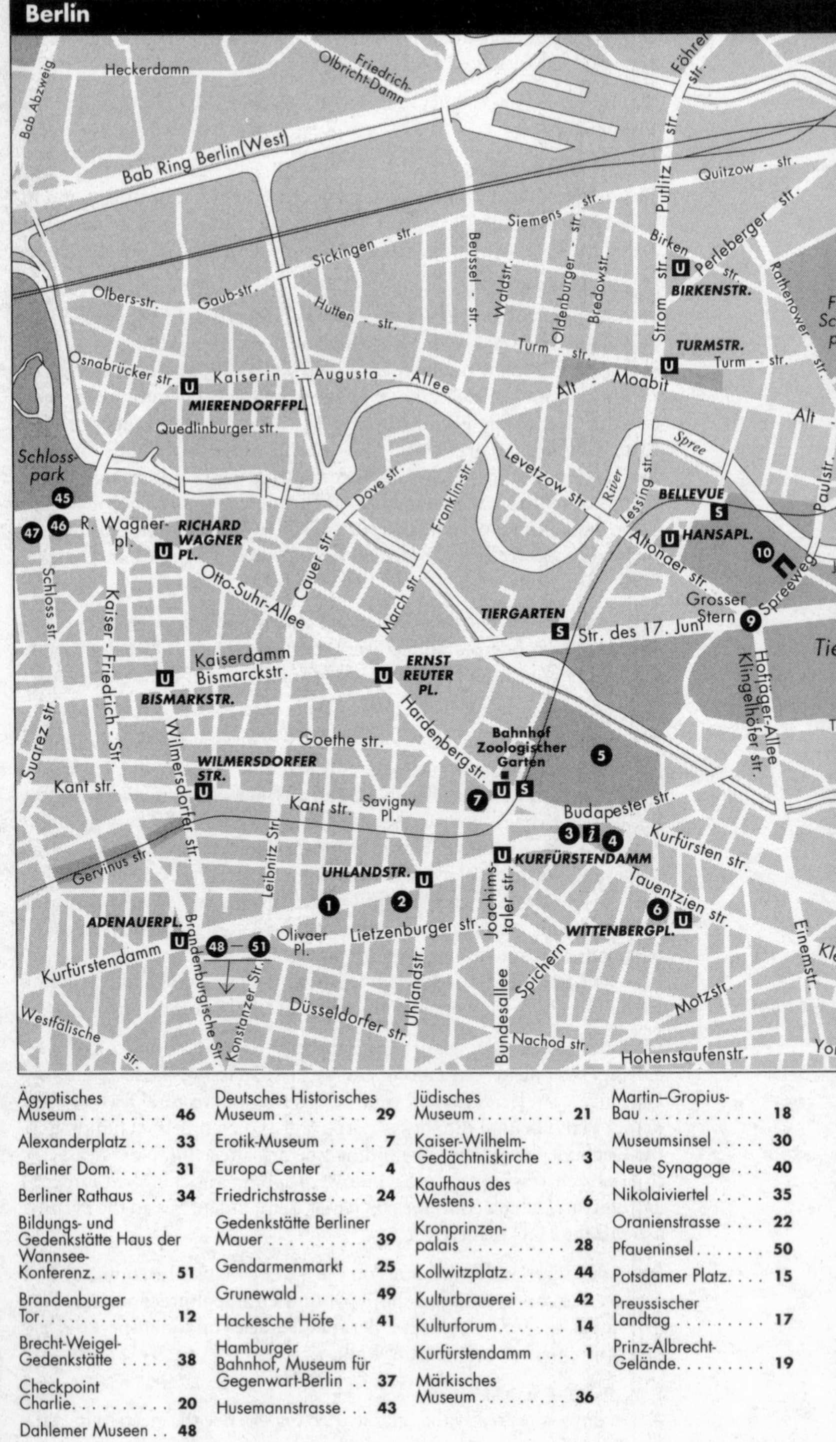

Ägyptisches Museum . . . 46
Alexanderplatz . . . 33
Berliner Dom . . . 31
Berliner Rathaus . . . 34
Bildungs- und Gedenkstätte Haus der Wannsee-Konferenz . . . 51
Brandenburger Tor . . . 12
Brecht-Weigel-Gedenkstätte . . . 38
Checkpoint Charlie . . . 20
Dahlemer Museen . . . 48
Deutsches Historisches Museum . . . 29
Erotik-Museum . . . 7
Europa Center . . . 4
Friedrichstrasse . . . 24
Gedenkstätte Berliner Mauer . . . 39
Gendarmenmarkt . . . 25
Grunewald . . . 49
Hackesche Höfe . . . 41
Hamburger Bahnhof, Museum für Gegenwart-Berlin . . . 37
Husemannstrasse . . . 43
Jüdisches Museum . . . 21
Kaiser-Wilhelm-Gedächtniskirche . . . 3
Kaufhaus des Westens . . . 6
Kronprinzenpalais . . . 28
Kollwitzplatz . . . 44
Kulturbrauerei . . . 42
Kulturforum . . . 14
Kurfürstendamm . . . 1
Märkisches Museum . . . 36
Martin–Gropius-Bau . . . 18
Museumsinsel . . . 30
Neue Synagoge . . . 40
Nikolaiviertel . . . 35
Oranienstrasse . . . 22
Pfaueninsel . . . 50
Potsdamer Platz . . . 15
Preussischer Landtag . . . 17
Prinz-Albrecht-Gelände . . . 19

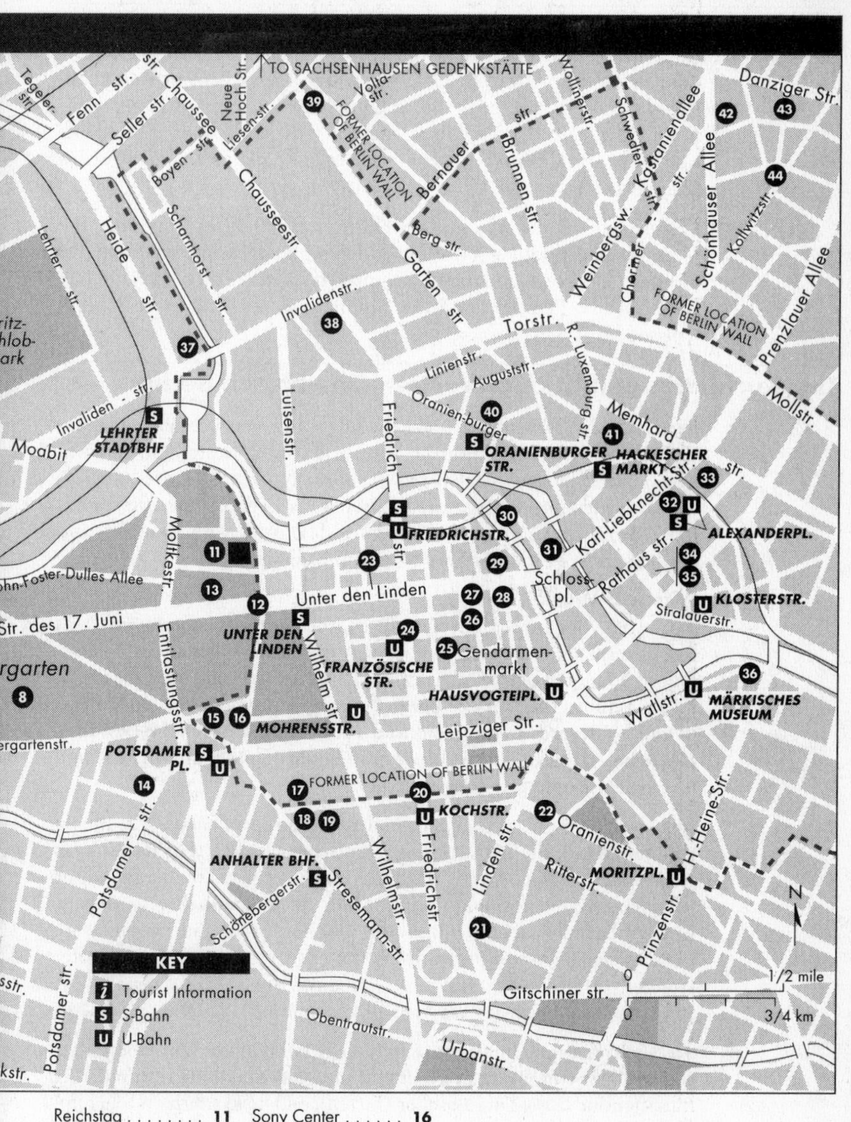

Reichstag **11**

Sammlung Berggruen **47**

St. Hedwigs-kathedrale **26**

St. Marienkirche . . . **32**

Schloss Bellevue . . . **10**

Schloss Charlottenburg **45**

Siegessäule **9**

Sony Center **16**

Sowjetisches Ehrenmal **13**

Staatsoper Unter den Linden **27**

The Story of Berlin . . . **2**

Tiergarten. **8**

Unter den Linden . . . **23**

Zoologischer Garten. **5**

Begin your fourth day in the district of Kreuzberg. See if the current exhibit interests you at the Martin-Gropius-Bau and then head next door to the Prinz-Albrecht-Gelände, where former Nazi prison cellars were excavated. Proceed to one of Berlin's cold-war hot spots—Checkpoint Charlie, the former border station at the Berlin Wall. Before hitting the heart of Kreuzberg via Oranienstrasse, detour to the Jüdisches Museum.

Spend your last day in southern Berlin at the Dahlem Museums, the Gedenk- und Bildungsstätte Haus der Wannsee-Konferenz, and the Grunewald (forest) and the Pfaueninsel. If you have time left, you may want to visit Potsdam and the summer-palace grounds of Schloss Sanssouci.

The Kurfürstendamm and Western Downtown Berlin

Ku'damm, as Berliners affectionately call the tree-lined Kurfürstendamm, stretches for 3 km (2 mi) through the heart of the western downtown. The popular thoroughfare is full of shops, department stores, art galleries, theaters, movie houses, and hotels, as well as some 100 restaurants, bars, clubs, and sidewalk cafés. It bustles with shoppers and strollers most of the day and far into the night.

A Good Walk

Start your tour on the far western end of the **Kurfürstendamm** ①, at Adenauerplatz. As you make your way east along the boulevard, stopping at boutiques or one of the cafés along the way, you'll pass the multimedia exhibit, **The Story of Berlin** ②. Farther down, almost at the end of the boulevard, is the memorial ruin of **Kaiser-Wilhelm-Gedächtniskirche** ③, the very heart of western Berlin. The square surrounding it is prime people-watching territory.

Just steps away from the memorial is the **Europa Center** ④, a dowdy shopping mall; the Berlin tourist information office is at its back on Budapester Strasse. Across from the tourist office is the Elefantentor (Elephant Gate), the main entrance to the **Zoologischer Garten** ⑤, western Berlin's zoo and aquarium. The boulevard Tauentzienstrasse (Tauentzien) runs southeast from the corner of the Europa Center straight to Europe's largest and Germany's most elegant department store, the **Kaufhaus des Westens** ⑥, nicknamed KaDeWe.

To reach the tour's final stop, catch the U-bahn at the Wittenbergplatz station, first completed in 1913 and now painstakingly restored. Get out after one stop (Zoologischer Garten), and head south on Joachimstaler Strasse to the **Erotik-Museum** ⑦, a tasteful exhibition on the art and culture of sexuality.

TIMING

A leisurely walk from the western end of the Kurfürstendamm down to its beginning at Breitscheidplatz takes at least two hours, including a breakfast or lunch. Amid the urban buzz, you could easily spend two hours around the Kaiser-Wilhelm-Gedächtniskirche and in the shops along Tauentzien. Set aside two hours for the admirable zoo and aquarium—watching feeding times and monkey-play is worth skipping some shopping. The Ku'damm is extremely crowded on Saturday morning.

Sights to See

❼ **Erotik-Museum.** The culture and art of human sexuality in all its sometimes peculiar manifestations are on display here, though primarily in paintings and other works of art from Europe and Asia. One exhibit documents the history of German scientist Magnus Hirschfeld, whose institute for sexuality was destroyed by the Nazis. Another recounts Berlin painter Heinrich Zille's humorous tales of sexual behavior in the city's working-class tenements. The museum is extremely tasteful, but it is owned and run by the Beate Uhse company, Germany's largest retailer of X-rated videos and other bedroom paraphernalia. Only adults over 18 years of age are admitted. ✉ *Kantstr. (corner Joachimstaler Str.), Western Downtown,* ☎ *030/886–0666.* 🎫 *€5.* ⏲ *Daily 9 AM–midnight.*

❹ **Europa Center.** This shopping and business complex was erected on the site of the renowned Romanisches Café, the hot spot for writers and actors during the Roaring '20s. The 22-story tower built in the 1960s—nicknamed "Pepper's Manhattan" after its owner—is a remarkable though somewhat shabby leftover from the good old days of West Berlin, when the city was pampered with federal money and business boomed around Kurfürstendamm. The center houses more than 100 shops, restaurants, and cafés; two cinemas, a comedy club, and the Verkehrsamt (tourist information center). Two pieces of the Berlin Wall stand by the Tauentzienstrasse entrance. The plaza in front of the mall is where hippies, homeless people, young punks, and tourists mingle in summer. ✉ *Breitscheidpl., Western Downtown,* ☎ *030/348–008,* WEB *www.europa-center-berlin.de.*

★ ❸ **Kaiser-Wilhelm-Gedächtniskirche** (Kaiser Wilhelm Memorial Church). A dramatic reminder of World War II's destruction, the ruined bell tower is all that remains of the once-imposing church, which was built between 1891 and 1895 and originally dedicated to the emperor, Kaiser Wilhelm I. On the hour the tower chimes out a melody composed by the last emperor's great-grandson, the late Prince Louis Ferdinand von Hohenzollern.

In stark contrast to the old bell tower, dubbed the "hollow tooth," are the adjoining Memorial Church and Tower, designed by the noted German architect Egon Eiermann in 1959–61. These ultramodern octagonal structures, with their myriad honeycomb windows, have nicknames as well: the lipstick and the powder box. Brilliant, blue stained-glass from Chartres dominate the interiors. Church music and organ concerts are presented in the church regularly.

An exhibition within the bell tower focuses on the devastation of World War II throughout Europe. Nails recovered from the ashes of Coventry Cathedral in England, destroyed in a German bombing raid in November 1940, make up the cross inside. ✉ *Breitscheidpl., Western Downtown,* ☎ *030/218–5023,* WEB *www.gedaechtniskirche.com.* 🎫 *Free.* ⏲ *Old Tower Mon., Sat. 10–4, Tues.–Fri. 10–6:45; Memorial Church daily 9–7.*

★ ❻ **Kaufhaus des Westens** (Department Store of the West). The KaDeWe isn't just Berlin's classiest department store; it's also Europe's largest, a grand-scale emporium in modern guise. Its seven floors hold an enormous selection, but it is best known for its two top floors' food and delicatessen counters, restaurants, champagne bars, and beer bars, and for its crowning rooftop winter garden. ✉ *Tauentzienstr. 21, Western Downtown,* ☎ *030/21210,* WEB *www.kadewe.de.*

NEED A BREAK? In a country known for its love of cars, it was only a matter of time before people started dining amidst shining hot rods. At **Daimler's** (✉ Kurfürstendamm 203, Western Downtown, ☎ 030/3901–1698) people dig into huge portions or hearty snacks of Southern German cuisine right alongside juiced-up Mercedes-S-Class monsters.

❶ **Kurfürstendamm.** This grand boulevard, nicknamed the Ku'damm, is certainly the liveliest and most exciting stretch in Berlin. The busy thoroughfare was first laid out in the 16th century as the path by which the elector Joachim II of Brandenburg traveled from his palace on the Spree River to his hunting lodge in the Grunewald. The Kurfürstendamm (Elector's Causeway) was developed into a major route in the late 19th century, thanks to the initiative of Bismarck, Prussia's Iron Chancellor.

Even in the 1920s, the Ku'damm was still relatively new and by no means elegant; it was fairly far removed from the old heart of the city, which was Unter den Linden in Mitte. The Ku'damm's prewar fame was due mainly to the rowdy bars and dance halls that studded much of its length and its side streets. Along with the rest of Berlin, the Ku'damm suffered severe wartime bombing. Almost half of its 245 late-19th-century buildings were destroyed in the 1940s, and the remaining buildings were damaged in varying degrees. What you see today (as in most of western Berlin) is either restored or was newly constructed. Some of the 1950s buildings have been replaced by skyscrapers, in particular at the corner of Kurfürstendamm and Joachimstaler Strasse.

❷ **The Story of Berlin.** In a city with such a turbulent history, this multimedia show and museum built over a nuclear shelter (which is the most eerie part of the exhibition) has plenty of rich material to represent. The unusual mixture of history museum, theme park, and movie theater covers 800 years of city history on four floors, from the first settlers to the fall of the Wall. Many original artifacts are woven together in an interactive design that is both entertaining and informative. ✉ *Ku'damm Karree, Kurfürstendamm 207–208, Western Downtown,* ☎ *030/8872–0100,* WEB *www.story-of-berlin.de.* 🎫 *€9.30.* ⏲ *Daily 10–8 (last admission: 6).*

★ ❺ **Zoologischer Garten** (Zoological Gardens). Germany's oldest zoo opened in 1844, and today holds more species than any other. The zoo is home to more than 14,000 animals belonging to 1,400 different species, and has been successful at breeding rare and endangered species. The animals' enclosures are designed to resemble their natural habitats as closely as possible. The Asian-style **Elefantentor** (Elephant Gate) is the main entrance to the zoo and is also next to the aquarium. ✉ *Hardenbergpl. 8 and Budapester Str. 34, Western Downtown,* ☎ *030/254–010,* WEB *www.zoo-berlin.de.* 🎫 *Zoo or aquarium €8, combined ticket €13.* ⏲ *Zoo Nov.–Feb., daily 9–5; Mar., daily 9–5:30; Apr.–late Sept., daily 9–6:30; Oct., daily 9–6; aquarium daily 9–6.*

NEED A BREAK? A variety of exotic coffees scent the air at **Café Einstein** (✉ Kurfürstenstr. 58, Tiergarten, ☎ 030/261–5096). The Viennese-style coffeehouse is in the beautiful 19th-century mansion of German silent-movie star Henny Porten.

Tiergarten and the Government District

The Tiergarten, a beautifully laid-out, 630-acre park with lakes and paths, is the "green lung" of Berlin. In the 17th century it served as the hunting grounds of the Great Elector. Now it's swamped in summer with sunbathers and family barbecues. Its eastern end, between the grandiose landmarks of the Reichstag and the Brandenburger Tor, serves as the center of Germany's federal government. The new and stunning Chancellery, embassies, and modern office buildings make this one of the architecturally most interesting areas in all of Berlin.

A Good Walk

From the Hardenbergplatz entrance to the Zoologischer Garten, you can set off diagonally through the greenery of the idyllic **Tiergarten** ⑧. At the center of the park is the traffic circle Grosser Stern (Big Star), so called because five roads meet here. The **Siegessäule** ⑨ column provides a lookout from the center of the rotary. Follow the Spreeweg Road from the Grosser Stern to **Schloss Bellevue** ⑩, the residence of Germany's president. Next head east along John-Foster-Dulles Allee, keeping the Spree River in sight on your left. You'll soon pass the former Kongresshalle (Congress Hall), which houses cultural exhibitions.

Continuing east, you'll reach the monumental **Reichstag** ⑪, the German Empire's old parliament building that has been refitted to house the federal parliament. Just south of the Reichstag, where Strasse des 17. Juni meets Unter den Linden, is the mighty **Brandenburger Tor** ⑫, probably the most significant icon of German triumph and defeat.

Back in the park, along Strasse des 17. Juni—a name that commemorates the 1953 uprising of East Berlin workers that was quashed by Soviet tanks—you'll see the **Sowjetisches Ehrenmal** ⑬. Turn south from the memorial onto Entlastungsstrasse and cross the tip of the Tiergarten to nearby Kemperplatz, with its **Kulturforum** ⑭, a complex of fascinating museums and galleries.

TIMING

You can do the whole tour in a day, provided you take Bus 100. It starts at the U-bahn station Zoologischer Garten and makes several stops in the western downtown and Tiergarten area. You can leave and reboard the bus whenever you like. All buildings in the Tiergarten, with the exception of the former Kongresshalle, are closed to the public, so you can explore the park in less than two hours, even if you walk. Reserve at least three hours for the Kulturforum museums around Kemperplatz.

Sights to See

★ ⓬ **Brandenburger Tor** (Brandenburg Gate). Once the pride of imperial Berlin and the city's premiere landmark, the Brandenburger Tor was left in a desolate no-man's-land when the Wall was built. Since the Wall's dismantling, the stone arched gateway has become the focal point of much celebrating and is the nation's central party venue for New Year's Eve. This is the sole remaining gate of 14 built by Carl Langhans in 1788–91, designed as a triumphal arch for King Frederick Wilhelm II. Its virile classical style pays tribute to Athens's Acropolis. The quadriga, a chariot drawn by four horses and driven by the Goddess of Victory, was added in 1794. Troops paraded through the gate after successful campaigns—the last time in 1945, when victorious Red Army troops took Berlin. The upper part of the gate, together with its chariot and Goddess of Peace, was destroyed in the war. In 1957 the original molds were discovered in West Berlin, and a new quadriga was cast in copper and presented as a gift to the people of East Berlin. The square behind the gate, **Pariser Platz,** has regained its traditional, prewar design: to the north is the Dresdner Bank and the French embassy. To the south is the DG bank designed by Frank O. Gehry and the city's famous **Akademie der Künste** (Academy of Arts), with its historic facade visible behind a modern glass front. At the historic address of "Unter den Linden No. 1," (now Unter den Linden No. 77) stands the rebuilt **Hotel Adlon Berlin,** the meeting point of Europe's jet set in the 1920s and today's unofficial guest house for state visitors and royalty. South of the Brandenburg Gate, the **Holocaust Mahnmal,** Germany's national Holocaust memorial, will honor the more than six million Jewish victims when completed in late 2003. Designed by American architect Peter

Eisenman, it will consist of 2,600 concrete pillars and house an information center about the Holocaust.

14 **Kulturforum** (Cultural Forum). With its unique ensemble of museums, galleries, and the Philharmonic Hall, the complex is considered one of Germany's cultural jewels. The **Gemäldegalerie** reunites formerly separated collections from East and West Berlin. It is one of Germany's finest art galleries and has an extensive selection of European paintings from the 13th to the 18th centuries. Seven rooms are reserved for paintings by German masters, among them Dürer, Cranach the Elder, and Holbein. A special collection has works of the Italian masters—Botticelli, Titian, Giotto, Lippi, and Raphael—as well as paintings by Dutch and Flemish masters of the 15th and 16th centuries: Van Eyck, Bosch, Brueghel the Elder, and van der Weyden. The museum also holds the world's second-largest Rembrandt collection. ✉ *Matthäikirchpl. 8, Tiergarten,* ☎ *030/2660; 030/2090–5555 for all state museums in Berlin,* WEB *www.smb.spk-berlin.de.* €6. ⏲ *Tues.–Wed. and Fri.–Sun. 10–6, Thurs. 10–10.*

Steps away from the Gemäldegalerie are two examples of ultramodern architecture. The **Kunstbibliothek** (Art Library; ☎ 030/2660 or 030/2090–5555; ⏲ Mon. 2–8, Tues.–Fri. 9–8) contains art posters, a costume library, ornamental engravings, and a commercial art collection. The exhibitions at the **Kupferstichkabinett** (Drawings and Prints Collection) include European woodcuts, engravings, and illustrated books from the 15th century to the present. Also on display are several pen-and-ink drawings by Dürer, 150 drawings by Rembrandt, and a photographic archive. Another building displays paintings dating from the late Middle Ages to 1800. ✉ *Matthäikirchpl. 6, Tiergarten,* ☎ *030/2660 or 030/2090–5555,* WEB *www.smb.spk-berlin.de.* €3. ⏲ *Tues.–Fri. 10–6, weekends 11–6.*

Inside the **Kunstgewerbemuseum** (Museum of Decorative Arts) are European arts and crafts from the Middle Ages to the present. Among the notable exhibits are the Welfenschatz (Welfen Treasure), a collection of 16th-century gold and silver plates from Nürnberg, as well as ceramics and porcelains. ✉ *Matthäikirchpl. 8, Tiergarten,* ☎ *030/266–2902,* WEB *www.smb.spk-berlin.de.* *€3; free 1st Sun. of every month.* ⏲ *Tues.–Fri. 10–6, weekends 11–6.*

The glass-and-steel **Neue Nationalgalerie** (New National Gallery) was designed by Mies van der Rohe and built in the mid-1960s. The collection comprises paintings, sculptures, and drawings from the 19th and 20th centuries, with an accent on works by such impressionists as Manet, Monet, Renoir, and Pissarro. Other schools represented are German Romantics, realists, expressionists, and surrealists. The gallery frequently showcases outstanding international art exhibitions. ✉ *Potsdamer Str. 50, Tiergarten,* ☎ *030/266–2662,* WEB *www.smb.spk-berlin.de.* *€4–€7, depending on exhibit.* ⏲ *Tues., Wed. 10–6, Thurs. 10–10, Fri. 10–8, weekends 11–8.*

The **Staatsbibliothek** (National Library; ✉ Postdamer Str. 33, ☎ 030/266–2303) is one of the largest libraries in Europe.

The roof that resembles a great tent belongs to the **Philharmonie** (Philharmonic Hall), home to the renowned Berlin Philharmonic Orchestra since 1963. The Philharmonie and the smaller Chamber Music Hall adjoining it were designed by Hans Scharoun. The Philharmonie's **Musikinstrumenten-Museum** (Musical Instruments Museum) has a fascinating collection of keyboard, string, wind, and percussion instruments. Wurlitzer organ presentations take place the first Saturday of the month at noon. ✉ *Museum: Tiergartenstr. 1, Tiergarten,* ☎ *030/*

2548–1129, WEB *www.sim.spk-berlin.de.* 🎫 *€3; free 1st Sun. of every month; tour €2.* ⏲ *Tues.–Fri. 9–5, weekends 10–5; guided tour Sat. at 11.*

11 **Reichstag** (Parliament Building). The Bundestag, Germany's federal parliament, returned to its traditional seat in the spring of 1999. British architect Sir Norman Foster did extensive remodeling to the gray monolithic structure, adding its glass dome, which quickly became one of the city's main attractions: you can circle up a gently rising ramp while taking in a spectacular view of Berlin. Visit either in the early morning or evening to avoid the longest lines.

The Reichstag was erected between 1884 and 1894 to house the imperial German parliament and later served a similar function during the ill-fated Weimar Republic. On the night of February 28, 1933, the Reichstag burned down under mysterious circumstances, an event that provided the Nazis with a convenient pretext for outlawing all opposition parties. It was rebuilt but again badly damaged in 1945. The graffiti of the victorious Russian soldiers can still be seen on some of walls in the hallways. The building is surrounded by ultramodern new federal government offices, such as the boxlike **Bundeskanzleramt,** the German Federal Chancellery, nicknamed the *Waschmaschine* (washing machine) by Berliners. Built by Axel Schultes, it is one of the very few new buildings in the government district by a Berlin architect. Behind the cube and extending across the Spree River is the **Kanzlergarten** (Chancellor Garden). ✉ *Reichstag, Pl. der Republik 1, Tiergarten,* ☎ *030/2270,* WEB *www.bundestag.de.* 🎫 *Free.* ⏲ *Daily 8 AM–midnight.*

10 **Schloss Bellevue** (Bellevue Palace). This small palace has served as the official residence of Germany's federal president since 1959 and is closed to the public. It was built on the Spree River in 1785 for Frederick the Great's youngest brother, Prince August Ferdinand. To the left of the palace is the egg-shape executive building—all marble, glass, and steel. Erected in 1998, it was the first new building built by the federal government in Berlin. It's powered by solar-energy panels on the roof. ✉ *Schloss Bellevue Park, Tiergarten.*

9 **Siegessäule** (Victory Column). The 227-ft-high granite, sandstone, and bronze column has a splendid view across much of Berlin. It was erected in front of the Reichstag in 1873 to commemorate Prussia's military successes and then moved to the Tiergarten in 1938–39. The climb of 285 steps up through the column to the observation platform can be tiring, but the view is rewarding. ✉ *Am Grossen Stern, Tiergarten,* ☎ *030/391–2961.* 🎫 *€1.20.* ⏲ *Nov.–Mar., Mon.–Thurs. 9:30–5:30, Fri.–Sun. 9.30–6; Apr.–Oct., daily 9:30–6:30 (last admission 1 hr before closing).*

13 **Sowjetisches Ehrenmal** (Soviet Memorial). Built directly after World War II, this semicircular monument stands as a reminder of the bloody Soviet victory over the shattered German army in Berlin in May 1945. It features a bronze statue of a soldier atop a marble plinth taken from Hitler's former Reichkanzlei (headquarters). The memorial is flanked by what are said to be the first two T-34 tanks to have fought their way into the city in the last days of the war. ✉ *Str. des 17. Juni, Tiergarten.*

8 **Tiergarten** (Animal Garden). For Berliners the quiet greenery of the 630-acre Tiergarten is a beloved oasis. In summer the park, with some 23 km (14 mi) of footpaths, playgrounds, and white marble sculptures, becomes the embodiment of multicultural Berlin: Turkish families gather in the meadows for spicy barbecues, children play soccer, and gay couples sunbathe. The inner park's 6½ acres of lakes and ponds were landscaped by garden architect Joseph Peter Lenné in the mid-

1800s. On the shores of the lake in the southwestern part of the park, you can relax at the **Café am Neuen See,** a café and beer garden. In the center of the Tiergarten is the former **Kongresshalle** (✉ John-Foster-Dulles Allee 10, ☎ 030/397–870, ⏲ Tues.–Sun. 9–6, WEB www.hkw.de), referred to as the "pregnant oyster" for its design; it's now home to the **Haus der Kulturen der Welt,** the World Culture House.

In the past few years the tranquillity of the Tiergarten has been disturbed by the construction of a huge autobahn, railway, and metro tunnel, the multibillion-dollar **Nord-Süd-Tunnel.** It will redirect downtown traffic when all branches of the federal government have finally settled in and the new central train station at **Lehrter Stadtbahnhof** is finished in 2005.

Potsdamer Platz to Kreuzberg

World War II and the division of Berlin reduced bustling Potsdamer Platz to a sprawling, empty lot at the southeastern end of the Tiergarten. In the mid-1990s it became Europe's largest construction site, with corporate giants such as debis, the software subsidiary of DaimlerChrysler, and Sony erecting headquarters next to malls devoted to shopping and entertainment. Today the square and its surrounding narrow streets are a modern version of prewar Potsdamer Platz, then the epitome of the urbane Berlin of the Roaring '20s. Neighboring Kreuzberg is still one of the most lively of Berlin's districts. A largely Turkish population lives cheek-by-jowl with a variegated assortment of political radicals, New Agers, down-at-the-heel artists real and fake, and bohemians of all nationalities.

A Good Walk

Begin at **Potsdamer Platz** ⑮, at the center of which is the **Sony Center** ⑯, one of the city's most striking new buildings, surrounded by an entertainment complex with plenty of eateries. From here head southeast along Stresemannstrasse and turn left on Niederkirchnerstrasse, where the Berlin Wall once ran; the fragment of the wall here is one of only four sections still standing.

This is yet another strip of German history, with the old **Preussischer Landtag** ⑰, the seat of Berlin's parliament, the **Martin-Gropius-Bau** ⑱, and the **Prinz-Albrecht-Gelände** ⑲—containing the underground ruins of Nazi SS headquarters—one after the other. Cross Wilhelmstrasse and continue east on Kochstrasse until you reach the corner of Friedrichstrasse. Gripping stories of the Wall, refugees, and spies are told in the museum at the former **Checkpoint Charlie** ⑳. From here continue east on Kochstrasse and detour right onto Lindenstrasse for the **Jüdisches Museum** ㉑, Germany's largest museum of Jewish culture. To find a place to unwind, head north on Lindenstrasse and turn right on **Oranienstrasse** ㉒. This is the heart of the offbeat Kreuzberg district, with Turkish shops; progressive, hip cafés; and nearby street markets.

TIMING

The sights are very close to one another until you set off for the Jüdisches Museum, which you should see from the outside even if you don't plan to view the exhibits. Due to it's small size and popularity, you may experience a wait or slow line at the Checkpoint Charlie museum if you visit any time other than the morning.

Sights to See

★ ⑳ **Checkpoint Charlie.** This famous crossing point between the two Berlins is where American and Soviet tanks faced off in the tense months of the Berlin blockade (1948–49). All evidence of the crossing point disappeared along with the Wall, but the **Haus am Checkpoint Charlie**

(House at Checkpoint Charlie—The Wall Museum) is still here to tell the Wall's fascinating stories. The museum reviews the events leading up to its construction and displays actual tools and equipment, records, and photographs documenting methods used by East Germans to cross over to the West (one of the most ingenious instruments of escape was a miniature submarine). Come early in the day to avoid the multitude of visitors dropped off by tour buses. ✉ *Friedrichstr. 43–45, Kreuzberg,* ☎ *030/253–7250,* WEB *www.mauer-museum.com.* €7. *Daily 9* AM*–10* PM*.*

NEED A BREAK? Try your best to conjure up an image of the Wall from a window seat at **Café Adler** (✉ Friedrichstr. 206, Kreuzberg, ☎ 030/251–8965), which once bumped right up against it. The soups and salads are all tasty and cheap.

OFF THE BEATEN PATH **EAST SIDE GALLERY** – This stretch of concrete went from guarded border to open-air gallery within three months. Between February and June of 1990, 118 artists from around the globe created unique works of art on the longest remaining section of the Berlin Wall; its 1.3 km (.8 mi) length has been declared a historic monument. Much of the paint is now peeling or fading. One of the best-known works, by Russian artist Dmitri Vrubel, depicts Brezhnev and Honnecker (the former East German leader) kissing, with the caption "My God. Help me survive this deadly love." Warschauer Strasse is the nearest S- and U-bahn station. ✉ *Mühlenstr./Oberbaumbrücke, Friedrichshain.*

21 **Jüdisches Museum.** (Jewish Museum). The life and history of Germany's Jews from the Middle Ages through today is chronicled here, from explanations of religious traditions to exhibits on prominent historical figures and the evolution of laws regarding Jews' participation in civil society. The highly conceptual building designed by American architect Daniel Libeskind is the real star attraction. Various physical "voids" represent the loss German society faces due to the Holocaust, and a portion of the exhibits document the Holocaust as well. You'll need at least three hours to do the museum justice. Devote more time to the second floor if you're already familiar with basic aspects of Judaica, which makes up much of the third floor. ✉ *Lindenstr. 9–14, Kreuzberg,* ☎ *030/2599–3300,* WEB *www.jmberlin.de.* €5. *Daily 10–8.*

Mariannenplatz. Restored 19th-century tenement houses surround this square, the highlight of which is the **Künstlerhaus Bethanien,** a former deaconesses' hospital, where artists from around the world are given studio space. A gallery presents their works. Turn north on Mariannenstrasse from Oranienstrasse to reach the square. ✉ *Mariannenpl. 2, Kreuzberg,* ☎ *030/616–9030,* WEB *www.bethanien.de.* *Wed.–Sun. 2–7 (hrs vary depending on exhibition).*

18 **Martin-Gropius-Bau.** This renowned, magnificent exhibition hall once housed Berlin's Arts and Crafts Museum and dates back to 1877. Its architect, Martin Gropius, was the uncle of Walter Gropius, a Bauhaus architect. For the past 20 years, many of Berlin's most spectacular art and history exhibits have been staged here. It stands opposite the Preussischer Landtag. ✉ *Niederkirchnerstr. 7, Kreuzberg,* ☎ *030/2548–6101 or 030/254–860,* WEB *www.berlinerfestspiele.de.* *Weekdays 10–8 (hrs vary depending on exhibit).*

22 **Oranienstrasse.** The spine of life in the Kreuzberg district, Oranienstrasse and its hard-core appeal have tempered into funkiness since re-

unification. When Kreuzberg literally had its back against the Wall, West German social outcasts, punks, and the radical left made this old working-class street their hideout. Since the 1970s the population has been largely Turkish, and many of yesterday's outsiders have turned into successful owners of trendy shops and restaurants. Oranienstrasse is a good case study of West Berlin's past and the slow changes that have taken place since the Wall fell. You'll find a curious mixture of Muslim culture, alternative lifestyles, offbeat clothing stores, and hip restaurants.

To the south of Oranienstrasse is the depressing and seedy Kottbusser Platz. Its social housing projects date to the 1970s, and there's drug dealing in the area (stay away from both the dealers and drug addicts and do not give them any money).

15 **Potsdamer Platz** (Potsdam Square). The once-divided capital is rejoined on this square, which was Berlin's inner-city center and Europe's busiest plaza before World War II. Today's buildings of steel, glass, and concrete make it hard to imagine the square was once a no-man's-land divided by the infamous Wall. On the streets, a line of cobblestones painted red traces the old border. Where the British, American, and Russian sectors once met, Sony, debis, Asea Brown Boveri, and other companies have built their headquarters.

The two high-rise towers dominating the square are part of the headquarters of debis, the software subsidiary of DaimlerChrysler, and other companies. The debis center was designed by star architect Renzo Piano.

The **Potsdamer Platz Arkaden** (⊠ Alte Potsdamer Str. 7, Tiergarten, ☎ 030/2559–2766; ⊙ weekdays 9:30–8, Sat. 9:30–4) is a shopping and entertainment mecca covering 40,000 square yards and housing 140 shops and restaurants on three levels. Right next to it are the Grand Hyatt Berlin, the movie complex Cinemaxx, and a **3D-IMAX cinema** (⊠ Marlene-Dietrich-Pl. 4, Tiergarten, ☎ 030/4431–6131; ⊙ daily 10 AM–midnight), as well as the Berlin casino and Germany's largest musical theater.

16 **Sony Center.** This light glass-and-steel construction is wrapped around a spectacular 4,800-square-yard forum. The architectural jewel designed by German-American architect Helmut Jahn is one of the most stunning buildings of Berlin's new center, filled with restaurants, cafés, movie theaters, apartments, and the European headquarters of Sony. The one reminder of more glorious days gone by is the meticulously integrated old **Kaisersaal** (Emperor's Hall). The hall originally stood some 50 yards away in the Grand Hotel Esplanade (built in 1907), but was moved here lock, stock, and barrel. Its restored interior houses a restaurant and cafés.

Also in the center is the **Filmmuseum Berlin** (⊠ Potsdamer Str. 2, Tiergarten, ☎ 030/300–9030, WEB www.filmmuseum-berlin.de; 🎫 €6; ⊙ Tues.–Sun. 10–6, Thurs. 10–8), presenting the history of movie-making and memorabilia of many German movie stars, including personal belongings of Marlene Dietrich.

17 **Preussischer Landtag** (Prussian State Legislature). The monumental parliament building houses Berlin's House of Deputies and is one of Germany's most impressive 19th-century administration buildings. Even if the house isn't in session, take a look inside and admire the huge entrance hall. ⊠ *Niederkirchnerstr. 3–5, Kreuzberg,* ☎ *030/23250,* WEB *www.parlament-berlin.de.* ⊙ *Weekdays 9–6.*

19 **Prinz-Albrecht-Gelände** (Prince Albrecht Grounds). The headquarters of the SS, the Main Reich Security Office, and other Nazi security or-

Close-Up

COPING WITH THE PAST

IN THE 21ST CENTURY, will Germany shed decades of self-loathing about the Holocaust and World War II? Critical self-examination began as late as the 1960s, when an angry young generation pointedly questioned what their parents did during the 12 years of fascism. This generation has now grown up and seems comfortable declaring its slate clean.

Baby boomers now hold key positions in the media, politics, science, and culture. They've opened the door for Germans wishing for a normalcy they feel has long eluded the country. The first administration (1998–2002) of chancellor Gerhard Schröder (born 1944) marked a historic shift in leadership: Schröder was the first postwar chancellor not to have experienced World War II. He and his generation are well aware of Germany's past but do not seem burdened by its weight. His left-wing government was straightforward, outspoken, and less apt to worry that the ever-wary world will hold Germany's history over its head. This open, unpretentious approach is a political style that has gone over well with Germany's neighbors, most significantly Poland and France.

But the past is never far from German consciousness, as American historian Daniel J. Goldhagen's book *Hitler's Willing Executioners* triggered the most profound shock wave of *Vergangenheitsbewältigung* (coping with the past) the nation has felt since World War II. Goldhagen reminded people that the Holocaust was carried out by ordinary Germans, not just by a minority of fanatical Nazis.

Between 1999 and 2001, Germany simultaneously faced reunification and revisited debates over the Holocaust. As historians and politicians argued over how to express German responsibility, shame, and guilt, plans for a national Holocaust memorial derailed, and controversy surrounded Berlin's Jewish Museum. Some of the country's most respected elder writers and politicians stressed the importance of examining the German traits that allowed the genocide to occur. This renewed reflection on the idea of a national character flaw once again aroused the country's insecurities. The construction of the disputed memorial for the victims of the Holocaust is finally being completed in late 2003 next to the Brandenburg Gate. The Jewish Museum, operating with great success under an American director, Michael W. Blumenthal, is one of the country's most popular museums. Even before its official opening, the building, designed by American architect Daniel Libeskind, attracted thousands of visitors. They inspected the daring style of jagged, irregular shapes that symbolize both a broken Star of David and the many links between the Jewish past and future in Germany. It thus is also a memorial to Jewish suffering and hopes in Germany.

Germany continues to address issues of its past. The much-feared political successes of right-wing parties that had appeared so imminent in the mid-1990s did not materialize. However, right-wing attacks on foreign workers continue, and the German government's attempt to attract foreign professionals to live and work in Germany is largely failing. But while many outside Germany look upon this country with suspicion and doubt, most Germans are slowly accepting the changing racial face of their society. And a revised citizenship and immigration law has begun to (at least legally) integrate Germany's alien residents. Finally, German corporations have established reparation funds for World War II slave-laborers. These days, accepting and exploring Germany's past has taken a somewhat quieter and more balanced approach. And that is probably the best sign that the nation is beginning to truly accept its history.

— Jürgen Scheunemann

ganizations were based on this site from 1933 until 1945. After the war the buildings were leveled. The grounds remained untouched until 1987, when the basements of the buildings, once used as "house prisons" by the SS, were excavated, and an open-air exhibit on their history and Nazi atrocities was opened—the Topography of Terror. Tours are available by appointment. ✉ *Niederkirchnerstr. 8, Kreuzberg,* ☎ *030/254–5090,* WEB *www.topographie.de.* 🎫 *Free.* ⏲ *Oct.–Apr., daily 10–6; May–Sept., daily 10–8.*

OFF THE BEATEN PATH — **TÜRKENMARKT** (Turkish Market) – On Tuesday and Friday from noon to 6:30 you can find the country's best selection of Arab and Turkish foods along the Landwehrkanal. Vendors line the bank roads of Maybachufer and the Paul-Lincke-Ufer. You can walk here from Kreuzberg's Kottbusser Tor U-bahn station via Kottbusser Damm. The cafés and restaurants on Paul-Lincke-Ufer are great places for a cup of coffee.

Unter den Linden to Alexanderplatz

Unter den Linden and Friedrichstrasse, the main streets of eastern Berlin, proudly roll out restored landmarks, museums, and upscale malls. The old boulevards were once almost forgotten in the shadow of the Wall. Some rather unattractive office buildings along Unter den Linden, hastily erected in the 1970s, are reminders that the boulevard was remodeled by Communist East Germany. At the very end of Unter den Linden, around the vast Alexanderplatz, eastern Berlin's handful of skyscrapers cluster around one of the city's premier landmarks, the Berlin TV tower. Northeast of it, the old working-class district of Prenzlauer Berg is home to wonderfully restored 19th-century tenement houses.

A Good Walk

Begin your walk at Pariser Platz, right behind the Brandenburger Tor, and take a long walk east down **Unter den Linden** ㉓. This eastern and older counterpart to Kurfürstendamm is both more historic and more elegant, with landmarks such as the famous Hotel Adlon next to the Brandenburger Tor. On your way, you'll pass several parliamentary offices and consulates, among them the Russian embassy and souvenir shops. From the turn of the 20th century until the beginning of World War II, the intersection of Unter den Linden and **Friedrichstrasse** ㉔ was the busiest in all Berlin. Turn right here, passing both quaint and fancy shops, then left at Französische Strasse to reach **Gendarmenmarkt** ㉕, one of Europe's finest early 19th-century plazas.

Head farther down Französische Strasse to **St. Hedwigskathedrale** ㉖, Berlin's leading Catholic church, and the **Staatsoper Unter den Linden** ㉗, the city's premier opera house. These buildings, along with the **Kronprinzenpalais** ㉘—which adjoins the opera house—and Humboldt University, form the Forum Fridericianum, the model of Prussian glory, designed by Frederick the Great himself. Back on Unter den Linden, opposite the Kronprinzenpalais and next to the university, is the **Deutsches Historisches Museum** ㉙. Turn left to follow the Spree Canal to **Museumsinsel** ㉚, the site of Berlin's two original medieval settlements. From the museum complex follow the Spree Canal back to Unter den Linden and turn left to reach the enormous cathedral **Berliner Dom** ㉛ and the adjacent Schlossplatz, the site of Berlin's destroyed city palace.

Follow Karl-Liebknecht-Strasse to take a look at the 13th-century **St. Marienkirche** ㉜ and the bordering **Alexanderplatz** ㉝, a wide-open square. Walk across the southern end of the square past the **Berliner Rathaus** ㉞, the city's town hall, and to the **Nikolaiviertel** ㉟, Berlin's historic quarter with the medieval St. Nikolaikirche (St. Nicolas

Church). To reach the **Märkisches Museum** (36), which displays the history of Berlin, wander down Spreeufer to the Mühlendamm, turn right onto this boulevard and cross the Spree River. Turn left into onto Fischerinsel, and then make another left onto Wallstrasse.

TIMING

The walk down Unter den Linden to Alexanderplatz and the St. Nikolaiviertel takes about two hours if you don't look closely at any museums or highlights. Allow at least two hours for the Museumsinsel. You won't regret one minute. Most of the other sights can be seen in less than one hour each. The Museumsinsel, Friedrichstrasse, and the Galeries Lafayette are crowded on weekends, so try to visit there early in the day or during the week.

Sights to See

33 **Alexanderplatz.** This square once formed the hub of East Berlin. German writer Alfred Döblin dubbed it the "heart of a world metropolis." It's a bleak sort of place today, open and windswept and surrounded by grim modern buildings, with no hint of its prewar activity—a reminder not just of the results of Allied bombing but of the ruthlessness practiced by the East Germans when they demolished the remains of the old buildings.

Finding Alexanderplatz is no problem; just head toward the **Berliner Fernsehturm,** the soaring TV tower, completed in 1969 and 1,198 ft high (not accidentally 710 ft higher than western Berlin's broadcasting tower and 98 ft higher than the Eiffel Tower in Paris). You can get the best view of Berlin from the tower's observation platform; on a clear day you can see for 40 km (25 mi). You can also enjoy a coffee break up there in the city's highest café, which rotates for your panoramic pleasure. ⊠ *Panoramastr. 1a, Mitte,* ☎ *030/242–3333,* WEB *www.berliner-fernsehturm.de.* *€6.* *Nov.–Mar., daily 10 AM–midnight; Apr.–Oct., daily 9 AM–1 AM (last admission at 11:30 PM).*

★ 31 **Berliner Dom** (Berlin Cathedral). The impressive 19th-century cathedral, with its enormous green copper dome, is one of the great ecclesiastical buildings in Germany. There's an observation balcony that allows a view of the cathedral's ceiling and interior. More than 80 sarcophagi of Prussian royals are on display in the cathedral's catacombs. ⊠ *Am Lustgarten, Mitte,* ☎ *030/2026–9136,* WEB *www.berlinerdom.de.* *€4 (combined ticket for church, crypt, and imperial staircase); with balcony €5.* *Church Mon.–Sat. 9–7, Sun. noon–7; balcony Oct.–Mar., daily 9–3.30; Apr.–Sept., daily 9–7 (last admission: 1 hr before closing); imperial staircase and crypt Mon.–Sat. 10–6, Sun. noon–6.*

34 **Berliner Rathaus** (Red Town Hall). A redbrick design and friezes depicting the city's history are the distinguishing features of city hall. It's largely considered a pompous symbol of Berlin's 19th-century self-importance. ⊠ *Jüdenstr. at Rathausstr., Mitte,* ☎ *030/90260.* *Free.* *Weekdays 9–6.*

29 **Deutsches Historisches Museum** (German History Museum). This magnificent baroque building, constructed between 1695 and 1730, was once the Prussian arsenal (Zeughaus). It now serves as Germany's National History Museum, which chronicles German history from the Middle Ages to the present. A new, modern wing designed by I. M. Pei holds special exhibits, often about 20th-century history. ⊠ *Unter den Linden 2, Mitte,* ☎ *030/203–040,* WEB *www.dhm.de.* *Free.* *Fri.–Wed. 10–6, Thurs. 10–10.*

★ 24 **Friedrichstrasse.** No other street in eastern Germany has changed as dramatically as Friedrichstrasse. The once-bustling 5th Avenue of prewar Berlin has risen from the rubble of war and Communist negligence to recover its glamour of old, though it doesn't offer the sheer number of establishments as the competing Ku'damm.

Heading south on Friedrichstrasse, you'll pass various new business buildings, including the **Lindencorso** and the **Rosmarin-Karree,** which are worth a look both for their architecture and fancy shops. The jewel of this street is the **Friedrichstadtpassagen,** a gigantic complex of three buildings praised for their completely different designs. An underground mall of elegant shops and eateries connects the buildings. At the corner of Französische Strasse a daring building, designed by French architect Jean Nouvel, houses the French department store **Galeries Lafayette** (✉ Französische Str. 23, ☎ 030/209–480). Its interior is dominated by a huge steel-and-glass funnel surrounded by four floors of merchandise.

★ 25 **Gendarmenmarkt.** Anchoring this large square are the beautifully reconstructed 1818 **Schauspielhaus,** one of Berlin's main concert halls, and the **Deutscher Dom and Französischer Dom** (German and French cathedrals). The Französischer Dom contains the **Hugenottenmuseum** (✉ Gendarmenmarkt 5, Mitte, ☎ 030/229–1760; 🎫 €1.60; ⏲ Tues.–Sat. noon–5, Sun. 11–5), with exhibits charting the history and art of the Protestant refugees from France—the Huguenots—expelled at the end of the 17th century by King Louis XIV. Their energy and commercial expertise did much to help boost Berlin during the 18th century.

The **Deutscher Dom** (✉ Gendarmenmarkt 1, Mitte, ☎ 030/2273–0431; 🎫 Free; ⏲ Sept.–May, Wed.–Sun. 10–5, Tues. 10–10; June–Aug., Wed.–Sun. 10–6, Tues. 10–10) has an extensive historical exhibition sponsored by the German parliament. It's worth a visit if you're interested in an official view of German history with a particular accent on the cold war and the division of Germany.

28 **Kronprinzenpalais** (Crown Prince's Palace). A former state guest house and a temporary exhibition hall for the Deutsches Historisches Museum until early 2003, this magnificent baroque-style building was originally constructed in 1732 by Philippe Gerlach for Crown Prince Friedrich (later Frederick the Great). ✉ *Unter den Linden 3, Mitte.*

36 **Märkisches Museum** (Brandenburg Museum). This redbrick showcase for Berlin's history includes exhibits on the city's theatrical past, its guilds, its newspapers, and the March 1848 revolution. Paintings capture the look of the city before it crumbled in World War II. The fascinating collection of mechanical musical instruments is demonstrated on Sunday at 3 PM. ✉ *Am Köllnischen Park 5, Mitte,* ☎ *030/308–660,* WEB *www.stadtmuseum.de.* 🎫 *€4, instrument demonstration €2.* ⏲ *Tues.–Sun. 10–6.*

★ 30 **Museumsinsel** (Museum Island). On the site of one of Berlin's two original settlements, this unique complex of four state museums is an absolute must. The completely restored **Alte Nationalgalerie** (Old National Gallery, entrance on Bodestrasse) houses an outstanding collection of 18th-, 19th-, and early 20th-century paintings and sculptures. Works by Cézanne, Rodin, Degas, and one of Germany's most famous portrait artists, Max Liebermann, are part of the permanent exhibition. Its **Galerie der Romantik** (Gallery of Romanticism) collection has masterpieces from such 19th-century German painters as Karl Friedrich Schinkel and Caspar David Friedrich, the leading members of the German Romantic school. The **Altes Museum** (Old Museum, entrance at Am Lustgarten), an austere neoclassical building just north of the old Lustgarten, features antique sculptures, clay figurines, and bronze art, that are part of the **Antikensammlung** (Antiquities Collection). It also is home to everyday utensils from ancient Greece and Rome and a number of Greek vases from the 6th to 4th centuries. Another part of the Antikensammlung is housed in the Pergamonmuseum.

Even if you think you aren't interested in the ancient world, make an exception for the **Pergamonmuseum** (entrance on Am Kupfergraben), one of the world's greatest museums. The museum's name is derived from its principal display, the Pergamon Altar, a monumental Greek temple discovered in what is now Turkey and dating from 180 BC. The altar was shipped to Berlin in the late 19th century. Equally impressive is the Babylonian processional way in the Asia Minor department. ✉ *Entrance to Museumsinsel: Am Kupfergraben, Mitte.* ☎ *030/209–5577 Museumsinsel; 030/2090–5560,* WEB *www.smb.spk-berlin.de.* 🎫 *Each museum €6; free 1st Sun. of every month; Tageskarte applicable.* 🕓 *Pergamonmuseum Fri.–Wed. 10–6, Thurs. 10–10; Alte Nationalgalerie and Altes Museum Tues.–Sun. 10–6.*

35 **Nikolaiviertel** (Nicholas Quarter). This tiny quarter of cobblestone streets grew up around Berlin's oldest parish church, the medieval, twin-spire **St. Nikolaikirche** (St. Nicholas Church), dating from 1230. The adjacent Fischerinsel (Fisherman's Island) area was the heart of Berlin 750 years ago, and retains some of its medieval character. At Breite Strasse you'll find two of Berlin's oldest buildings: No. 35 is the **Ribbeckhaus,** the city's only surviving Renaissance structure, dating from 1624, and No. 36 is the early baroque **Marstall,** built by Michael Matthais between 1666 and 1669. Life goes on here, and the area is filled with stores, cafés, and restaurants. ✉ *Church: Nikolaikirchpl., Mitte,* ☎ *030/240–020,* WEB *www.stadtmuseum.de.* 🎫 *€1.50.* 🕓 *Tues.–Sun. 10–6.*

26 **St. Hedwigskathedrale** (St. Hedwig's Cathedral). Similar to the Pantheon in Rome, this substantial circular building is Berlin's premier Catholic church. When the cathedral was erected in 1747, it was the first Catholic church built in resolutely Protestant Berlin since the Reformation. It was Frederick the Great's effort to appease Prussia's Catholic population after his invasion of Catholic Silesia. ✉ *Bebelpl., Mitte,* ☎ *030/203–4810,* WEB *www.hedwigs-kathedrale.de.* 🕓 *Weekdays 10–5, Sun. 1–5.*

32 **St. Marienkirche** (St. Mary's Church). This medieval church, one of the finest in Berlin, is worth a visit for its late-Gothic, macabre fresco *Der Totentanz* (*Dance of Death*). The cross on top of the church tower was an everlasting annoyance to Communist rulers, as its golden metal was always mirrored in the windows of the Berlin TV tower, the pride of socialist construction genius. ✉ *Karl-Liebknecht-Str. 8, Mitte,* ☎ *030/242–4467.* 🎫 *Tour free.* 🕓 *Mon.–Thurs. 10–noon, 1–4, weekends noon–4; tour Mon.–Tues. at 1, Sun. at 11:45.*

27 **Staatsoper Unter den Linden** (State Opera). Berlin's lavish, prime opera house lies at the heart of the Forum Fridericianum. This ensemble of buildings was designed by Frederick the Great himself to showcase the splendor of his enlightened rule. Daniel Barenboim is maestro of the house. ✉ *Unter den Linden 7, Mitte,* ☎ *030/2035–4555,* WEB *www.staatsoper-berlin.de.* 🕓 *Box office weekdays 11–7, weekends 2–7; reservations by phone Mon.–Sat. 10–8, Sun. 2–8.*

NEED A BREAK?

The **Opernpalais** (✉ Unter den Linden 5, Mitte, ☎ 030/202–683), right next to the opera house, is home to four restaurants and cafés, all famous for their rich German cakes, pastries, and original Berlin dishes.

23 **Unter den Linden.** The name of this major Berlin thoroughfare means "under the linden trees"—and as Marlene Dietrich once sang: "As long

as the old linden trees still bloom, Berlin is still Berlin." Once the most elegant and prestigious Berlin address, the grand boulevard is slowly regaining its old glamour. Lined by grand hotels, an opera house, some cafés and shops, parliamentary buildings, embassies, and consulates, the avenue reminds you that Berlin once was the proud capital of the German Empire. The **Kronprinzenpalais, Deutsches Historisches Museum,** and **Humboldt-Universität** (Humboldt University; ✉ Unter den Linden 6, Mitte, ☎ 030/20930) border the avenue. The university was built in 1766 as a palace for the brother of Friedrich II of Prussia. It became a university in 1810, and both Karl Marx and Friedrich Engels once studied here. The main hall of the university is open Monday–Saturday 6 AM–10 PM.

Next to the university is the **Neue Wache** (New Guardhouse). Constructed in 1818, it served as the Royal Prussian War Memorial until the declaration of the Weimar Republic in 1918. Badly damaged in World War II, it was restored by the East German state and rededicated as a memorial for the victims of militarism and fascism in 1960. After unification it was restored to its Weimar Republic appearance and later inaugurated as Germany's central war memorial. Inside is a copy of Berlin sculptor Käthe Kollwitz's *Pietà*, showing a mother mourning over her dead son on the battlefield.

Mitte and Prenzlauer Berg

Mitte (Middle) is close to the center of Berlin and served as the government district during the era of the Prussian kings, the German emperors, and, later, the German Democratic Republic governments. In 1999 Mitte resumed its role of yore when the German government relocated here from Bonn. The district includes Unter den Linden, Friedrichstrasse, and Alexanderplatz and abounds with landmarks on the grand boulevards.

But the atmosphere of this smallest of Berlin districts is best experienced in the alleyways of the Scheunenviertel (Barn Quarter), which also encompasses the former Spandauer Vorstadt (Jewish Quarter)—the streets around and to the west of Oranienburger Strasse. During the second half of the 17th century, artisans, small businessmen, and Jews moved into this area at the encouragement of the Great Elector, who sought to improve his financial situation through their skills. As industrialization intensified, the quarter became poorer, and in the 1880s many East European Jews escaping pogroms settled here.

North of Mitte, the old working-class district of Prenzlauer Berg used to be one of the poorest sections of Berlin. In socialist East Germany, the old (and mostly run-down) tenement houses attracted the artistic avant-garde, who transformed the area into a refuge for alternative lifestyles. Today both Mitte and Prenzlauer Berg charm with their blend of rugged, turn-of-the-20th-century architecture and the city's liveliest nightlife.

A Good Walk

From the S-bahn station of Lehrter Stadtbahnhof, walk east on Invalidenstrasse, passing the **Hamburger Bahnhof, Museum für Gegenwart–Berlin** ㊲, Berlin's museum for contemporary art. At the intersection of Invalidenstrasse and Chausseestrasse, turn right and walk south to find the **Brecht-Weigel-Gedenkstätte** ㊳, a museum in the living quarters of playwright Bertolt Brecht, and the adjacent graveyard, where many famous figures are buried. A short walk back toward Invalidenstrasse, and farther to the northeast, on Bernauer Strasse, is the **Gedenkstätte Berliner Mauer** ㊴, the only section of the Berlin Wall still in its original form and location. From here you can continue south on Gartenstrasse, Kleine Hamburger Strasse, and Auguststrasse to reach the heart of the Mitte district, Oranienburger Strasse. This is also the center of the old Jewish quarter (Spandauer Vorstadt), spread around the massive **Neue Synagoge** ㊵. From here continue east on Oranienburger Strasse to the **Hackesche Höfe** ㊶, an art deco warehouse complex. Jump on the nearby S-bahn to Alexanderplatz and transfer to the subway (U–2), getting off two stops later at Senefelderplatz station in Prenzlauer Berg. It's an easy walk north on Schönhauser Allee to the fringe art and culture center **Kulturbrauerei** ㊷, an old brewery and a typical example of late-19th-century industrial architecture. Finally, to take in some local flavor, follow the small Sredzkistrasse to the east until you reach the center of Berlin's old working-class district, the completely restored 19th-century **Husemannstrasse** ㊸ and **Kollwitzplatz** ㊹.

TIMING

If you want to indulge in the art exhibitions at Hamburger Bahnhof or relax at any of the many cafés along the way, reserve a full day for Mitte and Prenzlauer Berg. It's also possible to take in all spots along the tour within four hours.

Sights to See

38 **Brecht-Weigel-Gedenkstätte** (Brecht-Weigel Memorial Site). You can visit the former working and living quarters of playwright Bertolt Brecht and his wife, Helene Weigel, and scholars can browse the Brecht library by appointment only). The downstairs restaurant serves Viennese cuisine using Weigel's recipes. Brecht is buried next door, along with his wife and more than 100 other celebrated Germans, in the **Dorotheenstädtischer Friedhof** (Dorotheenstadt Cemetery). ✉ *Chausseestr. 125, Mitte,* ☎ *030/2830–57044; 030/461–7279 cemetery,* WEB *www.adk.de.* 🎫 *Apartment €3, library free.* ⏲ *Apartment Tues.–Wed. and Fri. 10–noon, Thurs. 10–noon and 5–7, Sat. 9:30–noon and 12:30–2, Sun. 11–6; tours every ½ hr, every hr on Sun.; cemetery Apr.–Oct., daily 8–8; Nov.–Mar., daily 8–4.*

★ 39 **Gedenkstätte Berliner Mauer** (Berlin Wall Memorial Site). This is the only nearly original piece of the Berlin Wall border system left in the city. The memorial took almost seven years to realize, as most East Berliners living nearby didn't want a reminder of German separation right in front of their homes. It includes a 230-ft-long piece of the whole Wall system, which consisted of two walls separated by a control path. Standing behind one wall, you can look through narrow gaps to the other. A modern chapel and a center with photos, television and radio excerpts, and documents on the Wall are also on site. ✉ *Bernauer Str. 111, Wedding,* ☎ *030/464–1030,* WEB *www.berliner-mauer-gedenkstaette.de.* 🎫 *Free.* ⏲ *Wed.–Sun. 10–5.*

★ 41 **Hackesche Höfe** (Hacke Warehouses). Built in 1905–07, the completely restored Hackesche Höfe are the finest example of art nouveau industrial architecture in Berlin. The huge complex is comprised of eight courtyards connected by narrow passageways. Most of the buildings are covered with white tiles and decorated with blue and gray mosaics. Today the Hackesche Höfe are the center of nightlife in Mitte, drawing crowds with several style-conscious bars and pubs, the restaurant Hackescher Hof, the variety theater Chamäleon Varieté, a drama stage, and a movie theater. On warm weekend nights in summer, the courtyards are packed. ✉ *Rosenthaler Str. 40–41, Mitte,* WEB *www.hackesche-hoefe.com.*

37 **Hamburger Bahnhof, Museum für Gegenwart–Berlin** (Museum of Contemporary Art). The best place in Berlin to survey Western art after 1960

is in this light-filled remodeled train station. The new wing is worth a visit itself for its stunning interplay of glass, steel, colorful decor, and sunlight coming through skylights. You can see installations by German artists Joseph Beuys and Anselm Kiefer as well as paintings by Andy Warhol, Cy Twombly, Robert Rauschenberg, and Robert Morris. Marcel Duchamp and Marcel Broodthaers are exhibited on the second floor. ✉ *Invalidenstr. 50–51, Tiergarten,* ☎ *030/397–8340,* WEB *www.smb.spk-berlin.de.* *€6; free 1st Sun. of every month; Tageskarte applicable.* ⏲ *Tues.–Wed. and Fri. 10–6, Thurs. 10–10, weekends 11–6.*

43 **Husemannstrasse.** This completely restored cobblestone street in the old part of Prenzlauer Berg gives a vivid impression of the late 19th century. With their squat advertising pillars, wrought-iron parapets on the balconies, and stucco decorations, the houses evoke a time when handicrafts and small shops flourished amid the large tenements built for the working class. The socialist East German government began renovating the street in 1987, and it's full of pubs, restaurants, and shops today.

NEED A BREAK? For coffee and cake or a good German beer, stop by **Restauration 1900** (✉ Husemannstr. 1, Prenzlauer Berg, ☎ 030/442–2494), one of the few popular cafés and restaurants from socialist times still in business today.

44 **Kollwitzplatz** (Kollwitz Square). Named for the painter, sculptor, and political activist Käthe Kollwitz (1867–1945) who lived nearby, the square is the center of the old working-class district of Prenzlauer Berg. It is dominated by a sculpture by Kollwitz, whose many art works portray the life and hard times of ordinary people living here.

OFF THE BEATEN PATH **JÜDISCHER FRIEDHOF** (Jewish Cemetery) – More than 150,000 graves make this peaceful retreat in Berlin's Weissensee district Europe's largest Jewish cemetery. The cemetery and tombstones are in excellent condition—a seeming impossibility, given its location in the heart of the Third Reich. To reach the cemetery, take Tram 2, 3, 4, 23, or 24 from Hackescher Markt to Berliner Allee and head south on Herbert-Baum-Strasse. ☎ *030/925–3330.* ⏲ *Apr.–Oct., Sun.–Thurs. 8–5, Fri. 8–3; Nov.–Mar., Sun.–Thurs. 8–4, Fri. 8–3.*

42 **Kulturbrauerei** (Culture Brewery). The redbrick buildings of the old Schultheiss brewery now house a fringe arts and entertainment center, containing a movie center, art galleries, pubs, and a concert hall. Parts of the brewery were built in 1842. Around the turn of the 20th century the complex was expanded to include the main brewery of Berlin's famous Schultheiss beer, then the largest brewery in the world. The buildings are completely restored, though no beer is brewed here now. ✉ *Schönhauser Allee 36–39, Prenzlauer Berg,* ☎ *030/443–150,* WEB *www.kulturbrauerei.de.*

40 **Neue Synagoge** (New Synagogue). This meticulously restored landmark, built between 1859 and 1866, is an exotic amalgam of styles, the whole faintly Middle Eastern. When its doors opened, it was the largest synagogue in Europe, with 3,200 seats. The synagogue was largely ruined on November 9, 1938 (*Kristallnacht*—Night of the Broken Glass), when Nazi looters rampaged across Germany, burning synagogues and smashing the few Jewish shops and homes left in the country. Further destroyed by Allied bombing in 1943, it remained untouched until restoration began under the East German government in the mid-1980s. The building is connected to the modern **Centrum Judaicum,** a center for Jewish culture and learning that sponsors exhibitions and

other cultural events. ✉ *Oranienburger Str. 28–30, Mitte,* ☎ *030/2840–1316,* WEB *www.cjudaicum.de.* ⏲ *Sun.–Thurs. 10–6, Fri. 10–2.*

Palaces, Parks, and Museums in Outer Berlin

The city's outlying areas abound with palaces, lakes, and museums set in lush greenery. Central to the former West Berlin but now a western district of the united city, Charlottenburg was once an independent and wealthy city that only became a part of Berlin in 1920. It holds the baroque Charlottenburg Palace and several important museums. The vast Grunewald (forest) covers most of southwestern Berlin; it's an ideal spot for hiking or for relaxing on one of the lake's islands. Some of the city's most intriguing museums are in the well-to-do neighborhood of Dahlem.

A Good Tour

Begin at the museums of **Schloss Charlottenburg** ㊺ and the adjacent **Ägyptisches Museum** ㊻ and **Sammlung Berggruen** ㊼. Richard-Wagner-Platz (U–7) is the nearest subway station to the palace. Spot its dome and follow Otto-Suher-Allee northwest towards it. (From Zoologischer Garten the total U-bahn ride to Richard-Wagner-Platz takes about 20 minutes.)

The four **Dahlemer Museen** ㊽ lie south of Charlottenburg in the neighborhood of Dahlem. To reach them from Richard-Wagner-Platz, take the U–7 in the direction of Rudow until you reach the stop Fehrbelliner Platz. Change trains here and take U–1 in the direction of Krumme Lanke to Dahlem-Dorf. The trip from the palace to the museums takes about 45 minutes.

After placard reading, it's time for the great outdoors in the **Grunewald** ㊾. From the Dahlem Museums it's a short ride on the U–1 to the Krumme Lanke station. Change trains at the suburban railway station at nearby Mexikoplatz and take a ride on the S-bahn No. 1 (in the direction of Wannsee) to the Nikolassee or Wannsee station. If you want to continue to the Grunewald station, change trains and take S-bahn 7 (in the direction of Friedrichstrasse). Each of these stations serves as a starting point for hour-long hikes through the greenbelt of the Grunewald and Wannsee lakes with the **Pfaueninsel** ㊿ and its romantic small palace. A grim reminder of the area's past is the **Bildungs- und Gedenkstätte Haus der Wannsee-Konferenz** (51), an old villa where the Holocaust was planned. You can reach the Pfaueninsel by taking Bus A16 or 316; the Haus der Wannsee-Konferenz can be reached on Bus 114. All buses depart from the Wannsee S-bahn station.

TIMING

Because of travel distances, you will need at least one full day for the outer Berlin attractions; spend the morning at Schloss Charlottenburg and the Dahlem Museums and the rest of the day in the Grunewald area. Even if you skip the museums at Schloss Charlottenburg and Dahlem, still allot a full day to visit the other places.

Sights to See

★ ㊻ **Ägyptisches Museum** (Egyptian Museum). The former east guardhouse and residence of the Prussian king Friedrich I's bodyguard is now home to the exquisite portrait bust of Queen Nefertiti. The 3,300-year-old sculpture of the Egyptian queen is the centerpiece of a collection of works that traces Egypt's history from 4000 BC and includes some of the best-preserved mummies outside Cairo. The museum is across from Schloss Charlottenburg. ✉ *Schlossstr. 70, Charlottenburg,* ☎ *030/343–5730,* WEB *www.smpk.de.* 🎫 *€6; free 1st Sun. of every month.* ⏲ *Tues.–Sun. 10–6.*

51 **Bildungs- und Gedenkstätte Haus der Wannsee-Konferenz** (Wannsee Conference Memorial Site). The lovely lakeside setting of this Berlin villa belies the unimaginable Holocaust atrocities planned here. This elegant edifice hosted the fateful conference held on January, 20, 1942, at which Nazi leaders and German bureaucrats under SS leader Reinhard Heydrich planned the systematic deportation and mass extinction of Europe's Jewish population. Today this so-called *Endlösung der Judenfrage* ("final solution of the Jewish question") is illustrated with an exhibition that documents the conference, and more extensively, the escalation of persecution against Jews, and the Holocaust itself. Upstairs is a research center with source materials in English. Allow at least two hours for a visit. ✉ *Am Grossen Wannsee 56–58, Zehlendorf,* ☎ *030/805–0010,* WEB *www.ghwk.de.* 🎫 *Free.* ⏲ *Daily 10–6.*

48 **Dahlemer Museen** (Dahlem Museums). This complex of four museums includes the **Ethnologisches Museum** (Ethnographic Museum) as well as museums for Indian, East Asian, and early European art. It is internationally known for its art and artifacts from Africa, Asia, the South Seas, and the Americas. The large collection of Maya, Aztec, and Incan ceramics and stone sculptures should not be missed. ✉ *Lansstr. 8, Zehlendorf,* ☎ *030/830–1438,* WEB *www.smb.spk-berlin.de.* 🎫 *€3; free 1st Sun. of every month.* ⏲ *Tues.–Fri. 9–6, weekends 11–6.*

49 **Grunewald.** Together with its Wannsee lakes, this splendid forest is the city's most popular retreat. In good weather Berliners come out in force, swimming, sailing their boats, tramping through the woods, and riding horseback. In winter a downhill ski run and even a ski jump operate on the modest slopes of Teufelsberg Hill. Excursion steamers ply the water wonderland of the Wannsee and the Havel River.

★ 50 **Pfaueninsel** (Peacock Island). Prussian king Friedrich Wilhelm II whisked his mistresses away to this small island oasis on the Great Wannsee. **Schloss Pfaueninsel,** the small palace, was erected in 1794 according to the ruler's plans and—in accordance with the taste of his era—was built as a fake ruin. In the early 19th century, garden architect Joseph Peter Lenné designed an English garden on the island, which ultimately became western Berlin's favorite summer getaway. ✉ *Pfaueninselchaussee, Zehlendorf,* ☎ *0331/969–4202,* WEB *www.spsg.de.* 🎫 *€3, and €1 for ferry service.* ⏲ *Ferry to Pfaueninsel Nov.–Feb., daily 10–4; Mar. and Oct., daily 9–5; Apr. and Sept., daily 8–6; May–Aug., daily 8–8; Palace Apr.–Oct., Tues.–Sun. 10–5.*

OFF THE BEATEN PATH

SACHSENHAUSEN GEDENKSTÄTTE (Sachsenhausen Memorial) – The only Nazi concentration camp near the Third Reich capital was established in 1936, later becoming a Soviet internment and prison camp for German soldiers. In 1961 the camp was made into a memorial to its more than 100,000 victims. The area has a few preserved facilities and barracks, as well as a memorial and museum. To reach Sachsenhausen, take the S-bahn 1 from Friedrichstrasse to Oranienburg, the last stop. The ride will take 45–50 minutes. From the station it's a 25-minute walk, or you can take a taxi. Oranienburg is 35 km (22 mi) north of Berlin. ✉ *Str. der Nationen 22, Oranienburg,* ☎ *03301/2000.* 🎫 *Free.* ⏲ *Apr.–Sept., daily 8:30–6; Oct.–Mar., daily 9–4:30 (last admission 30 mins before closing).*

★ 47 **Sammlung Berggruen** (Berggruen Collection). This small museum in the historic Stüler-Bau (once a museum of ancient art) focuses on the history of modern art, with representative work from such artists as Van Gogh and Cézanne, Picasso, Giacometti, Klee, and more contemporary artists. Heinz Berggruen, a businessman who emigrated to the United States in the 1930s, collected the excellent paintings on display and later sold them to the city of Berlin. Opened in 1996, the intimate museum has become one of Berlin's most beloved art venues. ✉ *Schlossstr. 1, Charlottenburg,* ☎ *030/326–9580,* WEB *www.smpk.de.* 🎫 *€6.* ⏲ *Tues.–Fri. 10–6, weekends 11–6.*

45 **Schloss Charlottenburg** (Charlottenburg Palace). The most monumental reminder of imperial days, this showplace served as a city residence for the Prussian rulers. The gorgeous palace started as a modest royal summer residence in 1695, built on the orders of King Friedrich I for his wife, Sophie-Charlotte. In the 18th century Frederick the Great made a number of additions, such as the dome and several wings designed in the rococo style. By 1790 the complex had evolved into a massive royal domain that could take a whole day to explore. Behind heavy iron gates, the Court of Honor—the front courtyard—is dominated by a baroque statue of the Great Elector on horseback.

The **Altes Schloss,** also called the Nering-Eosander-Bau (☎ 030/3209–1275, 🎫 €8 [with tour]; ⏲ Tues.–Sun. 10–5), is the main building with the suites of Friedrich I and his wife. Paintings include royal portraits by Antoine Pesne, a noted court painter of the 18th century. On the first floor you can visit the Oak Gallery, the early 18th-century palace chapel, and the suites of Friedrich Wilhelm II and Friedrich Wilhelm III, furnished in the Biedermeier style.

The **Neuer Flügel** (New Wing; ☎ 030/3209–1202, 🎫 €5, ⏲ Tues.–Fri. 10–6, weekends 11–5), where Frederick the Great once lived, is also called the Knobbeldorff-Flügel. The 138-ft-long Goldene Galerie (Golden Gallery) was the palace's ballroom. West of the staircase are the rooms of Frederick, in which the king's extravagant collection of works by Watteau, Chardin, and Pesne are displayed. Visits to the royal apartments are by guided tour only; tours leave every hour on the hour from 9 to 4.

The park behind the palace was laid out in the French baroque style beginning in 1697 and was transformed into an English garden in the early 19th century. In it stand the Schinkel Pavilion and the **Belvedere teahouse** (☎ 030/320–911; 🎫 €2; ⏲ Nov.–Mar., Tues.–Fri. noon–4, weekends noon–5; Apr.–Oct., daily 10–5), which overlooks the lake and the Spree River and holds a collection of Berlin porcelain.

The **Museum für Vor- und Frühgeschichte** (Museum of Pre- and Early History; ⏲ Tues.–Fri. 10–3, weekends 11–4) traces the evolution of mankind from 1 million BC to the Bronze Age. It's in the western extension of the palace opposite Klausener Platz. ✉ *Luisenpl., Charlottenburg,* ☎ *030/326–7480,* WEB *www.smpk.de.* 🎫 *Museum: €3, free 1st Sun. of month. A Tageskarte (day card) for €7 covers the admission for all buildings.*

DINING

Diversity defines the scene in Berlin, with a few top dining rooms, many good ethnic eateries, and ever-opening hot spots where trends are launched. Most any restaurant-café you find will provide very decent meals.

CATEGORY	COST*
$$$$	over €20
$$$	€15–€20
$$	€10–€15
$	under €10

**per person for a main course at dinner*

Berlin Dining and Lodging

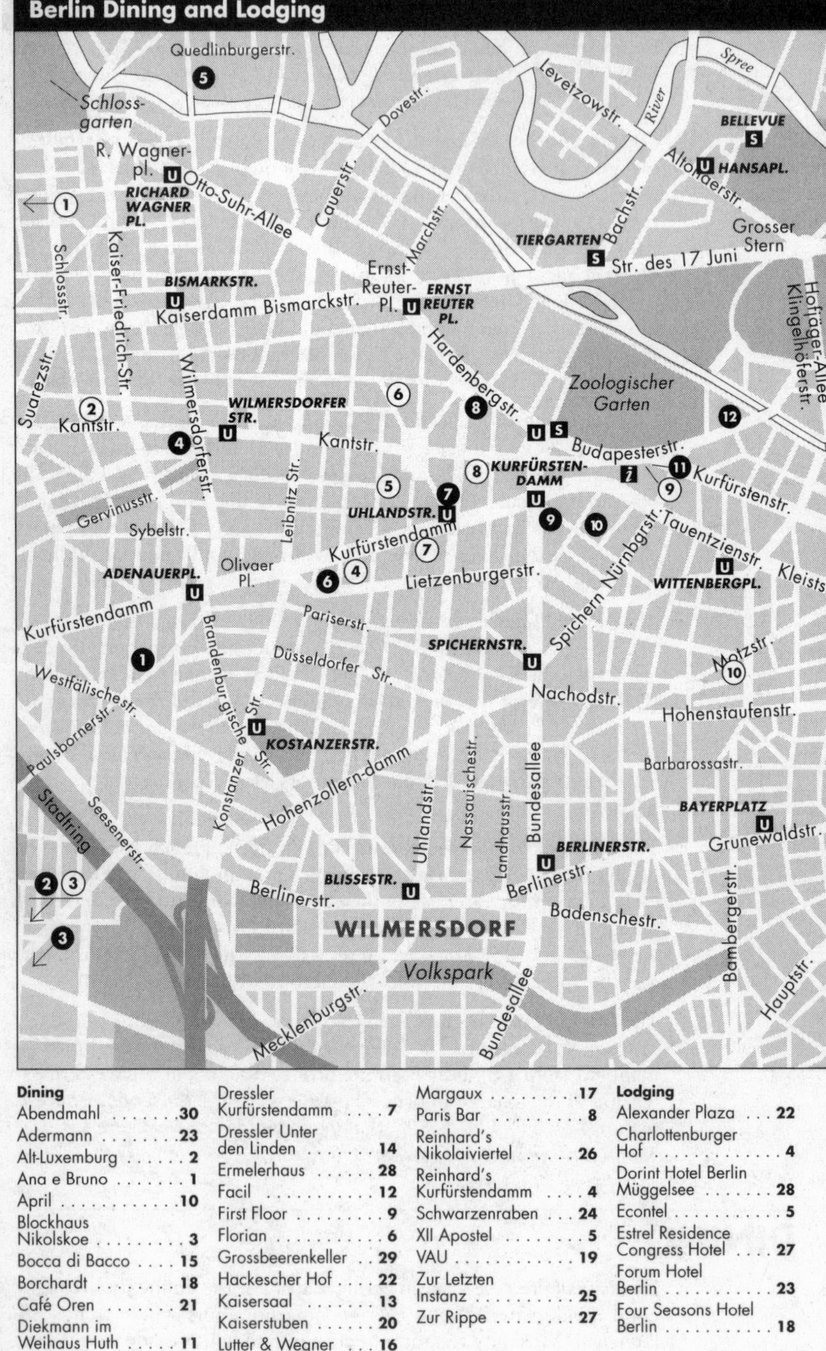

Dining
Abendmahl 30
Adermann 23
Alt-Luxemburg 2
Ana e Bruno 1
April 10
Blockhaus Nikolskoe 3
Bocca di Bacco 15
Borchardt 18
Café Oren 21
Diekmann im Weihaus Huth 11
Dressler Kurfürstendamm 7
Dressler Unter den Linden 14
Ermelerhaus 28
Facil 12
First Floor 9
Florian 6
Grossbeerenkeller . . 29
Hackescher Hof 22
Kaisersaal 13
Kaiserstuben 20
Lutter & Wegner . . . 16
Margaux 17
Paris Bar 8
Reinhard's Nikolaiviertel 26
Reinhard's Kurfürstendamm 4
Schwarzenraben . . . 24
XII Apostel 5
VAU 19
Zur Letzten Instanz 25
Zur Rippe 27

Lodging
Alexander Plaza . . . 22
Charlottenburger Hof 4
Dorint Hotel Berlin Müggelsee 28
Econtel 5
Estrel Residence Congress Hotel 27
Forum Hotel Berlin 23
Four Seasons Hotel Berlin 18

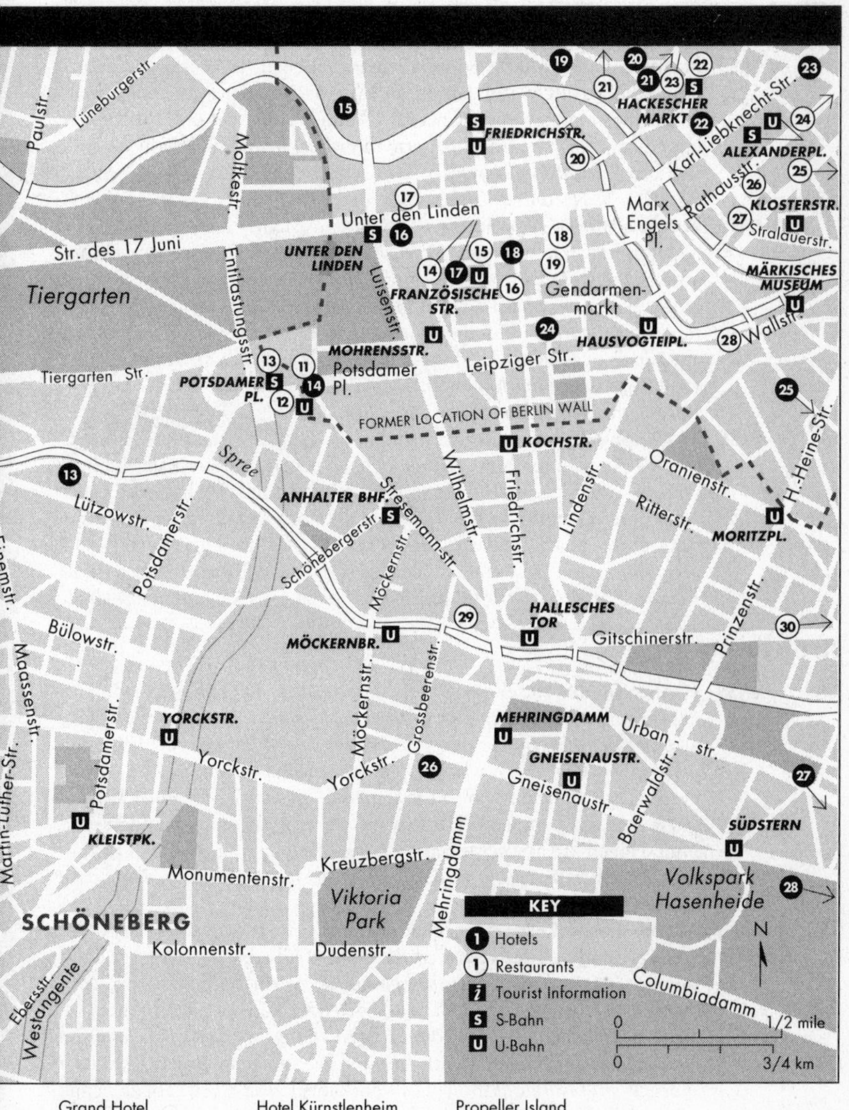

Grand Hotel Esplanade **13**
Grand Hyatt Berlin **14**
Heinrich-Heine City-Suites **25**
Hilton Berlin **24**
Hotel Adlon Berlin **16**
Hotel am Scheunenviertel **19**
Hotel Astoria **8**
Hotel Hackescher Markt **20**
Hotel Kürnstlenheim Luise **15**
Hotel Palace **11**
Hotel-Pension Dittberner **6**
Hotel-Pension Kastanienhof **21**
Inter-Continental Berlin **12**
Kempinski Hotel Bristol Berlin **7**
Landhaus Schlachtensee **2**
Propeller Island City Lodge **1**
Riehmers Hofgarten **26**
The Regent Schlosshotel Berlin **3**
Steigenberger Berlin **10**
Swissôtel Berlin **9**
Westin Grand Hotel **17**

Charlottenburg

$$$$ ★ ✕ **Alt-Luxemburg.** This popular restaurant has 19th-century-style furniture and wrought-iron lamps, and attentive service is one of the benefits of the intimate setting. Chef Karl Wannemacher uses only the freshest ingredients for his nouvelle German dishes, including his divine lobster lasagna. ✉ *Windscheidstr. 31, Charlottenburg,* ☎ *030/323–8730. AE, DC, V. No lunch. Closed Sun.*

$$$–$$$$ ★ ✕ **Ana e Bruno.** A Berlin classic with consistently high-quality offerings, this Italian restaurant is expensive but maintains a warm and homey atmosphere thanks to the hospitality of the owners Bruno and Ana. Don't expect hearty home cooking, though: the chef favors a low-calorie reinterpretation of Mediterranean cuisine and prefers fresh vegetables and salads over pasta. The four-course meals and daily specials are good value. ✉ *Sophie-Charlotten-Str. 101, Charlottenburg,* ☎ *030/325–7110. Reservations essential. AE. Closed Sun. and Mon.*

$–$$ ✕ **XII Apostel.** One of the nicest and liveliest Italian restaurants in Berlin, the XII Apostel made its debut with 12 pizzas, one for each biblical apostle—the biggest (and tastiest) is called the Judas. These and other pizzas are outstanding for their thin and crunchy crust; most people flock to this place, however, simply because it's hip. The colorful walls are reminiscent of Renaissance decorations in Italian churches. ✉ *Bleibtreustr. 49, Charlottenburg,* ☎ *030/312–1433. No credit cards.*

Kreuzberg

$–$$ ✕ **Abendmahl.** The exquisite vegetarian cuisine here proves that an inexpensive, meatless meal doesn't have to leave you hungry. Hearty creations have playful names such as *Flammendes Inferno* (Flaming Inferno), a fish curry whose spiciness means business. The campy desserts are particularly over the top, like *The Day I Shot Andy Warhol* (an ice cream sampler). Healthy eaters such as Wim Wenders and Nina Hagen are among the artsy crowd frequenting the small restaurant. ✉ *Muskauer Str. 9, Kreuzberg,* ☎ *030/612–5170. No credit cards.*

$ ★ ✕ **Grossbeerenkeller.** This cellar restaurant, with its massive, dark-oak furniture and decorative antlers, is undoubtedly one of the most quaint dining spots in town. Its old-fashioned, warm Berlin hospitality is hard to find elsewhere. Owner and bartender Ingeborg Zinn-Baier presents such dishes as *Sülze vom Schweinekopf mit Bratkartoffeln und Remoulade* (diced pork with home fries and herb sauce), *Kasseler Nacken mit Grünkohl* (boiled salt pork meat with green cabbage), and other traditional Berlin meals. Her fried potatoes are famous. ✉ *Grossbeerenstr. 90, Kreuzberg,* ☎ *030/251–3064. No credit cards. Closed Sun. and holidays.*

Mitte

$$$$ ★ ✕ **Adermann.** Nestled in an old city mansion in the Scheunenviertel, the Adermann brings some glamour to a district that still bears the peculiar charm of decay from the grim days of post-World War II. The French restaurant, which was awarded its first Michelin-star in 2001, is on the second floor, the so-called *bel étage*. The doors are decorated with gold leaf, and the wooden parquet floor is so precious it's protected under glass. The menu prepared by chef Wolfgang Müller changes daily, but the emphasis is definitely on French fish and game dishes (including fresh oysters at very reasonable prices). ✉ *Oranienburger Str. 27, Mitte,* ☎ *030/2838–7371. Reservations essential. AE, DC, MC, V. No lunch. Closed Mon.*

$$$$ ★ ✕ **Bocca di Bacco.** Hip Bocca di Bacco, the city's newest Italian restaurant, is the talk of the town primarily because of its down-to-earth yet high-quality blend of charming atmosphere and cuisine. Homemade pasta dishes, surprisingly hearty Northern Italian classics (with an emphasis on wild-game and fish) and an equally tasty assortment of desserts make for authentic Italian cooking—perhaps even Berlin's finest. The unbeatable three-course prix-fixe lunch is just €18. ✉ *Friedrichstr. 167–168, Mitte,* ☎ *030/2067–2828. AE, DC, MC, V.*

$$$$ ★ ✕ **Borchardt.** This is one of the most fashionable celebrity meeting places that have sprung up in Mitte. The high ceiling, red-plush benches, art nouveau mosaic (discovered during renovations), and columns create the impression of a 1920s café. The cuisine is high-quality French-Mediterranean, including several dishes with fresh fish, veal, and some of Berlin's best (and most tender) beef classics. ✉ *Französische Str. 47, Mitte,* ☎ *030/2038–7110. Reservations essential. AE, V.*

$$$$ ✕ **Ermelerhaus.** Within the artotel Berlin, the Ermelerhaus is two restaurants under one roof. The more traditional Raabediele and its Tabaklounge cook up good old German dishes. The Ermelerhaus à la carte restaurant relies on an exceptional Mediterranean cuisine (with an accent on seafood) to attract both a style-oriented and a more conservative business clientele. Of the four rococo dining rooms, the lavish Rosenzimmer is one of the nicest historic dinner settings in Berlin. ✉ *Märkisches Ufer 10, Mitte,* ☎ *030/2406–2904. AE, DC, MC, V.*

$$$$ ★ ✕ **Kaiserstuben.** Next to the Pergamonmuseum, soft candlelight spills onto the cobblestone street, inviting diners to make their way down into the Kaiserstuben's half-basement. The restaurant (German for "Emperor's Parlor") serves ingeniously prepared cuisine that carefully balances regional heritage with influences from all over the world. Chef Christian Ramlau, a rising star in Berlin's gourmet firmament, surprises guests with constantly changing combinations such as *Zweierlei vom Lammcarré auf Balsamicolinsen* (variation of lamb carré on balsamico lentils). The wine list is one of the most extensive in Berlin. This is the perfect place in Mitte to dine in a sophisticated yet cozy environment. ✉ *Am Kupfergraben 6a, Mitte,* ☎ *030/2045–2980. AE, MC, V. Closed Sun. and Mon. No lunch.*

$$$$ ★ ✕ **Margaux.** Margaux's eclectic cuisine comes with a touch of French and plenty of imagination. Here, asparagus is not cooked, but fried; chicken breast is not broiled, but cooked in an aspic jelly, placed in a puff pastry and topped with fresh fruits. Any dinner should be complemented with wine—the experienced sommelier is happy to help you choose one from a list of almost 750 vintages. The interior design is urban in its stylishness and minimalism. ✉ *Unter den Linden 78, Mitte,* ☎ *030/2265–2611. Reservations essential. AE, DC, MC, V. Closed Sun.*

$$$$ ★ ✕ **VAU.** Trendsetter VAU ushered in the movement of expensive and hip restaurants to the Mitte district several years ago. The excellent German fish and game dishes prepared by Chef Kolja Kleeberg earned him a Michelin star. Daring combinations include *Ente mit gezupftem Rotkohl, Quitten und Maronen* (duck with selected red cabbage, quinces, and sweet chestnuts) and *Steinbutt mit Kalbbries auf Rotweinschalotten* (turbot with veal sweet bread on shallots in red wine). The VAU's cool interior is all style and modern art: it was designed by one of Germany's leading industrial designers. ✉ *Jägerstr. 54/55, Mitte,* ☎ *030/202–9730. Reservations essential. AE, DC, MC, V. Closed Sun.*

$$$–$$$$ ★ ✕ **Lutter & Wegner.** One of the city's oldest vintners (it has produced *Sekt*, German champagne, first developed here by actor Ludwig Devrient, since 1811), Lutter & Wegner has returned to its old historic location off Gendarmenmarkt. The dark wood-panelled walls, an equally elegant parquet floor and the charming service takes you back

to 19th-century Vienna. In fact, the cuisine is mostly Austrian with superb game dishes in winter (the lamb neck with a crust of fresh cheese is unbeatable) and, of course, a Wiener schnitzel with potato salad. ✉ *Charlottenstr. 56, Mitte, ☎ 030/202–9540. AE, MC, V.*

$$–$$$ ✕ **Reinhard's.** Friends meet here in the Nikolaiviertel to enjoy the carefully prepared entrées and to sample spirits from the amply stocked bar, all served by friendly, colorful tie–wearing waiters. The honey-glazed breast of duck, *Adlon,* is one its specialties. If you just want to hug the bar but find no room, don't despair; head two doors down to Italian Marcellino's (under the same management). Reinhard's second restaurant on Ku'damm is much smaller but more elegant. Both the menu and prices are the same. ✉ *Poststr. 28, Mitte, ☎ 030/242–5295;* ✉ *Kurfürstendamm 190, Western Downtown, ☎ 030/881–1621. Reservations essential. AE, DC, MC, V.*

$–$$$ ✕ **Hackescher Hof.** The restaurant's setting in the hopping Hackesche Höfe makes it without question one of the most *in* restaurants in Mitte and a great place to experience the upswing in the old East. With oversize industrial lamps, the large, high-ceiling rooms have an urban and breathless atmosphere. The food is a mixture of international nouvelle cuisine and beefy German cooking—there is also a special dinner menu with more refined dishes. Reservations are advised. ✉ *Rosenthaler Str. 40/41, Mitte, ☎ 030/283–5293. AE, MC, V.*

$–$$ ✕ **Café Oren.** This popular part-vegetarian eatery next to the Neue Synagoge buzzes with loud chatter all evening, and the atmosphere and service are friendly. The traditional Jewish cooking, long absent from the old Jewish quarter of Berlin, includes gefilte fish and *Bachsaibling in schämender Butter* (red-meat trout in hot butter). The small backyard is a wonderful spot to enjoy a cool summer evening or a warm autumn afternoon. ✉ *Oranienburger Str. 28, Mitte, ☎ 030/282–8228. AE, V.*

$–$$ ★ ✕ **Zur Letzten Instanz.** Established in 1621, Berlin's oldest restaurant combines the charming atmosphere of old Berlin with a limited (but very tasty) menu. Napoléon is said to have sat alongside the tile stove in the front room, and Mikhail Gorbachev sipped a beer here during a visit in 1989. The emphasis is on beer, both in the recipes and in the mugs. Service can be erratic, though always engagingly friendly. ✉ *Waisenstr. 14–16, Mitte, ☎ 030/242–5528. AE, DC, MC, V.*

$–$$ ✕ **Zur Rippe.** This popular place in the Nikolaiviertel serves wholesome food in an intimate setting of oak paneling and ceramic tiles. Specialties include the cheese platter and a herring casserole. ✉ *Poststr. 17, Mitte, ☎ 030/242–4248. AE, DC, MC, V.*

Prenzlauer Berg

$–$$$$ ★ ✕ **Schwarzenraben.** No other restaurant in Berlin exemplifies the arrival of the New East better than the Schwarzenraben. At its white-clothed tables, uncomfortably squeezed together in a long, narrow room, the rich and beautiful of the capital gather to enjoy their success. The environment is noisy and not very elegant. The cooking lets you discover new Italian recipes such as risotto made of quail breast and leg, port wine, and goat cheese. ✉ *Neue Schönhauser Str. 13, Prenzlauer Berg, ☎ 030/2839–1698. Reservations essential. AE, MC, V.*

Schöneberg

$$$$ ★ ✕ **First Floor.** Few hotel-restaurants are so outstanding that they become a sensation, but this Michelin star–holder is unique. It's even more unusual that Chef Matthias Buchholz succeeds with traditional German fare, and not with the typically favored spread of light nouvelle cuisine. The menu changes according to the season and the chef's moods, but most dishes are new interpretations of heavy German dishes such as *Müritzlammrücken in Olivenkruste mit Bohnenmelange* (Müritz lamb back in olive crust, served with green beans). ✉ *Hotel Palace, Budapester Str. 42, Schöneberg,* ☎ *030/2502–1020. Reservations essential. AE, DC, MC, V. No lunch Sat.*

$–$$ ★ ✕ **April.** In an old city mansion, April is far away from the hustle and bustle of Schöneberg's restaurant and bar scene. The clientele and service is unpretentious, and that holds true for the cuisine—a mixture of Italian, Turkish, French, and German cooking—as well. The cost of the consistently delicious meals is amazingly reasonable. One of the best deals is the *Vorspeisenteller* (selection of appetizers) for two, which is a full meal in itself, and includes couscous, marinated tomatoes, and other spicy finger foods from Mediterranean countries. Reservations are advised. ✉ *Winterfeldstr. 56, Schöneberg,* ☎ *030/216–8869. No credit cards.*

Tiergarten

$$$–$$$$ ✕ **Kaisersaal.** A century ago, Prussian princes used to dine here with gusto. These days, all are welcome to experience the several splendid rooms of the demolished, pre-war Grand Hotel Esplanade, whose remains have been integrated into the sleek Sony Center. Even though the Kaisersaal offers fine German cuisine with a French twist, people tend to come here more for the ambience than for the food. The 400 wines and the three-course prix-fixe menu for only €60 are this establishment's real gems. Its interior is crowned by a portrait of the last German Kaiser, His Majesty Wilhelm II, which keeps a watchful eye on the dining patrons. ✉ *Bellevuestr. 1, Tiergarten,* ☎ *030/2575–1454. AE, DC, MC, V.*

$$–$$$$ ★ ✕ **Facil.** If you can take your focus off your Mediterranean-inspired dish—perhaps fish, lobster, or squid—you might notice the exquisite design of this fifth-floor restaurant. The glass roof can retract, the wood is mahogany, and the floor is made of stone–an interior designer's dream that cost the hotel a whopping 3 million U.S. dollars. Chef René Conrad's light, minimalist cuisine is clearly directed at getting his first Michelin star as soon as possible. He certainly deserves one. ✉ *Hotel Madison, Potsdamer Str. 3, Tiergarten,* ☎ *030/5900–51234. AE, MC, V. Closed weekends.*

$$ ✕ **Diekmann im Weinhaus Huth.** The Dieckmann is a fascinating place to eat, not so much for the ordinary French cooking, as for its location. The old Weinhaus Huth once was the last building standing in the no-man's-land of Potsdamer Platz. Now it's surrounded by the shiny company headquarters of Sony and debis. The interior tries to imitate a Paris bistro but lacks some warmth, though service is smooth and friendly. One outstanding exception on the reliable menu is the fresh oysters and shrimp, which is less expensive than elsewhere in Berlin. ✉ *Alte Potsdamer Str. 5, Tiergarten,* ☎ *030/2529–7524. AE, MC, V.*

Western Downtown

$$$–$$$$ ✕ **Paris Bar.** Just off the Ku'damm, this trendy restaurant attracts a polyglot clientele of film stars, artists, entrepreneurs, and executives to whom food plays second fiddle to socializing. The cuisine, including such delights as Jacques oysters and lamb chops with Provençal herbs, is reliably French. ✉ *Kantstr. 152, Western Downtown,* ☎ *030/313–8052. AE.*

$$–$$$ ✕ **Dressler.** Both in its cuisine and in its service, the Dressler is a mixture of French brasserie culture and German down-to-earth reliability. Accordingly, the dishes are conceived for a wide range of palates: duck with red cabbage or cod with Pommery mustard sauce, for example. The menu changes according to season. Compared to other French restaurants in Germany, the Dressler's *plateaux de fruits de mer,* with oysters, lobster, and clams, is a good value and beautiful to behold as well. Of the two (very similar) Dressler establishments, the one on Kurfürstendamm is livelier, with a genuinely French atmosphere. Reservations are advised. ✉ *Kurfürstendamm 207/208, Western Downtown,* ☎ *030/883–3530;* ✉ *Unter den Linden 39, Mitte,* ☎ *030/204–4422. AE, DC, MC, V.*

$$–$$$ ★ ✕ **Florian.** In a big city such as Berlin, the idea of creating a series of dishes based on down-home Franconian cuisine might have seemed a joke were there not so many successful Swabians in Berlin. Florian has turned out to be one of the most popular restaurants in town. The food, a high-gear combination of Swabian cuisine with a slight French accent, is only one of the little place's draws: most come for the warm, relaxed atmosphere and the people-watching opportunities. ✉ *Grolmanstr. 52, Western Downtown,* ☎ *030/313–9184. Reservations essential. MC, V.*

Zehlendorf

$–$$ ✕ **Blockhaus Nikolskoe.** Prussian king Frederick Wilhelm III built this Russian-style wooden lodge for his daughter Charlotte, wife of Russian czar Nicholas I. South of the city, in Glienecker Park, it offers open-air, riverside dining in summer. Game dishes are the main specialty. Wannsee is the closest S-bahn station. ✉ *Nikolskoer Weg 15, Zehlendorf,* ☎ *030/805–2914. DC, MC, V. Closed Thurs.*

LODGING

As a European metropolis, Berlin attracts all major international first-class hotel chains. Even the luxurious ones are but a faint reminiscence of the prewar past, when Berlin was considered Europe's hospitality capital. Elegance and style were bombed to rubble during World War II, and only a few native havens were rebuilt. Moderately priced pensions and small hotels offering good value are common in such western districts as Charlottenburg, Schöneberg, or Wilmersdorf; many of them date from the turn of the 20th century.

Year-round business conventions and the influx of summer tourists mean you should make reservations well in advance. If you arrive without reservations, consult hotel boards at airports and train stations, which show hotels with vacancies; or go to the tourist offices at Tegel Airport, at the Ostbahnhof or Zoologischer Garten train stations, or in the Europa Center for help with reservations.

CATEGORY	COST*
$$$$	over €225
$$$	€150–€225
$$	€75–€150
$	under €75

**All prices are for two people in a double room, including tax and service.*

Charlottenburg

$$ 🏨 **Econtel.** This family-oriented hotel is within walking distance of Charlottenburg Palace. The spotless rooms have a homey feel. Family rooms have four beds and are especially decorated for children. A crib, bottle warmer, and kiddie toilet are available on request free of charge. The breakfast buffet provides a dazzling array of choices to fill you up for a day of sightseeing. ✉ *Sömmeringstr. 24–26, Charlottenburg, D–*

10589, ☎ *030/346–810,* FAX *030/3468–1163,* WEB *www.econtel.de. 205 rooms. Restaurant, no a/c, in-room safes, cable TV, bar, baby-sitting, dry cleaning, laundry service, meeting room, parking (fee), some pets allowed (fee), no-smoking rooms. AE, MC, V.*

$–$$ ★ **Charlottenburger Hof.** A convenient location across from the Charlottenburg S-bahn station makes this low-key hotel a great value for no-fuss travelers. The variety of rooms, all brightened by primary-color schemes and prints by Kandinsky, Miró, and Mondrian, can suit travelers from friends to couples to families. Whether facing the street or the courtyard, all rooms receive good light; room amenities include hair dryers. The 24-hour café serves healthy dishes and draws locals, too. The Ku'damm is a 10-minute walk, taxis are easy to catch at the S-bahn station, and the bus to and from Tegel Airport stops a block away. ✉ *Stuttgarter Pl. 14, Charlottenburg, D–10627,* ☎ *030/329–070,* FAX *030/323–3723,* WEB *www.charlottenburger-hof.de. 46 rooms. Restaurant, no a/c, in-room safes, cable TV, lounge, laundry facilities, laundry service, parking (fee), some pets allowed (fee), no-smoking rooms. MC, V.*

$–$$ ★ **Propeller Island City Lodge.** One of Berlin's most eccentric accommodations is the creation of multitalented artist Lars Stroschen. Within his home are wildly creative rooms, such as the dizzying Symbol Room and the monastic Orange Room. Only children get to escape to the low-ceilinged Gnome Room, which keeps out those over 4′ 8″. There's use of a shared kitchen. ✉ *Albrecht-Achilles-Str. 58, Charlottenburg, D–10709,* ☎ *030/891–9016,* FAX *030/8928–721,* WEB *www.propeller-island.de. 27 rooms. No TV in some rooms, no room phones, some pets allowed. V.*

Köpenick

$$ **Dorint Hotel Berlin Müggelsee.** In the southeastern outskirts of the city, Berlin's largest and some say most beautiful lake is just beyond your balcony here. Rooms are comfortable and fairly spacious, and each floor has a different style; rooms on the ground floor are furnished with heavy, dark German woods; the second floor, which many guests find the most attractive for its airy environment, has an Italian accent (with elegant cherrywood furniture); and the third floor is reminiscent of a Japanese house. This a good alternative to the first-class hotels in the downtown areas; Unter den Linden is only a 20-minute drive away. ✉ *Am Grossen Müggelsee, Köpenick D–12559,* ☎ *030/658–820,* FAX *030/6588–2267,* WEB *www.dorint-berlin.de. 172 rooms, 4 suites. 2 restaurants, room service, in-room data ports, in-room safes, minibars, cable TV with movies, tennis court, hair salon, health club, massage, sauna, steam room, boating, bicycles, billiards, bowling, bar, dry cleaning, laundry service, convention center, meeting rooms, free parking, some pets allowed (fee), no-smoking rooms. AE, DC, MC, V.*

Mitte

$$$$ ★ **Four Seasons Hotel Berlin.** One of Berlin's best hotels, the Four Seasons combines turn-of-the-20th-century luxury (reminiscent of the *Grand Hotel* of Vicki Baum's novel) with such modern conveniences as portable phones for the business traveler. The large guest rooms have first-class amenities, including free newspapers, overnight dry cleaning, and valet parking. Behind the modern facade, thick red carpets; heavy crystal chandeliers; and a romantic restaurant, complete with an open fireplace, create a sophisticated and serene aura. ✉ *Charlottenstr. 49, Mitte, D–10117,* ☎ *030/20338,* FAX *030/2033–6119,* WEB *www.fourseasons.com. 162 rooms, 42 suites. Restaurant, room service, in-room data ports, minibars, cable TV with movies and video games,* *gym, massage, sauna, bar, baby-sitting, dry cleaning, laundry service, concierge, business services, meeting room, parking (fee), some pets allowed (fee), no-smoking rooms. AE, DC, MC, V.*

$$$$ **Hilton Berlin.** All the right touches are here, from heated bathtubs to special rooms for businesswomen and travelers with disabilities. It is also one of the few German first-class hotels offering discounts to parents traveling with children. Executive floor guests enjoy a private lounge, free breakfast, late check-in, and larger rooms. When making a reservation, ask for a second-floor room, which has classic Italianate furnishings. The Hilton overlooks the Gendarmenmarkt. ✉ *Mohrenstr. 30, Mitte D–10117,* ☎ *030/20230,* FAX *030/2023–4324,* WEB *www.hilton.com. 543 rooms, 46 suites. 2 restaurants, cafeteria, room service, in-room data ports, minibars, cable TV with movies and video games, pool, gym, massage, sauna, bar, baby-sitting, dry cleaning, laundry service, concierge, business services, meeting room, parking (fee), some pets allowed (fee), no-smoking rooms. AE, DC, MC, V.*

$$$$ ★ **Hotel Adlon Berlin.** Berlin's premiere hotel lives up to its almost mythical predecessor, the old Hotel Adlon, which, until its destruction during the war, was considered to be Europe's ultimate luxury resort, hosting the likes of Kaiser Wilhelm II and Greta Garbo. These days, the Adlon has become the unofficial guest house of the German government. The lobby is large and light, thanks to its creamy marble and limestone and its stained-glass cupola. The dark blue, garnet, and ocher color scheme continues in the guest rooms. All are identically furnished in 1920s style with cherrywood trim, myrtle-wood furnishings, and elegant bathrooms in black marble. The more expensive rooms overlook the Brandenburger Tor. ✉ *Unter den Linden 77, Mitte D–10117,* ☎ *030/22610,* FAX *030/2261–2222,* WEB *www.hotel-adlon.de. 337 rooms, 82 suites. 3 restaurants, café, room service, in-room data ports, in-room safes, minibars, room TVs with movies and video games, pool, hair salon, health club, massage, sauna, spa, 2 bars, shops, baby-sitting, dry cleaning, laundry service, concierge, business services, meeting room, parking (fee), some pets allowed (fee), no-smoking floor. AE, DC, MC, V.*

$$$–$$$$ ★ **Alexander Plaza.** In the heart of the Scheunenviertel, the Alexander Plaza is an ingenious combination of a 19th-century hotel and ultramodern and highly functional design. All rooms are done in bright earthy colors, using only natural materials for the parquet floors and fine curtains. The contrast between stucco ceiling and the old mosaic floor elsewhere in the hotel, along with the steel and glass, is striking. The hotel has evolved as a prime destination for a mostly European, trendy clientele. For €280, you can get one of the Executive Suites, which are large corner rooms in the four turrets. ✉ *Rosenstr. 1, Mitte, D–10178,* ☎ *030/240–010,* FAX *030/2400–1777,* WEB *www.alexander-plaza.com. 84 rooms, 9 suites. Restaurant, bar, minibars, in-room data ports, room service, massage, sauna, gym, baby-sitting, dry cleaning, laundry service, concierge, business services, meeting rooms, parking (fee), some pets allowed (fee). AE, DC, MC, V.*

$$$–$$$$ ★ **Grand Hyatt Berlin.** Europe's first Grand Hyatt is probably also the most modern first-class hotel on the continent. The hotel's minimalist-style yet elegant architecture is a mix of Japanese and Bauhaus design elements. Large guest rooms (they start at 406 square ft) feature dark cherrywood furniture and marble bathrooms (accessed through Asian-style sliding doors). You'll get a wonderful view of Berlin from the top-floor gym and swimming pool, and businesspeople check into the Regency Club floor for special services. The hotel's Vox restaurant serves international and Asian cuisine; it whets the appetite with a "show kitchen," where you can watch the chef preparing your dinner. ✉ *Marlene-Dietrich-Pl. 2, Mitte, D–10785,* ☎ *030/2553–1234,* FAX *030/2553–1235,* WEB *berlin.hyatt.com. 327 rooms, 16 suites. Restaurant,*

café, room service, in-room data ports, in-room safes, minibars, room TVs with movies and video games, pool, gym, massage, sauna, spa, bar, baby-sitting, dry cleaning, laundry service, concierge, business services, meeting room, parking (fee), some pets allowed (fee), no-smoking floor. AE, DC, MC, V.

$$$–$$$$ **Westin Grand Hotel.** The service sometimes lacks a genuine first-class approach, but the setting and architecture of this grand hotel make it a preferred choice among American travelers. The neoclassical pink-marble lobby, with its soaring six-story atrium, has polished brass accents, stuccowork, and richly decorated wallpaper. Standard rooms are tastefully decorated in muted tones; bathrooms have large tubs. ✉ *Friedrichstr. 158–164, Mitte D–10117,* ☎ *030/20270,* FAX *030/2027–3419,* WEB *www.westin-grand.com. 358 rooms, 35 suites. 2 restaurants, room service, in-room data ports, minibars, room TVs with movies and video games, pool, hair salon, hot tub, sauna, bar, lobby lounge, shops, baby-sitting, children's programs, laundry service, concierge, business services, convention center, meeting room, parking (fee), some pets allowed (fee), no-smoking floor. AE, DC, MC, V.*

$$–$$$$ **Forum Hotel Berlin.** With its 40 stories, this hotel (owned by Inter-Continental) at the top of Alexanderplatz competes with the nearby TV tower for the title of tallest downtown landmark. As one of the city's largest hotels, it is understandably less personal, at times even unfriendly. The bright Swiss birchwood furniture has erased any reminders that this was once socialist East Berlin's showcase hotel. The casino is open until 3 AM. ✉ *Alexanderpl. 8, Mitte, D–10178,* ☎ *030/23890,* FAX *030/2389–4305,* WEB *www.interconti.com. 994 rooms, 12 suites. 3 restaurants, room service, in-room data ports, minibars, room TVs with movies, gym, massage, sauna, bar, casino, baby-sitting, dry cleaning, laundry service, concierge, business services, meeting rooms, parking (fee), some pets allowed (fee), no-smoking floor. AE, DC, MC, V.*

$$$ **Hotel Hackescher Markt.** Not far from the nightlife around the Hackescher Markt and Rosenthaler Platz, this hotel provides discreet and inexpensive first-class services. The hotel doesn't have its own gym or pool, but guests can use the facilities of the Hotel Alexander-Plaza nearby. Unlike those of many older hotels in eastern Berlin, guest rooms here are spacious and light and furnished with bright pine furniture in the rustic but charming English cottage style. In winter, you'll appreciate the underfloor heating in your room, and in summer, you can enjoy a coffee in the small courtyard. The staff is quite friendly and attentive. ✉ *Grosse Präsidentenstr. 8, Mitte, D–10178,* ☎ *030/280–030,* FAX *030/2800–3111,* WEB *www.hackescher-markt.com. 28 rooms, 3 suites. No a/c, room service, in-room data ports, in-room safes, minibars, cable TV, bar, baby-sitting, dry cleaning, laundry service, parking (fee), some pets allowed (fee), no-smoking rooms. AE, DC, MC, V.*

$$ **Heinrich-Heine City-Suites.** Named after rebellious German poet Heinrich Heine, this apartment hotel close to the historic Nikolai Quarter primarily caters to business travelers on an extended stay. Even if you only want to spend a couple of days, the junior suites are a great deal. All rooms are tastefully decorated with timeless furniture and have a full kitchen as well a minioffice. The wide variety of extra services include a newspaper and fresh German rolls every morning. ✉ *Heinrich-Heine-Pl. 11, Mitte, D–10179,* ☎ *030/278–040,* FAX *030/2780–4780. 38 apartments. No a/c, room service, cable TV, kitchenettes, concierge, parking (fee), some pets allowed (fee), no-smoking rooms. AE, DC, MC, V.*

$$ ★ **Hotel-Pension Kastanienhof.** This small hotel in a 19th-century tenement house represents the working-class counterpart to the more luxurious pensions in the western part of Berlin. The rooms are simply furnished, but spacious and equipped with amenities usually found only in first-class hotels. The Kastanienhof is an excellent deal for those bent on exploring the hip nightlife in Prenzlauer Berg and Mitte. ✉ *Kastanienallee 65, Mitte, D–10119,* ☎ *030/443–050,* FAX *030/4430–5111,* WEB *www.hotel-kastanienhof-berlin.de. 34 rooms, 2 apartments. No a/c, in-room safes, cable TV, bicycles, bar, dry cleaning, laundry service, meeting room, parking (fee), no-smoking rooms. MC, V.*

$–$$ **Hotel am Scheunenviertel.** This simply furnished but well-kept small hotel is a good alternative to equally inexpensive pensions in western Berlin. It offers personal service, a wonderful breakfast buffet, and three restaurants (Mexican, Russian, and German) under one roof. The biggest advantage is its location in the old Jewish neighborhood around the Neue Synagogue. If you want to indulge in Berlin's hip nightlife, you'll be near the major cultural and entertainment hot spots. ✉ *Oranienburger Str. 38, Mitte, D–10117,* ☎ *030/282–2125,* FAX *030/282–1115. 18 rooms with shower. 3 restaurants, no a/c, cable TV, dry cleaning, laundry service, parking (fee), some pets allowed (fee). AE, DC, MC, V.*

$–$$ ★ **Hotel Künstlerheim Luise.** This hotel's name, which means "home for artists," suggests little more than a run-down bohemian commune, but nothing could be farther from the truth. The Künstlerheim is one of Berlin's most originalboutique hotels, with 30 rooms each designed and furnished by a different German artist. The fantastically creative room designs range from pop to sober classicism to modern minimalism. A small French breakfast is included in the price, and the location of the 1825 house makes it perfect for exploring the Scheunenviertel. ✉ *Luisenstr. 19, D–10117,* ☎ *030/284–480,* FAX *030/2844–8448,* WEB *www.kuenstlerheim-luise.de. 32 rooms, 1 suite. Brasserie, no a/c, no TV in some rooms, in-room data ports, in room safes, cable TV, some pets allowed. AE, DC, MC, V.*

Neukölln

$$ **Estrel Residence Congress Hotel.** Europe's biggest hotel may seem huge and anonymous, but it's the best deal in town for upscale rooms and service. The hotel is in the unappealing working-class district of Neukölln, some 20 minutes away from the downtown areas. But the modern hotel offers all amenities you can think of and guarantees quiet efficiency and smooth comfort at incredibly low prices. Rooms are decorated with Russian art. The lobby hall is a breathtakingly bright atrium with water basins, plants, and huge trees. The festival center adjoining the hotel features musicals. ✉ *Sonnenallee 225, Neukölln, D–12057,* ☎ *030/68310,* FAX *030/6831–2345,* WEB *www.estrel.com. 1,045 rooms, 80 suites. 6 restaurants, in-room data ports, minibars, cable TV with movies, gym, hair salon, sauna, bar, lobby lounge, theater, baby-sitting, children's programs, dry cleaning, laundry service, concierge, business services, convention center, parking (fee), some pets allowed (fee), no-smoking floor. AE, DC, MC, V.*

Schöneberg

$$$$ **Grand Hotel Esplanade.** The Grand Hotel Esplanade exudes luxury in its uncompromisingly modern design, its stylish rooms, and its artworks by some of Berlin's most acclaimed artists. Many rooms on the upper floors have panoramic views of the city, though the furnishings, a homage to the cool Bauhaus style, may not be to everyone's taste. Superb facilities and impeccable service are at your disposal. The enormous Panorama grand suite comes complete with fireplace, two bedrooms, sauna, whirlpool, and a grand piano—for €2,000 per night. ✉ *Lützowufer 15, Schöneberg, D–10785,* ☎ *030/254–780,* FAX *030/*

2547–88617, WEB *www.esplanade.de. 347 rooms, 39 suites. 3 restaurants, room service, in-room data ports, minibars, room TVs with movies, pool, gym, hot tub, sauna, steam room, bicycles, bar, lobby lounge, piano, shops, baby-sitting, dry cleaning, laundry service, concierge, business services, convention center, meeting room, parking (fee), some pets allowed (fee), no-smoking rooms. AE, DC, MC, V.*

$$ ★ **Riehmers Hofgarten.** The small rooms may be too spartan for many travelers, but they are modern, quiet, and functional. The Riehmers's true appeal comes from its location in an impressive, late-19th-century tenement house in the Kreuzberg district and in its special courtyard. The architecture, with its richly decorated facade, hints that 100 years ago the aristocratic officers of Germany's imperial army lived here. ✉ *Yorckstr. 83, Kreuzberg, D–10965,* ☎ *030/7809–8800,* FAX *030/7809–8808,* WEB *www.hotel-riehmers-hofgarten.de. 20 rooms. Restaurant, no a/c, room service, cable TV, bar, laundry service, parking (fee), some pets allowed (fee), no-smoking room. AE, MC, V.*

Western Downtown

$$$$ ★ **Hotel Palace.** This is the only first-class hotel directly in the heart of the western downtown, and probably the only hotel of its calibre with each guest room individually decorated. The interior is mostly done in dark blues or reds and dark-color woods. The spacious business and corner suites are a good deal; you might also want to ask for the special Panda-Suite or the Zackebarsch-Suite, both personally designed by the hotel's directors. Due to its low profile, the hotel is a favorite among international film stars who attend the Berlin Film Festival in February. ✉ *Europa-Center, Budapester Str. 26, Western Downtown, D–10789,* ☎ *030/25020,* FAX *030/2502–1197,* WEB *www.palace.de. 239 rooms, 43 suites. 3 restaurants, room service, in-room data ports, in-room safes, minibars, room TVs with movies and video games, pool, hair salon, health club, hot tub, massage, sauna, steam room, 2 bars, shops, baby-sitting, dry cleaning, laundry service, concierge, business services, convention center, meeting room, parking (fee), some pets allowed (fee), no-smoking floor. AE, DC, MC, V.*

$$$$ **Inter-Continental Berlin.** Probably no other hotel epitomizes old West Berlin more than the "Interconti," which has recently undergone a much needed facelift. With new and larger rooms and a huge spa area with several sauna facilities, the "Interconti" hopes to draw tourists in addition to its usual crowd of business travelers. Still, it still lacks warmth and has a bland atmosphere. Rooms in the new east wing have large windows that overlook the Tiergarten, an intricate lighting system, and walk-in closets. Rooms in the older west wing are more classically decorated. The Club Inter-Continental rooms on the 7th and 8th floors come with their own lounge, meeting rooms, as well as many other extras amenities. ✉ *Budapester Str. 2, Western Downtown, D–10787,* ☎ *030/26020,* FAX *030/2602–2600,* WEB *www.berlin.interconti.com. 510 rooms, 67 suites. 3 restaurants, room service, in-room data ports, minibars, room TVs with movies and video games, pool, gym, hot tub, sauna, bar, baby-sitting, dry cleaning, laundry service, concierge, business services, convention center, meeting room, parking (fee), some pets allowed (fee), no-smoking floor. AE, DC, MC, V.*

$$$$ **Kempinski Hotel Bristol Berlin.** Destroyed in the war and rebuilt in 1952, the "Kempi" is a renowned Berlin classic. It has the best shopping at its doorstep on Ku'damm and some fine boutiques of its own. All rooms and suites are luxuriously decorated and have marble bathrooms. Reserve a room in the "superior" category, which will give you all the elegance you'll need at a fair rate. Children under 12 stay for free if they share their parents' room. ✉ *Kurfürstendamm 27, West-*

ern Downtown, D–10719, ☎ *030/884–340,* FAX *030/8843–4805,* WEB *www.kempinski-berlin.de. 301 rooms, 52 suites. 2 restaurants, room service, in-room data ports, minibars, cable TV with movies and video games, pool, gym, hair salon, massage, sauna, bar, lobby lounge, shops, baby-sitting, dry cleaning, laundry service, concierge, business services, meeting room, parking (fee), some pets allowed (fee), no-smoking rooms. AE, DC, MC, V.*

$$$$ **Swissötel Berlin.** This ultra-modern hotel opened in mid-2001 and goes the distance in delivering its reputable Swiss hospitality. Rooms here are larger than at comparable hotels, and the Swiss food is high-quality. The biggest advantage here, however, may be the location at the corner of Ku'damm and Joachimsthaler Strasse. Don't worry about the traffic noise: all rooms have sound-proof windows, and the nightly view of the high-rises and bright city lights is fantastic. ✉ *Augsburger Str. 44 (corner of Kurfürstendamm, Western Downtown, D–10789,* ☎ *030/220–100,* FAX *030/2201–02222,* WEB *www.swissotel.com. 315 rooms, 31 suites. Restaurants, room service, in-room data ports, minibars, cable TV with movies and video games, health club, hot tub, massage, sauna, bar, baby-sitting, dry cleaning, laundry service, concierge, business services, meeting rooms, parking (fee), some pets allowed (fee), no-smoking rooms. AE, DC, MC, V.*

$$$–$$$$ **Steigenberger Berlin.** This exemplary hotel is very central, only steps from the Ku'damm, but remarkably quiet. Little things that can make your day are the umbrella on loan, extra-large towels, double sinks, and 24-hour room service. Bathrobes and a keyboard to access the Internet through the TV are available on request. The 6th-floor Executive Club rooms include late check-out, ironing and shoe-shine service, and a lounge where complimentary breakfast, afternoon tea, and evening cocktails are served. ✉ *Los-Angeles-Pl. 1, Western Downtown, D–10789,* ☎ *030/21270,* FAX *030/212–7799,* WEB *www.steigenberger.de. 397 rooms, 11 suites. 2 restaurants, bar, piano bar, room service, in-room data ports, Internet, in-room safes, minibars, cable TV with movies and video games, pool, massage, sauna, baby-sitting, dry cleaning, laundry service, concierge, meeting room, parking (fee), some pets allowed, no-smoking floor. AE, DC, MC, V.*

$$ **Hotel Astoria.** This privately owned and run hotel is one of the most traditional in Berlin. It provides every service with a personal touch. Rooms are spacious, though the 1980s furniture may seem outdated. The location is good for exploring the Ku'damm area, yet it's a quiet side street. Weekend specials offer discounts of €11 (single) or €3 (double) per night for a two-night stay. There's also several package deals for stays of up to six nights. ✉ *Fasanenstr. 2, Western Downtown, D–10623,* ☎ *030/312–4067,* FAX *030/312–5027. 31 rooms, 1 suite. No a/c, cable TV, room service, in-room safes, minibars, bar, dry cleaning, laundry service, parking (fee), some pets allowed, no-smoking rooms. AE, DC, MC, V.*

$$ ★ **Hotel-Pension Dittberner.** If you want to stay in a real Berlin pension, this is the place to go. The Dittberner, close to Olivaer Platz and next to the Ku'damm, is a typical, family-run, small hotel in a turn-of-the-20th-century house. The service sometimes may be a bit disorganized, and some of the furniture in the large rooms a little worn, but the warm atmosphere, breakfast buffet, and good rates more than make up for it. ✉ *Wielandstr. 26, Western Downtown, D–10707,* ☎ *030/884–6950,* FAX *030/885–4046. 22 rooms. No a/c, cable TV, dry cleaning, laundry service, concierge, meeting room, pets allowed. No credit cards.*

Zehlendorf

$$$$ **The Regent Schlosshotel Berlin.** The small but extremely luxe Schlosshotel regained its lofty reputation after being taken over by the Regent hotel group. In the beautiful, verdant setting of the Grunewald, the palacelike hotel is full of classic style and is lavishly decorated. You might be reminded of a late 19th-century château. It was designed by Chanel's Karl Lagerfeld, who also completed a special suite for himself, which is made available to guests if the master himself is not staying in Berlin. The service is amazingly personal but never intruding. ✉ *Brahmsstr. 10, Zehlendorf, D–14193,* ☎ *030/895–840,* FAX *030/8958–4800,* WEB *www.regenthotels.com. 54 rooms. Restaurant, room service, cable TV, in-room data ports, minibars, pool, gym, hair salon, massage, sauna, bar, lobby lounge, baby-sitting, dry cleaning, laundry service, concierge, business services, meeting room, parking (fee), no-smoking rooms. AE, DC, MC, V.*

$$ **Landhaus Schlachtensee.** This villa bed-and-breakfast offers personal and efficient service, well-equipped rooms, and a quiet location. The nearby Schlachtensee and Krumme Lanke lakes beckon you to swim, boat, or walk along their shores. ✉ *Bogotastr. 9, Zehlendorf D–14163,* ☎ *030/809–9470,* FAX *030/8099–4747. 18 rooms. No a/c, cable TV, free parking, some pets allowed. AE, MC, V.*

NIGHTLIFE AND THE ARTS

The Arts

Today's Berlin has a tough task living up to the reputation it gained from the film *Cabaret.* In the 1920s it was said that in Berlin, if you wanted to make a scandal in the theater, you had to have a mother committing incest with *two* sons; one wasn't enough. Even if nightlife has toned down since the 1920s and '30s, the arts and the avant-garde still flourish. Detailed information about events is covered in the *Berlin Programm,* a monthly tourist guide to Berlin arts, museums, and theaters. The magazines *Prinz, tip,* and *zitty,* which appear every two weeks, provide full arts listings. For the latest information on Berlin's bustling house, techno, and hip-hop club scene, pick up *(030),* a free weekly. The only English-language magazine available is *Berlin–the magazine,* published four times a year by the city's tourist information center.

The **Berlin Festival Weeks,** held annually from August through September, include concerts, operas, ballet, theater, and art exhibitions. For information and reservations, write Berliner Festspiele GmbH (Kartenbüro, ✉ Schaperstr. 24, D–10719 Berlin, ☎ 030/2548–9100, FAX 030/2548–9230, WEB www.berlinerfestspiele.de).

If your hotel can't book a seat for you, you can go to one of several ticket agencies. **Showtime Konzert- und Theaterkassen** (✉ KaDeWe, Tauentzienstr. 21, Western Downtown, ☎ 030/217–7754; ✉ Wertheim, Kurfürstendamm 181, Western Downtown, ☎ 030/882–2500) has offices within the major department stores. The **Theaterkasse Centrum** (✉ Meinekestr. 25, Western Downtown, ☎ 030/882–7611) is a small agency, but employs a very informed and helpful staff. The **Hekticket offices** (✉ Karl-Liebknecht-Str. 12, off Alexanderpl., Mitte, ☎ 030/2431–2431; ✉ At Zoo-Palast, Hardenbergstr. 29a, Western Downtown, ☎ 030/230–9930) offers discounted and last-minute tickets. The magazine **tip** (✉ Potsdamer Str. 89, Tiergarten, ☎ 030/2404–0111, ⏲ weekdays 7–8, Sat. 7–2) operates a central ticket phone hot line.

Concerts

Among the major symphony orchestras and orchestral ensembles in Berlin is one of the world's best, the Berliner Philharmonisches Orchester, which resides at the **Philharmonie mit Kammermusiksaal** (✉ Herbert-von-Karajan-Str. 1, Tiergarten, ☎ 030/2548–8132 or 030/2548–8301). The Kammermusiksaal is dedicated to chamber music.

Grosser Sendesaal des SFB (✉ Haus des Rundfunks, Masurenallee 8–14, Charlottenburg, ☎ 030/30310) is part of the Sender Freies Berlin, one of Berlin's broadcasting stations, and the home of the Radio Symphonic Orchestra. **Konzerthaus Berlin**'s (✉ Schauspielhaus, Gendarmenmarkt, ticket office behind the building, at Charlottenstr. 56, 2nd floor, Mitte, ☎ 030/2030–92101) beautifully restored hall is a prime venue for classical music concerts. The concert hall of the **Universität der Künste** (University of Arts; ✉ Hardenbergstr. 33, Charlottenburg, ☎ 030/3185–2374) is Berlin's second largest.

Dance, Musicals, and Opera

Berlin's three opera houses also have their own ballet companies and host renowned guest productions and companies from around the world. The ballet at **Deutsche Oper Berlin** (✉ Bismarckstr. 34–37, Charlottenburg, ☎ 030/3410–249 or 030/343–8401) maintains a reputation for young, fresh, quasi-contemporary work. The opera company is solid and the staging grand. Most of the operas are sung in German at the **Komische Oper** (✉ Behrenstr. 55–57, Mitte, ☎ 030/4799–7400 or 01805/304–168). On the day of the performance, half-price tickets are sold at the box office on Unter den Linden 41. The small and alternative **Neuköllner Oper** (✉ Karl-Marx-Str. 131–133, Neukölln, ☎ 030/6889–0777) has showy, fun performances of long-forgotten operas as well as humorous musical productions. Tickets at the historic **Staatsoper Unter den Linden** (✉ Unter den Linden 7, Mitte, ☎ 030/2035–4555) are hard to come by, so book early. Maestro Daniel Barenboim's opera house primarily offers Wagner, but also fascinating symphony concerts.

For musicals such as *West Side Story* and *Cabaret* (all in German), head for the **Stella Musical Theater** (✉ Marlene-Dietrich-Pl. 1 Tiergarten, ☎ 01805/4444). The **Theater des Westens** (✉ Kantstr. 12, Western Downtown, ☎ 030/882–2888), one of Germany's best musical theaters, features popular American musicals staged by US companies and mediocre German copies. New musicals with German themes are also occasionally staged at the **Schiller-Theater** (✉ Bismarckstr. 110, Charlottenburg, ☎ 0800/248–9842).

One of the leading cultural institutions of Berlin's alternative scene has found a new home in Kreuzberg behind ruins of Anhalter Bahnhof. The **Neues Tempodrom** (✉ Askanischer Platz 4,, Kreuzberg, ☎ 030/6110–1313) features international rock and folk stars. Modern-dance performances as well experimental music and electronic and multimedia art are presented at the **Podewil** (✉ Klosterstr. 68–70, Mitte, ☎ 030/2474–9777). The renowned **Tanzfabrik** (✉ Möckernstr. 68, Kreuzberg, ☎ 030/786–5861) is still Berlin's best venue for young dance talents and the latest from Europe's avant-garde. The **Theater am Halleschen Ufer** (✉ Hallesches Ufer 32, Kreuzberg, ☎ 030/251–0941) is one of the best places in Europe to see contemporary dance. It also hosts fringe theater and solo performers, some in English.

Film

International and German movies are shown in the big theaters on Potsdamer Platz, and around the Ku'damm; the off-Ku'damm theaters show less-commercial films. Unless a film is marked OF or OV (Originalfassung or original version) or OmU (original with subtitles), it is probably dubbed. In February Berlin hosts the **Internationale Filmfestspiele** (☎ 030/254–890), a festival at which the Golden Bear award is bestowed on the best films, directors, and actors.

For undubbed, but often subtitled independent movies in English, go to the **Babylon** (✉ Dresdnerstr. 126, Kreuzberg, ☎ 030/614–6316). To watch the mainstream US, British, and French productions in their original and mostly not subtitled versions, head for the sleek **Sony Cinestar** (✉ Sony Center, Potsdamer Str. 4, Tiergarten, ☎ 030/2606–6260).

The latest blockbuster movies fill the 19 theaters (three of which always show American movies in their original versions) of the high-tech **Cinemaxx am Potsdamer Platz** (✉ Potsdamer Pl. 5, Tiergarten, ☎ 030/4431–6313).

Theater

Theater in Berlin is outstanding, but performances are usually in German. The exceptions are operettas and the (nonliterary) cabarets. The theater most renowned for both its modern and classical productions is the **Deutsches Theater** (✉ Schumannstr. 13, Mitte, ☎ 030/2844–1222 or 030/2844–1225). It has an excellent studio theater next door, the Kammerspiele (☎ 030/2844–1226), which has evolved as a thrilling playground for the country's most promising young directors, writers, and actors. Once the city's most experimental stage, the rebellious actors at the **Schaubühne am Lehniner Platz** (✉ Kurfürstendamm 153, Western Downtown, ☎ 030/890–023) have somewhat mellowed, but are still up to great performances.

The **Berliner Ensemble** (✉ Bertolt Brecht-Pl. 1, Mitte, ☎ 030/282–3160) is dedicated to Brecht and works of other international playwrights. The **Hebbel Theater** (✉ Stresemannstr. 29, Kreuzberg, ☎ 030/259–00427) showcases international theater and dance troupes. The **Renaissance-Theater** (✉ Hardenbergstr. 6, Charlottenburg, ☎ 030/312–4202) shows German productions of international hit drama plays. The plays at the small **Theater Zerbrochene Fenster** (✉ Fidicinstr. 3, Kreuzberg, ☎ 030/691–2932) tend to be heavy; there are sometimes performances in English. The shabby but popular **Volksbühne am Rosa-Luxemburg-Platz** (✉ Rosa-Luxemburg-Pl., Mitte, ☎ 030/247–6772 or 030/2406–5661) is unsurpassed for its aggressively experimental style. The program changes daily and the name of the day's play is posted on a large banner outside the theater.

For children's theater head for the world-famous **Grips Theater** (✉ Altonaer Str. 22, Tiergarten, ☎ 030/3974–7477), whose musical hit *Linie 1* about life in Berlin is still playing. In Kreuzberg, exquisite puppets bring fairy tales to life for young children at Berlin's oldest puppet theater, **Berliner Figuren Theater** (✉ Yorkstr. 59, Kreuzberg, ☎ 030/786–9815).

For English-language theater try the **Friends of Italian Opera** (✉ Fidicinstr. 40, Kreuzberg, ☎ 030/691–1211), presenting both classical British and American drama as well as modern productions.

Variety Shows, Comedy, and Cabaret

Berlin's variety shows can include magicians, circus performers, musicians, and classic cabaret stand-ups. Intimate and intellectually entertaining is **Bar jeder Vernunft** (✉ Spiegelzelt, Schaperstr. 24, Wilmersdorf, ☎ 030/883–1582), whose name is a pun, literally meaning "devoid of any reason." The **Chamäleon Varieté** (✉ Rosenthaler Str. 40/41, Mitte, ☎ 030/282–7118) has risen to stardom in the city's offbeat scene thanks to its extremely funny shows, and is fairly accessible to non-German speakers. The world's largest variety show takes place at the **Friedrichstadtpalast** (✉ Friedrichstr. 107, Mitte, ☎ 030/2326–2326), a glossy showcase for revues, famous for its female dancers. The **Wintergarten** (✉ Potsdamer Str. 96, Tiergarten, ☎ 030/2308–8230 or 030/2500–8888) pays romantic homage to the old days of Berlin's original variety theater in the 1920s.

Social and political satire has a long tradition in cabaret theaters. The **BKA–Berliner Kabarett Anstalt** (✉ Mehringdamm 34, Kreuzberg, ☎ 030/251–0112), not only features guest performances by Germany's leading young comedy talents, but also *Chanson* vocalists. Eastern Berlin's traditional cabaret is the **Distel** (✉ Friedrichstr. 101, Mitte, ☎ 030/204–4704). The **Grüner Salon** (✉ Freie Volksbühne, Rosa-Luxemburg-Pl., Mitte, ☎ 030/2859–8936) is one of Berlin's hip venues for live music, cabaret, dancing, and drinks. The programs change almost daily. The **Stachelschweine** (✉ Europa Center, Breitscheidpl., Western Downtown, ☎ 030/261–4795), Berlin's most traditional and oldest cabaret, carries on tradition with biting wit and style. The **Die Wühlmäuse** (✉ Pommernallee 2–4, offTheodor-Heus-Pl., Charlottenburg, ☎ 030/213–7047) is owned by one of Germany's most popular TV comedians.

Nightlife

In Berlin, as in most German big cities, the term "bar" connotes a somewhat upscale setting, where tall drinks and cocktails are served but not food or snacks. Most people frequent bars later in the evening, past 10 PM. Kneipen, by contrast, are more down-to-earth places and comparable to English pubs. Many of the places listed are open until the wee hours of the morning. For a midday beer, try the Tiergarten's beer garden on Lichtensteinallee. There's food available and the picnic tables are shaded by trees.

Bars

In general, the most elegant bars and lounges in Berlin congregate around Mitte's Gendarmenmarkt. The cocktail menu is the size of a small guidebook at **Bar am Lützowplatz** (✉ Am Lützowpl. 7, Tiergarten, ☎ 030/262–6807) and the blonde-wood bar has the longest counter in town. Watch the attractive clientele sauntering in from an outdoor table. The Grand Hotel Esplanade's **Harry's New York Bar** (✉ Am Lützowufer 15, Tiergarten, ☎ 030/2547–8821) is the best lobby bar in town. It's also one of the few in the city that provides live piano music. Businessmen try to relax under the portraits of American presidents on the walls.

Kumpelnest 3000's (✉ Lützowstr. 23, Tiergarten, ☎ 030/261–6918) reputation is as wild as its red carpeted walls. Adventurous nightclubbers can mingle on the improvised dance floor with the crowd of both gays and heteros. There's no tap beer and the Caipirinhas are among the better mixed drinks. In a former coal cellar, the hip **Lore.Berlin** (✉ Neue Schönhauser Str. 20, Mitte, ☎ 030/2804–5134) turns into a dancing club on Friday and Saturday nights, and is the best example of Berlin's hip lounge culture. The most stylish bar in Mitte, **Newton** (✉ Charlottenstr. 57, Mitte, ☎ 030/2061–2999) stretches Helmut Newton's larger-than-life photos of nude women across its 12-ft-high walls. The minimalist **Riva** (✉ Dirckstenstr/S-Bahnbogen No. 142., Mitte, ☎ 030/2477–2688 is the hot spot for Berlin's beautiful and young party crowd.

Casinos

On Potsdamer Platz, **Spielbank Berlin** (✉ Marlene-Dietrich-Pl. 1, Tiergarten, ☎ 030/255–990, WEB www.spielbank-berlin.de) is Berlin's posher casino. You can try your luck at roulette tables, three blackjack tables, and slot machines from 2 PM to 3 AM. The **Casino Berlin** (✉ Alexanderpl., Mitte, ☎ 030/2389–4113, WEB www.casino-berlin.de) isn't as fashionable and international as Spielbank Berlin, but it's worth a visit for its breathtaking location on top of the Forum Hotel at Alexanderplatz.

Clubs

High-tech **Blu** (✉ Marlene-Dietrich-Pl. 4, Tiergarten, ☎ 030/8261–882), high above Potsdamer Platz, plays soul and funk music on three floors. The crowd is mixed—teenagers from East Berlin dance next to young managers. The view of the Berlin skyline is magnificent. The mood at **Golgatha** (✉ Dudenstr. 48–64, in Viktoriapark, Kreuzberg, ☎ 030/785–2453) is easy-going and extremely flirtatious. A large student crowd splits up between the beer garden, pub, and a small dance floor every weekend.

A young crowd interested in experimentation turns out at **Cox Orange** (✉ Dircksenstr. 40, Mitte, ☎ 030/281–0508) for DJs and performers of underground, drum 'n' bass, and electronic music. DJs spin every night of the week at **Delicious Doughnuts** (✉ Rosenthaler Str. 9, Mitte, ☎ 030/283–3021), which has surly bouncers and really does serve doughnuts.

Berlin's largest disco, **Metropol** (✉ Nollendorfpl. 5, Schöneberg, ☎ 030/217–3680) also stages concerts, and is a magnet for younger Berliners and tourists. The dance floor upstairs is the scene of a magnificent laser light show. Its occasional (Sunday afternoon) gay dances and exhibitionist Kit-Kat-Club nights are hugely popular. The disco is open Friday and Saturday only.

Jam-packed **90 Grad** (✉ Dennewitzstr. 37, Tiergarten, ☎ 030/2300–5954) plays hip-hop, soul, and some techno and really gets going around 2 AM. Women come fashionably dressed and go right in, but men usually have to wait outside until they get picked by the doorman. **Sage-Club** (✉ Köpenicker Str. 78, Mitte, ☎ 030/278–9830, WEB www.sage-club.de) is the most popular of Berlin's venues for young professionals who dance to hip-hop, fusion, and some techno music.

Gay and Lesbian Bars

Berlin is unmistakably Germany's gay capital, and many Europeans come to partake in the diverse scene, which is concentrated in Schöneberg (around Nollendorfplatz) and Kreuzberg, and growing in Mitte and Prenzlauer Berg. Check out the magazines *Siegessäule, (030),* and *Sergej* (free and available at the places listed below as well as many others around town).

A gay thirtysomething crowd frequents the upscale **Lenz** (✉ Eisenacher Str. 3, Schöneberg, ☎ 030/217–7820). Close to Wittenbergplatz, the dance club **Connection** (✉ Welserstr. 24, Schöneberg, ☎ 030/218–1432) provides heavy house music and lots of dark corners. It's open Friday and Saturday, midnight until 6 AM. The decor and the energetic crowd at **Hafen** (✉ Motzstr. 18, Schöneberg, ☎ 030/211–4118) make it ceaselessly popular and a favorite singles mixer. At 4 AM people move next door to Tom's Bar, open until 6 AM.

You can get extensive information on gay life, groups, and events at **Mann-O-Meter** (✉ Bülowstr. 106, Schöneberg, ☎ 030/216–8008). Talks are held in the café, which has a variety of books and magazines. It's open weekdays 3–11, Saturday 3–10. **Schwuz** (✉ Mehringdamm 61, Kreuzberg, ☎ 030/693–7025) sponsors various events. Every Saturday starting at 11 PM there's an "open evening" for talk and dance.

Kneipen

Bars and pubs all come under the heading of *Kneipen*—the place around the corner where you stop in for a beer, a snack, and conversation—and sometimes to dance. Other than along Ku'damm and its side streets, the happening places in western Berlin are around Savignyplatz in Charlottenburg, Nollendorfplatz and Winterfeldplatz in Schöneberg, Ludwigkirchplatz in Wilmersdorf, and along Oranienstrasse and Wienerstrasse in Kreuzberg, as well as Lützowplatz in Tiergarten. In Mitte most of the action is north of and along Oranienburger Strasse, and around Rosenthaler Platz and the Hackesche Höfe. Kollwitzplatz is the hub in Prenzlauer Berg.

The city's hip and wildly dressed crowd gets together for outstanding cocktails at **Green Door** (⊠ Winterfeldstr. 50, Schöneberg, ☎ 030/215–2515), a Schöneberg classic. **Hackbarths** (⊠ Augustr. 49a, Mitte, ☎ 030/282–7706) is only one of many similar alternative bars and clubs in the Oranienburger Strasse neighborhood, mostly frequented by students. The understated and cool setting of **Keyser Soze** (⊠ Tucholskystr. 31, Mitte, ☎ 030/2859–9489) make it one of Berlin's trendiest pubs. The service may be sluggish, but the drinks and the atmosphere are just great. Old-World **E. & M. Leydicke** (⊠ Mansteinstr. 4, Schöneberg, ☎ 030/216–2973) is a must for out-of-towners. The proprietors operate their own distillery and have a superb selection of sweet wines and liqueurs.

Jazz Clubs

Berlin's lively music scene is dominated by jazz and rock. For jazz enthusiasts *the* events of the year are the summer **Jazz in the Garden** festival and the autumn international **Jazz Fest Berlin.** For information call the **Haus der Kulturen der Welt** (☎ 030/397–870).

A-Trane Jazzclub (⊠ Pestalozzistr. 105, Charlottenburg, ☎ 030/313–2550, WEB www.a-trane.de) is often used for live radio broadcasts or recordings. **B-Flat** (⊠ Rosenthaler Str. 13, Mitte, ☎ 030/280–6349, WEB www.b-flat.freepage.de) presents mostly young German artists almost every night. The jam sessions focus on free and experimental jazz. On Sunday, dancers come for tango night; call for details. The sizzling jazz at **Flöz** (⊠ Nassauische Str. 37, Wilmersdorf, ☎ 030/861–1000, WEB www.floez-berlin.de) sometimes accompanies theater presentations. **Quasimodo** (⊠ Kantstr. 12a, Charlottenburg, ☎ 030/312–8086, WEB www.quasimodo.de), the most established and popular jazz venue in the city, has a great basement atmosphere and a good seating arrangement.

OUTDOOR ACTIVITIES AND SPORTS

Biking

There are bike paths throughout the downtown area and the rest of the city. **Fahrradstation** (⊠ Bergmannstr. 9, Kreuzberg, ☎ 030/215–1566; ⊠ Rosenthaler Str. 40–41, Mitte, ☎ 030/2859–9895, WEB www.fahrradstation) rents mostly green bikes. You must leave your passport as a security deposit. Bikes are usually €10 a day. The company also offers reduced weekend rates. Call for their other Mitte locations. **Fahrrad Vermietung Berlin** (☎ 030/261–2094) rents black bikes with baskets, which they keep in front of the Marmorhaus movie theater on Kurfürstendamm, opposite the Gedächtniskirche. Bikes are rented by the day (not 24 hours). Rates are usually €10 a day, and you must leave either a €100 deposit or your passport as security. If no one is there, just wait; the attendant will return shortly.

Golf

Berlin's leading club is the **Golf- und Land Club Berlin-Wannsee e.V.** (✉ Am Golfweg 2, Zehlendorf, ☎ 030/806–7060), with a par-72, 18-hole course and a 9-hole course.

Jogging

The Tiergarten is the best place for jogging in the downtown area. Run down the paths parallel to Strasse des 17 Juni and back, and you'll have covered 8 km (5 mi). Joggers can also take advantage of the grounds of Charlottenburg Palace, 3 km (2 mi) around. For longer runs, anything up to 32 km (20 mi), make for the Grunewald. In general, all of these woods are safe.

Squash and Tennis

Ask your hotel to direct you to the nearest tennis court and squash center. **Tennis & Squash City** (✉ Brandenburgische Str. 53, Charlottenburg, ☎ 030/873–9097) has four tennis courts and nine squash courts. At **Tennisplätze am Ku'damm** (✉ Cicerostr. 55A, Charlottenburg, ☎ 030/891–6630), you can step right off the Ku'damm and onto a tennis court.

Swimming

There are public pools throughout the city, so there's bound to be at least one near where you're staying. For full listings ask at the tourist office. The Wannsee, the Halensee, and the Plötzensee all have beaches that get crowded during summer weekends. The huge, lakeside park **Strandbad Wannsee** (✉ Wannseebad-weg 25, Zehlendorf, ☎ 030/803–5612) attracts as many as 40,000 Berliners to its fine, sandy beach on a summer weekend. The **Olympia-Schwimmstadion** (✉ Olympischer Pl., Charlottenburg, ☎ 030/3081–3249, U-bahn: Olympiastadion) was made for the 1936 Olympic games and is overlooked by sculptures of athletes. The **Blub Badeparadies** lido (✉ Buschkrugallee 64, Neuköulln, ☎ 030/606–6060, U-bahn: Grenzallee) has indoor and outdoor pools, a sauna garden, hot whirlpools, and a solarium.

SHOPPING

Berlin is a city of alluring stores and boutiques. Despite its cosmopolitan gloss, shop prices are generally lower than in cities such as Munich and Hamburg.

Shopping Districts

Charlottenburg

The city's liveliest and most-famous shopping area is along Kurfürstendamm and its side streets, especially between Olivaer Platz and Breitscheidplatz. For trendier clothes try the boutiques along Fasanenstrasse, Knesebeckstrasse, Mommsenstrasse, Bleibtreustrasse, Schlüterstrasse, and Uhlandstrasse. Kantstrasse, west of the corner of Uhlandstrasse, has reemerged as a stylish shopping area. Most shops here offer home furniture and accessories or designer stationery.

Running east from Breitscheidplatz is Tauentzienstrasse, practically an extension of Ku'damm. At the end of it is Berlin's most celebrated department store, the Kaufhaus des Westens, or KaDeWe.

Mitte

The most elegant shops in historic Berlin are springing up along Friedrichstrasse, including the French Galeries Lafayette department store. Nearby Unter den Linden has a mix of expensive boutiques, including a Meissen ceramic showroom and tourist souvenir shops. Many smaller clothing and specialty stores populate the old district, Nikolaiviertel.

Department Stores and Arcades

The smallest and most luxurious department store in town, **Department Store Quartier 206** (✉ Friedrichstr. 71, Mitte, ☎ 030/2094–6240) offers primarily French women's and men's designer clothes, perfumes, and home accessories. **Galeries Lafayette** (✉ Französische Str. 23, Mitte, ☎ 030/209–480) is an intimate and elegant counterpart to KaDeWe. It carries almost exclusively French products, including designer clothes, perfume, and all the French produce you might need for preparing your own haute cuisine at home. At the north end of Alexanderplatz, **Galeria Kaufhof** (✉ Alexanderpl. 9, Mitte, ☎ 030/247–430, WEB www.kaufhof.de) is worth a visit for its food department.

The largest department store in Europe, classy **Kaufhaus des Westens** (KaDeWe; ✉ Tauentzienstr. 21, Western Downtown, ☎ 030/21210, WEB www.kadewe.de) even surpasses London's Harrods. It has a grand selection of goods on seven floors, as well as food and deli counters, champagne bars, restaurants, and beer bars on its two upper floors. The city's newest mall, **Potsdamer Platz Arkaden** (✉ Potsdamer Pl., Tiergarten, ☎ 030/255–9270), has shops such as Benetton, Esprit, and Eddie Bauer under high glass ceilings. All the upscale shops on the four floors of **Stilwerk** (✉ Kantstr. 17, Charlottenburg, ☎ 030/315–150, WEB www.stilwerk.de/berlin) cater to stylish home furnishings and accessories.

The elegant **Uhland-Passage** (✉ Uhlandstr. 170, Western Downtown) has leading name stores as well as cafés and restaurants. The **Kempinski Plaza** (✉ Uhlandstr. 181–183, Western Downtown) features exclusive boutiques and a pleasant atrium café.JS: yes, that's ok. Downtown **Wertheim** (✉ Kurfürstendamm 181, Western Downtown, ☎ 030/883–8152) is neither as big nor as attractive as KaDeWe, but offers a large selection of fine wares.

Gift Ideas

If you long to have the Egyptian Museum's Queen Nefertiti bust on your mantelpiece at home, check out the state museum's shop, **Gipsformerei der Staatlichen Museen Preussischer Kulturbesitz** (✉ Sophie-Charlotten-Str. 17-18, Charlottenburg, ☎ 030/326–7690), open weekdays 9–4. It sells plaster casts of treasures from the city's museums. All the books, posters, and souvenirs focus on the city at **Berlin Story** (✉ Unter den Linden 10, Mitte, ☎ 030/2045–3842). Fine porcelain is still produced by **Königliche Porzellan Manufaktur** (✉ Kurfürstendamm 27, Western Downtown, ☎ 030/886–7210; ✉ Unter den Linden 35, Mitte, ☎ 030/206–4150), the former Royal Prussian Porcelain Factory, also called KPM. You can buy this delicate handmade, hand-painted china at KPM's two stores, but it may be more fun to visit the factory salesroom (✉ Wegelystr. 1, Charlottenburg, ☎ 030/3900–9215), which also sells seconds at reduced prices. You can buy kitschy props, costumes, and imitation antiques from the Komische Oper at **Kunstsalon** (✉ Unter den Linden 41, Mitte, ☎ 030/2045–0203).

Puppenstube im Nikolaiviertel (✉ Propststr. 4, Mitte, ☎ 030/242–3967) is the ultimate shop for any kind of (mostly handmade) dolls, including designer models as well as old-fashioned German dolls. Tucked under the elevated tram tracks, **Scenario** (✉ Savignypassage, Bogen 602, Western Downtown, ☎ 030/312–9199) sells stationery articles, gifts of any kind, and a lot of leather wares and jewelry. The designs here are always what's state-of-the-art in Europe. For stylish European furnishings, lamps, glass, porcelain, or stationery items, shop 'til you drop at **Wohnart Berlin** (✉ Uhlandstr. 179–180, Western Downtown, ☎ 030/882–5252).

Specialty Stores

Antiques

Not far from Wittenbergplatz lies Keithstrasse, a street full of antiques stores. Eisenacher Strasse, Fuggerstrasse, Kalckreuthstrasse, Motzstrasse, and Nollendorfstrasse—all close to Nollendorfplatz—have many antiques stores of varying quality. Another good street for antiques is Suarezstrasse, between Kantstrasse and Bismarckstrasse.

Berliner Antik- und Flohmarkt (☎ 030/208–2645) is one of the largest, more established, and expensive areas dealing in antique art. The series of stores offers everything from costly lamps to bargain books. Other antiques stores are found under the tracks at the Friedrichstrasse station, open Monday and Wednesday–Sunday 11–6. On weekends from 10 to 5, the colorful and lively **Berliner Kunstmarkt** (Berlin Art Market) on Strasse des 17. Juni swings into action. Don't expect to pick up many bargains. **Villa Grisebach** (✉ Fasanenstr. 25, Western Downtown, ☎ 030/885–9150, WEB www.villa-grisebach.de), one of the city's most classic arts and antiques auction houses, also hosts exhibitions and special events at which you can buy paintings.

Jewelry

Bucherer (✉ Kurfürstendamm 26a, Western Downtown, ☎ 030/880–4030, WEB www.bucherer.de) carries fine handcrafted jewelry, watches, and other stylish designer accessories. German designers featured at **Klaus Kaufhold** (✉ Kurfürstendamm 197, Western Downtown, ☎ 030/8847–1790) share a philosophy of sleek minimalism. Rubber and diamond rings and matte platinum and diamond pieces are conscious understatements of pure taste.

Men's Clothing

For guys who envy the diversity of wares offered to gals, **Boyz 'R' Us** (✉ Maassenstr. 8, Schöneberg, ☎ 030/2363–0640) is your chance to grab a pink-gingham shirt or spangly turquoise top. Patterned jeans and loud tartan pants make this store a magnet for gay and straight clubbers. Labels include Coration, the Berlin designers collective. Handmade and timeless shoes and brogues, mostly from England, Austria, and Hungary are sold at **Budapester Schuhe** (✉ Kurfürstendamm 199, Western Downtown, ☎ 030/881–1707, Friedrichstr. 81–82, Mitte, ☎ 030/2038–8110). The gentlemen's outfitter **Mientus** (✉ Wilmersdorfer Str. 73, Western Downtown, ☎ 030/3276–5430; ✉ Kurfürstendamm 52, Western Downtown, ☎ 030/323–9077, WEB www.mientus.com) stocks Armani, Jean Paul Gaultier, and Boss and has an in-house tailor.

Women's Clothing

The designs of **Anette Petermann** (✉ Bleibtreustr. 49, Western Downtown, ☎ 030/323–2556) are a delight of Berlin haute couture. Roses are her trademark, ruched into pinstripe jackets or taffeta stoles. Crushed organza evening wear or functional wool and fur are popular with local celebrities. The creations of Berlin's top avant-garde designer **Claudia Skoda** (✉ Kurfürstendamm 50, Western Downtown, ☎ 030/885–1009; ✉ Linienstr. 154, Mitte, ☎ 030/280–7211) are presented and sold in two locations. The shop on Linienstrasse has trendy fashion for younger women. The flagship store of German designer **Jil Sander** (✉ Kurfürstendamm 185, Western Downtown, ☎ 030/886–7020) carries her complete line of understated clothes. **Peek und Cloppenburg** (✉ Tauentzienstr. 19, Western Downtown, ☎ 030/212–900), or "P and C," stocks women's, men's, and children's clothes on five floors. Don't miss the Joop! designer store on the top floor and the international designer department in the basement.

SIDE TRIPS FROM BERLIN

A trip to Berlin wouldn't be complete without paying a visit to Potsdam and its Palace of Sanssouci, just a half-hour trip from Berlin via public transportation. The state of Brandenburg's lovely countryside is a pleasant surprise, with green meadows to the north and pine barrens to the east and south. The two rivers of the region, the Havel and the Spree, offer miles of unspoiled shores for walking.

Potsdam

Potsdam still retains the imperial character lent it by the many years during which it served as a royal residence and garrison quarters. The Alter Markt and Neuer Markt show off stately Prussian architecture, and both are easily reached from the main train station by any tram heading into the town center. Karl Friedrich Schinkel designed the Alter Markt's domed **Nikolaikirche.** In front of it stands an Egyptian obelisk erected by Schloss Sanssouci architect von Knobelsdorff. The gilded figure of Atlas tops the tower of the old **Rathaus,** built in 1755. In summer 2003, the region's history museum, the **Haus der Brandenburg-Preussischen Geschichte,** will open in the royal stables of the Neuen Markt. ✉ *Schlossstr. 1,* ☎ *0331/201–3949.* 🎫 *Fee varies.* ⏲ *Daily 10–6.*

The center of the small **Holländisches Viertel** (Dutch Quarter) is an easy walk north along Friedrich-Ebert-Strasse to Mittelstrasse. Friedrich Wilhelm I built the settlement in 1732 to entice Dutch artisans who could support the city's rapid growth. Few Dutch came, and the gabled, mansard-roof brick houses were largely used to house staff. Stores and restaurants inhabit the buildings now and the area is Potsdam's most visited.

NEED A BREAK? Fine coffee blends and rich cakes are offered at the **Wiener Restaurant-Café** (✉ Luisenpl. 4, ☎ 0331/967–8314), an old-style European coffeehouse opposite the Grünes Gitter entrance to Sanssouci. A favorite here is their *Sanssouci-Torte.*

Prussia's most famous king, Friedrich II—Frederick the Great—spent more time at his summer residence, **Sanssouci** in Potsdam, than in the capital Berlin. Its name means "without a care" in French, the language Frederick tried to cultivate in his own private circle and within the court. Some experts believe Frederick actually named the palace "Sans, Souci," which they translate as "with and without a care," a more apt name; its construction caused him a lot of trouble and expense and sparked furious rows with his master builder, Georg Wenzeslaus von Knobelsdorff. His creation nevertheless became one of Germany's greatest tourist attractions. To reach the palace from downtown, you can walk westward down Gutenbergstrasse or Brandenburger Strasse.

Executed according to Frederick's impeccable French-influenced taste, the palace, built between 1745 and 1747, is extravagantly rococo, with scarcely a patch of wall left unadorned. To the west of the palace are the **New Chambers** (☎ 0331/969–4206; 🎫 guided tour €3; ⏲ Apr.–mid-May, weekends 10–5; mid-May–mid-Oct., Tues.–Sun. 10–5), which housed guests of the king's family after its beginnings as a greenhouse. Just east of Sanssouci Palace is the **Bildergalerie** (Picture Gallery;

Berlin Side Trips

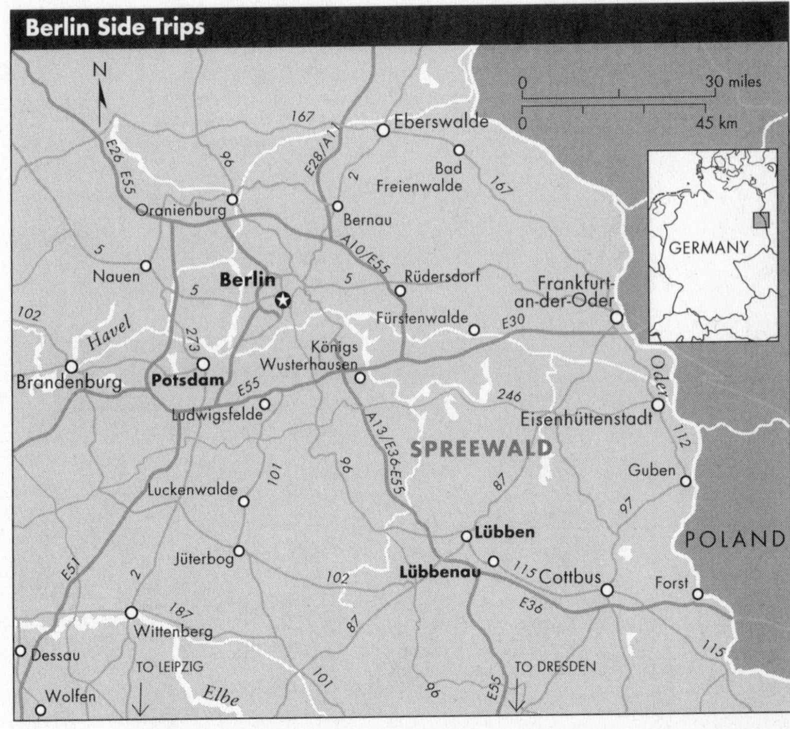

☎ 0331/969–4181; guided tour €3; mid-May–mid-Oct., Tues.–Sun. 10–5), with expensive marble from Siena in the main cupola. The gallery displays Frederick's collection of 17th-century Italian and Dutch paintings, including works by Caravaggio, Rubens, and Van Dyck. ✉ *Sanssouci Central Visitor Information, Besucherzentrum an der Historischen Mühle, Sanssouci,* ☎ *0331/969–4200; 0331/969–4201; 0331/969–4204 for recorded information,* WEB *www.spsg.de.* *Guided tour €8, entrance to park is free.* *Apr.–Oct., daily 9–5; Nov.–Mar., Tues.–Sun. 9–4.*

The **Neues Palais** (New Palace), a much larger and grander palace than Sanssouci, stands at the end of the long, straight avenue that runs through Sanssouci Park. It was built after the Seven Years' War (1756–63), when Frederick loosened the purse strings. It's said he wanted to demonstrate that the state coffers hadn't been depleted too severely by the long conflict. The Neues Palais has much of interest, including an indoor grotto hall with walls and columns set with shells, coral, and other aquatic decor. The upper gallery contains paintings by 17th-century Italian masters and a bijou court theater in which drama and opera performances are still staged. ✉ *Strasse am Neuen Palais, Sanssouci,* ☎ *0331/969–4255,* WEB *www.spsg.de.* *€6, including guided tour.* *Apr.–Oct., Tues.–Sun. 9–5; Nov.–Mar., Tues.–Sun. 9–4.*

Schloss Charlottenhof stands on its own grounds in the southern part of Sanssouci Park. After Frederick died in 1786, the ambitious Sanssouci building program ground to a halt, and the park fell into neglect. It was 50 years before another Prussian king, Frederick William IV, restored Sanssouci's earlier glory. He engaged the great Berlin architect Karl Friedrich Schinkel to build this small palace for the crown prince. Schinkel gave it a classical, almost Roman appearance, and he let his imagination loose in the interior, too—decorating one of the rooms as a Roman tent, with its walls and ceiling draped in striped canvas. ☎

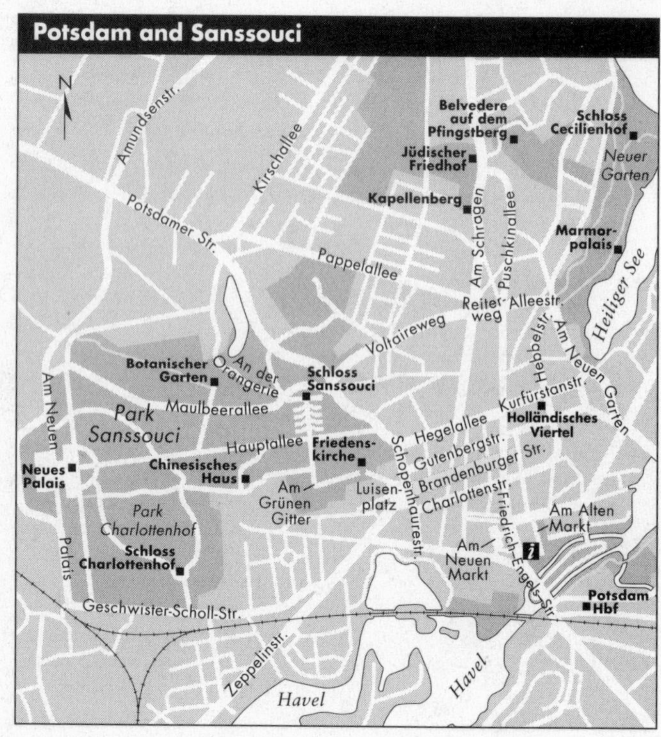

0331/969–4228. Guided tour €4. Mid-May–mid-Oct., Tues.–Sat. 10–5.

Just north of Schloss Charlottenhof on the path back to Sanssouci are later additions to the park. In 1836 Friedrich Wilhelm IV built the **Römische Bäder** (Roman Baths; ☎ 0331/969–4224; €2; mid-May–mid-Oct., Tues.–Sun. 10–5). The **Orangerie** (☎ 0331/969–4280; guided tour €3; mid-May–mid-Oct., Tues.–Sun. 10–5) was completed in 1860; its two massive towers linked by a colonnade evoke an Italian Renaissance palace. Today it houses 47 copies of paintings by Raphael. The **Chinesisches Teehaus** (Chinese Teahouse; ☎ 0331/969–4222; €1; mid-May–mid-Oct., Tues.–Sun. 10–5) was erected in 1757 in the Chinese style, which was then the rage. The **Italianate Peace Church** (1845–48) houses a 12th-century Byzantine mosaic taken from an island near Venice.

NEED A BREAK?

Halfway up the park's Drachenberg Hill, above the Orangerie, stands the curious **Drachenhaus** (Dragon House), modeled in 1770 after the Pagoda at London's Kew Gardens and named for the gargoyles ornamenting the roof corners. It now houses a popular café.

Resembling a rambling, half-timber country manor house, **Schloss Cecilienhof** (Cecilienhof Palace), the final addition to Sanssouci Park, was built for Crown Prince Wilhelm in 1913 in a newly laid-out stretch of the park bordering the Heiliger See, called the New Garden, on the northeastern side of the city. It was here that the Allied leaders Truman, Attlee, and Stalin hammered out the fate of postwar Germany at the 1945 Potsdam Conference. From Sanssouci you can reach the New Garden with any tram or bus going toward the Neuer Garten station. *☎ 0331/969–4244, WEB www.spsg.de/ehtdoc/Homepage3.ht. €5, including guided tour (in German). Apr.–Oct., Tues.–Sun. 9–5; Nov.–Mar., Tues.–Sun. 9–4.*

On a small hill called **Pfingstberg** in the park's western section, are the dark ruins of the palacelike building the **Belvedere.** Built in 1849–52 as an observation platform for the royals, the building is currently being restored. The spectacular view from the hill, however, can be enjoyed from the rooftop of the small **Pomonatempel** below the Belvedere.

Dining and Lodging

$$$ ✕ **Juliette.** In a city proud of its past French influences, the intimate Juliette serves as a homage to great French cuisine. Its home in a Dutch Quarter building is complete with old-fashioned brick walls and fireplace. The menu offers hearty country dishes from Brittany and Normandy such as wild hare pie with hot peppered cherries. Its extensive wine list invites you to experience more than just dinner. ✉ *Jägerstr. 39,* ☎ *0331/270–1791. DC, MC, V.*

$$–$$$ ★ **Hotel am Luisenplatz.** This intimate hotel hides a warm, upscale elegance and friendly, personal service behind a somber-looking facade. The large rooms are decorated in typically Prussian colors—dark-blue and yellow—and all have a bathtub. The biggest draw, however, is the hotel's location, offering a spectacular view of historic Luisenplatz and its restored Prussian city mansions. ✉ *Luisenpl. 5, D–14471,* ☎ *0331/971–900,* FAX *0331/971–9019,* WEB *www.hotel-luisenplatz.de. 22 rooms, 3 suites. No a/c, in-room safes, minibars, cable TV, dry cleaning, laundry service, meeting room, parking (fee), some pets allowed. AE, DC, MC, V.*

$$–$$$ **Steigenberger Maxx Hotel Sanssouci.** The terrace of this fine hotel overlooks the palace and park of Sanssouci. The Maxx, a slimmed down version of the luxurious Steigenberger chain, doesn't offer Old World royal luxury, but the movie-theme rooms (complete with Hollywood and Babelsberg vintage photos and memorabilia) are nice and spacious. The terra-cotta floors and rattan furniture lend a comfortable, casual feel. The hotel restaurant serves solid food, a mixture of American and German dishes. ✉ *Allee nach Sanssouci 1, D–14471,* ☎ *0331/90910,* FAX *0331/909–1904,* WEB *www.steigenberger.de. 133 rooms, 4 suites. Restaurant, bar, no a/c, in-room data ports, minibars, cable TV, health club, massage, sauna, spa, shops, baby-sitting, dry cleaning, laundry service, meeting room, parking (fee), some pets allowed (fee), nosmoking floor. AE, DC, MC, V.*

Potsdam A to Z

Potsdam is virtually a suburb of Berlin, some 20 km (12 mi) southwest of the city center and a half-hour journey by car, bus, or S-bahn. City traffic is heavy, however, and a train journey is recommended. The most effortless way to visit Potsdam and its attractions is to book a tour with one of the big Berlin operators.

BOAT TRAVEL

Boats leave the Wannsee S-bahn station harbor four times a day between April and September. A roundtrip tickets costs €8.50.

➤ CONTACT: **Stern- und Kreisschiffahrt** (✉ Puschkinallee 15, Berlin, ☎ 030/5363–600, WEB www.sternundkreis.de).

BUS TRAVEL

From Berlin there is regular service from the bus station at the Funkturm on Messedamm 8 (U–1 U-bahn: Kaiserdamm). You can also take Bus 118 from Wannsee to the Jagdhausstrasse in Potsdam, and then continue with Bus 106 to Potsdam's Bassanplatz, Hauptbahnhof, and other stations. From Spandau (U–7 U-bahn: Rathaus Spandau), take Bus 638 to Potsdam. From Potsdam's train station, Bus 695 goes to Sanssouci.

CAR TRAVEL

From central Berlin (Strasse des 17. Juni), take the Potsdamer Strasse south until it becomes Route 1 and then follow the signs to Potsdam. A faster way is taking the highway from Funkturm through Zehlendorf to Potsdam.

TOURS

All major sightseeing companies (☞ Tours *in* Berlin A to Z) offer three- to four-hour tours of Potsdam and Sanssouci for €28. The Potsdam Tourist Office runs two tours from April through October. Its three-hour tour, including Sanssouci, costs €20; the 1½-hour tour of the city alone is €14. Both tours are offered in English and German.

TRAIN TRAVEL

Take the S-bahn 7 line to Potsdam-Stadt (for the city and Schloss Sanssouci). Change there for the short rail trip to the Potsdam-Charlottenhof (for Schloss Charlottenhof) and Wildpark (for Neues Palais) stations. Two regional trains, RE 1 and RE 3 also connect Berlin's major train stations to Potsdam. From the Potsdam train station, take Tram 90, 92, or 95 into the city.

VISITOR INFORMATION

The Potsdam tourist office has information on tours, attractions, and events, and also reserves hotel rooms for tourists. Their branch office at Brandenburger Strasse 18 also sells tickets for the Neues Palais theater. Offices are open weekdays 10–6 and weekends 10–2.
➤ TOURIST OFFICE: **Potsdam tourist office** (✉ Touristenzentrum am Alten Markt, Friedrich-Ebert-Str. 5, Postfach 601220, D–14467 Potsdam, ☎ 0331/275–580 or 01805/535–3800, FAX 0331/2755–899; ✉ Brandenburger Str. 18, Potsdam, ☎ 0331/275–5888, WEB www.potsdam.de).

Spreewald

The Spreewald is a unique natural conservation area southeast of Berlin. This almost pristine landscape of wetlands, dark forests, canals, and uncharted waterways, rivers, and lakes covers nearly 500 square mi and is one of the most popular getaways for Berliners. Summer weekends are very crowded. The Spreewald is also known for its people, a blend of Germans and the Slavic Sorben, and for specialties such as freshwater fish and *Spreewald-Gurken* (pickles), and the many fairy tales that have come from this rugged and mysterious area.

From one of the region's major towns, **Lübben,** or **Lübbenau,** explore the narrow, shallow rivers by boarding one of the flat-bottom wooden boats called *Kähne,* which are punted along with long poles. You can have lunch or dinner when your boat docks at one of the hidden forest islands that have a restaurant. Smaller villages with ports such as **Straupitz** or **Raddusch** offer more personal tours with paddleboats or gondolas.

Lübben, the region's old residence of the Saxon prince electors, is also home to **Schloss Lübben,** a castle whose main defense tower is the only accessible building. ✉ *Ernst-von-Houwald-Damm, Lübben.* ⏲ *Tues.–Sun. 10–5.*

The city of Lübbenau has the largest harbor in the Spreewald region. Before boarding a boat here, follow the nature trail to the **Freilandmuseum Lehde** (Lehde Open-Air Museum), which features three old farmhouses typical of the Spreewald, historic handicrafts, traditional costumes, and one of the area's oldest barge-building shops. ✉ *Lehde, An der Gliglitza, Lübbenau,* ☎ *03542/2472.* 🎟 *€3.* ⏲ *Apr.–Oct., daily 10–6; Nov.–Mar., by appointment only.*

The small but fascinating **Spreewald-Museum** features local artwork and many historic craft-work items. ✉ *Torhaus, Am Topfmarkt 12, Lübbenau,* ☎ *03542/2472.* 🎫 *€3.* ⏲ *Apr.–mid-Sept., Tues.–Sun. 10–6; mid-Sept.–mid-Oct., Tues.–Sun. 10–5; mid-Oct.–Mar., by appointment only.*

The sleepy village of **Straupitz** has three mills under one roof: the Holländermühle has a grandiose waterwheel that once powered a sawmill, an oil mill, and a corn mill. A closer inspection of the inside is possible, but you must register in advance for a tour. ✉ *Lassower Str. 11a, Straupitz,* ☎ *035475/16997,* WEB *www.windmuehle-straupitz.de.* 🎫 *€2.*

Dining and Lodging

$$$ ★ ✗🏨 **Romantikhotel zur Bleiche.** One of the largest and most beautifully located hotels in the Spreewald region, the extensive Hotel zur Bleiche not only features various open-air restaurants on the river banks, but also a perfect wellness and swimming pool area. Guest rooms are furnished in a sophisticated country style and include all the amenities you would expect from a first-class resort. Room rates always include a five-course gourmet meal. ✉ *Bleichestr. 16, Burg, D–03096,* ☎ *035603/620,* FAX *035603/60292,* WEB *www.hotel-zur-bleiche.de. 83 rooms, 7 suites. 7 restaurants, bar, no a/c, in-room data ports, minibars, no-smoking floor, room service, cable TV, indoor pool, hot tub, massage, sauna, steam room, health club, baby-sitting, dry cleaning, laundry service, concierge, business services, meeting rooms, parking (fee), some pets allowed (fee). No credit cards.*

Spreewald A to Z

CAR AND TRAIN TRAVEL

The Spreewald is 60 km (37 mi) southeast of Berlin and easily accessible with a 45-minute ride on the A–13 toward Cottbus. To reach Lübben, take B–87 to the north; smaller villages such as Straupitz and Raddusch can be reached via B–320 and B–115, respectively.

Trains to Lübbenau depart from Berlin's Alexanderplatz station and the Ostbahnhof (train Lines RB 41 and RE 2).

TOURS

The Spreewald region is meant to be explored by boat. In Straupitz, boats depart from the barge dock at the village church. Tours depart from the Grosser Hafen in Lübbenau, cost €2.50 for one hour, and can last as long as eight hours. Larger boat tour operators are to be found at the Kahnabfahrtsstelle Am Holzgraben, in Lübbenau. You can rent your own paddleboat by the hour or day from Bootsverleih Petrick or Bootsverleih Ingrid Hannemann (April–October, daily 8–7).

➤ RENTALS AND TOURS: **Bootsverleih Ingrid Hannemann** (✉ Am Wasser 1, Lübbenau, ☎ 03542/3647). **Bootsverleih Petrick** (✉ Am Schlosspark, Lübbenau, ☎ 03542/3620). **Kahnabfahrtsstelle Am Holzgraben** (✉ Dammstr. 72, Lübbenau, ☎ 03542/2221).

VISITOR INFORMATION

➤ TOURIST OFFICES: **Fremdenverkehrsverein Lübben** (✉ Ernst-von-Houwald-Damm 15, D–15907 Lübben, ☎ 03546/3090, FAX 03546/2543, WEB www.luebben.com). **Fremdenverkehrsverein Lübbenau** (✉ Ehm-Welk-Str. 15, D–03222 Lübbenau, ☎ 03542/3668, FAX 03542/46770, WEB www.spreewald-online.de). **Heimat- und Fremdenverkehrsverein Straupitz** (✉ Lübbener Str. 28, D–15913 Straupitz, ☎ 035475/16771). **Tourismusverband Spreewald e.V.** (✉ Lindenstr. 1, D–03226 Raddusch, ☎ 035433/72299, FAX 035433/7228, WEB www.spreewald-tourist.de).

BERLIN A TO Z

To research prices, get advice from other travelers, and book travel arrangements, visit www.fodors.com.

AIR TRAVEL TO AND FROM BERLIN

Airlines serve western Berlin's Tegel Airport after a first stop at a major European hub (such as Frankfurt). The former military airfield at Tempelhof is used as an alternate airport for commuter flights to western Germany. Eastern Berlin's Schönefeld Airport is about 24 km (15 mi) outside the downtown area and is used principally by charter airlines. The three airports share a central phone number).

➤ AIRPORT INFORMATION: **Central airport service** (☏ 0180/500–0186, WEB www.berlin-airport.de).

AIRPORTS AND TRANSFERS

Tegel Airport is only 6 km (4 mi) from the downtown area. The express X9 airport bus runs at 10-minute intervals between Tegel and Bahnhof Zoologischer Garten (Zoo Station), the center of western Berlin. From here you can connect to bus, train, or subway. The trip takes 25 minutes; the fare is €3.10, or an additional €1 if you already have a regular metro or bus ticket. Alternatively, you can take Bus 128 to Kurt Schumacher Platz or Bus 109 to Jakob Kaiser Platz and change to the subway, where your bus ticket is also valid. Expect to pay about €14 for a taxi from the airport to the western downtown area. If you rent a car at the airport, follow the signs for the Stadtautobahn into Berlin. The Halensee exit leads to Kurfürstendamm.

Tempelhof is linked directly to the city center by the U–6 subway line. From Schönefeld a shuttle bus leaves every 10–15 minutes for the nearby S-bahn station; S-bahn trains leave every 20 minutes for the Friedrichstrasse station, in downtown eastern Berlin, and for the Zoo station, in downtown western Berlin. Bus 171 also leaves every 20 minutes for the western Berlin Rudow subway station. A taxi ride from the Schönefeld airport takes about 40 minutes and will cost around €28. By car, follow the signs for Stadtzentrum Berlin.

BIKE TRAVEL

Bike paths are generally marked by red pavement or white markings on the walkways. Be careful when walking on bike paths or crossing them. Many stores that rent or sell bikes carry the Berlin biker's atlas. Call the Allgemeiner Deutscher Fahrrad-Club, ADFC for information and rental locations, or rent your bikes at some of the major hotels for approximately €15 for 24 hours.

➤ BIKE RENTALS: **Allgemeiner Deutscher Fahrrad-Club, ADFC** (✉ Brunnenstr. 28, Prenzlauer Berg, ☏ 030/448–4724, WEB www.adfc-berlin.de).

BUS TRAVEL TO AND FROM BERLIN

The Omnibusbahnhof is the central bus terminal, where you can make reservations at ZOB-Reisebüro or BerlinLinienBus.

➤ BUS INFORMATION: **Zentrale Omnibusbahnhof** (✉ Masurenallee 4–6 at Messedamm, Charlottenburg, ☏ 030/302–5361 for information; 030/301–0380 for reservations).

CAR RENTAL

➤ MAJOR AGENCIES: **Avis** (✉ Schönefeld Airport, Brandenburg, ☏ 030/6091–5710; ✉ Tegel Airport, Reinickendorf, ☏ 030/4101–3148; ✉ Tempelhof Airport, Kreuzberg, ☏ 030/6951–2340; ✉ Budapester Str. 41, at Europa Center, Western Downtown, ☏ 030/230–9370; ✉ Holzmarktstr. 15–18, Friedrichshain, ☏ 030/240–7940). **Europcar** (✉

Schönefeld Airport, Brandenburg, ☎ 030/634–9160; ✉ Tegel Airport, Reinickendorf, ☎ 030/417–8520; ✉ Kurfürstenstr. 101–104, Tiergarten, ☎ 030/235–0640). **Hertz** (✉ Schönefeld Airport, Brandenburg, ☎ 030/6091–5730; ✉ Tegel Airport, Brandenburg, ☎ 030/4170–4674; ✉ Tempelhof Airport, Kreuzberg, ☎ 030/6981–9892; ✉ Budapester Str. 39, Western Downtown, ☎ 030/261–1053). **Sixt** (✉ Schönefeld Airport, Brandenburg, ☎ 030/6091–5690; ✉ Tegel Airport, Reinickendorf, ☎ 030/4101–2886; ✉ Tempelhof Airport, Kreuzberg, ☎ 030/6951–3816; ✉ Nürnberger Str. 65, Western Downtown, ☎ 030/212–9880; ✉ Kaiserdamm 40, Charlottenburg, ☎ 030/4117–987; ✉ Leipziger Str. 104, Mitte, ☎ 030/243–9050).

CAR TRAVEL

Berliners are known to be reckless drivers, so exploring the city by car can be extremely frustrating for out-of-towners. Due to the many construction sites, traffic on many streets is often detoured, and rush hour is stop-and-go for every driver. It's best to leave your car at the hotel and take the public transit system.

DISABILITIES AND ACCESSIBILITY

All major S- and U-bahn stations have elevators, and most buses have hydraulic lifts. Check the public transportation maps or call the Berliner Verkehrsbetriebe. The Service-Ring-Berlin e.V. runs a special bus service for travelers with physical disabilities. The Verband Geburts- und anderer Behinderter e.V. provides information and van and wheelchair rentals.

➤ LOCAL RESOURCES: **Berliner Verkehrsbetriebe** (☎ 030/19449, WEB www.bvg.de). **Service-Ring-Berlin e.V.** (☎ 030/859–4010). **Verband Geburts- und anderer Behinderter e.V.** (☎ 030/341–1797).

EMBASSIES

☞ See Embassies *in* Smart Travel Tips A to Z.

EMERGENCIES

Pharmacies in Berlin offer late-night service on a rotating basis. Every pharmacy displays a notice indicating the location of the nearest shop with evening hours.

➤ EMERGENCY SERVICES: **Police** (☎ 030/110). **Ambulance** (☎ 030/112). **Dentist** (☎ 030/8900–4333). **Emergency poison assistance** (☎ 030/19240).

ENGLISH-LANGUAGE MEDIA

BOOKS

➤ BOOKSTORES: **Books in Berlin** (✉ Goethestr. 69, Charlottenburg, Charlottenburg, ☎ 030/313–1233, WEB www.firstweb.de/books_in_berlin). **Buchhandlung Kiepert** (✉ Hardenbergstr. 4–5, Charlottenburg, ☎ 030/311–880, WEB www.kiepert.de). **Dussmann Kulturkaufhaus** (✉ Friedrichstr. 90, Mitte, ☎ 030/20250, WEB www.kulturkaufhaus.de). **Hugendubel** (✉ Tauentzienstr. 13, Western Downtown, ☎ 030/214–060, WEB www.hugendubel.de). **Marga Schoeller Bücherstube** (✉ Knesebeckstr. 33, Western Downtown, ☎ 030/881–1112).

TAXIS

The base rate is €2.50, after which prices vary according to a complex tariff system. Figure on paying around €8 for a ride the length of the Ku'damm. If you've hailed a cab on the street and are taking a short ride of less than 2 km (1 mi), ask the driver as soon as you start off for a special fare (€3) called *Kurzstreckentarif*. Groups of more than five people pay an additional (total) fee of €1.50. There is no additional fee if you call a cab by phone. You can also get cabs at taxi stands or order one by calling. U-bahn employees will call a taxi for passengers after 8 PM.

Students operate *Velotaxis,* a rickshaw service system, along Kurfürstendamm, in Tiergarten, Friedrichstrasse, and Unter den Linden. Just hail one of the cabs on the street or look for the VELOTAXI-STAND signs along the boulevards mentioned. The fare is €2.50 for up to 1 km (½ mi), €2.50 for a tour between sightseeing landmarks (for example, Europa Center to the Brandenburger Tor), and €7.50 for 30 minutes of travel. Velotaxis operate April–October, daily 1–8.
➤ TAXI COMPANIES: **Taxis** (☎ 030/210–101, 030/210–202, 030/443–322, or 030/261–026). **Velotaxis** (✉ Schönhauser Allee 8, Prenzlauer Berg, ☎ 030/4435–8990 or 0172/328–8888).

TOURS

BOAT TOURS

Tours of downtown Berlin's canals give you upclose and unusual views of sights such as Charlottenburg Palace, the Reichstag, and the Berliner Dom. Tours usually depart twice a day from several bridges and piers in Berlin, such as Hansabrücke in Tiergarten, Kottbusser Tor in Kreuzberg, Potsdamer Brücke, and Haus der Kulturen der Welt in Tiergarten. Make sure to have plenty of film, and be assured that plenty of beer and wursts are available during the narrated trips.

A tour of the Havel Lakes is the thing to do in summer. Trips begin at Wannsee (S-bahn: Wannsee) and at the Greenwich Promenade in Tegel (U-bahn: Tegel). You'll sail on either the whale-shape vessel *Moby Dick* or the *Havel Queen,* a Mississippi-style boat, and cruise 28 km (17 mi) through the lakes and past forests (Stern- und Kreisschiffahrt). Tours last 4½ hours and cost between €10 and €13. There are 20 operators.
➤ FEES AND SCHEDULES: **Reederei Bruno Winkler** (✉ Mierendorffstr. 16, Charlottenburg, ☎ 030/349–9595). **Reederei Riedel** (✉ Planufer 78, Kreuzberg, ☎ 030/693–4646). **Stern- und Kreisschiffahrt** (✉ Puschkinallee 15, Treptow, ☎ 030/536–3600).

BUS TOURS

Four companies offer more or less identical tours (in English) covering all major sights in Berlin, as well as all-day tours to Potsdam, Dresden, and Meissen. The Berlin tours cost €17–€23; those to Potsdam, €25–€36; and to Dresden and Meissen, approximately €51.

Berliner Bären Stadtrundfahrten tours depart from the corner of Rankestrasse and Kurfürstendamm and, in eastern Berlin, from Alexanderplatz, opposite the Forum Hotel. Berolina Berlin-Service tours depart from the corner of Kurfürstendamm and Meinekestrasse and, in eastern Berlin, from Alexanderplatz, opposite the Forum Hotel. Bus Verkehr Berlin tours leave from Kurfürstendamm 225. Severin Kühn tours leave from clearly marked stops along the Kurfürstendamm. The Stadtrundfahrtbüro Berlin organizes sightseeing tours in historic, open double-decker buses. Tours in English and German depart in front of the Marmorhaus on Kurfürstendamm, at the corner of Rankestrasse.
➤ FEES AND SCHEDULES: **Berliner Bären Stadtrundfahrten** (BBS; ✉ Seeburgerstr. 19b, Charlottenburg, ☎ 030/3519–5270, WEB www.sightseeing.de). **Berolina Berlin-Service** (✉ Kurfürstendamm 220, corner Meinekestr., Western Downtown, ☎ 030/8856–8030, WEB www.berolina-berlin.com). **Bus Verkehr Berlin** (BVB, ✉ Kurfürstendamm 225, Western Downtown, ☎ 030/885–9880, WEB www.bvb.net). **Severin & Kühn** (✉ Kurfürstendamm 216, Western Downtown, ☎ 030/880–4190, WEB www.severin-kuehn-berlin.de). **Stadtrundfahrtbüro Berlin** (✉ Kurfürstendamm 236, Western Downtown, ☎ 030/2612–001, WEB www.stadtrundfahrtbuero-berlin.de).

WALKING TOURS

Insider Tours offers an introductory tour of the city that runs for just over three hours and takes in all the major sights. Brit Terry Brewer's firsthand accounts of divided and reunified Berlin are a highlight of the six-hour Brewer's Best of Berlin tour. Berlin Walks offers theme tours such as Third Reich sites and Jewish life in addition to their introductory Discover Berlin tour. Tours cost from €7.50–€15. Printable discount coupons are also available on the tour operators' Web sites.

StattReisen's weekend tours cost approximately €7.50. Tours include "Jewish History" and "Prenzlauer Berg Neighborhoods" and are in German; English tours are offered upon request.

➤ FEES AND SCHEDULES: **Berlin Walks** (☎ 030/301–9194, WEB www.berlinwalks.de). **Insider Tours** (☎ 030/692–3149, WEB www.insidertour.de). **Brewer's Best of Berlin** (✉ Circus Hostel, Am Weinbergsweg 1a, off Rosenthaler Pl., Mitte, ☎ 030/2839–1433). **StattReisen** (✉ Malplaquetstr. 5, Wedding, ☎ 030/455–3028, WEB www.stattreisen.berlin.de).

TRANSPORTATION AROUND BERLIN

The city has one of the most efficient public-transportation systems in Europe, a smoothly integrated network of subway (U-bahn) and suburban (S-bahn) train lines, buses, trams (in eastern Berlin only). Get a map from any information booth. Don't be afraid to try and figure out the bus schedules posted—a bus can often cut the most direct path to your destination. U-bahn service stops around midnight during the week. All-night bus and tram service operates seven nights a week (indicated by the letter *N* next to route numbers).

The easiest and most inexpensive way to see most of both West and East Berlin's downtown areas is a ride on bus line No. 100 or 200, which run from the Zoologischer Garten to Alexanderplatz (No. 100), and from Zoologischer Garten to Potsdamer Platz and on to Alexanderplatz and Prenzlauer Allee (No. 200), passing (and stopping at) almost all major sightseeing spots on the way.

A €2.10 ticket covers only the downtown areas (fare Zones A and B), a ticket for these fare zones and the outlying areas (fare Zone C) is €2.30, and allows you to make an unlimited number of changes between trains, buses, and trams within two hours.

If you are just making a short trip, buy a Kurzstreckentarif. It allows you to ride six bus stops or three U-bahn or S-bahn stops for €1.20. The best deal for visitors who plan to travel around the city extensively is the day card, for €6.10, good until 3 AM next day after validation on all trains and buses. (It's €6.30 for all three zones.) A seven-day tourist pass costs €22 and allows unlimited travel on all city buses and trains for fare Zones A and B; €28 buys all three fare zones. The Berlin WelcomeCard entitles one adult and up to three children (under 14) to three days of unlimited travel for €16.36, as well as free admission or reductions of up to 50% for sightseeing trips, museums, theaters, and other events and attractions both in Berlin and Potsdam.

All tickets are available from vending machines at U-bahn and S-bahn stations. Punch your ticket into the red machine on the platform. For information about public transportation, call the Berliner Verkehrsbetriebe or go to the BVG-information office on Hardenbergplatz, directly in front of the Bahnhof Zoo train station. If you're caught without a ticket, the fine is €31. Additional information about S-Bahn connections can be obtained at the S-Bahn Berlin GmbH.

Information about all public transport by subway, bus, train, S-Bahn, and Deutsche Bahn both in Berlin and Brandenburg (with a special emphasis on connecting traffic between the two states) is provided by the region's central transit authority, the VBB.

➤ CONTACTS: **Berliner Verkehrsbetriebe** (☎ 030/19449, WEB www.bvg.de). **S-Bahn Berlin GmbH** (☎ 030/2971–9843, WEB www.s-bahn-berlin.de). **VBB** (✉ Hardenbergpl. 2, Western Downtown, ☎ 030/2541–4141, WEB www.vbbonline.de).

TRAVEL AGENCIES

➤ LOCAL AGENT REFERRALS: **Euroaide** (✉ Hardenbergpl., inside the Zoologischer Garten train station, Western Downtown, ☎ 030/2974–9241). **Reiseland American Express Reisebüro** (✉ Wittenbergerpl., Bayreuther Str. 37, Western Downtown, ☎ 030/2149–8363, WEB www.reiseland-american-express.de; ✉ Friedrichstr. 172, Mitte, ☎ 030/238–4102).

VISITOR INFORMATION

The Berlin Tourismus Marketing (main tourist office) is in the heart of the city in the Europa Center. If you want materials on the city before your trip, write Berlin Tourismus Marketing GmbH. For information on the spot, the office in the Europa Center is open Monday–Saturday 8 AM–10 PM, Sunday 9–9. Other offices are found at the Brandenburger Tor, open Monday–Saturday 9:30–6, and at Tegel Airport, open daily 5 AM–10:30 PM.

The Berlin-Hotline provides the latest tourist information via phone for hotel and ticket information and reservation) or fax.

For information in English on all aspects of the city, pick up a copy of *Berlin—the magazine* (€1.80) from any tourist office.

A Tageskarte (day card) for one-day admission to all of Berlin's state museums is available for €6 at all state museums; a Dreitageskarte is sold for €8 and covers admission for three days. The Tageskarte is valid at all museums on Museum Island, the Kulturforum, the Dahlem museum complex, and the Hamburger Bahnhof.

➤ TOURIST INFORMATION: **Berlin Tourismus Marketing GmbH** (✉ Am Karlsbad 11, Tiergarten, D–10785 Berlin, ☎ no phone, WEB www.btm.de). **Berlin-Hotline** (☎ 0190/754–040 €1.20 per minute; 030/250–025 for hotel and ticket information, FAX 030/2500–2424, WEB www.berlin.de).

17 SAXONY, SAXONY-ANHALT, AND THURINGIA

These three states in eastern Germany have a great many secrets in store and some gems of German culture. Treasures of art and music lie in Dresden and Leipzig, and milestones of history are found in Weimar and Wittenberg, the cities of Goethe and Martin Luther. An old-world state of mind is found here, the likes of which you will never find in western Germany.

Updated by Jürgen Scheunemann

THE SMALL TOWNS in the eastern states of Saxony, Saxony-Anhalt, and Thuringia will reveal much more about an older Germany than the pace of Frankfurt, Hamburg, or Köln can afford. Communism never penetrated the culture here as deeply as did the American influence in West Germany. The German Democratic Republic (GDR, commonly referred to by its German acronym—DDR) clung to its German heritage, proudly preserving connections with such national heroes as Luther, Goethe, Schiller, Bach, Handel, Wagner, and the Hungarian-born Liszt. Towns in the regions of the Thüringer Wald (Thuringian Forest) or the Harz Mountains—long considered the haunt of witches—are drenched in history and medieval legend.

East Germans rebuilt extensively after World War II bombings devastated most of their cities; though you will see eyesores of industrialization and stupendously bland housing projects, many historic centers were restored to their old glamour. Some of Europe's most famous palaces and cultural wonders—the Zwinger and Semperoper in Dresden, the Wartburg at Eisenach, the Schiller and Goethe houses in Weimar, Luther's Wittenberg—await the long-delayed traveler.

Traditional tourist sights aside, eastern Germany is also worth visiting precisely because it still *is* in transition. In 1989 the resolute people of Leipzig, with their now legendary *Montagsdemonstrationen* (Monday demonstrations) through the streets of their proud city, startled the East German regime and triggered the peaceful revolution. A year later the initiative for unification came as much from the West as it did from the East, and many former East Germans have not been altogether happy with the results. The closing of factories and a shrunken welfare system have left many jobless.

But apart from economic woes that still haunt parts of the region, a new class of entrepreneurs has transformed such cities as Leipzig and Dresden. It's all part of a wave of start-up businesses that benefit from the region's traditional work ethic. Consider this upswing in light of the past. When the GDR was communism's "Western Front," it was largely isolated from Western ideas. Saxony's Dresden area, in particular, was nicknamed *Tal der Ahnungslosen* (Valley of the Know-Nothings), as residents there couldn't receive Western television or radio signals.

The three states described here survived under a harsh political regime and have now embarked on a new and mostly promising future. Eastern Germany used to move very slowly, but nowadays the pace of cities such as Leipzig or Dresden has overtaken that of their West German counterparts.

Pleasures and Pastimes

Dining

Enterprising young managers and chefs are beginning to establish themselves in the east, so look for new and mostly small restaurants along the way. Some successfully blend nouvelle German cuisine with such regional specialties as *Thüringer Sauerbraten mit Klössen* (roast corned beef with dumplings), spicy *Thüringer Wurst* (sausage), *Bärenschinken* (cured ham), *Harzer Köhlerteller mit Röstkartoffeln* (charcoal-grilled meat with fried potatoes), *Harze Käse* (a strong-smelling cheese), and *Moskgauer Bauerngulasch mit Klump* (goulash with dumplings).

CATEGORY	COST*
$$$$	over €25
$$$	€20–€25
$$	€15–€20
$	under €15

**per person for a main course at dinner*

Lodging

All major hotel chains are present in the larger cities, most of them within beautifully restored mansions. Smaller and family-run hotels often combine a good restaurant with fairly good accommodations. In an effort to further improve tourism, most big hotels offer special (weekend) or activity-oriented packages that aren't found in the western part of the country.

During the trade fairs and shows of the **Leipziger Messe,** particularly in March and April, most Leipzig hotels increase their prices.

CATEGORY	COST*
$$$$	over €225
$$$	€150–€225
$$	€75–€150
$	under €75

**All prices are for two people in a standard double room, including tax and service charge.*

Old Railway Engines and Boats

Eastern Germany is a treasure-house of old steam-driven tractors, factory engines, train engines, and riverboats, many lovingly restored by enthusiasts. Deutsche Bahn (German Railways) regularly runs trains from the years 1899–1930 on a small-gauge line that penetrates deep into the Saxon countryside and the Fichtelberg Mountains. In Saxony-Anhalt you can ride the steam-powered narrow-gauge Brockenbahn to the Harz Mountains' highest point. The world's largest and oldest fleet of paddle steamers (Weisse Flotte) plies the Elbe. Eight old steamers (all of them under historic preservation orders) and two reconstructed ships ply up and down the Elbe, following the Saxon Wine Route as far as the Czech Republic.

Outdoor Activities and Sports

You can canoe on the Elbe, Gera, and Saale rivers and seldom see another paddler. Contact the tourist offices in Dresden, Gera, or Halle for rental information.

Hiking is good in the Harz Mountains, particularly around Thale and Wittenberg. Maps and guides to bicycle and walking trails are available in most hotels and bookstores. The Thale and Wernigerode tourist offices and the Wittenberg District Rural Information Office have great resources. Braunlage, in the Harz, offers good family skiing.

The elevated, dense Thuringian Forest is a popular holiday destination in summer and in winter. Its center is Suhl, administrative heart of an area where every 10th town and village is a spa or mountain resort. The region south of Erfurt, centering around Oberhof, has comfortable hotels and full sports facilities.

Wine

Saxony has cultivated vineyards for more than 800 years and is known for its dry red and white wines, among them Müller-Thurgau, Weissburgunder, Ruländer, and the spicy Traminer. The Sächsische Weinstrasse (Saxon Wine Route) follows the course of the Elbe River from Diesbar-Seusslitz (north of Meissen) to Pirna (southeast of Dresden).

Meissen, Radebeul, and Dresden have upscale wine restaurants, and wherever you see a green seal with the letter *S* and grapes depicted, good local wine is being served. Most of the hotels and restaurants reviewed in this chapter have their own wine cellars.

Exploring Saxony, Saxony-Anhalt, and Thuringia

These three states cover the southeastern part of the former East Germany, and some of the old and now run-down industrial towns will remind you of its communist past. But Germany's most historically important cities are here, and reconstruction programs are slowly restoring them. Dresden is promoting its reputation as the "Florence of the Elbe," and, just downstream, Meissen has undergone an impressive facelift. Weimar, one of the continent's old cultural centers, and Leipzig, in particular, have washed off their grime and have almost completely restored historic city centers.

Numbers in the text correspond to numbers in the margin and on the Saxony, Saxony-Anhalt, and Thuringia; Leipzig; and Dresden maps.

Great Itineraries

IF YOU HAVE 3 DAYS

Spend your first day and night in **Dresden** ①–⑭, with its impressive Zwinger complex and fine museums. Set out the next afternoon for **Meissen** ⑰, to see how its famous porcelain is produced. Continue northwest to spend the next two nights in **Leipzig** ⑳–㉝, where Bach once resided.

IF YOU HAVE 5 DAYS

Spend your first day and night in **Dresden** ①–⑭. Finish taking in its splendors in the morning and continue to **Meissen** ⑰, stopping long enough for a visit to the porcelain factory, before closing the day in **Leipzig** ⑳–㉝. When you've explored your fill, head north to the birthplace of Martin Luther and the Reformation, **Wittenberg** ㉞. An indirect route takes you on the third day to the old Harz Mountain towns of **Quedlinburg** ㊲, **Wernigerode,** and **Goslar** ㊳, the unofficial capital of the Harz region. Skirt through the Harz Mountains and drive south to **Eisenach** ㊵, where you can prowl through the Wartburg Castle, where Luther translated the Bible in hiding. The final stops are **Erfurt** ㊶, a city of towers that mostly managed to escape wartime bombing, and **Weimar** ㊷, where you might want to peek into its most famous hotel, the charming and luxurious Elephant.

IF YOU HAVE 7 DAYS

Your first day should be fully devoted to the various sights in **Dresden** ①–⑭, before exploring the **Sächsische Schweiz** ⑮, a mountainous region south of the city, the next day. Depending on how long you hiked through the mountains, you will still have enough time to drive to the Polish-border town of **Görlitz** ⑯. Spend the night there and travel to **Meissen** ⑰, and then follow a northern route on the A–14 autobahn to **Leipzig** ⑳–㉝ and spend the rest of the day there. Leave enough time in Leipzig for visits to its outstanding museums, including the Grassimuseum complex and the Museum der Bildenden Künste. On your fourth and fifth days, from Leipzig, drive back to the sights at **Halle** ㊱ before touring the old towns of **Wittenberg** ㉞ and **Quedlinburg** ㊲. You can spend the nights in any of the Harz towns and venture into the mountains for some fresh air. The sixth day is best spent at the Wartburg in **Eisenach** ㊵, which can be reached either by following the country roads or the autobahn from the Harz Mountains toward the south, and then on to **Erfurt** ㊶ and **Weimar** ㊷. Spend your last day either in both cities

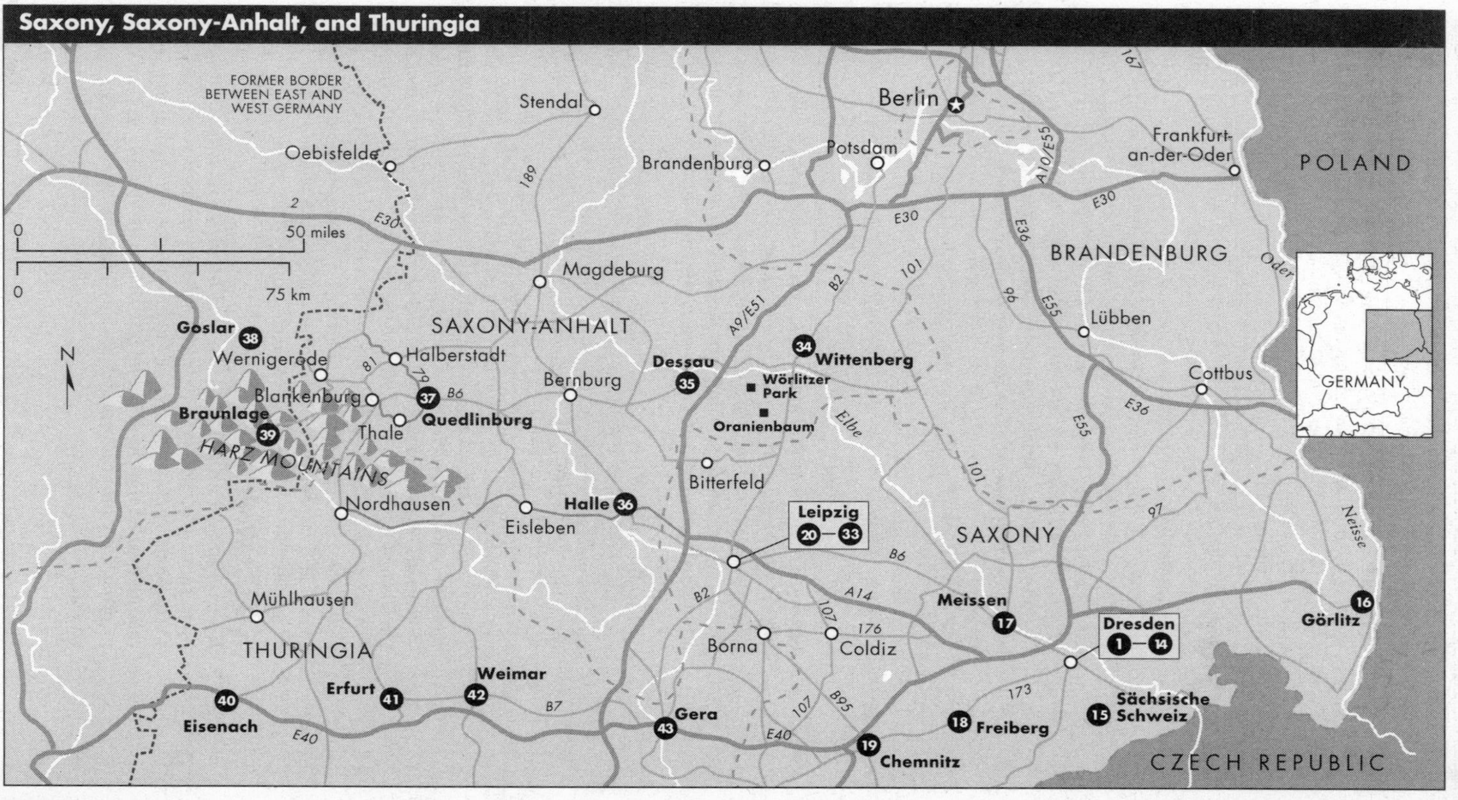

Saxony, Saxony-Anhalt, and Thuringia
FORMER BORDER BETWEEN EAST AND WEST GERMANY
Stendal
Berlin
Frankfurt-an-der-Oder
POLAND
Oebisfelde
Brandenburg
Potsdam
0
50 miles
75 km
Magdeburg
BRANDENBURG
Oder
GERMANY
SAXONY-ANHALT
Lübben
Goslar 38
Wernigerode
Halberstadt
Dessau 35
34 Wittenberg
Cottbus
N
Blankenburg
37 Quedlinburg
Bernburg
Wörlitzer Park
Braunlage 39
Thale
Oranienbaum
Elbe
HARZ MOUNTAINS
Bitterfeld
Nordhausen
Halle 36
Eisleben
Leipzig 20—33
SAXONY
Neisse
Mühlhausen
Meissen 17
Dresden 1—14
Görlitz 16
Borna
Coldiz
THURINGIA
Weimar 42
Erfurt 41
40 Eisenach
43 Gera
18 Freiberg
15 Sächsische Schweiz
19 Chemnitz
CZECH REPUBLIC
E30
E36
E55
E40
A10/E55
A9/E51
A14
B2
B6
B7
B95
2
79
81
96
97
101
107
167
173
176
189

or concentrate fully on the culture and museums in Weimar. If time permits, also detour to **Gera** ㊸.

When to Tour Saxony, Saxony-Anhalt, and Thuringia

Winters in this part of Germany can be cold, wet, and dismal, so unless you plan to ski in the Harz Mountains or the Thüringer Wald, visit in late spring, summer, or early autumn. Avoid Leipzig at trade fair times, particularly in March and April.

SAXONY

The people of Saxony, a once almost-forgotten corner of Germany near the Czech and Polish borders, identify themselves more as Saxon than German, and their somewhat indecipherable dialect is the target of endless jokes and puns. However, Saxon pride is rebuilding three cities magnificently: Dresden and Leipzig—the showcase cities of eastern Germany—and the smaller town of Görlitz, on the Neisse River. If you make your way toward Dresden from Freiberg, you can follow the Freital road or first cut north to the Elbe River and the enchanting little city of Meissen. The area has recovered well since the Elbe flooded in August 2002.

Dresden

205 km (127 mi) south of Berlin.

Saxony's capital city sits in baroque splendor on a wide sweep of the Elbe River, and its proponents are working with German thoroughness to recapture the city's old reputation as the "Florence of the North." Its yellow and pale green facades are enormously appealing, and their mere presence is even more overwhelming when you compare what you see today with photographs of Dresden from February 1945, after an Allied bombing raid destroyed the city overnight. Dresden was the capital of Saxony as early as the 15th century, although most of its architectural masterpieces date from the 18th century and the reigns of Augustus the Strong and his son, Frederick Augustus II. Both were widely traveled and sought out architects and designers capable of creating monuments like those they admired in Italy.

Though some parts of the city center still look halfway between demolition and construction, the present city is an enormous tribute to Dresdeners' skills and dedication. Despite lack of funds, the people of Dresden succeeded in rebuilding what was once one of Europe's architectural and cultural treasures. The resemblance of today's riverside to Dresden cityscapes painted by Canaletto in the mid-1700s is remarkable. Unfortunately, the war-inflicted gaps in the urban landscape elsewhere are too big to be closed any time soon.

A Good Walk

It's easy to cover the downtown area of Dresden on foot. From the main railway station (which has adequate parking), you'll first have to cross a featureless expanse surrounded by postwar high-rises to reach the old part of the city. Pick up any materials you like at the tourist information office on pedestrians-only Pragerstrasse (No. 8).

Buildings representing several centuries of architecture border the **Altmarkt** ①. At the square's southeast side, take a look at the **Kreuzkirche** ②, before heading east, into Wilsdruffer Strasse, until you reach the **Stadtmuseum Dresden im Landhaus** ③ with its historic exhibits. Continue east toward Pirnaischer Platz, and make a sharp left turn into Landhausstrasse, which connects to Dresden's historic heart, the Neumarkt (New Market). On your left is the baroque **Frauenkirche** ④, rising up from its rubble. Just behind the church, off Brühlsche Gasse, stands the

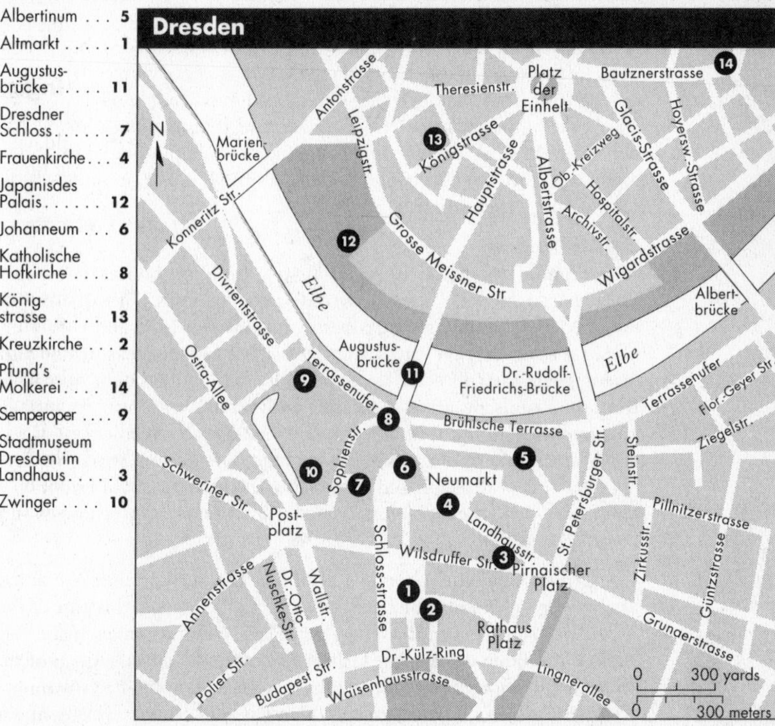

impressive **Albertinum** ⑤, which has one of the world's leading art galleries. If you leave the Albertinum by the Brühlsche Terrasse exit, you'll find yourself on what was once known as the "Balcony of Europe," a terrace high above the Elbe, carved from a 16th-century stretch of the city fortifications; from the terrace, a breathtaking vista of the Elbe River and the Dresden skyline opens up. From here, you can detour to **Schloss Pillnitz** and its museum. Back at the Neumarkt, you'll see the **Johanneum** ⑥ on its northwestern corner. The historic building is part of the former palace that now houses a transportation museum. The outside wall of the Johanneum has a unique porcelain-tile painting of a royal procession; walk along the wall, and at the end of the street you'll reach the **Dresdner Schloss** ⑦, which is still under reconstruction.

Next walk a short distance north on any of the small paths from the Neumarkt, crossing Augustusstrasse in the direction of Terrassenufer; cross Schlossplatz and then turn left, where you'll encounter Sophienstrasse. If you turn left, you can't miss Saxony's largest church, the **Katholische Hofkirche** ⑧. Just opposite the church on the Theaterplatz is the architecturally wondrous **Semperoper** ⑨, one of Europe's finest opera houses. Theaterplatz has as its centerpiece a proud equestrian statue of King Johann, who ruled Saxony when Gottfried Semper was at work. Don't be misled by Johann's confident pose in the saddle—he was terrified of horses and never learned to ride. Five minutes south of the Semperoper is the world-famous **Zwinger** ⑩, a richly decorated baroque palace with an entrance off Ostra-Allee. From the Zwinger, walk north, crossing the Elbe River on the **Augustusbrücke** ⑪, and then turn left on Grosse Meissner Strasse. You'll pass the **Japanisches Palais** ⑫, a baroque-classicist palace, on your left before crossing Albertplatz to reach **Königstrasse** ⑬, one of Dresden's most beautiful, historic little streets. To get a further glimpse of Dresden's magnificent past, cross Albertplatz and then continue down Bautzener Strasse to **Pfund's Molkerei** ⑭, an old dairy specialty shop.

TIMING

A full day is sufficient for a quick tour of historic Dresden, but if you plan to explore any of the museums, such as the Zwinger, or take a guided tour of the Semperoper, you'll need more than a day. Allow at least two hours each for the Zwinger, the Johanneum, and the Albertinum. In summer, schedule some time to relax in one of the cafés along the Elbe River. In winter and early spring, it can get quite windy on the wide, open squares.

Sights to See

5 **Albertinum.** This massive, imperial-style building houses Dresden's leading art museum, one of the world's great galleries. The Albertinum is named after Saxony's King Albert, who between 1884 and 1887 converted a royal arsenal into a suitable setting for the treasures he and his forebears had collected. The upper story of the Albertinum, accessible from the Brühlsche Terrasse, houses 19th- and 20th-century paintings and sculpture in the **Gemäldegalerie Neue Meister** (Gallery of Modern Masters). Permanent exhibits include outstanding work by German masters of the 19th and 20th centuries (Caspar David Friedrich's haunting *Das Kreuz im Gebirge* is here), and French Impressionists and Postimpressionists.

The **Grünes Gewölbe** (Green Vault) draws the most attention. Named after a green room in the palace of Augustus the Strong, this part of the Albertinum (entered from Georg-Treu-Platz) contains an exquisite collection of unique objets d'art fashioned from gold, silver, ivory, amber, and other precious and semiprecious materials. Among the crown jewels are the world's largest "green" diamond, 41 carats in weight, and a dazzling group of tiny gem-studded figures called *Hofstaat zu Delhi am Geburtstag des Grossmoguls Aureng-Zeb* (The Court at Delhi during the Birthday of the Great Mogul Aureng-Zeb). The unwieldy name gives a false idea of the size of the work, dating from 1708; some parts of the tableau are so small they can be admired only through a magnifying glass. Somewhat larger and less delicate is the drinking bowl of Ivan the Terrible, perhaps the most sensational artifact in this extraordinary museum. Next door is the **Skulpturensammlung** (Sculpture Collection), which includes ancient Egyptian and classical works and examples by Giovanni da Bologna and Adriaen de Vries. ✉ *Am Neumarkt, Brühlsche Terrasse,* ☎ *0351/491–4619,* WEB *www.staatl-kunstsammlungen.dresden.de.* 🎟 *€4.50, including admission to Gemäldegalerie Neue Meister, Grünes Gewölbe, Münzkabinett (coin collection), and Skulpturensammlung.* ⏲ *Fri.–Wed. 10–6.*

1 **Altmarkt** (Old Market Square). Although dominated by the nearby unappealing Kulturpalast (Palace of Culture), a concrete leftover from the 1970s, the broad square and its surrounding streets are the true center of Dresden. Its colonnaded beauty (from the Stalinist-era architecture of the early 1950s) survived the disfiguring efforts of city planners to turn it into a huge outdoor parking lot. The rebuilt **Rathaus** is here, as well as the yellow-stucco, 18th-century Landhaus, which contains the Stadtmuseum Dresden im Landhaus.

11 **Augustusbrücke** (Augustus Bridge). This bridge, which spans the river in front of the Katholische Hofkirche, is a reconstruction of a 17th-century baroque bridge blown up by the SS shortly before the end of World War II. The bridge was restored and renamed for Georgi Dimitroff, the Bulgarian Communist accused by the Nazis of instigating the Reichstag fire; after the fall of communism the original name, honoring August the Strong, was reinstated.

OFF THE BEATEN PATH **DEUTSCHES HYGIENE-MUSEUM DRESDEN** – A unique museum (even in a country with a national tendency for excessive cleanliness), the museum relates the history of public health and often features special art exhibits. ✉ *Lingnerpl. 1,* ☎ *0351/48460,* WEB *www.dhmd.de.* *€2.50.* ⏲ *Tues., Thurs., Fri. 9–5; Wed. 9–8; weekends 10–6.*

7 **Dresdner Schloss** (Dresden Palace). Restoration work is still under way behind the Renaissance facade of this former royal palace, much of which was built between 1709 and 1722. Some of the finished rooms in the **Georgenbau** host historical exhibitions, among them an excellent one on the reconstruction of the palace itself. The palace's main gateway, the Georgentor, has an enormous statue of the fully armed Saxon count George. From April through October, the palace's old **Hausmannsturm** (Hausmann Tower) offers a wonderful view of the city and the Elbe River. The palace housed August the Strong's Grünes Gewölbe before it was moved in its entirety to the Albertinum. ✉ *Schlosspl.,* ☎ *0351/491–4619.* *€2.60.* ⏲ *Tues.–Sun. 10–6.*

4 **Frauenkirche** (Church of Our Lady). Germany's greatest Protestant church was reduced to jagged ruins after the infamous February 1945 Allied bombing raid of World War II. The once mighty baroque church was so sturdily built that it had withstood a three-day bombardment during the Seven Years' War. A painstaking reconstruction of the Frauenkirche is under way; it is hoped that it can be reconsecrated in the year 2006, the 800th anniversary of the founding of Dresden. The church has also evolved as a symbol of German–British reconciliation. The golden church cross (worth U.S. $400,000) was donated to the building by a British foundation. Daily tours of the church's completed sections and the construction site start at entrance F of the church (northern facade). Try to avoid the always-crowded weekend tours. ✉ *An der Frauenkirche,* ☎ *0351/498–1131,* WEB *www.frauenkirche-dresden.org.* *Free (donation).* ⏲ *Daily 10–4 (tour every hr).*

12 **Japanisches Palais** (Japanese Palace). This baroque palace was built in 1715–1733 to hold August's collection of fine china. One of the city's most magnificent buildings, it features Asian architectural elements such as porticos and courtyard statues as well as a roof reminiscent of a pagoda. Today, the palace houses the **Museum für Völkerkunde** (Museum of Ethnology; ☎ 0351/814–4840) and the **Museum für Vorgeschichte** (Prehistoric Museum; ☎ 0351/814–450). Those who have already visited similar museums in Berlin may wish to skip these. Nonetheless, special exhibits may make them worth your while. ✉ *Palaispl. 11.* WEB *www.archsax.sachsen.de.* *€2 for each museum.* ⏲ *Tues.–Sun. 10–6.*

6 **Johanneum.** At one time the royal stables, this 16th-century building now houses the **Verkehrsmuseum** (Transportation Museum), a collection of historical conveyances, including vintage automobiles and engines. The former **stable exercise yard,** behind the Johanneum and enclosed by elegant Renaissance arcades, was used during the 16th century as an open-air festival ground. A ramp leading up from the courtyard made it possible for royalty to reach the upper story to view the jousting below without having to dismount. You'll find the scene today much as it was centuries ago, complete with jousting markings in the ground. More popular even than jousting in those days was *Ringelstechen,* a risky pursuit in which riders at full gallop had to catch small rings on their lances. Horses and riders often came to grief in the narrow confines of the stable yard.

On the outside wall of the Johanneum is a remarkable example of **Meissen porcelain art**: a Meissen tile mural of a royal procession, 336 ft long. More than 100 members of the royal Saxon house of Wettin, half of them on horseback, are represented on the giant mosaic of 25,000 porcelain tiles, painted in 1904–07 after a design by Wilhelm Walther. The Johanneum is reached by steps leading down from the Brühlsche Terrasse. ✉ *Am Neumarkt at Augustusstr. 1,* ☎ *0351/86440,* WEB *www.verkehrsmuseum.sachsen.de.* 🎟 *€3.* ⏲ *Tues.–Sun. 10–5.*

8 **Katholische Hofkirche** (Catholic Court Church). The largest church in Saxony is also known as the Cathedral of St. Trinitatis. Frederick Augustus II (reigned 1733–63) brought architects and builders from Italy to construct a Catholic church in a city that had been the first large center of Lutheran Protestantism (like his father, Frederick Augustus II had to convert to Catholicism to be eligible to wear the Polish crown). They worked in secret, so the story goes, and Dresden's Protestant citizens were presented with a fait accompli when the church was finally consecrated in 1754. Seventy-eight statues of historical and biblical figures decorate the baroque facade; inside, the treasures include a beautiful stone pulpit by the royal sculptor Balthasar Permoser and a painstakingly restored 250-year-old organ said to be one of the finest ever to come from the mountain workshops of the famous Silbermann family. In the cathedral's crypt are the tombs of 49 Saxon rulers and a precious vessel containing the heart of August the Strong. Due to restoration work, the cathedral's opening hours may change. ✉ *Schlosspl.,* ☎ *0351/484–4712.* 🎟 *Free.* ⏲ *Weekdays 9–5, Sat. 10–5, Sun. noon–4:30.*

13 **Königstrasse.** (King Street). The grand estates lining this historic boulevard attest to Dresden's bygone wealth. The street itself was once an important thoroughfare of a residential city quarter founded by August the Strong in the mid-18th century. Some of the meticulously restored buildings house restaurants, shops, and art galleries in their lovely open courtyards. ✉ *Between Grosse Meissner Str. and Albertpl.*

2 **Kreuzkirche** (Cross Church). Soaring high above the Altmarkt, the richly decorated tower of the baroque Kreuzkirche dates back to 1792. The city's main Protestant church is still undergoing post-war restoration, but the tower and church hall are open to the public; the plain gray interior reflects the traditional simplicity of German Lutherism. The Kreuzchor, a boys' choir, performs here almost every Saturday at 6 PM and during service on Sunday (at 10 AM). ✉ *Altmarkt,* ☎ *0351/439–390,* WEB *www.dresdner-kreuzkirche.de.* 🎟 *Tower €1.* ⏲ *Mon.–Sat. 10–5, Sun. noon–5.*

14 **Pfund's Molkerei.** (Pfund's Dairy Shop). This decorative 19th century shop has been a Dresden institution since 1880 and offers a wide assortment of cheese and other goods. Its intricate tile mosaics on its floor and walls has made it renowned for its decor. Pfund's is also famous for introducing pasteurized milk to the industry; it invented milk soap and specially treated milk for infants as early as 1900. ✉ *Bautzener Str. 79,* ☎ *0351/808–080,* WEB *www.pfunds.de.* ⏲ *Mon.–Fri. 10–6, Sat. 10–3.*

OFF THE BEATEN PATH

RADEBEUL – Follow the road along the north bank of the Elbe to Meissen. The small town of Radebeul, on the way, is a mecca for fans of Westerns. Radebeul is the birthplace of Germany's well-loved novelist Karl May, who wrote highly popular, convincing Westerns without once visiting America. A museum here explains just how he did it. ✉ *Karl-May-Str. 5,* ☎ *0351/837–300.* 🎟 *€5.* ⏲ *Mar.–Oct., Tues.–Sun. 9–5:30; Nov.–Feb., Tues.–Sun. 10–3:30.*

SCHLOSS PILLNITZ – This romantic baroque palace, once a summer retreat for King August the Strong, was built in 1720–22 and is surrounded by a landscaped garden and two smaller palaces, the Wasserpalais and the Bergpalais. Both buildings were designed in Germany's late baroque faux-Chinese pagoda style. Today, they house the **Kunstgewerbemuseum**, which showcases baroque furniture and craft, but also modern design. To get to Schloss Pillnitz, take Tram 10 from the central train station toward Striesen, exit there and continue with Tram 12 (to Schillerplatz), change there again and take Bus 83 to Pillnitz. ✉ *Kleinzschachwitz,* ☎ *0351/261–3201,* WEB *www.staatl-kunstsammlungen-dresden.de.* 🎫 *€1.50.* ⏲ *May–Oct., daily 10–6. Bergpalais closed Mon.; Wasserpalais closed Tues.*

★ 9 **Semperoper** (Semper Opera House). One of Germany's best-known and most popular theaters, this magnificent opera house saw the premieres of Richard Wagner's *Rienzi, Der fliegende Holländer,* and *Tannhäuser,* and Richard Strauss's *Salome, Elektra,* and *Der Rosenkavalier.* The Dresden architect Gottfried Semper built the house in 1838–41 in Italian Renaissance style, then saw his work destroyed in a fire caused by a careless lamplighter. Semper had to flee Dresden after participating in a democratic uprising, so his son Manfred rebuilt the theater in the neo-Renaissance style you see today. Even Manfred Semper's version had to be rebuilt after the devastating bombing raid of February 1945. On the 40th anniversary of that raid—February 13, 1985—the Semperoper reopened with a performance of *Der Freischütz,* by Carl Maria von Weber, another artist who did much to make Dresden a leading center of German music and culture. Even if you're no opera buff, the Semper's lavish interior can't fail to impress. Velvet, brocade, and well-crafted imitation marble create an atmosphere of intimate luxury (it seats 1,323). Guided tours of the building are offered throughout the day, depending on the opera's rehearsal schedule. Tours begin at the entrance to your right as you face the Elbe River. ✉ *Theaterpl. 2,* ☎ *0351/491–1496,* WEB *www.semperoper.de.* 🎫 *Tour €5.* ⏲ *Tours usually start weekdays at 1:30, 2, and 3; weekends at 10.*

3 **Stadtmuseum Dresden im Landhaus** (Dresden City Museum at the Country Mansion). The city's small but fascinating municipal museum tells the ups and downs of Dresden's turbulent past—from the dark Middle Ages to the dark period of the 20th century, such as the bombing of Dresden in February 1945. There are many peculiar exhibits on display, such as an American 250-kg bomb and a stove made from Allied bomb casing. Presenting furniture, medals and uniforms, clothes, and other products from Dresden's Socialist *VEBs* (state-run companies), the museum also gives a look at daily life in former East Germany between 1945 and 1990. ✉ *Wilsdruffer Str. 2,* ☎ *0351/498–660,* WEB *www.stmd.de.* 🎫 *€2.50.* ⏲ *Sat.–Thurs. 10–6 and Wed. 10–8 (May–Sept. only).*

★ 10 **Zwinger** (Bailey). Dresden's magnificent baroque showpiece is entered by way of the mighty Kronentor (Crown Gate), off Ostra-Allee. Augustus the Strong hired a small army of artists and artisans to create a "pleasure ground" worthy of the Saxon court on the site of the former bailey, part of the city fortifications. The artisans worked under the direction of the architect Matthäus Daniel Pöppelmann, who came reluctantly out of retirement to design what would be his greatest work, begun in 1707 and completed in 1728. Completely enclosing a central courtyard filled with lawns, pools, and fountains, the complex is made up of six linked pavilions, one of which boasts a carillon of Meissen bells, hence its name: Glockenspielpavillon.

The Zwinger is quite a scene—a riot of garlands, nymphs, and other baroque ornamentation and sculpture. Wide staircases beckon to galleried walks and to the romantic Nymphenbad, a coyly hidden courtyard where statues of nude women perch in alcoves to protect them from a fountain that spits unexpectedly. The Zwinger once had an open view of the riverbank, but the Semper Opera house now closes in that side. Stand in the center of this quiet oasis, where the city's roar is kept at bay by the outer wings of the structure, and imagine the court festivities held here.

The **Sempergalerie** (Semper Gallery), in the northwestern corner of the complex, was built to house portions of the royal art collections. It contains the world-renowned Gemäldegalerie Alte Meister (Old Masters Gallery). The Zwinger Palace complex also contains a porcelain collection, a zoological museum, and the Mathematisch-Physikalischer Salon, which displays old scientific instruments.

Among the priceless paintings in the Sempergalerie collection are works by Dürer, Holbein, Jan van Eyck, Rembrandt, Rubens, van Dyck, Hals, Vermeer, Raphael (*The Sistine Madonna*), Titian, Giorgione, Veronese, Velázquez, Murillo, Canaletto, and Watteau. On the wall of the entrance archway you'll see an inscription in Russian, one of the few amusing reminders of World War II in Dresden. It reads, in rhyme: "Museum checked. No mines. Chanutin did the checking." Chanutin, presumably, was the Russian soldier responsible for checking one of Germany's greatest art galleries for anything more explosive than a Rubens nude. ☎ *0351/491–4619*, WEB *www.staatl-kunstsammlungen-dresden.de*. 🎫 *€3.60*. ⏲ *Tues.–Sun. 10–6.*

The Zwinger's **Porzellansammlung** (Porcelain Collection; ☎ 0351/491–4619; 🎫 €2; ⏲ Fri.–Wed. 10–6), stretching from the curved gallery that adjoins the Glockenspielpavillon to the long gallery on the east side, is considered one of the best of its kind in the world. The focus, naturally, is on Dresden and Meissen china, but there are also outstanding examples of Japanese, Chinese, and Korean porcelain. The **Rüstkammer** (armory; ☎ 0351/491–4619; 🎫 €1.50; ⏲ Tues.–Sun. 10–6) holds medieval and Renaissance suits of armor and weapons. The **Zoologisches Museum** (Zoological Museum; ☎ 0351/495–2503; 🎫 €2; ⏲ Wed.–Mon. 10–6) has a small but very interesting collection of natural history exhibits, including skeletons of wild animals that once roamed the Elbe Valley. The **Staatlicher Mathematisch-Physikalischer Salon** (State Mathematics and Physics Salon; ☎ 0351/491–4660; 🎫 €1.50; ⏲ Fri.–Wed. 10–6) is packed with rare and historic scientific instruments. ✉ *Zwinger entrance, Ostra-Allee.*

Dining and Lodging

$–$$$ ★ ✕ **Ars Vivendi.** Serving high-quality Italian and French dishes prepared with the freshest ingredients, this restaurant is a perfect mixture of Saxon hospitality and Mediterranean gusto. The Ars Vivendi also attracts wine connoisseurs with one of the best wine lists in town. In summer locals spend a casual evening around tables in the small but lush garden. ✉ *Bürgerstr. 14*, ☎ *0351/840–0969. AE, MC, V.*

$–$$$ ★ ✕ **Marcolinis Vorwerk.** This old villa with a picturesque garden is frequented by a hip, young crowd with a taste for fine wine. The restaurant/art gallery serves Italian dishes with an original spin on meat dishes, such as veal chops served with blue cheese, or chicken baked in a honey-nut crust. In summer, terrace dining provides a spectacular view of Dresden's skyline and the Elbe river. ✉ *Bautzner Str. 96*, ☎ *0351/899–6356. AE, DC, MC, V.*

$–$$$ ✕ **Ristorante Bellotto im Italienischen Dörfchen.** The name of the restaurant refers to the fact that this historic building on the bank of the Elbe once housed Italian craftsmen. They had been brought to Dresden to work on the Hofkirche. Today the lavishly restored, colorful rooms offer a warm welcome. Choose between the beer tavern, café, or the shady garden. The menu is mostly Saxon; the Bellotto restaurant upstairs serves upscale, but not Italian, cuisine. ✉ *Theaterpl. 3,* ☎ *0351/498–160. AE, DC, MC, V.*

$$ ★ ✕ **Sophienkeller.** One of the most lively restaurants in town re-creates an 18th-century beer-cellar atmosphere in the basement of the Taschenberg Palace. Waitresses wear period costumes, and the furniture and porcelain are as rustic as the food is traditional, including the typically Saxon *Gesindeessen* (rye bread, panfried with mustard, slices of pork, and mushrooms, baked with cheese). The Sophienkeller is very popular with larger groups; you might have to wait if you're a party of three or less. ✉ *Taschenbergpalais, Taschenberg 3,* ☎ *0351/497–260. AE, DC, MC, V.*

$–$$ ★ ✕ **Ballhaus Watzke.** One of the city's oldest micro-breweries, the Ballhaus Watzke offers a great panorama view of Dresden from outside the historic downtown area. Several different beers are on tap (you can even help brew one). The extensive menu is made up of mostly hearty local dishes, and also has a great variety of Saxon deserts such as *Apfelparfait im Marzipanmantel an knusprigem Kartoffelreibekuchen* (apple creme baked in marzipan, on crispy potato pancakes). In summer, the beer garden is open for seating. ✉ *Koetzschenbroderstr. 1,* ☎ *0351/852–920. AE, MC, V.*

$$$ ★ ✕🏨 **Hotel Bülow-Residenz.** One of the most intimate first-class hotels in eastern Germany, the Bülow-Residenz is in a baroque palace built in 1730 by a wealthy Dresden city official. Each spacious room is tastefully decorated with thick carpets and mostly dark, warm cherrywood furniture, and has individual accents and modern amenities. In summer the verdant courtyard is a romantic setting for dinner. The Caroussel restaurant ($$$$) holds Saxony's sole Michelin star, and serves a large variety of sophisticated fish and game dishes. ✉ *Rähnitzg. 19, D–01097,* ☎ *0351/80030,* FAX *0351/800–3100,* WEB *www.buelow-residenz.de. 25 rooms, 5 suites. Restaurant, bar, no a/c in some rooms, room service, in-room safes, minibars, cable TV with movies, baby-sitting, dry cleaning, laundry service, concierge, meeting room, parking (fee), some pets allowed (fee), no-smoking floor. AE, DC, MC, V.*

$$$$ ★ 🏨 **Kempinski Hotel Taschenbergpalais Dresden.** Destroyed in wartime bombing but now rebuilt, the historic Taschenberg Palace—the work of the Zwinger architect Matthäus Daniel Pöppelmann—is Dresden's premier address and the last word in luxury, as befits the former residence of the Saxon crown princes. Rooms are as big as city apartments, although suites earn the adjective palatial; they are all furnished with bright elm-wood furniture and have several phone lines, as well as fax machines and data ports. ✉ *Taschenberg 3, D–01067,* ☎ *0351/49120,* FAX *0351/491–2812,* WEB *www.kempinski-dresden.de. 188 rooms, 25 suites. 3 restaurants, 2 bars, room service, in-room data ports, in-room safes, minibars, cable TV with movies, pool, hair salon, massage, sauna, shops, baby-sitting, dry cleaning, laundry service, concierge, business services, meeting room, parking (fee), some pets allowed (fee), no-smoking rooms. AE, DC, MC, V.*

$$–$$$$ 🏨 **artotel Dresden.** The artotel keeps the promise of its rather unusual name. It's all modern, designed by Italian interior architect Denis Santachiara and decorated with more than 600 works of art by Dresden-born painter and sculptor A. R. Penck. It's definitely a place for the artsy crowd; you might find the heavily styled rooms a bit much. The Kunsthalle Dresden and its exhibits of modern art is right next door.

Apart from offering art, the hotel's rooms and service have genuine first-class appeal at lower than usual prices. ✉ *Ostra-Allee 33, D–01067,* ☎ *0351/49220,* FAX *0351/492–2777,* WEB *www.artotel.de. 158 rooms, 16 suites. 2 restaurants, bar, room service, in-room data ports, in-room safes, minibars, cable TV, pool, gym, massage, sauna, steam room, babysitting, dry cleaning, laundry service, concierge, business services, meeting room, parking (fee), some pets allowed (fee), no-smoking rooms. AE, DC, MC, V.*

$$–$$$ 🏨 **Westin Bellevue Dresden.** Across the river from the city core, this modern hotel cleverly incorporates an old restored mansion, which also has the best rooms. From the outside the hotel may look unappealing, but most rooms on the upper floors have spectacular views of the city skyline and Elbe River. If you don't get a room with a view, you can enjoy vistas from the fitness club's panoramic windows. Guest rooms and suites in the old mansion are furnished with restored or reproduced pieces in the 18th-century style. ✉ *Grosse Meissner Str. 15, D–01097,* ☎ *0351/8050,* FAX *0351/805–609,* WEB *www.westin.com. 323 rooms, 16 suites. 3 restaurants, café, bar, room service, in-room data ports, in-room safes, minibars, cable TV with movies, pool, gym, hair salon, massage, sauna, children's programs, concierge, meeting room, parking (fee), pets allowed (fee), no-smoking rooms. AE, DC, MC, V.*

$$ 🏨 **Rothenburger Hof.** One of Dresden's smallest and oldest luxury hotels, the historic Rothenburger Hof opened in 1865, and is only a few steps away from the city's sightseeing spots. A highlight is the dining room, which gives you an impression of how Dresden's wealthy wined and dined some 150 years ago. The rooms are not very large, but comfortable and nicely decorated with furniture that looks antique, but, in fact, is reproduction. The breakfast buffet is rich even by German standards. ✉ *Hauptstr. 3, D–01099,* ☎ *0351/81260,* FAX *0351/812–6222,* WEB *www.dresden-hotel.de. 26 rooms, 13 apartments. Restaurant, no a/c, room service, minibars, cable TV, pool, health club, sauna, Turkish bath, bar, dry cleaning, laundry service, meeting room, free parking, no-smoking rooms. AE, MC, V.*

$$ ★ 🏨 **Schlosshotel Dresden-Pillnitz.** On the grounds of Schloss Pillnitz, this small four-star hotel in the countryside still keeps you close to the city. The beautifully restored mansion is run by the Zepp family, which extends extremely personal service. The airy rooms are decorated with bright colors and timeless, elegant country furniture. Just a few hundred yards from the hotel is a pier from which to depart on an Elbe River cruise. The spa "Vitalzentrum zum goldenen Apfel" is a short walk away. ✉ *August-Böckstiegel-Str. 10, D–01326,* ☎ *0351/26140,* FAX *0351/261–4400,* WEB *www.schlosshotel-pillnitz.de. 42 rooms, 3 suites. Restaurant, minibars, cable TV, bar, dry cleaning, laundry service, meeting rooms, free parking, some pets allowed (fee), no-smoking floor. AE, MC, V.*

Nightlife and the Arts

Dresdeners are known for their industriousness and very efficient way of doing business, but they also know how to spend a night out. Most of Dresden's pubs, bars, and *Kneipen* are in the **Äussere Neustadt** district and along the buzzing **Münzgasse** (between Frauenkirche and Brühlsche Terrasse). Folk and rock music are regularly featured at **Bärenzwinger** (✉ Brühlscher Garten, ☎ 0351/496–5153). One of the best bars in town is the groovy and hip **Aqualounge** (✉ Louisenstr. 36, ☎ 0351/810–6116). The name of the **Planwirtschaft** (✉ Louisenstr. 20, ☎ 0351/801–3187) ironically refers to the Socialist economic system and attracts an alternative crowd. The hip dance club **Dance Factory** (✉ Bautzner Str. 118, ☎ 0351/802–0066) is in an old Stasi garrison. The **Motown Club** (✉ St. Petersburger Str. 9, ☎ 0351/487–4150) attracts a young and stylish crowd.

The opera in Dresden regained its international reputation when the **Semper Opera House** (Sächsische Staatsoper Dresden; ✉ Theaterpl.) reopened in 1985 following an eight-year reconstruction. Tickets are reasonably priced but also hard to get; they're often included in package tours. Try your luck at the evening box office (Abendkasse, left of the main entrance; ☎ 0351/491–1705) about a half hour before the performance. If you're unlucky, take one of the opera house tours.

Dresden's fine **Philharmonie Dresden** (Philharmonic Orchestra Dresden; ✉ Kulturpalast am Altmarkt, ☎ 0351/486–6286) takes center stage in the city's annual music festival, from mid-May to early June. In addition to the annual film festival in April, open-air **Filmnächte am Elbufer** (Elbe Riverside Film Nights; ✉ Am Königsufer, next to the State Ministry of Finance, ☎ 0351/899–320) take place on the bank of the Elbe from late June to late August.

May brings an annual international Dixieland **jazz** festival, and the Jazz Autumn festival follows in October. Jazz musicians perform most nights of the week at the friendly, laid-back **Tonne Jazz Club** (✉ Waldschlösschen, Am Brauhaus 3, ☎ 0351/802–6017).

Shopping

Dresden is almost as famous as Meissen for its porcelain. It's manufactured outside the city in **Freital,** where there's a showroom and shop (Sächsische Prozellan-Manufaktur Dresden, ✉ Bachstr. 16, Freital, ☎ 0351/647–130), open weekdays 9–6. Within Dresden you'll find exquisite Meissen and Freital porcelain at the **Karstadt** department store (✉ Prager Str. 12, ☎ 0351/490–6833). The **Kunststube am Zwinger** (✉ Hertha-Lindner-Str. 10–12, ☎ 0351/490–4082) sells wooden toys and the famous Saxon *Rächermännchen* (Smoking Men) and *Weihnachtspyramiden* (Christmas Lights Pyramids) manufactured by hand in the Erzbirge Mountains.

Sächsische Schweiz

⓯ *42 km (26 mi) southeast of Dresden.*

True mountain climbers may smile at the name of the Sächsische Schweiz (Saxon Switzerland), the mountainous region southeast of Dresden. The highest summit is a mere 182 ft, but the scenery in this region, a mixture of cliffs, gorges, and small canyons, certainly has drama. The stone formations are at least 100 million years old and are a geological leftover of the Elbe River's sandstone deposits. In time, the soft stone was sculpted by wind and water into often grim but fantastic-looking tall columns of stone.

The **Nationalpark** covers 97 square km (37 square mi) of the region. Thanks to its inaccessibility, Saxon Switzerland is home to game and many other wild animals (such as the lynx), which are otherwise extinct in Germany. The park is divided into two parts which can be explored by foot, either following marked routes or by registering with the park rangers for guided tours. To reach the park from Dresden, drive southeast on the B–172 toward Pirna, or take the S-bahn from the central train station to Königsstein or Bad Schandau; both towns are served by buses and minitrains. The train ride itself takes close to an hour. ✉ *Nationalparkverwaltung Sächsische Schweiz, An der Elbe 4, D–01814 Bad Schandau,* ☎ *035022/90060,* WEB *www.nationalpark-saechsische-schweiz.de.* 🎫 *Free.* ⏲ *Free guided walking tours mid-Apr.–Oct., Mon. 10 AM, at Bad Schandau; Tues. 10 AM, at Kurort Rathen; Wed. 10:20 AM at Hinterhermsdorf; Thurs. 10 AM at Wehlen. Call for exact meeting points.*

Görlitz

 *60 km (38 mi) northeast of Dresden, 265 km (165 mi) southeast of Berlin.*

Quiet, narrow cobblestone alleys and late-medieval and Renaissance structures make Görlitz one of the most charming finds in eastern Germany. Once a major commercial hub between Dresden and Wroclaw, Germany's easternmost city fell into small-town oblivion after World War II. The Germans blew up all of the city's bridges over the Neisse River in the last days of the war (the eastern bank of the city now belongs to Poland), but Görlitz was barely touched by Allied bombings.

A vivid reminder of the city's wealthy past is the richly decorated Renaissance homes and warehouses on the **Obermarkt** (Upper Market). During the late Middle Ages, the most common merchandise here was cloth, which was bought and sold from covered wagons and the first floors of many buildings. On **Verrätergasse** (Traitors' Alley), off the Obermarkt, is the **Peter-Liebig-Haus** where the city's cloth makers secretly met in 1527 to plan a rebellion against the city council. Their plans were uncovered, and the plotters were hanged. The initials of the first four words of their meeting place, *Der verräterischen Rotte Tor* (The treacherous gang's gate) were inscribed above the door.

The **Städtische Kunstsammlung** (Municipal Art Collection) has two locations. The massive **Kaisertrutz** (Emperor's Fortress; ✉ Am Obermarkt) once protected the western city gates and now houses late-Gothic and Renaissance art from the area around Görlitz. The **Barockhaus Neissestrasse** (✉ Neissestr. 30) mostly displays furniture and art from the 17th to the 19th centuries. ☎ *03581/671–351.* €1.50. ⏲ *Tues.–Sun. 10–5. Kaisertrutz closed Nov.–Apr.*

The city's oldest section surrounds the **Untermarkt** (Lower Market), whose most prominent building is the **Rathaus.** Its winding staircase is as peculiar as the statue of the goddess of justice, whose eyes—contrary to European tradition—are not covered. The corner house on the square, the **Alte Ratsapotheke** (Old Council Pharmacy) has a sundial on the facade (painted in 1550) based on the 12 signs of the zodiac.

The **Schlesisches Museum** (Silesian Museum) at the magnificent Schönhof building, one of Germany's oldest *Patrizierhäuser,* showcases the history (primarily 17th–19th century) and art of formerly German Silesia. The museum will serve as Germany's central Silesian museum and is adding many new exhibits to its collections of furniture, fine porcelain, art, gold and silverware, jewelry, and sculptures. ✉ *Brüderstr. 8, off Untermarkt,* ☎ *03581/406–215.* WEB *www.schlesisches-museum.de.* €1. ⏲ *Tues.–Sun. 10–5.*

The **Karstadt** department store off busy Marienplatz dates to 1912–13 and is Germany's only original art nouveau department store. The main hall has a colorful glass cupola and several stunning freestanding staircases. ✉ *An der Frauenkirche 5,* ☎ *03581/4600.*

Perched high above the river is the **Kirche St. Peter und Paul** (Sts. Peter and Paul Church), one of Saxony's largest late-Gothic churches, dating to 1423. The real draw of the church is its famous organ, built in 1703 by Eugenio Casparini. Its full and deep sound can be heard during guided tours (which must be prearranged by phone). ✉ *Bei der Peterkirche 5,* ☎ *03581/409–590.* *Free.* ⏲ *Mon.–Sat. 10:30–4, Sun. 11:30–4; guided tours Thurs. and Sun. at noon.*

OFF THE BEATEN PATH

KULTURINSEL EINSIEDEL – This handcrafted amusement park transformed wood, rubber, and cement into a delightful wonderland of ships, forts, games, and mazes. Massive tree trunks stand upside down, roots pointed skyward. Kids descend into tunnels and can choose between various routes that lead to surprising places. This topsy-turvy world is mirrored in the Expressionist-like design of the outdoor stage, restaurant, and covered buildings. Various international arts festivals are held throughout the year. A family entry price includes a credit towards snacks. ✉ *Zentdendorfer Str., Zentendorf, 17 km (11 mi) north of Görlitz* ☎ *035891/4910.* WEB *www.kulturinsel.de.* €*10.* ⏲ *Apr.–Oct., daily 10–6.*

Dining and Lodging

$ ✕ **Le Trou Normand.** Behind the thick walls of a historic baroque buildingt, this charming little restaurant serves the cuisine of northern France. The wine list is impressive, the atmosphere friendly and familial. ✉ *Untermarkt 13,* ☎ *03581/417–037. MC, V. Mon.*

$$–$$$ ★ ✕ **Romantik-Hotel Tuchmacher.** The city's best hotel is also its most modern accommodation in antique disguise. In a mansion dating to 1528, guest rooms with wooden floors and thick ceiling beams are sparsely furnished with modern dark-cherrywood furniture. The colorful ceilings may remind you of Jackson Pollock paintings, but they are original ornaments from the Renaissance. The Schneider-Stube ($–$$$) serves traditional Saxon dishes. All room prices include a luxurious breakfast buffet. ✉ *Peterstr. 8, D–02826,* ☎ *03581/47310,* FAX *03581/473–179,* WEB *www.tuchmacher.de. 42 rooms, 1 suite. Restaurant, bar, room service, minibars, cable TV, gym, sauna, dry cleaning, laundry service, meeting room, free parking, some pets allowed (fee), no-smoking rooms. AE, DC, MC, V.*

Meissen

17 *25 km (16 mi) northwest of Dresden.*

This romantic city on the Elbe River is known the world over for its porcelain, bearing the trademark crossed blue swords. The first European porcelain was made in this area in 1708, and in 1710 the Royal Porcelain Workshop was established in Meissen, close to the local raw materials.

The story of how porcelain came to be produced in Meissen reads like a German fairy tale: the Saxon elector Augustus the Strong, who ruled from 1694 to 1733, urged his court alchemists to find the secret of making gold, something he badly needed to refill a state treasury depleted by his extravagant lifestyle. The alchemists failed to produce gold, but one of them, Johann Friedrich Böttger, discovered a method for making something almost as precious: fine hard-paste porcelain. Already a rapacious collector of Oriental porcelains, Prince August put Böttger and a team of craftsmen up in a hilltop castle—Albrechtsburg—and set them to work. Augustus hoped to keep their formula a state secret, but within a few years fine porcelain was being produced in many parts of Europe.

The **Albrechtsburg,** where the story of Meissen porcelain began, sits high above Old Meissen, towering over the Elbe River far below. The 15th-century castle is Germany's first truly residential one, a complete break with the earlier style of fortified bastions. It fell into neglect as nearby Dresden rose to prominence, but it's still an imposing collection of late-Gothic and Renaissance buildings. In the central *Schutzhof,* a typical Gothic courtyard protected on three sides by high rough-stone walls, is an exterior spiral staircase, the **Wendelstein,** a masterpiece of early masonry hewn in 1525 from a single massive stone block. The ceilings of the castle halls are richly decorated, although many date only from a restoration in 1870. Adjacent to the castle is an early Gothic cathedral. It's a bit of a climb up Burgstrasse and Amtsstrasse to the castle, but a bus runs regularly up the hill from the Marktplatz. ☎ *03521/47070,* WEB *www.albrechtsburg-meissen.de.* *€3.50; €5 with tour.* ⏲ *Mar.–Oct., daily 10–6; Nov.–Feb., daily 10–5. Closed Jan. 10–31.*

A set of porcelain bells at the late-Gothic **Frauenkirche** (Church of Our Lady) on the central Marktplatz was the first of its kind anywhere when installed in 1929. Nearby the Frauenkirche is the 1569 **Alte Brauerei** (Old Brewery), graced by a Renaissance gable and now housing city offices.

The city's medieval past is recounted in the museum of the **Franziskanerkirche** (St. Francis Church), a former monastery. ✉ *Heinrichspl. 3,* ☎ *03521/458–857.* *€2.50.* ⏲ *Daily 11–5.*

The **Staatliche Porzellan-Manufaktur Meissen** (Meissen Porcelain Works) outgrew its castle workshop in the mid-19th century, and today is on the southern outskirts of town. One of its buildings has a demonstration workshop and a museum whose Meissen collection rivals that of the Porcelain Museum in Dresden. ✉ *Talstr. 9,* ☎ *03521/468–700,* WEB *www.meissen.de.* *Museum €3; workshop €2.50, including guided tour.* ⏲ *May–Oct., daily 9–6; Nov.–Apr., daily 9–5.*

Near the porcelain works is the **Nikolaikirche** (St. Nicholas Church; ✉ Neumarkt 29), which holds the largest set of porcelain figures ever crafted (8.2 ft) and also has remains of early Gothic frescoes.

Dining and Lodging

$ ✕ **Domkeller.** Part of the centuries-old complex of buildings ringing the town castle, this ancient and popular hostelry is the best place to enjoy fine wines and hearty German dishes in Meissen. It's also worth a visit for the sensational view of the Elbe River valley from its large dining room and tree-shaded terrace. ✉ *Dompl. 9,* ☎ *03521/457–676. AE, DC, MC, V.*

$$ ✕ **Mercure Parkhotel Meissen.** This art nouveau villa on the bank of the Elbe, across from the hilltop castle, serves nouvelle cuisine in a dining room ($$) with original stained glass and elegantly framed doors. Although most of the luxuriously furnished and appointed rooms are in the newly built annexes, try for one in the villa—and for an unforgettable experience book the *Hochzeitssuite* (wedding suite), on the top floor (€194 a night) with a stunning view. ✉ *Hafenstr. 27–31, D–01662,* ☎ *03521/72250,* FAX *03521/722–904,* WEB *www.mercure.de. 97 rooms, 4 suites. Restaurant, bar, no a/c, room service, in-room data ports, minibars, cable TV, gym, hot tub, massage, sauna, babysitting, dry cleaning, laundry service, meeting room, parking (fee), some pets allowed (fee), no-smoking rooms. AE, DC, MC, V.*

Nightlife and the Arts

Meissen's cathedral, the **Dom** (✉ Dompl. 7, ☎ 03521/452–490), has a year-long music program, with organ and choral concerts every Saturday during the summer. Regular **concerts** (☎ 03521/47070) are held at the Albrechtsburg castle, and in early September the *Burgfestspiele*—open-air evening performances—are staged in the castle's romantic courtyard.

Shopping

Meissen porcelain can be bought directly from the **Staatliche Porzellan-Manufaktur Meissen** (✉ Talstr. 9, ☎ 03521/468–700) and in every china and gift shop in town. To wine connoisseurs, the name *Meissen* is associated with vineyards producing top-quality wines much in demand throughout Germany—try a bottle of Müller-Thurgau, Weissburgunder, or Goldriesling. They can be bought at the from the producer **Sächsische Winzergenossenschaft Meissen** (✉ Bennoweg 9, ☎ 03521/780–970).

Freiberg

18 *40 km (25 mi) south of Meissen.*

Once a prosperous silver-mining community, Freiberg's highlights are two picturesque Gothic town squares, the Upper and Lower markets. The late-Gothic cathedral, with its Golden Gate, constructed in 1230, has a richly decorated interior and a Silbermann organ dating from 1711.

The **Stadt- und Bergbaumuseum** (City and Mining Museum), on central Domplatz, vividly describes the history of silver mining in and around Freiberg. ✉ *Am Dom 1,* ☎ *03731/20250.* *€2.50.* *Tues.–Sun. 10–5.*

En Route Take the winding Freital Valley road (follow the B–173, and then take the country road in Oberschöna towards Frankenstein) west to Chemnitz. You'll pass through the village called **Frankenstein** on the way. It has no relation to Mary Shelley's fictional scientist-baron, but there are some ancient castle ruins in the vicinity.

Chemnitz

19 *35 km (22 mi) west of Freiberg, 80 km (50 mi) southeast of Leipzig.*

On older maps Chemnitz may appear as Karl-Marx-Stadt, an appellation imposed on the city in 1953 to remind the East German working community of the man who really started it all. In 1990 the inhabitants, free to express a choice, overwhelmingly voted to restore the original name. Still, in front of the district council building in the new city center is one of the few remaining Karl Marx memorials in eastern Germany (thanks to the hard-fighting pro-Marx lobby), a massive stylized head sculpted by the Soviet artist Lew Kerbel. Behind it is the motto WORKING MEN OF ALL COUNTRIES, UNITE!—in German, Russian, French, and English. Badly damaged during World War II, Chemnitz has revived as a center of heavy industry, but it never had the architectural attractions of other cities in the area.

Chemnitz's main visual attraction is its 12th-century **Rote Turm** (Red Tower; ✉ off Strasse der Nationen) in the center of the city. The **Altes Rathaus** (Old City Hall; ✉ Marktpl.), dating from 1496–98, incorporates a variety of styles from many reconstructions. Outside the city museum (which is not particularly interesting) on Theaterplatz is a group of 250-million-year-old **petrified tree trunks,** unique in Europe and looking for all the world like a modern work of sculpture.

Dining and Lodging

$$ **Günnewig Hotel Chemnitzer Hof.** This city-center hotel was built in 1930 in early Bauhaus style, in which ornamentation was discarded in favor of abstract design (it is now on the National Historic Register). The spacious rooms are furnished with fine veneers and attractive shades of blue. The restaurant Opera ($$) serves international beef dishes and has an extensive menu of local fish. ✉ *Theaterpl. 4, D–09111,* ☎ *0371/6840,* FAX *0371/676–2587,* WEB *www.guennewig.de. 89 rooms, 3 apartments. Restaurant, bar, no a/c, room service, in-room safes, minibars, cable TV, hair salon, sauna, dry cleaning, laundry service, meeting room, parking (fee), some pets allowed (fee), no-smoking rooms. AE, DC, MC, V.*

$–$$ ✕🏨 **Adelsberger Parkhotel Hoyer.** The first hotel built in Chemnitz after reunification has a modern, graceful exterior and elegant, comfortable guest rooms. The apartments under the steeply sloping eaves are particularly attractive, especially where sunlight streams through large dormer windows. The restaurant's ($–$$) royal-blue-and-white furnishings are flooded with light from floor-to-ceiling bay windows. The imaginative menu includes international cuisine and some hearty Saxon specialties. ✉ *Wilhelm-Busch-Str. 61, D–09127,* ☎ *0371/773–303,* FAX *0371/773–377,* WEB *www.adelsberger-parkhotel.de. 23 rooms, 3 suites. Restaurant, no a/c, room service, minibars, cable TV, gym, sauna, baby-sitting, dry cleaning, laundry service, meeting room, free parking, some pets allowed (fee). AE, MC, V.*

En Route Bundestrasse 95 leads to Leipzig, but for a scene out of World War II, detour at Borna for 176 to **Colditz.** A pretty river valley holds the town whose name still sends a chill through Allied veterans. During the war the Germans converted the town's massive, somber castle into what they believed would be an escape-proof prison for prisoners regarded as security risks. But many managed to flee, employing a catalog of ruses that have since been the stuff of films and books. The castle is now a home for the elderly, but the courtyards and some of the installations used during the war can be visited. You can continue to Leipzig via 107 to the autobahn.

Leipzig

80 km (50 mi) northwest of Chemnitz, 32 km (20 mi) southeast of Halle.

With a population of about 560,000, Leipzig is the second-largest city in eastern Germany (after Berlin) and has long been a center of printing and bookselling. Astride major trade routes, it was an important market town in the Middle Ages, and it continues to be a trading center, thanks to the *Leipziger Messe* (trade and fair shows throughout the year) that bring together buyers from east and west.

Those familiar with music and German literature associate Leipzig with the great composer Johann Sebastian Bach (1685–1750), who was organist and choir director at the Thomaskirche. The 19th-century composer Richard Wagner was born here in 1813; and German poets Goethe and Schiller both lived and worked in the area.

World War II left little of old Leipzig intact. Restoration conveys touches of the city's Renaissance character and art nouveau flair, although some of the newer buildings (notably the university's skyscraper tower) distort the perspective and proportions of the old city.

A Good Walk

Start your tour of downtown Leipzig at the gigantic **Hauptbahnhof** ⑳, the city's main train station and premier shopping mall. Cross the broad expanse of Willy-Brandt-Platz to walk south on Goethestrasse. On your left you'll see the modern **Opernhaus** ㉑, whose socialist facade is a sad contrast to the magnificent old architecture of the Hauptbahnhof. Turn right onto Grimmaischestrasse and after a short walk turn right onto Nikolaistrasse, where you can visit the **Nikolaikirche** ㉒. Returning south, Nikolaistrasse turns into Universitätstrasse, where the rather unappealing **Leipziger Universitätsturm** ㉓ looms above every other building in the city center. On its east side, the tower faces the vast Augustusplatz; across this square stands the **Neues Gewandhaus** ㉔, home of the city's renowned orchestra. Return north to Grimmaischestrasse and walk west; on your left you'll pass by the **Mädlerpassage** ㉕, one of the city's finest shopping arcades, which dates to the turn of the 20th century. Continue a bit farther west, and just off the street on your right

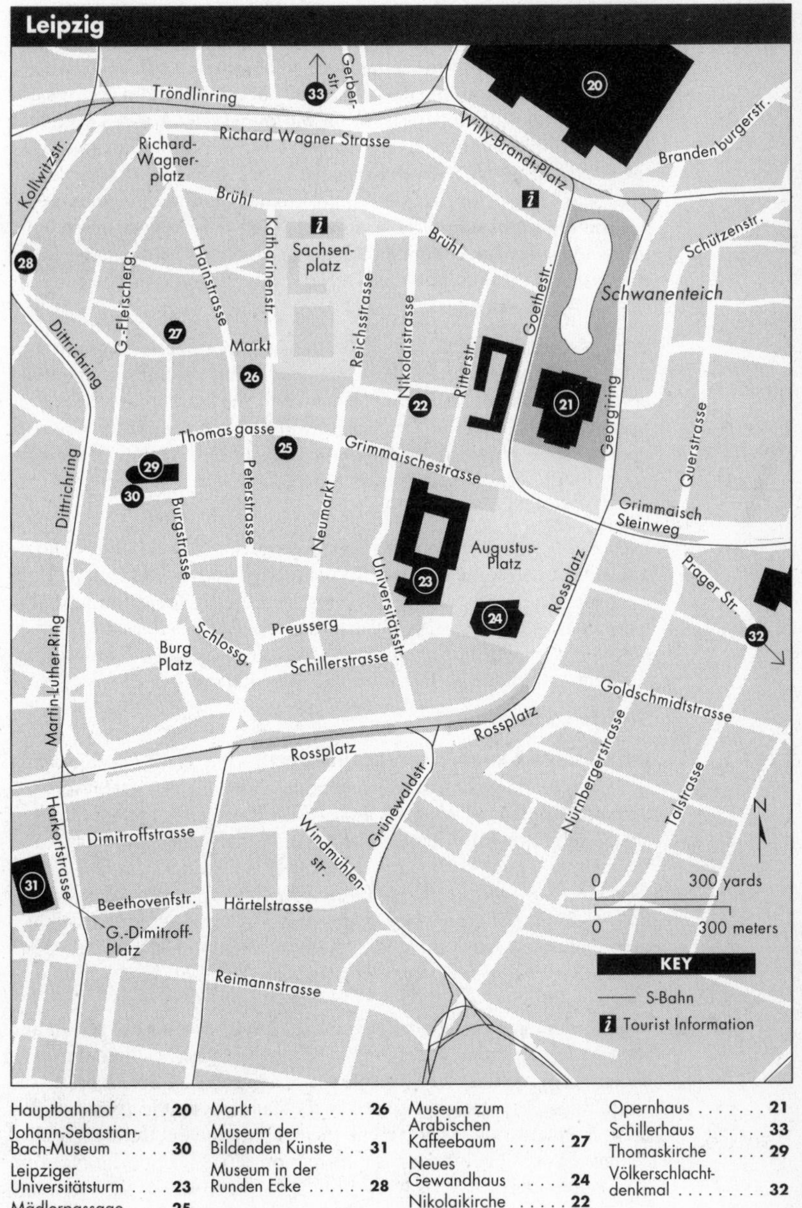

Hauptbahnhof 20	Markt 26	Museum zum Arabischen Kaffeebaum 27	Opernhaus 21
Johann-Sebastian-Bach-Museum 30	Museum der Bildenden Künste . . . 31	Neues Gewandhaus 24	Schillerhaus 33
Leipziger Universitätsturm 23	Museum in der Runden Ecke 28	Nikolaikirche 22	Thomaskirche 29
Mädlerpassage 25			Völkerschlacht-denkmal 32

is the market square, the **Markt** ㉖, with the old city hall and its museum devoted to Leipzig's past. Not far away, off the narrow Barfussgässchen, is the **Museum zum Arabischen Kaffeebaum** ㉗, a coffeehouse and museum devoted to the bitter bean. From here it's just a five-minute walk northwest to the **Museum in der Runden Ecke** ㉘, a special exhibition about East Germany's secret police, the Stasi. Take the Dittrichring to **Thomaskirche** ㉙, where Johann Sebastian Bach once worked as choirmaster. Opposite the church is the **Johann-Sebastian-Bach-Museum** ㉚. Follow Dittrichring and Harkortstrasse south to the **Museum der Bildenden Künste** ㉛, the city's leading art gallery. Right next to the museum stands a 19th-century neo-Gothic monstrosity that serves as Leipzig's city hall.

Leipzig's other main sights are on the city's periphery. Take a streetcar (No. 21, or No. 15 to Meusdorf) from Hauptbahnhof to the **Völkerschlachtdenkmal** ㉜, a huge memorial to the battle that marked the beginning of Napoléon's final defeat in 1815. For another side trip, take streetcar No. 6 to the **Schillerhaus** ㉝, once the home of German poet and playwright Friedrich Schiller.

TIMING

It's possible to walk around the downtown area in just about three hours and still stop in some of the sights mentioned above. The churches can be inspected in less than 20 minutes each. But if you're interested in German history and art, you'll need perhaps two full days because you can spend a whole day just visiting the museums. The Völkerschlachtdenkmal is perfect for a half-day side trip.

Sights to See

OFF THE BEATEN PATH

BOTANISCHER GARTEN (BOTANICAL GARDEN) – This set of splendid open-air gardens and greenhouses incorporates Germany's oldest university botanical garden, which dates from 1542. The journey to the Botanischer Garten stop takes about 15 minutes on Tram 2 or 21 (get off at the Johannisallee stop). ✉ *Linnestr. 1,* ☎ *0341/973–6850.* 💴 *Free.* ⏲ *Gardens: Nov.–Mar., daily 9–4; Apr. and Oct., daily 9–6; May–Sept., daily 9–8. Greenhouses: Nov.–Feb., daily 9–4; Mar.–Apr. and Oct., daily 9–6; May–Sept., daily 9–8. Butterfly house: Apr.–Oct., Tues.–Sun. 10–6. Greenhouse hours can vary according to events.*

⑳ **Hauptbahnhof.** Leipzig's main train station is a major attraction and with its 26 platforms, the station is Europe's largest. Its huge shopping center has more than 150 upscale shops and eateries. But its fin de siècle grandeur remains, particularly in the staircases that lead majestically up to the platforms. As you climb them, take a look at the great arched ceilings high above. A tourist information office is opposite Platform 3, open weekdays 9–5. ✉ *Willy-Brandt-Pl.,* ☎ *0341/141–270 for mall.*

㉚ **Johann-Sebastian-Bach-Museum.** The Bach family home, the old Bosehaus, stands opposite the Thomaskirche and is now a museum devoted to the composer's life and work. Musical instruments on display date to Bach's time. The exhibits are in German only; an English-language guide can be purchased in the shop. ✉ *Thomaskirchhof 16,* ☎ *0341/91370.* 💴 *€3, €6 with guided tour.* ⏲ *Daily 10–5.*

㉓ **Leipziger Universitätsturm** (Leipzig University Tower). Towering over Leipzig's city center is this 470-ft-high structure, which houses administrative offices and lecture rooms. Some of the University of Leipzig students have dubbed it the "Jagged Tooth"; students were also largely responsible for changing the university's name, replacing the postwar title of Karl Marx University with its original one. The **Augustusplatz** spreads out below the university tower like a space-age campus.

25 **Mädlerpassage** (Mädler Mall). This shopper's paradise is Leipzig's finest arcade, where the ghost of Goethe's Faust lurks in every marble corner. Goethe set one of the scenes of *Faust* in the famous Auerbachs Keller restaurant, at No. 2. A bronze group of characters from the play, sculpted in 1913, beckons you down the stone staircase to the restaurant. A few yards away down the arcade is a delightful art nouveau bar called Mephisto, done in devilish reds and blacks. The **Museum für Völkerkunde** (Ethnological Museum; ✉ Grimmaische Str. 2–4, ☎ 0341/268–9568; WEB www.mvl-grassimuseum.de; 🎫 €2; ⏲ Tues.–Fri. 10–6, Sat., Sun. 10–5) is showing its exhibits here while its main home is renovated. ✉ *Grimmaische Str.*

26 **Markt.** Leipzig's showpiece is its huge, old market square. One side is occupied completely by the Renaissance city hall, the **Altes Rathaus,** which houses the **Stadtgeschichtliches Museum,** where Leipzig's past is well documented. ✉ *Markt 1,* ☎ *0341/965–130.* 🎫 *€2.50.* ⏲ *Tues.–Sun. 10–6.*

★ 31 **Museum der Bildenden Künste** (Museum of Fine Arts). The city's leading art gallery occupies the ground floor of the former Reichsgericht, the court where the Nazis held a show trial against the Bulgarian Communist Georgi Dimitroff, accused of masterminding the burning of the Reichstag in 1933. The museum has more than 2,700 paintings representing the German Middle Ages to contemporary American art; one of its finest collections focuses on Cranach the Elder. ✉ *Grimmaische Str. 1–7,* ☎ *0341/216–990.* 🎫 *€2.50; free 2nd Sun. of month.* ⏲ *Tues. and Thurs.–Sun. 10–6, Wed. 1–9:30.*

Museum für Kunsthandwerk (Museum of Handicrafts). Changing exhibits of Leipzig's and East Germany's proud tradition of handicrafts—such as exquisite porcelain, fine tapestry art, or modern Bauhaus design—are presented here. This location is temporary due to the reconstruction of the original Grassimuseum, and exhibits tend to be rather small. A museum shop and café are on the first floor. ✉ *Neumarkt 20,* ☎ *0341/268–9568,* WEB *www.grassimuseum.de.* 🎫 *€4.* ⏲ *Thurs.–Sun. 10–6, Wed. 10–8.*

★ 28 **Museum in der Runden Ecke** (Museum in the Round Corner). The museum may have a comical name, but behind its thick walls lies one of the darkest chapters of post-war Leipzig history: the building once served as the headquarters of the city's secret police, the dreaded *Staatssicherheitsdient.* The exhibition, *Stasi—Macht und Banalität* (Stasi—Power and Banality), not only presents the offices and surveillance work of the Stasi, but also shows hundreds of documents revealing the magnitude of its interests in citizens' private lives. The material is written in German, but the items and the atmosphere still give an impression of how life under such a regime might feel. ✉ *Dittrichring 24,* ☎ *0341/961–2443.* 🎫 *Free, €3 with tour, daily at 3.* ⏲ *Daily 10–6.*

27 **Museum zum Arabischen Kaffeebaum** (Arabic Coffee Tree Museum). This museum and café tells the fascinating history of coffee culture in Europe, particularly in Saxony. The café, on the first floor, is one of the oldest on the Continent and once proudly served a cup of good coffee to such luminaries as Lessing, Schumann, Goethe, and Liszt. The museum features many paintings, Arabian coffee vessels, and coffeehouse games. It also explains the basic principles of roasting coffee. ✉ *Kleine Fleischerg. 4,* ☎ *0341/960–2632.* 🎫 *Free.* ⏲ *Daily 11–7.*

Musikinstrumentenmuseum. This museum of musical instruments has made a small, temporary home next to the Thomaskirchhof. The exhibit showcases 75 musical instruments, mostly from the Renaissance, including the world's oldest Clavichord, constructed in 1543 in Italy.

There are also spinets, flutes, and lutes. Sample sounds of these instruments can be heard while looking at them. The new *Klanglabor* (sound laboratory) is a small special area, where you can try to create your own sounds. ✉ *Thomaskirchhof 20,* ☎ *0341/268–9568,* WEB *www.uni-leipzig.de/museum/musik.* 🎫 *€3.* ⏲ *Tues.–Sun. 11–5.*

24 **Neues Gewandhaus** (New Orchestra Hall). In the shadow of the Leipziger Universitätsturm is the glass-and-concrete home of the city orchestra, one of Germany's greatest. Kurt Masur, is a former director and Herbert Blomstedt is currently at the helm. The statue of Beethoven that stands in the foyer, by sculptor Max Klinger, won first prize at the 1912 World Art Exhibition in Vienna. On the foyer's ceiling, a staggering allegorical painting by Sighard Gilles is devoted to the muse of music. Owing to the world-renowned acoustics of the concert hall, a tone resonates here for a full two seconds. ✉ *Augustuspl. 8,* ☎ *0341/127–0280.*

★ 22 **Nikolaikirche** (St. Nicholas Church). This church with its undistinguished facade was center stage during the demonstrations that helped bring down the Communist regime. Every Monday for months before the government collapsed, thousands of citizens gathered in front of the church chanting, "*Wir sind das Volk*" ("We are the people"). Inside is a soaring Gothic choir and nave. Note the unusual patterned ceiling supported by classical pillars that end in palm tree–like flourishes. Luther is said to have preached from the ornate 16th-century pulpit. ✉ *Nikolaikirchhof,* ☎ *0341/960–5270.* 🎫 *Free.* ⏲ *Mon.–Sat. 10–6; Sun. services 9:30, 11:15, and 5.*

21 **Opernhaus** (Opera House). Leipzig's stage for operas was the first postwar theater to be built in Communist East Germany. Its solid, boxy style is the subject of ongoing local controversy. ✉ *Opposite Gewandhaus, on north side of Augustuspl.*

33 **Schillerhaus** (Schiller House). This small country residence was for a time the home of the German poet and dramatist Friedrich Schiller. While staying here in 1785, Schiller wrote parts of his *Don Carlos* and the first draft of his world-famous *Ode an die Freude* (Ode to Joy). Documenting the 18th-century country lifestyle, the small museum contains period furniture, personal items, and other objects. To reach the Schillerhaus, take streetcar Line 6, 20, or 24 to Menckestrasse or Fritz-Seger-Strasse. ✉ *Menckestr. 42,* ☎ *0341/566–2170.* 🎫 *€1.50.* ⏲ *Apr.–Oct., Tues.–Sun. 11–6; Nov.–Mar., Wed.–Sun. 10–4.*

★ 29 **Thomaskirche** (St. Thomas's Church). Bach was choirmaster at this Gothic church for 27 years, and Martin Luther preached here on Whitsunday 1539, signaling the arrival of Protestantism in Leipzig. Originally the center of a 13th-century monastery, the tall church (rebuilt in the 15th century) now stands by itself, but the names of adjacent streets recall the cloisters. Bach wrote most of his cantatas for the church's famous boys' choir, the Thomasknabenchor, which was founded in the 13th century; the church continues as the choir's home as well as a center of Bach tradition.

The great music Bach wrote during his Leipzig years commanded little attention in his lifetime, and when he died, he was given a simple grave, without a headstone, in the city's Johannisfriedhof (St. John Cemetery). It wasn't until 1894 that an effort was made to find where the great composer lay buried, and after a thorough, macabre search his coffin was removed to the Johanniskirche. That church was destroyed by Allied bombs in December 1943, and Bach subsequently found his final resting place in the church he would have selected: the Thomaskirche. His gravestone below the high altar is never without a floral tribute. Fresh flowers also constantly decorate the statue of Bach that stands before the church, erected on the initiative of the composer Mendelssohn, who performed his own music in the church and revered its great master. You can listen to the famous boys' choir during the *Motette,* a service with a special emphasis on choral music.

Bach's 12 children and the infant Richard Wagner were baptized in the early 17th-century font; Karl Marx and Friedrich Engels also stood before this same font, godfathers to Karl Liebknecht, who grew up to be a revolutionary as well. ✉ *Thomaskirchhof, off Grimmaischestr.,* ☎ *0341/960–2855,* WEB *www.thomaskirche.org.* *Free; €1 for Motette.* ⏲ *Daily 9–6; Motette, Fri. 6* PM*, Sat. 3.*

32 **Völkerschlachtdenkmal** (Memorial to the Battle of the Nations). On the city's outskirts, Prussian, Austrian, Russian, and Swedish forces stood ground against Napoléon's troops in the Battle of the Nations of 1813, a prelude to the French general's defeat two years later at Waterloo. An enormous monument erected on the site in 1913 commemorates the battle. The somber, gray pile of granite and concrete is more than 300 ft high. Despite its ugliness, the site is well worth a visit, if only to wonder at the lengths—and heights—to which the Prussians went to celebrate their military victories and to take in the view from a windy platform (provided you can climb the 500 steps to get there). The Prussians did make one concession to Napoléon in designing the monument: a stone marks the spot where he stood during the three-day battle. An exhibition hall explains the history of the memorial. The memorial can be reached via Streetcar 15 or 21 (leave the tram at the Probstheida station). ✉ *Prager Str.,* ☎ *0341/878–0471.* *€3, €3.50 with tour.* ⏲ *Nov.–Apr., daily 10–4; May–Oct., daily 10–6; tour daily at 10:30, 1:30, and 2:30.*

Dining and Lodging

$$$ ★ ✕ **Kaiser Maximilian.** Leipzig's best Mediterranean restaurant serves inventive Italian and French dishes in a setting dominated by a cool design with high, undecorated walls and black, leather seats. The "Maximilian" is known for its pasta dishes such as *Schwarze Lachstortelloni im Safransud* (black salmon tortelloni cooked in saffron juice), but French classic recipes are equally good. ✉ *Neumarkt 9–19,* ☎ *0341/998–6900. Reservations essential. AE, MC, V.*

$$–$$$ ✕ **Barthels Hof.** This beamed and paneled Gasthaus is a local favorite. The hearty Saxon food has an international touch; some dishes try to be nouvelle German cuisine but lack inspiration and spices. Still, the Barthels Hof is a place to have dinner and a cold beer (or heavy Saxon red wine). The breakfast buffet is impressive, too. If you don't understand the menu, which employs German puns, ask one of the waitresses for an explanation. ✉ *Hainstr. 1,* ☎ *0341/141–310. AE, DC, MC, V.*

$$–$$$ ✕ **Paulaner Restaurant Hutter Culinaria.** Munich's Paulaner Brewery returned to its Leipzig subsidiary of prewar times and transformed the building into a vast complex, with restaurants, a banquet hall, a café, and a beer garden. There's something here for everyone, from intimate dining to noisy, Bavarian-style tavern-table conviviality. The food, such as *Schweinshaxen mit* (salty pork with sauerkraut), is a mix of Bavarian and Saxon. The Paulaner beer is a perfect accompaniment. ✉ *Klosterg. 3–5,* ☎ *0341/211–3115. AE, DC, MC, V.*

$–$$$ ✕ **Auerbachs Keller.** The most famous of Leipzig's restaurants has been around since 1530, and Goethe immortalized one of the several vaulted, historic rooms in his *Faust*. The menu features regional dishes from Saxony, mostly hearty, roasted meat recipes. There is also a good wine list. ✉ *Mädlerpassage, Grimmaische Str. 2–4,* ☎ *0341/216–100. Reservations essential. AE, MC, V.*

$-$$ ✕ **Apels Garten.** This elegant little restaurant in the city center pays homage to nature with landscape paintings on the wall, floral arrangements on the tables, and fresh produce on the imaginative menu. In winter the wild-duck soup with homemade noodles is an obligatory starter; in summer try the *Räucherfischsuppe* (smoked fish soup)—you won't find another soup like it in Leipzig. ✉ *Kolonnadenstr. 2,* ☎ *0341/960–7777. AE, MC, V. No dinner Sun.*

$-$$ ★ ✕ **Zill's Tunnel.** The "tunnel" refers to the barrel-ceiling ground-floor restaurant, where foaming glasses of excellent local beer are served with a smile. The friendly staff will also help you decipher the Old Saxon descriptions of the menu's traditional dishes. Upstairs there's a larger wine restaurant with an open fireplace. In December, goose prepared in a variety of ways (including marinated in heavy brown sauce with wild berries, then oven-baked) is a staple. ✉ *Barfussgässchen 9,* ☎ *0341/960–2078. AE, MC, V.*

$$$-$$$$ ★ **Hotel Fürstenhof Leipzig.** The city's grandest hotel is inside the renowned Löhr-Haus, a revered old mansion. The stunning banquet section is the epitome of 19th-century grandeur, with red wallpaper and dark mahogany wood; the bar is a lofty meeting area under a bright glass cupola. Rooms are spacious and decorated with dark cherrywood designer furniture. The incredible fitness facilities include a dreamy swimming pool, a Finnish sauna, and a Roman steam bath. Service throughout the hotel is attentive and impeccable. ✉ *Tröndlinring 8, D–04105,* ☎ *0341/1400,* FAX *0341/140–3700,* WEB *www.arabellasheraton.com. 84 rooms, 8 suites. Restaurant, bar, piano bar, room service, in-room data ports, in-room safes, minibars, cable TV with movies, pool, gym, massage, sauna, spa, baby-sitting, dry cleaning, laundry service, concierge, business services, meeting room, parking (fee), some pets allowed (fee), no-smoking rooms. AE, DC, MC, V.*

$$-$$$$ **Renaissance Leipzig Hotel.** One of the largest hotels in this city of fairs, the Renaissance Leipzig wins business travelers with its quiet atmosphere. It has large, elegant rooms—with fashionable bathrooms in dark marble. When making a reservation, ask for a room on the Club Floor: for about €12 a day, you get access to the Club Lounge. The hotel's restaurant, Four Seasons, serves light nouvelle German cuisine. The Renaissance is in the heart of old Leipzig, a perfect spot from which to explore the city on foot. ✉ *Grosser Brockhaus 3, D–04103,* ☎ *0341/12920,* FAX *0341/129–2800,* WEB *www.renaissancehotels.com. 295 rooms, 61 suites. Restaurant, bar, room service, in-room data ports, minibars, cable TV, pool, gym, massage, sauna, dry cleaning, laundry service, concierge, business services, meeting room, parking (fee), some pets allowed (fee), no-smoking floor. AE, DC, MC, V.*

$$$ **InterContinental.** Although the hotel's service is outstanding, the high-rise edifice and its accommodations lack true atmosphere. Rooms do offer every luxury, including bathrooms with marble floors and walls and full air-conditioning. The Japanese owners have included a Japanese restaurant and garden. The hotel is convenient to the main train station. ✉ *Gerberstr. 15, D–04105,* ☎ *0341/9880,* FAX *0341/988–1229,* WEB *www.interconti.com. 447 rooms, 27 suites. 3 restaurants, bar, room service, in-room data ports, in-room safes, minibars, cable TV with movies, pool, gym, hair salon, massage, sauna, spa, bowling, shops, baby-sitting, dry cleaning, laundry service, concierge, business services, meeting room, parking (fee), some pets allowed (fee), no-smoking rooms. AE, DC, MC, V.*

$$ **Park Hotel-Seaside Hotel Leipzig.** A few steps from the central train station, the Park Hotel is primarily geared toward the business traveler. The modern rooms may lack some individuality and are definitely not designed for romantic weekends, but the warm service and exceptional bathrooms and swimming pool area make for a pleasant stay.

The Orient Express restaurant, a reconstruction of the famous 19th-century train, is another plus. ✉ *Richard-Wagner-Str. 7, D–04109,* ☎ *0341/98520,* FAX *0341/985–2750,* WEB *www.seaside-hotels.de. 281 rooms, 9 suites. Restaurant, bar, no a/c, room service, in-room safes, minibars, cable TV, health club, hot tub, sauna, baby-sitting, dry cleaning, laundry service, concierge, meeting room, parking (fee), some pets allowed (fee), no-smoking floor. AE, DC, MC, V.*

$$ **Ringhotel Adagio Leipzig.** The quiet Adagio, tucked away behind the facade of a 19th-century city mansion, is centrally located between the Grassimuseum and the Neues Gewandhaus. All rooms are individually furnished; when making a reservation, ask for a "1920s room," which features the style of the Roaring '20s and bathtubs almost as large as a whirlpool. The Champagner-Offerte package includes a dinner in the hotel's restaurant and a city tour. ✉ *Seeburgstr. 96, D–04103,* ☎ *0341/216–699,* FAX *0341/960–3078,* WEB *www.hotel-adagio.de. 30 rooms, 1 suite, 1 apartment. Restaurant, bar, no a/c, cable TV, dry cleaning, laundry service, meeting room, parking (fee), some pets allowed (fee), no-smoking rooms. AE, DC, MC, V.*

Nightlife and the Arts

The *Kneipenszene* (pub scene) of Leipzig is centered around the **Drallewatsch** (a Saxon slang word for "going out"), the small streets and alleys around Grosse and Kleine Fleischergasse. A magnet for young people is the **Moritzbastei** (✉ Universitätsstr. 9, ☎ 0341/702–590), reputedly Europe's largest student club, with bars, a disco, a café, a theater, and a cinema. Nonstudents are welcome. One of the city's top dance clubs is the hip **Spizz Keller** (✉ Markt 9, ☎ 0341/960–8043). In the august setting of the city theater, the Schauspielhaus, is the **Tanzpalast** (✉ Dittrichring, ☎ 0341/960–0596), which attracts a thirtysomething crowd. The upscale **Weinstock** bar, pub, and restaurant (✉ Markt 7, ☎ 0341/1406–0606) is in a Renaissance building and offers a huge selection of good wines. A favorite hang-out among the city's new business elite is the **Schauhaus** (✉ Bosestr. 1, ☎ 0341/960–0596), a stylish bar serving great cocktails.

The **Neues Gewandhaus** (✉ Augustuspl. 8, D–04109, ☎ 0341/127–0280), a controversial piece of architecture, is home to an undeniably splendid orchestra. Tickets to concerts are very difficult to obtain unless you reserve well in advance and in writing only. Sometimes spare tickets are available at the box office a half hour before the evening performance. Leipzig's annual music festival, **Music Days,** is in June.

One of Germany's most famous cabarets, the **Leipziger Pfeffermühle** (✉ Thomaskirchhof 16, ☎ 0341/960–3196) has a lively bar off a courtyard opposite the Thomaskirche. On pleasant evenings the courtyard fills with benches and tables, and the scene rivals the indoor performance for entertainment. The variety theater **Krystallpalast** (✉ Magazinstr. 4, ☎ 0341/140–660) features a blend of circus, vaudeville, and comedy.

The **Gohliser Schlösschen** (✉ Menckestr. 23, ☎ 0341/589–690), a small rococo palace outside Leipzig's center, frequently holds concerts. It's easily reached by public transportation: Take streetcar No. 20 or No. 24, then walk left up Poetenweg; or take streetcar No. 6 to Menckestrasse. Daytime tours can be arranged for groups.

Shopping

Leading off the Markt, small streets attest to Leipzig's rich trading past. Tucked in among them are glass-roof arcades of surprising beauty and elegance, among them the wonderfully restored **Specks Hof,** the **Barthels Hof,** the **Jägerhof,** and the **Passage zum Sachsenplatz.** Invent a headache and step into the *Apotheke* (pharmacy) at Hainstrasse 9—it is spectacularly art nouveau, with finely etched and stained glass and rich mahogany. For more glimpses into the past, check out the antiquarian bookshops of the nearby **Neumarkt Passage.**

The **Hauptbahnhof** (☒ Willy-Brandt-Pl.) offers more than 150 shops, restaurants, and cafés. All shops are open Monday through Saturday 9:30 AM–10 PM, and many shops are also open on Sunday, with the same hours. Thanks to the historic backdrop, it's one of the most beautiful and fun shopping experiences in eastern Germany.

SAXONY-ANHALT

The central state of Saxony-Anhalt is a region rich in natural attractions. In the Altmark, on the edge of the Harz Mountains, fields of grain and sugar beets stretch to the horizon. In the mountains themselves are the deep gorge of the Bode River and the stalactite-filled caves of Rubeland. The songbirds of the Harz are renowned, and though pollution has taken its toll, both the flora and fauna of the Harz National Park (which includes much of the region) are coming back. Atop the Brocken, the Harz's highest point, legend has it that witches convene on Walpurgis Night. When Germany was divided, the Brocken was a grim frontier area closed to visitors, but today large numbers of tourists come to see its Alpine flowers and the views on clear days.

Saxony-Anhalt's Letzlinger Heide (Letzling Heath), another home to rare birds and animals, is one of Germany's largest tracts of uninhabited land. The Dübener Heide (Düben Heath), south of Wittenberg, has endless woods of oaks, beeches, and evergreens that are wonderful to explore by bike or on foot. In and around Dessau are magnificent parks and gardens.

Architecturally, Saxony-Anhalt abounds in half-timber towns and Romanesque churches. Quedlinburg has both the oldest half-timber house in Germany and the tomb of Germany's first king, 10th-century Henry I. In Dessau the Bauhaus School pointed the world to modern architecture and design just before the start of World War II. Music has thrived in Saxony-Anhalt as well. Among its favorite sons are the composers Georg Philipp Telemann, of Magdeburg; Georg Friedrich Handel, of Halle; and in modern times, Kurt Weill, of Dessau. And it was in Wittenberg that Martin Luther nailed his 95 Theses to a church door.

Wittenberg

 *107 km (62 mi) southwest of Berlin, 67 km (40 mi) north of Leipzig.*

Protestantism was born in the little town of Wittenberg (also called Lutherstadt-Wittenberg). In 1508 the fervent, idealistic young Martin Luther, who had become a priest only a year earlier, arrived to study and teach at the new university founded by Elector Frederick the Wise. Nine years later, enraged that the Roman Catholic Church was pardoning sins in exchange for the sale of indulgences, Luther posted his 95 Theses attacking the policy on the door of the Castle Church. Thereafter, Europe became a very different place.

Martin Luther is still the center of attention in Wittenberg, and sites associated with him are marked with plaques and signs. Post-Communist Wittenberg, however, is also an increasingly sprightly home of art galleries, clothing shops, and business travelers' hotels and restaurants that take advantage of the town's historic draw. Menus offer such dishes as *Luthersuppe* (soup of tomatoes, herbs, and croutons) and *Melanch-*

thontaler (a plate of pasta filled with venison; the name refers to a colleague of Luther's). You can see virtually all of historic Wittenberg on a 2-km (1-mi) stretch of Collegienstrasse and Schlossstrasse that begins at the railroad tracks and ends at the Schlosskirche (Castle Church).

In a small park where Weserstrasse meets Collegienstrasse, the **Luthereiche** (Luther Oak) marks the spot where in 1520 Luther burned the papal bull excommunicating him for his criticism of the Church. The present oak was planted in the 19th century.

Within **Lutherhalle** (Luther Hall) is the Augustinian monastery where Martin Luther lived both as a teacher-monk and later, after the monastery was dissolved, as a married man. Today it is a museum dedicated to Luther and the Reformation. (Due to renovation, it will be closed until March 2003. Parts of the exhibit are on display at the Marktplaz and Cranachhaus.) Visitors enter Lutherhalle through a garden and an elegant door with a carved stone frame; it was a gift to Luther from his wife, Katharina von Bora. Inside the much-restored structure is the monks' refectory, where works of Luther's contemporary, the painter Lucas Cranach the Elder, are displayed. The room that remains closest to the original is the dark, wood-paneled Lutherstube. The Luthers and their six children used it as a living room, study, and meeting place for friends and students. In it is a pulpit Luther is believed to have used. Prints, engravings, paintings, manuscripts, coins, and medals relating to the Reformation and Luther's translation of the Bible into the German vernacular are displayed throughout the house. ✉ *Collegienstr. 54,* ☎ *03491/42030,* WEB *www.martinluther.de.* 🎫 *€3.50.* ⏲ *Apr.–Oct., daily 9–6; Nov.–Mar., Tues.–Sun. 10–5.*

In the elegantly gabled Renaissance **Melanchthonhaus** (Melanchthon House), the humanist teacher and scholar Philipp Melanchthon corrected Luther's translation of the New Testament from Greek into German. Luther was shut up in the Wartburg in Eisenach at the time, and as each section of his manuscript was completed it was sent to Melanchthon for approval. (Melanchthon is a Greek translation of the man's real name, Schwarzerdt, which means "black earth"; humanists routinely adopted such classical pseudonyms.) The second-floor furnishings have been painstakingly re-created after period etchings. A green tile stove in his study is thought to have been made after a Cranach design. In the tranquil back garden, a little fountain has been bubbling from a spring ever since Melanchthon's day. ✉ *Collegienstr. 60,* ☎ *03491/403–279,* WEB *www.martinluther.de.* 🎫 *€2.50.* ⏲ *Apr.–Oct., Mon.–Sun. 9–6; Nov.–Mar., Tues.–Sun. 10–5.*

From 1514 until his death in 1546, Martin Luther preached two sermons a week in the twin-tower **Stadtkirche St. Marien** (Parish Church of St. Mary). He and Katharina von Bora were married here (Luther broke with monasticism in 1525 and married the former nun). The altar triptych by Lucas Cranach the Elder includes a self-portrait as well as portraits of Luther wearing the knight's disguise he adopted when hidden away at the Wartburg; Luther preaching; Luther's wife and one of his sons; Melanchthon; and Lucas Cranach the Younger. Also notable is the 1457 bronze baptismal font by Herman Vischer the Elder. On the church's southeast corner, you'll find a discomforting juxtaposition of two Jewish-related monuments: a 1304 mocking caricature called the Jewish Pig, erected at the time of the expulsion of the town's Jews, and, on the cobblestone pavement, a contemporary memorial to the Jews who died at Auschwitz. ✉ *Kirchpl.,* ☎ *03491/404–415.* 🎫 *€1.50, including tour.* ⏲ *May–Oct., Mon.–Sat. 9–5, Sun. 11:30–5; Nov.–Apr., Mon.–Sat. 10–4, Sun. 1–4.*

Two statues are the centerpiece of the **Marktplatz** (market square): an 1821 statue of Luther by Johann Gottfried Schadow, designer of the quadriga and Victory goddess and atop Berlin's Brandenburg Gate, and an 1866 statue of Melanchthon by Frederick Drake. Their backdrop is the handsome white High Renaissance **Rathaus** (town hall), showcasing some of the exhibits from the Lutherhalle. Gabled Renaissance houses containing shops line part of the square. ✉ *Markt 26,* ☎ *03491/421–720,* 🎫 *€2.* ⏲ *Apr.–Oct., daily 9–6; Nov.–Mar., Tues.–Sun. 10–5.*

The **Cranachhaus** is believed to have been the first home in town of Lucas Cranach the Elder, the court painter, printer, mayor, pharmacist, and friend of Luther's. His son, the painter Lucas Cranach the Younger, was born here. Some of the interior has been restored to its 17th-century condition. It is now a gallery of changing art exhibits. Until March 2003, it will present many of Cranach the Elder's original paintings, which are usually on display at the Lutherhalle. ✉ *Markt 4,* ☎ *03491/420–1915,* WEB *www.home.t-online.de/home/cranach-hoefe.* 🎫 *€2.* ⏲ *Apr.–Oct., daily 9–6; Nov.–Mar., Tues.–Sun. 10–5.*

Renaissance man Lucas Cranach the Elder probably the wealthiest man in Wittenberg in his day, lived in two different houses during his years in town. In a second **Cranachhaus,** near the Schlosskirche (Castle Church), he not only lived and painted but also operated a print shop, which has been restored, and an apothecary. The courtyard, where it is thought he did much of his painting, remains much as it was in his day. Children attend the **Malschule** (drawing school) here. ✉ *Schlossstr. 1,* ☎ *03491/410–919.* 🎫 *Free.* ⏲ *Mon.–Thurs. 8–4, Fri. 8–3.*

In 1517 the indignant Martin Luther affixed to the doors of the **Schlosskirche** (Castle Church) his 95 Theses attacking the Roman Catholic Church's policy of selling indulgences. Written in Latin, the theses might have gone unnoticed had not someone—without Luther's knowledge—translated them into German and distributed them. In 1521, the Holy Roman Emperor Charles V summoned Luther to Worms when Luther refused to retract his position. It was on the way home from his confrontation with the emperor that Luther was "captured" by his protector, Elector Frederick the Wise, and hidden from papal authorities in Eisenach for the better part of a year. The church's original wooden doors have been replaced by bronze ones that reproduce the Latin text of the theses. Inside the church, simple bronze plaques mark the burial places of Luther and Melanchthon. ✉ *Schlosspl.,* ☎ *03491/402–585.* 🎫 *€1.50.* ⏲ *May–Oct., Mon.–Sat. 10–5, Sun. 11:30–5; Nov.–Apr., Mon.–Sat. 10–4, Sun. 11:30–4.*

Dining and Lodging

$–$$ ✕ **Schlosskeller.** At the back of the Schlosskirche, this restaurant with historic atmosphere specializes in German dishes, such as *Schlosskellerpfanne* (pork fillets with fried potatoes, tomatoes, and pepper bells). ✉ *Schlosspl. 1,* ☎ *03491/480–805. AE, MC, V.*

$ ★ ✕ **Luther-Schenke.** Dressed in costumes of Luther's day, waiters serve the beer and the dishes they think the reformer might have eaten—roast boar and pigs' knuckles with sauerkraut—as well as such fare as salsa, pasta, lamb, or chicken roasted on a spit. The brick-vaulted beer cellar has a laid-back ambience. ✉ *Markt 2,* ☎ *03491/406–592. AE, DC, MC, V.*

$$ 🏨 **Best Western Stadtpalais Wittenberg.** In an old city mansion just a few steps from the Lutherhaus, this hotel presents modern style and high-quality service. The elegant lobby and upscale rooms may suggest high prices, but the rates are more than reasonable. The best deals are the special "executive double rooms," which are 330 square ft and have many extras. The rooms lack individuality, but their shiny look and the quality furniture make up for the blandness. ✉ *Collegienstr. 56–57, D–06886,* ☎ *03491/4250,* FAX *03491/425–100,* WEB *www.bestwestern.de. 78 rooms. Restaurant, bar, no a/c in some rooms, minibars, cable TV, sauna, steam room, baby-sitting, dry cleaning, laundry service, meeting room, parking (fee), some pets allowed (fee), no-smoking rooms. AE, DC, MC, V.*

$ **Hotel Grüne Tanne.** Four hundred years ago a knight's estate stood on the land occupied today by this cozy country hotel. A hostelry since 1871, the Grüne Tanne is a starting place for walks and bicycle and horseback rides into the countryside. The outside terrace is used for summer dining. A shuttle service goes to the Wittenberg train station. ✉ *Am Teich 1, D–06896 Wittenberg/Reinsdorf,* ☎ *03491/6290,* FAX *03491/629–250,* WEB *www.gruenetanne.de. 40 rooms, 1 apartment, 2 suites. Restaurant, no a/c, cable TV, sauna, free parking, some pets allowed (fee). AE, DC, MC, V.*

En Route From Wittenberg take B–187 west for 13 km (8 mi), then turn onto B–107 south for 8 km (5 mi) to Wörlitz. Leopold III Friedrich Franz of Anhalt-Dessau loved gardens and sought to create a garden kingdom in his lands. He had **Wörlitz Park** laid out between 1765 and 1802, largely in the naturalistic English style. It was the first such garden created in central Europe, with meadowlands and a lake, canals and woods, rocks and grottoes. You can walk or bicycle the 42 km (26 mi) to Dessau through the park.

From Wörlitz continue another 5 km (3 mi) on B–107 to the **Oranienbaum-Park.** Leopold enlarged his garden kingdom by incorporating Oranienbaum—a 17th-century baroque palace—and adding an English-Chinese garden with a teahouse as well as a pagoda inspired by the one in England's Kew Gardens. He further developed Park Lusium on the Elbe River, which he redesigned with fountains, sculptures, and bridges, and an orangery. After visiting Oranienbaum, go west on the road that becomes B–185 in Dessau.

On B–185 9 km (5½ mi) outside Dessau you'll come to Mosigkau and its 18th-century late-baroque **Schloss Mosigkau** (Mosigkau Palace). Prince Leopold of Anhalt-Dessau commissioned the palace for his favorite daughter, Anna Wilhelmine. Never married, she lived there alone, and when she died, she left the property to an order of nuns. They immediately tore up the formal grounds to make an English-style park, and after a post–World War II attempt to restore the original baroque appearance, money and enthusiasm ran out. The palace itself, however, was always well maintained. Only a quarter of the rooms can be visited, but they include one of Germany's very few baroque picture galleries. Its stucco ceiling is a marvel of rococo decoration, a swirling composition of pastel-color motifs. ✉ *Knobelsdorffallee 3, Dessau,* ☎ *0340/521–139.* *Palace €3; gardens free.* ⏲ *Apr. and Oct., Tues.–Sun. 10–4:30; May–Sept., Tues.–Sun. 10–6.*

Dessau

35 *35 km (22 mi) southwest of Wittenberg.*

The name *Dessau* is known to every student of modern architecture. In 1925–26 architect Walter Gropius set up his highly influential Bauhaus school of design here. Gropius hoped to replace the dark and inhumane tenement architecture of the 1800s with standardized yet spacious and bright apartments. His ideas and methods were used in building 316 villas in the city's Törten section in the 1920s. For a contrast to the no-nonsense Bauhaus architecture, look at downtown

Dessau's older buildings, including the Dutch baroque **St. George's Church** (✉ Georgenstr. 15), built in 1712.

Architectural styles that would influence the appearance of such cities as New York, Chicago, and San Francisco were conceived in the **Bauhaus Building.** The architecture school is still operating, and the building can be visited. Other structures designed by Gropius and the Bauhaus architects, among them the Meisterhäuser, are open for inspection off Ebertallee and Elballee. ✉ *Gropiusallee 38,* ☎ *0340/650–8251,* WEB *www.bauhaus-dessau.de.* *€4.* *Daily 10–6. Meisterhäser, Nov.–Mar., Tues.–Sun. 10–5; Apr.–Oct., Tues.–Sun. 10–6.*

Halle

36 *52 km (32 mi) south of Dessau.*

This 1,000-year-old city, built on the salt trade, has suffered from the shortfalls of Communist urban planning. The hastily built residential area, Halle-Neustadt, was cynically nicknamed "Hanoi." Yet the Old City has an unusual beauty, particularly its spacious central marketplace, the **Markt,** its northern side bristling with five distinctive sharp-steepled towers.

Of the four towers belonging to the late-Gothic **Marienkirche** (St. Mary's Church), two are connected by a vertiginous catwalk bridge. Martin Luther preached in the church; George Friedrich Handel (Händel in German), born in Halle in 1685, was baptized at its font and went on to learn to play the organ beneath its high, vaulted ceiling. The Markt's fifth tower is Halle's celebrated **Roter Turm** (Red Tower; ✉ Markt), built between 1418 and 1506 as an expression of the city's power and wealth. It houses a carillon and the local tourist office.

The **Marktschlösschen** (Market Palace), a late-Renaissance structure just off the market square, has an interesting collection of historical musical instruments, some of which could have been played by Handel and his contemporaries. ✉ *Markt 13,* ☎ *0345/202–9141.* *Free.* *Weekdays 10–5, weekends 10–6.*

Handel's birthplace, the **Händelhaus,** is now a museum devoted to the composer. The entrance hall displays glass harmonicas, curious musical instruments perfected by Benjamin Franklin in the 1760s. ✉ *Grosse Nikolaistr. 5,* ☎ *0345/500–900.* *€2.60, free Thurs.* *Fri.–Wed. 9:30–5:30, Thurs. 9:30–7.*

The **Moritzburg** (Moritz Castle) was built in the late 15th century by the archbishop of Magdeburg after he had claimed the city for his archdiocese. The typical late-Gothic fortress with a dry moat and a sturdy round tower at each of its four corners was a testament to Halle's early might, which vanished with the Thirty Years' War. Prior to World War II the castle contained a leading gallery of German Expressionist paintings, which were ripped from the walls by the Nazis and condemned as "degenerate." Some of the works are back in place at the **Staatliche Galerie Moritzburg,** together with some outstanding late 19th- and early 20th-century art. You'll find Rodin's famous sculpture *The Kiss* here. ✉ *Friedemann-Bach-Pl. 5,* ☎ *0345/212–590,* WEB *www.moritzburg.halle.de.* *€4.* *Tues. 11–8:30, Wed.–Sun. 10–6.*

Halle's only early Gothic church, the **Dom** (cathedral) stands about 200 yards southeast of the Moritzburg. Its nave and side aisles are of equal height, a characteristic of much Gothic church design in this part of Germany. ✉ *Dompl. 3,* ☎ *0345/202–1379.* *Free.* *June–Oct., Mon.–Sat. 2–4.*

The former archbishop's home, the 16th-century **Neue Residenz** (New Residence), houses the **Geiseltalmuseum** and its world-famous collection of fossils dug from brown coal deposits in the Geisel Valley near Halle. ✉ *Domstr. 5,* ☎ *0345/552–6135.* 🎟 *Free.* ⏲ *Weekdays 9–noon and 1–5; every 2nd and 4th Sat. and Sun. 9–1.*

The salt trade on which Halle built its prosperity is documented in the **Technisches Halloren- und Salinemuseum** (Technical Mine Museum). The old method of evaporating brine from local springs is sometimes demonstrated. A replica salt mine shows the salt-mining process, and the exquisite silver goblet collection of the Salt Workers' Guild is on display. The museum is on the south side of the Saale River (cross the Schiefer Bridge to get there). ✉ *Mansfelderstr. 52,* ☎ *0345/202–5034.* 🎟 *€2.10.* ⏲ *Tues.–Sun. 10–5.*

Dining and Lodging

$–$$$ ✕ **Restaurant Mönchshof.** Hearty German fare in hearty portions is served in the high-ceiling, dark-wood surroundings. Lamb from Saxony-Anhalt's Wettin region and venison are specialties in season, but there are always fish and crisp roast pork on the menu. The wine list is extensive, with international vintages. ✉ *Talamstr. 6,* ☎ *0345/202–1726. AE, DC, MC, V.*

$$ ✕🏨 **Ankerhof Hotel.** Stone walls and old wooden beams are a reminder of the tollhouse that once stood here beside the saltworks. The hotel's Alter Zollkeller restaurant ($–$$) serves both regional and international dishes, such as *Schweinemedaillons an Metaxasauce* (roast pork medallions with Metaxa sauce—a Greek schnapps). ✉ *Ankerstr. 2a, D–06108,* ☎ *0345/232–3200,* FAX *0345/232–3219,* WEB *www.ankerhofhotel.de. 50 rooms, 5 suites. 2 restaurants, in-room safes, minibars, cable TV, health club, sauna, bowling, free parking, some pets allowed (fee), no-smoking rooms. AE, DC, MC, V.*

$$$ 🏨 **Kempinski Hotel Rotes Ross.** Behind a 265-year-old facade in the city center, this friendly, well-equipped modern hotel has a certain old-fashioned elegance in its rooms. The modern wing lacks the old-world atmosphere of the original main building. ✉ *Leipziger Str. 76, D–06108,* ☎ *0345/29220,* FAX *0345/292–2222,* WEB *www.kempinski.com. 75 rooms, 14 suites. Restaurant, Weinstube, room service, in-room safes, minibars, cable TV with movies, health club, hot tub, sauna, baby-sitting, dry cleaning, laundry service, concierge, convention center, meeting room, free parking, some pets allowed (fee), no-smoking rooms. AE, DC, MC, V.*

Nightlife and the Arts

The city of Händel is of course an important music center, and Halle is famous for its opera productions, orchestral concerts, and particularly for its choirs. For schedules, prices, and reservations of opera performances staged at the city's renowned **Opernhaus,** call 0345/5110–0355. The city's main orchestra, the **State Philharmonic Orchestra,** performs at the Konzerthalle (✉ Brauhausstr. 26, ☎ 0345/221–3026 for concert information and tickets). The annual **Händel Festival** (☎ 0345/5009–0222) takes place in the first half of June, and two youth-choir festivals occur in May and October.

En Route To reach Quedlinburg in the Harz, you can take E–49 directly, or take a somewhat longer route via E–80 to **Eisleben** first. Martin Luther came into and out of this world here. Both the square Franconian house with the high-pitched roof that was his birthplace and the Gothic patrician house where he died are open to the public, as are, on request, the Petri-Pauli Kirche (Church of Sts. Peter and Paul), where he was baptized, and the Andreaskirche (St. Andrew's Church), where his funeral was held. From Eisleben take B–180 north to join with E–49 to Quedlinburg.

Quedlinburg

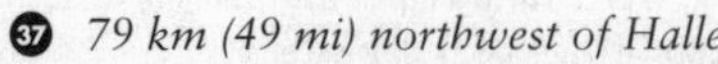

37 *79 km (49 mi) northwest of Halle.*

This medieval Harz town has more half-timber houses than any other town in Germany: more than 1,600 of them line the narrow cobblestone streets and squares. The town escaped World War II unscathed, and in GDR days, though not kept up, Quedlinburg was treasured, so it remains much as it was centuries ago. Today it is a UNESCO World Heritage Site.

For nearly 200 years Quedlinburg was a favorite imperial residence and site of imperial diets, beginning with the election in 919 of Henry the Fowler as Henry I, first Saxon king of Germany. It became a major trading city and a member of the Hanseatic League, equal in stature to Köln.

The Altstadt (Old Town) is full of richly decorated half-timber houses, particularly along Mühlgraben, Schuhof, the Hölle, Breitestrasse, and Schmalstrasse. Notable on the **Marktplatz** are the Renaissance Rathaus (town hall), with a 14th-century statue of Roland signifying the town's independence, and the baroque 1701 Haus Grünhagen. Street and hiking maps and guidebooks (almost all in German) are available at the information office at the Rathaus. ⊠ *Markt 2,* ☎ *03946/90550.* 🎫 *Free.* ⏲ *Mon.–Sat. 9–3; tour by appointment only.*

The oldest half-timber house in Quedlinburg, built about 1310, is now the **Ständerbau Fachwerkmuseum,** a museum of half-timber construction. ⊠ *Wordg. 3,* ☎ *03946/3828.* 🎫 *€2.* ⏲ *Fri.–Wed. 11–5.*

Placed behind half-timber houses so as not to affect the town's medieval feel is the sophisticated, modern **Lyonel Feininger Gallery.** When the art of American-born painter Lyonel Feininger, a Bauhaus teacher in both Weimar and Dessau, was declared "decadent" by the Hitler regime in 1938, the artist returned to America. Left behind with a friend were engravings, lithographs, etchings, and paintings. The most comprehensive Feininger print collection in the world is displayed here. ⊠ *Finkenherd 5a,* ☎ *03946/2238.* 🎫 *€6.* ⏲ *Apr.–Oct., Tues.–Sun. 10–6; Nov.–Mar., Tues.–Sun. 10–5.*

On top of the Schlossberg (Castle Hill), with a terrace overlooking woods and valley, perch Quedlinburg's largely Renaissance castle buildings—a church, an abbess's dwelling (Henry I's widow, Mathilde, founded a convent school here), and the building that once housed the abbey kitchens and workshops, now the **Schlossmuseum** (Castle Museum). Exhibits feature the history of the town and the castle, artifacts of the Bronze Age, and the wooden cage in which a captured 14th-century robber baron was put on public view. Restored 17th- and 18th-century rooms give an impression of castle life at that time. ⊠ *Schlossberg 1,* ☎ *03946/2730.* 🎫 *€2.50.* ⏲ *Daily 10–5.*

The simple, graceful **Stiftskirche St. Servatius** (Collegiate Church of St. Servatius) is one of the most important and best preserved 12th-century Romanesque structures in Germany. Henry I and his wife, Mathilde, are buried in its crypt. The renowned Quedlinburg Treasure of 10th-, 11th-, and 12th-century gold and silver and bejeweled manuscripts were also kept here. Some of this treasure was stolen by an American soldier in 1945 and returned to the church in 1993. In Nazi days SS leader Heinrich Himmler made the church into a shrine dedicated to the SS, insisting that it was only appropriate since Henry I was the founder of the first German Reich. ⊠ *Schlossberg 1,* ☎ *03946/709–900.* 🎫 *€3.* ⏲ *May–Oct., Tues.–Fri. 10–6, Sat. 10–4, Sun. noon–6; Nov.–Apr., Tues.–Sat., 10–4, Sun. noon–4.*

Dining and Lodging

$$ ✕🏨 **Hotel Zum Bär.** There are stuffed bears in the hall and a bear motif in the maroon stair carpet of this 250-year-old half-timber hostelry that has views out onto the marketplace. The French Provincial furniture is painted white and gold. Careful detail has gone into the interior decorating, and no two rooms are alike. The restaurant is known for its filling local dishes. ✉ *Markt 8–9, D–06484,* ☎ *03946/7770,* FAX *03496/700–268,* WEB *www.hotelzumbaehr.de. 50 rooms, 1 suite. Restaurant, no a/c, minibars, free parking, some pets allowed (fee). No credit cards.*

$$ ✕🏨 **Romantik Hotel Theophano.** This 1668 baroque half-timber merchant's house was the seat of the tanners' guild in the 18th century, a restaurant-coffeehouse in the early 20th century, and a domestic linen store until the Communists "deprivatized" the business. Now restored with care, its elegant rooms have country antiques. The vault-ceiling restaurant ($$–$$$$) serves such dishes as Harz trout and local wild boar. ✉ *Markt 13–14, D–06484,* ☎ *03946/96300,* FAX *03946/963–036,* WEB *www.hoteltheophano.de. 22 rooms. Restaurant, no a/c, cable TV, free parking, some pets allowed (fee). AE, MC, V.*

$–$$ ★ ✕🏨 **Hotel Zur Goldenen Sonne.** Rooms in this baroque half-timber inn are furnished in a pleasing, rustic fashion. The cozy restaurant ($–$$) offers such Harz fare as venison stew with plum sauce and potato dumplings, and local smoked ham in apricot sauce. ✉ *Steinweg 11, D–06484,* ☎ *03946/96250,* FAX *03946/962–530,* WEB *www.hotelzurgoldenensonne.de. 27 rooms. Restaurant, no a/c, minibars, cable TV, free parking, some pets allowed (fee), no-smoking rooms. AE, MC, V.*

En Route The most scenic way to go from Quedlinburg to Braunlage is via Blankenburg, with its hilltop castle, and Wernigerode, 28 km (20 mi) away. Half-timber **Wernigerode** has a colorful twin-towered Rathaus on the marketplace, and the neo-Gothic castle above it is a starting point for walks in the Harz. Also departing from here is the steam-powered narrow-gauge **Harzequerbahn** to the heights (3,745 ft) of the Brocken. From Wernigerode take B–244 south 10 km (6 mi) to Elbingerode; then turn onto B–27 west and continue another 17 km (10 mi) along mountain roads through spruce forests to Braunlage.

Goslar

38 *48 km (30 mi) northwest of Quedlinburg.*

Goslar, the lovely, unofficial capital of the Harz region, is one of Germany's oldest cities and is known for the medieval glamour expressed in the fine Romanesque architecture of the Kaiserpfalz, an imperial palace of the German Empire. Thanks to the deposits of ore close to the town, Goslar was one of the country's most wealthy hubs of trade during the Middle Ages. In this town of 46,000 today, time seems to have stood still among the hundreds of well-preserved (mostly typical northern German half-timber) houses that were built during the course of seven centuries.

Despite Goslar's rapid decline after the breakup of the medieval German empire, the city—thanks to the ore—maintained all its luxury and worldliness born of economic success. The **Rathaus** with its magnificent Huldigungssaal (Hall of Honor) dates to 1450 and testifies to the wealth of Goslar's merchants. ✉ *Markt 1,* ☎ *05321/704–241.* 🎫 €2. ⏲ *Daily 11–4.*

The impressive **Kaiserpfalz,** set high above the historic downtown area, dates to the early Middle Ages. It once was the center of German imperial glory, when emperors held their regular diets here. Among the rulers who frequented Goslar were Heinrich III (1039–1056) and his successor, Heinrich IV (1056–1106), who was also born in Goslar. You can visit an exhibit about the German medieval kaisers who stayed here, inspect the small chapel where the heart of Heinrich III is buried (the body is in Speyer), or view the beautiful ceiling murals in the Reichssaal (Imperial Hall). ✉ *Kaiserbleek 6,* ☎ *05321/704–358.* €4.50. *Apr.–Oct., daily 10–5; Nov.–Mar., daily 10–4.*

The source of the town's riches is outside the city in the **Erzbergwerk Rammelsberg,** the world's only silver mine in continuous operation for more than 1,000 years. It stopped operating in 1988, but you can now inspect the many tunnels and shafts of this old mine. ✉ *Bergtal 19,* ☎ *05321/7500,* WEB *www.rammelsberg.de.* *€8.50, including tour.* *Daily 9–6, last tour at 4:30.*

Dining and Lodging

$$ **Kaiserworth-Hotel und Restaurant.** Hidden behind the reddish-brown walls of a 500-year-old house, the seat of medieval tailors and merchants, the hotel offers small but pleasantly furnished and bright rooms. The front rooms have windows on the medieval city market. The restaurant ($$) offers reliable German food. ✉ *Markt 3, D–38640,* ☎ *05321/7090,* FAX *03521/709–345,* WEB *www.kaiserworth.de. 66 rooms. Restaurant, no a/c, room service, cable TV, baby-sitting, dry cleaning, laundry service, meeting room, parking (fee), some pets allowed (fee), no-smoking rooms. AE, DC, MC, V.*

Braunlage

39 *34 km (21 mi) south of Goslar.*

One of the oldest winter-sports centers in central Germany, Braunlage gets snow from December to March and is the best spot for skiing in the Harz. In spring, summer, and fall, hiking on mountain trails is a favorite pastime, and the bald top of the Brocken is a 16-km (10-mi) walk. In the days of a divided Germany, this small resort was little more than 2 km (1 mi) from the border. Guest houses, restaurants, and ski shops are everywhere. A year-round attraction is the indoor skating rink.

Dining and Lodging

$$ ★ **Romantik Hotel Zur Tanne.** Built in 1725, this is one of the oldest buildings in Braunlage. Most rooms have balconies and banquette corners. The historic house connects to a modern annex, and a less expensive guest house on the outskirts of the village opens out to forest and mountains. When making a reservation, ask for a room in the *Bachhaus* building. Diners can choose between hearty mountain dishes or lighter fare in the restaurant ($–$$). ✉ *Herzog-Wilhelm-Str. 8, D–38700,* ☎ *05520/93120,* FAX *05520/3992,* WEB *www.romantikhotels.com/braunlage. 19 rooms, 3 suites. Restaurant, no a/c, room service, in-room safes, minibars, cable TV, health club, massage, sauna, steam room, baby-sitting, dry cleaning, laundry service, meeting room, free parking, some pets allowed (fee), no-smoking rooms. AE, D, V.*

Outdoor Activities and Sports

SKIING

Innumerable cross-country trails (lighted at night for after-dark skiing) wend their way through the evergreen forests of Braunlage. Alpine skiers have five ski slopes and a ski jump. The jump was closed until the Wall fell—because the bottom of it was in the GDR. For Alpine skiing, a cable car rises to the top of the 3,237-ft-high Wurmberg. It has three ski lifts. There are also toboggan runs, horse-drawn sleigh rides, ski instruction, and equipment rentals. Contact the tourist office for more information.

THURINGIA

The tiny state of Thuringia is one of Germany's most historic regions, with a rich cultural past still present in small villages, medieval cities, and country palaces throughout the hilly countryside. In the 14th century traders used the 168-km (104-mi) Rennsteig ("fast trail") through the dark depths of the Thuringian Forest, and cities such as Erfurt, Eisenach, and Gera evolved as major commercial hubs. Today the forests and the Erzgebirge Mountains are a remote paradise for hiking and fishing. The city of Weimar is one of Europe's old cultural centers, and the short-lived German democracy, the Weimar Republic, was established here in 1918. Already a prime vacation spot during Communist times, Thuringia boomed when it attracted investors after reunification.

Eisenach

40 *126 km (79 mi) south of Braunlage, 95 km (59 mi) northeast of Fulda (nearest ICE rail station).*

When you stand in Eisenach's ancient market square, it's difficult to imagine this half-timber town as an important center of the eastern German automobile industry, home of the now-shunned Wartburg. This solid, noisy staple of the East German auto trade was named after the famous castle that broods over Eisenach, atop one of the foothills of the Thuringian Forest. Today West German auto maker Opel is continuing the tradition. The GM company built one of Europe's most modern car-assembly lines on the outskirts of Eisenach.

★ Begun in 1067 (and expanded through the centuries), the mighty **Wartburg** has hosted a parade of German historical celebrities. Hermann I (1156–1217), count of Thuringia and count palatine of Saxony, was a patron of the poets Walther von der Vogelweide (1170–1230) and Wolfram von Eschenbach (1170–1220). Legend has it that this is where Walther, the greatest lyric poet of medieval Germany, prevailed in the celebrated *Minnesängerstreit* (minnesinger contest), which features in Richard Wagner's *Tannhäuser.*

Within the castle's stout walls, Frederick the Wise (1486–1525) shielded Martin Luther from papal proscription from May 1521 until March 1522, even though he did not share the reformer's beliefs. Luther completed the first translation of the New Testament from Greek into German while in hiding, an act that paved the way for the Protestant Reformation. You can peek into the simple study in which Luther worked. Over the centuries souvenir hunters scarred its walls by scratching away the plaster and much of the wood paneling.

Frederick was also a patron of the arts. Lucas Cranach the Elder's portraits of Luther and his wife are on view in the castle, as is a very moving sculpture, the *Kneeling Angel,* by the great 15th-century artist Tilman Riemenschneider. The 13th-century great hall is breathtaking; it's here that the minstrels sang for courtly favors. Don't leave without climbing the belvedere for a panoramic view of the Harz Mountains and the Thuringian Forest. ☎ *03691/77073,* WEB *www.wartburg-eisenach.de.* 🎫 *€6, including guided tour.* ⏲ *Nov.–Feb., daily 9–3:30; Mar.–Oct., daily 8:30–5.*

The **Lutherhaus** in downtown Eisenach has many fascinating exhibits illustrating the life of Luther, who lived here as a student. ✉ *Lutherpl. 8,* ☎ *03691/29830.* 🎫 *€2.50.* ⏲ *Apr.–Oct., daily 9–5; Nov.–Mar., daily 10–5.*

Johann Sebastian Bach was born in Eisenach in 1685. The **Bachhaus** has exhibits devoted to the entire lineage of the musical Bach family and includes a collection of historical musical instruments. ✉ *Frauenplan 21,* ☎ *03691/79340,* WEB *www.bachhaus.de.* 🎫 *€2.50.* ⏲ *Apr.–Sept., Mon. noon–6, Tues.–Sun. 9–6; Oct.–Mar., Mon. 1–5, Tues.–Sun. 9–5.*

Composer Richard Wagner gets his due at the **Reuter-Wagner-Museum,** which has the most comprehensive exhibition on Wagner's life and work outside Bayreuth. Concerts take place in the old Teezimmer (tearoom), a hall with wonderfully restored French wallpaper. The Erard piano dating from the late 19th century is occasionally rolled out. ✉ *Reuterweg 2,* ☎ *03691/743–293.* 🎫 *€3.* ⏲ *Tues.–Sun. 10–5.*

At Johannesplatz 9, look for what is said to be the **narrowest house** in eastern Germany, built in 1890; its width is just over 6 ft, 8 inches; its height, 24½ ft; and its depth, 34 ft.

Dining and Lodging

$$ ✕🏨 **Best Western Hotel Kaiserhof.** One of the oldest hotels in town, the Kaiserhof maintains an elegant late-19th-century atmosphere. The lobby and dining room are extraordinarily beautiful and are fine examples of German Landhaus architecture. The mansion has been renovated several times, so rooms are modern, spacious, and equipped with all amenities. The Turmschänke restaurant ($$$) serves local dishes. ✉ *Wartburgallee 2, D–99817,* ☎ *03691/213–513,* FAX *03691/203–653,* WEB *www.kaiserhof-eisenach.bestwestern.de. 64 rooms. 2 restaurants, bar, no a/c, room service, minibars, cable TV, hair salon, sauna, dry cleaning, laundry service, meeting room, car rental, free parking, some pets allowed (fee), no-smoking rooms. AE, DC, MC, V.*

$–$$ ✕🏨 **Hotel Glockenhof.** At the base of Wartburg Castle, this former church-run hostel has blossomed into a handsome hotel, cleverly incorporating the original half-timber city mansion into a modern extension. The excellent restaurant ($–$$) has been joined by a brasserie. ✉ *Grimmelg. 4, D–99817,* ☎ *03691/2340,* FAX *03691/234–131,* WEB *www.glockenhof.de. 38 rooms, 2 suites. Restaurant, no a/c, room service, cable TV, meeting room, parking (fee), some pets allowed (fee), no-smoking rooms. AE, MC, V.*

$$$–$$$$ ★ 🏨 **Hotel auf der Wartburg.** In this castle hotel, where Martin Luther, Johann Sebastian Bach, and Richard Wagner were guests, you'll get a splendid view over the town and the countryside. The standard of comfort is above average, and antiques and Oriental rugs mix with modern furnishings. The hotel runs a shuttle bus to the rail station and parking lot of the Wartburg. ✉ *Wartburg, D–99817,* ☎ *03691/7970,* FAX *03691/797–100,* WEB *www.wartburghotel.de. 33 rooms, 2 apartments. Restaurant, no a/c, room service, in-room safes, minibars, cable TV, dry cleaning, laundry service, meeting room, free parking, some pets allowed (fee), no-smoking rooms. AE, DC, MC, V.*

Erfurt

41 *55 km (34 mi) east of Eisenach.*

The "flowers and towers" city of Erfurt emerged from World War II relatively unscathed, with most of its innumerable towers intact. Flowers? Erfurt is a center of horticultural trade and Europe's largest flower- and vegetable-seed producer. Local botanist Christian Reichart pioneered the trade in the 19th century with his seed research. The outskirts of the city are covered with greenhouses and plantations, and the annual Internationale Gartenbauaustellung, or horticultural show, takes place here from the end of March through September.

The city's highly decorative and colorful facades are easy to admire on a walking tour (though you can also take an old-fashioned horse-drawn open carriage tour of the Old Town center every weekend, leaving from the cathedral's entrance at Mettengasse between 10 and 4). Downtown Erfurt is a photographer's delight, with narrow, busy ancient streets dominated by a magnificent 14th-century Gothic cathedral, the Mariendom. The **Domplatz** (Cathedral Square) is bordered by houses dating from the 16th century and by the **Rathaus.** The pedestrian-zone **Anger** is also lined with restored Renaissance houses. The **Bartholomäusturm** (Bartholomew Tower), the base of a 12th-century tower, holds a 60-bell carillon.

The **Mariendom** (Erfurt Cathedral) is reached by a broad staircase from the expansive Cathedral Square. Its Romanesque origins (foundations can be seen in the crypt) are best preserved in the choir's glorious stained-glass windows and beautifully carved stalls. The cathedral's biggest bell, the Gloriosa, is the largest free-swinging bell in the world. Cast in 1497, it took three years to install in the tallest of the three sharply pointed towers, painstakingly lifted inch by inch with wooden wedges. No chances are taken with this 2-ton treasure; its deep boom resonates only on special occasions, such as Christmas and New Year's. ✉ *Dompl.,* ☎ *0361/646–1265.* 🎫 *Tour €1.50.* ⏲ *May–Oct., weekdays 9–11:30 and 12:30–5, Sat. 9–11:30 and 12:30–4:30, Sun. 2–4; Nov.–Apr., Mon.–Sat. 10–11:30 and 12:30–4, Sun. 2–4.*

The Gothic church of **St. Severus** has an extraordinary font, a masterpiece of intricately carved sandstone that reaches practically to the ceiling. It is linked to the cathedral by a 70-step open staircase.

Behind the predominantly neo-Gothic Rathaus, you'll find Erfurt's most outstanding attraction spanning the Gera River, the **Krämerbrücke** (Shopkeepers' Bridge). Like Florence, Erfurt has a Renaissance bridge incorporating shops and homes. Built in 1325 and restored in 1967–73, the bridge served for centuries as an important trading center. Today antiques shops fill the majority of the timber-frame houses built into the bridge, some dating from the 16th century. The area around the bridge, crisscrossed with old streets lined with picturesque and often crumbling homes, is known as **Klein Venedig** (Little Venice) simply for the recurrent flooding it endures.

The young Martin Luther spent his formative years in the **St. Augustin Kloster** (St. Augustine Monastery; ✉ Gotthardstr.), today a seminary. Erfurt's interesting local-history museum is in a late-Renaissance house, **Zum Stockfisch.** ✉ *Johannesstr. 169,* ☎ *0361/655–5644.* 🎫 *Museum €4.50.* ⏲ *Tues.–Sun. 10–6.*

Dining and Lodging

$–$$$ ★ ✕ **Faustus Restaurant.** In the heart of historic Erfurt the stylish Faustus defines fine Thuringian dining. This restaurant is in an old mansion, with both an inviting summer terrace and a bright, airy dining room. An after-dinner drink at the superb bar is an absolute must. ✉ *Wenigermarkt 5,* ☎ *0361/540–0954. AE, DC, MC, V.*

$–$$ ✕ **Paganini im Gildehaus.** This Italian restaurant in one of the city's oldest (and most beautiful) historic mansions serves a wide variety of both basic country cooking and complex fish dishes. In summer the restaurant opens its beer garden, where Thuringian specialties are served—but the focus is on Italian cooking, whose quality is far better than that of the German dishes. The chef, after all, is Italian. ✉ *Fischermarkt 13–16,* ☎ *0361/643–0692. AE, DC, MC, V.*

$ ✕ **Dasdie.** Wolfgang Staub's Dasdie combines restaurant, bistro, bar, cabaret stage, and dance floor under one roof, so you can dine here (for less than €11), return later (or simply hang loose at the bar) for a show, and end the evening with a dance. The food is hit-and-miss, but the place is always lively and prices are low. Make sure to call ahead about schedules and programs. ✉ *Marstallstr. 12,* ☎ *0361/646–4666. No credit cards.*

$$ **Radisson SAS Hotel Erfurt.** Since the SAS group gave the ugly highrise Kosmos a face-lift, the socialist-realist look of the GDR years no longer seriously intrudes on Hotel Erfurt. The hotel underwent several renovations; rooms now have bright, modern colors and fabrics (including leather-upholstered furniture). The Classico restaurant ($$) serves mostly local dishes and is one of Erfurt's best. ✉ *Juri-Gagarin-Ring 127, D–99084,* ☎ *0361/55100,* FAX *0361/551–0210,* WEB *www.radisson.com/erfurtde. 314 rooms, 3 suites. Restaurant, bar, room service, minibars, cable TV, bicycles, baby-sitting, dry cleaning, laundry service, meeting room, car rental, parking (fee), some pets allowed (fee), no-smoking floor. AE, DC, MC, V.*

Weimar

42 *21 km (13 mi) east of Erfurt.*

Sitting prettily on the Ilm River between the Ettersberg and Vogtland hills, Weimar occupies a place in German political and cultural history completely disproportionate to its size (population 63,000). It's not even particularly old by German standards, with a civic history that started as late as 1410. By the early 19th century the city had become one of Europe's most important cultural centers, where poets Goethe and Schiller wrote, Johann Sebastian Bach played the organ for his Saxon patrons, Carl Maria von Weber composed some of his best music, and Franz Liszt was director of music, presenting the first performance of *Lohengrin.* In 1919 Walter Gropius founded his Staatliche Bauhaus here, and behind the classical pillars of the National Theater, the German National Assembly drew up the constitution of the Weimar Republic, the first German democracy. After the collapse of the ill-fated Weimar government, Hitler chose the little city as the site for the first national congress of his Nazi party. On the outskirts of Weimar the Nazis built—or forced prisoners to build for them—the infamous Buchenwald concentration camp.

Much of Weimar's greatness is owed to the widowed countess Anna Amalia, whose home, the **Wittumspalais** (Wittum Mansion), is surprisingly modest. In the late 18th century the countess went talent hunting for cultural figures to decorate the glittering court her Saxon forebears had established. Goethe was one of her finds, and he served the countess as a counselor, advising her on financial matters and town design. Schiller followed, and he and Goethe became valued visitors to the countess's home. Within this exquisite baroque house you can see the drawing room in which she held soirees, complete with the original cherrywood table at which the company sat. The east wing of the house contains a small museum that is a fascinating memorial to those cultural gatherings. ✉ *Frauentorstr. 4,* ☎ *03643/545–377.* *€3.* *Nov.–Mar., Tues.–Sun. 9–4; Apr.–Oct., Tues.–Sun. 9–6.*

A statue on **Theaterplatz,** in front of the National Theater, shows Goethe placing a paternal-like hand on the shoulder of the younger Schiller. Goethe spent 57 years in Weimar, 47 of them in a house two blocks south of Theaterplatz that has since become a shrine for millions of visitors. The **Goethe Nationalmuseum** (Goethe National Museum) consists of several houses, including the **Goethehaus,** where Goethe lived. It shows an exhibit about life in Weimar around 1750 and contains writings that illustrate not only the great man's literary might but his interest in the sciences, particularly medicine, and his administrative skills (and frustrations) as minister of state and Weimar's exchequer. You'll see the desk at which Goethe stood to write (he liked to work standing up) and the modest bed in which he died. The rooms are dark and often cramped, but an almost palpable intellectual intensity seems to illuminate them. ✉ *Frauenplan 1,* ☎ *03643/545–320,* WEB *www.weimar-klassik.de.* 🎫 *€5.* ⏲ *Nov.–Mar., Tues.–Sun. 9–4; Apr.–Oct., Tues.–Sun. 9–6.*

The **Schillerhaus,** a sturdy, green-shutter residence, and also part of the Goethe National Museum, is on a tree-shaded square not far from Goethe's house. He and his family spent a happy, all-too-brief three years here (Schiller died here in 1805). Schiller's study is tucked underneath the mansard roof, a cozy room dominated by his desk, where he probably completed *Wilhelm Tell.* Much of the remaining furniture and the collection of books were added later, although they all date from around Schiller's time. ✉ *Schillerstr. 17,* ☎ *03643/545–350,* WEB *www.weimar-klassik.de.* 🎫 *€3.* ⏲ *Nov.–Mar., Tues.–Sun. 9–4; Apr.–Oct., Tues.–Sun. 9–6.*

Goethe's beloved **Gartenhaus** (Garden House), a modest country cottage where he spent many happy hours, wrote much poetry, and began his masterly classical drama *Iphigenie,* is set amid meadowlike parkland on the bank of the River Ilm. Goethe is said to have felt very close to nature here, and you can soak up the same rural atmosphere on footpaths along the peaceful little river. ✉ *Goethepark,* ☎ *03642/545–375,* WEB *www.weimar-klassik.de.* 🎫 *Cottage €2.50.* ⏲ *Nov.–Mar., Tues.–Sun. 9–4; Apr.–Oct., Tues.–Sun. 9–6.*

Goethe and Schiller are buried in the **Historischer Friedhof** (Historic Cemetery), a leafy cemetery where virtually every gravestone commemorates a famous citizen of Weimar. Their tombs are in the vault of the classical-style chapel. The cemetery is a short walk past Goethehaus and Wieland Platz. 🎫 *Goethe-Schiller vault €2.* ⏲ *Nov.–Mar., Wed.–Mon. 10–1, 2–4; Apr.–Oct., Wed.–Mon. 9–1, 2–6.*

On the central town square, the **Herderkirche** (two blocks east of Theaterplatz), you'll find the home of Lucas Cranach the Elder. Cranach lived here during his last years, 1552–53. Its wide, imposing facade is richly decorated and bears the coat of arms of the Cranach family. It now houses a modern art gallery. The Marktplatz's late-Gothic **Herderkirche** (Herder Church) has a large winged altar started by Lucas Cranach the Elder and finished by his son in 1555.

Weimar's 16th-century **Stadtschloss,** the city castle, is around the corner from the Hederkirche. It has a finely restored classical staircase, a festival hall, and a falcon gallery. The tower on the southwest projection dates from the Middle Ages but received its baroque overlay circa 1730. The **Kunstsammlung** (art collection) here includes several works by Cranach the Elder and many early 20th-century pieces by such artists as Böcklin, Liebermann, and Beckmann. ✉ *Burgpl. 4,* ☎ *03643/5460,* WEB *www.kunstsammlungen-weimar.de.* 🎫 *€4.* ⏲ *Apr.–Nov., Tues.–Sun. 10–6; Dec.–Mar., Tues.–Sun. 10–4:30.*

The city's latest addition to its rich cultural scene is the **Neues Museum Weimar** (New Museum Weimar), which is also eastern Germany's first museum exclusively devoted to contemporary art. The building, dating back to 1869, was carefully restored and converted to hold collections of American minimalist and conceptual art, and works by German installation artist Anselm Kiefer and American painter Keith Haring. In addition, it regularly presents international modern art exhibitions. ✉ *Burgpl. 4,* ☎ *03643/546–163,* WEB *www.kunstsammlungen-weimar.de.* 🎫 *€3.* ⏲ *Apr.–Oct., Tues.–Sun. 10–6; Nov.–Mar., Tues.–Sun. 10–4:30.*

OFF THE BEATEN PATH

BELVEDERE PALACE – Just 8 km (5 mi) south of Weimar, the lovely 18th-century yellow-stucco Belvedere Palace once served as a hunting and pleasure castle; today you'll find a baroque museum and an interesting collection of coaches and other historic vehicles inside. The formal gardens were in part laid out according to Goethe's concepts. ✉ *Belvederer Allee,* ☎ *03643/546–162,* WEB *www.weimar-klassik.de.* 🎫 *€2.* ⏲ *Apr.–Oct., Tues.–Sun. 10–6.*

GEDENKSTÄTTE BUCHENWALD – In the Ettersberg Hills just north of Weimar is a blighted patch of land that contrasts cruelly with the verdant countryside that so inspired Goethe: Buchenwald, one of the most infamous Nazi concentration camps. Sixty-five thousand men, women, and children from 35 countries met their deaths here through forced labor, starvation, disease, and gruesome medical experiments. Each is commemorated by a small stone placed on the outlines of the barracks, which have long since disappeared from the site, and by a massive memorial tower. Besides exhibits, tours are available. To reach Buchenwald, you can take the public bus (No. 6), which leaves every 10 minutes from Goetheplatz in downtown Weimar. The one-way fare is €1.25. ☎ *03643/4300,* WEB *www.buchenwald.de.* 🎫 *Free.* ⏲ *May–Sept., Tues.–Sun. 9:45–5:15; Oct.–Apr., Tues.–Sun. 8:45–4:15.*

Dining and Lodging

$–$$ ✕ **Ratskeller.** This is one of the region's most authentic city hall–cellar restaurants, its whitewashed, barrel-vaulted ceiling witness to centuries of tradition. At the side is a cozy bar where you can enjoy a preprandial drink beneath a spectacular art nouveau skylight. The delicious *Sauerbraten* (roast beef) is the highlight of the Thuringian menu. If venison is in season, try it—likewise the wild duck or wild boar in red-wine sauce. ✉ *Am Markt 10,* ☎ *03643/850–573. MC, V.*

$ ✕ **Hotel Thüringen.** The plush elegance of the Thüringen's restaurant, complete with velvet drapes and chandeliers, makes it seem expensive, but the regional dishes served are remarkably moderate in price. An excellent Thüringer roast beef, for instance, costs less than €11. ✉ *Brennerstr. 42,* ☎ *03643/903–675. AE, DC, MC, V.*

$ ★ ✕ **Scharfe Ecke.** Thuringia's traditional *Knödel* (dumplings) are at their best here—but be patient, they're made to order and take 20 minutes. The *Klösse* are salty and less dense than the Knödel and come with just about every dish, from roast pork to venison stew, and the wait is well worth it. The ideal accompaniment to anything on the menu is one of the three locally brewed beers on tap. ✉ *Eisfeld 2,* ☎ *03643/202–430. AE, DC, MC, V. Closed Mon.*

$$$ ★ ✕🏨 **Grand Hotel Russischer Hof.** The historic, classicist hotel, once a hallmark of the European nobility and intellectual society, continues to be a luxurious gem in the heart of Weimar. Tolstoy, Liszt, Schumann, Turgenev, and others once stayed at this former Russian city palace, whose (partly historic) rooms are decorated today with antique French tapestries, linens, and furniture. The service is impeccable. The atmosphere is casual yet serene and elegant. The restaurant Anastasia ($$) serves fine Austrian-Thuringian cuisine. ✉ *Goethepl. 2, D–99423,* ☎ *03643/7740,* FAX *03643/774–840,* WEB *www.russischerhof.com. 119 rooms, 6 suites. Restaurant, bar, room service, in-room safes, minibars, cable TV with movies, baby-sitting service, dry cleaning, laundry service, concierge, meeting room, parking (fee), some pets allowed (fee), no-smoking floor. AE, DC, MC, V.*

$$–$$$ ★ 🏨 **Hotel Elephant.** The historic Elephant, dating from 1696, is famous for its charm—even through the Communist years. Book here (well in advance), and you'll follow the choice of Goethe, Schiller, Herder, Liszt (after whom the hotel bar is named)—and Hitler—all of whom have been guests. Behind the sparkling white facade are comfortable modern rooms decorated in beige, white, and yellow in a timeless blend of art deco and Bauhaus styles. A sense of the past is ever present. ✉ *Markt 19, D–99423,* ☎ *03643/8020,* FAX *03643/802–610,* WEB *www.arabellasheraton.com. 97 rooms, 5 suites. 2 restaurants, piano bar, no a/c, room service, in-room safes, minibars, cable TV, dry cleaning, laundry service, meeting room, parking (fee), some pets allowed (fee), no-smoking rooms. AE, DC, MC, V.*

$$ 🏨 **Amalienhof VCH Hotel.** Book far ahead to secure a room at this friendly little hotel central to Weimar's attractions. The historic and officially protected building began in 1826 as a church hostel. Double rooms are furnished with first-rate antique reproductions; public rooms have the real thing. ✉ *Amalienstr. 2, D–99423,* ☎ *03643/5490,* FAX *03643/549–110,* WEB *www.vch.de. 22 rooms, 9 apartments. No a/c, cable TV, free parking, some pets allowed (fee). MC, V.*

Nightlife and the Arts

Weimar's lively after-dark scene concentrates around piano bars and nightclubs around the Marktplatz in bars like **Shakespeares** (✉ Windischenstr. 4–6, ☎ 03643/901–285), a Bauhaus-style bar and restaurant.

Gera

43 *65 km (40 mi) east of Weimar.*

Once a princely residence and center of a thriving textile industry, the city has largely been rebuilt since World War II. Gera had often been compared with old Vienna, although today you have to search long and hard to discover any striking similarities between the German provincial town and the Habsburg capital. But some ornate and beautifully restored house facades hint at Gera's rich past.

Although the palace in which prince-electors once held court was destroyed in the final weeks of World War II and never rebuilt, the palace's 16th-century **Orangerie** does still stand in the former Küchengarten in the suburb of Untermhaus. It's an imposing semicircular baroque pavilion, irreverently dubbed the "roast sausage" by the people of Gera, which now houses the **Kunstsammlung,** the city's official art gallery. ✉ *Küchengartenallee 4,* ☎ *0365/832–2147.* 🎫 *€2.50.* ⏲ *Tues. 1–8, Wed.–Fri. 10–5, weekends 10–6.*

Gera's real claim to fame is artist Otto Dix (1891–1969). The residence where the satirical Expressionist painter was born is now known as the **Otto-Dix-Haus** (Otto Dix House). It has a gallery of his work and a permanent exhibition on his life. ✉ *Mohrenpl. 4,* ☎ *03643/832–4927.* 🎫 *€2.50; €3.50, including admission to Orangerie.* ⏲ *Tues., 1–8, Wed.–Fri. 10–5, weekends 10–8.*

Don't leave Gera without checking out the **Marktplatz.** The Renaissance buildings surrounding it were restored with rare care. The 16th-century **Rathaus** has a vividly decorated entrance and a vaulted cellar restaurant. Note the weird angles of the lower-floor windows; they follow the incline of the staircase winding up the interior of the building's picturesque 185-ft-high tower.

Lodging

$$ 🏨 **Best Western Hotel Regent Gera.** The city's best hotel is also a good deal. Despite a modern facade, the shiny lobby and the newly remod-

eled rooms create the feel of a sophisticated English retreat. The furnishings are mostly in red and dark green colors, the classic furniture is made of fine dark woods. Most rooms are quiet, as the hotel is in a cul-de-sac in a nice neighborhood, and the city's sights are within a 10-minute walk. ✉ *Schülerstr. 22, D–07545,* ☎ *0365/91810,* FAX *0365/9181–100,* WEB *www.regent-gera.bestwestern.de. 102 rooms, 6 suites. Restaurant, bar, room service, minibars, gym, massage, sauna, steam room, baby-sitting, dry cleaning, laundry service, meeting room, parking (fee), no-smoking floor. AE, DC, MC, V.*

SAXONY, SAXONY-ANHALT, AND THURINGIA A TO Z

To research prices, get advice from other travelers, and book travel arrangements, visit www.fodors.com.

AIR TRAVEL

Your best bet is flying into Berlin and renting a car from there. Dresden Flughafen is about 10 km (6 mi) north of Dresden. Leipzig's Flughafen Leipzig-Halle is 12 km (8 mi) northwest of the city.

➤ AIRPORT INFORMATION: **Dresden Flughafen** (☎ 0351/8810, WEB www.dresden-airport.de). **Flughafen Leipzig-Halle** (☎ 0341/2240, WEB www.leipzig-halle-airport.de).

BUS TRAVEL

Long-distance buses travel to Dresden and Leipzig. Bus service within the area is infrequent and mainly connects with rail lines. Check schedules carefully at central train stations or call the service phone number of Deutsche Bahn at local railway stations.

CAR RENTALS

Cars can be rented at Dresden's and Leipzig's airports and train stations and through all major hotels. Be aware that you are not allowed to take rentals into Poland or the Czech Republic.

➤ LOCAL AGENCIES: **Avis** (✉ Dresden Airport, Dresden, ☎ 0351/881–4600; ✉ Friedrichstr. 24–26, Dresden, ☎ 0351/490–9613; ✉ Torgauer Str. 231, Leipzig, ☎ 0341/459–480; ✉ Leipzig-Halle Airport, Leipzig, ☎ 0341/224–1804; ✉ Hauptbahnhof, Georgiring 14, Leipzig, ☎ 0341/961–1400; MediaCity, ✉ Altenburger Str. 13, Leipzig, ☎ 0341/3500–3550, WEB www.avis.de). **Hertz** (✉ Dresden Airport, Dresden, ☎ 0351/881–4580; ✉ Antonstr. 39, Dresden, ☎ 0351/452–630; ✉ Leipzig-Halle Airport, Leipzig, ☎ 034204/14317; ✉ Hauptbahnhof, Reisezentrum, Leipzig, ☎ 0341/477–9712; WEB www.hertz.de). **Europcar** (✉ Dresden Airport, Dresden, ☎ 0351/884–770; ✉ Hauptbahnhof, Dresden, ☎ 0351/877–320; ✉ Leipzig-Halle Airport, Leipzig, ☎ 034204/7700; ✉ Wittenberger Str. 19, Leipzig, ☎ 0341/904–440; ✉ Hauptbahnhof, Leipzig, ☎ 0341/141–160; WEB www.europcar.de). **Sixt** (✉ Dresden Airport, Dresden, ☎ 01805/252–525; ✉ Hilton Hotel, An der Frauenkirche 5, Dresden, ☎ 0351/490–5781; ✉ Hamburger Str. 36–38, Dresden, ☎ 0351/495–4105; ✉ Leipzig-Halle Airport, Leipzig, ☎ 01805/252–525; ✉ Löhrstr. 2 [next to Fürstenhof Hotel], Leipzig, ☎ 0341/984–840; WEB www.sixt.de).

CAR TRAVEL

Expressways connect Berlin with Dresden (the A–13) and Leipzig (A–9). Both journeys take about two hours. The A–4 stretches east–west across the southern portion of Thuringia and Saxony.

A road-construction program in eastern Germany is ongoing, and you should expect traffic delays on any journey of more than 300 km (186 mi). The Bundesstrassen throughout Eastern Germany are narrow, tree-lined country roads, often jammed with traffic. Roads in the western part of the Harz Mountains are better and wider.

TRAIN TRAVEL

The fastest and most inexpensive way to explore the region is by train. All cities are connected by a network of trains and some—Dresden and Meissen, for example—by commuter trains. Slower D- and E-class or InterRegio trains link smaller towns. From Dresden a round-trip ticket to Chemnitz costs about €21 (a 1½-hour journey one-way); to Görlitz, €31 (a 1½-hour ride). Trains connect Leipzig and Halle or Erfurt and Eisenach within 40 minutes, and tickets cost around €10 each way. The train ride between Erfurt and Gera (1½-hours) costs €12.40 one-way.

TOURS

BOAT TOURS

Viking K–D has two luxury cruise ships on the Elbe River. It operates a full program of cruises of up to eight days in length from mid-April until late October that go from Hamburg as far as Prague. All the historic cities of Saxony and Thuringia are ports of call—including Dresden, Meissen, Wittenberg, and Dessau. For details *see* Cruise Travel *in* Smart Travel Tips A to Z.

Weisse Flotte's historic paddle-steam tours depart from and stop in Dresden, Meissen, Pirna, Pillnitz, Königsstein, and Bad Schandau. Besides tours in the Dresden area, boats also go into the Czech Republic. For more information contact the Sächsische Dampfschiffahrt.

➤ FEES AND SCHEDULES: **Sächsische Dampfschiffahrt** (✉ Hertha-Lindner-Str. 10, D–01067 Dresden, ☎ 0351/866–090, WEB www.saechsische-dampfschiffahrt.de).

BUS TOURS

Dresden bus tours (in German and English, run by the Dresdner Verkehrsbetriebe) leave from Postplatz (April–September, daily 9:30–5 every 30 minutes; October–March, daily 10–3, every hour); the Stadtrundfahrt Dresden bus tours, leaving from Augustusbrücke/Schlossplatz, stop at most sights.

Guided bus tours of Leipzig (in English) run April–October, daily every 30 minutes from 9:30–5; November–March, Saturday, every 30 minutes, 10–5. Tours leave from outside the opera house, on Goethestrasse.

➤ FEES AND SCHEDULES: **Dresdner Verkehrsbetriebe AG** (☎ 0351/857–2201, WEB www.dvb.de). **Stadtrundfahrt Dresden** (☎ 0351/8995–650, WEB www.dresden.de).

CANOE AND PADDLE TOURS

Tour operators and boat rental companies can be found throughout the region. One of the largest operators is Saaletours, which runs canoe tours on the rivers Saale and Unstrut. In Dresden, contact the Kanuverein Laubegast e.V., an association that offers canoe rentals and guided tours on the Elbe River. A good choice for the rivers Elster and Saale is the Kiesling Bootsverleih near Gera, which rents canoes for €25 a day. For canoe rental and tours on the Elbe River starting near Meissen, try Sachsenboote Marlies Trepte.

➤ FEES AND SCHEDULES: **Kanuverein Laubegast e.V.** (✉ Laubegaster Ufer 35, Dresden, ☎ 0351/252–5613). **Kiesling Bootsverleih** (✉ Dahlbach 7, D–07973 Greiz, ☎ 0172/350–7245). **Saaletours** (✉ Campingplatz Blütengrund, D–06618 Naumburg, ☎ 03445/202–051). **Sachsenboote Marlies Trepte** (✉ Niedermuschützer Str. 20, D–01665 Zehren, ☎ 035247/51215).

TRAIN TOURS

In Saxony, two historic narrow gauge trains still operate on a regular schedule. Both the *Lössnitzgrundbahn,* which connects Ost-Radebeul-Ost and Radeburg, as well as the *Weisseritzelbahn,* which operates between Freital-Hainsberg and Kurort Kipsdorf, are perfect for taking in some of Saxony's romantic countryside and Fichtelberg Mountains. A two-way ticket is between €6.60 and €10.70, depending on the length of the ride. For schedule and information contact Deutsche Bahn's regional Dresden office.

The famous steam locomotive *Harzquerbahn* connects Nordhausen-Nord with Wernigerode and Gernerode in the Harz mountains. The most popular track of this line is the *Brockenbahn,* a special narrow gauge train transporting tourists to the top of Northern Germany's highest mountain. For schedule and further information contact the Harzer Schmalspurbahnen GmbH.

➤ FEES AND SCHEDULES: **Deutsche Bahn** (☎ 0351/461–8634 Dresden office). **Harzer Schmalspurbahnen GmbH** (✉ Bahnhof Westerntor, Unter den Zindeln, Wernigerode, ☎ 03943/5580 or 03943/558–163, WEB www.hsb-wr.de).

WALKING TOURS

A walking tour of Leipzig (in English) sets off from the tourist office May–September, daily 1:30; October–April, Saturday 1:30 and Sunday 10:30.

TRAVEL AGENCIES

Information on travel and tours to and around eastern Germany is available from most travel agents. Most Berlin tourist offices carry brochures about travel in eastern Germany.

➤ CONTACT INFORMATION: **Berolina Berlin-Service** (✉ Meinekestr. 3, D–10719 Berlin, ☎ 030/8856–8030). **DER** (Deutsches Reisebüro GmbH; ✉ Augsburger Str. 27, D–12309 Berlin, ☎ 030/2199–8400). **Reiseland American Express** (✉ Willy-Brandt-Pl. 5, D–04109 Leipzig, ☎ 0341/961–7373; ✉ Dohnaer Str. 246, D–01239 Dresden, ☎ 0351/288–1109; WEB www.americanexpress.de).

VISITOR INFORMATION

Most of the region's larger cities offer special tourist (exploring) cards such as the Dresdencard, Hallecard, Leipzigcard, or Weimarcard, which include discounts at museums, concerts, hotels, and restaurants or special sightseeing packages for up to the three days. For details, call the cities' tourist information offices. State tourism offices may have more English-language resources than the tourist offices of smaller towns.

➤ STATE TOURIST OFFICES: **Saxony–Anhalt** (Sachsen–Anhalt, ✉ Am Alten Theater 6, D–39104 Magdeburg, ☎ 0391/567–7080, FAX 0391/567–7081, WEB www.sachsen-anhalt.de). **Thuringia** (Thüringen, ✉ Weimarische Str. 45, D–99099 Erfurt, ☎ 0361/37420, FAX 0361/374–2299, WEB www.thueringen-tourismus.de).

➤ LOWER SAXONY TOURIST OFFICES: **Braunlage** (✉ Elbingeröder Str. 17, D–3700, ☎ 05520/19433 or 05520/93070, FAX 05520/930–720, WEB www.braunlage.de). **Goslar** (✉ Tourist-Information, Markt 7, D–38640, ☎ 05321/78060, FAX 05321/780–644, WEB www.goslarinfo.de).

➤ SAXONY TOURIST OFFICES: **Chemnitz** (✉ City-Management und Tourismus GmbH Chemnitz, Bahnhofsstr. 6, D–09111, ☎ 0371/19433, FAX 0371/690–6830, WEB www.chemnitz.de). **Dresden** (✉ Tourist-Information, Prager Str. 10, D–01069, ☎ 0351/491–920, FAX 0351/4919–2116, WEB www.dresden-tourist.de). **Freiberg** (✉ Fremdenverkehrsamt Freiberg, Obermarkt 24, D–09599, ☎ 03731/273–266, FAX 03731/273–260, WEB www.freiberg.de). **Görlitz** (✉ Tourist-Information, Obermarkt

29, D–02826, ☎ 03581/47570, FAX 03581/475–727, WEB www.goerlitz.de). **Leipzig** (✉ Leipzig Tourist Service e.V., Richard-Wagner-Pl. 1, D–04109, ☎ 0341/710–4310, FAX 0341/710–4301, WEB www.leipzig.de). **Meissen** (✉ Tourist-Information Meissen, Markt 3, D–01662, ☎ 03521/41940, FAX 03521/419–419, WEB www.meissen.de).

➤ SAXONY-ANHALT TOURIST OFFICES: **Dessau** (✉ Tourist-Information Dessau, Zerbster Str. 2c, D–06844, ☎ 0340/204–1442, FAX 0340/204–1142, WEB www.dessau.de). **Halle** (✉ Tourist-Information, Marktpl., D–06108, ☎ 0345/472–330, FAX 0345/472–3333, WEB www.halle-tourist.de). **Quedlinburg** (✉ Tourismus-Marketing GmbH, Markt 2, D–06484, ☎ 03946/905–624, FAX 03946/905–629, WEB www.quedlinburg.de). **Thale** (✉ Tourist-Information, Rathaustr. 1, D–06502, ☎ 03947/2597, FAX 03947/2277, WEB www.thale.de). **Wernigerode** (✉ Tourist-Information, Nikolaipl. 1, D–38855, ☎ 03943/633–035, FAX 03943/632–040, WEB www.wernigerode.de). **Wittenberg** (✉ Tourist-Information, Schlosspl. 2, D–06886 Wittenberg, ☎ 03491/498–610, FAX 03491/498–611, WEB www.wittenberg.de). **Wittenberg District Rural Information Office** (✉ Mittelstr. 33, D–06886, ☎ 03491/402–610, FAX 03491/405–857). **Wörlitz** (✉ Wörlitz-Information, Neuer Wall 103, D–06786, ☎ 034905/21704, FAX 034905/20216, WEB www.woerlitz.de).

➤ THURINGIA TOURIST OFFICES: **Eisenach** (✉ Eisenach-Information, Markt 2, D–99817, ☎ 03691/79230, FAX 03691/792–320, WEB www.eisenach-tourist.de). **Erfurt** (✉ Tourist-Information, Benediktsplatz 1, D–99084, ☎ 0361/66400, FAX 0361/664–0290, WEB www.erfurt-tourist-info.de). **Freiberg** (✉ Fremdenverkehrsamt Freiberg, Obermarkt 24, D–09599, ☎ 03731/273–266, FAX 03731/273–260, WEB www.freiberg.de). **Gera** (✉ Gera-Information, Ernst-Toller-Str. 14, D–07545, ☎ 0365/800–7030, FAX 0365/800–7031, WEB www.gera-tourismus.de). **Suhl** (✉ Tourist-Information Suhl, Kongresszentrum, Friedrich-König-Str. 7, D–98527, ☎ 03681/720–052, FAX 03681/720–052, WEB www.suhl.com). **Weimar** (✉ Tourist-Information Weimar, Markt 10, D–99421, ☎ 03643/24000 or 03643/19443, FAX 03643/240–040, WEB www.weimar.de).

18 BACKGROUND AND ESSENTIALS

CHRONOLOGY

ca. 5000 BC Indo-Germanic tribes settle in the Rhine and Danube valleys

ca. 2000–800 BC Distinctive German Bronze Age culture emerges, with settlements ranging from coastal farms to lakeside villages

ca. 450–50 BC Salzkammergut people, whose prosperity is based on abundant salt deposits (in the area of upper Austria), trade with Greeks and Etruscans; Salzkammerguts spread as far as Belgium and have first contact with the Romans

9 BC–AD 9 Roman attempts to conquer the "Germans"—the tribes of the Cibri, the Franks, the Goths, and the Vandals—and are only partly successful; the Rhine becomes the northeastern border of the Roman Empire (and remains so for 300 years)

212 Roman citizenship is granted to all free inhabitants of the Empire

ca. 400 Pressed forward by Huns from Asia, such German tribes as the Franks, the Vandals, and the Lombards migrate to Gaul (France), Spain, Italy, and North Africa, scattering the Empire's populace and eventually leading to the disintegration of central Roman authority

486 The Frankish kingdom is founded by Clovis; his court is in Paris

497 The Franks convert to Christianity

Early Middle Ages

776 Charlemagne becomes king of the Franks

800 Charlemagne is declared Holy Roman Emperor; he makes Aachen capital of his realm, which stretches from the Bay of Biscay to the Adriatic and from the Mediterranean to the Baltic. Under his enlightened patronage there is an upsurge in art and architecture—the Carolingian renaissance

843 The Treaty of Verdun divides Charlemagne's empire among his three sons: West Francia becomes France; Lotharingia becomes Lorraine (territory to be disputed by France and Germany into the 20th century); and East Francia takes on, roughly, the shape of modern Germany

911 Five powerful German dukes (of Bavaria, Lorraine, Franconia, Saxony, and Swabia) establish the first German monarchy by electing King Conrad I; Henry I (the Fowler) succeeded Conrad in 919

962 Otto I is crowned Holy Roman Emperor by the pope; he establishes Austria—the East Mark. The Ottonian renaissance is marked especially by the development of Romanesque architecture

Middle Ages

1024–1125 The Salian dynasty is characterized by a struggle between emperors and the Church that leaves the Empire weak and disorganized; the great Romanesque cathedrals of Speyer, Trier, and Mainz are built

1138–1254 Frederick Barbarossa leads the Hohenstaufen dynasty; there is temporary recentralization of power, underpinned by strong trade and Church relations

1158 Munich, capital of Bavaria, is founded by Duke Henry the Lion; Henry is deposed by Emperor Barbarossa, and Munich is presented to the House of Wittelsbach, which rules it until 1918

1241 The Hanseatic League is founded to protect trade; Bremen, Hamburg, Köln, and Lübeck are early members. Agencies are soon established in London, Antwerp, Venice, and along the Baltic and North seas; a complex banking and finance system results

mid-1200s The Gothic style, exemplified by the grand Köln Cathedral, flourishes

1349 Black Death plague kills one-quarter of German population

Renaissance and Reformation

1456 Johannes Gutenberg (1400–68) prints first book in Europe

1471–1553 Renaissance flowers under influence of painter and engraver Albrecht Dürer (1471–1528); Dutch-born philosopher and scholar Erasmus (1466–1536); Lucas Cranach the Elder (1472–1553), who originates Protestant religious painting; portrait and historical painter Hans Holbein the Younger (1497–1543); and landscape painting pioneer Albrecht Altdorfer (1480–1538). Increasing wealth among the merchant classes leads to strong patronage of the revived arts

1517 The Protestant Reformation begins in Germany when Martin Luther (1483–1546) nails his 95 Theses to a church door in Wittenberg, contending that the Roman Church has forfeited divine authority through its corrupt sale of indulgences. Luther is outlawed, and his revolutionary doctrine splits the Church; much of north Germany embraces Protestantism

1524–30 The (Catholic) Habsburgs rise to power; their empire spreads throughout Europe (and as far as North Africa, the Americas, and the Philippines). Erasmus breaks with Luther and supports reform within the Roman Catholic church. In 1530 Charles V (a Habsburg) is crowned Holy Roman Emperor; he brutally crushes the Peasants' War, one in a series of populist uprisings in Europe

1545 The Council of Trent marks the beginning of the Counter-Reformation. Through diplomacy and coercion, most Austrians, Bavarians, and Bohemians are won back to Catholicism, but the majority of Germans remain Lutheran; persecution of religious minorities grows

Thirty Years' War

1618–48 Germany is the main theater for the Thirty Years' War. The powerful Catholic Habsburgs are defeated by Protestant forces, swelled by disgruntled Habsburg subjects and the armies of King Gustav Adolphus of Sweden. The bloody conflict ends with the Peace of Westphalia (1648); Habsburg and papal authority are severely diminished

Absolutism and Enlightenment

1689 Louis XIV of France invades the Rhineland Palatinate and sacks Heidelberg. At the end of the 17th century, Germany consolidates its role as a center of scientific thought

1708 Johann Sebastian Bach (1685–1750) becomes court organist at Weimar and launches his career; he and Georg Friederic Handel (1685–1759) fortify the great tradition of German music. Baroque and, later, rococo art and architecture flourish

1740–86 Reign of Frederick the Great of Prussia; his rule sees both the expansion of Prussia (it becomes the dominant military force in Germany) and the spread of Enlightenment thought

ca. 1790 The great age of European orchestral music is raised to new heights in the works of Joseph Haydn (1732–1809), Wolfgang Amadeus Mozart (1756–91), and Ludwig van Beethoven (1770–1827)

early 1800s Johann Wolfgang von Goethe (1749–1832) is part of the *Sturm und Drang* movement that leads to Romanticism. Painter Caspar David Friedrich (1774–1840) leads early German Romanticism. Other luminary cultural figures include writers Friedrich Schiller (1759–1805) and Heinrich von Kleist (1777–1811); the composers Robert Schumann (1810–56), Hungarian-born Franz Liszt (1811–86), Richard Wagner (1813–83), and Johannes Brahms (1833–97). In architecture, the severe lines of neoclassicism become popular

Road to Nationhood

1806 Napoléon's armies invade Prussia; it briefly becomes part of the French Empire

1807 The Prussian prime minister Baron vom und zum Stein frees the serfs, creating a new spirit of patriotism; the Prussian army is rebuilt

1813 The Prussians defeat Napoléon at Leipzig

1815 Britain and Prussia defeat Napoléon at Waterloo. At the Congress of Vienna, the German Confederation is created as a loose union of 39 independent states, reduced from more than 300 principalities. The *Bundestag* (national assembly) is established at Frankfurt. Already powerful Prussia increases its territory, gaining the Rhineland, Westphalia, and most of Saxony

1848 The "Year of the Revolutions" is marked by uprisings across the fragmented German Confederation; Prussia expands. A national parliament is elected, taking the power of the Bundestag to prepare a constitution for a united Germany

1862 Otto von Bismarck (1815–98) becomes prime minister of Prussia; he is determined to wrest German-populated provinces from Austro-Hungarian (Habsburg) control

1866 Austria-Hungary is defeated by the Prussians at Sadowa; Bismarck sets up the Northern German Confederation in 1867. A key figure in Bismarck's plans is Ludwig II of Bavaria. Ludwig—a political simpleton—lacks successors, making it easy for Prussia to seize his lands

1867 Karl Marx (1818–83) publishes *Das Kapital*

1870–71 The Franco-Prussian War: Prussia lays siege to Paris. Victorious Prussia seizes Alsace-Lorraine but eventually withdraws from all other occupied French territories

1871 The four south German states agree to join the Northern Confederation; Wilhelm I is proclaimed first kaiser of the united Empire

Modernism

1882 The Triple Alliance is forged between Germany, Austria-Hungary, and Italy. Germany's industrial revolution blossoms, enabling it to catch up with the other great powers of Europe. Germany establishes colonies in Africa and the Pacific

ca. 1885 Daimler and Benz pioneer the automobile

1890 Kaiser Wilhelm II (rules 1888–1918) dismisses Bismarck and begins a new, more aggressive course of foreign policy; he oversees the expansion of the navy

1890s A new school of writers, including Rainer Maria Rilke (1875–1926), emerges. Rilke's *Sonnets to Orpheus* give German poetry new lyricism

1905 Albert Einstein (1879–1955) announces his theory of relativity

1906 Painter Ernst Ludwig Kirchner (1880–1938) helps organize *Die Brücke,* a group of artists who, along with *Der Blaue Reiter,* create the avant-garde art movement Expressionism

1907 Great Britain, Russia, and France form the Triple Entente, which, set against the Triple Alliance, divides Europe into two armed camps

1914–18 Austrian Archduke Franz-Ferdinand is assassinated in Sarajevo. The attempted German invasion of France sparks World War I; Italy and Russia join the Allies, and four years of pitched battle ensue. By 1918 the Central Powers are encircled and must capitulate

Weimar Republic

1918 Germany is compelled by the Versailles Treaty to give up its overseas colonies and much European territory (including Alsace-Lorraine to France) and to pay huge reparations to the Allies; Kaiser Wilhelm II repudiates the throne and goes into exile in Holland. The tough terms leave the new democracy (the Weimar Republic) shaky

1919 The Bauhaus school of art and design, the brainchild of Walter Gropius (1883–1969), is born. Thomas Mann (1875–1955) and Hermann Hesse (1877–1962) forge a new style of visionary intellectual writing

1923 Germany suffers runaway inflation. Adolf Hitler's Beer Hall Putsch, a rightist revolt, fails; leftist revolts are frequent

1925 Hitler publishes *Mein Kampf* (*My Struggle*)

1932 The Nazi party gains the majority in the *Reichstag* (parliament)

1933 Hitler becomes chancellor; the Nazi "revolution" begins. In Berlin, Nazi students stage the burning of more than 25,000 books by Jewish and other politically undesirable authors

Nazi Germany

1934 President Paul von Hindenburg dies; Hitler declares himself Führer (leader) of the Third Reich. Nazification of all German social institutions begins, spreading a policy that is virulently racist and anticommunist. Germany recovers industrial might and rearms

1936 Germany signs anticommunist agreements with Italy and Japan, forming the Axis; Hitler reoccupies the Rhineland

1938 The *Anschluss* (annexation): Hitler occupies Austria. Germany occupies the Sudetenland in Czechoslovakia. *Kristallnacht* (Night of Broken Glass), in November, marks the Nazis' first open and direct terrorism against German Jews. Synagogues and Jewish–owned businesses are burnt, looted, and destroyed in a night of violence

1939–40 In August Hitler signs a pact with the Soviet Union; in September he invades Poland; war is declared by the Allies. Over the next three years, there are Nazi invasions of Denmark, Norway, the Low

Countries, France, Yugoslavia, and Greece. Alliances form between Germany and the Baltic states

1941–45 Hitler launches his anticommunist crusade against the Soviet Union, reaching Leningrad in the north and Stalingrad and the Caucasus in the south. In 1944 the Allies land in France; their combined might brings the Axis to its knees. In addition to the millions killed in the fighting, more than 6 million Jews and other victims die in Hitler's concentration camps. Germany is again in ruins. Hitler kills himself in April, 1945. East Berlin and what becomes East Germany are occupied by the Soviet Union

The Cold War

1945 At the Yalta Conference, France, the United States, Britain, and the Soviet Union divide Germany into four zones; each country occupies a sector of Berlin. The Potsdam Agreement expresses the determination to rebuild Germany as a democracy

1946 East Germany's Social Democratic Party merges with the Communist Party, forming the SED, which would rule East Germany for the next 40 years

1948 The Soviet Union tears up the Potsdam Agreement and attempts, by blockade, to exclude the three other Allies from their agreed zones in Berlin. Stalin is frustrated by a massive airlift of supplies to West Berlin

1949 The three Western zones are combined to form the Federal Republic of Germany; the new West German parliament elects Konrad Adenauer as chancellor (a post he held until his retirement in 1963). Soviet-held East Germany becomes the Communist German Democratic Republic (GDR)

1950s West Germany, aided by the financial impetus provided by the Marshall Plan, rebuilds its devastated cities and economy—the *Wirtschaftswunder* (economic miracle) gathers speed. The writers Heinrich Böll, Wolfgang Koeppen, and Günter Grass emerge

1957 The Treaty of Rome heralds the formation of the European Economic Community (EEC); West Germany is a founding member

1961 Communists build the Berlin Wall to stem the outward tide of refugees

1969–74 The vigorous chancellorship of Willy Brandt pursues *Ostpolitik,* improving relations with Eastern Europe, the Soviet Union, and acknowledging East Germany's sovereignty

mid-1980s The powerful German Green Party emerges as the leading environmentalist voice in Europe

Reunification

1989 Discontent in East Germany leads to a flood of refugees westward and to mass demonstrations; Communist power collapses across Eastern Europe; the Berlin Wall falls

1990 In March the first free elections in East Germany bring a center-right government to power. The Communists, faced with corruption scandals, suffer a big defeat but are represented (as Democratic Socialists) in the new, democratic parliament. The World War II victors hold talks with the two German governments, and the Soviet Union gives its support for reunification. Economic union takes place on July 1, with full political unity on October 3. In December, in the first democratic national German elections in 58 years, Chancellor Helmut Kohl's three-party coalition is reelected

1991 Nine months of emotional debate end on June 20, when parliamentary representatives vote to move the capital from Bonn—seat of the West German government since 1949—to Berlin, the capital of Germany until the end of World War II

1998 Helmut Kohl's record 16-year-long chancellorship of Germany ends with the election of Gerhard Schröder. Schröder's Social Democratic Party (SPD) pursues a coalition with the Greens in order to replace the three-party coalition of the Christian Democratic Union, Christian Social Union, and Free Democratic Party

1999 The Bundestag, the German parliament, returns to the restored Reichstag in Berlin on April 19. The German federal government also leaves Bonn for Berlin, making Berlin capital of Germany again

1999–2002 For the first time since 1945, the German army (the Bundeswehr) is deployed in combat missions in the former Yugoslavia and Afghanistan

2000 Hannover hosts Germany's first world's exposition, EXPO 2000, the largest ever staged in the 150-year history of the event

GERMAN VOCABULARY

	English	German	Pronunciation
Basics			
	Yes/no	Ja/nein	yah/nine
	Please	Bitte	**bit**-uh
	Thank you (very much)	Danke (vielen Dank)	**dahn**-kuh (**fee**-lun-dahnk)
	Excuse me	Entschuldigen Sie	ent-**shool**-de-gen zee
	I'm sorry.	Es tut mir leid.	es toot meer lite
	Good day	Guten Tag	**goo**-ten tahk
	Good bye	Auf Wiedersehen	auf **vee**-der-zane
	Mr./Mrs.	Herr/Frau	hair/frau
	Miss	Fräulein	**froy**-line
Numbers			
	1	ein(s)	eint(s)
	2	zwei	tsvai
	3	drei	dry
	4	vier	fear
	5	fünf	fumph
	6	sechs	zex
	7	sieben	**zee**-ben
	8	acht	ahkt
	9	neun	noyn
	10	zehn	tsane
Days of the Week			
	Sunday	Sonntag	**zone**-tahk
	Monday	Montag	**moan**-tahk
	Tuesday	Dienstag	**deens**-tahk
	Wednesday	Mittwoch	**mit**-voah
	Thursday	Donnerstag	**doe**-ners-tahk
	Friday	Freitag	**fry**-tahk
	Saturday	Samstag/ Sonnabend	**zahm**-stakh/ **zonn**-a-bent
Useful Phrases			
	Do you speak English?	Sprechen Sie Englisch?	**shprek**-hun zee **eng**-glish?
	I don't speak German.	Ich spreche kein Deutsch.	ich **shprek**-uh kine doych
	Please speak slowly.	Bitte sprechen Sie langsam.	**bit**-uh **shprek**-en-zee **lahng**-zahm
	I am American/ British	Ich bin Amerikaner(in)/ Engländer(in)	ich bin a-mer-i-**kahn**-er(in)/ **eng**-glan-der(in)
	My name is . . .	Ich heiße . . .	ich **hi**-suh
	Where are the restrooms?	Wo ist die Toilette?	vo ist dee twah-**let**-uh

Left/right	links/rechts	links/rechts
Open/closed	offen/geschlossen	O-fen/geh-**shloss**-en
Where is . . . the train station? the bus stop? the subway station? the airport? the post office? the bank? the police station? the Hospital? the telephone	Wo ist . . . der Bahnhof? die Bushaltestelle? die U-Bahn-Station? der Flugplatz? die Post? die Bank? die Polizeistation? das Krankenhaus? das Telefon	**vo** ist **dare bahn-hof** **dee booss-hahlt-uh-**shtel-uh dee oo-bahn-**staht-**sion dare **floog**-plats dee **post** dee **banhk** dee po-lee-tsai-**staht-**sion dahs **krahnk**-en-house **dahs te-le-fone**
What is your . . . address? phone number? fax number?	Was ist Ihre Adresse Telefon Nummer Fax Nummer	vas ist **ear**-eh ah-**drehs**-seh tay-lay-**fon num**-mer fax **num**-mer
I'd like . . . a room the key a map a ticket	Ich hätte gerne . . . ein Zimmer den Schlüssel eine Stadtplan eine Karte	ich **het**-uh gairn . . . ein **tsim**-er den **shluh**-sul **I**-nuh **staht**-plahn **I**-nuh cart-uh
How much is it?	Wieviel kostet das?	**vee-feel cost**-et dahs?
I am ill/sick	Ich bin krank	ich bin krahnk
I need . . . a doctor the police help Stop!	Ich brauche . . . einen Arzt die Polizei Hilfe Halt!	ich **brow**-khuh **I-nen** artst dee po-li-**tsai** **hilf-uh** **hahlt**
Fire!	Feuer!	**foy**-er
Look out/Caution!	Achtung!/Vorsicht!	**ahk**-tung/for-zicht

Dining Out

A bottle of . . .	eine Flasche . . .	I-nuh **flash**-uh
A cup of . . .	eine Tasse . . .	I-nuh **tahs**-uh
A glass of . . .	ein Glas . . .	ein glahss
Ashtray	der Aschenbecher	dare **Ahsh**-en-bekh-er
Bill/check	die Rechnung	dee **rekh**-nung
Do you have . . .?	Haben Sie . . .?	**hah**-ben zee
I am a vegetarian.	Ich bin Vegetarier(in)	ich bin ve-guh-**tah**-re-er
I'd like to order . . .	Ich möchte . . . bestellen	ich **mohr**-shtuh . . . buh-**shtel**-en
Menu	die Speisekarte	dee **shpie**-zeh-car-tuh
Napkin	die Serviette	dee zair-vee-**eh**-tuh

MENU GUIDE

English	German
Made to order	Auf Bestellung
Side dishes	Beilagen
Extra charge	Extraaufschlag
When available	Falls verfügbar
Entrées	Hauptspeisen
Homemade	Hausgemacht
(not) included	. . .(nicht) inbegriffen
Depending on the season	je nach Saison
Local specialties	Lokalspezialitäten
Set menu	Menü
Lunch menu	Mittagskarte
Desserts	Nachspeisen
style	. . . nach .. . . Art
at your choice	. . . nach Wahl
at your request	. . . nach Wunsch
Prices are . . .	Preise sind . . .
Service included	*inklusive Bedienung*
Value added tax included	*inklusive Mehrwertsteuer (Mwst.)*
Specialty of the house	Spezialität des Hauses
Soup of the day	Tagessuppe
Appetizers	Vorspeisen
Is served from . . . to . . .	Wird von . . . bis . . . serviert

Breakfast

Bread	Brot
Roll(s)	Brötchen
Butter	Butter
Eggs	Eier
Hot	heiß
Cold	kalt
Decaffeinated	koffeinfrei
Jam	Konfitüre
Milk	Milch
Orange juice	Orangensaft
Scrambled eggs	Rühreier
Bacon	Speck
Fried eggs	Spiegeleier
White bread	Weißbrot
Lemon	Zitrone
Sugar	Zucker

Soups

Stew	Eintopf
Semolina dumpling soup	Grießnockerlsuppe
Goulash soup	Gulaschsuppe
Chicken soup	Hühnersuppe
Potato soup	Kartoffelsuppe
Liver dumpling soup	Leberknödelsuppe
Oxtail soup	Ochsenschwanzsuppe

Tomato soup	Tomatensuppe
Onion soup	Zwiebelsuppe

Methods of Preparation

Blue (boiled in salt and vinegar)	Blau
Baked	Gebacken
Fried	Gebraten
Steamed	Gedämpft
Grilled (broiled)	Gegrillt
Boiled	Gekocht
Sauteed	In Butter geschwenkt
Breaded	Paniert
Raw	Roh

When ordering steak, the English words "rare, medium, (well) done" are used and understood in German.

Fish and Seafood

Eel	Aal
Oysters	Austern
Trout	Forelle
Flounder	Flunder
Prawns	Garnelen
Halibut	Heilbutt
Herring	Hering
Lobster	Hummer
Scallops	Jakobsmuscheln
Cod	Kabeljau
Crab	Krabbe
Crayfish	Krebs
Salmon	Lachs
Spiny lobster	Languste
Mackerel	Makrele
Mussels	Muscheln
Red sea bass	Rotbarsch
Sole	Seezunge
Squid	Tintenfisch
Tuna	Thunfisch

Meats

Mutton	Hammel
Veal	Kalb(s)
Lamb	Lamm
Beef	Rind(er)
Pork	Schwein(e)

Cuts of Meat

Example: For "Lammkeule" see "Lamm" (above) + ". . . keule" (below)

breast	. . . brust
scallopini	. . . geschnetzeltes
knuckle	. . . haxe
leg	. . . keule
liver	. . . leber
tenderloin	. . . lende

kidney	. . . niere
rib	. . . rippe
Meat patty	Frikadelle
Meat loaf	Hackbraten
Cured pork ribs	Kasseler Rippchen
Spicey meatloaf	Leberkäse
Ham	Schinken

Game and Poultry

Duck	Ente
Pheasant	Fasan
Goose	Gans
Chicken	Hähnchen (Huhn)
Hare	Hase
Deer	Hirsch
Rabbit	Kaninchen
Capon	Kapaun
Venison	Reh
Pigeon	Taube
Turkey	Truthahn
Quail	Wachtel

Vegetables

Eggplant	Aubergine
Red cabbage	Blaukraut
Cauliflower	Blumenkohl
Beans	Bohnen
green	*grüne*
white	*weiße*
Button mushrooms	Champignons
Peas	Erbsen
Cucumber	Gurke
Cabbage	Kohl
Lettuce	Kopfsalat
Leek	Lauch
Asparagus, peas and carrots	Leipziger Allerlei
Corn	Mais
Carrots	Mohrrüben
Peppers	Paprika
Chanterelle mushrooms	Pfifferlinge
Mushrooms	Pilze
Brussels sprouts	Rosenkohl
Red beets	Rote Beete
Celery	Sellerie
Asparagus (tips)	Spargel(spitzen)
Tomatoes	Tomaten
Cabbage	Weißkohl
Onions	Zwiebeln
Spring Onions	Frühlingszwiebeln

Condiments

Basil	Basilikum
Vinegar	Essig
Spice	Gewürz

Garlic	Knoblauch
Herbs	Kräuter
Caraway	Kümmel
Bay leaf	Lorbeer
Horseradish	Meerettich
Nutmeg	Muskatnuß
Oil	Öl
Parsley	Petersilie
Saffron	Safran
Sage	Salbei
Chives	Schnittlauch
Mustard	Senf
Artificial sweetener	Süßstoff
Cinnamon	Zimt
Sugar	Zucker
Salt	Salz

Cheese

Mild	Allgäuer Käse, Altenburger (goat cheese), Appenzeller, Greyerzer, Hüttenkäse (cottage cheese), Kümmelkäse (with caraway seeds), Quark, Räucherkäse (smoked cheese), Sahnekäse (creamy), Tilsiter, Ziegekäse (goat cheese).
Sharp	Handkäse, Harzer Käse, Limburger.
curd	frisch
hard	hart
mild	mild

Fruits

Apple	Apfel
Orange	Apfelsine
Apricot	Aprikose
Blueberry	Blaubeere
Blackberry	Brombeere
Strawberry	Erdbeere
Raspberry	Himbeere
Cherry	Kirsche
Grapefruit	Pampelmuse
Cranberry	Preiselbeere
Raisin	Rosine
Grape	Weintraube
Banana	Banane
Pear	Birne
Kiwi	Kiwi

Drinks

with/without ice	mit/ohne Eis
with/without water	mit/ohne Wasser
straight	pur
brandy	. . . geist
liqueur	. . . likör
Mulled claret	Glühwein

Caraway-flavored liquor	Kümmel
Fruit brandy	Obstler

When ordering a Martini, you have to specify "gin (vodka) and vermouth," otherwise you will be given a vermouth (Martini & Rossi).

Beer and Wine

non-alcoholic	Alkoholfrei
A dark beer	Ein Dunkles
A light beer	Ein Helles
A mug (one quart)	Eine Maß
Draught	Vom Faß
Dark, bitter, high hops content	Altbier
Strong, high alcohol content	Bockbier (Doppelbock, Märzen)
Wheat beer with yeast	Hefeweizen
Light beer, strong hops aroma	Pils(ener)
Wheat beer	Weizen(bier)
Light beer and lemonade	Radlermaß
Wines	Wein
Rosé wine	Rosëwein
Red wine	Rotwein
White wine and mineral water	Schorle
Sparkling wine	Sekt
White wine	Weißwein
dry	herb
light	leicht
sweet	süß
dry	trocken
full-bodied	vollmundig

Non-alcoholic Drinks

Coffee	Kaffee
decaffeinated	*koffeinfrei*
with cream/sugar	*mit Milch/Zucker*
black	*schwarz*
Lemonade	Limonade
Milk	Milch
Mineral water	Mineralwasser
carbonated/non-carbonated	*mit/ohne Kohlensäure*
juice	. . . saft
(hot) Chocolate	(heiße) Schokolade
Tea	Tee
iced tea	*Eistee*
herb tea	*Kräutertee*
with cream/lemon	*mit Milch/Zitrone*

INDEX

Icons and Symbols

★ Our special recommendations
✕ Restaurant
🏨 Lodging establishment
✕🏨 Lodging establishment whose restaurant warrants a special trip
🦆 Good for kids (rubber duck)
☞ Sends you to another section of the guide for more information
✉ Address
☎ Telephone number
⏲ Opening and closing times
🎫 Admission prices

Numbers in white and black circles ③ ❸ that appear on the maps, in the margins, and within the tours correspond to one another.

A

B

C

I

J